GET ON TOP OF THIS COURSE
AND STAY THERE

Student Workbook to Accompany
TOPICS IN MANAGEMENT SCIENCE
Second Edition
prepared by Marc J. Schniederjans
University of Nebraska-Lincoln

This useful workbook has been developed especially to increase the effectiveness of the Markland text. Read it before class. Use it to organize your note taking and to review for quizzes and exams. Save time and increase your learning efficiency!

Copies should be available at your college store. If not, ask your bookstore manager to order one for you now—don't wait until the first exam!

Ask for the **STUDENT WORKBOOK TO ACCOMPANY TOPICS IN MANAGE-MENT SCIENCE, Second Edition,** by **Robert Markland,** prepared by **Marc J. Schniederjans.**

From John Wiley & Sons, Inc.

Topics in Management Science

Topics in Management Science

Second Edition

Robert E. Markland

John Wiley & Sons

New York Chichester Brisbane Toronto Singapore

Cover design by Kevin J. Murphy
Interior Design by Jim Wall

Library of Congress Cataloging in Publication Data:

Markland, Robert E.
    Topics in management science.

    Includes bibliographies and index.
    1. Management science. I. Title. II. Series.
T56.M275 1983   658.4   82-20273
ISBN 0-471-09830-2

Printed in the United States of America

10 9 8 7 6 5 4 3 2 1

To my mother, the memory of my father, Mylla, Kevin and Keith

Preface

This edition of *Topics in Management Science* surveys the subject matter encompassed by the field of management science. Management science concerns both a number of quantitative techniques and a logical methodology for applying those quantitative techniques to decision making. Thus, the text is oriented toward the application of the theory and techniques of management science as they are currently being employed in modern organizations. Specifically, the book is designed for the introductory survey course in management science that, more and more, is becoming a requirement in undergraduate and graduate programs in business administration. This has occurred because the increased emphasis on the quantitative skills of business students has necessitated the inclusion of management science as an integral part of the business administration degree programs at most colleges and universities. In certain instances it can also be used as an introductory text for undergraduate or graduate students in economics, engineering, health administration, liberal arts, and public administration. Furthermore, the extensive topical coverage provided here will also allow it to be used in a more in-depth course in management science.

OBJECTIVES OF THE BOOK

The main objective of this edition is to provide a basic understanding of the usefulness and limitations of a wide range of management science techniques. It is likely that most readers will not become specialists in the field of management science. Instead, many of them will become managers or administrators. Thus, they will principally be users of the results of management science studies. As such, they will need the ability to:

1. Recognize problem situations in which management science could be applied.
2. Participate intelligently in the problem formulation process and in the specification of data requirements for the solution to the problem.
3. Communicate with a technical specialist (for example, the management science analyst) who would actually be responsible for modeling the problem and obtaining its solution.
4. Understand and assess the results of a management science study so that a decision with respect to the original problem can be made.

The book provides this managerially oriented group with insights on how they can utilize management science to make more effective decisions. Thus, a principal theme is to survey the major ideas and concepts of management science as they relate to decision making. Chapter 1 introduces this decision-making orientation within the framework of the scientific method. The following 15 chapters emphasize this decision-making orientation, while considering a broad range of management science techniques. Finally, Chapter 17 considers the important managerial problem of implementing the results of management science studies.

For the group of students who may decide to seek a professional career in management science, this textbook provides a comprehensive and insightful overview of management science that will motivate and prepare them for advanced study. In this second edition, we have provided an even more comprehensive review of the ideas and methods of management science that are fundamental to its practice.

This edition continues to be oriented toward providing the student with a thorough coverage of those management science techniques that are of the greatest practical significance in both the private and public sectors. It has a strong *application focus* toward the users of management science studies. It includes a great many application examples, clarifying definitions, case studies, and completely worked problems, which are couched as real-world scenarios. Also it discusses the use of various computerized management science models. At the end of the chapters are discussion questions and numerical problems that provide the student with an opportunity to gain a skill and an understanding of various management science concepts and techniques.

MAJOR CHANGES IN THE SECOND EDITION

As in the first edition, the primary focus is on problem formulation and model building, with a strong managerial emphasis. However, numerous major changes have been made as a result of my own classroom use of the book, suggestions from users of the first edition, and reviewers' comments. These changes are described below.

New Chapter on Goal Programming.   A completely new chapter on the important topic of goal programming has been added and integrated within a comprehensive treatment of mathematical programming. This new chapter provides an introduction to multiple-objective decision making within a goal programming context and includes a wide range of illustrative model formulations and solution procedures.

Addition of Glossaries of Terms.   A glossary of important terms has been added for each of the chapters. Each glossary clarifies the key terminology used in a particular chapter and provides a thorough recapitulation of important terms.

Addition of Case Studies. This textbook stresses the managerial aspects of problem formulation, model building, and interpretation of solution results. In the current edition this managerial emphasis has been enhanced by the addition of actual case studies at the end of most chapters. These case studies detail challenging and interesting management science applications and add a further dimension of realism for students. The cases are particularly useful in the classroom and help students to interrelate management science with real managerial situations.

Addition of New Problems. Approximately 200 new problems have been added, making a total of over 500 problems. Answers to all even-numbered problems are included in the back of the book.

Addition of Discussion Questions. A set of discussion questions is included at the end of each chapter. Moreover there are more than 240 discussion questions that review the key concepts of the various chapters and reinforce and challenge the student's understanding of the material.

Thorough Updating of Previous Edition. Several portions of the first edition have been rewritten or revised, as a result of classroom use, suggestions from adopters, or reviewers' comments. Some of the topics that have been clarified are degeneracy and unbounded solutions in linear programming (Chapter 4), duality theory (Chapter 5), the stepping-stone and modified distribution algorithms (Chapter 7), the transshipment problem (Chapter 7), the shortest-route problem (Chapter 8), and the branch-and-bound technique (Chapter 9). Almost all chapters received changes of some kind. The bibliographic references have also been updated. Finally, there are many more illustrative examples, figures, and tables.

New Student Workbook. A new Student Workbook accompanies the second edition, prepared by Marc Schniederjans of the University of Nebraska. It contains completely worked-out problems and study hints for the text, supplements the text discussion, and helps students to increase their learning ability.

MATHEMATICAL PREREQUISITES

The only mathematical prerequisites assumed for the text are the understanding of basic algebra and probability and statistics. The book uses algebra, probability, and statistics extensively in developing various management science techniques and models. It assumes a level of mathematical sophistication comparable to that acquired in a standard college course in finite mathematics and probability and statistics. A brief review of probability and statistics is provided in Appendix A.

A basic background in matrix algebra would be most helpful. However, since a course in matrix algebra is not commonly found in most business school curricula, a review of the "Fundamentals of Linear Algebra" is included as the second chapter in the textbook.

An introductory course in calculus would also be desirable, although such a course is not considered to be essential for an understanding and use of the book. Calculus is used only in Chapters 10, 11, 12, and 13, and is employed only to derive results that can then be applied without its further use. A brief review of differential and integral calculus is provided in Appendix B.

TOPICAL COVERAGE AND STRUCTURE OF THE BOOK

The sequencing of the 17 chapters of the textbook is indicated in the table of contents. Following Chapter 1, which involves an introduction to management science, Chapters 2 to 12, basically deal with deterministic models (i.e., models that do not involve probability considerations within their structure). Stochastic models (i.e., models that specifically treat probability considerations within their structure) are analyzed in Chapters 13–16. Chapter 17 then provides a synthesis for the textbook in terms of the implementation of management science.

Initially, we would like to indicate that while this book is organized in terms of a series of mathematical techniques, management science is more than just a set of techniques. Our feeling in this regard is that beginning students of a broad and complex area of study, such as management science, can best gain an initial understanding of it by concentrating on the formal structure of decision-making techniques rather than on the formulation and model building aspects of some particular problem. Thus, we are hopeful that students who become familiar with the basic management science techniques can then effectively apply them as they become more experienced in their working environment. However, throughout the book we do attempt to verbalize various decision-making situations to indicate how various management science techniques facilitate decision making, and to show the possible shortcomings associated with a particular method. Also, we do indicate several approaches to solving the same problem at various points in the book.

Our personal judgment has obviously been used in topical selection and the depth of treatment given to the various topics. This judgment has been guided by consulting experience gained over some 15 years in a wide variety of businesses and governmental organizations. Many of the examples and problems in the text are derived from real problems that the author has encountered. The depth of coverage and sequence of topics presented is reflective of the author's experience as to what is useful and important in a real world context. For example, we have emphasized mathematical programming in this textbook simply because it is widely and successfully used. In contrast, we have omitted material concerning game theory because we have not found it to be useful in real-world decision-making situations.

SUGGESTIONS TO STUDENTS USING THE BOOK

The major suggestion offered to students using the book is to be prepared for really getting involved with the material. Initially, you will be required to do a great deal of patient reading to gain an understanding of the text material. Furthermore, you will need to study the details of the many numerical examples that are presented and discussed. Additionally, you should devote a considerable amount of time to solving a substantial number of the problems presented at the end of the chapters. Remember that what you are studying is basically an *applied* mathematics course, and you must develop a problem solving skill to master the course. You can only develop this skill by "rolling up your sleeves and putting a pencil (with a good eraser) to paper!"

Your instructor will typically make homework assignments involving a few problems at the end of a particular chapter. You will find it instructive and useful to allow yourself several study sessions to complete such assignments. A typical problem assignment of four or five problems can be extremely tiring, and often frustrating, if you attempt to complete it the evening before it is to be collected.

Some of the problems presented at the end of the chapters are already formulated. These problems are designed for drill purposes, that is, to provide you with practice in developing computational skills for various management science techniques. Many other problems involve verbal descriptions of various decision-making situations. These problems are designed to develop your reasoning and analytical skills, as well as to provide further computational problems. Herein you may expect some ambiguity in terms of problem formulation. Although it is not possible to completely resolve this formulation ambiguity you will usually find that much of your dilemma can be eliminated if you simply state explicitly on paper the assumptions you are using, and then proceed. Remember that these formulation exercises are designed to enhance your analytical skills and by forcing you to make explicit assumptions such analytical skills can be improved.

Although the emphasis in management science—as evidenced in this book—is on quantitative techniques, the student should also strive to develop an understanding of the concepts and terminology of the field. Extensive glossaries of important terms are provided at the end of each chapter as a reference, and they should be consulted regularly. A set of discussion questions is also included at the end of each chapter. The instructor may include some discussion questions as a part of your homework assignment or, if not, you may want to review these discussion questions with your classmates in order to enhance your overall understanding of the text material.

SUGGESTIONS TO INSTRUCTORS USING THE BOOK

As noted previously, this textbook is designed primarily to be used for a one-semester course in management science. Obviously, the entire book is not meant to be covered in such a one-semester course. Rather, the broad topic coverage included in the book has been designed to give the instructor a great deal of freedom and flexibility in choosing the areas to be stressed.

In a one-semester management science course in which the students have some background in matrix algebra and probability theory, it is suggested that the following priority scheme be adopted. Within this priority framework the individual instructor can then make decisions as to the extent of coverage to be given to any particular topic.

In a typical two-quarter course the instructor might cover the introduction to management science (Chapter 1), linear programming (Chapters 3–5), goal programming (Chapter 6), and the transportation and assignment problems (Chapter 7) in the first quarter. Network models (Chapter 8), integer programming (Chapter 9), dynamic programming (Chapter 11), inventory models (Chapter 12), simulation modeling (Chapter 15), and implementation (Chapter 17) could be considered in the second quarter.

In a two-semester management science course the entire textbook would be used with sequencing generally following the order of the chapters as they are currently presented. For a one-semester course on mathematical programming models, the instructor would probably include Chapters 1 through 9, and selected material from Chapters 10 and 11.

Priority Framework—*Topics in Management Science*—One-Semester Course

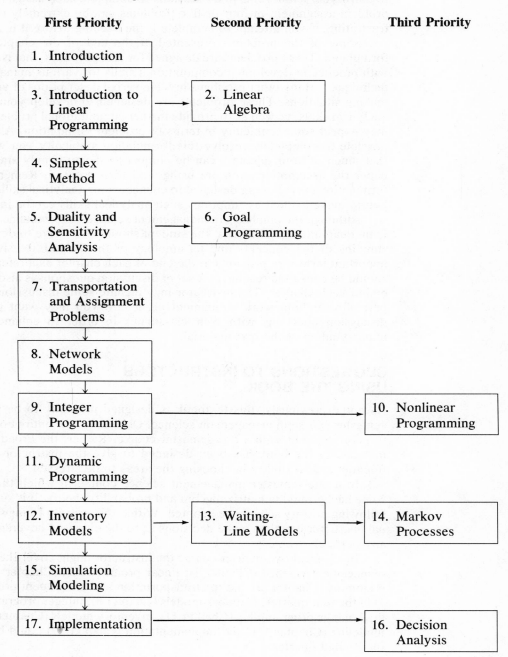

The second edition includes over 500 problems, many of which have multiple parts. These problem sets are arranged in the same order as the material is presented in the various chapters. Each problem set is divided into two major parts: computational exercises and formulation exercises. The computational exercises provide drill problems for applying computational algorithms. The formulation exercises require the student to translate a verbal problem statement into a mathematical model, and then solve this mathematical model. A typical homework assignment given to students would probably include problems of both types.

Discussion questions can also be included as a part of the homework assignment, and they afford a particularly good method for encouraging students to really think about some of the underlying concepts and theories of management science.

ACKNOWLEDGMENTS

I am deeply indebted to a number of individuals for their assistance. Academic colleagues offering valuable suggestions included James Patterson, L. Douglas Smith, Robert Nauss, Joseph Martinich, Richard Rosenthal, Sharad Chitgopekar, and Everett Adam. I particularly appreciate the many suggestions made by James Swiegart, a fellow professor at the University of South Carolina, who has used the first edition for several MBA classes. Administrative support was provided by Dean James F. Kane, and typing was done by Julia Moton. I must also thank the large number of students who used the first edition, offered helpful suggestions, and indicated where corrections or changes were needed. A current student, Shawnee Vickery, provided tremendous assistance with this edition by developing and solving new problems, structuring case studies, and performing numerous editorial duties. I am also grateful for the editorial assistance of Nina R. Lewis, my editor at Wiley and for the many suggestions made by the reviewers: Ed Wasil (University of Maryland), Richard Discenza (Northern Arizona University), Billy M. Thornton (Colorado State University), Philip R. Swenson (Utah State University), and Marc Schniederjans (University of Nebraska).

Finally, I deeply appreciate the continuing support of my wife, Mylla, and of my two boys, Kevin and Keith.

Robert E. Markland

ABOUT THE AUTHOR

Robert E. Markland is the Academic Program Director for Management Science, and a Professor of Management Science, in the College of Business Administration at the University of South Carolina. Previously, he was Associate Dean, Director of Graduate Studies, and Professor of Management Science, at the University of Missouri—St. Louis, where he taught for eight years. He has also taught at Arizona State University and Washington University. Dr. Markland has developed and taught undergraduate and graduate courses in management science, production and operations management, simulation modeling, computer programming, and statistics during his thirteen-year career.

Professor Markland is a native of St. Louis, Missouri, where he earned his D.B.A. in management science from Washington University, while a Ford Foundation Doctoral Fellow. An active member of the American Institute of Decision Sciences, the Institute of Management Sciences, and the Operations Research Society of America, he has held a number of offices in these organizations, and is a reviewer for their journals. He is also a member of Beta Gamma Sigma, Alpha Iota Delta, and Chi Epsilon honor societies. A frequent contributor to professional and academic journals, he has also been a Research Fellow in the Center of Community and Metropolitan Studies at the University of Missouri—St. Louis, has directed several research grants, and has been the recipient of an AMOCO Foundation Excellence in Teaching Award.

Much of the material presented in *Topics in Management Science* evolved from Dr. Markland's research and consulting activities. He has worked with modelers and decision makers in food processing, communications, automotive manufacturing, computer services, consulting, banking, police, and state and local government organizations. In particular, Professor Markland has worked extensively with Ralston Purina Company on a series of production–distribution problems, a number of simulation models, and various financial decision-making problems. From these real-world consulting activities many of the concepts, problems, and cases for this textbook were developed.

Contents

I INTRODUCTION

Chapter 1 An Introduction to Management Science

II DETERMINISTIC MODELS

Chapter 2 Fundamentals of Linear Algebra

Chapter 3 An Introduction to Linear Programming

Chapter 10   Nonlinear Programming

Chapter 11   Dynamic Programming

III STOCHASTIC MODELS

Chapter 13 Waiting-Line Models

Chapter 14 Markov Processes

IV   SYNTHESIS

Chapter 17   Implementation of Management Science

Introduction

An Introduction to Management Science

1.1 THE ORIGINS AND DEVELOPMENT OF MANAGEMENT SCIENCE

Management science is concerned with the application of the scientific method to decision making in business, industrial, governmental, and military organizations. It encompasses a methodology and a set of techniques derived from the physical sciences and mathematics with an objective of improving the quality of managerial decisions. Improved decisions by executives are crucial to the survival of the firm in our competitive economic environment. Such decisions concern the acquisition and utilization of the basic factors of production: human beings, materials, machines, and capital. As such decisions are made, the firm's market position either improves or worsens, and the value of the executive to the firm is judged accordingly. Consequently, the modern manager must have a basic understanding of the central ideas, techniques, accomplishments, and limits of management science.

The practice of management science is based on the application of the **scientific method** to the study of managerial problems. The foundations of the scientific method can be found in the writings of Aristotle and Plato, who fostered the idea that the methods used in mathematical reasoning—that is, that all propositions that are not self-evident should be derived from others that are self-evident—should be extended to all branches of inquiry. The scientific method was perhaps structured first by Sir Francis Bacon, who in 1620 set forth its basic principles in the *Novum Organum*. According to Bacon, the scientific method was built around four major elements:

1. Observation and description of form.
2. Hypothesis and model building.

3.   Hypothesis testing and analysis.
4.   Model modification and refinement.

Bacon's principles were widely debated, and to some extent, refined by other scientific philosophers, such as Hume and Mill. Additionally, they were widely used by pure scientists and researchers during the ensuing two centuries. At the same time, the Industrial Revolution was giving birth to the large-scale, functionally oriented enterprise that was not capable of being managed by a single individual. During the Industrial Revolution there were several notable applications of the scientific method. Foremost among these were the work of Eli Whitney concerning mass production in the cotton industry and the classic book by Charles Babbage, *On The Economy of Machinery and Manufactures*, which dealt with the systematic choice between alternatives and comparative cost analyses.

In the early 1900s Frederick W. Taylor provided a major impetus to the use of science in management through his classic book, *The Principles of Scientific Management*, which described studies of work capacities. Taylor also had a number of followers who expanded the use of his techniques within modern industrial organizations. Among the more noteworthy of these early "management scientists" were Henry L. Gantt, Harrington Emerson, and Frank and Lillian Gilbreth. Gantt is best known for his work in production scheduling, Emerson achieved significant results in cost reduction in the railroad industry, and the Gilbreths are recognized as the founders of the principles of motion study and additionally were the first to use motion pictures to analyze industrial operations.

By 1912, George Babcock had formulated some basic principles for establishing the economical size of a production lot of parts. In 1915, his work was expanded into a prototype inventory model by F. W. Harris of the Westinghouse Company. During World War I, Thomas Edison studied antisubmarine warfare; his work included compiling statistics for determining the best methods for evading and for destroying submarines, and analyzing the value of zigzagging as a method for protecting merchant shipping. Another important contributor to the application of scientific principles to management was the Danish engineer, A. K. Erlang, who performed experiments concerning the fluctuations of demand for telephone facilities upon automatic dialing equipment.

Other major achievements continued this early work. T. C. Fry applied probability theory to engineering problems; Walter Shewart pioneered the methods of statistical quality control; L.H.C. Tippett proposed a method for measuring delays in textile operations based on probability theory; and Horace C. Levison applied relatively sophisticated mathematical models to complex consumer behavior data.

During World War II the scientist entered the environment of military decision making. The first notable use of scientific research in military operations occurred in Great Britain, under the direction of the distinguished physicist P.M.S. Blackett.[1] This type of scientific activity was called "operational research" in England, since it was primarily concerned with problems associated with the operational use of radar. By 1942 the same type of scientific activity had been introduced within the United States military environment. In the U.S. Air Force, it became known as "operational analysis" and in the U.S. Army and Navy it was called "operations research and operations evaluation." Thus, during

---

[1] J. G. Crowder, and R. Widdington, *Science at War* (London: Her Majesty's Stationery Office, 1947).

World War II, numerous interdisciplinary study teams of mathematicians and scientists were formed to assist in the analysis of military operations. Notable achievements were made in determining how to protect a convoy, how to organize radar defenses, and how to most effectively drop bombs to destroy submarines.

Following World War II, industrial operations research groups were formed in both England and the United States, as an attempt was made to transfer the newly developed, and successfully applied, techniques of military operations research to the industrial decision-making environment. During this same time, a general industrial expansion was occurring, and decision making in many organizations was increasing in complexity. In England, in particular, new types of management problems, caused by the nationalization of industry and the wartime destruction of industrial facilities, were approached using operations research techniques.

At least three other major factors can be identified as providing strong impetus to the growth of the field of operations research during the post-World War II time period. First, the growth, product diversity, technological developments, and competitive and social pressures of the postwar industrial environment all served to enhance the need for precision in decision making and implementation. A second important factor was the growth and widespread interest in basic research in the field. This lead to rapid and important advances in the state of the art following World War II. A prime example of this type of advancement was the development of the simplex method for the solution of linear programming problems, as accomplished by George Dantzig in 1947. A third factor that provided a great thrust to the field was the development of the high-speed digital computer in this same time period. This development enabled the very complex problems that often resulted from operations research studies to be solved.

Operations research as a field of study also found its way into university curricula. In 1948, the Massachusetts Institute of Technology established a course in the nonmilitary applications of operations research. In the spring of 1952, Columbia University presented its first course in operations research, and similar courses were also developed by the Case Institute of Technology and Johns Hopkins University.[2] Several professional societies, composed of individuals actively working in the field, soon were formed. Rapid proliferation of knowledge concerning the field also occurred, through numerous books, and journals, such as *Operations Research, Operational Research Quarterly, Naval Research Logistics Quarterly,* and *Management Science.*

1.2 WHAT IS MANAGEMENT SCIENCE OR OPERATIONS RESEARCH?

From the foregoing discussion of the origins and development of operations research a general understanding of its nature may have been gained. However, let us now attempt to further our understanding of the field of study, which is the concern of this book. As we begin let us immediately acknowledge that several terms are often used as synonyms to describe this type of work. Principal among these are operations research, or operational research in England, and manage-

---

[2] Florence N. Trefethen, "A History of Operations Research," in *Operations Research for Management,* vol. 1, eds., Joseph F. McCloskey and Florence N. Trefethen (Baltimore: The Johns Hopkins Press, 1954), pp. 3–35.

ment science. Other less common terms sometimes used to describe the same general approach to management decision making include: systems analysis, systems engineering, managerial analysis, operations analysis, and planning research. Thus, the reader should be aware of minor semantic differences as we begin the development of an understanding of the field.

Several good definitions of **operations research** have been suggested, and provide valuable insights concerning its basic nature. Among these useful definitions are the following:

> Operations research is the application of scientific methods, techniques, and tools to problems involving the operation of a system so as to provide those in control of the system with optimum solutions to the problems (Churchman, Ackoff, and Arnoff 1957, p. 18).

Operations research (OR) can be considered as being:

1. The application of scientific method
2. by interdisciplinary teams
3. to problems involving the control of organized (man-machine) systems so as to provide solutions which best serve the purpose of the organization as a whole (Ackoff and Sasieni 1968, p. 6).

> The term operations research today refers to the application of scientific methodology of several different disciplines to problems related to the functioning or operating of some unit . . . business, governmental, or institutional (Levin and Kirkpatrick 1975, p. 13).

> Operations research may be described as a scientific approach to decision making that involves the operations of organizational systems (Hillier and Lieberman 1980, p. 3).

From a managerial viewpoint, the key element of these definitions is the application of the *scientific method* and its techniques and tools to the *study of systems*, with a focus on *decision making*, often directed to finding an *optimal solution* or *best course of action*, that is, to maximize or minimize some set of well-defined objectives. The methodology employed consists primarily of defining the system under consideration, constructing a mathematical model of the system, and manipulating the variables of the model to obtain an optimal solution to the problem of interest. Thus, the major focus of operations research is toward scientific problem solving involving total systems. However, operations research has become more than just a scientific approach to solving complex problems. It is also more than just a collection of mathematical and statistical techniques. Essentially, operations research is a philosophy of quantification that rests upon the ability to identify and quantify the pertinent variables and to discover the interrelationships that exist among these variables in a particular system or subsystem. It is an attempt to understand and to be able to manipulate industrial phenomena so as to select the optimum course of action from those available to the decision maker and to develop new course of action so as to further the objective of the organization. This broader definition has led many to refer to the application of the scientific method to the mathematical analysis of business problems as **management science** rather than the more esoteric title of **operations research**. Indeed, the term ''management science'' is suggestive of a philosophy built on the need for a more rigorous analysis of the complicated problems of management. In addition, the term ''operations research'' is suggestive of research concerning operational problems, which would tend to be of a short-run nature. In reality, much of the practical work that has been done in this area deals with strategic problems, or problems of a more long-run nature. The possible distinction between operations research and management science has been noted by Schellenberger (1969, pp. 29–30), who states:

> If management science has any distinguishable features from operations research, it is its concern with policy level decisions. Management science tends to focus more heavily than operations research on human and man-machine situations. Management science tends to be more cognitive of market or demand conditions. Management science relies heavily on the same kind of analytical tools as operations research, but it is also cognitive of analytical tools oriented toward psychological and economic analysis.

In spite of the possible distinction between operations research and management science, most practitioners, researchers, and writers in the field use the terms synonymously. Consequently, although personal preference is that of the broader term management science, we will use the terms interchangeably throughout this textbook.

In summary, the practice of management science can be characterized as follows:

1. The analysis should utilize the principles of the scientific method.
2. The analysis should consider the goals and objectives of the organization in which the study is being made.
3. The analysis should recognize the relationships between the significant variables of the system being analyzed.
4. The analysis should be oriented toward achieving optimality for the system.
5. The results of the analysis should be reproducible and verifiable.
6. Where possible, a team approach should be utilized in making the analysis.
7. The analysis will often utilize a digital computer to manipulate data, perform computations, and deal with the complexity of the problem.

1.3 THE METHODOLOGY OF MANAGEMENT SCIENCE

The methodological process of management science is based on the previously discussed scientific method. The foundation of the scientific method is the belief that natural phenomena do have a cause, and that by rigorous analysis this causal mechanism can be identified. Prior to making a management science study, the analyst must recognize that, although identification of this causal mechanism in a perfect sense is likely to be unattainable, it must be described in sufficiently accurate terms; and the management scientist must be prepared to repeat the steps of the scientific method until a satisfactory solution is obtained.

The methodological process of management science is depicted pictorially in Fig. 1.1. It thus proceeds according to the following steps:

1. *Analysis of the System and Problem Formulation.* The analysis begins by detailed observation of a real world system, and from this observation a

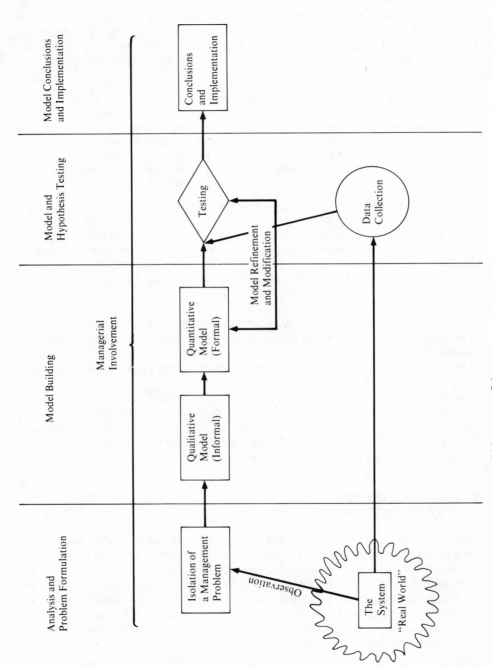

FIGURE 1.1 The Methodological Process of Management Science

specific management problem is isolated. Additionally, the analyst attempts to specify the objectives of the study in a rigorous manner. This requires an examination of the characteristics of the system being studied. Major parameters and variables of the system are identified, and the extent to which they are subject to control is determined. Often, analysis of the system will be accompanied by an overall feasibility study, in which questions are asked concerning:

(a) *Technical Feasibility.* Do management science techniques exist that are capable of solving the problem?

(b) *Economic Feasibility.* Is solution of the problem possible with the given level of economic inputs?

(c) *Operational Feasibility.* Can the solution procedure be made operationally viable on a continuing basis?

Such a feasibility study is designed to appraise the difficulty of the study, measure its probable costs, and determine its probability of success. The usual result of an affirmative answer to the feasibility question is a detailed research plan that sets forth the various phases of the work that will be done in the study.

2. *Model Building.* Based on the previous analysis of the system and problem formulation, the second phase of the study concerns model building. Initially, model building may be qualitative in nature, involving a rather informal descriptive approach. From this informal **qualitative model**, a formal **quantitative model** is developed. This quantitative model must mathematically depict the real system so that the model, rather than the physical system, can be manipulated. In addition, a typical management science model must express the effectiveness of the system under study as a function of a set of variables at least one of which is subject to control.

A typical quantitative model contains the following elements:

(a) A set of **decision variables.** The decision variables are the unknowns that are to be determined by solving the model. A specific decision is made when decision variables take on specific values.

(b) The **objective function.** The objective function changes value as a result of changes in the values of the decision variables. The objective function measures the desirability of the consequences of a decision.

(c) A set of **constraints.** The constraints may be in the form of equations, or they may be a set of inequalities. Usually, the constraints restrict the range of the decision variables as a result of technological, economic, or physical constraints on the system.

(d) A set of **parameters.** The parameters are the known values, or constants, of the model that relate the decision variables to the constraints and objective function of the model.

Model structuring will also generally require some type of computer formulation. Most meaningful management science modeling efforts are of a scope and complexity that requires computerization for testing and solution. Computer formulation is typically done in BASIC, FORTRAN, or PL-1 because of the mathematical and scientific nature of most management science models. Although this textbook does not stress the computer-programming aspects of management science modeling, it should be obvious that a computer-programming capability is important for a management science practitioner.

3. *Model and Hypothesis Testing.*   After model building has been completed, its structure must be verified experimentally. Actual experimentation must necessarily be preceded by data collection. Experimentation is usually of two types. The first type of experimentation simply involves manipulating the model in a fashion that produces a relevant set of information. From this set of information various model refinements and modifications may be suggested. These modifications can then lead to further experimentation in a feedback looping manner. At some point in time, the analyst must exercise judgment as to the modeling effort's validity. Then a second type of experimentation is done, in which a solution is derived for the model. Commonly, we say that an ''optimal'' solution is derived for the model. Indeed, much of the remainder of this book is devoted to the study of techniques designed to obtain optimal solutions for certain kinds of problems. It should be emphasized, however, that such solutions are optimal only with respect to the type of model being employed. All models are necessarily abstractions of the real world, and thus the optimal solution with respect to the model may not be the optimal solution for the real world problem. However, if the model is well-formulated, and if experimentation and model refinement are done prior to the determination of the optimal solution, it is reasonable to expect that the resulting solution will be a good approximation for the real world problem.

The solution to the model typically will employ an **algorithm**. An algorithm is a set of procedures or rules that is followed in a step-by-step, or iterative, manner that provides, or converges to, the best solution for a given model. It is important to note that a particular algorithm has a specific set of rules that apply only to a specific problem. Thus, there are a large number of algorithms in existence in management science, and many more are being developed currently. Since an algorithm is iterative in nature and converges to a solution, it will quite often be useful to program the algorithm on a digital computer. In this manner, the digital computer can be used to perform the calculations within the iterative process.

4. *Model Conclusions and Implementation.*   The final phase of a management science study involves drawing conclusions from the solution of the model and then implementing these conclusions. This phase is critical to any management science study, since the benefits of the study are realized only if this phase is successfully accomplished. Implementation itself involves several steps. First, the solution to the model and the conclusions drawn from this solution must be presented to operating management in a clear and logical manner. This step represents a detailing of the *technical* aspects of the model. Next, the management science analyst works with operating management to develop the procedures necessary to insure that the solution and conclusions are used on a continuing basis. This step focuses on the *operating* aspects of the model. Finally, the management science analyst should seek to develop mechanisms by which changes to the model can be made if future use of the model indicates that such changes should be made. Implementation of management science, an important and complex subject, will be treated in a more detailed manner in the final chapter of this book.

Throughout the methodological process of management science there should be involvement with operating management. Thus, in the analysis and problem formulation phase, the analyst should seek the advice and assistance of the operating manager in order that the manager's real problem is considered. Likewise, the model-building phase should involve a continuing dialogue between the analyst and the manager, so that the model that is constructed becomes a realistic and accurate representation of the real-world problem. During model and hypothesis testing, the manager will be asked to verify or validate the results produced by the model, and to suggest model refinements and modifications where necessary. Finally, in the conclusion and implementation phase the operating manager actually has to make decisions using the results of the study, and may need to provide a mechanism for continued use of the results of the study. In summary, managerial involvement and interest is essential to the success of the application of the methodology of management science.

1.4 MODEL FORMULATION IN MANAGEMENT SCIENCE

As you study this text remember that you should be concentrating on the formulation, analysis, and solution of models. One of the most important tasks of the manager, in either the private or public sector, is problem solving. The management science approach to problem solving is through model building. Proficiency in model formulation and analysis is probably the most important aspect of the modeling process. Thus, we will focus our attention on model formulation, using small-scale problems and case studies of real-world management problems. In many instances we will observe that the solution of the model, in practice, is obtained using the digital computer.

Model formulation is at the heart of management science. Formulation of a model allows the analyst to consider the complexities and uncertainties of a decision-making situation, and it requires that a logical structure be developed in order for the formal analysis and solution of the model to proceed.

Model building is certainly nothing that is really new. A model is nothing more than an abstraction or representation of a real-life system. Most of us, in our earlier days, had some sort of experience with **iconic models**, which are physical representations of real systems, to scale. For example, a toy automobile or a toy doll is an iconic model. Perhaps some readers have studied civil, chemical, or electrical engineering and have employed **analog models**. An analog model utilizes one physical property to represent another physical property. For example, the author, in his undergraduate studies, used an electrical network as an analog model of fluid flows. Finally, virtually all of us have been exposed to a **symbolic** or **mathematical model** in which we have used a set of mathematical symbols and functional relationships to represent some physical situation. For example, the translation of a verbal description of a problem situation into a set of linear equations is a very common undertaking in high school algebra. In management science, the models we employ are virtually always of a mathematical nature. As such, they should be our best approximation of the real-world problem situation.

In the practice of management science four major types of mathematical models are employed. The first is a **descriptive model**, in which the modeler attempts to represent some particular physical situation but does not indicate any preferred course of action. The **waiting-line model** described in Section 1.5 of this chapter is a descriptive model, in that the modeler determines certain output characteristics of the waiting line, given certain input characteristics. Another very important type of descriptive model that is utilized heavily in management science work is the **simulation model**, which generally is a mathematical model that is programmed for a computer and then used to replicate the behavior of the real-world system using the computer. Statistics describing the performance of the simulated system are accumulated as the simulation model is run on the computer, often using varying input conditions. The modeler then decides upon a course of action by examining the descriptive statistics that are generated. It is important to note that the results obtained from a simulation model are inferential in nature, and not general, such as would be obtained from other mathematical models.

The second major type of mathematical model that is employed is the **normative** or **optimization model**. The normative model is prescriptive in nature, in that it prescribes the course of action that the decision maker should select to achieve some defined objective. Most mathematical models employed in management science are normative in nature, and thus have an objective function that is optimized (maximized or minimized) subject to constraints that utilize decision variables (i.e., the unknowns of the model) and parameters. The major characteristc of the normative model is that it allows the modeler to determine the best course of action. We will concentrate our work in this book on the study of a series of normative management science models.

A third type of mathematical model that is commonly employed in management science work is the **heuristic model**. Heuristic models are basically models that employ intuitive rules or ''rules of thumb'' in the hope of generating ''good'' solutions. This is in contrast to optimization models that seek to generate the best solution. An example of a heuristic model might be an inventory model that simply states: ''Carry an inventory equal to $1/52$ of the average yearly demand for the last three years.'' Obviously, the modeler can think of a myriad of intuitive rules that might be applied to a problem situation. Thus, there are virtually an unlimited number of heuristic models that could be derived. We will not focus our attention on heuristic models in this text; however, they will be illustrated at several places in future chapters.

A fourth type of mathematical model that is commonly employed in management science is the **predictive model**, which typically is used to make a forecast of the future. A time series forecasting model, or a linear regression model that forecasts future sales as a function of several variables are examples of predictive models. Predictive models will not be addressed in this text to any great extent, since they are typically studied in the statistics course that should be taken prior to a course in management science.

1.4.1   Model Subclassifications in Management Science

Several types of model subclassifications are often employed in describing management science models. One common subclassification is the **deterministic model** versus the **stochastic model**. In a deterministic model the functional relationships and parameters of the model are known with certainty. The linear programming model to be discussed in Section 1.5 is a good example of a deterministic model, because the coefficients of its objective function and constraint set, and the physical limitations on the system are all assumed to be known with certainty. If, instead, we were uncertain as to the profits associated with the two products being produced in this situation, we would then have to use a stochastic model that would incorporate this uncertainty in terms of a specified probability of achieving a certain profitability for each product. The models we will discuss in Chapters 3 to 11 will basically be deterministic in nature while those discussed in Chapters 12 to 16 will basically be stochastic in nature.

A second common type of model subclassification used in management science is the **linear** versus the **nonlinear model**. A linear model is one in which all of the functional relationships between the variables in the model are expressed in linear terms. Obviously, a linear programming model is an example of a linear model in that its objective function and constraint function are all linear relationships. A nonlinear model utilizes one or more curvilinear or nonproportional functional relationships. In these nonlinear functional relationships the variables may be raised to a power other than one, or they may be expressed as the product of two or more variables. The solution processes required to solve nonlinear models are much more complex than those required for linear models. In this text we will emphasize the use of linear models in managerial decisions, but various kinds of nonlinear models are considered in detail in Chapters 9 to 11.

A third subclassification of models employed in management science is the **static** versus the **dynamic model**. A static model is defined at a particular point in time and encompasses a particular time period. For example, we may want to develop and solve an inventory model to determine the order quantity to purchase for the forthcoming month, with this decision being made on the last working day of the current month. In this modeling process we normally will assume that the demand conditions are static, that is, the demand expected next month is the same as the demand experienced in the current month. A dynamic model differs from a static model in the sense that the modeler examines a multiple time period horizon in order to select the optimal course of action. Thus, a sequence of interrelated decisions are made that encompass several time periods. Dynamic programming, in particular, considers the characteristics and solution processes for such dynamic models.

1.5 EXAMPLES OF MANAGEMENT SCIENCE PROBLEMS IN MINIATURE

Before we attempt to classify the problem areas that have been investigated using management science, let us consider three highly simplified illustrations of how management science models are constructed to represent specific problem situations. In each of these examples we will simply sketch out the model formulation without attempting to obtain a solution.

EXAMPLE 1   *A Production-Planning Problem.*   The Ace Screwdriver Company manufactures two products, 6-in. and 12-in. screwdrivers. Currently, it has organized its production effort to produce a batch of a *single* type of screwdriver in alternating weeks. Each type of screwdriver requires processing on three machines. A young management scientist recently hired by the company has suggested that it may be more profitable, and more efficient in terms of machine utilization, to produce some of *both* types of screwdrivers during each week.

As the first step in considering this production-planning problem, the operating management of the company, working in team fashion with the management scientist has investigated the technical, operational, and economic feasibility of altering its current production process. This team has concluded that it may indeed be desirable to attempt to devise a more efficient and more economical production process.

As the second step of the management science study, an attempt is made to construct a mathematical model of the system. First, a set of decision variables is specified. Thus, let:

Decision variables
$$x_1 = \text{the (unknown) number of production lots (i.e., 1000 units) of 6-in. screwdrivers to be manufactured in a week.}$$

$$x_2 = \text{the (unknown) number of production lots (i.e., 1000 units) of 12-in. screwdrivers to be manufactured in a week.}$$

(1-1)

Next, attention is focused on the construction of an objective function. The decision is made to attempt to maximize the total marginal profit resulting from production of these two products. As a result of an accounting analysis, the net profit for a production lot (i.e., 1000 units) of 6-in. screwdrivers is found to be \$20, while the net profit for a production lot of 12-in. screwdrivers is \$50. Thus, the model's objective function can be expressed as:

Objective function parameters

Objective function { Maximize (total net profit) $P = \$20\,(x_1) + \$50\,(x_2)$ (1-2)

The next consideration is that of defining a set of constraints that restrict the ranges of the decision variables as a result of the physical limitations of the production system. To accomplish this objective, the basic time data for the production process are tabulated, as shown:

Machine	Hours Required to Produce One Lot		Capacity Machine (Hours)
	Product 1	Product 2	
1	1	2	35
2	2	1	40
3	1	3	37

From this tabular data, the following set of constraint inequalities can be constructed:

Constraint set parameters

Constraints
Machine 1: $1x_1 + 2x_2 \le 35$

Machine 2: $2x_1 + 1x_2 \le 40$ (1-3)

Machine 3: $1x_1 + 3x_2 \le 37$

Note that this constraint set describes the manner in which each of the three machine resources are linearly combined to produce the two products. The entire mathematical model of the production system can then be rewritten as:

$$\text{Maximize (total net profit) } P = 20x_1 + 50x_2$$

$$\text{subject to:} \quad \begin{aligned} 1x_1 + 2x_2 &\leq 35 \\ 2x_1 + 1x_2 &\leq 40 \\ 1x_1 + 3x_2 &\leq 37 \end{aligned} \qquad (1\text{--}4)$$

$$\text{with} \quad x_1 \geq 0, x_2 \geq 0$$

Note that, both $x_1 \geq 0$ and $x_2 \geq 0$, since negative production has no meaning in this problem. This mathematical model is a **linear programming** representation of the production-planning problem.

The remaining steps required for concluding the management science study will not be discussed further here, as our main concern has been in developing a mathematical representation (model) of the problem situation. For this problem, the values of x_1 and x_2 that produce the largest value of the objective function could be determined very easily by simple graphical methods. Implementation of these results would then simply require the adoption of a production plan using the solution values for x_1 and x_2. It should also be apparent that it would not be desirable to make all of one product in alternate weeks, and that the optimal solution would result in the production of some of each of the two products during each week.

EXAMPLE 2   *An Inventory Control Problem.*   Ms. Karen Silverton is the owner and manager of a candle shop in Sausalito, California. She has been experiencing difficulty in maintaining an adequate supply of plain white (12-in.) candles. She would like to apply a management science approach to the problem of determining how many white (12-in.) candles to order so that lost sales are avoided. She has concluded that it is technically, economically, and operationally feasible to replenish inventory on a more scientific basis.

Ms. Silverton has decided to denote the unknown order quantity as Q. Her analysis of the problem further indicates that she sells 300 white (12-in.) candles per month, and that this sales rate is constant. The inventory situation can be pictured as shown in Fig. 1.2.

In proceeding to attempt to quantify this situation, Ms. Silverton concludes that she should try to choose Q in a fashion that achieves a balance between the

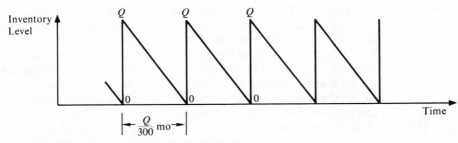

FIGURE 1.2   Inventory Level—Candle Example

inventory holding cost and the cost of making a replenishment order of size Q. Denoting the replenishment ordering cost as K and the inventory holding cost by h, and the per-item purchasing cost as c, the average cost per month can be expressed as:

Average cost per month = replenishment ordering cost
+ purchasing cost + inventory holding cost

$$= K \left(\frac{300}{Q}\right) + c(300) + h \left(\frac{Q}{2}\right) \qquad (1-5)$$

The contribution that is due to replenishment ordering is $K(300/Q)$, since there will be $(300/Q)$ orders per month. The contribution due to purchasing costs is $c(300)$, since 300 candles are sold each month. Finally, the contribution that is due to inventory holding costs is $h(Q/2)$, since $Q/2$ is the average inventory level, as can be seen in Fig. 1.2.

The mathematical model for this inventory control problem can be stated in terms of finding a value of Q that minimizes the average cost per month, as given by Equation 1–5. This value of Q can be determined by differential calculus by setting the derivative of the average cost per month with respect to Q equal to 0, and solving for Q. This model is known as the **economic lot size** for inventory control under a constant demand rate, with an instantaneous replenishment, and no ''out of stock'' allowed. We will not discuss the actual solution of the model at this point, but it will be considered further in a later chapter.

EXAMPLE 3   *A Waiting-Line Problem.*   Mr. Bill Pitcor is the manager of the reservation office of the Memorial Arena, a large multipurpose auditorium and sports arena in suburban Kansas City. He currently employs two reservation clerks. Each reservation clerk answers phone calls and takes incoming ticket reservations from two phone lines.

Mr. Pitcor has observed the reservation process during the course of several days. His survey indicates that incoming phone calls are made at the rate of three calls per minute, and that an average call will require 1 minute of the clerk's time for making the reservation. He is concerned that potential customers will encounter busy phone lines, become discouraged, and potential business may be lost. He estimates that about one-half the callers that encounter a busy line will be ultimately lost as customers, and he feels that each lost customer represents a $1 loss in profits. However, he has also determined that the hiring of an additional reservation clerk, and the installation and servicing of two additional phone lines will require an additional yearly expenditure of $7500.

The mathematical model required for this situation would attempt to balance the cost associated with the customer's inability to reach an open phone against the cost associated with that of the additional reservation clerk and phone equipment. Determination of the probabilities of having customers unable to reach an open phone line, for both the present system (two clerks) and the proposed system (three clerks), would use a **queueing** or **waiting-line** model. These probabilities would then be used to determine the losses, or savings, attributable to the present and proposed reservation systems. Again, we will not attempt to perform such an analysis here, but will consider waiting lines in detail in a future chapter.

1.6 PROBLEM-SOLVING MODELS IN MANAGEMENT SCIENCE

There is no unique set of problems that can be attacked using management science. There are, however, several broad classifications of types of problems that are encountered under many circumstances or across several industries. Thus, various management science models, or techniques, can be grouped into several basic classes. It should be recognized that any of these basic problem-solving models may have a number of variations. Additionally, the development of a specific management science model will often require the use of material from probability theory, statistics, applied mathematics, engineering, and the physical sciences.

This textbook will be structured around a series of management science models, or techniques. At this point we will provide an introductory, verbal description of these management science models. Their mathematical structure will be discussed in subsequent chapters. The problem-solving management science models, or techniques, to be studied in this textbook can be classified as follows:

1. **Mathematical Programming Models.** Allocation problems arise when there are alternative ways of accomplishing objectives or when resources or facilities are not available for accomplishing each objective in the most effective manner. The allocation problem then becomes one of combining resources and activities in a manner that optimizes overall effectiveness. Most of the techniques used to solve allocation problems are of a type known as **mathematical programming**. A **linear programming model** is applicable when the objective function, such as profit, cost, or quantities of goods, can be expressed as a linear function, and the restrictions on resources (constraints) can be expressed as a system of linear equalities, or inequalities. If any of the constraints, or the objective function, are nonlinear, a **nonlinear programming model** is required. In other instances the solution values, or decision variables, for the problem may be restricted to being integer values. This restriction necessitates the use of an **integer programming model**. Another useful type of allocation model involves the assignment of a certain number of activities to an equal number of resources. Such a model is called simply an **assignment model**. This allocation problem type becomes more complex if the activities require more than one resource and if the resources can be used for more than one activity. The allocation model applied to such problems is called the **transportation model**. Finally, an allocation model may be structured in a manner that allows consideration of multiple goals within its objective function. This type of allocation model is called a **goal programming model**.

2. **Network Models.** Network models are closely related to allocation models. They have proven to be particularly useful in the analysis of transportation and logistics systems, research and development projects, and information theory. One basic problem that is encountered in network analysis involves finding the **shortest route** through a network. A similar network problem is that of choosing a set of connections that provides a route between any two points of a network in a way to minimize the total length of these connections. This type of network model is called a **minimum spanning tree model**. A third basic problem in network analysis involves allocating flows within a network,

from a source to a destination, in a manner that maximizes the total flow for the network. This type of network model is termed a **maximal-flow model**. Project planning and control is a fourth problem area that has been successfully analyzed using network techniques, especially **PERT** (Program Evaluation and Review Technique) and **CPM** (Critical Path Method).

3. **Dynamic Programming Models.**   Dynamic programming is a direct outgrowth of mathematical programming, and is particularly useful for problem situations having a structure involving a sequence of interrelated decisions. Dynamic programming models are very valuable for analyzing decision processes that extend over a number of time periods or events.

4. **Inventory Models.**   Inventory problems involve two decisions: how much to order at a point in time, and at what point in time to place an order. Inventory models thus require the balancing of inventory carrying costs against one or more of the following: order or run set-up costs, shortage or delay costs, and costs associated with changing the level of production or purchasing.

5. **Waiting-Line Models.**   Waiting-line, or queueing, models are concerned with situations in which random arrivals are occurring at a servicing or processing facility of limited capacity. Thus, a product or customer requiring service is waiting for this service, or a service facility capable of providing the service is idle. The objective of waiting-line models is to determine the optimum number of personnel or facilities necessary to service customers or products that arrive at some random rate, while balancing the cost of service and the cost of waiting.

6. **Markovian Decision Models.**   Markovian decision models are applicable to problems involving the analysis of the current movement of some variable in an attempt to predict the future movement of that same variable. Markovian analysis has recently become very important in marketing research as a tool for examining and forecasting the behavior of customers from the standpoint of their loyalty to one brand and their switching patterns to other brands.

7. **Decision Analysis Models.**   Decision analysis models are broadly applied to problems involving decision making under uncertainty. The main elements found in decision analysis models include:

   (a)   A set of alternative courses of action.
   (b)   A set of different possible consequences associated with each course of action.
   (c)   A measurement of the degree of uncertainty associated with each possible consequence associated with each course of action.
   (d)   A decision criterion to be used in choosing a single course of action.

Decision analysis models focus on the optimal selection of a course of action, given the possible consequences and their associated probability of occurrence.

8. **Simulation Models.**   Simulation models are used to evaluate the merits of alternative courses of action by experimenting with a mathematical model that is a representation of the real-world problem situation. The mathematical model is designed to indicate the functional relationships between the decision variables. Repeated simulation experiments provide an indication of the consequences of adopting alternative courses of action with respect to the decision variables. Simulation models are thus experimental in nature, as

distinguished from the previously discussed models, which are analytical in structure.

1.7 SURVEYS OF MANAGEMENT SCIENCE ACTIVITIES AND APPLICATIONS

Management science has been applied in virtually every type of military, governmental, business, and industrial organization. Primarily utilized within military organizations in its early days, it has more recently been used extensively in the petroleum, paper, chemical, metal processing, brewing, food manufacturing, aircraft, rubber, transportation and distribution, mining, and textile industries. Financial- and corporate-planning uses of management science have also become important.

Since its inception, numerous researchers and scholars have conducted surveys concerning its usage. In 1965 Schumacher and Smith[3] reported findings from a survey of operations research activities as determined from a mail questionnaire sent to 168 companies in *Fortune* magazine's top 500. This study indicated heavy usage of operations research in production scheduling, inventory control, and forecasting.

Prasad,[4] in 1966, reported the results of a content analysis of 354 articles that were published in the journal *Management Science* during the period January 1955 through September 1964. The greatest frequency of application for these articles was seen to be in the production functional area.

A large-scale field study was conducted by Radnor, Rubenstein, and Bean[5] during the mid-1960s within 66 major U.S. corporations. Their findings indicated that management science activities began in the early 1950s in research and development, engineering, manufacturing, and financial areas of most corporations. Then, their findings suggested that there was a contraction of management science activities in all functional areas except finance and corporate planning during the 1960s. As Radnor, Rubenstein, and Bean indicate this is probably not surprising since the finance function usually has control of the important data sources that are required by the management science function. Also, in many corporations the location of the computer operation in the controller's area has given impetus to the development of management science.

An interesting survey of the uses of management science was made by Turban,[6] and involved 107 of the largest corporations in the United States. Turban traced the activities of management science groups over time and concluded that more sophisticated and difficult problems had been considered as management science became a more mature activity.

---

[3] C. C. Schumacher, and B. E. Smith, "A Sample Survey of Industrial Operations Research Activities II," *Operations Research,* 13: no. 6 (November–December 1965). 1023–27.

[4] S. Benjamin Prasad, "Problem-Solving Trends in Management Science," *Management Science,* 13: no. 1 (October 1966): C10–16.

[5] Michael Radnor, Albert H. Rubenstein, and Albert S. Bean, "Integration and Utilization of Management Science Activities in Organizations," *Operational Research Quarterly,* 19: no. 2 (June 1968): 117–41.

[6] Efraim Turban, "How They're Planning OR at the Top," *Industrial Engineering,* 1: no. 12 (December 1969): 16–20; also "A Sample Survey of Operations-Research Activities at the Corporate Level," *Operations Research,* 20: no. 3 (May–June 1972): 708–21.

The original Radnor, Rubenstein, and Bean study was updated by Radnor. Rubenstein, and Tansik in 1970[7] and by Radnor and Neal in 1973.[8] This later article indicated that operations research/management science activities were still in a transitional state within most organizations, with their position undergoing fairly steady improvement in terms of significance and acceptance. Radnor and Neal also found that there was an increasing diffusion of operations research/ management science techniques into various functional areas within business organizations, particularly in capital intensive industries. They concluded that the most important finding from their latest study was that operation research/management science was in a "success phase" in its development history.

In 1976, Fabozzi and Valente[9] reported on a survey of the *Fortune* 500 firms in the United States concerning the use of mathematical programming. Their survey findings indicated that the most important area of application of mathematical programming was in production management (determination of product mix, production scheduling, and plant, equipment, and manpower scheduling). The second most important area of application was financial and investment planning (capital budgeting, cash flow analysis, portfolio analysis, cash management). Linear programming was found to produce good results for 76 percent of the firms responding, nonlinear programming was found to produce good results for 57 percent of the firms responding, and dynamic programming was found to produce good results for 53 percent of the firms responding.

In 1977, Ledbetter and Cox[10] reported on a survey of the *Fortune* 500 firms listed in 1975. One hundred seventy-six of these firms responded and indicated that regression analysis, linear programming, and simulation were the most frequently used operations research techniques in their firms. Their findings were quite similar to those reported by Turban, and are summarized in Table 1.1.

TABLE 1.1 Use of Operations Research Techniques (Ledbetter and Cox Survey)

		Degree of Use (%)				
Techniques	*Number of Respondents*	*Never 1*	*2*	*3*	*4*	*Very Frequently 5*
Regression analysis	74	9.5	2.7	17.6	21.6	48.6
Linear programming	78	15.4	14.1	21.8	16.7	32.0
Simulation (in production)	70	11.4	15.7	25.7	24.3	22.9
Network models	69	39.1	29.0	15.9	10.1	5.8
Queueing theory	71	36.6	39.4	16.9	5.6	1.4
Dynamic programming	69	53.6	36.2	7.2	0.0	2.9
Game theory	67	69.7	25.4	8.9	6.0	0.0

[7] Michael Radnor, Albert H. Rubenstein, and David A. Tansik, "Implementation in Operations Research and R and D in Government and Business," *Operations Research,* 18: no. 7 (1970): 967–91.

[8] Michael Radnor, and Rodney D. Neal, "The Progress of Management-Science Activities in Large U.S. Industrial Corporations," *Operations Research,* 21: no. 2 (March–April 1973): 427–50.

[9] F. J. Fabozzi, and J. Valente, "Mathematical Programming in American Companies: A Sample Survey," *Interfaces,* vol. 7, no. 1 (November 1976), 93–98.

[10] W. N. Ledbetter, and J. F. Cox, "Are OR Techniques Being Used?" *Industrial Engineering* (February 1977), 19–21. Reprinted with permission from *Industrial Engineering* Magazine, February 1977. Copyright © Institute of Industrial Engineers, Inc., 25 Technology Park/Atlanta, Norcross, GA 30092.

1.8 THE INSTITUTIONALIZATION OF MANAGEMENT SCIENCE

Because of the rapid growth and development of management science, several professional societies devoted to this area of inquiry and its related activities have been founded in the United States. The prominent professional societies are:

1. *The Operations Research Society of America (ORSA).* This group was founded in 1952, and according to its constitution: "The purposes of the Society shall be the advancement of operations research through exchange of information, the establishment and maintenance of professional standards of competence for work known as operations research, the improvement of methods and techniques of operations research, and the encouragement and development of students of operations research."[11] By 1980, its membership had grown to over 14,000. Its principal publication is the bi-monthly journal titled *Operations Research.*
2. *The Institute of Management Sciences (TIMS).* TIMS was founded in 1953 as: "An international society to identify, extend and unify scientific knowledge pertaining to management."[12] By 1980 it had over 9000 members. It publishes a monthly journal titled *Management Science.*
3. *The American Institute for Decision Sciences (AIDS).* This group, primarily composed of academicians, was founded in 1969 as: "an organization to promote *the* development and application of quantitative methodology to functional and behaviorial problems of administration. . ."[13] In spite of its young age, it currently has a membership of over 3500 and publishes a quarterly journal, titled *Decision Sciences.*

In addition to these professional societies, which are U.S. based, there are similar groups in 40 foreign countries. Many of these other groups print journals. Additionally, a number of other technical and trade journals regularly publish articles having a management science viewpoint. A listing of the major periodicals containing articles of interest to the student or practitioner of management science is as follows:

1. *Periodicals having major emphasis on management science/operations research:*

   > AIIE Transactions
   > Canadian Operational Research Society Journal
   > Computers and Operations Research
   > Decision Sciences
   > European Journal of Operational Research
   > Industrial Engineering
   > INFOR
   > Interfaces
   > International Journal of Production Research

---

[11] *Constitution,* Operations Research Society of America.

[12] *Constitution,* The Institute of Management Sciences.

[13] *Constitution,* American Institute for Decision Sciences.

Journal of Financial and Quantitative Analysis
Journal of Operations Management
Journal of the Operational Research Society
Management Science
Mathematical Programming
Mathematics of Operations Research
Naval Research Logistics Quarterly
Networks
Omega-International Journal of Management Science
Operations Research
Operational Research Quarterly
Production and Inventory Management
Society for Industrial and Applied Mathematics Review
Simulation
Transportation Science

2. *Periodicals having an occasional article on management science/operations research:*

Accounting Review
American Economic Review
Bell Journal of Economics
Computers and Urban Society
Datamation
Econometrica
Financial Management
Harvard Business Review
IBM Journal of Research and Development
Journal of the Association for Computing Machinery
Journal of Business
Journal of Finance
Journal of Marketing
Journal of Marketing Research
Journal of Optimization Theory and Applications
Journal of Regional Science
Journal of Systems Management
Marketing Science
Sloan Management Review
Technometrics

3. *Periodicals having abstracting service in management science/operations research:*

Operations Research/Management Science

Management science also has been institutionalized into colleges and universities. Most of the major American universities currently offer course work in the field of management science, and many offer advanced degrees. Such courses may be found in more than one department within a university, including Departments of Business Administration, Industrial Engineering, Applied Mathematics, Computer Science, Economics, and Electrical Engineering, as well as in Departments of Management Science and Operations Research. The traditional academic disciplines that have provided entry to the field of operations research/ management science, include business administration, engineering, economics, and mathematics.

The growth in management science as an academic field has been accompanied by a proliferation of textbooks. There are probably more than 100 textbooks now in existence in management science, and many more are in the process of being written. Additionally, numerous textbooks have been written that deal with a particular management science technique, that is, linear programming or inventory control. Presented at the end of this chapter is an extensive set of textbook references for the broad field of management science. Subsequently, at the end of each of the chapters of this textbook similar sets of references will be presented that deal with a specific management science technique.

1.9 WHY STUDY MANAGEMENT SCIENCE?

Before we begin our study of management science, it may be useful to consider the question: "Why study management science?" First, as has been noted previously in this chapter there has been a tremendous proliferation and acceptance of the use of operations research/management science techniques throughout business, government, and industry in the last three decades. Thus, whatever your personal career may be you will probably be exposed to management science. For example, as a manager you may be required to make a decision concerning the location of new warehousing facilities on the basis of a report done by one of your staff members in which a mathematical programming model has been used to determine the most cost-effective warehouse locations. Thus, although you might not directly be using management science techniques, it is quite likely that you will be involved in decision making using management science. Management science is, and will increasingly be, an important facet of the decision-making process for the modern manager.

Second, because of the great growth in operations research/management science, career opportunities in this field are truly outstanding. The demand for well-trained, highly motivated analysts far exceeds the supply. One can expect very good starting positions, with rapid advancement possibilities. The nature of management science work is such that it necessarily projects the management science analyst throughout the organization, giving him or her valuable and widespread exposure. The work of the management science analyst is challenging, interesting, and of an important strategic nature to the organization. Thus, the management science analyst tends to be in a very good position to move into higher-level management positions within the organization. In summary, management science is a good place to begin working in an organization and an excellent position from which the move on to higher-level managerial responsibilities.

Third, some of you may seek careers involving basic research in management science. The course encompassed by this textbook is an introduction to this field. If you are particularly interested in management science from a research perspective, you will want to broaden your studies considerably. Specialized courses in various aspects of operations research/management science are offered in many departments at most universities. The research-oriented management scientist will want to pursue specialized training in fields such as mathematics, statistics, industrial engineering, business, or economics. This text affords a foundation for these advanced studies.

1.10 OVERVIEW OF THE BOOK

This textbook is intended to provide an introduction to the major topics of management science. The book is organized in the following manner:

1. Chapter 1 provides a general, nonquantitative introduction to management science.
2. Chapter 2 presents a review of the fundamentals of linear algebra, and develops a foundation for the understanding of linear programming.
3. Chapters 3, 4, and 5 explore linear programming including model formulation, graphical solutions, the simplex method, and duality and sensitivity analysis.
4. Chapter 6 treats goal programming, which facilitates the consideration of multiple goals or objectives.
5. Chapter 7 describes the transportation model and the assignment problem.
6. Chapter 8 considers a series of network models.
7. Chapters 9 and 10 treat advanced topics in mathematical programming, namely integer programming and nonlinear programming. Some of the material in Chapters 9 and 10 may be omitted if the instructor feels that it is inappropriate for the level of the course.
8. Chapter 11 discusses dynamic programming, and its use in sequential, interrelated decision making.
9. Chapter 12 investigates inventory control problems requiring decisions of when and how much to order.
10. Chapters 13 and 14 deal with problems of a probabilistic nature. Waiting-line models are examined in Chapter 13 and Markov processes are considered in Chapter 14. Portions of these chapters contain advanced material that may be omitted at the discretion of the instructor.
11. Chapter 15 investigates ill-structured problems, using the tools of computer simulation.
12. Chapter 16 presents material concerning decision analysis and its use in terms of problems involving uncertainty.
13. Chapter 17 completes the book with a discussion of the various problems and procedures involved in implementing management science.

Throughout the book, emphasis is placed on presenting and illustrating those management science techniques that have been successfully applied in business, government, and the military. Numerous examples, illustrations, and case studies are provided. A glossary of important terms is included at the end of each chapter.

Probability concepts and statistical techniques are utilized throughout the textbook. Although it is likely that you will have already had a course in probability and statistics prior to studying management science, a review of probability and statistics is provided in Appendix A.

Calculus is employed in a few instances in this textbook, in an expository manner. However, it is not necessary for the student to know calculus to successfully utilize this textbook. A brief review of differential and integral calculus is provided in Appendix B.

Numerous computational problems and exercises are provided at the end of Chapters 2 to 16. Answers to the even-numbered problems for these chapters are included at the end of the book. Appropriate tables to facilitate the solution of these problems are provided in Appendix C. Two of these tables (Tables 1 and 2) provide a glossary of the mathematical notation and symbols used throughout the book. Discussion questions are also included at the end of each of the chapters of the book.

GLOSSARY OF TERMS

Algorithm   A set of procedures, which is followed in an iterative manner, and which converges to the optimum solution for a specific model.

Analog Model   A model in which one physical property is used to represent another physical property.

Assignment Model   An allocation model that is characterized by a special structure in that it involves the assignment of a certain number of activities to an equal number of resources.

Constraint   A mathematical function that limits or restricts resource utilization or allocation with respect to the decision variables of the model.

Decision Analysis Models   A class of management science models designed to select an optimal course of action from a set of alternative courses of action given the possible consequences associated with each alternative and their associated probabilities of occurrence.

Decision Variables   The unknowns that are to be determined by solving the model.

Descriptive Model   A model that describes some problem situation but does not indicate any preferred course of action.

Deterministic Model   A model in which the functional relationships and parameters are known with certainty.

Dynamic Programming Model   A model that considers a multiple time period horizon in which the decisions made over time are interrelated.

Economic Lot Size Model   An inventory control model that balances the inventory holding cost and the cost of making (purchasing) a replenishment order of a particular size.

Feasibility Study   A comprehensive examination of the technical, economic, and operational aspects of a proposed problem-solving endeavor in order to appraise its difficulty, estimate its cost, and determine its probability of success.

Goal Programming Model   A mathematical programming model that allows the consideration of multiple objectives or goals.

Heuristic Model   A model that employs an intutitive rule or generates a ''good,'' but not necessarily optimum, decision.

Iconic Model   A scaled physical representation of a real system.

Integer Programming Model   A linear programming model in which one or more of the decision variables are restricted to assume integer values.

Inventory Models   A class of management science models that determines how much of a given item to order and at what point in time to place the order so as to minimize costs.

Linear Model   A mathematical model characterized by strictly linear relationships between the variables in the model.

Linear Programming Model   A mathematical programming model in which the objective function can be represented as a linear function and the restrictions on resources can be expressed as a system of linear equalities and/or inequalities.

Management Science   Encompasses a methodology and a set of techniques derived from the physical sciences and mathematics with an objective of improving the quality of managerial decisions.

Markovian Decision Models   A class of management science models that involves the analysis of the current movement of a given variable in an attempt to predict the future movement of the same variable.

Mathematical Model   A model in which a set of mathematical symbols and functional relationships are used to represent some physical situation.

Mathematical Programming Models   A class of management science models that seeks to combine resources and activities in a manner that optimizes the overall effectiveness of the systems being modeled.

Maximal-Flow Model   A model that allocates flows within a network, from a source to a destination, in order to maximize the total flow for the network.

Minimum Spanning Tree Model   A variation of the shortest route model that determines a minimum length set of connections that provides a route between any two points of a network.

Network Models   Graphical representations of problem situations that are frequently utilized in the analysis of transportation and logistics systems, research and development projects, and information theory.

Nonlinear Model   A mathematical model that employs one or more curvilinear or nonproportional functional relationships.

Nonlinear Programming Model   A mathematical programming model in which the objective function and/or one or more of the constraints are nonlinear functions.

Normative Model   A model that describes the functional relationships between the variables of a system and prescribes a course of action for the decision maker to follow in meeting some defined objective.

Objective Function   A mathematical function defining the relationships among the decision variables in terms of optimizing some measure of effectiveness.

Operations Research   The application of scientific methods, techniques, and tools to problems involving the operation of a system so as to provide those in control of the system with optimum solutions to the problems.

Predictive Model   A model used to make a forecast of the future.

Qualitative Model   An informal descriptive model of the real system.

Quantitative Model   A formal mathematical model of the real system.

Scientific Method   A rigorous analytical approach to the study of natural phenomena that encompasses observation and description of form, hypothesis and model building, hypothesis testing and analysis, and model refinement and modification.

Shortest-Route Model   A network model that determines the minimum length path through a network.

Simulation Model   A model in which the behavior of a real-world system is replicated, often using a digital computer.

Static Model A model that is defined at a fixed point in time and that considers a fixed period of time.

Stochastic Model A model that incorporates uncertainty in its functional relationships. ·

Transportation Model A special type of linear programming model that involves the transportation of goods and services from several supply origins to several demand destinations.

Waiting-Line or Queueing Models A class of management science models that is concerned with situations in which random arrivals are occurring at a servicing or processing facility of limited capacity. The objective of these models is to determine the optimum number of personnel or facilities necessary to serve customers or products that arrive at some random rate, while balancing the cost of service and the cost of waiting.

SELECTED REFERENCES

MANAGEMENT
SCIENCE

Ackoff, Russell L., and Patrick Rivett. 1963. *A Manager's Guide to Operations Research.* New York: John Wiley & Sons, Inc.

————, and Maurice W. Sasieni. 1968. *Fundamentals of Operations Research.* New York: John Wiley & Sons, Inc.

Anderson, David R., Dennis J. Sweeney, and Thomas A. Williams. 1982. *An Introduction to Management Science.* St. Paul: West Publishing Company.

Baumol, William J. 1972. *Economic Theory and Operations Analysis.* Englewood Cliffs, N.J.: Prentice-Hall, Inc.

Bell, Colin E. 1977. *Quantitative Methods for Administration.* Homewood, Ill.: Richard D. Irwin, Inc.

Bierman, Harold, Charles P. Bonini, and Warren H. Hausman. 1977. *Quantitative Analysis for Business Decisions.* Homewood, Ill.: Richard D. Irwin, Inc.

Budnick, Frank S., Richard Mojena, and Thomas E. Vollman. 1977. *Principles of Operations Research for Management.* Homewood, Ill.: Richard D. Irwin, Inc.

Buffa, Elwood S., and James S. Dyer. 1981. *Management Science/Operations Research.* New York: John Wiley & Sons, Inc.

Cabot, A. Victor, and Donald L. Harnett. 1977. *An Introduction to Management Science.* Reading, Ma.: Addison-Wesley Publishing Company.

Churchman, C. W., R. L. Ackoff, and E. L. Arnoff. 1967. *Introduction to Operations Research.* New York: John Wiley & Sons.

Cook, Thomas M., and Robert A. Russell. 1977. *Introduction to Management Science.* Englewood Cliffs, N.J.: Prentice-Hall, Inc.

Daellenbach, Hans G., and John A. George. 1978. *Introduction to Operations Research Techniques.* Boston: Allyn and Bacon, Inc.

Dannenbring, David G., and Martin K. Starr. 1981. *Management Science: An Introduction.* New York: McGraw-Hill Book Company.

Davis, K. Roscoe, and Patrick G. McKeown. 1981. *Quantitative Models for Management.* Boston: Kent Publishing Company.

Dinkel, John J., Gary A. Kochenberger, and Donald R. Plane. 1978. *Management Science: Text and Applications.* Homewood, Ill.: Richard D. Irwin, Inc.

Di Roccaferrera, Giuseppe M. Ferrero. 1969. *Operations Research Models for Business and Industry.* Cincinnati: Southwestern Publishing Company.

Dunn, Robert A., and Kenneth D. Ramsing. 1981. *Management Science.* New York: Macmillan Publishing Co., Inc.

Eck, Roger. 1976. *Operations Research for Business*. Belmont, Calif.: Wadsworth Publishing Company.

Eppen, Gary D., and F. J. Gould. 1979. *Quantitative Concepts for Management*. Englewood Cliffs, N.J.: Prentice-Hall, Inc.

Giffin, Walter C. 1971. *Introduction to Operations Engineering*. Homewood, Ill.: Richard D. Irwin, Inc.

Gillett, Billy E. 1976. *Introduction to Operations Research: A Computer-Oriented Algorithmic Approach*. New York: McGraw-Hill Book Company.

Gue, Ronald L., and Michael E. Thomas. 1968. *Mathematical Methods in Operations Research*. New York: Macmillan Publishing Company.

Gupta, Shiv K., and John M. Cozzolino. 1974. *Fundamentals of Operations Research for Management*. San Francisco: Holden-Day, Inc.

Hartley, Ronald V. 1976. *Operations Research: A Managerial Emphasis*. Pacific Palisades, Calif.: Goodyear Publishing Company.

Heinze, David. 1978. *Management Science—Introductory Concepts and Applications*. Cincinnati: Southwestern Publishing Company.

Hesse, Rick, and Gene Woolsey. 1980. *Applied Management Science*. Chicago: Science Research Associates, Inc.

Hillier, Frederick S., and Gerald J. Lieberman. 1980. *Introduction to Operations Research*. San Francisco: Holden-Day, Inc.

Horowitz, Ira. 1972. *An Introduction to Quantitative Business Analysis*. New York: McGraw-Hill Book Company.

Johnson, Ross H., and Paul R. Winn. 1976. *Quantitative Methods for Management*. Boston, Ma.: Houghton Mifflin Company.

Krajewski, Lee J., and Howard E. Thompson. 1981. *Management Science: Quantitative Methods in Context*. New York: John Wiley & Sons, Inc.

Lapin, Lawrence. 1976. *Quantitative Methods for Business Decisions*. New York: Harcourt Brace Jovanovich, Inc.

Lee, S. M., and L. J. Moore. 1975. *Introduction to Decision Science*. New York: Petrocelli/Charter.

Lee, Sang M., Laurence J. Moore, and Bernard W. Taylor. 1981. *Management Science*. Dubuque, Iowa: Wm. C. Brown Company Publishers.

Levin, Richard I., and C. A. Kirkpatrick. 1978. *Quantitative Approaches to Management*. New York: McGraw-Hill Book Company.

Miller, David W., and Martin K. Starr. 1969. *Executive Decisions and Operations Research*. Englewood Cliffs, N.J.: Prentice-Hall, Inc.

Moskowitz, Herbert, and Gordon P. Wright. 1979. *Operations Research Techniques for Management*. Englewood Cliffs, N.J.: Prentice-Hall, Inc.

Paik, C. M. 1973. *Quantitative Methods for Managerial Decisions*. New York: McGraw-Hill Book Company.

Plane, D. R., and G. A. Kochenberger. 1972. *Operations Research for Managerial Decisions*. Homewood, Ill.: Richard D. Irwin, Inc.

Render, Barry, and Ralph M. Stair. 1982. *Quantitative Analysis for Management*. Boston: Allyn and Bacon, Inc.

Riggs, James L., and Michael S. Inoue. 1975. *Introduction to Operations Research and Management Science*. New York: McGraw-Hill Book Company.

Sasieni, M. W., A. J. Yaspan, and L. Friedman. 1967. *Operations Research: Methods and Problems*. New York: John Wiley & Sons, Inc.

Shamblin, J. E., and G. J. Stevens, Jr. 1974. *Operations Research: A Fundamental Approach*. New York: McGraw-Hill Book Company.

Shore, Barry, 1978. *Quantitative Methods for Business Decisions: Text and Cases*. New York: McGraw-Hill Book Company.

Siemens, N., C. H. Marting, and F. Greenwood. 1973. *Operations Research*. New York: The Free Press.

Taha, Hamdy A. 1976. *Operations Research*. New York: Macmillan Publishing Co.

Thierauf, Robert J., and Robert C. Klekamp. 1975. *Decision Making Through Operations Research*. New York: John Wiley & Sons, Inc.

Thompson, Gerald E. 1976. *Management Science: An Introduction to Modern Quantitative Analysis and Decision Making*. New York: McGraw-Hill Book Company.

Trueman, Richard E. 1981. *An Introduction to Quantitative Methods for Decision Making*. New York: Holt, Rinehart & Winston, Inc.

Turban, Efraim, and Jack R. Meredith. 1981. *Foundations of Management Science*. Plano, Tex.: Business Publications, Inc.

Wagner, Harvey M. 1975. *Principles of Operations Research*. Englewood Cliffs, N.J.: Prentice-Hall, Inc.

———. 1975. *Principles of Management Science*. Englewood Cliffs, N.J.: Prentice-Hall, Inc.

Wu, Nesa L., and Jack W. Wu. 1980. *Introduction to Management Science*. Chicago: Rand McNally Publishing Company.

DISCUSSION QUESTIONS

1. Briefly review the origins and development of operations research/management science.
2. Develop a comprehensive working definition of operations research/management science.
3. What are the major elements in the methodology of management science?
4. What is the significance and importance of model building in management science?
5. What are the major elements in a typical model?
6. What questions are important in making a feasibility study of a particular system?
7. What are the important aspects of implementing the conclusions of a management science study?
8. What is the difference between a descriptive and a normative model?
9. What is the difference between a deterministic and a stochastic model?
10. What is the difference between a linear programming model and a nonlinear programming model?
11. What is the difference between a static and dynamic model?
12. What are the major characteristics of a simulation model?
13. What are some of the prominent professional societies in the field of operations research/management science?
14. What post-World War II factors were important in the development of operations research/management science?
15. Why is the study of management science of importance to the prospective manager?
16. What are the basic elements of the scientific method?
17. What are the major elements in the practice of management science?
18. What are some of the job possibilities in operations research/management science? Consult the "help-wanted" ads in the *Wall Street Journal* and your local newspaper.

II

Deterministic Models

2 Fundamentals of Linear Algebra

2.1 INTRODUCTION

Linear, or matrix, algebra is a very important area of study in mathematics, engineering, economics, and business. The increasing utilization of quantitative methods in all these fields and the adaptation of high-speed digital computers to matrix methods are two of the major reasons for this development. In business decision making, linear algebra has become a very important tool for representing and manipulating large amounts of data in the functional areas of production, marketing, and finance.

An understanding of matrix algebra is also important for developing an understanding of linear programming, which is one of the most important and most heavily utilized techniques of management science. In this chapter we will try to introduce the fundamentals of linear algebra relevant to the study of linear programming. Two points should be mentioned in this regard. First, linear programming is all too often taught in "cookbook" fashion, without exposing the student to the underlying principles of linear algebra upon which linear programming is based. This teaching practice can cause a lack of real understanding of linear programming. Second, it should be emphasized that this chapter only reviews the principles of matrix algebra that are most important in the study of linear programming. Matrix algebra, which is a broad field of study, is applicable to many areas other than linear programming. Thus, this chapter presents a basic review of this subject; and the more inquisitive student is referred to the comprehensive references provided at the end of the chapter.

EXAMPLE   To introduce the subject, let us consider a simple example of a matrix. Consider the following price chart for 2- × 4-in. lumber:

	6 ft	*8 ft*	*10 ft*
Pine	0.79	0.99	1.09
Oak	1.10	1.40	1.60
Redwood	1.15	1.50	1.70

Such rectangular arrays of data are examples of matrices. The matrix shown above indicates the price of various lengths of 2- × 4-in. lumber according to the type of wood. Note that an important characteristic of a matrix is that the position of each number within the matrix is significant, as is the magnitude of the number. For example, the cost for an 8-ft oak 2- × 4-in., $1.40, is indicated uniquely by the intersection of the "Oak" row and the "8-ft" column. Later in this chapter we shall see that certain algebraic operations can be performed on matrices. Matrix algebra thus enables us to manipulate rectangular arrays of numbers as single entities.

Before discussing matrices and matrix algebra, we shall briefly review linear functions and systems of linear equations. These two subjects are important to our future discussion of the use of matrix algebra in linear programming.

2.2 THE LINEAR FUNCTION

The most elementary means of describing a mathematical relationship is by use of a **function**. A function is defined as a mathematical relationship in which the values of a single dependent variable are determined by a relationship to the values of one or more independent variables. In a function, one set of independent variable values is associated with no more than *one* dependent variable value. The simplest **linear function** has the form:

$$f(x) = a + bx \tag{2-1}$$

where $f(x)$ = the dependent variable.

a = the value of the dependent variable $f(x)$ when the independent variable x has a value of zero.

b = the rate of change of the linear function; that is, the increase in $f(x)$ associated with a unit change of x.

x = the independent variable.

In this simple linear function, the dependent variable $f(x)$, varies linearly (i.e., in a straight-line relationship) with the single independent variable, x. Also, the independent variable, x, is expressed to the first power in this linear function.

To illustrate the properties of a linear function, consider the following profit function for ¼-in. rubber faucet washers:

$$f(p) = -5 + 3p \qquad\qquad (2\text{-}2)$$

where p = number of washers sold.

This linear profit function is shown in Fig. 2.1. Note in Fig. 2.1 that, for each value of the independent variable p, there is one corresponding value of the dependent variable $f(p)$. The value of $f(p)$ is uniquely specified by the linear function $f(p) = -5 + 3p$. Since both $f(p)$ and p are permitted to take on different numerical values, they are designated as variables. For this linear function, there is an infinite number of possible values for these variables. This infinite number of possible values traces out the straight line depicting the function $f(p) = -5 + 3p$.

The permissible values of the independent variable are termed the **domain** of the function. Assume, for example, that we are interested in all positive values of the independent variable (including zero). The function plotted in Fig. 2.1 could then be expressed as:

$$f(p) = -5 + 3p \qquad \text{for } p \geq 0 \qquad\qquad (2\text{-}3)$$

where $p \geq 0$ is the domain of the function, and consists of all positive numbers. The domain is the possible number of washers that can be sold.

The permissible values of the dependent variable are termed the **range** of the function. Thus, the range of the function becomes those numbers that the dependent variable assumes as the independent variable takes on all values in the domain. The range of $f(p)$ for the function plotted in Fig. 2.1 consists of all numbers along the continuum from $f(p) = -5$ to $f(p) = +\infty$, corresponding to the

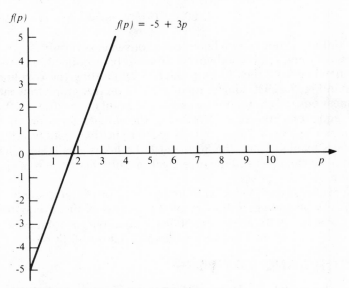

FIGURE 2.1   A Simple Linear Function

domain of the function, which consists of all numbers along the continuum from $p = 0$ to $p = +\infty$. The range is the profitability from sales of various numbers of washers.

2.3 SYSTEMS OF LINEAR EQUATIONS

Systems of linear equations arise as linear models are used to represent physical systems. A **linear equation** is a linear function in which no distinction is made between the dependent and independent variable(s). In a functional relationship one of the variables is considered to be the function of or to depend on the other variable. This relationship does not have to be present in the case of an equation. A system of linear equations consists of one or more linear equations with one or more independent variables.

The use of a set of linear equations to describe a physical system is illustrated by the following example.

EXAMPLE The Ace Metalworking Company produces woodworking files and metalworking files. Each unit (1000-file lot) of woodworking files requires 3 manhours of labor and each unit (1000-file lot) of metalworking files requires 5 manhours of labor. Furthermore, each unit of woodworking files requires 2 hours of metal lathe time, and each unit of metalworking files requires 5 hours of metal lathe time. We will now develop the system of linear equations to describe this physical production process, assuming that 100 manhours of labor and 80 hours of metal lathe time are available. Let x_1 represent the number of units of woodworking files to be produced, and let x_2 represent the number of units of metalworking files to be produced. The system of linear equations describing the production functions for these two variables is as follows:

$$3x_1 + 5x_2 = 100 \quad \text{(Labor manhours available)}$$

$$2x_1 + 5x_2 = 80 \quad \text{(Metal lathe time available)}$$

(2-4)

For this system of two linear equations in two variables, we can determine the number of units x_1 of woodworking files to be produced, and the number of units x_2 of metalworking files to be produced by plotting the two linear equations, as shown in Fig. 2.2. The single, unique, point on this graph that satisfies both of the two linear equations simultaneously is the point ($x_1 = 20$, $x_2 = 8$) at which the two linear equations intersect. Note that the unique solution to these two linear equations (i.e., $x_1 = 20$, $x_2 = 8$) is the output that exactly utilizes the 100 labor manhours available and the 80 metal lathe hours available. The method of substitution can also be used to solve algebraically this system of simultaneous linear equations.

While this type of system of linear equations is quite common, a great deal of complexity arises when the size of the system of linear equations increases and when the solution to the system of linear equations is not unique. These complications will be discussed further in the material that follows.

2.4 VECTORS AND MATRICES

For small systems of linear equations (e.g., two or three variable systems of equations), the process of describing and solving the system algebraically, or

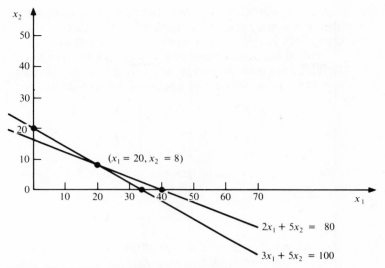

FIGURE 2.2   A System of Two Linear Equations

graphically, is not difficult. However, for larger systems of linear equations (e.g., 50 variables and 50 equations) the solution is very difficult to determine, and the process of describing the system of equations algebraically becomes laborious. To facilitate solution of the latter problem, a "shorthand" notational procedure, known as **matrix notation**, has been developed. This notational procedure is then used in conjunction with matrix algebra techniques for solving larger systems of linear equations.

To illustrate, a system of three linear equations in three variables may be written in algebraic form, as follows:

$$\begin{aligned} a_{11}x_1 + a_{12}x_2 + a_{13}x_3 &= b_1 \\ a_{21}x_1 + a_{22}x_2 + a_{23}x_3 &= b_2 \\ a_{31}x_1 + a_{32}x_2 + a_{33}x_3 &= b_3 \end{aligned} \qquad (2\text{-}5)$$

The variables (unknowns) in this system of linear equations are designated as x_1, x_2, x_3. The coefficients for these unknowns within this system are designated by the notation a_{ij}, where the first subscript i refers to the corresponding row number, and the second subscript j refers to the corresponding column number. The b_i refer to the right-hand sides of the system of equations.

Next, the various sets of symbols are collected into groups. First, the a_{ij}, the ordered numerical coefficients of the unknowns within the system, are designated as a **matrix**:

$$[\mathbf{A}] = \begin{bmatrix} a_{11} & a_{12} & a_{13} \\ a_{21} & a_{22} & a_{23} \\ a_{31} & a_{32} & a_{33} \end{bmatrix} \quad \text{(Dimensions: 3 rows} \times \text{3 columns)} \qquad (2\text{-}6)$$

This [**A**] matrix is called a (3×3) coefficient matrix, since it has dimensions of three rows and three columns. The horizontal lines of the matrix are called **rows**, and the vertical lines of the matrix are called **columns**. The a_{ij} entries of a matrix are called the **elements** of the matrix. In this text we shall assume that the entries of the matrix are simply **scalar** numbers. If all the entries of a matrix are real numbers, the matrix is called a **real matrix**. If all the entries of a matrix are zero, the matrix is called the **zero matrix** or the **null matrix**, commonly designated as $[\phi]$.

The variables (unknowns) in this system are described by a **vector** or **array**. This variables vector (vector of unknowns) is designated as:

$$\mathbf{x} = \begin{bmatrix} x_1 \\ x_2 \\ x_3 \end{bmatrix} \tag{2-7}$$

In this instance, $\mathbf{x}$ is a column vector, but it could have been written alternatively as a row vector:

$$\mathbf{x} = (x_1, x_2, x_3) \tag{2-8}$$

In similar fashion, the right-hand side of this system of equations can be described by a vector of constants, and written as:

$$\mathbf{b} = \begin{bmatrix} b_1 \\ b_2 \\ b_3 \end{bmatrix} \tag{2-9}$$

We have thus developed a standardized notational procedure for the three elements of any system of linear equations. These three elements are:

1. The coefficient matrix $[\mathbf{A}]$.
2. The variables vector (array) $\mathbf{x}$.
3. The right-hand side vector (array) $\mathbf{b}$.

Note finally that a vector (array) is nothing more than a column or row from a matrix. Conversely, a matrix is nothing more than a set of column or row vectors (arrays). A vector (array) may be a real vector (composed entirely of real numbers) or a null vector (composed entirely of zeroes).

Let us now apply this notational system to a numerical example.

EXAMPLE   Assume that we have the following system of linear equations:

$$\begin{aligned} 2x_1 + 5x_2 + 3x_3 + 7x_4 &= 10 \\ 9x_1 + 3x_2 + 1x_3 + 11x_4 &= 4 \\ 6x_1 + 2x_2 + 5x_3 + 2x_4 &= 7 \\ 4x_1 + 3x_2 + 6x_3 + 1x_4 &= 2 \end{aligned} \tag{2-10}$$

Describe this system, using matrix and vector notation. This is accomplished as follows:

$$\begin{array}{l} [\mathbf{A}] = \\ \text{(Coefficient matrix)} \end{array} \begin{bmatrix} 2 & 5 & 3 & 7 \\ 9 & 3 & 1 & 11 \\ 6 & 2 & 5 & 2 \\ 4 & 3 & 6 & 1 \end{bmatrix} \text{(Dimensions: } 4 \text{ rows} \times 4 \text{ columns)}$$

$$\mathbf{x} = \begin{bmatrix} x_1 \\ x_2 \\ x_3 \\ x_4 \end{bmatrix} \quad \text{and} \quad \mathbf{b} = \begin{bmatrix} 10 \\ 4 \\ 7 \\ 2 \end{bmatrix} \quad (2\text{-}11)$$

(Variables vector)   (Right-hand side vector)

In some instances we may need to employ the **transpose** of a matrix. The transpose of a matrix [**A**] is a matrix that is formed by interchanging the rows and columns of the matrix [**A**]. The ith row of the matrix [**A**] becomes the ith column of the transpose of the matrix [**A**]. The transpose of the matrix [**A**] will be denoted as [**A**]'. Similarly, we can form the transpose of vector by interchanging the rows and columns of the vector (i.e., the transpose of a column vector is a row vector, and vice versa). Examples of the transpose of a matrix and a vector are as follows:

$$[\mathbf{A}] = \begin{bmatrix} 3 & -1 & 5 \\ 7 & 2 & -4 \\ -1 & 0 & 2 \end{bmatrix} \qquad [\mathbf{A}]' = \begin{bmatrix} 3 & 7 & -1 \\ -1 & 2 & 0 \\ 5 & -4 & 2 \end{bmatrix} \quad (2\text{-}12)$$

$$\mathbf{x} = \begin{bmatrix} -1 \\ 3 \\ 5 \end{bmatrix} \qquad \mathbf{x}' = \begin{pmatrix} -1 & 3 & 5 \end{pmatrix}$$
$$(3 \times 1) \qquad\qquad\qquad (1 \times 3) \quad (2\text{-}13)$$
$$\text{(Column vector)} \qquad\qquad \text{(Row vector)}$$

The transpose of a vector and a matrix will be utilized subsequently in our work in linear programming.

As noted earlier, the matrix provides a convenient method for representing large quantities of data. To illustrate, consider the following example.

EXAMPLE   The Ace Screwdriver Company produces three types of screwdrivers at each of its three plants. Its monthly production plan can be conveniently written in matrix form as follows:

	4-in. screwdriver	6-in. screwdriver	8-in. screwdriver	
Plant 1	1000	3000	5000	
Plant 2	2000	2000	2000	(2-14)
Plant 3	6000	2000	4000	

This matrix indicates that Plant 1 produces 1000 screwdrivers 4 in. long, 3000 screwdrivers 6 in. long, and 5000 screwdrivers 8 in. long in a month. The monthly production for Plants 2 and 3 can be evaluated similarly. In total, 9000 screwdrivers 4 in. long are produced, that is, 1000 at Plant 1; 2000 at Plant 2; and 6000 at Plant 3. Total production of 6-in. screwdrivers and 8-in. screwdrivers can be evaluated similarly.

Again, observe that within a matrix both the position and the magnitude of a number are important. For example, the entry of 2000 in row 3, column 2 of the above matrix indicates that Plant 3 produces 2000 screwdrivers 6 in. long in this month. The position of the number in the matrix defines the specific screwdriver type and production location, while the magnitude of the number specifies the size of the quantity of a specific screwdriver produced at a specific plant.

2.5 MATRIX ALGEBRA

Matrix algebra, or **linear algebra**, is the set of rules developed for performing operations on matrices that are analogous to arithmetic operations. Since a matrix is nothing more than a set of column vectors (or row vectors), the rules we will study for matrices can just as readily be applied to the vectors that make up a matrix.

2.5.1 Matrix Addition and Subtraction

The rules of matrix algebra for the addition and subtraction of matrices are analogous to those of ordinary algebra, providing that the matrices being added or subtracted are conformable. Matrices are conformable for addition and subtraction if they have the same dimensions. A matrix, when its dimensions are equal, is called a **square matrix**. The **main diagonal** of a square matrix consists of the entries $a_{11}, a_{22}, a_{33}, \ldots, a_{nn}$. Thus, a two-row by two-column (2 × 2) matrix may be added or subtracted from a (2 × 2) matrix, or a (5 × 4) matrix may be added or subtracted from a (5 × 4) matrix. The addition or subtraction is performed by adding or subtracting the corresponding components from the original two matrices. This results in a new matrix of exactly the same dimension. The following example illustrates matrix addition and subtraction operations.

EXAMPLES   Assume that we are given two (4 × 3) matrices.

$$\begin{matrix} [\mathbf{A}] = \\ (4 \times 3) \end{matrix} \begin{bmatrix} -2 & 1 & 7 \\ 6 & -4 & 3 \\ 9 & 4 & 2 \\ 3 & 1 & -8 \end{bmatrix} \quad \begin{matrix} [\mathbf{B}] = \\ (4 \times 3) \end{matrix} \begin{bmatrix} -7 & 1 & 2 \\ 0 & 4 & 1 \\ 3 & 2 & 4 \\ 9 & 6 & -7 \end{bmatrix} \qquad (2\text{-}15)$$

Determine [**A** + **B**] and [**A** − **B**].

$$\begin{matrix} [\mathbf{A} + \mathbf{B}] = \\ (4 \times 3) \end{matrix} \begin{bmatrix} -2 + (-7) & 1 + 1 & 7 + 2 \\ 6 + 0 & -4 + 4 & 3 + 1 \\ 9 + 3 & 4 + 2 & 2 + 4 \\ 3 + 9 & 1 + 6 & -8 + (-7) \end{bmatrix} = \begin{bmatrix} -9 & 2 & 9 \\ 6 & 0 & 4 \\ 12 & 6 & 6 \\ 12 & 7 & -15 \end{bmatrix} \qquad (2\text{-}16)$$

$$\begin{matrix} [\mathbf{A} - \mathbf{B}] = \\ (4 \times 3) \end{matrix} \begin{bmatrix} -2 - (-7) & 1 - 1 & 7 - 2 \\ 6 - 0 & -4 - 4 & 3 - 1 \\ 9 - 3 & 4 - 2 & 2 - 4 \\ 3 - 9 & 1 - 6 & -8 - (-7) \end{bmatrix} = \begin{bmatrix} 5 & 0 & 5 \\ 6 & -8 & 2 \\ 6 & 2 & -2 \\ -6 & -5 & -1 \end{bmatrix} \qquad (2\text{-}17)$$

A null matrix can also be employed in matrix addition and subtraction. The sum or difference of any real matrix and a conformable null matrix is the original matrix.

EXAMPLES

$$[\mathbf{A}] = \begin{bmatrix} 1 & -2 & 4 \\ 2 & 0 & -6 \end{bmatrix} \quad \text{and} \quad [\boldsymbol{\phi}] = \begin{bmatrix} 0 & 0 & 0 \\ 0 & 0 & 0 \end{bmatrix} \quad (2\text{-}18)$$

$$[\mathbf{A}] + [\boldsymbol{\phi}] = \begin{bmatrix} 1 & -2 & 4 \\ 2 & 0 & -6 \end{bmatrix} = [\mathbf{A}] \quad (2\text{-}19)$$

$$[\mathbf{A}] - [\boldsymbol{\phi}] = \begin{bmatrix} 1 & -2 & 4 \\ 2 & 0 & -6 \end{bmatrix} = [\mathbf{A}] \quad (2\text{-}20)$$

2.5.2 Matrix Multiplication

The simplest type of multiplication operation involving a matrix is that of mulitplication of a matrix by a scalar. For this case, a matrix may be multiplied by a scalar by multiplying each component in the original matrix by the scalar. The resulting matrix will be of the same size and order as the original matrix. To illustrate, consider the following example.

EXAMPLE
Multiply the matrix $[\mathbf{A}] = \begin{bmatrix} 4 & 1 \\ 3 & 7 \end{bmatrix}$

by the scalar $K = 3$.

$$K \cdot [\mathbf{A}] = 3 \begin{bmatrix} 4 & 1 \\ 3 & 7 \end{bmatrix} = \begin{bmatrix} 12 & 3 \\ 9 & 21 \end{bmatrix} \quad (2\text{-}21)$$

The multiplication of two matrices is a more complicated operation. Here two matrices may be multiplied together only if the number of columns in the first (left) matrix equals the number of rows in the second (right) matrix. Such matrices are said to be comformable for multiplication. The matrix resulting from this multiplication will have dimensions equal to the number of rows in the first matrix and the number of columns in the second matrix. For example, a (2×3) matrix can be multiplied times a (3×3) matrix with the resulting matrix having dimensions of (2×3). However, a (3×3) matrix cannot be multiplied times a (2×3) matrix because such matrices are not conformable.

The actual matrix multiplication operation proceeds as follows. The components of the new matrix are formed by the sum of the products of the rows of the first matrix and the columns of the second matrix. To illustrate, consider the following example.

EXAMPLE
$$[\mathbf{A}] = \begin{bmatrix} a_{11} & a_{12} \\ a_{21} & a_{22} \end{bmatrix} \quad [\mathbf{B}] = \begin{bmatrix} b_{11} & b_{12} & b_{13} \\ b_{21} & b_{22} & b_{23} \end{bmatrix} \quad (2\text{-}22)$$
$$(2 \times 2) \qquad\qquad (2 \times 3)$$

Find the matrix $[\mathbf{A} \cdot \mathbf{B}]$.

Since $[\mathbf{A}]$ is a (2×2) matrix and $[\mathbf{B}]$ is a (2×3) matrix, the matrices are conformable for multiplication, and the resulting matrix $[\mathbf{A} \cdot \mathbf{B}]$ will have dimensions (2×3). The matrix multiplication proceeds as follows.

$$[\mathbf{A} \cdot \mathbf{B}] = \begin{bmatrix} a_{11} b_{11} + a_{12} b_{21} & a_{11} b_{12} + a_{12} b_{22} & a_{11} b_{13} + a_{12} b_{23} \\ a_{21} b_{11} + a_{22} b_{21} & a_{21} b_{12} + a_{22} b_{22} & a_{21} b_{13} + a_{22} b_{23} \end{bmatrix} \quad (2\text{-}23)$$
$$(2 \times 3)$$

It should be noted that, in general, $[\mathbf{A} \cdot \mathbf{B}] \neq [\mathbf{B} \cdot \mathbf{A}]$. In fact, in this example the matrix multiplication [**A** · **B**] is possible while the matrix multiplication [**B** · **A**] is not. A second example illustrates matrix multiplication for two numerical matrices.

EXAMPLE

$$[\mathbf{A}] = \begin{bmatrix} 3 & 1 \\ -2 & 9 \\ 4 & -6 \end{bmatrix} \quad [\mathbf{B}] = \begin{bmatrix} -1 & 6 & -2 \\ 4 & 7 & 0 \end{bmatrix} \quad (2\text{-}24)$$

Find the matrix [**A** · **B**].

$$[\mathbf{A} \cdot \mathbf{B}] = \begin{bmatrix} 3 \cdot (-1) + 1 \cdot 4 & 3 \cdot 6 + 1 \cdot 7 & 3 \cdot (-2) + 1 \cdot 0 \\ -2 \cdot (-1) + 9 \cdot 4 & -2 \cdot 6 + 9 \cdot 7 & -2 \cdot (-2) + 9 \cdot 0 \\ 4 \cdot (-1) + (-6) \cdot 4 & 4 \cdot 6 + (-6) \cdot 7 & 4 \cdot (-2) + (-6) \cdot 0 \end{bmatrix}$$

$$= \begin{bmatrix} 1 & 25 & -6 \\ 38 & 51 & 4 \\ -28 & -18 & -8 \end{bmatrix} \quad (2\text{-}25)$$

A null matrix can also be employed in matrix multiplication. The product of a real matrix and a conformable null matrix is a null matrix.

EXAMPLE

$$[\mathbf{A}] = \begin{bmatrix} 23 & 7 \\ -15 & 11 \\ 27 & -1 \end{bmatrix} \quad \text{and} \quad [\boldsymbol{\phi}] = \begin{bmatrix} 0 & 0 & 0 \\ 0 & 0 & 0 \end{bmatrix} \quad (2\text{-}26)$$

$$[\mathbf{A}] \cdot [\boldsymbol{\phi}] = \begin{bmatrix} 0 & 0 & 0 \\ 0 & 0 & 0 \\ 0 & 0 & 0 \end{bmatrix} \quad (2\text{-}27)$$

2.5.3 Matrix Inversion

The fourth basic operation of ordinary algebra, division, is not defined for matrix algebra. However, the inverse of a matrix is employed in matrix algebra in an analogous manner to division in ordinary algebra.

Recall that, in ordinary algebra, if we wish to solve the algebraic equation $ax = b$, we determine x by dividing both sides of the equations by a to give $x = b/a$ or $x = b(1/a)$. The quantity $1/a$ is called the reciprocal or the inverse of a. The inverse a^{-1} of any number $a \neq 0$, is itself a number that satisfies the relationship $a \cdot a^{-1} = 1$. For example, if $a = 3$ then $a^{-1} = 1/3$, or if $a = 1/5$ then $a^{-1} = +5$.

In matrix algebra, the **inverse** of a matrix bears the same relationship to that matrix that the reciprocal of a number bears to that number in ordinary algebra. Thus, in matrix algebra the product of a matrix [**A**], and its inverse [**A**$^{-1}$] is the identity matrix **I**, that is, [**A** · **A**$^{-1}$] = [**I**].

The identity matrix [**I**] is a matrix having properties analogous to the number 1 in ordinary algebra. Recall that the product of a number and its inverse (reciprocal) in ordinary algebra was the number 1. Analogously, in matrix algebra, the product of a matrix and its inverse is the identity matrix that consists entirely of zeroes, except for ones down the main diagonal. For example:

EXAMPLE $[\mathbf{I_2}] = \begin{bmatrix} 1 & 0 \\ 0 & 1 \end{bmatrix}$ is a (2×2) identity matrix $(a_{11} = 1, a_{22} = 1)$ (2-28)

and $[\mathbf{I_3}] = \begin{bmatrix} 1 & 0 & 0 \\ 0 & 1 & 0 \\ 0 & 0 & 1 \end{bmatrix}$ is a (3×3) identity matrix $(a_{11} = 1,$ (2-29)
$\qquad\qquad a_{22} = 1, a_{33} = 1)$

Note that an identity matrix has the property that multiplication of another matrix by it yields that original matrix. For example:

EXAMPLE $[\mathbf{A} \cdot \mathbf{I}] = \begin{bmatrix} 2 & 1 \\ 7 & 3 \end{bmatrix} \begin{bmatrix} 1 & 0 \\ 0 & 1 \end{bmatrix} = \begin{bmatrix} 2 & 1 \\ 7 & 3 \end{bmatrix} = [\mathbf{A}]$ (2-30)

We thus define the inverse of a matrix $[\mathbf{A^{-1}}]$ as being a matrix that satisfies the relationships:

$$[\mathbf{A} \cdot \mathbf{A^{-1}}] = [\mathbf{I}] = [\mathbf{A^{-1}} \cdot \mathbf{A}]$$ (2-31)

This definition indicates that the order of multiplication involving a matrix and its inverse does not matter. It should, therefore, be apparent that only **square** matrices (i.e., matrices having equal numbers of rows and columns) can have inverses. This is true because we must be able to multiply a matrix and its inverse in any order, the result being an identity matrix. This is only possible if we are dealing with a matrix whose inverse is of the same dimension as the original matrix. At this point, however, it should be cautioned that all square matrices do not necessarily have inverses. We shall discuss this point more fully after we have discussed the concept of the rank of a square matrix.

The properties of a matrix and its inverse are shown in the following example:

EXAMPLE $[\mathbf{A}] = \begin{bmatrix} 3 & 5 \\ 2 & 6 \end{bmatrix}$ $[\mathbf{A^{-1}}] = \begin{bmatrix} \frac{3}{4} & -\frac{5}{8} \\ -\frac{1}{4} & \frac{3}{8} \end{bmatrix}$ (2-32)

$[\mathbf{A} \cdot \mathbf{A^{-1}}] = \begin{bmatrix} 3 & 5 \\ 2 & 6 \end{bmatrix} \begin{bmatrix} \frac{3}{4} & -\frac{5}{8} \\ -\frac{1}{4} & \frac{3}{8} \end{bmatrix} = \begin{bmatrix} 1 & 0 \\ 0 & 1 \end{bmatrix} = [\mathbf{I}]$ (2-33)

$[\mathbf{A^{-1}} \cdot \mathbf{A}] = \begin{bmatrix} \frac{3}{4} & -\frac{5}{8} \\ -\frac{1}{4} & \frac{3}{8} \end{bmatrix} \begin{bmatrix} 3 & 5 \\ 2 & 6 \end{bmatrix} = \begin{bmatrix} 1 & 0 \\ 0 & 1 \end{bmatrix} = [\mathbf{I}]$ (2-34)

The question now becomes: "How do we obtain the inverse of a square matrix?" One convenient means for computing the inverse of a matrix is known as the **Gauss-Jordan elimination method.** The procedure commences with the augmentation of the square matrix $[\mathbf{A}]$ with the identify matrix $[\mathbf{I}]$, that is, we form

$$[\mathbf{A} \mid \mathbf{I}]$$ (2-35)

The Gauss-Jordan elimination method then involves performing a series of "row operations" to obtain concurrently an identity matrix $[\mathbf{I}]$ on the left side of the vertical line and the desired inverse $[\mathbf{A^{-1}}]$ on the right side of the vertical line. Thus, the Gauss-Jordan elimination method involves transforming $[\mathbf{A} \mid \mathbf{I}]$ to $[\mathbf{I} \mid \mathbf{A^{-1}}]$

by row operations. To verify that this process will work, recall the properties associated with the inverse of a matrix $[A^{-1}]$. If the inverse matrix $[A^{-1}]$ were known, we could multiply the matrices on both sides of the vertical line by $[A^{-1}]$, obtaining:

$$[A \cdot A^{-1} | I \cdot A^{-1}] = [I | A^{-1}] \qquad (2\text{-}36)$$

However, since we do not know the value of the inverse matrix, we employ the Gauss-Jordan elimination procedure to obtain the identity matrix on the left side of the vertical line.

The term ''row operation'' as used in this method refers to the application of simple algebraic operations to the rows of this matrix. The three basic row operations are defined as follows:

1. Any two rows of a matrix may be interchanged.
2. Any row of a matrix may be multiplied by a nonzero constant.
3. Any multiple of one row of a matrix may be added to another row of that matrix, element by element.

To illustrate the Gauss-Jordan elimination method, let us now determine the inverse of:

EXAMPLE

$$[A] = \begin{bmatrix} 3 & 5 \\ 2 & 6 \end{bmatrix} \qquad (2\text{-}37)$$

First, augment the matrix $[A]$ with the identity matrix $[I]$.

$$[A|I] = \begin{bmatrix} 3 & 5 & | & 1 & 0 \\ 2 & 6 & | & 0 & 1 \end{bmatrix} \qquad (2\text{-}38)$$

Next, multiply the first row by $\frac{1}{3}$ (divide first row by 3).

$$\begin{bmatrix} 1 & \frac{5}{3} & | & \frac{1}{3} & 0 \\ 2 & 6 & | & 0 & 1 \end{bmatrix} \qquad (2\text{-}39)$$

Next, add -2 times the first row to the second row.

$$\begin{bmatrix} 1 & \frac{5}{3} & | & \frac{1}{3} & 0 \\ 0 & \frac{8}{3} & | & -\frac{2}{3} & 1 \end{bmatrix} \qquad (2\text{-}40)$$

Next, multiply the second row by $\frac{3}{8}$ (divide second row by $\frac{8}{3}$).

$$\begin{bmatrix} 1 & \frac{5}{3} & | & \frac{1}{3} & 0 \\ 0 & 1 & | & -\frac{1}{4} & \frac{3}{8} \end{bmatrix} \qquad (2\text{-}41)$$

Finally, add $-\frac{5}{8}$ times the second row to the first row.

$$[I|A^{-1}] = \begin{bmatrix} 1 & 0 & | & \frac{3}{4} & -\frac{5}{8} \\ 0 & 1 & | & -\frac{1}{4} & \frac{3}{8} \end{bmatrix} \qquad (2\text{-}42)$$

Since we have obtained an identity matrix [I] on the left side of the vertical line, the desired inverse [A^{-1}] will be found to the right of the vertical line. The reader will recall from our previous example that we have already verified that [$A \cdot A^{-1}$] = [I] and [$A^{-1} \cdot A$] = [I] for this matrix and its inverse.

2.6 REPRESENTING SYSTEMS OF LINEAR EQUATIONS USING MATRICES

One of the most important uses of matrices is in the representation of systems of linear equations. To illustrate, consider again the set of three linear equations.

$$\begin{aligned} a_{11}x_1 + a_{12}x_2 + a_{13}x_3 &= b_1 \\ a_{21}x_1 + a_{22}x_2 + a_{23}x_3 &= b_2 \\ a_{31}x_1 + a_{32}x_2 + a_{33}x_3 &= b_3 \end{aligned} \tag{2-43}$$

Matrix notation can be used to write these three equations conveniently as:

$$[A] \cdot x = b \tag{2-44}$$

where [A] is the **coefficient matrix**:

$$[A] = \begin{bmatrix} a_{11} & a_{12} & a_{13} \\ a_{21} & a_{22} & a_{23} \\ a_{31} & a_{32} & a_{33} \end{bmatrix} \tag{2-45}$$

x is the (unknown) **solution vector**:

$$x = \begin{bmatrix} x_1 \\ x_2 \\ x_3 \end{bmatrix} \tag{2-46}$$

and b is the **right-hand side vector**:

$$b = \begin{bmatrix} b_1 \\ b_2 \\ b_3 \end{bmatrix} \tag{2-47}$$

Note that the product [A] $\cdot$ x is obtained by matrix multiplying the (3 $\times$ 3) coefficient matrix [A] times the (3 $\times$ 1) solution vector x. This system of linear equations is termed **homogeneous** in those cases in which b = 0. Conversely, a system of linear equations in which b $\neq$ 0 is termed **nonhomogeneous**.

2.7 SOLVING SYSTEMS OF LINEAR EQUATIONS

The Gauss-Jordan elimination method can also be used for solving a system of linear equations. Moreover, as we shall see in Chapter 4, the Gauss-Jordan elimination method is an integral part of the simplex procedure for solving linear programming problems. To apply this method we first augment the coefficient matrix [A] with the right-hand side vector b. The solution to the system of equations is determined by applying row operations to the rows of this augmented matrix. These row operations are performed with the objective of obtaining an identity matrix in the position originally occupied by the coefficient matrix [A]. Once an identity matrix is determined for the position originally occupied by [A], the solution to the system of equations appears in the position originally occupied by the right-hand side vector. To see that this is true, consider the following set of matrix operations:

1. Both sides of the matrix equation $[A]x = b$ are multiplied by $[A^{-1}]$:

$$[A^{-1} \cdot A]x = [A^{-1}]b \qquad (2\text{-}48)$$

2. Since $[A^{-1} \cdot A] = I$, the equation reduces to:

$$[I]x = [A^{-1}]b \qquad (2\text{-}49)$$

3. Since $[I]x = x$, the solution vector is given by:

$$x = [A^{-1}] \cdot b \qquad (2\text{-}50)$$

To illustrate the use of the Gauss-Jordan elimination procedure in solving a system of linear equations, consider the following example.

EXAMPLE

$$\begin{aligned} 2x_1 + 3x_2 + 4x_3 &= 6 \\ 1x_1 + 2x_2 + 3x_3 &= 5 \\ 4x_1 + 1x_2 + 5x_3 &= 2 \end{aligned} \qquad (2\text{-}51)$$

$$[A\,|\,b] = \begin{bmatrix} 2 & 3 & 4 & | & 6 \\ 1 & 2 & 3 & | & 5 \\ 4 & 1 & 5 & | & 2 \end{bmatrix} \qquad (2\text{-}52)$$

STEP 1   Divide row one by 2.

$$\begin{bmatrix} 1 & \frac{3}{2} & 2 & | & 3 \\ 1 & 2 & 3 & | & 5 \\ 4 & 1 & 5 & | & 2 \end{bmatrix} \qquad (2\text{-}53)$$

Multiply row one by -1 and add to row two. Multiply row one by -4 and add to row three.

$$\begin{bmatrix} 1 & \frac{3}{2} & 2 & | & 3 \\ 0 & \frac{1}{2} & 1 & | & 2 \\ 0 & -5 & -3 & | & -10 \end{bmatrix} \qquad (2\text{-}54)$$

In this first step we have obtained a one as the element in the first row and first column, and zeroes as the elements in the first column for all other rows.

STEP 2   Divide row two by ½.

$$\begin{bmatrix} 1 & \frac{3}{2} & 2 & 3 \\ 0 & 1 & 2 & 4 \\ 0 & -5 & -3 & -10 \end{bmatrix} \qquad (2\text{-}55)$$

Multiply row two by $-\frac{3}{2}$ and add to row one. Multiply row two by 5 and add to row three.

$$\begin{bmatrix} 1 & 0 & -1 & -3 \\ 0 & 1 & 2 & 4 \\ 0 & 0 & 7 & 10 \end{bmatrix} \qquad (2\text{-}56)$$

In this second step we have obtained a one as the element in the second row and second column, for all other rows.

STEP 3   Divide row three by 7.

$$\begin{bmatrix} 1 & 0 & -1 & -3 \\ 0 & 1 & 2 & 4 \\ 0 & 0 & 1 & \frac{10}{7} \end{bmatrix} \qquad (2\text{-}57)$$

Multiply row three by 1 and add to row one. Multiply row three by -2 and add to row two.

$$\begin{bmatrix} 1 & 0 & 0 & -\frac{11}{7} \\ 0 & 1 & 0 & \frac{8}{7} \\ 0 & 0 & 1 & \frac{10}{7} \end{bmatrix} \qquad (2\text{-}58)$$

In this third step we have obtained a one as the element in the third row and third column, and zeroes as the elements in the first column for all other rows.

This process, sometimes also referred to as diagonalization, has resulted in the determination of an identity matrix for the position originally occupied by the coefficient matrix [A].

Thus, the solution to this set of three linear equations is:

$$\mathbf{x} = \begin{bmatrix} x_1 \\ x_2 \\ x_3 \end{bmatrix} = \begin{bmatrix} -\frac{11}{7} \\ \frac{8}{7} \\ \frac{10}{7} \end{bmatrix} \qquad (2\text{-}59)$$

EXAMPLE   As a second example, consider the following situation. A certain job uses a metal lathe and a drill press to produce two products: bearings and shim plates. The metal lathe can be operated 16 hours per day and the drill press can be operated 100 hours per day. Each bearing that is produced requires 2 hours of work on the metal lathe and 1 hour of work on the drill press. Each shim plate that is produced requires 3 hours on the metal lathe and 2 hours on drill press. The management of the company wants to determine the number of bearings and shim plates that should be produced each day to keep the metal lathe and the drill press working to capacity.

To solve this problem let us define:

x_1 = number of bearings to be produced daily.
x_2 = number of shim plates to be produced daily.

Assuming that the metal lathe is used to capacity, the following production equation is obtained:

$$2 \text{ hours} \cdot x_1 + 3 \text{ hours} \cdot x_2 = 16 \text{ hours} \qquad \text{(Metal lathe)} \qquad (2\text{-}60)$$

Assuming that the drill press is operated at its capacity, the following production equation is obtained:

$$1 \text{ hour} \cdot x_1 + 2 \text{ hours} \cdot x_2 = 10 \text{ hours} \qquad \text{(Drill press)} \qquad (2\text{-}61)$$

The two production equations can be expressed in matrix notation as:

$$[\mathbf{A}]\mathbf{x} = \mathbf{b} \text{ where } [\mathbf{A}] = \begin{bmatrix} 2 & 3 \\ 1 & 2 \end{bmatrix} \quad \text{and} \quad \mathbf{b} = \begin{bmatrix} 16 \\ 10 \end{bmatrix} \qquad (2\text{-}62)$$

Using the Gauss-Jordan elimination method to obtain a solution to this sytem of linear equations, we proceed as follows:

$$[\mathbf{A}\,|\mathbf{b}] = \begin{bmatrix} 2 & 3 & | & 16 \\ 1 & 2 & | & 10 \end{bmatrix} \qquad (2\text{-}63)$$

Divide row one by 2.

$$\begin{bmatrix} 1 & \frac{3}{2} & | & 8 \\ 1 & 2 & | & 10 \end{bmatrix} \qquad (2\text{-}64)$$

Multiply row one by -1 and add to row two.

$$\begin{bmatrix} 1 & \frac{3}{2} & | & 8 \\ 0 & \frac{1}{2} & | & 2 \end{bmatrix} \qquad (2\text{-}65)$$

Multiply row two by 2.

$$\begin{bmatrix} 1 & \frac{3}{2} & | & 8 \\ 0 & 1 & | & 4 \end{bmatrix} \qquad (2\text{-}66)$$

Multiply row two by $-3/2$ and add to row one.

$$\begin{bmatrix} 1 & 0 & | & 2 \\ 0 & 1 & | & 4 \end{bmatrix} \qquad (2\text{-}67)$$

Thus, x_1 = two bearings and x_2 = four shim plates should be produced daily.

2.8 RANK

A system of m linear equations in n unknowns may:

1. Have no solution, in which case it is called an **inconsistent** system.
2. Have exactly one solution, called a unique solution.
3. Have an infinite number of solutions.

In the latter two cases the system is termed **consistent**.

The concept of **rank** may be used to develop a method for determining if a system of linear equations is consistent or inconsistent; and if consistent, if the system has a unique solution or an infinite number of solutions. We shall begin by discussing the concept of the rank of a matrix.

2.8.1 Rank of a Matrix

The rank of a matrix is defined to be the number of linearly independent rows (or alternatively, columns) in the matrix. Two or more rows (or columns) of a matrix are **linearly independent** if none of them can be expressed as a linear combination of the other rows (or columns). Two or more rows (or columns) of a matrix are **linearly dependent** if they can be expressed as a linear combination of the other rows (or columns). To illustrate linear independence consider the following (3×3) matrix:

EXAMPLE

$$[\mathbf{A}] = \begin{bmatrix} 2 & 7 & 3 \\ 1 & -9 & 6 \\ 4 & 2 & -1 \end{bmatrix} \quad \text{(Linear independence)} \quad (2\text{-}68)$$

(All three rows and columns are linearly independent.) To illustrate linear dependence consider the following (3×3) matrix:

EXAMPLE

$$[\mathbf{B}] = \begin{bmatrix} 2 & 3 & 6 \\ 1 & -2 & 4 \\ 4 & -1 & 14 \end{bmatrix} \quad \text{(Linear dependence)} \quad (2\text{-}69)$$

(Row three can be expressed as the sum of row one plus twice the sum of row two.) The rank of a matrix may be determined by applying row operations to the matrix with the objective of obtaining as many all zero rows (or columns) as possible. The number of rows (or columns) in the matrix that cannot be reduced to all zeroes is the number of linearly independent rows in the matrix, or the rank of the matrix.

To illustrate the determination of the rank of a matrix, consider the following example.

EXAMPLE

$$\begin{bmatrix} 1 & 3 & -6 \\ 5 & -3 & 4 \\ 6 & 0 & -2 \end{bmatrix} \quad (2\text{-}70)$$

Add -5 times row one to row two.

$$\begin{bmatrix} 1 & 3 & -6 \\ 0 & -18 & 34 \\ 6 & 0 & -2 \end{bmatrix} \tag{2-71}$$

Add -6 times row one to row three.

$$\begin{bmatrix} 1 & 3 & -6 \\ 0 & -18 & 34 \\ 0 & -18 & 34 \end{bmatrix} \tag{2-72}$$

Add -1 times row two to row three.

$$\begin{bmatrix} 1 & 3 & -6 \\ 0 & -18 & 34 \\ 0 & 0 & 0 \end{bmatrix} \tag{2-73}$$

Now, because there is a one in the first column of row one and a zero in the first column of row two, no further combinations of row operations can reduce all the elements of row one or all the elements of row two to zero. Thus, the rank of this matrix is 2, and this matrix has two linearly independent rows (columns).

2.8.2 Rank of a System of Linear Equations

The concept of rank can be extended to a system of linear equations. Thus, we define the rank of a system of linear equations as the number of linearly independent equations in the system. To determine the rank of the system of linear equations, $[A]x = b$, the coefficient matrix $[A]$ is first augmented with the right-hand side vector to form $[A\,|\,b]$. Row operations are then performed on the augmented matrix $[A\,|\,b]$ to try to produce all zero rows. The number of nonzero rows in the augmented matrix is the rank of the system of linear equations. To illustrate, consider the following example.

EXAMPLE

$$\begin{aligned} 1x_1 + 3x_2 - 6x_3 &= 2 \\ 5x_1 - 3x_2 + 4x_3 &= 5 \\ 6x_1 \qquad\;\; - 2x_3 &= 7 \end{aligned} \tag{2-74}$$

$$[A\,|\,b] = \begin{bmatrix} 1 & 3 & -6 & 2 \\ 5 & -3 & 4 & 5 \\ 6 & 0 & -2 & 7 \end{bmatrix} \tag{2-75}$$

Add -5 times row one to row two.

$$\begin{bmatrix} 1 & 3 & -6 & 2 \\ 0 & -18 & 34 & -5 \\ 6 & 0 & -2 & 7 \end{bmatrix} \tag{2-76}$$

Add -6 times row one to row three.

$$\begin{bmatrix} 1 & 3 & -6 & \bigm| & 2 \\ 0 & -18 & 34 & \bigm| & -5 \\ 0 & -18 & 34 & \bigm| & -5 \end{bmatrix} \tag{2-77}$$

Add -1 times row two to row three.

$$\begin{bmatrix} 1 & 3 & -6 & \bigm| & 2 \\ 0 & -18 & 34 & \bigm| & -5 \\ 0 & 0 & 0 & \bigm| & 0 \end{bmatrix} \tag{2-78}$$

Once again, no further combinations of row operations can reduce all the elements of row one or all of the elements of row two to zero. Thus, the rank of this system of linear equations is 2. This means that the number of linearly independent equations in this system of linear equations is also 2.

2.8.3 The Nature of Solutions to Systems of Linear Equations

The rank concept may be used to analyze a system of linear equations. As noted earlier, a system of linear equations may be consistent or inconsistent, and a consistent system of linear equations may have a unique or an infinite number of solutions. These possibilities may be investigated by applying the following two rules, which employ the rank concept:

RULE 1 *A system of linear equations is consistent if, and only if, the rank of the augmented matrix for this system is equal to the rank of the coefficient matrix for this system. This rank is termed the* rank of the system.

RULE 2 *A system of linear equations has a unique solution if, and only if, the rank of the coefficient matrix for this system equals the number of variables in the system.*

When these rules are applied to a system of linear equations, the three possibilities that may exist can be summarized by the following diagram shown in Fig. 2.3. To illustrate these rules, consider the following numerical examples:

EXAMPLE

$$\begin{aligned} 3x_1 + 2x_2 &= 6 \\ 1x_1 + 4x_2 &= 3 \end{aligned} \tag{2-79}$$

$$[\mathbf{A}] = \begin{bmatrix} 3 & 2 \\ 1 & 4 \end{bmatrix} \qquad [\mathbf{A}|\mathbf{b}] = \begin{bmatrix} 3 & 2 & \bigm| & 6 \\ 1 & 4 & \bigm| & 3 \end{bmatrix} \tag{2-80}$$

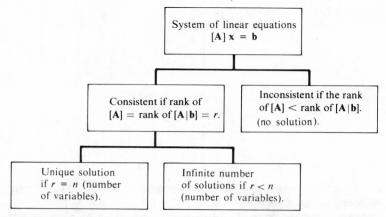

FIGURE 2.3   Solutions to a System of Linear Equations

Performing row operations, we first divide row one by 3.

$$[A] = \begin{bmatrix} 1 & \frac{2}{3} \\ 1 & 4 \end{bmatrix} \qquad [A|b] = \begin{bmatrix} 1 & \frac{2}{3} & 2 \\ 1 & 4 & 3 \end{bmatrix} \tag{2-81}$$

Multiply row one by -1 and add to row two.

$$[A] = \begin{bmatrix} 1 & \frac{2}{3} \\ 0 & \frac{10}{3} \end{bmatrix} \qquad [A|b] = \begin{bmatrix} 1 & \frac{2}{3} & 2 \\ 0 & \frac{10}{3} & 1 \end{bmatrix} \tag{2-82}$$

Multiply row two by $^3/_{10}$.

$$[A] = \begin{bmatrix} 1 & \frac{2}{3} \\ 0 & 1 \end{bmatrix} \qquad [A|b] = \begin{bmatrix} 1 & \frac{2}{3} & 2 \\ 0 & 1 & \frac{3}{10} \end{bmatrix} \tag{2-83}$$

Multiply row two by $-^2/_3$ and add to row one.

$$[A] = \begin{bmatrix} 1 & 0 \\ 0 & 1 \end{bmatrix} \qquad [A|b] = \begin{bmatrix} 1 & 0 & \frac{9}{5} \\ 0 & 1 & \frac{3}{10} \end{bmatrix} \tag{2-84}$$

No further row operations can now be performed to obtain all zero rows in either $[A]$ or $[A|b]$. Thus, the rank of $[A] = $ rank of $[A|b] = r = 2 = $ number of variables. We thus have a consistent set of linear equations having a unique solution, namely $x_1 = {}^9/_5$, $x_2 = {}^3/_{10}$.

EXAMPLE

$$\begin{aligned} 1x_1 + 2x_2 &= 2 \\ 3x_1 + 6x_2 &= 6 \end{aligned} \tag{2-85}$$

$$[A] = \begin{bmatrix} 1 & 2 \\ 3 & 6 \end{bmatrix} \qquad [A|b] = \begin{bmatrix} 1 & 2 & 2 \\ 3 & 6 & 6 \end{bmatrix} \tag{2-86}$$

Performing row operations, we multiply row one by -3 and add it to row two.

$$[\mathbf{A}] = \begin{bmatrix} 1 & 2 \\ 0 & 0 \end{bmatrix} \qquad [\mathbf{A}|\mathbf{b}] = \begin{bmatrix} 1 & 2 & | & 2 \\ 0 & 0 & | & 0 \end{bmatrix} \qquad (2\text{-}87)$$

No further row operations can now be performed to obtain all zero rows in either $[\mathbf{A}]$ or $[\mathbf{A}|\mathbf{b}]$. Thus, the rank of $[\mathbf{A}]$ = rank of $[\mathbf{A}|\mathbf{b}] = r = 1$. Since $r = 1 < n = 2$ (number of variables), we have a consistent set of linear equations having an infinite number of solutions.

EXAMPLE

$$\begin{aligned} 3x_1 + 2x_2 + 6x_3 &= 1 \\ 1x_1 + 2x_2 + 1x_3 &= 3 \\ 2x_1 + 4x_2 + 2x_3 &= 7 \end{aligned} \qquad (2\text{-}88)$$

$$[\mathbf{A}] = \begin{bmatrix} 3 & 2 & 6 \\ 1 & 2 & 1 \\ 2 & 4 & 2 \end{bmatrix} \qquad [\mathbf{A}|\mathbf{b}] = \begin{bmatrix} 3 & 2 & 6 & | & 1 \\ 1 & 2 & 1 & | & 3 \\ 2 & 4 & 2 & | & 7 \end{bmatrix} \qquad (2\text{-}89)$$

Performing row operations, we multiply row two by -2 and add to row 3.

$$[\mathbf{A}] = \begin{bmatrix} 3 & 2 & 6 \\ 1 & 2 & 1 \\ 0 & 0 & 0 \end{bmatrix} \qquad [\mathbf{A}|\mathbf{b}] = \begin{bmatrix} 3 & 2 & 6 & | & 1 \\ 1 & 2 & 1 & | & 3 \\ 0 & 0 & 0 & | & 1 \end{bmatrix} \qquad (2\text{-}90)$$

No further row operations can now be performed to obtain all zero rows in either $[\mathbf{A}]$ or $[\mathbf{A}|\mathbf{b}]$. The rank of $[\mathbf{A}] = 2$ and the rank of $[\mathbf{A}|\mathbf{b}] = 3$. We thus have an inconsistent of linear equations, and it has no solution.

In summary, we can employ elementary row operations to analyze the nature of solutions to systems of linear equations. The concept of the rank of a matrix is employed in this process.

2.9 NONSINGULAR AND SINGULAR SQUARE MATRICES

We noted earlier that a square matrix $[\mathbf{A}]$ and its inverse $[\mathbf{A}^{-1}]$ may be used to solve a system of linear equations $[\mathbf{A}]\mathbf{x} = \mathbf{b}$. Thus, since only square matrices can have inverses, the use of the matrix inverse method to solve systems of simultaneous linear equations is possible only for square systems of linear equations, where the number of unknowns equals the number of equations. However, it must be cautioned that having a square system of equations does not guarantee that such a system of equations has a solution. Because there are as many equations as variables does not guarantee that the coefficient matrix $[\mathbf{A}]$ will have an inverse. If the coefficient matrix of a square matrix has an inverse it is termed **nonsingular**, and if it does not have an inverse it is termed **singular**.

A singular matrix arises for a square system of linear equations when one or more of the equations in the system is linearly dependent on one or more of the other equations in the system. The rank of a nonsingular square matrix will always be equal to the size of the square matrix, while the rank of a singular square matrix will always be less than the size of the square matrix. To illustrate, consider the following example:

EXAMPLE

$$
\begin{aligned}
1x_1 + 2x_2 + 4x_3 &= 2 \\
2x_1 + 1x_2 + 6x_3 &= 1 \\
4x_1 + 5x_2 + 14x_3 &= 5
\end{aligned}
\tag{2-91}
$$

The coefficient matrix of this system of equations has no inverse, since the third equation is linearly dependent on the first two equations. The third equation can be written as the sum of twice the first equation plus one times the second equation.

To summarize, any square matrix whose rows (columns) are linearly dependent does not have an inverse, and is termed singular. Similarly, a square matrix does not have an inverse if its rows (columns) are linearly dependent.

2.10   BASIC SOLUTIONS

Let us now consider systems of linear equations in which there are more unknowns than equations. Such systems, in which the number of unknowns, n, is greater than the number of equations, m, are called **underdetermined** or **rectangular**. Such rectangular systems are either consistent or inconsistent. If they are consistent, since $m < n$, $r < n$ and there will be an infinite number of solutions. If they are inconsistent there will be no solution.

In Section 2.5 of this chapter we noted that, if a square matrix has linearly independent rows and columns, we can compute its inverse, and then use this inverse to compute the unique solution to its underlying system of equations. Now, a system of linear equations with more columns than rows does not have a square matrix, and thus it cannot be inverted. However, assume that we can select a subset of linearly independent columns from the set of columns available. If the number of linearly independent columns that is selected is exactly equal to the number of rows in the original set of matrix equations, we have formed a square matrix that we know has an inverse (i.e., we have formed a nonsingular square matrix). Assume further, that for our set of equations, rank of $[A]$ = rank of $[A|b] = m$. After determining the inverse $[A^{-1}]$, we can compute a solution to the original set of matrix equations using

$$
\mathbf{x} = [A^{-1}]\mathbf{b}
\tag{2-92}
$$

where $[A]$ is the m by m nonsingular matrix, and $n - m$ variables (unknowns) have arbitrarily been set equal to zero. This type of solution to a system of linear equations is called a **basic solution**.

BASIC SOLUTION   *Given a system of* m *simultaneous linear equations in* n *unknowns,* $[A]\mathbf{x} = \mathbf{b}$ *(*m < n*) and rank of* $[A]$ = m. *If any* m × m *nonsingular matrix is chosen from* $[A]$, *and if all the* n − m *variables not associated with the columns of this matrix are set equal to zero, the solution to the resulting set of equations is called a* basic *solution.*

In a basic solution $n - m$ variables are set equal to zero, and the remaining m

variables are then uniquely determined since the matrix of their coefficients is nonsingular. A basic solution thus has no more than m nonzero variables, and these m variables are called **basic variables**. The $n - m$ variables set equal to zero are called **nonbasic variables**. Furthermore, a **basic feasible solution** is defined as a basic solution in which all m basic variables are nonnegative (≥ 0), and a **basic nonfeasible solution** is defined as a basic solution in which one, or more, of the basic variables are negative (< 0). Finally, a **nondegenerate basic feasible solution** is defined as a basic feasible solution in which all m basic variables are positive (> 0), and a **degenerate basic feasible solution** is defined as a basic feasible solution in which one, or more, of the m basic variables are equal to zero.

Let us now illustrate the definitions presented above, using a numerical example.

EXAMPLE Given the following rectangular system of linear equations

$$
\begin{aligned}
1x_1 + 2x_2 + 1x_3 & & & = 12 \\
1x_1 + 1x_2 & + 1x_4 & & = 10 \\
1x_1 & & + 1x_5 & = 8
\end{aligned}
\tag{2-93}
$$

For this rectangular system of linear equations we have $m = 3$ equations in $n = 5$ unknowns. The maximum number of basic solutions possible for a system of m linear equations having n unknowns is given by the number of combinations of n items taken m at a time, or:[1]

$$
\begin{aligned}
\text{Number of basic solutions} \\
(m \text{ equations, } n \text{ unknowns})
\end{aligned}
= \binom{n}{m} = \frac{n!}{m!\,(n - m)!}
\tag{2-94}
$$

Thus, for this system of $m = 3$ linear equations in $n = 5$ unknowns we would have

$$
\begin{aligned}
\text{Number of basic solutions} \\
(m = 3, n = 5)
\end{aligned}
= \binom{5}{3} = \frac{5!}{3!\,(5 - 3)!} = 10
\tag{2-95}
$$

The ten basic solutions to this rectangular system of linear equations can be determined by setting $n - m = 5 - 3 = 2$ of the variables equal to zero and solving for the remaining $m = 3$ variables.

BASIC
SOLUTION 1 To illustrate, one basic solution can be determined by setting $x_1 = 0$, $x_2 = 0$, and solving:

$$
\begin{aligned}
1x_3 & & & = 12 \\
& + 1x_4 & & = 10 \\
& & + 1x_5 & = 8
\end{aligned}
\tag{2-96}
$$

Thus, the initial basic solution is: (Set $x_1 = 0, x_2 = 0$); $x_3 = 12, x_4 = 10, x_5 = 8$. This initial basic solution is a basic feasible solution that is nondegenerate.

---

[1] Note that as we set $n - m$ of the variables equal to zero and attempt to solve the resulting set of m linear equations in m unknowns, it may not be possible to obtain a particular basic solution. This situation will occur when the chosen set of m linear equations in m unknowns is inconsistent, and in this instance the $m \times m$ square matrix chosen from [A] will be singular and will not have an inverse.

BASIC
SOLUTION 2
A second basic solution can be determined by setting $x_1 = 0$, $x_3 = 0$, and solving:

$$
\begin{aligned}
2x_2 & & &= 12 \\
1x_2 &+ 1x_4 & &= 10 \\
 & &+ 1x_5 &= 8
\end{aligned}
$$

(2-97)

Using the Gauss-Jordan elimination method:

$$
[\mathbf{A} \,|\, \mathbf{b}] = \begin{bmatrix} 2 & 0 & 0 & | & 12 \\ 1 & 1 & 0 & | & 10 \\ 0 & 0 & 1 & | & 8 \end{bmatrix}
$$

(2-98)

Divide row one by 2.

$$
[\mathbf{A} \,|\, \mathbf{b}] = \begin{bmatrix} 1 & 0 & 0 & | & 6 \\ 1 & 1 & 0 & | & 10 \\ 0 & 0 & 1 & | & 8 \end{bmatrix}
$$

(2-99)

Multiply row one by -1 and add it to row two.

$$
[\mathbf{A} \,|\, \mathbf{b}] = \begin{bmatrix} 1 & 0 & 0 & | & 6 \\ 0 & 1 & 0 & | & 4 \\ 0 & 0 & 1 & | & 8 \end{bmatrix}
$$

(2-100)

Thus, a second basic solution is: (Set $x_1 = 0$, $x_3 = 0$); $x_2 = 6$, $x_4 = 4$, $x_5 = 8$. This second basic solution is a basic feasible solution that is nondegenerate.

Proceeding in similar fashion, setting combination of $n - m = 2$ variables equal to zero and solving for the remaining $m = 3$ variables, using the Gauss-Jordan elimination method, the remaining eight basic solutions are as follows (*note*: for the sake of brevity we are omitting the computational details of these eight solutions—the more interested reader can verify these computations):

BASIC
SOLUTION 3
(Set $x_1 = 0$, $x_4 = 0$); $x_2 = 10$, $x_3 = -8$, $x_5 = 8$. This is a basic nonfeasible solution, since $x_3 = -8$.

BASIC
SOLUTION 4
(Set $x_1 = 0$, $x_5 = 0$); no basic solution possible. In this instance, we are attempting to solve

$$
\begin{aligned}
2x_2 + 1x_3 & & &= 12 \\
1x_2 &+ 1x_4 & &= 10 \\
 & &+ 1x_5 &= 8
\end{aligned}
$$

(2-101)

$$
\begin{array}{cc}
1x_1 & \\
\| & \| \\
0 & 0
\end{array}
$$

This is obviously an inconsistent set of linear equations, and we cannot obtain a nonsingular square matrix involving the variables x_2, x_3, and x_4.

BASIC
SOLUTION 5
(Set $x_2 = 0$, $x_3 = 0$); $x_1 = 12$, $x_4 = -2$, $x_5 = -4$. This is a basic nonfeasible solution, since $x_4 = -2$ and $x_5 = -4$.

BASIC SOLUTION 6 (Set $x_2 = 0$, $x_4 = 0$); $x_1 = 10$, $x_3 = 2$, $x_5 = -2$. This is a basic nonfeasible solution, since $x_5 = -2$.

BASIC SOLUTION 7 (Set $x_2 = 0$, $x_5 = 0$); $x_1 = 8$, $x_3 = 4$, $x_4 = 2$. This is a basic feasible solution.

BASIC SOLUTION 8 (Set $x_3 = 0$, $x_4 = 0$); $x_1 = 8$, $x_2 = 2$, $x_5 = 0$. This is a degenerate basic feasible solution, since $x_5 = 0$.

BASIC SOLUTION 9 (Set $x_3 = 0$, $x_5 = 0$); $x_1 = 8$, $x_2 = 2$, $x_4 = 0$. This is a degenerate basic feasible solution, since $x_4 = 0$.

BASIC SOLUTION 10 (Set $x_4 = 0$, $x_5 = 0$); $x_1 = 8$, $x_2 = 2$, $x_3 = 0$. This is a degenerate basic feasible solution, since $x_3 = 0$.

In summary, for this rectangular system of $m = 3$ linear equations in $n = 5$ unknowns we obtained the following basic solutions.

Basic Solution[a]					Feasible/Nonfeasible	Degenerate/Nondegenerate
x_1	x_2	x_3	x_4	x_5		
(0)	(0)	12	10	8	Feasible	Nondegenerate
(0)	6	(0)	4	8	Feasible	Nondegenerate
(0)	10	−8	(0)	8	Nonfeasible	Nondegenerate
(0)				(0)	No basic solution possible—inconsistent set of equations	
12	(0)	(0)	−2	−4	Nonfeasible	Nondegenerate
10	(0)	2	(0)	−2	Nonfeasible	Nondegenerate
8	(0)	4	2	(0)	Feasible	Nondegenerate
8	2	(0)	(0)	0	Feasible	Degenerate
8	2	(0)	0	(0)	Feasible	Degenerate
8	2	0	(0)	(0)	Feasible	Degenerate

[a]Variables set equal to zero are enclosed in parentheses.

Thus, of the ten possible basic solutions, we could obtain nine basic solutions. Of these nine basic solutions, there were six basic feasible solutions. It is important to observe that the number of basic *feasible* solutions we obtained was less than the number of possible basic solutions. Of these six basic feasible solutions, three were degenerate basic feasible solutions.

Linear programming, which we will study in detail in the following three chapters, generally involves underdetermined systems of linear equations. Because underdetermined systems of linear equations are usually difficult to solve, and may indeed involve an infinite number of solutions, we utilize basic solutions in linear programming to reduce underdetermined systems to determined systems that can be solved more easily. Furthermore, in the solution process for linear programming we restrict our consideration to only basic feasible solutions. Thus, the determination of basic feasible solutions is the key to the solution of linear programming problems.

2.11   CONVEX SETS

In this section we will consider some fundamental properties of convex sets. These properties of convex sets will be very important in our future study of linear programming, as they will be utilized in the determination of the solution to the linear programming problem.

First, a **convex set** is defined as follows.

DEFINITION   *A* convex set *is a collection of points such that, for each pair of points in the collection of points, the entire line segment joining the two points will also be in the collection of points.*

The definition indicates that if x_1 and x_2 are points in the set X, then every point

$$x = \lambda x_2 + (1 - \lambda)x_1, \qquad 0 \le \lambda \le 1 \tag{2-102}$$

must also be in the set X. The expression given by Equation 2–102 is often referred to as a **convex combination** of x_1, x_2 (for a given λ). A set is convex if every convex combination of any two points in the set is also in the set. To illustrate the distinction between a convex set and nonconvex set, consider Fig. 2.4, below. In Fig. 2.4*a, b,* and *c,* line segment AB lies entirely within the boundary of the collection of points that forms the convex set. The palette-shaped figure shown in Fig. 2.4*d* is reentrant, and is thus nonconvex since line segment AB does not lie entirely in the set. Likewise, Figure 2.4*e* is nonconvex, since line segment AB does not lie entirely in the set. Figure 2.4*f* is nonconvex because of the presence of the circular "hole," which is another cause of nonconvexity. Generally speaking, a convex set cannot have any "holes" in it, and its boundary must not be reentrant, or indented anywhere.

Second, an **extreme point,** or **vertex,** of a convex set is defined as follows.

DEFINITION   *An* extreme point, *or* vertex, *of a convex set is a point in the convex set that does not lie on any line that joins two other points in the convex set.*

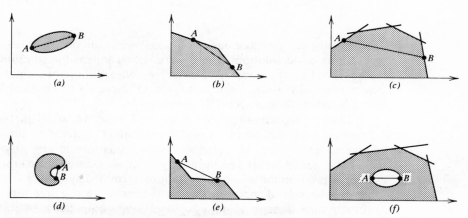

FIGURE 2.4   Convex and Nonconvex Sets. (*a***)** Convex Set. (***b***)** Convex Set. (***c***)** Convex Set. (***d***)** Nonconvex Set. (***e***)** Nonconvex Set. (***f***)** Nonconvex Set.

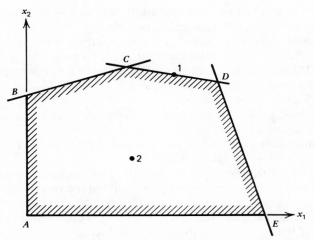

FIGURE 2.5   Extreme and Nonextreme Points of a Convex Set

This definition indicates that a point $\mathbf{x}$ is an extreme point of a convex set X if, and only if, there do not exist points $\mathbf{x}_1$, $\mathbf{x}_2$ ($\mathbf{x}_1 \neq \mathbf{x}_2$) in the convex set such that:

$$\mathbf{x} = \lambda \mathbf{x}_2 + (1 - \lambda)\mathbf{x}_1, \qquad 0 < \lambda < 1 \qquad (2\text{-}103)$$

Note that strict inequalities are imposed on λ. Thus, an extreme point cannot be "between" any other two points of the convex set, that is, it cannot be on the line segment joining the points $\mathbf{x}_1$ and $\mathbf{x}_2$. To illustrate extreme and nonextreme points of a convex set, consider Fig. 2.5. The extreme points of the convex set (crosshatched area) shown in Fig. 2.5 are at A, B, C, D, and E. Points 1 and 2 are nonextreme points of the convex set.

2.12   CONCLUSION

This chapter has provided an introduction to the rudiments of linear, or matrix algebra. Particular emphasis has been placed on those concepts of linear algebra that are useful in the development of an understanding of linear programming. In subsequent chapters we will utilize the material reviewed in this chapter, particularly the material dealing with the Gauss-Jordan elimination procedure. Again, it must be emphasized that this introduction to linear algebra is not intended to be definitive or exhaustive. The more interested student should consult one or more of the selected references in linear algebra that follow.

GLOSSARY OF TERMS

Basic Feasible Solution   A basic solution in which all m of the basic variables are nonnegative (≥ 0).

Basic Nonfeasible Solution   A basic solution in which one, or more, of the m basic variables are negative (< 0).

Basic Solutions   The basic solutions for a system of m linear equations in n

($m < n$) unknowns are determined by setting $n - m$ variables equal to zero and solving for the remaining m variables.

Basic Variables   The m variables of a basic solution whose values must be determined after $n - m$ variables are set equal to zero.

Coefficient Matrix   A matrix that consists of the ordered numerical coefficients of the unknowns within a linear system.

Columns   Vertical lines of the matrix.

Consistent System   A system of linear equations that has exactly one solution (unique solution) or an infinite number of solutions.

Convex Combination   The relationship between points x_1 and x_2 in the set X given by: $x = \lambda x_2 + (1 - \lambda)x_1, \quad 0 \leq \lambda \leq 1$.

Convex Set   A collection of points such that, for each pair of points in the collection of points, the entire line segment joining the two points will also be in the collection of points.

Degenerate Basic Feasible Solution   A basic feasible solution in which one, or more, of the m basic variables are equal to zero.

Domain of the Function   The permissible values of the *dependent* variable.

Extreme Point of a Convex Set   A point in the convex set that does not lie on any line that joins two other points in the convex set.

Elements   The individual entries in a matrix that are identified by means of their position within the matrix. For example, the ith, jth element refers to the number located in the ith row and jth column of the matrix.

Function   A mathematical relationship in which the values of a single dependent variable are determined by a relationship to the values of one or more independent variables. In a function, one set of independent variables values is associated with no more than *one* dependent variable.

Gauss-Jordan Elimination Method   A method used for inverting a matrix or solving a system of linear equations.

Homogeneous System   A system of linear equations $Ax = b = 0$.

Identity Matrix   A matrix whose diagonal elements are ones, and whose remaining elements are zeros.

Inconsistent System   A system of linear equations that has a solution.

Inverse   The product of a matrix $[A]$ and its inverse $[A^{-1}]$ is the identity matrix $[I]$, that is, $[A \cdot A^{-1}] = [I]$.

Linearly Dependent   Two or more rows (columns) of a matrix are *linearly dependent* if one of them can be expressed as a linear combination of the other rows (columns).

Linear Equation   A linear function in which no distinction is made between the dependent and independent variable(s).

Linear Function   A function that is defined in most basic terms by an expression of the form $f(x) = a + bx$, where a and b are real numbers.

Linearly Independent   Two or more rows (columns) of a matrix are *linearly independent* if none of them can be expressed as a linear combination of the other rows (columns).

Main Diagonal   The ith, jth entries of a square matrix where $i = j$.

Matrix   A set of numbers schematically arranged in rows (columns) of equal length.

Matrix Algebra or Linear Algebra   The set of rules developed for performing operations on matrices that are analogous to arithmetic operations.

Matrix Notation   The symbolic representation of matrices and matrix operations.

Nonbasic Variables   The $n - m$ variables set equal to zero in order to determine a basic solution for the remaining m variables.

Nondegenerate Basic Feasible Solution   A basic feasible solution in which all m of the basic variables are positive (> 0).

Nonhomogeneous System   A system of linear equations $[A]x = b$ where $b \neq 0$.

Nonsingular Matrix   A square matrix that has an inverse.

Range of the Function   The permissible values of the dependent variable.

Rank of a Matrix   The number of linearily independent rows (columns) in the matrix.

Rank of a System of Linear Equations   The number of linearly independent equations in the system.

Real Matrix   A matrix in which all the entries are real numbers.

Right-Hand Side Vector   A vector of constants that corresponds to the right-hand side of a system of linear equations.

Rows   Horizontal lines of the matrix.

Row Operations   The application of simple algebraic operations to the rows of a matrix.

Scalar   A real number.

Singular Matrix   A square matrix that has no inverse.

Solution Vector   The vector of unknowns in a matrix representation of a system of linear equations.

Square Matrix   A matrix having an equal number of rows and columns.

System of Linear Equations   A system consisting of one or more linear equations with one or more independent variables.

Transpose (of a Vector or Matrix)   The vector or matrix that is obtained by interchanging the rows and/or columns of a specified vector or matrix.

Underdetermined or Rectangular Systems   A system in which the number of unknowns is greater than the number of equations.

Variables Vector   A vector that consists of the unknowns of a linear system.

Vector   A single row (column) of numbers within a matrix.

Zero or Null Matrix [0]   A matrix in which all the entries are zeroes.

SELECTED REFERENCES

LINEAR
ALGEBRA

Ayres, Frank Jr. 1962. *Theory and Problems of Matrices*. Schaum's Outline Series. New York: McGraw-Hill Book Company.

Beaumont, Ross A. 1966. *Introduction to Modern Algebra and Matrix Theory*. New York: Holt, Rinehart & Winston, Inc.

Bellman, Richard E. 1970. *Introduction to Matrix Analysis*. New York: McGraw-Hill Book Company.

Bowman, Robert L. 1962. *An Introduction to Determinants and Matrices*. Princeton, N.J.: Van Nostrand Company.

Campbell, Hugh G. 1965. *An Introduction to Matrices, Vectors, and Linear Programming*. New York: Appleton-Century-Crofts.

————. 1968. *Matrices With Applications*. New York: Appleton-Century-Crofts.

Childress, Robert L. 1974. *Sets, Matrices, and Linear Programming*. Englewood Cliffs, N.J.: Prentice-Hall, Inc.

Davis, Phillip J. 1965. *The Mathematics of Matrices; A First Book of Matrix Theory and Linear Algebra*. New York: Blaisdell Publishing Company.

Eves, Howard W. 1966. *Elementary Matrix Theory*. Boston: Allyn and Bacon, Inc.

Fuller, Leonard E. 1962. *Basic Matrix Theory*. Englewood Cliffs, N.J.: Prentice-Hall, Inc.

Hadley, George. 1961. *Linear Algebra*. Reading, Ma.: Addison-Wesley Publishing Company, Inc.

Hohn, Franz H. 1967. *Elementary Matrix Algebra*. New York: Macmillan Publishing Company, Inc.

Lipschutz, Seymour. 1968. *Linear Algebra*. Schaum's Outline Series. New York: McGraw-Hill Book Company.

Pease, Marshall C. 1965. *Methods of Matrix Algebra*. New York: Academic Press, Inc.

Reiner, Irving. 1967. *Introduction to Matrix Theory and Linear Algebra*. New York: Macmillan Publishing Company, Inc.

Searle, S. R., and W. H. Hausman. 1970. *Matrix Algebra for Business and Economics*. New York: John Wiley & Sons, Inc.

DISCUSSION QUESTIONS

1. What is the difference between a dependent and an independent variable?
2. What do we mean by a "system of simultaneous linear equations"?
3. Why do only square matrices have inverses?
4. Would the Gauss-Jordan elimination method also work if we used only column operations instead of row operations? Why or why not?
5. Why do you have to use "diagonalization" to solve a system of linear equations by the Gauss-Jordan elimination method? Do the elements on the diagonal of the first [A]-matrix all have to be ones? Why or why not?
6. Is the concept of "rank" only relevant to "square" matrices? Why or why not?
7. Does a system, which has as many equations as variables, guarantee us a solution? Why or why not?
8. Why are "singular" matrices only relevant with respect to "square" matrices? (i.e.: why can a singular matrix only arise from a "square" system of linear equation?)
9. Can a system of linear equations in which there are more unknowns than equations be a "consistent" system? Why or why not?
10. How can we find a basic solution to an underdetermined or rectangular system of linear equations?

PROBLEM SET

1. Plot the linear profit function

$$f(p) = 4p - 3$$

2. State the linear function $f(x)$ shown in the graph at the top of the next page.
3. Plot the following linear functions and specify the slope of each function:
   (a) $f(x) = -2x + 5$
   (b) $f(x) = -0.6x + 3$
   (c) $f(x) = 5$
   (d) $f(x) = {}^x/_{10} + 5$
   (e) $f(x) = 2x$
4. Plot linear functions, $f(x) = a + bx$, that satisfy the following conditions:
   (a) $x = -1, f(x) = -3; x = 1, f(x) = 3$
   (b) $x = 2, f(x) = 2; b = 1$
   (c) $x = -3, f(x) = 2; x = 2, f(x) = 5$
   (d) $x = -2, f(x) = 2, b = -0.5$

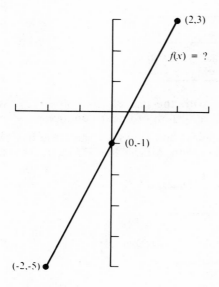

5. (a) Plot $f(x) = 0$.
    (b) Determine the linear functions $f_1(x)$ and $f_2(x)$ shown in the following graph.

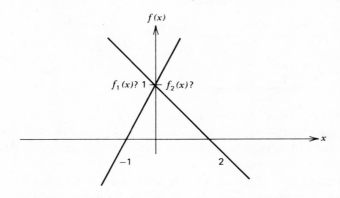

6. State, in mathematical terms, linear functions that describe the following verbal relationships:
    (a) Fixed costs are $10 and variable costs are $2.50 per unit produced.
    (b) Total costs are $100 for 10 units and $125 for 15 units.
    (c) An individual invests $1000 with the expectation that it will increase by $250 per year.
    (d) An individual invests $1000 with the expectation that it will increase by 25 percent per year.
    (e) One thousand bushels of corn can be sold at $2.00 per bushel, and 2000 bushels of corn can be sold at $1.25 per bushel.

7. Rusty Pipe, Professional Plumber, is considering installation of two types of pipes in any of three types of installations. Each installation requires a different length of pipe as follows.

	6 in.	*12 in.*	*18 in.*
Pipe 1: iron	$2.00	$5.00	$7.00
Pipe 2: plastic	4.00	6.00	8.00

Expenditures can total $25 with the use of iron pipe; $27, with plastic pipe. Describe this situation using a system of linear equations.

8. Abbie Seller has oranges, apples, and pears for sale. She has two buyers, Mr. X and Mrs. Y. Mr. X has $50 to spend; Mrs. Y has $75 to spend. The costs for Abbie Seller's fruit are as follows.

	$ Per Bushel
Oranges	3
Apples	4
Pears	6

Describe this situation using a system of linear equations.

9. Factory A and Factory B produce items 1, 2, and 3, in the following manner:

	Number Per Day	
Item	*Factory A*	*Factory B*
1	4	2
2	3	5
3	1	6

Describe this production situation in matrix form.

10. Sam's Used Car Lot has 25 Chevrolets, 22 Fords, and 19 Plymouths. Amy's Used Car Lot has 33 Chevrolets, 42 Fords, and 15 Plymouths. Describe this inventory situation in matrix form.

11. State, in mathematical terms, a linear total cost function that describes the following verbal relationship. Fixed cost is 500 and variable costs are:

3 per unit produced if you don't produce more than 500
2 per unit produced if you produce more than 500 but less than 1000
1 per unit produced if you produce 1000 or more

12. We seek to manufacture products A, B, and C.
A uses 20 lb of material a
      40 lb of material b
      10 lb of material c
B uses 10 lb of material a
      50 lb of material b
      20 lb of material c
C uses 5 lb of material a
      0 lb of material b
      10 lb of material c

The maximum amount available of materials a, b, c for production of A, B, C is 100, 200, and 300, respectively. Describe the situation using a system of linear equations, when all materials a, b, c are used fully.

13. Assume that we are given two matrices.

$$[\mathbf{A}] = \begin{bmatrix} 2 & 1 \\ 0 & 4 \end{bmatrix} \quad \text{and} \quad [\mathbf{B}] = \begin{bmatrix} 3 & 1 \\ 2 & 4 \end{bmatrix}$$

Determine the following:
(a) $[\mathbf{A}] + [\mathbf{B}]$
(b) $[\mathbf{A}] - [\mathbf{B}]$
(c) $3[\mathbf{A}] - 2[\mathbf{B}]$
(d) $2[\mathbf{A}] + 2[\mathbf{B}]$

14. Assume that we are given two matrices.

$$[\mathbf{A}] = \begin{bmatrix} 3 & 2 \\ 1 & 4 \end{bmatrix} \quad \text{and} \quad [\mathbf{C}] = \begin{bmatrix} 3 & 6 & -1 \\ 2 & -4 & 5 \end{bmatrix}$$

Can we determine $[\mathbf{A}] + [\mathbf{C}]$? Explain your answer.

15. A candy manufacturer produces a candy called "Chocolate Delight." The costs for the raw material costs and the transportation associated with producing 1 lb of this candy at each of two plants are given by the following matrices.

		Cost	
	Raw Material	*Transportation*	*Ingredient*
Plant **A** =	0.67	0.11	Chocolate
	0.92	0.13	Sugar
	0.33	0.09	Nuts
Plant **B** =	0.72	0.15	Chocolate
	0.88	0.18	Sugar
	0.42	0.12	Nuts

Determine the matrix representing the total raw material cost and the total transportation cost of each ingredient.

16. Given $[\mathbf{A}] = \begin{bmatrix} 1 & -3 \\ 5 & -2 \end{bmatrix}$ and $[\mathbf{B}] = \begin{bmatrix} 2 & 1 \\ -7 & 4 \end{bmatrix}$

Determine the following:
(a) $2[\mathbf{A}]$
(b) $-3[\mathbf{B}]$
(c) $[\mathbf{A}] + 2[\mathbf{B}]$
(d) $\frac{1}{2}[\mathbf{B}] - 3[\mathbf{A}]$

17. Given $[\mathbf{A}] = [2 \quad 3 \quad 4]$ and $[\mathbf{B}] = \begin{bmatrix} 4 \\ 3 \\ 2 \end{bmatrix}$

Determine the following:

(a) [**AB**]

(b) [**BA**]

18.
Let $[\mathbf{A}] = \begin{bmatrix} 2 & -1 \\ 1 & 3 \\ -3 & 5 \end{bmatrix}$ and $[\mathbf{B}] = \begin{bmatrix} 1 & 0 & -2 \\ 2 & 3 & 1 \end{bmatrix}$

Find:

(a) [**AB**]

(b) [**A**]

19. Using the matrices $[\mathbf{A}] = \begin{bmatrix} 2 & 1 \\ 3 & -2 \\ 1 & 0 \end{bmatrix}$ $[\mathbf{B}] = \begin{bmatrix} 3 & -1 \\ 2 & -2 \end{bmatrix}$, and

$[\mathbf{C}] = \begin{bmatrix} 1 & 3 \\ -1 & 4 \end{bmatrix}$

verify that [**A**]([**B**] + [**C**]) = [**AB**] + [**AC**] and [**A**]([**B**] − [**C**]) = [**AB**] − [**AC**].

20. Using the matrices $[\mathbf{A}] = \begin{bmatrix} 5 & 1 \\ 2 & 8 \end{bmatrix}$ and $[\mathbf{B}] = \begin{bmatrix} 0 & 5 \\ 2 & 3 \\ 6 & 4 \end{bmatrix}$

Can we determine [**A**] · [**B**]? Explain your answer.

21. Using the matrices $[\mathbf{A}] = \begin{bmatrix} 1 & 2 & 3 \end{bmatrix}$, $[\mathbf{B}] = \begin{bmatrix} 1 \\ 2 \\ 3 \end{bmatrix}$, and $[\mathbf{C}] = [5]$

Determine:

(a) [**A**] · [**B**] · [**C**]

(b) [**C**] · [**A**] · [**B**]

22. Using the matrix $[\mathbf{A}] = \begin{bmatrix} 1 & 2 \\ 2 & 1 \end{bmatrix}$

Calculate $[\mathbf{A}]^3$.

23. Using the matrices $[\mathbf{A}] = \begin{bmatrix} 1 & 2 \\ 2 & 1 \end{bmatrix}$, $[\mathbf{B}] = \begin{bmatrix} 0 & 1 & 5 \\ 6 & 3 & 2 \end{bmatrix}$, and

$[\mathbf{C}] = \begin{bmatrix} 1 & 0 \\ 0 & 1 \\ 2 & 3 \end{bmatrix}$

verify that [**A**][**BC**] = [**AB**][**C**].

24. Find the inverse of the following matrix, using the Gauss-Jordan elimination method.

$$[\mathbf{A}] = \begin{bmatrix} 2 & 4 \\ 1 & 5 \end{bmatrix}$$

25. Find the inverse of the following matrix, using the Gauss-Jordan elimination method.

$$[\mathbf{A}] = \begin{bmatrix} 3 & 2 & -1 \\ 4 & 7 & 3 \\ 2 & 1 & 2 \end{bmatrix}$$

26. (a) Find the inverse of the following matrix where a, b, $c > 0$, using the Gauss-Jordan elimination method.

$$\begin{bmatrix} a & 0 & 0 \\ 0 & b & 0 \\ 0 & 0 & c \end{bmatrix}$$

(b) Suppose $b = 0$; how does this change the answer?

27. (a) Given the matrix $[\mathbf{A}] = \begin{bmatrix} 5 & 1 \\ 2 & 8 \end{bmatrix}$

determine the inverse of $\lambda[\mathbf{A}]$ where $\lambda > 0$, using the Gauss-Jordan elimination method.

(b) Does $[\lambda\mathbf{A}]^{-1} = \frac{1}{\lambda}[\mathbf{A}^{-1}]$?

28. Solve the following system of linear equations, using the Gauss-Jordan elimination method.

$$1x_1 + 3x_2 = 2$$
$$2x_1 + 2x_2 = 3$$

29. Solve the following system of linear equations, using the Gauss-Jordan elimination method.

$$3x_1 + 2x_2 - 1x_3 = 4$$
$$4x_1 + 7x_2 + 3x_3 = 2$$
$$2x_1 + 1x_2 + 2x_3 = 6$$

30. Solve the following system of linear equations, using the Gauss-Jordan elimination method.

$$2x_1 + 4x_2 + x_3 \qquad = 6$$
$$x_2 \qquad + x_4 = 2$$
$$x_1 + 2x_2 \qquad = 4$$
$$x_2 + 2x_3 \qquad = 8$$

31. Determine the ranks of the following matrices.

(a) $\begin{bmatrix} 2 & 6 \\ 3 & 1 \end{bmatrix}$

(b) $\begin{bmatrix} 2 & 6 \\ 1 & 3 \end{bmatrix}$

(c) $\begin{bmatrix} 1 & 0 & 0 \\ 0 & 2 & 0 \\ 0 & 0 & 3 \end{bmatrix}$

(d) $\begin{bmatrix} 4 & -2 & 2 \\ 2 & 8 & 10 \\ 6 & 4 & 10 \end{bmatrix}$

(e) $[2]$

(f) $\begin{bmatrix} 1 \\ 2 \\ 3 \end{bmatrix}$

(g) $\begin{bmatrix} 3 & 2 & 9 \\ 1 & 4 & 2 \end{bmatrix}$

32. Determine the rank of the following matrices.
     (a) $[-1 \quad 2]$

(b) $\begin{bmatrix} 3 & 1 \\ 6 & 2 \end{bmatrix}$

33. (a) Determine the rank of the following matrix.

$$\begin{bmatrix} \frac{1}{3} & 1 & -2 \\ \frac{5}{3} & -1 & \frac{4}{3} \\ 2 & 0 & -\frac{2}{3} \end{bmatrix}$$

(b) Is the matrix a singular or nonsingular matrix?

34. Using the concept of rank, determine whether or not the following systems of equations are consistent or inconsistent. For those systems of equations that are consistent, determine if there is a unique solution or an infinite number of solutions.
     (a) $2x_1 + 3x_2 = 6$
        $1x_1 + 4x_2 = 3$
     (b) $2x_1 + 1x_2 = 1$
        $6x_1 + 3x_2 = 3$
     (c) $1x_1 + 3x_2 - 1x_3 = 2$
        $1x_1 + 2x_2 + 1x_3 = 3$
        $3x_1 + 7x_2 + 1x_3 = 7$

35. Using the concept of rank, determine whether or not the following systems of equations are consistent or inconsistent. For those systems of equations that are consistent, determine if there is a unique solution or an infinite number of solutions.

(a) $2x_1 + 4x_2 + 3x_3 = 2$
      $3x_1 - 1x_2 + 5x_3 = 3$
      $-2x_1 + 4x_2 - 3x_3 = 7$

(b) $2x_1 - 1x_2 + 4x_3 = 1$
      $6x_1 - 3x_2 + 12x_3 = 3$
      $1x_2 - \frac{1}{2}x_2 + 2x_3 = \frac{1}{2}$

(c) $3x_1 + 2x_2 + 6x_3 = 2$
      $1x_1 + 2x_2 + 1x_3 = 5$
      $1x_1 + 2x_2 + 1x_3 = 3$

36. Determine whether the following system of equations is consistent or not; if consistent, determine if there is a unique or an infinite number of solutions.

$$\frac{1}{3}x_1 + x_2 - 2x_3 = \frac{2}{3}$$
$$\frac{5}{3}x_1 - x_2 + \frac{4}{3}x_3 = \frac{5}{3}$$
$$2x_1 \qquad - \frac{2}{3}x_3 = \frac{7}{3}$$

37. Show that is [A] is nonsingular, then [A][B] = [A][C] implies [B] = [C].

38. Find all basic solutions to the following rectangular system of linear equations. For each basic solution indicate whether it is a basic feasible solution or not. For each basic feasible solution indicate whether it is degenerate or not.

$$2x_1 + 3x_2 + 7x_3 = 4$$
$$3x_1 + 4x_2 + 2x_3 = 2$$

39. Find all basic solutions to the following rectangular system of linear equations. For each basic solution indicate whether it is a basic feasible solution or not. For each basic feasible solution indicate whether it is degenerate or not.

$$1x_1 + 1x_2 + 2x_3 - 2x_4 = 5$$
$$3x_1 + 2x_2 - 4x_3 - 3x_4 = 2$$

40. Find all basic solutions to the following rectangular system of linear equations. For each basic solution indicate whether it is a basic feasible solution or not. For each basic feasible solution indicate whether it is degenerate or not.

$$2x_1 \qquad + 1x_3 + 1x_4 = 4$$
$$1x_1 \qquad + 2x_3 \qquad = 2$$
$$\qquad + 1x_2 \qquad + 2x_4 = 4$$

41. Find all basic solutions to the following rectangular system of linear equations. For each basic solution indicate whether it is a basic feasible solution or not. For each basic feasible solution indicate whether it is degenerate or not.

$$3x_1 + 5x_2 + 1x_3 = 7$$
$$2x_1 + 6x_2 + 4x_3 = 2$$

42. Find all basic solutions to the following rectangular system of linear equations. For each basic solution indicate whether it is a basic feasible solution or not. For each basic feasible solution indicate whether it is degenerate or not.

$$4x_1 + 3x_2 + 7x_3 = 36$$
$$2x_1 + 2x_2 + 4x_3 = 18$$

43. Find all basic solutions to the following rectangular system of linear equations. For each basic solution indicate whether it is a basic feasible solution or not. For each basic feasible solution indicate whether it is degenerate or not.

$$1x_1 + 2x_2 + 4x_3 + 2x_4 = 16$$
$$3x_1 + 2x_2 + 1x_3 + 1x_4 = 24$$

44. Which of the following figures are convex sets?

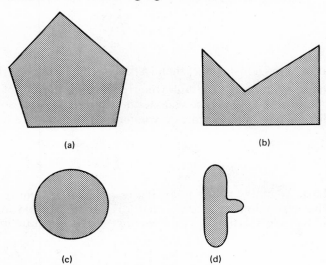

    (a)   (b)

    (c)   (d)

45. Which of the following figures are convex sets?

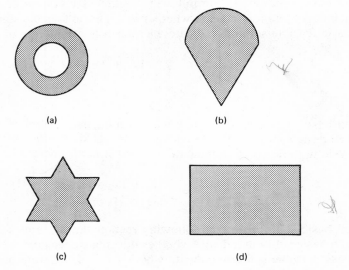

    (a)   (b)

    (c)   (d)

3 An Introduction to Linear Programming

3.1 INTRODUCTION

Linear programming is perhaps the most widely used technique in management science. Since the development of the simplex method for solving linear programming problems by George Dantzig in 1947, there has been an increasing use of the technique in a myriad of applications. Basically, **linear programming** is concerned with the problem of allocating limited resources among competing activities in an optimal manner. This type of problem arises naturally in a number of situations, such as scheduling production, manufacturing an item at a minimum cost, selecting an optimum portfolio of investments, blending of chemicals, and allocating salesman to sales territory. In each of these situations, it should be noted that the common ingredient is the requirement that some type of scarce or limited resource must be allocated to some specific activity. Since the resources employed generally incur costs and produce profits, the linear programming problem becomes that of allocating the scarce resources to the activities in such a manner that profits are a maximum or, alternatively, that costs are a minimum.

In this chapter we will introduce the basic concepts of linear programming, emphasizing the problem formulation process. We will also illustrate the use of a graphical procedure for solving linear programming problems having only two variables. The graphical representation of a two-variable linear programming problem will be used to illustrate the basic concepts, definitions, and terminology of linear programming. Next, the special cases that may arise in linear programming will be exhibited and discussed. Finally, several applications of linear programming will be presented, and the focus of these applications will again be on the problem formulation process.

A general solution technique for linear programming problems, termed the *simplex method*, will be developed in Chapter 4. This technique is based upon the Gauss-Jordan elimination procedure, which was discussed earlier in Chapter 2.

3.2 FORMULATION OF LINEAR PROGRAMMING PROBLEMS

We will begin our discussion by illustrating the formulation of two typical, but simplified, linear programming problems.

EXAMPLE 1   *Profit Maximization–Production Scheduling.*   The Crafty Machine Works produces machined metal parts to customer specifications and operates in "job shop" fashion. Management of the company is concerned with allocating excess production capacity to either, or both, of two new products:

Product 1:   bearing plate
Product 2:   gear

The excess capacity that is available but might limit production is given in the following table:

constraints

Machine Type	Available Excess Capacity (Machine Hours/Week)
Milling machine	60
Metal lathe	40

The number of machine hours required to produce each unit of the two products is given in the following table:

I/0. coefficients
(parameters)

Machine Type	Required Machine Hours (Machine Hours/Unit)	
	Product 1	Product 2
Milling machine	5	10
Metal lathe	4	4

The firm's marketing department has determined that the bearing plate can be priced to produce a unit profit of $6 while the gear can be priced to produce a unit profit of $8.

This problem situation can be formulated into a linear programming model, as follows. Let $x_j (j = 1,2)$ be the number of units (unknown) of product j to be produced in a week, where x_1 = number of bearing plates produced per week and x_2 = number of gears produced per week. The x_j are the *decision variables*, whose values we seek to determine as we solve the problem. We are interested in maximizing profitability, so that the profit function for the model can be written as:

$$\text{Maximize } Z = \$6x_1 + \$8x_2 \qquad (3\text{-}1)$$

This is the *objective function* for our problem formulation. In this objective function the values \$6 and \$8 are the profit *parameters*, or coefficients of the objective function.

The resource availabilities in this situation are the available excess capacities on the two machines. Thus, a constraint must be developed for each of these two resource availabilities. These resource availabilities are referred to as **right-hand side values**, or coefficients, and are resource availability parameters.

The mathematical statement of the two resource availability constraints is:

$$\begin{array}{ll} 5x_1 + 10x_2 \le 60 \text{ hours} & \text{(Milling machine constraint)} \\ 4x_1 + 4x_2 \le 40 \text{ hours} & \text{(Metal lathe constraint)} \end{array} \qquad (3\text{-}2)$$

This is the **constraint set** for our problem formulation. The first constraint states that 5 hours per unit times the number of units of bearing plates that are produced plus 10 hours per unit times the number of units of gears that are produced must be less than, or equal to, the 60 hours of available excess capacity for the milling machine. The second constraint states that 4 hours per unit times the number of units of bearing plates that are produced plus 4 hours per unit times the number of units of gears that are produced must be less than, or equal to, the 40 hours of available excess capacity for the metal lathe. In each of these constraints, the coefficients of the decision variables x_1 and x_2 are the **physical rates of usage** or **physical rates of substitution**. These physical rates of usage are the parameters of the constraint set. They tell us the rate at which the resources (milling machine hours or metal lathe hours) are used in the production of the desired end products (x_1 = bearing plates, x_2 = gears).

Finally, we must define the **nonnegativity restrictions** for our problem formulation:

$$x_1 \ge 0, \qquad x_2 \ge 0 \qquad (3\text{-}3)$$

These nonnegativity restrictions simply state that nonnegative amounts of each of the two products must be made.

EXAMPLE 2 *Cost Minimization–Chemical Requirements.* A photographic development company has determined the chemical requirements for blending a developer for a particular type of film. The company is able to purchase two brands of dry developing compounds that contain the required chemicals. The chemical requirements and the chemical contents and costs of the development compounds are shown in the following table:

Chemical Required	Developing Compound		Units Required
	Brand 1	*Brand 2*	
Chemical A	6 Units per bag	3 Units per bag	18 Units
Chemical B	2 Units per bag	4 Units per bag	12 Units
Chemical C	2 Units per bag	8 Units per bag	16 Units
Cost per bag	$5.00	$4.00	

[handwritten: Step 1]

This problem situation can be formulated into a linear-programming problem in the following manner. Let x_j ($j = 1,2$) be the number of bags (unknown) of developing compound j to be purchased. We are interested in minimizing cost; therefore, the cost function for the model can be written as:

[handwritten: Step 2: x_j ($j = 1,2$) = no. bags developing compound j to produce]

$$\text{problem:} \qquad \text{Minimize } Z = \$5x_1 + \$4x_2 \tag{3-4}$$

The resource requirements in this situation are the unit requirements for chemicals A, B, and C, respectively. A constraint must be developed for each of the three chemical requirements. The mathematical statement of the three resource requirement constraints is:

[handwritten: s.t.]

$$\begin{aligned} 6x_1 + 3x_2 &\geq 18 \quad &(\text{Chemical } A) \\ 2x_1 + 4x_2 &\geq 12 \quad &(\text{Chemical } B) \\ 2x_1 + 8x_2 &\geq 16 \quad &(\text{Chemical } C) \end{aligned} \tag{3-5}$$

[handwritten: $x_1, x_2 \geq 0$]

The first constraint states that 6 units per bag times the number of bags of developing compound 1 plus 3 units per bag times the number of bags of developing compound 2 must be equal to, or greater than, the 18 units of chemical A that are required. The second constraint states that 2 units per bag times the number of bags of developing compound 1 plus 4 units per bag times the number of bags of developing compound 2 must be equal to, or greater than, the 12 units of chemical B that are required. The third constraint states that 2 units per bag times the number of bags of developing compound 1 plus 8 units per bag times the number of bags of developing compound 2 must be equal to, or greater than, the 16 units of chemical C that are required.

Finally, there are the nonnegativity restrictions:

$$x_1 \geq 0, x_2 \geq 0 \tag{3-6}$$

These nonnegativity restrictions indicate that only nonnegative amounts of the two developing compounds can be purchased.

It is important to stress that every **linear programming problem formulation** requires a linear objective function (which we seek to maximize or minimize), a linear constraint set, and a set of nonnegativity restrictions. All three of these parts of the linear programming problem are defined in terms of a set of decision variables whose values are determined as the problem is solved.

One of the most difficult aspects of applying linear programming successfully involves model formulation. Unfortunately, model formulation cannot be taught in an easy manner. It is essentially an "art" that comes from experience and the diligent study of a number of applications and problem situations. However, some general guidelines to problem formulation can perhaps be identified:

1. Focus on the broad general objective of the problem, identifying what is the basic objective of the problem and how it is related to the factors (decision variables) over which the decision maker has control.
   (a) Identify the decision variables (the x_j's) of the problem and define the units of measure to be used with the decision variables.
   (b) Determine the values of the objective function coefficients and define the units of measure to be used with the objective function coefficients.
   (c) Formulate the objective function and make sure that it is stated consistently in terms of units of measure.
2. Focus on the physical usage of resources associated with the problem.
   (a) Identify the physical rate of usage coefficients and define the units of measure to be used with these coefficients.
   (b) Identify the available resources, or the right-hand side coefficients, and define the units of measure to be used with these coefficients.
   (c) Formulate the constraint set and make sure that each constraint is stated consistently in terms of units of measure.
3. Define the nonnegativity conditions associated with the decision variables.

Following these general procedural steps should help you to avoid making errors in the formulation process such as specifying inconsistent constraints or defining an objective function whose terms are not stated in the same units of measure.

As you begin to formulate linear programming problems you will quickly observe that there may be alternative ways of defining the objective function, some, or all, of the constraints, or indeed the entire problem. Do not let this trouble you unnecessarily, for there may be equally acceptable alternative ways of formulating a problem and any of the alternative formulations may be considered "correct." In the linear programming model formulations that follow in this and subsequent chapters, and in the answers given at the end of the book, a workable, acceptable formulation will be given. If you do not obtain exactly the same formulation, do not conclude that your formulation is incorrect. Instead, check your formulation for consistency in terms of meeting the requirements of the problem.

3.3   MATHEMATICAL STRUCTURE OF LINEAR PROGRAMMING PROBLEMS

Based on our previous illustrations the general mathematical structure of linear programming problems can now be stated. We seek to determine the values of x_j; $j = 1, 2, \ldots, n$, which maximize the linear function:

$$\text{Maximize} \quad Z = c_1 x_1 + c_2 x_2 + \cdots + c_n x_n \tag{3-7}$$

subject to the linear restrictions:

parameters

$$a_{11}x_1 + a_{12}x_2 + \cdots + a_{1n}x_n \leq b_1$$
$$a_{21}x_1 + a_{22}x_2 + \cdots + a_{2n}x_n \leq b_2$$
$$\begin{array}{ccccc} \cdot & \cdot & \cdot & \cdot & \cdot \\ \cdot & \cdot & \cdot & \cdot & \cdot \\ \cdot & \cdot & \cdot & \cdot & \cdot \end{array} \tag{3-8}$$
$$a_{m1}x_1 + a_{m2}x_2 + \cdots + a_{mn}x_n \leq b_m$$

with $x_1 \geq 0, x_2 \geq 0, \ldots, x_n \geq 0$ $\qquad\qquad$ (3-9)

where a_{ij}, b_i, and c_j are known (given) constants or *parameters* of the model. The c_j are the parameters of the objective function, the a_{ij} are the parameters of the constraint set, and the b_i are the right-hand side parameters. The linear function being maximized is the *objective function*. The linear restrictions given by (3-8) are the *constraint set*. The conditions given by (3-9) are the *nonnegativity restrictions* for the *decision variables*, the x_j.

This linear-programming model can be written more compactly as:

$$\text{Maximize} \quad Z = \sum_{j=1}^{n} c_j x_j \quad \text{(Objective function)} \tag{3-10}$$

subject to: $\quad \sum_{j=1}^{n} a_{ij}x_j \leq b_i \quad \text{for } i = 1,2, \ldots, m \quad \text{(Constraint set)} \tag{3-11}$

with $x_j \geq 0 \quad \text{for } j = 1,2, \ldots, n \quad \text{(Nonnegativity restrictions)} \tag{3-12}$

Or, using the matrix notation introduced in Chapter 2:

$$\text{Maximize} \quad Z = \mathbf{cx} \quad \text{(Objective function)} \tag{3-13}$$

subject to: $\quad \mathbf{Ax} \leq \mathbf{b} \quad \text{(Constraint set)} \tag{3-14}$

with $\mathbf{x} \geq \mathbf{0} \quad \text{(Nonnegativity restrictions)} \tag{3-15}$

where $\mathbf{c} = (c_1, c_2, \ldots, c_n)$ is a row vector, $\mathbf{x} = (x_1, x_2, \ldots, x_n)$ is a column vector, $\mathbf{A} = [a_{ij}]$ is an $(m \times n)$ matrix, $\mathbf{b} = (b_1, b_2, \ldots, b_m)$ is a column vector, and $\mathbf{0}$ is an n-dimensional null column vector.

We should immediately note that the general linear programming model presented above can have other forms. First, we may seek to minimize, rather than maximize, the objective function. Second, the constraints need not be of the form "less than or equal to" ($\leq$), but instead can be of the form "greater than or equal to" ($\geq$), or they can be strict "equalities" ($=$). Third, it is possible to delete the nonnegativity restrictions for some of the decision variables and allow them to be unrestricted ($+$ or $-$) in sign. These various other forms of the linear programming model will be presented and discussed in detail in the material that follows.

In the linear programming formulation given by 3-7, 3-8, and 3-9, all of the mathematical functions that are used are linear functions of the decision variables, (i.e., the x_j are all expressed to the first power). In later chapters of the book (Chapters 9 and 10) we will consider nonlinear programming problems that have the same structure as linear programming problems, with the important exception that the mathematical functions used are not linear functions of the decision variables (e.g., a nonlinear programming problem may have terms such as x_1^2, $2\sqrt{x_3}$).

3.3.1   Economic Interpretation— Activity Analysis Problem

The word *programming* in the name *linear programming* does not refer to computer programming at all, although many computer programs have been written and are used to solve linear programming problems. In the title *linear programming*, the word *programming* refers to the planning of activities in a manner that achieves some "optimal" result, under restrictions of resources availability.

The production scheduling linear programming problem formulated earlier in Section 3.2 is an example of an activity analysis problem in which we seek to allocate scarce resources among competing activities. The economic interpretation of the problem is as follows: given n competing activities, the decision variables, $x_1, x_2, \ldots, x_n$, represent the levels of these activities. In a typical production scheduling problem, each activity is the production of a certain number of units of the jth product during a given period of time. The c_j represent the unit profits associated with unit increases in the x_j. The number of relevant scarce resources is m, and each of the m linear inequalities in the constraint set corresponds to a restriction on the availability of one of these resources. Thus, the b_i are the amounts of resources available for the m activities, and the a_{ij} represent the amount of resource i consumed by each unit of product j. The constraint set, in total, represents the total usage of the respective resources. The nonnegativity restrictions ($x_j \geq 0; j = 1, 2, \ldots, n$) preclude the possibility of negative activity levels (i.e., we cannot produce a negative quantity of any product).

3.4   A GRAPHICAL APPROACH TO LINEAR PROGRAMMING

For simple two-variable linear programming problems,[1] a graphical approach can be used to obtain a solution. Additionally, the graphical solution provides a comprehensive illustration of the basic concepts of linear programming. However, the reader should be cautioned that the graphical procedure is limited to two-variable problems, and the simplex procedure is used for problems whose size exceeds two variables. We will now illustrate the graphical procedure, using the previously discussed production scheduling (maximization) and chemical requirements (minimization) problems. Recall first from the previous section of this chapter that the problem formulation for the production scheduling problem was as follows:

$$\text{Maximize } Z = 6x_1 + 8x_2 \quad \text{(Objective function)} \tag{3-16}$$

$$\text{subject to: } \begin{array}{l} 5x_1 + 10x_2 \leq 60 \\ 4x_1 + 4x_2 \leq 40 \end{array} \quad \text{(Constraint set)} \tag{3-17}$$

$$\text{with} \quad x_1 \geq 0, x_2 \geq 0 \quad \text{(Nonnegativity restrictions)} \tag{3-18}$$

In Fig. 3.1 a graphical representation of this production scheduling problem is presented. Several important facets of linear programming can be illustrated by

---

[1] Strictly speaking, three-variable linear programming problems can also be solved graphically. However, it is very difficult to obtain such a solution graphically because of the complexity associated with drawing in three dimensions.

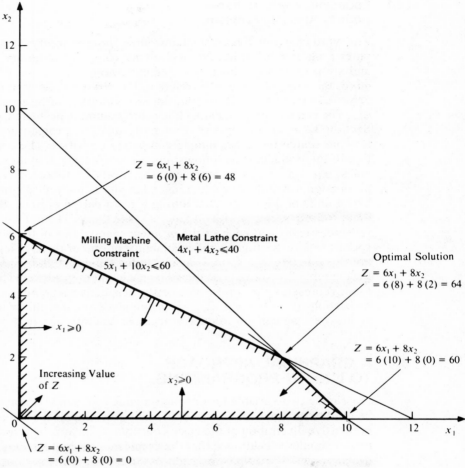

FIGURE 3.1   Graphical Representation—Production-Scheduling Problem

Fig. 3.1. First, observe that the constraint set is composed of two linear inequalities, which can be represented by straight lines that form boundaries for permissible values of the decision variables, the x_j. Each of the two constraints (inequalities) can be plotted from two intercept points. Thus, the intercept points $(x_1 = 0, x_2 = 6)$ and $(x_1 = 12, x_2 = 0)$ are used to plot the straight line representing the first constraint. This first constraint states that no (x_1, x_2) value can lie above the line $5x_1 + 10x_2 = 60$, in Fig. 3.1. Similarly, the intercept points $(x_1 = 0, x_2 = 10)$ and $(x_1 = 10, x_2 = 0)$ are used to plot the straight line representing the second constraint. This second constraint signifies that no (x_1, x_2) value can lie above the line $4x_1 + 4x_2 = 40$, in Fig. 3.1. Second, the nonnegativity restrictions are plotted as all values of $x_1 \geq 0$, and all values of $x_2 \geq 0$. These restrictions are simply all values, including and to the right of the straight lines, $x_1 = 0$ (x_2-axis), and all values, including and above the straight line, $x_2 = 0$ (x_1-axis). These restrictions correspond to the vertical and horizontal axes of the graph. Third, the objective function is graphed as a series of straight lines (often referred to as **iso-profit**, or ''equal profit,'' **lines** in a profit maximization problem) beginning at the origin (x_1

$= 0, x_2 = 0$), where the objective function has a value of $Z = 6x_1 + 8x_2 = 6(0) + 8(0) = 0$, and continuing upward and to the right to the point $(x_1 = 8, x_2 = 2)$ where the objective function has a value of $Z = 6x_1 + 8x_2 = 6(8) + 8(2) = 64$.

Now, let us introduce three important definitions.

DEFINITIONS

1. *Any set of x_j that satisfies the contraint set is termed a* solution *to the linear-programming model.*
2. *Any set of x_j that satisfies the constraint set and the nonnegativity restrictions is termed a* feasible solution *to the linear-programming model.*
3. *Any set of x_j that satisfies the constraint set and the nonnegativity restrictions and optimizes (maximizes and minimizes) the objective function, is termed an* optimal feasible solution.

These definitions are illustrated by referring to the graphical representation of Fig. 3.1. First, the **solution space** is defined by the constraint set that is bounded by the two straight lines, $5x_1 + 10x_2 = 60$, and $4x_1 + 4x_2 = 40$. Next, the **feasible solutions** are points within the **feasible solution space** that is defined by the two constraints and the two nonnegativity restrictions, $x_1 \geq 0$ and $x_2 \geq 0$. The feasible solution space in Fig. 3.1 has been crosshatched. Finally, the **optimal feasible solution** is seen to be the point $(x_1 = 8, x_2 = 2)$ within the feasible solution space at which the value of the objective function is the largest (i.e., $Z = 6x_1 + 8x_2 = 6(8) + 8(2) = 64$). Note how the values of the objective function, Z, are traced over the feasible solution space, beginning at the origin $(x_1 = 0, x_2 = 0)$, with a straight line having the slope of the objective function (Slope $= -c_1/c_2 = -6/8 = -3/4$). At the origin the value of the objective function is obviously, $Z = 0$. As the *iso-profit* line with slope $= -3/4$ is moved upward and to the right, the point $(x_1 = 0, x_2 = 6)$ is reached and at this point, $Z = 48$. Moving further right and upward we obtain the point $(x_1 = 10, x_2 = 0)$, at which the value of $Z = 60$. Finally, we move to the point $(x_1 = 8, x_2 = 2)$ producing the optimal feasible solution, $Z = 64$. Thus, to maximize profits we have moved the iso-profit line (objective function) as far as possible from the origin, increasing the values of x_1 and x_2, but have still remained within the feasible solution space.

As seen in Fig. 3.1, the optimal feasible solution to the linear programming problem is at a point on the boundary of the feasible solution space. Obviously, there are an infinite number of points on, or within, the feasible solution space (crosshatched area), and it would be virtually impossible to evaluate each point in our search for optimality. Fortunately, we greatly restrict our search procedure in linear programming, by utilizing four important theorems of linear programming:

Theorem 1   *The set of feasible solutions (feasible solution space) to a linear programming problem, if a feasible solution exists, is a convex set.*

Theorem 2   *Within the feasible solution space, basic feasible solutions correspond to the extreme points of the feasible solution space.*

Theorem 3   *There are a finite number of basic feasible solutions within the feasible solution space.*

Theorem 4   *The optimal feasible solution, if it exists, will occur at one, or more, of the extreme points.*

The proofs of these theorems are long and tedious. Consequently, they will not be developed here; the more interested reader is referred to advanced texts on linear programming.[2] However, by referring to Fig. 3.1 we can illustrate their use in solving linear programming problems. *First*, the feasible solution space (cross-hatched area) of Fig. 3.1 is definitely a convex set, in this instance a four-sided polygon.

Second, the **extreme points** of this convex set are the basic feasible solutions to the linear programming problem. Recall from Chapter 2 that for a system of m linear equations in n unknowns, basic solutions are obtained by setting $n - m$ variables equal to zero and solving for the remaining m variables. The constraint set for this production-scheduling problem, given by (3–17), consists of two inequalities. Basic solutions and basic feasible solutions can be obtained only for systems of linear equalities. To convert the two inequalities to two equalities we add one additional variable to each of the two inequalities, as follows.

Original Inequalities $\Rightarrow$	Resulting Equalities	
$5x_1 + 10x_2 \le 60$	$5x_1 + 10x_2 + 1x_3 \qquad = 60$	
$4x_1 + 4x_2 \le 40$	$4x_1 + 4x_2 \qquad + 1x_4 = 40$	(3–19)

(Note: the variables that are added are called *slack* variables, and their physical interpretation will be discussed in detail in Chapter 4. For now, we are interested in them only as a means of converting our set of linear inequalities to a set of linear equalities.) Observe that the resulting set of linear equalities is underdetermined since we have $m = 2$ equations in $n = 4$ unknowns. The maximum number of basic solutions to this system of linear equations is:

$$\frac{n!}{m!\,(n - m)!} = \frac{4!}{2!\,(4 - 2)!} = 6 \qquad (3\text{–}20)$$

These six basic solutions are determined by reducing this underdetermined system of linear equations to a determined system of linear equations, that is, by setting $n - m = 4 - 2 = 2$ variables equal to zero and solving for the remaining $m = 2$ variables. The six basic solutions, determined using the Gauss-Jordan elimination method, are as follows:

Basic Solutions[a]				Feasible/Nonfeasible	Value of Objective Function
x_1	x_2	x_3	x_4		
(0)	(0)	60	40	Feasible	$Z = 0$
(0)	6	(0)	16	Feasible	$Z = 48$
(0)	10	−40	(0)	Nonfeasible	—
12	(0)	(0)	−8	Nonfeasible	—
10	(0)	10	(0)	Feasible	$Z = 60$
8	2	(0)	(0)	Feasible	$Z = 64$

[a] Variables set equal to zero are shown in parentheses.

Observe that among the six basic solutions there are four basic feasible solutions. These four basic feasible solutions are the four extreme points labeled in Fig. 3.1, namely:

[2] See, for example: George B. Dantzig, *Linear Programming and Extensions* (Princeton, N.J.: Princeton University Press, 1963); George Hadley, *Linear Programming* (Reading, Ma.: Addison-Wesley, 1962).

Basic Feasible Solution 1: $(x_1 = 0, x_2 = 0, Z = 0)$ (Origin)
Basic Feasible Solution 2: $(x_1 = 0, x_2 = 6; Z = 48)$
Basic Feasible Solution 3: $(x_1 = 10, x_2 = 0; Z = 60)$ (3-21)
Basic Feasible Solution 4: $(x_1 = 8, x_2 = 2; Z = 64)$ (Optimal basic
                                                                feasible solution)

Third, it is evident that the feasible solution space has a finite number of extreme points (four). *Fourth*, the optimal basic feasible solution is seen to be at one of these extreme points ($x_1 = 8, x_2 = 2$, Maximum $Z = 64$). The fact that the feasible solution space is a convex set is also employed in determining the optimal solution because, in effect, we move the iso-profit line representing the objective function through the feasible solution space remaining within the convex set, and ultimately must reach the extreme point of the feasible region that produces the optimum value of the objective function. The optimal solution indicates that eight bearing plates and two gears should be produced with the excess capacity in order to maximize profit.

The importance of the fact that the feasible solution space of a linear programming problem constitutes a convex set should be emphasized. To illustrate consider the nonconvex set presented below in Fig. 3.2.

As can be seen in Fig. 3.2, if the objective function is moved through the nonconvex set we eventually move to an extreme point (Z_4), which lies completely outside the feasible solution space delineated by the other two constraints and the nonnegativity restriction. Thus, the optimal solution for this nonconvex set would not be an optimal *feasible* solution.

To further illustrate the graphical approach to linear programming recall the chemical requirements problem, which was formulated as follows:

$$\text{Minimize } Z = 5x_1 + 4x_2 \qquad \text{(Objective function)} \qquad (3\text{-}22)$$

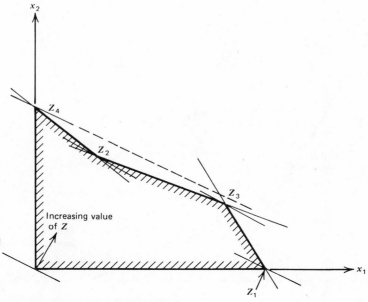

FIGURE 3.2 Nonconvex Set Example

subject to: $6x_1 + 3x_2 \geq 18$
                $2x_1 + 4x_2 \geq 12$ (Constraint set)   (3-23)
                $2x_1 + 8x_2 \geq 16$

with $x_1 \geq 0, x_2 \geq 0$ (Nonnegativity restrictions)   (3-24)

In Fig. 3.3 a graphical representation of this chemical requirements problem is presented. First, observe that the solution space for this problem is defined by the three inequalities given by 3-23. Second, the feasible solution space is then defined by the three constraint inequalities and the two nonnegativity restrictions, and has been crosshatched. Third, the objective function is graphed as a series of straight lines (often referred to as **iso-cost**, or "equal cost," **lines** in a cost minimization problem) at the point $(x_1 = 8, x_2 = 0)$ in the feasible solution space where the objective function has a value of $Z = 5x_1 + 4x_2 = 5(8) + 4(0) = 40$, and continuing downward and to the left to the point $(x_1 = 2, x_2 = 2)$ where the objective function has a value of $Z = 5x_1 + 4x_2 = 5(2) + 4(2) = 18$. In this problem, we seek to minimize cost and thus must move our objective function (Slope $= -c_1/c_2 = -\frac{5}{4}$) downward and to the left (i.e., in the direction of decreasing values of x_1 and x_2). As the objective function is moved through the feasible solution space, four extreme points, or basic feasible solutions are encountered. These extreme points, indicated in Fig. 3.3, are:

Basic Feasible Solution 1: $(x_1 = 8, x_2 = 0; Z = 40)$
Basic Feasible Solution 2: $(x_1 = 4, x_2 = 1; Z = 24)$
Basic Feasible Solution 3: $(x_1 = 0, x_2 = 6; Z = 24)$ (3-25)
Basic Feasible Solution 4: $(x_1 = 2, x_2 = 2; Z = 18)$ (Optimal basic feasible solution)

Thus, the feasible solution space for this minimization problem has a finite number

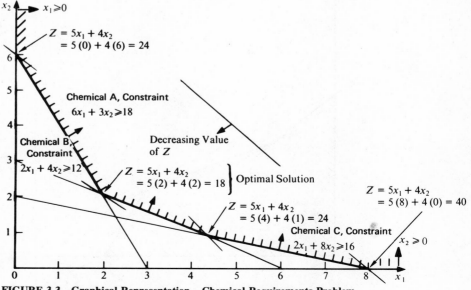

FIGURE 3.3   Graphical Representation—Chemical Requirements Problem

of extreme points (four) and the optimal basic feasible solution is found at one of these extreme points ($x_1 = 2$, $x_2 = 2$; Minimum $Z = 18$). The optimal solution indicates that two bags each of Brand 1 and Brand 2 of the dry developing compounds should be purchased to satisfy the chemical requirements at a minimum cost.

3.5 PROPERTIES OF THE LINEAR PROGRAMMING MODEL

Having considered the formulation, the mathematical structure, and the graphical solution approach to linear programming problems, let us now review the salient features of the linear programming model. To illustrate these features we will refer to our production scheduling example, whose structure has been reproduced in the following table.

| | Requirements or Profits Per Unit | | |
Item	Product 1 Bearing Plate	Product 2 Gear	Total Resource Availabilities
Milling machine hours	5	10	60 hours
Metal lathe hours	4	4	40 hours
Unit Profit ($)	6	8	Maximize
Production level	x_1	x_2	—

Linearity. The basic requirement in every linear programming model is that the objective function and every constraint must be linear with respect to the decision variables. In our production scheduling problem the property of **linearity** means that the marginal measure of profitability, as given by the objective function, and the marginal usage of each resource, as given by the constraints, are considered to be constant over the entire range of productive activity. In economic terms, linearity implies a "constant return to scale," regardless of the level of production. To illustrate, referring to the previous table, production of two bearing plates ($x_1 = 2$) and three gears ($x_2 = 3$) requires 2 bearing plates times 5 milling machine hours per bearing plate plus 3 gears times 10 milling machine hours per gear equals 40 milling machine hours; 2 bearing plates times 4 metal lathe hours per bearing plates plus 3 gears times 4 metal lathe hours per gear equals 20 metal lathe hours, and yields 2 bearing plates times $6 profit per bearing plate plus 3 gears times $8 profit per gear equals $36. The linearity property is really a result of three other important properties of the linear programming model, namely proportionality, additivity, and continuity.

Proportionality. The **proportionality** property means that the measure of effectiveness employed in the objective function (e.g., profit in our production scheduling example) and the amount of each resource used in each constraint must be proportional to the value of each decision variable considered individually. In this example, the objective function increases as a linear combination of the number of units being produced of each of the two products (i.e., $Z = 6x_1 + $

$8x_2$). The rate of increase in the objective function is proportional to the unit profit level associated with each product. Similarly, the constraint set provides for linear restrictions on resource usage. Again, resource usage is proportional to the level of activity associated with the production of each product. Thus, the bearing plate requires 5 hours of milling machine time, and 4 hours of metal lathe time. This requirement would have to be met, regardless of the number of bearing plates being manufactured. To facilitate an understanding of the proportionality principle, let's consider an example in which this property is violated. Suppose that the metal lathe is rather old and that increased usage results in a reduction in profit per unit for each additional unit produced due to higher maintenance costs and downtime. The objective function might then appear as follows:

$$\text{Maximize} \quad Z = (6 - 0.01x_1)x_1 + (8 - 0.01x_2)x_2$$
$$\text{or}$$
$$\text{Maximize} \quad Z = 6x_1 - 0.01x_1^2 + 8x_2 - 0.01x_2^2 \tag{3-26}$$

In this case, the rate of increase in the objective function is not proportional to the unit profit level associated with each product and thus we have a nonlinear objective function.

More will be said about linear programming problems in which some or all of the decision variables are required to have integer values, as *integer linear programming* is discussed in detail in Chapter 9.

Additivity.   In addition to proportionality, it is required that each of the activities be "additive" with respect to the measure of resource usage, as specified by the constraint set, and to the measure of effectiveness, as specified by the objective function. Thus, the manufacture of the first product cannot affect the profitability associated with manufacture of the second product, and vice versa. In essence, the total profitability and each total resource usage that results from the joint production of the two products must be the respective sum of the quantities resulting from the products being produced individually. From the preceding table, the production of one bearing plate ($x_1 = 1$) and one gear ($x_2 = 1$) requires ($5 + 10 = 15$ hours) of milling machine time, ($4 + 4 = 8$ hours) of metal lathe time, and yields ($\$6 + 8 = \$14$) profit.

Violation of the **additivity** property would introduce a crossproduct term or terms into the model since interactions between activities would be allowed. For example, if the manufacture of the bearing plate had a dampening effect on the profitability of the gear, the objective function might be formulated as:

$$\text{Maximize} \quad Z = 6x_1 + (8 - 0.05x_1)x_2$$
$$\text{or}$$
$$\text{Maximize} \quad Z = 6x_1 + 8x_2 - 0.05x_1x_2 \tag{3-27}$$

The additivity property prohibits the appearance of such a crossproduct term ($0.5x_1x_2$) in the objective function and the constraints of the model.

Continuity.   **Continuity**, or divisibility, means that fractional levels of the decision variables, the x_j, are possible. Similarly, fractional amounts of resource usage are also possible. This property is to be expected, as the linear equations that form the feasible solution space are themselves continuous linear functions. Thus, the extreme points of the feasible region, and the optimal feasible solution, need not have integer values.

Deterministic Coefficients.　All of the coefficients in the linear programming model (the a_{ij}, b_i, and c_j) are assumed to be **deterministic** (known) constants, or parameters. Usually, these parameters are determined from production, marketing, or accounting data. It should be obvious that there will be many cases in which such coefficients may be neither a known quantity nor a constant. In such cases, the skill and judgment of the management science analyst is required to determine a set of coefficients that will allow the solution of the model in a fashion that produces a useful, rational decision. In Chapter 5 we will study *sensitivity analysis* in which we will examine the sensitivity of the optimal solutions of a linear program to variations in the input data. Sensitivity analysis is concerned with determining how much the various coefficients of a linear programming model can vary before the optimal solution changes.

3.6　SPECIAL CASES IN LINEAR PROGRAMMING

Each of the linear programming problems discussed in the preceding section of this chapter had a unique optimal solution. If the linear programming problem has been properly formulated, this will usually be the case. However, it is possible for three other special cases to arise in linear programming. These special cases include:

1.　Alternative optimal solutions.
2.　Unbounded solution.
3.　Infeasible solution.

As will be shown in Chapter 4, the simplex method will always terminate with an indication that a unique optimal solution has been obtained, or that one of these special cases has occurred. Each of these special cases will now be illustrated graphically and discussed.

3.6.1　Alternative Optimal Solutions

Suppose that, in the production scheduling example, the unit profits associated with the two products had been $c_1 = \$5$ instead of \$6 and $c_2 = \$10$ instead of \$8. The graphical solution in Fig. 3.4 shows that the new objective function, $Z = 5x_1 + 10x_2$ now has the same slope (Slope $= -c_1/c_2 = -\frac{1}{2}$) as the first constraint, $5x_1 + 10x_2 \leq 60$. Thus, although the extreme point ($x_1 = 8, x_2 = 2$) is still optimal, the extreme point ($x_1 = 0, x_2 = 6$) is also optimal, and indeed the entire line segment between these two extreme points is optimal. The objective function is $Z = 60$ for all points along this straight line. The maximum profit is \$60 at either extreme point, or at any convex combination of these extreme points. A convex combination of these extreme points is any point of the form $\lambda x_2 + (1 - \lambda)x_1$, where $0 \leq \lambda \leq 1$, and $x_1 = (0,8)$ and $x_2 = (6,2)$.

As will be shown in Chapter 4, the simplex method stops as soon as one optimal solution is obtained. Additionally, for the case in which **alternative optimal solutions** exist, the simplex method provides a definite indication that such alternative optima are present.

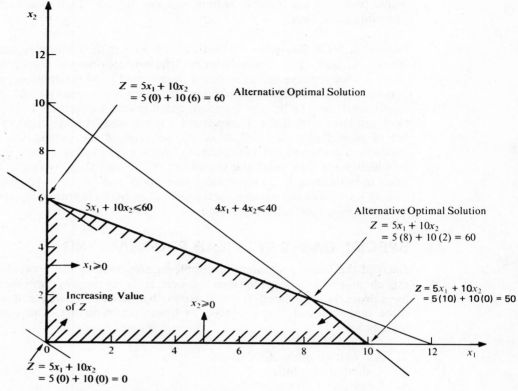

FIGURE 3.4 Alternative Optimal Solutions

3.6.2 An Unbounded Solution

Consider the following simple, two-variable, linear programming model.

$$\text{Maximize } Z = 2x_1 + 1x_2 \tag{3-28}$$

subject to:
$$\begin{aligned} 1x_2 &\le 5 \\ 1x_1 - 1x_2 &\ge -1 \end{aligned} \tag{3-29}$$

with $x_1 \ge 0, x_2 \ge 0$ (3-30)

This problem is shown graphically in Fig. 3.5. As can be seen in the figure, while $x_2 \le 5$, x_1 can be increased indefinitely, that is $x_1 \to +\infty$. Thus, the optimal solution is $x_1 = +\infty$, $x_2 = 5$, and $Z = +\infty$. Such a solution is termed an **unbounded solution**. It should be emphasized, however, that this solution, although unbounded, is feasible, since all of the basic variables in the optimal solution are nonnegative. Thus, linear programming problems that exhibit unbounded solutions *do* have feasible solutions. Again, the simplex procedure will provide a clear indication that an unbounded solution is present. If the problem formulation has physical significance, the presence of an unbounded solution will generally indicate that one or more important constraints were omitted.

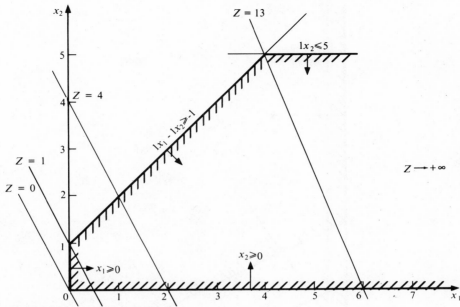

FIGURE 3.5   An Unbounded Solution

3.6.3   An Infeasible Solution

Consider first the following simple, two-variable linear programming model.

$$\text{Maximize } Z = 3x_1 - 2x_2 \qquad (3\text{-}31)$$

subject to: $\qquad 1x_1 + 2x_2 \le 2 \qquad\qquad\qquad (3\text{-}32)$
$\qquad\qquad\qquad 2x_1 + 4x_2 \ge 8$
with $\qquad x_1 \ge 0, x_2 \ge 0 \qquad\qquad\qquad\qquad (3\text{-}33)$

This problem is depicted graphically in Fig. 3.6. As shown in the figure, the two inequalities that form the constraint set are inconsistent. Thus, there is no feasible region, or convex set, formed by these two constraints in conjunction with the nonnegativity restrictions. Consequently, it is impossible to determine a feasible solution because we do not have a feasible region to examine. Again, this condition will clearly be indicated by the simplex procedure. Such a condition generally indicates that the linear programming problem has been misformulated, and it is called an **infeasible solution** (i.e., there is no feasible solution).

Secondly, consider the following simple, two-variable linear programming model.

$$\text{Minimize} \quad Z = 2x_1 + 3x_2 \qquad (3\text{-}34)$$

subject to: $\qquad x_1 - x_2 \ge 1 \qquad\qquad\qquad (3\text{-}35)$
$\qquad\qquad\qquad 2x_1 + 2x_2 \le -4$

with $\qquad x_1 \ge 0, x_2 \ge 0 \qquad\qquad\qquad\qquad (3\text{-}36)$

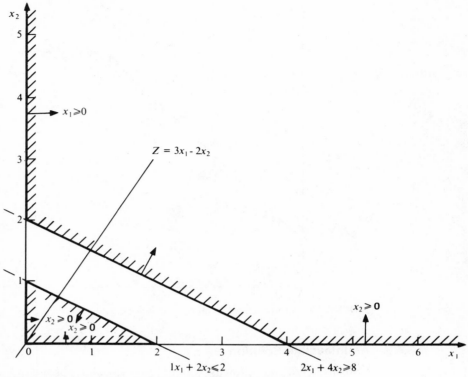

FIGURE 3.6   Infeasible Solution—Inconsistent Constraint Set

This problem is depicted graphically in Fig. 3.7. As shown in the figure, while the two inequalities that form the constraint set are consistent, there is no point that will satisfy the two constraints and also satisfy the nonnegativity conditions. Consequently, it is again impossible to determine a feasible solution, and this condition will clearly be indicated by the simplex procedure. Reformulation of the problem is necessary under this circumstance, as the linear programming model must be formulated in a manner so that the nonnegativity conditions can be satisfied.

3.7   REDUNDANT CONSTRAINT

In a properly formulated linear programming problem each of the constraints will define a portion of the boundary of the feasible solution space. Whenever a constraint does not define a portion of the boundary of the feasible solution space, it is labeled a **redundant constraint**. A redundant constraint is extraneous or unnecessary for the problem and may be omitted from the problem formulation. To illustrate, consider the following simple, two-variable linear programming problem.

$$\text{Maximize} \quad Z = 3x_1 + 5x_2 \tag{3-37}$$

subject to:
$$2x_1 + 4x_2 \leq 16$$
$$4x_1 + 2x_2 \leq 16 \tag{3-38}$$

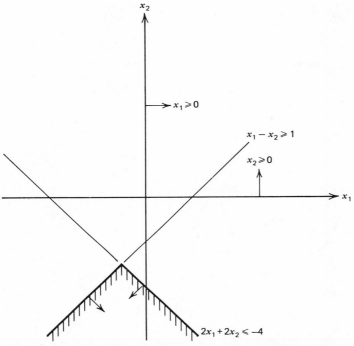

FIGURE 3.7 **An Infeasible Solution—Nonnegativity Conditions Violated**

$$3x_1 + 3x_2 \leq 30 \qquad \text{(Redundant constraint)}$$

with $\quad x_1 \geq 0, x_2 \geq 0$ $\hspace{8cm}$ (3–39)

This problem is depicted graphically in Fig. 3.8. The optimal solution for this problem is seen to be $x_1 = {}^8/_3$, $x_2 = {}^8/_3$, Maximum $Z = 21{}^1/_3$. As shown in Fig. 3.8, the third constraint is redundant since it does not contribute to defining the boundary of the feasible solution space. All values of x_1 and x_2 that satisfy the first two contraints will also satisfy the third constraint. Thus, the third constraint can be removed from the problem formulation as it will not affect the solution to the problem.

A redundant constraint can be detected, prior to beginning the solution process, for linear programming problems that can be solved graphically (i.e., linear programming problems involving three or less variables). However, for larger linear programming problems it will generally not be possible to identify redundant constraints, nor will the simplex procedure identify these redundant constraints.

3.8 APPLICATIONS OF LINEAR PROGRAMMING—FORMULATION EXAMPLES

One of the most important aspects in gaining a thorough understanding of linear programming concerns developing the ability to recognize and analyze problem situations that are amenable to formulation and solution using linear program-

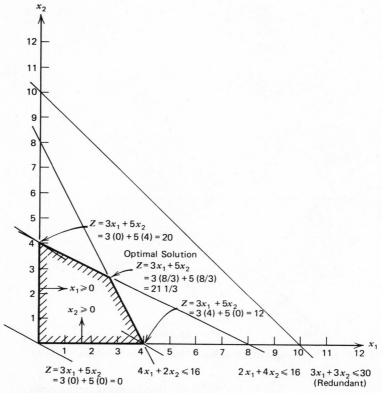

FIGURE 3.8   Redundant Constraint Example

ming. Although it is difficult, if not impossible, to teach someone what specific problem situations are amenable to solution using linear programming, it is very useful and instructive to consider a number of illustrative applications of linear programming. By developing an understanding based on these applications, the reader can perhaps begin to learn how to formulate problems using the framework of linear programming.

In this section of the chapter we concentrate on problem formulation, using the procedural framework outlined above. The analytical method used to solve linear programming problems will be discussed in detail in Chapter 4. However, to enhance our general understanding of linear programming and the problem formulation process in particular, we present a summary of the solutions for each of the applications presented. It is recommended that the student use these solutions to check the consistency of the problem formulations. Note finally that two important applications of linear programming, namely production scheduling and raw material blending, have already been discussed.

3.8.1   The Diet Problem

The Falston Company is a major manufacturer of dog food. It is considering the production of a new dog food "Enriched Wow." This new dog food must meet certain standards with respect to its calorie, protein, and vitamin content, and it can be blended from three basic ingredients. The standards for the dog food and for the calorie, protein, and vitamin content of the three basic ingredients are shown in the following table. Note also that the cost per pound for each of the three ingredients is shown in this table. The objective of the linear programming formulation is to ascertain the quantities of the various ingredients that should be blended to meet the standards established for the dog food, while minimizing its cost. We will assume that the formulation will be based on producing a 1.0 lb. unit of dog food.

Required Nutritional Element	*Units of Nutritional Elements per Pound of Ingredient*			*Total Nutritional Requirement per Pound of Dog Food*
	Ingredient 1	*Ingredient 2*	*Ingredient 3*	
Calories	430	550	480	≤ 2000
Protein	210	290	230	≥ 250
Vitamin A	100	75	110	≥ 70
Vitamin C	85	100	90	≥ 85
Vitamin E	110	50	70	≥ 55
Cost per Pound	$0.17	$0.23	$0.16	

Let x_j (j = 1, 2, 3) represent the number of pounds (unknown) of ingredients 1, 2, and 3 to be blended in a pound of dog food. The linear programming model for this problem can be written as:

$$\text{Minimize} \quad Z = 0.17x_1 + 0.23x_2 + 0.16x_3 \tag{3-40}$$

subject to:

$$
\begin{aligned}
430x_1 + 550x_2 + 480x_3 &\leq 2000 &&\text{(Calories)} \\
210x_1 + 290x_2 + 230x_3 &\geq 250 &&\text{(Protein)} \\
100x_1 + 75x_2 + 110x_3 &\geq 70 &&\text{(Vitamin A)} \\
85x_1 + 100x_2 + 90x_3 &\geq 85 &&\text{(Vitamin C)} \\
110x_1 + 50x_2 + 70x_3 &\geq 55 &&\text{(Vitamin E)} \\
x_1 + x_2 + x_3 &= 1.0 &&\text{(1-lb production unit)}
\end{aligned}
\tag{3-41}
$$

with $\quad x_1 \geq 0, x_2 \geq 0,$ and $x_3 \geq 0$ $\tag{3-42}$

Note that this problem formulation involves the minimization of cost, rather than the maximization of profits. Also, the first constraint provides for an upper limit (maximum) of 2000 calories per unit of dog food, while the following four constraints provide for lower limits (minimum) for protein, vitamin A, vitamin C, and vitamin E. The final constraint states that the sum of the ingredients used must total to 1.0 (lb), which is the amount of dog food we are trying to produce. Thus, the first constraint is expressed as a "less than or equal to" constraint, the next four constraints are expressed as "greater than or equal to constraints," and the final constraint is expressed as an "equality" constraint.

The minimum-cost dog food blending plan is summarized in the following table.

Ingredient	Pounds Used	Calories	Protein	Vitamin A	Vitamin C	Vitamin E	Cost Per Pound of Dog Food
No. 1	—	—	—	—	—	—	—
No. 2	0.333	183.33	96.67	25.00	33.33	17.67	0.076
No. 3	0.667	320.00	153.33	73.33	60.00	46.67	0.107
Total	1.000	503.33	250.00	98.33	93.33	64.34	$0.183

Note that this minimum-cost dog food blending problem does not utilize any of ingredient 1, and that 1.0 lb of dog food is blended from 0.333 lb of ingredient 2 and 0.667 lb. of ingredient 3. Observe also how the constraints of this problem are satisfied by the optimal solution.

3.8.2   The Fluid Blending Problem

A problem that is somewhat related to the diet problem involves the blending of fluids, such as chemicals, plastics, or oils, to form a desired end product. Each of the fluids (resources) included in the blend has certain blending properties and an associated cost. The objective of the blending problem is to produce the final product in a manner that minimizes its costs while still meeting the criteria established for its blending. As will be shown, the blending problem also illustrates the use of doubly subscripted notation in the linear programming formulation. Consider now the following highly simplified example of gasoline blending.

The Hexxon Company sells three brands of gasoline: Supreme, Regular, and Unleaded. Each brand of gasoline is composed of one or more of four blending constituents. The relevant data concerning the four blending constituents are shown in the following table. The supply per day figures shown in this table represent the maximum supply per day available for each of the four blending constituents.

Blending Constituent	Octane Rating	$ Cost (per Barrel)	Supply per Day (Barrels)
1	102	5.00	2500
2	96	4.00	3000
3	93	3.00	3500
4	110	8.00	2000

Now, each of the three brands of gasoline must meet a minimum standard for octane rating, and each of the three brands of gasoline sells at different price and has a different demand rate. The relevant data concerning the three brands of gasoline are shown in the following table. The demand per day figures shown in this table represent the minimum demand per day required for each of the three brands of gasoline.

Brand of Gasoline	Minimum Octane Standard	$ Selling Price (per Barrel)	Demand per Day (Barrels)
Supreme	100	7.50	3000
Regular	96	6.00	4000
Unleaded	90	5.50	2000

For simplicity it will be assumed that we are interested in making a blending decision for a single day, and that all gasoline blended during this day can be either sold or stored at negligible cost.

To formulate this linear programming model, let x_{ij} ($i = 1,2,3,4$ and $j = 1,2,3$) represent the barrels of blending component i used in gasoline brand j. Observe that the use of this doubly subscripted notation greatly enhances the model's formulation, as it makes specification of the variables much simpler than if singly subscripted variables had been employed. Using this doubly subscripted notation, the objective function for this model can be written as:

$$\text{Maximize } Z = (7.50 - 5.00)x_{11} + (7.50 - 4.00)x_{21}$$
$$+ (7.50 - 3.00)x_{31} + (7.50 - 8.00)x_{41}$$
$$+ (6.00 - 5.00)x_{12} + (6.00 - 4.00)x_{22}$$
$$+ (6.00 - 3.00)x_{32} + (6.00 - 8.00)x_{42} \tag{3-43}$$
$$+ (5.50 - 5.00)x_{13} + (5.50 - 4.00)x_{23}$$
$$+ (5.50 - 3.00)x_{33} + (5.50 - 8.00)x_{43}$$

The objective function indicates that there is a $2.50 profit on each barrel of blending component 1 used in Supreme, a $3.50 profit on each barrel of blending component 2 used in Supreme, a $4.50 profit on each barrel of blending component 3 used in Supreme, and a loss of $0.50 on each barrel of component 4 used in Supreme, and so forth. These numbers are obtained by subtracting the cost of blending constituents $i = 1,2,3,4$ from the selling price ($7.50) associated with brand $j = 1$ (Supreme). For example, blending component $i = 1$ costs $5.00 per barrel, and Supreme (brand $j = 1$) sells for $7.50 per barrel, giving a profit of $2.50, as indicated by the coefficient of the first term in the objective function.

Next, we formulate a set of constraints to satisfy the minimum octane rating required for each brand of gasoline. These constraints are "ratio constraints" of the form:

Octane rating constraints
$$\begin{cases} \dfrac{102x_{11} + 96x_{21} + 93x_{31} + 110x_{41}}{x_{11} + x_{21} + x_{31} + x_{41}} \geq 100 & \text{(Minimum octane standard-Supreme; } j = 1) \\[2mm] \dfrac{102x_{12} + 96x_{22} + 93x_{32} + 110x_{42}}{x_{12} + x_{22} + x_{32} + x_{42}} \geq 96 & \text{(Minimum octane standard-Regular, } j = 2) \\[2mm] \dfrac{102x_{13} + 96x_{23} + 93x_{33} + 110x_{43}}{x_{13} + x_{23} + x_{33} + x_{43}} \geq 90 & \text{(Minimum octane standard-Unleaded, } j = 3) \end{cases}$$

$$(3-44)$$

The ratio constraints given by (3-44) are not in a particularly convenient form for a linear programming model. Employing simple algebra, they can be written first as:

$$102x_{11} + 96x_{21} + 93x_{31} + 110x_{41} \geq 100(x_{11} + x_{21} + x_{31} + x_{41})$$
$$102x_{12} + 96x_{22} + 93x_{32} + 110x_{42} \geq 96(x_{12} + x_{22} + x_{32} + x_{42}) \qquad (3\text{-}45)$$
$$102x_{13} + 96x_{23} + 93x_{33} + 110x_{43} \geq 90(x_{13} + x_{23} + x_{33} + x_{43})$$

and then as:

$$2x_{11} - 4x_{21} - 7x_{31} + 10x_{41} \geq 0$$
$$6x_{12} \phantom{+ 00x_{00}} - 3x_{32} + 14x_{42} \geq 0 \qquad (3\text{-}46)$$
$$12x_{13} + 6x_{23} + 3x_{33} + 20x_{43} \geq 0$$

This latter form (3-46) would actually be employed in solving such a linear programming model.

Proceeding, we formulate a set of constraints to restrict the four blending constituents used in the three brands of gasoline to the daily supply availability of those four blending constituents. These four daily-supply availability constraints are written simply as:

Supply availability constraints
$$\begin{cases} x_{11} + x_{12} + x_{13} \leq 2500 & (\text{Blending constituent, } i = 1) \\ x_{21} + x_{22} + x_{23} \leq 3000 & (\text{Blending constituent, } i = 2) \\ x_{31} + x_{32} + x_{33} \leq 3500 & (\text{Blending constituent, } i = 3) \\ x_{41} + x_{42} + x_{43} \leq 2000 & (\text{Blending constituent, } i = 4) \end{cases} \quad (3\text{-}47)$$

Next, we formulate a set of constraints to satisfy the daily demand requirement. These constraints are written simply as:

Demand requirement constraints
$$\begin{cases} x_{11} + x_{21} + x_{31} + x_{41} \geq 3000 & (\text{Supreme brand, } j = 1) \\ x_{12} + x_{22} + x_{32} + x_{42} \geq 4000 & (\text{Regular brand, } j = 2) \\ x_{13} + x_{23} + x_{33} + x_{43} \geq 2000 & (\text{Unleaded brand, } j = 3) \end{cases} \quad (3\text{-}48)$$

Finally, we must specify nonnegativity restrictions of the form:

$$x_{ij} \geq 0, \quad \text{for} \quad i = 1, 2, 3, 4 \quad \text{and} \quad j = 1, 2, 3 \qquad (3\text{-}49)$$

The maximum-profit gasoline blending plan is summarized in the following table.

Blending Constituent i, Used in Gasoline j	Barrels Used	Profit per Barrel	Contribution to profit
x_{11}	2450	$2.50	$6,125
x_{12}	50	1.00	50
x_{22}	3000	2.00	6,000
x_{31}	700	4.50	3,150
x_{32}	800	3.00	2,400
x_{33}	2000	2.50	5,000
x_{42}	150	−2.00	−300
Totals	9,150	Maximum $Z =$ $22,425	

Note that in this maximum-profit gasoline blending plan we utilize 150 barrels of blending constituent 4 in gasoline 2, (i.e., $x_{42} = 150$) even though this reduces the value of the objective function. This must be done to satisfy the second octane-rating constraint and the second demand requirement constraint. It is suggested that the reader verify the fact that each of the constraints of this problem are satisfied, using the values of the decision variables shown in the table above.

3.8.3 A Multiperiod Investment Problem

Linear programming can be readily applied to problems having a nonstationary or multiperiod time horizon. To illustrate, consider the following multiperiod investment problem. A wealthy investor has three investment opportunities available at the beginning of each of the next 5 years, and also has a total of $500,000 available for investment at the beginning of year one. A summary of the financial characteristics of the three investment alternatives is presented in the following table.

Investment	Allowable Size of Initial Investment	Return (%)	Timing of Return	Immediate Reinvestment Possible
1	$100,000	9	1 year later	Yes
2	Unlimited	6	2 years later	Yes
3	$ 50,000	10	3 years later	Yes

This wealthy investor wishes to determine the investment plan that will maximize the amount of money that can be accumulated by the beginning of the sixth year in the future.

Let x_{ij} ($i = 1,2,3$ and $j = 1,2,3,4,5$) represent the unknown amount to be invested in alternative i at the beginning of year j. Similarly, let y_i represent the unknown amount not invested in any of the alternatives in period j.

The linear programming model of this problem situation is:

$$\text{Maximize} \quad Z = 1.09x_{15} + 1.06x_{24} + 1.10x_{33} + y_5 \qquad (3\text{-}50)$$

subject to:

Yearly cash flow constraints
$$\begin{cases} (\text{Year 1})x_{11} + x_{21} + x_{31} + y_1 & = 500{,}000 \\ (\text{Year 2}) - y_1 - 1.09x_{11} + x_{12} + x_{22} + x_{32} + y_2 & = 0 \\ (\text{Year 3}) - y_2 - 1.06x_{21} - 1.09x_{12} + x_{13} + x_{23} + x_{33} + y_3 & = 0 \\ (\text{Year 4}) - y_3 - 1.10x_{31} - 1.06x_{22} - 1.09x_{13} + x_{14} + x_{24} + x_{34} + y_4 & = 0 \\ (\text{Year 5}) - y_4 - 1.10x_{32} - 1.06x_{23} - 1.09x_{14} + x_{15} + x_{25} + x_{35} + y_5 & = 0 \end{cases}$$
$$(3\text{-}51)$$

Size of investment constraints
$$\begin{cases} x_{11} \le 100{,}000 \quad & x_{31} \le 50{,}000 \\ x_{12} \le 100{,}000 \quad & x_{32} \le 50{,}000 \\ x_{13} \le 100{,}000 \quad & x_{33} \le 50{,}000 \\ x_{14} \le 100{,}000 \quad & x_{34} \le 50{,}000 \\ x_{15} \le 100{,}000 \quad & x_{35} \le 50{,}000 \end{cases}$$

with $x_{ij} \geq 0$, $y_j \geq 0$ for $i = 1,2,3; j = 1,2,3,4,5$ (3-52)

The first five constraints apply to the cash flows for years $j = 1,2, \ldots, 5$. Thus, in year $j = 1$, the sum of the amount invested in the three alternatives plus the amount not invested must exactly equal the total amount, \$500,000, initially available for investment. In year $j = 2$, the following situation would be possible.

$$\frac{\text{Investment alternatives}}{x_{12} + x_{22} + x_{32} + y_2} = \frac{\text{Available funds}}{y_1 + 1.09x_{11}}$$

or $-y_1 - 1.09x_{11} + x_{12} + x_{22} + x_{32} + y_2 = 0$ (3-53)

Note that the available funds at the beginning of year $j = 2$ are the sum of the funds not invested in year $j = 1$, that is, y_1, plus the original investment and its associated return for alternative $i = 1$ in period $j = 1$, that is, $1.09x_{11}$. Thus, (3-53) is essentially a "balance of funds" equality that must be satisfied. Years $j = 3$, 4, and 5 can be evaluated similarly. The final 10 constraints apply to the maximum size of investment allowed for alternatives 1 and 3. The objective function to be maximized is that obtained from the optimal possible return from the three alternatives, taking into account the timing of the returns from each of the three alternatives. Since all funds available at the beginning of the year $j = 5$ may not necessarily be committed, the term y_5 must also be included in the objective function.

In addition to demonstrating how a linear programming model can be constructed for a multiperiod problem, it indicates that constraints can also be of the "strict equality" variety. The use of strict equalities in this problem formulation was necessary to insure the total commitment of funds, if desirable, in each year.

The solution to the multiperiod investment problem is summarized in the following table.

Yearly Investment Plan

Year 1	$x_{11} + x_{21} + x_{31} + y_1$	= 500,000
	$100,000 + 38,700 + 50,000 + 311,300$	= 500,000
Year 2	$-y_1 - 1.09x_{11} + x_{12} + x_{22} + x_{32} + y_2$	= 0
	$-311,300 - 109,000 + 100,000 + 320,300 + 0 + 0$	= 0
Year 3	$-y_2 - 1.06x_{21} - 1.09x_{12} + x_{13} + x_{23} + x_{33} + y_3$	= 0
	$0 - 41,000 - 109,000 + 100,000 + 0 + 50,000 + 0$	= 0
Year 4	$-y_3 - 1.10x_{31} - 1.06x_{22} - 1.09x_{13} + x_{14} + x_{24} + x_{34} + y_4$	= 0
	$-0 - 55,000 - 339,500 - 109,000 + 100,000 + 403,500 + 0 + 0$	= 0
Year 5	$-y_4 - 1.10x_{32} - 1.06x_{23} - 1.09x_{14} + x_{15} + x_{25} + x_{35} + y_5$	= 0
	$-0 - 0 - 0 - 109,000 + 100,000 + 0 + 0 + 9,000$	= 0

Maximum $Z = 1.09x_{15} + 1.06x_{24} + 1.10x_{33} + y_5$
$= 1.09(100,000) + 1.06(403,500) + 1.10(50,000) + 9,000$
$= 109,000 + 427,710 + 55,000 + 9,000 = \$600,710$

3.8.4 A Portfolio Selection Problem

A problem commonly faced by institutional and individual investors is that of the selection of a portfolio of investments from a number of investment opportunities. In making such a selection, a number of factors, such as risk, working capital liquidity, growth potential, rate of return, and diversification requirements, must often be considered. The use of linear programming in portfolio selection will be illustrated by the following example.

The Imprudential Insurance Company had developed a list of seven investment alternatives, with corresponding financial factors, for a 10-year investment horizon. These investments, and their corresponding financial factors, are presented in the following table. Within this table, the meaning of the various financial factors is as follows. The *length of investment* is the expected number of years required for the annual rate of return to be realized taking into account the possibility of reinvestment. The *annual rate of return* is the expected rate of return over the 10-year investment horizon. The *risk coefficient* is a subjective, dimensionless estimate representing the portfolio manager's appraisal of the relative safety of each alternative, based on an ordinal scale of 10. The *growth potential*, expressed as a percentage, is again a subjective estimate representing the portfolio manager's appraisal of the potential increase in the value of the investment alternative for the 10-year period.

Investment Alternative	Length of Investment (Year)	Annual Rate of Return (%)	Risk Coefficient	Growth Potential (%)
1. Treasury bills	4	3	1	0
2. Common stock	7	12	5	18
3. Corporation bonds	8	9	4	10
4. Real estate	6	20	8	32
5. Growth mutual fund	10	15	6	20
6. Savings and Loan	5	6	3	7
7. Cash	0	0	0	0

The Imprudential Insurance Company seeks to maximize the return on its portfolio of investments, subject to the following restrictions on the selection of the portfolio.

1. The average length of the investment for the portfolio should not exceed 7 years.
2. The average risk for the portfolio should not exceed 5.
3. The average growth potential for the portfolio should be at least 10 percent.
4. At least 10 percent of all available funds must be retained in the form of cash at all times in order to maintain working capital liquidity.
5. The proportions of funds invested in the various alternatives must sum to 1.00.

The linear programming model for this problem situation can be constructed as follows. Let x_j $(j = 1,2,3,4,5,6,7)$ represent the proportion of funds to be invested in the jth investment alternative. The objective function and constraints for the linear programming model can then be written as:

$$\text{Maximize } Z = 0.03x_1 + 0.12x_2 + 0.09x_3 + 0.20x_4 \\ + 0.15x_5 + 0.06x_6 + 0.00x_7 \tag{3-54}$$

subject to:

$$\begin{array}{ll} 4x_1 + 7x_2 + 8x_3 + 6x_4 + 10x_5 + 5x_6 + 0x_7 \leq 7 & \text{(Length of investment)} \\ 1x_1 + 5x_2 + 4x_3 + 8x_4 + 6x_5 + 3x_6 + 0x_7 \leq 5 & \text{(Risk level)} \\ 0.00x_1 + 0.18x_2 + 0.10x_3 + 0.32x_4 + 0.20x_5 & \text{(Growth} \\ \qquad\qquad + 0.07x_6 + 0.00x_7 \geq 0.10 & \quad\text{potential)} \\ x_7 \geq 0.10 & \text{(Cash requirement)} \\ x_1 + x_2 + x_3 + x_4 + x_5 + x_6 + x_7 = 1.00 & \text{(Proportion of funds)} \end{array} \tag{3-55}$$

with $x_1 \geq 0, x_2 \geq 0, x_3 \geq 0, x_4 \geq 0, x_5 \geq 0, x_6 \geq 0$ $\qquad\qquad$ (3-56)

The first constraint restricts the length of the investment for the portfolio to be less than, or equal to, 7 years. The second constraint provides a similar restriction on the risk level for the portfolio. The third constraint provides for a lower bound, which must be exceeded, for the average growth potential for the portfolio. The fourth constraint provides for the maintenance of at least 10 percent of the portfolio in the form of cash. The final constraint specifies that the proportions of funds invested in the various alternatives must sum to 1.00.

This linear programming model formulation illustrates the mixing of constraints ($\leq$, $\geq$, and $=$) within a single problem, a very common occurrence. Note also that the various constraints are expressed in different units. The first constraint is defined in terms of years, the second constraint is defined in terms of a dimensionless risk measure, the third and fourth constraints are defined in terms of percentages, and the fifth constraint is defined in terms of proportions that must sum to 1.00. This constraint set illustrates the fact that all measures of resource usage need not be the same for all constraints. Rather, each constraint must express a consistent, linear measure of usage for each of the activities present in the constraint. In essence, this model illustrates a common situation in which the linear programming problem is constrained by a number of factors, each of which is measured in different units.

The solution to the portfolio selection problem is summarized in the following table.

Investment Alternative	Proportion of Funds Invested	Annual Rate of Return	Contribution to Total Rate of Return
Treasury bills, x_1	0.3143	0.03	0.0094
Real estate, x_4	0.5857	0.20	0.1171
Cash, x_7	0.1000	0.00	0.0000
Totals	1.0000		Maximum $Z = 0.1266$

The reader should verify that the values for the decision variables given in the table above satisfy each of the constraints of the problem.

3.8.5 A Multiperiod Scheduling Problem

Linear programming can often be used for scheduling production over several time periods rather than for a single time period as illustrated previously. In such multiperiod scheduling situations, the manufacturer may seek to balance the cost of overtime production against the cost associated with carrying inventories from period to period.

To illustrate multiperiod scheduling, consider the following problem situation. Dudley Manufacturing Company produces diesel engines. The contract that it has signed with a large truck manufacturer calls for the following 4-month shipping schedule.

Month	Number of Diesel Engines to be Shipped
January	3000
February	4000
March	5000
April	5000

Dudley Manufacturing can manufacture 3000 diesel engines per month on a regular time basis and 2000 diesel engines per month on an overtime basis. Its production cost is $1500 for a diesel engine produced on regular time and $2500 for a diesel engine produced on overtime. Its monthly inventory holding cost is $50.

The linear programming model for this problem situation can be constructed as follows. Let x_{ijk}; $i = 1, 2, 3, 4$; $j = 1, 2$ and $k = 1, 2, 3, 4$, represent the number of engines manufactured in month i using shift j and shipped in month k. Note that, in this case, we are using a triply subscripted variable. For example, x_{123} would represent the number of engines manufactured in January ($i = 1$), on an overtime shift basis ($j = 2$), and shipped in March ($k = 3$). The objective function and constraints for this problem can now be written as:

$$\text{Minimize } Z = \overbrace{\$1500 \,(x_{111} + x_{112} + x_{113} + x_{114} + x_{212} + x_{213} + x_{214}}^{\text{Regular Time Production Costs}}$$

$$+ x_{313} + x_{314} + x_{414}) + \overbrace{\$2500 \,(x_{121} + x_{122} + x_{123} + x_{124} + x_{222} + x_{223} + x_{224}}^{\text{Overtime Production Costs}}$$

$$+ x_{323} + x_{324} + x_{424}) + \overbrace{\$50 \,(x_{112} + x_{122} + x_{213} + x_{223} + x_{314} + x_{324})}^{\text{One Month Inventory Cost}}$$

$$\overbrace{+ 100 \,(x_{113} + x_{123} + x_{214} + x_{224})}^{\text{Two Month Inventory Cost}} + \overbrace{\$150 \,(x_{114} + x_{124})}^{\text{3 Month Inventory Cost}} \tag{3-57}$$

subject to:

$$
\begin{aligned}
x_{111} + x_{112} + x_{113} + x_{114} &\leq 3{,}000 \\
x_{212} + x_{213} + x_{214} &\leq 3{,}000 \\
x_{313} + x_{314} &\leq 3{,}000 \\
x_{414} &\leq 3{,}000
\end{aligned}
\left.\vphantom{\begin{aligned}a\\a\\a\\a\end{aligned}}\right\}
\begin{aligned}
&\text{Monthly} \\
&\text{Regular time} \\
&\text{Production} \\
&\text{Constraints}
\end{aligned}
$$

$$
\begin{aligned}
x_{121} + x_{122} + x_{123} + x_{124} &\leq 2{,}000 \\
x_{222} + x_{223} + x_{224} &\leq 2{,}000 \\
x_{323} + x_{324} &\leq 2{,}000 \\
x_{424} &\leq 2{,}000
\end{aligned}
\left.\vphantom{\begin{aligned}a\\a\\a\\a\end{aligned}}\right\}
\begin{aligned}
&\text{Monthly} \\
&\text{Overtime} \\
&\text{Production} \\
&\text{Constraints}
\end{aligned}
$$

(3–58)

$$
\begin{aligned}
x_{111} + x_{121} &= 3{,}000 \\
x_{112} + x_{122} + x_{212} + x_{222} &= 4{,}000 \\
x_{113} + x_{123} + x_{213} + x_{223} + x_{313} + x_{323} &= 5{,}000 \\
x_{114} + x_{124} + x_{214} + x_{224} + x_{314} + x_{324} + x_{414} + x_{424} &= 5{,}000
\end{aligned}
\left.\vphantom{\begin{aligned}a\\a\\a\\a\end{aligned}}\right\}
\begin{aligned}
&\text{Monthly} \\
&\text{Demand} \\
&\text{Constraints}
\end{aligned}
$$

with all $x_{ijk} \geq 0$

(3–59)

Note that in the objective function that we first account for the regular time production costs. Next, the overtime production costs are considered. Then, we successively consider the inventory holding costs for 1 month, 2 months, and 3 months, that is, to the end of the production scheduling horizon. The constraints for this problem are obtained in a straightforward manner, as indicated.

The solution to the multiperiod-scheduling problem is summarized in the following table.

Engines Manufactured in Month i, Using Shift j, and Shipped in Month k	Number of Units	Objective Function Cost Contribution
x_{111}	3000	$4,500,000
x_{212}	3000	4,500,000
x_{313}	3000	4,500,000
x_{414}	3000	4,500,000
x_{222}	1000	2,500,000
x_{323}	2000	5,000,000
x_{424}	2000	5,000,000
Totals	17,000	Minimum Z = $30,500,000

The reader should verify that the values for the decision variables given in the table above satisfy each of the constraints of the problem.

3.8.6   A Media Selection Problem

Another type of allocation problem arises in the selection of various media to be employed in an advertising campaign. The usual objective in such an advertising campaign is to maximize its total effective advertising exposures, subject to monetary constraints and constraints upon the number of exposures possible for the individual communication media.

To illustrate the use of linear programming in media selection, consider the following problem situation. The Edward Belk Advertising Agency is preparing an advertising campaign for a group of travel agencies. These travel agencies have decided that their "target customer" should have the following characteristics, with relative importance indicated in parenthesis.

1. Female, married (0.2).
2. Age: 25–40 (0.3).
3. Household Income: above $20,000 annually (0.5).

Furthermore, they do not want to spend more than $50,000 for their advertising campaign.

In formulating an advertising campaign for these travel agencies, the Belk Agency has made a careful analysis of three available media and has compiled the following set of relevant data.

Data Item	Media		
	No. 1-Women's Magazine	No. 2-Radio	No. 3-Television
Reader characteristics			
1. Female, married	80%	70%	60%
2. Age: 25–40	60%	50%	45%
3. Income: $20,000, or more annually	40%	35%	25%
Cost per advertisement	$1,500	$2,000	$4,000
Minimum number of ads allowed	10	5	5
Maximum number of ads allowed	20	10	10
Audience size/media	750,000	1,000,000	1,500,000

In this problem situation the objective is to maximize the total effective exposures for all the advertising employed. Now the coefficients of the objective function are the products of the audience sizes for the various media multiplied by the "effectiveness coefficients" for the various media. The effectiveness coefficients for the three possible media are computed as follows:

Effectiveness coefficient-media no. 1 = 0.80(0.2) + 0.60(0.3) + 0.40(0.5) = 0.54
Effectiveness coefficient-media no. 2 = 0.70(0.2) + 0.50(0.3) + 0.35(0.5) = 0.465
Effectiveness coefficient-media no. 3 = 0.60(0.2) + 0.45(0.3) + 0.25(0.5) = 0.38

$$(3-60)$$

Then, the coefficients of the objective function can be computed as the products of the effectiveness coefficients and the audience sizes. For example, the objective function coefficient c_1, for media no. 1, is computed as:

$$c_1 = 0.54(750,000) = 405,000 \qquad (3-61)$$

The linear programming model for this problem situation can then be constructed in the following manner. Let x_j, $j = 1, 2, 3$, represent the number of advertisements made using the jth advertising media. The objective function and constraints for the model can be written as

$$\text{Maximize } Z = 405,000x_1 + 465,000x_2 + 570,000x_3 \qquad (3\text{-}62)$$

subject to:

$$
\begin{array}{llll}
\$1,500x_1 + \$2,000x_2 + \$4,000x_3 \leq \$50,000 & \text{(Total spending constraint)} \\
x_1 \geq 10 \\
 x_2 \geq 5 \\
 x_3 \geq 5
\end{array}
\left.\vphantom{\begin{array}{l}1\\2\\3\end{array}}\right\} \begin{array}{l}\text{(Minimum number of ads}\\ \text{constraints)}\end{array} \qquad (3\text{-}63)
$$

$$
\begin{array}{llll}
x_1 \leq 20 \\
 x_2 \leq 10 \\
 x_3 \leq 10
\end{array}
\left.\vphantom{\begin{array}{l}1\\2\\3\end{array}}\right\} \begin{array}{l}\text{(Maximum number of ads}\\ \text{constraints)}\end{array}
$$

with $x_j \geq 0,$ for $j = 1, 2, 3$ $\qquad (3\text{-}64)$

The solution to the media selection problem is summarized in the following table.

Media Alternative	Number of Advertisements To Be Made	Contribution-Effective Advertising Exposures
Women's Magazine	13.33	5,400,000
Radio	5.00	2,325,000
Television	5.00	2,850,000
	Maximum $Z = 10,575,000$	

The reader should verify that the values for the decision variables given in the table above satisfy each of the constraints of the problem.

3.8.7 The Least-Cost Shipping Network Problem

The management of the Aegis Pharmaceutical Corporation must determine the minimum-cost shipping route from its production unit in Kansas City, Missouri, to its East Coast storage facility in Spartanburg, South Carolina. The shipping manager has prepared the following network (Fig. 3.9), which depicts the most attractive alternatives and indicates the cost of shipping 100 units of product for each route segment. In this shipping network each major city is shown as a circled number (or "node"). The costs associated with shipping one hundred units of product for the various route segments (or "branches") between the various cities are shown as the numbered arrows.

The linear programming model for this problem situation can be constructed as follows. Let x_{ij} ($i = 1, 2, 3, 4, 5, 6$; $j = 2, 3, 4, 5, 6, 7$) represent the "flow" of 100 units of product from node i to node j, where $x_{ij} = 0$ signifies no flow and $x_{ij} =$

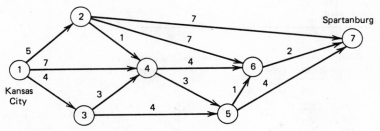

FIGURE 3.9   Shipping Network

1 signifies the flow of 100 units. The objective function and constraints for the problem can then be written as:

$$\text{Minimize } Z = 5x_{12} + 4x_{13} + 7x_{14} + 1x_{24} + 7x_{26} + 7x_{27} \\ + 3x_{34} + 4x_{35} + 3x_{45} + 4x_{46} + 1x_{56} + 4x_{57} + 2x_{67} \quad (3\text{-}65)$$

subject to:

$$
\begin{array}{llr}
\text{Node 1:} & x_{12} + x_{13} + x_{14} & = 1 \\
\text{Node 2:} & -1x_{12} + 1x_{24} + 1x_{26} + 1x_{27} & = 0 \\
\text{Node 3:} & -1x_{13} + 1x_{34} + 1x_{35} & = 0 \\
\text{Node 4:} & -1x_{14} - 1x_{24} - 1x_{34} + 1x_{45} + 1x_{46} & = 0 \\
\text{Node 5:} & -1x_{35} - 1x_{45} + 1x_{56} + 1x_{57} & = 0 \\
\text{Node 6:} & -1x_{26} - 1x_{46} - 1x_{56} + 1x_{67} & = 0 \\
\text{Node 7:} & x_{27} + x_{57} + x_{67} & = 1 \\
\end{array}
\quad (3\text{-}66)
$$

with all $x_{ij} \geq 0$ $\quad\quad\quad\quad\quad\quad\quad\quad\quad\quad\quad\quad\quad\quad\quad\quad\quad\quad\quad\quad\quad\quad\quad$ (3-67)

The constraint for Node 1 indicates that there must be flow out of one, and only one, of the branches leading out of Node 1. Similarly, the constraint for Node 7 indicates that there must be flow into one, and only one, of the branches leading into Node 7. At Nodes 2 through 6, the constraints are "conversion of flow" constraints indicating that the flow into the node must equal flow out of the node. For example, at node 2:

$$\frac{\text{Flow into Node 2}}{1x_{12}} = \frac{\text{Flow out of Node 2}}{1x_{24} + 1x_{26} + 1x_{27}}$$
$$(3\text{-}68)$$

or $\quad\quad\quad\quad\quad -1x_{12} + 1x_{24} + 1x_{26} + x_{27} = 0$

The solution to the least-cost shipping network problem is summarized in the following table.

Shipping Route Segment	Value	Cost per 100 units ($)
x_{12}	0	0
x_{13}	1	4
x_{14}	0	0 _(continued)_

(continued)

Shipping Route Segment	Value	Cost per 100 units ($)
x_{24}	0	0
x_{26}	0	0
x_{27}	0	0
x_{34}	0	0
x_{35}	1	4
x_{45}	0	0
x_{46}	0	0
x_{56}	1	1
x_{57}	0	0
x_{67}	1	2

Minimum $Z = \$11$

The minimum-cost shipping network is thus:

$$①→③→⑤→⑥→⑦$$

CASE STUDY: AUDITOR ASSIGNMENT PROBLEM[3]

As a final application let us consider an actual case study involving the assignment of auditors to audits. This study was done for the St. Louis office of the Army Audit Agency, a federal agency that is responsible for auditing various branches of the U.S. Army. At the time of the study, 1975, the St. Louis Army Audit Agency office staff was composed of 23 auditors, categorized as follows.

GS Level	Audit Role	Number of Auditors
14	Managing Auditor	1
13	Supervisor Auditor	2
12	Auditor-in-Charge (AIC)	6
11	Lead Auditor (LA)	8
9	Junior Auditor (JA)	2
5/7	Auditor Trainee (TA)	4

The managing auditor and the two supervisory auditors performed administrative functions, and the actual audits were accomplished by the remaining 20 auditors.

Annually, the managing auditor received a "Schedule of Audits" for the coming fiscal year, which outlined the audit coverage proposed by Army management for the period. The desired depth and scope of coverage for each audit was identified in the schedule by the number of proposed "workdays." Audit workdays ranged from 20 or 30 for small jobs to 600 or more for large, complex audits. In addition, the schedule listed proposed start dates (month only) for the audits. Because the schedule was only a planning document—and as such, listed audit requirements in broad terms—the

[3] The author would like to acknowledge the original work done on this problem by James A. McQuality, a MBA student at the University of Missouri, St. Louis.

managing auditor for each office was provided a great deal of flexibility in scheduling and staffing the audits. For example, a 40-workday audit could be performed by one auditor over a 2-month period of time, or it could be performed in 1 week by assigning eight auditors to the job. Another factor to be considered was that not all auditors of the same grade level (GS) performed equally. This fact was an important consideration for the assignment problem for two reasons. First, audit workday estimates were based on standard auditor productivity. Consequently, if a 300-workday audit was staffed with highly productive auditors, then one could expect the job to be completed in less than the time allowed. The converse would hold true for audits staffed with auditors of less than average productivity. The second aspect of the auditor performance problem dealt with the role assignment. As noted above, a GS-12 auditor was typically assigned the role of "auditor-in-charge" (AIC). It might appear, therefore, that the number of audits that could be conducted at any given time would be limited to the number of available AIC's In practice, however, some GS-11's had the necessary experience to be auditor-in-charge for certain jobs, while other jobs were so complex that at least two GS-12's were required. Also, it obviously was not possible to staff an audit entirely with auditor trainees.

The most critical aspect of the problem was to determine what benefits the St. Louis District office could expect to receive by assigning auditor i to audit j. If this factor were not important, then staffing could readily be accomplished by matching available resources to available audits on a first-come, first-serve basis. However, no two auditors were alike, as they differed in grade level and productivity. Some auditors had greater experience in some areas, and job requirements differed from audit to audit. For instance, results from an audit of a very complex area, such as data-processing management, could be expected to be more substantive if members of the staff had prior audit experience in that area.

The auditor assignment problem was modeled using a linear programming approach. The notation at the top of the next page was used in model formulation.

The linear programming model was constructed to make auditor assignments for four audits scheduled to be performed during the month of January 1976. Additionally, the model allowed for an auditor to be assigned to a fifth activity, training, during the scheduling period. The first set of constraints dealt with the maximum number of workdays during the month that each auditor could be assigned. Each auditor i was available to work on any assignment j up to D_i number of days during the month. The month of January 1976 had 20 working days for federal employees, and this is the figure used for the right-hand side values (D_i) for the constraints pertaining to 18 of the 20 auditors. Two auditors were to be transferred out of the office during January 1976 and were only available for 5 working days. This set of constraints was written as:

$$\sum_{j=1}^{5} x_{ij} \leq D_i \qquad (3\text{-}69)$$

for $i = 1, 2, \ldots, n = 20$ auditors

It was not necessary to constrain the minimum number of days each auditor had to work since the objective of this model (described later) was to maximize auditor utility. In addition, the total number of available auditor workdays (370) was less than the total workdays (386) required for the four audits.

The second set of constraints dealt with the maximum number of "standard workdays" that could be charged

n Number of auditors.

m Number of audit activities in which the staff could be engaged during the scheduling period. These activities included audits, professional education, vacations, etc.

x_{ij} Actual days to be worked during the scheduling period by the ith auditor on the jth activity.

B_j Maximum "standard audit workdays" that may be charged to the jth activity.

D_i The maximum number of actual days that the ith staff member would be available to engage in all audit activities.

E_i The minimum number of days the ith staff member would be available to engage in all audit activities.

A_{ij} The ratio of the number of days a "standard" auditor spends on the jth activity to the number of actual days spent by the ith auditor on the same activity to accomplish the same work.

C_{ij} The aggregate measure in dollar equivalents of the benefits to audit office as a result of the ith auditor working on the jth activity.

R_{ij} The billing rate in dollars of the ith auditor on the jth activity.

S_{ij} The dollar benefit of assigning auditor "i" to activity "j" for one day due to the special experience that auditor has on that type of audit.

T_{ij} The dollar benefit of assigning the ith auditor to the jth activity in order that auditor may gain experience on that type of audit.

to each audit. This set of constraints was written as:

$$\sum_{i=1}^{20} A_{ij}x_{ij} \le B_j$$
$$\text{for } j = 1,2,3,4 \text{ audits} \qquad (3-70)$$

The A_{ij} coefficients were determined from data previously collected by the St. Louis District Army Audit Agency. One constraint was required for each of the four audits. The right-hand sides of each constraint reflected the number of audit workdays specified in the original schedule.

The third and fourth sets of constraints dealt with professional training. Training was a necessary, yet low-priority, function of the St. Louis office. Twenty-six workdays of training

were specified for four specific auditors during this period. The actual auditors had already been selected, and therefore this condition was established by four equality constraints of the form:

$$x_{i5} = Y_i$$
$$\text{for } i = 1,2,3,4 \text{ auditors} \qquad (3-71)$$

Y_i represented the number of training workdays programmed for that specific auditor. These constraints could be ignored if the right-hand side of the first set of constraints were reduced by the number of training workdays for the auditors concerned. Training also served as a "catchall" in the event available auditor workdays exceeded programmed audit workdays (which they did not in this month). In this case, those auditors offering the least contribution to the programmed audits would be scheduled for optional training courses. These constraints appeared as:

$$\sum_{i=1}^{20} x_{i5} \geq B_5$$

$$(\text{i.e.,} \sum_{i=1}^{4} Y_i = 26 = B_5)$$ (3-72)

The A_{ij} coefficients were not required in these sets of constraints since the

Army Audit Agency considered all auditors equally productive in training. The objective of the model was to maximize certain predetermined office and Agency benefits by having auditor i work on activity j. Thus, the objective function was defined as:

$$\text{Maximize } Z = \sum_{i=1}^{n} \sum_{j=1}^{m} C_{ij} x_{ij}$$

(Net benefit to Army Audit Agency office from auditor assignment)

TABLE 3.1 Auditor Assignment Problem Formulation

Objective Function   (Net benefit to Army Audit Agency Office from auditor assignment)

Maximize $Z = 191x_{1,1} + 159x_{1,2} + 159x_{1,3} + 159x_{1,4} + 127x_{1,5} +$
$159x_{2,1} + 159x_{2,2} + 191x_{2,3} + 143x_{2,4} + 127x_{2,5} + \ldots +$
$113x_{20,1} + 113x_{20,2} + 86x_{2,3} + 113x_{20,4} + 77x_{20,5}$

Auditor Workday Constraints   (Maximum number of workdays during the month that each auditor could be assigned)

Auditor 1	$x_{1,1} + x_{1,2} + x_{1,3} + x_{1,4} + x_{1,5}$	$\leq$ 20 workdays
Auditor 2	$x_{2,1} + x_{2,2} + x_{2,3} + x_{2,4} + x_{2,5}$	$\leq$ 5 workdays
.	.	.
.	.	.
.	.	.
Auditor 20	$x_{20,1} + x_{20,2} + x_{20,3} + x_{20,4} + x_{20,5}$	$\leq$ 20 workdays

Auditor Workday Constraints   (Maximum number of "standard" workdays chargeable to each audit)

Audit 1	$x_{1,1} + x_{2,1} + x_{3,1} + x_{4,1} + 1.2x_{5,1} + \ldots + x_{20,1}$	$\leq$ 90 workdays
Audit 2	$x_{1,2} + x_{2,2} + x_{3,2} + x_{4,2} + 1.2x_{5,2} + \ldots + x_{20,2}$	$\leq$ 120 workdays
Audit 3	$x_{1,3} + x_{2,3} + x_{3,3} + x_{4,3} + 1.2x_{5,3} + \ldots + x_{20,3}$	$\leq$ 90 workdays
Audit 4	$x_{1,4} + x_{2,4} + x_{3,4} + x_{4,4} + 1.2x_{5,4} + \ldots + x_{20,4}$	$\leq$ 60 workdays

Professional Training Constraints   (Professional training requirements)

Auditor 16	$x_{16,5} =$ 20 workdays
Auditor 17	$x_{17,5} =$ 2 workdays
Auditor 19	$x_{19,5} =$ 2 workdays
Auditor 20	$x_{20,5} =$ 2 workdays

Assignment of "Excess" Workdays to Training Constraint   (All workdays not assigned to auditors are assigned to training)

Activity 5 $x_{1,5} + x_{2,5} + x_{3,5} + \cdots + x_{20,5} \geq 26$ workdays

Nonnegativity restrictions

$$x_{i,j} \geq 0 \text{ for all } i \text{ and } j$$

where $C_{ij} = R_{ij} + S_{ij} + T_{ij}$ (3-73)

R_{ij} was the "heaviest weight" of the C_{ij} elements. As indicated above, this element represented the auditor's billing rate. All GS-12's had the same R_{ij}; GS-11's had the same R_{ij} etc., regardless of job assignment. Similar to private industry, the R_{ij} was used in the government to insure that the highest paid (and generally more experienced) auditors are used whenever possible. This element also allowed for the "pyramiding" technique of audit staffs since the highest paid auditors were the fewest in number.

S_{ij} and T_{ij} were relative benefits of having certain auditors assigned to certain audits. There were numerous possible S_{ij}, T_{ij} combinations. For instance, if the office policy was to have auditors become experienced on all types of audits, then S_{ij} would generally be of low value. If, on the other hand, certain auditors were required to gain expertise in selected areas of Army management (i.e., data processing, procurement, etc.), then S_{ij} would probably have a greater weight than T_{ij}. In the model, we treated these two elements as relative to one another in such a fashion that their sum would never

TABLE 3.2 Optimal Solution—Auditor Assignment Problem

Type of Auditor	Workday Assignments					Total Workdays Assigned (Auditors)
	Audit 1	Audit 2	Audit 3	Audit 4	Professional Training	
GS 12 (AIC's)						
AUDITOR 1	20					20
2		5				5
3	20					20
4	20					20
5		20				20
6		4		16		20
GS 11 (LA's)						
AUDITOR 7				20		20
8			20			20
9			20			20
10				20		20
11		20				20
12		20				20
13		5				5
14		20				20
GS 9 (JA's)						
AUDITOR 15	15			5		20
16					20	20
GS 5/7 (TA's)						
AUDITOR 17			18		2	20
18		5.25			14.75	20
19	18				2	20
20			18		2	20
Total Workdays Assigned (Activities)	93	112.25	63	61	40.75	370

Optimal value of objective function = $53,000.

exceed one-half of the billing rate of each x_{ij}. This was done because the office wanted to preclude the possibility that, for example, a well-experienced junior auditor would be assigned to lead an audit dealing with his or her area of experience. The Agency's decision rule was that, under all circumstances, the highest-paid auditors would always be the more productively utilized.

The linear programming model constructed according to the details presented above consisted of some 30 constraints involving 100 decision variables. The mathematical formulation of the auditor assignment problem is presented below in Table 3.1. Because of the size and complexity of the model, it was solved using IBM's Mathematical Program Systems (MPS), a commercial linear programming computer software package. The optimal assignment of the 20 auditors to the four audits and professional training, for the month of January 1976, is presented below in Table 3.2. Note that combinations of three different grades (GS levels) of auditors were assigned to each of the four audits. However, the optimal solution assigned only "junior auditors" and "training auditors" to professional training. The optimal value of the objective function for this solution was $53,000 (i.e., net benefit to Army Agency office from auditor assignment).

3.9 CONCLUSION

In this chapter we have attempted to introduce the basic concepts of linear programming, and to illustrate how a solution to simple, two-variable linear programming problems can be obtained graphically. We have presented and discussed the properties of the linear programming model, and have analyzed graphically a number of special cases that may arise in applying linear programming. Additionally, a number of applications of linear programming have been presented, in an attempt to facilitate the reader's understanding of the use of linear programming in "real world" problem solving. In the following chapter we will focus our efforts on the development of a computational method, the simplex algorithm, that can be used to solve linear programming problems.

GLOSSARY OF TERMS

Additivity A property of a linear programming model stipulating that each of the activities must be additive with respect to the measure of resource usage, as specified by the constraint set, and the measure of effectiveness specified by the objective function.

Alternative Optimal Solutions In linear programming we may encounter simultaneously one or more extreme points that provide an (identical) optimal value of the objective function.

Constraint Set A collection of equalities and/or inequalities that along with the nonnegativity restrictions define the feasible region for a linear programming problem.

Continuity A property of a linear programming model that allows for fractional levels of the decision variables.

Deterministic Coefficients A property of a linear programming model which specifies that all coefficients in the model are known constants.

Extreme Points   The points of the convex set formed by the constraints and the nonnegativity restrictions of a linear programming problem that constitute the basic feasible solutions to the problem.

Feasible Solution   Any set of x_j that satisfies the constraint set and the nonnegativity restrictions of the linear programming problem.

Feasible Solution Space   The region defined by the constraint set and the nonnegativity restrictions of the linear program.

Infeasible Solution   A solution to a linear programming problem in which it is not possible to obtain feasible values for the decision variables because of (a) an inconsistent constraint set, or (b) violation of the nonnegativity restrictions.

Iso-cost Line   Equal cost line (objective function) in a cost minimization problem.

Iso-profit Line   Equal profit line (objective function) in a profit maximization problem.

Linearity   A property of a linear programming model that means the marginal measure of profitability, and the marginal usage of each resource, are being considered as constants over the entire range of productive activity.

Linear Programming   A linear, deterministic model used to solve the problem of allocating limited resources among competing activities.

Linear Programming Problem Formulation   In linear programming, problem formulation requires the determination of a linear objective function, a set of linear constraints, and the specification of nonnegativity restrictions on the decision variables.

Nonnegativity Restrictions   The conditions that require the values of the decision variables to be nonnegative ($x_j \geq 0, j = 1, \ldots, n$).

Optimal Feasible Solution   Any set of x_j that satisfies the constraint set and the nonnegativity restrictions and optimizes the objective function.

Physical Rates of Usage or Physical Rates of Substitution   The parameters of the constraint set; they specify the rate at which resources are used in the production of desired end products in a classical allocation problem.

Proportionality   A property of a linear programming model which means that the measure of effectiveness employed in the objective function and the amount of each resource used in each constraint must be proportional to the value of each decision variable considered individually.

Redundant Constraint   A constraint that does not form a boundary for the feasible solution space of the linear programming problem.

Right-Hand Side Values   Parameters in the linear programming formulation; they specify the amounts of resources available for various activities in a classical resource allocation problem.

Solution   A set of x_j that satisfies the constraint set of the linear programming problem.

Solution Space   The region defined by the constraint set of the linear program.

Unbounded Solution   A solution to a linear programming problem in which one (or more) of the basic variables can be increased indefinitely ($\to +\infty$), so that the objective function goes either to $+\infty$ or $-\infty$.

SELECTED REFERENCES

LINEAR PROGRAMMING   Anderson, David R., Dennis Sweeney, and Thomas A. Williams. 1974. *Linear Programming for Decision Making.* St. Paul, Minn.: West Publishing Co.

Bazaraa, Mokthar, S., and John J. Jarvis. 1977. *Linear Programming and Network Flows*. New York: John Wiley & Sons, Inc.

Beale, E.M.L. 1968. *Mathematical Programming in Practice*. London: Putnam.

Bradley, Stephen P., Arnoldo C. Hax, and Thomas L. Magnanti, 1977. *Applied Mathematical Programming*. Reading, Mass.: Addison-Wesley Publishing Company.

Charnes, A., and W. W. Cooper. 1961. *Management Models and Industrial Applications of Linear Programming*. vols. 1 and 2. New York: John Wiley & Sons, Inc.

Cooper, Leon, and David Steinberg. 1974. *Methods and Applications of Linear Programming*. Philadelphia: W. B. Saunders Company.

Daellenbach, Hans G., and Earl J. Bell. 1978. *User's Guide to Linear Programming*. Englewood Cliffs, N.J.: Prentice-Hall, Inc.

Dantzig, George B. 1963. *Linear Programming and Extensions*. Princeton, N.J.: Princeton University Press.

Frazer, J. Ronald. 1968. *Applied Linear Programming*. Englewood Cliffs, N.J.: Prentice-Hall, Inc.

Garvin, Walter W. 1960. *Introduction to Linear Programming*. New York: McGraw-Hill Book Company.

Gass, Saul I. 1969. *Linear Programming: Methods and Applications*. New York: McGraw-Hill Book Company.

Hadley, G. 1962. *Linear Programming*. Reading, Mass.: Addison-Wesley Publishing Company, Inc.

Hughes, Ann J., and Dennis E. Grawoig. 1973. *Linear Programming: An Emphasis on Decision Making*. Reading, Mass.: Addison-Wesley Publishing Company, Inc.

Ignizo, James P. 1982. *Linear Programming In Single- & Multiple Objective Systems*. Englewood Cliffs, N.J.: Prentice-Hall, Inc.

Kim, Chaiko. 1971. *Introduction to Linear Programming*. New York: Holt, Rinehart & Winston, Inc.

Kwak, N. K. 1973. *Mathematical Programming with Business Applications*. New York: McGraw-Hill Book Company.

Levin, Richard I., and Rudolph P. Lamone. 1969. *Linear Programming for Management Decisions*. Homewood, Ill.: Richard D. Irwin, Inc.

Loomba, Narendra P., and Efraim Turban. 1974. *Applied Programming for Management*. New York: Holt, Rinehart & Winston, Inc.

Luenberger, David G. 1973. *Introduction to Linear and Non-Linear Programming*. Reading, Mass.: Addison-Wesley Publishing Company, Inc.

Naylor, T. H., E. T. Byrne, and J. M. Vernon. 1971. *Introduction to Linear Programming: Methods and Cases*. Belmont, Calif.: Wadsworth Publishing Company.

Simmons, Donald M. 1972. *Linear Programming for Operations Research*. San Francisco: Holden-Day, Inc.

Strum, J. E. 1971. *Introduction to Linear Programming*. San Francisco: Holden-Day, Inc.

Thompson, Gerald E. 1971. *Linear Programming: An Elementary Introduction*. New York: Macmillan Publishing Company, Inc.

DISCUSSION QUESTIONS

1. Give the economic interpretation of a production scheduling problem in linear programming format.
2. What is the difference between a solution, a feasible solution, a basic feasible solution, and an optimal feasible solution with respect to a linear programming problem?
3. Why would the feasible solution space in an linear programming model have to constitute a "convex" set?

4. Is there a difference between an "optimal feasible solution" and an "optimal basic feasible solution"? If so, what is the difference?
5. Why would the optimal solution always be determined at one (or more) extreme point(s) of the feasible solution space?
6. How can you graphically determine that you have more than one optimal solution?
7. Is the assumption of "additivity" in linear programming realistic with respect to the real world?
8. How can you graphically determine that you have an unbounded solution?
9. How can you graphically see that you are not going to get a feasible solution to the problem, and what does it indicate?
10. How do you transform "ratios constraints" to a more convenient form so that they can be used in linear programming?

PROBLEM SET

1. Graph each of the following constraints and indicate whether the solution space associated with each of them lies "above," "below," "to the right," "to the left," or "directly on" the constraint.
   (a) $5x_1 \leq 10$
   (b) $2x_2 \geq 6$
   (c) $3x_1 + 4x_2 \leq 12$
   (d) $-4x_1 + 2x_2 \leq 16$
   (e) $3x_1 + 5x_2 = 30$

2. Given the following linear programming problem:

   Maximize $Z = 4x_1 + 6x_2$

   subject to: $2x_1 + 3x_2 \leq 150$
   $4x_1 + 2x_2 \leq 80$

   with $x_1 \geq 0, x_2 \geq 0$

   (a) Find the optimal solution to this problem using the graphical method.
   (b) How many extreme points are on your graph? Identify each of these extreme points, and the corresponding value of the objective function, in order to indicate the optimal solution.
   (c) Is there a redundant constraint for this problem? If so, identify it.

3. Given the following linear programming problem:

   Maximize $Z = 5x_1 + 3x_2$

   subject to: $x_1 \leq 12$
   $x_2 \leq 12$
   $x_1 + x_2 \leq 14$

   with $x_1 \geq 0, x_2 \geq 0$

   (a) Graph the feasible region for this problem.
   (b) Identify each of the extreme points, and the corresponding value of the objective function.
   (c) Determine the optimal solution.

(d) If the objective function of the problem was changed to Maximize $Z = 3x_1 + 5x_2$, what would the optimal solution be?

4. Given the following linear programming problem:

Maximize $Z = 6x_1 + 3x_2$

subject to:
$$2x_1 + 1x_2 \leq 8$$
$$3x_1 + 3x_2 \leq 18$$
$$1x_2 \leq 3$$

with $x_1 \geq 0, x_2 \geq 0$

(a) Solve the problem graphically.
(b) Does this problem have more than one optimal solution? If it does, identify the alternative optimal solutions. Explain what the line segment connecting the alternative optimal solutions means.
(c) Does this problem have a redundant constraint? If it does, identify it.

5. Given the following linear programming problem:

Maximize $Z = 4x_1 + 6x_2$

subject to:
$$2x_1 + 3x_2 \leq 12$$
$$6x_1 + 2x_2 \leq 18$$

with $x_1 \geq 0, x_2 \geq 0$

(a) Solve this problem graphically.
(b) Does this problem have more than one optimal solution? If it does, identify the alternative optimal solutions. Explain what the line segment connecting the alternative optimal solutions means.

6. Given the following linear programming problem:

Maximize $Z = 1x_1 + 4x_2$

subject to:
$$-1x_1 + 2x_2 \leq 14$$
$$-2x_1 + 1x_2 \leq 2$$

with $x_1 \geq 0, x_2 \geq 0$

Solve this problem graphically and state what your solution indicates.

7. Given the following linear programming problem:

Maximize $Z = 3x_1 + 1x_2$

subject to:
$$2x_1 + 5x_2 \geq 10$$
$$3x_1 + 1x_2 \geq 6$$

with $x_1 \geq 0, x_2 \geq 0$

Solve the problem graphically and state what your solution indicates.

8. Given the following linear programming problem:

Maximize $Z = 2x_1 + 3x_2$

subject to:
$$1x_1 - 1x_2 \geq 4$$
$$1x_1 + 1x_2 \geq 6$$
$$1x_1 \qquad \leq 2$$

with $x_1 \geq 0, x_2 \geq 0$

Solve this problem graphically and state what your solution indicates.

9. Given the following linear programming problem:

Maximize $Z = 3x_1 + 5x_2$

subject to:
$$4x_1 + 4x_2 \leq 20$$
$$7x_1 + 3x_2 \leq 21$$
$$1x_1 \qquad \geq 5$$

with $x_1 \geq 0, x_2 \geq 0$

Solve this problem graphically and state what your solution indicates.

10. For the following constraint set and nonnegativity conditions the corresponding graph is presented. Answer the questions below the graph.

$$3x_1 + 2x_2 \leq 12$$
$$-1x_1 + 1x_2 \leq 2$$

$$x_1 \geq 0, x_2 \geq 0$$

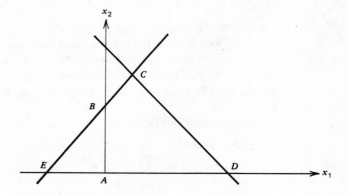

(a) Complete the following table:

Extreme Point	Value of	
	x_1	x_2
A		
B		
C		
D		
E		

(b) Which of these extreme points are feasible solutions? Have any extreme points been omitted?

(c) If the objective function for the problem is Maximize $Z = 2x_1 + 4x_2$, what are the objective function values at extreme points A, B, C, and D?

(d) What is the optimal solution to this problem, and at what extreme point does it occur.

11. Which of the following mathematical relationships could be found in a properly structured linear programming model and which could not? For those mathematical relationships that are unacceptable for a linear programming model, state the reason why.

(a) $2x_1 + 6x_2 = 400$

(b) Maximize $Z = 3x_1 + x_2^2 - 3x_3$

(c) $2.5x_1 - 1x_1 \geq 10$

(d) $2x_1x_3 \leq 20$

(e) $1x_1 + 6x_2 \geq 0$

(f) Minimize $Z = 4x_1 - 3\sqrt{x_2}$

12. Solve the following problem graphically.

Maximize $Z = 3x_1 - 1x_2$

subject to: $\quad 4x_1 + 2x_2 \leq 8$
$\quad\quad\quad\quad 3x_1 + 1x_2 \leq 10$

with $\quad x_1 \geq 0, x_2 \geq 0$.

13. Solve the following problem graphically.

Minimize $Z = x_1 + 2x_2$

subject to: $\quad 2x_1 - 3x_2 \leq 7$
$\quad\quad\quad\quad 1x_1 + 2x_2 \leq 10$

with $\quad x_1 \geq 0, x_2 \geq 0$.

14. Solve the following problem graphically.

Maximize $Z = 1x_1 + 6x_2$

subject to: $\quad 4x_1 + 8x_2 \leq 32$
$\quad\quad\quad\quad 5x_1 + 7x_2 \leq 35$
$\quad\quad\quad\quad -3x_1 + 3x_2 \leq 9$

with $\quad x_1 \geq 0, x_2 \geq 0$

15. Solve the following problem graphically.

Minimize $Z = 4x_1 + 8x_2$

subject to: $\quad 7x_1 + 1x_2 \geq 7$
$\quad\quad\quad\quad 2x_1 - 3x_2 \leq 6$
$\quad\quad\quad\quad 3x_1 + 2x_2 \geq 6$
$\quad\quad\quad\quad 1x_1 + 4x_2 \geq 4$

with $\quad x_1 \geq 0, x_2 \geq 0$

16. Mrs. Minnie Fingers has a basement macrame shop in which she weaves two types of macrame products: hanging flowerpot holders and wall hangings. Each of these macrame items must be made using a combination of four ropes, but each rope type is available in a limited quantity. The rope availability is as follows:

Rope Type	Rope Availability (ft)
A	150
B	210
C	130
D	190

The rope requirement to manufacture the two items is as follows:

	Rope Requirement (ft)	
Rope Type	Flower-Pot Holder	Wall Hanging
A	17	5
B	109	13
C	3	18
D	6	8

Mrs. Fingers believes that she can sell her hanging flowerpot holders for $3 each, and her wall hangings for $4 each. She can sell all that she produces. Formulate as a linear programming model.

17. Ye Olde Smokehouse, Ltd. prepares and packages three Christmas gift packages containing sausages and cheeses. The "Taster's Delight" gift package will contain 3 sausages and 6 cheeses; the "Succulent Delight" will contain 5 sausages, and 4 cheeses; and the "Gourmet Delight" will contain 6 sausages and 5 cheeses. The firm has 2500 sausages and 3000 cheeses available for packaging, and they believes that all gift packages can be sold (based on previous demand). Profits are estimated at $2.50 for the "Taster's Delight" gift package, $3.50 for the "Succulent Delight" gift package, and $4.00 for the "Gourmet Delight" gift package. Formulate as a linear programming model.

18. The Leather Boot Sporting Goods Company manufactures two types of leather soccer balls: "Competition Ball," and "Professional Ball." Each type of ball requires work by both of two types of employees: semiskilled, and skilled. Basically, the semiskilled employees employ machines in the manufacture of the soccer balls, while the skilled employees hand sew the soccer balls. The available time (per week) for each type of employee and the time requirement for each type of soccer ball are given below.

Type of Employee	Manufacturing Time Requirement (hr)		Time Availability (hr/week)
	"Competition Ball"	"Professional Ball"	
Semiskilled	2	3	80
Skilled	4	6	150

The cost of an hour of semiskilled labor is $5.50, and the cost of an hour of skilled labor is $8.50. To meet weekly demand requirements, at least 15 "Competition" balls and at least 10 "Professional" soccer balls must be manufactured. Formulate as a linear programming model.

19. Ms. Betty Pan, RN, is trying to develop a diet plan for her patients. The required nutritional elements, and the total daily requirements of each nutritional element are as follows.

Required Nutritional Element	Total Daily Requirement
Calories	Not more than 2700 calories
Carbohydrates	Not less than 300 grams
Protein	Not less than 250 grams
Vitamins	Not less than 60 grams

Ms. Pan has four basic food types to use in planning her menus. The units of nutritional elements per unit of food types are shown in the following table. Note that the cost associated with a unit of ingredient is also shown at the bottom of this table.

Required Nutritional Element	Units of Nutritional Elements per Unit of Food Type			
	Milk	*Meat*	*Bread*	*Vegetable*
Calories	160	210	120	150
Carbohydrates	110	130	110	120
Protein	90	190	90	130
Vitamins	50	50	75	70
Cost per unit	$0.42	$0.68	$0.32	$0.17

Formulate as a linear programming model.

20. The Hippocrates Pharmaceutical Company has developed a new pill to be taken by smokers that will make them nauseated if they smoke. This new pill is a combination of four ingredients that are costly and in limited supply. The supply availabilities and costs are as follows.

Ingredient	Supply Availability (lb)	Cost ($ per lb)
1	22	28.00
2	18	35.00
3	20	52.00
4	24	26.00

Blending requirements for this new pill are as follows:

(a) Ingredient 1 must be at least 45 percent of the total, but cannot exceed 60 percent of the total.

(b) Ingredients 2 and 3 must each comprise at least 10 percent of the mixture, but their combined percentage cannot exceed 25 percent of the total.

(c) Ingredient 4 must be not more than 50 percent of the total.

Additionally, at least 25 lb of the pill must be produced. Formulate as a linear programming model.

21. The Stavrakos Candy Company mixes three types of chocolate to produce its two major candy lines. The mixing requirements for these two candy lines are as follows.

Candy Line	Ingredients	Selling Price ($ per lb)
Premium	Not less than 30%, Chocolate A Exactly 25%, Chocolate B Not more than 40%, Chocolate C	2.50
Par Excellence	Exactly 25%, Chocolate A Not less than 50%, Chocolate B Not more than 35%, Chocolate C	3.50

The supply availabilities of the three types of chocolate and their associated costs are as follows.

Chocolate	Supply Availability (lb)	Cost ($ per lb)
A	500	1.20
B	750	1.40
C	625	1.10

To satisfy its demand forecast the Stavrakos Candy Company would like to produce at least 600 lbs. of Premium Candy and at least 800 lbs. of Par Excellence Candy. Formulate as a linear programming problem to maximize profits.

22. The Slippery Oil Company produces three brands of oils: Regular, Multigrade, and Supreme. Each brand of oil is composed of one or more of four crude stocks, each having a different viscosity index. The relevant data concerning the crude stocks is shown below.

Crude Stock	Viscosity Index	$ Cost per Barrel	Supply per Day (barrels)
1	20	7.10	1000
2	40	8.50	1100
3	30	7.70	1200
4	55	9.00	1100

Each brand of oil must meet a minimum standard for viscosity index, and each brand thus sells at different price. The relevant data concerning the three brands of oil is shown below.

Brand of Oil	Minimum Required Viscosity Index	Selling Price ($ per barrel)	Demand per Day (barrels)
Regular	25	8.50	2000
Multigrade	35	9.00	1500
Premium	50	10.00	750

You may assume that we are interested in determining a production plan for a single day, and that all oil produced during this day can be either sold or stored at negligible cost. Formulate as a linear programming model to maximize profits.

23. The Torn Tread Tire Company manufactures two brands of tires: "Spartans" and "Invincibles." It has developed a 6-month sales forecast for these two brands of tires, as follows.

	Sales Forecast	
Month	"Spartans"	"Invincibles"
January	500	750
February	750	1000
March	1000	800
April	900	800
May	750	900
June	800	1000

It seeks to exactly meet these sales forecasts over the 6-month time period. At the end of December, the company had an inventory of 100 "Spartans" tires and 250 "Invincibles" tires. It wishes to have the same inventory levels for these two brands of tires at the end of June. The direct cost associated with tire production are as follows.
1. $5.50 per hour for labor.
2. $0.50 per tire per month for inventory holding.
Additionally, the company has 1750 labor hours available each month. A "Spartan" tire requires 1.0 labor hours to produce while an "Invincible" tire requires 1.5 hours to produce. Formulate as a linear programming model, to minimize production and inventory holding costs.

24. The Slick Copy Advertising Company employs linear programming in allocating its clients' resources among various advertising media. One particular client is particularly interested in the advertising reaching an audience having the following characteristics.
(a) Female, aged 25–35, married.
(b) College graduate.
(c) Family income > $20,000.
(d) Own home.
Slick Copy has isolated four possible advertising vehicles, having the following characteristics.

	Advertising Vehicle			
	1 *Women's* *Magazine*	*2* *Radio*	*3* *Television*	*4* *Newspaper*
Characteristic				
Reader traits				
Female, age 25–35, married (%)	90	55	65	42
College graduate (%)	30	20	25	38
Family income > $20,000 (%)	10	6	5	13
Own home (%)	21	23	27	30
Cost per advertisement ($)	$1000	$1500	$3500	$500
Potential audience size	250,000	750,000	1,500,000	800,000
Minimum number of advertisements required	10	5	3	15

Additionally, the client has specified that the relative importance of the reader traits should be weighted as follows:

Reader Trait	**Weight**
Female, age 25–35, married	5
College graduate	3
Family income > $20,000	2
Own home	2

The client has $100,000 to spend at this point in time. Formulate the linear programming model to maximize the effective exposure level.

25. The Shiny Jewel Company, which imports silver jewelry from Mexico, deals in four pieces of jewelry and has received quotes for each piece of jewelry from four Mexican suppliers, as follows.

Mexican *Supplier*	Jewelry Item			
	Necklace	*Bracelet*	*Earrings*	*Belt*
Ole	$10.00	$8.00	$7.50	$5.00
Zapata	9.50	8.10	6.90	4.30
Juarez	11.00	9.00	8.00	3.00
Carta Blanca	8.00	9.50	6.00	6.00

With $1000 currently available to finance its jewelry purchases, the company would like to order at least $150 worth of jewelry from each of the four suppliers and feels that it cannot possibly sell more than 100 necklaces, 200 bracelets, 300 earrings, and 50 belts. Formulate as a linear programming model.

26. Major governmental officials in the St. Louis metropolitan region have become increasingly concerned with air pollution problems. In particular they wish to reduce the annual emission rates for three major air pollutants as follows.

Pollutant	Desired Reduction in Annual Emission Rate (million pounds)
Hydrocarbons	50
Sulfur dioxides	60
Particulate matter	70

The governmental officials have contracted a local university to suggest feasible alternatives for reducing air pollution in the region. After a long and rigorous study the university researchers have arrived at the following set of recommendations and associated reductions of pollutants (in million pounds):

	Recommendations		
Pollutant	*Reduce Automobile Traffic*	*Electrostatic Precipitation for all Smokestacks*	*Improved Fuels for Energy and Automobiles*
Hydrocarbons	60	40	50
Sulfur dioxides	75	60	40
Particulate matter	60	90	80

Additionally, the university researchers have specified the following sets of costs for each major alternative.

Alternative	Abatement Cost (million $)
Reduce automobile traffic	15
Electrostatic precipitation	30
Improved fuels	20

Formulate as a linear programming model in terms of an aggregate plan composed of various percentages of the three recommendations.

27. The managers of several cattle feed lots are interested in determining how many of each of several types of livestock feeds to purchase in order to satisfy the nutritional requirements for their livestock. They wish to purchase these feeds in a manner that minimizes the cost of feeding their livestock. Relevant cost and nutritional data are as follows.

Required Nutrient	Units of Nutritional Elements per unit of Food Type				Minimum Nutrient Requirement
	Alfalfa	Corn	Soybeans	Sorghum	
Nutrient A	40	50	30	60	500
Nutrient B	30	60	35	40	750
Nutrient C	25	30	25	50	600
Cost per unit	$1.00	$1.25	$0.95	$1.35	

Formulate as a linear programming model.

28. Olney Company manufactures paint at two plants. Firm paint orders have been received from three large contractors. The firm has determined that the following shipping cost data is appropriate for these three contractors with respect to its two plants.

Contractor	Order Size (gallon)	Shipping Cost per Gallon ($)	
		From Plant 1	From Plant 2
Master Builder	750	1.80	2.00
Zippy Homes, Inc.	1500	2.60	2.20
Well-Bilt, Ltd.	1500	2.10	2.25

Each gallon of paint must be blended and tinted. The company's costs with respect to these two operations at each of the two plants are as follows.

Plant/Operation	Hours Required per Gallon	$ Cost per Hour	Hours Available
No. 1-Blending	0.10	$3.80	300
No. 1-Tinting	0.25	$3.20	360
No. 2-Blending	0.15	$4.00	600
No. 2-Tinting	0.20	$3.10	720

Formulate as a linear programming model.

29. Boatman's Bank of Cape Girardeau, Missouri, is trying to select an investment portfolio for a wealthy Missouri "Bootheel" cotton farmer. The bank has determined a set of five investment alternatives, with subjective estimates of rates of return and risk, as follows.

Investment	Annual Rate of Return (%)	Risk
Tax-free municipal bonds	6.0	1.3
Corporate bonds	8.0	1.5
High-grade common stock	5.0	1.9
Mutual fund	7.0	1.7
Real estate	15.0	2.7

The bank officer in charge of selecting the portfolio would like to maximize the average annual rate of return on the portfolio. However, the wealthy investor has specified that the average risk of the portfolio should not exceed 2.0 and does not want more than 20 percent of the investment to be put into real estate. Formulate as a linear programming model.

30. The Bold Safari Tea Company is trying to create a blend of tea that will maximize profitability. The company can sell 5000 tea bags daily of this blend of tea and each tea bag produces $0.05 sales revenue. The blend of tea is made from four types of teas having the following characteristics.

Tea	$ Cost per Bag	Oiliness Coefficient	Bitterness Coefficient	Daily Purchase Availability (Bags)
Ceylon	0.03	2	6	2000
Indonesian	0.02	4	5	2000
Malaysian	0.04	1	4	1000
Indian	0.01	6	2	3000

A top-quality bag of blended tea should have an average oiliness coefficient that is not more than 4, and an average bitterness coefficient that is not more than 5. Additionally, each bag of blended tea can contain no more than 30 percent of "Indonesian" tea. Formulate as a linear programming model.

31. The Homespun Company produces an air conditioner/heating unit for use in recreational vehicles. The company currently has firm orders for 6 months in the future. The company can schedule its production over the next 6 months to meet these orders on either a regular (≤ 500 units per month) or an overtime (≤ 300 units per month) basis. Customer orders and the associated production costs for the next 6 months are as follows.

Month	Orders	Cost per unit Regular Production	Cost per Unit Overtime Production
January	590	$50	$62
February	610	52	58
March	650	51	63
April	700	55	60
May	500	47	55
June	700	50	52

At the beginning of January the company has 75 air conditioners in inventory. At the end of June it wishes to have at least 100 air conditioners in inventory. The inventory carrying cost for the air conditioners is $10 per unit per month. Formulate as a linear programming model.

32. The Fairview school district has two high schools that serve the needs of its four major neighborhood areas. Each of its two high schools have a capacity of 4000 students. Its four neighborhoods have sizes and minority student percentages as follows.

Neighborhood	Number of Students	Percent of Minority Students
1	2200	10
2	2100	20
3	1500	50
4	1800	70

The distances from the approximate center of each of the neighborhoods to each of the two schools are as follows.

From	To	
	High School A	High School B
Neighborhood 1	1.7	1.3
Neighborhood 2	2.6	2.3
Neighborhood 3	2.5	2.7
Neighborhood 4	2.6	3.2

A court-ordered desegregation plan has specified that each high school can have no more than 50 percent minority enrollment and not less than 25 percent minority enrollment. You have been asked by this school district to devise a school busing plan that will meet these integration requirements while minimizing the number of student miles of busing required. Additionally, no student may be bused more than 3 miles. Formulate as a linear programming model.

33. The Thin Paper Company produces rolls of paper used in cash registers. Each roll of paper is 500 ft in length and can be produced in widths of 1-, 2-, 3-, and 5-in. The company's production process results in 500-ft. rolls that are 12-in. wide. Thus, the company must cut its 12-in. rolls to the desired widths. It has six basic cutting alternatives, as follows.

Cutting Alternative	Number of Rolls				Waste (inches)
	1-in.	2-in.	3-in.	5-in.	
1	6	3	0	0	0
2	0	3	2	0	0
3	1	1	1	1	1
4	0	0	2	1	1
5	0	4	1	0	1
6	4	2	1	0	1

The minimum demand requirements for the four rolls are as follows.

Roll Width (inches)	Demand Requirements (rolls)
1	3000
2	2000
3	1500
5	1000

The company wishes to minimize the waste generated by its production process, while meeting its demand requirements. Formulate as a linear programming problem.

34. The Never Sink Shipping Company operates on a route from Charleston, South Carolina, to Miami, Florida, offering a cargo transportation service. Its ships are of a uniform size and have capacity limits on both weight and space for three storage compartments, as follows.

Storage Compartment	Weight Capacity (tons)	Space Capacity (cu ft)
Front	15	10,000
Center	20	16,000
Back	12	12,000

A prospective customer would like to ship part, or all, of the following four cargoes on a forthcoming trip.

Cargo	Weight (tons)	Volume (cu ft per ton)	Profit (to Never Sink) ($ per ton)
1	20	500	125
2	18	800	160
3	22	600	130
4	10	400	110

To balance the ship for flotation purposes, the weight of the cargoes allocated to the respective compartments must be the same proportion of that compartment's weight capacity. Formulate a linear programming model to determine how much (if any) of each cargo should be accepted, and how to distribute the cargo among the compartments to maximize the total profit for the voyage for the Never Sink Shipping Company.

35. The True-Strung Corporation is a leading producer of tennis rackets. It manufactures three types of tennis rackets, an all-graphite racket, a graphite-wood composition racket, and a wooden racket. It sells the graphite racket for $40 profit, the graphite-wood racket for $30 profit, and the wooden racket for $10 profit. The production process for these tennis rackets is composed of three major processes,

and all three rackets require all of the three manufacturing processes. The following set of production information has been collected.

Production Process	Production Time Requirement (hours per racket)			Monthly Production Hours Available
	Graphite	Graphite-Wood	Wood	
Forming	0.50	1.00	1.25	18,000
Lamination/ Curing	3.50	1.75	1.25	20,000
Painting/ Finishing	0.75	1.25	1.00	22,000

To avoid out of stock conditions, the company has adopted a policy that states at least 1000 rackets of each type will be produced each month. The marketing manager for the company has indicated that it can expect to sell no more than 5000 wooden rackets per month. The graphite racket and the graphite-wood racket sell for approximately the same price at retail. Their combined demand is expected to be not more than 8000 rackets each month. Formulate as a linear programming model to determine the number of each type of tennis rackets to be produced monthly to maximize profit for the True-Strung Corporation.

36. Bill and Karen Scanlon are the proud new owners of a "Ticky-Tacky-Taco" franchised reptaurant in Myrtle Beach, South Carolina. They now face the problem of determining how many "Mexican food preparation specialists" (i.e., taco slingers) to hire and train during the next 6 months. Their requirements, expressed in terms of production hours, are 1000 in January, 1000 in February, 1000 in March, 1500 in April, 1500 in May, and 1500 in June. The Scanlons have 13 trained taco slingers available from the previous owner's employees.

Each taco slinger can work up to 100 hours per month. However, one month of training is required before a taco slinger can be put to work on a regular basis. Because of local labor market conditions, it is unrealistic to expect to hire more than four new people into the training program during any month. Additionally, approximately 20 percent of the workers who are required on a regular basis either quit or are fired each month. Those individuals in the training program normally do not quit, and are not fired, during their 1-month training program.

The monthly training cost is $1000 per worker for the first 3 months and $1250 per work for the last 3 months. The monthly salary of a worker is $400. An employee who is hired in one month but does not begin work until a later month costs the Scandon's $50 for each month that he or she is idle.

Formulate a linear programming model to determine a minimum cost hiring schedule for the 6-month period.

37. A benevolent corporation in a major Midwestern city has 15 acres of idle land near its corporate headquarters. It has agreed to permit a neighborhood civic association to grow vegetables on all or part of this idle land. Furthermore, the company will buy up to certain amounts of the vegetables produced from the neighborhood civic assocation, but also will allow them to produce and keep whatever they need for their own use. The civic association has decided to grow corn, tomatoes,

cucumbers, and potatoes. The table below summarizes their expectations with respect to the four crops.

Crop	Expected Civic Association Demand	Maximum Expected Corporation Demand	Expected Profit from Sale to Corporation (per pound)	Expected Yield per Acre
Corn	15,000 lb	25,000 lb	$0.20/lb	10,000 lb
Tomatoes	15,000 lb	20,000 lb	$0.25/lb	6,000 lb
Cucumbers	25,000 lb	20,000 lb	$0.30/lb	12,000 lb
Potatoes	50,000 lb	60,000 lb	$0.10/lb	18,000 lb

The civic association has decided that its major priority is producing the vegetables required to exactly satisfy its own expected demand. Formulate the linear programming model to allocate land to each crop to maximize total profit, realizing that this profit applies only to the produce sold to the corporation in excess of that used to satisfy the civic association demand.

38. Mr. Able Tiller owns and operates a large farm near Armstrong, Missouri. To feed his livestock for the next year he must produce wheat, corn, and alfalfa. His projected demand for wheat requires at least 225 acres of land. Similarly, at least 160 acres of land are required for corn, and at least 275 acres of land are required for alfalfa. The total amount of land available for wheat, corn, and alfalfa are 200 acres in Plot A, 500 acres in Plot B, and 260 acres in Plot C. The labor-hour requirements per acres for each crop, for the three plots of land, are as follows.

	Wheat	Corn	Alfalfa
Plot A	12	15	14
Plot B	15	10	16
Plot C	18	13	12

The labor costs per hour for each crop for the three plots of land are as follows.

	Wheat	Corn	Alfalfa
Plot A	$10	$15	$12
Plot B	14	16	10
Plot C	9	11	14

Formulate as a linear programming problem to minimize the total labor cost while satsifying the projected demand requirements.

39. The Rivers Company manufactures four types of running shoes: the "Super," the "Super-GT," and "Flyer," and the "Flyer-GT." Each of the four types of shoes require time to assemble, laminate soles, and do finish stitching. The time requirements for these operations, by type of shoe, are shown below, together with an estimate of the time available for these operations for the next month.

Production Operation	Type of Shoe and Time Requirements (hours per pair of shoes)				Monthly Production Hours Available
	"Super"	"Super-GT"	"Flyer"	"Flyer-GT"	
Assembly	0.5	0.75	1.0	1.25	2000
Lamination	1.0	1.0	1.5	1.75	2700
Finish stitching	0.5	0.5	1.0	1.5	1500

In addition, due to a strike at the factory that produces the soles for the running shoes, there is a shortage of soles. The supplier has indicated that he will not be able to supply more than a total of 1500 pairs of soles next month and that, of these, not more than 800 could be used on the "Flyer" or "Flyer-GT" type of shoes. The marginal profits associated with the four types of shoes are $6, $8, $11, and $13, respectively. Formulate the linear programming model to determine the most profitable production schedule for the forthcoming month.

40. Catch-A-Crook, Inc., is experiencing a sizeable growth in demand for its home protection systems. It produces a "Clamp" system and a "Vise" system, which it sells through department stores, discount stores, and hardware retailers. It has recently entered into negotiations with a large Southeastern discount store chain, "Poorways," which wishes to purchase at least 14,000 "Clamp" systems and at least 11,500 "Vise" systems each month. Unfortunately, Catch-A-Crook, Inc., does not have sufficient production capacity to supply Poorways in the near future. It can, however, subcontract the production of some of its home protection systems to another rival manufacturer. Production, cost, and price information for Catch-A-Crook, Inc., are summarized below.

Production Operation	Hours Required per Unit		Production Hours Available per Week
	"Clamp"	"Vise"	
Manufacture components	0.15	0.17	2400
Assemble components	0.12	0.15	2700
Test and package	0.10	0.14	3000
Price per Unit	$170	$225	
Cost per unit	$125	$175	

The subcontractor can supply any combination of the "Clamp" and "Vise" units up to 10,000 units total each month. The cost of purchasing these units from the subcontractor is $140 for the "Clamp" system and $200 for the "Vise" system. Formulate the linear programming model that will allow Catch-A-Crook, Inc., to determine the number of units of each system to produce and buy so as to maximize total profit.

41. A group of MBA students has been hired by a marketing professor at the University of Missouri, St. Louis. They have been directed to conduct a survey among the residents of two St. Louis county suburbs, Clayton and Ladue. The following conditions must be met by the survey.
(a) A total of 1000 households must be contacted.

(b) At least 400 married couple households with children must be contacted.
(c) At least 200 married couple households with no children must be contacted.
(d) At least 100 households composed of a single person must be contacted.
(e) The total number of households contacted during the evening must be at least as great as the number contacted during the day.
(f) At least 100 married couple households with children must be contacted during the day and at least 100 married couple households with children must be contacted during the evening.

The marketing professor will pay the MBA students on the following basis:

Household Type	Interview Cost	
	Day	Evening
Married couple, children	$10	$12
Married couple, no children	6	8
Single person	4	5

Formulate a linear programming model that could be used to determine how many households of each type should be contacted during the day and evening so as to minimize the total cost of the survey.

42. An investment manager, Mr. Max Dollar, has recently attended at a local university a seminar concerned with the use of management science techniques in financial decision making. He has returned to his job in the bank and is faced with making a decision concerning what investments should be purchased for the bank's portfolio for the forthcoming year. The investment manager has the following set of investment opportunities for the next year.

Investment Opportunity	Projected Yearly Rate of Return (%)
Public utility stocks	8
Public utility bonds	10
Government securities	7
Industrial stocks	11
Industrial bonds	12
Municipal bonds	9
Real estate trust	15

The following investment restrictions have been placed on Mr. Dollar by the bank.
(a) Industrial stocks are limited to be less than 10 percent of the portfolio.
(b) The investment in the real estate trust is limited to be less than 7 percent of the portfolio.
(c) Public utility bonds must account for at least 35 percent of the portfolio.
(d) Government securities must account for at least 25 percent of the portfolio.
(e) The total investment in public utility or industrial securities (stocks or bonds) cannot exceed 50 percent of the portfolio.

Formulate the investment manager's decision as a linear programming problem in which the return on the portfolio is maximized.

43. Georgette Carter, an investor, has income producing activities A and B available at the beginning of each of the next 6 years. Each dollar invested in Activity A at the beginning of a year returns $1.40 2 years later, and this amount of money can then be reinvested. Each dollar invested in activity B at the beginning of a year returns $1.55 3 years later, and this amount of money can then be reinvested.

At the beginning of the third year, investment opportunity C will become available. Each dollar invested in activity C will produce $1.60 at the end of the fifth year, and this amount of money can then be reinvested. At the beginning of the fifth year, investment opportunity D will become available. Each dollar invested in activity D will produce $1.30 at the end of the sixth year. Finally, at the beginning of the sixth year, investment opportunity E will become available. It will produce $1.20 at the end of year 6.

Assuming that the investor begins with $100,000, formulate the linear programming model that will allow her to determine an investment plan that maximizes the amount of money she can accumulate at the beginning of the seventh year.

44. Sandy Dillon, an MBA student at the University of South Carolina, faces a dilemma as she begins to plan her study schedule for a fall weekend. On Monday she must turn in a written paper in her Organizational Behavior class, as well as take exams in Financial Management and Quantitative Methods II (Management Science). She is approximately three-fourths finished with her paper and estimates that if she hands it in as is she will receive a grade of 70. With another 4 hours of work she feels that she would receive a grade of 85, and with 8 hours of work she feels she would get a grade of 100.

Without studying at all for the Financial Management test she feels that she would score 60. With an additional 5 hours of study she feels she would score 80, and with an additional 10 hours of study she feels she would score 100.

Quantitative Methods II is Sandy's hardest course. Without studying for the test she predicts she would score 40. With an additional 10 hours of study she feels she would score 70, and with an additional 20 hours of study she feels she would score 100.

The paper will be counted as 50 percent of the final grade in Organizational Behavior, the exam will be counted as 25 percent of the final grade in Financial Management, and the exam will be counted as 20 percent of the final grade in Quantitative Methods II. All three courses are 3-credit-hour courses.

Sandy estimates that she has at most 20 hours of study time available on the weekend, since she also has a date for the South Carolina versus Clemson football game.

Formulate Sandy's decision situation as a linear programming problem in which time is allocated to maximize her overall grade point average, while still achieving at least a grade of 70 in each of the three assignments (i.e., paper and exams).

45. The University of South Carolina is considering the purchase of three types of planes for use of its administrators, faculty, and athletic teams. The purchase price would be $3 million for each large plane, $1.5 million for each medium-sized plane, and $300,000 for each small plane. The trustees of the university have authorized a total expenditure of $10 million for these aircraft.

   The University has enough trained pilots to staff 10 airplanes total. Its mainte-nance facilities can handle the equivalent of 12 of the small airplanes. However, each medium-sized plane has a maintenance equivalence of 1.5 small planes, and each large plane has a maintenance equivalence of 2 small planes. Additionally, the University has decided that it must purchase at least 1 large plane, at least 2 medium-sized planes, and at least 3 small planes.

   Formulate the linear programming model that would be used to determine how many planes of each type to purchase in order to minimize the total purchase cost.

46. Joe Parker owns a 300 acre farm near Greenwood, South Carolina. He is in-terested in trying to plan the operations of his farm for the forthcoming year. He has $25,000 available for investment in the forthcoming year, and he estimates that he has 1500 manhours of labor available for the fall-winter months (October–March) and 5000 man-hours of labor available for the spring-summer months (April–September). If any of these manhours are not required, they may be used in working at a local farmer's cooperative, at a rate of $2.35 per hour during the fall-winter months and $3.50 per hour during the spring-summer months. Mr. Parker obtains income from the production of wheat, soybeans, peaches, cows, and hogs. His estimates of the labor manhour requirements per acre are as fol-lows.

	Wheat	Soybeans	Peaches
Fall-Winter manhour requirement per acre	20	15	(not grown)
Spring-Summer manhour requirement per acre	40	35	50

Estimated annual incomes per acre from the three crops are as follows.

	Wheat	Soybeans	Peaches
Annual income per acre	$350	$250	$400

Estimated annual investments per acre for the three crops are as follows.

	Wheat	Soybeans	Peaches
Annual investment per acre	$4	$2	$1

The corresponding estimates for the two types of livestock are as follows.

	Cows	Hogs
Fall-Winter manhour requirements per head	30	20
Spring-Summer manhour requirements per head	15	10
Annual investment per head	$250	$125
Annual income per head	$450	$200

Additionally, Mr. Parker estimates that each cow raised requires 2 acres of land, and each pig raised requires 1 acre of land. He would like to limit (yearly) his cow herd to a maximum of 50 cows and his pig herd to a maximum of 100 pigs. Formulate the linear programming model for Mr. Parker's farm operations planning problem.

47. The Malachite Foundry is attempting to cast a lightweight brake drum using a new alloy composed of 60-percent aluminum, 30-percent tin, and 10-percent zinc. It can blend this new alloy from one or more of several existing alloys that have the following metallic properties.

Metallic Property	Existing Alloy				
	A	B	C	D	E
Percentage aluminum	60	30	70	20	40
Percentage tin	20	50	20	40	50
Percentage zinc	20	20	10	40	10

The cost per pound for each of these alloys is as follows.

	A	B	C	D	E
Cost per pound	$15.00	$13.50	$17.10	$12.00	$14.25

Formulate the linear programming model to be used to determine the proportions of the alloys that should be blended to produce the new alloy at a minimum cost.

48. The Ready-Rider Bus Company is attempting to plan the amounts of diesel fuels to purchase for its bus fleet for the forthcoming year. It services cities throughout the Southeastern United States, and refuels at four major cities. In each of these cities, diesel fuel may be purchased from Conch Oil, Puxico Oil, or Immobil Oil Company. For the forthcoming year Conch Oil has agreed to supply up to 450,000 gallons of diesel fuel, Puxico Oil has agreed to supply up to 700,000 gallons of diesel fuel, and Immobil Oil has agreed to furnish up to 800,000 gallons of diesel fuel. The requirements at the four "refueling" cities are 350,000 gallons, 400,000 gallons, 450,000 gallons, and 500,000 gallons, respectively. Each of the three companies has specified a bid price per gallon of diesel fuel for the four cities, as follows.

	Conch Oil	Puxico Oil	Immobil Oil
City 1	0.80	0.90	0.92
City 2	0.87	0.75	0.70
City 3	0.75	0.70	0.92
City 4	0.90	0.85	0.80

Formulate the linear programming model to determine the minimum cost diesel fuel purchase plan for the Ready-Rider Bus Company.

49. Trashland Oil Company has one refinery that is wholly devoted to the production of two types of unleaded fuels: Unleaded Premium, and Unleaded Regular. This refinery can currently purchase four different crudes, which have the following chemical analyses and costs.

Crude Type	Percent of Blending Ingredient			Cost per Gallon	Supply Availability (gallons)
	A	B	C		
No. 1	0.90	0.07	0.03	$0.70	4000
No. 2	0.70	0.20	0.10	$0.50	6000
No. 3	0.10	0.70	0.20	$0.65	5000
No. 4	0.60	0.30	0.10	$0.85	5000

The Unleaded Premium gasoline is priced at $1.00 to the refinery's customers, and it must contain at least 60 percent of A. at least 20 percent of B, and not more than 10 percent of C. The Unleaded Regular gasoline is priced at $0.90 to the refinery's customers, and it must contain at least 50 percent of A, at least 15 percent of B, and not more than 15 percent of C. The company has a forecasted demand of 6000 gallons of Unleaded Premium and 9000 gallons of Unleaded Regular. Formulate the linear programming model that could be used to determine the number of gallons of each crude type to be used in each gasoline in order to maximize profit.

50. A metalworking firms uses three machines to manufacture three products. Each unit of product A requires 4 hours on machine 1, 2 hours on machine 2, and 1 hour on machine 3. Each unit of product B requires 3 hours on machine 1, 5 hours on machine 2, and 2 hours on machine 3. Each unit of product C requires 2 hours on machine 1, 4 hours on machine 2, and 5 hours on machine 3. The profits associated with the three products are $35, $45, and $40 per unit, respectively. One hundred eighty hours of machine 1 time, 150 hours of machine 2 time, and 160 hours of machine 3 time are available for scheduling. Formulate a linear programming model that could be used to schedule the two products on the three machines in a manner that maximizes profit.

51. A local discount store is attempting to plan its advertising expenditures for the forthcoming year. With $100,000 to spend for its advertising, it seeks to reach the maximum number of potential customers with this amount. The following planning data has been collected.

Characteristics	Advertising Medium		
	Newspapers	*Radio*	*Television*
Number of persons reached per unit	50,000	100,000	150,000
Number of persons above average income per unit	20,000	30,000	50,000
Number of married households per unit	15,000	20,000	40,000
Maximum units available	100	150	50
Minimum units available	25	30	30
Cost per unit	300	150	1,500

As a part of its advertising campaign, the discount store would like to meet the following objectives.

(a) To reach at least 2.5 million persons in the area.

(b) To reach at least 1 million persons in the area with above average income.

(c) To reach at least 500,000 married households in the area.

Formulate the linear programming model that could be used to determine the discount store's most effective advertising plan for the forthcoming year.

52. The Studley Manufacturing Company has projected its desired shipping levels for the first 6 months of the year as follows.

Month	Desired Level of Shipments
January	1,000
February	4,000
March	3,000
April	2,000
May	3,500
June	2,500
Total	16,000

The Studley Manufacturing Company has a regular monthly production capacity of 1700 and an overtime monthly production capacity of 1100. Its manufacturing costs are $8 per unit for those items produced during regular time and $10 per unit for those items produced during overtime. The company is beginning the year with no inventory on hand, and it does not wish to have any inventory on hand at the end of June. However, any inventory accumulated in the interim period costs $2 per unit per month. Formulate a linear programming model that could be used to determine a 6-month production plan which will minimize total production and inventory carrying cost.

53. Susie McWilliams manages the computer center at a major Midwestern university. She has just received four jobs from faculty members that require keypunching of data. Fortunately, she has exactly four keypunchers to which the jobs can be assigned. However, because of the nature of the four keypunch jobs and the difference in the skill levels of the four keypunchers, she would like to make the assignment in some optimal manner. She has made the following estimates of job completion times (hours).

	Job			
Keypuncher	No. 1	No. 2	No. 3	No. 4
A	1.1	1.4	2.0	3.2
B	1.7	1.0	2.2	3.1
C	1.3	1.2	2.0	3.1
D	1.5	1.3	2.1	2.9

Formulate the linear programming model that could be used to determine the allocation of the four keypunchers to the four jobs in a manner that minimizes the overall completion time for the jobs.

54. Capitol City Bakery of Columbia, South Carolina, has customers in the cities of Newberry, Aiken, and Sumter. The distances between these cities are summarized below.

	To			
From	Columbia	Newberry	Aiken	Sumter
Columbia	—	50	75	60
Newberry	50	—	90	120
Aiken	75	90	—	135
Sumter	60	120	135	—

The manager of the bakery would like to visit the major retail stores in each of these cities, beginning and ending in Columbia. Formulate the linear programming model that could be used to determine the minimum distance route that should be selected.

55. World Books, Incorporated, publishes and sells sets of books, using a door-to-door sales force. It sells a set of encyclopedias producing $100 gross profit, a set of religious books producing $75 gross profit, and a set of "Classics of Literature" producing $130 gross profit. In addition to its door-to-door sales effort, it also advertises heavily in the Sunday supplement of various newspapers and in magazines. It has made the following estimates with respect to the advertising and selling costs associated with its three major sets of books.

Set of Books	Estimated Advertising Cost per Set	Estimated Selling Cost per Set
Encyclopedias	$5	$10
Religious books	$8	$20
"Classics of Literature"	$10	$35

The firm has established a budget of $100,000 for advertising for the forthcoming year and $500,000 for door-to-door selling for the forthcoming year. Its current yearly production capacity is 12,000 sets of books, which may be divided in any manner among the three types of book sets in its product line. However, it feels that it must sell at least 2000 sets of each type of book annually. Formulate the linear programming model that could be used to solve this marketing planning problem.

4 The Simplex Method

4.1 INTRODUCTION

The **simplex method** is the name given to the *solution algorithm* for solving linear programming problems developed by George Dantzig in 1947. A **simplex** is an n-dimensional convex figure that has exactly $n + 1$ extreme points. For example, a simplex in two dimensions is a triangle; and in three dimensions it is a tetrahedron. The simplex method refers to the idea of moving from one extreme point to another on the convex set that is formed by the constraint set and nonnegativity conditions of the linear programming problem. By solution algorithm we refer to an iterative procedure having fixed computational rules that leads to a solution to the problem in a finite number of steps (i.e., converges to an answer). The simplex method is algebraic in nature, and is based upon the Gauss-Jordan elimination procedure, which was discussed earlier in Chapter 2. Although the procedure is relatively straightforward, it does require some patience and skill to execute manually. Consequently, in practice, the algorithm is usually programmed and executed on a digital computer. Many computer codes embodying the essence of the simplex method are in existence. The widespread development and use of these codes attests to the importance of linear programmming in decision making.

In this chapter we will develop a manual technique that utilizes the simplex method for solving linear programming problems. The more inquisitive student might ask the question: "Why is it necessary to learn how to manually solve linear programming problems using the simplex method when, in practice, most linear programming problems are solved using computerized linear programming codes?" It is our feeling that the student should thoroughly understand the underlying principles of linear programming, as contained in the simplex method, before attempting to effectively utilize the results of a linear program analysis in a managerial situation. Similarly, it is essential for the manager to understand the key ideas that form the basis of linear programming. The manager should have a fundamental knowledge of linear programming in order to communicate effectively with the management scientist, develop the input data for applications of linear programming, and interpret and utilize the output produced by computerized linear programming codes. A fundamental understanding of linear programming can perhaps best be gained by manually working through linear programming problems using the simplex method. Thus, the objective of this chapter will be to develop a firm understanding of linear programming through the vehicle of the simplex algorithm.

4.2 AN ALGEBRAIC APPROACH TO LINEAR PROGRAMMING

Consider the linear programming formulation of the production-scheduling problem presented earlier in Chapter 3. Recall that the formulation of this problem was the following.

$$\text{Maximize } Z = 6x_1 + 8x_2 \tag{4-1}$$

subject to:

$$\left.\begin{array}{l} 5x_1 + 10x_2 \le 60 \\ 4x_1 + 4x_2 \le 40 \end{array}\right\} \quad \text{where} \quad \begin{array}{l} x_1 = \text{\# of bearing plates to be produced} \\ x_2 = \text{\# of gears to be produced} \end{array} \tag{4-2}$$

with $\quad x_1 \ge 0, x_2 \ge 0$ (4-3)

Recall also that we showed graphically in Figure 3.1 that the optimal solution to this linear programming problem was at one of the extreme points ($x_1 = 8, x_2 = 2$) of the feasible solution space, which was composed of the constraint set and the nonnegativity restrictions. We observed that this optimal solution was obtained as we traced out basic feasible solutions by examining the extreme points of the solution space.

The introduction to this chapter stated that the simplex method was an algebraically based algorithm. What needs to be done then is to develop a linkage between the geometrical solution procedure illustrated in the previous chapter and the algebraic procedure, which is the simplex method. This linkage can be developed in an efficient manner by employing the *Gauss-Jordan elimination procedure* that we studied earlier in the context of matrix algebra.

The key to solving the linear programming problem lies in the identification of the basic feasible solutions (extreme points) in an algebraic manner. Observe immediately that this is greatly complicated by the fact that the linear programming model formulation, as entailed in (4-1), (4-2) and (4-3), contains inequalities rather than equalities. Unfortunately, algebraic manipulations with inequalities are much more difficult to perform than algebraic manipulations with equalities. Thus, the first step that we must take is to convert the constraint set to a system of linear equalities. This conversion process involves the use of **slack variables.**

Consider first the inequality $5x_1 + 10x_2 \leq 60$. Recall that this inequality represents the resource restriction associated with the production of the two products on the milling machine. We now define a slack variable, x_3, as follows.

$$x_3 = 60 - 5x_1 - 10x_2 \qquad (4\text{-}4)$$

x_3 thus becomes the difference or slack between the two sides of the inequality. The first slack variable x_3 physically represents unused milling machine time. The original inequality can be rewritten as

$$5x_1 + 10x_2 + 1x_3 = 60 \qquad (4\text{-}5)$$

with $x_3 \geq 0$, since unused or slack milling machine time must be equal to or greater than zero. If $5x_1 + 10x_2$ equals 60, then x_3 has the value 0. If, conversely, $5x_1 + 10x_2$ is less than 60, then x_3 must assume the positive value equal to the difference between $5x_1 + 10x_2$ and 60.

The second inequality in the constraint set is treated in identical manner. Recall that this inequality represents the resource restriction associated with production of the two products on the metal lathe. We now define a slack variable, x_4, as follows.

$$x_4 = 40 - 4x_1 - 4x_2 \qquad (4\text{-}6)$$

The second slack variable physically represents unused metal lathe time. The original inequality can be rewritten as

$$4x_1 + 4x_2 + 1x_4 = 40 \qquad (4\text{-}7)$$

with $x_4 \geq 0$, since unused or slack metal lathe time must be equal to or greater than zero.

The original linear programming model can now be replaced by the equivalent model:

$$\text{Maximize } Z = 6x_1 + 8x_2 + 0x_3 + 0x_4 \qquad (4\text{-}8)$$

subject to:
$$\begin{aligned} 5x_1 + 10x_2 + 1x_3 \quad\;\; &= 60 \\ 4x_1 + \;\; 4x_2 \quad\quad\; + 1x_4 &= 40 \end{aligned} \qquad (4\text{-}9)$$

with $\quad x_1 \geq 0, x_2 \geq 0, x_3 \geq 0, x_4 \geq 0 \qquad (4\text{-}10)$

The model given by (4-8), (4-9), and (4-10) in which slack variables are introduced in the objective function, constraints—that is, to convert the original "less than or equal to" inequalities to equalities—and nonnegativity conditions, is often termed a reformulation of the original problem in *standard linear programming format.*

Observe that both slack variables are restricted to be equal to or greater than zero. However, slack variables have no effect on the objective function, that is,

$c_3 = 0$, $c_4 = 0$, since they are not associated with real products. Note further that we do nothing to the original nonnegativity restrictions, although technically they are also inequalities. This is because these nonnegativity restrictions only provide that the values that the decision variables may assume must be positive. Thus, the nonnegativity restrictions on all the variables must be stated in the form $x_j \geq 0$, $j = 1, 2, \ldots, n$.

The problem formulation given above by (4–8), (4–9), and (4–10) is identical to that given by (4–1), (4–2), and (4–3). The values of x_1 and x_2 that optimize (4–8) also optimize (4–1). However, the second problem formulation is now much more amenable to the algebraic manipulations required for Gauss-Jordan elimination.

Let us now analyze how we can obtain an initial basic feasible solution algebraically. Observe that the constraint set given by (4–9) is composed of $m = 2$ equalities in $n = 4$ unknowns. Remember from Chapter 2 that a *basic solution* to this set of m equations in n variables ($n > m$) was obtained by setting ($n - m$) variables equal to zero, and solving the resulting system of m equations in m variables. The m variables were referred to as the ''basic'' variables or as the variables ''in the **basis**.'' The ($n - m$) variables were referred to as the ''nonbasic'' variables or as the variables ''not in the basis.'' We further defined a *basic feasible solution* as being a basic solution where all m of the basic variables were nonnegative (≥ 0). Finally, we defined a *nondegenerate basic feasible solution* as a basic solution where all m of the basic variables were positive (> 0).

It should be emphasized that the number of basic solutions to a system of m linear equations in n unknowns, as given by (2–94), provides an upper bound on the number of basic feasible solutions to a system of m linear equations in n unknowns. As shown previously in Chapter 3, the constraint set given by (4–9), is a system of $m = 2$ equations in $n = 4$ unknowns that has six basic solutions, as follows.

Basic Solutions					Value of
x_1	x_2	x_3	x_4	Feasible/Nonfeasible	Objective Function
0	0	60	40	Feasible	$Z = 0$
0	6	0	16	Feasible	$Z = 48$
0	10	−40	0	Nonfeasible	—
12	0	0	− 8	Nonfeasible	—
10	0	10	0	Feasible	$Z = 60$
8	2	0	0	Feasible	$Z = 64$

Since the number of basic feasible solutions is bounded by $\binom{n}{m}$, we might conclude that we could simply list all of the basic feasible solutions and then pick the one which produced the optimal value of the objective function (e.g., $x_1 = 8$, $x_2 = 2$, Maximum $Z = 64$, in this instance). This complete enumeration approach is not generally satisfactory, for a number of reasons. First, the number of basic feasible solutions, while bounded by $\binom{n}{m}$, grows too large for a complete enumeration approach, even for moderate values of m and n. Second, the complete enumeration approach will not indicate the special case in which the problem is unbounded. Finally, we would have to enumerate all of the basic solutions in order to be able to detect the special case in which the problem has an inconsistent constraint set (i.e., no feasible solution).

Four of the six basic solutions are feasible; the other two are nonfeasible. The feasible basic solutions are, of course, the extreme points of the feasible solution space that was previously identified in Fig. 3.1. To facilitate our future discussion, Fig. 3.1 has been reproduced, and appears in this chapter as Fig. 4.1. The corresponding values of the objective function for these basic feasible solutions are also indicated. While we could proceed by trial and error to find an initial basic solution that is also feasible, a much easier procedure is available. Using this procedure, the initial basic feasible solution is chosen to include exactly the m slack variables. By this we mean that we select

$$x_3 = 60 - 5x_1 - 10x_2$$
$$x_4 = 40 - 4x_1 - 4x_2$$

$(4–11)$

with $x_1 = 0$ and $x_2 = 0$. Thus, our first basic feasible solution is obtained very

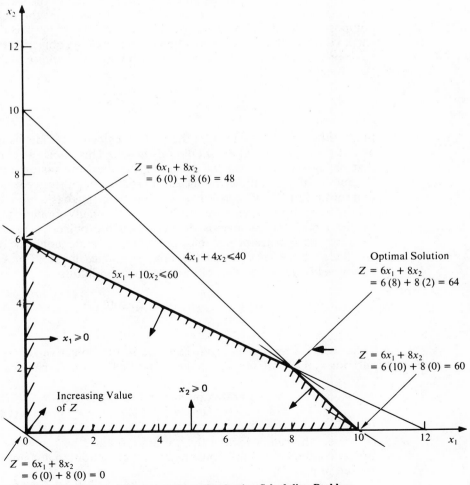

FIGURE 4.1 Graphical Representation—Production Scheduling Problem

simply as $x_1 = 0$, $x_2 = 0$, $x_3 = 60$, and $x_4 = 40$. It should also be apparent that we have selected the origin of the feasible region (refer to Fig. 4.1), or the first basic solution tabled above, as our initial extreme point.

Having selected the initial basic feasible solution, the algebraic procedure selects an adjacent extreme point that increases the value of the objective function. This is equivalent to finding another (alternative) basic feasible solution that has all but one of the same basic variables in the basis. Thus, finding the next basic feasible solution requires two operations.

1. *One* presently nonbasic variable must be selected to enter the current basis, thus becoming basic.
2. *One* presently basic variable must be selected to leave the current basis, thus becoming nonbasic.

The first operation proceeds in an intuitively simple manner. The objective function is examined and the effect of entering each of the variables in the objective function is measured. Remember that at this point the objective function is composed entirely of nonbasic variables since the initial basic variables are the slack variables that have no effect on the value of the objective function. Thus, the two nonbasic variables that are candidates for entry in this case are x_1 and x_2, since the objective function is:

$$Z = 6x_1 + 8x_2 \qquad (4\text{--}12)$$

Since either x_1 or x_2 could enter the basis, we need some means for selecting which one of these two variables should be chosen. This choice is made as the variable that appears to increase the objective function the fastest on the basis of the magnitude of its coefficient. Since x_2 increases the objective function at the rate of unit produced, x_2 is chosen to be the entering basic variable. It should be cautioned that this procedure, while computationally simple, may not be necessarily the most efficient means of increasing the objective function. This is true because the constraint set may prevent a specific nonbasic variable from becoming as large as some of the other variables might. For example, the constraint set might force the following set of conditions.

$$\begin{aligned} 0 \le x_1 \le 10 \\ 0 \le x_2 \le 5 \end{aligned} \qquad (4\text{--}13)$$

Thus, while a greater per-unit increase in the objective function is obtained by entering x_2 the *total* increase in the objective function is made by entering x_1, since

$$\begin{aligned} \$6 \cdot 10 \text{ (Maximum possible increase in } x_1) = \$60 \\ \$8 \cdot 5 \text{ (Maximum possible increase in } x_2) = \$40 \end{aligned} \qquad (4\text{--}14)$$

However, the rule selecting the variable to enter as being the variable with the largest coefficient is both convenient and computationally simple, and therefore, is used in practice.

The choice of the variable to leave the basis or be replaced by x_2 requires further analysis. The candidates for the leaving variables are the two slack variables x_3 and x_4. In the initial basis, each of these variables is at a positive level, that is

$$x_3 = 60 \quad \text{and} \quad x_1 = 0 \atop x_4 = 40 \qquad \qquad x_2 = 0 \tag{4-15}$$

For one of these variables to leave the basis it must be driven to zero. No variable can become less than zero or an infeasible solution will result. Consequently, the variable chosen to leave the basis is the one that is driven to zero *first* as the entering basic variable, x_2 in this case, is increased. This effectively increases the objective function as much as is possible while maintaining a feasible solution. With reference to Fig. 4.1, what we are doing is moving from one extreme point of the feasible solution space to another extreme point of the feasible solution space. The algebraic analysis that is required is illustrated by the following table.

Constraint Equation	*Maximum Possible Increase in x_2*
(1) $x_3 = 60 - 5x_1 - 10x_2$	$(x_1 = 0, x_3 \to 0)$ Solve: $0 = 60 - 10x_3 \Rightarrow x_2 = 6$
(2) $x_4 = 40 - 4x_1 - 4x_2$	$(x_1 = 0, x_4 \to 0)$ Solve: $0 = 40 - 4x_2 \Rightarrow x_2 = 10$

Thus, it is seen that x_3 should be chosen as the variable to leave the basis (i.e., $x_3 = 0$), or become nonbasic, with x_2 becoming basic, or being increased to six. The variable x_3 is chosen to be removed, because it is the first of the two variables to become zero as x_2 increases.

We must now solve for the new value of the remaining basic variable x_4, which results from entering x_2 into the basis and removing x_3 from the basis. This is accomplished using the Gauss-Jordan elimination procedure that we studied earlier in our discussion of matrix algebra. What we seek to do is to manipulate the constraint equations and the objective function algebraically until the entering basic variable x_2 appears only in the second constraint equation, and all the other constraints (and the objective function) are expressed in terms of the other variables. To summarize, we manipulate the constraint equations until each basic variable appears in only one equation and this equation contains no other basic variable. The entering basic variable is also eliminated from the algebraic formulation of the objective function. To illustrate this process, consider the original objective function and constraint set, written as follows.

(Objective function) (0) $Z - 6x_1 - 8x_2 \qquad = 0$ First

(First constraint) (1) $5x_1 + 10x_2 + 1x_3 \qquad = 60$ Basic Feasible $\tag{4-16}$ Solution:

(Second constraint) (2) $4x_1 + 4x_2 + 1x_4 = 40$ $x_1 = 0 \quad x_3 = 60$ $x_2 = 0 \quad x_4 = 40$

Now, x_2 is to replace x_3 in the new basis, that is, $x_2 \to 6$ and $x_3 \to 0$. The new basic variable x_2 thus replaces x_3 in Equation 4-16(1). The new basic variables are now x_2, and x_4. However, in order to determine the proper resulting values for the remaining basic variables, x_4 and x_2, x_2 must be eliminated from the equation 4-16(2) and the objective function 4-16(0) in which it appears. This is done by Gauss-Jordan elimination, namely, by adding or subtracting the appropriate multiple of equation 4–16(1) to or from the other equations. The Gauss-Jordan elimination process proceeds as follows.

STEP 1   Obtain $+1$ as the coefficient of x_2 in equation 4–16(1) (i.e., divide by 10).

$$\text{New eq. (1)} \quad \tfrac{5}{10}x_1 + \tfrac{10}{10}x_2 + \tfrac{1}{10}x_3 = \tfrac{60}{10}$$
$$\tfrac{1}{2}x_1 + 1x_2 + \tfrac{1}{10}x_3 = 6$$

STEP 2   Eliminate -8 as the coefficient of x_2 in equation 4–16(0).

$$
\begin{array}{ll}
\text{Old eq. (0)} & Z - 6x_1 - 8x_2 \qquad\qquad = 0 \\
8 \times \text{New eq. (1)} & \underline{\qquad 4x_1 + 8x_2 + \tfrac{4}{5}x_3 = 48} \\
\text{New eq. (0)} & Z - 2x_1 \qquad\quad + \tfrac{4}{5}x_3 = 48
\end{array}
\qquad (4\text{–}17)
$$

STEP 3   Eliminate $+4$ as the coefficient of x_2 in equation 4–16(2).

$$
\begin{array}{ll}
\text{Old eq. (2)} & 4x_1 + 4x_2 \qquad\qquad + 1x_4 = 40 \\
-4 \times \text{New eq. (1)} & \underline{-2x_1 - 4x_2 - \tfrac{2}{5}x_3 \qquad\quad = -24} \\
\text{New eq. (2)} & 2x_1 \qquad\quad - \tfrac{2}{5}x_3 + 1x_4 = 16
\end{array}
$$

The new (second) set of equations can be written as

$$
\left.
\begin{array}{ll}
(0)\; Z - 2x_1 \qquad\quad + \tfrac{4}{5}x_3 \qquad\quad = 48 \\[4pt]
(1) \qquad\quad \tfrac{1}{2}x_1 + 1x_2 + \tfrac{1}{10}x_3 \qquad\quad = 6 \\[4pt]
(2) \qquad\quad 2x_1 \qquad\quad - \tfrac{2}{5}x_3 + 1x_4 = 16
\end{array}
\right\}
\begin{array}{l}
\text{Second} \\
\text{basic} \\
\text{feasible} \\
\text{solution:} \\
x_1 = 0 \quad x_3 = 0 \\
x_2 = 6 \quad x_4 = 16
\end{array}
\qquad (4\text{–}18)
$$

This second set of equations is completely equivalent to the first set of equations. However, the second basic feasible solution is $x_1 = 0$, $x_2 = 6$, $x_3 = 0$, and $x_4 = 16$, yielding a value of the objective function, $Z = 48$. Referring to Fig. 4.1, we have moved from the origin extreme point ($x_1 = 0$, $x_2 = 0$; $Z = 0$), vertically to the extreme point ($x_1 = 0$, $x_2 = 6$; $Z = 48$).

We next examine this second basic feasible solution to see if we have obtained the optimal basic feasible solution. Note that the original objective function $Z = 6x_1 + 8x_2$ has been transformed to the objective function $Z = 2x_1 - \tfrac{4}{5}x_3 + 48$. It can thus be concluded that, by increasing the value of x_1 (with x_3 remaining nonbasic, i.e., $x_3 = 0$), we can further increase the value of the objective function. The current basic feasible solution is not optimal, and we must use the Gauss-Jordan elimination procedure to make at least one more iteration.

At this point in our work it should be obvious that only variable x_1 can enter the basis. Given our current expression of the objective function, only the insertion of x_1 into the basis will improve the value of the objective function. The only other variable in the expression of the objective function, namely x_3, is a slack variable; hence it does not need to be considered further because it has no effect on the objective function (i.e., $c_3 = 0$).

The choice of the variable to leave the basis (i.e., to be driven to zero) as x_1 enters the basis is determined exactly as before. The algebraic analysis that is required is shown by the following table.

Constraint Equation	Maximum Possible Increase in x_1
(1) $\frac{1}{10}x_3 = 6 - \frac{1}{2}x_1 - 1x_2$	$(x_2 \to 0,\ x_3 = 0)$ Solve: $0 = 6 - \frac{1}{2}x_1 \Rightarrow x_1 = 12$
(2) $x_4 = 16 - 2x_1 + \frac{2}{5}x_3$	$(x_3 = 0,\ x_4 \to 0)$ Solve: $0 = 16 - 2x_1 \Rightarrow x_1 = 8$

Thus, it is seen that x_4 should be chosen to be removed because it is the first of the two variables to become zero as x_1 increases. The Gauss-Jordan elimination process proceeds as follows.

STEP 1   Obtain $+1$ as the coefficient of x_1 in equation 4–18(2) (i.e., divide by 2).

$$\text{New eq. (2)}\ \frac{2}{2}x_1 - \frac{2}{5}/2x_3 + \frac{1}{2}x_4 = \frac{16}{2}$$
$$+1x_1 - \frac{1}{5}x_3 + \frac{1}{2}x_4 = 8$$

STEP 2   Eliminate -2 as the coefficient of x_1 in equation 4–18(0).

$$\begin{array}{lll}
\text{Old eq. (0)} & Z - 2x_1 + \frac{4}{5}x_3 \qquad\qquad = 48 \\
2 \times \text{New eq. (2)} & \underline{\quad + 2x_1 - \frac{2}{5}x_3 + 1x_4 = 16} \\
\text{New eq. (0)} & Z \qquad\qquad + \frac{2}{5}x_3 + 1x_4 = 64
\end{array} \qquad (4\text{–}19)$$

STEP 3   Eliminate $\frac{1}{2}$ as the coefficient of x_1 in equation 4–18(1).

$$\begin{array}{lll}
\text{Old eq. (1)} & \frac{1}{2}x_1 + 1x_2 + \frac{1}{10}x_3 \qquad\qquad = 6 \\
-\frac{1}{2} \times \text{New eq. (2)} & \underline{-\frac{1}{2}x_1 \qquad + \frac{1}{10}x_3 - \frac{1}{4}x_4 = -4} \\
\text{New eq. (1)} & 1x_2 + \frac{1}{5}x_3 - \frac{1}{4}x_4 = 2
\end{array}$$

The new (third) set of equations can be written as:

$$\left.\begin{array}{ll}
(0)\ Z \qquad\qquad + \frac{2}{5}x_3 + 1x_4 = 64 \\[4pt]
(1) \qquad\quad 1x_2 + \frac{1}{5}x_3 - \frac{1}{4}x_4 = 2 \\[4pt]
(2) \qquad 1x_1 \qquad\quad - \frac{1}{5}x_3 + \frac{1}{2}x_4 = 8
\end{array}\right\} \begin{array}{l} \text{Third} \\ \text{basic} \\ \text{feasible} \\ \text{solution:} \\ x_1 = 8 \quad x_3 = 0 \\ x_2 = 2 \quad x_4 = 0 \end{array} \qquad (4\text{–}20)$$

This third set of equations is completely equivalent to the first two sets of equations. However, the third basic feasible solution is now: $x_1 = 8$, $x_2 = 2$, $x_3 = 0$, $x_4 = 0$, yielding a value of the objective function $Z = 64$. Referring to Fig. 4.1, we have moved downward from the extreme point ($x_1 = 0$, $x_2 = 6$; $Z = 48$) to the extreme point ($x_1 = 8$, $x_2 = 2$; $Z = 64$).

The question at this point is: "Have we obtained the optimal feasible solution?" The answer is yes, since we have transformed the original objective function $Z = 6x_1 + 8x_2$ to an objective function having the form $Z = 64 - \frac{2}{5}x_3 - 1x_4$. Thus, an attempt to insert either of the current nonbasic variables x_3 and x_4 into the solution will cause a reduction in the objective function since they both have negative coefficients. We have obtained the optimal feasible solution with $x_1 = 8$ (produce eight bearing plates), $x_2 = 2$ (produce two gears), $x_3 = 0$ (no unused milling machine time), and $x_4 = 0$ (no unused metal lathe time). This solution has an optimal objective function (profit) value of $64.

4.3 THE SIMPLEX ALGORITHM

The *simplex algorithm*, or *simplex method*, is an iterative procedure that embodies the same steps that we previously employed in our algebraic approach to linear programming. The simplex algorithm, however, provides a more structured method for moving from one basic feasible solution to another, always maintaining or improving the objective function, until an optimal solution is obtained. The major steps in the simplex algorithm are as follows.

STEP 1 Given the problem formulation with m equalities in n unknowns, select a set of m variables that yields an initial basic feasible solution.

STEP 2 Analyze the objective function to see if there is a nonbasic variable that is equal to zero in the initial basic feasible solution, but which would improve the value of the objective function if made positive. If no such variable can be found the current basic feasible solution is optimal, and the simplex algorithm stops. If, however, such a variable can be found, the simplex algorithm continues to Step 3.

STEP 3 Using the nonbasic variable selected in Step 2, determine how large it can become before *one* of the m variables in the current basic feasible solution becomes zero. Eliminate (drive to zero) this current basic variable and replace (increase to the maximum permissible value) the nonbasic variable selected in Step 2.

STEP 4 Solve the problem using the Gauss-Jordan elimination procedure, for the current m variables. Return to Step 2.

Given that a feasible solution exists and that the optimal value of the objective function is finite, the simplex algorithm, as outlined in the steps above, will lead to an optimal solution in a finite number of iterations. We will now proceed to develop a tabular approach for the simplex algorithm. The advantage of using this tableau format is that it provides a more structured method for moving from one basic feasible solution to another and allows us to avoid the task of constantly rewriting all of the variables and equations of the problem.

4.3.1 Setting Up the Initial Simplex Tableau

In developing a tabular approach for the simplex algorithm, we will attempt to use an instructive and consistent set of notation (Hadley 1962). To enhance the reader's understanding of this tabular approach, we will first apply it to the production scheduling problem that we have been studying, namely

$$\text{Maximize } Z = 6x_1 + 8x_2 \tag{4-21}$$

subject to:
$$5x_1 + 10x_2 \le 60 \tag{4-22}$$
$$4x_1 + 4x_2 \le 40$$

with
$$x_1 \ge 0, x_2 \ge 0 \tag{4-23}$$

Once again, the first step in developing the tabular approach for the simplex algorithm is to transform the constraint set (inequalities) to a set of equalities by adding slack variables. The reformulated linear programming problem is thus rewritten as

$$\text{Maximize } Z = 6x_1 + 8x_2 + 0x_3 + 0x_4 \tag{4-24}$$

subject to:
$$\begin{array}{rl} 5x_1 + 10x_2 + 1x_3 = 60 \\ 4x_1 + 4x_2 + 1x_4 = 40 \end{array} \tag{4-25}$$

with $\quad x_1 \geq 0, x_2 \geq 0, x_3 \geq 0, x_4 \geq 0 \tag{4-26}$

The coefficients of the objective function, the coefficients of the transformed constraint set, and the right-hand side values of the constraint set are than transferred to the initial simplex tableau. This initial simplex **tableau** is presented in table 4.1. At the far-right-hand-side of this tableau a set of descriptions for the various rows of the tableau is provided. These descriptions will be explained in detail in the material that follows.

The first row of the tableau indicates the values of the c_j, the coefficients of the objective function. These coefficients are transferred directly from the objective function, and indicate the per-unit contributions to the objective function of each of the variables. The values of c_j shown in this row remain the same in successive simplex tableaus, and they are used in determining the variable to be entered into the basis, as will be shown below.

The second row of the tableau provides the major column headings for the tableau. These column headings remain the same in succeeding tableaus and apply to the values listed in successive m rows. The first column, heading by "$\mathbf{c}_b$," lists the objective function coefficients of the *current* basic variables. The $\mathbf{c}_b$ values are used in the computation of the decrease in the value of the objective function that will result if one unit of the jth variable is brought into solution. This computation will be illustrated below. The "**Variables in Basis**" are listed in the second column; and in the initial tableau, the basic variables are the slack variables x_3 and x_4. Referring back to column one, the cost coefficients for these two initial basic variables are $c_3 = 0$ and $c_4 = 0$, respectively. The next column, headed by "**Solu-**

TABLE 4.1 The Initial Simplex Tableau—Production Scheduling Problem

Pivot column ↓

		c_j	6	8	0	0	Contribution per Unit
c_b	Variables in Basis	Solution Values, x_b	a_1	a_2	a_3	a_4	Column Headings
Pivot row→ 0	x_3	60	5	(10)	1	0	Coefficients
0	x_4	40	4	4	0	1	
	Z_j	0	0	0	0	0	Contribution Loss per Unit
	$c_j - Z_j$		6	8	0	0	Net Contribution per Unit

Pivot element

decrease in value — of obj. function if 1 unit of jth var. is brought into the soln.

tion Values, x_b,'' presents the current value of the corresponding solution vector. For the initial basic feasible solution, the solution vector is

$$\mathbf{x}_b = \begin{bmatrix} x_3 \\ x_4 \end{bmatrix} = \begin{bmatrix} 60 \\ 40 \end{bmatrix} \tag{4-27}$$

The next four columns, headed by "$\mathbf{a}_1$, $\mathbf{a}_2$, $\mathbf{a}_3$, and $\mathbf{a}_4$," are the coefficients of the constraint set. Thus, $\mathbf{a}_1$ refers to the vector of coefficients corresponding to the first variable x_1 in the constraint set, that is:

$$\mathbf{a}_1 = \begin{bmatrix} 5 \\ 4 \end{bmatrix} \tag{4-28}$$

Observe that the column vectors $\mathbf{a}_3$ and $\mathbf{a}_4$, which correspond to the current basic variables x_3 (slack variable) and x_4 (slack variable), form a **basis matrix** [**B**] that is an identity matrix.

$$\mathbf{a}_3(x_3) \quad \mathbf{a}_4(x_4)$$
$$[\mathbf{B}] = \begin{bmatrix} 1 & 0 \\ 0 & 1 \end{bmatrix} = [\mathbf{I}] \tag{4-29}$$

The current basic variables must always form an identity matrix within the simplex tableau.

The row labeled "Z_j" is computed as the vector product of the coefficients of the current basic variables (i.e., the numbers in the $\mathbf{c}_b$ column) times the coefficients in the corresponding $\mathbf{a}_j$ columns, and the column marked, "**Solution Values**," $\mathbf{x}_b$. What we are really doing is the following vector multiplication.

$$\mathbf{Z}_j = [\mathbf{c}_b]' \cdot [\mathbf{a}_j] \tag{4-30}$$

Note that to perform this vector multiplication we utilize $[\mathbf{c}_b]'$ the (1×2) null row vector that is the transpose of the original (2×1) null column vector $[\mathbf{c}_b]$. Recall, from Chapter 2, that the transpose of a vector is a vector formed by interchanging the rows and columns of the original vector. We must employ the transpose in this vector multiplication in order for the two vectors to be conformable for vector multiplication.

To illustrate:

$$Z_1 = [\mathbf{c}_b]' \cdot [\mathbf{a}_1] = \begin{matrix}(0 \quad 0) \\ (1 \times 2)\end{matrix} \cdot \begin{matrix}\begin{bmatrix} 5 \\ 4 \end{bmatrix} \\ (2 \times 1)\end{matrix}$$
$$= [(0 \cdot 5) + (0 \cdot 4)]$$
$$= [0]$$
$$(1 \times 1) \tag{4-31}$$

Observe that all the values in the Z_j row are zero for this initial tableau. This must be the case obviously, because we are performing a vector multiplication in which $[\mathbf{c}_b]'$ is a null row vector (i.e., composed entirely of zeroes).

A value in the Z_j row represents the *decrease* in the value of the objective function that will result if one unit of the jth variable is brought into the solution.

The Z_j values can be thought of as the "objective function contribution loss per unit produced." Each Z_j value is determined by summing the vector products of the profits and physical rates of substitution associated with that variable. For example, Z_1 represents the decrease in profit that will result if one unit of x_1 is brought into solution. Consider why a decrease in profits might result if the non-basic variable x_1 is brought into the solution (i.e., x_1 is made basic). If one unit of x_1 is produced, we will need to change the value of some of the current basic variables in order to satisfy the constraint equations, and maintain feasibility. In the first constraint equation, we have

$$5x_1 + 10x_2 + 1x_3 = 60 \tag{4-32}$$

Thus, if we make x_1 some positive value, we will then have to reduce x_2 and/or x_3 in order to satisfy the constraint. Since x_2 is already zero (x_2 is a nonbasic variable), it cannot be reduced any further. The value of x_3 (x_3 is a basic variable) must therefore be reduced if x_1 is made a positive value. As the basic variable x_3 is reduced, a reduction in the value of the objective function may also occur. This reduction will be dependent upon the coefficient of x_3 in the objective function. In this instance, x_3 is a slack variable having a coefficient of zero in the objective function. Thus, reducing x_3 will not decrease the value of the objective function.

Note that there is an entry in the Z_j row in the column labeled "**Solution Values, x_b**" and it is also zero. This value is the current value of the objective function, denoted as Z_0. It is computed as follows.

$$Z_0 = [\mathbf{c}_b]' \cdot [\mathbf{x}_b] = (0 \quad 0) \cdot \begin{bmatrix} 60 \\ 40 \end{bmatrix} = [0] \tag{4-33}$$

Thus, Z_0 is computed as the vector product of the coefficients of the current basic variables transposed times the current solution values of the basic variables.

The final row; the $c_j - Z_j$ row, is determined by subtracting the appropriate Z_j value from the corresponding objective function coefficient, c_j for that column. This value is the difference between the contribution (c_j) and the loss (Z_j) that results from one unit of x_j being produced. Each unit of x_j brought into the solution will improve the value of the objective function by the amount c_j. For example, every unit of x_1 (bearing plate) that is produced will improve the objective function by the amount c_1, which is the $6 profit associated with each bearing produced. However, as we observed previously, the value of the objective function will also decrease by an amount Z_1 for each unit of x_1 that is produced. Thus, the net change in the objective function that results from one unit of x_1 being produced is $c_1 - Z_1 = \$6 - 0 = \$6$. Each value in the $c_j - Z_j$ row represents the *net profit*, or *net contribution*, that is added by producing one unit of product j (if $c_j - Z_j$ is positive) or the *net profit*, or *net contribution*, that is subtracted by producing one unit of product j (if $c_j - Z_j$ is negative). Since there is no c_0 value, we do not compute $c_0 - Z_0$. Furthermore, since all the Z_j values ($j = 1, 2, \ldots, 4$) are equal to zero in the initial tableau, the $c_j - Z_j$ values in this example are identical to the coefficients in the c_j row. The use of the $c_j - Z_j$ row in performing an iteration will be illustrated below.

4.3.2   Changing the Basis

We know that we have begun our solution process by selecting the two slack variables x_3 and x_4 as the initial basic variables. The initial value of the objective function is zero at this point, and we have already seen that we can improve our present solution by moving to an adjacent extreme point, that is, by inserting one of the current nonbasic variables into the basis and removing one of the current basic variables. This process is called "changing the basis" or **iterating**.

Now, the $c_j - Z_j$ row is used to determine which variable should be inserted into the basis. Since we are maximizing profit in this example, the numbers in the $c_j - Z_j$ row represent the *net* profit, which is added by producing one unit of j. Thus, referring to the initial tableau, the $c_j - Z_j$ row shows that the objective function will increase by \$6 for each unit of x_1 that is made, and by \$8 for each unit of x_2 that is produced. Since we are seeking to maximize profit, we naturally select x_2 to enter the basis because this choice will cause the greatest increase in net profit. This **variable entry criterion** can be summarized as follows.

VARIABLE
ENTRY
CRITERION

The variable entry criterion is based upon the values in the $c_j - Z_j$ row of the simplex tableau. For a maximization problem, the variable selected for entry is the one having the largest (most positive) value of $c_j - Z_j$. When all values of $c_j - Z_j$ are zero or negative, the optimal solution has been obtained. For a minimization problem, the variable selected for entry is the one having the smallest (most negative) value of $c_j - Z_j$. When all values of $c_j - Z_j$ are zero or positive, the optimal solution has been obtained. For either maximization or minimization problems, if there are ties for the entering $c_j - Z_j$ value, the tie can be broken arbitrarily (i.e., simply choose one of the corresponding variables for entry).

Applying the variable entry criterion to our present maximization example, the largest $c_j - Z_j$ value is $c_2 - Z_2 = 8$. Thus, x_2, is chosen as the variable to enter the basis.

The "**Solution Values, x_b**" column and the column vector $\mathbf{a}_2$, which contains the constraint equation coefficients for the entering variables x_2, are used to determine the variable to be removed from the basis as x_2 enters. Remember from our algebraic procedure that what we must do is determine which current basic variable is *first* driven to zero as we allow the current nonbasic variable x_2 to become basic. This is accomplished by using the following **variable removal criterion**.

VARIABLE
REMOVAL
CRITERION

*The variable removal criterion is based upon the ratios formed as the values in the "**Solution Values, x_b**" column are divided by the corresponding values (coefficients of x_j in the $\mathbf{a}_j$ column vector for the variable selected to enter the basis. Ignore any values in the $\mathbf{a}_j$ column vector that are zero or negative (i.e., do not compute the ratio). The variable chosen to be removed from the basis is the one having the smallest ratio. In the case of ties for the smallest ratio between two or more variables, break the tie arbitrarily (i.e., simply choose one of the variables for removal). This variable removal criterion remains the same for both maximization and minimization problems.*

In the variable removal criterion stated above it is important to stress that we do not compute the ratios for any values in the $\mathbf{a}_j$ column (i.e., the denominators of the ratios) that are zero or negative. Essentially, ratios involving either a zero or a negative number in the denominator are ignored because they would not allow the introduction of a variable into the basis at a finite positive level.[1] To illustrate, suppose that the following ratios were obtained.

Ratios

$$\frac{6}{0} = +\infty$$
$$\frac{10}{2} = 5 \tag{4-34}$$
$$-\frac{9}{3} = -3$$

The first ratio would be ignored (i.e., it does not need to be calculated) because entry of the variable associated with this ratio into the basis could only be accomplished if the entering variable were allowed to assume an infinitely large value. Alternatively, we could say that this ratio is ignored because it will always be larger (i.e., $+\infty$) than any other ratio possible. The third ratio is ignored because it is negative and would result in a variable entering the basis at a negative level. This cannot be done because we would not have the basic feasible solution required for the simplex method.

Note further that because the simplex method operates on a series of basic feasible solutions, we will not encounter a ratio having a negative value in the numerator (i.e., the values in the "**Solution Values, x_b**" column must remain positive). However, we may encounter a ratio having a zero value in the numerator and a nonzero positive value in the denominator. This ratio is zero, and is obviously the minimum ratio possible. What this means is that this variable will enter the basis, but at a value equal to zero. This results in a *degenerate basic feasible solution*. Degeneracy will be discussed in a later section of this chapter.

Applying the variable removal criterion to our present problem, the following ratios are formed.

Current Basic Variables	Solution Values, x_b	÷	a_2	Ratios
x_3	60	÷	10	6 (Smallest)
x_4	40	÷	4	10

Thus, the current basic variable x_3 is replaced by the current nonbasic variable x_2. This occurs because the ratios we have formed, as shown in the table above, indicate that x_3 is driven to zero first as x_2 is increased. The meaning of this ratio of "6" is that 6 units of entering product x_2 can be produced before the first constraint (corresponding to the current basic variable x_3) becomes binding. Thus, when $x_2 = 6$ and $x_3 = 0$, the first constraint is exactly satisfied, that is,

$$5x_1 + 10x_2 + 1x_3 = 60$$
$$5(0) - 10(6) + 1(0) = 60 \tag{4-35}$$

If $x_2 > 6$, this constraint will obviously be violated.

---

[1] The situation in which all of the ratios are zero or negative will be discussed in a later section of this chapter.

Observe that what we have accomplished so far is to identify the current nonbasic variable x_2, which will cause the greatest increase in profitability, and determine the current basic variable x_3 to be removed from the basis (driven to zero) as x_2 is increased to the maximum possible value of 6. Referring to Fig. 4.1, in graphical terms we have moved vertically from the extreme point $x_1 = 0$, $x_2 = 0$, to the extreme point $x_1 = 0$, $x_2 = 6$. These two steps have been done in a manner that maintains the feasibility of our solution. The next step in our basis-changing process requires the determination of our new solution through "pivoting" x_2 into the basis and "pivoting" x_3 out of the basis.

The **pivoting** process is really nothing more than performing Gauss-Jordan row operations on the rows of the simplex tableau to solve the system of constraint equations in terms of the new set of basic variables. We initiate the pivoting process by identifying the variable x_2, (vector $\mathbf{a}_2$) to be entered into the basis by denoting the **pivot column** (refer back to Table 4.1). Similarly, we identify the variable x_3 to be removed from the basis by specifying the **pivot row** (refer back to Table 4.1). The element at the intersection of the pivot column and the pivot row is circled, and is identified as the **pivot element**. The pivot element is the number "10" in the simplex tableau, which is at the intersection of the row corresponding to leaving variable x_3 and the column $\mathbf{a}_2$ corresponding to entering variable x_2 (refer back to Table 4.1).

The actual pivoting operation involves two steps that are performed to obtain an identity matrix as the coefficient matrix of the new set of basic variables x_2 and x_4. Recall from our earlier discussion that we indicated that the current basic variables must always form an identity matrix within the simplex tableau. Since x_4 was a basic variable in our previous solution nothing needs to be done to its corresponding column. However, in the *pivot column* corresponding to the variable x_2 we need to obtain a one as the pivot element and zeroes in all other positions. The two-step pivoting process proceeds as follows.

STEP 1 To convert the pivot element to one simply requires that we divide all values in the pivot row by 10. This new row is entered immediately in the second tableau, Table 4.2. Remember that each row in the simplex tableau represents a constraint equation, so all we are doing algebraically is dividing an equation by a constant. For our problem, the calculations are

Column Heading	Pivot Row Calculation		
"Solution Values, x_b"	$\frac{60}{10} = 6$		
"$\mathbf{a}_1$"	$\frac{5}{10} = \frac{1}{2}$		
"$\mathbf{a}_2$"	$\frac{10}{10} = 1$	(Pivot element)	(4–36)
"$\mathbf{a}_3$"	$\frac{1}{10} = \frac{1}{10}$		
"$\mathbf{a}_4$"	$\frac{0}{10} = 0$		
	New pivot row		

STEP 2 The objective of the second step is to obtain zeroes in all the elements of the pivot column, except of course, for the pivot element itself. This is done by elementary row operations involving adding or subtracting the appropriate multiple of the new

pivot row to or from the other original rows. Again, all we are doing is using the Gauss-Jordan elimination procedure to obtain a zero in the appropriate position in the pivot column. For our problem, the detailed calculations are as follows.

Row 2 (Variable x_4): Multiply the new pivot row by -4
and add to old row 2 to obtain
new row 2.

Old Row 2	+	$(-4 \cdot$ New Pivot Row$)$	=	New Row 2	
40	+	$(-4 \cdot 6)$	=	16	
4	+	$(-4 \cdot \frac{1}{2})$	=	2	
4	+	$(-4 \cdot 1)$	=	0	(4–37)
0	+	$(-4 \cdot \frac{1}{10})$	=	$-\frac{2}{5}$	
1	+	$(-4 \cdot 0)$	=	1	

Note that the pivoting process is equivalent to solving the system of constraint equations for the new basic variables x_2 and x_4, with $x_1 = 0$ and $x_3 = 0$. The system of equations representing this second solution can be written as:

$$
\begin{aligned}
1x_2 + 0x_4 &= 6 \\
0x_2 + 1x_4 &= 16
\end{aligned}
\quad \text{with} \quad
\begin{aligned}
x_1 &= 0 \\
x_3 &= 0
\end{aligned}
\qquad (4\text{–}38)
$$

The values of the basic variables can be immediately identified as $x_2 = 6$, $x_4 = 16$. The second simplex tableau can be constructed as shown in Table 4.2.

TABLE 4.2 The Second Simplex Tableau—Production Scheduling Problem

			Pivot column ↓			
		c_j	*6*	*8*	*0*	*0*
c_b	*Variables in Basis*	*Solution Values*, x_b	a_1	a_2	a_3	a_4
8	x_2	6	$1/2$	1	$1/10$	0
Pivot row → 0	x_4	16	②	0	$-2/5$	1
	Z_j	48	4	8	$4/5$	0
	$c_j - Z_j$		2	0	$-4/5$	0

Pivot element

Observe that the column vectors a_2 and a_4, which correspond to the current basic variables x_2 (real variable) and x_4 (slack variable), form a basis matrix $[\mathbf{B}]$ that is an identity matrix. Once again, the Z_j values in the second tableau are computed in exactly the same manner as in the initial simplex tableau, using the relationship $Z_j = [\mathbf{c}_b]' \cdot [\mathbf{a}_j]$. To illustrate:

$$Z_0 = [c_b]' \cdot [x_b] = (8 \quad 0) \begin{bmatrix} 6 \\ 16 \end{bmatrix} = 48 \qquad \text{(Current value of the objective function)}$$

$$Z_1 = [c_b]' \cdot [a_1] = (8 \quad 0) \begin{bmatrix} \frac{1}{2} \\ 2 \end{bmatrix} = 4$$

$$Z_2 = [c_b]' \cdot [a_2] = (8 \quad 0) \begin{bmatrix} 1 \\ 0 \end{bmatrix} = 8 \qquad (4\text{-}39)$$

$$Z_3 = [c_b]' \cdot [a_3] = (8 \quad 0) \begin{bmatrix} \frac{1}{10} \\ -\frac{2}{5} \end{bmatrix} = \frac{4}{5}$$

$$Z_4 = [c_b]' \cdot [a_4] = (8 \quad 0) \begin{bmatrix} 0 \\ 1 \end{bmatrix} = 0$$

The $c_j - Z_j$ values are computed by subtracting the corresponding Z_j values just computed from the c_j values shown in the top row of the tableau. We immediately observe that $c_1 - Z_1 = 2$ (positive) so we know that we are not yet optimal and must make at least one more iteration.

The selection of the next variable to enter the basis is again made using the variable entry criterion. The choice is very simple in this instance as only by entering the variable x_1 into the solution can profit be improved (i.e., the only positive $c_j - Z_j$ value is $c_1 - Z_1 = 2$). Thus, the variable x_1 is selected to enter the basis.

The selection of the variable to leave the basis is again made using the variable removal criterion. Applying this criterion, the following ratios are formed.

Current Basic Variables	Solution Values, x_b	÷	a_1	Ratios
x_2	6	÷	$1/2$	12
x_4	16	÷	2	8 (Smallest)

Thus, the current basic variable x_4 is replaced by the current nonbasic variable x_1. The element located at the intersection of the row corresponding to x_4 and the column corresponding to x_1, the value "2," becomes the pivot element.

Pivoting is accomplished in exactly the same manner as before. First, the pivot element 2 is converted to the value one, as follows.

Column Heading	Pivot Row Calculation	
"Solution Values, x_b"	$\frac{16}{2} = 8$	
"a_1"	$\frac{2}{2} = 1$	(Pivot element)
"a_2"	$\frac{0}{2} = 0$	(4-40)
"a_3"	$(-\frac{2}{5})/2 = -\frac{1}{5}$	
"a_4"	$\frac{1}{2} = \frac{1}{2}$	

Next, we proceed to obtain zeroes for the remaining elements of the pivot column, except of course for the pivot element itself. Using row operations on the first row, we obtain:

Row 1 (Variable x_2): Multiply the new pivot row by $-\frac{1}{2}$ and add to old row 1 to obtain new row 1.

Old Row 1	**+**	$(-\frac{1}{2} \cdot$ **New Pivot Row)**	**=**	**New Row 1**	
6	+	$(-\frac{1}{2} \cdot 8 = -4)$	=	2	
$\frac{1}{2}$	+	$(-\frac{1}{2} \cdot 1 = -\frac{1}{2})$	=	0	
1	+	$(-\frac{1}{2} \cdot 0 = 0)$	=	1	(4-41)
$\frac{1}{10}$	+	$(-\frac{1}{2} \cdot -\frac{1}{5} = \frac{1}{10})$	=	$\frac{1}{5}$	
0	+	$(-\frac{1}{2} \cdot \frac{1}{2} = -\frac{1}{4})$	=	$-\frac{1}{4}$	

We can now construct the third simplex tableau, as shown in Table 4.3.

TABLE 4.3 The Third Simplex Tableau (Optimal Solution)— Production-Scheduling Problem

c_b	*Variables in Basis*	*Solution Values,* x_b	a_1	a_2	a_3	a_4
		c_j	6	8	0	0
8	x_2	2	0	1	$1/5$	$-1/4$
6	x_1	8	1	0	$-1/5$	$1/2$
	Z_j	64	6	8	$2/5$	1
	$c_j - Z_j$		0	0	$-2/5$	-1

The Z_j values and the $c_j - Z_j$ values for this tableau are computed in exactly the same manner as they were for the previous two tableaus. The details of these computations will not be repeated here.

Observe that in this third simplex tableau all $c_j - Z_j$ values are either zero or negative. We have thus obtained the optimal solution with $x_1 = 8, x_2 = 2, x_3 = 0$, $x_4 = 0$ and the optimal value of $Z = 64$. This is exactly the same optimal solution we obtained by using the algebraic procedure embodying the Gauss-Jordan elimination procedure. The coefficients in Table 4.3 are also identical to those obtained for the third set of equations we derived by the Gauss-Jordan elimination procedure. The optimal solution tells the decision maker that profit will be maximized when eight bearing plates (product 1) and two gears (product 2) are produced.

4.4 MINIMIZATION—AN EXAMPLE

As shown in Chapter 3, a number of resource allocation problems involve the minimization of a function, such as costs, rather than the maximization of a function such as profits. Fortunately, the simplex algorithm applies just as readily to minimization problems as to maximization problems. First, it should be apparent that any minimization problem can be easily converted into an equivalent maximization problem. Thus,

$$\text{Minimizing } Z = \sum_{j=1}^{n} c_j x_j$$

is equivalent to   (4–42)

$$\text{Maximizing } Z' = \sum_{j=1}^{n} (-c_j) x_j$$

For example,

$$\text{Minimize } Z = 5x_1 + 2x_2$$

is equivalent to   (4–43)

$$\text{Maximize } Z' = -5x_1 - 2x_2$$

The reason that these two formulations are equivalent is that the smaller Z is, the larger Z' must become. Since both formulations have the same feasible solution space, the smallest value of Z in this solution space must be equal to the largest value of $Z' = -Z$ in this same solution space.

If we do not choose to employ this conversion, the only difference in the application of the simplex algorithm is that in solving minimization problems we select the nonbasic variable with the smallest (i.e., most negative) $c_j - Z_j$ value to enter the basis. The variable removal criterion and the pivoting computations are the same for both maximization and minimization problems. In minimization problems, we know that optimality has been reached when all $c_j - Z_j$ values are zero or positive.

To illustrate the use of the simplex algorithm in a minimization problem, and at the same time to consider some of the problems that can arise in the formulation of linear programming problems, consider the following situation. The Nelly Bly Candy Company uses two types of chocolate in the production of its "Giant Chewy Gooey" candy bar. The blending requirements for the candy bar can be summarized as follows.

Type of Requirement	Units of Requirement of Chocolate Ingredient (per ounce)		Total Requirements
	Chocolate 1	Chocolate 2	
Calories	2	4	Less than 12 calories
Sweetness	2	2	Exactly 10 units
Protein	5	2	Greater than 10 units

Chocolate 1 costs 5 cents per ounce and chocolate 2 costs 3 cents per ounce. Letting $x_j; j = 1,2$ represent the number of ounces (unknown) of chocolate 1 and chocolate 2 to be blended in a "Giant Chewy Gooey" candy bar, this situation can be formulated as the following linear programming problem.

$$\text{Minimize } Z = 5x_1 + 3x_2 \qquad (4–44)$$

subject to:
$$2x_1 + 4x_2 \leq 12$$
$$2x_1 + 2x_2 = 10 \qquad (4\text{-}45)$$
$$5x_1 + 2x_2 \geq 10$$

with $\quad x_1 \geq 0, x_2 \geq 0 \qquad\qquad\qquad\qquad (4\text{-}46)$

To enhance our understanding of this problem we shall briefly illustrate again the graphical approach to the solution of a linear programming problem having only two variables. A graphical representation of this minimization example is shown below in Fig. 4.2. Since we are minimizing, the objective function $Z = 5x_1 + 3x_2$ must be moved downward and to the left. As this is done the following extreme points (basic feasible solutions) are traced out.

Extreme Points	Value of Objective Function $Z = 5x_1 + 3x_2$
$x_1 = 5, x_2 = 0$	$Z = 25$
$x_1 = 4, x_2 = 1$	$Z = 23$ (Optimal)

In the graphical representation shown in Fig. 4.2 note that the second constraint $2x_1 + 2x_2 = 10$ must be represented as all points lying on the straight line that

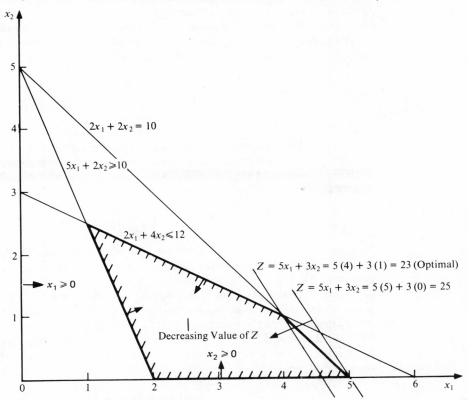

FIGURE 4.2   Graphical Representation—Minimization Example

represents this equality. The third constraint $5x_1 + 2x_2 \geq 10$ is represented graphically by all points upward and to the right of, and including, the straight line $5x_1 + 2x_2 = 10$. The first constraint $2x_1 + 4x_2 \leq 12$ is represented graphically by all the points downward and to the left of and including the straight line $2x_1 + 4x_2 = 12$. The graphical solution to the problem is indicated in Fig. 4.2 as being the extreme point $x_1 = 4, x_2 = 1$, where the minimum value of the objective function is $Z = 23$.

We shall now solve this problem using the simplex algorithm. Again, our first step will be to determine an initial basic feasible solution. Observe that for this latter problem our constraint set is composed of one "less than or equal to" inequality, one equality, and one "greater than or equal to" inequality, unlike the former problem, whose constraint set was composed of three "less than or equal to" inequalities. This means that for this latter problem we cannot employ three slack variables to generate the initial basic feasible solution. Rather, we will utilize a slack variable for the first constraint (i.e., for the "less than or equal to" constraint) an **artificial variable** for the second constraint (i.e., the equality constraint), and a **surplus variable** and an artificial variable for the third constraint (i.e., the "greater than or equal to" constraint). An artificial variable, as we shall demonstrate below, provides a convenient means for identifying the initial basis feasible solution that is the starting point for the application of the simplex method. An artificial variable has no physical meaning to the solution of the problem, and we will also illustrate the procedure that is employed to insure that artificial variables do not remain as basic variables in the final simplex tableau.

Recall that our initial basic feasible solution, and indeed all subsequent basic feasible solutions, must be composed of $m = 3$ variables whose associated column vectors form a (3×3) basis matrix that is also an identity matrix, namely,

$$[\mathbf{B}] = \begin{bmatrix} 1 & 0 & 0 \\ 0 & 1 & 0 \\ 0 & 0 & 1 \end{bmatrix} = [\mathbf{I}] \tag{4-47}$$

Proceeding to obtain an initial basic feasible solution we observe that the first constraint is a "less than or equal to" inequality. We thus introduce a slack variable x_3 as the basic variable for this first constraint and rewrite it as the equality:

$$2x_1 + 4x_2 + 1x_3 = 12 \tag{4-48}$$

with $x_3 \geq 0$, and with $c_3 = 0$ in the objective function. The column vector, $\mathbf{a}_3$, associated with this slack variable, x_3, will thus be the first column of our initial basis matrix, $[\mathbf{B}]$.

The second constraint is already an equality, and it is not possible to add a slack variable to it since both sides of the equation are already equal. Since we have just introduced a slack variable to the first constraint, our initial basic feasible solution would have $x_1 = 0, x_2 = 0, x_3 = 12$. Observe that if nothing further were done, in the second constraint the equality $2x_1 + 2x_2 = 10$ would obviously be violated, that is,

$$2(0) + 2(0) \neq 10 \tag{4-49}$$

The difficulty is resolved by introducing an artificial variable as the basic variable for this second constraint. Denoting the artificial variable as x_4, we rewrite the second constraint as

$$2x_1 + 2x_2 + 1x_4 = 10 \qquad (4-50)$$

with $x_4 \geq 0$. The column vector, $\mathbf{a}_4$, associated with this artificial variable, x_4, will thus be the second column of our initial basis matrix [**B**].

An initial basic feasible solution for the problem, as formulated thus far with only the first two constraints, would be $x_1 = 0$, $x_2 = 0$, $x_3 = 12$, and $x_4 = 10$. However, it should be apparent that this basic solution, in which the artificial variable x_4 has a value of 10 is not a basic feasible solution to the original problem. In essence, the effect of introducing the artificial variable x_4 has been to expand the original set of feasible solutions. At this point we have no assurance that the optimal solution for the revised problem will be a feasible solution for the original problem. To overcome this deficiency we resort to assigning a large penalty to any feasible solution to the expanded problem that lies outside the set of feasible solutions to the original problem. Remember that our expanded feasible solution space is identical to the original feasible solution space when $x_4 = 0$. Thus, we structure our objective function as

$$\begin{array}{ccc} & \text{Slack} & \text{Artificial} \\ & \downarrow & \downarrow \end{array}$$
$$\text{Minimize } Z = 5x_1 + 3x_2 + 0x_3 + Mx_4 \qquad (4-51)$$

where M is some very large number (usually 10^4 or 10^5 in computerized versions of the simplex algorithm). By doing this, the simplex procedure itself will tend to drive the artifical variable to zero as we move to optimality. Thus, x_4 will be used as an initial basic variable, but because of its large positive coefficient in the objective function we are seeking to minimize, it will be replaced rapidly as the pivoting process proceeds.

Consider finally the third constraint that is a "greater than or equal to" inequality. To convert this type of constraint to an equality we define a surplus variable, x_5, as follows.

$$-x_5 = 10 - 5x_1 - 2x_2 \qquad \text{or} \qquad x_5 = 5x_1 + 2x_2 - 10 \qquad (4-52)$$

x_5 is the additional amount or surplus between the two sides of the inequality. The original inequality can now be rewritten as

$$5x_1 + 2x_2 - 1x_5 = 10 \qquad (4-53)$$

with $x_5 \geq 0$, and with $c_5 = 0$ in the objective function.

However, by converting the third constraint from a "greater than or equal to" inequality to an equality by the use of the surplus variable x_5, we have created a further difficulty since the constraint equation coefficient for x_5 is -1. Thus, our initial basic solution would be $x_1 = 0$, $x_2 = 0$, $x_3 = 12$, $x_4 = 10$, and $x_5 = -10$. This initial basic solution is nonfeasible, and the simplex algorithm can proceed only from an initial basic feasible solution. To overcome this difficulty we again resort to introducing an artificial variable to the equality, which already contains the surplus variable x_5. We thus rewrite this equality as

$$5x_1 + 2x_2 - \underset{\underset{\text{Surplus}}{\uparrow}}{1x_5} + \underset{\underset{\text{Artificial}}{\uparrow}}{1x_6} = 10 \tag{4-54}$$

with $x_5 \geq 0$ and $x_6 \geq 0$, and with $c_5 = 0$ and $c_6 = +M$ in the objective function.

Again, the artificial variable is introduced into the third constraint only as a means of allowing the quick and simple determination of an initial basic feasible solution. The column vector, $\mathbf{a}_6$, associated with the artificial variable, x_6, will thus be the third column of our initial basis matrix, [**B**].

The complete problem formulation, with slack, surplus, and artificial variables identified for convenience, can now be rewritten as:

$$\text{Minimize } Z = 5x_1 + 3x_2 + 0\underset{\underset{\text{Slack}}{\uparrow}}{x_3} + M\underset{\underset{\text{Artificial}}{\uparrow}}{x_4} + 0\underset{\underset{\text{Surplus}}{\uparrow}}{x_5} + M\underset{\underset{\text{Artificial}}{\uparrow}}{x_6} \tag{4-55}$$

for max. (−) (−)

subject to:

$$2x_1 + 4x_2 + \underset{\underset{\text{Slack}}{\uparrow}}{1x_3} \qquad\qquad = 12$$

$$2x_1 + 2x_2 \qquad + \underset{\underset{\text{Artificial}}{\uparrow}}{1x_4} \qquad\qquad = 10 \tag{4-56}$$

$$5x_1 + 2x_2 \qquad\qquad\quad - \underset{\underset{\text{Surplus}}{\uparrow}}{1x_5} + \underset{\underset{\text{Artificial}}{\uparrow}}{1x_6} = 10$$

with $\quad x_1 \geq 0, x_2 \geq 0, x_3 \geq 0, x_4 \geq 0, x_5 \geq 0, x_6 \geq 0 \tag{4-57}$

The model given by (4-55), (4-56), and (4-57), which utilizes slack, surplus, and artificial variables in the objective function, constraints, and nonnegativity conditions, is again called a reformulation of the original problem in *standard linear programming format*.

Given this problem formulation, an obvious initial basic feasible solution is $x_1 = 0, x_2 = 0, x_3 = 12, x_4 = 10, x_5 = 0, x_6 = 10$. Our initial basic feasible solution is composed of one slack variable x_3 and two artificial variables x_4 and x_6.

Observe that the column vectors $\mathbf{a}_3$, $\mathbf{a}_4$, and $\mathbf{a}_6$, which correspond to the current basic variables x_3 (slack variable), x_4 (artificial variable), and x_6 (artificial variable), form a basis matrix [**B**] that is an identity matrix.

$$\begin{array}{ccc} \mathbf{a}_3(x_3) & \mathbf{a}_4(x_4) & \mathbf{a}_6(x_6) \end{array}$$
$$[\mathbf{B}] = \begin{bmatrix} 1 & 0 & 0 \\ 0 & 1 & 0 \\ 0 & 0 & 1 \end{bmatrix} = [\mathbf{I}] \tag{4-58}$$

We can now construct our initial simplex tableau, as shown in Table 4.4.

TABLE 4.4 The Initial Simplex Tableau—Minimization Example

			Pivot column ↓					
		c_j	5	3	0	+M	0	+M
c_b	Variables in Basis	Solution Values, x_b	a_1	a_2	a_3	a_4	a_5	a_6
0	x_3	12	2	4	1	0	0	0
Pivot +M	x_4	10	2	2	0	1	0	0
row → +M	x_6	10	⑤	2	0	0	−1	1
	Z_j	20M	7M	4M	0	M	−M	M
	$c_j - Z_j$		5 − 7M	3 − 4M	0	0	+M	0

Pivot element

Observe that our initial basis for this example is composed of the slack variable x_3, and the two artificial variables x_4 and x_6. The slack variable has an objective function coefficient of 0, while the two artificial variables have objective function coefficients of +M. The current value of the objective function is thus 20M, or a very large number. Since we are minimizing, we must seek to reduce this objective function.

It should be emphasized that the artificial variables are used only as a mathematical convenience to obtain an initial basic feasible solution. The effect of these artificial variables on the final solution to the problem is nullified by their extremely large coefficients in the objective function. This perhaps clarifies the name "artificial" given to these variables since they are fictitious and have no physical meaning for the original problem.

Applying our variable entry criterion, remembering that we are minimizing, we select the smallest value of $c_j - Z_j$. This value is $c_1 - Z_1 = 5 - 7M$ (since $M \gg 0$, $5 - 7M < 3 - 4M$). Thus, x_1 becomes our entering basic variable.

The current basic variable to be removed as x_1 becomes positive is chosen using the variable removal criterion. We form the following ratios.

Current Basic Variables	Solution Values, x_b	÷	a_1	Ratios
x_3	12	÷	2	6
x_4	10	÷	2	5
x_6	10	÷	5	2 (Smallest)

The current basic variable x_6, which is an artifical variable, is replaced by the current nonbasic variable x_1.

The pivoting operation proceeds in exactly the same manner as it did previously for the maximization example. First, we obtain a "1" as the pivot element, by dividing row three of the initial tableau (corresponding to the variable x_6, which is being removed from the basis) by 5. We then proceed to obtain zeroes as all the other elements of the pivot column, using elementary row operations involving the adding or subtracting or the appropriate multiple of the new pivot row to or from the other original rows.

The results of this two-step pivoting process leads to the construction of the second simplex tableau, which is shown in Table 4.5.

TABLE 4.5 The Second Simple Tableau—Minimization Example

			c_j	5	3	0	$+M$	0	$+M$
	c_b	Variables in Basis	Solution Values, x_b	a_1	a_2	a_3	a_4	a_5	a_6
Pivot →	0	x_3	8	0	$16/5$	1	0	$2/5$	$-1/5$
row	$+M$	x_4	6	0	$6/5$	0	1	$2/5$	$-2/5$
	5	x_1	2	1	$2/5$	0	0	$-1/5$	$1/5$
		Z_j	$6M + 10$	5	$6/5M + 2$	0	M	$2/5M - 1$	$-2/5M + 1$
		$c_j - Z_j$		0	$-6/5M + 1$	0	0	$-2/5M + 1$	$7/5M - 1$

Pivot column ↓ (over a_2)

Pivot element (pointing to $16/5$)

Observe that the column vectors a_3, a_4, and a_1, which corresponds to the current basic variables x_3 (slack variable), x_4 (artificial variable), and x_1 (real variable), form a basis matrix [**B**] that is an identity matrix.

Since all the $c_j - Z_j$ are not zero or positive, we know that the optimal solution has not been obtained. Indeed, our present solution still contains an artificial variable, that is, $x_4 = 6$. We thus proceed to make another simplex iteration.

Applying the vector entry criterion, the current smallest $c_j - Z_j$ is $c_2 - Z_2 = -6/5M + 1$. Thus, x_2 becomes the entering basic variable.

The current basic variable to be removed as x_2 becomes positive is chosen using the variable removal criterion. We form the following ratios.

Current Basic Variables	Solution Values, x_b	÷	a_2	Ratios
x_3	8	÷	$16/5$	$5/2$ (Smallest)
x_4	6	÷	$6/5$	5
x_1	2	÷	$2/5$	5

Thus, the current basic variable x_3 is replaced by the current nonbasic variable x_2.

The pivoting operation is performed exactly as has been done previously. The results of this two-step pivoting process lead to the construction of the third simplex tableau, which is shown in Table 4.6.

TABLE 4.6 The Third Simplex Tableau—Minimization Example

				Pivot column ↓					
		c_j	5	3	0	+M	0	+M	
	Variables in Basis	*Solution Values,* x_b	a_1	a_2	a_3	a_4	a_5	a_6	
c_b									
Pivot 3	x_2	$5/2$	0	1	$5/16$	0	$1/8$	$-1/8$	
row → +M	x_4	3	0	0	$-3/8$	1	$(1/4)$	$-1/4$	
5	x_1	1	1	0	$-1/8$	0	$-1/4$	$1/4$	
	Z_j	$3M + 12.5$	5	3	$-3/8M + 5/16$	M	$1/4M - 7/8$	$-1/4M + 7/8$	
	$c_j - Z_j$		0	0	$+3/8M - 5/16$	0	$-1/4M + 7/8$	$+5/4M - 7/8$	

Pivot element

Observe that the column vectors a_2, a_4, and a_1, which correspond to the current basic variables x_2 (real variable), x_4 (artificial variable), and x_1 (real variable), form a basis matrix [**B**] that is an identity matrix.

In this third simplex tableau, we observe that not all the $c_j - Z_j$ are positive; hence, the optimal solution has not been obtained. Applying our vector entry criterion, the current smallest $c_j - Z_j$ is $c_5 - Z_5 = -1/4 M + 7/8$. Thus, x_5 becomes the variable to be entered into the basis.

Applying the vector removal criterion, the following ratios are formed.

Current Basic Variables	*Solution Values,* x_b	÷	a_2	*Ratios*
x_2	$5/2$	÷	$1/8$	20
x_4	3	÷	$1/4$	12 (Smallest)
x_1	1	÷	$-1/4$	Ignored, since denominator is negative

Thus, the current basic variable x_4 (the last artificial variable remaining in the basis) is replaced by x_5. Applying our two pivoting operations, the fourth simplex tableau can be constructed as shown in Table 4.7.

In this fourth simplex tableau we immediately observe that all the $c_j - Z_j$ values are zero or positive (remember that $M \gg 0$). We are thus optimal, with a solution of $x_1 = 4$, $x_2 = 1$, $x_5 = 12$; Minimum $Z = 23$. The Nelly Bly Candy Company should utilize 4 ounces of chocolate 1 and 1 ounce of chocolate 2 in the production of its "Giant Chewy Gooey" candy bar, at a minimum cost of $0.23 per candy bar. This optimal solution can readily be compared to the optimal solution shown in Fig. 4.2.

As a final note, it should be mentioned that the structure of a particular set of constraints may preclude the need for the use of artificial variables to obtain

TABLE 4.7   The Fourth Simplex Tableau (Optimal Solution)—Minimization Example

c_b	Variables in Basis	Solution Values, x_b	c_j 5 a_1	3 a_2	0 a_3	+M a_4	0 a_5	+M a_6
3	x_2	1	0	1	$1/2$	$-1/2$	0	0
0	x_5	12	0	0	$-3/2$	4	1	-1
5	x_1	4	1	0	$-1/2$	1	0	0
	Z_j	23	5	3	-1	$7/2$	0	0
	$c_j - Z_j$		0	0	$+1$	$+M - 7/2$	0	$+M$

an initial basic feasible solution. To illustrate this point, consider the following example.

$$\text{Maximize } Z = -1x_2 + 3x_3 + 2x_4 \tag{4-59}$$

subject to:
$$
\begin{aligned}
1x_1 + 2x_2 + 4x_3 \quad\quad &= 9 \\
-3x_2 + 3x_3 + 1x_4 &= 11
\end{aligned}
\tag{4-60}
$$

with
$$x_1 \geq 0, x_2 \geq 0, x_3 \geq 0, x_4 \geq 0 \tag{4-61}$$

Observe that while the constraint set for this problem is composed of two equalities, the structure of the constraint set precludes the need for use of artificial variables. Thus, an initial basic feasible solution can be obtained as $x_1 = 9$, $x_2 = 0$, $x_3 = 0$, $x_4 = 11$, that is, by using the real variables x_1 and x_4 that both appear in only one constraint and have $+1$ as their coefficient in the constraint.

4.5   FURTHER COMPLICATIONS IN APPLYING THE SIMPLEX METHOD

We have presented examples of both maximization and minimization problems, and have shown how to use the simplex method for "greater than," "less than," and "equality" constraints. Let us now consider some of the other complications that may arise in applying the simplex method.

4.5.1   Nonpositive Right-Hand Side Values

In some instances one or more of the right-hand side values, the $b_i, i = 1, 2, \ldots,$ m may be negative. For example, consider the following constraints.

$$-2x_1 + 7x_2 \leq -10 \tag{4-62}$$

Now, if we add a slack variable, x_3, and select this slack variable as an initial basic variable, we would set $x_3 = -10$. However, this is not permissible in the application of the simplex method, that is, we must maintain feasibility with all $x_j \geq 0$.

The easiest way to handle such a complication is to convert the right-hand side to a positive value, and then add either a slack variable, or a surplus and artificial variable, as required. To illustrate, consider our previous constraint in which we now desire to have $+10$ as the right-hand side. To achieve this we multiply both sides of the inequality by -1 and reverse the direction of the inequality, as follows.

$$+2x_1 - 7x_2 \geq 10 \qquad (4\text{–}63)$$

This new constraint is exactly equivalent to the old constraint. However, to make the new constraint into an equality, we must add both a surplus and an artificial variable, as follows.

$$\overset{\text{Surplus}}{\underset{\downarrow}{}} \overset{\text{Artificial}}{\underset{\downarrow}{}}$$

$$+2x_1 - 7x_2 - 1x_3 + 1x_4 = 10 \qquad (4\text{–}64)$$

The simplex method then proceeds in normal fashion.

4.5.2 Unconstrained Variables

In many practical situations we may want to allow one or more of the decision variables, the x_j, to be unconstrained in sign, that is, either positive or negative. We have already noted that use of the simplex method requires that all the decision variables must be nonnegative at each iteration. However, by some simple algebraic manipulations we can convert a linear programming problem involving variables that are unconstrained in sign into an equivalent problem having only nonnegative variables. This is accomplished by expressing each of the **unconstrained variables** as the difference of two nonnegative variables. To illustrate, assume that we want to let the variable x_1 be unconstrained in sign. To accomplish this, we define two new variables $x_1' \geq 0$ and $x_1'' \geq 0$, and let $x_1 = x_1' - x_1''$. Thus, when $x_1' \geq x_1''$ then $x_1 \geq 0$ and when $x_1' \leq x_1''$ then $x_1 \leq 0$, and the desired result has been achieved. Obviously, the unconstrained variable must be replaced by the two new variables wherever it appears in the linear programming model, that is, in both the objective function and the constraint set.

To illustrate the treatment of an unconstrained variable, consider the following situation. The Ace Bicycle Tire Company is considering the production rate for two new types of bicycle tires, in addition to a third bicycle tire that is currently being produced. In this situation we would want to let x_1 represent the unknown number of lots of 100 the first type of tire to be produced, x_2 represent the unknown number of lots of 100 of the second type of tire to be produced, and x_3 represent the change (either an increase or decrease) in the production rate of lots of 100 for the third type of tire that is currently being produced. Assume that the first type of bicycle tire sells for $400 per lot, the second type of bicycle tire sells for $200 per lot, and the third type of bicycle tire sells for $100 per lot. The production process for this situation can be represented by the following table.

Production Process	Required Production Process Time per lot			Process Time Availability (excess)
	Tire 1	Tire 2	Tire 3	
Mixing	3	2	4	10 hours
Molding	2	1	−3	7 hours
Curing	9	−4	1	3 hours

The negative entries in this table indicate production-process-time savings that are possible. This problem situation can now be represented by the following linear programming formulation.

$$\text{Maximize } Z = 400x_1 + 200x_2 + 100x_3 \tag{4-65}$$

subject to:
$$\begin{array}{l} 3x_1 + 2x_2 + 4x_3 \le 10 \\ 2x_1 + 1x_2 - 3x_3 \le 7 \\ 9x_1 - 4x_2 + 1x_3 \le 3 \end{array} \tag{4-66}$$

with $x_1 \ge 0, x_2 \ge 0, x_3$ unconstrained $\tag{4-67}$

To solve this problem using the simplex method, we reformulate the problem as follows.

$$\text{Let } x_3 = x_3' - x_3'' \tag{4-68}$$

$$\text{Maximize } Z = 400x_1 + 200x_2 + 100x_3' - 100x_3'' \tag{4-69}$$

subject to:
$$\begin{array}{l} 3x_1 + 2x_2 + 4x_3' - 4x_3'' \le 10 \\ 2x_1 + 1x_2 - 3x_3' + 3x_3'' \le 7 \\ 9x_1 - 4x_2 + 1x_3' - 1x_3'' \le 3 \end{array} \tag{4-70}$$

with $x_1 \ge 0, x_2 \ge 0, x_3' \ge 0, x_3'' \ge 0$ $\tag{4-71}$

This reformulated problem can now be solved in the normal fashion using the simplex method. The initial and final (optimal) simplex tableaus are presented below in Tables 4.8 and 4.9.

TABLE 4.8   Unconstrained Variables Example—Initial Simplex Tableau

		c_j	*400*	*200*	*100*	*−100*	*0*	*0*	*0*
c_b	*Variables in Basis*	*Solution Values,* x_b	a_1	a_2	a_3'	a_3''	a_4	a_5	a_6
0	x_4	10	3	2	4	−4	1	0	0
0	x_5	7	2	1	−3	3	0	1	0
0	x_6	3	⑨	−4	1	−1	0	0	1
	Z_j	0	0	0	0	0	0	0	0
	$c_j - Z_j$		400	200	100	−100	0	0	0

The optimal solution indicates that $x_1 = 1.673$ lots of the first type of bicycle tire should be produced, $x_2 = 2.956$ lots of the second type of tire should be produced, while the production of the third type of tire changes by $x_3 = x_3' - x_3'' = 0.00 - 0.23 = -0.23$ lots.

4.5.3   Tie for Entering Basic Variable

Quite often in applying the simplex method we will encounter a situation in which there is a tie between two or more variables for entering the basis. This will be indicated by these variables having exactly the same $c_j - Z_j$ value. The question

TABLE 4.9 Unconstrained Variables Example—Final Simplex Tableau (Optimal Solution)

c_b	Variables in Basis	Solution Values, x_b	c_j 400 a_1	200 a_2	100 a_3'	−100 a_3''	0 a_4	0 a_5	0 a_6
200	x_2	470/159	0	1	0	0	29/159	11/53	−17/159
−100	x_3''	37/159	0	0	−1	1	−17/159	10/53	−1/159
400	x_1	266/159	1	0	0	0	11/159	6/53	10/159
	Z_j	196700/159	400	200	100	−100	11900/159	3600/53	700/159
	$c_j − Z_j$		0	0	0	0	−11900/159	−3600/53	−700/159

becomes: How should this tie be broken? Fortunately, this question can be answered very simply as the choice between two or more variables tying for entry can be made arbitrarily. Thus, it does not matter which variable is chosen for entry into the basis, as we will ultimately arrive at the optimal solution, regardless of the initial choice among the tied variables.

4.5.4 Tie for Leaving Basic Variable—Degeneracy

In applying the simplex method we can encounter a situation in which a tie occurs between two or more variables, in terms of selecting the minimum nonnegative ratio for the variable to leave the basis. This situation will be indicated by these variables having exactly the same (minimum nonnegative) ratio formed as the values in the "**Solution Values, x_b**" column are divided by the corresponding values in the a_j column. When this occurs, the variable selected for removal from the basis will be driven to zero by the pivoting process. Additionally, the other tying variable(s) will be driven to zero, but will remain in the basis. This will result in a *degenerate basic feasible solution*, having one, or more, of the basic variables equal to zero.

To illustrate degeneracy, let us reconsider our original production scheduling problem, modified by the addition of a third constraint and a change in the coefficients of the objective function.

$$\text{Maximize } Z = 10x_1 + 5x_2 \qquad (4\text{–}72)$$

subject to:
$$5x_1 + 10x_2 \le 60$$
$$4x_1 + 4x_2 \le 40 \qquad (4\text{–}73)$$
$$5x_1 \qquad\quad \le 40$$

with $\quad x_1 \ge 0, x_2 \ge 0 \qquad (4\text{–}74)$

A graphical solution to this problem is presented in Fig. 4.3. In this graphical solution observe that the (degenerate) optimal solution occurs at $x_1 = 8$, $x_2 = 2$, Maximum $Z = 10(8) + 5(2) = 90$. The point that produces the optimal solution is at the intersection of all three of the constraints of the problem. This means that all three of the constraints will be satisfied exactly, and that the three slack variables associated with the three constraints will all be equal to zero in the optimal solution. Thus, we will obtain a degenerate optimal solution in which less than

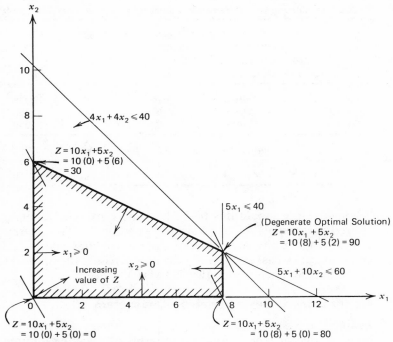

FIGURE 4.3   Degeneracy Example

$m = 3$ of the basic variables will be greater than zero (i.e., we can see graphically that the optimal solution will have only $x_1 = 8$, $x_2 = 2$).

The initial simplex tableau for this problem is presented in Table 4.10.

TABLE 4.10   Degeneracy Example—Initial Simplex Tableau

c_b	Variables in Basis	Solution Values, x_b	a_1	a_2	a_3	a_4	a_5
		c_j	*10*	*5*	*0*	*0*	*0*
0	x_3	60	5	10	1	0	0
0	x_4	40	4	4	0	1	0
0	x_5	40	⑤	0	0	0	1
	Z_j	0	0	0	0	0	0
	$c_j - Z_j$		10	5	0	0	0

In this initial simplex tableau the real variable x_1 enters the basis and the slack variable x_5 is removed from the basis. The second simplex tableau is presented in Table 4.11.

TABLE 4.11 Degeneracy Example—Second Simplex Tableau

c_b	Variables in Basis	Solution Values, x_b	c_j a_1	10 a_2	5 a_3	0 a_4	0 a_5	0
0	x_3	20	0	⑩	1	0	-1	
0	x_4	8	0	4	0	1	$-4/5$	
10	x_1	8	1	0	0	0	$1/5$	
	Z_j	80	10	0	0	0	2	
	$c_j - Z_j$		0	5	0	0	-2	

Applying the variable removal criterion to this second simplex tableau, the following ratios are formed.

Current Basic Variables	Solution Values, x_b	$\div$	a_2	Ratios
x_3	20	$\div$	10	2
x_4	8	$\div$	4	2
x_1	8	$\div$	0	Ignore

Thus, we have a tie between slack variables x_3 and x_4 for removal from the basis as the real variable x_2 enters the basis. Breaking this tie arbitrarily let us choose x_3 as the variable to be removed from the basis. The third simplex tableau (degenerate optimal solution) is presented in Table 4.12. Observe that in this tableau we not only removed x_3 from the basis as we inserted x_2 into the basis during the pivoting process, but we also drove x_4 to zero. Thus, we have obtained a degenerate optimal solution in which less than $m = 3$ of the basic variables are greater than zero (i.e., one of the basic variables $x_4 = 0$). Whenever we have a tie in the ratios used to select the variable to leave, there will always be a basic variable equal to zero in the next tableau. In this instance, since we have obtained the optimal solution we do not really care that the slack variable x_4 is in solution at a zero value.

TABLE 4.12 Degeneracy Example—Final Simplex Tableau (Degenerate Optimal Solution)

c_b	Variables in Basis	Solution Values, x_b	c_j a_1	10 a_2	5 a_3	0 a_4	0 a_5	0
5	x_2	2	0	1	$1/10$	0	$-1/10$	
0	x_4	0	0	0	$-2/5$	1	$-2/5$	
10	x_1	8	1	0	0	0	$1/5$	
	Z_j	90	10	5	$1/2$	0	$3/2$	
	$c_j - Z_j$		0	0	$-1/2$	0	$-3/2$	

Theoretically, if there is a tie between two or more variables to be removed from the basis at some iteration prior to reaching the optimal solution, a situation known as **cycling** can occur. The following sequence of events could occur causing cycling. First, the arbitrary choice between the tied variables for a variable to be removed from the basis will always generate a degenerate basic feasible solution in which all of the tied variables reach zero simultaneously as the entering basic variable is increased. Second, if one of these degenerate basic variables retains its value of zero until it is chosen at a later iteration to be a leaving basic variable, then the corresponding entering basic variable must then also enter at a value of zero (i.e., the entering basic variable could not enter at a value greater than zero without making the leaving variable negative). This means that the value of the objective function would remain unchanged at that iteration. Third, if the value of the objective function remained unchanged rather than increasing at each iteration it would then be possible for the simplex method to cycle in a loop, repeating the same sequence of degenerate basic feasible solutions without ever reaching *the* degenerate optimal basic feasible solution. Note that this did not happen in our previous example, because optimality was achieved at the same time that degeneracy occurred. Examples have been constructed, however, to show that cycling can occur.[2]

Fortunately, cycling has not been seen to occur frequently in practice. However, Kotiah and Steinberg recently reported encountering cycling in a relatively small (15 constraints, 20 variables) practical linear programming problem involving a queueing model.[3] Avoiding the possibility of cycling can be accomplished in several ways. Perhaps the simplest and best method was developed by Bland.[4] Specifically, his method indicates that if a tie is encountered between leaving basic variables, first examine the $c_j - Z_j$ row to see if another nonbasic variable can be selected to enter the basis. Select as the entering variable that variable with the smallest column subscript (j) among all nonbasic variables whose $c_j - Z_j$ values are positive (in a maximization problem). Then, if there is still a tie among leaving basic variables, select as the variable to leave solution that variable with the smallest row subscript (i). (See Bland 1977 for a proof of this method.) Other methods to avoid cycling are also in existence, such as the perturbation method of Charnes,[5] and the lexicographic ordering method of Dantzig, Orden, and Wolfe,[6] but they are more complicated than the method outlined above.

In summary, since cycling has not been seen to occur very frequently in practice, and since it can be avoided in several ways, we will not consider it any further. If ties do occur between the leaving basic variables as you are using the

[2] See: G. Hadley, *Linear Programming* (Reading, Mass: Addison-Wesley Publishing Company, Inc., 1962), pp. 190–195; and S. T. Gass, *Linear Programming: Methods and Applications,* (New York: McGraw-Hill Book Company, 1975), 69–70.

[3] T. C. Kotiah, and D. I. Steinberg, "On the Possibility of Cycling with the Simplex Method," *Operations Research,* vol. 26 (1978), 374–375.

[4] R. G. Bland, "New Finite Pivoting Rules for the Simplex Method," *Mathematics of Operations Research,* vol. 2 (1977), 103–107.

[5] A. Charnes, "Optimality and Degeneracy in Linear Programming," *Econometrica,* vol. 20 (1952), 160–172.

[6] G. B. Dantzig, A. Orden, and P. Wolfe, "The Generalized Simplex Method for Minimizing a Linear Form Under Linear Inequality Constraints," *Pacific Journal of Mathematics,* vol. 5 (1955), 183–195.

simplex method, simply break the tie arbitrarily, or apply Bland's method, recognizing that subsequent solutions may be degenerate.

4.6 TERMINATION OF THE SIMPLEX METHOD—TYPES OF SOLUTIONS

Thus far we have considered examples in which the simplex method terminated in normal fashion, that is, the optimal feasible solution was obtained in a finite number of steps. This will occur in the vast majority of practical cases. However, as noted in Chapter 3 there are three situations in which abnormalities do occur. Each of these abnormal types of solution will now be discussed in terms of how the termination of the simplex method occurs in each instance.

4.6.1 Alternative Optimal Solutions

The simplex method provides a clear indication of the presence of alternative, or multiple, optimal solutions upon its termination. These alternative optimal solutions can be recognized by considering the $c_j - Z_j$ row. Assume that we are maximizing, and remember that when all $c_j - Z_j$ values are zero or negative we know that an optimal solution has been obtained. Now, the presence of an alternative optimal solution will be indicated by the fact that for some variable not in the basis, the corresponding $c_j - Z_j$ value will equal zero. Thus, this variable can be entered into the basis, the appropriate variable can be removed from the basis, and the value of the objective function will not change. In this manner, the various alternative optimal solutions can be determined.

As an example of a problem having alternative optimal solutions consider the production scheduling problem discussed in section 3.6.1 of the previous chapter, namely

$$\text{Maximize } Z = 5x_1 + 10x_2 \tag{4-75}$$

subject to:
$$5x_1 + 10x_2 \leq 60 \tag{4-76}$$
$$4x_1 + 4x_2 \leq 40$$

with $\quad x_1 \geq 0, x_2 \geq 0$ $\hfill$ (4-77)

The graphical solution to this problem was presented in Fig. 3.4. Consider now the final simplex tableau for this problem, which is presented in Table 4.13.

TABLE 4.13 Alternative Optimal Solutions Example—Final Simplex Tableau

c_b	Variables in the Basis	c_j Solution Values, x_b	5 a_1	10 a_2	0 a_3	0 a_4
10	x_2	6	½	1	$1/10$	0
0	x_4	16	2	0	$-2/5$	1
	Z_j	60	5	10	1	0
	$c_j - Z_j$		0	0	-1	0

The optimal solution indicated in this final tableau is $x_1 = 0, x_2 = 6, x_3 = 0, x_4 = 16$, and $Z = 60$. Furthermore, in this final simplex tableau, $c_1 - Z_1 = 0$, and x_1 is not in the basis (i.e., $x_1 = 0$). Thus, we have an indication that an alternative optimal solution exists. The variable x_1 can be entered into the basis, and the variable x_4 can be removed from the basis, with the resulting alternative optimal solution having exactly the same value for its objective function. Performing the necessary iteration to obtain this alternative optimal solution, we obtain the simplex tableau shown in Table 4.14.

TABLE 4.14   Alternative Optimal Solutions Example—Final Simplex Tableau

c_b	Variables in the Basis	c_j Solution Values, x_b	5 a_1	10 a_2	0 a_3	0 a_4
10	x_2	2	0	1	$1/5$	$-1/4$
5	x_1	8	1	0	$-1/5$	$1/2$
	Z_j	60	5	10	1	0
	$c_j - Z_j$		0	0	-1	0

The optimal solution indicated in this final simplex tableau is $x_1 = 8, x_2 = 2, x_3 = 0$, $x_4 = 0$, and $Z = 60$. Observe also that in this final simplex tableau, $c_4 - Z_4 = 0$, and x_4 is not in the basis (i.e., $x_4 = 0$). Thus, we have an indication that an alternative optimal solution exists. This alternative optimal solution is, of course, the solution shown previously in Table 4.13.

4.6.2   An Unbounded Solution

In the case of an unbounded solution, the simplex method will terminate with the indication that the entering basic variable can do so only if it is allowed to assume a value of infinity, $+\infty$. Specifically, for a maximization problem we will encounter a simplex tableau having a nonbasic variable whose $c_j - Z_j$ row value is strictly greater than zero (i.e., $c_j - Z_j > 0$ for some variable x_j that is not in the basis), and for this same variable all of the a_{ij} elements in its column will be zero or negative (i.e., *every* coefficient in the pivot column will be either negative or zero). Thus, in performing the ratio test for the variable removal criterion it will be possible only to form ratios having negative numbers or zeroes as denominators. Negative numbers in the denominators cannot be considered, since this would result in the introduction of a basic variable at a negative level (i.e., an infeasible solution would result). Zeroes in the denominator would produce a ratio having a value of $+\infty$, and would indicate that the entering basic variable could be increased indefinitely (i.e., infinitely) without any of the current basic variables being driven from the basis. Therefore, if we have an unbounded solution, *none* of the current basic variables can be driven from solution by the introduction of a new basic variable, even if that new basic variable assumes an infinitely large value. Generally, arriving at an unbounded solution indicates that the problem was originally misformulated within the constraint set, and needs reformulation.

As an example of a problem having an unbounded solution, consider the problem presented in Section 3.6.2 of the previous chapter, namely

$$\text{Maximize } Z = 2x_1 + 1x_2 \qquad (4\text{-}78)$$

subject to:
$$1x_2 \leq 5$$
$$1x_1 - 1x_2 \geq -1 \quad \text{or} \quad -1x_1 + 1x_2 \leq 1 \qquad (4\text{-}79)$$

with $\quad x_1 \geq 0, x_2 \geq 0 \qquad (4\text{-}80)$

The graphical solution to this problem was presented in Figure 3.5. The initial simplex tableau for this problem is shown in Table 4.15.

TABLE 4.15 Unbounded Solution Example—Initial Simplex Tableau

		c_j	*2*	*1*	*0*	*0*
c_b	*Variables in the Basis*	*Solution Values*, x_b	a_1	a_2	a_3	a_4
0	x_3	5	0	1	1	0
0	x_4	1	-1	1	0	1
	Z_j	0	0	0	0	0
	$c_j - Z_j$		2	1	0	0

$\uparrow$
Pivot column

As can be seen in this initial tableau, $c_1 - Z_1 = 2$ (positive), and using the standard variable entry criterion we would attempt to insert the variable x_1 into the basis. However, when we apply the standard variable removal criterion to this problem, the following ratios are formed.

Current Basic Variables	*Solution Values*, x_b	$\div$	a_1	*Ratios*
x_3	5	$\div$	0	$+\infty$
x_4	1	$\div$	-1	(Negative $\rightarrow$ Infeasible)

The variable x_4 cannot be considered for removal from the basis as this would result in an infeasible solution. The variable x_3 can be considered for removal from the basis only if x_1 enters the basis at an infinite level. This will produce an unbounded solution, with an infinitely large objective function. To further illustrate why we have an unbounded solution, let us write out the set of equations that forms the basic feasible shown in the initial simplex tableau. These equations are as follows.

$$\begin{aligned} 1x_2 + 1x_3 \quad\;\;\;\; &= 5 \\ -1x_1 + 1x_2 \quad\;\; + 1x_4 &= 1 \end{aligned} \qquad (4\text{-}81)$$

The initial basic feasible solution for this problem is $x_1 = 0, x_2 = 0, x_3 = 5, x_4 = 1$. If we now attempt to remove x_3 from the basis (i.e., drive x_3 to 0) while introducing x_1 into the basis (i.e., allow x_1 to become positive), observe what happens. Keeping the nonbasic variable $x_2 = 0$ in both equations, we observe first that we cannot remove x_3 from the basis (i.e., $x_3 = 5$ in the first equation). Second, we observe that $x_1 \to +\infty$ and $x_4 \to +\infty$, *simultaneously*, in the second equation. Since the variable x_1 has a positive coefficient in the objective function, this would produce an unbounded solution with an infinitely large objective function.

The question might asked: What about the fact that the other nonbasic variable, x_2, has $c_2 - Z_2 = 1$ (positive) in the initial simplex tableau? To illustrate what would happen, let us assume that we chose to make our initial pivot using the variable x_2 as entering the basis. The series of simplex tableaus that would result is shown in Tables 4.16, 4.17, and 4.18.

TABLE 4.16   Unbounded Solution Example—Initial Simplex Tableau (Variable x_2 Chosen to Enter Basis)

c_b	Variables in the Basis	Solution Values, x_b	c_j 2 a_1	1 a_2	0 a_3	0 a_4
0	x_3	5	0	①	1	0
0	x_4	1	−1	1	0	1
	Z_j	0	0	0	0	0
	$c_j - Z_j$		2	1	0	0

TABLE 4.17   Unbounded Solution Example—Second Simplex Tableau

c_b	Variables in the Basis	Solution Values, x_b	c_j 2 a_1	1 a_2	0 a_3	0 a_4
0	x_3	4	①	0	1	−1
1	x_2	1	−1	1	0	1
	Z_j	1	−1	0	0	1
	$c_j - Z_j$		3	0	0	−1

TABLE 4.18   Unbounded Solution Example—Final Simplex Tableau

c_b	Variables in the Basis	Solution Values, x_b	c_j 2 a_1	1 a_2	0 a_3	0 a_4
2	x_1	4	1	0	1	−1
1	x_2	5	0	1	1	0
	Z_j	13	2	1	3	−2
	$c_j - Z_j$		0	0	−3	2

↑
Pivot Column

Note that in the final tableau, $c_4 - Z_4 = 2$ (positive), and using the standard variable entry criterion, we would attempt to insert the variable x_4 into the basis. But, again, we see that all of the a_{ij} elements in column 4 are negative or zero indicating that an unbounded condition is present. To further illustrate why we have again obtained an unbounded solution, let us once again write out the set of equations that forms the basic feasible solution shown in this final simplex tableau. These equations are as follows.

$$1x_1 \qquad + 1x_3 - 1x_4 = 4$$
$$1x_2 + 1x_3 \qquad = 5$$

(4–82)

If we now attempt to remove x_2 from the basis (i.e., drive x_2 to 0) while introducing x_4 into the basis (i.e., allow x_4 to become positive), observe what happens. Keeping the nonbasic variable $x_3 = 0$ in both equations, we observe first that we cannot remove x_2 from the basis (i.e., $x_2 = 5$ in the second equation). Second, we observe that $x_1 \to +\infty$ and $x_4 \to +\infty$, *simultaneously*, in the first equation. This would again produce an unbounded solution, indeed the same unbounded solution we obtained previously in Table 4.15.

It is important to stress the fact that, in a linear programming maximization problem, *whenever* we encounter a simplex tableau having a nonbasic variable with a corresponding $c_j - Z_j > 0$, with all of the associated $a_{ij} \leq 0$, we have an unbounded solution. It is not necessary to search for other nonbasic variables having positive $c_j - Z_j$ row values and make further pivots. As we have illustrated in the example above, we will eventually reach a situation in which no additional pivots are possible and the indication of an unbounded condition will be present. Finally, in a minimization problem, an unbounded solution will be indicated *whenever* we encounter a simplex tableau having a nonbasic variable whose $c_j - Z_j < 0$, with all of the associated $a_{ij} \leq 0$.

4.6.3 An Infeasible Solution

The final type of abnormal situation occurs when the linear programming problem has an infeasible solution. Once again, the simplex method will provide a clear indication that no feasible solution is possible. The indication that no feasible solution is possible will be given by the fact that at least one of the artificial variables, which should be driven to zero by the simplex method, will be present as a positive basic variable in the solution that appears to be optimal. For example, assume we are solving a maximization problem in which artificial variables are required. Then, at some iteration we achieve a solution in which all the $c_j - Z_j$ values are zero or negative, but which has one or more artificial variables as positive basic variables. Alternatively, the fact that no feasible solution exists may be indicated simply by the inability to remove one or more artificial variables from the basis, using the standard simplex procedure.

When an infeasible solution is indicated the management science analyst should carefully reconsider the construction of the model, because the model is either improperly formulated or two or more of the constraints are incompatible. Reformulation of the model is mandatory for cases in which the no feasible solution condition is indicated.

As an example of a problem having no infeasible solution, consider the first problem presented in Section 3.6.3, namely

$$\text{Maximize } Z = 3x_1 - 2x_2 \qquad (4\text{-}83)$$

subject to: $\qquad 1x_1 + 2x_2 \leq 2$

$\qquad\qquad\qquad 2x_1 + 4x_2 \geq 8 \qquad\qquad\qquad\qquad (4\text{-}84)$

with $\qquad x_1 \geq 0, x_2 \geq 0 \qquad\qquad\qquad\qquad\qquad\qquad (4\text{-}85)$

The graphical solution to this problem was presented in Fig. 3.6. The last two simplex tableaus for this problem are shown in table 4.19.

TABLE 4.19   Infeasible Solution Example—Final Simplex Tableaus

Pivot column ↓

	c_b	Variables in the Basis	Solution Values, x_b	c_j 3 a_1	−2 a_2	0 a_3	0 a_4	−M a_5
Pivot row →	−2	x_2	1	½	1	½	0	0
	−M	x_5	4	0	0	−2	−1	1
		Z_j	−4M − 2	−1	−2	−1 + 2M	+M	−M
		$c_j - Z_j$		4	0	−2M + 1	−M	0

Pivot element

	c_b	Variable in the Basis	Solution Values, x_b	c_j 3 a_1	−2 a_2	0 a_3	0 a_4	−M a_5
	3	x_1	2	1	2	1	0	0
	−M	x_5	4	0	0	−2	−1	1
		Z_j	−4M + 6	3	6	3 + 2M	+M	−M
		$c_j - Z_j$		0	−8	−3 − 2M	−M	0

In the next to last tableau, we observe that $c_1 - Z_1 = 4$ (positive) so we insert x_1 into the basis and remove x_2 from the basis. Note that the artificial variable x_5 remains in the basis. The resultant final tableau now has all $c_j - Z_j$ negative. We now have an indication that the optimal solution has been obtained. However, the artifical variable x_5 has not been removed from the basis, and we have an indication that no feasible solution exists for this problem.

As a second example of a problem having an infeasible solution, consider the second problem presented in Section 3.6.3, namely

$$\text{Minimize } Z = 2x_1 + 3x_2 \qquad (4\text{-}86)$$

subject to: $\qquad 1x_1 - 1x_2 \geq 1$

$\qquad\qquad 2x_1 + 2x_2 \leq -4 \qquad$ (rewritten as $-2x_1 - 2x_2 \geq 4$) $\qquad (4\text{-}87)$

with $\qquad x_1 \geq 0, x_2 \geq 0 \qquad\qquad\qquad\qquad\qquad\qquad (4\text{-}88)$

The graphical solution to this problem was presented in Fig. 3.7. The initial (and final) simplex tableau for this problem is shown in Table 4.20.

TABLE 4.20 Infeasible Solution Example—Final Simplex Tableau

c_b	Variables in the Basis	c_j Solution Values, x_b	2 a_1	3 a_2	0 a_3	+M a_4	0 a_5	+M a_6
+M	x_4	1	1	−1	−1	1	0	0
+M	x_6	4	−2	−2	0	0	−1	1
	Z_j	5M	−M	−3M	−M	+M	−M	+M
	$c_j − Z_j$		2 + M	3 + 3M	+M	0	+M	0

In this initial (and final) simplex tableau all of the $c_j − Z_j$ values are positive, and we have an indication that the optimal solution has been obtained. However, both artificial variables, x_4 and x_6, have not been removed from the basis, and we have an indication that no feasible solution exists for this problem.

In summary, a linear programming problem is infeasible if there is no solution that satisfies all of the constraints and nonnegativity conditions simultaneously. In applying the simplex method, this will be indicated by the presence of one or more artificial variables in the basis at a positive level for a solution satisfying the optimality conditions. Finally, it should also be noted that for linear programming problems with all constraints of "less than or equal to" form, and all right-hand sides nonnegative, there will always be a feasible solution, since the origin will always be a feasible solution. Additionally, such problems will never require the use of artificial variables, and therefore an artificial variable could not be present in the final simplex tableau.

4.7 REDUNDANT CONSTRAINT

As noted previously in Section 3.7, a redundant constraint can be removed from the problem formulation as it will not affect the solution to the problem. To illustrate what will occur in applying the simplex method, let us reconsider the redundant constraint problem discussed earlier in Section 3.7, namely

$$\text{Maximize } Z = 3x_1 + 5x_2 \tag{4-89}$$

subject to:
$$\begin{align} 2x_1 + 4x_2 &\le 16 \\ 4x_1 + 2x_2 &\le 16 \\ 3x_1 + 3x_2 &\le 30 \qquad \text{(Redundant constraint)} \end{align} \tag{4-90}$$

with $\quad x_1 \ge 0, x_2 \ge 0$ $\hfill$ (4-91)

The graphical solution to this problem was presented in Fig. 3.8. The final simplex tableau for this problem, including the redundant constraint, is presented in Table 4.21.

TABLE 4.21   Redundant Constraint Example (Redundant Constraint Included)—Final Simplex Tableau

		c_j	3	5	0	0	0
c_b	Variables in the Basis	Solution Values, x_b	a_1	a_2	a_3	a_4	a_5
3	x_2	$8/3$	0	1	$1/3$	$-1/6$	0
5	x_1	$8/3$	1	0	$-1/6$	$1/3$	0
0	x_5	$9/5$	0	0	$-1/2$	$-1/2$	1
	Z_j	$64/3$	3	5	$1/6$	$7/6$	0
	$c_j - Z_j$		0	0	$-1/6$	$-7/6$	0

In this final simplex tableau $x_1 = {}^8/_3, x_2 = {}^8/_3, x_3 = 0, x_4 = 0, x_5 = {}^9/_5$, and Maximum $Z = {}^{64}/_3$. Observe that the redundant constraint (i.e., the third constraint) is satisfied as follows.

$$
\begin{array}{ccccccc}
\text{real} & & \text{real} & & \text{slack} \\
\downarrow & & \downarrow & & \downarrow \\
3x_1 & + & 3x_2 & + & 1x_5 & = & 30 \\
3(^8/_3) & + & 3(^8/_3) & + & 1(^9/_5) & = & 30 \checkmark
\end{array}
\qquad (4\text{--}92)
$$

Thus, the slack variable, x_5, associated with the redundant constraint is in the basis at a positive level in the final simplex tableau.

The final simplex tableau for the same problem, except having the redundant constraint excluded, is presented in Table 4.22.

TABLE 4.22   Redundant Constraint Example (Redundant Constraint Excluded)—Final Simplex Tableau

		c_b	3	5	0	0
c_b	Variables in the Basis	Solution Values, x_b	a_1	a_2	a_3	a_4
3	x_2	$8/3$	0	1	$1/3$	$-1/6$
5	x_1	$8/3$	1	0	$-1/6$	$1/3$
	Z_j	$64/3$	3	5	$1/6$	$7/6$
	$c_j - Z_j$		0	0	$-1/6$	$-7/6$

In this final simplex tableau $x = {}^8/_3, x_2 = {}^8/_3, x_3 = 0, x_4 = 0$, and Maximum $Z = {}^{64}/_3$. These are, of course, exactly the same values we obtained for the two real variables, x_1 and x_2, and the objective function in the previous version of the problem in which the redundant constraint was included. Thus, we have demonstrated that exactly the same solution to the problem is obtained, regardless of whether or not the redundant constraint is included. Obviously, the problem formulation without the redundant constraint is preferable, since it results in simplex tableaus that have one less row requiring transformation during the pivoting process.

It should be stressed that while we have illustrated that a redundant constraint can be eliminated from the linear programming problem formulation, for problems involving more than two variables (i.e., problems that cannot be solved graphically) it will generally be very difficult, a priori, to determine that a redundant constraint is present.

4.8 USING THE COMPUTER TO SOLVE LINEAR PROGRAMMING PROBLEMS

In the previous chapter we have examined how to formulate linear programming problems to represent various managerial decision-making situations, and we have seen how certain simple linear programming problems can be solved graphically. In this chapter we have studied the simplex algorithm, a solution procedure that can be applied to larger, more complex linear programming problems. By this time, you have probably gained some experience in manually using the simplex algorithm. However, in order for linear programming to be really useful to the decision maker, it must be easily applicable to real-world problems of some complexity and size. Thus, in practice we would not want to have to manually apply the simplex method in order to obtain a solution to a large linear programming model.

Fortunately, the evolution of linear programming has been paralleled by the evolution of the high-speed digital computer. Thus, as linear programming has developed, a number of computer programming (software) packages for solving linear programming problems have been designed.

Two basic types of computer programming packages for linear programming are in existence. The first of these is called a **batch program**. A batch program requires the user to prepare the input in advance, usually on a set of punched cards. The input data, together with a set of control cards specifying certain parameters for the program, are then directly input to the computer using a card reader. The program output is then printed at a later time and retrieved by the user. Many batch programs (linear programming codes) are available and are commonly obtainable from computer vendors. One prominent example of a batch linear programming code is MPS-360 (Mathematical Programming System - 360), available on large IBM installations. This code can be used to solve very large linear programming problems very quickly. However, it requires a fairly complicated and highly structured input data format and is generally not used for classroom instruction.

The second type of package is generally referred to as a **time-shared** or **interactive package**. To use this type of package, the user provides input and receives output via a remote terminal, normally a cathode-ray tube (CRT) or teletype. Data for using the program is thus submitted directly through the terminal.

There are numerous computer programs in existence for solving linear programming problems. We will now attempt to illustrate how to use one simple type of batch linear programming package. Your instructor can provide you complete details concerning the use of this linear programming package by referring to material concerning the code provided at the back of the Instructor's Manual that accompanies this text. The package we will describe below probably will not be identical to the one in use at your institution. However, they both should have several common features, and by studying it you should be able to transfer your learning to your own computer system. In order to use this, or any computerized linear programming package, there are three major considerations: (1) gaining access to the computer code, (2) providing input data, and (3) interpreting the output data. Each of these items will be discussed below.

4.8.1   Gaining Access to the Computer Code

The linear programming code discussed herein is a batch-processing code designed for solving linear programming problems having up to 30 constraints, and up to 79 variables (including slack and artificial variables). Thus, access to the program is gained by means of input data and control cards (often called job control cards), which are read into the card reader. The job control cards will vary by computer installation, but the input data cards are standardized. Your instructor can provide you with details on access requirements tailored to your computer system.

4.8.2   Providing Input Data

As noted above, input data for the linear programming problem is provided in a structured manner. To illustrate the process of providing input data, let us reconsider the formulation of our production scheduling problem, namely

$$\text{Maximize } Z = 6x_1 + 8x_2 \tag{4-93}$$

subject to:
$$\begin{aligned} 5x_1 + 10x_2 &\le 60 \\ 4x_1 + 4x_2 &\le 40 \end{aligned} \tag{4-94}$$

with $x_1 \ge 0, x_2 \ge 0$ $\tag{4-95}$

The input data corresponding to this problem formulation is as follows (in punched card format) on the top of the next page. Again, your instructor can provide you with complete details on how to specify the input data.

4.8.3   Interpreting Output Data

The computer output for the production scheduling problem is shown below in Fig. 4.4 and Fig. 4.5. The computer output initial tableau is presented in Fig. 4.4, and corresponds to the initial simplex tableau presented in Table 4.1. Note that there are some minor differences between the two tableaus, but, in general, they

FIGURE 4.4   Computer Output—Initial Tableau

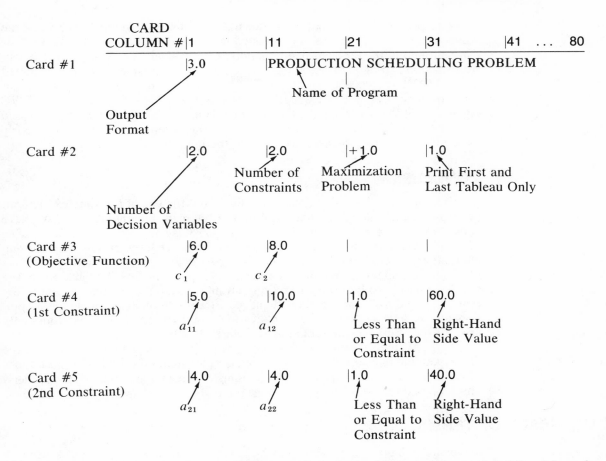

are the same. The computer output final tableau is presented in Fig. 4.5, and corresponds to the final simplex tableau presented in Table 4.3.

Observe that the computer output tableaus do not have a Z_j row, however, the $(c_j - Z_j)$ row is present, and is denoted as "DELTA." The optimal tableau (Fig. 4.5) is listed as "TABLEAU NUMBER 2," and at the bottom of this tableau there is an indication that it is the "FINAL TABLEAU ** OPTIMUM ** SOLUTION." In this optimal tableau, the basic variables are indicated as variables "2" (x_2) and "1" (x_1) listed under the column marked "P(I)."

FIGURE 4.5 COMPUTER OUTPUT-FINAL TABLEAU
                    PRODUCTION SCHEDULING PROBLEM
TABLEAU NUMBER 2   VALUE = 6.4000000E+01

         2 DECISION VARIABLES   2 CONSTRAINTS   THE OBJECT IS TO MAXIMIZE VALUE OF OBJECTIVE FUNCTION

      P(I)   1   2   3   4

        2   0.0   1.000E+00 2.000E-01 -2.500E-01 2.000E+00
        1   1.000E+00   0.0   -2.000E-01 5.000E-01 8.000E+00

   REAL VAR. C(J) 6.00000   8.00000   0.0   0.0

      SOLUTION   8.0000E+00 2.0000E+00 0.0   0.0

      DELTA   0.0   0.0   -4.000E-01 -1.000E+00

FINAL TABLEAU   **OPTIMUM** SOLUTION

FIGURE 4.5 Computer Output—Final Tableau

Interpreting this final output we see that the value of variable $x_1 = 8.0$ and the value of $x_2 = 2.0$. These values are listed in the row marked "SOLUTION," or can be found in the far-right-hand column of the tableau. The value of the objective function is found at the top-right-hand corner of the tableau and is designated as "VALUE = 6.4000000E+01" or $Z = 64$. Below this is an indication that for this problem: "THE OBJECT IS TO MAXIMIZE VALUE OF OBJECTIVE FUNCTION." Observe finally that all of the numbers in the tableau are expressed in scientific notation, and the user must use this scientific notation to properly assign the respective decimal positions in the numbers.

4.9 CONCLUSION

In this chapter we have developed and illustrated the use of the simplex method, perhaps the most powerful analytical tool of the management scientist. We have shown that the simplex method is an organized, systematic means for solving linear programming problems that embodies the procedures of the Gauss-Jordan elimination process to perform elementary row operations as we move from one basic feasible solution to another in the search for optimality. Applications of the simplex method to both maximization and minimization problems, having "less than," "equal to," and "greater than" constraints, have been presented. Additionally, we have reviewed the complications and their resolution that commonly arise in real world linear programming work. Finally, we have summarized the four types of solutions that can arise in linear programming and have discussed the corresponding indication provided by the simplex method for each of these types of solutions. To strengthen an understanding of the simplex method, the reader's attention is directed to the problems at the end of this chapter.

GLOSSARY OF TERMS

Artificial Variable A variable that has no physical meaning, which is used to obtain an initial basic feasible solution to a linear programming problem.

Basis The set of m basic variables that comprises a basic feasible solution to a linear programming problem.

Basis Matrix The matrix formed by the column vectors that correspond to the basic variables. The basis matrix will be a $(m \times m)$ identity matrix at each iteration of the simplex method.

Batch Programming Package A computer programming package that requires the user to prepare the input in advance, usually on a set of punched cards.

Cycling A situation in which the simplex method goes round in a loop repeating the same sequence of basic feasible solutions without ever reaching the optimal basic feasible solution.

Degeneracy A condition that occurs when there is a tie for leaving the basis between two variables, the result being that the variable remaining basic is driven to zero as pivoting is implemented.

Iterating Changing the basis, inserting one of the current nonbasic variables into the basis and removing one of the current basic variables.

Pivot Column A column of the simplex tableau associated with the variable selected for entry into the basis at a given iteration.

Pivot Element The element in the simplex tableau at the intersection of the pivot column and the pivot row.

Pivoting Performing Gauss-Jordan row operations on the rows of the simplex tableau to solve the system of constraint equations in terms of the new set of basic variables.

Pivot Row A row of the simplex tableau that corresponds to the variable selected for removal from the basis at a particular iteration.

Simplex An n-dimensional convex figure that has exactly $n + 1$ extreme points.

Simplex Algorithm or **Simplex Method** A structured method for solving linear programming problems which involves moving from one basic feasible solution to another, always maintaining or improving the objective function, until an optimal solution is obtained.

Simplex Tableau Setting up the linear programming problem in a tabular form, such that the simplex algorithm can be applied.

Slack Variable A variable used to convert a "less than or equal to" constraint into an equality constraint by adding it to the left-hand side of the original constraint.

Surplus Variable A variable used to convert a "greater than or equal to" constraint into an equality constraint by subtracting it from the left-hand side of the original constraint.

Time-Shared or Interactive Programming Package A computer programming package where the user provides input and receives output via a remote terminal (e.g., CRT) and the data is submitted directly through the terminal.

Unconstrained Variable A variable that is unconstrained in sign and thus can be positive, negative, or zero.

Variable Entry Criterion A criterion that determines which variable will enter the basis in a given iteration of the simplex method.

Variable Removal Criterion A criterion that determines which variable will leave the basis in a given iteration of the simplex method.

SELECTED REFERENCES

THE SIMPLEX METHOD Refer to those references provided at the end of Chapter 3, "An Introduction to Linear Programming."

DISCUSSION QUESTIONS

1. Why are "slack variables" used in the simplex method?
2. How does the simplex method move from one extreme point to another?
3. How are the basic variables in the first iteration of the simplex method determined?
4. Is the rule of selecting the variable to enter the basis as being the variable with the largest $c_j - Z_j$ value "always" going to increase the objective function by the largest amount at that particular iteration? If not, why not?
5. Explain the reasoning behind the rule that determines which variable is chosen to leave the basis at a particular iteration?
6. What does the Gauss-Jordan elimination procedure do at a particular iteration in the simplex method?
7. How do you determine when you have obtained the optimal solution?
8. Why must the basis matrix (the matrix formed by the column vectors that correspond to the current basic variables) always form an identity matrix within the simplex tableau?
9. Why must the pivot column corresponding to the entering variable in a particular

iteration of the simplex method have a "one" as the pivot element and zeroes in all other positions?

10. By performing different iterations in the simplex method could you obtain the same basis twice? Why or why not?

11. What happens to the entry and removal criteria if you have to deal with a minimization instead of a maximization problem?

12. What is the difference between an artificial and a surplus variable?

13. Why are artificial variables used, what do they do, and what are their implications on the simplex method?

14. Can an artificial variable ever appear in the final (optimal) tableau as a basic variable? Why or why not?

15. Why can't you have negative right-hand sides in the initial simplex tableau?

16. With respect to the number of calculations, does it matter which variable you choose when there is a tie between two or more variables for entering the basis?

17. How does a tie for leaving basic variable cause degeneracy?

18. How are multiple optimal solutions indicated in a final tableau?

19. How can you determine from the final tableau that you have an unbounded solution?

20. How does the final tableau indicate a nonfeasible solution?

PROBLEM SET

1. Solve the following linear programming problem by determining the value of the objective function for all basic solutions to the problem.

$$\text{Maximize } Z = 3x_1 - 1x_2$$

subject to: $4x_1 + 2x_2 \leq 8$
$3x_1 + 1x_2 \leq 10$

with $x_1 \geq 0, x_2 \geq 0$

2. Solve the following linear programming problem by determining the value of the objective function for all basic solutions to the problem.

$$\text{Maximize } Z = 1x_1 + 2x_2$$

subject to: $2x_1 - 3x_2 \leq 7$
$1x_1 + 2x_2 \leq 10$

with $x_1 \geq 0, x_2 \geq 0$

3. Solve the following linear programming problem by determining the value of the objective function for all basic solutions to the problem.

$$\text{Maximize } Z = 5x_1 - 3x_2$$

subject to: $7x_1 + 3x_2 \leq 16$
$4x_1 + 2x_2 \leq 20$

with $x_1 \geq 0, x_2 \geq 0$

4. Solve the following problem by determining the value of the objective function for all basic solutions to the problem.

$$\text{Maximize } Z = 3x_1 + 5x_2$$

subject to: $2x_1 + 3x_2 \le 90$
$4x_1 + 3x_2 \le 60$

with $x_1 \ge 0, x_2 \ge 0$

5. Solve the following problem by determining the value of the objective function for all basic solutions to the problem.

$$\text{Maximize } Z = 3x_1 + 5x_2$$

subject to: $x_1 \qquad \le 12$
$x_2 \le 12$
$x_1 + x_2 \le 14$

with $x_1 \le 0, x_2 \le 0$

6. Solve the following problem by determining the value of the objective function for all basic solutions to the problem.

$$\text{Minimize } Z = 3x_1 + 7x_2$$

subject to: $2x_1 + 5x_2 \ge 10$
$3x_1 + 1x_2 \ge 8$

with $x_1 \ge 0, x_2 \ge 0$

7. Solve the following problem by determining the value of the objective function for all basic solutions to the problem.

$$\text{Minimize } Z = 2x_1 + 5x_2$$

subject to: $4x_1 + 4x_2 \ge 20$
$3x_1 + 8x_2 \ge 24$

with $x_1 \ge 0, x_2 \ge 0$

8. Solve the following problem by determining the value of the objective function for all basic solutions to the problem.

$$\text{Minimize } Z = 4x_1 + 2x_2$$

subject to: $5x_1 + 2x_2 \ge 10$
$2x_1 + 2x_2 \ge 12$
$1x_1 + 6x_2 \ge 12$

with $x_1 \ge 0, x_2 \ge 0$

9. Solve the following problem by determining the value of the objective function for all basic solutions to the problem.

$$\text{Minimize } Z = 3x_1 + 5x_2 + 1x_3$$

subject to: $8x_1 + 2x_2 + 4x_3 \ge 6$
$6x_1 + 3x_2 - 1x_3 \ge 9$

with $x_1 \ge 0, x_2 \ge 0, x_3 \ge 0$

10. Solve the following problem by determining the value of the objective function for all basic solutions to the problem.

$$\text{Minimize } Z = 2x_1 + 6x_2 + 3x_3$$

subject to: $7x_1 + 3x_2 + 5x_3 \geq 9$
$2x_1 + 4x_2 - 1x_3 \leq 11$

with $x_1 \geq 0, x_2 \geq 0, x_3 \geq 0$

11. Solve Problem 1, using the Gauss-Jordan elimination procedure (algebraic approach).

12. Solve Problem 2, using the Gauss-Jordan elimination procedure (algebraic approach).

13. Solve Problem 3, using the Gauss-Jordan elimination procedure (algebraic approach).

14. Solve Problem 4, using the Gauss-Jordan elimination procedure (algebraic approach).

15. Solve Problem 5, using the Gauss-Jordan elimination procedure (algebraic approach).

16. Solve Problem 1, using the simplex algorithm.

17. Solve Problem 2, using the simplex algorithm.

18. Solve Problem 3, using the simplex algorithm.

19. Solve Problem 4, using the simplex algorithm.

20. Solve Problem 5, using the simplex algorithm.

21. Solve Problem 6, using the simplex algorithm.

22. Solve Problem 7, using the simplex algorithm.

23. Solve Problem 8, using the simplex algorithm.

24. Solve Problem 9, using the simplex algorithm.

25. Solve Problem 10, using the simplex algorithm.

26. Solve the following linear programming problem, using the simplex algorithm.

$$\text{Maximize } Z = 2x_1 - 1x_2 + 5x_3$$

subject to: $3x_1 \qquad - 2x_3 \leq 16$
$2x_1 + 5x_2 \qquad \leq 10$
$3x_2 + 1x_3 \leq 12$

with $x_1, x_2, x_3 \geq 0.$

27. Solve the following problem, using the simplex algorithm.

$$\text{Minimize } Z = 4x_1 + 3x_2 + 2x_3$$

subject to: $4x_1 + 1x_2 + 1x_3 \geq 10$
$3x_1 \qquad - 1x_3 \leq 4$
$2x_1 + 2x_2 - 8x_3 \leq 3$

with $x_1 \geq 0, x_2 \geq 0, x_3 \geq 0$

28. Solve the following linear programming problem, using the simplex algorithm.

$$\text{Maximize } Z = 4x_1 + 2x_2$$

subject to:
$$3x_1 + 2x_2 \leq 8$$
$$-4x_1 + 3x_2 \geq -7$$
$$7x_1 + 2x_2 = 14$$

with $x_1 \geq 0, x_2 \geq 0.$

29. Solve the following linear programming problem, using the simplex algorithm.

$$\text{Minimize } Z = 2x_1 + 5x_2 + 3x_3$$

subject to:
$$9x_1 - 3x_2 + 2x_3 = 4$$
$$-3x_1 + 4x_2 - x_3 \geq 10$$
$$5x_1 + 3x_3 \leq 9$$

with $x_1, x_2, x_3 \geq 0.$

30. Solve the following linear programming problem, using the simplex algorithm.

$$\text{Minimize } Z = 5x_1 + 4x_2$$

subject to:
$$6x_1 + 3x_2 \geq 18$$
$$2x_1 + 4x_2 \geq 12$$
$$2x_1 + 8x_2 \geq 16$$

with $x_1 \geq 0, x_2 \geq 0$

31. Solve the following problem using the simplex algorithm.

$$\text{Minimize } Z = 12x_1 - 20x_2 + 14x_3$$

subject to:
$$5x_1 - 3x_2 + 3x_3 \geq 80$$
$$3x_1 + 2x_2 + 6x_3 \leq 120$$

with $x_1 \geq 0, x_2 \geq 0, x_3 \geq 0$

32. Solve the following problem, using the simplex algorithm.

$$\text{Maximize } Z = 4x_1 + 2x_2 + 5x_3$$

subject to:
$$2x_1 + 4x_2 + 5x_3 \leq 24$$
$$1x_1 + 1x_2 + 2x_3 \leq 14$$

with $x_1 \geq 0, x_2 \geq 0, x_3 \geq 0$

33. Solve the following problem, using the simplex algorithm.

$$\text{Minimize } Z = 10x_1 + 20x_2$$

subject to:
$$30x_1 + 60x_2 \geq 600$$
$$-8x_1 + 16x_2 \leq -48$$
$$20x_1 + 30x_2 = 480$$

with $x_1 \geq 0, x_2 \geq 0$

34. Consider the following linear programming problem.

$$\text{Maximize } Z = 3x_1 + 4x_2 + 6x_3$$

subject to: $2x_1 + 3x_2 \qquad \le 30$
$5x_1 + 2x_2 + 3x_3 = 40$
$8x_1 + \qquad 10x_3 \ge 40$

with $x_1, x_2 \ge 0, x_3$ unconstrained in sign.

(a) Reformulate the problem in standard linear programming format.
(b) Construct the complete first simplex tableau and identify the corresponding initial basic feasible solution.
(c) Perform two iterations, using the simplex algorithm.

35.   Consider the following linear programming problem.

$$\text{Minimize } Z = 9x_1 + 7x_2 + 11x_3 - 1x_4$$

subject to: $5x_1 + 3x_2 + 4x_3 + 7x_4 \ge 21$
$3x_1 + 1x_2 + 2x_3 + 9x_4 = 30$
$1x_1 - 2x_2 - 1x_3 - 3x_4 \le -12$

with $x_1, x_2, x_3 \ge 0, x_4$ unconstrained in sign.

(a) Reformulate the problem in standard linear programming format.
(b) Construct the complete first simplex tableau and identify the corresponding initial basic feasible solution.
(c) Perform two iterations, using the simplex algorithm.

36.   Consider the following linear programming problem.

$$\text{Minimize } Z = 1x_1 - 3x_2 + 3x_3$$

subject to: $2x_1 - 1x_2 - 1x_3 \le -18$
$1x_1 + 1x_2 + 3x_3 \ge 36$
$-1x_1 + 3x_2 + 1x_3 = 24$

with $x_1 \ge 0, x_2 \ge 0, x_3 \ge 0$

(a) Reformulate the problem in standard linear programming format.
(b) Construct the complete first simplex tableau and identify the corresponding initial basic feasible solution.
(c) Perform two iterations, using the simplex algorithm.

37.   Consider the following linear programming problem.

$$\text{Minimize } Z = 2x_1 - 5x_2 + 3x_3$$

subject to: $3x_1 + 10x_2 + 5x_3 = 15$
$33x_1 - 10x_2 - 9x_3 \ge 12$
$x_1 + 2x_2 + x_3 \ge 4$

with $x_1 \ge 0, x_2 \ge 0, x_3 \ge 0$

(a) Reformulate the problem in standard linear programming format.
(b) Construct the complete first simplex tableau and identify the corresponding initial basic feasible solution.
(c) Perform two iterations, using the simplex algorithm.

38. Consider the following linear programming problem.

$$\text{Minimize } Z = 2x_1 - 1x_2 + 4x_3 - 3x_4$$

subject to:
$$1x_1 + 2x_2 + 4x_3 + 2x_4 = 8$$
$$1x_2 + 3x_4 \leq 10$$
$$-1x_1 - 1x_3 + 2x_4 \geq -5$$
$$5 \leq 2x_1 + 4x_2 - 3x_3 + 1x_4 \leq 15$$

with $x_1, x_2, x_3 \geq 0$, x_4 unconstrained in sign.

(a) Reformulate this problem in standard linear programming format.
(b) Construct the complete first simplex tableau and identify the corresponding initial basic feasible solution.
(c) Perform two iterations, using the simplex algorithm.

39. Consider the following linear programming problem.

$$\text{Maximize } Z = 5x_1 + 10x_2$$

subject to:
$$5x_1 + 10x_2 \leq 60$$
$$4x_1 + 4x_2 \leq 40$$
$$5x_1 \leq 40$$

with $x_1 \geq 0, x_2 \geq 0$.

Use the simplex algorithm to show that this problem has alternative optimal solutions.

40. Consider the following linear programming problem.

$$\text{Maximize } Z = 6x_1 + 3x_2$$

subject to:
$$2x_1 + 1x_2 \leq 8$$
$$3x_1 + 3x_2 \leq 18$$
$$1x_2 \leq 3$$

with $x_1 \geq 0, x_2 \geq 0$

Use the simplex algorithm to show that this problem has alternative optimal solutions.

41. Consider the following linear programming problem.

$$\text{Minimize } Z = 6x_1 + 12x_2$$

subject to:
$$6x_1 + 3x_2 \geq 18$$
$$2x_1 + 4x_2 \geq 12$$
$$2x_1 + 8x_2 \geq 16$$

with $x_1 \geq 0, x_2 \geq 0$

Use the simplex algorithm to show that this problem has alternative optimal solutions.

42. Consider the following linear programming problem.

$$\text{Minimize } Z = 2x_1 + 8x_2$$

subject to:
$$5x_1 + 1x_2 \geq 10$$
$$2x_1 + 2x_2 \geq 14$$
$$1x_1 + 4x_2 \geq 12$$

with $x_1 \geq 0, x_2 \geq 0$

Use the simplex algorithm to show that this problem has alternative optimal solutions.

43.   Consider the following linear programming problem.

$$\text{Minimize } Z = 2x_1 + 2x_2$$

subject to:
$$4x_1 + 4x_2 \geq 24$$
$$7x_1 + 1x_2 \geq 14$$
$$x_1 \quad\quad \leq 5$$

with $x_1 \geq 0, x_2 \geq 0$

Use the simplex algorithm to show that this problem has alternative optimal solutions.

44.   Consider the following linear programming problem.

$$\text{Maximize } Z = 3x_1 - 2x_2$$

subject to:
$$2x_1 - 1x_2 \leq 10$$
$$6x_1 - 4x_2 \leq 7$$

with $x_1 \geq 0, x_2 \geq 0$

Use the simplex algorithm to show that this problem has alternative optimal solutions.

45.   Consider the following linear programming problem.

$$\text{Maximize } Z = 2x_1 + 1x_2$$

subject to:
$$1x_2 \leq 5$$
$$1x_1 - 1x_2 \geq -1$$

with $x_1 \geq 0, x_2 \geq 0$

Use the simplex algorithm to show that this problem has an unbounded solution.

46.   Consider the following linear programming problem.

$$\text{Maximize } Z = -2x_1 + 3x_2$$

subject to:
$$x_1 \quad\quad \leq 5$$
$$2x_1 - 3x_2 \leq 6$$

with $x_1 \geq 0, x_2 \geq 0$

Use the simplex algorithm to show that this problem has an unbounded solution.

47. Consider the following linear programming problem.

$$\text{Maximize } Z = 1x_1 + 4x_2$$

subject to: $-1x_1 + 2x_2 \le 14$
$-2x_1 + 1x_2 \le 2$

with $x_1 \ge 0, x_2 \ge 0$

Use the simplex algorithm to show that this problem has an unbounded solution.

48. Consider the following linear programming problem.

$$\text{Maximize } Z = 3x_1 + 1x_2$$

subject to: $2x_1 + 5x_2 \ge 10$
$3x_1 + 1x_2 \ge 6$

with $x_1 \ge 0, x_2 \ge 0$

Use the simplex algorithm to show that this problem has an unbounded solution.

49. Consider the following linear programming problem.

$$\text{Minimize } Z = 2x_1 - 5x_2 + 3x_3$$

subject to: $3x_1 + 10x_2 + 5x_3 = 15$
$33x_1 - 10x_2 - 9x_3 \ge 12$
$1x_1 + 2x_2 + 1x_3 \ge 4$

with $x_1 \ge 0, x_2 \ge 0, x_3$ unconstrained in sign

Use the simplex algorithm to show that this problem has an unbounded solution.

50. Consider the following linear programming problem.

$$\text{Maximize } Z = 4x_1 - 3x_2 + 5x_3 + 2x_4$$

subject to: $1x_1 + 5x_2 + 9x_3 - 6x_4 \ge -2$
$3x_1 - 1x_2 + 1x_3 + 3x_4 \le 10$
$-2x_1 - 3x_2 + 7x_3 - 8x_4 \ge 0$

with $x_1 \ge 0, x_2 \ge 0, x_3 \ge 0, x_4 \ge 0$

Use the simplex algorithm to show that this problem has an unbounded solution.

51. Consider the following linear programming problem.

$$\text{Maximize } Z = -3x_1 - 2x_2$$

subject to: $1x_1 + 2x_2 \le 2$
$2x_1 + 4x_2 \ge 8$

with $x_1 \ge 0, x_2 \ge 0$

Use the simplex algorithm to show that this problem has no feasible solution.

52. Consider the following linear programming problem.

$$\text{Maximize } Z = 2x_1 + 3x_2$$

subject to:
$$
\begin{aligned}
1x_1 - 1x_2 &\ge 4 \\
1x_1 + 1x_2 &\le 6 \\
1x_1 &\le 2
\end{aligned}
$$

with $x_1 \ge 0, x_2 \ge 0$

Use the simplex algorithm to show that this problem has no feasible solution.

53. Consider the following linear programming problem.

$$\text{Maximize } Z = 3x_1 + 5x_2$$

subject to:
$$
\begin{aligned}
4x_1 + 4x_2 &\le 20 \\
7x_1 + 3x_2 &\le 21 \\
x_1 &\ge 5
\end{aligned}
$$

with $x_1 \ge 0, x_2 \ge 0$

Use the simplex algorithm to show that this problem has no feasible solution.

54. Consider the following linear programming problem.

$$\text{Maximize } Z = x_1 + 3x_2$$

subject to:
$$
\begin{aligned}
x_1 - x_2 &\ge 1 \\
3x_1 - 1x_2 &\le -3
\end{aligned}
$$

with $x_1 \ge 0, x_2 \ge 0$

Use the simplex algorithm to show that this problem has no feasible solution.

55. Consider the following linear programming problem.

$$\text{Minimize } Z = x_1 + 2x_2$$

subject to:
$$
\begin{aligned}
x_1 + x_2 &\le 3 \\
-x_1 + x_2 &\ge 6
\end{aligned}
$$

with $x_1 \ge 0, x_2 \ge 0$

Use the simplex algorithm to show that this problem has no feasible solution.

56. Consider the following linear programming problem.

$$\text{Maximize } Z = 3x_1 + 7x_2$$

subject to:
$$
\begin{aligned}
1x_1 - 1x_2 &\ge 0 \\
3x_1 - 1x_2 &\le -5
\end{aligned}
$$

with $x_1 \ge 0, x_2 \ge 0$

Use the simplex algorithm to show that this problem has no feasible solution.

The following problems are larger, in terms of the number of constraints and variables that those preceding. Thus, they are generally rather time consuming and difficult to solve by hand. It is recommended that a computer code, such as that included at the back of the Instructor's Manual, be used for obtaining solutions for the following problems.

57. Solve the following linear programming problem.

$$\text{Maximum } Z = 5x_1 + 1x_2 + 2x_3 + 3x_4 - 1x_5 + 7x_6$$

subject to:

$$1x_1 + 3x_2 + 2x_3 \leq 20$$
$$2x_5 - 1x_6 \leq 15$$
$$2x_1 - 1x_2 + 5x_3 + 1x_4 + 2x_5 + 1x_6 \leq 10$$
$$3 \leq x_4 \leq 9$$
$$x_5 + 3x_6 \leq 25$$
$$5x_1 - 1x_3 \leq 20$$
$$3x_1 + 1x_2 + 2x_4 + 3x_6 \leq 60$$
$$- 1x_1 + 2x_2 + 1x_3 \geq 10$$

with $x_1 \geq 0, x_2 \geq 0, x_3 \geq 0, x_4 \geq 0, x_5 \geq 0, x_6 \geq 0$

58. Solve the linear programming formulation you determined for Problem 3–16. (All of the following problems are based on the "Problem Set" section of Chapter 3.)

59. Solve the linear programming formulation you determined for Problem 3-17.

60. Solve the linear programming formulation you determined for Problem 3-18.

61. Solve the linear programming formulation you determined for Problem 3-19.

62. Solve the linear programming formulation you determined for Problem 3-20.

63. Solve the linear programming formulation you determined for Problem 3-21.

64. Solve the linear programming formulation you determined for Problem 3-22.

65. Solve the linear programming formulation you determined for Problem 3-23.

66. Solve the linear programming formulation you determined for Problem 3-24.

67. Solve the linear programming formulation you determined for Problem 3-25.

68. Solve the linear programming formulation you determined for Problem 3-26.

69. Solve the linear programming formulation you determined for Problem 3-27.

70. Solve the linear programming formulation you determined for Problem 3-28.

71. Solve the linear programming formulation you determined for Problem 3-29.

72. Solve the linear programming formulation you determined for Problem 3-30.

73. Solve the linear programming formulation you determined for Problem 3-31.

74. Solve the linear programming formulation you determined for Problem 3-32.

75. Solve the linear programming formulation you determined for Problem 3-33.

76. Solve the linear programming formulation you determined for Problem 3-34.

77. Solve the linear programming formulation you determined for Problem 3-35.

78. Solve the linear programming formulation you determined for Problem 3-36.

79. Solve the linear programming formulation you determined for Problem 3-37.

80. Solve the linear programming formulation you determined for Problem 3-38.

81. Solve the linear programming formulation you determined for Problem 3-39.

82. Solve the linear programming formulation you determined for Problem 3-40.

83. Solve the linear programming formulation you determined for Problem 3-41.

84. Solve the linear programming formulation you determined for Problem 3-42.

85.   Solve the linear programming formulation you determined for Problem 3-43.

86.   Solve the linear programming formulation you determined for Problem 3-44.

87.   Solve the linear programming formulation you determined for Problem 3-45.

88.   Solve the linear programming formulation you determined for Problem 3-46.

89.   Solve the linear programming formulation you determined for Problem 3-47.

90.   Solve the linear programming formulation you determined for Problem 3-48.

91.   Solve the linear programming formulation you determined for Problem 3-49.

92.   Solve the linear programming formulation you determined for Problem 3-50.

93.   Solve the linear programming formulation you determined for Problem 3-51.

94.   Solve the linear programming formulation you determined for Problem 3-52.

95.   Solve the linear programming formulation you determined for Problem 3-53.

96.   Solve the linear programming formulation you determined for Problem 3-54.

97.   Solve the linear programming formulation you determined for Problem 3-55.

Duality Theory and Sensitivity Analysis

5.1 INTRODUCTION

One of the most important concepts in linear programming is that of **duality theory**. It is of importance for several reasons. First, duality theory serves as a unifying concept that enables the manager to explore the interrelationships between a given linear programming problem (often called the *primal* problem) and a related linear programming problem (often called the *dual* problem). Second, an understanding of duality theory greatly enhances the general understanding of the structure of linear programming problems, particularly with respect to their economic ramifications. Third, duality theory provides the basis for the reformulation of linear programming problems, and such reformulation may allow for computational efficiencies for certain problems. Fourth, duality theory forms the foundation for the construction of several other linear programming algorithms, such as the **dual simplex algorithm**, which will be used in this chapter and in solving integer programming problems, and the modified distribution algorithm, which will be used to solve transportation problems. Finally, duality theory is utilized in the development of various sensitivity analysis techniques for linear programming.

The experienced management science practitioner usually is interested in a great deal more than simply the numerical values of the optimal linear programming solution. More often, the management scientist is concerned with examining the effect of changes in certain parameters of the linear programming problem upon the problem's optimal solution. Such an investigation is called **sensitivity analysis** or **postoptimality analysis**. Sensitivity analysis commonly concerns the following types of situations.

1. Changes in the coefficients of the objective function.
2. Changes in the right-hand side values of the constraint set.
3. Addition of a constraint (row) to the linear programming problem.
4. Addition of a variable (column) to the linear programming problem.

Both duality theory and sensitivity analysis will be discussed in detail in this chapter.

5.2 DUALITY THEORY

To initiate our discussion of duality theory we begin with the assumption that the *primal* linear programming problem can be stated in *standard form* as follows.

Primal Problem—Standard Form

$$\text{Maximize } Z_x = c_1 x_1 + c_2 x_2 + \cdots + c_n x_n \tag{5-1}$$

subject to:
$$
\begin{aligned}
a_{11} x_1 + a_{12} x_2 + \cdots + a_{1n} x_n &\leq b_1 \\
a_{21} x_1 + a_{22} x_2 + \cdots + a_{2n} x_n &\leq b_2 \\
&\ \ \vdots \\
a_{m1} x_1 + a_{m2} x_2 + \cdots + a_{mn} x_n &\leq b_m
\end{aligned}
\tag{5-2}
$$

with $\quad x_j \geq 0; \ j = 1, 2, \ldots, n \tag{5-3}$

This primal problem has an associated *dual* linear programming problem that can be stated in *standard form* as follows.

Dual Problem—Standard Form

$$\text{Minimize } Z_y = b_1 y_1 + b_2 y_2 + \cdots + b_m y_m \tag{5-4}$$

subject to:
$$
\begin{aligned}
a_{11} y_1 + a_{21} y_2 + \cdots + a_{m1} y_m &\geq c_1 \\
a_{12} y_1 + a_{22} y_2 + \cdots + a_{m2} y_m &\geq c_2 \\
&\ \ \vdots \\
a_{1n} y_1 + a_{2n} y_2 + \cdots + a_{mn} y_m &\geq c_n
\end{aligned}
\tag{5-5}
$$

with $y_i \geq 0; \ i = 1, 2, \ldots, m \tag{5-6}$

It should be mentioned that the problem formulation given by (5–1), (5–2), and (5–3) is commonly referred to as the **primal problem** of linear programming, and the problem formulation given by (5–4), (5–5), and (5–6) is typically referred to as the **dual problem** of linear programming. These names, while commonly employed, are arbitrary in nature.

At this point we should carefully note the following relationships between the primal problem and the dual problem.

1. The objective function is maximized in the primal problem and minimized in the dual problem.
2. The objective function coefficients in the dual problem are the right-hand side values in the primal problem. Similarly, the right-hand side values in the dual problem are the objective function coefficients in the primal problem.
3. The coefficients of the dual constraints are the same as those of the primal constraints, but with row and column coefficients interchanged. Thus, the coefficients of row $i = k$ in the primal problem become the coefficients of column $j = k$ in the dual problem.
4. The primal problem concerns a set of "less than or equal to" constraints while the dual problem concerns a set of "greater than or equal to" constraints.
5. For each variable in the primal problem there is a corresponding dual constraint. For each constraint in the primal problem there is a corresponding dual variable.

The correspondence between the primal problem and the dual problem is further illustrated in Fig. 5.1.

In this figure, the horizontal headings refer to the primal problem, and the vertical headings refer to the dual problem. Note that the coefficients of the objective function for either of these two problems are the right-hand side values for the other problem. Also, the row coefficients for the primal problem become the column coefficients for the dual problem. Finally, we maximize in the primal problem and minimize in the dual problem.

To numerically illustrate a primal problem and its corresponding dual problem, let us once again consider our production scheduling example.

		Primal Problem (Maximize $Z_x = c_1 x_1 + c_2 x_2 + \cdots + c_n x_n$)					
		Coefficient of				Right-Hand Side	
		x_1	x_2	$\cdots$	x_n		
Dual Problem (Minimize $Z_y = b_1 y_1 + b_2 y_2 + \cdots + b_m y_m$) — Coefficient of	y_1	a_{11}	a_{12}	$\cdots$	a_{1n}	$\leq b_1$	Coefficient of dual objective function (minimize)
	y_2	a_{21}	a_{22}	$\cdots$	a_{2n}	$\leq b_2$	
	$\vdots$	$\vdots$	$\vdots$	$\ddots$	$\vdots$	$\vdots$	
	y_m	a_{m1}	a_{m2}	$\cdots$	a_{mn}	$\leq b_m$	
Right-Hand Side		$\geq c_1$	$\geq c_2$	$\cdots$	$\geq c_n$		
		Coefficients of primal objective function (maximize)					

FIGURE 5.1 Primal-Dual Relationships

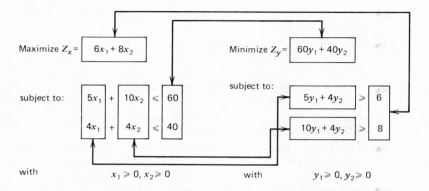

In this numerical example, the relationships between the two problems have been indicated by means of connecting arrows. The primal problem has two constraints and two decision variables. Likewise, the dual problem will have two decision variables and two constraints.

Substituting the parameters for the example into the format summarized in Fig. 5.1 yields Fig. 5.2 (explanatory headings have been deleted).

	x_1	x_2	
y_1	5	10	≤ 60
y_2	4	4	≤ 40
	≥ 6	≥ 8	

FIGURE 5.2   **Numerical Illustration of Primal-Dual Relationships**

5.2.1   The Dual Theorem of Linear Programming

The dual theorem of linear programming can be stated as follows.

DUAL THEOREM

1. *If x_j; $j = 1, 2, \ldots, n$ is a feasible solution for the primal problem and y_i; $i = 1, 2, \ldots, m$ is a feasible solution for the dual problem, then:*

$$Z_x = \sum_{j=1}^{n} c_j x_j \leq \sum_{i=1}^{m} b_i y_i = Z_y \tag{5-7}$$

2. *If both the primal and dual problems have feasible solutions, then the primal problem has an optimal solution x_j^*; $j = 1, 2, \ldots, n$ and the dual problem has an optimal solution y_i^*; $i = 1, 2, \ldots, m$, such that:*

$$Z_x^* = \sum_{j=1}^{n} c_j x_j^* = \sum_{i=1}^{m} b_i y_i^* = Z_y^* \tag{5-8}$$

To illustrate the meaning of the dual theorem, let x_j satisfy the primal constraints, and let y_i satisfy the dual constraints. Next, multiply the ith constraint in the primal problem by y_i, and add all the resultant constraints in the primal:

$$\sum_{i=1}^{m} y_i \left(\sum_{j=1}^{n} a_{ij} x_j \right) \leq \sum_{i=1}^{m} b_i y_i \qquad (5\text{-}9)$$

Then, multiply the jth constraint in the dual problem by x_j, and add all the resultant constraints in the dual:

$$\sum_{j=1}^{n} x_j \left(\sum_{i=1}^{m} a_{ij} y_i \right) \geq \sum_{j=1}^{n} c_j x_j \qquad (5\text{-}10)$$

Since $y_i \geq 0$ and $x_j \geq 0$, and we are adding like-direction inequalities, the direction of the two sets of inequalities does not change.

Now, the quantities on the left-hand sides of (5–9) and (5–10) are identical. Therefore, we can state:

$$\sum_{j=1}^{n} c_j x_j \leq \sum_{i=1}^{m} b_i y_i \qquad (5\text{-}11)$$

We have shown that the value of the objective function for a feasible solution to either the primal or the dual problem provides a bound, or limit, on the objective function value in the other problem for *any* feasible solution, including the optimal feasible solution. For the optimal (feasible) solution (5–11) will hold as a strict equality.

To illustrate numerically the dual theorem consider the example shown previously in section 5.2. Using the dual theorem, Part 1, given by (5–7) we can state,

$$Z_x = 6x_1 + 8x_2 \leq 60y_1 + 40y_2 = Z_y \qquad (5\text{-}12)$$

for any feasible primal solution and any feasible dual solution. One feasible solution to the primal problem is $x_1 = 0$, $x_2 = 6$, $x_3 = 0$, $x_4 = 16$, Maximum $Z_x = 48$. One feasible solution to the dual problem is $y_1 = 0$, $y_2 = 2$, $y_3 = 2$, $y_4 = 0$, $y_5 = 0$, $y_6 = 0$, Minimum $Z_y = 80$. Thus, by use of the dual theorem we know that the optimum value of the objective function for both the primal problem and the dual problem must lie within the range of $Z_x = 48$ to $Z_y = 80$. Furthermore, the optimal feasible solution to the primal problem is $x_1^* = 8$, $x_2^* = 2$, $x_3^* = 0$, $x_4^* = 0$, Maximum $Z_x^* = 64$. The optimal feasible solution to the dual problem is $y_1^* = \frac{2}{5}$, $y_2^* = 1$, $y_3^* = 0$, $y_4^* = 0$, $y_5^* = 0$, $y_6^* = 0$, Minimum $Z_y^* = 64$. Thus, we have verified that the dual theorem, Part 2, given by (5–8) holds as a strict equality for the optimal (feasible) solutions to the primal and dual problems.

5.2.2 Corollaries to the Dual Theorem

Several important corollaries to the dual theorem of linear programming can also be stated. One of the most interesting of these corollaries deals with the property known as **complementary slackness**.

COROLLARY 1 (Complementary Slackness.) *Let x_j^*, for $j = 1, 2, \ldots, n$, and y_i^*, for $i = 1, 2, \ldots, m$, be the corresponding basic feasible solutions to the primal problem and the dual problem, respectively. Then, the x_j^* and the y_i^* are optimal if, and only if:*

$$y_i^* \left(\sum_{j=1}^{n} a_{ij} x_j^* - b_i \right) = 0 \qquad \text{for } i = 1, 2, \ldots, m \qquad (5\text{-}13)$$

$$x_j^* \left(\sum_{i=1}^{m} a_{ij} y_i^* - c_j \right) = 0 \qquad \text{for } j = 1, 2, \ldots, n \qquad (5\text{-}14)$$

To understand the complementary slackness property it is first necessary to state the important relationships between the primal and dual problems that arise as a result of the direct correspondence between their basic solutions. The association between the variables in the primal problem (assumed to be in standard form) and the dual problem (assumed to be in standard form) can be summarized as follows.[1]

Primal Variable	Associated Dual Variable
(Original decision variable) $x_j; j = 1, 2, \ldots, n$	(Surplus Variable) $y_{m+j}; j = 1, 2, \ldots, n$
(Slack variable) $x_{n+i}; i = 1, 2, \ldots, m$	(Original decision variable) $y_i; i = 1, 2, \ldots, m$

Thus, the first primal decision variable is associated with the first dual surplus variable, the second primal decision variable is associated with the second dual surplus variable, and so forth. Likewise, the first primal slack variable is associated with the first dual decision variable, the second primal slack variable is associated with the second dual decision variable, and so forth.

The complementary slackness property states that each basic feasible solution in the primal problem has a complementary basic feasible solution in the dual problem, with a *complementary slackness* relationship as follows:

Primal Variable	Corresponding Dual Variable
Basic (> 0)	Nonbasic ($= 0$)
Nonbasic ($=0$)	Basic (>0)

Another way of stating the complementary slackness property is to indicate that, whenever a constraint in either one of the problems holds as a strict inequality so that there is slack (or surplus) in the constraint, the corresponding variable in the other problem equals zero. Conversely, whenever a constraint in either one of the problems holds as a strict equality so that there is no slack (or surplus) in the constraint, the corresponding variable in the other problem must be positive.

To illustrate the property of complementary slackness consider our production scheduling problem, which can be written in primal form as:

---

[1] Observe that we do not consider artificial variables in these relationships. Although artificial variables may be required in the dual problem to generate an initial basic feasible solution, they only change the feasible region temporarily and are forced out of the solution as we move towards optimality. Thus, there is no association for artificial variables.

Primal Problem

$$\text{Maximize } Z = 6x_1 + 8x_2 \tag{5-15}$$

subject to:
$$\begin{aligned} 5x_1 + 10x_2 &\leq 60 \\ 4x_1 + 4x_2 &\leq 40 \end{aligned} \tag{5-16}$$

with $x_1 \geq 0, x_2 \geq 0$ $\tag{5-17}$

The optimal solution to this primal problem is $x_1 = 8$, $x_2 = 2$, $x_3 = 0$, and $x_4 = 0$; Maximum $Z = 64$. Substitution of $x_1 = 8$ and $x_2 = 2$ into the two constraints indicates that both would hold as strict equalities so that no slack would be present in either constraint.

The corresponding dual problem is:

Dual Problem

$$\text{Minimize } Z' = 60y_1 + 40y_2 \tag{5-18}$$

subject to:
$$\begin{aligned} 5y_1 + 4y_2 &\geq 6 \\ 10y_1 + 4y_2 &\geq 8 \end{aligned} \tag{5-19}$$

with $y_1 \geq 0, y_2 \geq 0$ $\tag{5-20}$

The optimal solution to this dual problem is $y_1 = {}^2/_5$, $y_2 = 1$, $y_3 = 0$, $y_4 = 0$, $y_5 = 0$, and $y_6 = 0$; Minimum $Z' = 64$. Substitution of $y_1 = {}^2/_5$, $y_2 = 1$ into the two constraints indicates that both would hold as strict equalities so that no surplus would be present in either constraint.

For these two optimal solutions, the following complementary slackness relationships hold:

	Primal Variables		Corresponding Dual Variables	
Basic:	$x_1 = 8$ (First primal decision variable)	Nonbasic:	$y_3 = 0$	(First dual surplus variable)
	$x_2 = 2$ (Second primal decision variable)		$y_5 = 0$	(Second dual surplus variable)
Nonbasic:	$x_3 = 0$ (First primal slack variable)	Basic:	$y_1 = {}^2/_5$	(First dual decision variable)
	$x_4 = 0$ (Second primal slack variable)		$y_2 = 1$	(Second dual decision variable)

In the primal problem, the first and second constraints hold as strict equalities. Therefore, the first and second dual variables y_1 and y_2 must have positive values. In the dual problem, the first and second constraints hold as strict equalities. Consequently, the first and second primal variables x_1 and x_2 must also have positive values. These relationships illustrate complementary slackness.

A second important corollary of the dual theorem of linear programming is the following:

COROLLARY 2   *If the primal problem has an unbounded solution, then the dual problem has no feasible solution.*

To show that this corollary is true, recall that we indicated in our previous discussion of the dual theorem that

$$\sum_{j=1}^{n} c_j x_j \leq \sum_{i=1}^{m} b_i y_i \qquad (5\text{-}21)$$

or   Maximum $Z = \mathbf{c}\,\mathbf{x} \leq \mathbf{b}\,\mathbf{y}$ (5-22)

But our assumption is that the primal problem is unbounded; hence, maximum $Z = \infty$. This means that there is no feasible $\mathbf{y}$ whose components are all finite, and there is no feasible solution to the dual problem.

However, we must be careful not to conclude that, if the primal problem has no feasible solution, then the dual problem will have an unbounded solution. In this case the dual problem may be either unbounded or infeasible. Thus, four combinations of feasibility and infeasibility for the primal and the corresponding dual problems may occur. An example of each of these cases is presented in Table 5.1.

TABLE 5.1   Examples of Primal-Dual Solutions

Example	Primal Solutions	Dual Solutions
Ex. 1	*Primal Feasible* Maximize $Z_x = 3x_1 + 2x_2$ subject to: $2x_1 + 2x_2 \leq 6$ $3x_1 - 1x_2 \leq 4$ with $x_1 \geq 0, x_2 \geq 0$	*Dual Feasible* Minimize $Z_y = 6y_1 + 4y_2$ subject to: $2y_1 + 3y_2 \geq 3$ $2y_1 - 1y_2 \geq 2$ with $y_1 \geq 0, y_2 \geq 0$
Ex. 2	*Primal Feasible and Unbounded* Maximize $Z_x = 3x_1 + 2x_2$ subject to: $2x_1 - 2x_2 \leq 6$ $3x_1 - 1x_2 \leq 4$ with $x_1 \geq 0, x_2 \geq 0$	*Dual Infeasible* Minimize $Z_y = 6y_1 + 4y_2$ subject to: $2y_1 + 3y_2 \geq 3$ $-2y_1 - 1y_2 \geq 2$ with $y_1 \geq 0, y_2 \geq 0$
Ex. 3	*Primal Infeasible* Maximize $Z_x = 3x_1 + 2x_2$ subject to: $-2x_1 - 2x_2 \leq -6$ $3x_1 + 1x_2 \leq 2$ with $x_1 \geq 0, x_2 \geq 0$	*Dual Feasible and Unbounded* Minimize $Z_y = -6y_1 + 2y_2$ subject to: $-2y_1 + 3y_2 \geq 3$ $-2y_1 + 1y_2 \geq 2$ with $y_1 \geq 0, y_2 \geq 0$
Ex. 4	*Primal Infeasible* Maximize $Z_x = 3x_1 + 2x_2$ subject to: $-2x_1 + 2x_2 \leq -6$ $1x_1 - 1x_2 \leq 2$ with $x_1 \geq 0, x_2 \geq 0$	*Dual Infeasible* Minimize $Z_y = -6y_1 + 2y_2$ subject to: $-2y_1 + 1y_2 \geq 3$ $2y_1 - 1y_2 \geq 2$ with $y_1 \geq 0, y_2 \geq 0$

The nature of the solutions to the primal and the corresponding dual problems shown in Table 5.1 can be verified graphically. Additionally, in example 2 of Table 5.1 it is apparent that x_2 may be increased indefinitely without violating the constraints or the nonnegativity conditions, while at the same time the objective function becomes unbounded. The constraints of the dual problem for example 2 are clearly infeasible since the two constraints cannot be satisfied simultaneously. In example 3, the constraints of the primal problem cannot be satisfied simultaneously so it is infeasible. In the corresponding dual problem, both y_1 and y_2 can be simultaneously increased indefinitely without violating the constraints or the non-negativity conditions, while at the same time the objective function becomes unbounded. In example 4, the fact that neither the primal nor the dual problem is feasible can be easily verified by multiplying the first constraint of each problem by negative one.

The primal and dual problems may not always be couched in the standard form indicated by (5-1, 5-2, and 5-3) and (5-4, 5-5, and 5-6). Again, it should be emphasized that the "primal" and "dual" names are arbitrary in nature. Thus, whether in standard primal form or not, any linear programming problem possesses a dual. First, it is always possible to convert a nonstandard form into an equivalent standard primal form. Four such conversions that can be employed are

1. Minimize Z. Convert to maximize $(-Z)$.

2. $\sum_{j=1}^{n} a_{ij}x_j \geq b_i$. Convert to $- \sum_{j=1}^{n} a_{ij}x_j \leq -b_i$.

3. $\sum_{j=1}^{n} a_{ij}x_j = b_i$. Convert to $\sum_{j=1}^{n} a_{ij}x_j \leq b_i$ and $- \sum_{j=1}^{n} a_{ij}x_j \leq -b_i$.

4. x_j unconstrained in sign. Convert to $(x_j' - x_j'')$, with $x_j' \geq 0, x_j'' \geq 0$.

Thus, any nonstandard form can be converted into a standard primal form, and the problem can then be dualized in the usual way.

To illustrate this process let us consider the following dual problem, presented in standard form.

Dual Problem

$$\text{Minimize } Z_y = 7y_1 + 4y_2 + 6y_3 + 5y_4 + 8y_5 \qquad (5\text{-}23)$$

subject to:
$$2y_1 \qquad - 3y_3 + 3y_4 + 5y_5 \geq 3$$
$$3y_2 + 2y_3 + 4y_4 \qquad \geq 4 \qquad (5\text{-}24)$$

with $\quad y_1 \geq 0, y_2 \geq 0, y_3 \geq 0, y_4 \geq 0, y_5 \geq 0 \qquad (5\text{-}25)$

Now, convert this dual problem to the standard form for the primal problem.

Converted Problem

$$\text{Maximize } (-Z_y) = -7y_1 - 4y_2 - 6y_3 - 5y_4 - 8y_5 \qquad (5\text{-}26)$$

subject to:
$$-2y_1 \qquad + 3y_3 - 3y_4 - 5y_5 \leq -3$$
$$- 3y_2 - 2y_3 - 4y_4 \qquad \leq -4 \qquad (5\text{-}27)$$

with $\quad y_1 \geq 0, y_2 \geq 0, y_3 \geq 0, y_4 \geq 0, y_5 \geq 0 \qquad (5\text{-}28)$

Next, dualize this converted problem.

Dualized Problem

$$\text{Minimize } (-Z_x) = -3x_1 - 4x_2 \tag{5-29}$$

subject to:
$$
\begin{aligned}
-2x_1 & & \geq -7 \\
& -3x_2 & \geq -4 \\
+3x_1 & -2x_2 & \geq -6 \\
-3x_1 & -4x_2 & \geq -5 \\
-5x_1 & & \geq -8
\end{aligned}
\tag{5-30}
$$

with $x_1 \geq 0, x_2 \geq 0$ \tag{5-31}

Finally, convert this dualized problem to the standard form of the primal problem.

Primal Problem

$$\text{Maximize } Z_x = 3x_1 + 4x_2 \tag{5-32}$$

subject to:
$$
\begin{aligned}
2x_1 & & \leq 7 \\
& +3x_2 & \leq 4 \\
-3x_1 & +2x_2 & \leq 6 \\
3x_1 & +4x_2 & \leq 5 \\
5x_1 & & \leq 8
\end{aligned}
\tag{5-33}
$$

with $x_1 \geq 0, x_2 \geq 0$ \tag{5-34}

Thus, we have obtained the standard form of the primal problem. This indicates that, for any primal and dual problems, all relationships among them must be symmetrical because the dual of the dual problem is the primal problem.

The illustration presented above did not involve either equality constraints or variables unconstrained in sign. These two situations can be addressed by using two final corollaries to the dual theorem of linear programming. These corollaries are

COROLLARY 3   *If the ith constraint in the primal problem is a strict equality, then the ith dual variable is unrestricted in sign.*

COROLLARY 4   *If some variable x_j in the primal problem is unrestricted in sign, then the jth constraint of the dual problem will be a strict equality.*

To illustrate these two corollaries, consider the following problem.

Primal Problem

$$\text{Maximize } Z_x = 5x_1 + 7x_2 + 4x_3 \tag{5-35}$$

subject to:
$$
\begin{aligned}
3x_1 + 2x_2 + 5x_3 & \leq 6 \\
2x_1 \qquad\; + 4x_3 & \leq 9 \\
- 3x_2 + 1x_3 & = 5
\end{aligned}
\tag{5-36}
$$

with $x_1 \geq 0, x_2 \geq 0, x_3$ unrestricted in sign \tag{5-37}

Using the corollaries presented above, the dual of this problem is

Dual Problem

$$\text{Minimize } Z_y = 6y_1 + 9y_2 + 5y_3 \qquad (5-38)$$

subject to:

$$
\begin{aligned}
3y_1 + 2y_2 \quad\ & \geq 5 \\
2y_1 \quad\ - 3y_3 & \geq 7 \\
5y_1 + 4y_2 + 1y_3 & = 4
\end{aligned}
\qquad (5-39)
$$

with $y_1 \geq 0$, $y_2 \geq 0$, y_3 unrestricted in sign $\qquad (5-40)$

The third constraint in the primal is an equality and the third dual variable y_3 is unrestricted in sign. The third primal variable x_3 is unrestricted in sign and the third dual constraint is an equality.

The various duality relationships can be summarized as follows.

Primal (Maximize)	Dual (Minimize)
Objective Function Coefficients	Right-Hand Side Values
Right-Hand Side Values	Objective Function Coefficients
ith row of coefficients	ith column of coefficients
ith constraint $\leq$	ith variable ≥ 0
ith constraint $\geq$	ith variable ≤ 0
ith constraint $=$	ith variable unrestricted
jth column of coefficients	jth row of coefficients
jth variable ≤ 0	jth constraint $\leq$
jth variable ≥ 0	jth constraint $\geq$
jth variable unrestricted	jth constraint $=$

5.3 ECONOMIC INTERPRETATION OF THE DUAL PROBLEM

As noted earlier, one of the most important uses of the dual concerns the economic interpretation of linear programming problems. To illustrate how the dual is used to analyze the economics of linear programming problems, let us consider the production scheduling problem of Chapter 4. The primal formulation of this problem is as follows.

Primal Problem

	Unknown Level of Activity $j = 1$ (No. of units) $\downarrow$	Unknown Level of Activity $j = 2$ (No. of units) $\downarrow$	
Maximize $Z_x =$	$\$6x_1$ $+$	$\$8x_2$	$(5-41)$
(Total profit from all activities)	$\uparrow$ Unit Profit for Activity $j = 1$ ($\$$ per unit)	$\uparrow$ Unit Profit for Activity $j = 2$ ($\$$ per unit)	

subject to: 5 (hrs per unit)$x_1 + 10$ (hrs per unit)$x_2 \leq 60$ hours $(i = 1)$
                            4 (hrs per unit)$x_1 + 4$ (hrs per unit)$x_2 \leq 40$ hours $(i = 2)$

                            ↑   ↑   ↑   (5–42)
                            Amount of   Amount of   Total Amount
                            Resource i Resource i of Resource i
                            Used in   Used in   Available
                            Activity $j = 1$ Activity $j = 2$

with $x_1 \geq 0,$ $x_2 \geq 0$ (5–43)
            ↑   ↑
            Unknown   Unknown
            Level of   Level of
            Activity $j = 1$ Activity $j = 2$
            (No. of units)   (No. of units)

The corresponding dual problem is as follows.

Dual Problem

                                      Unknown   Unknown
                                      Marginal   Marginal
                                      Value of   Value of
                                      Resource $i = 1$ Resource $i = 2$
                                      ($ per hour)   ($ per hour)
                                            ↓   ↓
            Minimize $Z_y =$ 60 (hours)y_1 $+ 40$ (hours)y_2 (5–44)
                                ↑   ↑   ↑
      (Total value of all resources)   Total Amount of   Total Amount of
                                       Resource $i = 1$ Resource $i = 2$
                                       Available   Available

subject to: 5 (hr)y_1 $+$ 4 (hr)$y_2 \geq \$6$ $(j = 1)$
                            10 (hr)y_1 $+$ 4 (hr)$y_2 \geq \$8$ $(j = 2)$
                                                                                                         (5–45)
                            ↑   ↑   Unit
                            Amount of Resource $i = 1$ Amount of Resource $i = 2$ Profit
                            (Milling Machine) Hours   (Metal Lathe) Hours   for
                            Required for Activity j Required for Activity j Activity j
                                                                                      ($ per unit)

with $y_1 \geq 0,$ $y_2 \geq 0$ (5–46)
            ↑   ↑
            Unknown   Unknown
            Marginal   Marginal
            Value of   Value of
            Resource $i = 1$ Resource $i = 2$
            ($ per hour)   ($ per hour)

In the primal problem we are seeking to allocate quantities of resources to maximize profits. The x_j values in the primal problem are the activity levels (unknown) for activities $j = 1, 2, \ldots, n$. The c_j values in the primal problem are the unit profits associated with activities $j = 1, 2, \ldots, n,$ and the objective function represents the total profit associated with all the activities that are undertaken. The right-hand side values in the primal problem, the b_i, represent the amount of resources available. Finally, the coefficients of the constraints in the primal problem, the a_{ij}, represent the amounts of resources ($i = 1, 2, \ldots, m$) consumed by the activities ($j = 1, 2, \ldots, n$).

In the dual problem we are seeking to determine the marginal values of the resources to minimize the total value of all resources. The y_i values in the dual problem are the marginal values (unknown) of the resources $i = 1, 2, \ldots, m$. The objective function coefficients in the dual problem are the total amount of resources available and the objective function represents the total value of all resources. The right-hand side values in the dual problem represent the unit profits associated with activity j. Finally the coefficients of the constraints in the dual problem represent the amounts of resources ($i = 1$, milling machine hours; $i = 2$, metal lathe hours) required for the activities ($j = 1, 2$).

Note that, in the primal problem, we are seeking to allocate quantities of resources to maximize profits. Conversely, in the objective function of the dual problem we seek to minimize the value of these resources. Thus, the decision variables , the y_i, in the dual problem can be considered to be the marginal values of the resources. They represent the **opportunity costs** or **shadow prices** associated with milling machine time and metal lathe time, respectively. The marginal value of a resource can also be thought of as the change that occurs in the objective function of the primal problem as a result of utilizing an incremental unit of that resource. This marginal value, or shadow price, will hold as long as the change in the resource would not result in a new solution to the problem. Thus, the change in the resource must be sufficiently small to insure that the current set of basic variables remains optimal, since the shadow price changes if the set of basic variables changes.

It is also important to consider the interpretation of the constraint set for the dual problem. The first constraint states that the time to produce one unit of product x_1 on the milling machine (5 hours) times the opportunity cost of using the milling machine (y_1) plus the time to produce one unit of product x_1 on the metal lathe (4 hours) times the opportunity cost of using the metal lathe (y_2) must be equal to or greater than $6. This $6 is the objective function or profit coefficient of one unit of product x_1 in the primal function. It can also be thought of as the contribution margin of one unit of product x_1, and this constraint thus indicates that the value to the firm from allocating the scarce resources to manufacture one unit of product x_1 must be equal to, or greater than, the contribution margin of one unit of product x_1. Likewise, the first constraint indicates that the total opportunity cost for producing product x_1 is either going to be equal to the net profit (x_1 will be produced) or greater than the net profit (x_1 will not be produced).

The second constraint can be interpreted similarly. Thus, it can be observed that the dual solution does not allow the opportunity cost of producing either product to be less than the incremental profit of the product. These constraints show that the value to the firm of allocating its scarce resources to manufacure one unit of a product must be least equal the contribution margin for that product. The solutions to both the primal and dual formulations of the production-scheduling problem, are presented in side-by-side fashion in Table 5.2.

First, observe that the optimal value of the objective function $Z = 64$ is the same for both the primal problem and the dual problem. This illustrates our earlier statement of the dual theorem of linear programming. From our solution of this

TABLE 5.2 Primal Problem and Corresponding Dual Problem-Simplex Tableaus

Primal Problem—Simplex Tableaus | *Dual Problem—Simplex Tableaus*

Primal Problem: The Initial Simplex Tableau

c_b	Variables in Basis	Solution Values, x_b	c_j 6 a_1	8 a_2	0 a_3	0 a_4
0	x_3	60	5	⑩	1	0
0	x_4	40	4	4	0	1
	Z_j	0	0	0	0	0
	$c_j - Z_j$		6	8	0	0

Dual Problem: The Initial Simplex Tableau

c_b	Variables in Basis	Solution Values, y_b	c_j 60 a_1	40 a_2	0 a_3	+M a_4	0 a_5	+M a_6
+M	y_4	6	5	4	−1	1	0	0
+M	y_6	8	⑩	4	0	0	−1	1
	Z_j	14M	15M	8M	−M	+M	−M	+M
	$c_j - Z_j$		60 − 15M	40 − 8M	+M	0	+M	0

Primal Problem: The Second Simplex Tableau

c_b	Variables in Basis	Solution Values, x_b	c_j 6 a_1	8 a_2	0 a_3	0 a_4
8	x_2	6	1/2	1	1/10	0
0	x_4	16	②	0	−2/5	1
	Z_j	48	4	8	4/5	0
	$c_j - Z_j$		2	0	−4/5	0

Dual Problem: The Second Simplex Tableau

c_b	Variables in Basis	Solution Values, y_b	c_j 60 a_1	40 a_2	0 a_3	+M a_4	0 a_5	+M a_6
+M	y_4	2	0	②	−1	1	1/2	−1/2
60	y_1	4/5	1	2/5	0	0	−1/10	1/10
	Z_j	2M + 48	60	2M + 24	−M	+M	M/2 − 6	−M/2 + 6
	$c_j - Z_j$		0	16 − 2M	+M	0	−M/2 + 6	3M/2 − 6

Primal Problem: The Third Simplex Tableau (Optimal Solution)

c_b	Variables in Basis	Solution Values, x_b	c_j 6 a_1	8 a_2	0 a_3	0 a_4
8	x_2	2	0	1	1/5	−1/4
6	x_1	8	1	0	−1/5	1/2
	Z_j	64	6	8	2/5	1
	$c_j - Z_j$		0	0	−2/5	−1

Dual Problem: The Third Simplex Tableau (Optimal Solution)

c_b	Variables in Basis	Solution Values, y_b	c_j 60 a_1	40 a_2	0 a_3	+M a_4	0 a_5	+M a_6
40	y_2	1	0	1	−1/2	1/2	1/4	−1/4
60	y_1	2/5	1	0	1/5	−1/5	−1/5	1/5
	Z_j	64	60	40	−8	+8	−2	+2
	$c_j - Z_j$		0	0	8	M − 8	+2	M − 2

problem determined in Chapter 4, we know that a feasible solution with a finite valued objective function exists. From our solution to the dual problem we see that it also has a solution with the same finite valued objective function.

Now, consider the primal problem. Recall that we indicated earlier that the marginal value of a resource can be thought of as the change in the objective function of the primal problem that occurs as a result of utilizing an incremental unit of that resource. The marginal values of the resources are in the $c_j - Z_j$ row in the final (optimal) tableau. For the primal problem, x_3 and x_4 are the slack variables associated with the milling machine and metal lathe resources, respectively. In the optimal solution $x_3 = 0$, and $x_4 = 0$, which means that there is no slack present for either of these resources (i.e., all the available milling machine time and metal lathe time is being used in the production of the two products, bearing plates and gears). Observe in the optimal primal tableau that the $c_j - Z_j$ values for x_3 and x_4 are $c_3 - Z_3 = -2/5$ and $c_4 - Z_4 = -1$. These values are the marginal values, or shadow prices, of milling machine time and metal lathe time, respectively. They indicate that inserting one unit of x_3 in the basis (i.e., requiring 1 hour of slack milling machine time) would decrease the objective function by $0.40, and inserting one unit of x_4 in the basis (i.e., requiring 1 hour of slack metal lathe time) would decrease the objective function by $1.00. Alternatively, we can say that the values of these shadow prices indicate that the objective function will decrease by $0.40 if the availability of the milling machine resource b_1 is reduced by 1 hour from its present 60 hours, and the objective function will decrease by $1.00 if the availability of the metal lathe resource b_2 is reduced by 1 hour from its present 40 hours. Conversely, these shadow prices indicate that an additional hour of milling machine time is worth $0.40, and an additional hour of metal lathe time is worth $1.00, as long as there is no change in the variables that comprise the optimal solution (i.e., the current basic variables x_1 and x_2 remain in the optimal basis). Therefore, the shadow price can also be thought of as the value or worth of relaxing a constraint by acquiring an additional unit of the factor of production associated with that constraint.

Consider next the marginal values of the decision variables x_1 and x_2. These decision variables are in the optimal primal solution, and we have $x_1 = 8$ (produce eight bearing plates) and $x_2 = 2$ (produce two gears) as the best production plan. Observe in the optimal primal tableau that the $c_j - Z_j$ values for x_1 and x_2 are $c_1 - Z_1 = 0$ and $c_2 - Z_2 = 0$. These values are the marginal values, or opportunity costs, associated with the real products x_1 (bearing plates) and x_2 (gears). The fact that the opportunity costs are zero for both real products indicates that we are producing as much of each one as is possible given our resource constraints. Assume for a moment that our production planning problem involved a third real product and that, in the final tableau, we had obtained exactly the same solution as indicated in Table 5.1 except that we had an additional column for this third real product with a corresponding $c_j - Z_j$ value of -5. This would indicate that opportunity cost, or marginal value, of forcing production of one unit of this third real product would be $-$5.00. Thus, the $c_j - Z_j$ row can also be used to make an economic interpretation with respect to the decision variables.

Considering next the dual problem, observe that the optimal solution to this problem indicates that $y_1 = 2/5$, and $y_2 = 1$. This optimal dual solution indicates that the values of resource 1 (milling machine time) and resource 2 (metal lathe time) are $0.40 and $1.00, respectively. This is, of course, exactly what we observed by examining the $c_j - Z_j$ row of the optimal solution to the primal problem.

Additionally, we observed in the primal problem solution that \$64 of profit would be generated by the production of eight units of product 1 (bearing plate) and two units of product 2 (gear). Now, we also observe that, in the dual solution, the value of the resources used to generate this \$64 profit is also \$64. This is confirmed by the fact that the objective function value for the dual solution is $Z' = (\$0.40$ per hour of milling machine time) $\cdot$ (60 hours of milling machine time available) + (\$1.00 per hour of metal lathe time) $\cdot$ (40 hours of metal lathe time available) = \$64.

Observe further that the values $y_1 = {}^2/_5$ and $y_2 = 1$ in the dual solution are identical (except for the sign) to $c_3 - Z_3 = -{}^2/_5$ and $c_4 - Z_4 = -1$ in the primal solution. This is not a coincidence and indeed the solution values of the dual solution are uniquely the $c_j - Z_j$ values of the corresponding variables in the primal solution. The correspondence between the $c_j - Z_j$ values in the primal and the solution values of the variables in the dual is as follows.

1. The *first* primal decision variable is x_1, and thus the *first* dual surplus variable y_3 is associated with it. Since $c_1 - Z_1 = 0$ in the primal, $y_3 = 0$ in the dual.
2. The *second* primal decision variable is x_2, and thus the *second* dual surplus variable y_5 is associated with it. Since $c_2 - Z_2 = 0$ in the primal, $y_5 = 0$ in the dual.
3. The *first* primal slack variable is x_3, and thus the *first* dual decision variable y_1 is associated with it. Since $c_3 - Z_3 = -{}^2/_5$ in the primal, $y_1 = {}^2/_5$ in the dual.
4. The *second* primal slack variable is x_4, and thus the *second* dual decision variable y_2 is associated with it. Since $c_4 - Z_4 = -1$ in the primal, $y_2 = 1$ in the dual.

All these various associations make sense. For example, the dual variable y_1 represents the opportunity cost or the marginal value of 1 hour of milling machine time; the corresponding primal slack variable x_3 represents the unused capacity of the milling machine resource, and $c_3 - Z_3$ also represents the marginal value of the milling machine resource. Similarly, the solution values of the primal are uniquely the $c_j - Z_j$ values of the corresponding variables in the dual solution. The correspondence between the $c_j - Z_j$ values in the dual and the solution values of the variables in the primal is as follows:

1. The *first* dual decision variable is y_1, and thus the *first* primal slack variable x_3 is associated with it. Since $c_1 - Z_1 = 0$ in the dual, $x_3 = 0$ in the primal.
2. The *second* dual decision variable is y_2, and thus the *second* primal slack variable x_4 is associated with it. Since $c_2 - Z_2 = 0$ in the dual, $x_4 = 0$ in the primal.
3. The *first* dual surplus variable is y_3, and thus the *first* primal decision variable x_1 is associated with it. Since $c_3 - Z_3 = +8$ in the dual, $x_1 = 8$ in the primal.
4. The *second* dual surplus variable is y_5, and thus the *second* primal decision variable x_2 is associated with it. Since, $c_5 - Z_5 = +2$ in the dual, $x_2 = 2$ in the primal.

It should now be apparent that the final tableau of the primal problem solution provides both the optimal values of the primal decision variables, and through the $c_j - Z_j$ values, the values of the dual decision variables. Since $c_3 - Z_3 = -{}^2/_5$ and $c_4 - Z_4 = -1$ in the optimal primal tableau; we know that $y_1 = {}^2/_5$ and $y_2 = 1$ in the optimal dual tableau. The converse set of relationships hold for the final tableau of the dual problem. Since $c_3 - Z_3 = 8$ and $c_5 - Z_5 = 2$ in this optimal dual tableau, we know that $x_1 = 8$ and $x_2 = 2$ in the optimal primal tableau.

5.4 THE DUAL SIMPLEX ALGORITHM

As noted earlier, another one of the important uses of duality theory is in the construction of other types of linear programming algorithms. One such algorithm is the *dual simplex algorithm* in which we operate on the primal problem exactly as if the simplex method were being applied to the dual problem.

All basic solutions to a linear programming problem can be categorized according to two criteria.

1. Feasibility. All the basic variables in the current basic feasible solution are nonnegative (≥ 0).
2. Optimality. All the $c_j - Z_j$ values are nonpositive (maximization) or nonnegative (minimization).

These two criteria then lead to four classifications of basic solutions.

1. Optimal. Solution is both feasible and optimal.
2. Suboptimal. Solution is feasible but not optimal.
3. Superoptimal. Solution is not feasible but optimality conditions are met.
4. Neither feasible nor superoptimal. Solution is not feasible and optimality conditions are not met.

To illustrate these four classifications consider Table 5.3, which presents the six basic solutions for both the primal and dual formulations of our production scheduling problem. Recall that, in the application of the simplex method to the primal problem, we begin with a **suboptimal solution** (i.e., $x_1 = 0$, $x_2 = 0$, $x_3 = 60$, and $x_4 = 40$ in Table 5.3) and move toward the **optimal solution** by striving to satisfy the optimality criterion, at the same time maintaining feasibility. However, while the simplex method is iterating through a series of suboptimal solutions in the primal problem as it moves towards optimality, it is simultaneously treating a series of **superoptimal solutions** in the dual problem as it moves towards feasibility. The relationships between the complementary solutions in the primal and dual problems may be summarized as follows.

TABLE 5.3 Basic Solutions—Primal and Dual Formulations of Production-Scheduling Problem

	Primal Problem					Value of the Objective Function	Dual Problem[a]					
No.	Basic Solutions				Feasible/ Nonfeasible	Classification of Basic Solution		y_1	y_2	y_3	y_4	Feasible/ Nonfeasible	Classification of Basic Solution
	x_1	x_2	x_3	x_4									
1	0	0	60	40	Feasible	Suboptimal	0	0	0	-6	-8	Nonfeasible	Superoptimal
2	0	6	0	16	Feasible	Suboptimal	48	0	$3/2$	0	-2	Nonfeasible	Superoptimal
3	0	10	-40	0	Nonfeasible	Superoptimal	80	0	2	2	0	Feasible	Suboptimal
4	12	0	0	-8	Nonfeasible	Superoptimal	72	$6/5$	0	0	4	Feasible	Suboptimal
5	10	0	10	0	Feasible	Suboptimal	60	$4/5$	0	-2	0	Nonfeasible	Superoptimal
6	8	2	0	0	Feasible	Optimal	64	$2/5$	1	0	0	Feasible	Optimal

[a]*Note:* The basic solutions to the dual problem were determined without using artificial variables.

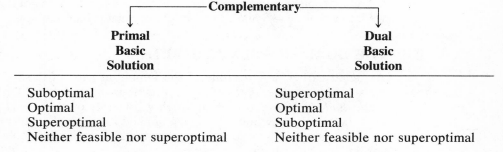

To illustrate these relationships consider the second basic solution to the primal problem, and the associated dual solution as shown in Table 5.3. For this basic solution we have

$$\text{Complementary}$$

Primal Basic Solution	Dual Basic Solution
$x_1 = 0$	$y_1 = 0$
$x_2 = 6$	$y_2 = {}^3/_2$
$x_3 = 0$	$y_3 = 0$
$x_4 = 16$	$y_4 = -2$
$Z_x = 48$ (Suboptimal)	$Z_y = 48$ (Superoptimal)

Now, it is sometimes more efficient to work with superoptimal basic solutions in the primal problem and move toward feasibility, and hence optimality. This is equivalent to using the simplex method to work with suboptimal basic solutions in the dual problem and moving toward optimality as feasibility is maintained. The dual simplex algorithm is designed to deal with superoptimal basic solutions and work toward feasibility. The algorithm works on the primal problem exactly as if the simplex method were being applied simultaneously to the dual problem.

The rules used for the dual simplex algorithm are very similar to those used for the simplex algorithm. The rules used to select the variable to leave the basis is as follows.

VARIABLE REMOVAL CRITERION *The variable removal criterion is based upon the solution values for the basic variables, the x_b. Examine the x_b and select for removal the basic variable with the largest negative value. If the solution values for all variables are zero, or positive, the current solution is the optimal solution.*

The rule used to select the variable to enter the basis is as follows.

VARIABLE ENTRY CRITERION *Form ratios of the number in the $c_j - Z_j$ row and the numbers in the row corresponding to the variable selected for removal from the basis. The numbers in the $c_j - Z_j$ row become the numerators in these ratios and the numbers in the row corresponding to the variable selected for removal become the denominators. Ignore ratios formed that have zero or positive numbers in the denominator. The* *column variable selected for entry is the one whose ratio has the minimum absolute value.*

The basic solutions that are traced out using the dual simplex algorithm will be infeasible (except for the final basic solution, which will be feasible and hence optimal) because some of the basic variables will be negative. The entries for the $c_j - Z_j$ will satisfy the conditions for optimality, and we will thus be considering a series of superoptimal, but infeasible, basic solutions as we move towards optimality and feasibility.

At each iteration the Gauss-Jordan elimination procedure is employed to enter one new variable into the basis and to remove one existing variable from the basis. This pivoting process is done in exactly the same manner as in the regular simplex method, after the variable removal and variable entry criteria described above have been used. After each iteration a check is made to see if all the basic variables are nonnegative. If they are, then the solution is feasible, and therefore optimal. If one or more variables are negative, we must use the dual simplex rules and continue to make iterations until the feasible conditions are met.

We shall now illustrate the dual simplex algorithm by applying it to the dual of our product mix problem. Recall that this dual problem was

$$\text{Minimize } Z_y = 60y_1 + 40y_2 \qquad (5\text{--}47)$$

subject to:
$$5y_1 + 4y_2 \geq 6$$
$$10y_1 + 4y_2 \geq 8 \qquad (5\text{--}48)$$

with
$$y_1, y_2 \geq 0 \qquad (5\text{--}49)$$

Expressing the constraints in $\leq$ form we obtain

$$\text{Miminize } Z_y = 60y_1 + 40y_2 \qquad (5\text{--}50)$$

subject to:
$$-5y_1 - 4y_2 \leq -6$$
$$-10y_1 - 4y_2 \leq -8 \qquad (5\text{--}51)$$

with
$$y_1 \geq 0, y_2 \geq 0 \qquad (5\text{--}52)$$

Utilizing two slack variables y_3 and y_4 the initial dual simplex tableau can now be constructed as in Table 5.4.

TABLE 5.4 Initial Dual Simplex Tableau

c_b	Variables in Basis	c_j Solution Values, y_b	60 a_1	40 a_2	0 a_3	0 a_4	
0	y_3	-6	-5	-4	1	0	
0	y_4	-8	-10	-4	0	1	← Leave
	Z_j	0	0	0	0	0	
	$c_j - Z_j$		60	40	0	0	

↑
Enter

Within Table 5.4 the variable selected to leave the basis is determined by examining the y_b column. The smallest value is $y_4 = -8$, so variable y_4 leaves the basis. The variable selected to enter the basis is determined by forming the ratio of the $c_j - Z_j$ row and the y_4 row. These ratios are

$$y_1 \left| \frac{60}{-10} \right| = 6 \quad \longleftarrow \quad \text{Minimum absolute value}$$
$$y_2 \left| \frac{40}{-4} \right| = 10 \tag{5-53}$$
$$y_3 \left| \frac{0}{0} \right| \text{ Ignore}$$
$$y_4 \left| \frac{0}{1} \right| \text{ Ignore}$$

Thus, y_1 is selected to enter the basis, and a simplex iteration is then performed, leading to the second dual simplex tableau shown in Table 5.5.

TABLE 5.5 Second Dual Simplex Tableau

		c_j	60	40	0	0	
$\mathbf{a}_b$	Variables in Basis	Solution Values, y_b	$\mathbf{a}_1$	$\mathbf{a}_2$	$\mathbf{a}_3$	$\mathbf{a}_4$	
0	y_3	-2	0	-2	1	$-1/2$	← Leave
60	y_1	$4/5$	1	$2/5$	0	$-1/10$	
	Z_j	48	60	24	0	-6	
	$c_j - Z_j$		0	16	0	6	

↑
Enter

Within Table 5.5 the variable selected to leave the basis is seen to be y_3, since $y_3 = -2$ is the only remaining negative value. The variable selected to enter the basis is determined by forming the ratio of the $c_j - Z_j$ row and the y_3 row. These ratios are

$$y_1 \left| \frac{0}{0} \right| \quad \text{Ignore}$$
$$y_2 \left| \frac{16}{-2} \right| = 8 \quad \longleftarrow \quad \text{Minimum absolute value} \tag{5-54}$$
$$y_3 \left| \frac{0}{1} \right| \quad \text{Ignore}$$
$$y_4 \left| \frac{6}{(-\frac{1}{2})} \right| = 12$$

Thus, y_2 is selected to enter the basis. Performing the corresponding simplex iteration we obtain the solution shown in Table 5.6. Since this solution is also feasible ($y_1 = 2/5$, $y_2 = 1$), we are optimal. Our optimal solution is, of course, exactly the same as that shown in the final tableau in Table 5.2.

TABLE 5.6   Third Dual Simplex Tableau (Optimal Solution)

c_b	Variables in Basis	c_j Solution Values, y_b	60 a_1	40 a_2	0 a_3	0 a_4
40	y_2	1	0	1	$-1/2$	$1/4$
60	y_1	$2/5$	1	0	$1/5$	$-1/5$
	Z_j	64	60	40	-8	-2
	$c_j - Z_j$		0	0	8	2

5.5   SENSITIVITY ANALYSIS

In Chapters 3 and 4 we analyzed the development and solution of linear programming problems. However, the overall goal of our study of linear programming is to develop an understanding and appreciation of the complex interrelationships that are present in linear programming models. You may recall that we alluded earlier to the fact that the manager and the management scientist are rarely interested in only the numerical values of the optimal solution to a linear programming problem. Generally, they are also interested in determining how far the input parameters of a linear programming model, the a_{ij}, b_i, and c_j, can vary before the optimal solution changes or is no longer optimal. This type of determination is called *sensitivity analysis* or *postoptimality analysis*.

Quite often we can perform a sensitivity analysis given the results shown in the final simplex tableau. We shall now consider four examples of sensitivity analysis.

1.   Changes in the coefficients of the objective function.
2.   Changes in the right-hand side values of the constraint set.
3.   Addition of a new constraint (row) to the linear programming problem.
4.   Addition of a new variable (column) to the linear programming problem.

Many of the other sensitivity analysis questions that could also be asked might require the use of a digital computer to ease the computations, but they would also tend to be based upon the use of the previous optimal solution.

The reasons for making a sensitivity analysis are numerous and important. First, some of the parameter values used in a linear programming problem may be estimates, based either on historical data or on predictions of future conditions. Second, the parameters may have been specified on the basis of achieving a particular set of objectives (e.g., the right-hand side resources might be the desired labor force level at a point in time). These objectives might change as a result of the solution to the linear programming problem. Furthermore, the analyst may want to know how sensitive the current optimal solution is to changes in the model's parameters so that management can be made particularly aware of areas needing further analysis and refinement. The manager is typically very interested in the sensitivity analysis data produced as a part of a linear programming study. The manager is faced with making decisions and allocating resources based on an uncertain knowledge of the future. Sensitivity analysis affords the manager a means of resolving some of the uncertainty surrounding various decisions. For example, sensitivity analysis involving a particular profit function coefficient might indiciate that a particular unlikely profit increase would have to occur before the current optimal solution would change. This would tend to reinforce the manager's confidence in a decision made on the basis of the current optimal solution.

5.5.1   Changes in the Coefficients of the Objective Function

The effect of changes in the coefficients of the objective function can be determined directly by considering the final simplex tableau. To illustrate, consider the final simplex tableau for our product mix example. This tableau is reproduced in Table 5.7. The sensitivity of the optimal solution to changes in a coefficient of the objective function is measured by adding a variable δ_j to the coefficient of the objective function. The new objective function coefficient becomes $c'_j = c_j + \delta_j$, and the magnitude of δ_j can be determined by analyzing the appropriate $c_j - Z_j$ value in the final simplex tableau. You will recall that the $c_j - Z_j$ values are zero for all basic variables in the optimal solution, and are nonpositive for all nonbasic variables in a maximization problem and are nonnegative for all nonbasic variables in a minimization problem. The sensitivity analysis is thus performed by calculating the values of δ_j for which these criteria are met.

TABLE 5.7   The Third Simplex Tableau (Optimal Solution)

c_b	Variables in Basis	Solution Values, x_b	a_1	a_2	a_3	a_4
		c_j	6	8	0	0
8	x_2	2	0	1	$1/5$	$-1/4$
6	x_1	8	1	0	$-1/5$	$1/2$
	Z_j	64	6	8	$2/5$	1
	$c_j - Z_j$		0	0	$-2/5$	-1

The optimal tableau shown above indicates that x_1 and x_2 are basic variables and that x_3 and x_4 are nonbasic variables. Consider first the sensitivity of the optimal solution to a change in the objective function coefficient of the first nonbasic variable, x_3. We add δ_3 to the objective function coefficient c_3, and the new objective function coefficient becomes $c'_3 = 0 + \delta_3$. The new final simplex tableau is shown in Table 5.8. In this tableau we see that our optimality criterion is met for $\delta_3 - 2/5 \le 0$ or $\delta_3 \le 2/5$. Thus, the objective function coefficient of x_3 can be increased by as much as $2/5$, that is, $c'_3 \le 0 + 2/5 \le 2/5$ before a change in the optimal solution can occur. As soon as x_3 is increased by more than $2/5$, $c'_3 - Z_3 > 0$, and x_3 will enter the basis. The sensitivity of the optimal solution to a change in the objective function coefficient for the variable x_4 (i.e., the second nonbasic variable) can be determined in similar fashion. Herein, the optimality criterion will be maintained for $\delta_4 \le 1$, or $c'_4 \le 0 + 1 \le 1$.

TABLE 5.8 The Third Simplex Tableau (Optimal Solution)—Change in c_3

c_b	Variables in Basis	Solution Values, x_b	a_1	a_2	a_3	a_4
		c_j	6	8	$0 + \delta_3$	0
8	x_2	2	0	1	$1/5$	$-1/4$
6	x_1	8	1	0	$-1/5$	$1/2$
	Z_j	64	6	8	$2/5$	1
	$c_j - Z_j$		0	0	$\delta_3 - 2/5$	-1

The procedure for determining the sensitivity of the optimal solution to changes in the objective function coefficients of the basic variables is slightly more complicated. Consider the sensitivity of the optimal solution to a change in the objective function coefficient of the second basic variable x_2. We add δ_2 to the objective function coefficient c_2, and the new objective function coefficient becomes $c_2' = 8 + \delta_2$. The new final simplex tableau is shown in Table 5.9. For the current solution to remain positive, all $c_j' - Z_j$ entries into the final row of this tableau must remain negative. The values of δ_2 that satisfy this requirement can be determined by solving the following system of linear inequalities.

$$-2/5 - \delta_2/5 \leq 0 \rightarrow -\delta_2/5 \leq 2/5 \rightarrow \delta_2 \geq -2$$
$$-1 + \delta_2/4 \leq 0 \rightarrow +\delta_2/4 \leq 1 \rightarrow \delta_2 \leq 4 \tag{5-55}$$

Thus, the solution is: $-2 \leq \delta_2 \leq 4$. The current optimal solution will not change as long as $(8 - 2) \leq c_2' \leq (8 + 4)$ or $6 \leq c_2' \leq 12$. If $c_2' < 6$ or if $c_2' > 12$ a change of basis is required, and this change of basis is made using the usual simplex procedures. A similar type of analysis can be made for the other basic variable x_1.

TABLE 5.9 The Third Simplex Tableau (Optimal Solution)—Change in c_2

c_b	Variables in Basis	Solution Values, x_b	a_1	a_2	a_3	a_4
		c_j	6	$8 + \delta_2$	0	0
$8 + \delta_2$	x_2	2	0	1	$1/5$	$-1/4$
6	x_1	8	1	0	$-1/5$	$1/2$
	Z_j	$64 + 2\delta_2$	6	$8 + \delta_2$	$2/5 + \delta_2/5$	$1 - \delta_2/4$
	$c_j - Z_j$		0	0	$-2/5 - \delta_2/5$	$-1 + \delta_2/4$

The sensitivity of the optimal solution to changes in each of the coefficients of the decision variables of the objective function is summarized in Table 5.10. The reader should review the computations underlying the entries shown in Table 5.10.

TABLE 5.10 Summary of Sensitivity Analysis—Objective Function Coefficients

Decision Variable	Change in δ_j	Change in c'_j
x_1 (Basic)	$-2 \leq \delta_1 \leq 2$	$4 \leq c'_1 \leq 8$
x_2 (Basic)	$-2 \leq \delta_2 \leq 4$	$6 \leq c'_2 \leq 12$
x_3 (Nonbasic)	$\delta_3 \leq {}^2/_5$	$c'_3 \leq {}^2/_5$
x_4 (Nonbasic)	$\delta_4 \leq 1$	$c'_4 \leq 1$

5.5.2 Changes in the Right-Hand Side Values

The sensitivity of the optimal solution to changes in the right-hand side values is of major importance to the practitioner because these values typically represent the available quantities of resources. Obviously, these resource availabilities could change either from natural causes, such as a lack of supply of a particular material or ingredient, or as a result of a particular management decision, such as an expansion of the work force or the purchase of new machinery.

The procedure that we employ to test the sensitivity of the optimal solution to changes in the right-hand side values is similar to that which we employed in measuring the sensitivity of the objective function coefficients. Using our familiar product mix example, assume that we seek to test the sensitivity of the first resource, milling machine time. To do this we begin by adding δ_1 to the *original* first resource value $b_1 = 60$, that is, $b'_1 = b_1 + \delta_1 = 60 + \delta_1$. The new right-hand side vector thus becomes

$$b'_1 = \begin{bmatrix} 60 + \delta_1 \\ 40 \end{bmatrix} \quad \text{(Milling machine time)} \atop \text{(Metal lathe time)} \tag{5-56}$$

Now, recall that in the optimal final tableau the basic variables were x_1 and x_2. We compute the limits of the first resource by solving for the values of δ_1 for which the basic variables x_1 and x_2 remain in the optimal solution.

The values of the basic variables for any iteration of the solution are given by:

$$\mathbf{x}_b = [\mathbf{B}^{-1}]\mathbf{b} \tag{5-57}$$

where $[\mathbf{B}]$ = the basis matrix for the initial basic solution to the problem. $[\mathbf{B}]$ is a square matrix whose columns (rows) are any m linearly independent columns (rows) from the constraint matrix $[\mathbf{A}]$.

   $\mathbf{b}$ = the original right-hand side vector.

   $\mathbf{x}_b$ = the solution vector.

In order to maintain the feasibility of the solution $\mathbf{x}_b \geq \mathbf{0}$ at each iteration. Thus, the upper and lower bounds for b'_1 are determined by solving

$$\mathbf{x}_{b'_1} = [\mathbf{B}^{-1}]\mathbf{b}'_1 \geq \mathbf{0} \tag{5-58}$$

Fortunately, the inverse of the basis matrix, $[\mathbf{B}^{-1}]$, can be found in any iteration of the simplex algorithm by examining the columns that correspond to the *original* basic variables used to initiate the simplex algorithm. Recall that we always begin the simplex procedure by selecting m column vectors that form an $m \times m$ identity matrix. For our current problem, the original two vectors that formed the identity matrix were $\mathbf{a}_3$ and $\mathbf{a}_4$, and

$$[\mathbf{B}] = \begin{matrix} \mathbf{a}_3 & \mathbf{a}_4 \\ \begin{bmatrix} 1 & 0 \\ 0 & 1 \end{bmatrix} \end{matrix} \tag{5-59}$$

At each iteration subsequently $[\mathbf{B}^{-1}]$ is given by the column vectors $\mathbf{a}_3$ and $\mathbf{a}_4$, which formed the original basic matrix. Remember that at each iteration we are solving the relationship $\mathbf{x}_b = [\mathbf{B}^{-1}]\mathbf{b}$ using the Gauss-Jordan elimination procedure.

Now let us refer once again to the optimal tableau, which is reproduced in Table 5.11.

TABLE 5.11   The Third Simplex Tableau (Optimal Solution)

c_b	Variables in Basis	Solution Values, $\mathbf{x}_b$	c_j 6 $\mathbf{a}_1$	8 $\mathbf{a}_2$	0 $\mathbf{a}_3$	0 $\mathbf{a}_4$
8	x_2	2	0	1	$1/5$	$-1/4$
6	x_1	8	1	0	$-1/5$	$1/2$
	Z_j	64	6	8	$2/5$	1
	$c_j - Z_j$		0	0	$-2/5$	-1

In this final tableau, the inverse of the original basis matrix is given by:

$$[\mathbf{B}^{-1}] = \begin{matrix} \mathbf{a}_3 & \mathbf{a}_4 \\ \begin{bmatrix} 1/5 & -1/4 \\ -1/5 & 1/2 \end{bmatrix} \end{matrix} \tag{5-60}$$

We can now solve for the values of δ_1 by solving the system of linear inequalities, $[\mathbf{B}^{-1}]\mathbf{b}_1' \geq \mathbf{0}$, or:

$$\begin{bmatrix} 1/5 & -1/4 \\ -1/5 & 1/2 \end{bmatrix} \cdot \begin{bmatrix} 60 + \delta_1 \\ 40 \end{bmatrix} \geq \begin{bmatrix} 0 \\ 0 \end{bmatrix} \tag{5-61}$$

which produces the following two inequalities.

$$\begin{aligned} 2 + \delta_1/5 \geq 0 \rightarrow \delta_1/5 \geq -2 \rightarrow \delta_1 \geq -10 \\ 8 - \delta_1/5 \geq 0 \rightarrow \delta_1/5 \leq 8 \rightarrow \delta_1 \leq 40 \end{aligned} \tag{5-62}$$

The value of δ_1 that satisfies these two inequalities is $-10 \leq \delta_1 \leq 40$. This means that the basic variables x_1 and x_2 remain in solution for $(60 - 10) \leq b_1' \leq (60 + 40)$ or $50 \leq b_1' \leq 100$.

The sensitivity of the optimal solution to a change in the second right-hand side value can be determined similarly. We replace the second resource value by $40 + \delta_2$, giving a new requirements vector:

$$\mathbf{b}_2' = \begin{bmatrix} 60 \\ 40 + \delta_2 \end{bmatrix} \tag{5-63}$$

The values of δ_2 are determined by solving, $[\mathbf{B}^{-1}]\mathbf{b}_2' \geq \mathbf{0}$, or

$$\begin{bmatrix} 1/5 & -1/4 \\ -1/5 & 1/2 \end{bmatrix} \cdot \begin{bmatrix} 60 \\ 40 + \delta_2 \end{bmatrix} \geq \begin{bmatrix} 0 \\ 0 \end{bmatrix} \tag{5-64}$$

which produces the following two inequalities.

$$\begin{aligned} 2 - \delta_2/4 \geq 0 &\rightarrow \delta_2/4 \leq 2 \rightarrow \delta_2 \leq 8 \\ 8 + \delta_2/2 \geq 0 &\rightarrow \delta_2/2 \geq -8 \rightarrow \delta_2 \geq -16 \end{aligned} \tag{5-65}$$

The value of δ_2 that satisfies these two inequalities is $-16 \leq \delta_2 \leq 8$. This means that the basic variables x_1 and x_2 remain in solution for $(40 - 16) \leq b_2' \leq (40 + 8)$ or $24 \leq b_2' \leq 48$.

In making changes in the coefficients of the objective function and the right-hand side values, we have considered only the change of a single objective function coefficient or a single right-hand side value at a time. Such changes led to simple systems of linear inequalities, involving a single unknown, which could then be easily solved to determine the range for the unknown. It should be mentioned that it is possible to change more than one objective function coefficient, or more than one right-hand side value at a time. However, such a process will lead to a much more complicated system of linear inequalities, involving two or more unknowns that must be solved simultaneously. Although certain computer codes in existence do incorporate this type of sensitivity analysis, it is considered to be beyond the scope of this text. Thus, we will consider only the change of a single objective function coefficient or a single right-hand side value at a time.

5.5.3 Adding a Constraint (Row)

The addition of a constraint to the original problem can occur for a number of reasons. First, the management science analyst may have simply overlooked the constraint in the original formulation of the problem. Second, new information or a new set of circumstances may have evolved that makes the addition of a constraint necessary. Finally, the management scientist may want to ''tighten'' the constraint set by adding a more restrictive constraint.

Fortunately, when a constraint is added to a linear programming problem it is not necessary to resolve the entire problem. First, assume that we are maximizing and that the new constraint is of the less than or equal to variety. This set of conditions will result in the need for the inclusion of a new slack variable in the basis for the constraint being added. Given the current values of the basic variables in solution, the value of this slack variable may be positive, zero, or negative. If the new slack variable has a positive or zero value, then the current basic optimal solution will remain optimal with the new slack variable in the solution with a positive or zero value. If the new slack variable has a negative value, the current basic solution will now be infeasible. Then, the new constraint can be added directly to the final tableau of the original problem, and the dual simplex algorithm can be employed to find the solution to the expanded problem.

To illustrate the sensitivity analysis procedure involving the addition of a constraint let us consider our original product mix problem with the addition of one new constraint. This expanded problem is as follows.

$$\text{Maximize } Z = 6x_1 + 8x_2 \tag{5–66}$$

subject to:
$$\begin{array}{l} 5x_1 + 10x_2 \le 60 \\ 4x_1 + 4x_2 \le 40 \\ 4x_1 + 3x_2 \le 24 \quad \text{(New constraint)} \end{array} \tag{5–67}$$

with $\quad x_1 \ge 0, x_2 \ge 0$ \hfill (5–68)

Expressing this new constraint as an equality, with the addition of the slack variable x_5 we obtain:

$$4x_1 + 3x_2 + 1x_5 = 24 \tag{5–69}$$

Substituting the current optimal values $x_1 = 8$, $x_2 = 2$ into (5–69) we have

$$\begin{array}{l} 4(8) + 3(2) + 1x_5 = \quad 24 \\ \qquad\qquad\qquad 1x_5 = -14 \end{array} \tag{5–70}$$

Thus, we observe that the addition of this constraint will result in the inclusion of a slack variable in the basis with a negative value. Thus, feasibility and optimality must be restored using the dual simplex method. The effect of adding this constraint to the optimal solution, in terms of the final simplex tableau, is shown in Table 5.12.

TABLE 5.12 Revised Simplex Tableau—Additional Constraint

c_b	Variables in Basis	Solution Values, x_b	c_j a_1	8 a_2	0 a_3	0 a_4	0 a_5
8	x_2	2	0	1	$1/5$	$-1/4$	0
6	x_1	8	1	0	$-1/5$	$1/2$	0
0	x_5	24	4	3	0	0	1
	Z_j	64	6	8	$2/5$	1	0
	$c_j - Z_j$		0	0	$-2/5$	-1	0

Now, for every other basic variable in this final tableau, x_1 and x_2, we must convert the corresponding coefficient in the new (x_5) row to zero using the usual simplex iterative procedure. This process involves creating an identity matrix within the final simplex tableau for the variables x_1, x_2, and x_5. The entries in the x_5 row are obtained as follows. First, reduce the x_5 row coefficient for column $a_1(x_1)$ to zero, using the usual simplex procedure.

	Old Row x_5	Row x_1		Intermediate Row x_5
Z	24	$-$	4(8)	$= -8$
x_1 (Basic)	4	$-$	4(1)	$= 0$
x_2 (Basic)	3	$-$	4(0)	$= 3$
x_3	0	$-$	$4(-1/5)$	$= 4/5$
x_4	0	$-$	$4(-1/2)$	$= -2$
x_5 (Basic)	1	$-$	4(0)	$= 1$

(5-71)

	Intermediate Row x_5	Row x_2		New Row x_5
Z	-8	$-$	3(2)	$= -14$
x_1 (Basic)	0	$-$	3(0)	$= 0$
x_2 (Basic)	3	$-$	3(1)	$= 0$
x_3	$4/5$	$-$	$3(1/5)$	$= 1/5$
x_4	-2	$-$	$3(-1/4)$	$= -5/4$
x_5 (Basic)	1	$-$	3(0)	$= 1$

(5-72)

TABLE 5.13   Revised Simplex Tableau—New Basic Solution

a_b	Variables in Basis	c_j Solution Values, x_b	6 a_1	8 a_2	0 a_3	0 a_4	0 a_5	
8	x_2	2	0	1	$1/5$	$-1/4$	0	
6	x_1	8	1	0	$1/5$	$1/2$	0	
0	x_5	-14	0	0	$1/5$	$-5/4$	1	← Leave
	Z_j	64	6	8	$2/5$	1	0	
	$c_j - Z_j$		0	0	$-2/5$	-1	0	

↑
Enter

We have now accomplished our objective of converting to zero the coefficients in the x_5 row that correspond to the basic variables x_1 and x_2. Since x_5 is in this new basic solution, it must have a coefficient of 1 in its row, which it does. The revised simplex tableau with the new basic solution is shown in Table 5.13.

Considering the tableau shown in Table 5.13 we observe that we have a new basic solution that is not feasible. However, we can easily restore feasibility, and hence optimality, by applying the dual simplex algorithm. Applying the dual simplex algorithm we select the variable x_5 to leave the basis, since $x_5 = -14$ is the only negative value in the x_b column. The variable to enter the basis is determined by forming the ratios:

$$x_1 \;\middle|\; {}^0/_0 \;\middle|\quad \text{Ignore}$$

$$x_2 \;\middle|\; {}^0/_0 \;\middle|\quad \text{Ignore}$$

$$x_3 \;\left|\; \frac{-(^2/_5)}{^1/_5} \;\right|\quad \text{Ignore} \tag{5-73}$$

$$x_4 \;\left|\; \frac{-1}{-(^5/_4)} \;\right| = {}^4/_5 \longleftarrow \text{Minimum absolute value}$$

$$x_5 \;\middle|\; {}^0/_1 \;\middle|\quad \text{Ignore}$$

x_4 is thus selected to enter the basis and a simplex iteration is performed. This leads to the second dual simplex tableau shown in Table 5.14.

TABLE 5.14 Second Dual Simplex Tableau (Optimal Solution)

c_b	Variables in Basis	Solution Values, x_b	c_j 6 a_1	8 a_2	0 a_3	0 a_4	0 a_5
8	x_2	$^{24}/_5$	0	1	$^4/_{25}$	0	$^1/_5$
6	x_1	$^{12}/_5$	1	0	$-^3/_{25}$	0	$^2/_5$
0	x_4	$^{56}/_5$	0	0	$-^4/_{25}$	1	$-^4/_5$
	Z_j	$52^4/_5$	6	8	$^{14}/_{25}$	0	$^4/_5$
	$c_j - Z_j$		0	0	$-^{14}/_{25}$	0	$-^4/_5$

Since this solution is also feasible ($x_1 = {}^{12}/_5$, $x_2 = {}^{24}/_5$, $x_3 = {}^{56}/_5$) we are optimal according to our dual simplex criterion. The addition of the constraint $4x_1 + 3x_2 \leq 24$, has changed our solution from $x_1 = 8, x_2 = 2, Z = 64$ to $x_1 = {}^{12}/_5, x_2 = {}^{24}/_5, Z = 52^4/_5$. The objective function value has been reduced and the optimal solution indicates that both products should be produced in fractional quantities, as a result of the addition of the new constraint.

5.5.4 Adding a Variable (Column)

Sensitivity analysis that involves the addition of a new variable (column) to the original problem is easily handled. First, if the variable x_{n+1}, with activity vector $\mathbf{a}_{n+1}$ and objective function coefficient c_{n+1}, is added to the original linear programming problem, we can check to see if this will change the current optimal solution. Thus, we compute

$$\mathbf{y}_{n+1} = [\mathbf{B}^{-1}]\mathbf{a}_{n+1} \tag{5-74}$$

and $\quad c_{n+1} - Z_{n+1} = c_{n+1} - \mathbf{c}_b'\mathbf{y}_{n+1} \tag{5-75}$

where $[\mathbf{B}]$ is again the basis matrix for the initial basic solution to the problem. For a maximization problem, if $c_{n+1} - Z_{n+1} \leq 0$, the present optimal solution remains optimal. If $c_{n+1} - Z_{n+1} > 0$, we must proceed with the simplex method and insert the variable x_{n+1} into the basis at the next step. For a minimization problem, if $c_{n+1} - Z_{n+1} \geq 0$, the present optimal solution remains optimal. If $c_{n+1} - Z_{n+1} < 0$, we must continue with the simplex method and insert the variable x_{n+1} into the basis at the next step.

To illustrate this type of sensitivity analysis let us consider our original product-mix problem with an additional variable added. This new problem is as follows.

$$\text{Maximize } Z = 6x_1 + 8x_2 + 12x_3 \tag{5-76}$$

subject to:
$$\begin{aligned} 5x_1 + 10x_2 + 4x_3 &\leq 60 \\ 4x_1 + 4x_2 + 2x_3 &\leq 40 \end{aligned} \tag{5-77}$$

with $x_1 \geq 0, x_2 \geq 0, x_3 \geq 0$ $\tag{5-78}$

The new column vector added to this problem is

$$\mathbf{a}_3 = \begin{bmatrix} 4 \\ 2 \end{bmatrix} \tag{5-79}$$

and the new objective function coefficient is $c_3 = 12$.

We begin by checking to see if the current solution will remain optimal.

$$\mathbf{y}_3 = [\mathbf{B}^{-1}]\mathbf{a}_3$$
$$= \begin{bmatrix} 1/5 & -1/4 \\ -1/5 & 1/2 \end{bmatrix} \cdot \begin{bmatrix} 4 \\ 2 \end{bmatrix} = \begin{bmatrix} 3/10 \\ 1/5 \end{bmatrix} \tag{5-80}$$

Next, we compute:

$$\begin{aligned} c_3 - Z_3 = c_3 - \mathbf{c}_b'\mathbf{y}_3 \\ = 12 - (8 \quad 6) \cdot \begin{bmatrix} 3/10 \\ 1/5 \end{bmatrix} \\ = 12 - 3\tfrac{3}{5} \\ = {}^{60}/_5 - {}^{18}/_5 = {}^{42}/_5 \end{aligned} \tag{5-81}$$

Since we are solving a maximization problem, and since we have determined that $c_3 - Z_3 = {}^{42}/_5$, we know that the addition of the variable x_3 (column vector $\mathbf{a}_3$) with objective function coefficient $c_3 = 12$ will change the present optimal solution.

Now, we must construct the simplex tableau with the added variable x_3 (column $\mathbf{a}_3$). Note that we have renumbered the original two slack variables (vectors) as follows.

Original Problem		New Problem
$(x_3)\mathbf{a}_3$	$\rightarrow$	$\mathbf{a}_4(x_4)$
$(x_4)\mathbf{a}_4$	$\rightarrow$	$\mathbf{a}_5(x_5)$

This was done for simplicity and to avoid redundancy, since we are considering the effect of adding a new real variable x_3, and in the original problem x_3 was the slack variable associated with the first constraint. This renumbering has no effect on the original basis matrix except that this original basis matrix would be represented by the column vectors corresponding to x_4 and x_5. The revised simplex tableau, with the additional variable (column) added, is shown below in Table 5.15.

TABLE 5.15 Revised Simplex Tableau—Variable Added

c_b	Variables in Basis	c_j	6	8	12	0	0
		Solution Values, $\mathbf{x}_b$	$\mathbf{a}_1$	$\mathbf{a}_2$	$\mathbf{a}_3$	$\mathbf{a}_4$	$\mathbf{a}_5$
8	x_2	2	0	1	$3/10$	$1/5$	$-1/4$
6	x_1	8	1	0	$1/5$	$-1/5$	$1/2$
	Z_j	64	6	8	$18/5$	$2/5$	1
	$c_j - Z_j$		0	0	$42/5$	$-2/5$	-1

Now, since $c_3 - Z_3 = {}^{42}/_5 > 0$, we must make another simplex iteration. Performing this simplex iteration we obtain the tableau shown in Table 5.16.

TABLE 5.16 Second Simplex Tableau—Variable Added

c_b	Variables in Basis	c_j	6	8	12	0	0
		Solution Values, $\mathbf{x}_b$	$\mathbf{a}_1$	$\mathbf{a}_2$	$\mathbf{a}_3$	$\mathbf{a}_4$	$\mathbf{a}_5$
12	x_3	$20/3$	0	$10/3$	1	$2/3$	$-5/6$
6	x_1	$20/3$	1	$-2/3$	0	$-1/3$	$2/3$
	Z_j	120	6	34	12	6	-6
	$c_j - Z_j$		0	-24	0	-6	$+6$

In Table 5.16, $c_5 - Z_5 = +6 > 0$, and we must make another iteration. Performing this simplex iteration we obtain the tableau shown in Table 5.17 below.

TABLE 5.17 Third Simplex Tableau (Optimal Solution)

c_b	Variables in Basis	c_j	6	8	12	0	0
		Solution Values, $\mathbf{x}_b$	$\mathbf{a}_1$	$\mathbf{a}_2$	$\mathbf{a}_3$	$\mathbf{a}_4$	$\mathbf{a}_5$
12	x_3	15	$5/4$	$5/2$	1	$1/4$	0
0	x_5	10	$3/2$	-1	0	$-1/2$	1
	Z_j	180	15	30	12	5	0
	$c_j - Z_j$		-9	-22	0	-3	0

In Table 5.17, all $c_j - Z_j \leq 0$. Therefore, we have obtained an optimal solution to the problem with the variable x_3 added. The optimal solution to this new problem is $x_3 = 15$, $x_5 = 10$, and maximum $Z = 180$.

5.6 CASE STUDY: IMPROVING FUEL UTILIZATION IN STEEL MILL OPERATIONS

This study was done for the Granite City Steel Division of the National Steel Corporation.[2] The National Steel Corporation, with its subsidiaries and affiliates, makes iron, steel, and aluminum products. It is the fourth-largest steel producer in the United States and has two major steel markets: the automobile and container industries. In 1979, steel and steel mill products accounted for 94 percent of the company's total sales and revenues, and the automobile and container industries encompassed about 27 and 18 percent, respectively, of total steel shipments by tonnage.

The principal steel products produced by the company are hot and cold rolled sheets and strip, tin plate, galvanized sheets, pig iron, nailable steel flooring, steel pipe and oil country goods, preengineered metal building systems and components, steel tubing, and highway and construction products. The Granite City Steel Division is a wholly owned subsidiary of the company, with its major production facility being located in Granite City, Illinois.

National Steel Corporation has maintained a strong record of production and cost reduction innovations. It introduced the first continuous hot-strip mill, the first big basic oxygen furnace, and the first 80-inch computerized hot-strip mill in the United States. More recently it brought into operation what is still the only cold-reduction mill in the United States, and it is presently converting all of its steel furnaces to a "top-and-bottom-blown" design that will further reduce costs.

All of these technological innovations have been coupled with continuous cost-reduction programs that have advanced productivity and efficiency. In the early 1970s National Steel Corporation became very concerned about its rapidly increasing raw material and operating costs. One particularly important element in its operating cost was the cost associated with fuels used in the steel-making process. An industrial engineering study completed in late 1975 at the Granite City steel mill indicated that considerable operating savings might be possible through the collection and use of two by-product gases, blast-furnace gas and coke-oven gas, throughout the steel-making process. In this environment, it was desired to fully investigate the general problem of efficiently allocating fuels throughout the production process.

The Granite City Steel mill used four types of fuels in eight locations throughout the blast furnace and steel works complex. The four fuels that were used and their associated costs at the time of the study (April 1976) were

1. Natural Gas (NG), (Outside Purchase—$1.090 per thousand cubic feet)
2. Fuel Oil (FO), (Outside Purchase—$0.310 per gallon)

[2] I would like to acknowledge the original work done in this area by David A. Page, an MBA student at the University of Missouri, St. Louis.

3. Blast-Furnace Gases (BG), (By-Product—$0.450 per thousand cubic feet)
4. Coke-Plant Gases (CG), (By-product—$0.048 per thousand cubic feet)

Note that the latter two gases were natural by-products of the production process and were available at a very low cost, in contrast to the first two fuels, which had to be purchased externally, and were considerably higher in cost.

The eight production units that consumed these fuels, and the fuels that could be utilized, were:

1. Blast-Furnace (BF)—The first step in the conversion of iron ore into steel takes place in the blast furnace where iron ore, coke, and limestone are transformed into pig iron. Natural gas and blast-furnace gas could be utilized in the blast furnace.
2. Basic Oxygen Furnaces (BOF)—Pig iron and scrap are mixed together in the basis oxygen furnace, and oxygen is injected into the bath of molten metal to produce steel. Natural gas is utilized to produce the necessary heat in the basic oxygen furnace.
3. Coke Plant [CP]—Coal is introduced into coke plant ovens, where it burns in the absence of air, driving gases from the coal to produce coke. Natural gas and coke gas may be utilized as fuels in this process.
4. Blast Furnace Boilers [BFB]—Used to produce great quantities of heated air that are blown up through the blast furnace to meet descending amounts of iron ore, coke, and flux stone. Natural gas, fuel oil, blast-furnace gas, and coke gas may be utilized to fire the blast-furnace boilers.

5. Sintering Plant [SP]—The sinter plant is used to agglomerate small or fine pieces of iron ores into larger "clinkers" of iron ore that can then be used as input to the blast furnace. Natural gas and coke gas can be used in the sintering plant.
6. Blooming Mill Soaking Pits [SOP]—In the blooming mill hot steel ingots are rolled into various semi-finished shapes (i.e., blooms, slabs, or billets). The blooming mill soaking pits are used to keep the steel blooms hot so that they can be rolled. Natural gas ans coke gas can be used in the blooming mill soaking pit.
7. Steelworks Boiler [SWB]—The steelworks boiler is used to produce steam and hot water, which is then used in several parts of the steelmaking process. Natural gas, fuel oil, and coke gas can be utilized in the steelworks boiler.
8. Hot-Strip Slab Furnaces [SF]—The hot-strip slab furnaces are used to heat the slabs prior to their being rolled into plates or sheets. Natural gas or fuel oil can be used in the hot-strip slab furnace.

A flow diagram of the steel mill fuel sources and uses is shown in Fig. 5.3 on the following page.

Note that not all of the production units were equipped to use all four of the fuels available. However, the fuel requirements of each unit could be expressed in terms of millions of BTU's, which provided a common denominator for the analysis of existing fuel utilization and for consideration of alternative fuel utilization configurations. Various resource constraints existed in specific areas, such as a minimum level of natural gas usage in the steelworks boilers, a limitation on the availability of natural gas and fuel oil in certain time periods, and a limitation on the availa-

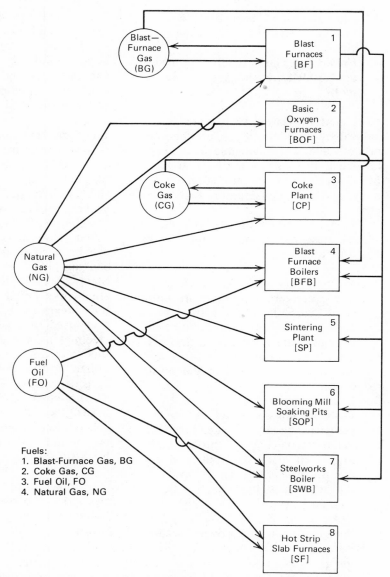

FIGURE 5.3 Flow Diagram—Steel Mill Fuel Sources and Uses

bility of the two by-product gases as a function of coke-plant and blast-furnace production levels.

A linear programming model was designed to minimize the total cost of fuel utilization:

Minimize total cost of fuel utilization =

$$\sum_{\text{all fuel types}} (\$ \text{ per unit of fuel} \times \text{units of fuel used}) \qquad (5\text{-}82)$$

subject to six types of constraints.

1. *Production fuel requirements* in millions of BTU's (MMBTU) taking into consideration the interchangeability of fuels at particular producing units. For example, referring to Fig. 5.3, natural gas or coke-plant gas may be used interchangeably to fuel the sintering plant.

2. *External natural gas requirements* (i.e., natural gas requirements for other than production). For example, external natural gas requirements for heating, power, etc. were 730,000 MCF per month.

3. *Base requirements of fuels per month* including minimum amounts of specific type fuels to be used at various producing units. For example, the pilots for the steelworks boiler required at least 1000 MCF per day, while the coke plant required at least 6700 MCF of natural gas per month.

4. *By-product fuel availability based on production.* For example, each ton of coke produced each month resulted in the production of 16.61 MCF of coke gas as a by-product.

5. *External fuel source supply constraints.* For example, at the time of the study the monthly supply availability of natural gas was in the range of 35,000–50,000 MCF per day.

6. *Restrictions on uses of certain fuels at certain production units.* For example, fuel oil could be used only at the blast-furnace boilers, the steelworks boilers, and the hot-strip slab furnace.

The mathematical formulation of the steel mill fuel-utilization model encompassing the variables and relationships described above was constructed in the following manner.

First we define:

x_{ij}: number of units of fuel i; $i = 1, 2, 3, 4$, used at production unit j; $j = 1, 2, 3, \ldots, 8$.

c_{ij}: cost ($ per unit) of fuel i used at production unit j.

As noted previously, at the time of the study, the base costs for the fuels were as follows.

Base Fuel Costs
_____

($i = 1$) Natural Gas—$1.090 per thousand cubic feet.

($i = 2$) Fuel Oil—$0.310 per gallon.

($i = 3$) Coke Gas—$0.450 per thousand cubic feet.

($i = 4$) Blast-Furnace Gas—$0.048 per thousand cubic feet.

The base fuel costs for the by-products, coke gas and blast-furnace gas, reflected the costs associated with their extraction, storage, and utilization. The base fuel costs for the externally purchased fuels reflected their average purchase cost during the time of the study.

The objective function for the steel mill fuel-utilization model was written as

$$\text{Minimize (Fuel Cost) } Z = \sum_{i=1}^{4} \sum_{j=1}^{8} c_{ij} x_{ij}$$

$$= \$1.090 \sum_{j=1}^{8} x_{1j}$$

$$+ \$0.310 \sum_{j=1}^{8} x_{2j}$$

$$+ \$0.450 \sum_{j=1}^{8} x_{3j}$$

$$+ \$0.048 \sum_{j=1}^{8} x_{4j}$$

$$(5-83)$$

Considering next the constraint set for the steel mill fuel-utilization model, the following *data conversion factors* were utilized, based on the engineering characteristics of the production process.

Data Conversion Factor

Natural Gas—1.0363 MMBTU per MCF.
Fuel Oil—0.1500 MMBTU per Gal.
Coke Gas—0.5250 MMBTU per MCF.
Blast-Furnace Gas—0.0923 MMBTU per MCF.

The constraints for the model were then written as follows.

1. Production Fuel Requirements and Interchangeability.
   (a) *Coke Plant* (MMBTU per Number Tons Production = 4.176)

$$(0.5252 \times \text{Coke Gas Utilized}) + (1.0363 \times \text{Natural Gas Utilized}) = 4.176 \times \text{Number Tons of Coke Production} \qquad (5\text{--}84)$$

   (b) *Blast-Furnaces* (MMBTU per Number Tons Production = 3.314)

$$(0.0923 \times \text{Blast Furnace Gas Utilized}) + (1.0363 \times \text{Natural Gas Utilized}) = 3.314 \times \text{Number Tons of Blast Furnace Production} \qquad (5\text{--}85)$$

   (c) *Sinter Plant* (MMBTU per Number Tons Production = 0.269)

$$(0.5250 \times \text{Coke Gas Utilized}) + (1.0363 \times \text{Natural Gas Utilized}) + 0.269 \times \text{Number Tons of Sinter Production} \qquad (5\text{--}86)$$

   (d) *Blast-Furnace Boilers* (MMBTU per M Number = 1.549)
   Steam Production (base) = 148,000 M Number

Steam Production (turbo blowers) = 0.895 × Wind Rate of Blast Furnaces

$$(0.5250 \times \text{Coke Gas Utilized}) + (0.0923 \times \text{Blast-Furnace Gas Utilized}) + (1.0363 \times \text{Natural Gas Utilized}) + (0.1500 \times \text{Fuel Oil Utilized}) = 1.549 \,[148,000 + 0.895 (\text{Wind Rate})] \qquad (5\text{--}87)$$

   (e) *Basic Oxygen Furnace*
   Natural Gas Utilization is a function of (4 MCF per Preheat) × (Average Minutes per Preheat) × (% preheats) × (Total Number of Heats Produced)

$$\text{Natural Gas Utilized} = 4 \times \text{Average Preheat Minutes} \times \% \text{ Preheats} \times \text{Heats Produced} \qquad (5\text{--}88)$$

   (f) *Blooming Mill Soaking Pits* (MMBTU per Number Ingot Tons Production = 0.601)

$$(0.520 \times \text{Coke Gas Utilized}) + (1.0363 \times \text{Natural Gas Utilized}) = 0.601 \times \text{Number Ingot Tons Produced} \qquad (5\text{--}89)$$

   (g) *Steelworks Boilers* (MMBTU per M Number − 1.442)
   M Number Production = 156,000 + 0.005 Fuel Oil Utilization at Slab Furnaces

$$(0.5250 \times \text{Coke Gas Utilized}) + (1.0363 \times \text{Natural Gas Utilized}) + (0.1500 \times \text{Fuel Oil Utilized}) = 1.442 \,(156,000 + 0.005 \text{ Fuel Oil Utilization at Slab Furnaces}) = 224,952 + 0.007 \text{ Fuel Oil Utilization at Slab Furnaces} \qquad (5\text{--}90)$$

   (h) *Slab Furnaces* (MMBTU per Number Tons Production = 3.690)

$$(1.0363 \times \text{Natural Gas Utilized}) + (0.1500 \times \text{Fuel Oil Utilized}) =$$

3.690 × Number Slab Tons Produced (5–91)

2. External Requirements for Natural Gas
Present Requirement = 730,000 MCF per Month (5–92)

3. Base Requirements of Fuels (per Month)
(a) *Natural Gas at Steelworks Boiler*
Present Requirement = 1,000 MCF per Day for Pilots

Natural Gas Utilization at Steelworks Boiler ≥ 1,000 × Days per Month (5–93)

(b) *Natural Gas at Blast-Furnace Boiler*
Present Requirement = 1,000 MCF per Day for Pilots

Natural Gas Utilization at Blast-Furnace Boiler ≥ 1,000 × Days per Month (5–94)

(c) *Natural Gas at Coke Plant*
Present Requirement = 6,700 MCF per Month

Natural Gas Utilization at Coke Plant ≥ 6,700 MCF per Month

4. By-Product Fuel Availability Based on Production
(a) *Coke Gas By-Product Availability*
Coke Gas Produced at a Rate of 16.61 MCF per Number Tons of Coke Production

Sum of Coke Gas Utilization at Coke Plant, Sinter Plant, Blast-Furnace Boiler, Blooming Mill Soaking Pits, and Steelworks Boiler ≤ 16.61 MCF × Number Tons Coke Produced (5–96)

(b) *Blast Furnace Gas By-Product Availability*
Blast Furnace Gas Produced at a Rate of 59.75 MCF per MCF Wind Rate

Sum of Blast Furnace Gas Utilization at Blast Furnace and Blast-Furnace Boiler ≤ 59.75 MCF × Wind Rate (5–97)

5. External Fuel Source Supply Constraints. The external fuel source supply constraints were varied for each run of the model. They were of very simple form, for example:

Monthly Natural Gas Supply Availability ≤ 45,000 MCF × (Days per Month) (5–98)

6. Restrictions on Uses of Fuels
(a) *Coke Gas*—Not used in blast furnace, basic oxygen furnace or slab furnace
(b) *Blast-Furnace Gas*—Not used in blast furnace, blast-furnace boilers
(c) *Fuel Oil*—Not used in blast-furnace boiler, steelworks boiler, slab furnace

A summary of the entire formulation of the steel mill fuel-utilization linear programming model is presented in Table 5.18.[3]
After the mathematical formulation of the linear programming model had been accomplished, it was calibrated and tested using data that closely approximated the actual operating condi-

[3] Complete details concerning the mathematical formulation of the model are presented in Robert E. Markland, ''Improving Fuel Utilization in Steel Mill Operations Using Linear Programming,'' *Journal of Operations Management,* vol. 1, no. 2, (November 1980), 95–102. Reprinted with permission of *The Journal of Operations Management*, November, 1980, American Production and Inventory Control Society.

TABLE 5.18 Linear Programming Formulation—Steel Mill Fuel-Utilization Model[a]

Rows \ Columns	Natural Gas									Fuel Oil						
	CP	BF	SIP	BFB	BOF	SOP	SWB	SF	EXT	CP	BF	SIP	BFB	SOP	SWB	SF
Objective function	1.0900	1.0900	1.0900	1.0900	1.0900	1.0900	1.0900	1.0900	1.0900	0.3100	0.3100	0.3100	0.3100	0.3100	0.3100	0.3100
Coke plant requirement	1.0363									0.1500						
Blast-furnace requirement		1.0363									0.1500					
Sintering plant requirement			0.0363									0.1500				
Blast-furnace boiler requirement				1.0363									0.1500			
Basic oxygen furnace requirement					1.0363											
Soaking pits requirement						1.0363								0.1500		
Steelworks boiler requirement							1.0363								0.1500	
Hot-strip furnace requirement								1.0363								0.1500
External requirement									1.0000							
Natural gas requirement—BF				1												
Natural gas requirement—SWB							1									
Natural gas requirement—CP	1															
Natural gas availability—NG	1	1	1	1	1	1	1	1	1							
Coke gas availability																
Blast-furnace gas availability																
Coke gas restriction	1							1								
Blast-furnace gas restriction		1	1	1												
Fuel oil restriction										1	1	1				−0.0070

[a]KEY: CP—Coke-Plant; BF—Blast-Furnace; SIP—Sintering Plant; BFB—Blast-Furnace Boilers; BOF—Basic Oxygen Furnace; SOP—Soaking Pits; SWB—Steelworks Boiler; SF—Slab Furnaces; EXT—External Requirements.

TABLE 5.18 (continued)

Rows	Coke Gas							Blast Furnace Gas							Type of Constraint	Right-Hand Side Values
	CP	BF	SIP	BFB	SOP	SWB	SF	CP	BF	SIP	BFB	SOP	SWB	SF		
Objective function	0.4500	0.4500	0.4500	0.4500	0.4500	0.4500	0.4500	0.0480	0.0480	0.0480	0.0480	0.0480	0.0480	0.0480		
Coke plant requirement	0.5250							0.0923							=	4.176 $\left(\begin{array}{c}\text{Number of Tons}\\\text{Coke Produced}\end{array}\right)$
Blast-furnace requirement		0.5250							0.0923						=	3.314 $\left(\begin{array}{c}\text{Number of Tons}\\\text{Hot Metal Produced}\end{array}\right)$
Sintering plant requirement			0.5250							0.0923					=	0.269 $\left(\begin{array}{c}\text{Number of Tons}\\\text{Sinter Produced}\end{array}\right)$
Blast-furnace boiler requirement				0.5250							0.0923				=	1.549 $\left(\begin{array}{c}148{,}000\;+\\0.895\,[\text{Wind Rate}]\end{array}\right)$
Basic oxygen furnace requirement															=	4 × Average Preheat Minutes × % Preheats × Heats Produced
Soaking pits requirement					0.5250							0.0923			=	0.601 (Ingot Tons Reheated)
Steelworks boiler requirement						0.5250							0.0923		=	224,952 BTU per Mo
Hot-strip furnace requirement							0.5250							0.0923	=	3.690 $\left(\begin{array}{c}\text{Number of Slab}\\\text{Tons Produced}\end{array}\right)$
External requirement															=	730,000 MCF per Mo
Natural gas requirement—BF															=	1000 MCF × No. Days per Mo
Natural gas requirement—SWB															=	1000 MCF × No. Days per Mo
Natural gas requirement—CP															=	6700 MCF per Mo
Natural gas availability—NG															≥	45,000 MCF × No. Days per Mo
Coke gas availability	1	1	1	1	1	1	1								≥	16.61 MCF × No. Tons Coke Produced
Blast-furnace gas availability								1	1	1	1	1	1	1	≥	59.75 MCF × Blast-Furnace Wind Rate
Coke gas restriction	1														≤	0
Blast-furnace gas restriction								1							≤	0
Fuel oil restriction								1							≤	0

tions for the steel mill at the time of the study. Numerous test runs of the fuel-utilization linear programming model described were made, using a monthly time horizon. In these test runs, various types of operating conditions were examined. Specific test results will now be presented for the following six operating conditions.

1. Baseline condition—current operating conditions for the steel mill.

2. No venting of coke-oven gas—utilize coke oven gas that was being vented.

3. Coke oven underfiring with blast-furnace gas, coke-oven gas used at the hot-strip slab furnaces—use of both by-product gases in the production process.

4. Natural gas availability assumed to be 50,000 MCF per day.

5. Natural gas availability assumed to be 40,000 MCF per day.

6. Natural gas availability assumed to be 35,000 MCF per day.

In Table 5.19, test results for these six operating conditions are presented for input data reflecting exising production levels at the time of the study.

Referring to Table 5.19, it can be seen that by using the coke gas that was being vented ("Run 2") a cost savings of $2,580,606 − $2,562,886 = $17,720 per month from the baseline condition (Run 1) was possible. The source of this savings can be analyzed by using our knowledge of duality theory. As can be seen in Table 5.19 the only differences between Runs 1 and 2 were the following.

Thus, 97,667 gallons of fuel oil were replaced with 27,905 MCF of previously vented coke gas, at the steelworks boiler. Referring to the optimal solution produced for Run 1, it was observed that the marginal value, or shadow price, of the by-product coke gas was $0.635/MCF. Thus, a savings of $0.0635 × 27,905 = $17,720 resulted. In addition, the optimal solution indicated that the shadow price of the by-product blast-furnace gas was $0.00 per MCF, which indicated that there was more blast-furnace gas available than could be utilized. Finally, the shadow price of natural gas was $1.15 per MCF. However, all of the natural gas available was being used to satisfy production requirements or the external requirements (i.e., there was no slack in any of these constraints).

The test run involving use of the blast-furnace gas at the coke ovens, and coke-oven gas at the hot-strip slab furnaces (Run 3) indicated that a savings of $258,134 per month from current operating conditions (Run 1) was possible. For this run, no fuel oil was required and an excess of approximately 88,500 MCF per month of natural gas existed. Also, due to the high cost of replacing fuel oil at the slab furnaces with coke gas, it became less expensive to use a small amount of natural gas at the sinter plant and blast furnaces, rather than either coke gas or blast-furnace gas.

The final three test runs summarized in Table 5.19 (Runs 4, 5, and 6) involved varying the natural gas availability under the baseline operating conditions. As can be observed in the last three columns of Table 5.19, the

	Run 1	Run 2	△
Fuel Oil (Gal)—Steelworks Boiler	271,132 gal	173,465 gal	− 97,667 gal
Coke Gas (MCF)—Steelworks Boiler	297,117 MCF	325,022 MCF	+ 27,905 MCF

TABLE 5.19 Test Results—Existing Production Levels

Results	Run 1– Baseline Conditions	Run 2– No Venting of Coke Gas	Run 3– Blast-Furnace Gas at Coke Plant	Run 4– Natural Gas Availability (= 50,000 MCF per day)	Run 5– Natural Gas Availability (= 40,000 MCF per day)	Run 6– Natural Gas Availability (= 35,000 MCF per day)
Value of Objective Function (Total Cost of Fuel Distribution)	$2,580,606	$2,562,886	$2,322,472	$2,440,116	$2,926,096	$3,098,840
Fuel Distribution Plan						
Coke gas (MCF)						
Coke plant	464,032	464,032	—	430,432	464,032	464,032
Sinter plant	35,577	35,577	—	—	35,577	35,577
Blast-furnace boilers	—	—	—	—	—	—
Soaking pits	176,769	176,769	176,769	176,769	176,769	176,769
Steelworks boilers	297,117	325,022	—	366,294	297,117	297,117
Slab furnaces	—	—	796,726	—	—	—
Blast-furnace gas (MCF)						
Coke plant	—	—	2,639,402	—	—	4,354,085
Blast furnace	4,354,085	4,354,085	4,111,531	4,354,085	4,354,085	4,354,085
Blast-furnace boilers	3,859,591	3,859,591	3,859,591	3,859,591	3,859,591	3,859,591
Natural gas (MCF)						
Coke plant	6,700	6,700	6,700	23,722	6,700	6,700
Blast furnace	—	—	21,603	18,023	—	—
Sinter plant	—	—	18,023	—	—	—
Blast-furnace boilers	31,504	31,504	31,504	31,504	31,504	31,504
BOF	25,403	25,403	25,403	25,403	25,403	25,403
Soaking pits	—	—	—	—	—	—
Steelworks boilers	31,504	31,504	217,072	31,504	31,504	31,504
Slab furnaces	524,889	524,889	211,247	614,877	224,889	74,889
Fuel oil (gal)						
Steelworks boilers	271,132	173,465	—	—	367,854	416,214
Slab furnaces	621,696	621,696	—	—	2,694,296	3,730,596

greatest fuel distribution cost increase occurred as the natural gas availability dropped from 50,000 MCF per day to 40,000 MCF per day, (i.e., $\triangle$ = $485,980 per 10,000 MCF per day = 48.60 per MCF per day).

This case has presented a linear programming approach to fuel utilization within the production environment of a large Midwestern steel mill. Test results involving various operating conditions indicated that considerable cost savings could be achieved by using a fuel allocation plan that more effectively utilized by-product gases produced in the steel-making process.

5.7 CONCLUSION

In Chapter 3 we studied the structure, formulation, and graphical solution approach to linear programming. In Chapter 4 we explored, using the simplex method, the mechanics of obtaining an optimal solution to the linear programming problem. In this chapter we have broadened our understanding of the interrelations in linear programming through the study of duality theory and sensitivity analysis.

Duality theory is important to the understanding of the interrelationships between the primal and dual formulations of the linear programming problem, to the construction of the dual simplex algorithm which may be more efficient for certain types of linear programming problems, and in analyzing the economic consequences of the solution to a linear programming analysis. Sensitivity analysis enables the manager and management scientist to work together in eliciting a great deal of pertinent information from the optimal solution. Included are the ramifications of changes that would result from changes to the various input data and parameters. Finally, we have seen that a thorough understanding of duality theory enhances the understanding of sensitivity analysis, and indeed leads to a much greater appreciation of the entire methodology of linear programming.

GLOSSARY OF TERMS

Complementary Slackness An important corollary to the dual theorem of linear programming, which indicates that each basic feasible solution in the primal problem has a complementary basic feasible solution in the dual problem, with specific relationships between the primal and dual variables.

Duality Theory A body of knowledge concerning the interrelationships between a primal linear programming problem and its dual and the economic significance of these relationships.

Dual Problem A linear programming problem that has some specific interrelationships with the primal linear programming problem.

Dual Simplex Algorithm A linear programming algorithm designed to deal with superoptimal basic solutions and work toward feasibility.

Dual Variables The variables associated with the dual problem.

Optimal Solution Solution that is both feasible and optimal.

Primal Problem A maximization linear programming problem with all less-than-or-equal-to constraints.

Sensitivity Analysis or Postoptimality Analysis Examining the effect of changes in certain parameters of the linear programming problem upon the problem's optimal solution.

Shadow Price-Opportunity Cost   The value or worth of relaxing a constraint by acquiring an additional unit of the factor of production associated with that constraint.

Suboptimal Solution   A feasible solution that is not yet optimal.

Superoptimal Solution   An optimal solution that is not yet feasible.

SELECTED REFERENCES

DUALITY THEORY   Refer to those references provided at the end of Chapter 3, "An Introduction to Linear
AND SENSITIVITY   Programming."
ANALYSIS

DISCUSSION QUESTIONS

1. Judge this statement: "The optimal solution to the primal problem corresponds with a basic feasible solution to the dual problem."
2. Explain the "complementary slackness" relationships.
3. If the primal problem has no feasible solution, what does this imply for the dual problem?
4. Do "Corollary 3" and the "complementary slackness conditions" contradict each other? Why or why not?
5. Discuss the economic interpretation of the objective function and constraints of the dual problem when the primal problem is stated as a "production-scheduling problem." In this context, what do we mean by a "shadow price"?
6. Show how you can obtain the values of the shadow prices directly from the optimal tableau of the primal problem.
7. In what sense can you compare the dual simplex algorithm to the simplex method?
8. When the optimal solution to the primal is unbounded, the dual solution is (a) suboptimal, (b) superoptimal, (c) neither a nor b.
9. In what situation do you think that it might be much more efficient to solve the dual problem instead of the primal problem? (That is, identify the type of situation with respect to the primal problem.)
10. Suppose you have a maximization problem and variable x_5 is basic in the optimal solution. Assume you increase the coefficient of x_5 in the objective function (this is the only change you make). Could you make some statement about x_5 with respect to the new optimal solution without performing any sensitivity analysis? If so, what statement and why?
11. Describe the different steps you would apply when dealing with an "equality constraint," where you want to transform the equality into two inequalities and you want to begin with a standard maximization problem.
12. When adding a constraint to the original problem, for what type of situation would you have to use the dual simplex algorithm?
13. In a minimization problem, when is the current optimal solution going to change if we add a variable?
14. How can the inverse of the basis matrix $[\mathbf{B}^{-1}]$ be determined at any iteration from the simplex tableau?
15. Discuss the variable removal criterion and variable entry criterion of the dual simplex algorithm.

PROBLEM SET

1. Construct the dual of the following linear programming problem.

$$\text{Maximize } Z = 2x_1 + 6x_2 + 3x_3$$

subject to:
$$1x_1 \qquad + 4x_3 \leq 12$$
$$2x_2 - 1x_3 \leq 8$$
$$3x_1 - 7x_2 \qquad \leq 4$$
$$2x_3 \leq 5$$

with $\quad x_1 \geq 0,\ x_2 \geq 0,\ x_3 \geq 0$

2. Construct the dual of the following linear programming problem.

$$\text{Maximize } Z = 1x_1 + 2x_2$$

subject to:
$$2x_1 - 3x_2 \leq 7$$
$$1x_1 + 2x_2 \leq 10$$

with $\quad x_1 \geq 0,\ x_2 \geq 0$

3. Construct the dual of the following linear programming problem.

$$\text{Minimize } Z = 5y_1 + 7y_2 + 4y_3 + 11y_4 + 2y_5$$

subject to:
$$2y_1 \qquad + 1y_3 + 3y_4 \qquad \geq 5$$
$$+ 1y_2 + 2y_3 + 1y_4 - 1y_5 \geq 2$$

with $\quad y_1 \geq 0,\ y_2 \geq 0,\ y_3 \geq 0,\ y_4 \geq 0,\ y_5 \geq 0$

4. Construct the dual of the following linear programming problem.

$$\text{Minimize } Z = 5y_1 + 4y_2$$

subject to:
$$6y_1 + 3y_2 \geq 18$$
$$2y_1 + 4y_2 \geq 12$$
$$2y_1 + 8y_2 \geq 16$$

with $\quad y_1 \geq 0,\ y_2 \geq 0$

5. Construct the dual of the following linear programming problem.

$$\text{Maximize } Z = 1x_1 + 4x_2$$

subject to:
$$4x_1 + 2x_2 \leq 7$$
$$3x_1 + 1x_2 = 4$$

with $\quad x_1 \geq 0,\ x_2 \geq 0$

6. Construct the dual of the following linear programming problem.

$$\text{Minimize } Z = 2y_1 + 3y_2 + 5y_3$$

subject to:
$$3y_1 + 2y_2 + 5y_3 \geq 7$$
$$2y_1 \qquad + 1y_3 \geq 5$$
$$4y_2 + 3y_3 \geq 8$$

with $\quad y_1 \geq 0,\ y_2 \geq 0,\ y_3 \geq 0$

7. Construct the dual of the following linear programming problem.

$$\text{Minimize } Z = 3y_1 - 2y_2 + 3y_3 - 4y_4$$

subject to:
$$1y_1 - 6y_2 + 3y_3 \qquad = 10$$
$$\qquad + 2y_2 \qquad - 2y_4 \le 10$$
$$3y_1 \qquad + 4y_3 + 2y_4 \ge 15$$

with $y_1 \ge 0$, $y_2 \ge 0$, y_3 unrestricted in sign, $y_4 \ge 0$

8. Construct the dual of the following linear programming problem.

$$\text{Maximize } Z = 1x_1 - 3x_2 + 5x_3 - 1x_4$$

subject to:
$$3x_1 + 2x_2 - 4x_3 - 2x_4 \ge 12$$
$$\qquad - 1x_2 \qquad + 4x_4 = 10$$
$$2x_1 + 1x_2 - 3x_3 \qquad \le 15$$

with x_1 unrestricted in sign, $x_2 \ge 0$, $x_3 \ge 0$, $x_4 \ge 0$

9. Construct the dual of the following linear programming problem.

$$\text{Maximize } Z = 4x_1 + 1x_2$$

subject to:
$$2x_1 + 4x_2 \ge 7$$
$$5x_1 - 1x_2 = 4$$
$$1x_1 + 2x_2 \le 2$$

with $x_1 \ge 0$, x_2 unrestricted in sign

10. Construct the dual of the following linear programming problem.

$$\text{Minimize } Z = -2y_1 + 4y_2 + 3y_3$$

subject to:
$$1y_1 - 3y_2 + 2y_3 \le 12$$
$$2y_2 + 1y_3 \ge 10$$
$$1y_1 \qquad - 2y_3 = 18$$

with $y_1 \ge 0$, $y_2 \ge 0$, y_3 unrestricted in sign

11. Given the following linear programming problem,

$$\text{Maximize } Z = 3x_1 + 7x_2$$

subject to:
$$-3x_1 + 7x_2 \ge 21$$
$$9x_1 - 3x_2 = 0$$
$$5x_1 + 4x_2 \le 40$$

with $x_1 \ge 0$, $x_2 \ge 0$

(a) Reformulate this problem in standard primal form.
(b) Now construct the dual to the primal problem you have determined.

12. Given the following linear programming problem,

$$\text{Maximize } Z = 5x_1 - 3x_2$$

subject to:
$$-2x_1 + 6x_2 \ge 20$$
$$6x_1 - 2x_2 = 2$$
$$4x_1 - 1x_2 \ge 0$$

with $x_1 \geq 0, x_2 \geq 0$

(a) Reformulate this problem in standard primal form.

(b) Now construct the dual to the primal problem you have determined.

13.   Given the following linear programming problem,

$$\text{Minimize } Z = 3x_1 - 6x_2$$

subject to: $-2x_1 + 5x_2 \leq 12$
$$4x_1 - 8x_2 \geq 8$$

with $x_1 \geq 0, x_2 \geq 0$

(a) Reformulate this problem in standard primal form.

(b) Now construct the dual to the primal problem you have determined.

14.   Given the following linear programming problem,

$$\text{Minimize } Z = 2x_1 - 5x_2 - 3x_3$$

subject to: $-2x_1 + 4x_2 - 3x_3 \leq 14$
$$- 1x_2 + 1x_3 = 10$$
$$4x_1 \qquad\quad - 2x_3 \geq -6$$

with $x_1 \geq 0, x_2 \geq 0, x_3 \geq 0$

(a) Reformulate this problem in standard primal form.

(b) Now construct the dual to the primal problem you have determined.

15.   Determine the optimal values of the primal and dual variables for Problem 5-1. For the two optimal solutions verify all of the complementary slackness relationships.

16.   Determine the optimal values of the primal and dual variables for Problem 5-2. For the two optimal solutions verify all of the complementary slackness relationships.

17.   Determine the optimal values of the primal and dual variables for Problem 5-3. For the two optimal solutions verify all of the complementary slackness relationships.

18.   Determine the optimal values of the primal and dual variables for Problem 5-4. For the two optimal solutions verify all of the complementary slackness relationships.

19.   Determine the optimal values of the primal and dual variables for Problem 5-5. For the two optimal solutions verify all of the complementary slackness relationships.

20.   Determine the optimal value of the primal and dual variables for Problem 5-6. For the two optimal solutions verify all of the complementary slackness relationships.

21.   The following linear programming problem, which is structured in standard primal form, has an unbounded solution. Show that the dual to this problem has no feasible solution.

$$\text{Maximize } Z = -2x_1 + 3x_2$$

subject to:
$$1x_1 \qquad \leq 5$$
$$2x_1 - 3x_2 \leq 6$$

with $\quad x_1 \geq 0, x_2 \geq 0$

22. The following linear programming problem, which is structured in standard primal form, has an unbounded solution. Show that the dual to this problem has no feasible solution.

$$\text{Maximize } Z = 2x_1 + 1x_2$$

subject to:
$$1x_2 \leq 5$$
$$-1x_1 + 1x_2 \leq 1$$

with $\quad x_1 \geq 0, x_2 \geq 0$

23. The following linear programming problem has an unbounded solution. Show that the dual to this problem has no feasible solution.

$$\text{Minimize } Z = 2x_1 - 5x_2 + 3x_3$$

subject to:
$$3x_1 + 10x_2 + 5x_3 = 15$$
$$33x_1 - 10x_2 - 9x_3 \geq 12$$
$$1x_1 + 2x_2 + 1x_3 \geq 4$$

with $\quad x_1 \geq 0, x_2 \geq 0, x_3$ unrestricted in sign

24. The following linear programming problem has an unbounded solution. Show that the dual to this problem has no feasible solution.

$$\text{Maximize } Z = 3x_1 + 1x_2$$

subject to:
$$2x_1 + 5x_2 \geq 10$$
$$3x_1 + 1x_2 \geq 6$$

with $\quad x_1 \geq 0, x_2 \geq 0$

25. The following linear programming problem has no feasible solution. Determine whether the dual to this problem has no feasible solution or has an unbounded solution.

$$\text{Maximize } Z = -3x_1 - 2x_2$$

subject to:
$$1x_1 + 2x_2 \leq 2$$
$$2x_1 + 4x_2 \geq 8$$

with $\quad x_1 \geq 0, x_2 \geq 0$

26. The following linear programming problem has no feasible solution. Determine whether the dual to this problem has no feasible solution or has an unbounded solution.

$$\text{Maximize } Z = 3x_1 + 5x_2$$

subject to:
$$4x_1 + 4x_2 \leq 20$$
$$7x_1 + 3x_2 \leq 21$$
$$1x_1 \qquad \geq 5$$

with $\quad x_1 \geq 0, x_2 \geq 0$

27. The following linear programming problem has no feasible solution. Determine whether the dual to this problem has no feasible solution or has an unbounded solution.

$$\text{Minimize } Z = 1x_1 + 2x_2$$

subject to:
$$1x_1 + 1x_2 \leq 3$$
$$-1x_1 + 1x_2 \geq 6$$

with $x_1 \geq 0, x_2 \geq 0$

28. The following linear programming problem has no feasible solution. Determine whether the dual to this problem has no feasible solution or has an unbounded solution.

$$\text{Maximize } Z = 1x_1 + 3x_2$$

subject to:
$$1x_1 - 1x_2 \geq 1$$
$$3x_1 - 1x_2 \leq -3$$

with $x_1 \geq 0, x_2 \geq 0$

29. Consider Example 2 presented in Section 3.2 of Chapter 3 as a primal problem.
    (a) Determine the optimal values of the primal and dual variables for this problem.
    (b) Verify all of the complementary slackness relationships.
    (c) Provide an economic interpretation summary for the primal problem.
    (d) Provide an economic interpretation summary for the dual problem.

30. Consider the diet problem presented in Section 3.8.1 of Chapter 3 as a primal problem.
    (a) Determine the optimal values of the primal and dual variables for this problem.
    (b) Verify all of the complementary slackness relationships.
    (c) Provide an economic interpretation summary for the primal problem.
    (d) Provide an economic interpretation summary for the dual problem.

31. Consider the fluid-blending problem presented in Section 3.8.2 of Chapter 3 as a primal problem.
    (a) Determine the optimal values of the primal and dual variables for this problem.
    (b) Verify all of the complementary slackness relationships.

32. Consider the multiperiod investment problem presented in Section 3.8.3 of Chapter 3 as a primal problem.
    (a) Determine the optimal values of the primal and dual variables for this problem.
    (b) Verify all of the complementary slackness relationships.

33. Consider the portfolio selection problem presented in Section 3.8.4 of Chapter 3 as a primal problem.
    (a) Determine the optimal values of the primal and dual variables for this problem.
    (b) Verify all of the complementary slackness relationships.

34. Consider the multiperiod-scheduling problem presented in Section 3.8.5 of Chapter 3 as a primal problem.

(a) Determine the optimal values of the primal and dual variables for the problem.
(b) Verify all of the complementary slackness relationships.

35. Consider the media selection problem presented in Section 3.8.6 of Chapter 3 as a primal problem.
(a) Determine the optimal values of the primal and dual variables for the problem.
(b) Verify all of the complementary slackness relationships.

36. Consider the Nelly Bly Candy Company problem discussed in Section 4.4 of Chapter 4 as a primal problem.
(a) Determine the optimal values of the primal and dual variables for the problem.
(b) Verify all of the complementary slackness relationships.

37. Solve the following problem using the dual simplex algorithm.

$$\text{Maximize } Z = 3x_1 + 4x_2$$

subject to:
$$2x_1 + 3x_2 \le 7$$
$$1x_1 + 4x_2 \ge 5$$
$$-3x_1 + 5x_2 \ge 6$$

with $x_1 \ge 0, x_2 \ge 0$

38. Solve the following problem using the dual simplex algorithm.

$$\text{Minimize } Z = 7y_1 + 5y_2 + 1y_3$$

subject to:
$$-5y_1 \qquad + 3y_3 \le -7$$
$$- 2y_2 + 5y_3 \le -4$$
$$1y_1 - 3y_2 \qquad \le \quad 3$$

with $y_1 \ge 0, y_2 \ge 0, y_3 \ge 0$

39. Solve the following problem using the dual simplex algorithm.

$$\text{Minimize } Z = 1y_1 + 2y_2$$

subject to:
$$2y_1 + 1y_2 \ge 3$$
$$1y_1 + 5y_2 \ge 7$$

with $y_1 \ge 0, y_2 \ge 0$

40. Solve the following problem using the dual simplex algorithm.

$$\text{Maximize } Z = -4x_1 - 2x_2 - 3x_3$$

subject to:
$$1x_1 + 2x_2 + 1x_3 \ge 7$$
$$2x_1 \qquad + 3x_3 \ge 5$$
$$3x_2 + 1x_3 \ge 9$$

with $x_1 \ge 0, x_2 \ge 0, x_3 \ge 0.$

41. Solve the following problem using the dual simplex algorithm.

$$\text{Maximize } Z = 4x_1 - 2x_2$$

subject to:
$$1x_1 + 1x_2 \ge 2$$
$$2x_1 + 3x_2 \ge 3$$

with $x_1 \ge 0, x_2 \ge 0$

42. Solve the following problem using the dual simplex algorithm.

$$\text{Minimize } Z = 4x_1 + 2x_2 + 1x_3$$

subject to:
$$2x_1 + 4x_2 + 5x_3 \geq 10$$
$$3x_1 - 1x_2 + 6x_3 \geq 3$$
$$5x_1 + 2x_2 + 1x_3 \geq 12$$

with $x_1 \geq 0,\ x_2 \geq 0,\ x_3 \geq 0$

43. A plastics company uses three extruding and curing machines in the manufacture of three types of children's toys. Toy 1 requires 4 hours on machine A, 1 hour on machine B, and 3 hours on machine C. Toy 2 requires 6 hours on machine A, 1½ hours on machine B, and 1 hour on machine C. Toy 3 requires 3 hours on machine A and 3 hours on machine B. At present there is an excess of 24 hours of machine A time, 12 hours of machine B time, and 12 hours of machine C time. Toy 1 produces $0.50 profit per unit, toy 2 produces $6.00 profit per unit, and toy 3 produces $5.00 profit per unit.

The linear programming formulation of this problem is

$$\text{Maximize } Z = \frac{1}{2}x_1 + 6x_2 + 5x_3$$

subject to:
$$4x_1 + 6x_2 + 3x_3 \leq 24$$
$$1x_1 + \frac{3}{2}x_2 + 3x_3 \leq 12$$
$$3x_1 + 1x_2 \qquad \leq 12$$

with $x_1 \geq 0,\ x_2 \geq 0,\ x_3 \geq 0$

The optimal tableau (solution) for this problem is shown below.

c_b	Variables in Basis	Solution Values, x_b	c_j	½	6	5	0	0	0
				a_1	a_2	a_3	a_4	a_5	a_6
6	x_2	8/3		2/3	1	0	2/9	−2/9	0
5	x_3	8/3		0	0	1	−1/9	4/9	0
0	x_6	28/3		7/3	0	0	−2/9	2/9	1
	Z_j	88/3		4	6	5	7/9	8/9	0
	$c_j - Z_j$			−7/2	0	0	−7/9	−8/9	0

(a) Perform a sensitivity analysis for each of the objective function coefficients.
(b) Perform a sensitivity analysis for each of the right-hand side values.
(c) Perform a sensitivity analysis for the addition of the constraint:

$$2x_1 + 4x_2 + 5x_3 \leq 16$$

(d) Perform a sensitivity analysis for the addition of the real variable x_4. *Note:* rearrange and renumber the original slack variables, x_4, x_5, x_6. The column vector corresponding to this new variable x_4 is

$$\mathbf{a}_4 = \begin{bmatrix} 4 \\ 1 \\ 2 \end{bmatrix}$$

The objective function coefficient corresponding to this new variable is $c_4 = 8$.

44. Using the optimal solution shown for Problem 5–16, answer the following questions.
    (a) What is the optimal production schedule for this firm? Are there any alternative optimal production schedules? If there are, what are they?
    (b) What are the optimal values of the dual decision variables, y_1, y_2, and y_3?
    (c) What are the optimal values of the dual surplus variables, y_4, y_5, and y_6?
    (d) What is the shadow price for an additional hour of time on machine A? machine B? machine C?
    (e) What is the opportunity cost associated with toy 1? How can this opportunity cost be interpreted?

45. Consider the following linear programming problem.

$$\text{Maximize } Z = -2x_1 + 1x_2 - 1x_3$$

subject to: $2x_1 + 1x_2 \qquad \le 7$
$1x_1 + 1x_2 + 1x_3 \ge 4$

with $x_1 \ge 0, x_2 \ge 0, x_3 \ge 0$

The optimal tableau (solution) for this problem is shown below.

		c_j	-2	1	-1	0	0	$-M$
c_b	Variables in Basis	Solution Values, x_b	$\mathbf{a}_1$	$\mathbf{a}_2$	$\mathbf{a}_3$	$\mathbf{a}_4$	$\mathbf{a}_5$	$\mathbf{a}_6$
0	x_5	3	1	0	-1	1	1	-1
1	x_2	7	2	1	0	1	0	0
	Z_j	7	2	1	0	1	0	0
	$c_j - Z_j$		-4	0	-1	-1	0	$-M$

(a) Perform a sensitivity analysis for each of the objective function coefficients.
(b) Perform a sensitivity analysis for each of the right-hand side values.
(c) Perform a sensitivity analysis for the addition of the constraint:

$$1x_1 + \tfrac{1}{2}x_2 - 2x_3 \le 3$$

(d) Perform a sensitivity analysis for the addition of the real variable x_4. *Note:* rearrange and renumber the original slack, surplus, and artificial variables x_4, x_5, and x_6. The column vector corresponding to this new variable x_4 is

$$\mathbf{a}_4 = \begin{bmatrix} 2 \\ 3 \end{bmatrix}$$

The objective function coefficient corresponding to this new variable is $c_4 = 3$.

46. A firm uses three machines in the manufacture of three products. Each unit of product 1 requires 3 hours on machine 1, 2 hours on machine 2, and 1 hour on machine 3. Each unit of product 2 requires 4 hours on machine 1, 1 hour on machine 2, and 3 hours on machine 3. Each unit of product 3 requires 2 hours on machine 1, 2 hours on machine 2, and 2 hours on machine 3. The contribution margin of the three products is \$30, \$40, and \$35 per unit, respectively. Available for scheduling are 90 hours of machine-1 time, 54 hours of machine-2 time, and 93 hours of machine-3 time.

The linear programming formulation of this problem is

$$\text{Maximize } Z = 30x_1 + 40x_2 + 35x_3$$

subject to:
$$3x_1 + 4x_2 + 2x_3 \leq 90$$
$$2x_1 + 1x_2 + 2x_3 \leq 54$$
$$x_1 + 3x_2 + 2x_3 \leq 93$$

with $x_1, x_2, x_3 \geq 0$

and the optimal tableau for the problem is

c_b	Variables in Basis	Solution Values, x_b	c_j 30 a_1	40 a_2	35 a_3	0 a_4	0 a_5	0 a_6
40	x_2	12	$1/3$	1	0	$1/3$	$-1/3$	0
35	x_3	21	$5/6$	0	1	$-1/6$	$2/3$	0
0	x_6	15	$-5/3$	0	0	$-2/3$	$-1/3$	1
	Z_j	1215	42.5	40	35	7.5	10	0
	$c_j - Z_j$		-12.5	0	0	-7.5	-10	0

(a) What is the optimal production schedule for this firm? Are there any other optimal production schedules indicated by the final tableau? If there are, what are they?

(b) What is the marginal value of an additional hour of time on machine 1? Over what range of time is this marginal value valid?

(c) What is the opportunity cost associated with product 1? What interpretation should be given to this opportunity cost?

(d) Suppose that the contribution margin for product 1 increased from \$30 to \$43. Would this change the optimum production plan? If it would, why would it?

(e) How much can the contribution margin for product 2 change before the current optimal solution is no longer optimal?

(f) What are the values of the dual decision variables, y_1, y_2, and y_3?

(g) Management of this firm is considering the introduction of a new product that will require 4 hours on machine 1, 2 hours on machine 2, and 3 hours on machine 3. This new product will have a contribution margin of \$55. Should it be produced? If it should, what will be the marginal value of producing one unit of this new product?

47. A small manufacturer of wooden doors has determined that it will have 30 excess hours of machine capacity, and 20 excess hours of labor capacity, in the following week. It makes two types of doors, as follows.

Door	Machine Time per Door	Labor Time per Door	Profit Contribution per Door
Deluxe	3	2	5
Supreme	5	3	8

(a) Formulate and solve the primal problem to determine the number of "Deluxe" and "Supreme" doors that should be produced.

(b) Formulate and solve the dual problem to determine the opportunity cost associated with an hour of machine time and an hour of labor time.

48. A pig farmer is attempting to analyze his feeding operation. The minimum daily requirements for the pigs of three nutritional elements and the number of units of each of these nutritional elements in two feeds is given in the following table.

Required Nutritional Element	Units of Nutritional Elements in Pounds		Minimum Requirement
	Feed 1	Feed 2	
Nutrient A	20	30	200
Nutrient B	40	25	350
Nutrient C	30	45	430
Cost per pound	$0.05	$0.03	

(a) Determine the minimum cost feed mix by formulating and solving a linear programming problem.

(b) What are the shadow prices associated with the three nutrients?

(c) Assume that the farmer can purchase a third feed at a cost of $0.02 per pound, which will provide 35 units of nutrient A, 30 units of nutrient B, and 50 units of nutrient C. Would this change the optimal mix of feeds? If so, how?

(d) Assume that the farmer decides that a fourth nutritional element is required for his pigs. Upon analysis of the two feeds being used, feed 1 is found to provide 20 units per pound of this required nutritional element and feed 2 is found to provide 30 units per pound of this required nutritional element. If a total of 250 units of this new nutrient are required, will the optimal solution change? If so, how?

49. Krypton Chemical Company produces three lawn fertilizers that vary according to their nitrate, phosphate, and potash content. Fertilizer 1 is 5 percent nitrate, 5 percent phosphate, and 10 percent potash. Fertilizer 2 is 10 percent nitrate, 10 percent phosphate, and 5 percent potash. Fertilizer 3 is 10 percent nitrate, 5

percent phosphate, and 5 percent potash. The company currently has an availability of 1000 tons of nitrates, 1000 tons of phosphates, and 2000 tons of potash. The profits associated with the three fertilizers are $17 per ton, $20 per ton, and $15 per ton, respectively. All of the fertilizer of each type that can be produced can be sold.

The linear programming formulation of this problem is

$$\text{Maximize } Z = 17x_1 + 20x_2 + 15x_3$$

subject to:
$$
\begin{array}{llll}
0.05x_1 + 0.10x_2 + 0.10x_3 \le 1000 & \text{(Nitrate)} & .075 \; X_4 \\
0.05x_1 + 0.10x_2 + 0.05x_3 \le 1000 & \text{(Phosphate)} & .05 \; X_4 \\
0.10x_1 + 0.05x_2 + 0.05x_3 \le 1500 & \text{(Potash)} & .05 \; X_4
\end{array}
$$

with $\quad x_1 \ge 0, \; x_2 \ge 0, \; x_3 \ge 0$

The final tableau (optimal solution) for this problem is shown below.

		c_j	17	20	15	0	0	0
c_b	Variables in Basis	Solution Values, x_b	a_1	a_2	a_3	a_4	a_5	a_6
20	x_2	$3,333\frac{1}{3}$	0	1	1	$40/3$	0	$-20/3$
0	x_5	0	0	0	$-\frac{1}{20}$	-1	1	0
17	x_1	$13,333\frac{1}{3}$	1	0	0	$-20/3$	0	$40/3$
	Z_j	293,333.33	17	20	20	$460/3$	0	$280/3$
	$c_j - Z_j$		0	0	-5	$-460/3$	0	$-280/3$

(a) Perform a sensitivity analysis for each of the objective function coefficients.
(b) Perform a sensitivity analysis for each of the right-hand side values.
(c) The company decides that it needs a weed killer constituent in each of the three fertilizers. It has 1000 tons of this weed killer available and fertilizer 1 requires 12 percent, fertilizer 2 requires 15 percent, and fertilizer 3 requires 10 percent of this weed killer. Formulate a new constraint based on this situation, and perform a sensitivity analysis for the addition of this new constraint.

$.12X_1 + .15X_2 + .10X_3 \le 1000$

(d) The company decides that it would like to produce a fourth fertilizer that it can sell at a profit of $25 per ton. This fourth fertilizer will require 7.5 percent nitrate, 5 percent phosphate, and 5 percent potash. Formulate a new column based on this situation, and perform a sensitivity analysis for the addition of the new real variable. *Note:* Ignore the addition of the new constraint from part *c*.

$25 X_4$

50. Using the optimal solution shown for Problem 5–49, answer the following questions.
(a) What are the optimal production amounts of the three fertilizers? Are there any alternative optimal solutions to this problem? If so, what are they?
(b) What are the optimal values of the dual decision variables, y_1, y_2, and y_3?
(c) What are the optimal values of the dual surplus variables y_4, y_6, and y_8?

(d) What is the shadow price for nitrate? for phosphate? for potash?

(e) What is the opportunity cost associated with fertilizer 3?

51. Mr. Slim Pickings operates a 600-acre truck farm near Columbia, Missouri. He currently raises tomatoes, corn, and cabbages, and can sell all of these three vegetables that he produces. In attempting to plan for the next growing season he has compiled the following set of data.

Crop	Days of Labor Needed per Acre	Gallons of Water Needed per Acre	Pounds of Fertilizer Needed per Acre
Tomatoes	4	10,000	30
Corn	3	6,000	50
Cabbages	6	8,000	60
Total availability	2,000	5,000,000	50,000

The average yield expected for the three crops if 2000 pounds per acre of tomatoes, 100 bushels per acre of corn, and 400 heads per acre of cabbage. Mr. Pickings expects to receive $.25 per pound for his tomatoes, $4.00 per bushel for his corn, and $.80 per head for his cabbages. He wishes to determine the number of acres to be allocated to each of the crops in order to maximize revenue.

The linear programming formulation of this problem is

Maximize Z = (2000 lb per acre)($.25 per lb)$x_1$ + (100 bushels per acre)
($4.00 per bushel)$x_2$ + (400 heads per acre)($.80 per head)
x_3 = ($500 per acre)$x_1$ + ($400 per acre)$x_2$ + ($320 per acre)$x_3$

subject to:
$$4x_1 + 3x_2 + 6x_3 \leq 2,000$$
$$10,000x_1 + 6,000x_2 + 8,000x_3 \leq 5,000,000$$
$$30x_1 + 50x_2 + 60x_3 \leq 50,000$$
$$x_1 + x_2 + x_3 \leq 600$$

with $x_1 \geq 0, x_2 \geq 0, x_3 \geq 0$

The final tableau (optimal solution) for this problem is shown below.

		c_j	500	400	320	0	0	0	0
c_b	Variables in Basis	Solution Values, x_b	a_1	a_2	a_3	a_4	a_5	a_6	a_7
500	x_1	200	1	0	3	1	0	0	−3
0	x_5	600,000	0	0	−10,000	−4,000	1	0	6,000
0	x_6	24,000	0	0	70	20	0	1	−110
400	x_2	400	0	1	−2	−1	0	0	4
	Z_j	260,000	500	400	700	100	0	0	100
	$c_j - Z_j$		0	0	−380	−100	0	0	−100

(a) Perform a sensitivity analysis for each of the objective function coefficients.

(b) Perform a sensitivity analysis for each of the right-hand side values.

(c) Mr. Pickings is worried about a predicted "grasshopper plague." He has decided that he must spray each of his three crops according to the following schedule.

Tomatoes	6 gallons of spray per acre
Corn	10 gallons of spray per acre
Cabbages	6 gallons of spray per acre

He has purchased 3600 gallons of spray for the entire truck farm. Formulate a new constraint based on this situation, and perfrom a sensitivity analysis for the addition of this new constraint.

(d) Mr. Pickings is considering growing a fourth crop, cucumbers, which he feels will yield 900 pounds per acre of cucumbers. He is confident that he can sell these cucumbers for $.50 per pound. The cucumber crop will require 3 days of labor per acre, 7000 gallons of water per acre, and 40 pounds of fertilizer per acre. Formulate a new column based on this situation, and perform a sensitivity analysis for the addition of the new variable. *Note:* Ignore the addition of the new constraint from part c.

52. Using the optimal solution shown for Problem 5–51, answer the following questions.

(a) What are the optimal number of acres to be allocated to the three crops? Are there any alternative optimal solutions to this problem? If so, what are they?

(b) What are the optimal values of the dual decision variables y_1, y_2, y_3, and y_4?

(c) What are the optimal values of the dual surplus variables y_5, y_7, and y_9?

(d) What is the shadow price for days of labor per acre? gallons of water per acre? pounds of fertilizer per acre?

(e) What is the opportunity cost associated with tomatoes? with corn? with cabbages?

53. Easy-Rider Truck Rental Company is considering the purchase of three tyr e⁻ of trucks for its rental fleet. The purchase price will be $25,000 for each large-sized truck, $20,000 for each medium-sized truck, and $10,000 for each small-sized truck. It has $400,000 available for purchasing these trucks. In order to balance its fleet it has decided that it must purchase at least 4 large-sized trucks, at least 5 medium-sized trucks, and at least 10 small-sized trucks. Its current storage facility can accommodate a total of 25 trucks. Its maintenance facilities can handle the equivalent of 40 small trucks. However, each medium-sized truck has a maintenance equivalence of 2 small trucks, and each large truck has the maintenance equivalence of 4 small trucks.

The linear programming formulation of this problem is

$$\text{Minimize } Z = 25{,}000x_1 + 20{,}000x_2 + 10{,}000x_3$$

$$\begin{aligned}
\text{subject to:} \quad 25{,}000x_1 + 20{,}000x_2 + 10{,}000x_3 &\leq 400{,}000 \\
x_1 \quad\quad\quad\quad\quad\quad &\geq 4 \\
x_2 \quad\quad\quad &\geq 5 \\
x_3 &\geq 10 \\
x_1 + x_2 + x_3 &\leq 25 \\
4x_1 + 2x_2 + 1x_3 &\leq 40
\end{aligned}$$

with $x_1 \geq 0,\ x_2 \geq 0,\ x_3 \geq 0$

c_b	Variables in Basis	Solution Values x_b	a_1 (25,000)	a_2 (20,000)	a_3 (10,000)	a_4 (0)	a_5 (0)	a_6 (+M)	a_7 (0)	a_8 (+M)	a_9 (0)	a_{10} (+M)	a_{11} (0)	a_{12} (0)
0	x_4	100,000	0	0	0	1	25,000	−25,000	20,000	−20,000	10,000	−10,000	0	0
25,000	x_1	4	1	0	0	0	−1	1	0	0	0	0	0	0
20,000	x_2	5	0	1	0	0	0	0	−1	1	0	0	0	0
10,000	x_3	10	0	0	1	0	0	0	0	0	−1	1	0	0
0	x_{11}	6	0	0	0	0	1	−1	1	−1	1	−1	1	0
0	x_{12}	4	0	0	0	0	4	−4	2	−2	1	−1	0	1
Z_j		300,000	25,000	20,000	10,000	0	−25,000	+25,000	−20,000	+20,000	−10,000	+10,000	0	0
$c_j - Z_j$		0	0	0	0	0	25,000	$M - 25,000$	+20,000	$M - 20,000$	+10,000	$M - 10,000$	0	0

The final tableau (optimal solution) for this problem is shown on page 251.
(a) Perform a sensitivity analysis for each of the objective function coefficients.
(b) Perform a sensitivity analysis for each of the right-hand side values.
(c) Easy-Rider Truck Rental Company has an opportunity to buy a group of large-sized, medium-sized, and small-sized trucks from one of its competitors who has gone bankrupt. It can purchase a mixture of the three types of trucks, but its purchases must be at least 22 trucks in total. Formulate a new constraint to describe this situation, and perform a sensitivity analysis for the addition of this new constraint.
(d) Easy-Rider Truck Rental Company is contemplating adding a diesel-powered type of truck to its fleet. The purchase price for each of these diesel-powered trucks will be $18,000. The diesel truck has a maintenance equivalence equal to that of the small truck. Formulate a new column corresponding to this situation, and perform a sensitivity analysis for the addition of the real variable. *Note:* Ignore the constraint formulated in part *c*.

54. Using the optimal solution shown for Problem 5–33, answer the following questions.
   (a) What is the optimum truck-purchasing schedule for this firm? Are there any alternative optimal purchasing schedules? If there are, what are they?
   (b) What are the optimal values of the dual decision variables y_1, y_2, y_3, y_4, y_5, and y_6?
   (c) What are the optimal values of the dual slack variables y_7, y_8, and y_9?
   (d) What is the shadow price for an additional dollar of purchasing funds? What is the shadow price for an additional unit of storage space? What is the shadow price of an additional unit of maintenance facility?
   (e) What is the opportunity cost associated with a large-sized truck? a medium-sized truck? a small-sized truck?

6 Goal Programming

6.1 INTRODUCTION

In previous chapters we have made an extensive study of linear programming. In formulating and solving linear programming problems the modeling process focused on a single objective, such as maximizing total profits or minimizing total costs. Thus, we inherently forced all of the objectives or goals of management into a single aggregate dimension. However, in many important "real world" decision-making situations it may not be feasible, nor desirable, to try to reduce all of the goals of an organization to a single objective. For example, rather than focusing only on maximizing profits, the corporation may simultaneously be interested in maintaining a stable workforce, increasing its share of market, and limiting price increases.

An important new technique for the analysis and solution of problems involving multiple goals or objectives has been developed to supplement linear programming. Called **goal programming**, it allows the decision maker the opportunity to include in the problem formulation multiple goals or objectives. Goal programming greatly enhances the flexibility of linear programming as it allows the inclusion of conflicting objectives while still yielding a solution that is optimal with respect to the decision maker's specification of goal priorities. The use of goal programming thus reflects a philosophy of trying to obtain an optimal compromise solution to a set of conflicting objectives. Goal programming has been applied to numerous multiobjective modeling situations, including linear or nonlinear functions and constraints, and both continuous and discrete variables. However, in this text we will limit our discussion to linear goal programming problems with continuous variables.

Goal programming is a multiobjective extension of linear, or nonlinear, programming. As we shall demonstrate below, formulation of a goal programming model is done in a manner similar to the formulation of a linear programming model. Thus, the decision variables of the model must first be defined. Then the managerial goals related to the problem must be specified and ranked in order of priority. Since it may be very difficult to rank these goals on a cardinal scale, an ordinal ranking is usually applied to each of the goals. A distinguishing characteristic of goal programming is that goals ranked in order of priority or importance by the decision maker, or manager, are satisfied in ordinal sequence by the goal programming solution procedure. Obviously, it may not always be possible to reach every goal specified by the decision maker. Thus, goal programming is often referred to as a **lexicographic** procedure in which the various goals are satisfied in order of their relative importance. Finally, goal programming is often called a **satisficing** procedure in that the goal programming approach involves the decision maker in a process that attempts to achieve a "satisfactory" level of multiple objectives, rather than an "optimal" outcome for a single objective (as in done in linear programming).[1]

The beginnings of goal programming can perhaps be traced to the pioneering work of Charnes and Cooper[2] who developed a goal programming approach to resolving infeasibility problems in linear programming problems that were caused by conflicting objectives. Charnes and Cooper considered only a linear multiobjective model, which they transformed into a conventional single-objective linear programming model by the use of weighted-goal deviational variables. Their approach is often referred to as **weighted linear goal programming**. One major advantage of this approach to goal programming is that it is very efficient computationally, because the weighted linear goal programming model can be solved using the usual linear programming procedures. One major disadvantage of

---

[1] This "satisficing" concept is discussed more fully in J. G. March, and H. A. Simon, *Organizations* (New York: John Wiley & Sons, Inc., 1958).

[2] A. Charnes, and W. W. Cooper, *Management Models and Industrial Applications of Linear Programming* (New York: John Wiley & Sons, Inc., 1961).

this approach is that it may be difficult, or impossible, to assign valid weights for various conflicting objectives in practical, real-world problems.

Both Ijiri[3] and Jaaskelainen[4] made further refinements to the technique of goal programming. Lee[5] contributed greatly to the advancement of goal programming by the development of the idea of **preemptive priority goal programming**. In this framework, achievement of a set of goals, at some priority P_1, is always preferred to the achievement of a set of goals at a lower-ranking priority, P_2. Additionally, it is possible to include several weighted goals within each ranking, if the goals within a ranking are **commensurable** (i.e., measured in the same units). This approach is often referred to as *lexicographic weighted goal programming*. Lee has provided extensive case study results from the application of lexicographic weighted goal programming. Ignizio[6] has further extended goal programming by developing and applying a number of exact integer goal programming algorithms, and has also done work in nonlinear goal programming.

6.2 GOAL PROGRAMMING CONCEPTS AND TERMINOLOGY

The basic idea in goal programming is to incorporate all managerial objectives into the goal programming formulation. An *objective* is any general statement of the desires of the decision maker, such as "maintain stable workforce" or "reduce energy costs." For each objective the decision maker then specifies a numerical **aspiration level** that serves to relate or transform the objective into a numerical **goal**. For example, the decision maker may seek to "reduce energy costs by at least 10 percent." Since all the aspiration levels cannot always be simultaneously satisfied, **deviations** from the goals can be expected. In goal programming a specific numerical goal is first established for each of the objectives. We then seek a solution that minimizes the (weighted) sum of the deviations of these objectives from their respective goals. In mathematical terms, let

$x_1, x_2, \ldots, x_n$ = the decision variables of the problem

K = the number of objectives being considered

c_{jk} = the coefficient of x_j ($j = 1, 2, \ldots, n$) in the objective function for each objective k ($k = 1, 2, \ldots, K$)

g_k = the goal for objective k

The solution to the goal programming problem that is sought is the one that comes as close as possible to attaining the goals:

---

[3] Y. Ijiri, *Management Goals and Accounting for Control* (Chicago: Rand-McNally, 1965).

[4] V. Jaaskelainen, *Accounting and Mathematical Programming* (Helsinki: Research Institute for Business and Economics, 1973).

[5] S. M. Lee, *Goal Programming for Decision Analysis* (Philadelphia: Auerbach Publishers, Inc., 1972).

[6] J. P. Ignizio, *Goal Programming and Extensions* (Lexington, Mass.: D. C. Heath and Company, 1976).

$$\sum_{j=1}^{n} c_{j1} x_j = g_1 \qquad \text{(Goal 1)}$$

$$\sum_{j=1}^{n} c_{j2} x_j = g_2 \qquad \text{(Goal 2)} \qquad\qquad (6\text{-}1)$$

$$\sum_{j=1}^{n} c_{jk} x_j = g_k \qquad \text{(Goal } K)$$

Now, it will generally not be possible to satisfy all of these goals simultaneously. Thus, we need to define an aggregate objective function for the goal programming model that allows for a compromise with respect to achieving the various goals. Assuming that positive or negative deviations from the respective goals are considered to be equally important, the aggregate objective function for the goal programming model can be written as

$$\text{Minimize (Sum of deviations from goals) } Z = \sum_{k=1}^{K} \left| \left(\sum_{j=1}^{n} c_{jk} x_j - g_k \right) \right| \quad (6\text{-}2)$$

Thus, the objective function of the goal programming model is expressed as a **preference function** or **achievement function** in terms of deviations from target goals. Unfortunately, the objective function given by Equation 6–2 is too complicated to be solved very easily. Now, the key notion in goal programming involves transforming the objective function given by Equation 6–2 into a linear programming format that will facilitate the solution of the problem. The first step in the transformation process involves the definition of the new variables.

$$d_k = \sum_{j=1}^{n} c_{jk} x_j - g_k, \qquad \text{for } k = 1, 2, \ldots, K \qquad\qquad (6\text{-}3)$$

so that the objective function becomes

$$\text{Minimize } Z = \sum_{k=1}^{K} |d_k| \qquad\qquad (6\text{-}4)$$

Since the d_k can be either positive or negative, we can replace each variable d_k by the difference of two new nonnegative variables (e.g., $d_k = d_k^+ - d_k^-$, where $d_k^+ \geq 0$, $d_k^- \geq 0$) such that[7]

$$|d_k| = |d_k^+ - d_k^-| = +d_k^+ + d_k^-, \qquad \text{for } k = 1, 2, \ldots, K \qquad (6\text{-}5)$$

Thus, d_k^+ and d_k^- are **deviational variables** that represent the degree of overachievement and underachievement of a goal, respectively. Since we cannot have

---

[7] Earlier, in Chapter 4, we represented unconstrained variables as $x_j' - x_j''$ where $x_j' \geq 0$ and $x_j'' \geq 0$. We are using exactly the same concept here, except that we are changing the notation to emphasize the positive and negative deviation concept of goal programming.

both underachievement and overachievement of a goal simultaneously, either one or both of these deviational variables will be equal to zero. That is,

$$d_k^+ \times d_k^- = 0 \tag{6-6}$$

The complete goal programming model can now be written as

$$\text{Minimize } Z = \sum_{k=1}^{K} (d_k^+ + d_k^-) \tag{6-7}$$

subject to: $\qquad \sum_{j=1}^{n} c_{jk} x_j - (d_k^+ - d_k^-) = g_k, \qquad \text{for } k = 1, 2, \ldots, K \tag{6-8}$

plus any original linear programming constraints involving the x_j

with $\qquad d_k^+ \geq 0, d_k^- \geq 0, x_j \geq 0 \qquad (j = 1, 2, \ldots, n) \tag{6-9}$

Observe that in this goal programming formulation each of the respective goals is included as an equality constraint. Each of these **goal constraints** has been rewritten in terms of nonnegative deviational variables (d_k^+ and d_k^-). This ensures that the auxiliary variables will satisfy their original definition, (Equation 6–3), in terms of the real variables of the problem, and allows us to incorporate the deviational variables into the objective function in a linear programming format.

The simplex method can now be used to solve the goal programming model given by (6–7), (6–8) and (6–9). The solution will provide values for all of the variables (including the x_j). The values of d_k^+ and d_k^- are used to determine the values of $d_k = d_k^+ - d_k^-$ and are then discarded.

In many practical situations deviations from certain goals may be much more important than deviations from other goals. Also, for a particular goal, a deviation in one direction may be much more important than a deviation in the opposite direction. These situations can be addressed by assigning **differential weights**, w_k^+ and w_k^- ($k = 1, 2, \ldots, K$) to the respective d_k^+ and d_k^- deviations, where the differential weights reflect the relative importance of the various deviations from the goals. The weighted goal programming model is written as

$$\text{Minimize } Z = \sum_{k=1}^{K} (w_k^+ d_k^+ + w_k^- d_k^-) \tag{6-10}$$

subject to:

$$\sum_{j=1}^{n} c_{jk} x_j - (d_k^+ - d_k^-) = g_k, \qquad \text{for } k = 1, 2, \ldots, K$$

or

$$\sum_{j=1}^{n} c_{jk} x_j - d_k^+ + d_k^- = g_k, \qquad \text{for } k = 1, 2, \ldots, K \tag{6-11}$$

plus any original linear programming constraints involving the x_j

with $\qquad d_k^+ \geq 0, d_k^- \geq 0, x_j \geq 0 \qquad (j = 1, 2, \ldots, n) \tag{6-12}$

Instead of seeking to satisfy a goal exactly, we may have a case of a **one-sided goal** where g_k will represent only a **bound** on the goal to be achieved. If g_k is a **lower-bound goal**, it is written as the following inequality constraint:

$$\sum_{j=1}^{n} c_{jk} x_j \geq g_k \qquad (6\text{-}13)$$

Then, any amount in excess of the goal g_k is acceptable, but any deviation below g_k should be avoided if possible. Thus, we would change the linear programming formulation of the goal programming model by deleting d_k^+ from the objective function, since we would only want to minimize the d_k^- deviation. However, both d_k^+ and d_k^- would still appear in the constraint for the goal g_k, since it would possible for both types of deviations to occur.

Similarly, if g_k is an **upper-bound goal**, it is written as the following inequality constraint:

$$\sum_{j=1}^{n} c_{jk} x_j \leq g_k \qquad (6\text{-}14)$$

Thus, any amount in excess of the goal g_k is unacceptable, but any deviation below g_k is acceptable. Thus, we would change the linear programming model by deleting d_k^- from the objective function, since we would only want to minimize the d_k^+ deviation. However, both d_k^+ and d_k^- would still appear in the constraint for the goal g_k, since it would be possible for either type of deviation to occur.

6.3 FORMULATING GOAL PROGRAMMING MODELS

The goal programming model given by (6-7), (6-8), and (6-9) has been applied to a number of real-world problems. In this section we will attempt to provide simple examples of some of the more common goal programming formulations. To gain a clear understanding of the relationship between linear programming and goal programming, we will initially consider a single-goal model.

6.3.1 Single-Goal Model

EXAMPLE 1 The Sonic Company produces two types of microwave ovens: (1) a "Dial Setting" model, and (2) a "Touch Setting" model. It currently is experiencing very strong demand for its microwave ovens and can sell all of these two microwave ovens that it can produce. The company makes a profit of $100 on the "Dial Setting" model and $150 on the "Touch Setting" model. The production capacities and processing times for the two major manufacturing steps required are shown in the following table.

Type of Microwave Oven	Processing Hours per Microwave Oven	
	Wiring and Component Subassembly	Final Assembly and Testing
Dial Setting	4	2
Touch Setting	2	2
Hours available per Day	80	60

Assume for the moment that the Sonic Company is interested in simply maximizing the total profit associated with the production of these two microwave ovens. If this were the case, this problem situation could be formulated as the following linear programming model.

$$\text{Maximize (Total Profit) } Z = 100x_1 + 150x_2 \qquad (6\text{-}15)$$

subject to: $\quad 4x_1 + 2x_2 \leq 80 \qquad$ (Wiring and component subassembly) $\quad (6\text{-}16)$
$\qquad\qquad\quad 2x_1 + 2x_2 \leq 60 \qquad$ (Final assembly and testing)

with $\quad x_1 \geq 0, x_2 \geq 0 \qquad\qquad\qquad\qquad\qquad\qquad\qquad\qquad (6\text{-}17)$

where: $\quad x_1$ = number of "Dial Setting" microwave ovens produced daily
$\qquad\quad x_2$ = number of "Touch Setting" microwave ovens produced daily

The optimal solution to this linear programming problem can be obtained easily (i.e., solved graphically) and is $x_1 = 0$ units per day, $x_2 = 30$ units per day with a total daily profit of \$4500. The graphical solution to this problem is shown in Fig. 6.1.

Assume now that the management of the Sonic Company is contemplating making a major capital investment to improve the efficiency of its two manufacturing processes. As it attempts to make a decision with respect to this capital investment, it feels that it can no longer simply seek to maximize profit. However,

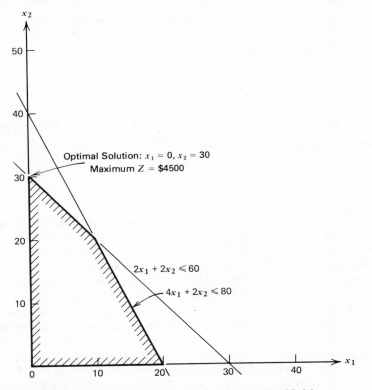

FIGURE 6.1   Graphical Solution—Linear Programming Model
(Microwave Oven Production)

it would like to achieve some satisfactory level of profits during the period of time for which the capital investment would be made. The management of the Sonic Company has decided that a daily profit goal of \$5000 during the capital expenditure period would be acceptable. It now wishes to determine, for the same production data, the product mix that would at least achieve this daily profit goal.

This new problem situation can be addressed by means of goal programming. To incorporate the \$5000 daily-profit goal into the goal programming model, we first define the following deviational variables.

d_1^+ Overachievement of the target daily profit (i.e., the amount by which the actual daily profit will exceed the target daily profit)

d_1^- Underachievement of the target daily profit (i.e., the amount by which the actual daily profit will fail to reach the target daily profit)

The daily profit goal is now written into the goal programming model, using these deviational variables, as the following profit goal constraint.

$$100x_1 + 150x_2 - (d_1^+ - d_1^-) = 5000 \qquad \text{(Profit goal constraint)}$$

or

$$100x_1 + 150x_2 - d_1^+ - d_1^- = 5000 \qquad \text{(Profit goal constraint)}$$

(6–18)

The entire goal programming model can be formulated as

$$\text{Minimize } Z = d_1^- \qquad \text{(Minimize underachievement of daily profit goal)}$$

(6–19)

$$
\begin{aligned}
4x_1 + 2x_2 &\le 80 && \text{(Wiring and component subassembly)} && \left.\begin{array}{l}\text{Resource or}\\ \text{Structural}\\ \text{Constraints}\end{array}\right. \\
2x_1 + 2x_2 &\le 60 && \text{(Final assembly and testing)} \\
100x_1 + 150x_2 - d_1^+ + d_1^- &= 5000 && \text{Daily Profit Goal Constraint}
\end{aligned}
$$

(6–20)

with $x_1, x_2, d_1^+, d_1^- \ge 0$

(6–21)

The major difference between the linear programming formulation given by (6–15), (6–16), and (6–17), and the goal programming formulation given by (6–19), (6–20), and (6–21) is in the objective function of the goal programming model where a deviational variable is employed, and in the daily profit goal constraint that is a part of (6–20). The objective function of the goal programming model, as given by Equation 6–19, contains only the deviational variable, d_1^-, reflecting the fact that our objective, in goal programming form, is to minimize the underachievement of the \$5000 daily-profit goal. Since underachievement of this goal is undesirable, we seek to drive d_1^- as close to zero as possible. The daily profit goal constraint utilizes both an overachievement deviational variable (d_1^+) and an underachievement deviational variable (d_1^-), thus recognizing that the actual daily profit level attainable may be above or below the \$5000 daily-profit goal. In most applications, both overachievement and underachievement variables will appear in the goal constraints. However, for each pair of deviational variables, at most only one will take on a positive value in any solution. For example, in this example it is not possible to underachieve the daily profit goal of $5000 at the same time, that it is overachieved. Therefore, if a goal is exactly achieved, both deviational variables will be zero, and if the goal cannot be achieved, then one or the other of the deviational variables will be zero. Observe finally, that the two **resource** or **structural constraints** for the goal programming model are exactly the same as the original constraints of the linear programming model.

6.3.2 Multiple-Goal Model—Goals Equally Ranked

EXAMPLE 2 Suppose that the Sonic Company has reconsidered its microwave oven production problem and has decided that it would like to achieve two equally important goals. Accordingly, it would like to achieve a daily sales goal of at least 15 "Dial Setting" microwave ovens and at least 15 "Touch Setting" microwave ovens. In both instances it wishes to avoid underachievement of the respective goals. The Sonic Company now wishes to determine, for the same production data, the production mix that would achieve, or most nearly achieve, both of the daily sales goals.

For this new problem situation let us first define the following deviational variables.

d_1^+ = overachievement of the target daily sales goal—"Dial Setting" microwave ovens

d_1^- = underachievement of the target daily sales goal—"Dial Setting" microwave ovens

d_2^+ = overachievement of the target daily sales goal—"Touch Setting" microwave ovens

d_2^- = underachievement of the target daily sales goal—"Touch Setting" microwave ovens

The entire goal programming model for this new problem situation can be written as

$$\text{Minimize } Z = d_1^- + d_2^- \quad \text{(Minimize underachievement of daily sales goals)} \tag{6-22}$$

subject to:

$$
\begin{array}{lll}
4x_1 + 2x_2 & \leq 80 & \text{(Wiring and component subassembly)} \left.\begin{array}{l}\end{array}\right\} \text{Resource} \\
2x_1 + 2x_2 & \leq 60 & \text{(Final assembly and testing)} \quad\;\; \text{Constraints} \\
x_1 \qquad - d_1^+ + d_1^- & = 15 & \text{(Daily sales goal constraint—"Dial Setting" microwave ovens)} \\
x_2 \qquad\; - d_2^+ + d_2^- & = 15 & \text{(Daily sales goal constraint—"Touch Setting" microwave ovens)} \tag{6-23}
\end{array}
$$

$$\text{with} \quad x_1, x_2, d_1^+, d_1^-, d_2^+, d_2^- \geq 0 \tag{6-24}$$

Note that only the underachievement deviational variables d_1^- and d_2^- appear in the objective function and both are assigned equal weights (i.e., cardinal weights of one). The goal programming formulation specified by (6–22), (6–23), and (6–24) is a *weighted linear goal programming model*, in which the management of the Sonic

Company wants to equally avoid underachievement of both of the two daily sales goals.

6.3.3 Multiple-Goal Model—Priority Ranking of Goals (Nonconflicting Goals)

EXAMPLE 3 Suppose now that the management of the Sonic Company has decided that it wishes to achieve a daily profit goal of at least $2400, a daily sales goal of at least 15 "Touch Setting" microwave ovens, and a daily sales goal of at least 5 "Dial Setting" microwave ovens. In each instance it wishes to avoid underachievement of the respective goal. Furthermore, it has decided that these three goals should be assigned priorities, which reflect their importance, as follows.

Goal	*Priority*
1. Produce to make a daily profit of at least $2400.	P_1
2. Produce to achieve daily sales of at least 15 "Touch Setting" microwave ovens.	P_2
3. Produce to achieve daily sales of at least 5 "Dial Setting" microwave ovens.	P_3

Observe that these three priority ranked goals are **incommensurable goals**, since they are not measured in the same units. The ordinal priority rankings here are called **preemptive priority factors** in goal programming. These priority factors have the relationship:

$$P_1 >>> P_2 >>> \cdots >>> P_j >>> P_{j+1} \tag{6-25}$$

where $>>>$ means "very much greater than."

Thus, the priority ranking is absolute, that is, the P_1 goal is so much more important than the P_2 goal that the P_2 goal will never be achieved until the P_1 goal is achieved. In mathematical terms, the preemptive priority relation implies that multiplication by a number $n > 0$, however large n may be, cannot make a lower-priority goal as important as a higher-priority goal (i.e., $P_j > n\, P_{j+1}$). These preemptive priority factors are incorporated into the objective function as weights for the deviational variables. The Sonic Company now wishes to determine, for the same production data, the product mix that would achieve, or most nearly achieve, the three priority ranked goals.

For this new problem situation let us first define the following deviational variables.

$d_1^+ =$ overachievement of the target daily profit
$d_1^- =$ underachievement of the target daily profit
$d_2^+ =$ overachievement of the target daily sales of "Touch Setting" microwave ovens

$d_2^- =$ underachievement of the target daily sales of "Touch Setting" microwave ovens

$d_3^+ =$ overachievement of the target daily sales of "Dial Setting" microwave ovens

$d_3^- =$ underachievement of the target daily sales of "Dial Setting" microwave ovens

The goal programming model for this new problem situation can then be reformulated as

$$\text{Minimize } Z = P_1 d_1^- + P_2 d_2^- + P_3 d_3^- \tag{6-26}$$

subject to:

$$
\begin{array}{rll}
4x_1 + 2x_2 & \leq & 80 \\
2x_1 + 2x_2 & \leq & 60 \\
100x_1 + 150x_2 - d_1^+ + d_1^- & = & 2400 \\
x_2 \qquad - d_2^+ + d_2^- & = & 15 \\
x_1 \qquad - d_3^+ + d_3^- & = & 5
\end{array}
\tag{6-27}
$$

with $\quad x_1, x_2, d_1^+, d_1^-, d_2^+, d_2^-, d_3^+, d_3^- \geq 0$ $\tag{6-28}$

The objective function for this goal programming model indicates that management first wishes to minimize the underachievement of the daily profit goal, then it wishes to minimize the underachievement of the daily sales goal for the "Touch Setting" microwave oven, and, finally, it wishes to minimize the underachievement of the daily sales goal for the "Dial Setting" microwave oven.

Observe one other very important characteristic of this problem. Although there are three priority-ranked goals for this problem, all three are inherently **nonconflicting goals**. This occurs because the achievement of the two sales goals (i.e., daily sales of 5 "Dial Setting" microwave ovens, and 15 "Touch Setting" microwave ovens) will also achieve the first priority goal (i.e., daily profit of $2400), since $100 ($x_1 = 5$) + $150 ($x_2 = 15$) = $2750. Thus, as long as the two resource constraints can be satisfied, all three of the priority-ranked goals can be achieved.

6.3.4 Multiple-Goal Model—Priority Ranking of Goals (Conflicting Goals)

EXAMPLE 4 Suppose now that the management of the Sonic Company is faced with multiple, conflicting goals because of a disagreement with one of its labor unions. Because of this labor disagreement, which involves total hours worked by employees daily, the hours available for wiring and component subassembly can be at most 45 hours per day, and the hours available for final assembly and testing can be at most 35 hours per day. Thus, for this situation management decides to rank its set of goals, with priorities as follows.

Goal	Priority
1. Utilize at most 45 hours per day in wiring and component subassembly and utilize at most 35 hours per day in final assembly and testing.	P_1
2. Produce to make a daily profit of at least $2400.	P_2
3. Produce to achieve daily sales of at least 15 "Touch Setting" microwave ovens.	P_3
4. Produce to achieve daily sales of at least 5 "Dial Setting" microwave ovens.	P_4

Observe that once again these four priority-ranked goals are incommensurable, since they are not measured in the same units. The Sonic Company now wishes to determine the product mix that would achieve, or most nearly achieve, the four priority-ranked goals.

For this new problem situation let us first define the following deviational variables.

d_1^+ = overachievement of the target daily profit

d_1^- = underachievement of the target daily profit

d_2^+ = overachievement of the target daily sales of "Touch Setting" microwave ovens

d_2^- = underachievement of the target daily sales of "Touch Setting" microwave ovens

d_3^+ = overachievement of the target daily sales of "Dial Setting" microwave ovens

d_3^- = underachievement of the target daily sales of "Dial Setting" microwave ovens

d_4^+ = overachievement of the target daily hours—wiring and component subassembly

d_4^- = underachievement of the target daily hours—wiring and component subassembly

d_5^+ = overachievement of the target daily hours—final assembly and testing

d_5^- = underachievement of the target daily hours—final assembly and testing

The goal programming model for this new problem situation can then be reformulated as

$$\text{Minimize } Z = P_1 d_4^+ + P_1 d_5^+ + P_2 d_1^- + P_3 d_2^- + P_4 d_3^- \qquad (6\text{–}29)$$

subject to: $\qquad (6\text{–}30)$

$$
\begin{array}{rcrcrcrcrcr}
100x_1 + 150x_2 - d_1^+ + d_1^- & & & & & & & & & = & 2400 \\
x_2 & - d_2^+ + d_2^- & & & & & & & & = & 15 \\
x_1 & & - d_3^+ + d_3^- & & & & & & = & 5 \\
4x_1 + 2x_2 & & & - d_4^+ + d_4^- & & & & = & 45 \\
2x_1 + 2x_2 & & & & - d_5^+ + d_5^- & = & 35
\end{array}
$$

with $\qquad x_1, x_2, d_1^+, d_1^-, d_2^+, d_2^-, d_3^+, d_3^-, d_4^+, d_4^-, d_5^+, d_5^- \geq 0 \qquad\qquad$ (6–31)

The objective function for this new formulation of the problem indicates the management of the Sonic Company first wishes to minimize usage of labor hours in both wiring and component subassembly and final assembly and testing, then it wishes to meet its daily profit goal, and then it wishes to meet its daily sales quota on "Touch Setting" and "Dial Setting" microwave ovens.

Observe very carefully the **conflicting goals** nature of this problem. Because the two resource constraint goals have been given the top priority, there is now inherently a conflict between satisfying the resource constraint goals and achieving the daily profit and sales goals. Obviously, it may not now be possible to achieve these conflicting goals, because the resource constraint goals have the top priority and the amounts of resource to be utilized have been reduced.

6.3.5 Multiple Goal Model—Weighted Priority Ranking of Goals (Conflicting Goals)

EXAMPLE 5 As a final situation suppose that the management of the Sonic Company is confronted with a similar set of prioritized goals as was developed in the previous example (see Section 6.3.4). However, with respect to the first priority factor, P_1, the management of the Sonic Company has determined that avoiding *overutilization* of 45 hours per day in wiring and component subassembly is twice as important as avoiding *underutilization* of 35 hours per day in final assembly and testing. Thus, the goal programming formulation for this situation involves the weighting of the deviational variables at the same priority level (P_1). This can be done since the deviational variables on the first priority level are commensurable (i.e., they are both measured in labor hours).

Using the same goals, priorities, and deviational variables as defined in Section 6.3.4, the goal programming model for this new problem situation can be reformulated as

$$\text{Minimize } Z = 2P_1d_4^+ + P_1d_5^- + P_2d_1^- + P_3d_2^- + P_4d_3^- \qquad (6\text{–}32)$$

subject to: $\qquad\qquad\qquad\qquad\qquad\qquad\qquad\qquad\qquad\qquad\qquad\qquad\quad$ (6–33)

$$
\begin{array}{lllllr}
100x_1 + 150x_2 - d_1^+ + d_1^- & & & & & = 2400 \\
x_2 & - d_2^+ + d_2^- & & & & = 15 \\
x_1 & & - d_3^+ + d_3^- & & & = 5 \\
4x_1 + \quad 2x_2 & & & - d_4^+ + d_4^- & & = 45 \\
2x_1 + \quad 2x_2 & & & & - d_5^+ + d_5^- & = 35
\end{array}
$$

with $\qquad x_1, x_2, d_1^+, d_1^-, d_2^+, d_2^-, d_3^+, d_3^-, d_4^+, d_4^-, d_5^+, d_5^- \geq 0 \qquad\qquad$ (6–34)

The objective function for this new formulation of the problem thus involves a weighted priority ranking of the deviational variables associated with the first priority goal. Additionally, the conflicting goals nature of the problem is also still present, because there is still an inherent conflict between satisfying the (weighted) resource constraint goals and achieving the daily profit and sales goals.

6.4 COMPUTATIONAL APPROACHES TO GOAL PROGRAMMING

There are several computational approaches that can be used to solve goal programming problems. Virtually all are based on the simplex method of linear programming. As we shall see in the discussion that follows, the choice of a computational approach for a specific goal programming problem is dependent on the structure of the goal programming model that is being used. Thus, we will discuss computational approaches to goal programming within the framework of the five goal programming models previously developed.

6.4.1 Single-Goal Model

Reconsider the first Sonic Corporation problem that was discussed earlier in Section 6.3.1. The linear programming formulation of this problem was solved graphically, as shown in Fig. 6.1, with a solution identified as $x_1 = 0, x_2 = 30$, with a total daily profit of $4500.

The goal programming formulation for this problem situation resulted in a single-goal model given by Equations 6–19, 6–20, and 6–21. The graphical solution to this single-goal model is shown in Fig. 6.2. To solve this problem graphically we plot all three constraints (i.e., two resource constraints plus one goal

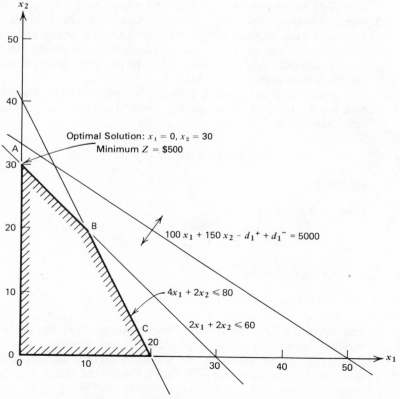

FIGURE 6.2   Graphical Solution—Single-Goal Model (Microwave Oven Production)

constraint) as shown. Ignoring for a moment the profit goal constraint, the feasible solution space is defined by area $OABC$. Next, taking into consideration the profit goal constraint and noting that profit can be less than, equal to, or greater than $5000, the feasible solution space can be on either side of the straight line defined by this constraint, as noted by the arrow signs pointing in two directions. Therefore, the feasible solution space is still defined by $OABC$, that is, by the two resource constraints that formed the constraint set of the original linear programming formulation.

The next step involves the analysis of the objective functon (i.e., Minimize $Z = d_1^-$), which states that we are seeking to minimize the underachievement (d_1^-) of the daily profit goal. To minimize this objective function, the optimal solution must lie at point A (i.e., $x_1 = 0$, $x_2 = 30$, Minimum $Z = d_1^- = 500$). This is the extreme point within the feasible solution space that is the closest to the profit goal constraint (as can be seen graphically).

The simplex method of linear programming can also be used to solve the single-goal model given by 6–19, 6–20, and 6–21. The initial tableau for this problem is shown in Table 6.1.

TABLE 6.1 Single-Goal Model—Initial Tableau

c_b	Variables in Basis	c_j Solution Values, x_b	0 a_1 (x_1)	0 a_2 (x_2)	0 a_3 (d_1^+)	1 a_4 (d_1^-)	0 a_5 (x_5)	0 a_6 (x_6)
0	x_5	80	4	2	0	0	1	0
0	x_6	60	2	(2)	0	0	0	1
1	d_1^-	5000	100	150	−1	1	0	0
	Z_j	5000	100	150	−1	1	0	0
	$c_j - Z_j$		−100	−150	1	0	0	0

In constructing this initial tableau, the first two resource constraints are converted to equalities using the usual slack variables. In the goal constraint the deviational variable d_1^+ represents a surplus variable and the deviational variable d_1^- represents a slack variable. Thus, the initial basic variables are x_5 (slack variable), x_6 (slack variable), and d_1^- (deviational variable). In this initial basic feasible solution $x_5 = 80$, $x_6 = 60$, and $d_1^- = 5000$. The profit contribution at $x_1 = 0$, $x_2 = 0$ is equal to zero, which is $5000 below the profit goal. This is indicated by the fact that the deviational variable $d_1^- = 5000$ and $Z_0 = 5000$.

Since we are minimizing the objective function we select the variable having the smallest $c_j - Z_j$ value to enter the basis (i.e., x_2 is selected to enter the basis since $c_2 - Z_2 = -150$). This means that the profit goal will be increased by $150 for each unit of x_2 produced. Pivoting is accomplished using the usual simplex procedure. The final simplex tableau for this problem is shown in Table 6.2.

This final tableau (optimal solution) indicates that underachievement of the daily profit goal of $5000 will be minimized by producing 0 units of x_1 and 30 units of x_2. This will result in a daily profit of (0 units) ($100 per unit) + (30 units) ($150 per unit) = $4500, which is the closest that we can come to the $5000 daily-profit goal. Note that the profit level achieved is identical to the solution to the standard linear programming formulation shown in Fig. 6.1.

TABLE 6.2   Single-Goal Model—Final Tableau (Optimal Solution)

c_b	Variable in Basis	c_j Solution Values, x_b	a_1 (x_1)	a_2 (x_2)	a_3 (d_1^+)	a_4 (d_1^-)	a_5 (x_5)	a_6 (x_6)
			0	0	0	1	0	0
0	x_5	20	2	0	0	0	1	-1
0	x_2	30	1	1	0	0	0	$\frac{1}{2}$
1	d_1^-	500	-50	0	-1	1	0	-75
	Z_j	500	-50	0	-1	1	0	-75
	$c_j - Z_j$		50	0	1	0	0	75

6.4.2 Multiple-Goal Model— Goals Equally Ranked

Reconsider the second Sonic Corporation problem that was discussed earlier in Section 6.3.2. The goal programming formulation of this problem was given by (6–22), (6–23), and (6–24).

The simplex method of linear programming can be used directly to solve this multiple-goal model where the goals are equally ranked (i.e., the coefficients of the deviational variables in the objective function are all $+1$).[8] The initial tableau for this problem is shown in Table 6.3. In constructing this initial tableau, the first two resource constraints are converted to equalities using the usual slack variables. In the first (daily sales) goal constraint the deviational variable d_1^+ represents a surplus variable and the deviational variable d_1^- represents a slack variable. In the second (daily sales) goal constraint the deviational variable d_2^+ represents a surplus variable and the deviational variable d_2^- represents a slack variable. Thus, the initial basic variables are x_7 (slack variable), x_8 (slack variable), d_1^- (deviational variable) and d_2^- (deviational variable). In this initial basic feasible solution $x_7 = 80$, $x_8 = 60$, $d_1^- = 15$, $d_2^- = 15$. This solution is 15 units below the daily sales goal for both the "Dial Setting" and "Touch Setting" microwave ovens. This is indi-

TABLE 6.3   Multiple-Goal Model—Initial Tableau (Goals Equally Ranked)

c_b	Variables in Basis	c_j Solution Values, x_b	a_1 (x_1)	a_2 (x_2)	a_3 (d_1^+)	a_4 (d_1^-)	a_5 (d_2^+)	a_6 (d_2^-)	a_7 (x_7)	a_8 (x_8)
			0	0	0	1	0	1	0	0
0	x_7	80	4	2	0	0	0	0	1	0
0	x_8	60	2	2	0	0	0	0	0	1
1	d_1^-	15	①	0	-1	1	0	0	0	0
1	d_2^-	15	0	1	0	0	-1	1	0	0
	Z_j	30	1	1	-1	1	-1	1	0	0
	$c_j - Z_j$		-1	-1	1	0	1	0	0	0

---

[8] It should also be noted that if the goals can be assigned cardinal weights (e.g., goal 1 is three times as important as goal 2, and so forth), then the simplex method of linear programming can again be employed.

cated by the fact that the deviational variables $d_1^- = 15$, $d_2^- = 15$, and Minimum $Z = 30$.

Since we are minimizing the objective function we select the variable having the smallest $c_j - Z_j$ value to enter the basis (i.e., x_1 is selected to enter the basis). Pivoting is accomplished using the usual simplex procedure, and the series of simplex tableaus that results are shown in Tables 6.4, 6.5, and 6.6. The final tableau (optimal solution) shown in Table 6.6 indicates that 12.5 units of x_1 ("Dial

TABLE 6.4 Multiple-Goal Model—Second Tableau (Goals Equally Ranked)

c_b	Variables in Basis	Solution Values, x_b	c_j 0 a_1 (x_1)	0 a_2 (x_2)	0 a_3 (d_1^+)	1 a_4 (d_1^-)	0 a_5 (d_2^+)	1 a_6 (d_2^-)	0 a_7 (x_7)	0 a_8 (x_8)
0	x_7	20	0	(2)	4	−4	0	0	1	0
0	x_8	30	0	2	2	−2	0	0	0	1
0	x_1	15	1	0	−1	1	0	0	0	0
1	d_2^-	15	0	1	0	0	−1	1	0	0
	Z_j	15	0	1	0	0	−1	1	0	0
	$c_j - Z_j$		0	−1	0	1	1	0	0	0

TABLE 6.5 Multiple-Goal Model—Third Tableau (Goals Equally Ranked)

c_b	Variables in Basis	Solution Values, x_b	c_j 0 a_1 (x_1)	0 a_2 (x_2)	0 a_3 (d_1^+)	1 a_4 (d_1^-)	0 a_5 (d_2^+)	1 a_6 (d_2^-)	0 a_7 (x_7)	0 a_8 (x_8)
0	x_2	10	0	1	2	−2	0	0	$1/2$	0
0	x_8	10	0	0	−2	2	0	0	−1	1
0	x_1	15	1	0	−1	1	0	0	0	0
1	d_2^-	5	0	0	−2	(2)	−1	1	$-1/2$	0
	Z_j	5	0	0	−2	2	−1	1	$-1/2$	0
	$c_j - Z_j$		0	0	2	−1	1	0	$1/2$	0

TABLE 6.6 Multiple-Goal Model—Final Simplex Tableau (Goals Equally Ranked)

c_b	Variables in Basis	Solution Values, x_b	c_j 0 a_1 (x_1)	0 a_2 (x_2)	0 a_3 (d_1^+)	1 a_4 (d_1^-)	0 a_5 (d_2^+)	1 a_6 (d_2^-)	0 a_7 (x_7)	0 a_8 (x_8)
0	x_2	15	0	1	0	0	−1	1	0	0
0	x_8	5	0	0	0	0	1	−1	$-1/2$	1
0	x_1	12.5	1	0	0	0	$1/2$	$-1/2$	$1/4$	0
1	d_1^-	2.5	0	0	−1	1	$-1/2$	$1/2$	$-1/4$	0
	Z_j	2.5	0	0	−1	1	$-1/2$	$1/2$	$-1/4$	0
	$c_j - Z_j$		0	0	1	0	$1/2$	$1/2$	$1/4$	0

setting'' microwave oven) and 15 units of x_2 (''Touch Setting'' microwave oven) should be produced. This will underachieve the first daily sales goal by 2.5 units, which is indicated by the fact that the underachievement deviational variable $d_1^- = 2.5$. The second daily sales goal of 15 units is exactly achieved. There is also 5 hours of slack in final assembly and testing. Since the first daily sales goal has not been achieved, by 2.5 units, the goal programming objective function composed of the two equally weighted deviational variables is minimized to a value of $1(d_1^- = 2.5) = 2.5$.

6.4.3 Multiple-Goal Model—Priority Ranking of Goals (Nonconflicting Goals)

Reconsider the third Sonic Corporation problem that was discussed earlier in Section 6.3.3. The goal programming formulation of this problem was given by (6–26), (6–27), and (6–28). Also recall that the priority rankings for this problem, P_1, P_2, and P_3, were preemptive. In solving this problem we thus seek to satisfy the minimization of all deviations involved with priority 1, then we seek to satisfy the minimization of all deviations involved with priority 2, and finally we seek to satisfy the minimization of all deviations involved with priority 3. To solve the problem in this fashion, we must modify the simplex procedure to take into account the priority rankings.

In Table 6.7, the initial goal programming simplex tableau for this problem is presented. Using this tableau, there are a number of characteristics of the **modified simplex method of goal programming** that we will now explain.

TABLE 6.7 Priority-Ranked Multiple-Goal Model—Initial Simplex Tableau (Nonconflicting Goals Model)

		c_j	0	0	0	P_1	0	P_2	0	P_3	0	0
c_b	Variables in Basis	Solution Values, x_b	a_1 (x_1)	a_2 (x_2)	a_3 (d_1^+)	a_4 (d_1^-)	a_5 (d_2^+)	a_6 (d_2^-)	a_7 (d_3^+)	a_8 (d_3^-)	a_9 (x_9)	a_{10} (x_{10})
0	x_9	80	4	2	0	0	0	0	0	0	1	0
0	x_{10}	60	2	2	0	0	0	0	0	0	0	1
P_1	d_1^-	2400	100	150	−1	1	0	0	0	0	0	0
P_2	d_2^-	15	0	①	0	0	−1	1	0	0	0	0
P_3	d_3^-	5	1	0	0	0	0	0	−1	1	0	0
P_3	Z_j	5	1	0	0	0	0	0	−1	1	0	0
	$c_j - Z_j$		−1	0	0	0	0	0	1	0	0	0
P_2	Z_j	15	0	1	0	0	−1	1	0	0	0	0
	$c_j - Z_j$		0	−1	0	0	1	0	0	0	0	0
P_1	Z_j	2400	100	150	−1	1	0	0	0	0	0	0
	$c_j - Z_j$		−100	−150	1	0	0	0	0	0	0	0

1. The variable entry criterion (i.e., select the variable having the most negative $c_j - Z_j$ value as the variable to enter the basis for a minimization problem) is no longer expressed as a single row at the bottom of the simplex tableau. Instead, there is a separate Z_j and $c_j - Z_j$ for each of the P_1, P_2, and P_3 preemptive priorities. This is necessary because we cannot add deviations from the profit goal to deviations from the "Touch Setting" microwave oven sales goal because the units are different. Thus, we need these separate priority rows to properly account for each of the priorities. The usual practice is to place the priority rows from bottom to top in the simplex tableau.

2. The $c_j - Z_j$ value for any *column* is shown in the priority rows at the bottom of the tableau. Thus, $c_1 - Z_1 = -1 P_3 - 100 P_1; c_2 - Z_2 = -1 P_2 - 150 P_1$, and so forth.

3. In selecting a variable to enter the basis, we begin with the most important priority, P_1, and select as the variable to enter the basis that variable having the most negative value in that row. Thus, in the initial goal programming simplex tableau variable x_2 is chosen to enter the basis, since $c_2 - Z_2 = -150$ is the most negative $c_j - Z_j$ value. If there was no negative $c_j - Z_j$ value in that row, we would have moved up in the tableau to the next most important priority, P_2, and would have examined the $c_j - Z_j$ values in that row. If there are no negative $c_j - Z_j$ values in any of the priority rows, the optimal solution has been obtained.

4. In selecting a variable to remove from the basis, the usual linear programming variable removal criterion is employed. Thus, we compute the appropriate ratios in column two, and $^{15}/_1 = 15$ is the smallest positive value. Thus, row four (variable d_2^-) will be replaced in the next tableau. The pivot element, "1," has been circled in Table 6.7.

5. If we encounter a negative $c_j - Z_j$ value in one of the priority rows that has a positive $c_j - Z_j$ in one of the priority rows underneath it, we do not consider it. This is done because the positive value means that deviations from the lower (and therefore more important) goal would be *increased* if we entered that variable into the basis. This must be avoided since it will not improve the solution, and in fact will make it worse.

From the initial goal programming simplex tableau shown in Table 6.7 we proceed in the manner encompassed by the five steps just discussed. The resulting goal programming simplex tableaus are shown below in Tables 6.8 to 6.11.

TABLE 6.8 Priority-Ranked Multiple-Goal Model—Second Simplex Tableau (Nonconflicting Goals Model)

c_b	Variables in Basis	c_j — Solution Values, x_b	0 a_1 (x_1)	0 a_2 (x_2)	0 a_3 (d_1^+)	P_1 a_4 (d_1^-)	0 a_5 (d_2^+)	P_2 a_6 (d_2^-)	0 a_7 (d_3^+)	P_3 a_8 (d_3^-)	0 a_9 (x_9)	0 a_{10} (x_{10})
0	x_9	50	4	0	0	0	2	-2	0	0	1	0
0	x_{10}	30	2	0	0	0	2	-2	0	0	0	1
P_1	d_1^-	150	100	0	-1	1	⑮⓪ (150)	-150	0	0	0	0
0	x_2	15	0	1	0	0	-1	1	0	0	0	0
P_3	d_3^-	5	1	0	0	0	0	0	-1	1	0	0
P_3 Z_j		5	1	0	0	0	0	0	-1	1	0	0
P_3 $c_j - Z_j$			-1	0	0	0	0	0	1	0	0	0
P_2 Z_j		0	0	0	0	0	0	0	0	0	0	0
P_2 $c_j - Z_j$			0	0	0	0	0	1	0	0	0	0
P_1 Z_j		150	100	0	-1	1	150	-150	0	0	0	0
P_1 $c_j - Z_j$			-100	0	1	0	-150	150	0	0	0	0

TABLE 6.9   Priority-Ranked Multiple-Goal Model—Third Simplex Tableau (Nonconflicting Goals Model)

c_b	Variables in Basis	Solution Values, x_b	0 a_1 (x_1)	0 a_2 (x_2)	0 a_3 (d_1^+)	P_1 a_4 (d_1^-)	0 a_5 (d_2^+)	P_2 a_6 (d_2^-)	0 a_7 (d_3^+)	P_3 a_8 (d_3^-)	0 a_9 (x_9)	0 a_{10} (x_{10})
0	x_9	48	$8/3$	0	$2/150$	$-2/150$	0	0	0	0	1	0
0	x_{10}	28	$2/3$	0	$2/150$	$-2/150$	0	0	0	0	0	1
0	d_2^+	1	$(2/3)$	0	$-1/150$	$1/150$	1	-1	0	0	0	0
0	x_2	16	$2/3$	1	$-1/150$	$1/150$	0	0	0	0	0	0
P_3	d_3^-	5	1	0	0	0	0	0	-1	1	0	0
P_3 {	Z_j	5	1	0	0	0	0	0	-1	1	0	0
	$c_j - Z_j$		-1	0	0	0	0	0	1	0	0	0
P_2 {	Z_j	0	0	0	0	0	0	0	0	0	0	0
	$c_j - Z_j$		0	0	0	0	0	1	0	0	0	0
P_1 {	Z_j	0	0	0	0	0	0	0	0	0	0	0
	$c_j - Z_j$		0	0	0	1	0	0	0	0	0	0

TABLE 6.10   Priority-Ranked Multiple-Goal Model—Fourth Simplex Tableau (Nonconflicting Goals Model)

c_b	Variables in Basis	Solution Values, x_b	0 a_1 (x_1)	0 a_2 (x_2)	0 a_3 (d_1^+)	P_1 a_4 (d_1^-)	0 a_5 (d_2^+)	P_2 a_6 (d_2^-)	0 a_7 (d_3^+)	P_3 a_8 (d_3^-)	0 a_9 (x_9)	0 a_{10} (x_{10})
0	x_9	44	0	0	$2/50$	$-2/50$	-4	4	0	0	1	0
0	x_{10}	27	0	0	$1/50$	$-1/50$	-1	1	0	0	0	1
0	x_1	$3/2$	1	0	$-1/100$	$1/100$	$3/2$	$-3/2$	0	0	0	0
0	x_2	15	0	1	0	0	-1	1	0	0	0	0
P_3	d_3^-	$7/2$	0	0	$(1/100)$	$-1/100$	$-3/2$	$3/2$	-1	1	0	0
P_3 {	Z_j	$7/2$	0	0	$1/100$	$-1/100$	$-3/2$	$3/2$	-1	1	0	0
	$c_j - Z_j$		0	0	$-1/100$	$1/100$	$3/2$	$-3/2$	1	0	0	0
P_2 {	Z_j	0	0	0	0	0	0	0	0	0	0	0
	$c_j - Z_j$		0	0	0	0	0	1	0	0	0	0
P_1 {	Z_j	0	0	0	0	0	0	0	0	0	0	0
	$c_j - Z_j$		0	0	0	1	0	0	0	0	0	0

The optimal solution to this goal programming problem is presented in the final goal programming simplex tableau shown as Table 6.11. From the optimal solution shown in it, all three of the nonconflicting goals have been entirely met. Thus, for this set of priority goals and resource constraints, the Sonic Corporation should produce (daily) 5 "Dial Setting" microwave ovens and 15 "Touch Setting" microwave ovens. If this is done, the profit goal will be overachieved, since

$$\$100(x_1 = 5) + 150(x_2 = 15) = \$2750 \ (>\$2400 \ \text{by} \ \$350) \tag{6-35}$$

TABLE 6.11 Priority-Ranked Multiple-Goal Model—Final Simplex Tableau (Nonconflicting Goals Model)

		c_j	0	0	0	P_1	0	P_2	0	P_3	0	0
c_b	Variables in Basis	Solution Values, x_b	a_1 (x_1)	a_2 (x_2)	a_3 (d_1^+)	a_4 (d_1^-)	a_5 (d_2^+)	a_6 (d_2^-)	a_7 (d_3^+)	a_8 (d_3^-)	a_9 (x_9)	a_{10} (x_{10})
0	x_9	30	0	0	0	0	2	−2	4	−4	1	0
0	x_{10}	20	0	0	0	0	2	−2	2	−2	0	1
0	x_1	5	1	0	0	0	0	0	−1	1	0	0
0	x_2	15	0	1	0	0	−1	1	0	0	0	0
0	d_1^+	350	0	0	1	−1	−150	150	−100	100	0	0
P_3 $\{$ Z_j		0	0	0	0	0	0	0	0	0	0	0
$\quad$ $c_j - Z_j$			0	0	0	0	0	0	0	1	0	0
P_2 $\{$ Z_j		0	0	0	0	0	0	0	0	0	0	0
$\quad$ $c_j - Z_j$			0	0	0	0	0	1	0	0	0	0
P_1 $\{$ Z_j		0	0	0	0	0	0	0	0	0	0	0
$\quad$ $c_j - Z_j$			0	0	0	1	0	0	0	0	0	0

This is shown in the final tableau by the fact that the deviational variable $d_1^+ = 350$. Note also that in this goal programming problem we are able to satisfy the two resource constraints, since

$$4(x_1 = 5) + 2(x_2 = 15) = 50(< 80 \text{ by } 30)$$
$$2(x_1 = 5) + 2(x_2 = 15) = 40(< 60 \text{ by } 20) \tag{6-36}$$

This is shown in the final tableau by the fact that slack variable $x_9 = 30$ and slack variable $x_{10} = 20$.

6.4.4 Multiple-Goal Model—Priority Ranking of Goals (Conflicting Goals)

Reconsider the fourth Sonic Corporation problem discussed earlier in Section 6.3.4. The goal programming formulation of this problem was given by (6–29), (6–30), and (6–31). Also recall that the priority rankings for this problem were preemptive. Finally, the daily sales and profit goals for this problem are in conflict with the goals that seek to minimize the usage of labor hours in both wiring and component subassembly and final assembly and testing.

The initial goal programming simplex tableau for this problem is shown in Table 6.12. From this initial tableau, this problem is solved as shown in Tables 6.13 to 6.16. Observe that the solution process employs a series of tableaus and a pivoting process that is the same as that employed for our previous example. This multiple-goal simplex tableau will be utilized whenever we encounter a goal programming situation involving multiple goals.

The optimal solution to this goal programming problem is presented in the final goal programming simplex tableau, which is shown in Table 6.16. For the fourth priority, P_4, observe that there are two negative $c_j - Z_j$ values, namely, $c_6 - Z_6 = -1$ and $c_{11} - Z_{11} = -1/2$. However, each of these negative $c_j - Z_j$ values

TABLE 6.12 Priority-Ranked Multiple-Goal Model—Initial Simplex Tableau (Conflicting Goals Model)

		c_j	0	0	0	P_2	0	P_3	0	P_4	P_1	0	P_1	0
c_b	*Variables in Basis*	*Solution Values,* x_b	a_1 (x_1)	a_2 (x_2)	a_3 (d_1^+)	a_4 (d_1^-)	a_5 (d_2^+)	a_6 (d_2^-)	a_7 (d_3^+)	a_8 (d_3^-)	a_9 (d_4^+)	a_{10} (d_4^-)	a_{11} (d_5^+)	a_{12} (d_5^-)
P_2	d_1^-	2400	100	150	−1	1	0	0	0	0	0	0	0	0
P_3	d_2^-	15	0	1	0	0	−1	1	0	0	0	0	0	0
P_4	d_3^-	5	1	0	0	0	0	0	−1	1	0	0	0	0
0	d_4^-	45	4	2	0	0	0	0	0	0	−1	1	0	0
0	d_5^-	35	2	2	0	0	0	0	0	0	0	0	−1	1
P_4	Z_j	5	1	0	0	0	0	0	−1	1	0	0	0	0
	$c_j - Z_j$		−1	0	0	0	0	0	1	0	0	0	0	0
P_3	Z_j	15	0	1	0	0	−1	1	0	0	0	0	0	0
	$c_j - Z_j$		0	−1	0	0	1	0	0	0	0	0	0	0
P_2	Z_j	2400	100	150	−1	1	0	0	0	0	0	0	0	0
	$c_j - Z_j$		−100	−150	1	0	0	0	0	0	0	0	0	0
P_1	Z_j	0	0	0	0	0	0	0	0	0	0	0	0	0
	$c_j - Z_j$		0	0	0	0	0	0	0	0	1	0	1	0

TABLE 6.13 Priority-Ranked Multiple-Goal Model—Second Simplex Tableau (Conflicting Goals Model)

		c_j	0	0	0	P_2	0	P_3	0	P_4	P_1	0	P_1	0
c_b	*Variables in Basis*	*Solution Values,* x_b	a_1 (x_1)	a_2 (x_2)	a_3 (d_1^+)	a_4 (d_1^-)	a_5 (d_2^+)	a_6 (d_2^-)	a_7 (d_3^+)	a_8 (d_3^-)	a_9 (d_4^+)	a_{10} (d_4^-)	a_{11} (d_5^+)	a_{12} (d_5^-)
P_2	d_1^-	150	100	0	−1	1	150	−150	0	0	0	0	0	0
0	x_2	15	0	1	0	0	−1	1	0	0	0	0	0	0
P_4	d_3^-	5	1	0	0	0	0	0	−1	1	0	0	0	0
0	d_4^-	15	4	0	0	0	2	−2	0	0	−1	1	0	0
0	d_5^-	5	2	0	0	0	2	−2	0	0	0	0	−1	1
P_4	Z_j	5	1	0	0	0	0	0	−1	1	0	0	0	0
	$c_j - Z_j$		−1	0	0	0	0	0	1	0	0	0	0	0
P_3	Z_j	0	0	0	0	0	0	0	0	0	0	0	0	0
	$c_j - Z_j$		0	0	0	0	0	1	0	0	0	0	0	0
P_2	Z_j	150	100	0	−1	1	150	−150	0	0	0	0	0	0
	$c_j - Z_j$		−100	0	1	0	−150	150	0	0	0	0	0	0
P_1	Z_j	0	0	0	0	0	0	0	0	0	0	0	0	0
	$c_j - Z_j$		0	0	0	0	0	0	0	0	1	0	1	0

TABLE 6.14 Priority-Ranked Multiple-Goal Model—Third Simplex Tableau (Conflicting Goals Model)

c_b	Variables in Basis	Solution Values, x_b	a_1 (x_1)	a_2 (x_2)	a_3 (d_1^+)	a_4 (d_1^-)	a_5 (d_2^+)	a_6 (d_2^-)	a_7 (d_3^+)	a_8 (d_3^-)	a_9 (d_4^+)	a_{10} (d_4^-)	a_{11} (d_5^+)	a_{12} (d_5^-)
	c_j		0	0	0	P_2	0	P_3	0	P_4	P_1	0	P_1	0
0	d_2^+	1	②/₃	0	$-1/150$	$1/150$	1	-1	0	0	0	0	0	0
0	x_2	16	$2/3$	1	$-1/150$	$1/150$	0	0	0	0	0	0	0	0
P_4	d_3^-	5	1	0	0	0	0	0	-1	1	0	0	0	0
0	d_4^-	13	$8/3$	0	$2/150$	$-2/150$	0	0	0	0	-1	1	0	0
0	d_5^-	3	$2/3$	0	$2/150$	$-2/150$	0	0	0	0	0	0	-1	1
P_4 { Z_j		5	1	0	0	0	0	0	-1	1	0	0	0	0
$c_j - Z_j$			-1	0	0	0	0	0	1	0	0	0	0	0
P_3 { Z_j		0	0	0	0	0	0	0	0	0	0	0	0	0
$c_j - Z_j$			0	0	0	0	0	1	0	0	0	0	0	0
P_2 { Z_j		0	0	0	0	0	0	0	0	0	0	0	0	0
$c_j - Z_j$			0	0	0	1	0	0	0	0	0	0	0	0
P_1 { Z_j		0	0	0	0	0	0	0	0	0	0	0	0	0
$c_j - Z_j$			0	0	0	0	0	0	0	0	1	0	1	0

TABLE 6.15 Priority-Ranked Multiple-Goal Model—Fourth Simplex Tableau (Conflicting Goals Model)

c_b	Variables in Basis	Solution Values, x_b	a_1 (x_1)	a_2 (x_2)	a_3 (d_1^+)	a_4 (d_1^-)	a_5 (d_2^+)	a_6 (d_2^-)	a_7 (d_3^+)	a_8 (d_3^-)	a_9 (d_4^+)	a_{10} (d_4^-)	a_{11} (d_5^+)	a_{12} (d_5^-)
	c_j		0	0	0	P_2	0	P_3	0	P_4	P_1	0	P_1	0
0	x_1	$3/2$	1	0	$-1/100$	$1/100$	$3/2$	$-3/2$	0	0	0	0	0	0
0	x_2	15	0	1	0	0	-1	1	0	0	0	0	0	0
P_4	d_3^-	$7/2$	0	0	$1/100$	$-1/100$	$-3/2$	$3/2$	-1	1	0	0	0	0
0	d_4^-	9	0	0	$6/150$	$-6/150$	-4	4	0	0	-1	1	0	0
0	d_5^-	2	0	0	③/₁₅₀	$-3/150$	-1	1	0	0	0	0	-1	1
P_4 { Z_j		$7/2$	0	0	$1/100$	$-1/100$	$-3/2$	$3/2$	-1	1	0	0	0	0
$c_j - Z_j$			0	0	$-1/100$	$1/100$	$3/2$	$-3/2$	1	0	0	0	0	0
P_3 { Z_j		0	0	0	0	0	0	0	0	0	0	0	0	0
$c_j - Z_j$			0	0	0	0	0	1	0	0	0	0	0	0
P_2 { Z_j		0	0	0	0	0	0	0	0	0	0	0	0	0
$c_j - Z_j$			0	0	0	1	0	0	0	0	0	0	0	0
P_1 { Z_j		0	0	0	0	0	0	0	0	0	0	0	0	0
$c_j - Z_j$			0	0	0	0	0	0	0	0	1	0	1	0

TABLE 6.16   Priority-Ranked Multiple-Goal Model—Final Simplex Tableau (Conflicting Goals Model)

c_b	Variables in Basis	c_j Solution Values, x_b	0 a_1 (x_1)	0 a_2 (x_2)	0 a_3 (d_1^+)	P_2 a_4 (d_1^-)	0 a_5 (d_2^+)	P_3 a_6 (d_2^-)	0 a_7 (d_3^+)	P_4 a_8 (d_3^-)	P_1 a_9 (d_4^+)	0 a_{10} (d_4^-)	P_1 a_{11} (d_5^+)	0 a_{12} (d_5^-)
0	x_1	$5/2$	1	0	0	0	1	-1	0	0	0	0	$-1/2$	$1/2$
0	x_2	15	0	1	0	0	-1	1	0	0	0	0	0	0
P_4	d_3^-	$5/2$	0	0	0	0	-1	1	-1	1	0	0	$1/2$	$-1/2$
0	d_4^-	5	0	0	0	0	-2	2	0	0	-1	1	2	-2
0	d_1^+	100	0	0	1	-1	-50	50	0	0	0	0	-50	50
P_4 $\{$	Z_j	$5/2$	0	0	0	0	-1	1	-1	1	0	0	$1/2$	$-1/2$
	$c_j - Z_j$		0	0	0	0	1	-1	1	0	0	0	$-1/2$	$1/2$
P_3 $\{$	Z_j	0	0	0	0	0	0	0	0	0	0	0	0	0
	$c_j - Z_j$		0	0	0	0	0	1	0	0	0	0	0	0
P_2 $\{$	Z_j	0	0	0	0	0	0	0	0	0	0	0	0	0
	$c_j - Z_j$		0	0	0	1	0	0	0	0	0	0	0	0
P_1 $\{$	Z_j	0	0	0	0	0	0	0	0	0	0	0	0	0
	$c_j - Z_j$		0	0	0	0	0	0	0	0	1	0	1	0

has a positive $c_j - Z_j$ value in one of the P rows underneath it. These positive values mean that deviations from the lower (and more important) goals would be *increased* if the corresponding variables were brought into the basic solution. This must be avoided, and therefore the optimal goal programming solution has been obtained. From the optimal solution shown in Table 6.16, three of the four priority goals have been satisfied. The top priority goal has been achieved exactly by the production of $2^1/2$ "Dial Setting" microwave ovens and 15 "Touch Setting" microwave ovens. These production levels satisfy the labor-hour utilization goal, since

$$4(x_1 = {}^5/_2) + 2(x_2 = 15) = 40 \ (<45 \text{ by } 5)$$
$$2(x_1 = {}^5/_2) + 2(x_2 = 15) = 35 \ (\text{exactly } 35) \tag{6-37}$$

Similarly, the second priority goal, namely that of making a daily profit of $2400 has been overachieved, since

$$100(x_1 = {}^5/_2) + 150(x_2 = 15) = 2500 \ (> \$2400 \text{ by } \$100) \tag{6-38}$$

This is indicated by the fact that the deviational variable, d_1^+, has a value of 100 in the final goal programming tableau. The third priority goal, namely that of achieving a daily sales goal of 15 "Touch Setting" microwave ovens has been exactly achieved, since $x_2 = 15$ in the final goal programming tableau. The fourth priority goal, namely that of achieving a daily sales goal of 5 "Dial Setting" microwave ovens, has been underachieved, since $x_1 = 2.5$ in the final goal programming goal. In summary, it is not possible, for this problem situation, to achieve all four of the conflicting priority goals.

6.4.5 Multiple-Goal Model—Weighted Priority Ranking of Goals (Conflicting Goals)

Reconsider finally the fifth Sonic Corporation problem discussed earlier in Section 6.3.5. The weighted priority goal programming formulation of this problem was given by (6–32), (6–33), and (6–34). Recall that the priority rankings for this problem were preemptive and that the deviational variables associated with the first priority factor, P_1, were weighted. Finally, the daily sales and profit goals for this problem were in conflict with the goals that sought to minimize the usage of labor hours in both wiring and component subassembly and final assembly and testing.

The initial goal programming simplex tableau for this problem is shown in Table 6.17. The modified simplex procedure discussed in the preceding two sections of this chapter is again used to solve the problem. For the sake of brevity, the intermediate goal programming simplex tableaus will not be illustrated. The final goal programming simplex tableau (optimal solution) is presented in Table 6.18.

The final goal programming simplex tableau shown in Table 6.18 indicates that priorities P_1, P_2, and P_3 have been satisfied. The optimal solution indicates that $x_1 = 3.75$ "Dial Setting" microwave ovens and $x_2 = 15$ "Touch Setting" microwave ovens should be produced. These production levels satisfy the labor hour utilization goals since

$$4(x_1 = 3.75) + 2(x_2 = 15) = 45 \text{ (exactly 45)}$$
$$2(x_1 = 3.75) + 2(x_2 = 15) = 37.5 \text{ (>35 by 2.5)}$$

(6–39)

Note that the weight of the deviational variables associated with the first priority has led to a solution in which the most heavily weighted first priority goal has

TABLE 6.17 Weighted Priority Ranked Multiple-Goal Model—Initial Simplex Tableau (Conflicting Goals Model)

c_b	Variables in Basis	Solution Values, x_b	0 a_1 (x_1)	0 a_2 (x_2)	0 a_3 (d_1^+)	P_2 a_4 (d_1^-)	0 a_5 (d_2^+)	P_3 a_6 (d_2^-)	0 a_7 (d_3^+)	P_4 a_8 (d_3^-)	$2P_1$ a_9 (d_4^+)	0 a_{10} (d_4^-)	0 a_{11} (d_5^+)	P_1 a_{12} (d_5^-)
P_2	d_1^-	2400	100	150	−1	1	0	0	0	0	0	0	0	0
P_3	d_2^-	15	0	1	0	0	−1	1	0	0	0	0	0	0
P_4	d_3^-	5	①	0	0	0	0	0	−1	1	0	0	0	0
0	d_4^-	45	4	2	0	0	0	0	0	0	−1	1	0	0
P_1	d_5^-	35	2	2	0	0	0	0	0	0	0	0	−1	1
P_4	Z_j	5	1	0	0	0	0	0	−1	1	0	0	0	0
	$c_j − Z_j$		−1	0	0	0	0	0	1	0	0	0	0	0
P_3	Z_j	15	0	1	0	0	−1	1	0	0	0	0	0	0
	$c_j − Z_j$		0	−1	0	0	1	0	0	0	0	0	0	0
P_2	Z_j	2400	100	150	−1	1	0	0	0	0	0	0	0	0
	$c_j − Z_j$		−100	−150	1	0	0	0	0	0	0	0	0	0
P_1	Z_j	35	2	2	0	0	0	0	0	0	0	0	−1	1
	$c_j − Z_j$		−2	−2	0	0	0	0	0	0	2	0	1	0

TABLE 6.18 Weighted Priority Ranked Multiple-Goal Model—Final Simplex Tableau (Conflicting Goals Model)

c_b	Variables in Basis	Solution Values, x_b	c_j: 0 a_1 (x_1)	0 a_2 (x_2)	0 a_3 (d_1^+)	P_2 a_4 (d_1^-)	0 a_5 (d_2^+)	P_3 a_6 (d_2^-)	0 a_7 (d_3^+)	P_4 a_8 (d_3^-)	$2P_1$ a_9 (d_4^+)	0 a_{10} (d_4^-)	0 a_{11} (d_5^+)	P_1 a_{12} (d_5^-)
0	d_5^+	2.5	0	0	0	0	1	1	0	0	$-1/2$	$1/2$	1	-1
0	d_1^+	225.0	0	0	1	-1	-100	100	0	0	-25	25	0	0
0	x_1	3.75	1	0	0	0	$-1/2$	$-1/2$	0	0	$1/4$	$1/4$	0	0
0	x_2	15.0	0	1	0	0	1	1	0	0	0	0	0	0
P_4	d_3^-	1.25	0	0	0	0	$1/2$	$1/2$	-1	1	$1/4$	$-1/4$	0	0
P_4 { Z_j		1.25	0	0	0	0	$-1/2$	$1/2$	-1	1	$1/4$	$-1/4$	0	0
$c_j - Z_j$			0	0	0	0	$1/2$	$-1/2$	1	0	$-1/4$	$1/4$	0	0
P_3 { Z_j		0	0	0	0	0	0	0	0	0	0	0	0	0
$c_j - Z_j$			0	0	0	0	0	1	0	0	0	0	0	0
P_2 { Z_j		0	0	0	0	0	0	0	0	0	0	0	0	0
$c_j - Z_j$			0	0	0	1	0	0	0	0	0	0	0	0
P_1 { Z_j		0	0	0	0	0	0	0	0	0	0	0	0	0
$c_j - Z_j$			0	0	0	0	0	0	0	0	2	0	0	1

been satisfied exactly. The second most heavily weighted first priority goal has been exceeded by 2.5 hours (i.e., $d_5^+ = 2.5$). The second priority goal, namely that of making a daily profit of \$2400 has been overachieved since

$$100(x_1 = 3.75) + 150(x_2 = 15) = 2625 \ (>2400 \text{ by } \$225) \tag{6-40}$$

This is indicated by the fact that the deviation variable $d_1^+ = 225$. The third priority goal, namely that of achieving a daily sales goal of 15 "Touch Setting" microwave ovens has been exactly achieved, since $x_2 = 15$ in the optimal solution. The fourth priority goal has been underachieved, since $x_1 = 3.75$ in the optimal solution. This is verified by the fact that the underachievement deviational variable associated with this goal, $d_3^- = 1.25$. In summary, for this problem situation three of the four conflicting priority goals have been achieved.

6.5 SPECIAL PROBLEMS IN GOAL PROGRAMMING

As evidenced in the examples presented in the preceding section of this chapter, the computational approaches used in goal programming are based upon the simplex algorithm of linear programming. Therefore, just as was the case for linear programming, a number of special problems can occur in the goal programming simplex solution process. These special problems will now be discussed in a goal programming context.

6.5.1 Alternative Optimal Solutions

Alternative optimal solutions can occur in goal programming, just as in linear programming, and will be indicated by the presence of an entire column of zeroes in the $c_j - Z_j$ rows for a nonbasic variable with the existence of at least one positive a_{ij} element in the corresponding column. The alternative optimal solution is determined by computing a new tableau, using the standard iterating procedure described above.

6.5.2 Unbounded Solutions

Unbounded solutions do not occur in goal programming, since every goal constraint (i.e., objective) has an associated right-hand side value. Subsequently, any given solution either does or does not satisfy this right-hand side value. Therefore, in the goal programming simplex process we only search for a solution that *satisfies* a given goal, not for a solution that absolutely optimizes the value of this goal. Thus, regardless of how much a right-hand side value is increased, the problem may still have an implementable solution. The presence of this type of situation will not be identified in a manner analogous to that in linear programming.

6.5.3 Infeasible Solutions

Infeasible solutions occur in linear programming where *absolute* constraints, which are always present, may be incompatible. In goal programming, infeasibility is generally not a problem, because deviational variables are employed in an attempt to *satisfy* various goals, which are written as constraints. Nevertheless, a type of infeasibility can occur in goal programming if we establish a set of absolute objectives at the highest priority level. An infeasibility for this situation represents an unimplementable solution and is indicated by a solution with a negative $c_j - Z_j$ value for some nonbasic variable associated with the highest priority level (i.e., with some absolute goal). This means that the satisfaction of this absolute objective was not completely achieved. In practice, this indicates that either the absolute objectives should be modified (i.e., they do not have to be as absolute as first stated) or that changes in the problem environment (e.g., increases in the limited resources) need to be considered.

6.5.4 Tie for Entering Basic Variable

A tie for the entering basic variable can occur between the $c_j - Z_j$ values in any row (i.e., for any priority level) of the goal programming tableau. As in linear programming, this tie can be broken arbitrarily.

6.5.5 Tie for Leaving Basic Variable

In the goal programming simplex process, the variable selected for removal from the basis is determined as the smallest nonnegative ratio that is computed when the coefficients of the incoming column are divided into the "**Right-Hand-Side Values, x_b**." If two or more rows have the same ratio, the tie may be broken by selecting the row having the highest associated priority level (i.e., by referring to the priority levels as indicated in the c_b column). However, in some instances the variables being considered for removal will not have associated priority levels. In such cases, the tie can be broken arbitrarily. Theoretically, this could cause degeneracy in the goal programming problem, but this has not occurred in practice.

6.5.6   Negative Right-Hand Side Values

In the goal programming simplex procedure, negative right-hand-side values are not permitted. We can avoid negative right-hand-side values by multiplying the entire goal constraint by -1. However, this modification should be done after the deviational variables have been added. For example, the goal constraint:

$$2x_1 - 5x_2 - d_1^+ + d_1^- = -100 \qquad (6\text{--}41)$$

would be changed to:

$$-2x_1 + 5x_2 + d_1^+ - d_1^- = 100 \qquad (6\text{--}42)$$

The correct variable to appear in the objective function is determined by analyzing the original constraint, rather than the new constraint. Thus, if our goal was to achieve or exceed -100, then d_1^- would appear in the objective function; if our goal was to underachieve -100, then d_1^+ would appear in the objective function.

6.6   DUALITY THEORY AND SENSITIVITY ANALYSIS IN GOAL PROGRAMMING

Just as was the case for linear programming, duality theory and sensitivity analysis can be considered in a goal programming context. These topics, although of interest and importance to goal programming, will be omitted here for the sake of brevity. The more interested reader can refer to textbooks by Lee (1972) and Ignizio (1976) for extensive discussions of these topics (see "Selected References," this chapter).

6.7   APPLICATIONS OF GOAL PROGRAMMING—FORMULATION EXAMPLES

Goal programming has been utilized in a large variety of decision-making situations. In marketing, it has been used for advertising media scheduling[9] and sales effort allocation.[10] In finance, it has been used for portfolio selection problems[11] and for capital-budgeting problems.[12] In accounting, it has been used for budgeting and break-even analysis[13] and for audit-sampling problems.[14] In the public

---

[9] C. A. DeKluyver, "An Exploration of Various Goal Programming Formulations with Application to Advertising Media Scheduling," *Journal of the Operational Research Society,* vol. 30, no. 2 (1979), 167–171.

[10] S. M. Lee and M. M. Bird, "A Goal Programming Model for Sales Effort Allocation," *Business Perspectives* (July 1970), 17–21.

[11] S. M. Lee and A. J. Terro, "Optimizing the Portfolio Selection for Mutual Funds," *The Journal of Finance* (December 1973), 1086–1101.

[12] J. P. Ignizio, "An Approach to the Capital Budgeting Problem with Multiple Objectives," *The Engineering Economist,* vol. 21, no. 4 (Summer 1976), 259–272.

[13] K. M. El-Sheshai, G. B. Harwood, and R. H. Hermanson, "Cost Volume Profit Analysis with Integer Goal Programming," *Management Accounting* (October 1977), 43–47.

[14] J. Blocher, "Sampling for Integrated Audit Objectives: A Comment," *The Accounting Review* (July 1978), 776–772.

sector, goal programming has been used for academic-planning problems,[15] and to determine school busing plans.[16]

In this section of the chapter we will present several examples that illustrate the formulation of goal programming models. Each of the formulations presented below will be based upon some actual application of goal programming. In addition to the problem formulation, we will summarize the solution for each of the applications presented. It is recommended that the student use these solutions to check the consistency of the problem formulations.

6.7.1 The Diet Problem

Sally Phillips has a choice of seven different food items from which to plan a daily diet menu: beef, milk, eggs, yogurt, bread, rice, and orange juice. The nutritional and cost information for the selected items are provided in the following table.

Vitamin/ Nutritional Element	Selected Food Items							Recommended Daily Allowance
	Beef (oz)	Milk (cup)	Eggs (each)	Yogurt (oz)	Bread (oz)	Rice (cup)	Orange Juice (cup)	
Vitamin A (IU)	7.0	380.0	590.0	300.0	0.0	0.0	500.0	7000.0
Iron (mg)	1.0	0.1	1.1	0.12	0.75	1.7	0.5	12.0
Protein (g)	9.0	9.0	7.0	7.0	2.5	15.0	2.0	75.0
Food energy (Calorie)	50.0	170.0	100.0	80.0	80.0	677.0	90.0	2600.0
Carbohydrates (g)	1.7	12.0	0.0	6.0	14.0	112.0	25.0	—
Cholesterol (Units)	1.0	5.0	10.0	0.0	0.0	0.0	0.0	—
Cost per unit	0.18	0.35	0.10	0.17	0.15	0.15	0.19	

In order to maintain a "balanced" diet, Sally's physician strongly recommends that she restrict her daily consumption each of the various food items to the following amounts: 8 ounces of beef, 6 cups of milk, 3 eggs, 8 ounces of yogurt, 6 ounces of bread, 3 cups of rice, and 4 cups of orange juice. Sally must also take into consideration that she has a budgeted amount of $7.00 per day with which to plan her menu. In light of these constraints, Sally desires to design a daily menu that satisfies certain daily nutritional requirements as well as her own preferences for the various food items. Her first priority, however, is to satisfy the recommended daily allowances for vitamin A, iron, protein, and food energy. Her second priority is to minimize her intake of cholesterol and carbohydrates. Lastly, Sally desires to incorporate her food preferences into her diet menu: her favorite food is beef, followed by milk, eggs, yogurt, bread, rice, and orange juice respectively. A goal programming model can be formulated to determine an appropriate

---

[15] R. G. Schroeder, "Resource Planning in University Management by Goal Programming," *Operations Research* (July–August 1974), 700–710.

[16] S. M. Lee and L. J. Moore, "Multi-Criteria School Busing Models," *Management Science*, vol. 23, (March 1977), 703–714.

diet menu. To construct this goal programming model, let x_j $(j = 1, \ldots, 7)$ represent the number of units of food type j to be included in Sally's daily diet plan. (Note that some of the units for various food items are incommensurable).

To initiate the formulation of this model, we define a set of constraints that are associated with the maximum allowable amounts of the food items recommended by her physician and the aforementioned budget limitation.

First we define the *maximum allowable consumption constraints*, as follows.

$$
\begin{aligned}
x_1 &\le 8 \quad \text{(Beef)} \\
x_2 &\le 6 \quad \text{(Milk)} \\
x_3 &\le 3 \quad \text{(Eggs)} \\
x_4 &\le 8 \quad \text{(Yogurt)} \\
x_5 &\le 6 \quad \text{(Bread)} \\
x_6 &\le 3 \quad \text{(Rice)} \\
x_7 &\le 4 \quad \text{(Orange juice)}
\end{aligned}
\tag{6-43}
$$

Then we define the *budget constraint*, as follows.

$$0.18x_1 + 0.35x_2 + 0.10x_3 + 0.17x_4 + 0.15x_5 + 0.15x_6 + 0.19x_7 \le 7.00 \tag{6-44}$$

The constraints given by (6–43) and (6–44) are the *resource constraints* for this goal programming model.

Next, we must formulate the goal constraints for this model. Note that the first set of goal constraints will be associated with Sally's foremost priority of meeting certain nutritional requirements. The recommended daily allowances of Vitamin A, iron, protein, and food energy serve as target or aspiration levels for these constraints.

$$
\text{Vitamin A} \{7.0x_1 + 380.0x_2 + 590.0x_3 + 300.0x_4 + 0.0x_5 + 0.0x_6 + 500.0x_7 + d_9^- - d_9^+ = 7000.0 \tag{6-45}
$$

$$
\text{Iron} \{1.0x_1 + 0.1x_2 + 1.1x_3 + 0.12x_4 + 0.75x_5 + 1.7x_6 + 0.5x_7 + d_{10}^- - d_{10}^+ = 12.0 \tag{6-46}
$$

$$
\text{Protein} \{9.0x_1 + 9.0x_2 + 7.0x_3 + 7.0x_4 + 2.5x_5 + 15.0x_6 + 2.0x_7 + d_{11}^- - d_{11}^+ = 75.0 \tag{6-47}
$$

$$
\text{Food energy} \{50.0x_1 + 170.0x_2 + 100.0x_3 + 80.0x_4 + 80.0x_5 + 677.0x_6 + 90.0x_7 + d_{12}^- - d_{12}^+ = 2600.0 \tag{6-48}
$$

The positive and negative deviational variables associated with these constraints will be assigned a priority factor of one (P_1) in the objective function in order to encourage conformance with the stated aspiration levels.

The next set of goal constraints are concerned with Sally's objective of minimizing her intake of cholesterol and carbohydrates. Consider that the positive deviational variables for both these constraints will appear at a priority level of two (P_2) in the objective function.

$$
\text{Carbohydrates} \{1.7x_1 + 12.0x_2 + 0.0x_3 + 6.0x_4 + 14.0x_5 + 112.0x_6 + 25.0x_7 - d_{13}^+ = 0 \tag{6-49}
$$

$$
\text{Cholesterol} \quad \{1.0x_1 + 5.0x_2 + 10.0x_3 + 0.0x_3 + 0.0x_4 + 0.0x_5 + 0.0x_6 + 0.0x_7 - d_{14}^+ = 0 \tag{6-50}
$$

Finally, we formulate a set of goal constraints that reflect Sally's preferences for the selected food items.

$$
\begin{aligned}
x_1 + d_{15}^- &= 8.0 \\
x_2 + d_{16}^- &= 8.0 \\
x_3 + d_{17}^- &= 8.0 \\
x_4 + d_{18}^- &= 8.0 \\
x_5 + d_{19}^- &= 8.0 \\
x_6 + d_{20}^- &= 8.0 \\
x_7 + d_{21}^- &= 8.0
\end{aligned}
\qquad (6\text{-}51)
$$

It should be mentioned that by minimizing each of these negative deviational variables at the appropriate priority levels in the objective function, we place an upward pressure on the values of the decision variables based on the indicated preference relationships. The right-hand-side value was set at 8 because that is the highest value a decision variable can assume based on the first seven constraints. The objective function for this model is specified as follows.

$$
\begin{aligned}
\text{Minimize } Z = \; & P_1\,(d_9^- + d_9^+ + d_{10}^- + d_{10}^+ + d_{11}^- + d_{11}^+ + d_{12}^- + d_{12}^+) + \\
& P_2\,(d_{13}^+ + d_{14}^+) + P_3 d_{15}^- + P_4 d_{16}^- + P_5 d_{17}^- + \\
& P_6 d_{18}^- + P_7 d_{19}^- + P_8 d_{20}^- + P_9 d_{21}^-
\end{aligned}
\qquad (6\text{-}52)
$$

Finally, we must restrict the values of our decision and deviational variables to be nonnegative:

$$
x_j \geq 0; j = 1, \ldots, 7 \; d_i^-, d_i^+ \geq 0; i = 1, \ldots, 21. \qquad (6\text{-}53)
$$

The optimal solution values for this goal programming model are given below.

(Beef, oz):	$x_1 = 0.0$
(Milk, cups):	$x_2 = 6.0$
(Eggs, each):	$x_3 = 3.0$
(Yogurt, oz):	$x_4 = 3.1667$
(Bread, oz):	$x_5 = 0.0$
(Rice, cups):	$x_6 = 0.98473$
(Orange juice, cups):	$x_7 = 4.00$

The aspiration levels associated with the vitamin A and food-energy requirement constraints were exactly achieved. The aspiration level associated with the iron requirement constraint was underachieved by 5.046 mg; however, the target level for protein was overachieved by 44.94 grams. The daily consumption level of carbohydrates was 301.29 grams, while the resulting intake of cholesterol was 60.0 units. The daily cost of Sally's diet menu was $3.85.

6.7.2 The School-Busing Problem

Carteret County is faced with the challenge of designing a busing program for the students in its three school districts in order to achieve racial desegregation in its three schools. The table below contains the busing cost and mileage data for every district-to-school combination and indicates the number of students of each race in each district as well as the total school-population capacities of the three schools.

	School 1		School 2		School 3		Number of Pupils by Race	
	Transportation Cost($)	Mileage	Transportation Cost($)	Mileage	Transportation Cost($)	Mileage	Black	White
District 1	39	4	71	8	103	12	450	80
District 2	47	5	63	7	119	14	250	100
District 3	87	10	31	3	47	5	20	500
School Capacity	400		500		500		1400 (combined black/ white total)	

The mileage figures represent the average miles traveled by a student within the county on the shortest route basis from strategic community bus stops to schools. The costs figures are based on the assumption that for the first mile there is a fixed transportation cost of $15.00 per student per year and an additional annual cost of $8.00 per student for every mile traveled beyond the initial mile.

The County School Board has delineated and prioritized the following goals for Carteret's school busing program.

Priority	Goal
1	Each child must be assigned to a school.
2	Achieve a racial balance in each school that corresponds to the racial proportions of Carteret County (i.e., if 50% of the citizens in the county are black, then 50% of the students in each of the schools must be black).
3	Avoid overcrowding or underutilization of any of the schools.
4	Minimize the total transportation cost of the school busing program.
5	Limit the distance (average) traveled by any student to 8 miles.

To formulate this goal programming model, let x_{ijk} ($i = 1,2; j = 1,2,3; k = 1,2,3$) represent the number of students of race i (where black is coded "1") from district j that are assigned to school k. The constraints for this goal programming problem can now be formulated. The constraints corresponding to the highest priority goal are written as follows.

$$\sum_{k=1}^{3} x_{11k} + d_1^- = 450$$

$$\sum_{k=1}^{3} x_{21k} + d_2^- = 80$$

$$\sum_{k=1}^{3} x_{12k} + d_3^- = 250$$

$$\sum_{k=1}^{3} x_{22k} + d_4^- = 100 \tag{6-54}$$

$$\sum_{k=1}^{3} x_{13k} + d_5^- = 20$$

$$\sum_{k=1}^{3} x_{23k} + d_6^- = 500$$

Note that the negative deviational variable d_i^- in each equation represents the number of unaccepted children of race i in district j assigned by the school system. To achieve the objective of assigning every child in the county to a school, the slack variable d_i^- must be minimized.

The racial balance constraints are formulated next since the achievement of racial balance in every school was the second-highest priority goal and in fact the main reason for instituting a school busing program. The objective is to ensure that the racial proportions in each school correspond to the racial proportions in the entire county. The target proportions are calculated below.

Population	Students	Proportion
Black Students	720	0.514
White Students	680	0.486
Total Population	1400	1.000

As indicated, the racial mix in each school should be 51.4 percent black and 48.6 percent white. Therefore the racial balance constraint for school 1, for example, was expressed as

$$\sum_{j=1}^{3} x_{1j1} + d_7^- - d_7^+ = 0.514 \left(\sum_{j=1}^{3} x_{1j1} + \sum_{j=1}^{3} x_{2j1} \right) \tag{6-55}$$

Note that this constraint requires that the number of black children in each of the districts assigned to school 1 $\left(\sum_{j=1}^{3} x_{1j1} \right)$ must equal 51.4 percent of the total number of students assigned to school 1 when the deviational variables d_7^- and d_7^+ are minimized. This constraint can be rewritten as follows.

$$0.486 \sum_{j=1}^{3} x_{1j1} - 0.514 \sum_{j=1}^{3} x_{2j1} + d_7^- - d_7^+ = 0 \tag{6-56}$$

The racial balance constraints for schools 2 and 3 are written as follows.

$$0.486 \sum_{j=1}^{3} x_{1j2} - 0.514 \sum_{j=1}^{3} x_{2j2} + d_8^- - d_8^+ = 0$$

$$\tag{6-57}$$

$$0.486 \sum_{j=1}^{3} x_{1j3} - 0.514 \sum_{j=1}^{3} x_{2j3} + d_9^- - d_9^+ = 0$$

The next goal in order of importance was to avoid overcrowding or under-utilization of any of the schools. The constraints associated with this objective can be expressed as

$$\sum_{i=1}^{3} \sum_{j=1}^{3} x_{ij1} + d_{10}^- - d_{10}^+ = 400$$

$$\sum_{i=1}^{2} \sum_{j=1}^{3} x_{ij2} + d_{11}^- - d_{11}^+ = 500 \tag{6-58}$$

$$\sum_{i=1}^{2} \sum_{j=1}^{3} x_{ij3} + d_{12}^- - d_{12}^+ = 500$$

Note that in the first of these constraints, the aspiration level for the number of students assigned to school 1 is the capacity of school 1. To avoid overcrowding or underutilization in school 1, both deviational variables must be minimized in the objective function. The same holds true for the second and third constraints of this constraint set.

Proceeding, we formulate a constraint for the minimization of total transportation cost. This objective can be achieved by minimizing the positive deviational variable in the following constraint.

$$\sum_{i=1}^{2} \sum_{j=1}^{3} \sum_{k=1}^{3} c_{jk} x_{ijk} - d_{13}^+ = 0 \tag{6-59}$$

where c_{jk} is the annual per-student transportation cost from district j to school k.

Lastly, the constraints associated with the lowest-priority goal were formulated. To limit the average distance traveled by any student to 8 miles, we must first identify all the decision variables that represent district-to-school combinations with a mileage factor greater than 8, and then minimize the values of these decision variables in the final solution. This can be accomplished by minimizing the positive deviational variables in the following constraints.

$$\begin{aligned}
x_{113} - d_{14}^+ &= 0 \\
x_{213} - d_{15}^+ &= 0 \\
x_{123} - d_{16}^+ &= 0 \\
x_{223} - d_{17}^+ &= 0 \\
x_{131} - d_{18}^+ &= 0 \\
x_{231} - d_{19}^+ &= 0
\end{aligned} \tag{6-60}$$

The constraint set for the model is completed by placing nonnegativity restrictions on the decision and deviational variables comprising the goal programming formulation. Finally, the objective function is constructed by minimizing the previously specified deviational variables with the appropriate preemptive priority factors assigned to them.

$$\text{Minimize } Z = P_1 \sum_{i=1}^{6} d_i^- + P_2 \sum_{i=7}^{9} (d_i^- - d_i^+) + P_3 \sum_{i=10}^{12} (d_i^- + d_i^+) \tag{6-61}$$

$$+ P_4 d_{13}^+ + P_5 (4d_{14}^+ + 4d_{15}^+ + 6d_{16}^+ + 6d_{17}^+ + 2d_{18}^+ + 2d_{19}^+)$$

Note that the cardinal weights associated with the last six positive deviational variables represent miles above 8 for the associated district-to-school combinations.

The optimal solution is presented in the following table.

District	Race	School 1	School 2	School 3	Total Number of Pupils
1	Black	206	7	237	450
	White	80	0	0	80
2	Black	0	250	0	250
	White	100	0	0	100
3	Black	0	0	20	20
	White	14	243	243	500
School Capacity		400	500	500	1400

The underachievement at each priority is provided below.

Priority	Underachievement
1	0.00 child
2	0.40 child (i.e., virtually 0)
3	0.00 child
4	$77,623.69
5	976.00 miles

Notice that the first three goals, which were assigned the highest priorities, were achieved at a total transportation cost of $77,623.69. The goal of limiting the average distance traveled by any student was not achieved, which is not surprising since it was the lowest-ranked objective in this model. The underachievement value of 976 miles results from the fact that 237 black students must travel an average distance that is 4 miles above the desired upper-bound average distance of 8 miles, and 14 white students must travel an average distance that exceeds the desired upper-bound distance by 2 miles (i.e., $[4 \times 237] + [2 \times 14] = 976$).

6.7.3   A Portfolio Selection Problem

The portfolio selection problem previously introduced in Section 3.7.4 can also be analyzed using a goal programming model. Recall that the Imprudential Insurance

Company was faced with a choice of seven investment alternatives over a 10-year time horizon. The investments and their associated financial factors are presented in the following table.

Investment Alternative	Length of Investment (year)	Annual Rate of Return (%)	Risk Coefficient	Growth Potential (%)
1. Treasury Bills	4	3	1	0
2. Common Stock	7	12	5	18
3. Corporation Bonds	8	9	4	10
4. Real Estate	6	20	8	32
5. Growth Mutual Fund	10	15	6	20
6. Savings and Loan	5	6	3	7
7. Cash	0	0	0	0

The various financial factors given in the table are explained as follows: The *length of the investment* is the expected number of years required for the annual rate of return to be realized, taking into account the possibility of reinvestment. The *annual rate of return* is the expected rate of return over the 10-year investment horizon. The *risk coefficient* is an ordinal estimate of the relative safety of each investment opportunity on a scale from 1 to 10. (The larger the integer, the higher is the perceived risk of the alternative.) The *growth potential*, expressed as a percentage, is also a subjective estimate and is indicative of the portfolio manager's appraisal of the potential increase in the value of the investment alternative over the 10-year time horizon.

Assume that Imprudential Insurance Company wants to determine the proportion of their available funds to invest in each alternative with a view toward achieving several prioritized objectives. These objectives are listed in order of their importance to the firm as follows.

1. Retain a target level of 9 percent of all available funds in the form of cash for the purpose of maintaining working capital liquidity.
2. Achieve an average annual rate of return of 14 percent or higher.
3. Achieve an average risk coefficient of 5 or lower.
4. Attain an average potential growth percentage of 14 or higher.
5. Achieve a targeted average length of the investment for the portfolio of 6 years.

A goal programming model for this problem situation can be formulated in the following manner. First of all we must define a set of choice variables $x_j (j = 1, \ldots, 7)$ to represent the proportion of available funds to be invested in the jth investment alternative. The next consideration involves the construction of the goal constraints. Recall that the first priority of the firm is to maintain a target level of 9 percent of all funds in the form of cash. The goal constraint that corresponds to this particular objective is presented as follows.

$$x_7 + d_1^- - d_1^+ = 0.09 \qquad (6\text{--}62)$$

Note that the achievement of this objective will be encouraged by the minimization of the negative and positive deviational variables in the objective function at the appropriate priority level (P_1).

The next goal constraint, associated with attaining an annual rate of return of 14 percent or higher, can be written as

$$0.03x_1 + 0.12x_2 + 0.9x_3 + 0.20x_4 + 0.15x_5 + 0.06x_6 + 0.0x_7 + d_2^- - d_2^+ = 0.14$$
$$(6\text{--}63)$$

In order to encourage conformance with the designated objective, the negative deviational variable d_2^- will be minimized (at a priority level of 2) in the objective function.

The third objective—to achieve a risk coefficient less than or equal to 5—is now subject to examination. The constraint associated with this particular prioritized goal can be expressed as

$$1x_1 + 5x_2 + 4x_3 + 8x_4 + 6x_5 + 3x_6 + 0x_7 + d_3^- - d_3^+ = 5.0 \qquad (6\text{--}64)$$

The positive deviational variable d_3^+ will be minimized in the objective function at a preemptive priority of 3 in order to encourage conformance with the specified objective.

The next constraint to be formulated is associated with the growth potential objective.

$$0.00x_1 + 0.18x_2 + 0.10x_3 + 0.32x_4 + 0.20x_5 + 0.07x_6 + 0.00x_7 + d_4^- - d_4^+ = 0.14$$
$$(6\text{--}65)$$

The negative deviational variable d_4^- will be minimized in the objective function at a priority level of 4. The final goal constraint to be constructed corresponds to the objective involving the average length of the investment.

$$4x_1 + 7x_2 + 8x_3 + 6x_4 + 10x_5 + 5x_6 + 0x_7 + d_5^- - d_5^+ = 6.0 \qquad (6\text{--}66)$$

Both the positive and negative deviational variables in this constraint will be assigned a priority factor of 5 and minimized in the objective function.

It should be clear to the reader that the single *structural constraint* in this goal programming model is concerned with restricting the sum of the proportion of funds invested in the various investment alternatives to equal one.

$$x_1 + x_2 + x_3 + x_4 + x_5 + x_6 + x_7 = 1.0 \qquad (6\text{--}67)$$

Equation 6–64, and the usual nonnegativity constraints on the decision and deviational variables, completes the constraint set for our goal programming problem, and we proceed to formulate the objective function.

$$\text{Minimize } Z = P_1(d_1^- + d_1^+) + P_2 d_2^- + P_3 d_3^+ + P_4 d_4^- + P_5(d_5^- + d_5^+) \qquad (6\text{--}68)$$

Note that the priority factors are assigned to the deviational variables to reflect the relative importance of the specified objectives of this model.

The results of this goal programming formulation are discussed next. The optimal solution values of the decision variables were as follows: $x_1 = 0.247$, $x_2 = 0.0$, $x_3 = 0.0$, $x_4 = 0.633$, $x_5 = 0.0$, $x_6 = 0.0$, and $x_7 = 0.09$. Thus, 24.7 percent of the available funds should be invested in treasury bills, 66.3 percent should be invested in real estate, and 9 percent should be retained to maintain working capital liquidity.

The optimal solution implies an expected annual rate of return of 14 percent for the investment portfolio, an average risk coefficient of 5.551, an average growth potential of 21.2 percent, and an average investment length of 4.97 years. Note that objectives 1, 2, and 4 were achieved, and that the average growth potential percentage exceeded the specified lower bound by 7 percent.

The third objective, however, was not achieved; the resulting risk coefficient was 0.551 higher than the specified upper bound on its value. Also, the average length of the investment was lower than the target value of 6 years. However, the deviations from aspiration levels in these instances were not unduly large.

6.8 CONCLUSION

Modern decision making inherently involves problems in which the decision maker would like to consider multiple (and often conflicting) goals or objectives. Goal programming allows the decision maker the opportunity to include in the problem formulation multiple goals or objectives. It represents an important approach for the solution of multiobjective decision-making problems. In this chapter we have demonstrated how several types of goal programming problems can be formulated and solved. Additionally, we have presented case study applications that demonstrate how goal programming has been used in practice.

GLOSSARY OF TERMS

Achievement Function The expressing of the objective function of a goal programming problem in terms of deviations from target goals.

Aspiration Level A numerical value that represents the decision maker's desired level of achievement for a given goal.

Bound A limit on a goal.

Commensurable Goals Goals that have a common unit of measure.

Conflicting Goals Two goals are conflicting if the level of achievement of one of the goals cannot be increased without simultaneously reducing the level of achievement of the other goal.

Deviational Variables Auxiliary variables in a goal constraint equation that measure the underachievement or overachievement of the specified aspiration level. A negative deviation variable ($d_i^- \geq 0$) reflects the amount by which aspiration level i is underachieved, while a positive deviational variable ($d_i^+ \geq 0$) indicates the amount by which aspiration level i is exceeded, where $d_i^- \cdot d_i^+ = 0$.

Deviations Failure to achieve a particular goal will result in a positive or negative deviation from that goal.

Differential Weights Cardinal weights used in weighted linear goal programming to weight deviational variables.

Goal A numerical expression of an objective in terms of the aspiration level associated with that objective.

Goal Constraints   A set of constraints that corresponds to the goals expressed by the decision maker.

Goal Programming   A technique that extends linear programming to allow the consideration of multiple objectives or goals, rather than the single objective of a linear programming formulation.

Incommensurable Goals   Goals that have no common units of measure.

Lexicographic   Ranked according to some ordinal scale.

Lower-Bound Goal   A goal from which a positive deviation is acceptable but a negative deviation is to be avoided.

Modified Simplex Method of Goal Programming   A modification of the simplex algorithm used in solving preemptive linear goal programming problems that allows for the achievement of the highest priority goal before considering the next-highest priority goal, and so on.

Nonconflicting Goals   Two goals are nonconflicting if the level of achievement of one of the goals can be increased without simultaneously reducing the level of achievement of the other goal.

Objective   A general statement of the desires of the decision maker.

One-Sided Goal   A goal from which a positive (negative) but not a negative (positive) deviation is acceptable.

Preemptive Priority Factors   Priority factors P_j ($j = 1, \ldots, K$; where K is the number of objectives in the model) that have the following relationship:

$$P_1 >>> P_2 >>> \cdots >>> P_j >>> P_{j+1}$$

where $>>>$ implies "infinitely greater than"

Preemptive Priority Goal Programming   A frequently used goal programming formulation in which the deviational variables in the objective function are assigned preemptive priority factors that represent an ordinal ranking of goals. Each of the goals is considered in order of priority; low-priority goals may be satisfied only after higher-priority goals have been satisfied to the fullest possible extent. Deviational variables in the objective function that are associated with incommensurable goals are assigned different priority factors.

Resource or Structural Constraints   The set of constraints involving resource utilization that are included in the goal programming formulation. These constraints are typically the same as those that would appear in the linear programming formulation of the problem.

Satisficing   A concept that states that the decision maker may often be satisfied with achieving a satisfactory level for multiple objectives rather than determining the optimal level for a single objective.

Upper-Bound Goal   A goal from which a negative deviation is acceptable but a positive deviation is to be avoided.

Weighted Linear Goal Programming   A goal programming formulation in which the deviational variables in the objective function are assigned cardinal weights, thus allowing solution by the simplex algorithm.

SELECTED REFERENCES

GOAL PROGRAMMING   Charnes, A., and W. W. Cooper. 1961. *Management Models and Industrial Applications of Linear Programming.* New York: John Wiley & Sons, Inc.

Cohen, J. L. 1978. *Multiobjective Programming and Planning.* New York: Academic Press.

Fatseas, V. A. 1973. *Multi-Goal Decision Model Solutions by Goal Programming.* Sydney: University of New South Wales.

Halter, A. N., and G. W. Dean. 1971. *Decisions Under Uncertainty.* Cincinnati, Ohio: South-Western Publishing Co..

Ignizio, J. P. 1976. *Goal Programming and Extensions.* Lexington, Mass.: D. C. Heath & Co.

Ignizio, J. P. 1982. *Linear Programming in Single & Multiple Objective Systems.* Englewood Cliffs, New Jersey: Prentice-Hall, Inc.

Ijiri, Y. 1965. *Management Goals and Accounting for Control.* Chicago: Rand-McNally.

Jaaskelainen, V. 1973. *Accounting and Mathematical Programming.* Helsinki: Research Institute for Business and Economics.

Lee, S. M. 1972. *Goal Programming for Decision Analysis.* Philadelphia: Auerbach Publishers, Inc.

Lee, S. M., and L. J. Moore. 1975. *Introduction to Decision Science.* New York: Petrocelli/Charter.

DISCUSSION QUESTIONS

1. Explain why the weighted linear goal programming formulation may not be appropriate in a problem where some of the objectives are expressed in noncommensurable units.

2. Explain why the following condition must always hold when one is using a simplex or simplex-based solution algorithm: $d_1^- \cdot d_1^+ = 0$.

3. Describe the advantages of preemptive linear goal programming over linear programming from the viewpoint of management.

4. Provide a brief description of the goal programming simplex method.

5. What are some of the limitations of linear preemptive goal programming?

6. Explain how you could use a standard linear programming computer package to solve the following preemptive linear goal programming problem using a sequential optimization methodology.

$$\text{Minimize } Z = P_1(d_1^- + d_1^+) + P_2 d_2^- + P_3 d_3^-$$

subject to:
$$a_{11}x_1 + a_{12}x_2 + d_1^- - d_1^+ = b_1$$
$$a_{21}x_1 + a_{22}x_2 + d_2^- - d_2^+ = b_2$$
$$a_{31}x_1 + a_{32}x_2 + d_3^- - d_3^+ = b_3$$

with $x_j, d_i^-, d_i^+ \geq 0 \qquad (j = 1,2; i = 1,2,3)$

7. Suppose the following two goal constraints involve the jth priority level objective of meeting the sales forecasts (SF) for two products, A and B.

$$x_A + d_1^- - d_1^+ = SF_A$$
$$x_B + d_2^- - d_2^+ = SF_B$$

Given that the contribution margin of product A is \$80 and the contribution margin of product B is \$40, show how the deviational variables associated with these constraints should appear in the objective function if differential weights are utilized.

8. Provide a brief summary of the steps involved in the formulation of a goal programming model.

9. Identify two conditions that prohibit the appearance of alternate optimal solutions in a preemptive goal programming solution.

10. What course of action should be taken when the final solution to a goal programming problem involving multiple conflicting goals yields zero deviations from all the goals?

PROBLEM SET

1. The Winthrop Corporation manufactures two flavors of mouthwash: spearmint and cinnamon. A batch (1000 bottles) of spearmint requires 10 production hours, while a batch (1000 bottles) of cinnamon requires 12 production hours. The sales forecast for the coming week for the spearmint mouthwash is 20,000 bottles (200 production hours), while the forecasted level of sales for the cinnamon mouthwash is 25,000 bottles (300 production hours). The regular time-available production capacity is 4500 hours. If more than 4500 hours are utilized, overtime costs are incurred. If less than 4500 hours are utilized, lay-off costs result. However, if the sales forecasts are not met, the company suffers from loss of goodwill, and if the sales forecasts are exceeded, inventory costs are incurred. Formulate this problem as a goal programming model, in order to minimize overtime, lay-offs, loss of goodwill, and inventory costs.

2. Hatteras Hammocks, Incorporated, produces some of the world's finest hammocks. The Hatteras production facility consists of two production lines. Production line A is staffed with skilled workers who can produce an average of three hammocks per hour. Production line B is staffed with less-experienced employees who are able to produce only two hammocks per hour. Regular working hours for each line for the next week are 40 hours. The operating costs of the two lines are almost identical. The production manager has prioritized the objectives for the coming week as follows.

    Produce 228 hammocks.
    Limit the overtime operation of line A to 5 hours.
    Avoid the underutilization of regular working hours for both lines (assign differential weights according to the productivity of each line).
    Limit the sum of the overtime operation of both lines (apply differential weights according to the productivity of each line).

    Formulate and solve as a goal programming model.

3. A production manager is faced with the problem of job allocation between his two production teams. The production rate of team X is 8 units per hour, while the production rate of team Y is 5 units per hour. The normal working hours for both teams are 40 hours per week. The production manager has prioritized the following goals for the coming week.

    P_1: Avoid underachievement of the desired producton level of 550 units.
    P_2: Any overtime operation of team X beyond 5 hours should be avoided.
    P_3: The sum of the overtime for both teams should be minimized. (Assign differential weights according to the relative cost of an overtime hour—assume that the operating costs of the two teams are identical.
    P_4: Any underutilization of regular working hours should be avoided; again, assign differential weights according to the relative productivity of the two teams.

    Formulate and solve as a goal programming model.

4. Sally Hefty has a choice of five different food items to include in her diet plan for the coming week: cottage, fruit, yogurt, bread, and carob candy bars. The calories and protein associated with each unit of these items and their unit cost are provided in the following table.

Food Item	Calories per Unit	Protein (mg) per Unit	Cost per Unit
Cottage cheese	225	0.15	$2.00
Fruit	200	0.25	0.10
Yogurt	175	0.15	1.10
Bread	150	0.05	0.08
Carob candy bar	400	0.08	0.75

Sally has a limited budget of $25.00, and she must restrict her intake of calories to at most 10,000 in order to lose weight (Sally weighs 200 pounds). Furthermore, she must consume at least 9.5 mg of protein in order to keep her strength up (Sally is a weight lifter). Sally has stated that her favorite diet item is the carob candy bar, followed by cottage cheese, fruit, bread, and yogurt, respectively. Formulate and solve this problem so as to maximize Sally's satisfaction subject to the aforementioned constraints.

5. The Trentwater Corporation has developed two new products that can be produced by making use of the excess productive capacity in their two production facilities. The principal reason for the development of the new products was to achieve complete utilization of excess production capacity on a profitable basis. Although Trentwater's plants usually operate at full capacity on their existing product lines, production at less than full capacity does occur occasionally, causing problems with the labor force. While the company does not need the full labor force during these slack periods, lay-offs would be costly and Trentwater's management wants to avoid this as much as possible.

Management also wants to balance the utilization of excess capacity between the two plants in order to equitably distribute the workload between the two plants.

For the current production-planning horizon, the plants have the following excess production capacities (in terms of units of new products) and available warehouse capacities allocated to the new products.

Plant	Excess Production Capacity (units)	Storage capacity (cubic ft)
1	800	27,500
2	700	20,000

Products 1 and 2 require 35 and 30 cubic feet per unit, respectively. The unit profit contributions of products 1 and 2 are $250 and $200, respectively. Sales forecasts indicate that Trentwater will sell at least 1200 and 1400 units of products 1 and 2, during the specified planning horizon.

Management has expressed the following goals in order of decreasing importance.

P_1: Achieve a profit of at least $145,000.

P_2: Use as much of the excess plant capacity as possible. Due to lower labor costs, management feels that it is twice as important to use the excess capacity in plant 1 than in plant 2.

P_3: Achieve a workload balance in the use of the excess capacity among all plants. Because of certain extra demands on plant-1 workers, management feels that if a workload imbalance occurs, it is twice as important to favor having plant 1 do less work than more work relative to plant 2.

P_4: Achieve the sales forecast for product 1, since it has the largest contribution per unit.

P_5: Produce a sufficient amount of product 2 to meet forecasted sales.

P_6: Avoid exceeding the available warehouse capacity.

Formulate and solve the goal programming model for the Trentwater Corporation production-planning problem.

6. A medium-size vegetable farm in southern Illinois is faced with the problem of choosing a 1-year cropping plan, such that initially the sum of the gross margins from all its crops grown are maximized. The farmer considers the following four cropping activities: (1) carrots, (2) celery, (3) cucumbers, and (4) peppers. The farmer must consider his decision subject to three resource constraints.

(1) The available acreage of land (200 acres).

(2) The hours of labor available (10,000 hours).

(3) A rotational and market outlet constraint (this requires that the total acreage of celery and peppers be less than or equal to the total acreage of carrots and cucumbers).

A time series of gross margins over the 6 most-recent years was obtained from a sample of actual fresh market vegetable farms in South Carolina and Georgia, and mean gross margins used as forecast values for the Illinois farmer's gross margins. These gross margins are provided in the following table.

	Activity Gross Margins per Acre			
Year	*Carrots*	*Celery*	*Cucumbers*	*Peppers*
1	292	−128	420	579
2	179	560	187	639
3	114	648	366	379
4	247	544	249	924
5	426	182	322	5
6	259	850	159	569

The number of hours of labor required per acre of carrots, celery, cucumbers, and peppers are 30, 45, 35, and 60, respectively.

(a) Formulate and solve as a linear programming model.

(b) Formulate and solve as a goal programming model where the farmer's goals in order of their priorities are

(1) Maximize gross margins.

(2) Utilize all available acreage.

(c) Now assume that it is possible for the farmer to acquire more land, but that he dislikes this 5 times more than he dislikes not using all his 200 acres.

(d) Compare and discuss your solution in part *c* with those of parts *a* and *b*.

7. Carteret County is faced with the challenge of designing a busing program for the students in its four districts to achieve racial desegregation in its three schools. The following table contains the busing cost and mileage data for every district-to-school combination, and also provides the number of student of each race in each district and the capacities of the three schools.

District	Race	School 1 Transportation Cost ($)	Miles	School 2 Transportation Cost ($)	Miles	School 3 Transportation Cost ($)	Miles	Total Number of Pupils
1	Black	39	4	71	8	103	12	450
	White	39	4	71	8	103	12	0
2	Black	47	5	63	7	119	14	250
	White	47	5	63	7	119	14	100
3	Black	87	10	31	3	47	5	20
	White	87	10	31	3	47	5	500
4	Black	63	7	47	5	31	3	0
	White	63	7	47	5	31	3	380
	School capacity	700		500		500		1700 / 1700

The mileage figures represent the average miles traveled by a student within the county on the shortest-route basis from strategic community bus stops to schools. The cost figures are based on the assumption that for the first mile there is a fixed transportation cost of $15.00 per student per year and an additional annual cost of $8.00 per student for every mile traveled beyond the initial mile.

The County School Board has the following goals for the busing program, which are listed in order of their importance.

(1) Achieve a racial balance in each school which corresponds to the racial proportions of Carteret County. (For example, if 50 percent of the students in the county are black, then 50 percent of the students in each of the schools must be black.)

(2) Avoid overcrowding or underutilization of any of the schools.

(3) Minimze the total transportation cost of the busing program.

(4) Limit the distance (average) traveled by students to eight miles.

The system constraints of the problem must ensure that every child is assigned to a school.

(a) Formulate this problem using the goal programming approach.

(b) Suppose the number of white children in district 4 is 300 instead of 380. This means that the total capacity of the school system exceeds the total number of children (1620 versus 1700). Suppose the objectives listed in order of importance are as follows.

(1)   Achieve racial balance. (Note that proportions will differ from those of part A because the number of white children in district 4 was decreased.)

(2)   Avoid overcrowding any of the schools.

(3)   Balance the underutilization of each of the schools by allocating students to schools in proportion to their capacities. That is, if 41.2 percent of the total capacity of the school system is accounted for by school 1, then assign 41.2 percent of the total number of students to school 1.

(4)   Minimize the total transportation cost of the busing program.

Formulate this revised problem as a goal programming model.

8.   The Ace Manufacturing firm uses three different resources in the manufacture of two products, A and B, which have contribution margins of $30 and $25, respectively. The following table indicates the requirements of material, labor, and equipment needed to produce a single unit of product A and a single unit of product B.

	Product A	*Product B*
Material (parts per unit)	7	5
Labor (hours per unit)	3	5
Equipment (hours per unit)	6	4

The general manager has prioritized the following goals.

P_1:   Manufacture at least 7 units of product A and 10 units of product B.

P_2:   Avoid using more than 95 parts of material, 125 worker hours, and 110 equipment hours.

P_3:   Achieve a target profit of $550.

Specify a production plan using a goal programming model.

9.   The editor of a publishing company must expedite the editing of a racy new novel entitled "Rita's Story." The 1400-page manuscript *must* be edited within 10 working days (8 hours per day), and the targeted total cost for this endeavor is $1500.00. The number-one company policy dictates that a published book of this size should have no more than 15 errors. The editor can assign a given number of pages to each of four freelance editors, Harry, Mickey, Joe, and Suzy. Their performance and relevant cost data are presented in the following table.

	1 *Harry*	*2* *Mickey*	*3* *Joe*	*4* *Suzy*
Speed (hours per page)	0.25	0.20	0.15	0.10
Accuracy (errors per page)	0.02	0.03	0.005	0.01
Wage rate ($ fee per page)	$1.25	1.19	1.29	1.30

Formulate and solve this problem using the goal programming methodology.

10.   The Atwater Corporation manufactures seven types of water skis from four basic

resources. Resource requirements for each ski type, available units of resources, sales forecasts, and contribution margins for each ski type are provided in the following table.

Number of Units of Resource i Needed to Manufacture One Pair of Skis	Water Ski Type, j							Available Units of Resource
	1	2	3	4	5	6	7	
Resource 1	3	3	2	7	5	5	3	600
Resource 2	2	2	1	3	4	2	2	350
Resource 3	5	5	4	4	3	2	1	450
Resource 4	3	2	3	3	2	2	1	300
Contribution margin	$100	$125	$275	$275	$350	$250	$125	
Sales forecast	10	40	40	40	30	30	30	

The Atwater Corporation must generate a profit of at least $30,000. Furthermore, the management wishes to minimize loss of goodwill costs associated with the failure to meet demand. Loss of goodwill costs are roughly equivalent for all ski types except for types 2 and 4. Minimizing loss of goodwill costs for these ski types is twice as important as for the other other ski types.

Formulate and solve as a weighted linear goal program. Discuss the results.

11. A company is considering undertaking three candidate marketing programs, each with a 2-year life. The total projected budget for year one is 8 units but it falls to 7 units in year two. Relevant data for each program are given in the following table.

Program	Units of Net Profit	Units of Market Share	Cost (yr 1)	Cost (yr 2)
1	5	3	7	3
2	4	3	1	1
3	5	2	4	1

The company has a goal of obtaining as much profit as possible and as great a market share as possible, while adhering as closely as possible to the projected budget. Formulate using a weighted linear goal programming model.

The Transportation and Assignment Problems

7.1 INTRODUCTION

A very interesting and important special type of linear programming problem arises frequently in the practice of management science. This special type of problem is called a **transportation problem** because it involves the transportation or physical distribution of goods and services from several **supply origins** to several **demand destinations**. In general, there will be a fixed amount or limited quantity of goods or services available at each supply location, or origin, and a fixed amount or required quantity of goods or services at each customer demand location, or destination. The structure of the transportation problem thus involves a variety of shipping routes, and associated costs, for the possible origin-to-destination movements. Solution of the transportation problem requires the determination of how many units should be shipped from each origin to each destination, in order to satisfy all of the destination demands, while minimizing the total associated cost of transportation. Transportation problems typically arise in situations involving physical movement of goods from plants to warehouses, warehouses to customers, wholesalers to retailers, or retailers to consumers. The transportation problem has a special structure and, because of this special structure, we will develop and utilize a special algorithm for its solution.

The **assignment problem** is closely related to the transportation problem. However, its structure is such that the resources are allocated to the various activities on a one-to-one basis. By this we mean that each resource is assigned to one, and only one, activity. Again, there is a cost or profit associated with each potential activity-resource pair, and the objective is to optimize the total cost or profit of completing all the activities using all of the resources. Typical assignment problems include the assignment of workers to tasks, jobs to machines, and service equipment to service routes. The assignment problem also has a special structure and, because of its special structure, we will develop and utilize a special algorithm for its solution.

7.2 MATHEMATICAL STRUCTURE OF THE TRANSPORTATION PROBLEM

The general transportation problem is structured to describe the following situation. A given product is available in known quantities at each of m origins. Known quantities of the same product are required at each of n destinations. The per-unit cost for shipping one unit of the given product from any origin to any destination is known. We seek to determine a shipping schedule that will satisfy the requirements at each of the destinations while minimizing the total cost of the shipments.

To develop the mathematical structure of the transportation problem we will proceed as follows. Let

a_i = the quantity of the product available at origin i.
b_j = the quantity of the product required at destination j.
c_{ij} = the unit cost associated with shipping one unit of product from origin i to destination j.
x_{ij} = the unknown quantity to be shipped from origin i to destination j.

The transportation problem can now be stated as solve for the x_{ij}, which:

$$\text{Minimize } Z = \sum_{i=1}^{m} \sum_{j=1}^{n} c_{ij} x_{ij} \quad \text{(Objective function)} \quad (7\text{--}1)$$

subject to:

$$\left.\begin{array}{ll} \sum_{j=1}^{n} x_{ij} = a_i & a_i > 0, i = 1, 2, \ldots, m \\ \sum_{i=1}^{m} x_{ij} = b_j & b_j > 0, j = 1, 2, \ldots, n \end{array}\right\} \quad \text{Constraint Set} \quad (7\text{--}2)$$

with $\quad x_{ij} \geq 0 \quad$ (Nonnegativity conditions) $\hspace{3cm}$ (7-3)

Additionally, in the **balanced transportation problem** it is assumed that

$$\sum_{i=1}^{m} a_i = \sum_{j=1}^{n} b_j \hspace{3cm} (7\text{-}4)$$

or that the total amount available at the m origins will exactly satisfy the quantity required at the n destinations. As we shall see later, this latter assumption (7-4) is really no more restrictive than one in which the constraints could have $\leq$ signs. However, for the present we will concentrate our efforts on the transportation problem couched in this form.

This balanced transportation problem can be written in the standard form for a linear programming problem as follows.

$$\text{Minimize } Z = c_{11}x_{11} + c_{12}x_{12} + \cdots + c_{mn}x_{mn} \hspace{2cm} (7\text{-}5)$$

subject to:

$$\left.\begin{array}{l} x_{11} + x_{12} + \cdots + x_{1n} \hspace{5cm} = a_1 \\ \hspace{1.5cm} x_{21} + x_{22} + \cdots + x_{2n} \hspace{3cm} = a_2 \\ \hspace{8cm} \vdots \\ \hspace{3cm} x_{m1} + x_{m2} + \cdots + x_{mn} = a_m \end{array}\right\} \begin{array}{l} \text{Origin} \\ \text{Constraints} \\ \\ (7\text{-}6) \end{array}$$

$$\left.\begin{array}{l} x_{11} \hspace{2cm} + x_{21} \hspace{1cm} \cdots \hspace{1cm} + x_{m1} \hspace{2.5cm} = b_1 \\ \hspace{0.7cm} x_{12} \hspace{2cm} + x_{22} \hspace{2cm} + x_{m2} \hspace{2cm} = b_2 \\ \hspace{10cm} \vdots \\ \hspace{1.5cm} x_{1n} \hspace{2cm} + x_{2n} \hspace{1cm} \cdots \hspace{1cm} + x_{mn} = b_n \end{array}\right\} \begin{array}{l} \text{Destination} \\ \text{Constraints} \end{array}$$

$$x_{ij} \geq 0 \quad \text{for } i = 1, 2, \ldots, m; j = 1, 2, \ldots, n \hspace{2cm} (7\text{-}7)$$

Note that the $[\mathbf{A}]$ matrix is an $(m + n) \times (m \cdot n)$ matrix. Also observe that each variable appears in two, and only two, of the constraints.

As an example, consider the situation in which we have two origins and three destinations. The standard matrix form of this problem becomes

EXAMPLE $\quad \text{Minimize } Z = c_{11}x_{11} + c_{12}x_{12} + c_{13}x_{13} + c_{21}x_{21} + c_{22}x_{22} + c_{23}x_{23} = \mathbf{cx} \hspace{1cm} (7\text{-}8)$

subject to:

$$
\underset{[\mathbf{A}]}{\begin{bmatrix} 1 & 1 & 1 & 0 & 0 & 0 \\ 0 & 0 & 0 & 1 & 1 & 1 \\ 1 & 0 & 0 & 1 & 0 & 0 \\ 0 & 1 & 0 & 0 & 1 & 0 \\ 0 & 0 & 1 & 0 & 0 & 1 \end{bmatrix}} \cdot
\underset{\mathbf{x}}{\begin{bmatrix} x_{11} \\ x_{12} \\ x_{13} \\ x_{21} \\ x_{22} \\ x_{23} \end{bmatrix}} =
\underset{\mathbf{b}}{\begin{bmatrix} a_1 \\ a_2 \\ b_1 \\ b_2 \\ b_3 \end{bmatrix}} \hspace{2cm} (7\text{-}9)
$$

with $\quad x_{ij} \geq 0 \quad$ for $i = 1, 2, \ldots, m; j = 1, 2, \ldots, n$, or $\mathbf{x} \geq \mathbf{0}$ $\hspace{1cm}$ (7-10)

Since we have cast the balanced transportation problem into the form of the standard linear programming problem, we could readily apply the simplex algorithm to solve such a transportation problem. However, as can be observed, the [A] matrix has a very simple and special structure. This special structure will be exploited in the development of two algorithms that can be used to solve transportation problems. As will be seen later in this chapter, these algorithms are much more efficient computational procedures than the simplex method.

EXAMPLE   Before we proceed with the development of the algorithm for solving transportation problems, let us consider a prototype example of the transportation problem. The Van Kemp Seafood Company has as its main product canned tuna fish. This product is prepared at three main canneries: San Diego, California; New Orleans, Louisiana; and Jacksonville, Florida. The tuna fish is then shipped to four major distribution warehouses that are located at Los Angeles, California; Kansas City, Missouri; Atlanta, Georgia; and Philadelphia, Pennsylvania. These shipping costs represent a major portion of the F.O.B. prices that are quoted to food wholesalers at these four major distribution warehouses. The demand expected at each of these four warehouses (in number of cases), for the forthcoming year, has been estimated as follows.

Warehouses	Estimated Yearly Demand (No. of cases)
Los Angeles, California	35,000
Kansas City, Missouri	20,000
Atlanta, Georgia	25,000
Philadelphia, Pennsylvania	45,000

Similarly, the yearly output (number of cases) expected to be available from each of the three canneries is estimated to be as follows.

Canneries	Estimated Yearly Output (No. of cases)
San Diego, California	40,000
New Orleans, Louisiana	50,000
Jacksonville, Florida	35,000

Finally, the per-case shipping cost for each origin-destination pair has been determined, as is shown in Table 7.1.

TABLE 7.1 Tuna Fish Shipping Costs

| *From Cannery* | To Warehouse | | | |
	Los Angeles	*Kansas City*	*Atlanta*	*Philadelphia*
San Diego	$ 1.00	$7.50	$8.50	$11.00
New Orleans	7.50	4.50	3.00	7.50
Jacksonville	10.00	6.50	1.00	6.00

Letting x_{ij} represent the unknown amount of tuna fish to be shipped from cannery i to warehouse j, this problem can be formulated as the following linear programming problem.

$$\text{Minimize } Z = \begin{aligned} &1.00x_{11} + 7.50x_{12} + 8.50x_{13} + 11.00x_{14} \\ &+ 7.50x_{21} + 4.50x_{22} + 3.00x_{23} + 7.50x_{24} \\ &+ 10.00x_{31} + 6.50x_{32} + 1.00x_{33} + 6.00x_{34} \end{aligned} \qquad (7\text{-}11)$$

subject to:

$$
\begin{array}{llll}
x_{11} + x_{12} + x_{13} + x_{14} & & & = 40{,}000 \\
& x_{21} + x_{22} + x_{23} + x_{24} & & = 50{,}000 \\
& & x_{31} + x_{32} + x_{33} + x_{34} & = 35{,}000 \\
x_{11} \quad\quad + x_{21} \quad\quad + x_{31} & & & = 35{,}000 \\
\quad x_{12} \quad\quad + x_{22} \quad\quad + x_{32} & & & = 20{,}000 \\
\quad\quad x_{13} \quad\quad + x_{23} \quad\quad + x_{33} & & & = 25{,}000 \\
\quad\quad\quad x_{14} \quad\quad + x_{24} \quad\quad + x_{34} & & & = 45{,}000
\end{array}
\qquad (7\text{-}12)
$$

[margin annotations: 3 (= m) origin constraints; 4 (= n) destination constraints]

with $\quad x_{ij} \geq 0 \quad (i = 1,2,3; j = 1,2,3,4)$ $\qquad\qquad\qquad (7\text{-}13)$

7.3 SOLVING THE TRANSPORTATION PROBLEM, THE STEPPING-STONE ALGORITHM

Having developed the mathematical structure of the transportation problem, we will now proceed to develop an algorithm for the solution of the transportation problem. The special structure of the transportation problem will be utilized in the construction of this algorithm. However, in developing this algorithm, we will find it convenient to focus our attention on a matrix tableau having m rows and n columns. Such a tableau is shown below in Table 7.2.

Each row in this tableau corresponds to an origin, and each column corresponds to a destination. The entries in the final column are the supply availabilities at the origins, and the entries in the bottom row are the demand requirements at the destinations. The x_{ij} entry in cell (i, j) denotes the allocation from origin i to destination j, and the corresponding cost per unit allocated is c_{ij}. The sum of the x_{ij}'s across row i must equal a_i in any feasible solution, and the sum of the x_{ij}'s down column j must equal b_j in any feasible solution. Finally, the lower-right-hand box reflects the fact that the total amount available at the m supply origins exactly satisfies the total quantity required at the n demand destinations.

7.3.1 Constructing an Initial Basic Feasible Solution

Before we begin the mechanics of constructing an initial basic feasible solution, let us reexamine the structure of the balanced transportation problem as shown in Equations 7-5, 7-6, and 7-7. We noted earlier that there were $(m + n)$ constraints and that each variable appears in two, and only two, of these constraints. The constraints of the transportation problem fall naturally into two sets.

1. The first m rows that come from the origin constraints.
2. The last n rows that come from the destination constraints.

Now, the sum of the first m rows is equal to the sum of the last n rows. The reader can easily verify this result for the specific case of $m = 2$ (origins) and $n = 3$ (destinations) by performing such an operation on the $[\mathbf{A}]$ matrix shown in Equation 7-9. Furthermore, any row of the constraint set of the transportation problem can be expressed as linear combination of the remaining $m + n - 1$ rows of the constraint set of the transportation problem. For example, in the constraint set for the tuna fish shipping problem given by Equation 7-12, the first constraint can be formed by summing the last four constraints and subtracting the second and third constraints. Therefore, only $m + n - 1$ of the constraints of the transportation problem are independent or we can remove any one constraint from the $m + n$ constraints of the transportation problem and the remaining $m + n - 1$ constraints will be independent. Thus, the set of $m + n$ constraints for the transportation problem always has one *redundant* constraint (i.e., any one of the constraints is automatically satisfied whenever the other $m + n - 1$ constraints are satisfied). These results occur because we are assuming that the "balance" between supply and demand, as given by Equation 7-4, is required. This means that any set of x_{ij} that satisfies all but one of the constraints must automatically satisfy this remaining constraint in order for Equation 7-4 to be satisfied.

TABLE 7.2   The Transportation Problem Tableau

	Destination						Origin Availability, a_i
Origin	D_1	D_2	...	D_j	...	D_n	
O_1	x_{11} $\quad c_{11}$	x_{12} $\quad c_{12}$	...	x_{1j} $\quad c_{1j}$	...	x_{1n} $\quad c_{1n}$	a_1
O_2	x_{21} $\quad c_{21}$	x_{22} $\quad c_{22}$	...	x_{2j} $\quad c_{2j}$	...	x_{2n} $\quad c_{2n}$	a_2
$\vdots$	$\vdots$	$\vdots$	$\vdots$	$\vdots$	$\vdots$	$\vdots$	$\vdots$
O_i	x_{i1} $\quad c_{i1}$	x_{i2} $\quad c_{i2}$	...	x_{ij} $\quad c_{ij}$	...	x_{in} $\quad c_{in}$	a_i
$\vdots$	$\vdots$	$\vdots$	$\vdots$	$\vdots$	$\vdots$	$\vdots$	$\vdots$
O_m	x_{m1} $\quad c_{m1}$	x_{m2} $\quad c_{m2}$	...	x_{mj} $\quad c_{mj}$	...	x_{mn} $\quad c_{mn}$	a_m
Destination Requirement, b_j	b_1	b_2	...	b_j	...	b_n	$\sum_{i=1}^{m} a_i = \sum_{j=1}^{n} b_j$

The results discussed above make it apparent that a basic feasible solution to a balanced transportation problem must contain exactly $m + n - 1$ basic variables.[1] Thus, a basic feasible solution to a balanced transportation problem would

---

[1] Assuming, of course, that it is not degenerate. Degeneracy in transportation problems will be discussed further in a later section of this chapter.

be represented in the transportation problem tableau (Table 7.2) as having exactly $(m + n - 1)$ *positive* x_{ij}'s (allocations), with the sum of the allocations for each row being equal to the a_i for that row, and with the sum of the allocations for each column being equal to the b_j for that column.

The general procedure for constructing an initial basic feasible solution involves selecting the $(m + n - 1)$ basic variables one at a time, with a value being assigned to the variable that will satisfy either a row or a column constraint (but not both). It is possible, of course, to satisfy both at a single point in time. Such a condition produces a degenerate basic feasible solution. For simplicity, this possibility will not be considered until later. After each selection and assignment of a value to a basic variable, one additional constraint has been satisfied. After $(m + n - 1)$ such assignments are made, the entire basic feasible solution will have been constructed in a manner that satisfies all the constraints. We will now proceed to develop several procedures for determining an initial basic feasible solution.

Northwest Corner Rule. The first procedure used to determine an initial basic feasible solution is called the **Northwest Corner Rule**. Using the Northwest Corner Rule, and referring to Table 7.2, we begin with cell (1,1), which is the northwest corner cell in the tableau, and we set $x_{11} = \min (a_1, b_1)$. At this first step we satisfy either an origin availability or a destination requirement. If $a_1 > b_1$, we then move to cell (1,2) and set $x_{12} = \min (a_1 - b_1, b_2)$. Conversely, if $b_1 > a_1$, we move to cell (2,1) and set $x_{21} = \min (b_1 - a_1, a_2)$. (Remember that, if $a_1 = b_1$, degeneracy will occur; this possibility will be considered later.) At this second step we will satisfy either the second origin availability or the second destination requirement. We continue in this way, satisfying either an origin availability or a destination requirement at each step in the process. Eventually, we must obtain a basic feasible solution with $(m + n - 1)$ positive values because after we have made $(m + n - 2)$ such allocations we are forced to make a single final allocation that satisfies the last row and last column simultaneously. Thus, after $(m + n - 1)$ steps, $(m + n - 1)$ of the constraints will be satisfied, and we noted earlier that a basic feasible solution must have exactly $(m + n - 1)$ positive allocations. Note, however, that the initial basic feasible solution obtained by application of the Northwest Corner Rule may be far from the optimal basic feasible solution, since the costs associated with the various origin-destination routes were completely ignored. We shall now attempt to make our description of the Northwest Corner Rule more complete by applying the procedure to our tuna fish shipping problem. The initial basic feasible solution for this problem, using the Northwest Corner Rule, is presented in Table 7.3.

Observe first that the format for Table 7.3 is exactly that which we introduced earlier in Table 7.2. Applying the Northwest Corner Rule, the first allocation is $x_{11} = 35,000$, the min ($a_1 = 40,000$; $b_1 = 35,000$). This exactly satisfies the destination requirement for column one (Los Angeles). Since $a_1 > b_1$, we then move to cell (1,2) and set $x_{12} = 5,000$, the min ($a_1 - b_1 = 40,000 - 35,000 = 5,000$; $b_1 = 20,000$). This completely utilizes the origin availability for row one (San Diego). We then proceed downward and to the right until all row (origin) availabilities have been utilized and all column (destination) requirements have been met. The arrows in Table 7.3 show the order in which the basic variables (allocations) are determined. Observe that the initial basic feasible solution obtained by use of the Northwest Corner Rule has $m + n - 1 = 3 + 4 - 1 = 6$ positive allocations. The total shipping cost associated with this initial basic feasible solution is as follows.

Shipping Route	Shipping Cost
San Diego → Los Angeles	35,000 cases × $1.00 per case = $ 35,000
San Diego → Kansas City	5,000 cases × $7.50 per case = $ 37,500
New Orleans → Kansas City	15,000 cases × $4.50 per case = $ 67,500
New Orleans → Atlanta	25,000 cases × $3.00 per case = $ 75,000
New Orleans → Philadelphia	10,000 cases × $7.50 per case = $ 75,000
Jacksonville → Philadelphia	35,000 cases × $6.00 per case = $210,000
	Total $500,000

TABLE 7.3   Initial Basic Feasible Solution—Northwest Corner Rule

	Destination				
Origin	D_1 Los Angeles	D_2 Kansas City	D_3 Atlanta	D_4 Philadelphia	Origin Availability
O_1 San Diego	(35,000) → 1.00	(5,000) 7.50	8.50	11.00	40,000
O_2 New Orleans	7.50	(15,000) → 4.50	(25,000) → 3.00	(10,000) 7.50	50,000
O_3 Jacksonville	10.00	6.50	1.00	(35,000) 6.00	35,000
Destination Requirement	35,000	20,000	25,000	45,000	125,000

Column Minima Rule.   A second procedure for determining an initial basic feasible solution involves the successive determination of *column minima*. Using the **Column Minima Rule** we begin with column one of the tableau and choose the minimum cost in this column. If a tie occurs, select the minimum cost having the smallest row index within this column. Assuming that the minimum cost is found in row r we set $x_{r1} = \min(a_r, b_1)$. If $x_{r1} = a_r$, we remove row r from further consideration, since this origin availability will have been satisfied, and select the next lowest cost in column one. Conversely, if $x_{r1} = b$, we eliminate column one from further consideration and move to column two and select the lowest cost in column two. Assume that the latter condition was present (i.e., $x_{r1} = a_r$), and assume that the next lowest cost in column one is found in row s. We then set $x_{s1} = \min(a_s, b - a_r)$ and continue in the same manner until the destination requirement for column one has been satisfied. When the requirement for column one has been met, eliminate column one from further consideration and repeat the procedure for column two. Continue this process until the requirement for column n (last column) is satisfied. If, at any point in the search process, the minimum cost in a column is not unique, simply select any one of the minima. This column minima procedure will produce an initial basic feasible solution that is usually better than that produced by application of the Northwest Corner Rule. Degeneracy can also occur during the application of the Column Minima Rule, and this problem will be discussed more fully later. Let us now apply the Column Minima

Rule to our tuna fish shipping problem. The initial basic feasible solution for this problem using the Column Minima Rule is presented below in Table 7.4.

TABLE 7.4 Initial Basic Feasible Solution—Column Minima Rule

Origin	Destination				Origin Availability
	D_1 Los Angeles	D_2 Kansas City	D_3 Atlanta	D_4 Philadelphia	
O_1 San Diego	1.00 (35,000)	7.50	8.50	11.00 (5,000)	40,000
O_2 New Orleans	7.50	4.50 (20,000)	3.00	7.50 (30,000)	50,000
O_3 Jacksonville	10.00	6.50	1.00 (25,000)	6.00 (10,000)	35,000
Destination Requirement	35,000	20,000	25,000	45,000	125,000

Applying the Column Minima Rule, the first allocation is $x_{11} = 35,000$, the min $(a_1 = 40,000; b_1 = 35,000)$, since $c_{11} = \$1.00$ is the lowest cost in column one. This allocation exactly satisfies the destination requirement for column one (Los Angeles). Since $x_{r1} = 35,000 = b_1$, we eliminate column one from further consideration and move to column two and select the lowest cost in column two, which is $c_{22} = \$4.50$. We then set $x_{22} = 20,000$, the min $(a_2 = 50,000; b_2 = 20,000)$. This satisfies the destination requirement for column two (Kansas City). We proceed in this fashion, as indicated by the arrows in table 7.4, until all of the basic variables (allocations) are determined. Observe that we have again made $m + n - 1 = 3 + 4 - 1 = 6$ positive allocations. The total shipping cost associated with this initial basic feasible solution is as follows.

Shipping Route	Shipping Cost
San Diego → Los Angeles	35,000 cases × $ 1.00 per case = $ 35,000
San Diego → Philadelphia	5,000 cases × $11.00 per case = $ 55,000
New Orleans → Kansas City	20,000 cases × $ 4.50 per case = $ 90,000
New Orleans → Philadelphia	30,000 cases × $ 7.50 per case = $225,000
Jacksonville → Atlanta	25,000 cases × $ 1.00 per case = $ 25,000
Jacksonville → Philadelphia	10,000 cases × $ 6.00 per case = $ 60,000
	Total $490,000

It should be intuitively obvious that we could employ a row minima procedure that would be identical to the column minima procedure, except for searching for the smallest cost in successive rows. The procedure will not be discussed further, but it certainly can be used instead of the column minima process.

Matrix Minima Rule.   A third procedure for determining an initial basic feasible solution involves the successive determination of *matrix minima*. Using the

Matrix Minima Rule, we begin by determining the smallest cost in the entire tableau. If a tie occurs, the tie may be broken arbitrarily. Assuming that this occurs for cell (i,j), we then set $x_{ij} = \min (a_i, b_j)$ and eliminate from further consideration either row i or column j, depending on which requirement is satisfied. Thus, if $x_{ij} = a_i$, we decrease b_j by a_i, and if $x_{ij} = b_j$, we decrease a_i by b_j. We then repeat this process throughout the remainder of the tableau. Whenever the search process reaches a point at which the minimum cost is not unique, an arbitrary choice among the minima can be made. Degeneracy can again occur, but this possibility will be discussed more fully later. Again, use of the Matrix Minima Rule will generally produce a better initial feasible solution than the Northwest Corner Rule. Applying the Matrix Minima Rule to our tuna fish shipping problem we obtain the initial basic feasible solution shown below in Table 7.5.

TABLE 7.5 Initial Basic Feasible Solution—Matrix Minima Rule

		Destination			
Origin	D_1 Los Angeles	D_2 Kansas City	D_3 Atlanta	D_4 Philadelphia	Origin Availability
O_1 San Diego	1.00 35,000	7.50	8.50	11.00 5,000	40,000
O_2 New Orleans	7.50	4.50 20,000	3.00	7.50 30,000	50,000
O_3 Jacksonville	10.00	6.50	1.00 25,000	6.00 10,000	35,000
Destination Requirement	35,000	20,000	25,000	45,000	125,000

Applying the Matrix Minima Rule, the first allocation is $x_{11} = 35,000$, the min $(a_1 = 40,000; b_1 = 35,000)$, since $c_1 = \$1.00$ is the minimum cost in the tableau. This allocation exactly satisfies the destination requirement for column one (Los Angeles), and we decrease a_1 by 35,000 also. The next smallest cost in the tableau is $c_{33} = \$1.00$. We thus make the second allocation as $x_{33} = 25,000$, the min $(a_3 = 35,000; b_3 = 25,000)$. We then decrease a_3 by $b_3 = 25,000$ and continue. This process is repeated throughout the remainder of the tableau, as indicated by the arrows in Table 7.5, until all the basic variables (allocations) are determined. Observe that we have again made $m + n - 1 = 3 + 4 - 1 = 6$ positive allocations. The total shipping cost associated with this initial basic feasible solution is as follows.

Shipping Route	Shipping Cost
San Diego → Los Angeles	35,000 cases × $ 1.00 per case = $ 35,000
San Diego → Philadelphia	5,000 cases × $11.00 per case = $ 55,000
New Orleans → Kansas City	20,000 cases × $ 4.50 per case = $ 90,000
New Orleans → Philadelphia	30,000 cases × $ 7.50 per case = $225,000
Jacksonville → Atlanta	25,000 cases × $ 1.00 per case = $ 25,000
Jacksonville → Philadelphia	10,000 cases × $ 6.00 per case = $ 60,000
	Total $490,000

Vogel's Method. A final procedure for determining an initital basic feasible solution is known as **Vogel's Method**.[2] This procedure evolves as follows. For each row, we determine the lowest cost c_{ij}, and the next lowest cost c_{it}. We then compute $c_{it} - c_{ij}$. This difference represents the "penalty" that will be incurred if, instead of shipping over the *best* route (i.e., the route having cost c_{ij}) we are forced to ship over the *second best* route (i.e., the route having cost c_{it}). This computation is made for each of the m rows and m numbers are obtained. The same process is then applied for each of the n columns and n numbers are obtained. We then select the largest of the $m + n$ values. If a tie occurs, the tie may be broken arbitrarily. Assume that the largest of these numbers is associated with column j, and that we have determined that cell (i, j) is the minimum cost cell for column j. We then set $x_{ij} = \min(a_i, b_j)$ and cross off either row i or column j, depending on which requirement is satisfied. What we are doing is making an allocation to the cell for which the penalty would be greatest if we did not select this cell or route. That is, we locate the row or column with the largest penalty and then allocate the maximum number of units possible to the lowest cost (i.e., the "best") cell in that row or column. We then repeat the entire process for the remaining rows and columns. This process continues until all the basic variables (allocations) are determined. Again, when the maximum difference is not unique, an arbitrary choice can be made. Degeneracy can again occur, and will be discussed more fully later. Vogel's Method usually produces an initial basic feasible solution that is superior to that produced by the Northwest Corner Rule. Applying Vogel's Method to our tuna fish shipping problem, we obtain the initial basic feasible solution shown in Table 7.6 on the following page. The steps taken in applying Vogel's Method are summarized as follows.

| | Differences, Δ | | | | | | | |
| | Row | | | Column | | | | Allocation |
Step	1	2	3	1	2	3	4	
1	6.50	1.50	5.00	6.50	2.00	2.00	1.50	$x_{11} = 35,000$ $\left\{\begin{array}{l}\text{Eliminate}\\ \text{column 1}\end{array}\right.$
2	1.00	1.50	5.00		2.00	2.00	1.50	$x_{33} = 25,000$ $\left\{\begin{array}{l}\text{Eliminate}\\ \text{column 3}\end{array}\right.$
3	3.50	3.00	0.50		2.00		1.50	$x_{12} = 5,000$ $\left\{\begin{array}{l}\text{Eliminate}\\ \text{row 1}\end{array}\right.$
4		3.00	0.50		2.00		1.50	$x_{22} = 15,000$ $\left\{\begin{array}{l}\text{Eliminate}\\ \text{column 2}\end{array}\right.$
5							1.50	$x_{24} = 35,000$ $\left\{\begin{array}{l}\text{Eliminate}\\ \text{column 4}\end{array}\right.$
								$x_{34} = 10,000$ $\left\{\text{row 2 \& 3}\right.$

In step 1 we first compute the $m + n$ row and column differences for the entire tableau. Observing that 6.50 in row 1 is the largest of these differences we then set $x_{11} = \min(a_1 = 40,000; b_1 = 35,000) = 35,000$. This eliminates column 1

[2] N. V. Reinfeld, and W. R. Vogel, *Mathematical Programming* (Englewood Cliffs, New Jersey: Prentice-Hall, Inc., 1958).

TABLE 7.6 Initial Basic Feasible Solution—Vogel's Method

Origin	Destination				Origin Availability
	D_1 Los Angeles	D_2 Kansas City	D_3 Atlanta	D_4 Philadelphia	
O_1 San Diego	1.00 (35,000)	7.50 (5,000)	8.50	11.00	40,000
O_2 New Orleans	7.50	4.50 (15,000)	3.00	7.50 (35,000)	50,000
O_3 Jacksonville	10.00	6.50	1.00 (25,000)	6.00 (10,000)	35,000
Destination Requirement	35,000	20,000	25,000	45,000	125,000

from further consideration. In step 2 we then compute the differences for the remaining columns (i.e., column 1 eliminated) and rows. Observing that 5.00 in row 3 is the largest of these differences we then set $x_{33} = \min (a_3 = 35,000; b_3 = 25,000) = 25,000$. This eliminates column 3 from further consideration. In step 3 we then compute the differences for the remaining columns (i.e., columns 1 and 3 eliminated) and rows. Observing that 3.50 in row 1 is the largest of these differences we then set $x_{12} = \min (a_1 - x_{11} = 5,000; b_2 = 20,000) = 5,000$. This eliminates row 1 from further consideration. In step 4 we then compute the differences for the remaining columns (i.e., columns 1 and 3 eliminated) and rows (i.e., row 1 eliminated). Observing that 3.00 in row 2 is the largest of these differences we then set $x_{22} = \min (a_2 = 50,000; b_2 - x_{12} = 15,000) = 15,000$. This eliminates column 2 from further consideration. In step 5 we have only column 4, and rows 2 and 3 remaining under consideration. We can make these final allocations by inspection, that is, $x_{24} = 35,000$ satisfying the remaining row requirement for row 2, and $x_{34} = 10,000$ satisfying the remaining row requirement for row 3. The sum of these two row allocations simultaneously satisfies the column requirement for column 4. Thus, we have obtained the initial basic feasible solution shown in Table 7.6. Again, our initial basic feasible solution contains $m + n - 1 = 3 + 4 - 1 = 6$ positive allocations. The total shipping cost associated with this initial basic feasible solution is as follows.

Shipping Route	Shipping cost	
San Diego → Los Angeles	35,000 cases × $1.00 per case =	$ 35,000
San Diego → Kansas City	5,000 cases × $7.50 per case =	$ 37,500
New Orleans → Kansas City	15,000 cases × $4.50 per case =	$ 67,500
New Orleans → Philadelphia	35,000 cases × $7.50 per case =	$262,500
Jacksonville → Atlanta	25,000 cases × $1.00 per case =	$ 25,000
Jacksonville → Philadelphia	10,000 cases × $6.00 per case =	$ 60,000
	Total	$487,500

7.3.2 Making an Iteration

In the previous section of this chapter we determined a basic feasible solution to the transportation problem having $m + n - 1$ of the basic variables, the x_{ij}, positive. We entered the values for the basic x_{ij} in the appropriate cells, and we circled the values to indicate that they were basic. Now, we must evaluate each of the unoccupied cells (unused shipping routes) to determine the effect upon the objective function of transferring one unit from an occupied cell to the unoccupied cell. The **stepping-stone algorithm** thus involves two steps.

1. All unoccupied cells are evaluated for the "net cost" effect of transferring one unit from an occupied cell to the unoccupied cell. This transfer is made in a manner that maintains the row and column balance of the transportation problem (i.e., each row availability is exactly allocated and each column requirement is exactly satisfied).
2. After the unoccupied cells have all been evaluated, a reallocation is made to the unoccupied cell for which it is indicated that the greatest per-unit "net cost" savings would occur.

The steps of the stepping-stone algorithm are employed repeatedly until there are no unoccupied cells for which an improvement in the objective function would occur.

To measure the effect on the objective function of transferring one unit to an unoccupied cell, we must find a closed loop or path between the unoccupied cell and selected occupied cells. This path consists of a series of "steps" leading from the unoccupied cell to the occupied cells ("stones") and back to the unoccupied cell. Since we are evaluating the effect of making a one-unit allocation to an unoccupied cell, this can be done by simply using the c_{ij}'s associated with the cells along the path.

The procedure for tracing out the closed loop is as follows.

1. Begin with the unoccupied cell to be evaluated and place a $+1$ in this unoccupied cell. This indicates that we are evaluating the effect of moving one unit into this unoccupied cell (i.e., moving one unit into this unoccupied cell (i, j) will incur a cost of $+c_{ij}$).
2. Draw an arrow from the unoccupied cell being evaluated to an occupied cell in the same row, or to an occupied cell in the same column. Place a -1 in the cell to which the arrow was drawn. This signifies that we are compensating for the $+1$ unit moved into the unoccupied cell by subtracting (shifting) one unit from either an occupied cell in its same row or an occupied cell in its same column (i.e., moving one unit from this occupied cell (k, j) will save a cost equal to c_{kj}). This shifting is necessary in order to maintain the row, or column, balance.
3. Move from the occupied cell just selected, horizontally or vertically (but never diagonally), to another occupied cell. Draw an arrow to this occupied cell and place a $+1$ in the cell to which the arrow was drawn, again to maintain the row, or column, balance.
4. Repeat the process of moving from occupied cell to occupied cell until we loop back to the original unoccupied cell. At each step of the looping process the $+1$ and -1 allocations are alternated in order to maintain the row, or column, balance.
5. Throughout the looping process we maintain the important restriction that there is exactly one positive allocation ($+1$) and exactly one negative allocation (-1) in any row or column through which the loop happens to pass.

Again, this restriction is necessary to maintain the row, or column, balance. Physically, this means that as we trace out the closed loop, **orthogonal** (90° or right-angle) **turns** will be made at only the occupied cells. It is also important to note that the number of cells involved in the closed loop process will always be an even integer equal to or greater than 4 (i.e., 4, 6, 8, . . .).

6. After the entire closed loop has been constructed the "net cost" associated with the unoccupied cell is determined by adding the c_{ij} values in all the cells marked with a +1 and subtracting the c_{ij} values in all the cells marked with a −1.

All of the unoccupied cells are evaluated in the manner described above. Then, the unoccupied cell in which the greatest per-unit "net cost" savings occurs is selected as the cell into which a reallocation is made. If two or more cells tie in the evaluation process, the tie may be broken arbitrarily. To summarize, the steps outlined above are the variable entry criterion for the transportation problem.

The variable removal criterion for the transportation problem involves the cells on the closed loop that are marked with a −1 during the evaluation process described above. Since the variable entry criterion involves a reallocation to a previously unoccupied cell, the variable removal criterion requires that the cells on the closed loop with an entry of −1 must be *decreased* to maintain the row and column balance. Thus, we must examine each of the cells marked with a −1, and the cell marked with a −1 having the *minimum* value will indicate how much the current nonbasic variable can be increased. The cell selected in this manner will decrease to zero (i.e., will become nonbasic), and the unoccupied cell selected using the variable entry criterion will increase to the amount that was originally in the cell marked with a −1 (i.e., will become basic). In this manner the row and column balance will also be maintained. This process is the variable removal criterion for the transportation problem.

In the procedure employed for tracing out the closed loop used to evaluate an unoccupied cell it should be emphasized that we begin by placing a +1 in the unoccupied cell being evaluated and then alternately place −1 and +1 in the occupied cells along the closed loop. Additionally, the assignment of the −1 and +1 values is uniquely specified in a manner that maintains the row and column balance. To illustrate, consider the following example.

EXAMPLE

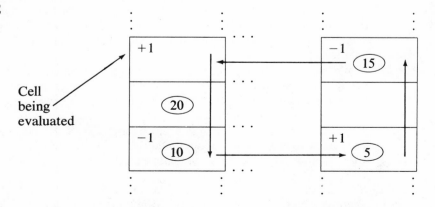

In this example a +1 is automatically assigned to the unoccupied cell being evaluated. Then the assignment of the -1 is uniquely determined as the cell occupied with the amount "10," since the assignment of -1 to this cell can be offset by the assignment of $+1$ to the cell occupied with the amount "5" (i.e., we can thus maintain the row-column balance). Note that we cannot make the assignment of the -1 to the cell occupied with the amount "20" because the row balance could not be maintained since there is no other occupied cell in the corresponding row. Note finally that the number of cells in the closed loop process is the even value four, that is, two occupied cells assigned -1 and two cells—one the unoccupied cell being evaluated and one the other occupied cell—assigned $+1$.

As the stepping-stone algorithm is applied we maintain a set of $m + n - 1$ occupied cells that forms a **basic tree**. A **tree** in the transportation tableau is a **connected set of cells** without loops, and a *basic tree* in the transportation tableau is that tree which consists of the $m + n - 1$ occupied cells that correspond to the current basic variables. A set of cells in the transportation tableau is said to be connected if there exists a directed path (and thus a **simple directed path**), involving only cells in the set, that joins any cell in the set to any other cell in the set. A *simple directed path* from cell (i, j) to cell (u, v) in the transportation tableau is a directed path such that in any row or column there are no more than two cells in the set of cells that define the path.

To illustrate the stepping-stone algorithm, we will solve the tuna fish shipping problem using the initial basic feasible solution determined by the Northwest Corner Rule. This tableau is reproduced below in Table 7.7.

TABLE 7.7   Tuna Fish Shipping Problem—Initial Basic Feasible Solution

	Destination				
Origin	D_1 *Los Angeles*	D_2 *Kansas City*	D_3 *Atlanta*	D_4 *Philadelphia*	*Origin* *Availability*
O_1 San Diego	1.00 (35,000)	7.50 (5,000)	8.50 +2.50	11.00 +0.50	40,000
O_2 New Orleans	7.50 +9.50	4.50 (15,000)	3.00 (25,000)	7.50 (10,000)	50,000
O_3 Jacksonville	10.00 +13.50	6.50 +3.50	1.00 −0.50	6.00 (35,000)	35,000
Destination *Requirement*	35,000	20,000	25,000	45,000	125,000

Note: Total shipping cost (initial basic feasible solution) = \$500,000.

We will begin our analysis by considering cell (1,3), which is currently unoccupied and represents the San Diego $\rightarrow$ Atlanta shipping route. In the case of cell (1,3) a closed path consists of steps from this cell (1,3) to cell (2,3), from cell (2,3) to cell (2,2), from cell (2,2) to cell (1,2), and from cell (1,2) back to cell (1,3). We are thus evaluating the effect of adding one unit to cell (1,3), which in turn must be compensated for by subtracting one unit from cell (2,3). This reduction in cell (2,3) must then be compensated for by adding one unit to cell (2,2). This addition to cell

(2,2) must then be compensated for by subtracting one unit from cell (1,2). This completes the reallocation along the closed path from cell (1,3) back to itself.

The net change in the objective function that corresponds to this reallocation can be determined by adding and subtracting the appropriate transportation costs. Following our closed path, these results are as follows.

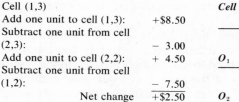

Cell (1,3)	
Add one unit to cell (1,3):	+$8.50
Subtract one unit from cell (2,3):	− 3.00
Add one unit to cell (2,2):	+ 4.50
Subtract one unit from cell (1,2):	− 7.50
Net change	+$2.50

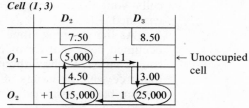

Thus, an allocation of one unit to cell (1,3) will result in a $2.50 increase in the objective function. This net increase is entered in cell (1,3) in the tableau.

The effect of allocating one unit to each of the other unoccupied cells is evaluated in the same manner. The computations for the other cells are shown below:

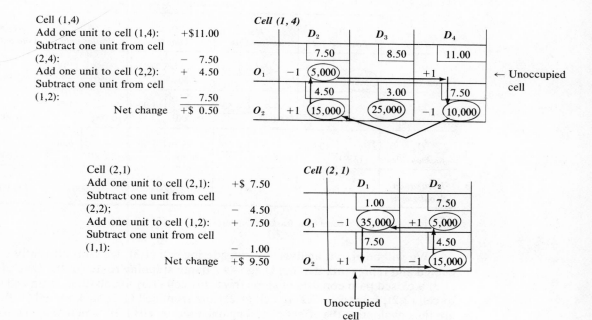

Cell (1,4)	
Add one unit to cell (1,4):	+$11.00
Subtract one unit from cell (2,4):	− 7.50
Add one unit to cell (2,2):	+ 4.50
Subtract one unit from cell (1,2):	− 7.50
Net change	+$ 0.50

Cell (2,1)	
Add one unit to cell (2,1):	+$ 7.50
Subtract one unit from cell (2,2):	− 4.50
Add one unit to cell (1,2):	+ 7.50
Subtract one unit from cell (1,1):	− 1.00
Net change	+$ 9.50

Cell (3,1)

Add one unit to cell (3,1):	+$10.00
Subtract one unit from cell (3,4):	– 6.00
Add one unit to cell (2,4):	+ 7.50
Subtract one unit from cell (2,2):	– 4.50
Add one unit to cell (1,2):	+ 7.50
Subtract one unit from cell (1,1):	– 1.00
Net change	+$13.50

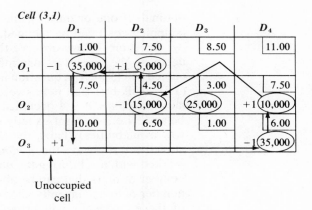

Cell (3,2)

Add one unit to cell (3,2):	+$ 6.50
Subtract one unit from cell (3,4):	– 6.00
Add one unit to cell (2,4):	+ 7.50
Subtract one unit from cell (2,2):	– 4.50
Net change	+$ 3.50

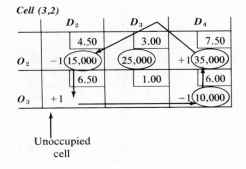

Cell (3,3)

Add one unit to cell (3,3):	+$ 1.00
Subtract one unit from cell (3,4):	– 6.00
Add one unit to cell (2,4):	+ 7.50
Subtract one unit from cell (2,3):	– 3.00
Net change	–$ 0.50

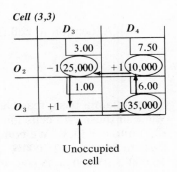

These net changes are entered in Table 7.7. They are equivalent to the $c_j - Z_j$ values we used earlier in the simplex algorithm. However, we are now solving a minimization problem. Thus, if all $c_{ij} - Z_{ij} \geq 0$, the basic feasible solution is optimal. If one or more of the $c_{ij} - Z_{ij} < 0$, the value of the objective function (shipping cost) can be reduced.

In Table 7.7 we observe that $c_{33} - Z_{33} = -0.50$, and we know that we can decrease the objective function by making an allocation to the currently unoccupied cell (3,3). The question now is: How large an allocation can we make to cell (3,3)? This question is answered by remembering that a basic feasible solution must have $m + n - 1$ occupied cells, and we must maintain our row and column balance (i.e., we must exactly satisfy the column requirements using exactly the row availabilities). Thus, the amount of the allocation to be made into an unoccupied cell is always the *minimum* amount in the cells on the closed loop that are marked with a -1 during the unoccupied cell evaluation process. The limit on the number of units that can be allocated to cell (3,3) is equal to the *minimum* of the number of units currently allocated to cell (2,3) and cell (3,4). This is because one of these two cells will provide the units that will move into cell (3,3). Diagramatically,

	D_3	D_4
O_2	-1 | 3.00 (25,000)	$+1$ | 7.50 (10,000)
O_3	$+1$ | 1.00	-1 | 6.00 (35,000)

or

	D_3	D_4
O_2	-1 | 3.00 (25,000)	$+1$ | 7.50 (10,000)
O_3	$+1$ | 1.00	-1 | 6.00 (35,000)

In these diagrams note that each of the cells along the closed loop has been marked with a $+1$ or a -1. The number of units to be allocated to cell (3,3) would be computed as

$$\text{Allocation to cell (3,3)} = \text{minimum} \left(\frac{\text{cell (2,3)}}{25,000}; \frac{\text{cell (3,4)}}{35,000} \right)$$
$$= 25,000 \tag{7-14}$$

To maintain a basic feasible solution and the row-column balance, the minimum value in these two cells must be selected. Thus, we move 25,000 units from cell (2,3) into cell (3,3). We compensate for this move by reducing the amount in cell (3,4) to $35,000 - 25,000 = 10,000$. Then we increase the amount in cell (2,4) to $10,000 + 25,000 = 35,000$. Finally, we reduce the amount in cell (2,3) to $25,000 - 25,000 = 0$. We have, of course, simply moved 25,000 units around the closed path that we used to originally evaluate cell (3,3). The new tableau, in which this change has been made, is shown below in Table 7.8.

To illustrate the determination of the amount of the allocation for a more complicated route refer back to Table 7.7 and assume for purposes of discussion that we had determined that an allocation should be made to cell (3,1). (Note that this would not really be the case since $c_{31} - Z_{31} = +13.50$.)

TABLE 7.8 Tuna Fish Shipping Problem—Second Basic Feasible Solution (Optimal Solution)

	Destination				
Origin	D_1 Los Angeles	D_2 Kansas City	D_3 Atlanta	D_4 Philadelphia	Origin Availability
O_1 San Diego	1.00 (35,000)	7.50 (5,000)	8.50 +3.00	11.00 +0.50	40,000
O_2 New Orleans	7.50 +9.50	4.50 (15,000)	3.00 +0.50	7.50 (35,000)	50,000
O_3 Jacksonville	10.00 +13.50	6.50 +3.50	1.00 (25,000)	6.00 (10,000)	35,000
Destination Requirement	35,000	20,000	25,000	45,000	125,000

Note: Total shipping cost (second basic feasible solution) = \$487,500.

Below, the closed loop used to make the evaluation for cell (3,1) in Table 7.7 is shown, and each of the cells involved in this closed loop is marked with a +1 or a −1.

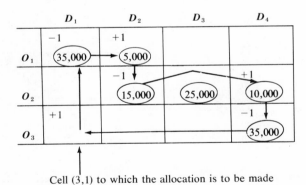

Cell (3,1) to which the allocation is to be made

The allocation to be made to cell (3,1) would be computed as

$$\text{Allocation to cell } (3,1) = \text{minimum}\left(\frac{\text{cell }(1,1)}{35,000}; \frac{\text{cell }(2,2)}{15,000}; \frac{\text{cell }(3,6)}{35,000}\right)$$

$$= 15,000 \qquad (7\text{-}15)$$

If this allocation were made the revised loop would appear as shown below.

Cell (2,2) from which allocation was made

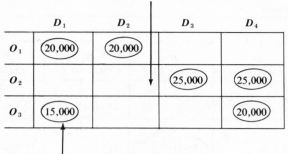

	D_1	D_2	D_3	D_4
O_1	(20,000)	(20,000)		
O_2			(25,000)	(25,000)
O_3	(15,000)			(20,000)

Cell (3,1) to which allocation was made

We must now evaluate the unoccupied cells in this second tableau (Table 7.8) to see if any further allocations that reduce the objective function can be made. The computations for these cells are as follow.

Cell (1,3)

Add one unit to cell (1,3):	+$8.50
Subtract one unit from cell (1,2):	− 7.50
Add one unit to cell (2,2);	+ 4.50
Subtract one unit from cell (2,4):	− 7.50
Add one unit to cell (3,4):	+ 6.00
Subtract one unit from cell (3,3):	− 1.00
Net change	+$3.00

Cell (1, 3)

Unoccupied cell

	D_1	D_2	D_3	D_4
	1.00	7.50	8.50	11.00
O_1		−1 (5,000)	+1	
	7.50	4.50	3.00	7.50
O_2		+1 (15,000)		−1 (35,000)
	10.00	6.50	1.00	6.00
O_3			−1 (25,000)	+1 (10,000)

Cell (1,4)

Add one unit to cell (1,4):	+$11.00
Subtract one unit from cell (2,4):	− 7.50
Add one unit to cell (2,2):	+ 4.50
Subtract one unit from cell (1,2):	− 7.50
Net change	+$ 0.50

Cell (1, 4)

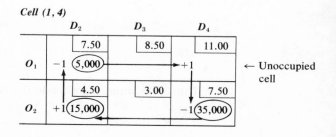

	D_2	D_3	D_4
	7.50	8.50	11.00
O_1	−1 (5,000)		+1
	4.50	3.00	7.50
O_2	+1 (15,000)		−1 (35,000)

← Unoccupied cell

Cell (2,1)

Add one unit to cell (2,1):	+$7.50
Subtract one unit from cell (2,2):	− 4.50
Add one unit to cell (1,2):	+ 7.50
Subtract one unit from cell (1,1):	− 1.00
Net change	+$9.50

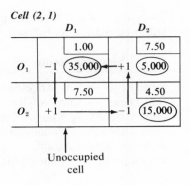

Cell (2, 1)

Unoccupied cell

Cell (2,3)

Add one unit to cell (2,3):	+$3.00
Subtract one unit from cell (2,4):	− 7.50
Add one unit to cell (3,4):	+ 6.00
Subtract one unit from cell (3,3):	− 1.00
Net change	+$0.50

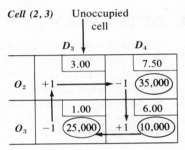

Cell (2, 3)   Unoccupied cell

Cell (3,1)

Add one unit to cell (3,1):	+$10.00
Subtract one unit from cell (3,4):	− 6.00
Add one unit to cell (2,4):	+ 7.50
Subtract one unit from cell (2,2):	− 4.50
Add one unit to cell (1,2):	+ 7.50
Subtract one unit from cell (1,1):	− 1.00
Net change	+$13.50

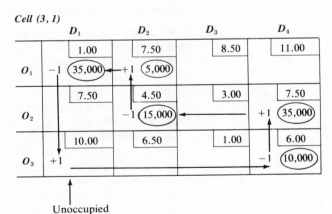

Cell (3, 1)

Unoccupied cell

Cell (3,2)

Add one unit to cell (3,2):	+$6.50
Subtract one unit from cell (3,4):	− 6.00
Add one unit to cell (2,4):	+ 7.50
Subtract one unit from cell (2,2):	− 4.50
Net change	+$3.50

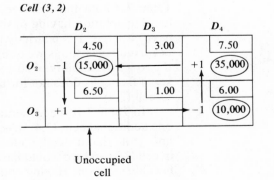

Cell (3, 2)

Unoccupied cell

Since $c_{ij} - Z_{ij} \geq 0$ for all unoccupied cells, we are optimal. The minimum-cost shipping plan is as follows.

Shipping Route	Shipping Cost
San Diego → Los Angeles	35,000 cases × \$1.00 per case = \$ 35,000
San Diego → Kansas City	5,000 cases × \$7.50 per case = \$ 37,500
New Orleans → Kansas City	15,000 cases × \$4.50 per case = \$ 67,500
New Orleans → Philadelphia	35,000 cases × \$7.50 per case = \$262,500
Jacksonville → Atlanta	25,000 cases × \$1.00 per case = \$ 25,000
Jacksonville → Philadelphia	10,000 cases × \$6.00 per case = \$ 60,000
	Total \$487,500

7.4 DEGENERACY

A feasible solution to a transportation problem is **degenerate** if less than $m + n - 1$ of the x_{ij} values are strictly positive. Degeneracy can occur as an initial basic feasible solution is determined, or it can occur as an iteration is made. In a practical sense, degeneracy in a transportation problem does not cause any great problem because no transportation problem has ever been known to cycle. However, for transportation problems we can employ a very simple technique to deal with degeneracy.

7.4.1 Degeneracy—Initial Basic Feasible Solution

First, let us consider the situation in which degeneracy occurs as an initial basic feasible solution is being determined. In this case degeneracy results because the method we are using to provide an initial solution yields a feasible solution with $k < m + n - 1$ of the $x_{ij} > 0$, and the cells associated with the positive x_{ij} do not form a basic tree. To construct an initial basic feasible solution, we simply add $m + n - 1 - k$ cells at a zero level in the tableau. These cells are added in a manner such that the resultant $m + n - 1$ cells form a basic tree. A zero is entered into the added cells, and these zero cells are circled to indicate that they are a part of the initial basic feasible solution. We then proceed to make iterations in the usual manner. However, in this case a variable can enter and leave the solution at a zero level, and we may ultimately arrive at a degenerate optimal feasible solution.

To illustrate a situation in which degeneracy occurs as an initial basic feasible solution is determined, consider the tableau shown in Table 7.9 in which the Northwest Corner Rule was used to select the initial basic feasible solution. In Table 7.9 note that the use of the Northwest Corner Rule results in an initial feasible solution having positive allocations to only five cells, whereas we must have $m + n - 1 = 6$ strictly positive x_{ij} for an initial basic feasible solution. This occurred because, as we assigned the value $x_{23} = 15$, we simultaneously satisfied the row 2 availability of 30 and the column 3 requirement of 15. Also note that this set of five cells does not form a connected tree, since we cannot connect cell (2,3) to cell (3,4).

In Table 7.10 a degenerate initial basic feasible solution is presented, in which one additional cell, (2,4), has been added at a zero level and circled with a dotted line. Note that instead of entering a zero in cell (2,4) we could have entered a zero in cell (3,3) and we would have alternatively constructed a degenerate initial basic feasible solution. Having obtained our initial (degenerate) basic feasible solution, we can now proceed to apply the stepping-stone algorithm. The second transportation tableau, which is the optimal solution to this problem, is presented below in Table 7.11. Observe that this optimal solution is no longer degenerate.

TABLE 7.9 Initial Feasible Solution Using Northwest Corner Rule

Origin	Destination				Origin Availability
	D_1	D_2	D_3	D_4	
O_1	2 ⑮	6	3	4	15
O_2	3 ⑤	1 ⑩	4 ⑮	2	30
O_3	3	6	3	2 ⑳	20
Destination Requirement	20	10	15	20	65

$Z = 115$

TABLE 7.10 Degenerate Initial Basic Feasible Solution

Origin	Destination				Origin Availability
	D_1	D_2	D_3	D_4	
O_1	2 ⑮	6 +6	3 0	4 +3	15
O_2	3 ⑤	1 ⑩	4 ⑮	2 ⓪	30
O_3	3 0	6 +5	3 −1	2 ⑳	20
Destination Requirement	20	10	15	20	65

$Z = 155$

TABLE 7.11 Optimal Solution (Nondegenerate)

Origin	Destination				Origin Availability
	D_1	D_2	D_3	D_4	
O_1	2 ⑮	6 +6	3 +1	4 +3	15
O_2	3 ⑤	1 ⑩	4 +1	2 ⑮	30
O_3	3 0	6 +5	3 ⑮	2 ⑤	20
Destination Requirement	20	10	15	20	65

Min $Z = 140$ (Optimal)

7.4.2   Degeneracy—Tie for Leaving Basic Variable

Degeneracy can also appear during any iteration of the solution process for the transportation problem in which there is a tie for the variable chosen to leave the basic solution. When such a tie occurs we can choose any one of the tied variables as the variable to leave the basis. However, at the next stage of the problem the variables that were tied with the variable chosen to be removed from the basis will also be driven to zero. Thus, we will have obtained a basic feasible solution with less than $m + n - 1$ of the cells having $x_{ij} > 0$ (i.e., a degenerate basic feasible solution will be generated). However, we can continue the iteration process by keeping these variables in solution, circled at a zero level.

To illustrate a situation in which degeneracy occurs as a result of a tie for the leaving basic variable, consider the transportation problem tableau shown in Table 7.12 in which the Northwest Corner Rule was used to generate an initial basic feasible solution.

TABLE 7.12   Initial Basic Feasible Solution (Tie for Leaving Basic Variable)

Origin	Destination				Origin Availability	
	D_1	D_2	D_3	D_4		
O_1	㉕ 5	⑮ 2	-4 1	-5 2	40	$Z = 340$
O_2	-3 4	⑳ 4	⑤ 7	-6 3	25	Tie for basic variable to leave solution
O_3	$+2$ 6	$+1$ 2	⑩ 4	⑤ 6	15	
Destination Requirement	25	35	15	5	80	

Each of the unoccupied cells has been evaluated and cell (2,4) would be chosen as the cell to which an allocation should be made. Now, however, there is a tie for the basic variable to be removed as either $x_{23} = 5$ or $x_{34} = 5$ can be replaced by x_{24}. Assume that we arbitrarily decide to replace x_{34}. The new feasible solution is shown in Table 7.13.

TABLE 7.13   New Feasible Solution, x_{34} and x_{23} Driven to Zero—Iteration 1

Origin	Destination				Origin Availability	
	D_1	D_2	D_3	D_4		
O_1	㉕ 5	⑮ 2	1	2	40	
O_2	4	⑳ 4	7	⑤ 3	25	$Z = 310$
O_3	6	2 ⑮	4	6	15	
Destination Requirement	25	35	15	5	80	

In Table 7.13, note that as we removed variable x_{34} from the basis, variable x_{23} was also driven to zero. We have $x_{ij} > 0$ for only five cells, and we require that $m + n - 1 = 3 + 4 - 1 = 6$ cells have positive allocations. We can proceed in the normal manner, however, by keeping variable x_{23} in the basis at a zero level (i.e., we can generate a degenerate basic feasible solution and proceed).

Many authors suggest the use of a cell marked with an "ϵ" (epsilon) instead of a cell containing a zero. This is perfectly acceptable as a means for treating degeneracy, and in this case the epsilon quantity can be thought of as being so small that it does not incur any cost but, at the same time, as being large enough to represent an allocation to a cell. If needed, the ϵ value is carried through subsequent manipulations as though it were a real value. Assuming this were done for the example given above, the series of tableaus shown below in Tables 7.14 to 7.18 would result.

TABLE 7.14   Degenerate Basic Feasible Solution ($x_{23} = \epsilon$)—Iteration 1

Origin	D_1		D_2		D_3		D_4		Origin Availability	
		5		2		1		2		
O_1	㉕		⑮		-4		$+1$		40	
		4		4		7		3		
O_2	-3		⑳		(ϵ)		⑤		25	$Z = 310$
		6		2		4		6		
O_3	$+2$		$+1$		⑮		$+6$		15	
Destination Requirement	25		35		15		5		80	

(Destination header spans D_1–D_4)

TABLE 7.15   Degenerate Basic Feasible Solution ($x_{13} = \epsilon$)—Iteration 2

Origin	D_1		D_2		D_3		D_4		Origin Availability	
		5		2		1		2		
O_1	㉕		⑮		(ϵ)		$+1$		40	
		4		4		7		3		
O_2	-3		⑳		$+4$		⑤		25	$Z = 310$
		6		2		4		6		
O_3	-2		-3		⑮		$+2$		15	
Destination Requirement	25		35		15		5		80	

(Destination header spans D_1–D_4)

Observe that the degeneracy that is introduced because of the tie between the leaving basic variables x_{23} and x_{24} (see Table 7.14) continues through the next two iterations (i.e., we carry the ϵ value along), but the degeneracy is removed as a result of the fourth iteration (see Table 7.17). However, in Table 7.17 there is again a tie for the basic variable to be removed as either $x_{11} = 5$ or $x_{24} = 5$ can be replaced by x_{14}. The final optimal (degenerate) solution is shown in Table 7.18, where x_{11} is driven to zero, and we let $x_{24} = \epsilon$.

TABLE 7.16 Degenerate Basic Feasible Solution ($x_{12} = \epsilon$) — Iteration 3

Origin	Destination D_1	D_2	D_3	D_4	Origin Availability	
O_1	㉕ 5	(ε) 2	⑮ 1	+1 2	40	
O_2	−3 4	⑳ 4	+4 7	⑤ 3	25	$Z = 265$
O_3	−1 6	⑮ 2	+3 4	+5 6	15	
Destination Requirement	25	35	15	5	80	

TABLE 7.17 Nondegenerate Basic Feasible Solution — Iteration 4

Origin	Destination D_1	D_2	D_3	D_4	Origin Availability	
O_1	⑤ 5	⑳ 2	⑮ 1	−2 2	40	
O_2	⑳ 4	+3 4	+7 7	⑤ 3	25	$Z = 205$
O_3	+1 6	⑮ 2	+3 4	+2 6	15	
Destination Requirement	25	35	15	5	80	

TABLE 7.18 Optimal (Degenerate) Solution — Iteration 5

Origin	Destination D_1	D_2	D_3	D_4	Origin Availability	
O_1	+2 5	⑳ 2	⑮ 1	⑤ 2	40	
O_2	㉕ 4	+1 4	+5 7	(ε) 3	25	*Min* $Z = 195$ (Optimal)
O_3	+3 6	⑮ 2	+3 4	+3 6	15	
Destination Requirement	25	35	15	5	80	

7.5 SOLVING TRANSPORTATION PROBLEMS USING THE MODIFIED DISTRIBUTION ALGORITHM (MODI METHOD)

Because of the special structure of the transportation problem another very powerful algorithm can be exploited for its solution. Known as the **modified distribution algorithm** or **MODI Method**, this algorithm offers an alternative approach to evaluating the unoccupied cells in a transportation tableau that is simpler than the stepping-stone algorithm.[3] The balanced transportation problem, written in the standard form for a linear programming problem, was given previously by Equations 7–5, 7–6, and 7–7. The tuna fish shipping problem was then expressed explicitly in this form by Equations 7–11, 7–12, and 7–13. Note that the tuna fish shipping problem has $m = 3$ origin (supply) constraints and $n = 4$ destination (demand) constraints. Let us now consider the tuna fish shipping problem as a primal linear programming problem. We can then construct the primal form transportation tableau as shown in Table 7.19.

TABLE 7.19   Primal Form Transportation Tableau—Tuna Fish Shipping Problem

	Origin 1 Variables				Origin 2 Variables				Origin 3 Variables				
	x_{11}	x_{12}	x_{13}	x_{14}	x_{21}	x_{22}	x_{23}	x_{24}	x_{31}	x_{32}	x_{33}	x_{34}	
Objective Function (Minimize)	c_{11}	c_{12}	c_{13}	c_{14}	c_{21}	c_{22}	c_{23}	c_{24}	c_{31}	c_{32}	c_{33}	c_{34}	
Origin (Supply) Constraints	1	1	1	1									$= a_1$
					1	1	1	1					$= a_2$
									1	1	1	1	$= a_3$
Destination (Demand) Constraints	1				1				1				$= b_1$
		1				1				1			$= b_2$
			1				1				1		$= b_3$
				1				1				1	$= b_4$

In this primal form transportation tableau, a c_{ij} value represents the unit cost associated with shipping one unit of product from origin i to destination j, an x_{ij} value represents the unknown quantity to be shipped from origin i to destination j, and we seek to minimize the total cost associated with shipping all products from origins to destinations.

Recall from Chapter 5 that every primal form linear programming problem has an associated dual. The transportation problem, being a specialized type of linear programming problem, thus can be written in either primal or dual form. Let us now dualize the primal linear programming problem given by Equations 7–11, 7–12, and 7–13. In our dual linear programming problem we will associate the three dual variables, u_1, u_2, and u_3 with the three origin (supply) constraints of the primal linear programming problem, and the four dual variables, v_1, v_2, v_3, and v_4 with the four destination (demand) constraints of the primal linear programming problem. We can then construct the dual form transportation tableau as shown in Table 7.20.

---

[3] Originally developed by George B. Dantzig, and first discussed in T. C. Koopmans, *Activity Analysis of Production and Allocation* (New York: John Wiley & Sons, Inc., 1951).

TABLE 7.20   Dual Form Transportation Tableau—Tuna Fish Shipping Problem

	Origin 1, 2, 3 Variables			*Destination 1, 2, 3, 4 Variables*				
	u_1	u_2	u_3	v_1	v_2	v_3	v_4	
Objective Function (Maximize)	a_1	a_2	a_3	b_1	b_2	b_3	b_4	
Origin 1— *Cost Constraints*	1			1				$\leq c_{11}$
	1				1			$\leq c_{12}$
	1					1		$\leq c_{13}$
	1						1	$\leq c_{14}$
Origin 2— *Cost Constraints*		1		1				$\leq c_{21}$
		1			1			$\leq c_{22}$
		1				1		$\leq c_{23}$
		1					1	$\leq c_{24}$
Origin 3— *Cost Constraints*			1	1				$\leq c_{31}$
			1		1			$\leq c_{32}$
			1			1		$\leq c_{33}$
			1				1	$\leq c_{34}$

From Table 7.20 it can be seen that the dual to the original transportation problem can be written as

$$\text{Maximize } Z = (a_1 u_1 + a_2 u_2 + a_3 u_3) + (v_1 b_1 + v_2 b_2 + v_3 b_3 + v_4 b_4) \quad (7\text{-}16)$$

subject to:

$$
\begin{aligned}
u_1 && + v_1 && && && &&\leq c_{11} \\
u_1 && && + v_2 && && &&\leq c_{12} \\
u_1 && && && + v_3 && &&\leq c_{13} \\
u_1 && && && && + v_4 &&\leq c_{14} \\
u_2 && + v_1 && && && &&\leq c_{21} \\
u_2 && && + v_2 && && &&\leq c_{22} \\
u_2 && && && + v_3 && &&\leq c_{23} \\
u_2 && && && && + v_4 &&\leq c_{24} \\
u_3 + v_1 && && && && &&\leq c_{31} \\
u_3 && + v_2 && && && &&\leq c_{32} \\
u_3 && && + v_3 && && &&\leq c_{33} \\
u_3 && && && + v_4 && &&\leq c_{34} \\
\end{aligned}
$$
$$(7\text{-}17)$$

with $u_1, u_2, u_3, v_1, v_2, v_3, v_4$ unrestricted in sign (since all the constraints in the primal problem were equalities). $\qquad (7\text{-}18)$

In this dual form transportation tableau the u_i and v_j dual variables are the implicit values (at a given solution stage of the problem) associated with the various origins and destinations. Thus, u_i is the value of one unit of the product at origin i, or the implicit worth of origin i (per unit). Similarly, v_j is the value of one unit of the product delivered at destination j, or the implicit worth of destination j (per unit). In the objective function of this dual problem, the a_i are the amounts available at the i origins, and the b_j are the amounts required at the j destinations. We thus seek to maximize the total value associated with the origins and destinations.

Observe the special structure of the constraints of the dual problem given by Equation 7-17. This special structure results from the unique arrangement of the "1" and "0" elements in the constraints of the primal problem. In the dual problem constraints, each constraint includes one u-variable and one v-variable only. Additionally, for each dual constraint, the subscript of u_i and v_j match the double subscript of c_{ij}, the right-hand side value. Thus, if u_i and v_j are the dual variables corresponding to the i origin constraints ($i = 1, 2, \ldots, m$) and the j destination constraints ($j = 1, 2, \ldots, n$), the corresponding dual to the transportation problem is given by

$$\text{Maximize } Z = \sum_{i=1}^{m} a_i u_i + \sum_{j=1}^{n} b_j v_j \qquad (7\text{-}19)$$

subject to: $\quad u_i + v_j \leq c_{ij} \qquad$ for all i, j $\hspace{2cm}$ (7-20)

with u_i, v_j unrestricted in sign $\hspace{5cm}$ (7-21)

As noted in our discussion of duality theory in Chapter 5, for each primal basic variable in any basic feasible solution, the corresponding dual constraint must be satisfied as an equality (i.e., according to the property of complementary slackness). This means that

$$u_i + v_j = c_{ij} \qquad \text{for all basic } x_{ij} (x_{ij} > 0)$$
$$\text{(i.e., for each occupied cell)}$$

and the remaining dual constraints will all be inequalities of the form: $\qquad$ (7-22)

$$u_i + v_j \leq c_{ij} \qquad \text{for all nonbasic } x_{ij} (x_{ij} = 0)$$
$$\text{(i.e., for each unoccupied cell)}$$

The value of $c_{ij} - u_i - v_j$ represents the amount by which each unit of x_{ij} would change the value of the objective function. The modified distribution algorithm, or MODI Method, is based on the dual formulation of the transportation problem. Specifically, it is based on the fact that there are $m + n - 1$ occupied cells in a basic feasible solution to a transportation problem, and that the dual constraints corresponding to the basic variables must be satisfied as strict equalities. Suppose that we designate $c_{ir}{}^B, c_{qr}{}^B, c_{qt}{}^B, \ldots, c_{ws}{}^B, c_{wj}{}^B$ as the $m + n - 1$ prices corresponding to the basic variables in the basic feasible solution to the transportation problem having m origins and n destinations. Suppose further that we express these values as $m + n - 1$ simultaneous linear equations, as follows.

$$\begin{aligned} u_i + v_r &= c_{ir}{}^B \\ u_q + v_r &= c_{qr}{}^B \\ u_q + v_t &= c_{qt}{}^B \\ &\vdots \qquad \vdots \\ u_w + v_s &= c_{ws}{}^B \\ u_w + v_j &= c_{wj}{}^B \end{aligned} \qquad (7\text{-}23)$$

We now have a set of $m + n - 1$ simultaneous linear equations in $m + n$ unknowns. Thus, we can assign an arbitrary value to any one of the u_i or v_j and solve for the remaining $m + n - 1$ variables. Furthermore, these linear equations are very easy to solve since they can be solved sequentially. For example, if we arbitrarily set $u_i = 0$, then $v_r = c_{ir}{}^B$ and $u_q = c_{qr}{}^B - v_r = c_{qr}{}^B - c_{ir}{}^B$. Once all the u_i and v_j have been determined, the entering basic variable (if there is one) can be determined by calculating $c_{ij} - u_i - v_j$ for each unoccupied cell. If $c_{ij} - u_i - v_j \geq 0$ for each unoccupied cell, then we are optimal. Otherwise, we make the maximum permissible allocation to the cell having the smallest (largest negative) value of $c_{ij} - u_i - v_j < 0$.

TABLE 7.21   Initial Tableau—MODI Method

Origin	Destination				Origin Availability	u_i
	D_1 Los Angeles	D_2 Kansas City	D_3 Atlanta	D_4 Philadelphia		
O_1 San Diego	1.00 (35,000)	7.50 (5,000)	8.50 +2.50	11.00 +0.50	40,000	0
O_2 New Orleans	7.50 +9.50	4.50 (15,000)	3.00 (25,000)	7.50 (10,000)	50,000	−3
O_3 Jacksonville	10.00 +13.50	6.50 +3.50	1.00 −0.50	6.00 (35,000)	35,000	−4.5
Destination Requirement	35,000	20,000	25,000	45,000	125,000	
v_j	1	7.5	6	10.5		

The savings in computational effort afforded by this method becomes apparent as we consider an actual problem situation. Thus, let us now apply the MODI Method to the initial basic feasible solution to our tuna fish shipping problem that we obtained by utilizing the Northwest Corner Rule. This initial tableau is shown in Table 7.21. Note that Table 7.21 has an additional column, which indicates the values of the u_i, and an additional row, which indicates the values of the v_j. The values of the u_i and v_j were computed in the following manner. The prices corresponding to the variables in the initial basic feasible solution are

$$
\begin{aligned}
c_{11} &= 1.00 \\
c_{12} &= 7.50 \\
c_{22} &= 4.50 \\
c_{23} &= 3.00 \\
c_{24} &= 7.50 \\
c_{34} &= 6.00
\end{aligned}
\tag{7-24}
$$

Thus, the set of simultaneous linear equations to be solved is

$$u_1 + v_1 = c_{11} = 1.00$$
$$u_1 + v_2 = c_{12} = 7.50$$
$$u_2 + v_2 = c_{22} = 4.50$$
$$u_2 + v_3 = c_{23} = 3.00 \qquad (7\text{-}25)$$
$$u_2 + v_4 = c_{24} = 7.50$$
$$u_3 + v_4 = c_{34} = 6.00$$

Arbitrarily setting $u_1 = 0$, we obtain

$$0 + v_1 = 1.00 \rightarrow v_1 = 1$$
$$0 + v_2 = 7.50 \rightarrow v_2 = 7.5$$
$$u_2 + 7.5 = 4.50 \rightarrow u_2 = -3$$
$$-3 + v_3 = 3.00 \rightarrow v_3 = 6 \qquad (7\text{-}26)$$
$$-3 + v_4 = 7.50 \rightarrow v_4 = 10.50$$
$$u_3 + 10.50 = 6.00 \rightarrow u_3 = -4.5$$

Now, for any cell $c_{ij} - Z_{ij} = c_{ij} - u_i - v_j$, and all the $c_{ij} - Z_{ij}$ for the unoccupied cells can be determined simply by subtracting the appropriate $u_i + v_j$ from the c_{ij} value. These computations are made as follows.

$$
\begin{aligned}
c_{13} - Z_{13} &= c_{13} - u_1 - v_3 = \ 8.50 - \quad 0 \ - \ 6 \ \ = +2.50 \\
c_{14} - Z_{14} &= c_{14} - u_1 - v_4 = 11.00 - \quad 0 \ - 10.5 = +0.50 \\
c_{21} - Z_{21} &= c_{21} - u_2 - v_1 = \ 7.50 - (-3) \ - \ 1 \ \ = +9.50 \\
c_{31} - Z_{31} &= c_{31} - u_3 - v_1 = 10.00 - (-4.5) - \ 1 \ \ = +13.50 \qquad (7\text{-}27) \\
c_{32} - Z_{32} &= c_{32} - u_3 - v_2 = \ 6.50 - (-4.5) - 7.5 = +3.50 \\
c_{33} - Z_{33} &= c_{33} - u_3 - v_3 = \ 1.00 - (-4.5) - \ 6 \ \ = -0.50
\end{aligned}
$$

These values are, of course, exactly the same as those obtained by use of the stepping-stone algorithm (refer to Table 7.7). However, our use of the MODI Method has required less work, and the chances for making numerical errors have been reduced.

As in the stepping-stone method, the value (-0.50) in cell $(3,3)$ indicates that the present solution is not optimal. The amount allocated to cell $(3,3)$ is determined in exactly the same manner as was done for the stepping-stone procedure. Accordingly, 25,000 units are allocated to cell $(3,3)$ resulting in the new tableau shown in Table 7.22.

At this stage, the u_i, v_j, and the values of the $c_{ij} - u_i - v_j$ for the unoccupied cells must be recomputed for this new tableau. This has been done for the tableau shown in Table 7.22. Since all of the unoccupied cells in this tableau are positive, we have obtained the optimal solution. This optimal solution is, of course, identical to the optimal solution to this same problem obtained earlier by application of the stepping-stone algorithm (refer to Table 7.8).

7.6   THE UNBALANCED TRANSPORTATION PROBLEM

Instead of the balanced transportation problem given by Equations 7–1, 7–2, 7–3, and 7–4, it is very common in practical applications to encounter an **unbalanced transportation problem** of the form

TABLE 7.22   Second Tableau—MODI Method (Optimal Solution)

Origin	D_1 Los Angeles	D_2 Kansas City	D_3 Atlanta	D_4 Philadelphia	Origin Availability	u_i
			Destination			
O_1 San Diego	1.00 (35,000)	7.50 (5,000)	8.50 +3.00	11.00 +0.50	40,000	0
O_2 New Orleans	7.50 +9.50	4.50 (15,000)	3.00 +0.50	7.50 (35,000)	50,000	−3.00
O_3 Jacksonville	10.00 +13.50	6.50 +3.50	1.00 (25,000)	6.00 (10,000)	35,000	−4.50
Destination Requirement	35,000	20,000	25,000	45,000	125,000	
v_j	1.00	7.50	5.50	10.50		

$$\text{Minimize } Z = \sum_{i=1}^{m}\sum_{j=1}^{n} c_{ij} x_{ij} \tag{7-28}$$

subject to:
$$\sum_{j=1}^{n-1} x_{ij} \le a_i \quad i = 1, \ldots, m \tag{7-29}$$

$$\sum_{i=1}^{m} x_{ij} = b_j \quad j = 1, \ldots, n-1$$

with
$$x_{ij} \ge 0 \quad \text{all } i, j \tag{7-30}$$

Note that in the first set of m constraints we sum from $j = 1$ to $n - 1$ rather than the usual $j = 1$ to n. The reasons for doing this will become apparent shortly. This first set of m constraints now contains a $\le$ sign rather than an equality sign. This means that we physically have more units available at the origins than are required at the destinations.

Now, the first m inequalities can be converted to m equalities by the addition of m slack variables. These slack variables are written as $x_{in}; i = 1, \ldots, m$. The constraint set becomes

$$\sum_{j=1}^{n-1} x_{ij} + x_{in} = a_i \quad i = 1, \ldots, m \tag{7-31}$$

$$\sum_{i=1}^{m} x_{ij} = b_j \quad j = 1, \ldots, n-1 \tag{7-32}$$

Furthermore, we can sum Equation 7-31 over i and subtract this result from the sum of Equation 7-32 over j, giving

$$\sum_{i=1}^{m} a_i - \sum_{j=1}^{n-1} b_j = \sum_{i=1}^{m} x_{in} \qquad (7\text{-}33)$$

Thus, the sum of the slack variables is a constant, and is equal to the difference between the origin availabilities and the destination requirements. To construct the transportation tableau we simply add one more column, that is, we add an additional destination having a requirement equal to the sum of the slack variables. This additional column is referred to as a **slack** or **dummy destination**. The costs associated with this dummy column, the c_{in} associated with the slack variables, the x_{in}, are all zero. Thus, we are considering the slack units as being shipped at no cost. Having made these modifications, this unbalanced transportation problem has been converted into a balanced transportation problem, and it can be solved in the usual manner.

To illustrate an unbalanced transportation problem in which supply exceeds demand, consider the following situation. The Missouri Farmers Association Co-op owns large wheat silos in six locations throughout Missouri. The storage capacities of these six silos (in millions of bushels of wheat) are as follows.

$$\left. \begin{array}{l} D_1 = 50 \\ D_2 = 20 \\ D_3 = 10 \\ D_4 = 35 \\ D_5 = 15 \\ D_6 = 50 \end{array} \right\} \quad \text{Storage capacity} = 180 \text{ (million bushels)} \quad \text{(Demands)} \qquad (7\text{-}34)$$

From the current wheat harvest the Co-op has obtained 245 million bushels of wheat, and currently has this amount of wheat temporarily stored at four locations, in the following manner.

$$\left. \begin{array}{l} A_1 = 45 \\ A_2 = 70 \\ A_3 = 30 \\ A_4 = 100 \end{array} \right\} \quad \text{Supply availability} = 245 \text{ (million bushels)} \quad \text{(Supplies)} \qquad (7\text{-}35)$$

The Co-op is faced with the problem of moving the wheat from the four temporary storage locations to the six large wheat silos. We will assume that the per unit (million bushels of wheat) costs of transporting the wheat from each of the temporary storage locations to each of the silos is known. Given this cost information the initial transportation tableau for this unbalanced problem can be constructed, and an initial basic feasible solution determined, as shown in Table 7.23. In Table 7.23 observe first that we have added one slack destination (column) with a requirement given by:

Slack destination requirement
$$\begin{aligned}
&= \sum_{i=1}^{m} a_i - \sum_{j=1}^{n-1} b_j \\
&= (45 + 70 + 30 + 100) - (50 + 20 + 10 + 35 + 15 + 50) \\
&= 245 - 180 \\
&= 65
\end{aligned} \qquad (7\text{-}36)$$

TABLE 7.23   Initial Basic Feasible Solution—Unbalanced Transportation Example

Origin	D_1	D_2	D_3	D_4	D_5	D_6	Slack Destination	Origin Availability	u_i
O_1	5 (45)	10 +2	15 +9	8 +4	9 +7	7 (10) −2	0 +4	45	0
O_2	14 +5	13 +1	10 (10)	9 +1	20 +14	21 +8	0 (60)	70	4
O_3	15 +7	11 (20)	13 +4	25 +18	8 +3	12 (10)	0 +1	30	3
O_4	9 (5)	19 +7	12 +2	8 (35)	6 (15)	13 (40)	0 (5)	100	4
Destination Requirement	50	20	10	35	15	50	65	245	
v_j	5	8	6	4	2	9	−4		

The costs associated with this slack destination column are all zero. Observe next that we have determined an initial basic feasible solution for this problem, with $m + n - 1 = 4 + 7 - 1 = 10$ cells occupied, using the matrix minima method. In determining this initial basic feasible solution two cells in the slack column are utilized. For this initial basic feasible solution, the cost of the shipping plan is $1600. Note finally that we have used the MODI Method to evaluate the costs associated with moving into the unoccupied cells for this initial basic feasible

TABLE 7.24   Second Basic Feasible Solution—Unbalanced Transportation Example

Origin	D_1	D_2	D_3	D_4	D_5	D_6	Slack Destination	Origin Availability	u_i
O_1	5 (5)	10 +4	15 +9	8 +4	9 +7	7 (40)	0 +4	45	0
O_2	14 +5	13 +3	10 (10)	9 +1	20 +14	21 +10	0 (60)	70	4
O_3	15 +5	11 (20)	13 +2	25 +16	8 +1	12 (10)	0 −1	30	5
O_4	9 (45)	19 +9	12 +2	8 (35)	6 (15)	13 +2	0 (5)	100	4
Destination Requirement	50	20	10	35	15	50	65	245	
v_j	5	6	6	4	2	7	−4		

solution. We see that per unit savings of $2 can be achieved by making an allocation to cell (1,6). Furthermore, we can determine that it is possible to move 40 units (millions of bushels of wheat) into cell (1,6). Making this reallocation, we obtain the second basic feasible solution shown in Table 7.24.

In this second basic feasible solution, the cost of the shipping plan is $1520. Again, employing the MODI Method to evaluate the costs associated with the unoccupied cells, we see that a per-unit savings of $1 can be achieved by making an allocation to cell (3,7) (i.e., row three, slack column). Furthermore, we can determine that it is possible to move 5 units (millions of bushels of wheat) into cell (3,7). Making this reallocation we obtain the third basic feasible solution shown in Table 7.25.

TABLE 7.25   Third Basic Feasible Solution (Optimal)—Unbalanced Transportation Example

	Destination								
Origin	D_1	D_2	D_3	D_4	D_5	D_6	Slack Destination	Origin Availability	u_i
O_1	5 ⓪	10 +4	15 +10	8 +4	9 +7	7 ㊻	0 +5	45	0
O_2	14 +4	13 +2	10 ⑩	9 0	20 +13	21 +9	0 ⑥⓪	70	5
O_3	15 +5	11 ⑳	13 +3	25 +16	8 +1	12 ⑤	0 ⑤	30	5
O_4	9 ㊿	19 +9	12 +3	8 ㉟	6 ⑮	13 +2	0 +1	100	4
Destination Requirement	50	20	10	35	15	50	65	245	
v_j	5	6	5	4	2	7	−5		

In this third basic feasible solution the $c_{ij} - Z_{ij} \geq 0$ for all the unoccupied cells. Thus, we have determined an optimal solution. The minimum cost shipping plan is as follows.

Shipping Route	Shipping Cost	
$O_1 \rightarrow D_1$	0 units × $5 per unit	= $ 0
$O_1 \rightarrow D_6$	45 units × $7 per unit	= 315
$O_2 \rightarrow D_3$	10 units × $10 per unit	= 100
$O_2 \rightarrow$ Slack destination	60 units × $0 per unit	= 0
$O_3 \rightarrow D_2$	20 units × $11 per unit	= 220
$O_3 \rightarrow D_6$	5 units × $12 per unit	= 60
$O_3 \rightarrow$ Slack destination	5 units × $0 per unit	= 0
$O_4 \rightarrow D_1$	50 units × $9 per unit	= 450
$O_4 \rightarrow D_4$	35 units × $8 per unit	= 280
$O_4 \rightarrow D_5$	15 units × $6 per unit	= 90
		$1515

Observe first that this optimal basic feasible solution is degenerate (i.e., less than $m + n - 1 = 10$ cells are occupied), since $x_{11} = 0$. Note that since supply exceeds demand by 65 units our optimal solution indicates that we must ship the excess 65 units to the slack destination. Given this problem situation, since no slack destination is in existence, this solution would simply indicate that we would have an excess of 60 units at origin O_2, and 5 units at origin O_3. These excess units should be sold at their respective origins since there is not enough storage capacity to accommodate this excess. It is important to recognize, however, that the optimal solution to this unbalanced transportation problem specifies the exact location and amounts of the excess availabilities.

A second type of unbalanced transportation problem has the form:

$$\text{Minimize } Z = \sum_{i=1}^{m} \sum_{j=1}^{n} c_{ij} x_{ij} \tag{7-37}$$

subject to:

$$\sum_{j=1}^{n} x_{ij} = a_i \qquad i = 1, \ldots, m - 1 \tag{7-38}$$

$$\sum_{j=1}^{m-1} x_{ij} \leq b_j \qquad j = 1, \ldots, n$$

$$x_{ij} \geq 0 \qquad \text{all } i, j \tag{7-39}$$

Now, we have a situation in which the resource requirements exceed the supply availabilities. Consequently, rather than introducing a slack or dummy destination to receive an unused supply, we must now introduce a **slack** or **dummy origin** from which we can obtain the unfilled demand capacity. We thus add one more row to the tableau, that is, we add an additional source having an availability equal to the difference between the destination requirements and the supply availability. In general, the costs associated with this dummy row, the c_{mj} associated with the slack variables, the x_{mj}, are set equal to zero. However, in this case we are really indicating that a certain amount of the requirement at the real destination will be satisfied from ficticious, or nonexistent, origins. Thus, it may be preferable to make the costs associated with this dummy origin equal to some reasonable set of "penalty" costs, which typically would be higher than the costs associated with the other (real) origins. Having made these modifications, we have converted this unbalanced transportation problem into a balanced transportation problem, and it can be solved in the usual manner.

7.7 OTHER COMMENTS ON THE TRANSPORTATION PROBLEM

Frequently, in practical transportation problems, it will be desirable to discourage or even prevent shipment of a product from a certain origin to a certain destination. This can be accomplished very simply by assigning an arbitrarily large cost, for example, $c_{ij} = +M$, as the cost coefficient associated with this allocation. The use of a $+M$ will effectively prevent the entry of the associated cell into the basis, and hence such an allocation will not be a part of the final solution.

Additionally, observe that once we have couched any transportation problem in the form given by Equations 7-1, 7-2, 7-3, and 7-4, we can replace each c_{ij} by

$c_{ij} + \delta$, for any constant δ, without changing the values of the x_{ij}, which yield an optimal solution. This can be done because the substitution of $c_{ij} + \delta$ for each c_{ij} will change only the value of the objective function by a constant amount, say K.

$$K = \delta \sum_{i=1}^{m} a_i \quad \text{or} \quad K = \delta \sum_{j=1}^{n} b_j \qquad (7\text{-}40)$$

For example, assume that we have solved a transportation problem involving truck shipments from 10 plants to 25 warehouses, and have determined that the minimum cost associated with shipping some 5,000 units of our product is $10,000. We then learn that a gasoline price increase will increase the unit cost associated with each origin → destination route by $0.05. We do not need to resolve the transportation problem to determine the values of the x_{ij}, which yield the optimal solution. They will remain as they are in the current solution, and the value of the objective function will simply increase by:

$$\begin{aligned} K &= \delta \sum_{j=1}^{n} b_i \\ &= (0.05)(5000) \\ &= \$250 \end{aligned} \qquad (7\text{-}41)$$

Also, note that the values of the x_{ij} for the optimal solution to a transportation problem do not change if a constant λ is added either to each cost in row i of the transportation tableau or to each cost in column j of the transportation tableau. The reason that this is true becomes apparent when we consider the nature of the stepping-stone algorithm used to solve the transportation problem. In making the evaluation of the effect of moving one unit into an unoccupied cell we move along a closed path from that unoccupied cell, to various occupied cells, back to the unoccupied cell, always using an even number of steps. This means that within any row or any column we will always be making exactly two steps, either from

1. The unoccupied cell to an occupied cell.
2. An occupied cell to another occupied cell.
3. Or an occupied cell back to the unoccupied cell.

Thus, in making this evaluation we will always be using exactly two c_{ij} values from any row or any column, and one c_{ij} value will be added in the computation and the other c_{ij} value will be subtracted in the computation. If we now add a constant λ to each of the c_{ij} values in row i or to each of the c_{ij} values in column j, the optimal solution will not change because, in evaluating each occupied cell involving row i or column j, the constant amount λ must be both added and subtracted one time. Once again, we do not need to resolve the transportation problem to determine the values of the x_{ij}, which yield the optimal solution. They will remain as they are in the current solution, and the value of the objective function will increase by:

$$K = \lambda \cdot a_i, \text{ if } \lambda \text{ is added to each } c_{ij} \text{ value in row } i \qquad (7\text{-}42)$$
$$K = \lambda \cdot b_j, \text{ if } \lambda \text{ is added to each } c_{ij} \text{ value in column } j \qquad (7\text{-}43)$$

As an example of this situation assume that we have a plant → warehouse transportation problem in which we want to include the variable production cost of \$0.25/unit for the 100 units produced at plant 2. We know that, when this variable production cost is added to row 2 of the tableau, the values of the x_{ij}, which yield the optimal solution, will not change. They will remain as they are in the current solution, and the value of the objective function will simply increase by:

$$K = \lambda \cdot a_i$$
$$= (\$0.25) \cdot (100) = \$25 \qquad (7\text{-}44)$$

In several practical transportation problems the structure of the problem may require the maximization of profits, rather than the minimization of costs. Such transportation problems can still be solved using either the stepping-stone algorithm or the MODI Method. However, one of the two following modifications must be made.

1. The profit maximization transportation problem is solved in exactly the same manner as the cost minimization transportation problem except that costs c_{ij} are replaced by profits p_{ij} and the test of optimality is reversed. Thus, if all $c_{ij} - Z_{ij} \le 0$, the basic feasible solution is optimal (i.e., all of the cell evaluations must be zero or negative).
2. The profit maximization problem is transformed by subtracting all of the p_{ij}'s from the largest p_{ij}. This transformation scales the original problem into a new problem involving *relative costs*. This new relative cost problem can be solved in the usual cost minimization manner. The total maximum profit is calculated by multiplying the optimal values of the basis variables, the x_{ij}, by the original profits, the p_{ij}.

Finally, it should be noted that a transportation problem can have more than one optimal solution (i.e., multiple alternative optimal solutions). This will be indicated by one, or more, of the unoccupied cells having $c_{ij} - Z_{ij} = 0$. Thus, a reallocation to the cell (route) having a net change equal to zero will have no effect on the total transportation cost. This reallocation will provide another solution with the same total transportation cost, but the routes employed will be different than those for the original optimal solution.

7.8 THE TRANSSHIPMENT PROBLEM

In certain situations it may not be economical to make all shipments directly from origins to destinations. Instead, it may be desirable to allow the product or commodity to pass through other sources or destinations (i.e., intermediate transfer points) before it eventually reaches its final destination. This situation is referred to as the **transshipment problem**.[4] It is basically a generalization, or extension, of the transportation problem in which there may be, not only pure origins and pure destinations, but also transshipment points that can be both origins and destinations. Thus, in the transshipment problem it is generally possible for any origin or any destination to ship to any other origin or any other

---

[4] The transshipment problem was first developed by A. Orden. For a discussion of its origination see: A. Orden, "The Transshipment Problem," *Management Science*, vol. 2 (1956), 276–285.

destination, and there may be many different ways of shipping a product or commodity from origin i to destination j in addition to the direct route used in the standard transportation problem. For example, rather than shipping a small quantity of product directly from city 1 to city 3, it may be more economical to include it with regular shipments made from city 1 to city 2, and then ship it on from city 2 to city 3.

We have previously studied two ways of solving transportation problems, the stepping-stone algorithm and the modified distribution algorithm. They cannot, however, be employed to solve the transshipment problem directly. Fortunately, there is a simple way of reformulating the transshipment problem to restructure it into the format of the standard transportation problem. Then, either the stepping-stone algorithm or the modified distribution algorithm can be used to solve the transshipment problem.

7.8.1 Transforming a Transshipment Problem into a Transportation Problem

A procedure for transforming a transshipment problem into a transportation problem can be illustrated by considering an actual problem situation. Consider the following transshipment problem. The Alton Fiber Company produces a specific type of polyester fiber at each of three plants, and ships the polyester fiber to four large distribution warehouses. The supply availabilities at the three plants are 40 tons per month, 50 tons per month, and 30 tons per month, respectively. The demand requirements at the four distribution warehouses are 20 tons per month, 40 tons per month, 30 tons per month, and 30 tons per month, respectively. In Table 7.26 the shipping costs per ton are given for the plant-to-warehouse shipments.

TABLE 7.26 Shipping Costs per Ton—Plant-to-Warehouse Shipments

From Plant	To Warehouse			
	A	*B*	*C*	*D*
1	70	110	40	80
2	60	100	30	90
3	50	90	20	100

For this problem situation we will assume that it is also possible to ship to plants *from* the warehouses at the same cost of shipping as from the plants *to* the warehouses. This might be desirable if excess storage space was available at the plants, or if the company's trucking fleet could be better utilized by allowing warehouse-to-plant shipments.

Now, let us further assume that shipping through intermediate locations (i.e., plant-to-plant or warehouse-to-warehouse) is also allowable in this problem situation. The shipping costs associated with such shipments are given below in Table 7.27 and 7.28.

With these transshipments being allowed, the transshipment problem is to find the shipping schedule that will minimize the total shipping cost.

With the cost data given in Tables 7.26, 7.27, and 7.28 we can easily construct

TABLE 7.27 Shipping Costs per Ton—Plant-to-Plant Shipments

	To Plant		
From Plant	1	2	3
1	0	20	30
2	20	0	25
3	30	25	0

TABLE 7.28 Shipping Costs per Ton—Warehouse-to-Warehouse Shipments

	To Warehouse			
From Warehouse	A	B	C	D
A	0	50	20	20
B	50	0	40	35
C	20	40	0	15
D	20	35	15	0

a combined cost matrix that will encompass all of the shipping routes allowable for the transshipment problem. This is the first step in transforming the transshipment problem into a transportation problem. The combined cost matrix for the transshipment problem is presented below in Table 7.29.

TABLE 7.29 Combined Cost Matrix—Transshipment Problem

	Plant			Warehouse				Supply
	1	2	3	A	B	C	D	
Plant								
1	0	20	30	70	110	40	80	40
2	20	0	25	60	100	30	90	50
3	30	25	0	50	90	20	100	30
Warehouse								
A	70	60	50	0	50	20	20	0
B	110	100	90	50	0	40	35	0
C	40	30	20	20	40	0	15	0
D	80	90	100	20	35	15	0	0
Demand	0	0	0	20	40	30	30	

The second step in the transformation process involves the determination of the appropriate modified supply amounts at the expanded set of origins and of the appropriate modified demand amounts at the expanded set of destinations. Now, in the transshipment problem each origin or destination represents a potential point of supply or demand. This means that any location (origin or destination) can serve as a supply or demand point for all other locations. Therefore, the key idea is that the total transshipment quantity allowed for a location should be included in *both* the supply for that location as an origin and in the demand for that location as a destination. This means that any location (origin or destination) can serve as a supply, or demand, point for all other locations. The quantity

$$S = \sum_{i=1}^{m} a_i = \sum_{j=1}^{n} b_j$$

serves[5] as an upper bound on the quantity to be transshipped, since it is the maximum supply (or demand) for the entire problem, and we would never transship through the same location more than once. For our problem $S = 40$ tons per month $+$ 50 tons per month $+$ 30 tons per month $=$ 120 tons per month. This upper bound amount is added to *both* the supply for the location as an origin and the demand for the location as a destination. Then the same slack variable is introduced into the location's supply and demand constraints, in order to allocate the excess. This single slack variable thus becomes both a dummy source and a dummy destination. For example, for location i, the slack variable would be x_{ii} and would represent the number of tons of polyester fiber (fictional) shipped from this location as a supply point to this location as a demand point (i.e., shipped from itself to itself). Thus, $(S - x_{ii}) = (120 - x_{ii})$ is the real number of tons of polyester fiber transshipped through location i. Since the quantity x_{ii} is a fictional shipment, its unit shipping cost $c_{ii} = 0$. We can now construct the transportation problem equivalent of the transshipment problem. The structure of the equivalent transportation problem is presented in Table 7.30.

TABLE 7.30 Transportation Problem Equivalent of the Transshipment Problem

From Origin	To Destination 1	2	3	A	B	C	D	Modified Supply
1	0	20	30	70	110	40	80	160
2	20	0	25	60	100	30	90	170
3	30	25	0	50	90	20	100	150
A	70	60	50	0	50	20	20	120
B	100	100	90	50	0	40	35	120
C	40	30	20	20	40	0	15	120
D	80	90	100	20	35	15	0	120
Modified Demand	120	120	120	140	160	150	150	

[5] If total supply does not equal total demand a dummy column (i.e., supply exceeds demand) or a dummy row (i.e., demand exceeds supply) must be added to balance supply and demand.

7.8.2 Solving the Transshipment Problem—Interpreting the Results

The transportation problem equivalent of the transshipment problem, as shown in Table 7.30, may now be solved using either the stepping-stone algorithm or the modified distribution algorithm. The optimal solution for this problem is presented below in Table 7.31.

TABLE 7.31 Optimal Solution—Transshipment Problem

From Origin	*To Destination* 1	2	3	A	B	C	D	*Modified Supply*
1	0 ⟨120⟩	20	30	70	110	40 ⟨40⟩	80	160
2	20	0 ⟨120⟩	25	60	100	30 ⟨50⟩	90	170
3	30	25	0 ⟨120⟩	50	90	20 ⟨30⟩	100	150
A	70	60	50	0 ⟨120⟩	50	20	20	120
B	110	100	90	50	0 ⟨120⟩	40	35	120
C	40	30	20	20 ⟨20⟩	40 ⟨40⟩	0 ⟨30⟩	15 ⟨30⟩	120
D	80	90	100	20	35	15	0 ⟨120⟩	120
Modified Demand	120	120	120	140	160	150	150	

The minimum-cost shipping plan is as follows:

Shipping Route	Shipping Cost
Plant 1 → Warehouse C	40 tons × $40 per ton = $1600
Plant 2 → Warehouse C	50 tons × $30 per ton = $1500
Plant 3 → Warehouse C	30 tons × $20 per ton = $ 600
Warehouse C → Warehouse A	20 tons × $20 per ton = $ 400
Warehouse C → Warehouse B	40 tons × $40 per ton = $1600
Warehouse C → Warehouse D	30 tons × $15 per ton = $ 450
Total	$6150

Note exactly what this solution indicates. First, a total of 120 tons of polyester fiber is shipped from the three plants to warehouse C. Then, 90 tons are transshipped from warehouse C to warehouses A, B, and D (i.e., 20 tons, 40 tons, and 30 tons, respectively). These transshipments exactly satisfy the demand requirements at warehouses A, B, and D. The remaining amount at warehouse C is 120 tons $-$ 90 tons $=$ 30 tons, which exactly satisfies the demand requirement at warehouse C. Thus, by using warehouse C as a transshipment point for 90 tons of the total 120 tons of demand, the lowest-cost shipping plan is obtained.

7.9 THE ASSIGNMENT PROBLEM

The assignment problem is a linear programming problem having a special structure in which each of n resources must be assigned to each of n activities, on a one-to-one basis. Thus, each resource must be assigned to one, and only one, activity. A cost c_{ij} is associated with using resource i for activity j, and the objective of the assignment problem is to minimize the total cost of assigning all resources to all activities.

The assignment problem occurs frequently in a variety of decision making situations. Typical assignment problems include the assigning of jobs to machines in a job shop, the assigning of the order of execution of programs on a computer, the assigning of salesmen to sales territories, and the assigning of workers to various projects.

The assignment problem can be stated mathematically, as follows.

$$\text{Minimize } Z = \sum_{i=1}^{n} \sum_{j=1}^{n} c_{ij} x_{ij} \quad \text{(Objective function)} \qquad (7\text{--}45)$$

$$\text{subject to:} \quad \left. \begin{aligned} \sum_{i=1}^{n} x_{ij} &= 1 \quad \text{for } j = 1, 2, \ldots, n \\[2mm] \sum_{j=1}^{n} x_{ij} &= 1 \quad \text{for } i = 1, 2, \ldots, n \end{aligned} \right\} \text{Constraint Set} \qquad (7\text{--}46)$$

with $\quad x_{ij} = 0 \text{ or } 1 \quad$ for all i and j $\qquad\qquad\qquad (7\text{--}47)$

where: $\quad x_{ij} =$ assignment of resource i to activity j

$\qquad\quad c_{ij} =$ cost associated with assignment of resource i to activity j

Observe that the assignment problem specified by Equations 7–45, 7–46, and 7–47 is a **balanced assignment problem** since the number of activities is exactly equal to the number of resources.

Note also that the assignment problem is a special case of the transportation problem in which $m = n$, supply availability $a_i = 1$ for $i = 1, 2, \ldots, n$, demand requirement $b_j = 1$ for $j = 1, 2, \ldots, m$, and

$$\sum_{i=1}^{n} a_i = \sum_{j=1}^{n} b_j = n.$$

The transportation tableau corresponding to the assignment problem is shown in Table 7.32 on the following page.

Several characteristics of the assignment problem should be noted. First, since $m = n$ in the assignment problem, it can always be structured in the form of a

TABLE 7.32   Transportation Tableau for the Assignment Problem

Resource	Activity A_1	A_2	$\ldots$	A_n	Availability
R_1	c_{11}	c_{12}	$\ldots$	c_{1n}	1
R_2	c_{21}	c_{22}	$\ldots$	c_{2n}	1
$\vdots$	$\vdots$	$\vdots$	$\ddots$	$\vdots$	$\vdots$
R_n	c_{n1}	c_{n2}	$\ldots$	c_{nn}	1
Requirement	1	1	$\ldots$	1	n

square matrix.[6] Second, the formulation of the assignment problem ensures that the decision variables, the x_{ij}, will always have values of either 0 or 1. This means that the optimal assignment will always involve a one-to-one matching of the n resources to the n activities. Thus, the number of solution variables $x_{ij} = 1$ in an $n \times n$ assignment problem is exactly n, and the assignment problem is inherently a degenerate form of a transportation problem. Third, the assignment problem containing n rows and n columns, with a one-to-one matching of resources and activities, has $n!$ possible assignments. This means that even for a small problem of, say, six resources and six activities, the number of alternative solutions is 6! = ~~240~~ 720. Thus, direct enumeration of all possible solutions is not an efficient way of solving the assignment problem.

7.9.1   Solving the Assignment Problem—The Hungarian Method

An efficient solution procedure has been developed for the assignment problem and is known as the **Hungarian method**.[7] The Hungarian method is based on two features of the structure of the assignment problem. First, each resource must be assigned to one and only one of the activities, and vice versa. Thus, in a solution we will have one $x_{ij} = 1$ in each row (and column). Second, as we noted earlier in Section 7.7, we can add or subtract any constant from all values in a row or column of the cost matrix without changing the values of the x_{ij} for the optimal solution of any transportation problem. The optimal solution values of the x_{ij} for the new cost matrix will also be the optimal solution values of the x_{ij} for the original cost matrix, and conversely. Thus, the relative cost of assigning resource i to activity j in the assignment problem will not be changed by the subtraction of a constant from either a row or column of the cost matrix.

The procedure for solving the assignment problem initially involves convert-

---

[6] If $m \neq n$ in the original assignment problem, we can make $m = n$ by adding either dummy resources (rows) or dummy activities (columns).

[7] Named after D. König, a Hungarian mathematician who first proved (1916) a theorem required for the development of the method. See: C. W. Churchman, R. L. Ackoff, and E. L. Arnoff, *Introduction to Operations Research* (New York: John Wiley & Sons, Inc., 1967), 347–368, for a discussion of the history and development of the Hungarian method.

ing the original cost matrix into an equivalent cost matrix having only positive or zero elements. This process is called **matrix reduction**, and results in changing the original cost matrix into a **total opportunity-cost matrix**. Matrix reduction is achieved by subtracting the smallest element in each row from every element in that row, and then, if necessary, subtracting the smallest element in each column from every element in that column. The zero entries in this total opportunity-cost matrix represent the minimum relative cost assignments of resources to activities, and vice versa. The assignments are then made to the zero element positions, and if it is possible to make one assignment in each row and each column we will have determined a set of assignments having zero total opportunity-cost that is optimal.

EXAMPLE 1   To illustrate the matrix reduction procedure, consider the following assignment problem. A certain small municipality owns four garbage trucks, which it must assign to each of four collection districts. However, these trucks have different physical characteristics, and the daily cost of assigning a truck to a collection district varies according to the following cost matrix. The problem is that of determining how to make the assignments in order to minimize the total daily garbage collection cost. The assignments must be made in a manner such that one, and only one, garbage truck is assigned to each collection district.

TABLE 7.33   Garbage Collection Cost Matrix

	Collection District			
Garbage Truck	*1*	*2*	*3*	*4*
1	10	7	8	12
2	9	13	12	10
3	8	11	6	13
4	11	12	14	9

Using the matrix reduction procedure we begin by row reducing the original cost matrix by subtracting the minimum cost element in each row from all other costs in that row. Table 7.34 presents the row-reduced cost matrix.

TABLE 7.34   Row-Reduced Cost Matrix

	Collection District				*Row*
Garbage Truck	*1*	*2*	*3*	*4*	*Reduction*
1	3	0	1	5	7
2	0	4	3	1	9
3	2	5	0	7	6
4	2	3	5	0	9

This row-reduced cost matrix has all of the zero elements necessary to obtain an optimal solution, and we do not need to make a column reduction. The optimal solution for this assignment problem is as follows. (*Note:* This optimal solution has one truck assigned to each district, and vice versa.)

Assignment	Cost
Truck 1 → District 2	$ 7
Truck 2 → District 1	9
Truck 3 → District 3	6
Truck 4 → District 4	9
Minimum total cost	$31

EXAMPLE 2   Unfortunately, the optimal assignment is not always obtained in as easy a manner. We will now consider a second assignment problem in which we must expand and modify our basic solution procedure. Consider the following cost matrix (Table 7–35) involving the assignment of five workers to five jobs.

TABLE 7.35   Worker Assignment to Job Cost Matrix

	Job				
Worker	1	2	3	4	5
A	7	5	9	8	11
B	9	12	7	11	10
C	8	5	4	6	9
D	7	3	6	9	5
E	4	6	7	5	11

Proceeding with our row reduction process, the minimum element in each row is subtracted from every entry in that row. The resultant row-reduced cost matrix is shown in Table 7.36.

TABLE 7.36   Row-Reduced Cost Matrix

	Job					Row
Worker	1	2	3	4	5	Reduction
A	2	0	4	3	6	5
B	2	5	0	4	3	7
C	4	1	0	2	5	4
D	4	0	3	6	2	3
E	0	2	3	1	7	4

In Table 7.36 it is not possible to make a complete set of assignments with zero elements. Thus, we column reduce Table 7.36, subtracting the minimum element in each column from every entry in that column. The resultant matrix, which has been both row- and column-reduced, is shown in Table 7.37.

Now, we attempt to make a complete set of assignments using only a single zero element in each row or column. We can make the assignments shown in Table 7.38.

1.   Assign $\boxed{A\text{-}2}$, which eliminates D-2.

TABLE 7.37 Row- and Column-Reduced Cost Matrix (Total Opportunity-Cost Matrix)

Worker	Job				
	1	*2*	*3*	*4*	*5*
A	2	0	4	2	4
B	2	5	0	3	1
C	4	1	0	1	3
D	4	0	3	5	0
E	0	2	3	0	5
Column Reduction	—	—	—	1	2

TABLE 7.38 Attempted Assignments

Worker	Job				
	1	*2*	*3*	*4*	*5*
A	2	[0]	4	2	4
B	2	5	[0]	3	1
C	4	1	⊠	1	3
D	4	⊠	3	5	[0]
E	[0]	2	3	⊠	5

2. Assign $\boxed{B\text{-}3}$, which eliminates C-3.

3. Assign $\boxed{D\text{-}5}$.

4. Assign $\boxed{E\text{-}1}$, which eliminates E-4.

Thus, it is possible to make only four of the five necessary assignments using the zero element positions. We therefore need to modify our procedure to create one more zero element.

The procedure for creating more zero elements first involves the determination of a *minimum* number of straight lines, drawn horizontally or vertically, which cover all of the zeros (including the zeros not used in the assignments) in the reduced-cost matrix. If we have used k zero cells in our assignments, then we can draw *exactly* k lines through the rows and/or columns of the reduced-cost matrix that cover all the zeros in the reduced cost matrix. Usually, the minimum number of covering lines can be obtained by inspection. However, if inspection cannot be used, the following steps can be employed.

1. Mark all rows that do not have any zero assignments.
2. Mark all columns that have zeros in the previously marked rows.
3. Mark all rows that have zero assignments in the previously marked columns.
4. Repeat steps 2 and 3 until no more rows or columns can be marked.
5. Draw a line through each unmarked row and each marked column.

Since we have made four zero assignments in our reduced cost matrix, four covering lines are required. The covering lines required for our reduced-cost matrix, obtained by inspection, are shown in Table 7.39. Since the minimum number of covering lines possible (four) is less than the number of required assignments (five), we do not have an optimal solution. Further reduction of our cost matrix is necessary to create additional zero elements to which an assignment could be made. The covering lines serve to "protect" the zero elements we have already obtained, while the uncovered elements become the candidates for further reduction. To make a further reduction we examine all of the elements that are not covered by a line. The minimum element not crossed out by a line is 1 in position B-5, C-2, and C-4. Therefore, subtracting 1 from every element in the entire table, from every row and column element, will create a zero in positions B-5, C-2, and C-4. Then, to restore the previous zero elements and to eliminate negative elements, we must add 1 to each row or column that is covered by a line, namely, rows A, D, and E and column 3. The results of this process are presented below in Table 7.40, shown in two steps, for simplicity. An alternative procedure for obtaining the matrix shown in Table 7.40 is to subtract 1 from the elements without a line through them and then add 1 to every element that lies at the intersection of two lines.

Using Table 7.40, we can now attempt to make another assignment having a complete set of zero element positions. Proceeding, we obtain Table 7.41.

TABLE 7.39   Covering Lines

Worker	Job 1	2	3	4	5
A	2	0	4	2	4
B	2	5	0	3	1
C	4	1	0	1	3
D	4	0	3	5	0
E	0	2	3	0	5

TABLE 7.40   Obtaining Another Zero Element

Worker	Job 1	2	3	4	5
A	1	−1	3	1	3
B	1	4	−1	2	0
C	3	0	−1	0	2
D	3	−1	2	4	−1
E	−1	1	2	−1	4

(Subtract 1 from every element— creates a zero in B-5, C-2, and C-4)

		Job			
Worker	1	2	3	4	5
A	2	0	5	2	4
B	1	4	0	2	0
C	3	0	0	0	2
D	4	0	4	5	0
E	0	2	4	0	5

(Add 1 to rows A, D, and E, and column 3)

TABLE 7.41   Optimal Solution

		Job			
Worker	1	2	3	4	5
A	2	☐0	5	2	4
B	1	4	☐0	2	✗
C	3	✗	✗	☐0	2
D	4	✗	4	5	☐0
E	☐0	2	4	✗	5

1.   Assign $\boxed{A\text{-}2}$, which eliminates C-2, and D-2.

2.   Assign $\boxed{B\text{-}3}$, which eliminates C-3, and B-5.

3.   Assign $\boxed{C\text{-}4}$, which eliminates E-4.

4.   Assign $\boxed{D\text{-}5}$.

5.   Assign $\boxed{E\text{-}1}$.

Since we have now obtained a complete set of assignments, we have determined an optimal solution. If we had not obtained a complete set of assignments, the above line-covering procedure would have to be repeated until such a complete set of assignments were possible. The minimum-cost assignment is as follows.

Assignment	Cost
A-2	$ 5
B-3	7
C-4	6
D-5	5
E-1	4
Minimum total cost	$27

The complete Hungarian method for solving the assignment problem can be summarized as follows.

1. Subtract the smallest element in each row from each element in that row of the original cost matrix and determine the row-reduced cost matrix.
2. Subtract the smallest element in each column of the row-reduced cost matrix from each element in that row-reduced cost matrix and determine the total opportunity-cost matrix.
3. Draw a minimum number of straight lines to cover all zero elements in the total opportunity-cost matrix. An optimal assignment is possible if the number of lines drawn equals the number of rows (columns).
4. If the number of lines drawn is less than the number of rows (columns), select the smallest uncovered element. Subtract this element from all uncovered elements and add this element to all covered elements where two lines intersect. All the other covered elements remain unchanged.
5. Repeat Steps 3 and 4 until an optimal assignment is possible.

7.9.2 The Unbalanced Assignment Problem

If the number of resources is not equal to the number of activities in an assignment problem, it is referred to as an **unbalanced assignment problem**. Since each of the resources must be assigned to each of the activities on a one-to-one basis, the unbalanced condition is removed by adding a row, or rows, of dummy resources or a column, or columns, of dummy activities, until the number of resources exactly equals the number of activities. The costs of all the elements of the dummy row(s) or column(s) are set equal to zero, since any assignment made to a dummy row or dummy column will not actually occur.

To illustrate this type of problem, consider the unbalanced assignment problem shown in Table 7.42. In this problem, there are four engineers to be assigned to three projects, with assignment costs as indicated.

TABLE 7.42 An Unbalanced Assignment Problem

Engineer	Project 1	Project 2	Project 3
Tom	8	14	15
Sue	9	16	19
Al	14	11	17
Jane	12	20	13

To apply the Hungarian method to this problem, a dummy column is added with zero costs, so that the original problem is expressed as a square matrix of size $n = 4$. This new cost matrix is shown in Table 7.43.

In the matrix shown in Table 7.43, the smallest element in each row is zero, and this matrix thus represents a row-reduced cost matrix. Performing a column reduction on Table 7.43 leads to the total opportunity cost matrix shown in Table 7.44.

TABLE 7.43   Balanced Assignment Problem
(Dummy Column Added)

Engineer	Project			
	1	*2*	*3*	*Dummy*
Tom	8	14	15	0
Sue	9	16	19	0
Al	14	11	17	0
Jane	12	20	13	0

TABLE 7.44   Total Opportunity Cost Matrix

Engineer	Project			
	1	*2*	*3*	*Dummy*
Tom	0	3	2	0
Sue	1	5	6	0
Al	6	0	4	0
Jane	4	9	0	0

This total opportunity cost matrix has all of the zero elements necessary to obtain an optimal solution. The optimal solution for this unbalanced assignment problem is

Assignment	Cost
Tom → Project 1	$ 8
Al → Project 2	11
Jane → Project 3	13
Sue → Dummy (Idle)	0
	$32

7.9.3   A Maximization Assignment Problem

Assignment problems that require the maximization of an objective function utilize the following solution procedure.

1. Select the largest cell value in the profit matrix.
2. Construct a new cost matrix by subtracting each of the cell values of the original profit matrix from the largest cell value in the profit matrix.
3. Proceed to find the assignment producing the optimum (minimum) cost for the converted problem, using the assignment algorithm discussed previously. This minimum-cost assignment for the converted problem will be the maximum-profit assignment for the original problem.

To illustrate this procedure, consider the maximization assignment problem shown below in Table 7.45.

TABLE 7.45 Maximization Assignment Problem

Salesperson	Territory		
	1	*2*	*3*
Sue	10	13	9
Jane	9	12	14
Alice	11	7	8

The largest cell value in this original profit matrix is 14, in cell (2,3). Subtracting all of the original cell values in the profit matrix from the value of 14, we obtain the converted cost matrix shown below in Table 7.46.

TABLE 7.46 Converted Cost Matrix

Salesperson	Territory		
	1	*2*	*3*
Sue	4	1	5
Jane	5	2	0
Alice	3	7	6

We now proceed to find the minimum-cost assignment for this converted cost matrix. Row reducing this cost matrix, we obtain

TABLE 7.47 Row-Reduced Cost Matrix

Salesperson	Territory		
	1	*2*	*3*
Sue	3	0	4
Jane	5	2	0
Alice	0	4	3

This row-reduced cost matrix has all of the zero elements necessary to obtain an optimal solution. The optimal solution for this maximization assignment problem is

Assignment	Minimum Cost (converted problem)	Maximum Profit (original problem)
Row 1—Column 2	$1	$13
Row 2—Column 3	0	14
Row 3—Column 1	3	11
	$4	$38

7.9.4 Other Comments on the Assignment Problem

In certain instances we may want to prohibit the assignment of a certain resource to a certain activity. This situation is handled in exactly the same manner as it was in the transportation problem. Thus, we would assign a very large positive cost (i.e., $+M$) to the unacceptable assignment in a cost minimization assignment problem, and a very large negative profit (i.e., $-M$) to the unacceptable assignment in a profit maximization assignment problem. Also, it is possible for the original cost matrix in a minimization assignment problem to have negative cell values. If this occurs, the original cost matrix must be converted to an equivalent cost matrix having all cells nonnegative, by adding the appropriate quantity to the appropriate row(s) and/or column(s).

Finally, it should be noted that an assignment problem can have more than one optimal solution (i.e., multiple optimal solutions). This will be indicated by there being more than the n required assignments possible in the reduced-cost matrix. For example, for a particular row of a matrix there will be two, or more, zero element positions that could be used in combination with other zero element positions in the matrix to make the required assignment. A simple example of a multiple optimal solution assignment problem is presented below in Table 7.48.

TABLE 7.48 Assignment Problem with Multiple Optimal Solutions

	1	2	3
A	0	2	0
B	1	0	4
C	0	5	0

($n = 3$ assignments required, $n + 2 = 5$ assignments possible)

First Optimal Solution: A-1, B-2, C-3
Alternative Optimal Solution: A-3, B-2, C-1

7.10 CASE STUDY—ANALYZING MULTICOMMODITY DISTRIBUTION NETWORKS HAVING MILLING-IN-TRANSIT FEATURES

This case study describes the development and implementation of a large-scale transportation model for the Ralston Purina Company, St. Louis, Missouri. The major use of this transportation model to date has been in situations in which the shipment of finished goods (animal food and human food) is functionally related to inbound raw materials by the privilege of "milling-in-transit" that is commonly granted to grain and ore processors by common carriers. Under milling-in-transit, the manufacturer is allowed to ship the raw material from its source to its plant, manufacture it into finished or intermediate goods, and then ship these products to a final destination, and it is charged freight for the entire movement as if it had shipped only raw material from the source to final destination without intermediate processing. The raw material purchases must ultimately be allocated to the end pro-

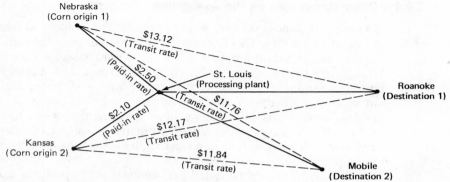

FIGURE 7.1 A Simple Milling-in-Transit Network

duction destinations, a process known as "transit billing."

In Figure 7.1, above, a simple milling-in-transit network is presented in which a single commodity (e.g., corn) can be purchased at either, or both, of two origins, and processed into finished goods that are in turn shipped to two destinations. Assume for the present that the purchase cost for the commodity is the same at either origin. Under milling-in-transit, the buyer and processor of the commodity would make the commodity-purchasing decision on the basis of minimizing the sum of the transit rate charges on the shipments from the two origins to the two destinations. This would be accomplished by purchasing "Nebraska transit corn" for the Mobile requirement, and "Kansas transit corn" for the Roanoke requirement.

The "transit billing" allocation is slightly more complicated, as the processor tends to reflect the difference between the transit freight rate

and the "paid-in" freight rate (origin to plant) in the price of the finished product as it is delivered to the end destination customer. This difference, known as the "transit balance rate," determines the allocation of the transit bills as the processor attempts to select the minimum transit balance rate associated with an origin-to-destination movement. Table 7.49, below, summarizes the transit-billing procedure that would result for the network shown in Figure 7.1.

As can be seen in Table 7.49, a "Nebraska corn" transit bill should be allocated to the Mobile customer, while a "Kansas corn" transit bill should be allocated to the Roanoke customer.

The complications to the pure milling-in-transit network, and the potential uses for the model, are several. First, the transit privilege extends only to certain end products. For example, consider the case in which 100 tons of raw material are processed into 75 tons of products having transit privileges

TABLE 7.49 Transit Billing Procedure

	Nebraska→ Mobile	Nebraska→ Roanoke	Kansas→ Mobile	Kansas→ Roanoke
Transit rate	$11.76	$13.12	$11.84	$12.17
Paid-in rate	2.50	2.50	2.10	2.10
Transit balance rate	9.26	10.62	9.74	10.07

and into 25 tons of products that do not have transit privileges. In this case, the processor is allowed the transit privilege on the 75-ton movement, but the 25-ton movement is said to be shipped along the "flat route," and its "flat rate" must be used in the allocation process.

Second, in many instances it may be advantageous to employ a commodity's flat route instead of its transit route. It is quite common for a transit route and a flat route to exist simultaneously, with the transit rate being applicable for a rail shipment and the flat rate being applicable for a truck shipment, and with either mode of transportation being possible. To illustrate, consider Fig. 7.2, below, which presents the Nebraska-to-Mobile transit situation of Fig. 7.1, with the addition of a corresponding flat route.

Note that the paid-in rate along the flat route in Fig. 7.2 is now $3.00. However, the sum ($11.50) of this paid-in rate ($3.00) and the flat rate ($8.50) to the destination along the flat route is still less than the transit rate ($11.76) from the origin to the destination. The processor would now purchase "Nebraska flat corn" for the Mobile requirement, since the cheapest delivered cost from origin to destination is along this flat route. The billing allocation would be made similarly, as the flat rate ($8.50) from plant to destination is less than the transit balance rate ($9.26) from plant to destination.

Third, the processor is allowed to substitute transit bills between com-

modities, and at the same time mix flat and transit bills within individual commodities in certain geographical areas (e.g., the eastern United States). As an example of transit bill substitution, a corn transit can be applied against the wheat transit portion of a shipment, and vice versa. However, when mixing of transit and flat shipments occurs in addition to substitution of transit bills, only transit shipments can be substituted between commodities. Thus, the processor can ship corn both transit and flat, and at the same time apply a wheat transit bill against a portion of the corn transit billing, but he cannot apply nontransit wheat against the corn portion of the shipment. In summary, mixing of flat and transit shipments is constrained within each individual commodity, but substitution of transit shipments can occur between any commodities.

An illustration of the mixed transit and flat situation in which transit billing substitution is allowed is presented in Table 7.50 below. In the simplified tableau shown in Table 7.50 there are $m = 12$ commodity origins, composed of multiple transit origins and one flat origin for each of three commodities, and $n = 9$ real destinations, composed of the requirements for each of the three commodities at three cities. Within each of the cells of the tableau, the appropriate per-ton cost of the associated movement is indicated (i.e., the transit rate for the transit shipments and the sum of the paid-in rate and the flat rate for the flat shipments). Ob-

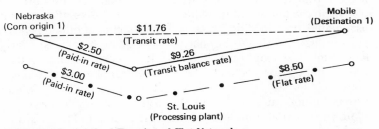

FIGURE 7.2 A Mixed Transit and Flat Network

TABLE 7.50   Tableau Structure—A Mixed Transit and Flat Network with Commodity Substitution Allowed

Origin \ Destination	Newark			Philadelphia			Baltimore			Origin Availability a_i
	Corn	Wheat	Soybean Meal	Corn	Wheat	Soybean Meal	Corn	Wheat	Soybean Meal	
Toledo										
Transit Corn	16.60	16.60	16.60	16.20	16.20	16.20	15.60	15.60	15.60	785
Battle Creek										
Transit Corn	18.40	18.40	18.40	18.00	18.00	18.00	17.60	17.60	17.60	710
Cincinnati										
Transit Corn	17.40	17.40	17.40	17.00	17.00	17.00	16.60	16.60	16.60	750
Toledo										
Flat Corn	17.10	M	M	15.50	M	M	15.10	M	M	750
New York										
Transit Wheat	11.20	11.20	11.20	11.00	11.00	11.00	12.20	12.20	12.20	200
Toledo										
Transit Wheat	16.60	16.60	16.60	16.20	16.20	16.20	15.60	15.60	15.60	170
Truck										
Flat Wheat	M	9.60	M	M	8.00	M	M	8.70	M	160
Decatur										
Transit Soybean Meal	23.50	23.50	23.50	23.10	23.10	23.50	22.70	22.70	22.70	200
Chicago										
Transit Soybean Meal	23.80	23.80	23.80	23.20	23.20	23.80	22.00	22.00	22.00	160
Lafayette										
Transit Soybean Meal	23.50	23.50	23.50	22.90	22.90	23.50	22.30	22.30	22.30	190
Louisville										
Transit Soybean Meal	23.40	23.40	23.40	22.90	22.90	22.90	21.80	21.80	21.80	200
Lafayette										
Flat Soybean Meal	M	M	24.00	M	M	20.80	M	M	18.20	210
Destination Requirement, b_j	295	79	73	246	66	60	197	52	49	$\Sigma a_i = 4485$ $\Sigma b_j = 1117$

Note: Slack column vectors are not shown, for simplicity.

serve first that the transit rate associated with the same origin-to-destination movement is identical for each of the possible transit bill substitutions allowed at a destination. Thus, "Toledo transit corn" can be used as transit billing for transit corn, transit wheat, or transit soybean meal at Newark, and its associated transit-billing rate is $16.60 per ton, irrespectively. Similarly, "Toledo transit wheat" can be used for transit billing for each of these three commodities at Newark, again at a transit-billing rate of $16.60 per ton. Note further that a number of the cells are blocked, by the use of a cost value

of M ($M >> 0$). This blocking of routes corresponds to the restrictions placed on the mixing of flat and transit shipments. For example, the "Truck flat wheat" routes and the "Lafayette flat soybean meal" routes are blocked for each of the corn destination columns, because the mixing of corn flat and transit billing is restricted solely to corn shipments. Similarly, the "Toledo flat corn" route is blocked against being applied to any commodity except corn (e.g., in the "Toledo flat corn" row, all columns except "corn" have an entry of M). The origin availabilities and the destination requirements shown in

Table 7.50 are simply the available and required commodity amounts in tons. As will be explained later, the dummy column requirements for each of the commodities (not shown in table) are defined in a manner that insures the satisfaction of the destination-commodity requirements.

From observation of Table 7.50, it is apparent that the addition of a restricted flat route for each commodity and the allowance of substitution of transit bills between commodities greatly increases the problem's size and complexity, in terms of the transportation tableau's density and the likely number of routes that must be evaluated in the determination of the optimum solution. The origins of the raw materials are the geographical areas from which the commodity requirements can be purchased. In general, a given plant will purchase C commodities, with each commodity c having I_c origins. Thus, the model must actually accommodate $C \cdot I_c$ origins. Each origin is capable of supplying the entire requirement of a particular commodity, but because of the difference between the raw material costs at the origins and the milling-in-transit privileges, certain origins are preferable. The destinations of the end products are the geographical areas served by the manufacturing facilities. Since the P end products are shipped to K destinations, the model must accommodate $P \times K$ destinations. The dummy destination requirement for each commodity is set equal to an amount equal to the sum of the availabilities of that commodity at all origins minus the sum of the requirements of that commodity at all destinations.

For the sake of brevity a detailed description of the mathematical formu-lation of the transportation model developed to solve the milling-in-transit situation will not be presented herein.[8] The crux of the model is a method of route labeling using set notation, which facilitates the structuring of the mixed flat and transit routes in which transit-billing occurs. Additionally, a route-blocking procedure is employed to restrict the mixing of flat and transit shipments to a single commodity at a time. In actually applying the model, it is divided into two sectors and a separate transportation problem is solved within each sector. The first sector of the model is used to make commodity-purchasing decisions, in terms of specifying the sources and associated quantities of commodities that must be purchased to satisfy the demands for the various end products at the various destinations. In this sector of the model, an objective function composed of the sum of the total purchase cost of the raw materials at the origins and the total transportation costs associated with origin-to-destination movements is minimized. The second sector of the model is used to make transit-billing allocation decisions in terms of specifying the sources and associated quantities of commodities that should be billed against the end product shipments made to various destinations. In this sector of the model, an objective function composed entirely of the transportation costs associated with plant-to-destination end product movements is minimized.

A typical milling-in-transit transportation problem in the Ralston Purina environment involved approximately 100 real origins and 200 real destinations. These problems were solved using a computerized transportation code, which employed the "out-of-

[8] Reprinted by permission of Robert E. Markland, "Analyzing Multi-Commodity Distribution Networks Having Milling-In-Transit Features," *Management Science,* vol. 21, no. 12, August 1975, copyright, 1975, The Institute of Management Sciences.

TABLE 7.51 Sample Output-Commodity Purchasing Model

(a) Commodity Purchasing Specification (Origin-Commodity Quantities)

| | | | Costs (per ton) | |
| | | Tons | Purchase | Freight |
Commodity	Origin	Purchased	Cost	Cost
Corn	Toledo-tr	770	$ 54.11	$15.10–$16.60
	Toledo-fl	55	$ 53.57	$14.20
Oats	Chicago-tr	94	$ 62.50	$15.60–$16.00
Wheat	New York-tr	195	$ 80.00	$10.70
Wheat midds	Buffalo-tr	19	$ 66.00	$11.40
Wheat germ	Buffalo-tr	20	$175.00	$11.40
Gluten meal	Chicago-tr	67	$268.00	$16.00
Gluten feed	Chicago-tr	66	$ 50.00	$16.00
Soybean meal	Danville-tr	252	$220.00	$23.10–$23.50
	Lafayette-fl	143	$222.00	$17.70–$20.40

(b) Commodity Purchasing Allocation (Destination-Commodity Quantities)

| | Shipment Requirement | | Purchasing Allocation | |
Destination	Commodity	Tons	Origin	Commodity
Boston	Corn	20	Danville-tr	Soybean meal
	Oats	2	Danville-tr	Soybean meal
	Wheat	5	Danville-tr	Soybean meal
	Gluten meal	2	Danville-tr	Soybean meal
	Gluten feed	2	Danville-tr	Soybean meal
	Soybean meal	10	Danville-tr	Soybean meal
Philadelphia	Corn	116	Toledo-tr	Corn
	Oats	13	Toledo-tr	Corn
	Wheat	27	Toledo-tr	Corn
	Wheat midds	3	Toledo-tr	Corn
	Wheat germ	3	Toledo-tr	Corn
	Gluten meal	3	Toledo-tr	Corn
	Gluten feed	3	Toledo-tr	Corn
	Soybean meal	56	Lafayette-fl	Soybean meal
Harrisburg	Corn	55	Toledo-fl	Corn
	Oats	6	Toledo-tr	Corn
	Wheat	13	Toledo-tr	Corn
	Wheat midds	1	Toledo-tr	Corn
	Wheat germ	1	Toledo-tr	Corn
	Gluten meal	4	Toledo-tr	Corn
	Gluten feed	4	Toledo-tr	Corn
	Soybean meal	26	Lafayette-fl	Soybean meal

kilter'' algorithm originally developed by Ford and Fulkerson.[9]

Typical output for the commodity purchasing sector of the model is presented in Table 7.51, above, in abbreviated form. Note that Table 7.51 is divided into two parts (*a* and *b*).

Table 7.51(*a*) shows the optimal pur-

---

[9] L. R. Ford, and D. R. Fulkerson, "Solving the Transportation Problem," *Management Science,* vol. 3, no. 1 (September 1956), 24–32.

chasing specifications, for eight commodities, at each of their respective commodity source origins. For example, the optimal solution indicates that 770 tons of "Toledo transit corn" and 55 tons of "Toldeo flat corn" should be purchased. Similarly, the optimal solution indicates that 252 tons of "Danville transit soybean meal" and 143 tons of "Lafayette flat soybean meal" should be purchased. All of the other commodities are purchased from their respective transit origins. Note further that only one or two origins were utilized for each commodity-purchasing specification. This will generally not be the case, and several origins will be utilized for each commodity. There were, for example, eight possible "oats" origins, but the "Chicago transit oats" origin was utilized for the entire 94-ton oat requirement on a minimum-cost basis.

The cost associated with the optimal-buying allocation are shown in the two right-hand columns of Table 7.51(*a*). The first of these two columns shows the purchase cost of the commodity at the respective origins. The second column shows the associated freight costs for the various origin-to-destination movements specified by the optimal-buying allocation. Observe that in several instances a range of freight costs is given. This simply indicates that a commodity being purchased at a particular origin is being allocated to a number of destinations, each of which have a different freight rate associated with the origin-to-destination movement.

Table 7.51(*b*) presents a portion of the optimal allocation of the commodity-purchasing specification presented earlier in Table 7.51(*a*). Observe that each of the commodity shipment requirements for Boston is optimally satisfied by the allocation of a portion of the "Danville transit soybean meal" purchasing specification. In Philadelphia, the shipment requirements for all

commodities except soybean meal are optimally satisfied by the allocation of a portion of the "Toledo transit corn" purchasing specification. The soybean meal shipment requirement at Philadelphia is optimally satisfied by the user of a portion of the "Lafayette flat soybean meal" purchasing specification. At Harrisburg, Pennsylvania, both the "Toledo flat corn" and "Toledo transit corn" purchasing specifications are utilized, with the "Toledo flat corn" specification being used to satisfy the corn shipment requirement, and the "Toledo transit corn" specification being used for all of the other commodity shipment requirements, except soybean meal. The soybean meal shipment requirement at Harrisburg is again satisfied by the allocation of a portion of the "Lafayette flat soybean meal" purchasing specification. In total, then, the commodity-purchasing allocation optimally satisfies the commodity shipment requirements at each destination by minimizing an objective function composed of the purchase costs of the various commodities at their respective origins plus the freight costs associated with the origin-to-destination movements.

Results obtained from the use of the transit-billing allocation sector of the model are quite similar, in both appearance and meaning, to those presented earlier for the purchasing allocation sector of the model. The transit-billing allocation sector of the model is run to minimize the freight costs (transit balance rates plus flat rates) for the outbound movement of finished products from the processing plants to the destinations. Output from the transit-billing allocation sector of the model specifies the optimum set of transit and nontransit bills (origin-commodity to destination) that should be utilized in meeting the end product demand at the various destinations. For the sake of brevity, output from the transit-billing allocation sector of the model will be omitted.

Both of the computational sectors of the model were embedded within a teleprocessing system that linked each of the company's 10 manufacturing facilities with the central computer facility in St. Louis, Missouri. Input and output for the model was accomplished using cathode ray tubes, with an interactive data base and the computational model being maintained at the central computer facility. Teleprocessing thus facilitated rapid communication between the widely scattered plants, at which the basic logistics decisions were made, and the central computer facility, which contained the data base and mathematical model.

The model described in this case study supplanted an existing manual system. The manual system was slow and cumbersome, was based almost exclusively on experience and judgment, and was not employed at all plants. Thus, the computerized model afforded a number of advantages.

1. It provided a standardized analytical tool that could be used at all manufacturing facilities.
2. It facilitated the consideration of a much larger number of purchasing-allocation alternatives within an objective framework.
3. It greatly reduced the computation time required for a typical analysis.
4. It improved overall computational accuracy.

Implementation of the model was achieved over approximately a 12-month period, in very close cooperation with the company's traffic and commodity-purchasing personnel. The general aspects of the model were first explained to the commodity buyers and traffic specialists. The model was then developed, using their expertise for data collection and editing, file structuring, and for the formatting of input forms and output reports. Actual model installation was done in a series of trips to each of the manufacturing facilities, by a team composed of management science analysts and traffic specialists. Throughout the model's development and implementation, strong support was afforded by the company's management. The cost of the model's development and implementation was recovered within the first year of its use, with some plants reporting savings of up to $1000 per week from its use.

7.11 CONCLUSION

In this chapter we have considered the transportation problem and the assignment problem. The transportation problem is one of the most frequently encountered applications in management science. The transportation or physical distribution of goods and services from several supply locations to several customer demand locations is an extremely common and important business problem. Solution of the transportation problem facilitates the specification of how many units should be shipped from each origin to each destination in order to satisfy all destination demands, while minimizing the total costs of transportation. The assignment problem is a special type of transportation problem in which allocations are made from source to destination on a one-to-one basis. The assignment problem is also frequently encountered in a wide variety of managerial decision-making situations. Assignments of jobs to machines, workers to various tasks or projects, salesmen to sales territories, and equipment to routes are examples of real-world situations having this particular problem structure. Solution of the assignment problem enables the determination of the one-to-one assignment of resources to tasks which optimizes the appropriate objective function. The special structures of both these problems allowed them to be solved by very efficient types of algorithms. We have presented, discussed, and shown applications of these algorithms in this chapter.

GLOSSARY OF TERMS

Assignment Problem   A linear programming problem having a special structure in which each of n resources must be assigned to each of n activities, on a one-to-one basis.

Balanced Assignment Problem   An assignment problem in which the number of activities is exactly equal to the number of resources.

Balanced Transportation Problem   A transportation problem in which the total amount available at the origins exactly satisfies the total amount required at the destinations.

Basic Tree   A tree that consists of $m + n - 1$ occupied cells that correspond to the current basic variables in a transportation tableau.

Column Minima Rule   A procedure used to determine an initial basic feasible solution to the transportation problem.

Connected Set of Cells   A set of cells in the transportation tableau is said to be connected if there exists a directed path, involving only cells in the set, that joins any cell in the set to any other cell in the set.

Degenerate Solution   A feasible solution to a transportation problem is degenerate if *less* than $m + n - 1$ of the x_{ij} values are strictly positive.

Demand Destination   A customer demand location characterized by a required quantity of goods or services.

Equivalent Cost Matrix   In the procedure of solving the assignment problem, the original cost matrix is converted into an equivalent cost matrix having only positive or zero cost elements.

Hungarian Method   An efficient solution procedure for the assignment problem that was developed by a Hungarian mathematician.

Matrix Minima Rule   A procedure used to determine an initial basic feasible solution to the transportation problem.

Matrix Reduction   Conversion of the original cost matrix of the assignment problem into an equivalent cost matrix having only positive or zero elements.

MODI Method or Modified Distribution Algorithm   An algorithm for the solution of the transportation problem.

Northwest Corner Rule   A procedure used to determine an initial basic feasible solution to the transportation problem.

Orthogonal Turns   Ninety-degree or right-angle turns made within a transportation tableau.

Simple Directed Path   A directed path such that in any row or column of the transportation tableau there are no more than two cells in the set of cells that defines the path.

Slack or Dummy Destination   The additional column added to a tableau in a transportation problem where supply exceeds demand, having a requirement equal to the excess supply.

Slack or Dummy Origin   An additional row added to a tableau in a transportation problem where demand exceeds supply, having a supply availability equal to the excess demand.

Stepping-Stone Algorithm   An algorithm for the solution of the transportation problem.

Supply Origin   A supply location having a fixed amount or limited quantity of goods or services.

Total Opportunity-Cost Matrix   The cost matrix that results from matrix reduction of the original cost matrix of the assignment problem.

Transportation Problem   A special type of linear programming problem that involves the transportation or physical distribution of goods and services from several supply origins to several demand destinations.

Transshipment Problem   A special type of transportation problem in which the product or commodity is allowed to pass through intermediate transfer points before it reaches its final destination.

Tree   A connected set of cells without loops in a transportation tableau.

Unbalanced Assignment Problem   An assignment problem where the number of resources is not equal to the number of activities.

Unbalanced Transportation Problem   A transportation problem in which we physically have more units available at the origins than are required at the destinations; or a transportation problem in which resource requirements exceed supply availabilities.

Vogel's Method   A procedure used to determine an initial basic feasible solution to the transportation problem.

SELECTED REFERENCES

TRANSPORTATION
AND
ASSIGNMENT
PROBLEM

Refer to those references provided at the end of Chapter 3.

DISCUSSION QUESTIONS

1. Why must a basic feasible solution to a balanced transportation problem with m origins and n destinations contain $m + n - 1$ basic variables, assuming the problem is not degenerate?

2. Judge this statement: "A degenerate basic feasible solution is produced by selecting the basic variables one at a time and assigning a value to the variable that will satisfy both a row and a column constraint."

3. Why will the "Column Minima Rule" usually produce a better basic feasible solution than the "Northwest Corner Rule"?

4. Will using a "Row Minima Rule" instead of a "Column Minima Rule" yield *exactly* the same basic feasible solution? Why or why not?

5. How can degeneracy occur in Vogel's Method?

6. In what sense are the computed "net changes" with the stepping-stone algorithm equivalent to the $c_j - Z_j$ values in a linear programming minimization problem?

7. Why does degeneracy cause problems in the stepping-stone algorithm? Does a degenerate optimal solution cause any problems?

8. Describe briefly how you balance a transportation problem in which you require more units at the destinations than are supplied at the origins?

9. Why will adding constant d either to each cost in row i or to each cost in column j of the transportation tableau *not* cause the value of the optimal x_{ij} to change? Will the value of the objective function change?

10. In general, why won't the optimal solution to an assignment problem be obtained by row reducing the original cost matrix and then making assignments to the zero element positions?

11. When the minimum number of lines necessary to cover all the zeros equal the required number of assignments, why is it that an optimal solution to the assignment problem has been obtained?

12. What type(s) of unbalanced assignment problem(s) can you have and how do you solve it (them)?

13. Discuss the theoretical basis of the modified distribution algorithm (MODI Method).

14. What are the two basic steps of the stepping-stone algorithm?

15. What are the basic differences between the transportation model and the assignment model?

PROBLEM SET

1. A potato chip manufacturer has three plants and four distribution warehouses. The shipping costs from each plant to the four distribution warehouses and the plant availabilities and destination requirements are shown below. The manufacturer seeks to develop a shipping schedule that minimizes her total shipping cost.

| Plant | Warehouse | | | | Plant Availability |
	1	2	3	4	
1	6.50	4.00	3.00	5.00	235
2	6.00	8.50	7.00	4.00	280
3	5.00	6.00	9.00	10.00	110
Warehouse Requirement	125	160	110	230	625

(a) Determine an initial basic feasible solution using the Northwest Corner Rule.
(b) Determine the optimal solution using the stepping-stone algorithm.

2. The Slippery Oil Company has three refineries that produce gasoline, which is then shipped to four large storage facilities. The total quantities (1000 barrels) produced by each refinery and the total requirements (1000 barrels) for each storage facility, as well as the associated shipping costs, are shown below. The Slippery Oil Company needs to determine a shipping schedule that minimizes its total shipping costs.
(a) Determine an initial basic feasible solution using the Northwest Corner Rule.
(b) Determine the optimal solution using the stepping-stone algorithm.

	Storage Facility				Refinery
Refinery	S_1	S_2	S_3	S_4	Availability
R_1	80	70	50	60	16
R_2	60	90	40	80	20
R_3	50	50	95	90	14
Storage Requirement	10	10	12	18	50

3. Solve the transportation problem having the following costs, origin availabilities, and destination requirements. Use the Northwest Corner Rule to obtain an initial basic feasible solution, and use the stepping-stone algorithm to obtain the optimal solution.

	Destination						Origin
Origin	D_1	D_2	D_3	D_4	D_5	D_6	Availability
O_1	2	3	2	5	6	4	40
O_2	4	4	3	2	5	2	60
O_3	4	3	5	9	6	2	85
O_4	4	2	8	4	5	7	30
Destination Requirement	25	50	35	15	60	30	215

4. Solve Problem 3 using the Row Minima Method to obtain an initial basic feasible solution. Use the stepping-stone algorithm to obtain the optimal solution.

5. Solve Problem 3 using the Column Minima Method to obtain an initial basic feasible solution. Use the stepping-stone algorithm to determine the optimal solution.

6. Solve Problem 3 using the Matrix Minima Method to obtain an initial basic feasible solution. Use the stepping-stone algorithm to determine the optimal solution.

7. Solve Problem 3 using Vogel's Method to obtain an initial basic feasible solution. Use the stepping-stone algorithm to determine the optimal solution.

8. Solve Problem 3 using the Northwest Corner Rule to obtain an initial basic

feasible solution. Use the modified distribution algorithm to determine the optimal solution.

9. Solve Problem 3 using a method of your choice to obtain an initial basic feasible solution. Use the modified distribution algorithm to determine the optimal solution.

10. Solve the transportation problem having the following costs, origin availabilities, and destination requirements. Use the Northwest Corner Rule to obtain an initial basic feasible solution, and use the stepping-stone algorithm to obtain the optimal solution.

Origin	Destination					Origin Availability
	D_1	D_2	D_3	D_4	D_5	
O_1	2	1	3	3	2	40
O_2	2	3	4	3	1	50
O_3	2	3	5	4	3	60
O_4	4	2	2	4	6	30
Destination Requirement	30	50	40	25	35	180

11. Solve Problem 10 using the Row Minima Method to obtain an initial basic feasible solution. Use the stepping-stone algorithm to determine the optimal solution.

12. Solve Problem 10 using the Column Minima Method to obtain an initial basic feasible solution. Use the stepping-stone algorithm to determine the optimal solution.

13. Solve Problem 10 using the Matrix Minima Method to obtain an initial basic feasible solution. Use the stepping-stone algorithm to determine the optimal solution.

14. Solve Problem 10 using Vogel's Method to obtain an initial basic feasible solution. Use the stepping-stone algorithm to determine the optimal solution.

15. Solve Problem 10 using the Northwest Corner Rule to obtain an initial basic feasible solution. Use the modified distribution algorithm to determine the optimal solution.

16. Solve Problem 10 using a method of your choice to obtain an initial basic feasible solution. Use the modified distribution algorithm to determine the optimal solution.

17. A state wildlife association wishes to stock its four major lakes with a fresh supply of largemouth bass. It has three fisheries which it can use to supply the four lakes. The transportation costs from each fishery to each lake and the fishery availabilities and lake requirements are shown below.

	Lake				Fishery Availability
Fishery	1	2	3	4	
1	6.50	4.00	3.00	5.00	300
2	6.00	8.50	7.00	4.00	350
3	5.00	6.00	9.00	10.00	150
Lake Requirement	150	250	125	275	800

(a) Determine an initial basic feasible solution using the Northwest Corner Rule.
(b) Determine a minimum transportation cost solution for this problem, using the MODI method.

18. Vermont Maple Sugar, Inc., has three refineries at which it produces maple syrup. The maple syrup is then shipped to four large bottling facilities, where it is bottled for shipment to wholesalers. The total quantities (1000 barrels) produced by each refinery and the total requirements (1000 barrels) for each bottling facility, as well as the associated shipping costs, are shown below.

	Bottling Facility				Refinery Availability
Refinery	S_1	S_2	S_3	S_4	
R_1	80	70	50	60	24
R_2	60	90	40	80	30
R_3	50	50	95	90	16
Bottling Facility Requirement	20	20	13	17	70

(a) Determine an initial basic feasible solution using the Northwest Corner Rule.
(b) Determine a minimum cost shipping schedule using the MODI Method.

19. Solve the transportation problem having the following costs, origin availabilities, and destination requirements. Use the Northwest Corner Rule to obtain an initial basic feasible solution, and use the MODI method to obtain the optimal solution.

Origin	Destination						Origin Availabilty
	D_1	D_2	D_3	D_4	D_5	D_6	
O_1	2	3	2	5	6	4	50
O_2	4	4	3	2	5	2	75
O_3	4	3	5	9	6	2	95
O_4	4	2	8	4	5	7	40
Destination Requirement	30	60	40	20	70	40	260

20. Solve the transportation problem given below, which involves a pinball machine manufacturer who has three distribution centers that supply four amusement park arcades. Determine the minimum-cost shipping schedule.

Distribution Center	Amusement Park Arcade				Availability
	APA_1	APA_2	APA_3	APA_4	
DC_1	11.0	8.0	11.5	10.0	20
DC_2	12.5	11.0	13.5	12.0	45
DC_3	11.0	9.5	11.5	11.0	10
Requirement	30	15	5	25	

21. Jim Pit, Manager of Ripe and Juicy Peach Enterprises, has three farm operations located in Elgin, McBee, and Bethune, South Carolina. These three peach farms supply peaches to three farmers' markets located in Columbia, Charleston, and Spartanburg, South Carolina. The transportation cost per truckload of peaches for every farm to market combination are given in the following cost matrix.

Farm	Market		
	Columbia	Charleston	Spartanburg
Elgin	40	70	50
McBee	20	30	20
Bethune	30	60	60

The supply availabilities of peaches (in truckloads) for the farm operations are as follows.

Elgin	30
McBee	50
Bethune	30

The demand requirements of each of the farmers' markets are given below.

Columbia	50
Charleston	20
Spartanburg	40

Develop a shipping schedule that minimizes total transportation cost.

22. Solve the following transportation problem using the modified distribution algorithm, using the Northwest Corner Rule to obtain an initial basic feasible solution. *Hint:* Use cells marked with a 0 or an ϵ to resolve degeneracy.

Origin	Destination						Origin Availability
	D_1	D_2	D_3	D_4	D_5	D_6	
O_1	11	9	7	5	3	5	30
O_2	8	13	11	9	6	8	40
O_3	7	9	12	14	9	7	10
O_4	5	4	9	11	15	14	80
Destination Requirement	50	20	10	30	20	30	160

23. Solve the plant-to-warehouse transportation problem whose initial basic feasible solution is shown in the following tableau. *Hint:* Use cells marked with a 0 or ϵ to resolve degeneracy.

Plant	Warehouse				Plant Availability
	W_1	W_2	W_3	W_4	
P_1	5 ㉕	2 ⑮	1	2	40
P_2	4	4 ⑳	7 ⑤	3	25
P_3	6	2	4 ⑩	6 ⑤	15
Warehouse Requirement	25	35	15	5	80

24. Solve the transportation problem that involves shipments of iron ore from a series of ports to a series of steel mills, and that has the following initial basic feasible solution. *Hint:* Use cells with a 0 or ϵ to resolve degeneracy.

Port	SM$_1$	SM$_2$	SM$_3$	SM$_4$	SM$_5$	SM$_6$	Port Availability
			Steel Mill				
P$_1$	3 (30)	1 (20)	2	5	2	6	50
P$_2$	4	2 (20)	1 (25)	6	3	4	45
P$_3$	4	5	3 (10)	4 (50)	7 (20)	1	80
P$_4$	5	2	1	3	2 (40)	1 (20)	60
Steel Mill Requirement	30	40	35	50	60	20	235

25. Solve the following transportation problem that involves a shoe manufacturer who has three distribution centers that must supply four shoe wholesalers. The initial feasible solution for this problem is as follows.

Distribution Center	W$_1$	W$_2$	W$_3$	W$_4$	Distribution Center Availability
		Warehouse			
DC$_1$	2 (15)	6	3	4	15
DC$_2$	3 (5)	1 (10)	4 (15)	2 (0)	30
DC$_3$	3	6	5	2 (20)	20
Warehouse Requirement	20	10	15	20	65

26. Solve the following transportation problem, using the MODI Method. Obtain an initial basic feasible solution using the Northwest Corner Rule and use cells marked with a 0 or ϵ to resolve degeneracy.

Origin	D$_1$	D$_2$	D$_3$	D$_4$	D$_5$	D$_6$	Origin Availability
			Destination				
O$_1$	11	9	7	5	3	5	50
O$_2$	8	13	11	9	6	8	60
O$_3$	7	9	12	14	9	7	20
O$_4$	5	4	9	11	15	14	90
Destination Requirement	70	40	20	30	20	40	220

27. The shipping manager of Yummy Catfood Ltd. has three plants and four distribution warehouses composing his operations network. The transportation costs from each plant to the four warehouses and the plant availabilities and destination requirements are shown below.

Plant	Warehouse 1	Warehouse 2	Warehouse 3	Warehouse 4	Availability
1	35	60	68	60	35
2	45	55	80	75	190
3	50	30	50	48	100
Requirements	50	175	65	35	325

Determine an optimal shipping schedule for Yummy Catfood Ltd.

28. Solve the transportation problem having the following costs, origin availabilities, and destination requirements. Use the Northwest Corner Rule to obtain an initial basic feasible solution.

Sources	Destination D_1	D_2	D_3	D_4	D_5	Availability
S_1	10	15	20	5	10	80
S_2	15	25	25	15	30	80
S_3	20	20	30	15	25	225
S_4	5	15	20	10	15	70
Requirement	80	200	70	55	50	455

29. For the tableau of Problem 1, assume that the plant availabilities are 250, 300, and 125, respectively, instead of the values shown. Add the necessary slack column and solve the problem using the MODI Method.

30. For the tableau of Problem 2, assume that the refinery availabilities are 20, 22, and 15 respectively, instead of the values shown. Add the necessary slack column and solve the problem using the stepping-stone algorithm.

31. For the tableau of Problem 3, assume that the origin availabilities are 50, 70, 90, and 35, respectively, instead of the values shown. Add the necessary slack column and solve the problem using the MODI Method.

32. A company has three warehouses containing 10,000, 7,500, and 12,000 units of its product. In the next month it must ship 3,500, 2,500, 7,000, 5,000, 500, and 3,500

units to six retail outlets. The unit cost of shipment from any warehouse to any retail outlet is contained in the following matrix. Determine the minimum-cost shipping plan.

	Destination					
Origin	D_1	D_2	D_3	D_4	D_5	D_6
O_1	10	9	16	3	10	26
O_2	17	23	18	9	11	19
O_3	20	15	20	6	13	15

33. The Runaway Railroad Company has a problem in connection with the distribution of its empty railroad cars. It has a shortage of railroad cars in certain cities and an oversupply of railroad cars in other cities. The imbalances are as follows.

City	Shortage	Overage
New York	—	50
Boston	—	75
Philadelphia	—	30
Atlanta	20	—
Miami	—	40
Washington, D.C.	30	—
Pittsburgh	40	—
Cleveland	25	—
Detroit	35	—

The costs associated with distributing the railroad cars are presented in the following table. Determine the minimum-cost shipping plan.

	To				
From	*Atlanta*	*Washington*	*Pittsburgh*	*Cleveland*	*Detroit*
New York	40	30	50	60	90
Boston	M	50	70	90	100
Philadelphia	30	10	20	40	60
Miami	30	50	60	70	M

34. A producer of microcomputers manufactures its product in Los Angeles, Dallas, San Francisco, and Denver, and maintains regional distribution centers in New York, Cleveland, Reno, and Tampa. The shipping cost per microcomputer for every manufacturer to distribution center combination is provided by the following cost matrix. Origin availabilities and destination requirements are also indicated. Determine a minimum-cost shipping plan for this firm.

Manufacturing Location	Regional Distribution Center				Availability
	New York	Cleveland	Reno	Tampa	
Los Angeles	45	20	20	30	200
Dallas	40	25	30	35	75
San Francisco	50	25	35	40	105
Denver	50	30	35	35	150
Requirement	90	75	100	195	

35. The Damascus Sword Razor Corporation has three warehouses containing 13,000, 15,000, and 8,000 units of its product, respectively. In the next week it must ship 20,000, 8,000, and 6,000 units to three retail outlets. The unit cost of shipment from any warehouse to any retail outlet is provided by the following matrix. Use this information to determine an optimal shipping schedule.

Warehouse	Retail Outlet			Availability
	R_1	R_2	R_3	
W_1	1	3	7	13,000
W_2	7	7	2	15,000
W_3	5	6	7	8,000
Requirement	20,000	8,000	6,000	

36. The farm districts surrounding Moscow, Minsk, Kiev, and Volgograd produce all the corn, barley, rye, and wheat for the USSR. The Soviet demand requirements for corn, barley, rye, and wheat (in hundred-thousand bushels) are as follows: 40, 115, 5, and 120. The total amounts of land allocated to these crops in the four farming districts (in hundred-thousand bushels) are: 25, 75, 100, and 40. The cost (per hundred-thousand bushels of crop) for each farm district in hundreds of rubles is given below.

	Corn	Barley	Rye	Wheat
Moscow	30	25	40	25
Minsk	45	25	45	35
Kiev	35	20	30	20
Volgograd	50	40	50	50

Determine the optimal allocation of acreage for each crop in each of the districts so as to meet Soviet food requirements at a minimum cost. Assume that the cost of importing each crop is double the highest domestic production cost for a hundred-thousand bushels of that crop.

37. Solve the transportation problem having the following costs, origins, availabilities, and destination requirements. Use a method of your choice to obtain an initial basic feasible solution, and use the modified distribution algorithm to determine the optimal solution.

Origin	Destination					Origin Availability
	D_1	D_2	D_3	D_4	D_5	
O_1	2	1	3	3	2	55
O_2	2	3	4	3	1	65
O_3	2	3	5	4	3	70
O_4	4	2	2	4	6	40
Destination Requirement	40	80	30	55	25	230

38. J. W. Bandit runs a moonshine operation in western North Carolina. He operates three stills located in North Wilkesboro, Boone, and Hendersonville. Bandit Enterprises has four major distributors located in Charlotte, Raleigh, Asheville, and Burlington. The cost of running a truckload of shine from each of the supply facilities to the demand destinations is given below.

	Charlotte	Burlington	Raleigh	Asheville
North Wilkesboro	$250	$350	$200	$250
Boone	200	350	350	350
Hendersonville	300	350	300	350

The supply availabilities at the stills in North Wilkesboro, Boone, and Hendersonville are 40, 30, and 25, respectively. The demand requirements for Charlotte, Burlington, Raleigh, and Asheville are 15, 35, 40, and 35. Determine an optimal shipping schedule for Bandit Enterprises.

39. Energon Industries is a large manufacturer of turbines with an international market for its product. Four of its production facilities are situated in the eastern United States and supply Energon's South American and Caribbean markets. These plants are located in New York, Norfolk, Jacksonville, and Miami; the markets are located in Caracas, Rio de Janeiro, Salvador, Santiago, and Lima (S.A.), and in San Juan (Caribbean). The cost of shipping a turbine from any of the port production locations to another is given by the following cost matrix.

	To			
From	**1** **Jacksonville**	**2** **Norfolk**	**3** **New York**	**4** **Miami**
1 Jacksonville	0	25	22	14
2 Norfolk	25	0	17	19
3 New York	22	17	0	55
4 Miami	14	19	55	0

The air transport cost per turbine from production unit to market is given by the following cost matrix.

	To					
From	**Caracas**	**Rio**	**Salvador**	**Santiago**	**Lima**	**San Juan**
Jacksonville	52	50	78	93	89	73
Norfolk	65	78	57	57	82	65
New York	75	100	82	95	57	90
Miami	43	33	25	37	52	49

The air transport cost per turbine from one market location to another is provided by the following cost matrix.

	To					
From	**5** **Caracas**	**6** **Rio**	**7** **Salvador**	**8** **Santiago**	**9** **Lima**	**10** **San Juan**
5 Caracas	0	25	17	25	33	24
6 Rio	25	0	5	35	20	57
7 Salvador	17	5	0	23	51	42
8 Santiago	25	35	23	0	45	38
9 Lima	33	20	51	45	0	27
10 San Juan	24	57	42	38	27	0

The supply availabilities at the production units in Jacksonville, Norfolk, New York, and Miami are 54, 30, 62, and 21 respectively. The demand requirements at the markets in Caracas, Rio de Janeiro, Salvador, Santiago, Lima, and San Juan are 30, 22, 51, 11, 7, and 46 respectively. Develop an optimum transshipment schedule utilizing the transportation algorithm.

40. Super Suction Ltd. manufactures vacuum cleaners for three department stores located in New York, Chicago, and Dallas. The manufacturing concern consists of three production facilities to serve the three department stores. The following shipping options are available to management to aid in getting cleaners to the three department stores.

(a) Ship from plant to department store.
(b) Ship from plant to one of two intermediate distribution centers.
(c) Ship from plant to plant.
(d) Ship from distribution center to distribution center.
(e) Ship from distribution center to department store.
(f) Ship from department store to department store.

The number of cartons available for shipment at plant 1 is 50, plant 2 is 90, and plant 3 is 35. The demand requirements for the three department stores are 75, 50, and 50. Derive an optimum shipping schedule given the following cost matrices.

Plant to Department Store:

Plant	Department Store		
	1	2	3
1	200	225	300
2	120	180	130
3	165	210	210

Plant to Distribution Center:

Plant	Distribution Center	
	1	2
1	75	180
2	75	100
3	95	125

Plant to Plant:

Plant	Plant		
	1	2	3
1	0	75	60
2	75	0	45
3	60	45	0

Distribution Center to Distribution Center:

Distribution Center	Distribution Center	
	1	2
1	0	25
2	25	0

Distribution Center to Department Store:

Distribution	Department Store		
Center	1	2	3
1	120	100	100
2	75	80	85

Department Store to Department Store:

Department	Department Store		
Store	1	2	3
1	0	100	70
2	100	0	30
3	70	30	0

41. A diesel engine manufacturing operation consists of three production facilities that supply three warehouses. The following network provides the cost per railcar shipment of engines for the factory-to-factory, warehouse-to-warehouse, and factory-to-warehouse combinations indicated. The supply of engines (in railcar shipments) for each production facility is as follows.

       Factory 1   30

       Factory 2   45

       Factory 3   50

The demand for engines (in railcar shipments) for each of the warehouses is as follows.

       Warehouse 1   25

       Warehouse 2   30

       Warehouse 3   70

Use the transportation algorithm to select an optimal shipping schedule for this transshipment scenario.

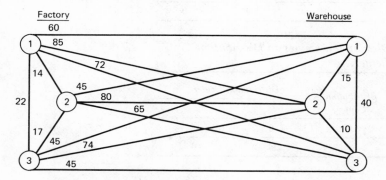

42. A light fixture manufacturing concern has three manufacturing facilities that supply four wholesale distributors. The production units are located in Boise, Idaho; Denver, Colorado; and Omaha, Nebraska. The wholesale distribution outlets are in Sacramento, California; Albuquerque, New Mexico; Houston, Texas; and Tampa, Florida. The cost matrices provided below give the cost per truckload of light fixtures for the various available shipping options.

Plant to Plant

	Boise	*Denver*	*Omaha*
Boise	0	70	95
Denver	80	0	30
Omaha	95	25	0

Wholesale Distributor to Wholesale Distributor

	Sacramento	*Albuquerque*	*Houston*	*Tampa*
Sacramento	0	90	65	150
Albuquerque	90	0	60	120
Houston	65	60	0	85
Tampa	150	120	85	0

Plant to Distributor

	Sacramento	*Albuquerque*	*Houston*	*Tampa*
Boise	60	115	175	155
Denver	50	45	120	200
Omaha	130	60	125	125

The distributor-to-plant shipping costs are the same as the plant-to-distributor shipping costs. The supply availabilities at Boise, Denver, and Omaha are 25, 75, and 50, respectively. The demand requirements at Sacramento, Albuquerque, Houston, and Tampa are 25, 30, 50, and 45, respectively. Develop an optimal shipping schedule for this transshipment problem.

43. Five auto mechanics in a garage must be assigned to five cars needing repair. From the type of repairs involved, the supervisor knows the time each mechanic needs to do the job. These times, in hours, are shown in the following table.

	Job				
Mechanic	*1*	*2*	*3*	*4*	*5*
Alice	3	5	2	4	6
June	4	6	4	3	7
Bob	2	7	3	4	5
Slim	5	4	7	3	6
Fats	3	4	4	5	5

Assuming that each mechanic can be assigned to only one job, determine the minimum-cost assignment.

44. A certain computer service bureau has six keypunching jobs that it wishes to assign to its six keypunchers. From the nature and length of the job, the manager of the service bureau can estimate the time each keypuncher requires to perform each job. These times, in hours, are shown in the following table.

Keypuncher	Job					
	1	2	3	4	5	6
Sue	4	6	9	7	10	5
Alice	7	2	3	6	4	8
Elton	5	5	6	10	7	10
Janet	8	4	2	4	11	3
Bill	5	6	4	9	3	8
Yvonne	3	2	7	9	6	5

Assuming that each keypuncher can be assigned to only one job, determine the minimum-cost assignment.

45. Mr. Speedy Limbs, the head track coach at the local university, needs to assign runners to a medley relay race involving four events. His four best runners and the fastest times (in seconds) they have achieved in each of the four races are as follows.

Race	Runner			
	Ken	Al	Gene	Janet
100-yd dash	9.7	9.8	10.1	9.9
220-yd dash	24.0	22.4	23.1	22.3
440-yd dash	50.3	48.9	48.6	48.3
880-yd dash	100.7	106.2	105.2	103.3

Each runner can run in only one event in the medley relay. Determine the best assignment of runners to the events.

46. Slick's Used Car lot currently has five prospective customers for its six available late-model Ford used cars. Each of the five customers is willing to pay a price, p_{ij} (or less) for the jth car. The values of the p_{ij} are given in the following table.

Customer	Car						
	1	2	3	4	5	6	
1	12	14	9	13	10	16	
2	11	13	15	17	13	11	
3	9	15	9	14	12	13	($, hundreds)
4	10	12	11	13	14	14	
5	13	10	15	10	16	15	

The management wishes to determine which car to offer to each customer at what price, so as to maximize its total revenues. Solve as an assignment problem.

47. Betty Edwards is a college student whose summer job involves selling magazine subscriptions. She currently has five magazine subscriptions available and, according to company policy, she can sell only one subscription to any customer. She currently has four prospective customers, and these four customers are willing to pay different prices for the subscriptions to the five magazines. The profit table associated with sales of the five magazine subscriptions to the four customers is as follows.

		Customer			
		1	2	3	4
	1	5	7	8	10
	2	8	6	9	11
Magazine	3	9	6	7	9
	4	11	8	10	7
	5	8	10	9	6

To which customers should Betty Edwards try to sell the magazine subscriptions, in order to maximize profits?

48. A certain equipment repair operation has seven repair jobs that it wishes to assign to its seven mechanics. The service manager has estimated the time each mechanic requires to fix each machine. These estimates, in hours, are provided by the following table.

	Job						
Mechanic	1	2	3	4	5	6	7
1	3	2	1	4	7	5	8
2	4	3	1	6	8	4	7
3	2	1	3	3	4	6	8
4	5	3	1	7	8	9	9
5	4	6	7	8	9	8	7
6	3	1	5	7	7	9	8
7	3	5	6	5	8	7	7

Assuming that each mechanic can be assigned to only one job, determine the minimum time assignment.

49. A law firm has five secretaries composing its support staff. A. J. Alimony has four divorce action documents that must be typed as accurately as possible. He knows the approximate number of errors each secretary will make in each of the documents. These error estimates are given in the following table.

	Errors			
Case Secretary	*1*	*2*	*3*	*4*
1	5	9	3	4
2	6	10	3	4
3	6	9	2	4
4	3	7	1	3
5	2	6	2	4

Assuming that each secretary can be assigned to only one job, determine the minimum error job assignment for this unbalanced problem.

8 Network Models

8.1 INTRODUCTION

For some time, network analysis has been an important tool in the study of electrical networks. Recently, there has been a growing awareness that various concepts and techniques of network theory are also very useful in business and economic analysis. For example, important applications of network theory have been made in information retrieval and processing, in the study of subway, highway, and transportation systems, and in the planning and control of research and development projects. Consequently, it is very important for the management science student and practitioner to have an understanding of some of the basic aspects of network modeling.

One typical network analysis problem involves allocating flows in a manner that maximizes the flow through a network connecting an origin and a destination. The maximum flow problem thus concerns the maximum amount of flow (e.g., liquids, electrical impulses, and vehicles) that can enter into and exit from some connected network during a given period of time. Another interesting network analysis problem, which is of great practical importance in the study of transportation systems, involves the determination of the shortest route through a network. The shortest-route problem involves the determination of the minimum total distance from the origin to the destination in a network. A third network problem requires the determination of the set of connections that provides a route between any two points in a network in a manner so as to minimize the total length of this set of connections. This situation is known as the minimal spanning tree problem and requires using the branches of the network to reach all the connecting points in the network in a manner that minimizes the total length of the branches used to reach these points. A final network problem entails the planning and control of activities or projects that can be presented as time-dimensioned networks. The network analysis procedures of the Critical Path Method (CPM) and the Program Evaluation and Review Technique (PERT) have been widely employed by managers in the planning and control of such time-dimensioned networks.

Each of the above four types of network problems will be analyzed and explained in detail in this chapter. We will also provide illustrations of applications of the various network models. Throughout this chapter we will employ various terms and concepts from the field of graph theory. This nomenclature will be useful in developing a good understanding of network modeling, and it is suggested that careful attention be paid to the various aspects of graph theory as they relate to network analysis. Finally, we will observe that three of these four network models have a special structure that facilitates their analysis and solution by means of very powerful, special-purpose algorithms.

8.2 BASIC TERMINOLOGY USED IN ANALYZING NETWORK PROBLEMS

Before we begin our study of network models it is instructive to define certain basic terms. Using the terminology of the theory of graphs,[1] a **graph** is defined as a set of junction points called **nodes** or **events** that are connected by lines called **branches** or **activities** (or "arcs," "links," "connectors," or "edges"). Fig. 8.1 is an example of a simple graph, in which the circles are the nodes and the lines connecting the circles are the branches.

We can attribute a sense of direction to a branch by indicating which node is to be considered the point of origin. Such a branch is called **directed**, or **oriented**, and when drawing a graph we indicate the orientation of a branch by an arrowhead. For example, in Fig. 8.1, "branch 1 to 2" is a directed branch, and in this branch the direction is from node 1 to node 2. A branch that does not have a sense of direction attached to it is called **undirected** and is not marked with an arrowhead. In Fig. 8.1, "branch 2 to 3" is an undirected branch. In most instances, we can replace an undirected branch with a pair of directed branches, whose directions are opposite.

A sequence of connecting branches between nodes i and j is called a **chain** from i and to j. In Fig. 8.1, one of the chains connecting node 1 and node 7 is the sequence of branches 1 to 2, 2 to 5, 5 to 7, or vice versa.

If the direction of travel, or flow, along a chain between two nodes is

---

[1] See, for example: R. G. Busacker and T. L. Saaty, *Finite Graphs and Networks* (New York: McGraw-Hill, 1964); and L. R. Ford and D. R. Fulkerson, *Flows in Networks* (Princeton, N. J.: Princeton University Press, 1962).

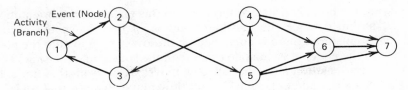

FIGURE 8.1   A Simple Graph

specified, it is called a **path**. In Fig. 8.1, one path between node 1 and node 7 is composed of the branches 1 to 2, 2 to 5, 5 to 4, and 4 to 7 (in that specific order).

A **cycle** is a chain that begins and ends at the same node. In Fig. 8.1, the chain $1 \to 2 \to 5 \to 4 \to 3 \to 1$ is a cycle.

A graph is called a **connected graph** if there is a path connecting every pair of nodes in the graph. The graph shown in Fig. 8.1 is a connected graph. However, if we removed branches 2 to 5 and 3 to 4 we would no longer have a connected graph.

An undirected, connected graph that contains no cycles is called a **tree**. Therefore, between any two nodes of the tree there is a unique chain joining the two nodes. For example, Fig. 8.1 would be a tree if its only branches were 1 to 2, 2 to 3, 2 to 5, 5 to 4, 5 to 6, and 4 to 7.

In many practical situations some sort of physical flow takes place in the branches of the graph. A **network** is defined as a graph such that flow can take place in the branches of the graph.[2] Examples of common networks involving physical flows are shown below in Table 8.1.

TABLE 8.1   Examples of Flow Networks

Nodes	*Branches*	*Flow*
Intersections	Highways	Automobiles
Valves	Pipeline segments	Natural gas
Ports	Shipping lanes	Ships
Cities	Rivers	Barges
Work stations	Conveyors	Products

The basic graph theory definitions presented above will be used throughout the material that follows. Additional definitions will be introduced with respect to specific network models.

8.3   THE MAXIMUM (-MAXIMAL) FLOW PROBLEM

In the **maximum-** or **maximal-flow problem** we consider a connected network consisting of a single origin (source), a single destination (sink), and branches connecting intermediate nodes. Within the maximum-flow network some, or all,

---

[2] This is the graph theory definition of a network, and this definition will be used as we analyze maximal-flow network problems. However, in later sections of this chapter, we will consider other generic ''network'' problems in which a network will simply be a collection of nodes connected by branches and will not have to involve physical flows.

of the branches may be directed. In this instance, the orientation of the branch is assumed to be the feasible direction of flow along the particular branch. We assume that there is conservation of flow (i.e., flow into the node equals flow out of the node) at each node other than the source and the sink. The source node has an orientation such that all flow moves away from that node, and the sink node has an orientation such that all flow moves toward that node. Additionally, it is important to recognize that a branch in a maximal-flow network need not be directed because it may be feasible to have flow in either direction along a branch. A two-way street is an example of a nonoriented branch, while a one-way street is an example of an oriented branch.

In the maximum-flow problem, the **flow capacity** of a branch in a specified direction is defined to be the upper limit to the feasible magnitude of the rate (or total quantity) of flow in the branch in that direction. The flow capacity of a branch may be any nonnegative quantity, including infinity. An oriented branch will have a flow capacity equal to zero in one direction, and a flow capacity equal to a nonnegative quantity in the other direction. The maximum-flow problem is to determine the feasible steady-state pattern of flows through the network that maximizes the total flow from the source to the sink.

One typical network flow problem involves the maximization of the flow through an oil pipeline network. The oil field becomes the source, the refinery the sink, and the various pipeline segments the branches of the network. Each node of the network is a valve, and there is no storage or transformation possible at the nodes. The problem becomes that of planning the pipeline network in a fashion that maximizes the total oil flow through the network.

A second typical network flow problem might involve the maximization of information flow through a computer network. The central processing unit would be the source, and some type of output device would become the sink. The branches of the network would then become the various channels between the central processing unit and the output device. The objective in this situation would be to plan the selection and utilization of the various channels in a manner that would maximize the total information flow through the network.

8.3.1 A Linear Programming Approach to the Maximum-Flow Problem

The maximum-flow problem can be formulated as a linear programming problem. Suppose that we have a network with N nodes, where nodes 1 and N are the source node and sink node, respectively. For each directed branch (i,j) let x_{ij} denote the rate of flow from node i to node j, and let c_{ij} be the flow capacity for the branch (i,j). We seek to send as much material (flow) as is possible from the source node to the sink node. A flow from source to sink is considered feasible if there is conservation of flow at every node except the source node and sink node and if the flow capacities are satisfied for all the branches. The linear programming formulation of the maximum-flow problem can be written as

$$\text{Maximize } Z = \sum_k x_{1k} \quad \text{or} \quad \text{Maximize } Z = \sum_k x_{kN} \qquad (8\text{--}1)$$

$$\|\qquad\qquad\qquad\qquad\qquad\|$$

Flow out of   Flow into
Source Node   Sink Node

subject to:

$$\sum_j x_{ij} - \sum_k x_{ki} = \begin{cases} \sum_k x_{kN} & \text{if } i = 1 \text{ (Source node)} \\[2ex] 0 \text{ otherwise} \\[2ex] -\sum_k x_{1j} & \text{if } i = N \text{ (Sink node)} \end{cases} \qquad (8\text{--}2)$$

with $\quad 0 \le x_{ij} \le c_{ij} \quad$ for each branch (i,j) $\qquad\qquad$ (8--3)

In the constraint set given by Equation 8–2, note that there is conservation of flow at every node except the source node and the sink node.

Although the maximum-flow problem can be formulated and solved using linear programming, a much simpler and more efficient solution procedure can be devised by following an intuitive solution approach. The following example will be used to explain this solution procedure.

8.3.2 Solution Procedure for the Maximum-Flow Problem

To illustrate the development and application of an efficient method for solving the maximum-flow problem, consider the Benzoil Company pipeline network presented in Fig. 8.2. The source node (oil field) and sink node (refinery) are nodes 1 and 7, respectively. The potential flow capacity for each pipeline segment c_{ij} is shown by the number along branch (i,j) nearest node i. Thus, the flow capacity of branch (1,2) is 7 and the flow capacity of branch (2,1) is 0. The maximum-flow problem is to determine the feasible flow in each branch in the network that will maximize F, the total flow out of the source or into the sink. Each node can be thought of as a valve that can be used to regulate flows through that node.

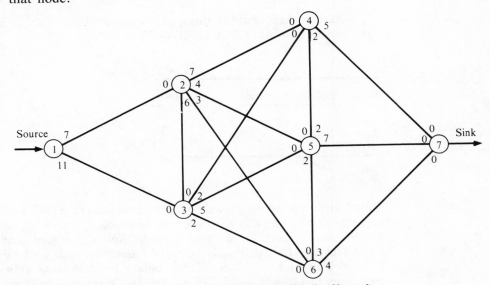

FIGURE 8.2 Maximum-flow example—Benzoil Company Pipeline Network

The intuitive solution procedure for the maximum-flow problem involves repeatedly selecting any path from source to sink and assigning the maximum feasible flow to that path, continuing the process until no more paths have strictly positive flow capacity. To begin this solution procedure we can immediately see that one feasible flow pattern is a flow of 5 along the path $1 \to 2 \to 4 \to 7$. This flow is limited by the capacity of branch $(4 \overset{\curvearrowright}{,} 7)$, $c_{47} = 5$. Assigning a flow of 5 to path $1 \to 2 \to 4 \to 7$ we obtain the following network.

Assign a flow of 5 to $1 \to 2 \to 4 \to 7$

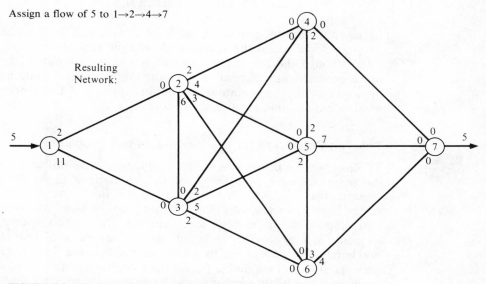

FIGURE 8.3   Maximum-flow example—First-flow Assignment

Note that, as a result of this assignment of a flow of 5, we have reduced the capacities in branches $(1 \overset{\curvearrowright}{,} 2)$, $(2 \overset{\curvearrowright}{,} 4)$, $(4 \overset{\curvearrowright}{,} 7)$ as follows.

Branch	Original Capacity	New Capacity
$(1 \overset{\curvearrowright}{,} 2)$	7	2
$(2 \overset{\curvearrowright}{,} 4)$	7	2
$(4 \overset{\curvearrowright}{,} 7)$	5	0

Note further that no additional flow can occur along the path $1 \to 2 \to 4 \to 7$ since the capacity of branch $(4 \overset{\curvearrowright}{,} 7)$ has been reduced to 0.

We now search for another feasible flow assignment, and observe that a second feasible flow pattern is a flow of 2 along the path $1 \to 3 \to 6 \to 7$. Assigning a flow of 2 to path $1 \to 3 \to 6 \to 7$, we obtain the following network. Again, the capacities in branches $(1 \overset{\curvearrowright}{,} 3)$, $(3 \overset{\curvearrowright}{,} 6)$, and $(6 \overset{\curvearrowright}{,} 7)$ are reduced, and we see that no additional flow can occur along the path $1 \to 3 \to 6 \to 7$, since the capacity of branch $(3 \overset{\curvearrowright}{,} 6)$ has been reduced to 0.

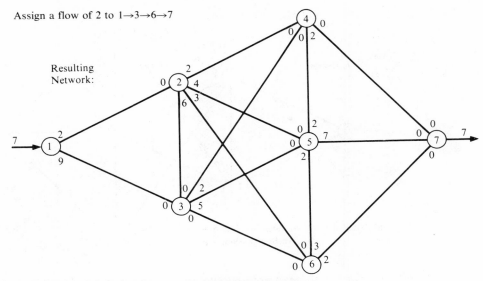

FIGURE 8.4   Maximum-flow example—Second-flow Assignment

This intuitive approach continues in similar fashion with the assignment of flows along the various paths until no more such paths can be found. This procedure is illustrated below in Figures 8.5 and 8.6. Observe that one flow assignment is made at each step and that the corresponding branch capacities are then reduced by the amount of this flow assignment. The assignment of flows is done in a purely arbitrary manner, based on the judgment of the analyst.

We now observe that no more paths with positive flow capacity remain. The question is: Has our intuitive approach yielded a flow pattern that is optimal? The

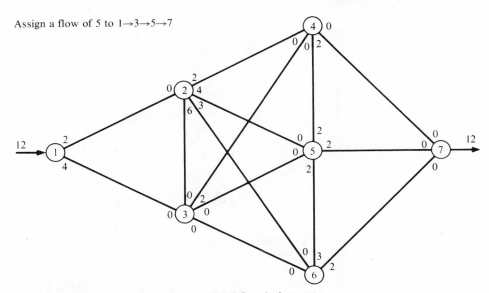

FIGURE 8.5   Maximum-flow example—Third-flow Assignment

Assign a flow of 2 to 1→2→4→5→6

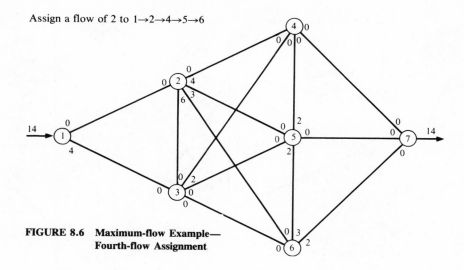

FIGURE 8.6 Maximum-flow Example—
Fourth-flow Assignment

answer for the example shown above, and in general, is no. Remember that we began our intuitive approach by arbitrarily assigning a flow of 5 along the path 1→2→4→7. This immediately reduced the flow capacity of branch (4→7) to 0, and no further flow through branch (4→7) was permitted. However, we could have just as easily chosen to make an initial assignment of a flow of 3 along the path 1→2→4→7 and a flow of 2 along the path 1→2→5→6→7. Thus, the total flow would remain equal to 5 as it did in our original assignment. Now, all subsequent assignments could be made as previously and we obtain this network.

Path	Flow Assignment
1→2→4→7	3
1→2→5→6→7	2
1→3→6→7	2
1→3→5→7	5
1→2→4→5→7	$\dfrac{2}{14}$

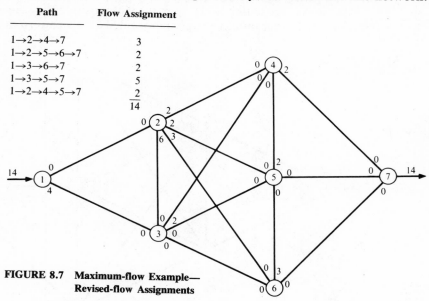

FIGURE 8.7 Maximum-flow Example—
Revised-flow Assignments

Note that, in this network, we can now assign an additional flow of 2 to the path 1→3→4→7, thus increasing the total flow from $F = 14$ to $F = 16$. The maximum flow for the Benzoil Company pipeline network is as shown in Fig. 8.8.

Path	Flow Assignment
1→2→4→7	3
1→2→5→6→7	2
1→3→6→7	2
1→3→5→7	5
1→2→4→5→7	2
1→3→4→7	2
	16

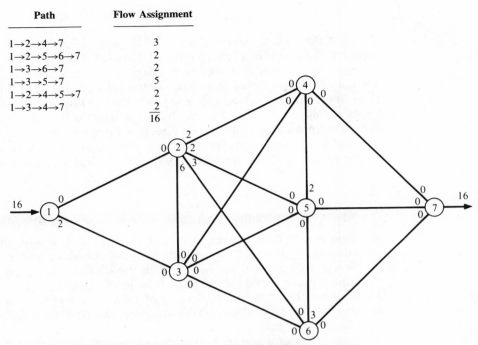

FIGURE 8.8   Maximum-flow—Benzoil Company Pipeline Network Problem

Comparing the suboptimal flow assignments in Fig. 8.6 and the optimal flow assignments in Fig. 8.8, it is apparent that we need to refine our intuitive approach slightly to guarantee an optimal solution. We need to permit a previously assigned flow to take an alternate route in order to open up new paths from the source to the sink with positive flow capacities. This is done in the following manner. We permit the assignment of fictional flows in the "wrong" direction, that is, in the direction of a zero flow capacity branch, when the real effect of this assignment is to cancel out part or all of the previously assigned flow in the "right" direction, that is, in the direction of a positive flow capacity branch. To demonstrate this procedure, consider the last network shown originally for our intuitive approach in which $F = 14$ was obtained. As we observed in our analysis of this network, it was possible to gain an improvement to $F = 16$ by increasing by 2 the flow along paths 1→2→5→6→7 and 1→3→4→7, and decreasing by 2 the flow in branch $(2\overset{\rightarrow}{,}4)$. Note, however, that this can also be accomplished by assigning a flow of 2 along the path 1→3→4→2→5→6→7. Now, the real effect of assigning a flow of 2 along branch $(4\overset{\rightarrow}{,}2)$ is to decrease the previously assigned flow along branch $(2\overset{\rightarrow}{,}4)$ by 2. For this to occur, our procedure should have increased the flow capacity by 5 in branch $(4\overset{\rightarrow}{,}2)$ when we made our original flow assignment of 5 to path 1→2→4→7, and by 2 in branch $(4\overset{\rightarrow}{,}2)$ when we made our original flow assignment of 2 to path 1→2→4→5→7. In summary, the refinement that we must make to our original intuitive approach is that of increasing the capacity of a branch in the opposite direction by the same quantity of flow being assigned to that branch. In addition, when this procedure is completed, only the net flow in a branch is relevant. We imagine that two flows, x'_{ij} and x'_{ji}, pass simultaneously in opposite directions through branch $(i\overset{\rightarrow}{,}j)$ and that the net flow is given by:

$$x_{ij} = x'_{ij} - x'_{ji} \geq 0 \qquad (8\text{-}4)$$

This net flow must satisfy Equation 8.4, and we are thus assuming that the capacity c_{ij} for flow in a branch refers to the *net* flow in that branch. In a problem-solving sense, when flow has been assigned to a branch in both directions, the smaller of the two flows should be subtracted from the capacities in both directions in the optimal network, leaving only the net flow as shown in Equation 8.4. Given a value of x'_{ij}, then x'_{ji} must be in the interval $0 \leq x'_{ji} \leq x'_{ij}$. This means we cannot impose a flow in the wrong direction along a branch unless we have at least as great a flow in the proper direction. Thus, there cannot be a net flow in the wrong direction. If we are given a value of x'_{ji}, then x'_{ij} must satisfy:

$$x'_{ji} \leq x'_{ij} \leq c_{ij} + x'_{ji} \qquad (8\text{-}5)$$

The modified solution procedure may now be summarized as follows.

1. Find a path from source to sink with positive flow capacity. Obviously, if none exists, the net flows already assigned constitute a maximal flow pattern.
2. Search this path for the branch with the smallest flow capacity. Denote this capacity as c_{ij}^*, and increase the flow in this path by c_{ij}^*.
3. Decrease by c_{ij}^* the flow capacity of each branch in the selected path.
4. Increase by c_{ij}^*, in the opposite direction, the flow capacity of each branch in the selected path.
5. Return to step 1 and repeat the procedure outlined in steps 2, 3, and 4 until no paths with positive flow capacity remain.
6. Compute the net flow in all branches for which flow(s) have been assigned in both directions.

Applying this modified solution procedure to the example given previously in Fig. 8.2 yields the results summarized below. No paths with positive flow capacity remain in the network shown in Fig. 8.11. Thus, the maximum flow is 16.

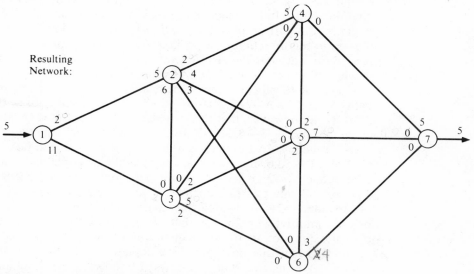

Resulting Network:

FIGURE 8.9 Modified Solution Procedure—First-Flow Assignment

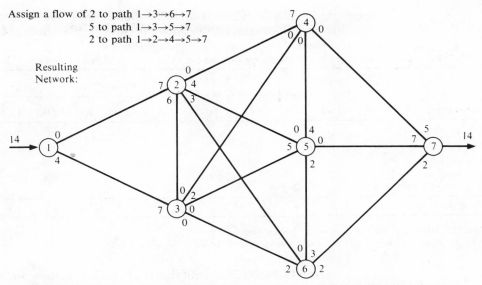

Assign a flow of 2 to path 1→3→6→7
5 to path 1→3→5→7
2 to path 1→2→4→5→7

Resulting
Network:

FIGURE 8.10 **Modified Solution Procedure—Second-, Third-, and Fourth-Flow Assignments**

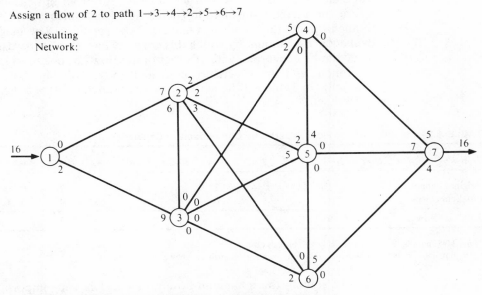

Assign a flow of 2 to path 1→3→4→2→5→6→7

Resulting
Network:

FIGURE 8.11 **Modified Solution Procedure—Fifth-Flow Assignment**

The maximum flow and its associated flow pattern are most easily identified by recording and accumulating the flow assignments as they are made. This is easily accomplished by making accumulations such as those shown in Table 8.2 as the flow assignments are made. Using this method, when flow has been assigned to a branch in both directions, the smaller of the two flows must be subtracted from the larger of the two flows to determine the net flow for that branch. For example, in Table 8.2, the net flow of 5 in branch (2↗4) is computed as the flow of 7 in branch (2↗4) minus the flow of 2 in branch (4↗2).

TABLE 8.2 Identification of Flow Patterns by Accumulation of Branch Flows

Assignments	Branch[a]												
	1→2	1→3	2→4	2→5	3→4	3→5	3→6	4→2	4→5	4→7	5→6	5→7	6→7
5 to 1→2→4→7	5		5							5			
2 to 1→3→6→7		2					2						2
5 to 1→3→5→7		5				5						5	
2 to 1→2→4→5→7	2		2						2			2	
2 to 1→3→4→2→5→6→7		2		2	2			2			2		2
Total net flow	7	9	7	2	2	5	2	2	2	5	2	7	4

Note: Maximum flow = 16; net flow = 7 − 2 = 5 in branch (2↗4).
[a] For simplicity, only those branches to which flows are assigned are shown in Table 8.2.

A second method for identifying the final flow pattern and the maximum flow involves comparing the remaining flow capacities of the optimal network with the flow capacities of the original network. Using this method one can construct a summary such as that shown in Table 8.3, after all flow assignments are made. Using this method, the direction of net flow in a branch is the same direction of the branch having the smallest remaining flow capacity. The magnitude of the flow will equal the amount by which this capacity has decreased. Using this method we need not be concerned with whether or not flow has occurred in both directions of a branch, and the procedure indicated above will hold for all situations. For example, in Table 8.3 the net flow of 5 in branch (2↗4) is indicated directly in the table itself.

TABLE 8.3 Identification of Flow Patterns by Comparison of Capacities

Branch[a]	1→2	1→3	2→4	2→5	3→4	3→5	3→6	4→2	4→5	4→7	5→6	5→7	6→7
Original capacity	7	11	7	4	2	5	2	0	2	5	2	7	4
Final capacity	0	2	2	2	0	0	0	5	0	0	0	0	0
Total net flow	7	9	5	2	2	5	2	−5	2	5	2	7	4

Note: Maximum flow = 16; net flow = 5 in branch (2↗4).
[a] For simplicity, only those branches to which flows are assigned are shown in Table 8.3.

In solving the maximum-flow problem it is very important to develop and utilize some systematic type of recordkeeping, or accounting, such as the two methods described previously. For small problems, either of these two methods can be executed in manual fashion. The author has a preference for the first method in which flows are accumulated as each flow assignment is made. This method essentially affords a check on each flow assignment and associated branch capacity as the assignments are made. The second method is satisfactory, provided the analyst keeps an accurate record of the reduced branch capacities throughout the analysis.

8.3.3   The Max Flow-Min Cut Theorem

The modified intuitive approach for determining the maximum flow in a network is a very straightforward and simple process. However, it would be more useful if one could ascertain when optimality had been reached, without having to conduct an exhaustive search for a nonexistent path. We now proceed to develop a method for determining when optimality has been reached, using an important theorem of network theory known as the **max cut-min flow theorem**. We shall begin by defining a **cut** in a network.

CUT   *A cut in a network is a collection of oriented branches such that every oriented path from source to sink contains at least one branch in the cut.*

To illustrate, consider the cuts shown in the original network of Fig. 8.2, which is redrawn as Fig. 8.12.

For any given network, the number of cuts is finite. If we sum the capacities of the branch in a cut, it is clear that the maximum flow cannot be greater than this sum, because the flow in every path is limited by the branch of lowest capacity, and every oriented path contains a branch of the cut. The sum of the flow capacities of the branches (in the direction of the orientation designated by the cut) is defined to be the **cut value** of the cut. The first cut value of 18 is obtained by adding the capacity of branch $(1\vec{,}2)$, 7, to the capacity of branch $(1\vec{,}3)$, 11. The second cut value of 16 is obtained by adding the capacity of branch $(1\vec{,}2)$, 7; the capacity of branch $(3\vec{,}2)$, 0; the capacity of branch $(3\vec{,}4)$, 2; the capacity of branch $(3\vec{,}5)$, 5; and the capacity of branch $(2\vec{,}6)$, 2. The cut values of the other cuts shown in Fig. 8.12 are computed in similar fashion.

The max flow-min cut theorem can be stated as follows.

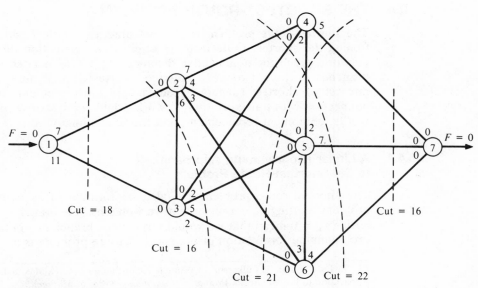

FIGURE 8.12   Illustrations of Cuts in a Network

MAX FLOW–MIN
CUT THEOREM

If, for any network, we find the cut value for each of the finite number of cuts that can be made in the network, then the smallest total capacity (cut value) is equal to the maximum flow in the network.

The max flow–min cut theorem simply states that the smallest of the cut values in a network is equal to the maximum value of F. In addition, any cut value provides an upper bound on F. Thus, if we can determine a cut in the original network whose value equals the value of F currently attained by the solution procedure, then the current flow pattern must be optimal. Equivalently, optimality has been obtained whenever there exists a cut in the current network whose value is zero with respect to the remaining flow capacities.

Notice that two cuts in the network shown in Fig. 8.12 have a minimal cut value equal to 16, which was later found to be the maximum value of F. Note further that, for the final network that resulted from our modified solution procedure, in which $F = 16$, each of these two corresponding cuts had cut values of zero with respect to the remaining flow capacities. Thus, we had achieved optimality, and could have recognized this fact from either, or both, of the two applications of the max flow–min cut theorem.

The modified intuitive solution procedure, accompanied by the max flow–min cut theorem provides an adequate, yet simple, method for solving maximum-flow problems of reasonable size. For large, complicated networks the modified intuitive procedure for finding the maximum-flow may be rather inconvenient. However, other more rigorous approaches have been developed. Ford and Fulkerson have suggested a branch-labeling technique, based on a straightforward algebraic expansion of the intuitive approach.[3] Hadley later expanded their work into a matrix approach to the problem.[4] Both of these procedures are beyond the level of this textbook, but the interested reader can consult the references given below for further details.

8.4   THE SHORTEST-ROUTE PROBLEM

The **shortest-route problem** is of great practical interest and is concerned with finding the shortest route from an origin to a destination through a connecting network, given the nonnegative distances $d_{ij} \geq 0$ associated with the respective branches of the network. In practice, shortest (time) routes are often of equal interest to shortest (distance) routes, and such problems arise frequently in connection with transportation networks, delivery systems, communications networks, equipment replacement, and the scheduling of complex projects.

8.4.1   A Linear Programming Approach to the Shortest-Route Problem

The shortest-route problem can also be formulated as a linear programming problem. Letting $x_{ij} = 1$ mean that we would include branch $i \rightarrow j$ in the route, and letting $x_{ij} = 0$ mean that we would not include branch $i \rightarrow j$ in the route, the linear programming formulation of the shortest-route problem is as follows.

---

[3] L. R. Ford and D. R. Fulkerson, "A Simple Algorithm for Finding Maximal Network Flows and an Application to the Hitchcock Problem," *Canadian Journal of Mathematics,* **9** (1955), 210–18.

[4] G. Hadley, *Linear Programming* (Reading, Mass.: Addison-Wesley Publishing Company, Inc. 1965), pp. 346–51.

$$\text{Minimize } Z = \sum_i \sum_j d_{ij} x_{ij} \quad \text{where } d_{ij} = \begin{array}{l} \text{direct distance} \\ \text{between nodes } i \text{ and } j \end{array} \quad (8\text{-}6)$$

$$\text{subject to: } \sum_j x_{ij} - \sum_k x_{ki} = \begin{cases} 1 & \text{if } i = 1 \text{ (Source node)} \\ 0 & \text{otherwise} \\ -1 & \text{if } i = N \text{ (Sink node)} \end{cases} \quad (8\text{-}7)$$

$$\text{with} \quad x_{ij} \geq 0, \text{ and } x_{ij} = 0 \text{ or } 1 \text{ for all } i \text{ and } j \quad (8\text{-}8)$$

The interpretation of the shortest-route problem is that we want to go from the source node to the sink node in a minimum distance. The constraint set imposed by Equation 8–7 indicates that we can take only one route out of the source node, and only one route into the sink node, and for every other node that is part of the shortest route we can take only one route into, and one route out of the node. Note that this last restriction does not mean that all nodes will necessarily be utilized in determining the shortest route (i.e., if a node is not part of the shortest route, all branches into the node and all branches out of the node would be equal to zero).

Although the shortest-route problem can be formulated and solved using linear programming, a more efficient solution procedure can be devised. This solution procedure will now be presented; it will then be illustrated by means of an example.

8.4.2 Solution Procedure for the Shortest-Route Problem

This solution procedure for the shortest-route problem was originally developed by Dijkstra.[5] It assumes that the direct distance, d_{ij}, between any two nodes in the network of n nodes is given, and that all such distances are nonnegative. Dijkstra's algorithm proceeds by assigning to all nodes a *label* that is either *temporary* or *permanent*. The temporary label represents the upper bound on the shortest distance from the source node to the node being evaluated. The permanent label is the actual shortest distance from the source node to the node being evaluated.

To begin, the source node is assigned a permanent label of zero. All of the other nodes are assigned temporary labels equal to the direct distance from the source node to the node being examined. If any node cannot be reached directly from the source node it is assigned a temporary label of $+\infty$. The algorithm then proceeds to examine the temporarily labeled nodes, and makes them, one at a time, permanent labels. As soon as the sink node receives a permanent label, the shortest route from the source node to the sink node has been determined.

The iterative steps of Dijkstra's algorithm can be summarized as follows.

STEP 0
Initialization
Step
A permanent label of zero is assigned to the source node. All other nodes are assigned temporary labels that are set equal to the direct distances from the source node to the nodes being examined. If any node cannot be reached directly from the source node it is assigned a temporary label of $+\infty$.

STEP 1 All of the nodes having temporary labels are examined and the node having the

---

[5] E. W. Dijkstra, "A Note On Two Problems in Connection with Graphs," *Numerische Mathematik*, vol. 1 (1959), 269–271.

minimum of the temporary labels is selected and declared permanent. If there are ties between temporary labels, break the tie arbitrarily.

STEP 2   Suppose that node T has been assigned a permanent label most recently. The remaining nodes with temporary labels are examined, by comparing, one at a time, the temporary label of each node to the *sum* of the permanent label of node T and the *direct distance* from node T to the node being examined. The minimum of these two distances is assigned as the new temporary label for that node. Note that if the old temporary label for the node being examined is still minimal, then it will remain unchanged during this step.

STEP 3   Now select the minimum of the temporary labels and declare it permanent. If there are ties, select one, but only one, and declare it permanent. If the node just declared permanent is the sink node, the algorithm terminates and the shortest route has been determined. Otherwise return to Step 2.

After the algorithm terminates, the shortest path is identified by retracing the path backward from the sink node to the source node, selecting the nodes that were permanently labeled at each step. Alternatively, the shortest path may be identified by determining which of the nodes have permanent labels that differ exactly by the length of the connecting arc.

Before illustrating Dijkstra's algorithm, we should emphasize that it can be applied to either a directed or nondirected graph, or network. In actuality the shortest-route problem involves finding which path connecting two specified nodes minimizes the sum of the branch distances along the path. Thus, it is not really necessary to travel in any specific direction along this path. It should also be mentioned that frequently d_{ij} does not equal d_{ji}, and some nodes may not be connected directly, a situation which can be indicated by letting the corresponding $d_{ij} = +\infty$.

The use of Dijkstra's algorithm will now be illustrated by means of an example.

8.4.3 A Shortest-Route Application

Consider the nine-city highway network shown in Fig. 8.13, and suppose that we are interested in driving from San Francisco to Cincinnati. As can be seen in Fig. 8.13, we could travel along any of several different routes in going from San Francisco to Cincinnati. The distances between the various cities (nodes) of this network are shown along its various branches. We are interested in determining the shortest (distance) route from San Francisco to Cincinnati.

Initially, Node O is permanently labeled as zero, and all other nodes are assigned temporary labels equal to their direct distance from Node O. Thus, the node labels at Step 0, denoted by $L(0)$, are

Nodes:	*O*	*A*	*B*	*C*	*D*	*E*	*F*	*G*	*S*
$L(0) =$	[0,	827,	759,	800,	$+\infty$,	$+\infty$,	$+\infty$,	$+\infty$,	$+\infty$,]
Preceding Node	—	*O*	*O*	*O*	—	—	—	—	—

Note that an asterisk (*) has been placed over Node O, indicating that Node O has

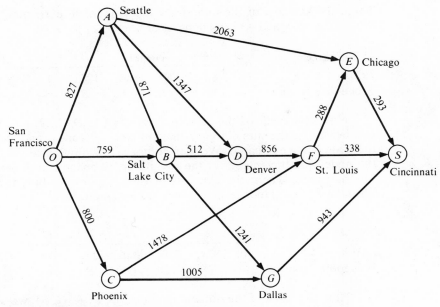

FIGURE 8.13   A Nine-City Highway Network

been permanently labeled. Additionally, we have included a row marked "Preceding Node," which indicates the preceding node on the route from the source node to the other nodes.

At Step 1 the smallest of the temporary labels is made permanent. Thus, Node B is assigned a permanent label equal to 759, and it is the shortest distance from Node O to Node B. This must be true because all branch distances are nonnegative (i.e., all $d_{ij} \geq 0$), and if we move from Node O to Node B through any intermediate node we cannot go less than the direct distance from Node O to Node B (i.e., the shortest distance from Node O to Node B is 759). Thus, the node labels at Step 1, denoted by L(1), are

Nodes:	$\overset{*}{O}$	A	$\overset{*}{B}$	C	D	E	F	G	S
L(1) =	[0,	827,	759,	800,	$+\infty$,	$+\infty$,	$+\infty$,	$+\infty$,	$+\infty$,]
Preceding Node	—	O	O	O	—	—	—	—	—

Now, for each of the remaining nodes (A, C, D, E, F, G, S), we compute a number that is the sum of the permanent label of Node B and the direct distance to the node being evaluated. We then compare this number to the temporary label of the node, and the smaller of the two numbers becomes the new temporary label for that node. To illustrate:

New temporary label for Node A = minimum of ($759 + 871 = 1630$, 827) = 827
New temporary label for Node D = minimum of ($759 + 512 = 1271$, ∞) = 1271
New temporary label for Node G = minimum of ($759 + 1241 = 2000$, ∞) = 2000

$$(8-9)$$

Then, the smallest of the temporary labels is made permanent. Thus, at Step 2, Node C is assigned a permanent label.

Nodes:	O	A	B*	C*	D	E	F	G	S
$L(2) =$	[0,	827,	759,	800,	1271,	$+\infty$,	$+\infty$,	2000,	$+\infty$]
Preceding Node	—	O	O	O	B	—	—	B	—

Now, for each of the remaining nodes (A, D, E, F, G, S), we compute a number that is the sum of the permanent label of Node C and the direct distance to the node being evaluated. We then compare this number to the temporary label of the node, and the smaller of the two numbers becomes the new temporary label for that node. Then, the smallest of the temporary labels is made permanent. Thus, at Step 3, Node A is assigned a permanent label.

Nodes:	O*	A*	B*	C*	D	E	F	G	S
$L(3) =$	[0,	827,	759,	800,	1271,	$+\infty$,	2278,	1805,	$+\infty$]
Preceding Node	—	O	O	O	B	—	C	C	—

Now, for each of the remaining nodes (D, E, F, G, S), we compute a number that is the sum of the permanent label of Node A and the direct distance to the node being evaluated. Thus, at Step 4, the permanent label of Node A is used to update the temporary label of Node E. Then, Node D is assigned a permanent label.

Nodes	O*	A*	B*	C*	D*	E	F	G	S
$L(4) =$	[0,	827,	759,	800,	1271,	2890,	2278,	1805,	$+\infty$]
Preceding Node	—	O	O	O	B	A	C	C	—

Using the permanent label of Node D, the comparison process is repeated. Then, Node G is assigned a permanent label.

Nodes	O*	A*	B*	C*	D*	E	F	G*	S
$L(5) =$	[0,	827,	759,	800,	1271,	2890,	2127,	1805,	$+\infty$]
Preceding Node	—	O	O	O	B	A	D	C	—

Using the permanent label of Node G, the comparison process is repeated. Then, Node F is assigned a permanent label.

Nodes	O*	A*	B*	C*	D*	E	F*	G*	S
$L(6) =$	[0,	827,	759,	800,	1271,	2890,	2127,	1805,	2748]
Preceding Node	—	O	O	O	B	A	D	C	G

Using the permanent label of Node F, the comparison process is repeated. Then, Node E is assigned a permanent label.

Nodes	$\overset{*}{O}$	$\overset{*}{A}$	$\overset{*}{B}$	$\overset{*}{C}$	$\overset{*}{D}$	$\overset{*}{E}$	$\overset{*}{F}$	$\overset{*}{G}$	S
$L(7) =$	[0,	827,	759,	800,	1271,	2415,	2127,	1805,	2465]
Preceding Node	—	O	O	O	B	F	D	C	F

Using the permanent label of Node E, the comparison process is repeated. Then, Node S is assigned a permanent label.

Nodes	$\overset{*}{O}$	$\overset{*}{A}$	$\overset{*}{B}$	$\overset{*}{C}$	$\overset{*}{D}$	$\overset{*}{E}$	$\overset{*}{F}$	$\overset{*}{G}$	$\overset{*}{S}$
$L(8) =$	[0,	827,	759,	800,	1271,	2415,	2127,	1805,	2465]
Preceding Node	—	O	O	O	B	F	D	C	F

We have now labeled the destination (sink) node so that algorithm terminates, and the shortest distance from Node O to Node S is 2465 miles. Actually, we have determined the shortest distance from Node O to every other node in the network since every node was labeled in Step 8.

To determine the sequence of nodes in the shortest route from Node O to Node S, we work backwards from Node S. The "Preceding Node" row can be used in this process. Thus, Node F is the immediate predecessor of Node S. Similarly, Node D precedes Node F, Node B precedes Node D, and the immediate predecessor of Node B is Node O. Therefore, the shortest route from Node O to Node S is $O{\rightarrow}B{\rightarrow}D{\rightarrow}F{\rightarrow}S$, with total distance of 2465 miles.

8.4.4 Applying the Shortest-Route Algorithm to Equipment Replacement

The Backgammon Taxicab Company operates a fleet of taxis in Tempe, Arizona. A small, but aggressive company, it is interested in planning replacements for its taxicab fleet over the next 5 years. It can replace its entire fleet at any point in time during the next 5 years. However, because its cabs receive heavy use, there is an increase in operating and maintenance costs over time. The following chart summarizes the company's estimates of the total net discounted cost of purchasing its cab fleet (purchase price minus trade-in allowance, plus operating and maintenance costs) at the end of year i and selling it at the end of year j. Year 0 represents the current point in time, and all entries are given in thousands of dollars.

Year Purchased, i	Year Sold (j)				
	1	2	3	4	5
0	10	13	15	26	36
1		12	14	20	26 ($,000)
2			10	16	24
3				10	21
4					10

Represents estimated total net discount cost of purchasing a cab fleet at the end of year i & selling at the end of year j.

The company wishes to determine the best time, or times, to replace its cab fleet

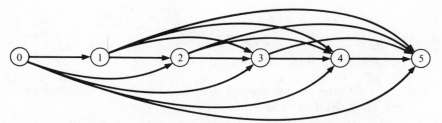

FIGURE 8.14   Shortest-Route Network—Equipment Replacement Problem

over the next 5 years. It wants to make this decision in a manner that minimizes the total net discounted cost of the cab fleet over the 5 years.

This equipment replacement situation can be couched in the form of the shortest-route problem by letting each of the years be the nodes of the network, and by letting the branches between the nodes represent the discounted cost of purchasing the cab fleet at the end of year i and selling the cab fleet at the end of year j. The shortest-route network for the problem can be constructed as shown in Fig. 8.14.

Using Dijkstra's algorithm, the solution to this shortest-route problem is obtained as follows.

Nodes	*0	1	2	3	4	5
$L(0) =$	[0	10	13	15	26	36]
Preceding Node	—	0	0	0	0	0

Nodes	*0	*1	2	3	4	5
$L(1) =$	[0	10	13	15	26	36]
Preceding Node	—	0	0	0	0	0

Nodes	*0	*1	*2	3	4	5
$L(2) =$	[0	10	13	15	26	36]
Preceding Node	—	0	0	0	0	0

Nodes	*0	*1	*2	*3	4	5
$L(3) =$	[0	10	13	15	25	36]
Preceding Node	—	0	0	0	3	0

Nodes	*0	*1	*2	*3	*4	5
$L(4) =$	[0	10	13	15	25	36]
Preceding Node	—	0	0	0	3	0

Nodes	*0	*1	*2	*3	*4	*5
$L(5) =$	[0	10	13	15	25	35]
Preceding Node	—	0	0	0	3	4

Using the "Preceding Node" row, the shortest route can be traced backward from

Node 5. Thus, Node 4 precedes Node 5, Node 3 precedes Node 4, and Node 0 precedes Node 3.

The shortest-route solution to this equipment replacement problem, therefore, indicates that the Backgammon Taxicab Company should buy a new fleet of cabs now, at the end of year 3, and at the end of year 4. This will result in a total minimum net discounted cost of $35,000 for the 5-year planning horizon.

8.5 THE MINIMUM SPANNING TREE PROBLEM

A very interesting variation of the shortest-route problem is known as the **minimum spanning tree problem**. Once again, we are given a network consisting of a set of nodes and branches, with the length of the various branches being known. However, the minimum spanning tree problem involves choosing the branches for the network that have the shortest total length while providing a route between each pair of nodes. In solving this problem, we choose the branches in a manner that the resulting network forms a tree, a connected network containing no cycles, that "spans" (i.e., is connected to) all the nodes of the given network. This spanning tree cannot have any "cycles," or sequences of branches connecting two nodes. In summary, the problem is simply to find the tree that reaches all the nodes of the network with a minimum total branch length.

The minimum spanning tree problem is important in a number of practical situations. Its most important application is in the planning of transportation networks, such as bus or subway systems. In such applications, the nodes of the network are the various terminals or stops and the branches are the distances between the nodes via highways, subway tracks, etc. The problem then, is to specify the transportation lanes that would serve all the terminals in a minimum total distance. Other applications of the minimum spanning tree problem arise in the planning of distribution networks and communication systems.

8.5.1 Solution Procedure for the Minimum Spanning Tree Problem

The minimum spanning tree problem can be solved in a simple, orderly manner. The steps involved in the solution procedure are as follows.

1. Select any node of the network arbitrarily and connect it to its nearest node, that is, choose the shortest possible branch to another node, without worrying about the effect this would have on a later decision.
2. Identify the unconnected node that is closest to a connected node, and then connect these two nodes.
3. Repeat Step 2 until all nodes have been connected.

The resulting network will be a minimal spanning tree.

Ties for the nearest node (Step 1) or for the closest unconnected node (Step 2) can be broken arbitrarily and the solution process will still yield an optimal solution. Such ties indicate that there *may* be multiple optimal solutions to the problem. Such multiple optimal solutions can be identified by tracing out the spanning trees for all possible ways of breaking ties.

We will now illustrate the solution procedure for the minimum spanning tree problem, using a graphical approach. Our illustration will utilize the highway network discussed previously, which is reproduced in Fig. 8.15. Assume that, for the network shown in Fig. 8.15, we are interested in specifying a set of commu-

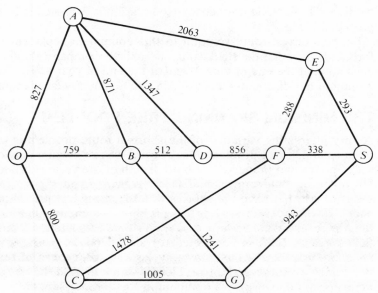

FIGURE 8.15   **Minimum Spanning Tree—Communications Network Example**

nication lines paralleling the branches of this highway network that will connect, or span, all of the nodes. Further assume that any unspecified distances in Fig. 8.15 are greater than the branch distances already shown. For example, no distance is specified for Branch *OE*, but it is assumed that the length of branch *OE* is greater than the lengths of branches *OA*, *OB*, and *OC*, respectively. Using the data summarized in Fig. 8.15, the step-by-step solution of the problem is summarized below.

Arbitrarily select Node *O* (source node) to start. The unconnected node closest to Node *O* is Node *B*. Connect Node *B* to Node *O*.

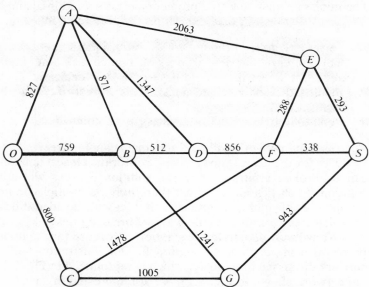

The unconnected node closest to Node O or Node B is Node D (closest to Node B). Connect Node D to Node B.

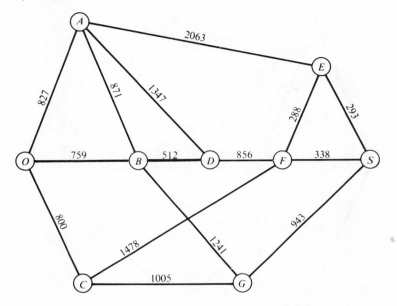

The unconnected node closest to Node O, B, or D is Node C (closest to Node O). Connect Node C to Node O.

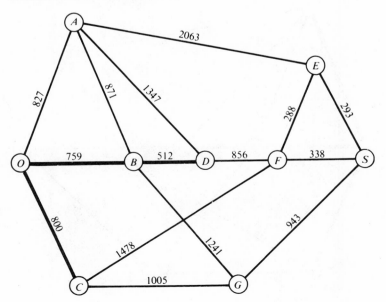

The unconnected node closest to node O, B, C, or D is node A (closest to Node O). Connect Node A to Node O.

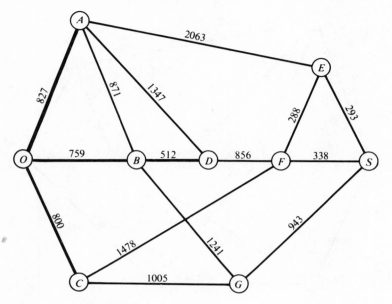

The unconnected node closest to Node O, A, B, C, or D is Node F (closest to Node D). Connect node F to Node D.

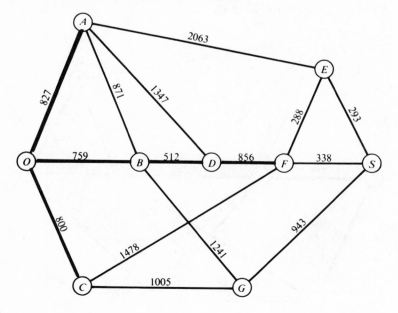

The unconnected node closest to Node O, A, B, C, D, or F is Node E (closest to Node F). Connect Node E to Node F.

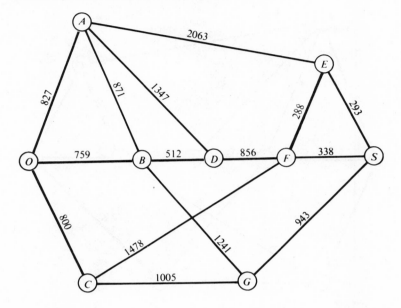

The unconnected node closest to Node O, A, B, C, D, E, or F is Node S (closest to Node E). Connect Node S to Node E.

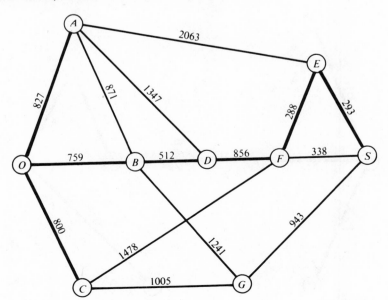

The unconnected node closest to Node O, A, B, C, D, E, F, or S is Node G (closest to Node S). Connect Node G to Node S.

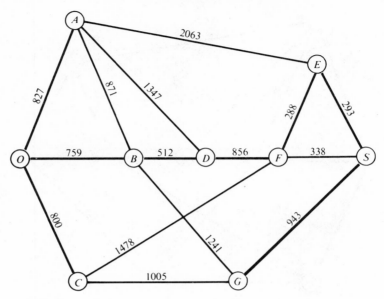

All nodes are now connected, so we have determined the desired solution to the problem. This minimum spanning tree, shown in Fig. 8.16, has a total branch length of 5278 miles.

It may appear that the choice of the starting node will affect the final solution and its total branch length. This does not occur, and it is suggested that the reader verify this fact by reworking the example, using a different starting node.

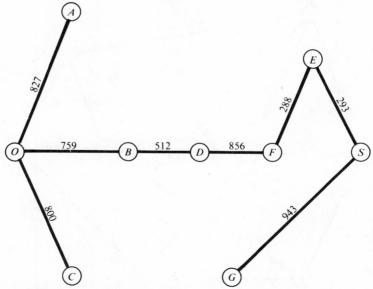

FIGURE 8.16   Minimum Spanning Tree—Communications Network Example

8.6 CRITICAL PATH METHOD (CPM) AND PROGRAM EVALUATION REVIEW TECHNIQUE (PERT)

In recent years, few management tools have been the subject of so many discussions, have had as much publicity, or have been the target for so much scrutiny as have the **Critical Path Method (CPM)** and the **Program Evaluation and Review Technique (PERT)**. The Critical Path Method originated in 1957, when consultants from the Remington Rand UNIVAC Division of the Sperry Rand Corporation were asked by the DuPont Corporation of Wilmington, Delaware, to help devise a scheduling technique to be used in the construction, maintenance, and shutdown of chemical process plants. The Program Evaluation Review Technique was developed in 1958 for the planning and control of the efforts involved in the development of the Fleet Ballistic Missile (Polaris) submarine.

CPM is typically used for construction projects in which a single, or deterministic, time estimate is made for each job or activity. PERT is used for projects that involve research and development work in which the planning effort and the manufacturing of component parts is new and is usually being attempted for the first time. Hence, the time estimates cannot be predicted with certainty, and probabilistic concepts are employed.

8.6.1 Fundamentals of CPM and PERT Networks

A project can be viewed as a group of jobs or operations that are performed in a certain sequence to reach an objective. Each one of the jobs or operations that make up a project is time and resource consuming and is usually referred to as an **activity**. Each activity has a beginning and an end point that are points in time. The points in time are known as **events**, and can be considered as milestones of the project. A mathematical model satisfying the previous definitions can then be visualized as a network in which nodes, corresponding to events, are joined by branches, corresponding to activities. This network thus becomes a convenient method of expressing the sequential nature of the project.

There are several important ground rules connected with the handling of events and activities in a network that should be followed in order to maintain the correct structure for the network. The following rules are most important.

1. Each defined activity is shown by a unique branch.
2. Branches show only the relationship between different activities; the length and bearing of the branches have no significance.
3. Branch direction indicates the general progression in time. The branch head represents the point in time at which an "activity completion event" takes place. In similar manner, the branch tail represents the point in time at which an "activity start event" occurs.
4. When a number of activities terminate at one event, this indicates that no activity starting from that event may start before all activities terminating at this event have been completed.
5. If one event takes precedence over another event that is not connected by a specific activity, a **dummy activity** is used to join the two events. Dummy activities have no duration or cost.
6. Events are identified by numbers. An effort should be made to have each event identified by a number higher than the immediately preceding event.

7. Activities are identified by the numbers of their starting event and ending events.

To illustrate these rules, consider the following examples.

EXAMPLE 1   When an activity is dependent on the completion of many other activities, the network should be structured as follows.

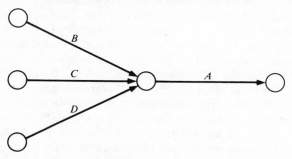

In this situation, Activity A is shown to start only after B, C, and D are completed.

EXAMPLE 2   If the completion of an activity is the milestone for the start of a number of activities, the network model will be shown as follows.

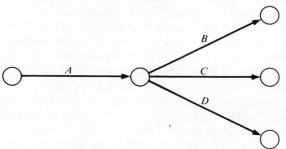

In this situation, B, C, D can start only after the completion of A.

EXAMPLE 3   If two activities in a project must be done concurrently, one way to present these activities would be to join two events by two or more branches corresponding to each activity. However, because all activities are identified by their beginning and ending event number, a dummy activity should be introduced and the ambiguity that would have arisen is eliminated, as follows.

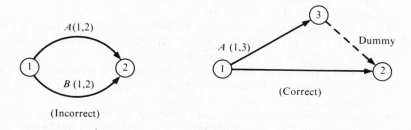

8.6.2 Activity Time Estimating Procedures

As previously mentioned, CPM deals with deterministic situations. Thus, only one time estimate for the completion of an activity is required. PERT is commonly employed for projects having a significant amount of time uncertainty. Herein, three time estimates are employed, as follows.

1. **Optimistic.** An estimate of the *minimum* time an activity will take; a result that will be obtained only if unusually good luck is experienced and everything goes according to plan.
2. **Most likely.** An estimate of the normal time an activity will take; a result that would occur most frequently if the same activity could be repeated a number of times.
3. **Pessimistic.** An estimate of the *maximum* time an activity will take; a result that can occur only if unusually bad luck is experienced. This estimate should reflect the possibility of initial failure and fresh start. However, the possibility of catastrophic events should not be considered unless they are an inherent risk of the activity.

In developing three time estimates for an activity, the statistical judgment of competent personnel should be utilized. The three time estimates are considered to be related in the form of a unimodal probability distribution, with m, the most likely time, being the modal value. Because a, the optimistic time, and b, the pessimistic time, may vary in their relationship to m, this probability distribution may be skewed to the right or to the left. These relationships are shown in Fig. 8.17.

After considerable research into the relationships between these three times, the original research team decided that the **beta distribution** seemed to fit these general properties. Thus, the beta distribution was chosen for determining the *mean* or *expected time*, t_e, and the *standard deviation*, $\sigma_{t,e}$, associated with the three time estimates.

Two basic assumptions are made in order to convert m, a, and b into estimates of the expected value and variance of the elapsed time required by the

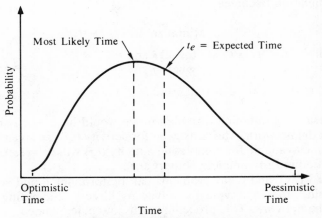

FIGURE 8.17 Probability Distribution of PERT Time Estimates

activity. The first of these assumptions is that $\sigma_{t,e}$, the standard deviation of the elapsed time required by the activity, is equal to one-sixth of the range of reasonably possible time requirements.

$$\sigma^2 = variance \qquad \sigma_{t,e} = \left[\frac{(b-a)}{6}\right] \qquad (8\text{–}10)$$

The underlying rationale for this assumption is that the tails of many probability distributions are known to lie at about three standard deviations from the mean, so that there would be a range of about six standard deviations between the tails.

The second basic assumption is that the activity times are beta distributed, as shown earlier in Fig. 8.17. Under this assumption, the expected activity time can be approximated as:

$$t_e = \frac{1}{6}[a + 4m + b] \qquad (8\text{–}11)$$

This equation is thus used to compute the estimated expected value of the elapsed time required for an activity.

8.6.3 A Linear Programming Formulation of a PERT/CPM Problem

Both PERT and CPM can be used to analyze project management problems. In a typical project management problem, the completion time of all project activities and the sequence in which they must be done is known. The manager is usually concerned with determining the minimum time in which the project can be completed, and with identifying the crucial jobs that can delay the entire project.

A project management problem can also be considered as a network problem that can be formulated in a linear programming format. Consider such a project network and let t_i represent the time at which event i occurs, where $i = 1, 2, 3, \ldots, N$. Thus, $(t_N - t_1)$ represents the time of completion of the entire project, and the objective is to minimize this time period. Further, let t_{ij} represent the time required to complete the activity between event i and event j. The linear programming formulation becomes

$$\text{Minimize } Z = (t_N - t_1) \qquad (8\text{–}12)$$

subject to: $\qquad t_j - t_i \geq t_{ij} \qquad$ for all i and j
$$\text{where } j > i \qquad (8\text{–}13)$$

with $\qquad t_i \geq 0, t_j \geq 0 \qquad$ for all i and j $\qquad (8\text{–}14)$

In this linear programming formulation we would have one constraint for every activity in the network. The constraint for activity (i,j), as given by (8–13) ensures that the time available for completing activity (i,j) will be greater than or equal to the time required to complete activity (i,j).

While PERT and CPM problems can be formulated and solved using linear programming, they are typically solved by directly computing the longest time path for the network. This procedure will now be explained.

8.6.4 Slack and Critical Path Concepts

Once time estimates have been made, the actual method of calculating the longest, or **critical path**, is the same for either PERT or CPM. To illustrate, consider the simple network shown in Fig. 8.18, where the numbers along the branches indicate the expected values of the elapsed times for the various activities. From this network, using our previous definitions, it is evident that events C and D cannot occur any earlier than 5 and 13 months hence, respectively, but that activity BC can be delayed 1 month without delaying events C and D. For any particular event, its **earliest time** T_E may be defined as the time at which the event will occur if the preceding activities are started as early as possible. Thus, the earliest times for events A, B, C, and D are 0, 0, 5, and 13, respectively. Similarly, the **latest time** for an event, T_L, may be defined as the latest time at which the event can occur without delaying the completion of the project beyond its earliest time. Consequently, the latest times for events A, B, C, and D are 0, 1, 5, and 13, respectively. Now, the slack concept defines the **slack** S for an event as the difference between its latest time and earliest time, $S = T_L - T_E$. Thus, the slacks for events A, B, C, and D are 0, 1, 0, 0, respectively. The slack value indicates how much delay in reaching an event can be tolerated without delaying project completion.

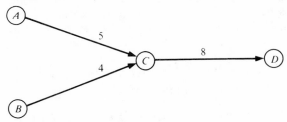

FIGURE 8.18 A Simple Network

When project activities are plotted according to the branch-diagramming technique described in the previous section, there can be numerous paths existing between the "start" and "end" of a project network. By adding the duration of all the various activities forming a path, various "durations for project completion" are obtained. The longest of these durations is the critical time for project completion, and the path associated with it is the *critical path*. Thus, the critical path controls the project completion time.

The critical path for the project can be defined as the path through the network defined such that the events on this path have zero slack. In the example above, the critical path is $A \rightarrow C \rightarrow D$. It is important to note that, in determining the critical path for the network, we are not optimizing anything. Rather, we are simply identifying the set of branches (activities) of the network that are most critical in terms of the time required for the project's completion.

8.6.5 A PERT Example

The concepts outlined above will now be utilized in the analysis of a simple PERT network. A typical PERT network is shown below in Fig. 8.19, with three time estimates given for each activity.

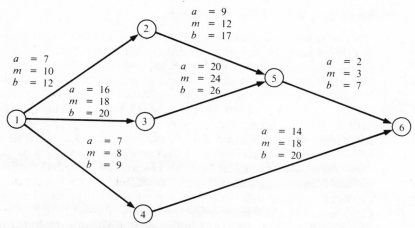

FIGURE 8.19   PERT Network Example

The input information required for the PERT analysis is contained in Fig. 8.19. Table 8.4 exhibits results obtained from the computation of the expected value, standard deviation, and variance of the elapsed times required by the various activities of this network. Determination of the values of t_e and $\sigma_{t,e}$ in Table 8.4 was done using Equations 8-10 and 8-11. For example, the PERT distribution parameters for Activity 1,2 were computed as follows.

$$t_{e;1,2} = \text{}^1/_6[a + 4m + b] = \text{}^1/_6[7 + 4 \cdot 10 + 12] = \text{}^{59}/_6 = 9.83$$

$$\sigma_{t_{e;1,2}} = \text{}^1/_6[b - a] = \text{}^1/_6[12 - 7] = \text{}^5/_6 = 0.83 \tag{8–15}$$

$$\sigma^2_{t_{e;1,2}} = [\text{}^1/_6(b - a)]^2 = [\text{}^5/_6]^2 = \text{}^{25}/_{36} = 0.69$$

The information shown in Table 8.4 can now be used to derive output information for the PERT network. This output information is shown in Table 8.5.

The derivation of the information shown in Table 8.5 will now be explained. First, it is assumed that the elapsed times for the individual activities of the network are statistically independent. This assumption is reasonable because the activities are themselves independent, each having a definite starting and ending point. The use of this assumption facilitates the computation of the mean and

TABLE 8.4   Computation of PERT Network Parameters

Activities		Time Estimates			Expected Elapsed Time, t_e	Std. Dev. $\sigma_{t,e}$	Variance $\sigma^2_{t,e}$
Predecessor Event	Successor Event	a	m	b			
1	2	7	10	12	9.83	0.83	0.69
1	3	16	18	20	18.00	0.67	0.45
1	4	7	8	9	8.00	0.33	0.11
2	5	9	12	17	12.33	1.33	1.77
3	5	20	24	26	23.67	1.00	1.00
4	6	14	18	20	17.67	1.00	1.00
5	6	2	3	7	3.50	0.83	0.69

TABLE 8.5   Output Information for the PERT Network

Event Number	Earliest Time, T_E		Latest Time, T_L		Slack $(T_L - T_E)$
	Expected Value	Variance	Expected Value	Variance	
1	0	0	0	2.14	0
2	9.83	0.69	29.34	2.46	+19.50
3	18.00	0.45	18.00	1.69	0
4	8.00	0.11	27.50	1.00	+19.50
5	41.67	1.45	41.67	0.69	0
6	45.17	2.14	45.17	0	0

variance of the earliest and latest times for the various events in the network that require the completion of two or more activities. For example, if there is only one path to an event in the network, it is evident from our earlier definition that the earliest time for the event is simply the sum of the estimated elapsed times of the activities leading to the event. For this case, the expected value and the expected variance of the earliest time are the sum of the expected values and the sum of the variances, respectively, of these activity time estimates. Similarly, the definition of latest time implies that, if there is only one path leading from a particular event to a terminal event, then the latest time for that event is the expected earliest time for the terminal event minus the sum of the elapsed times of the activities on the path back to the event under consideration. For this case, the expected value of the latest time would be the expected earliest time for the terminal event minus the sum of the expected values of the activity times along the path back to the event under consideration. The variance of the latest time will be the sum of the variances of the times of the activities from this terminal event back to the event under consideration.

To illustrate, consider the simple network shown in Fig. 8.20 having only a single path. In this network the expected value and variance of the earliest time for Event 4 are $(2 + 6 + 3) = 11$ and $(1 + 3 + 2) = 6$, respectively. The expected value and variance of the latest time for Event 3 are $(12 - 1 - 3) = 8$ and $(1 + 2) = 3$, respectively.

Unfortunately, difficulties arise when there is more than one path leading to an event. For example, in Fig. 8.19 there are two paths leading to Event 5. These paths are $1 \rightarrow 2 \rightarrow 5$ and $1 \rightarrow 3 \rightarrow 5$. The earliest time for Event 5, in this case, is the maximum of the total elapsed time along these two paths. In general, it is very difficult to find the *exact* expected value and variance for the maximum of the total elapsed times along multiple paths. Thus, a simplifying approximation is used in which it is assumed that the largest total elapsed time *always* occurs on the path with the largest *expected* total elapsed time. In our example above, the expected total elapsed time on Path $1 \rightarrow 2 \rightarrow 5$ is $(9.83 + 12.33) = 22.16$, and on Path $1 \rightarrow 3 \rightarrow 5$ is $(18.00 + 23.67) = 41.67$. Thus, Path $1 \rightarrow 3 \rightarrow 5$ has the largest value 41.67, and it is assumed that the largest total elapsed time occurs along this path.

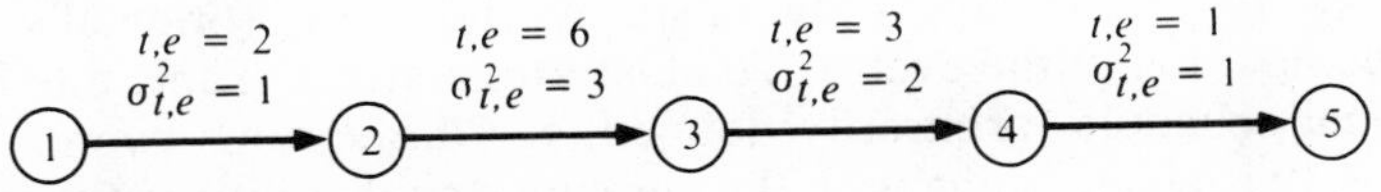

FIGURE 8.20   One-Path Network

It then follows that the expected value and variance of the total elapsed time for Event 5 are the expected value and variance of the total elapsed time along this path, $(18.00 + 23.67) = 41.67$ and $(0.45 + 1.00) = 1.45$, respectively.

When there is more than one path leading back to an event, the expected values and variances of the latest times are computed exactly as before for the single path case, with the exception that the simplifying assumption described above is used to determine the largest total elapsed time from the terminal event back to the event in question. For example, in Fig. 8.19 there are three paths leading from the terminal event, Event 6, back to the starting event, Event 1. The latest time for Event 1, in this case, is the minimum of expected earliest time for Event 6 minus the total elapsed times along the three paths back to event. The expected latest time for Event 1 is determined as follows.

Path	Expected Latest Time (Event 1)		
$6 \rightarrow 5 \rightarrow 2 \rightarrow 1$	$45.17 - 3.50 - 12.33 - 9.83 = 19.51$		
$6 \rightarrow 5 \rightarrow 3 \rightarrow 1$	$45.17 - 3.50 - 23.67 - 18.00 = 0.00$	(Minimum)	(8–16)
$6 \rightarrow 4 \rightarrow 1$	$45.17 - 17.67 - 8.00 = 19.50$		

The variance of the expected latest time for Event 1 is the sum of the variances along Path $6 \rightarrow 5 \rightarrow 3 \rightarrow 1$, namely $(0.69 + 1.00 + 0.45) = 2.14$. Note that the use of the simplification of considering only the path with the largest expected total elapsed time leading to (or from) the event has reduced the multiple-path problem to the one-path problem considered earlier.

Once the expected values for the earliest and latest times for the various events have been computed, the slacks for the events can be computed as the expected latest time minus the expected earliest time. These slacks are shown in Table 8.5, and the path having zero slack, $1 \rightarrow 3 \rightarrow 5 \rightarrow 6$, is immediately identified as the critical path.

8.6.6 Using the Output from a PERT Network Analysis

The output information from the PERT network can be utilized in a number of ways. For example, assume that we had established an original time schedule for the activities and events shown in Fig. 8.19. It is then possible to utilize the output information given in Table 8.5 to compute the probability of meeting the original schedule for the events in the network. This can be done in the following manner. First, the probability distribution of the earliest time must be specified, and under the PERT procedure this distribution is assumed to be normal. This assumption is a reasonable one, since the earliest time is the sum of many random variables, and under the Central Limit Theorem of classical probability theory, the distribution of the sum of independent variables (not necessarily randomly distributed) tends toward normality. From our computation of the output information for the PERT network, we know the values of the mean and variance of the earliest time. It is then a straightforward procedure to find the probability that a random variable (earliest time) will be less than a specified quantity (originally scheduled time for the completion of the event). To illustrate, consider Table 8.6, below, in which an original schedule (arbitrarily defined) for the various events of the network of Fig. 8.19 is given, along with the computed probabilities of meeting this schedule. For clarity we have also included the computed earliest times and their associated

TABLE 8.6   Probability of Meeting Schedule

| Event | Earliest Time, T_E | | T_S, Original Schedule | Probability of Meeting Schedule |
	Expected Value	Variance		
1	0	0	0	—
2	9.83	0.69	9	0.1587
3	18.00	0.45	17	0.0681
4	8.00	0.11	9	1.0000
5	41.67	1.45	42	0.6079
6	45.17	2.14	44	0.2119

variances for the various events from Table 8.5. To illustrate how the probabilities shown in Table 8.6 were computed, consider Event 2. Let $T_{E,2}$ be the earliest time for Event 2 and let $T_{S,2}$ be the originally scheduled time for Event 2. Then,

$$\text{Probability (meeting original schedule)} = P\,(T_{S,2} \le 9) \qquad (8\text{--}17)$$

To obtain this probability using a standardized normal table, we must compute

$$\text{Probability (meeting original schedule)} = P\!\left(Z \le \frac{T_{S,2} - T_{E,2}}{\sigma_{T_{E,2}}}\right) \qquad (8\text{--}18)$$

where Z is a standard normal deviate.

This probability is the cross-hatched area shown in Fig. 8.21.

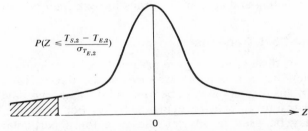

FIGURE 8.21   Probability (Meeting Original Schedule)

Using the numerical data shown in Table 8.5, this probability is computed as:

$$
\begin{aligned}
\text{Probability} \\
\text{(meeting original schedule)} &= P\!\left(Z \le \frac{9.00 - 9.83}{\sqrt{0.69}}\right) \\
&= P\!\left(Z \le \frac{-0.83}{0.83}\right) = P(Z \le -1.00) \\
&\doteq 0.1587
\end{aligned}
\qquad (8\text{--}19)
$$

The probabilities associated with meeting the scheduled times for other events in this network are computed similarly and are summarized in the final column of Table 8.6.

From the output information presented in Table 8.5, we readily identified the critical path by tracing through the events with zero slack. If we think of the expected elapsed times of the activities as distances, the critical path for the network can be interpreted as its longest route. Identification of the critical path of the network is of obvious significance, since we must put top priority on the activities along this path in order to reach the terminal event by its expected date. If any event on this path slips beyond its expected date of completion, then the terminal event will slip likewise by the same amount.

If the expected earliest time of the terminal event is not satisfactory, then we must concentrate our efforts on activities along the critical path. Note that events not on the critical path have positive slack, so that minor variances from the expected dates for accomplishing these events probably will not alter the project's critical path or completion date. Thus, we can often **crash activities** along the critical path by reassigning some of the manpower from activities not on the critical path (assuming transference of labor skills). For example, in our example, we could theoretically transfer up to 19.5 units of work force from Path $1\rightarrow2\rightarrow5$ to the Critical Path $1\rightarrow3\rightarrow5\rightarrow6$.

PERT has most often been used as a project-control device in which an attempt is made to review the project's status on a regular basis, as it moves to completion. Herein, PERT has proved to be very valuable in measuring and evaluating the current status of the project, and in determining the effect of a proposed change or the consequences of a slip in schedule. In most projects involving large networks, the PERT computations have been computerized in order to reduce the time required for the repetitious and somewhat tedious PERT calculations. Finally, it should be noted that there have been both successes and failures attributed to the application of PERT. Many of the failures can be attributed to the fact that PERT was sometimes poorly understood and misapplied to the vital planning and control functions for extremely costly projects.

8.6.7 Making Time-Cost Tradeoffs

In our previous discussion we have assumed that the time associated with completing an activity in a network was essentially fixed. However, it should be apparent that this may not always be true and the manager may have the ability to assign more resources to a particular activity. For example, more workers or overtime may be used to shorten the time for a particular project activity. Decreasing the project activity time will usually be accompanied by an increase in the activity cost, and thus, we must consider how to make appropriate time-cost tradeoffs.

To illustrate the procedure used in analyzing time-cost tradeoffs consider the home repair activity network shown in Fig. 8.22. Each of the activities within this network may be done in a regular manner, or on a "crash" basis involving overtime. The activity times (in weeks) and the activity costs for the regular and crash programs are shown in Table 8.7. For this activity network, the critical path is $1\rightarrow2\rightarrow5\rightarrow7$ and has a length of 8 weeks, under the assumption that regular programs are used for each activity. The total cost for the home repair job, using the activity costs in the regular program column is $3225.

Assume now that the homeowner decides that 8 weeks is too long for the home repair job and wishes to shorten it to 6 weeks or less by using overtime labor. Observe first that those activities that are not on the critical path already have slack time associated with their completion. Thus, there is no need to try to

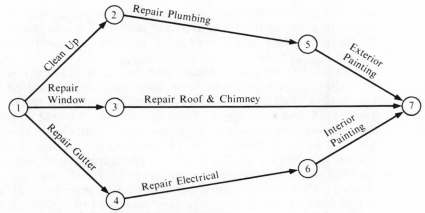

FIGURE 8.22   Home Repair Activity Network

hasten the completion time for these activities, since this would have no effect on the total time required for the home repair project's completion. This means that the homeowner needs only to consider those activities on the critical path since shortening any of these activities will shorten the total project time.

The three critical path activities, their incremental time savings, and incremental cost increases are shown in Table 8.8. From Table 8.8 it is apparent that the activity that can be shortened in the cheapest manner is activity $1\rightarrow2$ at an incremental cost of $150 per week. This would reduce the total project completion time to $8 - \frac{1}{2} = 7\frac{1}{2}$ weeks, at a total project cost of $3225 + $75 = $3300. Note that the critical path is still $1\rightarrow2\rightarrow5\rightarrow7$.

TABLE 8.7   Activity Times and Activity Costs

	Activity Time		Activity Cost	
Activity	Regular	Crash	Regular	Crash
$1\rightarrow2$	2	$1\frac{1}{2}$	200	275
$1\rightarrow3$	1	$\frac{1}{2}$	150	200
$1\rightarrow4$	1	$\frac{1}{2}$	175	250
$2\rightarrow5$	3	2	750	1000
$3\rightarrow7$	3	2	600	700
$4\rightarrow6$	2	1	500	650
$5\rightarrow7$	3	$1\frac{1}{2}$	500	1200
$6\rightarrow7$	2	1	350	400

TABLE 8.8   Incremental Time Savings and Cost Increases

Activity	Weeks Shortened by Crash Program	Incremental Cost of Crash Program ($)	Incremental Cost per Week ($)
$1\rightarrow2$	$\frac{1}{2}$	75	150
$2\rightarrow5$	1	250	250
$5\rightarrow7$	$1\frac{1}{2}$	700	467

Since the homeowner wishes to reduce the home repair project completion time to less than 6 weeks he would next put activity 2→5 on the crash program. This would reduce the total project completion time to $7\frac{1}{2} - 1 = 6\frac{1}{2}$ weeks, at a total project cost of $3300 + $250 = $3550.

Continuing the time reduction process, he would next attempt to put activity 5→7 on the crash program. Now, however, there would be two critical paths (1→4→6→7 and 1→2→5→7), both with a length of 5 weeks, since if activities 1→2; 2→5; and 5→7 are all crashed, 1→2→5→7 would take only 5 weeks. The total project cost associated with the crashed critical path (1→2→5→7) would be $3225 + $75 + $250 + $700 = $4250. Note further that it would no longer be necessary to have 1→2, 2→5, and 5→7 on a crash basis, since this would reduce the total project completion time to 5 weeks, which is below the 6 weeks minimum required. Thus, after deciding that activity 5→7 must be crashed, the homeowner would need to review activities 1→2 and 2→5 to see which of these activities could be put back on a regular program. If activities 1→2 and 5→7 are crashed, and activity 2→5 is not, then 1→2→5→7 would take 6 weeks at a cost of $3225 + $75 + $700 = $4000. If activities 2→5 and 5→7 are crashed, and activity 1→2 is not, then 1→2→5→7 would take $5\frac{1}{2}$ weeks at a cost of $3225 + $250 + $700 = $4175.

Since the time-cost tradeoff analysis has reduced the critical path to 6 weeks, which equals the 6 weeks maximum desired by the homeowner, no further activities would be crashed. However, this example should make apparent some of the complexities involved in analyzing time-cost tradeoffs. For example, were this analysis to proceed it would be necessary to consider crashing activities along both current critical paths (i.e., along 1→2→5→7 and along 1→4→6→7).

In Fig. 8.23 we have summarized the results of our time-cost tradeoff analysis. The time-cost tradeoff curve shown in Fig. 8.23 indicates the costs to the homeowner associated with the various project completion times.

8.7 CONCLUSION

In this chapter we have considered a group of problems that can be analyzed by constructing a network. Network problems arise in a wide variety of business decision making situations, including the planning of transportation and distribution systems, the structuring of flow systems such as pipelines, and the specification of terminals in a mass transit system. For three of these network problems, namely the maximum-flow problem, the shortest-route problem, and the minimum spanning tree problem, we developed and applied algorithms that were based on the unique structures of these particular problems.

In the final portion of this chapter we considered the planning and control of network projects using either the Critical Path Method (CPM) or the Program Evaluation Review Technique (PERT). Herein, we developed procedures that allowed the identification of the tasks that must be completed on schedule if the entire project is to be completed on schedule, and indicated how progress on the project could be reviewed. Furthermore, we studied how various activities within the project could be crashed, or completed in less time, and determined a procedure for evaluating the various time-cost tradeoffs possible in such networks. Our orientation in this area of study was toward overall project control rather than toward optimization with respect to some particular feature of the network.

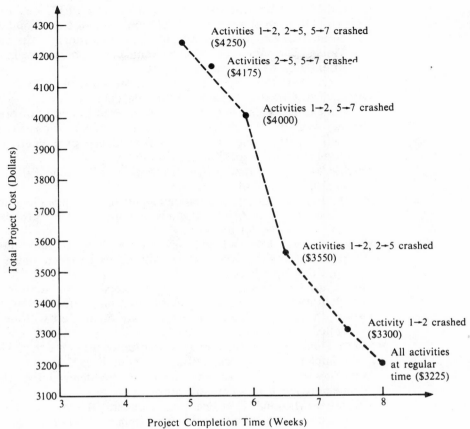

FIGURE 8.23   Time-cost Tradeoffs

GLOSSARY OF TERMS

Activity   In graph theory terminology an activity is simply a branch or connector between the nodes of the network; in PERT/CPM terminology an activity is one of the jobs or operations that makes up a project and consumes time and resources.

Beta Distribution   A continuous probability distribution used to describe the distribution of PERT time estimates.

Branch   A line connecting junction points in a graph.

Chain   A sequence of connecting branches between nodes i and j.

Connected Graph   A graph in which there is a path connecting every pair of nodes in the graph.

CPM (Critical Path Method)   A network procedure typically used for construction projects in which a single, or deterministic, time estimate is made for each job or activity.

"Crash" Activities   Reassigning some of the manpower from activities not on the critical path to activities on the critical path (assuming transference of labor skills).

Critical Path   The "longest" path in a CPM or PERT network.

Cut   A collection of oriented branches in a network such that every oriented path from source to sink contains at least one branch in the cut.

Cut Value   The sum of the flow capacities of the branches, in the direction of the orientation designated by the cut.

Cycle   A chain that begins and ends at the same node.

Directed or Oriented Branch   A branch characterized by a sense of direction indicating which node is to be considered the point of origin.

Dummy Activity   An activity that has no duration or cost, which is used to join two events if one event takes precedence over another event and is not connected by a specific activity.

Earliest Time   The time at which the event will occur if the preceding activities are started as early as possible.

Event   In graph theory terminology an event is simply a junction point or node of the network; in PERT/CPM terminology an event is the beginning or ending point, in time, for an activity.

Expected Time   In PERT, the mean of the optimistic time, most likely time, and pessimistic time where the relationship between these time estimates is specified by a beta distribution.

Flow Capacity   The upper limit to the feasible magnitude of the rate (or total quantity) of flow in the branch in that direction.

Graph   A set of *nodes* or *events* that are connected with certain pairs of lines called *branches* or *activities*.

Latest Time   The latest time at which the event can occur without delaying the completion of the project beyond its earliest time.

Max Flow–Min Cut Theorem   A method for determining when optimality has been reached in a network problem.

Maximum-(Maximal) Flow Problem   Concerns the maximum amount of flow that can enter into and exit from some connected network during a given period of time.

Minimum Spanning Tree Problem   Involves choosing the branches for the network that have the shortest total length while providing a route between each pair of nodes.

Most Likely Time   In PERT, an estimate of the normal time an activity will take.

Network   A graph with flow of some type between its nodes through its branches.

Node   A junction point in a graph.

Optimistic Time   In PERT, an estimate of the minimum time an activity will take.

Path   A chain between two nodes that has a direction of travel, or flow, attributed to it.

PERT (Program Evaluation Review Technique)   A project-scheduling network technique typically employed in research and development work in which a probabilistic time estimate is made for each job or activity.

Pessimistic Time   In PERT, an estimate of the maximum time an activity will take.

Shortest-Route Problem   Involves the determination of the minimum total distance from the origin to the destination in a network.

Slack   The slack for an event is the difference between its latest and earliest times; it indicates how much delay in reaching an event can be tolerated without delaying project completion.

Time-Cost Tradeoff Curve   Indicates the costs of a project associated with various project completion times.

Trees   An undirected, connected graph that contains no cycles.

SELECTED REFERENCES

NETWORK MODELS

Antill, James M., and Ronald Woodhead. 1970. *Critical Path Methods in Construction Practice*. New York: John Wiley-Interscience.

Archibald, Russell D., and Richard L. Villoria. 1967. *Network-Based Management Systems (PERT/CPM)*. New York: John Wiley & Sons, Inc.

Battersby, Albert. 1970. *Network Analysis for Planning and Scheduling*. New York: John Wiley & Sons, Inc.

Busacker, Robert G., and Thomas L. Saaty. 1960. *Finite Graphs and Networks: An Introduction with Applications*: New York: McGraw-Hill Book Company.

Conway, R. W., W. L. Maxwell, and L. W. Miller. 1967. *Theory of Scheduling*. Reading, Mass.: Addison-Wesley Publishing Co., Inc.

Elmaghraby, Salah E. 1970. *Some Network Models in Management Science*. Berlin; New York: Springer-Verlag.

Evarts, H. F. 1964. *Introduction to PERT*. Boston, Mass.: Allyn & Bacon, Inc.

Ford, Lester R., and Delbert R. Fulkerson. 1962. *Flows in Networks*. Princeton, New Jersey: Princeton University Press.

Frank, Howard, and Ivan T. Frisch, 1971. *Communication, Transmission and Transportation Networks*. Reading, Mass.: Addison-Wesley Publishing Co., Inc.

Hu, Te Chiang. 1969. *Integer Programming and Network Flows*. Reading, Mass.: Addison-Wesley Publishing Co., Inc.

Martino, R. L. 1970. *Critical Path Networks*. New York: McGraw-Hill Book Company.

Miller, Robert Wallace. 1963. *Schedule, Cost and Profit Control with PERT: A Comprehensive Guide for Program Management*. New York: McGraw-Hill Book Company.

Moder, Joseph J., and Cecil R. Phillips. 1970. *Project Management with CPM and PERT*. New York: D. Van Nostrand Company.

Riggs, James L., and Charles O. Heath. 1966. *Guide to Cost Reduction Through Critical Path Scheduling*. Englewood Cliffs, New Jersey: Prentice-Hall, Inc.

Wiest, J., and F. Levy, 1969. *A Management Guide to PERT-CPM*. Englewood Cliffs, New Jersey: Prentice-Hall, Inc.

DISCUSSION QUESTIONS

1. Why does the solution procedure for the maximum flow problem work with "net" flows to obtain an optimal solution?
2. How is the max cut–min flow theorem used?
3. What do we mean by "convergence" of the shortest-route algorithm?
4. What is the difference between the solution procedure of the shortest-route problem and the minimum spanning tree problem?
5. Is the solution procedure of the minimum spanning tree problem dependent on the choice of the starting node? Is this same question also relevant for the shortest-route problem? Why or why not?
6. What is the basic difference in assumptions between CPM and PERT?
7. When are "dummy" activities used and why are they used?
8. What are the two basic assumptions underlying the "expected time" estimate?

9. Would the "slack" concept be relevant in CPM? Why or why not?
10. How does the assumption of statistically independent activities facilitate the computation of the mean and variance of the earliest and latest times for the various events in the network that require the completion of two or more activities?
11. Describe briefly how you find the critical path. What assumption is made with respect to the "largest total elapsed time"?
12. Why is identification of the critical path so important?
13. What do we mean by "crashing" activities? When would you want to crash an activity?
14. What "time-cost tradeoff" might there exist in a PERT network? Can this tradeoff also occur in CPM? Why or why not?

PROBLEM SET

1.   For the following pipeline network, find the maximum oil flow from the source to the sink, given that the flow capacity from node i to node j is the number along branch (i, j) nearest node i.

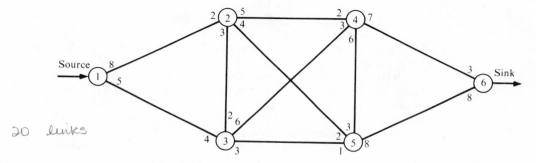

20 links

2.   For the following highway network, find the maximum vehicle flow from the source to the sink, given that the flow capacity from node i to node j is the number along branch (i, j) nearest node i.

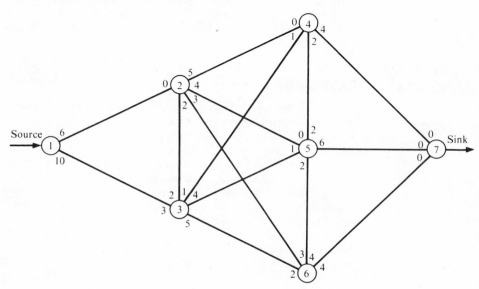

3. For the following pipeline network, find the maximum natural gas flow from the source to the sink, given that the flow capacity from node i to node j is the number along branch (i, j) nearest node i.

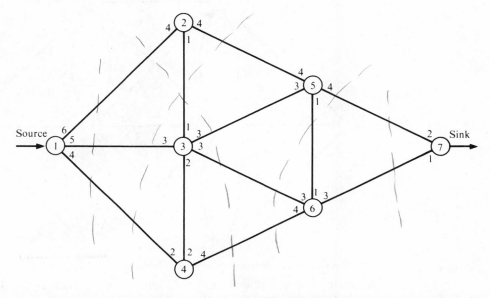

4. For the following electrical transmission network, find the maximum energy flow from the source to the sink, given that the flow capacity from node i to node j is the number along branch (i, j) nearest node i.

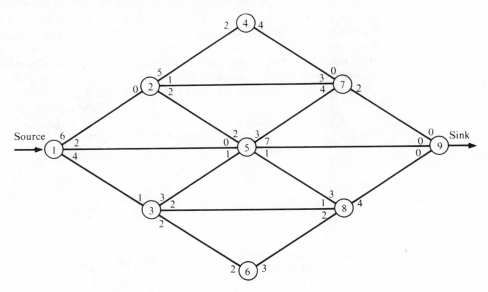

5. Eight Flags Over Arizona is attempting to plan a system of tramways for its proposed amusement park to be built in Apache Junction, Arizona. It has a single entrance and a single exit to and from the park. There are six major amusement

areas within the park. Potential flow capacities for the tramways are determined and structured in terms of the following network.

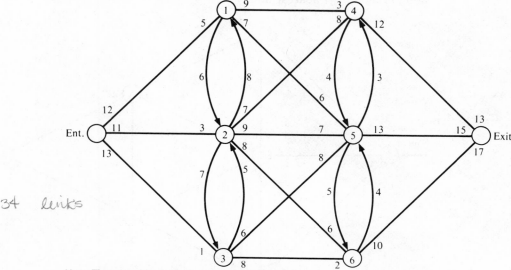

Note: Flow capacities are in thousands of persons per hour.

34 links

Determine the size (capacities) of tramways to be built to maximize the flow of people from the entrance to the exit. Specify the maximum flow.

6. The Arabco Oil conglomerate has a network of pipelines and intermediate storage facilities connecting its oil field in Northern Iraq to its oil refinery in Baghdad. Crude oil can be pumped from the oil field to any of three major intermediate storage facilities A, B, and C. The maximum capacity of each of the connecting pipelines from the field to A, B, and C is 20, 15, and 22 (thousand) barrels of oil per day, respectively. Oil can be pumped from these major intermediate facilities to other facilities and, finally, to the refinery. The pipeline branches comprising this network and their maximum flow capacities are given below. Determine the maximum flow from the oil field to the refinery.

field → A 20
→ B 15
↘ C 22

10 nodes
17 links

field = 1

A = 2
B = 3
C = 4
D = 5
E = 6
F = 7
G = 8
H = 9
Refinery = 10

Branches	Maximum Flow Capacity (thousand barrels)
$A \rightarrow B$	12
$A \rightarrow D$	18
$B \rightarrow D$	20
$B \rightarrow E$	20
$C \rightarrow B$	5
$C \rightarrow F$	18
$D \rightarrow G$	14
$D \rightarrow E$	10
$E \rightarrow G$	25
$E \rightarrow F$	5
$F \rightarrow H$	20
$G \rightarrow$ Refinery	30
$G \rightarrow H$	10
$H \rightarrow$ Refinery	25

7.   Determine the maximum flow for the following network.

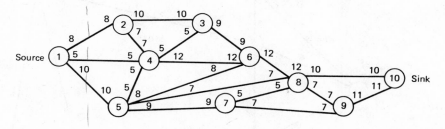

8.   The Sydney Zoo has decided to sell Beargrass Zoo a number of koala bears. The koala bears cannot be shipped directly to Beargrass Zoo but instead will be shipped first to one or more of three intermediate destinations. Six koala bears can be shipped by commercial jet from Sydney to intermediate Location 1; 2 koala bears can be shipped from Sydney to intermediate Location 2; and 3 koala bears can be shipped from Sydney Zoo to Location 3 by private aircraft. From intermediate Location 1 to intermediate Location 3, 2 koalas can be transferred by train. From intermediate Location 2 to intermediate Location 1, 4 koalas can be transferred by truck. From Locations 1, 2, and 3 to Beargrass Zoo, 5, 1, and 4 koalas respectively can be shipped by train. Determine the maximum number of koalas that can be transferred from Sydney Zoo to Beargrass Zoo in a 24-hour period.

9.   Find the shortest route for the following highway network, where the distances shown are in hundreds of miles.

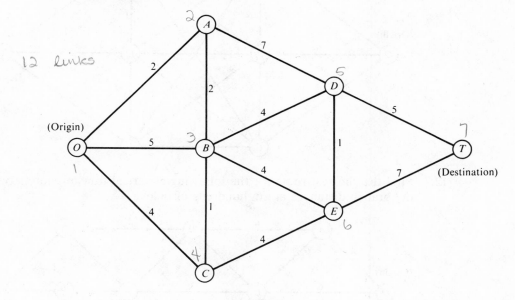

10. A hiker wishes to hike through a national park in as few days as possible. Possible branches between various ranger stations in this park are shown in the following network (branch numbers represent number of days required to hike between nodes of that branch). What route should be taken to minimize travel time?

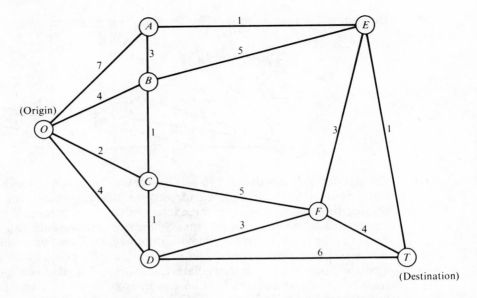

11. Find the shortest route for the following railroad network, where the branch distances are in hundreds of mile.

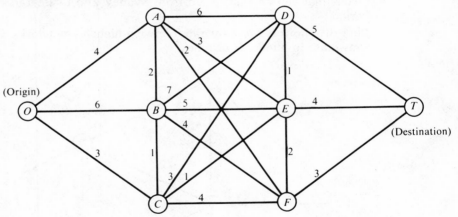

12. Find the shortest route for the following electrical transmission network, where the branch distances are in hundreds of miles.

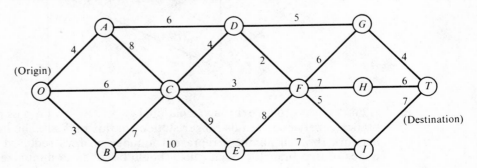

13. The Flying Horse Commuter Airline Company operates a fleet of small airplanes to provide commuter flights between a number of small Midwestern cities. The flight distances between these cities are shown below.

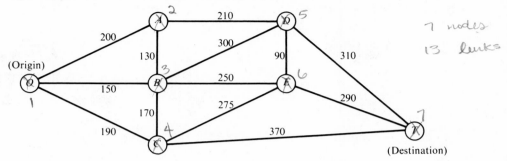

Find the shortest route from the origin to the destination.

14. The city of Metro has a comprehensive monorail system that connects eight of its major shopping areas as well as its two main cultural centers. Each monocab is assigned a round-trip route between two of the centers; every 5 minutes a monocab departs from one center to another. A one-way monorail trip between two centers averages 20 minutes. Determine the minimum route from the east side of Metro (Center 1) to the west side of Metro (Center 10) given the following list of Metro's mono-routes and the associated distances.

Mono-Route Connection	Distance (miles)
Center 1 to Center 2	1.0
Center 1 to Center 4	2.0
Center 1 to Center 5	5.5
Center 2 to Center 4	1.2
Center 2 to Center 3	1.5
Center 3 to Center 4	1.8
Center 3 to Center 6	2.2
Center 4 to Center 5	3.5
Center 4 to Center 6	2.5
Center 5 to Center 6	2.0
Center 5 to Center 7	1.2
Center 5 to Center 8	4.0
Center 6 to Center 8	3.5
Center 7 to Center 8	1.5
Center 7 to Center 9	2.0
Center 8 to Center 9	3.3
Center 8 to Center 10	2.5
Center 9 to Center 10	1.5

15. Using the flows capacities specified in Problem 6 as distances, determine the shortest route from the oil field to the refinery.

16. Beargrass Zoo has a network of paths that gives animal lovers easy access to all of the exhibits and also serves to connect 11 information and refreshment centers. A member of the Beargrass staff is stationed at each center to answer any questions

the public may have. The distances (in miles) between the centers is indicated on the paths in the diagram below. Determine the minimum-distance route from the entrance to the exit.

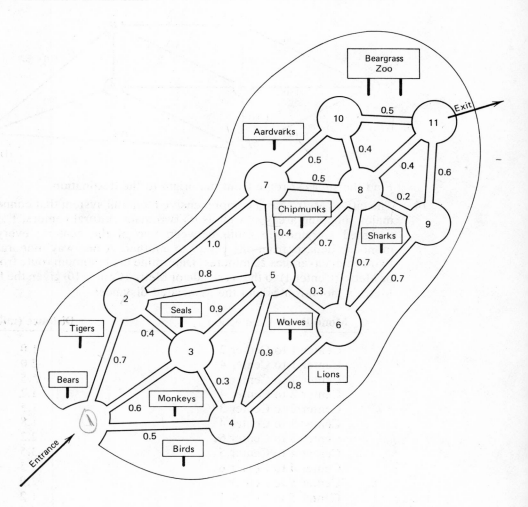

17. A Midwestern company which owns and manages a chain of automatic car washes is considering the replacement of the conveyor mechanisms in its car washes. It anticipates completely remodeling its car washes in 3 years, so the conveyor systems will not be needed after that time (i.e., the conveyor systems will be replaced by belt systems). However, because the car washes receive heavy usage, it still may be economical to repair the conveyor systems after 1 or 2 years. The following table indicates the total net discounted cost associated with purchasing the conveyor systems (purchase price minus salvage value, plus running and maintenance costs) at the end of year i and salvaging them at the end of year j (where year 0 is now).

	j			
i	2	3	4	
0 1	5	9	17	
1 2		6	12	($,000)
2 3			7	

4 nodes
6 links

What is the best repair plan?

18. The Parks and Recreation Department of Florissant, Missouri, is considerating the problem of planning the resurfacing of the 25 tennis courts at its various city parks. It can resurface these courts at any point in time over the next 4 years. However, since the courts are under increasingly heavy use because of the rising popularity of tennis, there will be an increase in resurfacing costs over time. The following table summarizes the Parks and Recreation Department's estimate of the costs associated with resurfacing again in year *j*. All entries are given in thousands of dollars.

Year of Initial Resurfacing, *i*	Year of Next Resurfacing, *j*				
	1	*2*	*3*	*4*	
0	20	26	33	57	
1		21	29	36	
2			22	29	($,000)
3				22	

What is the best resurfacing plan?

19. Find the minimum spanning tree for the network shown in Problem 9.
20. Find the minimum spanning tree for the network shown in Problem 10.
21. Find the minimum spanning tree for the network shown in Problem 11.
22. Find the minimum spanning tree for the network shown in Problem 12.
23. Find the minimum spanning tree for the network shown in Problem 13.
24. The Sunsmooch Citrus Company planted a large orange grove some 5 years ago in Mesa, Arizona. It plans on starting to harvest oranges from this grove next year and must make each of the 10 sections of the orange grove accessible to each of the other sections. Consequently, it needs to plan a system of roads that makes each section of the grove accessible from every other section. The distances (in miles) between every pair of sections of the grove are as follows.

| From | To Section | | | | | | | | | |
Section	1	2	3	4	5	6	7	8	9	10
1	—	3	8	6	5	7	8	7	9	4
2		—	4	2	3	5	6	8	10	12
3			—	5	5	9	9	11	8	6
4				—	6	10	9	12	4	5
5					—	8	4	13	9	13
6						—	11	5	7	10
7			(Symmetrical; i.e.,				—	4	5	9
8			values same as above					—	4	5
9			diagonal)						—	12
10										—

Solve as a minimum spanning tree problem.

25. The city of Metro (Problem 14) wishes to establish a minimum-cost communications system for its 10 centers so that every center is connected. Determine the minimal spanning tree for the communications network.

26. Suppose Arabco wishes to establish a communications network for its oil field, intermediary facilities, and refinery, so that communications lines connect all locations. The cost associated with establishing communications between any two of the facilities is a function of the distance between any two facilities as given below. Determine the optimal set of connections (minimum spanning tree).

Connection	Distance (miles)
Oil Field→A	105
Oil Field→B	115
Oil Field→C	125
A→B	135
A→D	120
B→D	100
B→E	114
C→B	122
C→F	117
D→G	140
D→E	143
E→G	121
E→F	113
F→H	109
G→Refinery	101
G→H	119
H→Refinery	121

27. Beargrass Zoo management wants to establish a communications system between each of the centers. The cost of establishing a communication line between each center is based on the distances between the centers. Determine the optimal communication network so all centers are connected at a minimum cost. (See diagram, Problem 16.)

28. Consider the following CPM network in which the time required (in hours) for each activity is known, and given by the number along the corresponding branch. Find the earliest time, latest time, and corresponding slack for each event. Identify the critical path for the system flow plan.

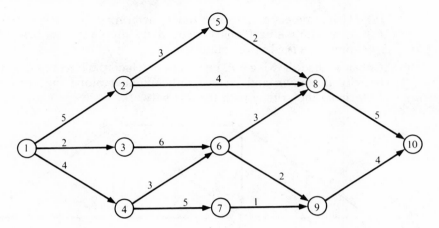

29. Consider the following PERT network.

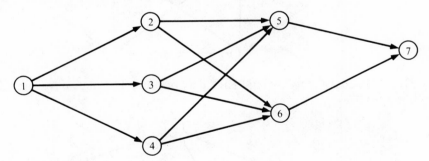

The PERT time estimates for each of these activities are:

Activity	Optimistic Estimate	Most Likely Estimate	Pessimistic Estimate
1→2	2	4	5
1→3	3	4	5
1→4	6	7	9
2→5	5	7	8
2→6	4	6	8
3→5	2	4	5
3→6	3	5	9
4→5	5	6	7
4→6	6	8	9
5→7	4	5	6
6→7	3	5	8

Designate the start of the project as time 0, and the scheduled time to complete the project (by contract) is 21 days.

(a) Using the three time estimates shown above, calculate the expected value and the standard deviation of the expected value of the time required for each activity.

(b) Using the expected value times, determine the critical path for the project.

(c) Compute the probability associated with the project being completed by the time specified in the contract

30. Consider the following CPM network in which the time required (in days) for each activity is known and given by the number along the corresponding branch. Determine the critical path for this network.

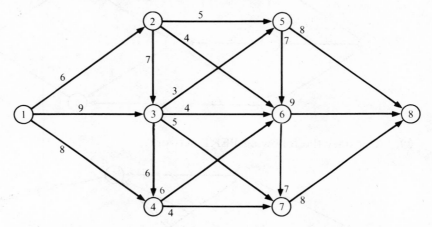

31. Consider the following PERT network that describes a research and development project.

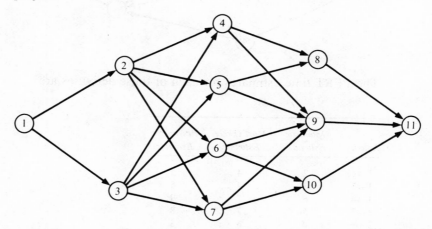

The PERT time estimates (in days) for each of the activities of this network are as shown on page 431.

(a) Using the three time estimates shown above, calculate the expected value and the standard deviation of the expected value of the time required for each activity.

Activity	a Optimistic Estimate	m Most Likely Estimate	b Pessimistic Estimate	Predecesor
1 1→2	3	6	8	—
2 1→3	4	6	7	—
3 2→4	5	9	10	1
4 2→5	6	8	9	1
5 2→6	9	10	12	1
6 2→7	8	11	13	1
7 3→4	7	10	12	2
8 3→5	11	13	15	2
9 3→6	8	10	12	2
10 3→7	9	12	13	2
11 4→8	5	7	9	3,7
12 4→9	3	5	6	3,9
13 5→8	2	4	5	4,8
14 5→9	7	9	10	4,8
15 6→9	8	9	10	5,9
16 6→10	10	12	15	5,9
17 7→9	6	7	11	6,10
18 7→10	5	9	11	6,10
19 8→11	7	8	12	11,13
20 9→11	8	10	13	12,14,15,17
21 10→11	3	5	8	16,18

(b) Using the expected value time, determine the critical path for the network.

(c) Assume that we would like to have this research and development project completed by 35 days from its initiation (time 0). Compute the probability of completing the project within 35 days.

32. Consider the following PERT network that describes the probable activities associated with staging a conference of university professors of management science.

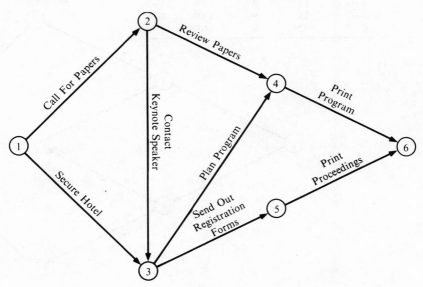

The PERT time estimates (in weeks) for each of these activities are

Activity	Optimistic Estimate	Most Likely Estimate	Pessimistic Estimate
1→2	3	4	6
1→3	1	2	4
2→3	1	3	5
2→4	6	8	12
3→4	2	3	5
3→5	1	2	4
4→6	4	5	9
5→6	4	6	11

(a) Using the three time estimates shown above, calculate the expected value and the standard deviation of the expected value of the time required for each activity.

(b) Using the expected value time, determine the critical path for the network.

(c) Assume that the conference planners would like to complete all of their planning activities within 16 weeks. What is the likelihood of this occurring?

33. The following data relate to the project network shown below.

	Activity	Activity Time (days)		Activity Cost	
		Regular	Crash	Regular	Crash
1	1→2	5	4	$ 500	$ 550
2	1→3	6	4	650	750
3	2→4	7	5	800	900
4	2→5	9	6	1000	1200
5	3→5	6	3	750	1000
6	3→6	8	5	900	1100
7	4→7	10	8	1200	1300
8	5→7	11	9	1300	1400
9	6→7	12	8	1400	1700

Handwritten left margin annotations:

Predecessor
- 1 —
- 2 —
- 3 1
- 4 1
- 5 2
- 6 2
- 7 3
- 8 4,5
- 9 6

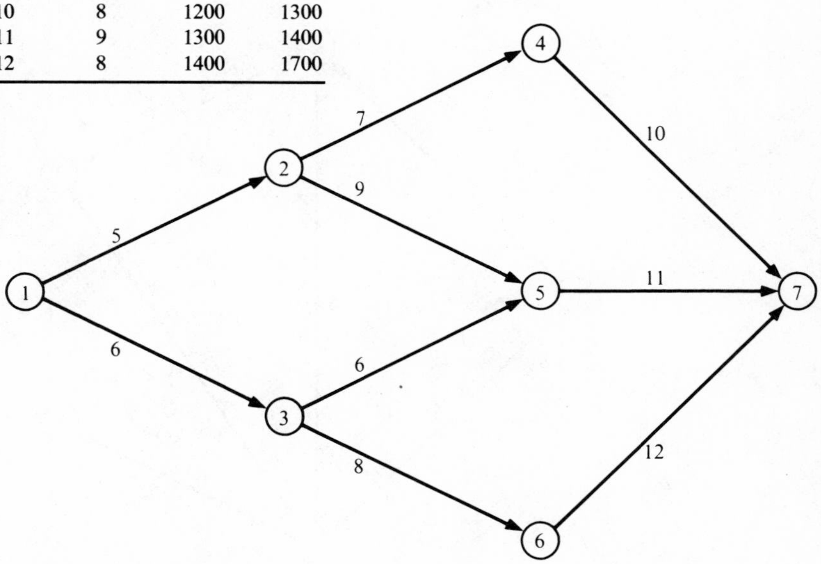

(a) Determine the critical path for this network.
(b) Assume that the project manager wants to reduce the total completion time for the project to 23 days. Determine the time-cost tradeoff curve, and associated activities to be crashed, to achieve this objective.

34. In a research and development project, the various activities can be crashed at various costs and with various time reductions. The following table lists the various activities and the associated time and cost information.

Activity	Regular Time (days)	Crash Time (days)	Daily "Crash" Cost
A→B	3	2	$100
A→C	4	2	150
B→D	3	3	200
B→E	6	4	125
C→D	7	5	175
C→E	5	4	225
D→F	8	5	200
D→G	9	5	180
D→H	10	7	200
E→F	9	7	190
E→G	8	6	150
E→H	11	9	175
F→I	7	5	225
G→I	8	5	210
H→I	9	6	200

(a) Draw the network diagram for this project and determine the critical path, assuming that no activities are crashed.
(b) Determine the least-cost sequence to crash activities in order to complete the project in 26 days. Determine the time-cost tradeoff curve and associated activities to be crashed to achieve this objective.

35. Southeastern University is attempting to organize an eight-team soccer tournament. It has determined that the following activities must be accomplished, and has made time estimates for each of the activities.

Activity		Immediate Predecessor	Time Estimate		
			Optimistic Time	Most Likely Time	Pessimistic Time
A	Select teams	—	2	3	5
B	Determine tournament site	A	3	5	8
C	Make invitations	B	10	13	20
D	Make team-housing arrangement	C	5	8	11
E	Print programs and tickets	B	4	7	8
F	Sell programs and tickets	E	17	20	21
G	Complete final planning	C	5	7	12
H	Schedule practices, games, and field	D	2	3	5
I	Schedule practice sessions	G,H	1	2	3
J	Conduct tournament	F,I	1	1	1

(a) Draw the PERT network for these activities.
(b) What is the expected time necessary to complete all activities (That is, what is the critical path)?
(c) What is the probability of organizing and conducting the soccer tournament within 30 days?

9 Integer Programming

9.1 INTRODUCTION

You will recall that in our previous discussion of linear programming (Chapters 3, 4, and 5) we allowed both the decision variables and the slack variables to assume nonnegative fractional values, or nonnegative integer values, in the optimal solution. We observed that one of the basic properties of linear programming is *continuity*, which means that fractional levels of the decision variables are possible in the solution to a linear programming model. In many of the problem situations we analyzed fractional values for the decision variables were obtained as an optimal solution was determined; and these fractional values were acceptable and appropriate in the context of the problem being considered. In general, it is quite possible to use a fractional amount of a resource to produce a fractional amount of a product.

EXAMPLE 1   However, there are also a number of important problem situations in which fractional answers are neither practical nor very meaningful. For example, consider the following production-planning situation. Pegasus Airframe Corporation manufactures three types of corporate jets. The selling prices for these three corporate jets are as follows.

Model A - $1,750,000
Model B - $2,000,000
Model C - $1,900,000

Yearly production of these three corporate jets is constrained by available work force, available machine time, and capital availability. The production conditions for the problem situation can be expressed as follows.

Constraint	Model A	Model B	Model C	Resource Availability
Work force	40 Workers	65 Workers	50 Workers	150 Workers
Machine time	6,000 Hours	10,000 Hours	8,000 Hours	30,000 Hours
Capital	$1,500,000	$1,000,000	$1,250,000	$3,500,000

Letting x_1 = number of Model A airplanes produced, x_2 = number of Model B airplanes produced, and x_3 = number of Model C airplanes produced, the standard linear programming formulation of this problem would be

$$\text{Maximize } Z = \$1,750,000x_1 + \$2,000,000x_2 + \$1,900,000x_3 \tag{9-1}$$

subject to:

$$
\begin{aligned}
40x_1 + 65x_2 + 50x_3 &\leq 150 \\
6,000x_1 + 10,000x_2 + 8,000x_3 &\leq 30,000 \\
1,500,000x_1 + 1,000,000x_2 + 1,250,000x_3 &\leq 3,500,000
\end{aligned} \tag{9-2}
$$

with $x_1 \geq 0,\ x_2 \geq 0,\ x_3 \geq 0$ $\qquad\qquad$ (9-3)

The linear programming solution to this problem is x_1 = 2.32 Model A airplanes, x_3 = 1.14 Model C airplanes, Z = $6,234,474. However, from the nature of the problem it is apparent that we could not allow the manufacture of a part of an airplane. In this production-scheduling situation the decision variables have relevance only if they have integer values.

EXAMPLE 2   In some practical applications, an integer solution to a particular linear programming problem can be obtained by simply "rounding off" the fractional values that appear in the optimal solution that is determined by application of the simplex algorithm. Unfortunately, this rounding procedure may cause two difficulties. First, this integer solution may not be feasible, particularly if some of the a_{ij} coefficients in the constraint set are negative. Second, even if the "rounded off" solution is feasible, it may not be the optimal solution. To illustrate the first problem, suppose that the constraint set for the problem is

$$
\begin{aligned}
x_1 + x_2 &\leq 7\tfrac{1}{3} \\
x_1 - x_2 &\leq \tfrac{2}{3}
\end{aligned} \tag{9-4}
$$

and that application of the simplex method has resulted in an optimal (noninteger) solution of $x_1 = 4$, $x_2 = 3^1/_3$. Observe that we cannot round off x_2 to either 3 or 4 and maintain feasibility. Indeed, we can round off x_2 only if we also change the integer value of x_1. Obviously, rounding off becomes even more impractical as the number of constraints and variables increases.

EXAMPLE 3   The second problem, as noted above, is that even though a feasible integer solution can be obtained by rounding off, it may not be the optimal integer solution. To illustrate, consider the following problem situation. The Tesla Transformer Company manufactures two large transformers. The 5-kilo-volt transformer sells for $1000 and the 25-kilo-volt transformer sells for $4000. Production of these transformers is constrained by the company's current stock of copper wire, which consists of some 18 rolls. Each 5-kilo-volt transformer requires 1 roll of copper wire and each 25-kilo-volt transformer requires 6 rolls of copper wire. Additionally, production of the 5-kilo-volt transformer is constrained to be equal to, or less than, three units because there are several unsold 5-kilo-volt transformers in inventory at the present time.

Letting x_1 = number of 5-kilo-volt transformers produced and x_2 = number of 25-kilo-volt transformers produced, the integer programming formulation of this problem would be

$$\text{Maximize } Z = \$1000x_1 + \$4000x_2 \qquad (9\text{-}5)$$

subject to:
$$
\begin{array}{rl}
x_1 + 6x_2 & \leq 18 \\
x_1 & \leq 3
\end{array}
\qquad (9\text{-}6)
$$

with $x_1 \geq 0$, $x_2 \geq 0$, and x_1 and x_2 integers   (9-7)

Referring graphically to Fig. 9.1, it can be seen that the optimal noninteger solution is $x_1 = 3$, $x_2 = 2.5$, $Z = 13$. To obtain an integer solution to this problem by rounding off, we would obtain $x_1 = 3$, $x_2 = 2$, $Z = 11$. However, the *optimal* integer solution is $x_1 = 0$, $x_2 = 3$, $Z = 12$, as can be seen in Fig. 9.1.

Practical applications of integer programming have become much more common in recent years. Because of this fact, and the problems associated with simply rounding off linear programming solutions, there has arisen a need for an efficient solution procedure for integer linear programming problems. Thus, in this chapter we shall study three approaches to integer programming, namely,

1.   The cutting-plane algorithm initially developed by Ralph Gomory.[1]
2.   The branch-and-bound algorithm initially developed by A. H. Land and A. G. Doig.[2]
3.   The additive algorithm developed by E. Balas.[3]

---

[1] Ralph E. Gomory, "An Algorithm for Integer Solutions to Linear Programs," in R. L. Graves and P. Wolfe (eds). *Recent Advances in Mathematical Programming* (New York: McGraw-Hill Book Company, 1963), 269–302.

[2] A. H. Land and A. G. Doig, "An Automatic Method of Solving Discrete Programming Problems," *Econometrica*, 28 (July 1960), 497–520.

[3] Egon Balas, "An Additive Algorithm for Solving Linear Programs with Zero-One Variables," *Operations Research*, 13, no. 4 (July–August 1965), 517–46.

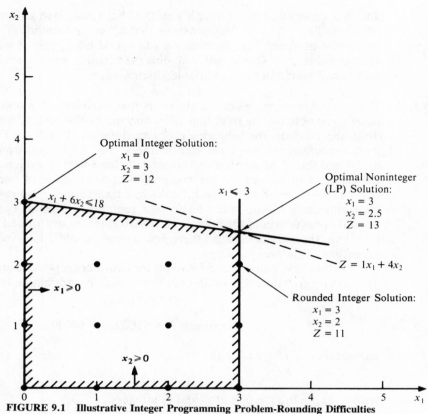

FIGURE 9.1   Illustrative Integer Programming Problem-Rounding Difficulties

These algorithms generally are applicable to small problems, because of computational difficulties. However, progress is being made in terms of developing more efficient algorithms and/or computer codes that are applicable to larger problems.

9.2   FORMULATING INTEGER PROGRAMMING MODELS

Integer programming problems arise in a wide variety of managerial decision-making situations. Many integer programming problems are essentially identical to linear programming problems with only the added requirement that some, or all, of the decision variables must assume integer values. Other problems situations have a structure such that they can be modeled accurately only if integer variables are employed. Still other problems have structures that can be reformulated in integer programming form. In the material that follows we will attempt to describe and discuss some of the integer programming formulations that are possible. It should be stressed that the integer programming formulation techniques described below can be used in a wide variety of applications.

9.2.1 Representing Yes-or-No Decisions Using Binary (Zero-One) Variables

One of the most common uses of integer programming involves decision-making situations in which a choice must be made concerning whether or not to undertake some activity or project. For example, we may need to decide whether or not to build a plant on a particular site, or whether or not to invest in a specific security, or whether or not to develop a new product.

In cases such as these a "yes-or-no" or "go-no-go" decision is required. Such decisions can be represented within an integer programming framework using **binary** (or **0-1**) **variables** (*Note:* such variables are also sometimes referred to as *bivalent* or *logical* variables). Thus, with just two choices, such decisions can be represented by decision variables that are restricted to just two values, namely 0 and 1. The jth yes-or-no decision would be represented by the decision variable x_j such that:

$$x_j = \begin{cases} 1, & \text{if decision } j \text{ is yes} \\ 0, & \text{if decision } j \text{ is no} \end{cases} \tag{9-8}$$

Many go-no-go decisions involve **multiple choice** or **mutually exclusive alternatives** in which only one decision in a group of decisions can be yes. In this situation, each group of alternatives would need a constraint having one of the following forms.

Mutually Exclusive: $\displaystyle\sum_{j=1}^{n} x_j \le 1$ (if *at most one* decision in the group must be yes)

or $\tag{9-9}$

Multiple Choice: $\displaystyle\sum_{j=1}^{n} x_j = 1$ (if *exactly one* decision in the group must be yes)

A slight extension of the idea of a multiple-choice constraint can be used to model situations in which k out of a set of n projects either must, or can, be selected. For example, assume that $x_1, x_2, x_3, x_4,$ and x_5 represent five investment opportunities. If exactly $k = 2$ investment opportunities had to be selected, the following constraint would be used.

$$x_1 + x_2 + x_3 + x_4 + x_5 = 2 \tag{9-10}$$

If no more than $k = 2$ investment projects could be selected, the following constraint would be used.

$$x_1 + x_2 + x_3 + x_4 + x_5 \le 2 \tag{9-11}$$

Other go-no-go decisions may involve **precedence** or **contingency relationships**. (*Note:* such relationships are also sometimes referred to as *conditional* or *dependence relationships*.) For example, x_2 might be a 0-1 variable signifying the acceptance ($x_2 = 1$) or rejection ($x_2 = 0$) of a building construction project in a particular part of the city that is in turn dependent on the acceptance of a building construction project in another part of the city. Denoting as x_1 the first project, then the fact that the second project cannot be accepted unless the first project has been accepted can be represented by the precedence constraint:

or $\quad \begin{aligned} x_2 &\leq x_1 \\ -x_1 + x_2 &\leq 0 \end{aligned}$ $\hspace{4cm}$ (9–12)

where x_1 and x_2 are $0 - 1$ variables.

In situations involving two projects that must be undertaken simultaneously, or not at all, a precedence constraint of the following form can be employed.

or $\quad \begin{aligned} x_1 &= x_2 \\ x_1 - x_2 &= 0 \end{aligned}$ $\hspace{4cm}$ (9–13)

where x_1 and x_2 are $0 - 1$ variables

EXAMPLE   *Construction Project Selection Problem.*   Carolina Pride Construction Company has an opportunity to build five shopping malls during the forthcoming year. The expected net profit and expected cost for each of the shopping malls is shown in the following table.

Shopping Mall	Expected Net Profit ($ thousands)	Expected Cost ($ thousands)
1	200	150
2	150	90
3	140	50
4	125	80
5	180	100

Because of cash flow problems, Carolina Pride Construction Company will have approximately $300,000 available for construction work during the next year. Also, due to various legal restrictions the following relationships among the projects must be met.

1. Exactly one of the three shopping malls 1, 2, and 5 must be constructed.
2. At most, only one of the two shopping malls 3 and 4 may be constructed.
3. If shopping mall 4 is constructed, then shopping mall 5 must also be constructed.

Carolina Pride Construction Company wants to select the feasible set of shopping malls to build in order to maximize total net profit.

    To formulate this problem as an integer programming model let x_j be the binary decision variables of the problem:

$$x_j = \begin{cases} 1, & \text{if shopping mall } j \text{ is built} \\ 0, & \text{if shopping mall } j \text{ is not built} \end{cases} \quad (j = 1,2,3,4,5) \quad (9–14)$$

Thus, this problem requires a yes-or-no or go–no go decision with respect to the project selection decision. Using these variables the objective function for the integer programming model can be written as:

$$\text{Maximize (Total Expected Net Profit)} = \$200{,}000x_1 + \$150{,}000x_2 + \$140{,}000x_3$$
$$+ \$125{,}000x_4 + \$180{,}000x_5 \qquad (9\text{-}15)$$

The cash flow restriction constraint for the problem can be written as:

$$\$150{,}000x_1 + \$90{,}000x_2 + \$50{,}000x_3 + \$80{,}000x_4$$
$$+ \$100{,}000x_5 \le \$300{,}000 \qquad (9\text{-}16)$$

The restriction that exactly one of the three shopping malls 1, 2, and 5 must be constructed can be written as the following constraint.

$$x_1 + x_2 + x_5 = 1 \qquad (9\text{-}17)$$

This is an example of a *multiple-choice* constraint, stating that the company wants to build exactly one shopping mall from the group of three shopping malls (i.e., 1, 2, and 5). The restriction that at most one of the two shopping malls 3 and 4 may be constructed can be written as the following constraint.

$$x_3 + x_4 \le 1 \qquad (9\text{-}18)$$

This is an example of a *mutually exclusive alternative* constraint, stating that the company wants to build at most one shopping mall from the group of two shopping malls (i.e., 3 and 4). The restriction stating that if shopping mall 4 is constructed then shopping mall 5 must also be constructed can be written as the following constraint.

$$\text{or} \quad \begin{array}{l} x_4 \le x_5 \\ x_4 - x_5 \le 0 \end{array} \qquad (9\text{-}19)$$

This is an example of a *precedence* constraint. Finally, we have the binary (0-1) restrictions on the decision variables, which can be written as:

$$x_j = 0 \text{ or } 1 \quad \text{for } j = 1, 2, \ldots, 5 \qquad (9\text{-}20)$$

9.2.2 The Fixed-Charge Problem

Many practical problems involve a situation in which a fixed-charge or setup cost is incurred if a particular activity is undertaken. In such situations the total cost of the activity will be the sum of the fixed charge for undertaking the activity plus the variable cost associated with the level of the activity. Thus, if the variable x_j represents the level of activity j, c_j represents the variable cost associated with activity j, and k_j represents the fixed charge associated with activity j, then the total cost of activity j will be given by:

$$\begin{array}{ll} (k_j + c_j x_j) & \text{if } x_j > 0 \\ 0 & \text{if } x_j = 0 \end{array} \qquad (9\text{-}21)$$

The corresponding objective function for a fixed charge problem can then be written as:

$$Z = f_1(x_1) + f_2(x_2) + \cdots + f_n(x_n) \tag{9-22}$$

where $\quad f_j(x_j) = \begin{cases} k_j + c_j x_j, & \text{if } x_j > 0 \\ 0, & \text{if } x_j = 0 \end{cases} \tag{9-23}$

where the x_j variables are nonnegative for $j = 1, 2, \ldots, n$.

Quite often the constraint set for a **fixed charge problem** will consist entirely of a set of linear constraints just as in a linear programming problem. Assuming that some or all of the fixed charges, the k_j, are strictly positive, the fixed charge problem can be formulated as an integer programming problem having the following form:

$$\text{Minimize } Z = \sum_{j=1}^{n} (c_j x_j + k_j y_j) \tag{9-24}$$

subject to: 1. The original set of linear constraints $\tag{9-25}$

2. $y_j \le 1$
   $y_j \ge 0$ $\tag{9-26}$
   y_j is an integer for $j = 1, 2, \ldots, n$

3. $x_j - My_j \le 0$ $\tag{9-27}$

where the x_j variables are nonnegative for $j = 1, 2, \ldots, n$.

In the objective function, the fixed-charge portion:

$$y_j = \begin{cases} 1, & \text{if } x_j > 0 \\ 0, & \text{if } x_j = 0 \end{cases} \tag{9-28}$$

Thus, in the constraint set we must constrain y_j to be an integer zero-one variable, as is done in Equation 9-26. Furthermore, by letting M be a very large number that exceeds the maximum feasible value of any $x_j (j = 1, 2, \ldots, n)$, then the constraints:

$$x_j \le My_j, \quad \text{for } j = 1, 2, \ldots, n \tag{9-29}$$

will ensure that $y_j = 1$ whenever $x_j > 0$. Note that these constraints allow y_j to be either zero or one when $x_j = 0$. However, recall that $k_j \ge 0$. If $k_j = 0$, the product $k_j \cdot y_j$ will also be zero in the objective function. When $k_j > 0$, and $x_j = 0$ so that the constraints will allow either $y_j = 0$ or $y_j = 1$, $y_j = 0$ must yield a smaller value for the objective function. Thus, the optimal solution to the problem will have $y_j = 0$ when $x_j = 0$.

EXAMPLE   *Fixed-Charge Problem.*   The River Falls Textile Company can use any, or all, of three different processes for weaving its standard white polyester fabric. Each of these production processes has a weaving machine setup cost and per-square-yard processing cost. These costs and the capacities of each of the three production processes are as follows.

Process Number	Weaving Machine Setup Cost	Processing Cost ($ per yd²)	Maximum Daily Capacity (yd²)
1	$ 50	$0.06	20,000
2	80	0.04	30,000
3	100	0.03	35,000

River Falls Textile Company forecasts a daily demand for its white polyester fabric of 40,000 square yards. The company's production manager wants to make a decision concerning which production processes to utilize to meet the daily demand forecast, and at what level of capacity, in order to minimize total production costs.

To formulate this problem as an integer programming model, let x_j ($j = 1,2,3$) represent the production level for process j, and let

$$y_j = \begin{cases} 1, & \text{if process } j \text{ is used; } j = 1,2,3 \\ 0, & \text{if process } j \text{ is not used; } j = 1,2,3 \end{cases} \tag{9-30}$$

Using these variables the objective function for the integer programming model can be written as:

$$\text{Minimize (Total Production Cost) } Z = \$0.06x_1 + \$0.04x_2 + \$0.03x_3 + \$50y_1 \\ + \$80y_2 + \$100y_3 \tag{9-31}$$

subject to:

$$\begin{array}{ll} x_1 + x_2 + x_3 = 40,000 \text{ (yd}^2\text{)} & \text{(Daily demand forecast)} \\ x_1 \quad\quad\quad \le 20,000 \text{ (yd}^2\text{)} & \text{(Capacity constraint-Process 1)} \\ \quad\quad x_2 \quad\quad \le 30,000 \text{ (yd}^2\text{)} & \text{(Capacity constraint-Process 2)} \\ \quad\quad\quad x_3 \le 35,000 \text{ (yd}^2\text{)} & \text{(Capacity constraint-Process 3)} \end{array} \tag{9-32}$$

Additionally, we must ensure that if any production process is used at a positive level, both the fixed weaving machine setup cost and the variable weaving machine processing cost will be incurred. For example, if we use production process 1 (i.e., $x_1 > 0$), then $y_1 = 1$ (i.e., we incur the fixed weaving machine setup cost associated with process 1). Thus, we must ensure that the following relationships are present in the integer programming model.

$$\begin{array}{lll} \text{For each production process:} & \text{If } x_j = 0, \text{ then } y_j = 0 \\ (j = 1,2,3) & \text{If } x_j > 0, \text{ then } y_j = 1 \end{array} \tag{9-33}$$

Fortunately, each of these relationships can be combined with the corresponding capacity constraint, to form one constraint. For example, for production process 1 we can utilize a constraint of the form:

$$x_1 \le 20,000y_1$$

$$\text{or} \quad x_1 - 20,000y_1 \le 0 \quad \text{where } y_1 \text{ is 0 or 1} \tag{9-34}$$

In using this constraint we want to insure that y_1 is either 0 or 1. If $x_1 > 0$, then

$20,000y_1 > 0$, and this can occur only if $y_1 = 1$. If $x_1 = 0$, then $y_1 = 0$ since we are minimizing total production cost and $y_1 = 0$ will yield a smaller value for the objective function.

Thus, the complete fixed-charge integer programming model for the River Falls Textile Company can be written as:

Minimize (Total Production Cost) $Z = \$0.06x_1 + \$0.04x_2 + \$0.03x_3 + \$50y_1$
$$+ \$80y_2 + \$100y_3 \qquad (9\text{--}35)$$

subject to:
$$
\begin{aligned}
x_1 + x_2 + x_3 &= 40,000 \text{ (yd}^2) \\
x_1 - 20,000y_1 &\leq 0 \\
x_2 - 30,000y_2 &\leq 0 \\
x_3 - 40,000y_3 &\leq 0 \\
y_1 &\leq 1 \\
y_2 &\leq 1 \\
y_3 &\leq 1 \\
y_1 &\geq 0 \\
y_2 &\geq 0 \\
y_3 &\geq 0
\end{aligned}
\qquad (9\text{--}36)
$$

with $x_1 \geq 0, x_2 \geq 0, x_3 \geq 0;\ y_1, y_2, y_3$ integers $(9\text{--}37)$

9.2.3 Either-Or Constraints

In some problem situations, a choice must be made between two constraints, so that one but not both constraints must hold. For example, assume that we have a blending situation in which either of two resources may be used to satisfy a resource requirement. Assume that we have formulated this situation with the constraints:

$$\text{Either} \qquad 5x_1 + 3x_2 \leq 15 \qquad (9\text{--}38)$$

$$\text{or} \qquad 4x_1 + 2x_2 \leq 11 \qquad (9\text{--}39)$$

Letting M be a very large number, the constraints given by (9–38) and (9–39) can be rewritten as:

$$5x_1 + 3x_2 \leq 15 + My \qquad (9\text{--}40)$$

$$4x_1 + 2x_2 \leq 11 + M(1 - y) \qquad (9\text{--}41)$$

$$y = 0 \text{ or } 1 \qquad (9\text{--}42)$$

Additionally, the integer variable y is assumed to have an objective function coefficient of zero.

When $y = 0$, the first constraint (9–40) reverts to its original form (9–38) and becomes binding. The second constraint (9–41) becomes redundant since M is very large and is, in effect, eliminated.

When $y = 1$, the second constraint (9–41) reverts to its original form

(9–39) and becomes binding. Since M is assumed to be very large the first constraint (9–40) becomes redundant and is, in effect, eliminated.

Thus, the formulation given by (9–40), (9–41), and (9–42) guarantees that one, and only one, of the original constraints must hold. This set of constraints would then simply be added to the original problem, and the resulting integer programming formulation would be solved using an appropriate algorithm.

9.2.4 *K* Out of *N* Constraints Must Be Met

Various problem situations require that some K out of N constraints must be met (assuming $K < N$). For example, a firm might decide to use a group of criteria such as cost, expected life, efficiency, and energy consumption with respect to a particular piece of equipment. Then, in making a decision as to purchasing a particular piece of equipment, the manager might want to try to specify that a minimum satisfactory level for a certain number of these criteria be achieved. This would be equivalent to specifying that K out of N constraints must be met.

The equivalent integer programming formulation of this problem situation can be constructed as follows.

$$
\begin{aligned}
f_1(x_1, x_2, \ldots, x_n) &\leq b_1 + My_1 \\
f_2(x_1, x_2, \ldots, x_n) &\leq b_2 + My_2
\end{aligned}
\tag{9-43}
$$

$$
\begin{aligned}
f_N(x_1, x_2, \ldots, x_n) &\leq b_N + My_N \\
y_i &\leq 1 \\
y_i &\geq 0
\end{aligned}
\tag{9-44}
$$

y_i is an integer, for $i = 1, 2, \ldots, N$

$$
\sum_{i=1}^{N} y_i = N - K
\tag{9-45}
$$

where it is assumed that M is a very large number.

This formulation assures that the y_i values will be zero or one. The constraint given by (9–45) guarantees that K of the y_i values will equal zero, and that $N - K$ of the y_i values will equal 1. This assures that K of the original constraints will be unchanged, and hence binding, while the remaining $N - K$ constraints will be eliminated.

To illustrate, assume that we have formulated a problem having the following four constraints:

$$
\begin{aligned}
2x_1 - 1x_2 + 3x_3 &\leq 11 \\
-3x_1 + 4x_2 &\leq 7 \\
2x_2 - 3x_3 &\leq 12 \\
2x_1 + 4x_2 - 1x_3 &\leq 10
\end{aligned}
\tag{9-46}
$$

and that we would like for three ($K = 3$) of these four ($N = 4$) constraints to be binding.

We would then reformulate this constraint set as the following.

$$2x_1 - 1x_2 + 3x_3 \leq 11 + My_1$$
$$-3x_1 + 4x_2 \qquad \leq 7 + My_2$$
$$2x_2 - 3x_3 \leq 12 + My_3 \qquad (9\text{-}47)$$
$$2x_1 + 4x_2 - 1x_3 \leq 10 + My_4$$
$$y_i = 0 \text{ or } 1, \quad \text{for } i = 1, 2, 3, 4 \qquad (9\text{-}48)$$
$$y_1 + y_2 + y_3 + y_4 = 4 - 3 = 1$$

9.2.5 Right-Hand Side of a Constraint Required to Assume One of Several Values

In certain problem situations, the right-hand side of a single constraint may be required to assume *one* of several values, that is,

$$f(x_1, x_2, \ldots, x_n) \leq b_1, b_2, \ldots, \text{ or } b_r \qquad (9\text{-}49)$$

The equivalent integer programming formulation of this constraint is

$$f(x_1, x_2, \ldots, x_n) \leq \sum_{k=1}^{r} b_k y_k$$

and

$$y_1 + y_2 + \ldots + y_r = 1 \qquad (9\text{-}50)$$

where
$$y_k = \begin{cases} 1, & \text{if } b_k \text{ is the right-hand side} \\ 0, & \text{otherwise} \end{cases} \qquad (9\text{-}51)$$

This is an equivalent formulation because exactly one y_k must equal 1, and all the other y_k must equal zero. This makes the r yes-or-no decisions on the selection of the respective b_k right-hand side values multiple-choice alternatives.

For example, assume that we have a situation in which we are manufacturing two products, denoted as x_1 and x_2, with 1½ hours required to manufacture product x_1 and ½ hour required to manufacture product x_2. Assume further that we have 80 labor hours available on our first shift, but if a second shift is employed this labor hour availability will increase to 120 labor hours. Thus, the right-hand side of the constraint corresponding to this situation can be either 80 hours or 120 hours. We can represent this situation in an integer programming format, as follows.

$$1.5x_1 + 0.5x_2 \leq 80y_1 + 120y_2$$
$$y_1 + y_2 = 1 \qquad (9\text{-}52)$$

where $x_1 \geq 0, x_2 \geq 0,$ and y_1, y_2 are $0 - 1$ (binary) variables

9.3 STRUCTURE AND ILLUSTRATIONS OF INTEGER PROGRAMMING PROBLEMS

Recall from our earlier discussions of linear programming that the set of feasible solutions was seen to be a convex set. The consequence of this fact was that the basic feasible solutions were then seen to be at the corners of this convex set, which were the intersections of the constraint boundaries. However, when we add to the linear programming problem the restriction that all decision variables may have only integer values, the intersection of the constraints will no longer specify feasible solutions, except by accident.

Consider Fig. 9.2, which presents the convex set formed by two constraints and the nonnegativity restrictions in a linear programming problem. Any point within this convex set represents a basic feasible solution. Now, assume that both decision variables x_1 and x_2 must be integers. This added restriction reduces the number of feasible solutions from infinity to 26, namely, those lattice points (integer values of x_1 and x_2) specified by dots that lie on the boundary or within the original constraint set. Thus, integer programming is concerned with discrete functions that exist for only integer values of the function.

There are basically three types of integer programming problems.

1. **An all-integer programming problem.** All the decision variables are constrained to integer values.
2. **A mixed-integer programming problem.** Some, but not all, of the decision variables are constrained to integer values.
3. **A zero-one integer programming problem.** All of the decision variables are constrained to the integer values zero or one.

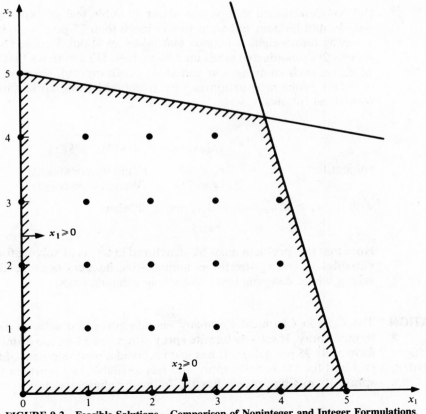

FIGURE 9.2 Feasible Solutions—Comparison of Noninteger and Integer Formulations.

All these types of integer programming problems are couched within the general format of what would otherwise be a linear programming problem. That is, the objective function and constraint set of the problem are linear functions, with only the additional restriction that the decision variables must be solved for as integers. As a result, some authors prefer the use of the term "integer linear programming" rather than just "integer programming." This distinction does not seem to be too important as long as the student understands the structure of the problem being considered.

Applications of integer programming within various decision making contexts are numerous and varied. Typical illustrations of the three basic types of integer programming problems will now be provided.

ILLUSTRATION 1
An All-Integer Programming Problem

Bill Dawes is returning from a late-summer fishing trip in Colorado. He has extra space in the back of his station wagon, and is interested in taking back two locally produced camping items to sell to friends. These two items are

$$x_1 = \text{camping tents}$$
$$x_2 = \text{sleeping bags}$$

Bill has determined that he has about 50 cubic feet of extra space in his station wagon, and he does not want to add more than 75 pounds to his current load. A camping tent weighs 9 pounds and takes up about 5 cubic feet. A sleeping bag weighs 2½ pounds and takes up 2 cubic feet. He estimates that he can make a $10 profit on each camping tent and an $8 profit on each sleeping bag.

This problem situation can be structured using an all-integer programming format, as follows.

$$\text{Maximize } Z = \$10x_1 + \$8x_2 \tag{9-53}$$

subject to: $5x_1 + 2x_2 \leq 50$ (Volume constraint)
$9x_1 + 2\tfrac{1}{2}x_2 \leq 75$ (Weight constraint) $\qquad(9\text{-}54)$

with $x_1 \geq 0,\ x_2 \geq 0,$ and x_1 and x_2 integers $\qquad(9\text{-}55)$

Note that this problem must be structured in terms of solving for both the decision variables x_1 and x_2 strictly as nonnegative integers because Bill is restricted to selling whole camping tents and whole sleeping bags.

ILLUSTRATION 2
A Mixed-Integer Programming Problem

The Gorgon Chemical Company manufactures and sells an extremely effective termite spray. It sells its termite spray either in a 55-gallon drum for $50, or in bulk form at $1.25 per gallon. It has just received a new shipment of the two chemicals required for the termite spray and has available two workers to mix the termite spray. Its mixing process has the following characteristics.

	Chemical Requirement per Drum	Chemical Requirement per Gallon	Chemical Availability
Chemical A	16.67 gal	0.444 gal	1000 gal
Chemical B	13.33 gal	0.250 gal	750 gal

	Labor requirement per drum	Labor requirement per gallon	Work force availability
	0.53 hr	0.04 hr	80 hr

If we let x_1 = number of 55-gallon drums of the termite spray produced and x_2 = number of gallons (in bulk form) of the termite spray produced, this problem situation can be represented by the following mixed-integer programming formulation.

$$\text{Maximize } Z = \$50x_1 + \$1.25x_2 \tag{9-56}$$

subject to:
$$\left.\begin{array}{r} 16.67x_1 + 0.444x_2 \le 1000 \\ 13.33x_1 + 0.250x_2 \le 750 \end{array}\right\} \quad \text{(Chemical availability constraints)} \tag{9-57}$$
$$0.53x_1 + 0.04x_2 \le 80 \quad \text{(Work force availability constraint)}$$

with
$$x_1 \ge 0, x_2 \ge 0, x_1 \text{ integer} \tag{9-58}$$

Note that only x_1 is required to be an integer since the variable x_1 represents the number of whole drums to be produced. The variable x_2 represents the bulk gallons of the termite spray produced and is thus not required to be integer valued.

ILLUSTRATION 3

A Zero-One Integer Programming Problem (Capital Budgeting)

Barbara Shade, the Controller of the Clover Manufacturing Company, is trying to determine which of 10 capital investment projects to fund for the coming year. Based on the discounted cash flow rate of return predicted for each project, she has assigned a value to that project on a scale of 1 to 100. For each project she has also determined the capital cost for the project.

Barbara would like to select a set of capital projects that maximizes the total discounted cash flow rate of return for the company. However, she is constrained by a capital expenditure budget of $750,000. Additionally, according to company policy she cannot spend more than $100,000 on any one project. Finally, she must either totally accept or totally reject each project (i.e., making a partial capital expenditure for a project is not possible).

Ms. Shade's preliminary evaluation of the potential projects is as follows.

Capital Investment Project	Capital Expenditure Requirement ($)	Project Value (scale: 1-100)
1	95,000	60
2	70,000	40
3	82,000	50
4	50,000	35
5	110,000	70
6	75,000	45
7	100,000	65
8	60,000	35
9	85,000	55
10	80,000	50

To formulate this problem we let $x_j; j = 1,2, \ldots , 10$ be zero-one integer decision variables. Thus, if $x_j = 0$, this indicates that project j is not funded. This problem situation can then be represented by the following zero-one integer programming formulation.

$$\text{Maximize } Z = 60x_1 + 40x_2 + 50x_3 + 35x_4 + 70x_5 + 45x_6 + 65x_7$$
$$+ 35x_8 + 55x_9 + 50x_{10} \tag{9-59}$$

subject to:

$$95,000x_1 + 70,000x_2 + 82,000x_3 + 50,000x_4 + 110,000x_5$$
$$+ 75,000x_6 + 100,000x_7 + 60,000x_8 + 85,000x_9 + 80,000x_{10} \tag{9-60}$$

$$\leq 750,000 \qquad \text{(Total capital expenditure constraint)}$$

$$
\begin{aligned}
95,000x_1 &\leq 100,000 \\
70,000x_2 &\leq 100,000 \\
82,000x_3 &\leq 100,000 \\
50,000x_4 &\leq 100,000 \\
110,000x_5 &\leq 100,000 \qquad \text{(Individual project capital} \\
75,000x_6 &\leq 100,000 \qquad \text{expenditure constraints)} \tag{9-61} \\
100,000x_7 &\leq 100,000 \\
60,000x_8 &\leq 100,000 \\
85,000x_9 &\leq 100,000 \\
80,000x_{10} &\leq 100,000
\end{aligned}
$$

$$x_j \geq 0, x_j = 0 \text{ or } 1 \qquad \text{for } j = 1,2, \ldots , 10 \tag{9-62}$$

Note that each of the x_j values are constrained to be either 1 or 0 in the optimal solution. Thus, we are restricted to a zero-one integer solution for this problem situation.

ILLUSTRATION 4
A Zero-One Integer Programming Problem (Routing)

An entire class of problems involving sequencing, scheduling, or routing inherently involves 0–1 integer programming problems. One very important scheduling problem is the **traveling salesman problem**, which is concerned with the determination of a routing that minimizes the total travel cost (with travel cost usually expressed as a function of distance or time). In the traveling salesman problem, the variable x_{ijk} equals 1 if the overall routing includes a trip from location i to location j in stage k of the routing, otherwise x_{ijk} equals 0. The parameter c_{ijk}

represents the cost associated with making a trip from location i to location j, in stage k of the routing.

To illustrate the formulation of a traveling salesman problem, consider the following situation involving a routing between five cities. An independent trucker has contracted to deliver vegetables to four locations in South Carolina: Spartanburg, Florence, Sumter, and Rock Hill. The produce will be loaded onto his truck at the Farmers' Market in Columbia, South Carolina, and after his final delivery he must return to this control supply location for another load. The trucker wants to determine a route that will minimize the total distance that he travels. He has obtained the following mileage data from the South Carolina Department of Transportation.

	Destination				
Origin	Columbia	Spartanburg	Florence	Sumter	Rock Hill
Columbia	0	93	82	44	68
Spartanburg	93	0	150	137	62
Florence	82	150	0	38	99
Sumter	44	137	38	0	88
Rock Hill	68	62	99	88	0

Note that this mileage data is symmetrical (e.g., the distance from Columbia to Spartanburg is the same as the distance from Spartanburg to Columbia). If the problem were couched in time units, or cost units, the data could be asymmetrical. This however, would not affect the formulation of the problem.

In the traveling salesman problem the idea is to begin from some home city, visit each of $(n - 1)$ other cities exactly once, and return home at a minimal distance (or cost, or time). Thus, a traveling salesman problem involves $(n - 1)!$ possible routings. In our example there are $(5 - 1)! = 4! = 24$ possible routings, with one such routing being Columbia→Spartanburg→Florence→Sumter→Rock Hill→Columbia.

This problem situation can be formulated as the following $0 - 1$ integer programming problem.

$$\text{Minimize } Z = \sum_{i=1}^{5} \sum_{j=1}^{5} \sum_{k=1}^{5} c_{ijk} x_{ijk} \quad \text{for } i \neq j \quad (9\text{-}63)$$

(Minimize total travel distance for the trip.)

$$\text{subject to:} \quad \sum_{j=2}^{5} x_{1j1} = 1 \quad (9\text{-}64)$$

(This constraint stipulates that the trip must begin in Columbia.)

$$\sum_{i=2}^{5} x_{i15} = 1 \quad (9\text{-}65)$$

(This constraint stipulates that the trip must end in Columbia.)

$$\sum_{i=2}^{5} \sum_{j=2}^{5} x_{ijk} = 1 \qquad \text{for } k = 2,3,4; i \neq j \qquad (9\text{-}66)$$

(These constraints specify that each stage of the routing is associated with a single routing segment.)

$$\sum_{j=1}^{5} \sum_{k=2}^{5} x_{ijk} = 1 \qquad \text{for } i = 2, \ldots, 5; i \neq j \qquad (9\text{-}67)$$

$$\text{If } j = 1, k = 5 \quad \text{or} \quad \text{if } k = 5, j = 1$$

(This set of constraints guarantees that there is exactly one departure from each of the five locations.)

$$\sum_{i=1}^{5} \sum_{k=1}^{4} x_{ijk} = 1 \qquad \text{for } j = 2, \ldots, 5; i \neq j \qquad (9\text{-}68)$$

$$\text{If } i = 1, k = 1 \quad \text{or} \quad \text{if } k = 1, i = 1$$

(This set of constraints ensures that only one stage of the trip ends at each of the five locations.)

$$x_{1j1} = \sum_{t=2}^{5} x_{jt2} \qquad \text{for } j = 2, \ldots, 5; i \neq j$$

$$\sum_{i=2}^{5} x_{ijk} = \sum_{t=2}^{5} x_{jtk+1} \qquad \text{for } j = 2, \ldots, 5; k = 2,3; i \neq j \qquad (9\text{-}69)$$

$$\sum_{t=2}^{5} x_{tj4} = x_{j15} \qquad \text{for } j = 2, \ldots, 5; i \neq j$$

(This final set of constraints guarantees that if stage k of the trip ends at location j, then stage $k + 1$ must start from the same location.)

Note that the last constraint set eliminates the possibility of disjoint subtours of the cities from occurring instead of a single trip or tour. That is, it prevents an infeasible solution such as the one depicted in Fig. 9.3 from resulting.

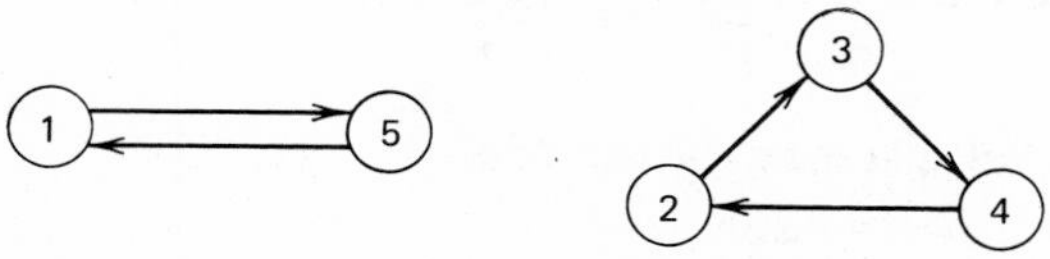

Infeasible Solution: $x_{151} = 1 \quad x_{424} = 1$
$x_{232} = 1 \quad x_{515} = 1$
$x_{343} = 1$

FIGURE 9.3 Disjoint Subtours

Consider that in Fig. 9.3 we have two disjoint subtours that involve all five cities. However, in the first subtour we start and end in city 1, and in the second subtour we start and end in city 2. Note that we do not have any linkage between city 5 and city 2. The constraints given by (9-69) ensure that such a linkage will always occur. For instance, $x_{151} = 1$ indicates that in stage 1 we are traveling to city 5. Therefore, a feasible solution would require that in stage 2 we depart from city 5. Note that in the infeasible solution given above we are departing from city 2 in stage 2.[4]

9.4 THE CUTTING-PLANE ALGORITHM

An algorithm for solving all-integer and mixed-integer programming problems has been developed by Ralph E. Gomory. In using this algorithm, the integer requirement is first relaxed and the resulting linear programming problem is solved in the usual manner. If all the decision variables have integer values, then this current linear programming solution is also the solution to the corresponding integer programming problem. However, if the current linear programming solution does not have integer values for the decision variables we proceed as follows. We modify the original linear programming problem by adding a new constraint that eliminates some noninteger solutions (including the previously optimal noninteger linear programming solution), but which does not eliminate any feasible integer solutions. (This procedure will be discussed in detail subsequently.)

We now proceed to find the optimal solution to the modified problem, using the dual simplex algorithm, since the addition of the new constraint will have made the previous optimal solution infeasible. If this optimal solution has all integer values for the decision variables, it is the integer solution to the problem. If it does not, we add another new constraint to the current modified problem and repeat the procedure.

Utilizing this **cutting-plane algorithm**, the optimal integer solution will eventually be obtained after all the noninteger solutions to the problem have been "cut" away. The key idea in the process is that we are searching for a new linear programming problem whose set of feasible integer solutions coincides with the set of feasible solutions for the integer programming problem that we are attempting to solve. If the optimal solution to this linear programming problem is an integer solution, then it must be the best feasible solution to the integer programming problem.

EXAMPLE We will now proceed to illustrate the procedure used to add a **cutting-plane constraint** at each iteration. Assume that we have used the simplex algorithm on an integer programming problem and have obtained a row in the final (optimal) simplex tableau that can be expressed algebraically in terms of the variables as:

$$1x_1 + 2\tfrac{1}{3}x_2 - \tfrac{1}{4}x_4 + 3\tfrac{1}{5}x_5 - 3\tfrac{1}{2}x_7 + 3x_9 = 3\tfrac{1}{3} \qquad (9\text{-}70)$$

and that $x_1 = 3\tfrac{1}{3}$ is the only noninteger value in the optimal solution to the current problem. We can now rewrite the coefficients of Equation 9-70 as the sum of an integer and a nonnegative fraction, namely as:

$$(1 + 0)x_1 + (2 + \tfrac{1}{3})x_2 + (-1 + \tfrac{3}{4})x_4 + (3 + \tfrac{1}{5})x_5 \\ + (-4 + \tfrac{1}{2})x_7 + (3 + 0)x_9 = 3 + \tfrac{1}{3} \qquad (9\text{-}71)$$

---

[4] For alternate formulations of the traveling salesman problem see: T. C. Hu, *Integer Programming and Network Flows* (Reading, Mass.: Addison-Wesley Publishing Company, 1970), p. 270; and Harvey M. Wagner, *Principles of Operations Research*, 2nd ed. (Englewood Cliffs, New Jersey: Prentice-Hall, 1975), p. 518.

By transposing the integer coefficients to the right-hand side we obtain:

$$\tfrac{1}{3}x_2 + \tfrac{3}{4}x_4 + \tfrac{1}{5}x_5 + \tfrac{1}{2}x_7 = \tfrac{1}{3} + (3 - 1x_1 - 2x_2 + 1x_4 - 3x_5 + 4x_7 - 3x_9) \quad (9\text{-}72)$$

Now, assume that *all* the variables are nonnegative integers.[5] Clearly, the left-hand side of the transposed version of Equation 9–72 is nonnegative since the simplex algorithm will generate only zero or positive values for the decision variables. Also, the right-hand side of Equation 9–72 must equal $\tfrac{1}{3}$ plus some integer. Additionally, it must be positive. Furthermore, it is apparent that the quantity in parentheses on the right-hand side of the equal sign is an integer (because we assumed that all the variables were nonnegative integers). This quantity in parentheses must be positive, or zero, because it would yield a negative sum when added to $\tfrac{1}{3}$ if it were any negative integer. This, in turn, would make the quantity on the left side of the equal sign negative, and we have already concluded that this cannot occur since all values are positive.

Therefore, since:

$$\tfrac{1}{3}x_2 + \tfrac{3}{4}x_4 + \tfrac{1}{5}x_5 + \tfrac{1}{2}x_7 = \tfrac{1}{3} + \text{some integer (positive or zero)} \quad (9\text{-}73)$$

and

$$\tfrac{1}{3}x_2 + \tfrac{3}{4}x_4 + \tfrac{1}{5}x_5 + \tfrac{1}{2}x_7 \geq 0 \quad (9\text{-}74)$$

for nonnegative integer valued variables, it now follows that:

$$\tfrac{1}{3}x_2 + \tfrac{3}{4}x_4 + \tfrac{1}{5}x_5 + \tfrac{1}{2}x_7 \geq \tfrac{1}{3} \quad (9\text{-}75)$$

Thus, the minimum possible value for the quantity on the left side of the equal sign is the quantity on the right side that results when the portion in parentheses on the right-hand side is equal to zero.

The condition shown by Equation 9–75 is the cutting plane constraint that is added to the original linear programming problem. Introducing a nonnegative slack variable, x_8, this new constraint can be written in equation form as:

$$-\tfrac{1}{3}x_2 - \tfrac{3}{4}x_4 - \tfrac{1}{5}x_5 - \tfrac{1}{2}x_7 + x_8 = -\tfrac{1}{3} \quad (9\text{-}76)$$

To obtain the next optimal solution we simply append Equation 9–76 as a row in the previously optimal solution, with $x_8 = -\tfrac{1}{3}$. The dual simplex algorithm is then applied with x_8 being selected as the initial basic variable to leave.

The above discussion assumed that only one variable had a noninteger value. It is, of course, quite possible that more than one, or indeed all variables, will be noninteger in the optimal solution. As a result, a choice must now be made as to which variable (and corresponding equation) will be used to derive the new constraint, as shown above. In practice, the noninteger variable (and associated equation) having the largest fractional part is selected to generate the additional constraint at each subsequent iteration until optimality is achieved.

---

[5] By *all* variables is meant original variables and slack variables. This condition will be assured if we scale the constraint set and the right-hand side vector so that all coefficients and b_j values are integers.

9.5 APPLICATION OF THE CUTTING-PLANE ALGORITHM— AN ALL-INTEGER PROGRAMMING PROBLEM

The cutting-plane algorithm will now be illustrated by applying it to the all-integer programming problem presented earlier, namely.

$$\text{Maximize } Z = 1x_1 + 4x_2 \qquad (9\text{--}77)$$

subject to:
$$\begin{aligned} 1x_1 + 6x_2 &\leq 18 \\ 1x_1 &\leq 3 \end{aligned} \qquad (9\text{--}78)$$

with $\quad x_1 \geq 0, x_2 \geq 0$, and x_1 and x_2 integers $\qquad (9\text{--}79)$

Application of the simplex method to this all-integer programming problem yields, in two iterations, the following optimal (noninteger) linear programming solution (refer also to Fig. 9-1).

TABLE 9.1 Third Simplex Tableau (Optimal LP Solution)

		c_j	1	4	0	0
c_b	Variables in Basis	Solution Values, x_b	a_1	a_2	a_3	a_4
1	x_1	3	1	0	0	1
4	x_2	$5/2$	0	1	$1/6$	$-1/6$
	Z_j	13	1	4	$2/3$	$1/3$
	$c_j - Z_j$		0	0	$-2/3$	$-1/3$

This optimal linear programming solution having $x_2 = 5/2$ is obviously not the optimal solution to the all-integer programming problem given by (9–77), (9–78), and (9–79). Since the variable x_2 is the only variable having a noninteger solution value, we refer to the second row of the optimal simplex tableau to specify the cutting-plane constraint. Expressing the second row of this simplex tableau algebraically in terms of the variables, we obtain:

$$0 + (1 + 0)x_2 + (0 + 1/6)x_3 + (-1 + 5/6)x_4 = 2\tfrac{1}{2} \qquad (9\text{--}80)$$

or
$$\tfrac{1}{6}x_3 + \tfrac{5}{6}x_4 = \tfrac{1}{2} + (2 - 1x_2 + 1x_4) \qquad (9\text{--}81)$$

The cutting-plane constraint is then written as:

$$\tfrac{1}{6}x_3 + \tfrac{5}{6}x_4 \geq \tfrac{1}{2} \qquad (9\text{--}82)$$

The cutting-plane constraint, with the addition of the nonnegative slack variable x_5 becomes

$$-\tfrac{1}{6}x_3 - \tfrac{5}{6}x_4 + x_5 = -\tfrac{1}{2} \qquad (9\text{--}83)$$

The appended first dual simplex tableau then becomes

TABLE 9.2 First Dual Simplex Tableau (with Appended Constraint)

c_b	Variables in Basis	Solution Values, x_b	c_j	1	4	0	0	0
				a_1	a_2	a_3	a_4	a_5
1	x_1	3		1	0	0	1	0
4	x_2	$5/2$		0	1	$1/6$	$-1/6$	0
0	x_5	$-1/2$		0	0	$-1/6$	$-5/6$	1
	Z_j	13		1	4	$2/3$	$1/3$	0
	$c_j - Z_j$			0	0	$-2/3$	$-1/3$	0

Applying the dual simplex algorithm we obtain the second dual simplex tableau, as follows.

TABLE 9.3 Second Dual Simplex Tableau

c_b	Variables in Basis	Solution Values, x_b	c_j	1	4	0	0	0
				a_1	a_2	a_3	a_4	a_5
1	x_1	$12/5$		1	0	$-1/5$	0	$6/5$
4	x_2	$13/5$		0	1	$1/5$	0	$-1/5$
0	x_4	$3/5$		0	0	$1/5$	1	$-6/5$
	Z_j	$12^4/5$		1	4	$3/5$	0	$2/5$
	$c_j - Z_j$			0	0	$-3/5$	0	$-2/5$

Thus, the first dual simplex iteration yields the optimal solution to the current linear programming problem, namely,

$$
\begin{aligned}
x_1 &= {}^{12}/_5 \\
x_2 &= {}^{13}/_5 \\
x_3 &= 0 \qquad \text{Maximum } Z = 12^4/_5 \\
x_4 &= {}^3/_5 \\
x_5 &= 0
\end{aligned}
\qquad (9\text{-}84)
$$

To illustrate what has occurred recall that our original constraints were

$$
\begin{aligned}
1x_1 + 6x_2 + 1x_3 \qquad\quad &= 18 \rightarrow 1x_3 = 18 - 1x_1 - 6x_2 \\
1x_1 \qquad\qquad\quad + 1x_4 &= 3 \rightarrow 1x_4 = 3 - 1x_1
\end{aligned}
\qquad (9\text{-}85)
$$

and that we appended to these constraints the first cutting-plane constraint:

$$
{}^1/_6 x_3 + {}^5/_6 x_4 \ge {}^1/_2 \quad \text{or} \quad x_3 + 5x_4 \ge 3 \qquad (9\text{-}86)
$$

Substituting the values of x_3 and x_4 from the original constraints into the first cutting-plane constraint, we obtain:

$$(18 - 1x_1 - 6x_2) + 5(3 - 1x_1) \geq 3 \qquad (9\text{-}87)$$

or
$$1x_1 + 1x_2 \leq 5$$

Thus, the first cutting-plane constraint is equivalent to the constraint $1x_1 + 1x_2 \leq 5$. Our original constraint set has now been expanded to the constraint set:

$$
\begin{aligned}
1x_1 + 6x_2 &\leq 18 \\
1x_1 &\leq 3 \qquad (9\text{-}88) \\
1x_1 + 1x_2 &\leq 5
\end{aligned}
$$

The graphical solution to this expanded problem is shown in Fig. 9.4. However, this optimal solution is not an integer solution, so a new variable and its corresponding equation (row) must be selected for generating a new constraint. Using the rule we previously discussed row 2, x_2, or row 3, x_4, are tied with the largest fractional parts. Choosing row 3, x_4, arbitrarily, yields the following new constraint.

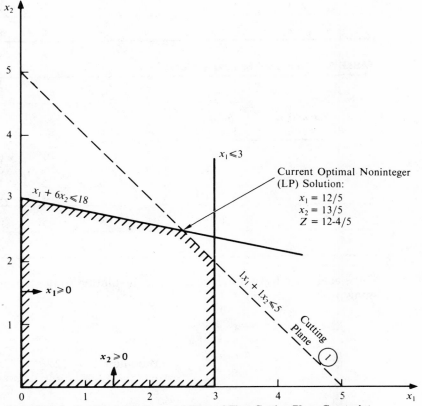

FIGURE 9.4 Graphical Solution—Addition of First Cutting-Plane Constraint

$$\tfrac{1}{5}x_3 + \tfrac{4}{5}x_5 \geq \tfrac{3}{5} \tag{9-89}$$

so the equation

$$-\tfrac{1}{5}x_3 - \tfrac{4}{5}x_5 + x_6 = -\tfrac{3}{5} \tag{9-90}$$

is appended to the current (second) dual simplex tableau. The appended second dual simplex tableau is shown in Table 9.4. Applying the dual simplex algorithm we obtain the third dual simplex tableau, as follows.

TABLE 9.4 Second Dual Simplex Tableau (with Appended Constraint)

c_b	Variables in Basis	Solution Values, x_b	c_j 1 a_1	4 a_2	0 a_3	0 a_4	0 a_5	0 a_6
1	x_1	$\tfrac{12}{5}$	1	0	$-\tfrac{1}{5}$	0	$\tfrac{6}{5}$	0
4	x_2	$\tfrac{13}{5}$	0	1	$\tfrac{1}{5}$	0	$-\tfrac{1}{5}$	0
0	x_4	$\tfrac{3}{5}$	0	0	$\tfrac{1}{5}$	1	$-\tfrac{6}{5}$	0
0	x_6	$-\tfrac{3}{5}$	0	0	$-\tfrac{1}{5}$	0	$-\tfrac{4}{5}$	1
	Z_j	$12\tfrac{4}{5}$	1	4	$\tfrac{3}{5}$	0	$\tfrac{2}{5}$	0
	$c_j - Z_j$		0	0	$-\tfrac{3}{5}$	0	$-\tfrac{2}{5}$	0

TABLE 9.5 Third Dual Simplex Tableau

c_b	Variables in Basis	Solution Values, x_b	c_j 1 a_1	4 a_2	0 a_3	0 a_4	0 a_5	0 a_6
1	x_1	$\tfrac{3}{2}$	1	0	$-\tfrac{1}{2}$	0	0	$\tfrac{3}{2}$
4	x_2	$\tfrac{11}{4}$	0	1	$\tfrac{1}{4}$	0	0	$-\tfrac{1}{4}$
0	x_4	$\tfrac{3}{2}$	0	0	$\tfrac{1}{2}$	1	0	$-\tfrac{3}{2}$
0	x_5	$\tfrac{3}{4}$	0	0	$\tfrac{1}{4}$	0	1	$-\tfrac{5}{4}$
	Z_j	$12\tfrac{1}{2}$	1	4	$\tfrac{1}{2}$	0	0	$\tfrac{1}{2}$
	$c_j - Z_j$		0	0	$-\tfrac{1}{2}$	0	0	$-\tfrac{1}{2}$

Once again, we have obtained an optimal solution to the current linear programming problem, namely,

$$
\begin{aligned}
x_1 &= \tfrac{3}{2} \\
x_2 &= \tfrac{11}{4} \\
x_3 &= 0 \\
x_4 &= \tfrac{3}{2} \qquad \text{Maximum } Z = 12\,\tfrac{1}{2} \\
x_5 &= \tfrac{3}{4} \\
x_6 &= 0
\end{aligned}
\tag{9-91}
$$

Illustrating what occurred, recall that our revised constraints were

$$
\begin{aligned}
1x_1 + 6x_2 + 1x_3 \qquad\qquad &= 18 \rightarrow 1x_3 = 18 - 1x_1 - 6x_2 \\
1x_1 \qquad\qquad + 1x_4 \qquad &= 3 \rightarrow 1x_4 = 3 - 1x_1 \\
1x_1 + 1x_2 \qquad\quad + 1x_5 &= 5 \rightarrow 1x_5 = 5 - 1x_1 - 1x_2
\end{aligned}
\tag{9-92}
$$

and that we appended to these constraints the second cutting-plane constraint:

$$
{}^1\!/_5 x_3 + {}^4\!/_5 x_5 \geq {}^3\!/_5 \qquad \text{or} \qquad x_3 + 4x_5 \geq 3
\tag{9-93}
$$

Substituting x_3 and x_5 from the revised constraints into the second cutting-plane constraint, we obtain:

$$
(18 - 1x_1 - 6x_2) + 4(5 - 1x_1 - 1x_2) \geq 3
\tag{9-94}
$$

or $\quad x_1 + 2x_2 \leq 7$

Thus, the second cutting-plane constraint is equivalent to the constraint $1x_1 + 2x_2 \leq 7$. The original constraint set has now been expanded to the constraint set:

$$
\begin{aligned}
1x_1 + 6x_2 &\leq 18 \\
1x_1 \qquad &\leq 3 \\
1x_1 + 1x_2 &\leq 5 \\
1x_1 + 2x_2 &\leq 7
\end{aligned}
\tag{9-95}
$$

The graphical solution to this problem is shown in Fig. 9.5. However, this optimal solution is not an integer solution, so a new variable and its corresponding equation (row) must be selected for generating a new constraint. Using the largest fractional part rule we have a tie between row 2, x_2, and row 4, x_5. Choosing row 2, x_2, arbitrarily, yields the following new constraint.

$$
{}^1\!/_4 x_3 + {}^3\!/_4 x_6 \geq {}^3\!/_4
\tag{9-96}
$$

so the equation

$$
-{}^1\!/_4 x_3 - {}^3\!/_4 x_6 + x_7 = -{}^3\!/_4
\tag{9-97}
$$

is appended to the current (third) dual simplex tableau. The appended third dual simplex tableau is shown in Table 9.6. Applying the dual simplex algorithm we obtain the fourth dual simplex tableau, as follows.

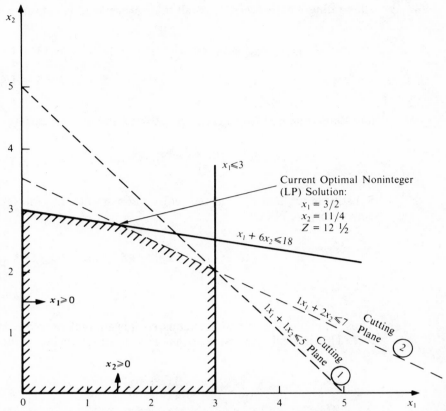

FIGURE 9.5 Graphical Solution—Addition of Second Cutting-Plane Constraint

TABLE 9.6 Third Dual Simplex Tableau (with Appended Constraint)

c_b	Variables in Basis	Solution Values, x_b	c_j a_1	a_2	a_3	a_4	a_5	a_6	a_7
			1	**4**	**0**	**0**	**0**	**0**	**0**
1	x_1	$3/2$	1	0	$-1/2$	0	0	$3/2$	0
4	x_2	$11/4$	0	1	$1/4$	0	0	$-1/4$	0
0	x_4	$3/2$	0	0	$1/2$	1	0	$-3/2$	0
0	x_5	$3/4$	0	0	$1/4$	0	1	$-5/4$	0
0	x_7	$-3/4$	0	0	$-1/4$	0	0	$\boxed{-3/4}$	1
	Z_j	$12\frac{1}{2}$	1	4	$1/2$	0	0	$1/2$	0
	$c_j - Z_j$		0	0	$-1/2$	0	0	$-1/2$	0

TABLE 9.7 Fourth Dual Simplex Tableau (Optimal Integer Solution)

c_b	Variables in Basis	Solution Values, x_b	c_j 1 a_1	4 a_2	0 a_3	0 a_4	0 a_5	0 a_6	0 a_7
1	x_1	0	1	0	-1	0	0	0	2
4	x_2	3	0	1	$1/3$	0	0	0	$-1/3$
0	x_4	3	0	0	1	1	0	0	-2
0	x_5	2	0	0	$2/3$	0	1	0	$-5/3$
0	x_6	1	0	0	$1/3$	0	0	1	$-4/3$
	Z_j	12	1	4	$1/3$	0	0	0	$2/3$
	$c_j - Z_j$		0	0	$-1/3$	0	0	0	$-2/3$

As can be seen in this tableau, the optimal integer solution has been obtained, namely,

$$
\begin{aligned}
x_1^* &= 0 \\
x_2^* &= 3 \\
x_3^* &= 0 \\
x_4^* &= 3 \\
x_5^* &= 2 \\
x_6^* &= 1
\end{aligned}
\qquad \text{Maximum } Z^* = 12 \qquad (9\text{–}98)
$$

Illustrating what has occurred, recall that our revised constraints were

$$
\begin{aligned}
1x_1 + 6x_2 + 1x_3 \qquad\qquad\qquad &= 18 \rightarrow 1x_3 = 18 - 1x_1 - 6x_2 \\
1x_1 \qquad\quad + 1x_4 \qquad\qquad\qquad &= 3 \rightarrow 1x_4 = 3 - 1x_1 \\
1x_1 + 1x_2 \qquad\quad + 1x_5 \qquad &= 5 \rightarrow 1x_5 = 5 - 1x_1 - 1x_2 \\
1x_1 + 2x_2 \qquad\qquad\quad + 1x_6 &= 7 \rightarrow 1x_6 = 7 - 1x_1 - 2x_2
\end{aligned}
\qquad (9\text{–}99)
$$

and that we appended to these constraints the third cutting-plane constraint:

$$
1/4 x_3 + 3/4 x_6 \geq 3/4 \qquad \text{or} \qquad x_3 + 3x_6 \geq 3 \qquad (9\text{–}100)
$$

Substituting x_3 and x_6 from the revised constraints into the third cutting-plane constraint, we obtain

$$
\begin{aligned}
(18 - 1x_1 + 6x_2) + 3(7 - 1x_1 - 2x_2) &\geq 3 \\
1x_1 + 3x_2 &\leq 9
\end{aligned}
\qquad (9\text{–}101)
$$

or

Thus, the third cutting-plane constraint is equivalent to the constraint $1x_1 + 3x_2 \leq 9$. The original constraint set has now been expanded to the constraint set:

$$
\begin{aligned}
1x_1 + 6x_2 &\leq 18 \\
1x_1 \quad\;\; &\leq 3 \\
1x_1 + 1x_2 &\leq 5 \\
1x_1 + 2x_2 &\leq 7 \\
1x_1 + 3x_2 &\leq 9
\end{aligned}
\qquad (9\text{–}102)
$$

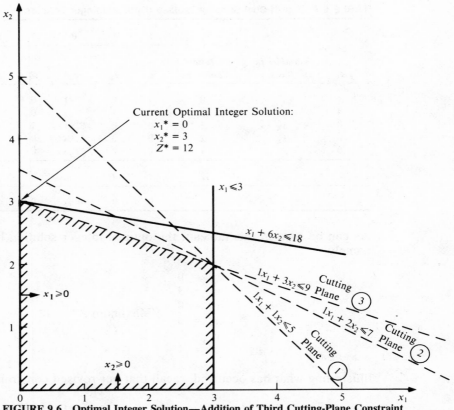

FIGURE 9.6 Optimal Integer Solution—Addition of Third Cutting-Plane Constraint

The graphical solution to this problem is shown in Fig. 9.6. Observe that all variables, both the real variables, x_1 and x_2, and the slack variables have zero or nonnegative integer values in the current optimal integer solution.

In terms of the original problem formulation for this situation, the Telsa Transformer Company will maximize revenue at \$12,000 by constructing three of the 25 kilo-volt transformers. This all-integer solution has a lower optimum value for its objective function than does the corresponding linear programming problem. However, the physical realities of the problem situation requires that all the solution values must be integers.

9.6 MIXED-INTEGER PROGRAMMING

In the illustrative problem of the last section, both the decision variables and the slack variables were restricted to being integers in the optimal solution. However, in many problems only a subset of the decision and slack variables needs to be restricted to integer values. This type of a problem is a *mixed-integer programming problem*.

Gomory[6] has also developed a cutting-plane procedure for mixed-integer

---

[6] Ralph E. Gomory, "An Algorithm for the Mixed Integer Problem," P-1885, The RAND Corporation, June 1960.

programming problems. The algorithm is very similar in most aspects to that discussed previously for all-integer programming problems. Once again, an optimal solution is obtained to the problem without the integrality requirements, using the simplex method of linear programming. If the solution so obtained is a feasible solution to the mixed-integer programming problem it must also be an optimal solution to the mixed-integer programming problem. If not, we again proceed to introduce cutting-plane constraints. However, these cutting-plane constraints are determined in a different manner than they were for all-integer programming problem.

To determine the cutting-plane constraint in mixed-integer programming we proceed as follows. Suppose that some basic variable x_{Bi} has a fractional value in the optimal simplex tableau, and that it must be an integer value in the mixed-integer programming problem. If the nonbasic variables are denoted as x_j, the basic variable has the following relationship with the nonbasic variables.

$$x_{Bi} = \hat{b}_i + \sum_{j=1}^{n} \hat{a}_{ij} x_j \quad \text{for } i = 1, 2, \ldots, m \tag{9-103}$$

$$\text{or} \quad x_{Bi} + \sum_{j=1}^{n} -\hat{a}_{ij} x_j = \hat{b}_i \tag{9-104}$$

where $\hat{a}_{ij}$ = transformed values of the original coefficients a_{ij}
$\hat{b}_i$ = transformed values of the original right-hand side values b_i

The coefficients $\hat{a}_{ij}$ and the constants $\hat{b}_i$ are divided into two parts:

Nonnegative fraction

$$\hat{a}_{ij} = \overset{\downarrow}{f(\hat{a}_{ij})} + \text{integer} \tag{9-105}$$

$$\hat{b}_i = \overset{\downarrow}{f(\hat{b}_i)} + \text{integer} \tag{9-106}$$

The Gomory cutting-plane constraint for mixed-integer programming is expressed as:

$$\sum_{j=1}^{n} f'(\hat{a}_{ij}) x_j = f(\hat{b}_i) + \text{integer} \quad \text{for } i = 1, 2, \ldots, m \tag{9-107}$$

Therefore:

$$\sum_{j=1}^{n} f'(\hat{a}_{ij}) x_j \geq f(\hat{b}_i) \tag{9-108}$$

where: $f'(\hat{a}_{ij})$ = newly obtained nonnegative fractional values.
The cutting-plane equation is then determined by introducing a slack variable x_s and rearranging, as follows.

$$x_s = -f(\hat{b}_i) + \sum_{j=1}^{n} f'(\hat{a}_{ij}) x_j \quad \text{for } i = 1, 2, \ldots, m \tag{9-109}$$

The value of $f'(\hat{a}_{ij})$ is determined by whether or not the nonbasic variables in the cutting-plane constraint are required to take on integer values. The rules for this determination are

---

RULE 1   *If the nonbasic variable* x_j *is restricted to take on an integer value, then:*

$$f'(\hat{a}_{ij}) = f(\hat{a}_{ij}) \qquad\qquad \text{for } f(\hat{a}_{ij}) \le f(\hat{b}_i) \qquad (9\text{-}110)$$

$$f'(\hat{a}_{ij}) = \frac{f(\hat{b}_i)}{1 - f(\hat{b}_i)}[1 - f(\hat{a}_{ij})] \qquad \text{for } f(\hat{a}_{ij}) > f(\hat{b}_i) \qquad (9\text{-}111)$$

RULE 2   *If the nonbasic variable* x_j *is not restricted to take on an integer value, then:*

$$f'(\hat{a}_{ij}) = \hat{a}_{ij} \qquad\qquad \text{for } \hat{a}_{ij} \ge 0 \qquad (9\text{-}112)$$

$$f'(\hat{a}_{ij}) = \frac{f(\hat{b}_i)}{1 - f(\hat{b}_i)}(-\hat{a}_{ij}) \qquad \text{for } \hat{a}_{ij} < 0 \qquad (9\text{-}113)$$

Once we have determined the Gomory cutting-plane equation, it is appended to the optimal simplex tableau of the original linear programming problem. The dual simplex procedure is then employed, just as was done previously for the all-integer programming problem. If the desired optimal solution is not obtained, a new Gomory cutting-plane constraint must be formulated, and the procedure is repeated until the desired optimal solution is obtained.

9.7   APPLICATION OF THE CUTTING-PLANE ALGORITHM— A MIXED-INTEGER PROGRAMMING PROBLEM

The modified cutting-plane algorithm will now be illustrated by applying it to the following mixed-integer programming problem.

$$\text{Maximize } Z = 4x_1 + 3x_2 \qquad (9\text{-}114)$$

subject to:
$$\begin{aligned} 3x_1 + 5x_2 &\le 11 \\ 2x_1 + \tfrac{1}{2}x_2 &\le 4 \end{aligned} \qquad (9\text{-}115)$$

$$x_1 \ge 0, x_2 \ge 0 \qquad x_1 \text{ an integer} \qquad (9\text{-}116)$$

The graphical solution to this problem is presented in Fig. 9.7, where it can be seen that the optimal noninteger (LP) solution is

$$\begin{aligned} x_1 &= {}^{20}/_{17} \\ x_2 &= {}^{29}/_{17} \\ \text{Maximum } Z &= 10{}^{6}/_{17} \end{aligned} \qquad (9\text{-}117)$$

and the optimal mixed-integer solution is

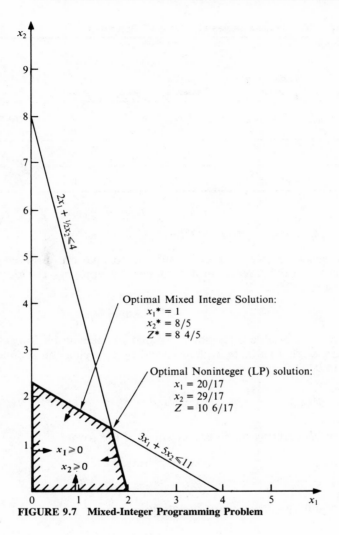

FIGURE 9.7   Mixed-Integer Programming Problem

$$x_1^* = 1$$
$$x_2^* = {}^8\!/_5$$
$$\text{Maximum } Z^* = 8{}^4\!/_5 \tag{9-118}$$

Application of the simplex method to this mixed-integer programming problems yields, in two iterations, the optimal (noninteger) linear programming solution shown in Table 9.8.

However, this optimal linear programming solution is not the optimal solution to the mixed-integer programming problem given by (9–114), (9–115), and (9–116), since $x_1 = {}^{20}\!/_{17}$ is not the required integer value.

Since the mixed-integer programming problem requires an integer value for x_1, the cutting-plane constraint will be generated from the x_1 row. The relationship of the basic variable x_1 to the nonbasic variables x_3 and x_4 is

TABLE 9.8 Third Simplex Tableau (Optimal LP Solution)

c_b	Variables in Basis	Solution Values, x_b	c_j			
			4	**3**	**0**	**0**
			a_1	a_2	a_3	a_4
3	x_2	$20/17$	0	1	$4/17$	$-6/17$
4	x_1	$29/17$	1	0	$-1/17$	$10/17$
	Z_j	$176/17$	4	3	$8/17$	$22/17$
	$c_j - Z_j$		0	0	$-8/17$	$-22/17$

$$x_1 = 29/17 - 1/17 x_3 + 10/17 x_4 \qquad (9\text{-}119)$$

or $\quad x_1 + 1/17 x_3 - 10/17 x_4 = 29/17$

The nonbasic variable x_3 is not restricted to take on an integer value, and the coefficient of this variable is determined by applying the first part of Rule 2 (Equation 9–112).

$$f'(x_3) = 1/17 \qquad \text{since } 1/17 \geq 0 \qquad (9\text{-}120)$$

The nonbasic variable x_4 is not restricted to take on an integer value, and the coefficient of this variable is determined by applying the second part of Rule 2 (Equation 9–113).

$$f'(x_4) = \frac{12/17}{1 - 12/17}[-(-10/17)] = 24/17 \qquad \text{since } -10/17 < 0 \qquad (9\text{-}121)$$

Therefore, the cutting-plane constraint is of the form:

$$1/17 x_3 + 24/17 x_4 \geq 12/17 \qquad (9\text{-}122)$$

or $\quad -1/17 x_3 - 24/17 x_4 \leq -12/17$

and the resulting cutting-plane equation is

$$-1/17 x_3 - 24/17 x_4 + 1 x_5 = -12/17 \qquad (9\text{-}123)$$

The appended tableau (first dual simplex tableau) then becomes

TABLE 9.9 First Dual Simplex Tableau (with Appended Constraint)

c_b	Variables in Basis	Solution Values	c_j				
			4	**3**	**0**	**0**	**0**
			a_1	a_2	a_3	a_4	a_5
3	x_2	$20/17$	0	1	$4/17$	$-6/17$	0
4	x_1	$29/17$	1	0	$-1/17$	$10/17$	0
0	x_5	$-12/17$	0	0	$-12/85$	$\left(-10/17\right)$	1
	Z_j	$176/17$	4	3	$8/17$	$22/17$	0
	$c_j - Z_j$		0	0	$-8/17$	$-22/17$	0

Applying the dual simplex algorithm, we obtain the second dual simplex tableau, as follows.

TABLE 9.10 Second Dual Simplex Tableau (Optimal Mixed-Integer Solution)

c_b	Variables in Basis	Solution Values	c_j 4 $\mathbf{a_1}$	3 $\mathbf{a_2}$	0 $\mathbf{a_3}$	0 $\mathbf{a_4}$	0 $\mathbf{a_5}$
3	x_2	$8/5$	0	1	$8/25$	0	$-3/5$
4	x_1	1	1	0	$-1/5$	0	1
0	x_3	$6/5$	0	0	$6/25$	1	$-17/10$
	Z_j	$44/5$	4	3	$4/25$	0	$11/5$
	$c_j - Z_j$		0	0	$-4/25$	0	$-11/5$

As can be seen in this tableau, dual feasibility has been achieved and we have obtained the optimal mixed-integer solution, namely,

$$x_1^* = 1, x_2^* = 8/5, x_3^* = 6/5 \qquad \text{Maximum } Z^* = 44/5 \qquad (9\text{--}124)$$

Illustrating what has occurred recall that our original constraints were

$$3x_1 + 5x_2 + 1x_3 = 11 \rightarrow x_3 = 11 - 3x_1 - 5x_2$$
$$2x_1 + \frac{1}{2}x_2 + 1x_4 = 4 \rightarrow x_4 = 4 - 2x_1 - \frac{1}{2}x_2 \qquad (9\text{--}125)$$

and that we appended to these constraints the cutting-plane constraint:

$$\frac{10}{85}x_3 + \frac{10}{17}x_4 \geq \frac{12}{17} \qquad \text{or} \qquad 12x_3 + 50x_4 \geq 60 \qquad (9\text{--}126)$$

Substituting the values of x_3 and x_4 from the original constraints into the cutting-plane constraint, we obtain

$$12(11 - 3x_1 - 5x_2) + 50(4 - 2x_1 - \frac{1}{2}x_2) \geq 60$$

or $\qquad\qquad\qquad 136x_1 + 85x_2 \qquad\qquad \leq 272 \qquad (9\text{--}127)$

Our original constraint set has been expanded to the constraint set:

$$3x_1 + 5x_2 \leq 11$$
$$2x_1 + \frac{1}{2}x_2 \leq 4 \qquad (9\text{--}128)$$
$$136x_1 + 85x_2 \leq 272$$

The graphical solution to this problem is shown in Fig. 9.8. Observe how the addition of the cutting-plane constraint yields the optimum mixed-integer programming solution.

9.8 THE BRANCH-AND-BOUND TECHNIQUE

The difficulties encountered in applying the cutting-plane algorithm, and the fact that any bounded integer program has only a finite number of feasible solutions,

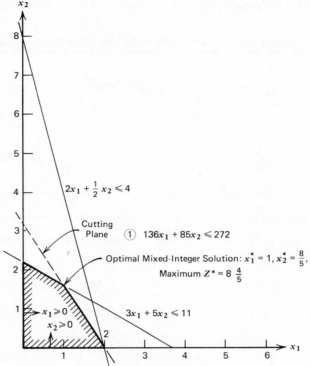

FIGURE 9.8 Optimal Mixed-Integer Solution

has led to the development of **implicit enumeration procedures** for finding the solution to such problems. One such implicit enumeration procedure is the **branch-and-bound technique** in which only a small fraction of the feasible solutions are explicitly examined.[7] The fact that the branch-and-bound technique involves enumeration of only a small percentage of the feasible solutions should be emphasized, because a relatively small problem involving 15 decision variables, each of which could assume 10 feasible values, could have as many as 10^{15} feasible solutions. Regardless of the fact that today's digital computers make arithmetic computations very rapidly, exhaustive or complete enumeration of all the feasible solutions to a problem such as this would be very time consuming and costly.

9.8.1 An Overview of the Branch-and-Bound Method

The branch-and-bound method employs a strategy in which the feasible region is divided into smaller and smaller subsets, with each successive subset being examined until that feasible solution which produces the optimal value of the objective function is obtained. In general, there are a number of ways of dividing the feasible region, and therefore there are a number of branch-and-bound algorithms

---

[7] A survey of branch-and-bound methods can be found in E. L. Lawler and J. D. Wood, "Branch-and-Bound Methods: A Survey," *Operations Research,* vol. 14 (1966), 619–719.

in existence. We will provide a brief overview of the branch-and-bound method in this section, and then we will illustrate its application to specific problems.

An integer linear programming problem is a continuous linear programming problem that has been further constrained by the imposition of integrality requirements on the decision variables. In a maximization problem, the optimal solution value to the continuous linear programming problem will always be an upper bound on the optimal solution value to the integer linear programming problem. Furthermore, any feasible point (i.e., any feasible integer solution) to the integer programming problem is always a lower bound on the optimal value of the objective function of the continuous linear programming problem. Now, the basic idea of the branch-and-bound method is to utilize these two fundamental observations to logically subdivide the continuous linear programming feasible region and to then seek feasible integer solutions to the integer programming problem.

The basic steps of the branch-and-bound method (for a maximization problem) can be summarized as follows.

1. **Initialization Step.** Given the integer programming problem, relax the integrality restrictions and solve the problem as a continuous linear programming problem. If the optimal solution results in integer values for all the variables that are constrained to be integers, the optimal integer programming solution has been obtained. If not, the optimal solution to the continuous linear programming problem represents the *initial upper bound* on the integer programming problem. The *initial lower bound* on the integer programming problem can be determined by rounding down to integers all of the noninteger variables in the optimal solution to the continuous linear programming problem. At this point the optimal integer programming solution is greater than or equal to the lower bound and less than or equal to the upper bound. Proceed to Step 2.

2. **Branch Step.** Select an integer-constrained variable that has a noninteger value in the optimal solution to the linear programming problem. *Partition,* or *branch*, the problem into two new subproblems using the variable selected. The branching is done by introducing two mutually exclusive constraints that satisfy integer requirements while preventing the exclusion of any feasible integer solution. If k is the integer portion of the current value of the noninteger selected for branching, the variable will be constrained to be less than or equal to k in one subproblem and greater than or equal to $k + 1$ in the other subproblem. Proceed to Step 3.

3. **Bound Step.** Determine the optimal solution for each of the newly created subproblems, using the usual linear programming procedures (i.e., disregarding the integer restrictions on the variables). In this manner a reasonable upper bound for each newly created subproblem is determined.

4. **Fathoming Step.** Each new subproblem is examined to determine if it is desirable to explore it any further. There are four possible outcomes for each subproblem:

    (a) If a subproblem has no feasible linear programming solution it is eliminated from further consideration, or said to be **fathomed by infeasibility**.

    (b) If a subproblem has a linear programming solution that is worse than the best integer solution obtained thus far (i.e., the current lower bound), it is eliminated from further consideration, or said to be **fathomed by bounding**.

(c)   If a subproblem has a linear programming solution that is also all-integer, the value of this integer solution is compared to the best integer solution obtained thus far (i.e., the current lower bound). If the integer solution for the subproblem is worse than the best integer solution obtained thus far, it is eliminated from further consideration, or said to be **fathomed by integrality**. If the integer solution for the subproblem is better than the best integer solution obtained thus far, it is specified as the current lower bound.

(d)   If a subproblem has a linear programming solution that does not have integer values for the integer-constrained variables, but which is better than any integer solution obtained thus far (i.e., the current lower bound) we then specify this solution value as the upper bound for this subproblem and return to Step 2 and branch on the subproblem.

5.   **Completion Step.**   The procedure outlined above in Steps 2, 3, and 4 is continued for each such subproblem until there are no further subproblems to be examined. At this juncture the integer solution corresponding to the current lower bound is the optimal integer programming solution, and the entire procedure stops.

We will now illustrate the branch-and-bound method, using a small, two-variable integer programming problem that can be solved using graphical procedures. Each of the steps described above will be illustrated by this example.

9.8.2   Application of the Branch-and-Bound Method to an All-Integer Programming Problem

To illustrate the branch-and-bound method let us first consider the following two-variable all-integer programming problem, which we will call Problem P_1.

$$\text{Maximize } Z = 3x_1 + 4x_2 \tag{9-129}$$

subject to:
$$\begin{array}{l} 2x_1 + 8x_2 \le 16 \\ 7x_1 + 2x_2 \le 14 \end{array} \tag{9-130}$$

with $x_1 \ge 0,\ x_2 \ge 0,\ x_1, x_2$ integer   (9-131)

This problem is presented below graphically in Fig. 9.9. Note that the feasible solution space for this problem has been cross-hatched, and the lattice points (integer values of x_1 and x_2) have been shown as dots within this feasible solution space.

Relaxing the integrality restrictions and solving the problem graphically, the optimal continuous (noninteger) linear programming solution is $x_1 = {}^{20}/_{13}$, $x_2 = {}^{21}/_{13}$, Maximum $Z = 11^1/_{13}$. This (noninteger) solution is the initial upper bound on the integer solution (i.e., $Z_U = 11^1/_{13}$). The initial lower bound on the integer solution is the solution with both x_1 and x_2 rounded down (i.e., $x_1 = 1$, $x_2 = 1$, $Z_L = 7$).

A convenient way of presenting the various solutions that are obtained while using the branch-and-bound method is by an **enumeration tree**. The enumeration tree for our problem at this point consists of a single node. The initial enumeration tree is shown in Fig. 9.10.

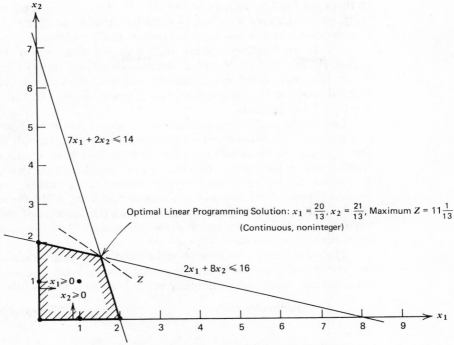

FIGURE 9.9 Two-Variable Integer Programming Problem (Problem P₁)

The continuous linear programming solution has $x_1 = {}^{20}/_{13}$ and $x_2 = {}^{21}/_{13}$. Both of these variables must be integer in the optimal integer programming solution, and we therefore need to subdivide the original problem into two parts in order to search for possible integer solution values for x_1 and x_2. Since both x_1 and x_2 are noninteger, we must select one of the two variables in order to make the first subdivision. Although no general rule exists for selecting among two, or more, noninteger variables, various **branching rules** can be used, such as:

1. Select the variable with the noninteger solution value that has the greatest fractional part.
2. Select the variable with the noninteger solution value whose objective function coefficient is largest.

For this problem the variable x_2 is initially selected by either of these two branching rules. Now, we subdivide the feasible region in an attempt to make x_2 integral.

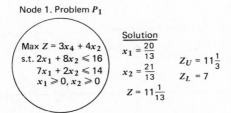

FIGURE 9.10 Enumeration Tree—Problem P₂

In this case the two integer values closest to $x_2 = {}^{21}/_{13}$ are 1 and 2. Thus, in any integer programming solution, x_2 must be either an integer ≤ 1 or an integer ≥ 2. Our first subdivision involves the two mutually exclusive constraints $x_1 \leq 1$ and $x_1 \geq 2$. These subdivisions are shown as the single point, P_2, and the shaded region, P_3, in Fig. 9.11. Note that the two added constraints eliminate all fractional values of x_2 between 1 and 2, thereby reducing the feasible solution space of the original problem in a manner so that a fewer number of finite integer solutions needs to be evaluated.

Inspection of the two new feasible regions that have been created from the original problem indicates the following. First, the original, continuous optimal linear programming solution to the problem has been eliminated (i.e., it is not feasible with respect to the feasible regions of either of the two new subproblems). Therefore, the optimal integer solution that we are seeking will be found in the feasible region of one of these two subproblems and will have a worse value (i.e., smaller value) of the objective function than the solution of the original problem. Second, any all-integer solution to the original problem is contained within one or the other of the two new subproblems.

The next step in the branch-and-bound method involves solving each of the two new subproblems with integer restrictions relaxed. The solutions to these two subproblems, obtained graphically using Fig. 9.11, are as follows.

Subproblem P_2	Subproblem P_3
$x_1 = 0$	$x_1 = 1^5/_7$
$x_2 = 2$	$x_2 = 1$
$Z = 8$	$Z = 9^1/_7$

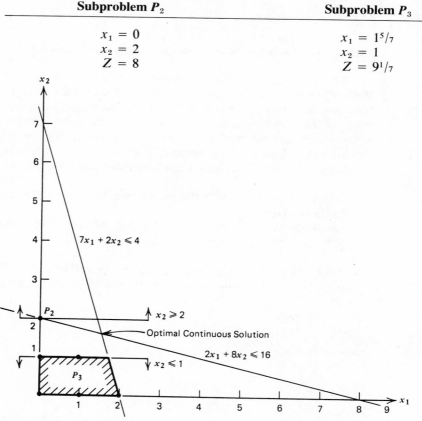

FIGURE 9.11   Subdividing Problem P_2 into Subproblems P_2 and P_3

The results up to this point are shown in the enumeration tree, presented as Fig. 9.12.

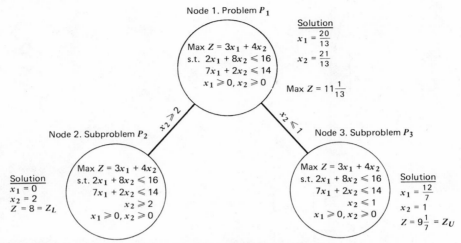

Node 1. Problem P_1

$\text{Max } Z = 3x_1 + 4x_2$
s.t. $2x_1 + 8x_2 \leqslant 16$
$7x_1 + 2x_2 \leqslant 14$
$x_1 \geqslant 0, x_2 \geqslant 0$

Solution
$x_1 = \dfrac{20}{13}$
$x_2 = \dfrac{21}{13}$

$\text{Max } Z = 11\dfrac{1}{13}$

$x_2 \geqslant 2$ $x_2 \leqslant 1$

Node 2. Subproblem P_2 Node 3. Subproblem P_3

Solution
$x_1 = 0$
$x_2 = 2$
$Z = 8 = Z_L$

$\text{Max } Z = 3x_1 + 4x_2$
s.t. $2x_1 + 8x_2 \leqslant 16$
$7x_1 + 2x_2 \leqslant 14$
$x_2 \geqslant 2$
$x_1 \geqslant 0, x_2 \geqslant 0$

$\text{Max } Z = 3x_1 + 4x_2$
s.t. $2x_1 + 8x_2 \leqslant 16$
$7x_1 + 2x_2 \leqslant 14$
$x_2 \leqslant 1$
$x_1 \geqslant 0, x_2 \geqslant 0$

Solution
$x_1 = \dfrac{12}{7}$
$x_2 = 1$
$Z = 9\dfrac{1}{7} = Z_U$

FIGURE 9.12   **Enumeration Tree-Problem P_1, Subproblems P_2, P_3**

Observe that Subproblem P_2 has yielded an all-integer solution whose objective function value, $Z = 8$, is better than the current lower bound, $Z_L = 7$. Thus, the current lower bound becomes $Z_L = 8$, and we do not need to make any further search in Subproblem P_2.

In Subproblem P_3, further search is required because its noninteger solution ($x_1 = {}^{12}/_7$, $x_2 = 9$, $Z = 9^1/_7$) is better than the current lower bound, $Z_L = 8$. Consequently, this further search may lead to an all-integer solution whose objective function value exceeds the lower bound obtained for Subproblem P_2. At this juncture we set the solution value for Subproblem P_3 as the upper bound for this subproblem (i.e., $Z_U = 9^1/_7$).

We next subdivide, or branch, Subproblem P_3 into two new subproblems, the first with the added constraint $x_1 \geq 2$, and the second with the constraint $x_1 \leq 1$. These subdivisions are shown as the single point, P_4, and the shaded region, P_5, in Fig. 9.13. Note that the two added constraints eliminate all fractional values of x_1 between 1 and 2.

Solving each of these two new subproblems with integer restrictions relaxed, the following solutions are obtained.

Subproblem P_4	**Subproblem P_5**
$x_1 = 2$	$x_1 = 1$
$x_2 = 0$	$x_2 = 1$
$Z = 6$	$Z = 7$

The results up to this point are summarized in the enumeration tree, presented as Fig. 9.14. Note that for both Subproblem P_4 and Subproblem P_5 we have obtained all-integer solutions. However, the objective function values for these subproblems ($Z = 6$ and $Z = 7$) are less than the current lower bound, $Z_L = 8$, which was obtained as the solution to Subproblem P_2. Consequently, Subproblem P_4 and Subproblem P_5 have been fathomed by integrality. There are no further

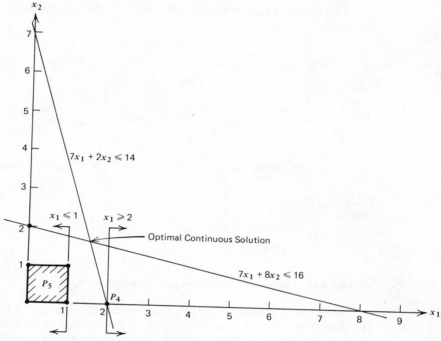

FIGURE 9.13   Subdividing Subproblem P_3 into Subproblems P_4 and P_5

subproblems to be examined, so the integer programming solution obtained for Subproblem P_2, (i.e., the current lower bound $Z_L = 8$) is the optimal integer programming solution. This solution is

$$x_1^* = 0, \; x_2^* = 2 \qquad \text{Maximum } Z^* = 8 \qquad (9-132)$$

In the two-variable all-integer programming problem we just solved, the various linear programming problems corresponding to the various subproblems were solved very easily using graphical methods. For larger problems involving many variables we need a procedure for efficiently solving a series of linear programming problems (which cannot be solved graphically). Fortunately, this procedure is readily available. Recall that when we branch to a subproblem, we add one constraint that cannot be satisfied by the linear programming solution to the subproblem that we branched from. Thus, we have added a constraint that renders the previous linear programming solution infeasible. However, this is another situation in which we can use the dual simplex algorithm to restore feasibility and, hence, obtain the optimal solution for the new subproblem with the added constraint. The use of the dual simplex algorithm in this manner will be shown in the following section of the chapter, as a mixed-integer programming problem is solved.

9.8.3 Application of the Branch-and-Bound Method to a Mixed-Integer Programming Problem

The branch-and-bound method described above can easily be used to solve mixed-integer programming problems in which some, but not all, of the variables

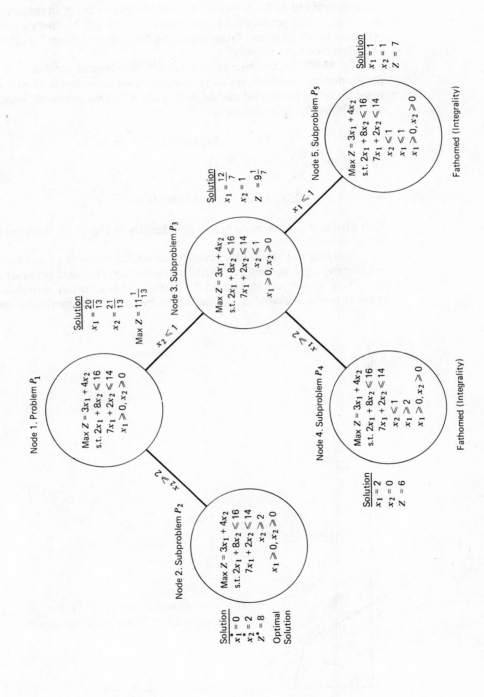

FIGURE 9.14   Enumeration Tree–Problem P_1, Subproblems P_2, P_3, P_4, P_5

are constrained to be integers. In mixed-integer programming problems the sub-divisions of the problem are generated exclusively by the variables that are constrained to be integers. Otherwise, the branch-and-bound method is the same as that described previously.

To illustrate the use of the branch-and-bound method for a mixed-integer programming problem, let us reconsider the two-variable mixed-integer programming problem presented earlier in Section 9.7. This problem, which we will denote as Problem P_1, is as follows.

$$\text{Maximize } Z = 4x_1 + 3x_2 \tag{9-133}$$

subject to:
$$
\begin{aligned}
3x_1 + 5x_2 &\leq 11 \\
2x_1 + {}^1\!/_2 x_2 &\leq 4
\end{aligned}
\tag{9-134}
$$

with $x_1 \geq 0, x_2 \geq 0$ x_1 an integer   (9-135)

This problem is presented below graphically in Fig. 9.15, with the feasible solution space cross-hatched.

Relaxing the integrality restrictions on the variable x_1 and solving the problem graphically, the optimal continuous (noninteger) linear programming solution is $x_1 = {}^{29}\!/_{17}$, $x_2 = {}^{20}\!/_{17}$, Maximum $Z = 10^6\!/_{17}$. This solution, which is noninteger with respect to the variable, x_1, is the upper bound on the mixed-integer solution (i.e.,

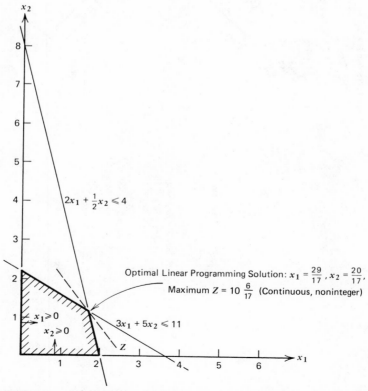

FIGURE 9.15   Two-Variable Mixed-Integer Programming Problem (Problem P_1)

$Z_U = 10^6/_{17}$). The initial lower bound on the mixed-integer solution is the solution with x_1 rounded down (i.e., $x_1 = 1$, $x_2 = {}^{20}/_{17}$, $Z_L = 7^9/_{17}$).

We will again employ an enumeration tree to trace out the branch-and-bound process. The enumeration tree for our problem at this point consists of a single node, and is shown in Fig. 9.16.

Node 1. Problem P_1

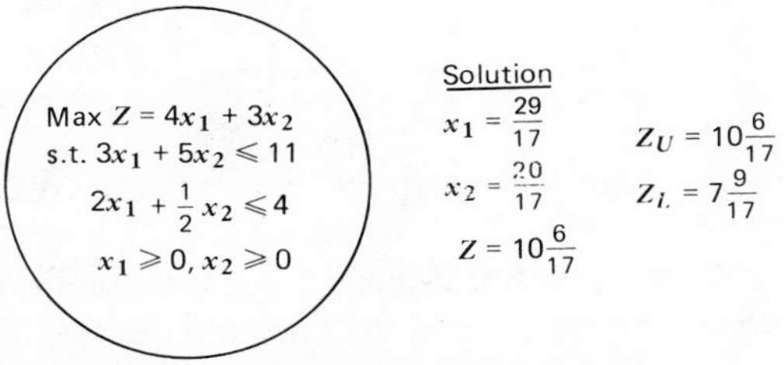

Max Z = 4x1 + 3x2
s.t. 3x1 + 5x2 ≤ 11
2x1 + 1/2 x2 ≤ 4
x1 ≥ 0, x2 ≥ 0
Solution
x1 = 29/17
x2 = 20/17
Z = 10 6/17
ZU = 10 6/17
ZL = 7 9/17

FIGURE 9.16 Enumeration Tree-Problem P_1

The continuous linear programming solution has $x_1 = {}^{29}/_{17}$, $x_2 = {}^{20}/_{17}$. However, only the variable x_1 must be an integer in the mixed-integer programming problem. Therefore, we must subdivide the original problem (P_1) into two parts in an attempt to make x_1 integral. Thus, our first subdivision involves the two mutually exclusive constraints $x_1 \leq 1$ and $x_1 \geq 2$. These subdivisions are shown as the single point P_2 and the shaded region P_3 in Fig. 9.17.

x2
8
7
6
5
4
3
2
1
2x1 + 1/2 x2 ≤ 4
x1 ≤ 1
x1 ≥ 2
P3
P2
3x1 + 5x2 ≤ 11
1
2
3
4
5
6
x1

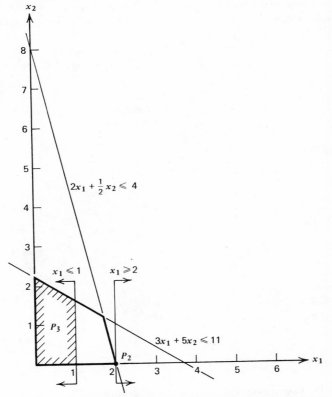

FIGURE 9.17 Subdividing Problem P_1 into Subproblems P_2 and P_3.

The next step in the branch-and-bound method involves solving each of the two new subproblems with integer restrictions relaxed. The solution to these two subproblems, obtained graphically using Fig. 9.17, are as follows.

Subproblem P_2	Subproblem P_3
$x_1 = 2$	$x_1 = 1$
$x_2 = 0$	$x_2 = {}^8/_5$
$Z = 8$	$Z = 8{}^4/_5$

The results up to this point are shown in an enumeration tree, presented in Fig. 9.18.

Examining the solution to Subproblem P_2 we immediately observe that the solution is integral with respect to x_1 (i.e., the variable required to be integral). The all-integer solution we have obtained for Subproblem P_2 has an objective function value $Z = 8$, which is better than the current lower bound $Z_L = 7{}^9/_{17}$. Thus, the current lower bound becomes $Z_L = 8$.

Examining the solution to Subproblem P_3 we immediately observe that the solution is integral with respect to x_1. The mixed-integer solution we have obtained for Subproblem P_3 has an objective function value $Z = 8{}^4/_5$, which is better than the current lower bound, $Z_L = 8$. Thus, the current lower bound becomes $Z_L = 8{}^4/_5$. Now, there are no further subdivisions to be examined, so the mixed-integer programming solution obtained for Subproblem P_3 (i.e., corresponding to the current lower bound $Z_L = 8{}^4/_5$) is the optimal mixed-integer programming solution. This solution is

$$x_1^* = 1, \; x_2^* = {}^8/_5 \qquad \text{Maximum } Z^* = 8{}^4/_5 \qquad (9\text{--}136)$$

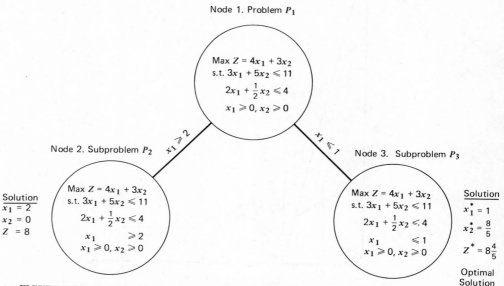

FIGURE 9.18   Enumeration Tree-Problem P_1, Subproblems P_2, P_3

To illustrate how the dual simplex algorithm would be used to solve the linear programming problems corresponding to the various subdivisions of the branch-and-bound method let us reconsider Subproblem P_3. Subproblem P_3 is as follows.

$$\text{Maximize } Z = 4x_1 + 3x_2 \qquad (9\text{--}137)$$

subject to:
$$
\begin{aligned}
3x_1 + 5x_2 &\leq 11 \\
2x_1 + {}^1\!/_2 x_2 &\leq 4 \\
x_1 &\leq 1 \quad \text{(New constraint)}
\end{aligned}
\qquad (9\text{--}138)
$$

with $\quad x_1 \geq 0, x_2 \geq 0 \qquad (9\text{--}139)$

Expressing this new constraint as an inequality, with the addition of the slack variable x_5, we obtain

$$x_1 \quad + 1x_5 = 1 \qquad (9\text{--}140)$$

Substituting the current optimal value $x_1 = {}^{29}\!/_{17}$ (i.e., the solution value of x_1 in Problem P_1) into Equation 9--140, we have

$$
\begin{aligned}
1({}^{29}\!/_{17}) \quad + 1x_5 &= 1 \\
x_5 &= -{}^{12}\!/_{17}
\end{aligned}
\qquad (9\text{--}141)
$$

Thus, we observe that the addition of this constraint will result in the inclusion of a slack variable in the basis with a negative value. Thus, feasibility and optimality must be restored using the dual simplex method.

Recall that we actually obtained a linear programming solution to Problem P_1 (i.e., the original problem without the added constraint $x_1 \leq 1$) earlier in Section 9.7 of this chapter (i.e., refer back to Table 9.8). Therefore, the effect of adding this new constraint to the optimal linear programming solution, in terms of the final simplex tableau, would be as shown in Table 9.11.

TABLE 9.11   Revised Simplex Tableau—Additional Constraint

c_b	Variables in Basis	Solution Values, x_b	c_j				
			4	**3**	**0**	**0**	**0**
			a_1	a_2	a_3	a_4	a_5
3	x_2	$^{20}/_{17}$	0	1	$^{4}/_{17}$	$-^{6}/_{17}$	0
4	x_1	$^{29}/_{17}$	1	0	$-^{1}/_{17}$	$^{10}/_{17}$	0
0	x_5	1	1	0	0	0	1
	Z_j	$^{176}/_{17}$	4	3	$^{8}/_{17}$	$^{22}/_{17}$	1
	$c_j - Z_j$		0	0	$-^{8}/_{17}$	$-^{22}/_{17}$	-1

Observe that the solution with the additional constraint, as presented in Table 9.11, is not a basic solution. We must, therefore, create an identity matrix within this simplex tableau for the basic variables x_1, x_2, and x_5. This means that for the other basic variables in this simplex tableau, x_1 and x_2, we must convert the corresponding coefficient in the new (x_5) row to zero using the usual Gauss-Jordan procedures (refer back to Chapter 5 for a review of the specifics). The revised simplex tableau, which is the new basic solution with the added constraint, is presented in Table 9.12.

TABLE 9.12   Revised Simplex Tableau—New Basic Solution

c_b	Variables in Basis	Solution Values, x_b	c_j 4 a_1	3 a_2	0 a_3	0 a_4	0 a_5
3	x_2	$20/17$	0	1	$4/17$	$-6/17$	0
4	x_1	$29/17$	1	0	$-1/17$	$10/17$	0
0	x_5	$-12/17$	0	0	$1/17$	$\left(-10/17\right)$	1
	Z_j	$176/17$	4	3	$8/17$	$22/17$	0
	$c_j - Z_j$		0	0	$-8/17$	$-22/17$	0

In Table 9.12 we observe that we have a new basic solution that is not feasible. However, we can easily restore feasibility, and hence optimality, by applying the dual simplex algorithm. Once this is done, we will have solved Subproblem P_3.

Applying the dual simplex algorithm, variable x_5 leaves the basis and variable x_4 enters the basis. An iteration is performed, and this leads to the second dual simplex tableau shown in Table 9.13.

TABLE 9.13   Second Dual Simplex Tableau (Optimal Solution)

c_b	Variables in Basis	Solution Values, x_b	c_j 4 a_1	3 a_2	0 a_3	0 a_4	0 a_5
3	x_2	$8/5$	0	1	$1/5$	0	$-3/5$
4	x_1	1	1	0	0	0	1
0	x_4	$6/5$	0	0	$-1/10$	1	$-17/10$
	Z_j	$44/5$	4	3	$3/5$	0	$11/5$
	$c_j - Z_j$		0	0	$-3/5$	0	$-11/5$

This solution is, of course, exactly the same solution we obtained graphically for Subproblem P_3. Subproblem P_2 could be solved in a similar manner using the dual simplex algorithm. In summary, the dual simplex algorithm is a convenient and efficient way of solving the linear programming problems that are created during the branching process of the branch-and-bound method.

9.8.4 Application of the Branch-and-Bound Method to a Zero-One Combinatorial Problem (Assignment Problem)

To further illustrate the use of the branch-and-bound method, let us reconsider the assignment problem discussed previously in Section 7.8.1 of Chapter 7. The cost table associated with the assignments of workers to jobs is reproduced below as Table 9.14.

TABLE 9.14 Cost Table—Assignment Problem Illustrating the Branch-and-Bound Technique

	Jobs				
Workers	1	2	3	4	5
A	7	5	9	8	11
B	9	12	7	11	10
C	8	5	4	6	9
D	7	3	6	9	5
E	4	6	7	5	11

Recall that the objective of this assignment problem was to assign each of the five workers to a unique job in a manner that minimized the total cost of doing all five jobs. This small ($n = 5$) assignment problem is a zero-one combinatorial problem (i.e., $x_{ij} = 1$ = worker i is assigned to job j; $x_{ij} = 0$ = worker i is not assigned to job j) which has $n! = 5! = 120$ *feasible* solutions. Recall that a feasible solution to an assignment problem requires the assignment of each resource to a single activity, and vice versa. We will now illustrate the branch-and-bound solution to this cost minimization assignment problem in an iterative manner.

ITERATION 0
Initialization

Using the 120 feasible solutions, we begin by determining a *lower bound* on the total cost of the assignment. This lower bound is the lowest possible cost associated with the assignment of the five workers to the five jobs. The lower bound can be determined by summing the minimum costs in the respective columns of the assignment cost matrix. When we do this, we obtain: $Z_L = 4 + 3 + 4 + 5 + 5 = 21$, which is not a feasible solution (i.e., the assignment for this solution is E-1, D-2, C-3, E-4, and D-5). Next, we specify an *upper bound* on the total cost of an assignment.[8] Initially, we set the upper bound $Z_U = +\infty$. In subsequent steps this upper bound will be reduced to the cost associated with the best feasible assignment obtained thus far. In this initialization step, we have determined both a lower bound and upper bound on the total cost of the assignment. However, in the assignment that produces our lower bound, worker D and worker E have been assigned to two jobs, and this assignment is not feasible. We must proceed to find the least-cost feasible solution.

---

[8] If a feasible solution is readily identifiable initially, the upper bound can be set equal to the total cost of this feasible solution. For example, we could have initially set $Z_U = 7 + 12 + 4 + 9 + 11 = 43$, which is the total cost associated with the feasible assignment A-1, B-2, C-3, D-4, and E-5.

ITERATION 1
Branching and
Bounding

In this iteration we partition the set of 120 feasible solutions into five branches, or subsets, which correspond to the five possible lowest-cost ways in which a worker can be assigned to job 1. The corresponding lower bounds (Z_L) for these five branches are computed as:

$$Z_{L_{A-1}} = {}^{(A-1)}7 + 3 + 4 + 5 + 5 = 24 \qquad \text{(Not feasible)}$$

$$Z_{L_{B-1}} = {}^{(B-1)}9 + 3 + 4 + 5 + 5 = 26 \qquad \text{(Not feasible)}$$

$$Z_{L_{C-1}} = {}^{(C-1)}8 + 3 + 6 + 5 + 5 = 27 \qquad \text{(Not feasible)} \qquad (9\text{-}142)$$

$$Z_{L_{D-1}} = {}^{(D-1)}7 + 5 + 4 + 5 + 9 = 30 \qquad \text{(Not feasible)}$$

$$Z_{L_{E-1}} = {}^{(E-1)}4 + 3 + 4 + 6 + 5 = 22 \qquad \text{(Not feasible)}$$

Each of these lower bounds are determined by assigning job 1 to a specific worker (row), and then adding the sum of the minimum costs (ignoring that row) for the remaining four columns. These results are summarized in the tree diagram shown in Fig. 9.19. Each of these five solutions is not feasible. Thus, our lower bound does not change, (i.e., $Z_L = 21$), our upper bound does not change (i.e., $Z_U = +\infty$), and we must further partition one of the five existing branches.

ITERATION 2
Branching and
Bounding

From the five branches created in Iteration 1, branch E is selected as the one to partition into new branches, since it has the smallest value of Z_L (i.e., $Z_{L_{E-1}} = 22$). The partitioning is done by assigning worker E to job 1 and then making the second assignment in each of four possible ways (i.e., A-2, B-2, C-2, or D-2). This partitions branch E into branches EA, EB, EC, and ED. The corresponding lower bounds for these four new branches are

$$Z_{L_{E-1, A-2}} = {}^{(E-1)}4 + {}^{(A-2)}5 + 4 + 6 + 5 = 24 \qquad \text{(Not feasible)}$$

$$Z_{L_{E-1, B-2}} = {}^{(E-1)}4 + {}^{(B-2)}12 + 4 + 6 + 5 = 31 \qquad \text{(Not feasible)}$$

$$Z_{L_{E-1, C-2}} = {}^{(E-1)}4 + {}^{(C-2)}5 + 6 + 8 + 5 = 28 \qquad \text{(Not feasible)} \qquad (9\text{-}143)$$

$$Z_{L_{E-1, D-2}} = {}^{(E-1)}4 + {}^{(D-2)}3 + 4 + 6 + 9 = 26 \qquad \text{(Not feasible)}$$

Each of these four new solutions is not feasible. Thus, our lower bound does not change (i.e., $Z_L = 21$), our upper bound does not change (i.e., $Z_U = +\infty$), and we must further partition one of the eight existing branches (i.e., A, B, C, D, EA, EB,

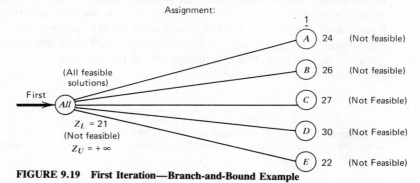

FIGURE 9.19   First Iteration—Branch-and-Bound Example

EC, and *ED*). These results are summarized in the tree diagram shown in Fig. 9.20.

ITERATION 3
Branching and
Bounding

For the eight existing branches we have a tie between branch *A* (i.e., $Z_{L_{A-1}} = 24$) and branch *EA* (i.e., $Z_{L_{E-1, A-2}} = 24$). Breaking this tie arbitrarily, assume that we select branch *EA* as the one to partition into new branches. The partitioning is done by assigning worker *E* to job 1, worker *A* to job 2, and then making the third assignment in each of three possible ways (i.e., $B - 3$, $C - 3$, and $D - 3$). The corresponding lower bounds for these three new branches are

$$Z_{L_{E-1, A-2, B-3}} = {}^{E-1}4 + {}^{A-2}5 + {}^{B-3}7 + 6 + 5 = 27 \qquad \text{(Feasible)}$$

$$Z_{L_{E-1, A-2, C-3}} = {}^{E-1}4 + {}^{A-2}5 + {}^{C-3}4 + 9 + 5 = 27 \qquad \text{(Not feasible)} \qquad (9\text{-}144)$$

$$Z_{L_{E-1, A-2, D-3}} = {}^{E-1}4 + {}^{A-2}5 + {}^{D-3}6 + 6 + 9 = 30 \qquad \text{(Not feasible)}$$

Since the lower bound $Z_L = 27$ for the *EAB* branch corresponds to a feasible solution (i.e., $E - 1$, $A - 2$, $B - 3$, $C - 4$, $D - 5$), 27 becomes the new upper bound (i.e., we set $Z_U = 27$) on the total value of the optimal solution. We have now determined the best feasible solution for branch *EA*, namely *EABCD*. Furthermore, we can discontinue further consideration of branches *C*, *D*, *EB*, and *EC* (i.e., we can "fathom" these branches), since the lower bound for each of these branches is equal to or greater than our new upper bound $Z_U = 27$ (i.e., for branch *C*, $Z_L = 27 = Z_U = 27$; for branch *D*, $Z_L = 30 > Z_U = 27$; for branch *EB*, $Z_L = 31 > Z_U = 27$; and for branch *EC*, $Z_L = 28 > Z_U = 27$). Thus, we need to consider further possible assignments using only branches *A*, *B*, and *ED*. These results are summarized in the tree diagram shown in Fig. 9.21.

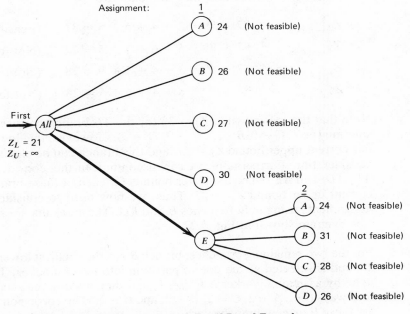

FIGURE 9.20 Second Iteration—Branch-and-Bound Example

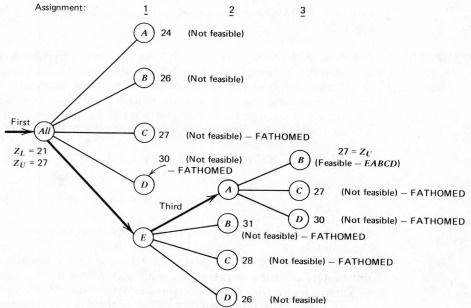

FIGURE 9.21   Third Iteration—Branch-and-Bound Example

ITERATION 4
Branching and
Bounding

For the three remaining branches, branch A has the smallest lowest bound (i.e., $Z_{L_{A-1}} = 24$) and is selected as the one to partition into new branches. This partitioning is done by assigning worker A to job 1, and then making the second assignment in four ways (i.e., $B-2, C-2, D-2$, and $E-2$). The corresponding lower bounds for these four new branches are

$$Z_{L_{A-1, B-2}} = {}^{(A-1)}7 + {}^{(B-2)}12 + 4 + 5 + 5 = 33 \qquad \text{(Feasible)}$$

$$Z_{L_{A-1, C-2}} = {}^{(A-1)}7 + {}^{(C-2)}5 + 6 + 5 + 5 = 28 \qquad \text{(Not feasible)}$$

$$Z_{L_{A-1, D-2}} = {}^{(A-1)}7 + {}^{(D-2)}3 + 4 + 5 + 9 = 28 \qquad \text{(Not feasible)} \qquad \text{(9–145)}$$

$$Z_{L_{A-1, E-2}} = {}^{(A-1)}7 + {}^{(E-2)}6 + 4 + 6 + 5 = 28 \qquad \text{(Not feasible)}$$

Note that the lower bound $Z_L = 33$ for the AB branch corresponds to a feasible solution (i.e., $A-1, B-2, C-3, D-5$). However, this lower bound exceeds our current upper bound $Z_U = 27$, and this branch can be eliminated from further consideration. Furthermore, we can discontinue further consideration of branches AC, AD, and AE, since the lower bounds for each of these branches exceeds our current upper bound $Z_U = 27$. Thus, we now need to consider further possible assignments using only branches B and ED. These results are summarized in the tree diagram shown in Fig. 9.22.

ITERATION 5
Branching and
Bounding

For the two remaining branches, branch B has the smallest lower bound (i.e., $Z_L = 26$) and is selected as the one to partition into new branches. This partitioning is done by assigning worker B to job 1, and then making the second assignment in four ways (i.e., $A-2, C-2, D-2$, and $E-2$). The corresponding lower bounds for these four new branches are

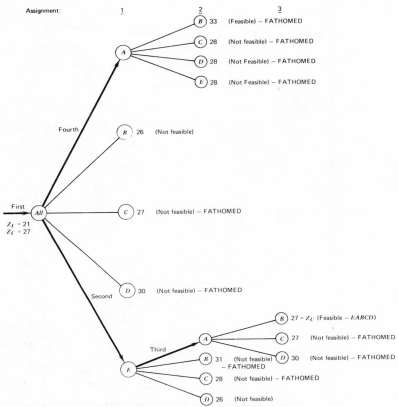

FIGURE 9.22 Fourth Iteration—Branch-and-Bound Example

$$Z_{L_{B-1,\,A-2}} = {}^{(B-1)}9 + {}^{(A-2)}5 + 4 + 5 + 5 = 28 \qquad \text{(Feasible)}$$

$$Z_{L_{B-1,\,C-2}} = {}^{(B-1)}9 + {}^{(C-2)}5 + 6 + 5 + 5 = 30 \qquad \text{(Not feasible)}$$

$$Z_{L_{B-1,\,D-2}} = {}^{(B-1)}9 + {}^{(D-2)}3 + 4 + 5 + 9 = 30 \qquad \text{(Not feasible)}$$

$$Z_{L_{B-1,\,E-2}} = {}^{(B-1)}9 + {}^{(E-2)}6 + 4 + 6 + 5 = 30 \qquad \text{(Not feasible)}$$

(9–146)

Note that the lower bound $Z_L = 28$ for the BA branch corresponds to a feasible solution (i.e., $B - 1$, $A - 2$, $C - 3$, $E - 4$, $D - 5$). However, this lower bound exceeds our current upper bound $Z_U = 27$, and this subset can be eliminated from further consideration. Additionally, we can discontinue further consideration of branches BC, BD, and BE, since the lower bounds for each of these branches exceeds our current upper bound $Z_U = 27$. Thus, we now need to consider further possible assignments using only branch ED. These results are summarized in the tree diagram shown in Fig. 9.23.

ITERATION 6
Branching and
Bounding

The only remaining branch, ED, is partitioned by assigning worker E to job 1, worker D to job 2, and then making the third assignment in each of three ways (i.e., $A - 3$, $B - 3$, $C - 3$). The corresponding lower bounds for these three new branches are

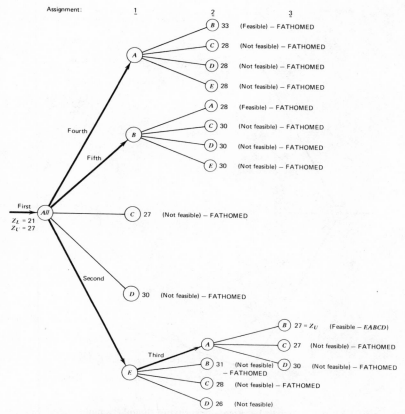

FIGURE 9.23 Fifth Iteration—Branch-and-Bound Example

$$Z_{L_{E-1,\ D-2,\ A-3}} = {}^{E-1}4 + {}^{D-2}3 + {}^{A-3}9 + 6 + 9 = 31 \quad \text{(Not feasible)}$$

$$Z_{L_{E-1,\ D-2,\ B-3}} = {}^{E-1}4 + {}^{D-2}3 + {}^{B-3}7 + 6 + 9 = 29 \quad \text{(Not feasible)} \quad (9\text{-}147)$$

$$Z_{L_{E-1,\ D-2,\ C-3}} = {}^{E-1}4 + {}^{D-2}3 + {}^{C-3}4 + 8 + 10 = 29 \quad \text{(Feasible)}$$

Since all of these lower bounds are greater than $Z_U = 27$, these three branches are immediately eliminated from further consideration. There are now no further branches remaining for consideration. Thus, the current feasible solution $E - 1$, $A - 2$, $B - 3$, $C - 4$, $D - 5$ must be optimal. Results from this sixth and final iteration are summarized in the tree diagram shown in Fig. 9.24. The complete sequence of iterations for the application of the branch-and-bound method to this assignment problem is summarized in Table 9.15.

In Table 9.15, note that we determined lower-bound solutions for 23 branches in total. Of these 23 solutions, 3 were feasible solutions, and 1 of these feasible solutions was the optimal solution. This illustrates the efficiency of the branch-and-bound method, as the complete enumeration of all the feasible solutions to this problem would have required the evaluation of 120 branches.

Several alternative branching rules have been suggested for zero-one combinatorial problems. The two most popular branching rules for selecting a subset to partition are the **best bound rule** and the **newest bound rule**. The best bound rule

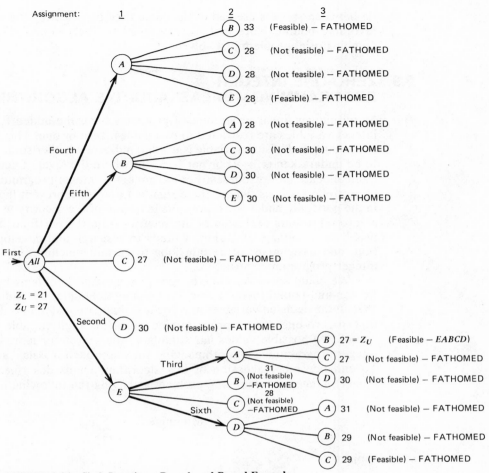

FIGURE 9.24 Sixth Iteration—Branch-and-Bound Example

says to select the subset having the most favorable bound (the smallest lower bound in the case of minimization) because this subset would seem to be most promising in terms of containing an optimal solution. The newest bound rule says to select the most recently created subset that has not been fathomed, breaking a

TABLE 9.15 Summary of Results—Branch-and-Bound Example

Iteration	New Branches (* = feasible)	Best Z_L	Z_U
0		21	$+\infty$
1	A, B, C, D, E,	21	$+\infty$
2	EA, EB, EC, ED,	21	27
3	EAB,* EAC, EAD	21	27
4	AB,* AC, AD, AE	21	27
5	AB,* BC, BD, BE	21	27
6	EDA, EDB, EDC	21	27

tie between subsets created at the same time by selecting the one with the most favorable bound. Note that we employed the best bound rule in the zero-one combinatorial problem just solved.

9.9 ZERO-ONE INTEGER PROGRAMMING—BALAS' ADDITIVE ALGORITHM

Many integer linear programming problems have the added feature that all the integer variables are restricted to two values: zero or one. This frequently occurs as the integer decision variable is used to indicate whether some possible action is to be undertaken ($x_j = 1$) or not ($x_j = 0$), where the level of activity represents a fixed allocation of resources. For example, 0-1 integer programming is often used in portfolio analysis, where the decision variables represent individual securities in the portfolio, and a one represents inclusion of the security in the portfolio, and a zero represents exclusion of the security from the portfolio. Similarly, various problems involving allocation of funds to research and development, site selection, and assignment of certain jobs to certain machines, all have a zero-one integer programming structure.

We could solve zero-one integer programming problems by using either the branch-and-bound method or cutting-plane technique, by adding the constraint that all the decision variables must be less than or equal to one. However, the fact that in zero-one integer programming problems each variable can take on only one of two possible values has stimulated the search for more efficient zero-one integer programming algorithms. One such approach is **Balas' additive algorithm**. To enhance our discussion of this algorithm, let us describe the zero-one (or binary) integer programming problem as having the following form.

$$\text{Minimize } Z = \sum_{j=1}^{n} c_j x_j \qquad (9\text{-}148)$$

subject to:
$$\sum_{j=1}^{n} a_{ij} x_j \geq b_i \qquad \text{for } i = 1, 2, \ldots, m \qquad (9\text{-}149)$$

and
$$x_j = 0 \text{ or } 1 \qquad \text{for } j = 1, 2, \ldots, n \qquad (9\text{-}150)$$

where
$$0 \leq c_1 \leq c_2 \leq \ldots \leq c_n$$

Note that this condition for the ordering of the c_j parameters is not restrictive at all because if $c_j < 0$, originally, then the corresponding x_j can be replaced by $(1 - x_j')$ where $x_j' = 0$ or 1. Then x_j' will have a positive coefficient in the objective function, and all the variables can be reordered as needed to array these coefficients in increasing order.

In general terms, given the binary programming problem in the form specified by (9-148), (9-149), and (9-150), with the objective function coefficients ordered as indicated, it should be apparent that the general objective of the algorithm should be to make the decision variables zero as much as possible, given the constraint set, and then to allow the decision variables to enter the solution at a value of one in the same order that the objective function coefficients are arrayed. Thus, it would seem reasonable to first check the feasibility (and optimality) of setting all the decision variables to zero. We could then proceed to check the feasibility (and optimality) of setting $x_1 = 1$, and then setting $x_1 = 1$ and $x_2 = 1$, and so forth. The algorithm thus proceeds to define subsets of solutions by assigning values to some of the variables, say $(x_1, x_2, \ldots, x_N)$. Letting N denote the number of assigned variables for the subset currently under consideration, we refer to the value of $(x_1, x_2, \ldots, x_N)$ as the *current* **partial solution**. Any complete solution $(x_1, x_2, \ldots, x_N, x_{N+1}, \ldots, x_n)$ starting out in this manner is then called a **completion** of this partial solution.

In the *branching step* a partial solution $(x_1, x_2, \ldots, x_N)$ may be selected for partitioning, and if so, it is then partitioned into two new subsets (partial solutions) by setting $x_{N+1} = 1$ and $x_{N+1} = 0$. The *newest bound rule* is used to make this selection. Within the *bound step*, the lower bound Z_L for a partial solution $(x_1, x_2, \ldots, x_N)$ is determined as:

$$
Z_L = \begin{cases} \displaystyle\sum_{j=1}^{N} c_j x_j & \text{if } x_N = 1 \text{ (or if } N = 0 \text{ or } N = n) \\ \displaystyle\sum_{j=1}^{N-1} c_j x_j + c_{N+1} & \text{if } x_N = 0 \end{cases} \tag{9-151}
$$

The reason for adding c_{N+1} if $x_N = 0$ is that the algorithm calculates this bound only if it had previously found that $(x_1, x_2, \ldots, x_{N-1}, x_N = 0, \ldots, x_n = 0)$ is infeasible. This occurs during the test of the *fathoming step* for the previous partial solution $(x_1, x_2, \ldots, x_m)$, where $M = \max\{j | x_j = 1\}$. Therefore, the bound is always smaller (or equal) for $x_N = 1$ than for $x_N = 0$, so the newest bound rule always selects the $x_N = 1$ partial solution first if neither has been fathomed. Because of this, the fathoming step is not even applied to the $x_N = 0$ partial solution until after the $x_N = 1$ partial solution has been fathomed (i.e., it may be necessary to fathom all of its subsequent subsets).

The fathoming step is applied to a partial solution as follows. For each new subset, obtain a lower bound Z_L on the value of the objective function for the feasible solutions in the subset. For each new subset, exclude it from further consideration if $Z_L \geq Z_U$, where Z_U is the current upper bound. Next, test to see if the subset is found to contain no feasible solutions by seeing whether any individual constraint cannot be satisfied by completion of the partial solution. Therefore, the partial solution is fathomed if

$$
\sum_{j=1}^{n} a_{ij} x_j + \sum_{j=N+1}^{n} \max\{a_{ij}, 0\} \leq b_i, \quad \text{for some } i = 1, 2, \ldots, m \tag{9-152}
$$

since $\max\{a_{ij}, 0\} = \max\{a_{ij} x_j | x_j = 0 \text{ or } 1\}$. Next, we test to see whether the solution corresponding to the lower bound Z_L (namely, the partial solution $x_{N+1} = 1 - x_N$ and the rest of the variables equal to zero) actually is feasible. Therefore, the third way in which the partial solution can be fathomed is if

$$
\sum_{j=1}^{N} a_{ij} x_j + a_{i,N+1}(1 - x_N) \geq b_i, \quad \text{for all } i = 1, 2, \ldots, m \tag{9-153}
$$

If this occurs and $Z_L < Z_U$, then we reset $Z_U = Z_L$ and store this solution as the current incumbent solution.

EXAMPLE   To illustrate this algorithm, consider the following problem.

$$\text{Minimize } Z = 2x_1 + 3x_2 + 5x_3 + 7x_4 + 9x_5 + 10x_6 \qquad (9\text{-}154)$$

subject to:
$$
\begin{aligned}
-2x_1 + 6x_2 - 3x_3 + 4x_4 + 1x_5 - 2x_6 &\geq +2 \\
-5x_1 - 3x_2 + 1x_3 + 3x_4 - 2x_5 + 1x_6 &\geq -2 \\
5x_1 - 1x_2 + 4x_3 - 2x_4 + 2x_5 - 1x_6 &\geq +2
\end{aligned}
\qquad (9\text{-}155)
$$

and $x_j = 0$ or 1,   for $j = 1, 2, \ldots, 6$ $\qquad (9\text{-}156)$

Results from the application of this algorithm are shown in Table 9.16. To begin the solution procedure, we observe that the complete set of solutions ($N = 0$) can not be fathomed at iteration 1[$Z_L \leq Z_U$], each constraint can be satisfied, but (0,0,0,0,0,0) is infeasible. The partial solution $x_1 = 1$ cannot be fathomed [$Z_L \leq Z_U$, each constraint can be satisfied, but (1,0,0,0,0,0) is infeasible]. Next, we observe that the partial solution (x_1, x_2) = (1,1) is fathomed because it has no completions, even (1,1,1,1,0,1), that satisfy the second constraint. At iteration 4 we observe that the partial solution (x_1, x_2) = (1,0) is not fathomed [$Z_L \leq Z_U$, each constraint can be satisfied, but as we noted above (1,0,0,0,0,0) is infeasible]. At interation 5 the partial solution (x_1, x_2, x_3) = (1,0,1) is fathomed, because it has no completions, even (1,0,1,1,1,0) that satisfy the second constraint. At iteration 6, the next partial solution (x_1, x_2, x_3) = (1,0,0), has at its *best* possible completion (1,0,0,1,0,0), which is also *feasible*. Thus, we have determined the first incumbent solution. Continuing in this manner, at iteration 9, we find that the best possible completion - (0,1,1,0,0,0) is also feasible with a lower Z_L, so it becomes the next incumbent solution. Subsequent iterations indicate that the remaining partial solutions cannot lead to better feasible solutions, so the optimal solution is $x_1 = 0$, $x_2 = 1, x_3 = 1, x_4 = 0, x_5 = 0, x_6 = 0$, minimum $Z = 8$.

TABLE 9.16   Solution—Application of Balas' Additive Algorithm to a Zero-One Integer Programming Problem

Iteration	Partial Solution	Z_L	Fathomed ?	Fathoming Test Passed	Z_U	Incumbent Solution
1	—	0	No		∞	—
2	(1)	2	No		∞	—
3	(1,1)	5	Yes	2	∞	—
4	(1,0)	7	No		∞	—
5	(1,0,1)	7	Yes	2	∞	—
6	(1,0,0)	9	Yes	3	9	(1,0,0,1,0,0)
7	(0)	3	No		9	
8	(0,1)	3	No		9	
9	(0,1,1)	8	Yes	3	8	(0,1,1,0,0,0)
10	(0,1,0)	10	Yes	1,2	8	
11	(0,0)	5	No		8	
12	(0,0,1)	5	No		8	
13	(0,0,1,1)	12	Yes	1	8	
14	(0,0,1,0)	14	Yes	1,2	8	
15	(0,0,0)	7	Yes	1	8	

9.10 CASE STUDY—THE LOCKBOX LOCATION PROBLEM

One of the most important aspects of cash management involves the development of an efficient accounts receivable collection system that makes it possible to collect payments quickly from a number of widespread customers. Thus, a company that collects payments from geographically dispersed customers will generally maintain "lockbox" accounts with banks in several strategically located cities. A bank that services lockbox accounts will provide a lockbox depository at the local post office to which checks can be sent, and will collect and process checks from this lockbox at regular time intervals throughout the day. The objective herein is to select a *set* of lockbox banks where customers can be assigned so that the company can minimize the opportunity costs of uncollected accounts receivable and lockbox service charges.

The lockbox location problem briefly described above may be more formally defined as selecting a set of lockbox banks and assigning customers to those banks such that the opportunity cost of uncollected funds and lockbox service charges is minimized. Initially, it is important to note that we must consider both the opportunity cost of uncollected funds (commonly referred to as "dollar-float") and the lockbox service charges, regardless of whether such charges are on a cash basis or on a compensating balance basis.

In order to formulate the model in a detailed fashion we first define two sets of indices. Let $J = \{1, 2, \ldots, n\}$ be the index set of prospective lockbox banks. Usually each index j represents a particular city, but it is also possible for each index to represent a particular bank. Thus, it is possible to have competing banks in the same city represented in the model.

Let $I = \{1, 2, \ldots, m\}$ be the index set of customer zones in the model. In the extreme case each corporate customer could be represented by a customer zone, resulting in a large value for m. To make the model more manageable it is usually desirable to aggregate a number of customers into one customer zone. The criterion of aggregation most often used in the United States is the postal zip code from which a customer check is mailed. For example, if the first two zip code digits represent a mailing area, then 100 customer zones are formed, starting with 00 and ending with 99. Federal Reserve banking districts are used to decide whether or not a customer should be placed into a zip code customer zone. First, each two-digit zip code is assigned to the Federal Reserve district where the zip code area is located. If a customer's check mailed from a certain zip code is drawn on a bank in that zip code's Federal Reserve district, then the customer belongs in the normal customer zip code zone. If the check is drawn on a bank not in that zip code's Federal Reserve district, it is then necessary to create a separate customer zone for that customer.

Given index i and j for customer zone and lockbox respectively, we can define the following terms. Let d_j be the fixed cost per time period associated with maintaining a lockbox account at bank j. Let s_j be the per-check processing charge at lockbox bank j. Let h_i be the expected number of checks received from customer zone i per time period. Let K be the maximum number of lockboxes that can be maintained. If there is no aritifical limit on the number of lockboxes, then K may be set to n. Next, let c_{ij} be the opportunity cost of dollar-float per time period if customer zone i checks are sent to lockbox j.

Finally, we define the following variables. Let y_j equal 1 if lockbox j is opened and 0 if it is not. Let x_{ij} equal 1 if checks from customer zone i are to be sent to lockbox j and 0 if not.

We can then formulate the lockbox problem as a $0 - 1$ integer programming model as follows.

$$\text{Minimize } Z = \sum_{i \in I} \sum_{j \in J} c_{ij} x_{ij} + \sum_{j \in J} d_j y_j$$
$$+ \sum_{i \in I} \sum_{j \in J} h_i s_j x_{ij} \quad (9\text{-}157)$$

subject to:
$$\sum_{j \in J} x_{ij} = 1, \, i \, \varepsilon \, I \quad (9\text{-}158)$$

$$\sum_{j \in J} y_j \le K \quad (9\text{-}159)$$

$$y_j \, \varepsilon \, \{0,1\}, j \, \varepsilon \, J \quad (9\text{-}160)$$

$$x_{ij} \, \varepsilon \, \{0,1\}, i \, \varepsilon \, I, j \, \varepsilon \, J \quad (9\text{-}161)$$

$$x_{ij} \le y_j, i \, \varepsilon \, I, j \, \varepsilon \, J \quad (9\text{-}162)$$

The objective function (Equation 9-157) that is being minimized is the sum of the opportunity costs of dollar-float of deposits made at all lockboxes for a specific time period, plus the fixed and variable costs associated with operating these lockboxes, for the same time period. Constraint (9-158) states that each customer zone i must be assigned to exactly one lockbox j. Constraint (9-159) simply requires K or fewer lockboxes to be open, and constraint (9-162) requires that a lockbox be open in order for a customer zone location to be assigned to that lockbox. Constraints (9-160) and (9-161) impose $0 - 1$ integrality conditions on the y_j and x_{ij} variables. It should also be noted that the x_{ij} variables may be treated as continuous variables since there always exists an optimal solution that has all x_{ij} either 0 or 1 regardless of whether or not the $x_{ij} \, \varepsilon \, \{0,1\}$ constraints are imposed.

One of the most important aspects involved in actually solving the lockbox location problem involves the data calculations required for properly defining its objective function coefficients. Calculation of the opportunity cost of dollar-float (the c_{ij} coefficients) is done as follows. First, there are three components that make up total collection time or total float.

1. m_{ij}: *Mail float*—The period of time from when a check from customer zone i is mailed to when it is received by lockbox bank j. (Such data may be obtained from Phoenix-Hecht, Inc., a private firm that collects such data, or can be determined independently.)

2. p_j: *Processing float*—The period of time from when a check is received by lockbox bank j to when it is deposited. (Such data may be obtained directly from banks.)

3. r_{jl}: *Clearing float*—The period of time from when a remittance is deposited in lockbox bank j to when it clears, where l denotes the bank upon which the check is drawn. Note that r_{jl} may depend on the size of the check, a_k, as some banks expedite clearing of checks over a particular dollar amount. (Such data may be obtained directly from banks.)

To calculate the clearing float, the hourly mail delivery schedule, lockbox (post office) pickup schedule, percentage of weekly mail received each day, and the check availability schedule for lockbox j are required. Finally, we must specify α, the current annual marginal interest rate for investment of corporate funds.

To illustrate the computation of the yearly opportunity cost of dollar-float, suppose that two checks for $5000 each are sent from Atlanta, Georgia, to St. Louis, Missouri, each day of the year. Assume further that one of the checks is drawn on an Atlanta, Georgia, bank, the other on a bank in Plains, Georgia.

For simplicity, suppose that an equal percentage of the mail received by the St. Louis lockbox is received each hour of the day and that mail pickups at the lockbox are made at 6 A.M., 2 P.M., and 4 P.M. Assume that the average mail time from Atlanta to St. Louis is 2 days, lockbox processing time is 2 hours, and the lockbox operation collects mail Monday through Friday, with 25 percent of the weekly mail collected on Monday, 15 percent on Tuesday, 19 percent on Wednesday, 20 percent on Thursday, and 21 percent on Friday. An assumed check availability schedule for the St. Louis lockbox is presented in Table 9.17 (for Atlanta checks) and Table 9.18 (for Plains checks). At the bottom of Tables 9.17 and 9.18 we pre-

sent the computation of the expected total float for the assumed availability schedules. Then, the yearly opportunity cost of dollar-float for Atlanta to St. Louis (for $\alpha = 6$ percent per year) is (.06 per year) ($5000 per day per year) (3.900 days) + (.06 per year) ($5000 per day per year)(5.185 days) = $2,725.50.

For a more general mail delivery schedule, a cumulative probability distribution, $M(t)$ should be used, where $M(t) = Pr$ (a piece of mail is delivered before t hundred hours). Thus $M(0) = 0$ and $M(24) = 1$. In the example above we have $M(0) = 0$, $M(1) = \frac{1}{24}$, $M(2) = \frac{2}{24}, \ldots , M(24) = 1$. Note also that processing float may or may not need to be included in the calculation depend-

TABLE 9.17   Expected Total Float Calculation—St. Louis, Missouri, Lockbox (Atlanta Checks)
Assumed Availability Schedule

Availability	*Cutoff Time Required to Achieve Availability*
1 day	If received by 4 P.M. on Mon., Tues., Wed., Thurs.
2 days	If received after 4 P.M. on Mon., Tues., Wed.
3 days	If received Friday
4 days	If received after 4 P.M. on Thurs.

Expected Total Float Calculation

	Day of Week							
	Mon.	*Tues.*	*Wed.*	*Thurs.*	*Fri.*	*Sat.*	*Sun.*	*Mon.*
Day Received (probability)	*Number of Days Availability (probability of availability cutoff time)*							
Monday (.25)	0 (0)	1 $(^{16}/_{24})$	2 $(^{8}/_{24})$	3 (0)	4 (0)	5 (0)	6 (0)	7 (0)
Tuesday (.15)		0 (0)	1 $(^{16}/_{24})$	2 $(^{8}/_{24})$	3 (0)	4 (0)	5 (0)	6 (0)
Wednesday (.19)			0 (0)	1 $(^{16}/_{24})$	2 $(^{8}/_{24})$	3 (0)	4 (0)	5 (0)
Thursday (.20)				0 (0)	1 $(^{16}/_{24})$	2 (0)	3 (0)	4 $(^{8}/_{24})$
Friday (.21)					0 (0)	1 (0)	2 (0)	3 $(^{24}/_{24})$

Expected Total Float = Expected Mail Float + Expected Processing Float + Expected Clearing Float

$= 2 + \frac{2}{24} + [(.25 + .15 + .19 + .20)(^{16}/_{24})(1) + (.25 + .15 + .19)(^{8}/_{24})(2) + (.20)(^{8}/_{24})(4)$

$+ (.21)(^{24}/_{24})(3)]$

$= 3.900$ days

TABLE 9.18 **Expected Total Float Calculation—St. Louis, Missouri, Lockbox (Plains Checks)**
Assumed Availability Schedule

Availability	*Cutoff Time Required to Achieve Availability*
2 days	If received by 2 P.M. on Mon., Tues., Wed.
3 days	If received after 2 P.M. on Mon., Tues.; by 2 P.M. on Friday
4 days	If received Thurs., and after 2 P.M. on Friday
5 days	If received after 2 P.M. Wednesday

Expected Total Float Calculation

	Day of Week								
	Mon.	*Tues.*	*Wed.*	*Thurs.*	*Fri.*	*Sat.*	*Sun.*	*Mon.*	*Tues.*
Day Received *(probability)*	*Number of Days Availability* *(probability of availability cutoff time)*								
Monday	0	1	2	3	4	5	6	7	8
(.25)	(0)	(0)	$(^{14}/_{24})$	$(^{10}/_{24})$	(0)	(0)	(0)	(0)	(0)
Tuesday		0	1	2	3	4	5	6	7
(.15)		(0)	(0)	$(^{14}/_{24})$	$(^{10}/_{24})$	(0)	(0)	(0)	(0)
Wednesday			0	1	2	3	4	5	6
(.19)			(0)	(0)	$(^{14}/_{24})$	(0)	(0)	$(^{10}/_{24})$	(0)
Thursday				0	1	2	3	4	5
(.20)				(0)	(0)	(0)	(0)	$(^{24}/_{24})$	(0)
Friday					0	1	2	3	4
(.21)					(0)	(0)	(0)	$(^{14}/_{24})$	$(^{10}/_{24})$

Expected Total Float = Expected Mail Float + Expected Processing Float + Expected Clearing Float

$$= 2 + {}^2/_{24} + [(.25 + .15 + .19)(^{14}/_{24})2 + (.25 + .15)(^{10}/_{24})3 + (.19)(^{10}/_{24})5 + (.20)(^{24}/_{24})4 +$$
$$(.21)(^{14}/_{24})(3) + (.21)(^{10}/_{24})(4)]$$
$$= 5.185 \text{ days}$$

ing on whether or not a bank's availability schedule states that a check must be received by the cutoff time or states that it must be received, say, V hours before the cutoff time. In addition, if a probability distribution for mail float is available rather than just average mail float, as well as a distribution for when during the week letters are mailed, a more detailed and realistic opportunity cost of dollar-float figure can be calculated.

The opportunity cost of dollar-float for one check of amount a_k drawn on bank l and mailed from customer zone i to lockbox j is

$$opc_k = \frac{\alpha}{365}(m_{ij} + p_j + r_{jl})a_k$$
(9–163)

Now suppose that in one year T checks for size a_k, $k = 1, \ldots, T$ were sent from customer zone i to lockbox j. The yearly opportunity cost of dollar-float for customer zone i to lockbox j is

$$c_{ij} = \sum_{k=1}^{T} opc_k \qquad (9\text{–}164)$$

Charges for lockbox services vary from bank to bank, but usually have two components: a fixed charge that is independent of lockbox activity, and a variable charge that depends on lockbox activity. Variable charges typically depend on the number of checks processed. Fixed charges are assessed on a periodic basis (daily, weekly, monthly, annually, etc.) regardless of the number of checks processed. Examples of fixed charges include monthly account maintenance, daily deposit fees, depository transfer checks, and/or daily wire transfer charges. Such periodic charges should be multiplied by appropriate factors to arrive at corresponding annual charges. For example, the daily fees should be multiplied by the number of working days per year.

Generally, payment for lockbox charges may be on a cash basis or on a compensating balance basis or some combination of the two. The method of payment affects the cost to the corporation (in opportunity dollars) of maintaining a lockbox at a particular bank, since this cost includes, not only cash payments made to the bank, but also the cost associated with keeping compensating balances at the bank when in fact these balances could be invested elsewhere earning additional funds for the corporation.

We shall give two examples of the calculation of total lockbox charges. First, consider the lockbox bank j^* that has a per-check charge of $0.20 and a fixed charge of $1000 per year. If 1000 checks are processed per year, the total lockbox cost is $1000 + $0.20 (1000) = $1200. If 2000 checks are processed, the total lockbox cost is $1400. Such a scheme may be easily incorporated into the model's objective function, as follows.

$$\text{Minimize } Z = \sum_{i \in I} \sum_{j \in J} c_{ij} x_{ij}$$
$$+ \sum_{j \in J} d_j y_j \quad (9\text{--}165)$$
$$+ \sum_{i \in I} \sum_{j \in J} h_i s_j x_{ij}$$

where $d_j^* = 1000$ and $s_j^* = .2$, and where h_i is the expected number of checks received annually from customer zone i at lockbox j^*.

A second example can be constructed using the charging scheme above, but with the requirement that compensating balances must be used to offset the charges. Suppose that the bank allows a 7-percent earning credit rate, which is to be applied against 8 percent of collected balances. Also suppose that the corporation has an $\alpha = .08$, and that 1000 checks are processed per year. For the fixed charge of $100 and a per-check charge of $0.20 we have the following calculation.

Equivalent Annual Fixed Charges =
$$\frac{\$1000}{(.85)(.07)}(.08) = \$1344$$
$$(9\text{--}166)$$

Equivalent Variable Charge
(for 1 check) $= \dfrac{(\$.20)}{(.85)(.07)}(.08) = \$.269$
$$(9\text{--}167)$$

Thus, in the objective function given above in Equation 9–165 $d_j^* = \$1344$, $s_j^* = \$0.269$, and h_i is the expected number of checks received annually from customer zone i at lockbox j^*.

An efficient branch-and-bound algorithm has been developed to solve the lockbox algorithm problem described above. The data calculations, solution algorithm, and an output report writer for the lockbox location problem have all been programmed in FORTRAN IV, and structured to form a *Lock Box Location Optimization System* (LBOS).[9] Three FORTRAN IV programs comprise LBOS. The first module is an optimal preprocessor that

---

[9] Further details concerning the development of this computerized system can be found in: Robert M. Nauss and Robert E. Markland, "Theory and Application of an Optimizing Procedure for Lock Box Location Analysis," *Management Science*, vol. 27, no. 8 (August 1981), 855–865; Copyright 1981, The Institute of Management Sciences and Robert M. Nauss and Robert E. Markland, "Solving Lock Box Location Problems," *Financial Management* (Spring 1979), 21–31, reprinted by permission.

TABLE 9.19 Summary of Results—Steel Company Lockbox Location Study

Model 1A Optimize on Mail Plus Availability Float—All Potential Lockboxes Are Allowed To Be in Solution

Output Data	11-Box Solution	10-Box Solution	9-Box Solution	8-Box Solution	7-Box Solution	6-Box Solution	5-Box Solution	4-Box Solution	3-Box Solution	2-Box Solution	1-Box Solution
	Atlanta Boston Chicago Cleveland Detroit Kansas City Milwaukee Minneapolis Pittsburgh St. Louis Tulsa	Atlanta Boston Chicago Cleveland Detroit Kansas City Milwaukee Minneapolis Pittsburgh St. Louis	Atlanta Chicago Cleveland Detroit Kansas City Milwaukee Minneapolis Pittsburgh St. Louis	Atlanta Chicago Cleveland Detroit Milwaukee Minneapolis Pittsburgh St. Louis	Atlanta Chicago Detroit Milwaukee Minneapolis Pittsburgh St. Louis	Atlanta Chicago Detroit Milwaukee Minneapolis St. Louis	Atlanta Chicago Detroit Milwaukee St. Louis	Atlanta Chicago Detroit Milwaukee	Atlanta Detroit Milwaukee	Chicago Detroit	Chicago
Average $-float per day	13,157,922	13,183,009	13,218,465	13,279,234	13,373,366	13,511,479	13,661,660	13,899,179	14,341,361	14,965,344	16,825,952
Opportunity cost of $-float per day	1,052,633	1,054,640	1,057,477	1,062,338	1,069,869	1,080,918	1,092,932	1,111,934	1,147,308	1,197,227	1,346,076
Opportunity cost of $-float per day plus lockbox charges	1,077,936	1,077,961	1,078,801	1,081,645	1,087,176	1,096,205	1,106,137	1,123,177	1,156,203	1,204,758	1,351,607

identifies remotely disbursed checks (mailed from one city but drawn on a bank in another city) and classifies them as separate customer zones, apart from checks drawn on a bank in the city from which they were mailed. The second module is a data preprocessor that calculates the expected mail time, expected processing time, and expected clearing time for each check to each potential lockbox site. These times and the check sample data are then used to calculate an opportunity-cost-of-float matrix that is input to the third module. This optimization program generates the optimal lockbox configuration and assigns customer zones to each lockbox.

To illustrate the use of the lockbox location model consider the actual case of a major steel producer in the United States who was employing a four-lockbox configuration involving banks in Atlanta, Detroit, Milwaukee, and New York. It wished to determine whether or not the number and locations of its lockbox banks were correct, and to study the effect of locating a lockbox in St. Louis, Missouri.

Each of the analyses undertaken was based on the following input data provided by the steel company.

1. A one-month sample of customer checks.
2. A marginal interest rate for investment of corporate funds of 8 percent.
3. A total of 24 potential lockbox sites.
4. A total of 143 actual customer zones.
5. Actual fixed and variable charges at the potential lockbox sites.

A series of lockbox location analyses were undertaken, using the lockbox location model previously described. Summary results from these analyses are presented below in Table 9.19 and Table 9.20.

Table 9.19 presents solutions in which all potential lockbox locations are allowed to be in solution. Note in Table 9.19 that the optimum solution has 11 lockboxes open, with a resultant minimum opportunity cost of dollar-float plus lockbox service charges of $1,077,936. Following the optimal solution, the lockbox location system determines a sequence of solutions in which the number of lockboxes open in solution is reduced by one. These results are also shown in Table 9.19, and it can be seen that the objective func-

TABLE 9.20 Comparison of Four Lockbox Solutions

Output Data	Solutions		
	4-Box Solution[a]	*4-Box Solution*[b]	*4-Box Solution*[c]
	Atlanta	Atlanta	Atlanta
	Chicago	Detroit	Detroit
	Detroit	Milwaukee	Milwaukee
	Milwaukee	St. Louis	New York
Average $-float per day	13,899,179	14,086,375	14,394,127
Opportunity cost of $-float per day	1,111,934	1,126,910	1,151,529
Opportunity cost of $-float per day plus lockbox charges	1,123,177	1,137,769	1,162,757

[a] Optimum 4-lockbox solution.

[b] Optimum 4-lockbox solution with St. Louis fixed in solution (i.e., a particular location fixed in solution).

[c] Current 4-lockbox configuration being used by the steel company.

tion increases as the number of lockboxes in solution decreases. For the sake of brevity we have not shown the actual assignments of customer zones to the various lockboxes that are produced as a part of the model's output. Additionally, for each of the solutions shown in Table 9.19 (i.e., for the 11 lockbox solution down to the 1 lockbox solution) three "next best" solutions based on a one-for-one swap of lockboxes are computed so that an incremental analysis can be made. The results are also omitted.

In Table 9.20 the optimum four-lockbox solution, the optimum four-lockbox solution with St. Louis, Missouri, fixed in solution, and the steel company's current four-lockbox configuration are presented. The steel company was particularly interested in a four-lockbox solution with St. Louis fixed in solution because it had a very favorable banking arrangement with a St. Louis bank. Note that the steel company's current four-lockbox configuration is worse than the four-lockbox solution with St. Louis fixed in solution, or the optimum four-lockbox solution.

In summarizing and comparing the results shown in Table 9.19 and Table 9.20 the following can be observed. Thus, an $84,821 (7.3 percent) savings could be achieved by adopting the optimum 11-lockbox configuration.

Solution	Table	Value of the Objective Function	Δ-$ Savings from Current	Δ-% Savings from Current
Steel company's current lockbox configuration	7	$1,162,757	—	—
Four-lockbox solution— St. Louis fixed in solution	7	1,137,769	$24,988	2.1
Optimum four-lockbox solution	6,7	1,123,177	39,580	3.4
Optimum solution	6	1,077,936	84,821	7.3

9.11 CONCLUSION

In this chapter we have considered the structure and solution of integer programming problems. Integer programming problems are frequently encountered in management science practice because some or all of the decision variables must be restricted to integer values. We have seen that such problems are much more difficult to solve than linear programming problems without integer restrictions. Three basic algorithms for solution of such problems have been presented in this chapter, namely the cutting-plane algorithm, the branch-and-bound algorithm, and Balas' additive algorithm. Computer codes for solution of integer programming problems are now commonly available in mathematical programming software packages. Such computer codes are generally based on the branch-and-bound algorithm, and improvement of the efficiency of various branch-and-bound algorithms continues to be an important research area in management science.

GLOSSARY OF TERMS

All-Integer Programming Problem   A mathematical programming problem in which all of the decision variables are constrained to assume integer values.

Balas' Additive Algorithm   An algorithm used to solve zero-one integer programming problems.

Best Bound Rule   Branching rule in which the subset of solutions having the most favorable bound is selected for partitioning.

Binary Variables   Zero-one $(0 - 1)$ variables.

Bound Step   The step in which a lower bound (for a minimization problem) is determined for the value of the objective function for the feasible solutions in the subset.

Branch-and-Bound Technique   An implicit enumeration procedure used to solve integer programming problems in which only a small fraction of the feasible solutions are examined.

Branch Step   The step in which some branching rule is used to select one of the remaining subsets (those neither fathomed nor partitioned) for partitioning into two or more new subsets of solutions.

Branching Rule   Rule used to determine the manner in which the partitioning of solutions into subsets will be done.

Completion   Any complete solution starting out from a particular partial solution, as obtained using Balas' additive algorithm.

Completion Step   The step in which the branch-and-bound procedure terminates (i.e., stop when there are no remaining unfathomed subsets).

Cutting-Plane Algorithm   An algorithm for solving all-integer and mixed-integer programming problems, which modifies the original linear programming problem by adding a new constraint that eliminates some noninteger solutions (including the previously optimal noninteger linear programming solution), but which does not eliminate any feasible integer solutions.

Cutting-Plane Constraint   A constraint that is added to a linear programming problem in order to cut away some of the noninteger solutions to the problem.

Enumeration Tree   A graphical presentation of the various solutions that are obtained using the branch-and-bound method.

Fathomed by Bounding   The elimination from further consideration of a subproblem (in a branch-and-bound context) that has a worse linear programming solution than the best integer solution obtained thus far.

Fathomed by Infeasibility   The elimination from further consideration of a subproblem (in a branch-and-bound context) that has no feasible solution.

Fathomed by Integrality   The elimination from further consideration of a subproblem (in a branch-and-bound context) that has a worse all-integer linear programming solution than the best all-integer solution obtained thus far.

Fathoming Step   The step in which each new subset is examined to see if it has been fathomed (i.e., can be excluded from further consideration).

Fixed-Charge Problem   A situation in which a fixed charge or setup cost is incurred if a particular activity is undertaken.

Implicit Enumeration Procedure   An optimization procedure that explicitly examines only a small fraction of the feasible solutions to a problem, but implicitly considers all of them.

Initialization Step   The beginning step of the branch-and-bound procedure; requires the determination of the initial upper bound and the initial lower bound for the integer programming problem.

Lower Bound   A value that is less than or equal to the value of the optimal solution (e.g., the value of any feasible integer solution for a maximization integer programming problem provides a lower bound).

Mixed-Integer Programming Problem A mathematical programming problem in which some, but not all, of the decision variables are constrained to assume integer values.

Multiple-Choice Alternatives A set of decisions in which exactly one decision in the group must be "yes."

Mutually Exclusive Alternatives A set of decisions in which at most one decision in the group must be "yes."

Newest Bound Rule Branching rule in which the subset of solutions that has most recently been created, and that has not been fathomed, is selected for partitioning.

Partial Solution A subset of solutions defined by Balas' algorithm at some point during the solution process.

Precedence or Contingency Relationships Relationships used to describe situations in which one decision is dependent upon another decision.

Traveling Salesman Problem An important scheduling problem that is concerned with the determination of a routing that minimizes total travel cost.

Upper Bound A value that is greater than or equal to the value of any feasible solution (e.g., the solution to the linear programming relaxation of an integer programming problem provides an upper bound for a maximization problem).

Zero-One Integer Programming Problem A mathematical programming problem in which all of the decision variables are constrained to assume integer values of zero or one.

SELECTED REFERENCES

INTEGER
PROGRAMMING

Abadie, J., ed. 1967. *Integer and Nonlinear Programming.* New York: American Elsevier Publishing Company (n.d.)

Garfinkel, Robert, and George L. Nemhauser. 1972. *Integer Programming.* New York: John Wiley & Sons, Inc.

Greenberg, Harold. 1971. *Integer Programming.* New York: Academic Press, Inc.

Hadley, George. 1964. *Nonlinear and Dynamic Programming.* Reading, Mass.: Addison-Wesley Publishing Company, Inc.

Hu, T. C. 1969. *Integer Programming and Network Flows.* Reading, Mass.: Addison-Wesley Publishing Company, Inc.

Loomba, Narenda P., and Efraim Turban. 1974. *Applied Programming for Management.* New York: Holt, Rinehart & Winston, Inc.

McMillan, Claude. 1975. *Mathematical Programming.* New York: John Wiley & Sons, Inc.

Muth, John, and G. Thompson. 1963. *Industrial Scheduling.* Englewood Cliffs, N.J.: Prentice-Hall, Inc.

Plane, Donald R., and Claude McMillan. 1971. *Discrete Optimization: Integer Programming and Network Analysis for Management Decisions.* Englewood Cliffs, N.J.: Prentice-Hall, Inc.

Saaty, Thomas L. 1970. *Optimization in Integers and Related Extremal Problems.* New York: McGraw-Hill Book Company.

Scott, Thomas L. 1971. *Combinatorial Programming, Spatial Analysis and Planning.* London: Methuen.

Taha, Hamdy A. 1975. *Integer Programming: Theory, Applications, and Computations.* New York: Academic Press, Inc.

Zionts, S. 1974. *Linear and Integer Programming.* Englewood Cliffs, N.J.: Prentice-Hall, Inc.

DISCUSSION QUESTIONS

1. What is the effect of the "integer" restriction of the decision variables on the solution space in integer programming problems?
2. Give a brief description of how the cutting-plane algorithm works.
3. Why does the addition of a cutting-plane constraint make the previous optimal solution infeasible (assuming the previous optimal solution is not integer)? How do we solve this problem?
4. Do you think the cutting-plane algorithm is an efficient technique for solving large integer programming problems? Why or why not? What alternative technique(s) could you use?
5. When do you know in the branch-and-bound technique that you have obtained an optimal solution to the integer programming problem?
6. What is one of the big advantages of using a branch-and-bound technique compared with other possible techniques in solving integer programming problems? Can the branch-and-bound technique also be used to solve $0 - 1$ integer programming problems? To solve mixed-integer programming problems?
7. What do we mean by the "current incumbent solution" in using Balas' additive algorithm.
8. Suppose you cannot find an incumbent solution in using Balas' additive algorithm. What does this indicate?
9. What changes in the solution procedure have to be made if you want to solve minimization instead of maximization integer programming problems by the branch-and-bound technique?
10. Why is the condition for the ordering of the objective function parameters in Balas' additive algorithm not restrictive?
11. What are the problems associated with simply "rounding off" a *continuous* optimal solution to an LP in order to obtain an *integer* solution.

PROBLEM SET

1. Solve the following all-integer programming problem, using Gomory's cutting-plane algorithm.

$$\text{Maximize } Z = 3x_1 + 4x_2$$

subject to: $3x_1 + 2x_2 \leq 8$
$1x_1 + 5x_2 \leq 9$

with $x_1 \geq 0, x_2 \geq 0, x_1, x_2$ integers.

2. Solve the following all-integer programming problem, using Gomory's cutting-plane algorithm.

$$\text{Maximize } Z = 2x_1 + 1.7x_2$$

subject to: $4x_1 + 3x_2 \leq 7$
$1x_1 + 1x_2 \leq 4$

with $x_1 \geq 0, x_2 \geq 0, x_1, x_2$ integers.

3. Daniel Bridger is going camping and is packing his knapsack. He likes sweets and is trying to decide between packing dehydrated packages of cake, or packages of candy. He prefers the cake to the candy in the ratio of 3 to 1. However, each tin of

cake weighs 0.55 pound and takes up 0.45 cubic foot of space. The candy weighs only 0.25 pound and takes up 0.17 cubic foot of space. He has 1 cubic foot space available in his knapsack and wants to restrict the weight of his sweet items to 2 pounds. Also, he feels that he must take at least one cake and one package of candy. Formulate and solve as an all-integer programming problem.

4. The St. Louis office of a major CPA firm is attempting to schedule its auditors for the next audit period. It has three major audits, each of which may be accomplished by using a mix of senior auditors, junior auditors, and clerks. The audit requirement for these jobs, and the "audit value" of the various personnel with respect to the various jobs is as follows:

Audit No.	"Audit Value" of Auditing Personnel (hours)			Audit Requirement (hours)
	Senior Auditors	Junior Auditors	Clerks	
1	5.0	3.0	1.0	20.0
2	4.0	2.5	0.5	15.0
3	4.5	2.0	1.5	18.0
				Total 53.0

There are 15 senior auditors available, 20 junior auditors available, and 25 clerks available. The per-job cost is $2500 for a senior auditor, $1500 for a junior auditor, and $500 for a clerk. No more than three of any of the auditing personnel can be assigned to any job. Formulate and solve as an all-integer programming problem.

5. A dietician for a hospital is trying to develop a menu plan. She would like to determine the quantities of certain foods that should be eaten to meet the nutritional requirements, at a minimum cost. Her present menu plan is limited to milk, beef, and eggs and to vitamins A, B, and D. Suppose that the number of milligrams of each of these vitamins contained within a purchasing unit for each of the three foods is as follows.

Vitamin	Milligrams per Purchasing Unit of Food			Minimum Requirement (mg)
	Milk (gal)	Beef (lb)	Eggs (dz)	
A	2	1	10	5
B	50	10	8	60
D	10	90	10	10

The cost for the food ingredients is $1.20 per gallon for milk, $1.50 per pound for beef, and $0.75 per dozen for eggs. Formulate and solve as an all-integer programming problem.

6. A small Midwestern college has just constructed one indoor court and one outdoor court, each of which may be used for handball or racquetball. The recreation director for the school estimates that there will be 12 playing hours per day available on the indoor court and 14 playing hours per day available on the outdoor court. Depending on the hours of operation and the weather, each of the two courts can be described by a "court-hour" requirement, which can then be related

to the game being played. The estimated court-hour requirement per court, by type of game being played, is as follows.

	Game	
Court	Handball	Racquetball
Indoor	1.0	0.75
Outdoor	1.25	1.33

In general, the recreation director would like to schedule at least twice as many racquetball games as handball games. He feels that this schedule must include at least 2 games daily of handball, both indoors and outdoors, and at least 3 games daily of racquetball, both indoors and outdoors. Formulate and solve the all-integer programming problem that will facilitate the scheduling of the greatest number of hours during a day.

7. Solve the following mixed-integer programming problem, using Gomory's cutting-plane algorithm.

$$\text{Maximize } Z = 4x_1 + 3x_2$$

subject to: $3x_1 + 5x_2 \leq 7$
$2x_1 + 1x_2 \leq 4$

with $x_1 \geq 0, x_2 \geq 0, x_1$ an integer.

8. Solve the following mixed-integer programming problem, using Gomory's cutting-plane algorithm.

$$\text{Maximize } Z = 1.5x_1 + 3x_2 + 4x_3$$

subject to: $2.5x_1 + 2x_2 + 4x_3 \leq 12$
$2x_1 + 4x_2 - 1x_3 \leq 7$

with $x_1 \geq 0, x_2 \geq 0, x_3 \geq 0, x_3$ an integer.

9. The Green-Lawn Service Company provides lawn maintenance service to suburban homeowners in St. Louis county. For its spring lawn spray it mixes boxes (10 lb) of dry chemical A with gallons of liquid chemical B. Each gallon of lawn spray that is produced must contain at least 500 units of weed killer and at least 400 units of crabgrass killer. The two chemicals provide the needed ingredients in the following manner.

	Number of Units of Ingredient		
Required Ingredient	Chemical A (per 10-lb box)	Chemical B (per gal)	Total Requirement
Weed killer	29	13	500 units
Crabgrass killer	17	27	400 units

The dry chemical costs $25 per 10-lb box and the liquid chemical costs $10 per gallon. At least one box of dry chemical must be used for every 5 gallons, or more, of liquid chemical that is used. Formulate and solve as a mixed-integer programming problem.

10. The dietician discussed earlier in problem 5 is considering a new breakfast menu involving oranges, milk, and cereal. This breakfast must meet minimum requirements for the vitamins A, B, and C. The number of milligrams of each of these vitamins contained in a purchasing unit for each of these foods is as follows.

	Milligrams per Purchasing Unit of Food			Minimum Requirements (mg)
Vitamin	Oranges (dz)	Milk (gal)	Cereal (box)	
A	30	35	17	100
B	20	40	11	200
C	17	31	9	160

The cost for the food ingredients is $1.10 per dozen for oranges, $1.25 per gallon for milk, and $1.00 per box for cereal. For dietary reasons, at least one unit of each food type must be used in the menu plan. Formulate and solve as a mixed-integer programming problem.

11. The Deep Six Quarry Company produces paving aggregate, gravel, and sand. Each of these products involves two operations: (1) crushing, and (2) washing and sorting. The production capacities and production requirements for the company are as follows.

	Capacity Required per Ton of Product (hours)			Available Capacity (hours)
Operation	Paving Aggregate	Gravel	Sand	
Crushing	9	11	13	≤ 50
Washing and sorting	5	8	11	≤ 75

The unit profits associated with the three products are $95 per ton for paving aggregate, $80 per ton for gravel, and $75 per ton for sand.

In the production process, at least two units of gravel and three units of sand must be produced for each unit of paving aggregate that is produced. Also, paving aggregate cannot be sold in fractional amounts. Formulate and solve as a mixed-integer programming problem.

12. Solve the asymmetric traveling salesman problem, whose cost matrix is given below, by the branch-and-bound method.

From City	To City				
	A	B	C	D	E
A	∞	210	420	150	300
B	70	∞	150	40	290
C	190	120	∞	310	50
D	200	150	230	∞	190
E	110	450	290	470	∞

Assume that the salesman's trip must start and finish at City *A*.

13. Solve the symmetrical traveling salesman problem portrayed in the illustration below, using the branch-and-bound method.

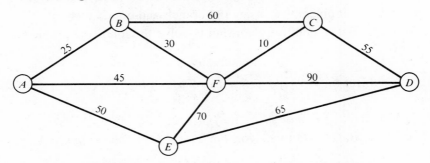

Assume that the salesman's trip must start and finish at City *A*.

14. The Brad-Dunge Paint Company mixes four colors of paint each production shift, using one large mixing vat. The vat changeover times (minutes) for the various colors are as follows.

From Color	To Color			
	Red	**Green**	**Blue**	**Yellow**
Red	—	11	15	14
Green	11	—	12	13
Blue	15	10	—	16
Yellow	17	8	16	—

Determine the optimum sequence of color production to minimize the vat changeover time for the production process (*Hint:* Solve by branch-and-bound).

15. A university professor is working as a consultant to an office of the Small Business Administration. She is currently planning a training and development program that will allow high school dropouts to move through various jobs, at increasing skill levels. In general the training and development time for any job is a function of the immediately preceding job. The following table indicates the training and development time (in weeks) associated with moving from one job to another.

From Job	To Job				
	Dropout	**A**	**B**	**C**	**D**
Dropout	—	6	5	3	1
A	0	—	4	3	1
B	0	4	—	2	2
C	0	2	1	—	1
D	0	4	3	5	—

The professor would like to determine the job sequence that minimizes the training and development time for all four stages of jobs. (*Hint:* Solve by branch-and-bound.)

16. Solve Problem 7–23, using the branch-and-bound method.
17. Solve problem 7–24, using the branch-and-bound method.
18. Solve Problem 9–1, using the branch-and-bound method.
19. Solve Problem 9–2, using the branch-and-bound method.
20. Use Balas' additive algorithm to solve the following problem.

$$\text{Maximize } Z = 2x_1 + 3x_2 + 5x_3 + 8x_4$$

subject to:
$$3x_1 - 2x_2 + 5x_3 - 4x_4 \leq 6$$
$$1x_1 - 1x_2 + 2x_3 + 2x_4 \leq 3$$

with $x_j = 0$ or 1, for $j = 1, 2, \ldots, 4$.

21. Use Balas' additive algorithm to solve the following problem.

$$\text{Maximize } Z = 7x_1 + 9x_2 + 10x_3$$

subject to:
$$1x_1 + 2x_2 - 1x_3 \geq 2$$
$$2x_1 + 1x_2 + 1x_3 \leq 3$$

with $x_j = 0$ or 1, for $j = 1, 2, 3$.

22. The personnel manager at a small plant has six applicants for production jobs involving two types of machines. From a series of tests, the ability of the applicants to operate these two types of machines has been determined to be the following.

Applicant	Index of Ability	
	Machine Type 1	Machine Type 2
1 (Male)	30	60
2 (Female)	60	50
3 (Female)	50	50
4 (Male)	55	45
5 (Male)	40	35
6 (Female)	25	70

Each applicant can be assigned to only one machine type. Additionally, no more than three applicants can be assigned to any one machine type. Finally, at least one female applicant must be assigned to each machine type. The personnel manager wishes the selection of applicants to maximize the overall ability of the applicants so chosen. Formulate and solve as a $0 - 1$ integer programming problem.

23. A large motel chain is considering opening motel complexes in some or all of eight Southwestern U.S. locations. It feels that it must construct at least five of these motels. These eight locations, with their respective discounted construction and operating costs and discounted cash flow rates of return are summarized in the following table.

Motel Location	Discounted Construction and Operating Cost ($)	Discounted Cash Flow Rate of Return (%)
Phoenix	500,000	25
Flagstaff	250,000	13
Tucson	450,000	21
Albuquerque	500,000	18
Gallup	280,000	16
Santa Fe	225,000	12
El Paso	350,000	22
Las Cruces	400,000	17

The company has a (discounted) construction and operating budget of $2 million. Additionally, if the motel in Phoenix is constructed, the motel in Tucson must also be constructed. Similarly, if the motel in Albuquerque is constructed, then the motel in El Paso must also be constructed. Formulate and solve as a 0 − 1 integer programming problem.

24. A food manufacturer is considering building five new plants over the next 4 years on already purchased land. Conceivably, the manufacturer could start and finish construction of any of the plants in any of the years, but the construction costs to do so will vary according to the following table.

Plant	Construction Year			
	1	*2*	*3*	*4*
A	$100,000	$125,000	$110,000	$130,000
B	$150,000	$125,000	$175,000	$140,000
C	$125,000	$110,000	$100,000	$170,000
D	$175,000	$200,000	$220,000	$250,000
E	$140,000	$105,000	$155,000	$135,000

The company is further constrained in its construction planning by the following conditions.
(a) Plants A and B cannot be started and finished after year 3.
(b) The company cannot spend more than $500,000 in total.
(c) Plants D and E must be built in the same year.
Formulate and solve as a 0 − 1 integer programming problem.

25. The Silent Meow Catfood Corp. must determine how many units of four types of dry catfood mixes to manufacture in order to satisfy their forecasted demand for the next 2 weeks and to minimize production cost. Four varieties of catfood mix can be produced: tuna, mackerel, chicken, and beef. The tuna and mackerel mixes have a high degree of substitutability; the minimum (combined) forecasted demand for these seafood mixes is 300,000 boxes. The beef and chicken mixes are also considered to be substitutes; minimum (combined) forecasted demand for these mixes is 200,000 boxes. The setup cost for a production run for each type mix and the variable cost per unit are given in the following table.

	Tuna	Mackerel	Chicken	Beef
Setup cost	$300.	450.	500.	450.
Variable cost per box	.003	.002	.002	.003

Formulate as an integer programming problem.

26. The Gingerbread Man Bakery specialized in three types of Christmas cakes: the Fudge Walnut Delight, which has a contribution margin of $5.25; the Angel Food Fantasy, which has a contribution margin of $5.89; and the Cherry Berry Frosted Surprise, which has a contribution margin of $5.75. The major ingredients are flour, sugar, and butter. The supply of each of these ingredients is listed below along with the number of cups of each ingredient that goes into each of the three Christmas cakes.

	Fudge Walnut	Angel Food	Cherry Berry	Supply
Flour	3	$3^3/_4$	$2^3/_4$	500
Sugar	1	$1^1/_4$	$1^3/_4$	425
Butter	$^3/_4$	$^1/_2$	$^7/_8$	300

The head baker has found that he can substitute honey for sugar and margarine for butter in the recipes. The requirements and supply availabilities are given below.

	Fudge Walnut	Angel Food	Cherry Berry	Supply
Honey	$^3/_4$	$1^1/_2$	$1^3/_8$	424
Margarine	$^5/_8$	$^3/_4$	$^3/_4$	299

However, he must decide to use either sugar or honey; to use both would be confusing to his apprentice bakers because of the measurement differences. The same goes for butter/margarine. Formulate as an integer programming problem that will determine how many of each type of Christmas cake to bake in order to maximize profit.

27. The production unit of Siba-Gegy Pharmaceuticals manufactures three different types of antibiotic topical ointments. The contribution margin of each of these products is as follows.

1. Polymycrin ointment $1.75
2. Neomycrox ointment   2.19
3. Bacimyxin ointment   1.99

In order to meet FDA standards for quality control, Siba-Gegy must adopt at least two of four possible inspection systems in the coming month. The number of workhours required per unit of each product for each of the systems is given in the table below.

Inspection System	Polymycrin	Neomycrox	Bacimyxin
1	0.50	0.60	0.75
2	0.81	0.50	0.45
3	0.38	0.68	0.77
4	0.59	0.82	0.53

The quality control laboratory director has promised to make 3500 workhours available for each of the possible inspection systems. However, if inspection system 4 is adopted, he will grant an additional 100 workhours of laboratory labor since he developed the system and has a definite preference for it. Formulate as a profit-maximizing integer programming problem that will indicate the number of units of each product that can be manufactured in the next month and satisfy FDA regulations.

28. The Morecash Corporation is faced with the selection of a number of potential investments. The controller for Morecash has assigned a value (from 1 to 10) to each potential investment based on the discounted cash flow rate of return that is expected for each investment. The Morecash Corporation desires to select a set of investments that maximizes the total discounted cash flow rate of return for the company, subject to its capital expenditure budget of $1,150,000. Each investment must be selected on a *go–no-go* basis. In addition, investment 3 (new product development) is contingent upon the selection of investment 5 (construction of a new plant). Also, since the last four investments are associated with the petroleum industry, only two of these investments can be accepted since the Morecash Corporation follows a diversification investment policy. The rating and capital expenditure requirement for each of the 10 potential investments is provided below.

Potential Investment	Capital Expenditure Requirement	Rating
1	$125,000	4.0
2	235,000	8.1
3	320,000	9.3
4	155,000	4.7
5	500,000	5.0
6	450,000	7.0
7	100,000	7.5
8	85,000	3.0
9	175,000	5.5
10	425,000	6.3

Formulate as an integer programming problem to maximize the total discounted cash flow rate of return for the company.

29. A hiker is going backpacking in the Great Smoky Mountains. He must select the items to include in his gear. The following list of items are available for selection, with the "utility" value (scale of 1 to 10) and weight of each provided.

Items		Utility	Weight (lb)
1.	Sleeping bag	10	1
2.	Ground cloth	9	$1^1/_2$
3.	Canteen (water)	10	$^1/_2$
4.	Canteen (whiskey)	3	$^1/_2$
5.	Matches	10	$^1/_8$
6.	Flashlight	9	1
7.	Coffee packet	8	$^1/_2$
8.	Frying pan	4	2
9.	Sauce pan	6	1
10.	Mosquito repellent	5	$^1/_4$
11.	Mosquito netting	2	$^1/_2$
12.	Millet packet	6	$^1/_2$
13.	Lentil packet	6	$^1/_2$
14.	Knife	10	$^3/_4$
15.	Shotgun and ammunition	8	5
16.	One clothes change	10	$2^1/_2$
17.	Long underwear	8	1
18.	Two clothes change	5	5
19.	Raingear	10	$1^1/_2$
20.	Fishing gear	8	$2^1/_2$
21.	Sugar packet	7	$^1/_8$
22.	Vegetable oil	4	$^1/_2$
23.	Salt	10	$^1/_2$

Note that it would be useless to carry coffee, millet, or lentils unless the hiker is also bringing a saucepan. Note also it would be useless to carry sugar unless the hiker is also bringing coffee. Finally, it is useless to carry vegetable oil unless the hiker is also bringing a frying pan. The hiker can only carry 18 lb comfortably. Formulate as an integer programming problem to maximize utility.

30. The Sharpshooter Corporation manufactures rifle scopes for the sporting goods departments of five major department stores. Johnny Target, the shipping manager for Sharpshooter, must decide which of five available warehouses to lease in order to meet the demand requirements of its customers. The following cost matrix provides the leasing cost for each warehouse (l_j); the per-carton operating cost at each warehouse (o_i); and the per-carton transportation cost for shipping from warehouse i to customer j (t_{ij}).

Warehouse	l_i	o_i	t_{i1}	t_{i2}	t_{i3}	t_{i4}	t_{i5}
1	500.	.50	.75	.71	.80	.50	.76
2	515.	.55	.82	.89	.75	.65	.75
3	530.	.45	.77	.65	.85	.45	.65
4	498.	.57	.71	.65	.95	.80	.59
5	505.	.48	.68	.55	.99	.82	.89

The demand requirements (d_j) of the five customers are given below (in cartons).

Customer	d_j
1	100
2	200
3	300
4	400
5	175

Formulate as a mixed integer programming problem, with a minimum-cost objective function.

31. The Deep Freeze Corporation produces ice cube trays for refrigerator manufacturers. Their production unit has seven machines that mold plastic inputs into ice cube trays. The newer molding machines are more cost efficient than the older molding machines. The setup cost for each machine, variable cost per tray, and production capacity (trays per week) are given below.

Molding Machine	Setup Cost	Var. Cost per Unit	Capacity
1	$50	$.03	4000
2	55	.04	4500
3	60	.01	5000
4	58	.05	5500
5	54	.02	4800
6	60	.05	4400
7	52	.01	4500

The forecasted minimum demand for the coming week is 20,000 ice cube trays. Formulate as a mixed integer programming problem to minimize production costs.

32. The population of Winnsboro is concentrated in five districts within the city. District 1 contains 5000 people, (p_i), district 2 contains 2000 people, district 3 contains 2500 people, district 4 contains 4500 people, and district 5 contains 3000 people. Preliminary land surveys have limited the potential location of fire stations to eight sites. The distance (in miles) from the center of district i to site j is given by the following table.

Districts	Sites							
	1	2	3	4	5	6	7	8
1	2	3	4	5	7	7	8	11
2	7	2	1	2	4	7	7	8
3	6	4	7	7	1	1	3	5
4	10	6	9	5	3	7	2	2
5	11	9	11	10	6	5	2	4

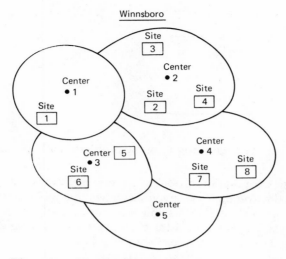

The cost of building a fire station at any location is a function of the number of people it will serve (m_j) plus a fixed cost.

Cost Function for Site j (C_j)

$$C_1(m_1) = 50,000 + 40\,m_1$$
$$C_2(m_2) = 55,000 + 50\,m_2$$
$$C_3(m_3) = 60,000 + 35\,m_3$$
$$C_4(m_4) = 45,000 + 45\,m_4$$
$$C_5(m_5) = 58,000 + 38\,m_5$$
$$C_6(m_6) = 48,000 + 35\,m_6$$
$$C_7(m_7) = 50,000 + 45\,m_7$$
$$C_8(m_8) = 52,000 + 40\,m_8$$

No more than 40,000 people can be assigned to any site and every district should be assigned to exactly one fire station. A total budget (B) of \$1 million has been allocated for firehouse construction. Determine the optimal site selection and assignment of districts to fire stations. The objective is to minimize the total distance traveled from the districts to the fire station sites to which they have been assigned. Let your decision variables include:

$$y_j = \begin{cases} 1 & \text{If site } j \text{ is selected} \\ 0 & \text{Otherwise} \end{cases}$$

and

$$x_{ij} = \begin{cases} 1 & \text{If district } i \text{ is assigned to site } j \\ 0 & \text{Otherwise} \end{cases}$$

Formulate as an integer programming problem.

33.   Starting from his home office in Columbia, a salesman wishes to visit Spartanburg, Charleston, and Orangeburg, and return home at minimal cost. The salesman must visit each city exactly once, and it costs c_{ij} to travel from city i to city j. What is

the optimal route? Formulate as an integer programming problem, using the following cost matrix.

	Columbia	Spartanburg	Charleston	Orangeburg
Columbia	M	10	15	5
Spartanburg	10	M	20	12
Charleston	15	20	M	14
Orangeburg	5	12	14	M

34. The Sportsworld Corporation is forming a five-man basketball team for participation in local competitions. The company wishes to select a starting lineup from seven available candidates in order to maximize the average height of the starting lineup. The candidates are the following employees.

Employee	No.	Height Above 5 ft. 10 in. (in inches)	Position
Johnny Jumpup	1	7	Center
Les Basket	2	5	Center
Joe Score	3	7	Forward
Too-Short Jones	4	1	Forward
Ed Leap	5	3	Guard
Mike Speed	6	5	Guard
Nick Toss	7	4	Guard

The starting lineup must satisfy the following requirements.

1. At least one forward must start.
2. At least one center must start.
3. No more than two centers can start.
4. At least one guard must start.
5. Either Joe Score or Nick Toss must be held in reserve.

Formulate as an integer programming problem.

10 Nonlinear Programming

10.1 INTRODUCTION

The importance and usefulness of linear programming has been discussed and illustrated in earlier chapters. In Chapter 3, Section 3.5, we discussed the linearity assumption of linear programming, observing that all the functions (objective function and constraints) of a linear programming problem were linear. However, in many practical problems it is necessary to deal with a nonlinear objective function and/or nonlinear constraints. For example, the objective function may need to be constructed in a manner that describes the nonlinear relationship of sales quantities or sales prices to volume. Similarly, the constraint relationships may need to be derived in a manner to represent nonlinear returns to scale as production volumes are increased. Finally, nonlinearities can arise when any of the coefficients in a mathematical programming model are considered as random variables. For example, the cost coefficients in a transportation model might be random variables that are functionally related to the quantities shipped from the origins to the destinations.

In this chapter we will consider some of the rudimentary aspects of nonlinear programming problems. Initially, the reader should be cautioned that nonlinear programming problems are considerably more difficult to solve than linear programming problems, primarily because of the complexity involved with general, nonlinear functions. Consequently, we will concentrate our discussions on a few of the nonlinear programming problems that can be solved. As we proceed with our study of nonlinear programming the reader is urged to review the material in the earlier chapters that dealt with linear programming. As we shall observe, many nonlinear programming problems are direct extensions of their linear analogs. Also, certain nonlinear programming solution methods are based directly upon linear programming procedures. Additionally, we shall find it necessary to introduce and/or review several mathematical concepts. These mathematical tools will be required in developing solution procedures for nonlinear problems. Finally, we will make use of differential calculus in several of the solution procedures presented. The reader who wishes to briefly review differential calculus may do so by referring to the material presented in Appendix B at the end of the book.

10.2 EXAMPLES OF NONLINEAR PROGRAMMING PROBLEMS

The following two examples illustrate how nonlinear programming problems can arise in practical managerial decision making situations.

EXAMPLE 1 *Portfolio Selection.* The manager of a trust fund for a wealthy investor is contemplating the reinvestment of $10,000 from the trust fund. Based on past historical data he has isolated two investments, which have an expected annual return of 18 and 13 percent, respectively. Additionally, the trust fund manager has determined that the variance of the total return resulting from investing in the two projects will be given by $3x_1^2 + 2x_2^2 + (x_1 + x_2)^2$, where x_1 is the amount allocated to the first investment (in thousands of dollars) and x_2 is the amount allocated to the second investment (in thousands of dollars). This variance measure thus expresses the risk associated with a portfolio composed of these two investments, and the expression for the variance of the portfolio suggests that the risk increases nonlinearly with the total investment and with the amount of each individual investment. Now, the trust fund manager would like to select his portfolio of investments in a manner that both maximizes the expected return and minimizes the risk. Unfortunately, these two objectives cannot generally be satisfied simultaneously.

One approach to this portfolio problem would be to select a dimensionless "risk coefficient," K, and formulate a model having the following form.

$$\text{Maximize } Z = 18x_1 + 13x_2 - K[3x_1^2 + 2x_2^2 + (x_1 + x_2)^2] \qquad (10-1)$$

subject to: $\quad x_1 + x_2 \le 10$ $\qquad\qquad\qquad\qquad\qquad\qquad\qquad (10-2)$

with $\quad x_1 \ge 0, x_2 \ge 0$ $\qquad\qquad\qquad\qquad\qquad\qquad\qquad\qquad (10-3)$

The objective function for this model is nonlinear, while the constraint set (a single constraint) is linear. This portfolio selection model is thus a nonlinear programming model. The risk coefficient K can be employed to weight the tradeoff between risk and expected return. If $K = 0$, risk is ignored and the model reverts to a very simple linear programming problem in which the trust fund manager will invest entirely in the investment having the greatest expected return. If K becomes very large, the objective function contribution due to the expected return will become negligible, and the trust fund manager would then be essentially minimizing the nonlinear risk term.

EXAMPLE 2   *Sales Effort Determination.*   The Lindsay Distributing Company sells two types of automotive tool kits. The first tool kit sells for $10 per unit, regardless of the number of units sold. However, sales revenue for the second tool kit declines as the number of units sold increases, according to the expression:

$$\text{Sales revenue} = \$15x_2 - \$0.15x_2^2 \qquad (10\text{-}4)$$

where x_2 = number of type 2 tool kits sold

This sales revenue expression was derived in terms of the total sales revenue from any number of units being sold as equaling the number of units sold, x_2, times the unit contribution ($\$15 - \$0.15x_2$).

The company has two restrictions upon its distribution efforts. First, its sales force is limited and has available 1000 sales hours total to devote to these two products in the next year. The company estimates that its sales time function is nonlinear and can be approximated by the function $1x_1 + 0.1x_1^2 + 2x_2 + 0.25x_2^2$. Second, it has limited availability of the two tool kits, and can secure 5000 tool kits total for the next year.

This sales effort determination problem can be formulated as the following problem.

$$\text{Maximize } Z = \$10x_1 + \$15x_2 - \$0.15x_2^2 \qquad (10\text{-}5)$$

subject to: $1x_1 + 0.1x_1^2 + 2x_2 + 0.25x_2^2 \leq 1000$ (Sales hours)   (10-6)

$\qquad\qquad\qquad x_1 \qquad + \qquad x_2 \leq 5000$ (Units available)

with $x_1 \geq 0, x_2 \geq 0$ (10-7)

The objective function for this problem is nonlinear, while the constraint set has one nonlinear and one linear constraint. Thus, we again have a nonlinear programming formulation.

With the improvement in high-speed computing capabilities, and the development of more efficient and powerful approaches for certain nonlinear programming problems, there has been an associated increasing interest in analyzing various problems as nonlinear models. In the remainder of this chapter we will attempt to provide other examples of nonlinear models. The reader who is particularly interested in applications of nonlinear programming should consult the books written by Bracken and McCormick (1968), Lavi and Vogel (1968), and McMillan (1975).

10.3   THE GENERAL NONLINEAR PROGRAMMING PROBLEM

The general form of a nonlinear programming problem can be stated as follows. Select n decision variables $x_1, x_2, \ldots, x_n$ from a given feasible region in a manner that optimizes (maximizes or minimizes) a given objective function.

$$Z = f(x_1, x_2, \ldots, x_n) \qquad (10\text{-}8)$$

subject to: $\quad g_1(x_1, x_2, \ldots, x_n) \; \{\leq, =, \geq\} \; b_1$

$$g_2(x_1, x_2, \ldots, x_n) \; \{\leq, =, \geq\} \; b_2$$

$$\vdots \qquad\qquad \vdots \quad\;\; \vdots \qquad\qquad (10\text{-}9)$$

$$g_m(x_1, x_2, \ldots, x_n) \; \{\leq, =, \geq\} \; b_m$$

with $\qquad \mathbf{x} = (x_1, x_2, \ldots, x_n) \geq 0 \qquad\qquad (10\text{-}10)$

where at least one of the functions $f(x_1, x_2, \ldots, x_n)$ or $g_i(x_1, x_2, \ldots, x_n)$ is nonlinear.

This general form of a nonlinear programming problem allows for a number of possible problem formulations. Thus, we have problems involving:

1. A linear objective function with some or all of the constraints nonlinear.
2. A nonlinear objective function with a linear constraint set.
3. A nonlinear objective function with some or all of the constraints nonlinear.

The complications afforded by these forms of nonlinear programming problems are numerous and difficult, particularly when a problem has a number of constraints and decision variables.

Earlier, in Chapter 3, we noted that the linear constraint set and the non-negativity restrictions in any linear programming problem form a convex set. We then noted that we could identify the extreme (corner) points of this convex set as being basic feasible solutions to the linear programming problem. Finally, we observed that one of these extreme points was the optimal basic feasible solution to the linear programming problem.

The optimal basic feasible solution in a linear programming problem is the **absolute** or **global maximum** value of the objective function. Now, a function, $y = f(x)$, is said to have an **absolute** or **global maximum** at a point $x = x'$ if $f(x')$ is greater than $f(x)$ for any other allowable value of x. To illustrate, consider Fig. 10.1. The global maximum in Fig. 10.1 occurs at point $x = x'$, where $f(x')$ is larger than $f(x)$ for any other value of x within the region $0 \leq x \leq x^\dagger$. Similarly, a function is said to have an **absolute** or **global minimum** at a point $x = x^*$ if $f(x^*)$ is less than $f(x)$ for any other allowable value of x. In Fig. 10.1, the global minimum occurs at point $x = x^*$, where $f(x^*)$ is less than $f(x)$ for any other value of x within the region $0 \leq x \leq x^\dagger$.

A function can also be said to have a **relative** or **local maximum** at a point $x = x''$ if $f(x'')$ is greater than the value of $f(x)$ for any adjacent value of x. Similarly, a function is said to have a **relative** or **local minimum** at a point $x = x^{**}$ if $f(x^{**})$ is less than the value of $f(x)$ for any adjacent value of x. In Fig. 10.1, a local maximum occurs at point $x = x''$, and a local minimum occurs at point $x = x^{**}$. From the definitions given and illustrated above it should be apparent that a local maximum or minimum of a function can also be a global maximum or minimum of that function.

Unfortunately, when we begin to consider nonlinear programming problems the fact that the constraint set can have some or all nonlinear functions means that we may no longer be dealing with a convex solution space. To illustrate, consider Fig. 10.2 which presents a nonconvex solution space. In Fig. 10.2 the nonconvex solution space is formed by one linear constraint, one nonlinear constraint, and

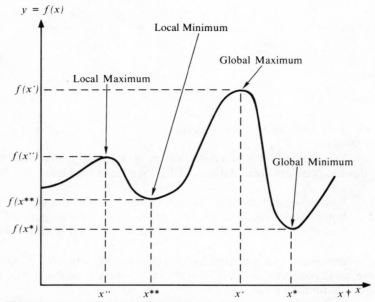

FIGURE 10.1 Local and Global Maxima and Minima

the nonnegativity restriction $x_1 \geq 0$, $x_2 \geq 0$. Assuming that we are solving a maximization problem with an objective function having the slope indicated, we observe that as we move the objective function upward and to the right through the nonconvex solution space, we first encounter a local maximum, Z' at point A, and then the global maximum, Z'' at point B. In linear programming the convex feasible solution space always resulted in the optimal basic feasible solution being selected at one of its extreme points. However, in nonlinear programming problems, as seen in Fig. 10.2, the optimal solution may occur at a corner point, at

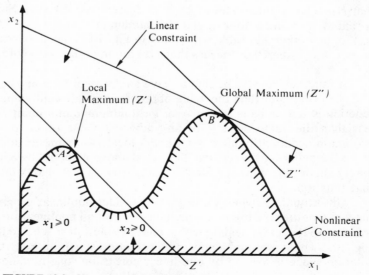

FIGURE 10.2 Nonconvex Solution Space-Local and Global Maximum

another boundary point of the nonconvex solution space, or at interior points within the nonconvex solution space. Additionally, as shown in Fig. 10.2, one may identify a local optimum, rather than a global optimum, as being *the* best solution (i.e., $Z' < Z''$). While it is easy to distinguish between a local optimum and the global optimum in this small graphical problem, it may be very difficult to do so in larger, more complicated, nonlinear programming problems.

No specific algorithm exists for solving the general nonlinear programming problem as defined by (10–8), (10–9), and (10–10). However, by making various assumptions about the function $Z = f(\mathbf{x})$ and the $g_i(\mathbf{x})$ functions, solution algorithms for important special cases of the general nonlinear programming problem have been developed. Work in this area of management science is actively evolving, but remains a large, uncharted area. Consequently, we shall not attempt to survey nonlinear programming completely, but rather, we will concentrate on some of the more useful results that have been obtained to date.

10.4   CONCAVE AND CONVEX FUNCTIONS

In the field of mathematical programming, linear functions are most often found. For this reason a great deal of the earlier portion of this textbook was devoted to the study of linear programming. As we now begin to study nonlinear programming we will observe the importance of functions that are defined as being **concave** or **convex**. Because of the importance of such functions in nonlinear programming we will now proceed to discuss their basic properties.

The properties of a **concave function** are given by the following definition.

DEFINITION   *A function of a single variable, say* f(x), *is a concave function if, for each pair of values of* x, *say* x' *and* x'':

$$f[\lambda x'' + (1 - \lambda)x'] \geq \lambda f(x'') + (1 - \lambda)f(x') \qquad (10\text{–}11)$$

for all values of λ *such that* $0 \leq \lambda \leq 1$. *It is a strictly concave function if the sign* $\geq$ *is replaced by the sign* $>$.

An example of a concave function would be a profit function in which the marginal returns decrease as the number of units sold increase. Thus, if sales doubled, profits would not double, if the profit function were concave.

Conversely, the properties of a **convex function** are given by the following definition.

DEFINITION   *A function of a single variable, say* f(x), *is a convex function if, for each pair of values of* x, *say* x' *and* x'':

$$f[\lambda x'' + (1 - \lambda)x'] \leq \lambda f(x'') + (1 - \lambda)f(x') \qquad (10\text{–}12)$$

for all values of λ *such that* $0 \leq \lambda \leq 1$. *It is a strictly convex function if the sign* $\leq$ *is replaced by the sign* $<$.

An example of a convex function would be a cost function in which the marginal costs increase as the number of units produced increase. Thus, if the number of units produced doubled, the production costs would more than double if the cost function were convex.

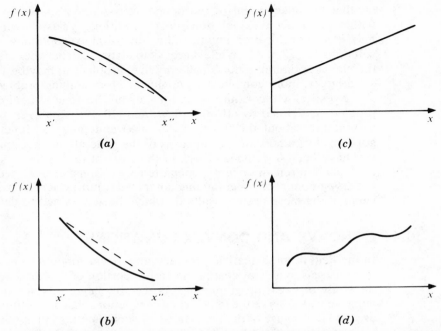

FIGURE 10.3 **Examples of Concavity and Convexity.** (*a*) **A Concave Function.** (*b*) **A Convex Function.** (*c*) **Both Concave and Convex.** (*d*) **Neither Concave nor Convex**

Geometric interpretations of concavity and convexity are shown in Fig. 10.3.

From Fig. 10.3 it can be seen that $f(x)$ is *concave* if, for each pair of points on the graph of $f(x)$, the line segment joining these two points lies entirely below the graph of the function. A concave function is like an umbrella and will shed water. Conversely, $f(x)$ is *convex* if, for each pair of points on the graph of $f(x)$, the line segment joining these two points lies entirely above the graph of the function. A convex function is thus like a bathtub and will hold water. A straight line, which we have for the objective function and constraints in a linear programming problem is both concave and convex, according to the above definition. In part (*d*) of Fig. 10.3, we have a nonlinear function that is both nonconvex and nonconcave.

For a single-variable function, in calculus terms, if $f(x)$ is continuous, and possesses a second derivative over the region of interest, then:

$f(x)$ is *concave* if, and only if, $d^2f(x)/dx \leq 0$.

$f(x)$ is *strictly concave* if, and only if, $d^2f(x)/dx < 0$.

$f(x)$ is *convex* if, and only if, $d^2f(x)/dx \geq 0$.

$f(x)$ is *strictly convex* if, and only if, $d^2f(x)/dx > 0$.

To illustrate strict convexity consider the function of $f(x) = 3x^2$, which is plotted in Fig. 10.4. Taking derivatives, we obtain

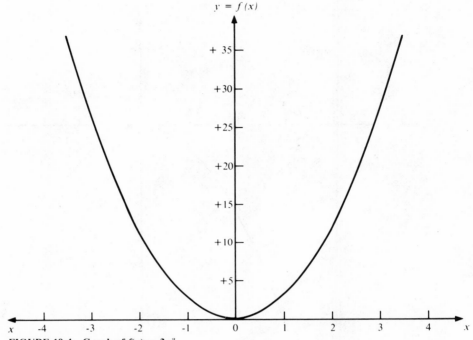

FIGURE 10.4 Graph of $f(x) = 3x^2$

$$\frac{df(x)}{dx} = 6x \tag{10-13}$$

$$\frac{d^2f(x)}{dx} = 6 > 0 \tag{10-14}$$

$\therefore f(x) = 3x^2$ is strictly convex

To illustrate strict concavity consider the function $f(x) = -3x^2$, which is plotted in Fig. 10.5.

$$\frac{df(x)}{dx} = -6x \tag{10-15}$$

$$\frac{d^2f(x)}{dx} = -6 < 0 \tag{10-16}$$

$\therefore f(x) = -3x^2$ is strictly concave

To illustrate a function that is both convex and concave, consider the function $f(x) = 2x^3 - 3x^2$, which is plotted in Fig. 10.6.

$$\frac{df(x)}{dx} = 6x^2 - 6x \tag{10-17}$$

$$\frac{d^2f(x)}{dx} = 12x - 6 \tag{10-18}$$

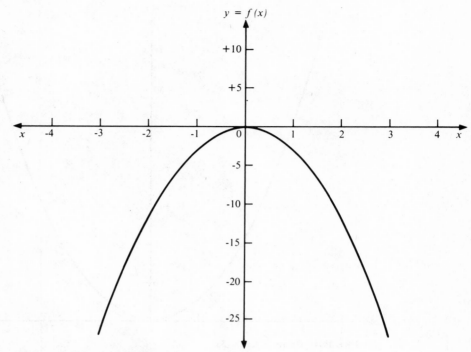

FIGURE 10.5   Graph of $f(x) = -3x^2$

Thus, for $x \geq \frac{1}{2}$, $f(x)$ is convex and for $x < \frac{1}{2}$, $f(x)$ is concave.

Other examples of convex functions of a single variable are x^4, e^x, or $-\log x$. Conversely, other examples of concave functions are $-x^4$, $-e^x$, or $+\log x$. Our definition of convexity implies that the sum of convex functions will also be a convex function, and that the nonnegative multiple of a convex function will be a convex function. Conversely, the sum of concave functions will also be a concave function, and the nonnegative multiple of a concave function will be a concave function.

The concept of concave and convex functions naturally generalizes to functions of more than one variable. Thus, if $f(x)$ is replaced by $f(x_1, x_2, \ldots, x_n)$, the definitions stated above still apply as long as x is replaced everywhere by $(x_1, x_2, \ldots, x_n)$. Second partial derivatives can be used to check functions of several variables for concavity and convexity properties, although the computational process involved is very time-consuming and tedious.

The concept of concave and convex functions is related to the concept of a **convex set**, which was formally defined in Chapter 2.

In our discussion of nonlinear programming methods that follows, local rather than global optima may be obtained unless certain convexity-concavity conditions are met. Therefore, assessing convexity-concavity properties is important. In summary, it can be shown that the following relationships for local and global maxima will hold.

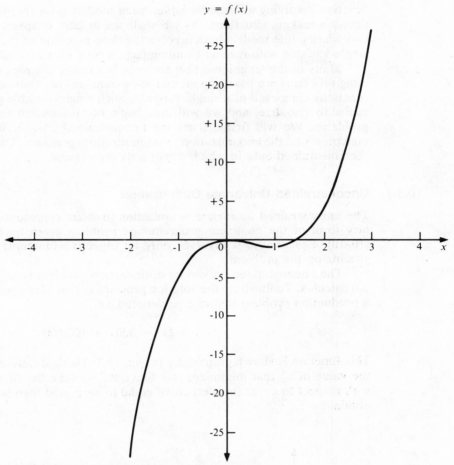

FIGURE 10.6   Graph of $f(x) = 2x^3 - 3x^2$

1. A local $\left\{\begin{matrix} \text{minimum} \\ \text{maximum} \end{matrix}\right\}$ of a $\left\{\begin{matrix} \text{convex} \\ \text{concave} \end{matrix}\right\}$ function on a

    convex set is also a global $\left\{\begin{matrix} \text{minimum} \\ \text{maximum} \end{matrix}\right\}$ of that function.

2. A local $\left\{\begin{matrix} \text{minimum} \\ \text{maximum} \end{matrix}\right\}$ of a strictly $\left\{\begin{matrix} \text{convex} \\ \text{concave} \end{matrix}\right\}$ function on

    a convex set is also the unique global $\left\{\begin{matrix} \text{minimum} \\ \text{maximum} \end{matrix}\right\}$ of that function.

10.5 OPTIMIZATION INVOLVING A SINGLE VARIABLE

The simplest type of nonlinear programming model is encountered in problem situations in which an optimum is sought with respect to a nonlinear objective function involving a single variable. Such models arise frequently in managerial decision-making situations. As we shall see in later chapters, inventory control and waiting-line models both involve the determination of the optimal value of a single variable with respect to minimizing a total cost function.

Many of the techniques that are used in solving complex nonlinear programming problems are based upon, and are extensions of, methods used to optimize functions composed of a single variable. Such single-variable problems are much easier to visualize, and we will thus begin our discussion with such univariate problems. We will first discuss the unconstrained case in which there are no constraints on the maximization (or minimization) problem. Then, we will analyze the constrained case in which constraints are present.

10.5.1   Unconstrained Univariate Optimization

The **unconstrained univariate optimization problem** represents the most elementary form of the nonlinear programming problem given by (10–8), (10–9), and (10–10). Essentially, it involves only an objective function; there are no constraints on the problem.

The unconstrained univariate optimization problem is solved using differential calculus. To illustrate the solution procedure, consider a total cost function for a production problem that can be denoted as:

$$f(x) = 2x^2 - 800x + 100,000 \qquad (10\text{--}19)$$

This function is shown graphically in Fig. 10.7. Using differential calculus to find the value of x^* that minimizes this function, we take the first derivative of $f(x)$ with respect to x, set this derivative equal to zero, and then solve for x. We thus obtain

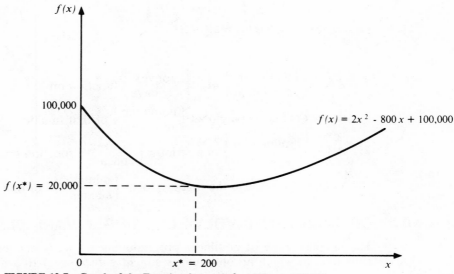

FIGURE 10.7   Graph of the Function $f(x) = 2x^2 - 800x + 100,000$

$$\frac{df(x)}{dx} = 4x - 800 \tag{10-20}$$

Letting $df(x)/dx = 0$ yields the optimal value, x^*

$$0 = 4x^* - 800 \tag{10-21}$$
$$x^* = 200$$

Thus, this production cost function will be minimized when 200 units are produced. The total (minimum) production cost for this production quantity is found by substituting 200 for x in the cost function, obtaining

$$\begin{aligned} f(200) &= 2(200)^2 - 800(200) + 100,000 \\ &= 80,000 - 160,000 + 100,000 \\ &= \$20,000 \end{aligned} \tag{10-22}$$

Our graphical representation of this problem in Fig. 10.7 clearly indicates that we have obtained the value of x that produces the minimum value of $f(x)$. However, in many other problems it may not be so apparent whether values of x^* obtained in this manner, called **stationary points**, produce maximum or minimum values of the function being analyzed. To determine whether a maximum or minimum has been found, the second derivative should be evaluated at the point x^*, using the following rule.

> **RULE** *If $d^2f(x)/dx$ is negative, then point x^* is a maximum.*
> *If $d^2f(x)/dx$ is positive, then point x^* is a minimum.*
> *If $d^2f(x)/dx$ is zero, the test is indeterminant.*

Thus, to verify that $x^* = 200$ in our production-cost problem is truly a minimum, we determine

$$\frac{d^2f(x)}{dx} = 4 \tag{10-23}$$

Since $d^2f(x)/dx$ is positive for all values of x we are assured that $x^* = 200$ is the minimum value of the function $f(x)$. This value is a global minimum for this function.

10.5.2 Constrained Univariate Optimization

The **constrained univariate optimization problem** involves an objective function, and one or more constraints. Quite often these constraints may be in the form of nonnegativity restrictions on the variable x in terms of a range for the variable x. To illustrate such a problem, first consider an unconstrained profit function that can be specified as:

$$f(x) = -2x^3 + 3x^2 + 12x + 15 \tag{10-24}$$

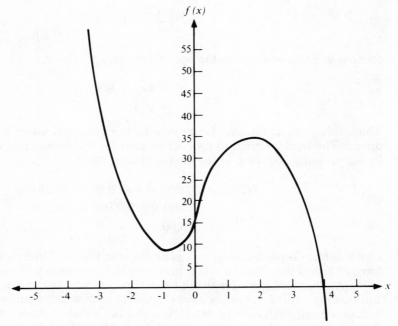

FIGURE 10.8   Graph of the Function $f(x) = -2x^3 + 3x^2 + 12x + 15$

This function is shown graphically in Fig. 10.8.

This univariate optimization problem is again solved using differential calculus. However, taking the first derivative of $f(x)$ and solving for x yields two different stationary points.

$$\frac{df(x)}{dx} = -6x^2 + 6x + 12$$
$$= -6(x^2 - 1x - 2) \quad (10\text{-}25)$$
$$= -6(x - 2)(x + 1)$$

Thus, $x^* = 2$ (First stationary point)   (10-26)

$x^* = -1$ (Second stationary point)

Taking the second derivative of this profit function we obtain

$$\frac{d^2f(x)}{dx} = -12x + 6 \quad (10\text{-}27)$$

Substituting $x^* = 2$ into this second derivative yields

$$\frac{d^2f(x)}{dx} = -12(2) + 6 = -18 \quad (10\text{-}28)$$

Thus, $x^* = 2$ is a maximum value.

Substituting $x^* = -1$ into this second derivative yields

$$\frac{d^2f(x)}{dx} = -12(-1) + 6 = +18 \qquad (10\text{-}29)$$

Thus, $x^* = -1$ is a minimum value.

Referring to Fig. 10.8, it can be seen that the stationary point $x^* = 2$ is a local maximum for this profit function. The stationary point $x^* = -1$ is a local minimum for this profit function.

Now, let us add a constraint to this problem that specifies that $-3 \le x \le 2$. In the constrained case, the global maximum of this profit function is at the boundary point $x^* = -3$, and the global minimum is at the stationary point $x^* = -1$.

Suppose instead that we had constrained the problem by specifying that $x \ge 0$, the typical form of a nonnegativity restriction. Now, the stationary point $x^* = 3$ is a global maximum.

In summary, in a constrained univariate optimization problem, a global optimum (if one exists) will always occur either at one of the stationary points or at one of the boundary points determined by the constraints. Differential calculus is again employed to determine the stationary points.

10.6 OPTIMIZATION INVOLVING MULTIPLE VARIABLES

A more difficult type of nonlinear programming problem involves a nonlinear objective function having n variables ($n \ge 2$). This multivariate optimization problem again requires the identification of the stationary points of the function and then the identification of which of these points represent local or global optima. Unfortunately, the identification of local or global optima is not necessarily easily done for some multivariate functions.

We will again separate our discussion of optimization involving multiple variables into two sections. First, we will consider the unconstrained case, and then we will consider the constrained case.

10.6.1 Unconstrained Multivariate Optimization

The **unconstrained multivariate optimization problem** represents a nonlinear programming problem composed of only an objective function, but this objective function has multiple variables. To illustrate a solution procedure for this type of problem, consider the following nonlinear profit function.

$$Z = f(x_1, x_2) = -(x_1 - 4)^2 - x_2^2 \qquad (10\text{-}30)$$

This function is shown graphically in Fig. 10.9. This three-dimensional graph indicates that the maximum of the function $Z = 0$ lies at the point $\mathbf{x} = (4,0)$.

Just as we did for the univariate optimization problem, the stationary points are found by setting the first derivatives equal to zero, and solving the resulting equations. For the multivariate problem having n variables there will be n first derivatives. Each of these n first derivatives will be a partial derivative taken with respect to that variable. This set of n partial derivatives is expressed in vector form as the **gradient** of the function $f(\mathbf{x}) = f(x_1, x_2, \ldots, x_n)$ and is denoted as:

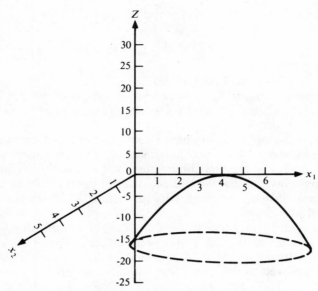

FIGURE 10.9   Three-Dimensional Graph of $Z = -(x_1 - 4)^2 - x_2^2$

$$\nabla f(\mathbf{x}) = \begin{bmatrix} \dfrac{\partial f(x_1, x_2, \ldots, x_n)}{\partial x_1} \\[2mm] \dfrac{\partial f(x_1, x_2, \ldots, x_n)}{\partial x_2} \\[2mm] \vdots \\[2mm] \dfrac{\partial f(x_1, x_2, \ldots, x_n)}{\partial x_n} \end{bmatrix} \qquad (10\text{-}31)$$

The gradient of the multivariate profit function we are considering is found by taking partial derivatives with respect to x_1 and x_2, namely,

$$\nabla f(\mathbf{x}) = \begin{bmatrix} \dfrac{\partial f(x_1, x_2)}{\partial x_1} \\[2mm] \dfrac{\partial f(x_1, x_2)}{\partial x_2} \end{bmatrix} = \begin{bmatrix} -2(x_1 - 4) \\[2mm] -2x_2 \end{bmatrix} \qquad (10\text{-}32)$$

Setting $\nabla f(\mathbf{x}) = 0$ then gives the coordinates of the stationary point for this function.

$$\begin{array}{llll} -2(x_1 - 4) = 0 & \text{or} & x_1 = 4 \\ -2x_2 \quad\ = 0 & \text{or} & x_2 = 0 \end{array} \qquad (10\text{-}33)$$

This stationary point can also be observed from Fig. 10.9, and can be seen to be a local maximum.

Given that we have found the stationary point(s) for the multivariate function, we still must determine whether these stationary points are either local or global maxima or minima, or neither a maximum nor a minimum.

From our discussion of univariate optimization recall that the second derivative was used to evaluate whether stationary points were maxima or minima. An analogous concept is used for multivariate optimization, and is based on the matrix of all possible second partial derivatives. A second derivative of the multivariate function $f(x_1, x_2, \ldots, x_n)$ can be taken with respect to each of the n first derivatives, for each of the n variables. This results in a $n \times n$ matrix of the second derivatives. This matrix of second derivatives is called a **Hessian matrix**, and is denoted as:

$$\mathbf{H(x)} = \begin{bmatrix} \dfrac{\partial f^2(\mathbf{x})}{\partial x_1 \partial x_1}, & \dfrac{\partial f^2(\mathbf{x})}{\partial x_1 \partial x_2}, & \cdots, & \dfrac{\partial f^2(\mathbf{x})}{\partial x_1 \partial x_n} \\[2mm] \dfrac{\partial f^2(\mathbf{x})}{\partial x_2 \partial x_1}, & \dfrac{\partial f^2(\mathbf{x})}{\partial x_2 \partial x_2}, & \cdots, & \dfrac{\partial f^2(\mathbf{x})}{\partial x_2 \partial x_n} \\[2mm] \vdots & \vdots & & \vdots \\[2mm] \dfrac{\partial f^2(\mathbf{x})}{\partial x_n \partial x_1}, & \dfrac{\partial f^2(\mathbf{x})}{\partial x_n \partial x_2}, & \cdots, & \dfrac{\partial f^2(\mathbf{x})}{\partial x_n \partial x_n} \end{bmatrix} \tag{10-34}$$

The Hessian matrix for the multivariate function we are considering, $f(x) = -(x_1 - 4)^2 - x_2^2$, is computed as:

$$\mathbf{H(x)} = \begin{bmatrix} -2 & 0 \\ 0 & -2 \end{bmatrix} \tag{10-35}$$

The Hessian matrix can be used to identify local maxima or minima. This is done by examining the **minors** of the Hessian matrix. Now, any $n \times n$ matrix has n minors. The first minor of the Hessian matrix is the element in the upper left corner of $\mathbf{H(x)}$. The second minor is composed of the elements in the first two rows and the first two columns of $\mathbf{H(x)}$. The total Hessian matrix is the nth minor.

Associated with each of the minors in $\mathbf{H(x)}$ is a number, called a **determinant**. The signs of the determinants of the minors of the Hessian matrix indicate the presence of maxima or minima for multivariate functions. A stationary point for a multivariate function will be a local maximum or a local minimum only if one of the two following conditions are met.

1. The signs of the determinants are all positive, in which case the Hessian matrix is termed **positive-definite**.
2. The sign of the first determinant is negative; the sign of the second determinant is positive; the sign of the third determinant is negative, etc.; in alternating fashion. In this case the Hessian matrix is termed **negative-definite**. In this case the stationary point is a local maximum.

If the signs of the determinants do not meet these two conditions, then the stationary points may be either a maximum or a minimum, or neither. In this instance the Hessian matrix is termed **semi-definite**.

To illustrate these results, consider the Hessian matrix we have just computed, namely,

$$\mathbf{H(x)} = \begin{bmatrix} -2 & 0 \\ 0 & -2 \end{bmatrix} \tag{10-36}$$

The determinant for the first minor is the same as the first minor. The first minor is composed of the single element -2 and thus the value of the determinant for this first minor is also -2. Thus, the sign of the first determinant is negative. The determinant for the second minor is obtained by performing the following multiplications and subtractions.

1.   Multiply the number in row one, column one (-2), times the number in row two, column two (-2).
2.   Multiply the number in row two, column one (0), times the number in row two, column one (0).
3.   Subtract the second product from the first product.

Thus, the second determinant in our example is computed as:[1]

$$(-2)(-2) - (0)(0) = +4 \qquad (10\text{-}37)$$

In some unconstrained nonlinear optimization problems it may be difficult to actually solve for the values of the variables at the stationary point.

Thus, a procedure must be used that will allow us to start at some point, and then move in a certain direction that will improve the value of the objective function, $f(\mathbf{x})$. The gradient $\nabla f(\mathbf{x})$ is employed in this procedure.

First, it is necessary to transpose the gradient. For example, using our earlier example, the transpose of the gradient of this function is given by:

$$\nabla f(\mathbf{x})' = (-2(x_1 - 4), -2x_2) \qquad (10\text{-}38)$$

Assume next that we seek to maximize $f(\mathbf{x})$. It can then be shown that $f(\mathbf{x})$ will increase if a direction d is selected such that the product of the transpose of the gradient and d is positive. Thus,

$$\nabla f(\mathbf{x})'d > 0 \qquad (10\text{-}39)$$

will increase $f(\mathbf{x})$. Now, in a typical unconstrained multivariate optimization problem there may be an infinite number of directions satisfying the condition given by (10-37). Thus, we need to find the direction d^* that produces the largest immediate increase in $f(\mathbf{x})$ as we move away from the point x. Again, it can be shown using the Cauchy-Schwartz inequality that the gradient itself points in the optimal *direction* to move in order to achieve the largest immediate increase in $f(\mathbf{x})$ (Hadley, p. 4). Since the gradient points in the direction that we should move from x in order to cause the greatest immediate increase in $f(\mathbf{x})$, the gradient is said to point in the direction of the *steepest ascent* for the function.

It is important to recognize that the gradient points only in the direction giving the largest immediate increase in $f(\mathbf{x})$. The gradient does not provide for the shortest route to the optimum. Thus, the gradient must be employed in a series of steps, involving movements of short distances from the current point.

Assume now that we have determined some arbitrary starting point $\mathbf{x}^1 = (x_1^1,$

---

[1] We have shown only the computation of a simple determinant. Calculation of determinants when $n > 2$ is much more difficult, and the reader should discuss one of the references on matrix algebra given in Chapter 2.

$x_2^1, \ldots, x_n^1$). As we search for a local optimum we will want to move to a second point that has the property $f(\mathbf{x}^2) > f(\mathbf{x}^1)$, for a maximization problem. We know that the direction to move is specified by the gradient, but we do not know how far to travel. Suppose that we now let the letter s represent the distance (unknown at this juncture) to be traveled in the direction $f(\mathbf{x})$. Thus, we will generate a new point.

$$\mathbf{x}^2 = \mathbf{x}^1 + s \, \nabla f(\mathbf{x}^1) \tag{10-40}$$

or in general

$$\mathbf{x}^{k+1} = \mathbf{x}^k + s \, \nabla f(\mathbf{x}^k) \tag{10-41}$$

The distance s, in the relationship given by (10-41) is called the *step size*. Unfortunately, there is no precise way to determine this step size. However, one method that has shown good computational results has been devised. Known as the **optimal gradient method**, it involves determining the step size in such a manner that we always move as far as possible from $\mathbf{x}^k$ in the direction $\nabla f(\mathbf{x}^k)$. This is then accomplished by determining the (positive) value of s, which maximizes $f(\mathbf{x}^k + s \, \nabla f(\mathbf{x}^k)$. Solving this maximization problem generally requires a search over discrete values of s. Numerous examples of search procedures can be found in books by Wilde (1964) and Himmelblau (1972).

Let us now consider the previous example in which we seek to maximize

$$\begin{aligned} Z = f(\mathbf{x}) &= -(x_1 - 4)^2 - x_2^2 \\ &= -x_1^2 + 8x_1 - 16 - x_2^2 \end{aligned} \tag{10-42}$$

Previously, we computed the gradient of this function to be

$$\nabla f(\mathbf{x}) = \begin{bmatrix} -2(x_1 - 4) \\ -2x_2 \end{bmatrix} = \begin{bmatrix} -2x_1 + 8 \\ -2x_2 \end{bmatrix} \tag{10-43}$$

To begin, let us start our search from the origin, that is, $\mathbf{x}^1 = (x_1^1 = 0, x_2^1 = 0)$. At this initial point the value of the gradient is

$$\nabla f(\mathbf{x}') = \nabla f(0,0) = \begin{bmatrix} -2(0 - 4) \\ -2(0) \end{bmatrix} = \begin{bmatrix} +8 \\ 0 \end{bmatrix} \tag{10-44}$$

To determine how far to move in the direction $\begin{bmatrix} +8 \\ 0 \end{bmatrix}$, we must solve the problem:

$$\underset{s>0}{\text{maximize}} \, f[\mathbf{x}^1 + s \, \nabla f(\mathbf{x}^1)], \tag{10-45}$$

where $\quad \mathbf{x}^1 = (0,0) \quad$ and $\quad \nabla f(\mathbf{x}^1) = \begin{bmatrix} +8 \\ 0 \end{bmatrix}$

Thus, we must substitute $x_1^2 = [0 + s(+8)]$ and $x_2^2 = [0 + s(0)]$ into Equation (10-42). Then we must solve:

$$\underset{s>0}{\text{maximize}} - (+8s)^2 + 8(+8s) - 16 - (0s)^2 = \underset{s>0}{\text{maximize}} - 64s^2 + 64s - 16 \tag{10-46}$$

Setting the first derivative (with respect to s) of this function equal to zero results in the following equation.

$$-128s + 64 = 0$$
$$s = {}^{64}/_{128} = \tfrac{1}{2} \tag{10-47}$$

The optimal distance s is thus $\tfrac{1}{2}$, and our second point is

$$\mathbf{x}^2 = \mathbf{x}^1 + s\,\nabla f(\mathbf{x}^1)$$

$$= \begin{bmatrix} 0 \\ 0 \end{bmatrix} + \tfrac{1}{2} \begin{bmatrix} +8 \\ 0 \end{bmatrix} = \begin{bmatrix} +4 \\ 0 \end{bmatrix} \tag{10-48}$$

At this second point, $x_1^2 = +4$, $x_2^2 = 0$, the value of the gradient is

$$\nabla f(\mathbf{x}^2) = \begin{bmatrix} 2(+4 - 4) \\ -2(0) \end{bmatrix} = \begin{bmatrix} 0 \\ 0 \end{bmatrix} \tag{10-49}$$

Thus, the local optimum has been obtained at $x_1^* = +4$, $x_2^* = 0$.

The process of minimizing a function using gradient techniques requires following the direction specified by the negative of the gradient. Thus, we seek to search for new coordinates defined by

$$\mathbf{x}^{k+1} = \mathbf{x}^k - s\,\nabla f(\mathbf{x}^k) \tag{10-50}$$

The remainder of the computational process proceeds in the manner previously illustrated.

10.6.2 Constrained Multivariate Optimization

Constrained multivariate optimization is the most difficult type of nonlinear programming. In this situation we may have a nonlinear objective function and/or nonlinear constraints, plus some type of nonnegativity restrictions. Depending on the nature and number of nonlinear functions, such problems may become very difficult, if not impossible, to solve.

In general, we can again employ the methods discussed earlier for unconstrained multivariate optimization. However, for many constrained optimization problems it may be difficult to solve for the stationary points. In addition, in the **constrained multivariate optimization problem**, the constraints may restrict the set of directions that are feasible as we search for new values of $\mathbf{x}$ that will increase $f(\mathbf{x})$. Thus, while we know that moving in a direction d, such that $\nabla f(\mathbf{x})'\,d > 0$, will increase $f(\mathbf{x})$, such a movement may also cause one of the m constraints of the nonlinear programming problem to be violated. The problem thus becomes one of determining what directions satisfying $f(\mathbf{x})'\,d > 0$ are feasible.

Solving this problem involves taking the gradient to a constraint. Since a constraint is itself a function, it is certainly possible to determine the gradient of a constraint in the same manner that we determined the gradient of the objective function $f(\mathbf{x})$. For example, consider a constraint $g_1(x_1, x_2) \leq b_1$. The left-hand side of this inequality is a function, whose gradient is $\nabla g_1(x_1, x_2)$. This gradient then points in the optimal direction we should move in order to increase the value of $g_1(x_1,x_2)$. However, we still do not know whether or not it is feasible to move in the direction indicated by the gradient of the constraint, $\nabla g_1(x_1,x_2)$. It can be shown that the set of feasible directions with respect to this constraint must satisfy

$$\nabla g_1(x_1,x_2)'d < 0 \qquad (10\text{--}51)$$

Thus, in order to explore optimality conditions in constrained multivariate optimization problems, we must be able to specify the necessary and sufficient conditions for these optimality conditions. We will now consider the Kuhn-Tucker conditions, which provide a set of necessary conditions for the extreme points in constrained optimization problems. Furthermore, we shall see that the Kuhn-Tucker conditions may be sufficient conditions for certain types of problems. As such, they may actually be used to solve certain types of nonlinear programming problems.

10.6.3 The Kuhn-Tucker Conditions

For the general nonlinear programming problem involving a nonlinear objective function and m constraints, a subset k of these constraints ($k \le m$) may be satisfied as equalities at a given feasible solution. However, if such a feasible point is a local optimum, then there must be no feasible direction (i.e., no values satisfying $\nabla g_i(\mathbf{x})'d < 0$ for the k constraints that are satisfied as equalities) that increases $f(\mathbf{x})$ (i.e., no values where $f(\mathbf{x})'d > 0$). To make such a determination, we rely on the **Kuhn-Tucker conditions** that represent necessary conditions under which a given point, x^*, is a local optimum for the general nonlinear programming problem.[2]

To begin our discussion consider the case in which the general nonlinear programming problem is reduced to:

$$\text{Maximize } Z = f(\mathbf{x}) \qquad (10\text{--}52)$$

where $f(\mathbf{x})$ is a differentiable function. In this case we have no constraints and no nonnegativity restrictions. Additionally, if this objective function contains only one variable we can state, using classical calculus, that $x_1 = x_1^*$ can maximize $f(x_1)$ only if $df/dx_1 = 0$ at $x_1 = x_1^*$. This is known as a necessary condition. Furthermore, if $f(x_1)$ is a concave function the above statement is also a sufficient condition.

Now, if the objective function in the nonlinear programming problem contains several variables, using classical calculus, we can state that $\mathbf{x}^* = (x_1^*, x_2^*, \ldots, x_n^*)$ can maximize $f(\mathbf{x})$ only if $\partial f/\partial x_j = 0$ at $x_j = x_j^*$ for $j = 1, 2, \ldots, n$. This again is a necessary condition that becomes a sufficient condition if $f(\mathbf{x})$ is a concave function.

If we next add the nonnegativity restrictions $\mathbf{x} \ge 0$ to the above problem in which the objective function contains several variables the only revision that must be made is that if $x_j^* = 0$, then the conditions $\partial f/\partial x_j = 0$ at $x_j = x_j^*$ are replaced by the conditions $\partial f/\partial x_j \le 0$ at $x_j = x_j^*$.

Now, consider the general nonlinear programming problem given by (10–8),

---

[2] H. W. Kuhn and A. W. Tucker, "Nonlinear Programming," in *Proceedings of the Second Berkeley Symposium on Mathematical Statistics and Probability*, Jerzy Neyman, ed. (Berkeley, Calif.: University of California Press, 1951), 481–92.

(10–9), and (10–10) and assume that $f(\mathbf{x}), g_1(\mathbf{x}), g_2(\mathbf{x}), \ldots, g_m(\mathbf{x})$ are differentiable functions that satisfy certain regularity conditions.[3] Then, according to a theorem derived by Kuhn and Tucker $\mathbf{x}^* = (x_1^*, x_2^*, \ldots, x_n^*)$ can be an optimal solution to the nonlinear programming problem only if there exists m numbers, $\lambda_1, \lambda_2, \ldots, \lambda_m$, such that all of the following conditions are satisfied.

Kuhn-Tucker Conditions

1. $\dfrac{\partial f(\mathbf{x})}{\partial x_j} - \displaystyle\sum_{i=i}^{m} \lambda_i \dfrac{\partial g_i(\mathbf{x})}{\partial x_j} \leq 0$ $\left.\right\}$ at $x_j = x_j^*,$ for $j = 1, 2, \ldots, n$ (10–53)

2. $x_j^* \left[\dfrac{\partial f(\mathbf{x})}{\partial x_j} - \displaystyle\sum_{i=1}^{m} \lambda_i \dfrac{\partial g_i(\mathbf{x})}{\partial x_j} \right] = 0$ (10–54)

3. $g_i(\mathbf{x}^*) - b_i \leq 0$ $\left.\right\}$ for $i = 1, 2, \ldots, m$ (10–55)
4. $\lambda_i (g_i(\mathbf{x}^*) - b_i) = 0$ (10–56)
5. $x_j^* \geq 0$ for $j = 1, 2, \ldots, n$ (10–57)
6. $\lambda_i \geq 0$ for $i = 1, 2, \ldots, m$ (10–58)

These six conditions are the Kuhn-Tucker conditions. They are **necessary conditions** but not **sufficient conditions** for optimality. The λ_i are commonly called generalized **Lagrange multipliers**, and are analogous to the values associated with the dual variables in a linear programming problem. We will make further use of these Lagrange multipliers in a later section of this chapter. The conditions given by (10–55) and (10–57) are essentially required only to help ensure the feasibility of the solution. The condition given by (10–56) is used to assure that only constraints that are binding, or satisfied as equalities, are used in the determination of the optimal solution. This is the complementary slackness property we discussed earlier in Chapter 5. Thus, this condition states that $\lambda_i = 0$ for each nonbinding constraint, and that $g_i(\mathbf{x}) - b_i = 0$ or $g_i(\mathbf{x}) = b_i$ for each binding constraint. The other conditions then serve to eliminate most of the other feasible solutions as possible candidates for the optimal solution.

Satisfying the Kuhn-Tucker conditions is only necessary for having an optimal solution. The sufficiency requirements for optimality are based upon certain properties being satisfied. Thus, the Kuhn-Tucker *sufficient conditions* are given by the following corollary (Mangasarian, pp. 92–112).

COROLLARY *Assume that* $\mathbf{f}(\mathbf{x})$ *is a concave function and that* $\mathbf{g}_1(\mathbf{x}), \mathbf{g}_2(\mathbf{x}), \ldots, \mathbf{g}_m(\mathbf{x})$ *are convex functions satisfying the regularity conditions. Then* $\mathbf{x}^* = (\mathbf{x}_1^*, \mathbf{x}_2^*, \ldots, \mathbf{x}_n^*)$ *is an optimal solution if, and only if, all of the conditions of the Kuhn-Tucker theorem are satisfied.*

Now that we have formally presented the Kuhn-Tucker conditions, we will demonstrate how these conditions can be used to solve various problems. First, we will use the Kuhn-Tucker conditions in the solution of a linear programming problem. Next, we will use the Kuhn-Tucker conditions on a more difficult nonlinear programming problem.

---

[3] In this theorem, "regularity conditions" refer to the behavior, or geometry of function, in a small region around the optimal point. See Olvi L. Mangasarian (pp. 92–112) for a more detailed discussion.

EXAMPLE 1   *Linear Programming Problem.*   To illustrate how the Kuhn-Tucker conditions can be used to solve a particular problem, let us consider first a simple linear programming problem. Remember that the general nonlinear programming problem does not restrict the structure of the objective function or the constraints. Consequently, a linear programming problem can be thought of as a special case of the general nonlinear programming problem.

A typical linear programming problem (for example, a maximization problem) originally having m inequality constraints, n variables, and n nonnegativity restrictions can be reformulated in the following form.

$$\text{Maximize } Z = f(\mathbf{x}) = \sum_{j=1}^{n} c_j \, x_j \tag{10-59}$$

$$\text{subject to: } \sum_{j=1}^{n} a_{ij} x_j \le b_i, \quad i = 1, 2, \ldots, m \tag{10-60}$$

$$\text{with} \quad -x_j \le 0, \quad j = 1, 2, \ldots, n \tag{10-61}$$

Observe that we now have $m + n$ constraints since each one of the nonnegativity restrictions in the original linear programming problem has been expressed as a constraint in the formulation given above.

In determining the Kuhn-Tucker conditions for this reformulated problem, we must first determine the gradient of the objective function. Since the objective function $f(\mathbf{x})$ has only first-degree terms, its gradient is composed of only constraints, and is computed as:

$$\nabla f(\mathbf{x}) = \begin{bmatrix} \dfrac{\partial f(\mathbf{x})}{\partial x_1} \\[2mm] \dfrac{\partial f(\mathbf{x})}{\partial x_2} \\ \vdots \\ \dfrac{\partial f(\mathbf{x})}{\partial x_n} \end{bmatrix} = \begin{bmatrix} c_1 \\ c_2 \\ \vdots \\ c_n \end{bmatrix} \tag{10-62}$$

We also need to determine the gradient of the m inequality constraints. These inequality constraints are also composed entirely of first-degree terms. Thus, the gradients of the constraints are given by:

$$\nabla g_1(\mathbf{x}) = \frac{\partial g_1(\mathbf{x})}{x_j} = \begin{bmatrix} a_{11} \\ a_{12} \\ \vdots \\ a_{1n} \end{bmatrix} \quad \nabla g_2(\mathbf{x}) = \begin{bmatrix} a_{21} \\ a_{22} \\ \vdots \\ a_{2n} \end{bmatrix} \ldots, \quad \nabla g_m(\mathbf{x}) = \begin{bmatrix} a_{m1} \\ a_{m2} \\ \vdots \\ a_{mn} \end{bmatrix} \tag{10-63}$$

The Kuhn-Tucker necessary conditions for a local optimum, x^*, for this linear programming problem can then be written as follows.

1. $\quad c_1 \quad - \quad \sum\limits_{i=1}^{m} \lambda_i a_{i1} \;\leq 0$

$\quad\quad c_2 \quad - \quad \sum\limits_{i=1}^{m} \lambda_i a_{i2} \;\leq 0$ $\qquad\qquad\qquad\qquad$ (10–64)

$$\vdots \qquad\qquad \vdots \qquad\qquad \vdots$$

$\quad\quad c_n \quad - \quad \sum\limits_{i=1}^{n} \lambda_i a_{in} \;\leq 0$

2. $\quad x_1^* \left[\nabla f(\mathbf{x}) - \sum\limits_{i=1}^{m} \lambda_i (\nabla g_i(\mathbf{x})) \right] + x_2^* \left[\nabla f(\mathbf{x}) - \sum\limits_{i=1}^{m} \lambda_i (\nabla g_i(\mathbf{x})) \right] = 0$ $\quad$ (10–65)

3. $\quad \sum\limits_{j=1}^{n} a_{ij} x_j - b_i \leq 0$ $\qquad\qquad\qquad\qquad\qquad\qquad$ (10–66)

$\qquad\qquad\qquad\qquad\qquad\qquad\qquad\qquad\qquad i = 1, 2, \ldots, m$

4. $\quad \lambda_i \left[\sum\limits_{j=1}^{n} a_{ij} x_j - b_i \right] = 0$ $\qquad\qquad\qquad\qquad\qquad$ (10–67)

5. $\quad x_j^* \geq 0, \qquad \text{for } j = 1, 2, \ldots, n$ $\qquad\qquad\qquad$ (10–68)

6. $\quad \lambda_i \geq 0, \qquad \text{for } i = 1, 2, \ldots, m$ $\qquad\qquad\qquad$ (10–69)

Consider now the production scheduling linear programming problem that we originally presented in Chapter 3. This linear programming problem was formulated as:

$$\text{Maximize (profit) } Z = 6x_1 + 8x_2 \qquad\qquad (10\text{–}70)$$

subject to: $\quad\quad 5x_1 + 10x_2 \leq 60 \quad\quad$ (Metal lathe time) $\qquad$ (10–71)
$\quad\quad\quad\quad\quad\quad 4x_1 + 4x_2 \leq 40 \quad\quad$ (Milling machine time)

with $\quad\quad x_1$ (number of gears) ≥ 0, x_2 (number of bearing plates) ≥ 0 $\quad$ (10–72)

Now, the gradient of the objective function and the two constraints are

$$\nabla f(\mathbf{x}) = \begin{bmatrix} c_1 \\ c_2 \end{bmatrix} = \begin{bmatrix} 6 \\ 8 \end{bmatrix} \qquad\qquad (10\text{–}73)$$

$$\nabla g_1(\mathbf{x}) = \begin{bmatrix} 5 \\ 10 \end{bmatrix} \; \nabla g_2(\mathbf{x}) = \begin{bmatrix} 4 \\ 4 \end{bmatrix} \qquad\qquad (10\text{–}74)$$

The Kuhn-Tucker conditions for this problem can be written as:

1a. $\quad 6 - 5\lambda_1 - 4\lambda_2 \leq 0$ $\qquad\qquad\qquad\qquad\qquad$ (10–75)
1b. $\quad 8 - 10\lambda_1 - 4\lambda_2 \leq 0$ $\qquad\qquad\qquad\qquad\qquad$ (10–76)
2a. $\quad x_1 (6 - 5\lambda_1 - 4\lambda_2) = 0$ $\qquad\qquad\qquad\qquad$ (10–77)
2b. $\quad x_2 (8 - 10\lambda_1 - 4\lambda_2) = 0$ $\qquad\qquad\qquad\qquad$ (10–78)
3a. $\quad 5x_1 + 10x_2 - 60 \leq 0$ $\qquad\qquad\qquad\qquad\qquad$ (10–79)
3b. $\quad 4x_1 + 4x_2 - 40 \leq 0$ $\qquad\qquad\qquad\qquad\qquad$ (10–80)
4a. $\quad \lambda_1 (5x_1 + 10x_2 - 60) = 0$ $\qquad\qquad\qquad\qquad$ (10–81)
4b. $\quad \lambda_2 (4x_1 + 4x_2 - 40) = 0$ $\qquad\qquad\qquad\qquad$ (10–82)

5. $x_1 \geq 0, \qquad x_2 \geq 0$ \hfill (10–83)

6. $\lambda_1 \geq 0, \qquad \lambda_2 \geq 0$ \hfill (10–84)

To actually solve these Kuhn-Tucker conditions we can proceed by graphing the problem, as shown in Fig. 10.10 (same as Fig. 3.1). From Fig. 10.10 it can be seen that the maximum occurs at $x_1^* = 8$, $x_2^* = 2$, maximum $Z = 64$. Furthermore, at the optimum solution, both constraints are active, that is are exactly satisfied. Thus, we must solve (1a) and (1b), simultaneously to determine the values of λ_1 and λ_2. Proceeding, we determine that $\lambda_1 = {}^2/_5$, $\lambda_2 = 1$, solves both (1a) and (1b) simultaneously. Thus, the solution to the Kuhn-Tucker conditions is: $x_1^* = 8$, $x_2^* = 2$, $\lambda_1^* = {}^2/_5$, $\lambda_2^* = 1$. These values satisfy the Kuhn-Tucker conditions, as follows.

1a.
$$6 - 5\lambda_1^* - 4\lambda_2^* = 0$$
$$6 - 5({}^2/_5) - 4(1) = 0$$
$$6 - 2 - 4 = 0 \quad \checkmark$$
\hfill (10–85)

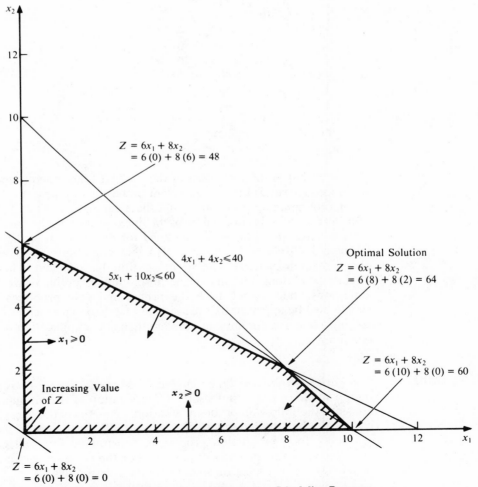

FIGURE 10.10 Graphical Representation—Production Scheduling Program

1b. $8 - 10\lambda_1^* - 4\lambda_2^* = 0$
$8 - 10(^2/_5) - 4(1) = 0$ (10–86)
$8 - \quad 4 \quad - \quad 4 \quad = 0$ ✔

2a. $x_1^* (6 - 5\lambda_1^* - 4\lambda_2^*) = 0$
$8[6 - 5(^2/_5) - 4(1)] = 0$ (10–87)
$8[6 - \quad 2 \quad - \quad 4 \quad] = 0$
$8[\quad\quad 0 \quad\quad] = 0$ ✔

2b. $x_2^* (8 - 10\lambda_1^* - 4\lambda_2^*) = 0$
$2[8 - 10(^2/_5) - 4(1)] = 0$ (10–88)
$2[8 - \quad 4 \quad - \quad 4 \quad] = 0$
$2[\quad\quad 0 \quad\quad] = 0$ ✔

3a. $5x_1^* + 10x_2^* - 60 \le 0$
$5(8) + 10(2) - 60 \le 0$ (10–89)
$40 + \quad 20 \quad - 60 = 0$ ✔

3b. $4x_1^* + 4x_2^* - 40 \le 0$
$4(8) + 4(2) - 40 \le 0$ (10–90)
$32 + \quad 8 \quad - 40 = 0$ ✔

4a. $\lambda_1^* (5x_1^* + 10x_2^* - 60) = 0$
$^2/_5 [5(8) + 10(2) - 60] = 0$ (10–91)
$^2/_5 [40 + \quad 20 \quad - 60] = 0$
$^2/_5 [\quad\quad 0 \quad\quad] = 0$ ✔

4b. $\lambda_2^* (4x_1^* + 4x_2^* - 40) = 0$
$1 [4(8) + 4(2) - 40] = 0$ (10–92)
$1 [32 + \quad 8 \quad - 40] = 0$
$1 [\quad\quad 0 \quad\quad] = 0$ ✔

5. $x_1^* = 8,$ $x_2^* = 2$ ✔   (10–93)

6. $\lambda_1^* = \frac{2}{5},$ $\lambda_2^* = 2$ ✔   (10–94)

Note that in the statement of the Kuhn-Tucker conditions for this problem, conditions (1*a*) and (1*b*) are equivalent to the constraints of the dual of the original linear programming problem. Thus, the Lagrange multipliers, λ_1 and λ_2 are the same as the variables in the dual of the linear program. The values of $\lambda_1 = {}^2/_5$, $\lambda_2 = 1$ are exactly the same as we obtained for the solution of the dual problem (see Chapter 5, Table 5.2). Observe also that conditions (4*a*) and (4*b*) satisfy the complementary slackness relationships for this problem. Therefore, the Kuhn-Tucker conditions for this linear programming problem are exactly the same conditions under which both the primal and dual problems are optimized. It should also be apparent that the simplex method is a much more efficient way of solving a linear programming problem than is the application of the Kuhn-Tucker conditions.

EXAMPLE 2   *Two-Variable Nonlinear Programming Problem with Linear Constraints.*   As a second example of the formulation and application of the Kuhn-Tucker conditions, consider the following problem situation: The Amesbury Health Food Company produces a health food involving two types of wheat germ in 100-pound-lot sizes. Its health food production process is constrained by available machine time, available work forces, and a requirement on the protein content of the wheat-germ blend. Data concerning these constraints is as follows.

Constraint	Requirement/Unit of Blended Health Food		Resource Availability (requirement)
	Wheat Germ, Type 1	Wheat Germ, Type 2	
Work force	½	1	4 Workers
Machine time	3	1	15 Machine hours
Protein	1	1	3 (Protein units)

In addition, it estimates that the total revenue produced by the blend of the two wheat germs is given by the nonlinear function $f(x) = 3(x_1 - 1.5)^2 + 6(x_2 - 1.5)^2$, where x_1 = 100-pound units of wheat germ 1, and x_2 = 100-pound units of wheat germ 2.

This problem situation can be structured as the following two-variable non-linear programming problem, with three linear constraints.

$$\text{Maximize } Z = f(x) = 3(x_1 - 1.5)^2 + 6(x_2 - 1.5)^2 \quad (10\text{-}95)$$

subject to:
$$\begin{aligned} \tfrac{1}{2}x_1 + 1x_2 &\leq 4 \\ 3x_1 + 1x_2 &\leq 15 \\ 1x_1 + 1x_2 &\geq 3 \end{aligned} \quad (10\text{-}96)$$

$$x_1, x_2 \geq 0 \quad (10\text{-}97)$$

In this problem $m = 3$, $n = 2$, and

$$\begin{aligned} g_1(\mathbf{x}) &= \tfrac{1}{2}x_1 + 1x_2 \\ g_2(\mathbf{x}) &= 3x_1 + 1x_2 \\ g_3(\mathbf{x}) &= 1x_1 + 1x_2 \end{aligned} \quad (10\text{-}98)$$

Since these constraints are straight lines they are clearly convex functions, and since the objective function traces out curves of constant Z that are ellipses with centers at $x_1 = 1.5$ and $x_2 = 1.5$ it is clearly a concave function. Thus, we know that an optimal solution can be obtained by solving the Kuhn-Tucker conditions. For this problem, these conditions are

1a. $6x_1 - 9 - \tfrac{1}{2}\lambda_1 - 3\lambda_2 - 1\lambda_3 \leq 0$ (10-99)
1b. $12x_2 - 18 - 1\lambda_1 - 1\lambda_2 - 1\lambda_3 \leq 0$ (10-100)
2a. $x_1(6x_1 - 9 - \tfrac{1}{2}\lambda_1 - 3\lambda_2 - \lambda_3) = 0$ (10-101)
2b. $x_2(12x_2 - 18 - \lambda_1 - \lambda_2 - \lambda_3) = 0$ (10-102)
3a. $\tfrac{1}{2}x_1 + 1x_2 - 4 \leq 0$ (10-103)
3b. $3x_1 + 1x_2 - 15 \leq 0$ (10-104)
3c. $1x_1 + 1x_2 - 3 \geq 0$ (10-105)
4a. $\lambda_1(\tfrac{1}{2}x_1 + 1x_2 - 4) = 0$ (10-106)
4b. $\lambda_2(3x_1 + 1x_2 - 15) = 0$ (10-107)
4c. $\lambda_3(1x_1 + 1x_2 - 3) = 0$ (10-108)
5. $x_1 \geq 0, x_2 \geq 0$ (10-109)
6. $\lambda_1 \geq 0, \lambda_2 \geq 0, \lambda_3 \geq 0$ (10-110)

To solve these Kuhn-Tucker conditions we proceed by first graphing the problem,

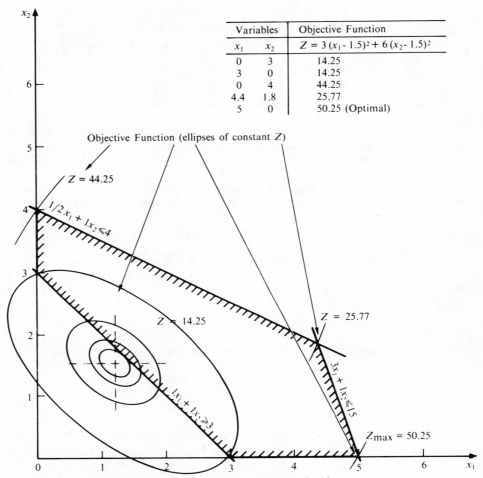

Variables		Objective Function
x_1	x_2	$Z = 3(x_1 - 1.5)^2 + 6(x_2 - 1.5)^2$
0	3	14.25
3	0	14.25
0	4	44.25
4.4	1.8	25.77
5	0	50.25 (Optimal)

FIGURE 10.11   Graphical Solution to Nonlinear Programming Problem

as shown in Fig. 10.11. From Fig. 10.11 it can be seen that the maximum occurs at $x_1^* = 5, x_2^* = 0, Z^* = 50.25$. Furthermore, only the second constraint is active at the point $x_1^* = 5, x_2^* = 0$, and therefore $\lambda_1^* = 0$ and $\lambda_3^* = 0$. We can then proceed to solve (1a), which must hold as a strict equality since $x_1^* > 0$.

1a.
$$6x_1 - 9 - \tfrac{1}{2}\lambda_1 - 3\lambda_2 - 1\lambda_3 = 0$$
$$6(5) - 9 - \tfrac{1}{2}(0) - 3\lambda_2 - 1(0) = 0 \qquad\qquad (10\text{--}111)$$
$$- 3\lambda_2 \qquad\quad = -21$$
$$+\lambda_2 = 7$$

Thus, the solution to this problem is $x_1^* = 5, x_2^* = 0, \lambda_1^* = 0, \lambda_2^* = 7, \lambda_3^* = 0$. These values satisfy the Kuhn-Tucker conditions as follows.

1a. $6x_1^* - 9 - \frac{1}{2}\lambda_1^* - 3\lambda_2^* - 1\lambda_3^* \leq 0$

$\ 6(5) - 9 - \frac{1}{2}(0) - 3(7) - 1(0) \leq 0$ (10-112)

$\ \ 30 - 9 \quad \frac{1}{2}(0) - 21 \qquad \leq 0 \ \checkmark$

1b. $12x_2^* - 18 - \lambda_1^* - \lambda_2^* - \lambda_3^* \leq 0$

$\ 12(0) - 18 - 0 - 7 - 0 \leq 0$ (10-113)

$\ \qquad\qquad\qquad\qquad\quad -25 \leq 0 \ \checkmark$

2a. $x_1^*(6x_1^* - 9 - \frac{1}{2}\lambda_1^* - 3\lambda_2^* - \lambda_3^*) = 0$ (10-114)

$\ 5(6 \cdot 5 - 9 - \frac{1}{2} \cdot 0 - 3 \cdot 7 - 1.0) = 0$

$\ \qquad\qquad\qquad\qquad\qquad 5(0) = 0$

2b. $x_2^*(12x_2^* - 18 - \lambda_1^* - \lambda_2^* - \lambda_3^*) = 0$

$\ 0(12 \cdot 0 - 18 - 0 - 7 - 0) = 0$ (10-115)

$\ \qquad\qquad\qquad\qquad 0(-25) = 0 \ \checkmark$

3a. $\frac{1}{2}x_1^* - 1x_2^* - 4 \leq 0$

$\ \frac{1}{2}(5) - 1(0) - 4 \leq 0$ (10-116)

$\ \ ^5/_2 - 0 - 4 \leq 0$

$\ \qquad\qquad\quad -\ ^3/_2 \leq 0 \ \checkmark$

3b. $3x_1^* + 1x_2^* - 15 \leq 0$

$\ 3(5) - 1(0) - 15 \leq 0$ (10-117)

$\ \qquad\qquad\quad 0 \leq 0 \ \checkmark$

3c. $1x_1^* + 1x_2^* - 3 \geq 0$

$\ 1(5) - 1(0) - 3 \geq 0$ (10-118)

$\ \qquad\qquad\quad 2 \geq 0 \ \checkmark$

4a. $\lambda_1^*(\frac{1}{2}x_1^* + 1x_2^* - 4) = 0$

$\ 0(^5/_2 + 0 - 4) = 0$ (10-119)

4b. $\lambda_2^*(3x_1^* + 1x_2^* - 15) = 0$

$\ 7(15 + 0 - 15) = 0 \ \checkmark$ (10-120)

4c. $\lambda_3^*(1x_1^* + 1x_2^* - 3) = 0$

$\ 0(5 + 0 - 3) = 0 \ \checkmark$ (10-121)

5. $x_1^* = 5, x_2^* = 0 \ \checkmark$ (10-122)

6. $\lambda_1^* = 0, \ \lambda_2^* = 7, \ \lambda_3^* = 0 \ \checkmark$ (10-123)

In many problems it may be difficult to derive the optimal solution by direct application of the Kuhn-Tucker conditions. Indeed, in the examples shown above we utilized a graphical approach to determine the values for x_1^* and x_2^* and then utilized the Kuhn-Tucker conditions to check the optimality of the proposed solution. Thus, the Kuhn-Tucker conditions are probably most useful in checking the optimality of various proposed solutions. Additionally, they are very useful in deriving special purpose algorithms, such as are encountered in the solution of quadratic programming problems. We will further *illustrate* the use of the Kuhn-Tucker conditions in discussing quadratic programming. Finally, it should be apparent that the usefulness of the Kuhn-Tucker conditions is highly dependent on the difficulty involved in determining $\nabla f(\mathbf{x})$ and the $\nabla g_i(\mathbf{x})$. In our previous two examples, these gradients were obtained rather easily, and the Kuhn-Tucker conditions were also not difficult to solve.

10.6.4 Lagrange Multiplier Method

The Kuhn-Tucker conditions are actually a generalization of the **Lagrange multiplier method**, which can be used to solve constrained nonlinear problems involving the optimization of a function subject to a constraint set composed entirely of equalities. The Lagrange multiplier method thus focuses on the following constrained nonlinear programming problems.

$$\begin{Bmatrix} \text{Maximize} \\ \text{Minimize} \end{Bmatrix} Z = f(\mathbf{x}) \tag{10-124}$$

subject to: $g_i(\mathbf{x}) = b_i \qquad i = 1, 2, \dots, m$ \hfill (10-125)

The Lagrange multiplier method involves combining the objective function and the constraints into a single function that, when optimized, yields a solution that is equivalent to the formulation given by (10-124) and (10-125). This single function is called the **Lagrangean function** $F(\mathbf{x}, \lambda)$, where

$$F(\mathbf{x}, \lambda) = f(\mathbf{x}) - \sum_{i=1}^{m} \lambda_i [g_i(\mathbf{x}) - b_i] \tag{10-126}$$

EXAMPLE   To illustrate the Lagrange multiplier method, let us consider the following problem situation. The Chitman Candy Company is experimenting with making a new chocolate candy by blending two types of raw cocoa. The blending function b, for the new chocolate candy is estimated to be

$$b = f(x_1, x_2) = 4.0x_1 - 0.2x_1^2 + 2.5x_2 - 0.1x_2^2 \tag{10-127}$$

where b is the quantity (pounds) of chocolate candy produced, and x_1 and x_2 indicate the input amount of the two types of raw cocoa. The company has \$100 available to spend for the experiment involving these two types of cocoa, and the per-pound price of the first type of cocoa is \$4, while the per-pound price of the second type of cocoa is \$2. The budgetary constraint may be expressed as:

$$\$4x_1 + \$2x_2 = \$100$$
or \hfill (10-128)
$$2x_1 + 1x_2 = 50$$

The complete nonlinear programming problem may now be written as:

$$\text{Maximize } Z = f(x_1 x_2) = 4.0x_1 - 0.2x_1^2 + 2.5x_2 - 0.1x_2^2 \tag{10-129}$$

subject to: $2x_1 + 1x_2 = 50$ \hfill (10-130)

This nonlinear programming problem has a single constraint (equality) and thus will involve a single Lagrange multiplier. The Lagrangean function is

$$F(\mathbf{x}, \lambda_1) = 4.0x_1 - 0.2x_1^2 + 2.5x_2 - 0.1x_2^2 - \lambda_1(2x_1 + 1x_2 - 50) \tag{10-131}$$

To maximize this Lagrangean function we must take its first partial derivative with respect to x_1, x_2, and λ_1; set each of these three partial derivatives to zero; and then solve the resulting three equations simultaneously.

Now, these three partial derivatives are computed as:

$$\frac{\partial F(\mathbf{x}, \lambda_1)}{\partial x_1} = 4 - 0.4x_1 - 2\lambda_1 = 0 \tag{10-132}$$

$$\frac{\partial F(\mathbf{x}, \lambda_1)}{\partial x_2} = 2.5 - 0.2x_2 - 1\lambda_1 = 0 \tag{10-133}$$

$$\frac{\partial F(\mathbf{x}, \lambda_1)}{\partial \lambda_1} = -2x_1 - 1x_2 + 50 = 0 \tag{10-134}$$

Note that these three partial derivatives are equivalent to stating

$$f(\mathbf{x}) = \sum_{i=1}^{m} \lambda_i \nabla g_i(\mathbf{x}) \tag{10-135}$$

Also, the last partial derivative (10–134) is the same as the original constraint for the problem. Solving the three equations, (10–132), (10–133), and (10–134) simultaneously, we obtain the optimal solution:

$x_1^* = 15.8$
$x_2^* = 18.4$ Maximum $Z = 4(15.8) - 0.2(15.8)^2 + 2.5(18.4) - 0.1(18.4)^2$
$\lambda_1^* = -0.59$ $= 63.20 - 49.93 + 46.00 - 33.86$ $\tag{10-136}$
                $= 25.41$

From this example it can be seen that the conditions we obtain by differentiating the Lagrangean function are very similar to the Kuhn-Tucker conditions. The major difference is that in using the Lagrange multiplier method, the $\lambda_i (i = 1, 2, \ldots, m)$ are unrestricted in sign. This is necessary because in a problem that we solve by the Lagrange multiplier method all the constraints are assumed to be equalities, while in the general nonlinear programming problem the constraints may be inequalities. Thus, when such constraints are all equalities the marginal change in $f(\mathbf{x})$ that would result from an increase in b_i could either be plus or minus, since the variables themselves could increase in value and the resulting change in the objective function value would depend on the sign associated with a particular variable. However, when the constraints are inequalities, an increase in b_i essentially "loosens" the constraint, and $f(\mathbf{x})$, can never decrease. In such a problem the λ_i cannot be negative.

10.7 QUADRATIC PROGRAMMING

A **quadratic programming problem** is a special type of constrained nonlinear programming problem having a set of linear constraints and an objective function that is composed of linear and quadratic (second-order) terms. Fortunately, from a solution standpoint, quadratic programming problems are more easily solved than most nonlinear programming problems. Additionally, a number of important problems, paricularly in the field of portfolio selection, can be solved using quadratic programming models. The quadratic programming problem can be stated as follows.

Find $\mathbf{x} = \{x_1, x_2, \ldots, x_n\}$ so as to

$$\text{Maximize } f(\mathbf{x}) = \left\{ \sum_{j=1}^{n} c_j x_j - \frac{1}{2} \sum_{j=1}^{n} \sum_{k=1}^{n} c_{jk} x_j x_k \right\} \tag{10-137}$$

subject to: $\displaystyle\sum_{j=1}^{n} a_{ij}x_j \le b_i$ for $i = 1, 2, \ldots, m$ $\hfill$ (10–138)

and $x_j \ge 0$ for $j = 1, 2, \ldots, n$ $\hfill$ (10–139)

where the c_{jk} are given constants such that $c_{jk} = c_{kj}$

In the quadratic programming problem formulation stated above, the set of feasible solutions to the linear constraints forms a convex set. Thus, if we can show that the objective function is a concave function, then any solution (relative maximum) to this problem is also a global maximum solution to the problem, according to the sufficiency corollary to the Kuhn-Tucker theorem. The objective function is the sum of a linear form (which is concave) and a quadratic form. As noted earlier, (Section 10.4), the sum of two concave functions is also concave so the objective function will be concave if $\sum_{j=1}^{n} \sum_{k=1}^{n} c_{jk}x_j x_k$ is a concave function. A way to verify that it is a concave function is to verify the equivalent condition that:

$$\sum_{j=1}^{n} \sum_{k=1}^{n} c_{jk}x_j x_k \ge 0 \hfill (10\text{–}140)$$

for $\mathbf{x} = \{x_1, x_2, \ldots, x_n\}$

In mathematical terms, the equivalent condition is that the term given by (10–140) is a positive semidefinite or positive definite form.

Assuming that the term given by (10–140) is concave, we can then proceed to develop the Kuhn-Tucker conditions as follows.

1. $\dfrac{\partial f(\mathbf{x})}{\partial x_j} - \displaystyle\sum_{i=1}^{m} \lambda_i \dfrac{\partial g_i(\mathbf{x})}{\partial x_j} \le 0$

$c_j - \displaystyle\sum_{k=1}^{n} c_{jk}x_k - \lambda_i \sum_{i=1}^{m} a_{ij} \le 0$ $\qquad$ for $j = 1, 2, \ldots, n$ $\hfill$ (10–141)

2. $\displaystyle\sum_{j=1}^{n} x_j^* \left(\dfrac{\partial f(\mathbf{x})}{\partial x_j} - \sum_{i=1}^{m} \lambda_i \dfrac{\partial g_i(\mathbf{x})}{\partial x_j} \right) = 0$

$x_j \left(c_j - \displaystyle\sum_{k=1}^{n} c_{jk}x_k - \lambda_i \sum_{i=1}^{m} a_{ij} \right) = 0$ $\qquad$ for $j = 1, 2, \ldots, n$ $\hfill$ (10–142)

3. $g_i(\mathbf{x}^*) - b_j \le 0$

$\displaystyle\sum_{j=1}^{n} a_{ij}x_j - b_i \le 0$ $\qquad$ for $i = 1, 2, \ldots, m$ $\hfill$ (10–143)

4. $\displaystyle\sum_{i=1}^{m} \lambda_i[g_i(\mathbf{x}^*) - b_i] = 0$

$\lambda_i \left(\displaystyle\sum_{j=1}^{n} a_{ij}x_j - b_i \right) = 0$ $\qquad$ for $i = 1, 2, \ldots, m$ $\hfill$ (10–144)

5. $x_j^* \ge 0,$ for $j = 1, 2, \ldots, n$ $\hfill$ (10–145)
6. $\lambda_i \ge 0,$ for $i = 1, 2, \ldots, m$ $\hfill$ (10–146)

Since the objective function is assumed to be concave and the constraint functions are linear and therefore convex, the corollary to the Kuhn-Tucker condition holds and $\mathbf{x} = (x_1, x_2, \ldots, x_n)$ is optimal if and only if all of the Kuhn-Tucker conditions hold. The quadratic programming problem thereby reduces to finding a feasible solution to these conditions.

We now proceed to rewrite the Kuhn-Tucker conditions shown above as follows. In (10–141), replace λ_i by y_{n+1} for $i = 1, 2, \ldots, m$ and let y_i denote the slack in the inequality. The condition given by (10–141) becomes

$$c_j - \sum_{k=1}^{n} c_{jk}x_k - \sum_{i=1}^{m} a_{ij}y_{n+1} + y_j = 0 \qquad (10\text{--}147)$$

$$y_j \geq 0 \qquad (10\text{--}148)$$

or $\quad \displaystyle\sum_{k=1}^{n} c_{jk}x_k + \sum_{i=1}^{m} a_{ij}y_{n+i} - y_j = c_j \qquad$ for $j = 1, 2, \ldots, n \qquad (10\text{--}149)$

$$y_j \geq 0 \qquad (10\text{--}150)$$

The condition given by Equation 10–142 is

$$x_j\left(c_j - \sum_{k=1}^{n} c_{jk}x_k - \sum_{i=1}^{m} \lambda_i a_{ij}\right) = 0 \qquad \text{for } j = 1, 2, \ldots, n \qquad (10\text{--}151)$$

or $x_j y_j = 0$, based on the rewritten statement of condition one. The condition given by (10–143) is

$$\sum_{j=1}^{n} a_{ij}x_j - b_i \leq 0 \qquad \text{for } i = 1, 2, \ldots, m \qquad (10\text{--}152)$$

or $\quad \displaystyle\sum a_{ij}x_j + x_{n+i} = b_i \qquad$ for $i = 1, 2, \ldots, m \qquad (10\text{--}153)$

$$x_{n+i} \geq 0 \qquad (10\text{--}154)$$

The condition given by (10–144) is

$$y_{n+i}\left(\sum_{j=1}^{n} a_{ij}x_j - b_i\right) = 0 \qquad \text{for } i = 1, 2, \ldots, m \qquad (10\text{--}155)$$

or $\quad y_{n+i}x_{n+i} = 0 \qquad (10\text{--}156)$

The condition given by (10–145) is

$$x_j \geq 0 \qquad \text{for } j = 1, 2, \ldots, n \qquad (10\text{--}157)$$

The condition given by (10–146) is

$$y_{n+i} \geq 0 \qquad \text{for } i = 1, 2, \ldots, m \qquad (10\text{--}158)$$

Combining these conditions yields

$$\sum_{k=1}^{n} c_{jk}x_k + \sum_{i=1}^{m} a_{ij}y_{n+i} - y_j = c_j \qquad \text{for } j = 1, 2, \ldots, n \qquad (10\text{--}159)$$

$$\sum_{j=1}^{n} a_{ij}x_j + x_{n+i} \qquad\qquad = b_i \qquad \text{for } i = 1, 2, \ldots, m \qquad (10\text{--}160)$$

$$x_j y_j = 0 \qquad \text{for } j = 1, 2, \ldots, n + m \qquad (10\text{--}161)$$

$$x_j \geq 0 \qquad \text{for } j = 1, 2, \ldots, n + m \qquad (10\text{-}162)$$
$$y_j \geq 0 \qquad \text{for } j = 1, 2, \ldots, n + m \qquad (10\text{-}163)$$

Note that with the exception of (10–160), these reformulated Kuhn-Tucker conditions are linear programming constraints involving $2(n + m)$ variables. The $x_j y_j = 0$ restriction given by (10–161) simply states that it is not permissible for both x_j and y_j to be basic variables when considering (nondegenerate) basic feasible solutions. Thus, the quadratic programming problem reduces to finding an optimal basic feasible solution to a linear programming problem having these constraints, subject to this additional restriction on the identity of basic variables.

The initial basic variables (10–160) would be the x_{n+i} (assuming that the b_i are positive). However, in (10–159), most or all the c_j are positive so it is not obvious what the other initial basic variables should be. We must, therefore, introduce artificial variables that are eventually driven to zero. Letting $z_1, z_2, \ldots, z_n$ be these artificial variables, the initial restriction on them is

$$z_j \geq 0, \qquad \text{for } j = 1, 2, \ldots, n \qquad (10\text{-}164)$$

The equations given by (10–159) are then

$$\sum_{k=1}^{n} c_{jk} x_k + \sum_{i=1}^{m} a_{ij} y_{n+i} - y_j + z_j = c_j \qquad \text{for } j = 1, 2, \ldots, n \qquad (10\text{-}165)$$

(except when the coefficient of z_j is -1 and $c_j < 0$.) Also this procedure will generate an artificial initial basic feasible solution.

$$z_j = c_j \qquad \text{for } j = 1, 2, \ldots, n \qquad (10\text{-}166)$$
$$x_{n+i} = b_i \qquad \text{for } j = 1, 2, \ldots, m \qquad (10\text{-}167)$$
$$x_j = 0 \qquad \text{for } j = 1, 2, \ldots, n + m \qquad (10\text{-}168)$$
$$y_j = 0 \qquad \text{for } j = 1, 2, \ldots, n + m \qquad (10\text{-}169)$$

However, since a feasible solution to the artificial problem is feasible for the real problem if and only if $z_j = 0$ for $j = 1, 2, \ldots, n$, we must decrease $\sum_{j=1}^{n} z_j$ to zero to obtain the desired feasible solution. To achieve this result, we begin with the artificial basic feasible solution given above and apply a modification of the simplex method to the problem.

$$\text{Minimize } f(x) = \sum_{j=1}^{n} z_j \qquad (10\text{-}170)$$

subject to:

$$\sum_{k=1}^{n} c_{jk} x_k + \sum_{i=1}^{m} a_{ij} y_{n+1} - y_j + z_j = c_j \qquad \text{for } j = 1, 2, \ldots, n \qquad (10\text{-}171)$$

$$\sum_{j=1}^{n} a_{ij} x_j + x_{n+i} = b_i \qquad \text{for } i = 1, 2, \ldots, m \qquad (10\text{-}172)$$

and
$$x_j \geq 0 \qquad \text{for } j = 1, 2, \ldots, n + m \qquad (10\text{-}173)$$
$$y_j \geq 0 \qquad \text{for } j = 1, 2, \ldots, n + m \qquad (10\text{-}174)$$
$$z_j \geq 0 \qquad \text{for } j = 1, 2, \ldots, n \qquad (10\text{-}175)$$

The modification required for this problem is that we do not permit y_j to become a basic variable whenever x_j is already a basic variable, and vice versa, for $j = 1, 2, \ldots, n + m$. This ensures that $x_j y_j = 0$ for each value of j. When the optimal solution $(x_1^*, x_2^*, \ldots, x_{n+m}^*, y_1^*, y_2^*, \ldots, y_{n+m}^*, z_1 = 0, z_2 = 0, \ldots, z_n = 0)$ has been obtained to this modified problem, then $(x_1^*, x_2^*, \ldots, x_n^*)$ is the desired optimal solution to the original quadratic programming problem.

To illustrate the formulation and solution of a quadratic programming problem consider the following portfolio selection situation. A mutual fund manager is trying to create a portfolio of two stocks that promise annual returns of 8 and 6 percent, respectively. Additionally, she estimates that the risk of each investment will vary directly with the square of the size of the investment. Each lot (100 shares) of the first stock costs \$3000, and each lot (100 shares) of the second stock costs \$2000. The total amount of cash available for investment is \$6000.

This portfolio selection situation can then be structured as the following quadratic programming problem.

$$\text{Maximize } Z = \overbrace{8x_1 + 10x_2}^{\text{Return}} - \overbrace{1x_1^2 - 1x_2^2}^{\text{Risk}} \qquad (10\text{–}176)$$

subject to:
$$3x_1 + 2x_2 \le 6 \qquad \text{(Capital constraint)} \qquad (10\text{–}177)$$

with $\quad x_1, x_2 \ge 0$ $\qquad\qquad\qquad\qquad\qquad\qquad\qquad\qquad (10\text{–}178)$

Rewriting the objective function we obtain

$$\text{Maximize } Z = 8x_1 + 10x_2 - \tfrac{1}{2}(2x_1^2 + 2x_2^2) \qquad (10\text{–}179)$$

and therefore $\quad c_{11} = 2, \; c_{12} = 0, \; c_{21} = 0, \; c_{22} = 2$ $\qquad\qquad (10\text{–}180)$

Thus, the problem to be solved by the modification of the simplex method is

$$\text{Minimize } Z' = \qquad\qquad\qquad\qquad\quad + z_1 \quad + z_2 \qquad (10\text{–}181)$$

subject to:
$$
\begin{aligned}
2x_1 \qquad\qquad + 3y_3 - y_1 + z_1 \qquad\qquad &= 8 \\
2x_2 \qquad + 2y_3 \qquad\qquad - y_2 + z_2 &= 10 \qquad (10\text{–}182) \\
3x_1 + 2x_2 + 1x_3 \qquad\qquad\qquad\qquad &= 6
\end{aligned}
$$

with all $\quad x_j \ge 0, \; y_j \ge 0, \; z_j \ge 0$ $\qquad\qquad\qquad\qquad (10\text{–}183)$

The resulting solution to this problem is

$$
\begin{aligned}
x_1 &= {}^4/_{13} \\
x_2 &= {}^{33}/_{13} \\
x_3 &= 0 \qquad \text{Maximum } Z = 21.30 \qquad (10\text{–}184) \\
y_1 &= 0 \\
y_2 &= 0 \\
y_3 &= {}^{32}/_{13}
\end{aligned}
$$

The reader should verify that $x_1 = {}^4/_{13}$, $x_2 = {}^{33}/_{13}$, $\lambda_1 = {}^{32}/_{13}$ satisfy the Kuhn-Tucker conditions given by Equations (10–53) through (10–58).

10.8 CASE STUDY—QUADRATIC PROGRAMMING APPLIED TO PRODUCT LINE EXPANSION

Frank J. Fabozzi has demonstrated how quadratic programming can be applied to a capital-budgeting problem to determine what product lines a firm should expand into in order to reduce its overall risk.[4] The risk of a portfolio of capital assets is not only a function of the variance of the returns of the individual capital assets in the portfolio but also of the covariance between the capital assets in the portfolio. Modern portfolio theory advocates the selection of capital assets that have negative covariances of return, or if such capital assets are not available, capital assets with low covariances of return for the investment portfolio. Such diversification is not only applicable to a portfolio of securities but also to a portfolio of capital-budgeting projects. From the variance/covariance structure of returns of the capital assets and the expected returns for each capital asset, a risk-reward tradeoff, or efficient frontier, can be generated. The tradeoff specifies the minimum risk that could be incurred to realize a designated rate of return for the portfolio.

An actual problem situation involving a distributor in the United States electrical industry is presented. The company is faced with a decision regarding the future expansion of its product lines. The expansion could be effected in one of three ways: by expanding its present product lines; by the expansion of its present product lines coupled with expansion into the electronics industry; and by the expansion of its present product lines in conjunction with expansion into the automotive industry. Eight product lines are being considered in the electronics industry, and six product lines in the automotive industry. Because of the nature of the distributorship, the firm's principals have decided to expand into only one of the two industries.

To generate the risk-reward relationships associated with each of the alternatives, the optimal allocation of funds that minimizes the total risk of a portfolio of product lines subject to the realization of a specified rate of return must be determined for each of the three portfolios of product lines under consideration. Quadratic programming is used to generate the optimal weights for allocating the total funds available to the firm between the product lines in a given portfolio. To illustrate how the quadratic programming model would be formulated for the alternative involving expansion into the automotive (A) industry, consider the expected return for the portfolio of product lines associated with this alternative, which is

$$E(R_A) = \sum_i w_{iA} E(r_{iA}) \qquad (10\text{–}185)$$

where $E(r_{iA})$ Denotes the expected rate of return on product line i if the firm expands into the automotive industry; and the range of the index i is defined to include existing product lines as well as the six additional automotive product lines being considered.

     w_{iA} Represents the per-

---

[4] For further details, see: Frank J. Fabozzi, "A Portfolio Approach to Capital Budgeting: An Application to the Expansion to Additional Product Lines," *Journal of the Operational Research Society,* vol. 29, no. 3 (1978), 245–249, Pergamon Press, Ltd., Oxford, England.

centage of product line i invested in total inventory if the firm elects to expand into the product lines of the automotive industry. (Note that $\sum_i w_{iA}$ is constrained to equal one in the quadratic programming formulation.)

The variance that measures the risk of the portfolio of product lines is then

$$\sigma_{RA}^2 = \sum_i \sum_k w_{iA} w_{kA} \sigma_{ikA} \qquad (10\text{–}186)$$

where σ_{ikA} Denotes the covariance of returns for product line i and k if the firm expands into the product lines of the automotive industry ($i \neq k$); and the variance of returns for product line i if i equals k.

Thus, the objective of the quadratic programming model is to minimize the portfolio risk, σ_{RA}^2, specified by (10–185) subject to a designated ex-

pected return $E(R_A)^*$ sought, and the restriction that the optimal weights must sum to one. Also included in the model are constraints to insure that the funds spent on present product lines are not reduced, and that the proportion of funds invested in each product line in terms of total inventory is not larger than the maximum value of each respective product line as given by forecasted maximum sales. The value for the expected portfolio return for this particular alternative can then be parameterized to obtain the risk-reward or efficient frontier. From the quadratic programming solutions associated with each of the three alternatives, the risk-reward relationships for each of the alternatives were constructed. The tradeoffs are depicted in Figure 10.12.

Note that the expansion of its present product lines coupled with expansion into the automotive industry results in a risk-reward tradeoff that dominates such expansion into the electronics industry. At every level of portfolio risk, a higher portfolio return can be expected by expanding into the automotive industry. The maximum expected

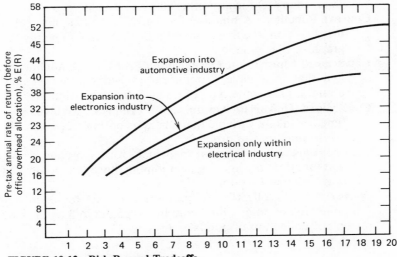

FIGURE 10.12 Risk Reward Tradeoffs

return that the company can obtain by expanding into the automotive industry is 50 percent compared with 39 percent in electronics. At the 38-percent portfolio return the level of risk is approximately one-third lower by expanding into the automotive industry compared with electronics. Fig. 10.12 also illustrates that expansion into the automo-tive industry substantially improves the risk-reward tradeoff from what it would have been if expansion was restricted to only the present product lines. Fabozzi states that the firm chose to expand into the automotive industry as well as expanding its present product lines, which is of course, the best alternative of the three under consideration.

10.9 CONCLUSION

In this chapter we have considered a few types of nonlinear programming problems. We have observed that nonlinear programming problems are invariably more difficult to solve than linear programming problems. We noted that computational procedures have been developed for only a very small fraction of the possible types of nonlinear progamming problems. We further observed that the solution procedures for various nonlinear programming problems are based upon the procedures which we studied earlier in linear programming.

It should be mentioned that a great variety of practical problems exist that can be formulated as nonlinear programming problems. Indeed, many of the practical problems that have been formulated in a linear programming mode are really nonlinear programming problems for which the nonlinearities were either ignored or approximated. Thus, it is very important for the management science student and practitioner to have some understanding of the rudiments involved in nonlinear programming.

GLOSSARY OF TERMS

Absolute or Global Maximum (Minimum)   A function $y = f(x)$ is said to have an absolute or global maximum (minimum) at a point $x = x'$ if $f(x')$ is greater (less) than $f(x)$ for any other allowable value of x.

Concave Function   A function for which, for each pair of points on the graph of that function, the line segment joining those two points lies entirely *below* the graph of that function.

Constrained Multivariate Optimization Problem   A nonlinear programming problem that may have a nonlinear objective function and/or nonlinear constraints, plus some type of nonnegativity restrictions.

Constrained Univariate Optimization Problem   Involves a nonlinear objective function in one variable that has to be optimized, where there are one or more constraints on the problem.

Convex Function   A function for which, for each pair of points on the graph of that function, the line segment joining those two points lies entirely *above* the graph of that function.

Convex Set   A collection of points such that, for each pair of points in the collection of points, the entire line segment joining the two points will also be in the collection of points.

Determinant   A specific number that can be assigned to a square matrix.

Gradient   The gradient of a function is the vector of partial derivatives associated with that function.

Hessian Matrix   A matrix of partial derivatives used in multivariate optimization problems to identify local maxima or minima.

Kuhn-Tucker Conditions   The necessary conditions under which a given point, x^*, is a local optimum for the general nonlinear programming problem.

Lagrangean Function   A function combining the objective function and the constraints into a single function.

Lagrange Multiplier Method   A method that can be used to solve constrained nonlinear problems involving the optimization of a function subject to a constraint set composed entirely of equalities.

Lagrange Multipliers   Variables utilized in deriving the Kuhn-Tucker necessary conditions that are analogous to the values associated with the dual variables in a linear programming problem.

Minors   Submatrices of the Hessian specified in a specific way.

Necessary Conditions   The conditions that must be satisfied for an optimal solution, but that do not guarantee that a particular solution is optimal.

Negative-Definite   A Hessian matrix is classified as negative-definite if the determinants of its minors alternate in sign, with the determinant of the first minor being negative.

Nonlinear Programming Problem   A mathematical programming problem in which the objective function and/or one or more constraints are not linear.

Optimal Gradient Method   A procedure for determining the optimum distance to move when utilizing the gradient in solving an unconstrained multivariate optimization problem.

Positive-Definite   A Hessian matrix is classified as positive-definite if the determinants of all of its minors are positive.

Quadratic Programming Problem   A special type of constrained nonlinear programming problem having a set of linear constraints and an objective function composed of linear and quadratic (second-order) terms.

Relative or Local Maximum (Minimum)   A function $y = f(x)$ is said to have a relative or local maximum (minimum) at $x = x''$ if $f(x'')$ is greater (less) than $f(x)$ for any adjacent value of x.

Semi-Definite   A Hessian matrix is classified as semi-definite if the determinants of its minors fail to meet the conditions specified for either a positive-definite or negative-definite Hessian matrix.

Stationary Point x^* of a Function $f(x)$ The point x^* that we find by setting the first derivative of $f(x)$ with respect to x equal to zero and solving for x.

Sufficient Conditions   The additional conditions that must be satisfied by a particular solution (i.e., in addition to satisfying the necessary conditions) to guarantee that the particular solution is also an optimal solution.

Unconstrained Multivariate Optimization Problem   A nonlinear programming problem composed of only an objective function, with this objective function having multiple variables.

Unconstrained Univariate Optimization Problem   The most elementary form of a nonlinear programming problem involving an objective function in a single variable.

SELECTED REFERENCES

NONLINEAR
PROGRAMMING

Aoki, Masanao, 1971. *Introduction to Optimization Techniques; Fundamentals and Applications of Nonlinear Programming*. New York: Macmillan Publishing Company.

Beveridge, Gordon S. G., and Robert S. Schecter. 1970. *Optimization: Theory and Practice*. New York: McGraw-Hill Book Company.

Bracken, J., and G. P. McCormick. 1968. *Selected Applications of Nonlinear Programming*. New York: John Wiley & Sons, Inc.

Bradley, Stephen P., Arlando C. Hax, and Thomas L. Magnanti. 1977. *Applied Mathematical Programming*. Reading, Mass.: Addison-Wesley Publishing Company.

Gottfried, Byron S., and Joel Wieseman. 1973. *Introduction to Optimization Theory*. Englewood Cliffs, N.J.: Prenctice-Hall, Inc.

Hadley, G. 1964. *Nonlinear and Dynamic Programming*. Reading, Mass.: Addison-Wesley Publishing Company, Inc.

Himmelblau, D. 1972. *Applied Nonlinear Programming*. New York: McGraw-Hill Book Company.

Kwak, N. K. 1973. *Mathematical Programming with Business Applications*. New York: McGraw-Hill Book Company.

Lavi, A., and T. Vogel. 1968. *Recent Advances in Optimization Techniques*. New York: John Wiley & Sons, Inc.

Luenberger, David G. 1973. *Introduction to Linear and Nonlinear Programming*. Reading, Mass.: Addison-Wesley Publishing Company, Inc.

McMillan, Claude. 1975. *Mathematical Programming*. New York: John Wiley & Sons, Inc.

Mangasarian, Olvi L. 1969. *Nonlinear Programming*. New York: McGraw-Hill Book Company.

Saaty, Thomas L., and Joseph Bram. 1964. *Nonlinear Mathematics*. New York: McGraw-Hill Book Company.

Wilde, D. 1964. *Optimum Seeking Methods*. Englewood Cliffs, N.J.: Prentice-Hall, Inc.

Zangwill, Willard I. 1969. *Nonlinear Programming: A Unified Approach*. Englewood Cliffs, N.J.: Prentice-Hall, Inc.

DISCUSSION QUESTIONS

1. What portion of the solution space is not a convex set in Fig. 10.2?
2. Give a real-world example of a convex and a concave cost function.
3. When is a global maximum of a function on a convex set "unique"?
4. What is the graphical representation of the first derivative of a single variable function, evaluated at some point x? How does this graphically appear if at point x the first derivative equals zero?
5. Do you always have a "global" optimum in a constrained univariate optimization problem? Why or why not?
6. Why would you want to use the "negative" of the gradient in the process of minimizing a function using gradient techniques (consider an unconstrained multivariate minimization problem)? What does the "step size" indicate?
7. What is the difference between a "necessary" and a "sufficient" condition?
8. When do you know you have obtained an optimal solution with respect to the Kuhn-Tucker conditions? In this case, are you assured you have a "global" optimum?
9. Describe in *detail* the particular type of situation in which the use of the Kuhn-Tucker conditions is appropriate.
10. What similarity exists between the Lagrange multipliers of the Kuhn-Tucker conditions and duality theory in linear programming, and when does this similarity exist?

11. How are the Kuhn-Tucker conditions usually applied?
12. Describe the situation in which the use of the Lagrange multiplier method is appropriate?
13. Could you also solve a maximization problem in quadratic programming whereby the objective function is convex? Why or why not?
14. Suppose you want to maximize a quadratic programming problem for which the objective function is concave. Why is it sufficient to find a feasible solution to the Kuhn-Tucker conditions in order to also obtain the optimal solution? In this situation, can the maximum be a "local" maximum? Why or why not?
15. In linear programming, the optimal solution occurs at a cornerpoint of the feasible region. Discuss where the optimal solution to a nonlinear program may occur.

PROBLEM SET

1. Determine the stationary points of the following functions and indicate whether the stationary points are local maxima or local minima.
   (a) $f(x) = -3x^2 + 2x - 1$
   (b) $f(x) = 6x^2 - 2x + 7$
   (c) $f(x) = 2x^3 - 3x^2 + x$
   (d) $f(x) = -\frac{1}{3}x^3 + \frac{3}{2}x^2 - 2x$

2. Determine the global maximum or global minimum for the following functions over the constrained range shown.
   (a) $f(x) = 3x^2 + 2$ $\qquad\qquad$ $-4 \le x \le +4$
   (b) $f(x) = -x + 3$ $\qquad\qquad$ $-2 \le x \le +2$
   (c) $f(x) = 2x^3 + 1x^2 - 5$ $\qquad$ $-5 \le x \le +5$
   (d) $f(x) = -3x^3 - 2x^2 + 10$ $\qquad$ $-3 \le x \le +3$

3. For the following functions, determine which are convex functions, which are concave functions, and which are neither concave nor convex.
   (a) $f(x) = \dfrac{1}{x}$, for $x > 0$

   (b) $f(x_1, x_2) = 2x_1^2 + 2x_2^2$
   (c) $f(x_1, x_2) = x_1^2 \cdot x_2^2$
   (d) $f(x) = e^{-x}$
   (e) $f(x) = \log(x)$, for $x > 0$
   (f) $f(x) = |x|$

4. Plot the function $f(x) = x^3 - 6x$, over the region $-4 \le x \le 4$. Identify the local maxima and local minima of $f(x)$ over the region. What is the global maxima and global minima over this region?

5. Use the optimal gradient method to solve the following problem.

$$\text{Minimize } Z = (x_1 - 3)^2 + (x_2 - 4)^2$$

6. Use the optimal gradient method to solve the following problem.

$$\text{Maximize } Z = -(x_1 - 2)^2 - 2x_2^2$$

7. Summarize the Kuhn-Tucker conditions for the following problem.

$$\text{Maximize } Z = 2(x_1 - 3)^2 + 4(x_2 - 2)^2$$

subject to:
$$1x_1 + 2x_2 \leq 6$$
$$3x_1 + 1x_2 \leq 15$$
$$1x_1 + 1x_2 \geq 1$$

with $x_1 \geq 0, x_2 \geq 0$

8.   Summarize the Kuhn-Tucker conditions for the following problem.

$$\text{Maximize } Z = 4x_1 + 3x_2$$

subject to: $(x_1 - 2)^2 + (x_2 - 1)^2 \leq 8$

with $x_1 \geq 0, x_2 \geq 0$

9.   Consider the following problem.

$$\text{Maximize } Z = x_2$$

subject to: $(1 - x_2)^3 - x_1 \geq 0$

with $x_1 \geq 0, x_2 \geq 0$

Show that the Kuhn-Tucker conditions do not hold for this problem.

10.   A firm produces and sells two glass products. The profit functions for these two products are given by:

$$c_1 = 0.1x_1^2 + 1.1x_1 + 25$$
$$c_2 = 0.2x_2^2 + 1.5x_2 + 20$$

where x_1 = number of units of glass product one sold
x_2 = number of units of glass product two sold

The firm also has limited resources that restrict its production process in the following manner.

$5x_1 + 7x_2 \leq 400$ (Production hours)
$1x_1 + 3x_2 \leq 120$ (Production work force)

Determine the optimal product mix using the Kuhn-Tucker conditions.

11.   Consider the following nonlinear programming problem.

$$\text{Maximize } Z = -3x_1^2 - 6x_1x_2 - 5x_2^2 + 7x_1 + 5x_2$$

subject to: $x_1 + x_2 = 5$

Solve this problem using the Lagrange multiplier method.

12.   Consider the following nonlinear programming problem.

$$\text{Minimize } Z = -2x_1^2 + 5x_1x_2 - 4x_2^2 + 18x_1$$

subject to: $x_1 + x_2 = 7$

Solve this problem using the Lagrange multiplier method.

13. Knock-Em-Out Bug Spray Company produces a termite spray consisting of two chemicals c_1 and c_2. The production function for the termite spray is estimated to be

$$Q = f(x_1, x_2) = 4.3x_1 - 0.3x_1^2 + 2.5x_2 - 0.1x_2^2$$

where Q = quantity (1000 gallons) of termite spray produced
x_1 = input (1000 gallons) of chemical c_1 used
x_2 = input (1000 gallons) of chemical c_2 used

The company currently has $1000 to spend on purchasing the two chemicals, which have unit prices (per 1000 gallons) of $300 and $200, respectively. Determine the chemical inputs to maximize the total quantity of termite spray produced using the Lagrange multiplier method.

14. Solve the following quadratic programming problem.

$$\text{Maximize } Z = 2x_1 + 3x_2 - x_1^2 - x_2^2$$

subject to: $2x_1 + 2x_2 \leq 4$

with $x_1 \geq 0, x_2 \geq 0$

15. Solve the following quadratic programming problem.

$$\text{Maximize } Z = 3x_1 + 4x_2 - 2x_2^2$$

subject to: $x_1 + 2x_2 \leq 4$
$x_1 + x_2 \leq 2$

with $x_1 \geq 0, x_2 \geq 0$

16. The Mellow Perfume Company produces two types of blended perfumes. The total profit function for the sale of these two types of blended perfumes is given by:

$$f = 8x_1 + 5x_2 - \tfrac{1}{100}x_1^2 - \tfrac{1}{50}x_2^2$$

where x_1 = gallons of "Mellow Yellow" perfume produced
x_2 = gallons of "Mellow Gold" perfume produced

The constraints on the resources used in the production process are as follows.

	Per-Gallon Requirement		Resource Availability per Requirement
Resource	"Mellow Yellow"	"Mellow Gold"	
Blend 1	2 Units	1 Unit	$\leq$ 50 Units
Blend 2	3 Units	3 Units	$\geq$ 75 Units
Distillation hours	3 Units	8 Units	$\geq$ 120 Units

How many gallons of each type of perfume should be produced if we are interested in maximizing the total profit? Formulate and solve this problem using quadratic programming.

Dynamic Programming

INTRODUCTION
AN ILLUSTRATION OF DYNAMIC PROGRAMMING
DYNAMIC PROGRAMMING UNDER CERTAINTY
    Dynamic Programming Applied to the Shortest-Route Problem
    A Multiperiod Production-Scheduling Problem
    Dynamic Programming with a Multiplicative Recursion Relationship
DYNAMIC PROGRAMMING UNDER UNCERTAINTY
    Probabilistic Lot Scheduling by Dynamic Programming
INFINITE-STATE DYNAMIC PROGRAMMING
    An Infinite-State Work-Force Employment Problem
CASE STUDY—DYNAMIC PROGRAMMING APPLIED TO CAPITAL BUDGETING
CONCLUSION
GLOSSARY OF TERMS
SELECTED REFERENCES—DYNAMIC PROGRAMMING
DISCUSSION QUESTIONS
PROBLEM SET

11.1 INTRODUCTION

Dynamic programming is a management science technique applicable to certain types of problems involving a sequence of decisions that are interrelated. Unlike linear programming, for which the simplex algorithm is used as a computational mechanism, there is no standard formulation of the dynamic programming problem. Thus, dynamic programming is really a general type of problem solving procedure that can be applied to sequential decision-making situations. The dynamic programming model, or set of equations, that is formulated must be developed uniquely for each problem solving situation. Therefore, the student of business should learn to analyze the general structure of sequential decision problems in order to determine whether or not the problem can be solved by dynamic programming, and how it would be done.

Dynamic programming developed initially as a result of studying the sequential decision stochastic programming problems that arose in inventory control theory. The name ''dynamic programming'' became associated with the computational technique that referred to the types of problems to which it was applied originally. The basic ideas of dynamic programming were developed by Richard Bellman in the 1950s.

In this chapter we will concentrate on presenting and discussing several applications of dynamic programming. This is necessary because, as noted previously, there is no standard problem formulation for dynamic programming, and it can perhaps be best understood by studying a number of situations to which it can be applied. The student should be aware that the study of dynamic programming requires the mastery of a set of structural characteristics and notation that is unique to dynamic programming. We will attempt to present, explain, and use these characteristics and notation throughout the expository examples that are presented in this chapter. The student should also be cautioned that advanced work in dynamic programming can be difficult, requiring the use of probability distributions and calculus in the solution of various problems. The latter part of this chapter will provide examples of these more difficult types of dynamic programming problems.

Numerous examples of practical applications of dynamic programming to business and managerial problems are in existence. For example, dynamic programming has been used in a variety of production-scheduling and inventory control decision-making situations. Similarly, dynamic programming has been used to solve problems involving spare parts level determination given space and weight constraints. Capital budgeting, allocation of research and development funds, and long-run corporate planning are other areas that have been analyzed by means of dynamic programming.

We will begin our discussion of dynamic programming by presenting and discussing a decision-making situation that can be analyzed very effectively using dynamic programming. This illustration will also be used to demonstrate the general structure and format of dynamic programming. Following this we will then consider various examples of dynamic programming under certainty, or deterministic dynamic programming. This discussion will be followed by the more difficult case of dynamic programming under uncertainty, or probabilistic or stochastic dynamic programming. Finally, an infinite-state dynamic programming problem will be discussed.

11.2 AN ILLUSTRATION OF DYNAMIC PROGRAMMING

In order to describe and explain the general approach used in dynamic programming, let us consider the following decision-making situation. The Roadrunner Transmission Company operates a transmission-rebuilding service in Gallup, New Mexico. It offers free tow-in service to its rebuilding shop, which is composed of three departments: inspection and diagnosis, disassembly and repair, and reassembly and testing. All transmission-rebuilding work must move through these three departments in this order, and each of the three departments has four identical work stations at which the particular work is done. However, since different workers, tools, and equipment are found at different work stations, there is a variation in the cost associated with a particular work station within a department. The cost associated with a particular work station in a department is also dependent on the work station in the previous department at which the last operation was done.

A late-model Cadillac has just been towed in, and it must now be scheduled, at a minimum total cost, at one work station in each of the three repair departments. The possible costs for the various departments are as follows.

	To Inspection and Diagnosis Station			
From Towing	*1*	*2*	*3*	*4*
	35	40	30	45

From Inspection and Diagnosis Station	To Disassembly and Repair Station			
	1	2	3	4
1	105	100	85	90
2	90	85	100	95
3	100	90	95	105
4	110	105	120	110

From Disassembly and Repair Station	To Reassembly and Testing Station			
	1	2	3	4
1	70	75	85	80
2	85	90	80	95
3	90	70	85	80
4	80	85	90	75

In analyzing this decison-making situation by means of dynamic programming, observe first that three basic characteristics are present in the structure of the problem itself. They are:

1. The dynamic programming problem can be divided into **stages**, with each stage requiring a standardized *policy decision*. Thus, dynamic programming problems require making a sequence of interrelated decisions, with each decision having a standardized format.

    In analyzing and solving this problem it will be subdivided, or decomposed, into a sequence of smaller subproblems representing the three stages of the problem. The idea of subdividing the problem into a sequence of stages, or subproblems, is illustrated in Fig. 11.1.

    In this problem there are three stages, with each stage representing one of the three departments in the transmission-rebuilding shop. At each stage in the transmission-rebuilding process a policy decision with respect to the assignment of a particular work station must be made.

    It should be mentioned that often the stages represent different time periods associated with the planning horizon of the problem, although this does not have to be the case. Thus, dynamic programming has often been used as a technique for analysis of problems requiring repetitive decisions at specific

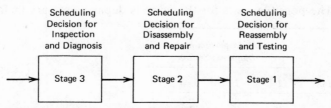

FIGURE 11.1   Subdivision of Roadrunner Transmission Company Problem into Stages

points in time. However, in the problem currently being analyzed the stages do not have time implications, since we are interested in making scheduling decisions that are independent of time.

2. Each stage in a dynamic programming problem has a number of **states** associated with it. Generally, these states are the various possible conditions in which the problem system may be at a point in time. The states provide the information required for analyzing the results that the current decision has upon future courses of action. The number of states may be finite, or infinite, for any stage of the decision process.

Each department (stage) in the transmission-rebuilding process has four work stations, or states, associated with it. This is an example of a finite number of states at each stage in the decision process.

3. As a policy decision is made at each stage in the solution process, the current state is transformed into a state that is interrelated to a state associated with the next stage of the process. This relationship may be described in deterministic terms, or it may be defined according to a probability distribution.

The multistage decision process is shown below in Fig. 11.2. At stage n of the problem, there are two inputs. These are the state (variable), s_n, and the decision (variable), x_n. The state variable is the state input to the present stage of the problem, and relates the present stage back to the previous stage. Given the current state, s_n, which provides complete information about the system when there are n stages to go, we seek to make the decision x_n that will optimize the total performance of the system over the remaining stages. The decision, x_n, which is selected from among the set of possible decisions, produces two outputs from this stage of the problem. These are the **return function** at stage n, which is denoted as $f_n(s, x_n)$, and the new state s_{n-1}.

The return function at any stage is the increase in profit (or decrease in cost) that occurs at that stage as a function of the state variable, s_n, and the decision variable, x_n. The state variable at the beginning of the next stage is determined by the **transition function**, $s_{n-1} = t_n(x_n, s_n)$. The transition function defines, as a functional relationship, the value of the state variable at each stage, and thus interconnects the stages of the dynamic programming problem. This new state is then a complete description of the system when there are $n - 1$ stages left in the decision process.

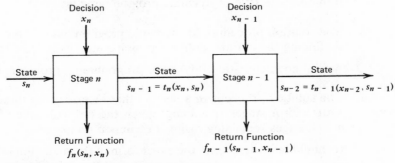

FIGURE 11.2 Multistage Decision Process

At each stage (department) in the decision process, a state (work station) is chosen. This choice of a work station is then interrelated to the choice of a work station in the next stage of the transmission-rebuilding process. The relationship is described in deterministic monetary terms, as shown in the cost tables previously summarized.

The solution of a dynamic programming problem having these three structural characteristics is based upon Bellman's **principle of optimality**:

PRINCIPLE OF
OPTIMALITY

An optimal policy must have the property that, regardless of the decision made to enter a particular state, the remaining decisions must constitute an optimal policy for leaving that state (Bellman 1957).

In our present problem this means that if we are at a particular state (work station) in a particular stage (department) of the transmission-rebuilding process, then our choice of the next state (work station) to be chosen in the next stage (department) is not dependent upon how we arrived at the current state in the present stage of the decision process. Thus, a fourth characteristic of dynamic programming problem is:

4. At each stage in the decision process, given the current state, an optimal policy for the remaining stages of the process is independent of the policy adopted in previous stages of the decision process.

To actually solve a dynamic programming problem we begin by first solving a one-stage problem, and then we sequentially add a series of one-stage problems that are solved until the overall optimum is found. Usually, this solution procedure is based on a **backward induction process**, where the first stage analyzed is the final stage of the problem and the solution of the problem proceeds by moving back one stage at a time until all stages in the problem are included. In our current example, we would initially focus on the selection of the minimum reassembly and testing cost, given that we have previously come from a particular disassembly and repair station. However, it should be mentioned that certain problems alternatively allow the use of a **forward induction process**, where the first stage analyzed is the initial stage of the problem and the solution of the problem proceeds by moving forward one stage at a time until all stages in the problem are included. In general, backward induction is probably more prevalent, and in dynamic programming problems involving uncertainty, backward induction will be required. Thus, a fifth characteristic of dynamic programming is:

5. The solution procedure for dynamic programming problems generally begins by finding the optimal policy for each state of the *last stage* of the process.

A final characteristic of dynamic programming problems is the following.

6. The solution proceeds in a fashion that identifies the optimal policy for each state with n stages remaining, given the optimal policy for each state with $n - 1$ stages remaining, using a **recursion relationship**.

It should be stressed that the exact form of the recursion relationship will vary according to the dynamic programming problem being analyzed. However, the recursion relationship will always be of the general form:

$$f_n^*(s_n) = \text{Max/Min } \{f_n(s_n, x_n)\} \tag{11-1}$$

The function $f_n(s_n, x_n)$ is the value associated with the best overall policy for the remaining stages of the problem, given that the system is in state s_n with n stages to go and the decision variable x_n is selected. The function $f_n(s_n, x_n)$ is written in terms of s_n, x_n, and $f_{n-1}^*(\cdot)$. For our current problem, this recursion relationship can be written as:

$$f_n^*(s_n) = \text{Min } \{f_n(s_n, x_n)\} = \text{Min } \{c_{s_n, x_n} + f_{n-1}^*(x_n)\} \tag{11-2}$$

The first term in this recursion relationship, c_{s_n, x_n} is the cost associated with the state variable, s_n, and the decision variable, x_n, for the current stage of the problem. The second term in this recursion relationship, $f_{n-1}^*(x_n)$, is the optimal cost from the previous stage of the problem, as a function of the decision variable, x_n, for the current stage of the problem.

In summarizing the computations associated with dynamic programming problems, it is useful to construct a table such as the following for each stage in the decision process.

	x_n	$f_n(s_n, x_n)$		
s_n		x_n	$f_n^*(s_n)$	x_n^*

Within this table s_n represents the states for the current stage of the decision process and the x_n are the decision variables for the current stage (stage $= n$) of the decision process. The function $f_n(s_n, x_n)$ is the value associated with the best overall policy for the remaining stages of the problem, given that the system is in state s_n with n stages to go and the decision variable x_n is selected. The value $f_n^*(s_n)$ is the maximum (minimum) value of $f_n(s_n, x_n)$ over all possible values of x_n for a particular s_n. The value x_n^* is the value of x_n producing the optimal value, $f_n^*)(s_n)$.

To illustrate the construction of this table consider the decisions that can be made with respect to the current (last) stage of the decision process. At this point there are $n = 1$ more stages to go. We can enter this stage (reassembly and testing) from stages $s_1 = 1, 2, 3, 4$ of the previous stage (disassembly and repair), and can make a decision to go to work stations $x_1 = 1, 2, 3, 4$. These decisions will then result in the following one-stage table ($n = 1$).

	x_1	$f_1(s_1, x_1) = c_{s_1, x_1}$					
s_1		*1*	*2*	*3*	*4*	$f_1^*(s_1)$	x_1^*
1		70	75	85	80	70	1
2		85	90	80	95	80	3
3		90	70	85	80	70	2
4		80	85	90	75	75	4

Each value of $f_1(s_1,x_1)$ in this table is simply the cost, $c_{s_1 x_1}$, associated with entering this stage of the decision process from state s_1 and making a selection of state x_1. The value of $f_1^*(s_1)$ is then the minimum value of $f_1(s_1,x_1)$ over all possible values of x_1 for a particular s_1. The value of x_1^* is the value of x_1 that produces the optimal (minimum) value, $f_1^*(s_1)$.

The next step in the solution of the dynamic programming problem involves moving backward one more stage, that is, considering the decision that must be made when there are $n = 2$ more stages to go. We can enter this stage (disassembly and repair) from states $s_2 = 1, 2, 3, 4$ of the previous stage (inspection and diagnosis), and can make a decision to go to work stations $x_2 = 1, 2, 3, 4$. These decisions will then result in the following two-stage table ($n = 2$).

s_2 \ x_2	$f_2(s_2,x_2) = c_{s_2 x_2} + f_1^*(x_2)$				$f_2^*(s_2)$	x_2^*
	1	*2*	*3*	*4*		
1	$105 + 70$ $= 175$	$100 + 80$ $= 180$	$85 + 70$ $= 155$	$90 + 75$ $= 165$	155	3
2	$90 + 70$ $= 160$	$85 + 80$ $= 165$	$100 + 70$ $= 170$	$95 + 75$ $= 170$	160	1
3	$100 + 70$ $= 170$	$90 + 80$ $= 170$	$95 + 70$ $= 165$	$105 + 75$ $= 180$	165	3
4	$110 + 70$ $= 180$	$105 + 80$ $= 185$	$120 + 70$ $= 190$	$110 + 75$ $= 185$	180	1

Each value of $f_2(s_2,x_2)$ in this table is the sum of the cost, $c_{s_2 x_2}$, associated with entering this stage of the decision process from state s_2 and making a selection of state x_2 *plus* the optimal cost $f_1^*(x_2)$ already determined for the one-stage problem. Note that the decision variable x_2 that is selected in this two-stage problem is identical to the entry state s_1 in the one-stage problem. Thus, we have expressed the function $f_2(s_2,x_2)$ to be minimized as a *recursion relationship* having a term $f_1^*(x_2)$ that is related to the one-stage problem.

In this two-stage table, $f_2^*(x_2)$ is the minimum value of $f_2(s_2,x_2)$ over all possible values of x_2 for a particular s_2. The value x_2^* is the value of x_2 that produces the optimal (minimum) value, $f_2^*(s_2)$.

The final step in using dynamic programming to solve this problem involves moving backward one more stage, that is, considering the decision that must be made when there are $n = 3$ more stages to go. Since there are only three stages in the entire transmission-rebuilding process, when we have obtained the optimal solution for the situation in which there are $n = 3$ more stages to go, we will have moved backward to the beginning of the decision process. We can enter this stage (inspection and diagnosis) only from the towing operation. However, we can still make a decision to go to work stations $x_3 = 1, 2, 3, 4$ within this stage. These decisions will then result in the following three-stage table.

s_3 \ x_3	$f_3(s_3,x_3) = c_{s_3 x_3} + f_2^*(x_3)$				$f_3^*(s_3)$	x_3^*
	1	*2*	*3*	*4*		
From towing	$35 + 155$ $= 190$	$40 + 160$ $= 200$	$30 + .165$ $= 195$	$45 + 180$ $= 225$	190	1

Each value of $f_3(s_3, x_3)$ in this three-stage table is the sum of the cost $c_{s_3 x_3}$ associated with entering this stage of the decision process from state s_3 and making a selection of work station x_3 plus the optimal cost $f_2^*(x_3)$ already determined for the two-stage problem. Thus, we have expressed the function $f_3(s_3, x_3)$ to be minimized as a recursion relationship having a term, $f_2^*(x_3)$, that is related to the two-stage problem. In this three-stage table, $f_3^*(s_3)$ is the minimum value of $f_3(s_3, x_3)$ over all possible values of x_3 for a particular s_3. The value of x_3^* is the value of x_3 that produces the optimal (minimum) value, $f_3^*(s_3)$.

We have now proceeded backward from the one-stage problem to the three-stage problem, or to the beginning of the decision process. Our dynamic programming solution is now complete. The three-stage table indicates that the optimal sequence of work stations for rebuilding the Cadillac's transmission will result in a minimum total cost of $190. The three-stage table also indicates work station 1 should be used for inspection and diagnosis ($x_3^* = 1$, from towing). Setting $x_3^* = 1 = s_2$ for the two-stage table, we observe that work station 3 should be used for disassembly and repair ($x_2^* = 3$, for $s_2 = 1$). Setting $x_2^* = 3 = s_1$ for the one-stage table, we see that work station 2 should be used for reassembly and repair ($x_1^* = 2$, for $s_1 = 3$). The optimal sequence of work stations, and the associated cost, is

		Inspection and Diagnosis		**Disassembly and Repair**		**Reassembly and Inspection**
Sequence { Towing	$\rightarrow$	1	$\rightarrow$	3	$\rightarrow$	2
Cost { Towing	$\rightarrow$	$35	+	85	+	70 = $190

11.3 DYNAMIC PROGRAMMING UNDER CERTAINTY

Dynamic programming under certainty, or **deterministic dynamic programming**, involves problem situations in which the state in the next stage of the decision process is completely determined by the interaction of the state and the policy decision, with respect to the decision variable, that occurs at the current stage. In deterministic dynamic programming there is no uncertainty and no probability distribution associated with what the next state in the decision process will be.

Assume that we are at stage n in the decision process and are in state s_n. Assume further that our policy decision has resulted in the choice of the decision variable x_n. This choice of the decision variable will then be reflected in some state s_{n+1} at stage $n + 1$. The objective function for the optimal policy for this next stage will be given by $f_{n+1}^*(s_{n+1}) = f_{n+1}(x_{n+1}, s_{n+1}) + f_n^*(s_n)$, where $f_n^*(s_n)$ has been determined for the present stage.

We will now consider three examples of dynamic programming under certainty.

11.3.1 Dynamic Programming Applied to the Shortest-Route Problem

An excellent illustration of dynamic programming under certainty can be obtained by considering the shortest-route problem that we studied previously in Chapter 8. We will now illustrate the methodology of dynamic programming by applying it to a shortest-route problem. Consider the network shown in Fig. 11.3, where the numbers along each branch represent the distances (in hundreds of miles)

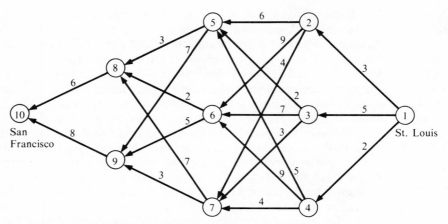

FIGURE 11.3 Shortest Route Network (St. Louis → San Francisco)

between the respective nodes. This shortest-route problem requires the determination of the minimum-distance route from node 1, St. Louis, to node 10, San Francisco.

One possible approach to solving this problem would be to resort to exhaustive enumeration, that is, determine the total distance along each route. To do this we would have to determine the total distance associated with $3 \times 3 \times 2 \times 1 = 18$ possible routes. A complete enumeration such as this would be a very time-consuming and tedious task. Fortunately, the shortest-route problem possesses the attributes necessary for the application of a dynamic programming procedure, which is much more efficient than exhaustive enumeration. Thus, let the decision variables x_n ($n = 1, 2, 3, 4$) be defined as the immediate destinations when there are n more stages to go. The route selected by the dynamic programming procedure would be $x_5 \rightarrow x_4 \rightarrow x_3 \rightarrow x_2 \rightarrow x_1$, where $x_5 = 1$ (start) and $x_1 = 10$ (finish), and x_4, x_3, and x_2 are unknown. Let $f_n(s_n, x_n)$ be the minimum total distance for the last n stages, given that we are in state s_n and select x_n as our immediate destination. Given state s_n and stage n, let x_n^* denote the value of x_n, which minimizes $f_n(s_n, x_n)$. Therefore, $f_n^*(s) = f_n(s_n, x_n^*)$. When we are able to compute $f_4^*(s_4)$ and its corresponding policy we have solved the problem. We do this by beginning at our destination and working backward to find the optimum path by successively finding $f_1^*(s_1), f_2^*(s_2), f_3^*(s_3), f_4^*(s_4)$. The recursion relationship for this problem can be written as follows.

$$f_n^*(s_n) = \operatorname*{Min}_{x_n} \{f_n(s_n, x_n)\} = \operatorname*{Min}_{x_n} \{d_{s_n, x_n} + f_{n-1}^*(x_n)\} \qquad (11\text{-}3)$$

In this recursion relationship the first term, d_{s_n, x_n}, is the distance associated with the state variable, s_n, and the decision variable, x_n, for the current stage of the problem. The second term, $f_{n-1}^*(x_n)$, is the optimal distance for the previous stage of the problem, expressed as a function of the decision variable, x_n.

The dynamic programming approach to this problem involves working backward, in stages, from the destination (San Francisco) to the origin (St. Louis). We begin our computational process by determining the shortest route to the destination node (node 10—San Francisco), from state $s_1 = 8$ (node 8) and state $s_1 = 9$ (node 9). At this point there are $n = 1$ more stages to go. We can enter this stage from states $s_1 = 8$ (node 8) and $s_1 = 9$ (node 9), and can make a decision only to go to node 10 (i.e., $x_1 = 10$). These decisions result in the following one-stage table ($n = 1$).

| x_1 | $f_1(s_1,x_1) = d_{s_1 x_1}$ | | |
s_1	10	$f_1^*(s_1)$	x_1^*
8	6	6	10
9	8	8	10

Within this one-stage table $x_1 = 10$ (node 10) is the immediate destination for stage $n = 1$. We can travel to this destination from either state $s_1 = 8$ or state $s_1 = 9$. Each value of $f_1(s_1,x_1)$ in this table is simply the distance, $d_{s_1 x_1}$, associated with entering this stage of the decision process from state s_1 and moving to the final destination, $x_1 = 10$. The value of $f_1^*(s_1)$ is the minimum value of $f_1(s_1,x_1)$ over all possible values of x_1 for a particular s_1. The value x_1^* is the value of x_1 that produces the optimal (minimum) value, $f_1^*(s_1)$.

The next step in the solution of this dynamic programming problem involves moving backward one more stage, that is, considering the decision that must be made when there are $n = 2$ more stages to go. The computational process for the two-stage problem becomes slightly more complicated. To illustrate, assume for the moment that we are at state $s_2 = 5$ (node 5). We can next go to either $x_2 = 8$ (node 8) or $x_2 = 9$ (node 9). The distances associated with these movements are $d_{58} = 3$ or $d_{59} = 7$. If we choose to go from state $s = 5$ to $x_2 = 8$, the minimum additional distance after reaching $x_2 = 8$ will be given in the table for the one-stage problem as $f_1^*(8) = 6$. Thus, the total distance for the decision is $d_{58} + f_1^*(8) = 3 + 6 = 9$. Similarly, the total distance if we choose to go from state $s_2 = 5$ to $x_2 = 9$ is $d_{59} + f_1^*(9) = 7 + 8 = 15$. As a result, we would decide to move from state $s_2 = 5$ to $x_2 = 8$, since this move yields the minimum total distance $f_2^*(5) = d_{58} + f_1^*(8) = 3 + 6 = 9$. We have thus determined a recursion relationship for the two-stage problem and this recursion relationship utilizes the optimal solution already obtained for the one-stage problem. This recursion relationship is again deterministic in that we are minimizing using a set of known (constant) distances. The two-stage table ($n = 2$) can now be constructed as:

| x_2 | $f_2(s_2,x_2) = d_{s_2 x_2} + f_1^*(x_2)$ | | | |
s_2	8	9	$f_2^*(s_2)$	x_2^*
5	9	15	9	8
6	8	13	8	8
7	13	11	11	9

Within this two-stage table, the entries for the values of $f_2(s_2,x_2)$ are obtained using the recursion relationship, as follows.

$$
\begin{aligned}
f_2(5,8) &= d_{58} + f_1^*(8) = 3 + 6 = 9 \\
f_2(5,9) &= d_{59} + f_1^*(9) = 7 + 8 = 15 \\
f_2(6,8) &= d_{68} + f_1^*(8) = 2 + 6 = 8 \\
f_2(6,9) &= d_{69} + f_1^*(9) = 5 + 8 = 13 \\
f_2(7,8) &= d_{78} + f_1^*(8) = 7 + 6 = 13 \\
f_2(7,9) &= d_{79} + f_1^*(9) = 3 + 8 = 11
\end{aligned}
\tag{11-4}
$$

The entries for the respective values of $f_2^*(s_2)$ are then obtained as the minimum values of the $f_2(s_2, x_2)$ for the respective states. The entries for the respective values of x_2^* are obtained by observing which destinations produced the values of $f_2^*(s_2)$.

Continuing this solution process we move backward one more stage, to the situation where there are $n = 3$ more stages to go. The solution for the three-stage problem is obtained in a similar fashion to the previous stages, except that we now employ a recursion relationship of the form: $f_3(s_3, x_3) = d_{s_3 x_3} + f_2^*(x_3)$. For example, assume that we are at state $s_3 = 2$. The recursion relationship gives the following results.

$$
\begin{aligned}
f_3(2,5) &= d_{25} + f_2^*(5) = 6 + 9 = 15 \\
f_3(2,6) &= d_{26} + f_2^*(6) = 9 + 8 = 17 \\
f_3(2,7) &= d_{27} + f_2^*(7) = 4 + 11 = 15
\end{aligned}
\tag{11-5}
$$

Thus, the minimum total distance from state $s_3 = 2$ onward is $f_3^*(2) = 15$, and the immediate destination is either $x_3^* = 5$ or $x_3^* = 7$. For the three-stage problem, the following is the complete three-stage table ($n = 3$).

x_3 / s_3	$f_3(s_3, x_3) = d_{s_3 x_3} + f_2^*(x_3)$			$f_3^*(s_3)$	x_3^*
	5	**6**	**7**		
2	15	17	15	15	5 or 7
3	11	15	14	11	5
4	14	17	15	14	5

The solution to the four-stage problem is obtained in similar fashion, except that our recursion relationship becomes: $f_4(s_4, x_4) = c_{s_4 x_4} + f_3^*(x_4)$. In the four-stage problem we have moved backward to the origin (node 1). Thus, in the four-stage problem we need to consider moving only from state $s_4 = 1$ to states $x_4 = 2$, 3, 4. These decisions will result in the following four-stage table ($n = 4$).

x_4 / s_4	$f_4(s_4, x_4) = d_{s_4 x_4} + f_3^*(x_4)$			$f_4^*(s_4)$	x_4^*
	2	**3**	**4**		
1	18	16	16	16	3 or 4

We have now proceeded backward from the one-stage problem to the four-stage problem, or from state $s_4 = 10$ (node 10, San Francisco) to state $s_1 = 1$ (node 1, St. Louis). Our dynamic programming solution is now completed. The four-stage table indicates that the minimum-distance route will be of length $= 16$

(hundreds of miles). The four-stage table also indicates that if we start at node 1 (St. Louis) we should then go to either node 3 or node 4. Setting $x_4^* = 3 = s_3$ for the three-stage table, we observe that we should then go from node 3 to node 5. Setting $x_4^* = 4 = s_3$ for the three-stage table, we observe that we should also go from node 4 to node 5. Setting $x_3^* = 5 = s_2$ for the two-stage table, we see that we should go from node 5 to node 8. Finally, setting $x_2^* = 8 = s_1$ for the one-stage table we see that we should go from node 8 to node 10. The optimal sequences of nodes, and their associated distances are

$$
\begin{array}{c}
\textbf{Nodes} \\
\hline
\end{array}
$$

		Nodes			
Sequences $\begin{cases} \\ \end{cases}$	1	3	5	8	10
	1	4	5	8	10

$$
\text{Distances} \begin{cases} 5 + 2 + 3 + 6 = 16 \\ 2 + 5 + 3 + 6 = 16 \end{cases} \tag{11-6}
$$

Thus, we have two (alternative) shortest routes for this problem, both having a minimum distance of 16 (hundreds of miles).

11.3.2 A Multiperiod Production-Scheduling Problem

One of the practical areas to which dynamic programming has been applied is that of multiperiod production scheduling. In such applications, dynamic programming has proven to be very useful in relating various production and inventory decisions over time. The example that we will now consider is simplified in terms of the length of its time horizon, and in terms of the variables and parameters that are employed. However, similar production scheduling models have been implemented with the aid of high-speed digital computers and have been of considerable economic benefit to many companies.

The Incredible Manufacturing Company is trying to establish a production schedule for one of its products for the next N months. This manufacturer is basically a job shop and usually receives firm orders on a monthly basis 6 to 9 months before a particular month's order must be shipped. We will assume that the company has an accurate forecast of the amount of production needed to meet demand for each of the N future periods, on the basis of firm orders it has received.

Incredible Manufacturing Company can manufacture the order to be shipped at the end of a given month in the month it is to be shipped. However, since order quantities vary considerably from month to month, considerable overtime would be required in some months to produce the order, while the quantity to be produced in other months might not justify the cost of a setup. At other times it might be desirable to produce enough to satisfy the demand for several months on a single production run and then inventory the excess output until it is needed. This would obviously increase the cost associated with the resultant inventory. This expense would be attributable to such factors as interest on capital borrowed for financing the inventory buildup, storage, rental fees, insurance, and maintenance.

The production-scheduling objective of the Incredible Manufacturing Company is to devise a schedule that meets all its demand requirements on time. For simplicity, we will assume that a production run can be made in each month, but that no more than one production run will be scheduled in a month.

We begin the dynamic programming formulation of this problem by developing a mathematical model of the situation posed above. Let S_n be the number of units that must be shipped at the end of the month n, x_n be the number of units produced in month n, and let i_n be the inventory at the end of the month n (including any units produced in month n). Further, let D_n be the demand requirement for month n, and assume that each D_n is a nonnegative integer known at the beginning of the planning horizon. Once again, this deterministic demand assumption is based on the fact that the Incredible Manufacturing Company is a job shop that operates on the basis of firm customer orders.

The cost of making x_n units in a single production run in month n will be written $A_n + C_n(x_n)$, where A_n is the setup cost (fixed) for a production run, and C_n is the variable cost per unit of production, $C_n(0) = 0$. The inventory holding cost in month n will be a function of $i_{n-1} + x_n - D_n$ and will be written as $g_n(i_{n-1} + x_n - D_n)$, where the precise form of the g_n is not specified. We can then write the total cost function as:

$$f_n(x_n, i_n) = \alpha_n[A_n\delta_n + C_n(x_n) + g_n(i_{n-1} + x_n - D_n)] \tag{11-7}$$

where α_n = a discount factor used to discount costs over time
$\delta_n = 0$ if $x_n = 0$
$\delta_n = 1$ if $x_n > 0$

Using the above definitions and assumptions, the total cost (discounted) over the planning horizon for a given set of x_n can be written as:

$$Z = \sum_{n=1}^{N} f_n(x_n, i_n) \tag{11-8}$$

We now place several constraints on the policy variables x_n and i_n. We first restrict production to be integer-valued in all time periods.

$$x_n = 0, 1, 2, 3, \ldots \text{ for all } n \in N \tag{11-9}$$

We further stipulate that each period's demand must be entirely satisfied, that is, demand in each month must be met entirely in the month scheduled. This condition is satisfied by two constraints. The first is "material balance" equation that states that:

Ending inventory for period n ≡ Beginning inventory for period n
+ production in period n
− demand in period n

or, notationally,

$$i_n = i_{n-1} + x_n - D_n \qquad \text{for } n = 1, 2, \ldots, N \tag{11-10}$$

Expressing this relationship in terms of satisfying demand we obtain

$$i_{n-1} + x_n - i_n = D_n \qquad \text{for } n = 1, 2, \ldots, N \qquad (11\text{-}11)$$

where we assume that i_0 is a specified (fixed) level of initial inventory at the beginning of the planning horizon, and $i_N = 0$, that is, management desires a policy in which the inventory level is zero at the end of period N. The second constraint we must impose to ensure that Incredible meets its demand requirements on time is that each period's beginning inventory and production must always be large enough to make ending inventory a nonnegative quantity. Thus, we require that:

$$i_n = 0, 1, 2, 3, \ldots \text{ for } n = 1, 2, \ldots, N \qquad (11\text{-}12)$$

Note that we have also restricted all inventory levels to integer values, since demands and production levels were specified as being integer-valued earlier.

Observe that the material balance Equation (11–10) is linear. If the total cost function, Equation 11–7, were linear we could easily solve this problem using a network-flow approach. But, as can be seen from an examination of Equation 11–7, the total cost function is nonlinear because of the "fixed charge" associated with the setup cost. To account for such nonlinearities in the $f_n(x_n, i_n)$ we utilize dynamic programming.

We again initiate our computational procedure at the end of the time horizon, when there is only one period left in the planning horizon, and we work backward until there are N periods to go. We will find it useful to utilize an indexing system in which the subscript $n = 1$ denotes the *end* of the planning horizon and the subscript $n = N$ denotes the *beginning* of the planning horizon. We thus redefine

D_n = the demand requirement in the period when there are n more periods to go,

$f_n(x_n, i_n)$ = the cost of producing x_n items and having i_n items in ending inventory in the period when there are n more periods to go

To illustrate our subscripting convention consider a planning horizon consisting of the months January through June, that is, $N = 6$. With January as the beginning of the time horizon, D_6 is January's demand, the demand when there are 6 more months to go until the end of the horizon. Similarly, D_2 refers to May's demand, or the demand when there are 2 months to go until the end of the horizon.

We next define

$f_n^*(i)$ = minimum total cost when *entering* inventory is at level i with n more periods to go,

$x_n^*(i)$ = a production level yielding $f_n^*(i)$

We previously noted that management desires to have a zero inventory level at the end of the time horizon. We can thus write

$$f_0^*(i) = 0 \qquad \text{for } n = 0 \qquad (11\text{-}13)$$

We next consider $n = 1$. The entering inventory i for this period can be any integer amount between the limits of 0 and D_1. Regardless of its level, the production amount must be $D_1 - i$ so that the final period's demand is exactly met. It thus follows that

$$f_1(i) = f_1(x_1, i + x_1 - D_1) + f_0^*(i) \qquad \text{for } i = 0, 1, \ldots, D_1 \qquad (11\text{-}14)$$
$$= f_1(x_1, i + x_1 - D_1) + 0$$

Consider next $n = 2$, with entering inventory denoted by i, and the production level by x_n. Then, the associated cost is

$$f_2(i) = f_2(x_2, i + x_2 - D_2) + f_1^*(i + x_2 - D_2) \qquad (11\text{-}15)$$

assuming that we have acted optimally for period $n = 1$. Note that the quantity $i + x_2 - D_2$ is the inventory existing at the end of period $n = 2$. Now, the value of i can be any integer amount between 0 and $D_1 + D_2$. Given i, the integer value of x_2 must be at least as large as $D_2 - i$ in order to meet the period's demand requirement, but no larger than $D_1 + D_2 - i$ because ending inventory must be 0. An optimal value of x_2 is one that minimizes the above sum. We can thus determine a minimum cost policy for period $n = 2$ by:

$$f_2^*(i) = \underset{x_2}{\text{minimum}} \; [f_2(x_2, i + x_2 - D_2) + f_1^*(i + x_2 - D_2)] \qquad (11\text{-}16)$$

where $i = 0, 1, \ldots, D_1 + D_2$, and the minimization is made over nonnegative integer values of x_2 in the range $D_2 - i \le x_2 \le D_1 + D_2 - i$.

Given the general process outlined above, once $f_2(i)$ is computed, it can be used to find $f_3(i)$, and so on, until $f_N(i_N)$ is computed, where i_N is the initial inventory. The general recursion relationship can be written as:

$$f_n^*(i) = \underset{x_n}{\text{minimum}} \; [f_n(x_n, i + x_n - D_n) + f_{n-1}^*(i + x_n - D_n)]$$
$$\text{for } n = 1, 2, \ldots, N \qquad (11\text{-}17)$$

where $i = 0, 1, \ldots, D_1 + \cdots + D_n$ and the minimization is made over the nonnegative integer values of x_n in the range $D_n - i \le x_n \le D_1 + D_2 + \cdots + D_n - i$.

Note that the entering inventory i is the state variable, and that the only independent decision variable in the recursion given by Equation 11-17 is x_n, since the ending inventory is always given by $(i + x_n - D_n)$. Further observe that $f_0(i)$ and $f_1(i)$ were easily computed using Equations 11-13 and 11-17, respectively. It is then a straight-forward process to calculate, in turn, $f_2(0), f_2(1), \ldots, f_2(D_1)$; then $f_3(0), f_3(1), \ldots, f_3(D_1 + D_2)$, and to continue for successively increasing values of n to find $f_{N-1}(0), f_{N-1}(1), \ldots, f_{N-1}(D_1 + D_2 + \cdots + D_{N-1})$, and finally to $f_N(i_N)$.

The optimal schedule is then determined by observing the production level $x_N(i_o)$, which yielded the value for $f_N(i_N)$. This is an optimal decision at the start of the horizon. For the next period, the entering inventory level will be $i_0 + x_N(i) - D_n$, and we simply find the production level that yields a value for $(i_0 + x_N(i_N) - D_n)$. This process continues over the time horizon.

We will now consider a numerical example to help explain the dynamic programming process we have discussed above. To keep our example reasonably simple we will assume stationarity over time in the demand requirements and cost functions, and will specify the length of the time horizon at $N = 6$. Specifically, we will let

$$D_n = 5 \text{ (constant demand)} \qquad \text{for } n = 1, 2, \ldots, N \qquad (11\text{–}18)$$

Next we will assume that in the total cost function given by Equation 11–7:

$$A_n(\text{setup cost}) = \$11 \text{ per set up} \qquad (11\text{–}19)$$

$$C_n(\text{variable production cost}) = \$2 \text{ per unit} \qquad (11\text{–}20)$$

$$g_n(i_{n-1} + x_n - D_n)(\text{variable inventory holding cost}) = g_n(i_n)$$
$$= \$1 \text{ per unit, that is, the variable holding cost is \$1 times} \qquad (11\text{–}21)$$
the ending inventory

and that we will not discount the total cost function over time, that is, $\alpha_n = 1.00$. For future ease of computation we will split out the production cost and storage cost portions of this total cost function as follows. Let

$$PC = \text{total cost of production of } x_n \text{ units.}$$

$$SC = \text{total cost of storage of } i_n \text{ units.}$$

Then
$$PC_{x_n} = [A_n\delta_n + C_n(x_n)] = [\$11 \ \delta_n + \$2(x_n)] \qquad (11\text{–}22)$$

$$SC_{i_n} = g_n(i_n) = g_n(i_{n-1} + x_n - D_n) \qquad (11\text{–}23)$$
$$= g_n(i_n) = \$1 \ (i_n)$$

We now tabulate the values of PC_n and SC_n for various values of x_n and i_n, as follows.

x_n	PC_{x_n}	i_n	SC_{i_n}
0	0	0	0
1	13	1	1
2	15	2	2
3	17	3	3
4	19	4	4
5	21	5	5
6	23	6	6
7	25		

The problem will be further constrained by the limited production capacity and storage space of the Incredible Manufacturing Company. Specifically,

$$x_n = 0, 1, 2, \ldots, 7, \text{ for } n = 1, 2, \ldots, N \qquad \text{(Production constraint)} \qquad (11\text{–}24)$$

$$i_n = 0, 1, 2, \ldots, 6, \text{ for } n = 1, 2, \ldots, N \qquad \text{(Storage constraint)} \qquad (11\text{–}25)$$

Observe that setup costs are high in relation to production and inventory holding costs. Thus, an optimal schedule will attempt to avoid frequent production runs (which require frequent setups). However, since production x_n cannot exceed 7 and demand D_n is always 5, no schedule can increase inventory i_n by more than two each period. If initial inventory is zero, we must have at least two setups in the first two periods. However, the optimum schedule of setups and production over the entire time horizon cannot be ascertained readily, and this is the reason we must resort to dynamic programming.

We can write the general recursion relationship for the problem as:

$$f_n^*(i) = \underset{x_n}{\text{minimum}} [PC_{x_n} + SC_{i_n} + f_{n-1}^* (i + x_n - D_n)] = \underset{x_n}{\text{minimum}} [A_n \delta_n + C_n(x_n)$$
$$+ \$1(i + x_n - 5) + f_{n-1}^*(i + x_n - 5)] \qquad \text{for } n = 1, 2, \ldots, N \qquad (11\text{-}26)$$

where $i = 0, 1, 2, \ldots, 6$ and minimization is carried out over only nonnegative values of the decision variable, x_n, in the range:

$$5 + i \leq x_n \leq \text{minimum } (7, 11 - i) \qquad (11\text{-}27)$$

Note that in this recursion relationship i is the *entering* inventory level where there are n more periods to go.

Given the above numerical data, we can now proceed with our analysis. For $n = 1$, the one-stage problem, we obtain

$$x_1(i) = (D_1 - i) = (5 - i) \qquad \text{for } i = 0, 1, \ldots, 5 \qquad (11\text{-}28)$$

since management wishes to have a zero inventory level at the end of the time horizon, and

$$f_1(i) = f_1(x_1, i + x_1 - D_1) + f_0^*(i) \qquad \text{for } i = 0, 1, \ldots, 5$$
$$= f_1(D_1 - i, 0) + 0 \qquad (11\text{-}29)$$
$$= f_1(5 - i)$$

Note that the production constraint given by Equation 11-24 keeps x_n from exceeding 7, and the storage constraint given by Equation 11-25 keeps x_n from exceeding $11 - i$.

We now proceed to develop a table of the variables of interest for the one-stage problem ($n = 1$).

| i | \multicolumn{8}{c}{$PC_{x_1} + SC_{i_1} + f_0^*(i + x_1 - D_1)$} | $x_1^*(i)$ | $f_1^*(i)$ |
	0	1	2	3	4	5	6	7		
0						21			5	21
1					19				4	19
2				17					3	17
3			15						2	15
4		13							1	13
5	0								0	0
6									—	—

In the table above, note that we cannot enter the final stage $n = 1$ with an entering inventory of $i = 6$, because this would make it impossible to have a zero inventory at the end of the time horizon. Similarly, $x_1 \leq 5$, in order to have a zero inventory at the end of the time horizon. Indeed, there is one, and only one production level x_n possible for each entering inventory level i. The entries in the table, the $f_1(i)$ values, were computed as follows.

$$f_1(0) = PC_{x_1=5} + SC_{i_1=0} + f_0(i = 0)$$
$$= 21 + 0 + 0 \qquad\qquad (11\text{-}30)$$
$$f_1(1) = PC_{x_1=4} + SC_{i_1=0} + f_0(i = 1)$$
$$= 19 + 0 + 0$$

and so forth. Observe that the storage cost term is always zero, because $i + x_1 - D_1 = 0$, that is, the ending inventory for $n = 1$ must be zero in all instances.

Proceeding similarly with the two-stage problem we obtain the following table ($n = 2$).

i \ x_2	0	1	2	3	4	5	6	7	$x_2^*(i)$	$f_2^*(i)$
				$PC_{x_2} + SC_{i_2} + f^*_1(i + x_2 - D_2)$						
0						21+0+21	23+1+19	25+2+17	5	42
1					19+0+21	21+1+19	23+2+17	25+3+15	4	40
2				17+0+21	19+1+19	21+2+17	23+3+15	25+4+13	3	38
3			15+0+21	17+1+19	19+2+17	21+3+15	23+4+13	25+5+0	7	30
4		13+0+21	15+1+19	17+2+17	19+3+15	21+4+13	23+5+0		6	28
5	0+0+21	13+1+19	15+2+17	17+3+15	19+4+13	21+5+0			0	21
6	0+1+19	13+2+17	15+3+15	17+4+13	19+5+0				0	20

Observe the detailed construction of this table. There are seven rows, one for each feasible value of the entering inventory. Similarly, there are eight columns, one for each feasible value of production, x_n. Note that several of the cells of the table are blanked out. For example, if $i = 0$, $x_n \geq 5$ in order for demand $D_2 = 5$ to be met. If $i = 4$, $x_n \leq 6$ in order for the ending inventory to be zero at the end of the time horizon.

The first entry in each of the occupied cells is the value of the production cost, PC_{x_n}, obtained from Equation 11-22. The second entry in each of the occupied cells is the value of the inventory holding cost, computed as the per-unit storage cost, \$1, times the number of units in ending inventory, as indicated by Equation 11-23. Recall that from the general recursive relationship the ending inventory for each period is computed as ($i + x_n - 5$). For example, if $i = 3$, and $x_n = 2$, then the ending inventory is $3 + 2 - 5 = 0$ units and the corresponding inventory holding cost is \$1 per unit $\times$ 0 units = \$0. If $i = 4$ and $x_n = 2$, then the ending inventory is $4 + 2 - 5 = 1$ unit, and the corresponding inventory-holding cost is \$1 per unit $\times$ 1 unit = \$1. The final term in each of the occupied cells is the value of $f^*_1(i + x_n - 5)$, which was computed for the previous table.

Given a level i, $f_2^*(i)$ is the minimum sum in the body of the table for that row, and $x_2^*(i)$ is the corresponding production level. Thus, if $i = 3$, with $n = 2$ periods to go, the best production level is $x_2^* = 7$, which yields a minimum cost of \$30 for these two periods.

We now consider the three-stage problem for which we obtain the following table ($n = 3$).

i \ x_3	0	1	2	3	4	5	6	7	$x_3^*(i)$	$f_3^*(i)$
					$PC_{x_3} + SC_{i_3} + f_2^*(i + x_3 - D_3)$					
0						21+0+42	23+1+40	25+2+38	5	63
1					19+0+42	21+1+40	23+2+38	25+3+30	7	58
2				17+0+42	19+1+40	21+2+38	23+3+30	25+4+28	6	56
3			15+0+42	17+1+40	19+2+38	21+3+30	23+4+28	25+5+21	7	51
4		13+0+42	15+1+40	17+2+38	19+3+30	21+4+28	23+5+21	25+6+20	6	49
5	0+0+42	13+1+40	15+2+38	17+3+30	19+4+28	21+5+21	23+6+20		0	42
6	0+1+40	13+2+38	15+3+30	17+4+28	19+5+21	21+6+20			0	41

In the above table, the first entry in each occupied cell is again the value of the production cost PC_{x_n} obtained from Equation 11–22. The second entry is again the inventory holding cost, computed in exactly the same fashion as for the previous table using Equation 11–23. The final entry is $f_2^*(i + x_n - 5)$ obtained directly from the previous table.

Note that, on the left-hand side of this table, several cells are again blanked out. This is necessary for the same reason as for the previous table. For example, if $i = 1$, then $x_3 \geq 4$ in order to satisfy $D_3 = 5$. Observe further, however, that three cells are now blanked out on the right-hand side of this table as opposed to one cell in the previous table. These cells must be blanked out because there are no values of $f_2(i + x_3 - 5)$ applicable from the previous table for these cells. Thus, we cannot compute the total cost for cell $i = 5$, $x_3 = 7$, because $f_2(5 + 7 - 5) = f_2(7)$ does not exist, that is, it was not possible to have an entering inventory of $i = 7$ in stage $n = 2$. Indeed it is not possible to have $i = 7$ in any stage of the problem.

We now present the tables for $n = 4$, 5, and 6, respectively. Students should

Four-stage problem ($n = 4$):

i \ x_4	0	1	2	3	4	5	6	7	$x_4^*(i)$	$f_4^*(i)$
					$PC_{x_4} + SC_{i_4} + f_3^*(i + x_4 - D_4)$					
0						21+0+63	23+1+58	25+2+56	6	82
1					19+0+63	21+1+58	23+2+56	25+3+51	7	79
2				17+0+63	19+1+58	21+2+56	23+3+51	25+4+49	6	77
3			15+0+63	17+1+58	19+2+56	21+3+51	23+4+49	25+5+42	7	72
4		13+0+63	15+1+58	17+2+56	19+3+51	21+4+49	23+5+42	25+6+41	6	70
5	0+0+63	13+1+58	15+2+56	17+3+51	19+4+49	21+5+42	23+6+41		0	63
6	0+1+58	13+2+56	15+3+51	17+4+49	19+5+42	21+6+41			0	59

Five-stage problem ($n = 5$):

i \ x_5	0	1	2	3	4	5	6	7	$x_5^*(i)$	$f_5^*(i)$
					$PC_{x_5} + SC_{i_5} + f_4^*(i + x_5 - D_5)$					
0						21+0+82	23+1+79	25+2+77	5 or 6	103
1					19+0+82	21+1+79	23+2+77	25+3+72	7	100
2				17+0+82	19+1+79	21+2+77	23+3+72	25+4+70	6	98
3			15+0+82	17+1+79	19+2+77	21+3+72	23+4+70	25+5+63	7	93
4		13+0+82	15+1+79	17+2+77	19+3+72	21+4+70	23+5+63	25+6+59	7	90
5	0+0+82	13+1+79	15+2+77	17+3+72	19+4+70	21+5+63	23+6+59		0	82
6	0+1+79	13+2+77	15+3+72	17+4+70	19+5+63	21+6+59			0	80

test their understanding of the recursive calculations required in this dynamic programming problem by verifying the entries in these tables.

Six-stage problem ($n = 6$):

i \ x_6	0	1	2	3	4	5	6	7	$x_6^*(i)$	$f_6^*(i)$
					$PC_{x_6} + SC_{i_6} + f_5^*(i + x_6 - D_6)$					
0						21+0+103	23+1+100	25+2+98	5 or 6	124
1					19+0+103	21+1+100	23+2+98	25+3+93	7	121
2				17+0+103	19+1+100	21+2+98	23+3+93	25+4+90	6 or 7	119
3			15+0+103	17+1+100	19+2+98	21+3+93	23+4+90	25+5+82	7	112
4		13+0+103	15+1+100	17+2+98	19+3+93	21+4+90	23+5+82	25+6+80	6	110
5	0+0+103	13+1+100	15+2+98	17+3+93	19+4+90	21+5+82	23+6+80		0	103
6	0+1+100	13+2+98	15+3+93	17+4+90	19+5+82	21+6+80			0	102

Using the tables we have constructed for each of the stages we can now construct the following summary table.

TABLE 11.1 Summary Table—Production-Scheduling Problem

Entering Inventory i	$n = 1$		$n = 2$		$n = 3$		$n = 4$		$n = 5$		$n = 6$	
	$x_1^*(i)$	$f_1^*(i)$	$x_2^*(i)$	$f_2^*(i)$	$x_3^*(i)$	$f_3^*(i)$	$x_4^*(i)$	$f_4^*(i)$	$x_5^*(i)$	$f_5^*(i)$	$x_6^*(i)$	$f_6^*(i)$
0	5	21	5	42	5	63	6	82	5 or 6	103	5 or 6	124
1	4	19	4	40	7	58	7	79	7	100	7	121
2	3	17	3	38	6	56	6	77	6	98	6 or 7	119
3	2	15	7	30	7	51	7	72	7	93	7	112
4	1	13	6	28	6	49	6	70	7	90	6	110
5	0	0	0	21	0	42	0	63	0	82	0	103
6			0	20	0	41	0	59	0	80	0	102

Let us now suppose that our planning horizon is from $N = 1$ to $N = 6$ months in length, and that the first month is January. We are interested in determining the optimal production sequences, as we allow the planning horizon to increase. We shall compute results for $N = 1, 2, 3, 4, 5$, and 6 under the assumption that the entering inventory level i_0 at the beginning of January is 0. The results derived from the data presented in Table 11.1 are shown below in Table 11.2.

TABLE 11.2 Optimal Production Schedules for Various Plannning Horizons

Planning Horizon N	Jan.	Feb.	Mar.	April	May	June	Cost	Cost per Month
1	5						21	21
2	5	5					42	21
3	5	5	5				63	21
4	6	7	7	0			82	$20\frac{1}{2}$
5	5	6	7	7	0		103	$20\frac{3}{5}$
	6	7	7	0	5		103	$20\frac{3}{5}$
6	5	5	6	7	7	0	124	$20\frac{2}{3}$
	5	6	7	7	0	5	124	$20\frac{2}{3}$
	6	7	7	0	5	5	124	$20\frac{2}{3}$

Assume for the moment that we are interested only in a 1-month planning horizon, that is, $N = 1$. Remember that our entering inventory level for January is always zero. Thus, the optimal production quantity for January, at which time there is an entering inventory level $i = 0$, and $n = 1$ month to go in the planning horizon, is $x_1^*(0) = 5$. This value is found in the first row ($i = 0$) of Table 11.1 under $n = 1$. The optimal (minimum) cost for this 1-month production schedule is $f_1^*(0) =$ \$21, as seen in Table 11.1.

Assume next that we are interested in a 2-month planning horizon, that is, $N = 2$. For this situation, the optimal production quantity for January, at which time there is an entering inventory level $i = 0$, and $n = 2$ months to go in the planning horizon, is $x_2^*(0) = 5$. This value is found in the first row ($i = 0$) of Table 11.1 under $n = 2$. The inventory entering February is then $i + x_2^*(0) - D_2 = 0 + 5 - 5 = 0$. Consequently, the optimal production quantity for February, at which time there is an entering inventory level $i = 0$, and $n = 1$ month to go in the planning horizon, is $x_1^*(0) = 5$. This value is found in the first row ($i = 0$) of Table 11.1 under $n = 1$. The optimal (minimum) cost for this 2-month production schedule is $f_2^*(0) =$ \$42, as seen in Table 11.1.

Now assume that we are interested in optimally scheduling production for the entire 6-month planning horizon, that is, $N = 6$. For this situation, the optimal production quantity for January, at which time there is an entering inventory level $i = 0$ and $n = 6$ months to go in the planning horizon, is $x_6^*(0) = 5$ or 6. This value is found in the first row ($i = 0$) of Table 11.1 under $n = 6$. The inventory entering February is then either $i + [x_6^*(0) = 5] - D_6 = 0 + 5 - 5 = 0$ or $i + [x_6^*(0) = 6] - D_6 = 0 + 6 - 5 = 1$. Consequently, the optimal production quantities for February, at which time there is an entering inventory of 0 or 1 and $n = 5$ months to go in the planning horizon, is $x_5^*(0) = 5$ or 6 and $x_5^*(1) = 7$. These values are found in the first row ($i = 0$) under $n = 5$ and in the second row ($i = 1$) under $n = 5$ of Table 11.1. The entering inventory for March is then either $i + [x_5^*(0) = 5] - D_5 = 0 + 5 - 5 = 0$, $i + [x_5^*(0) = 6] - D_5 = 0 + 6 - 5 = 1$, or $i + [x_5^*(1) = 7] - D_5 = 1 + 7 - 5 = 3$. Consequently, the optimal production quantities for March, at which time there is an entering inventory of 0, 1, or 3 and $n = 4$ months to go in the planning horizon, is $x_4^*(0) = 6$, $x_4^*(1) = 7$ and $x_4^*(3) = 7$. These values are found in the first row ($i = 0$) under $n = 4$, in the second row ($i = 1$), and in the fourth row ($i = 3$) under $n = 4$ of Table 11.1. The entering inventory for April is then either $i + [x_4^*(0) = 6] - D_4 = 0 + 6 - 5 = 1$, $i + [x_4^*(1) = 7] - D_4 = 1 + 7 - 5 = 3$, or $i + [x_4^*(3) = 7] - D_4 = 3 + 7 - 5 = 5$. Consequently, the optimal production quantities for April, at which time there is an entering inventory of 1, 3, and 5 and $n = 3$ months to go in the planning horizon, is $x_3^*(1) = 7$, $x_3^*(3) = 7$, and $x_3^*(5) = 0$. These values are found in the second row ($i = 1$) under $n = 3$ in the fourth row ($i = 3$) under $n = 3$, and in the sixth row ($i = 5$) under $n = 3$ of Table 11.1. The entering inventory for May is then either $i + [x_3^*(1) = 7] - D_3 = 1 + 7 - 5 = 3$, $i + [x_3^*(3) = 7] - D_3 = 3 + 7 - 5 = 5$, or $i + [x_3^*(5) = 0] - D_3 = 5 + 0 - 5 = 0$. Consequently, the optimal production quantities for May, at which time there is an entering inventory of 3, 5, or 0, and $n = 2$ months to go in the planning horizon is $x_2^*(3) = 7$, $x_2^*(5) = 0$, or $x_2^*(0) = 5$. These values are found in the fourth row ($i = 3$) under $n = 2$, in the sixth row under $n = 2$, and in the first row ($i = 0$) under $n = 2$ of Table 11.1. The entering inventory for June is then either $i + [x_2^*(3) = 7] - D_2 = 3 + 7 - 5 = 5$, $i + [x_2^*(5) = 0] - D_2 = 5 + 0 - 5 = 0$, or $i + [x_2^*(0) = 5] - D_2 = 0 + 5 - 5 = 0$. Consequently, the optimal production quantities for June, at which time there is an entering inventory 5, 0, or 0, and $n = 1$ month to go in the planning horizon, is $x_1^*(5) = 0$, $x_1^*(0) = 5$, or $x_1^*(0) = 5$. These values are found in the first row ($i = 0$) under $n = 1$, in the sixth row ($i = 5$) under $n = 1$, and in the first row ($i = 0$) under $n = 1$, of Table 11.1. Since we have reached the end of our planning horizon our solution is complete.

Our solution for the 6-month planning horizon indicates that there are three alternative optimal production schedules that can be utilized. Regardless of which plan is chosen we will produce 30 units over the 6-month planning horizon at a total cost of $124. This $124 is the value of $f_6^*(0)$, the optimal value in the six-stage table for an entering inventory of $i = 0$. An inventory and cost summary for the 6-month planning horizon is shown in Table 11.3.

TABLE 11.3 Inventory and Cost Summary—6-Month Planning Horizon

Month	Entering Inventory	Optimal Production	Ending Inventory	Production Cost	Storage Cost	Monthly Cost	Cumulative Cost
January	0	5	0	21	0	21	21
	0	6	1	23	1	24	24
February	0	5	0	21	0	21	42
	0	6	1	23	1	24	45
	1	7	3	25	3	28	52
March	0	6	1	23	1	24	66
	1	7	3	25	3	28	73
	3	7	5	25	5	30	82
April	1	7	3	25	3	28	94
	3	7	5	25	5	30	103
	5	0	0	0	0	0	82
May	3	7	5	25	5	30	124
	5	0	0	0	0	0	103
	0	5	0	21	0	21	103
June	5	0	0	0	0	0	124
	0	5	0	21	0	21	124
	0	5	0	21	0	21	124

11.3.3 Dynamic Programming with a Multiplicative Recursion Relationship

The Aviresearch Company produces a navigational guidance system for commercial airliners. The navigational guidance system consists of three major components, each of which must function properly in order for the entire system to operate properly. As in most commercial airliner systems, the reliability of the navigational guidance system can be improved by installing parallel units for each of the three system components. If this is done, the probability that the individual components will function if they have one, two, or three parallel units is as follows.

Number of Parallel Units	Component			Probability of Navigational System Functioning Properly
	Probability of Functioning Properly			
	1	*2*	*3*	
1	0.75	0.80	0.60	0.75 × 0.80 × 0.60 = 0.36
2	0.85	0.88	0.75	0.85 × 0.88 × 0.75 = 0.561
3	0.95	0.96	0.85	0.95 × 0.96 × 0.85 = 0.775

As seen in this table the probability that the navigational system will function properly is the product of the probabilities associated with the individual components functioning perfectly.

Each of the individual components of the navigational guidance system is costly and the Aviresearch Company would like to avoid installing any more parallel units than are necessary. The costs associated with installing one, two, or three parallel units, for each of the three components, is as follows.

Number of Parallel Units	Component		
	Cost of Installation		
	1	*2*	*3*
1	1000	2000	2500
2	1500	3100	3500
3	2000	3500	3750

The Aviresearch Company would like its navigational guidance system to cost not more than $7500. It is trying to use dynamic programming to determine the number of parallel units of each of three components that should be installed in order to maximize the probability that the navigational guidance system will function properly.

In this dynamic programming problem the stages are the three components for which we must determine the number of parallel units to be installed. Thus, the decision variables x_n ($n = 1, 2, 3$) are the number of parallel units that are to be installed at stage n. The cost of installing x_n parallel units at stage n will be denoted as $c_n(x_n)$, and the probability that the component will function properly if it has x_n parallel units will be denoted as $p_n(x_n)$. Finally, we will denote as s the dollars remaining to be spent as a function of the decision stage and the number of units being installed in parallel.

Now, let $f_n(s, x_n)$ be the maximum total probability that the navigational system will function properly for the last n components (stages), given that we are in state s and select x_n as the number of parallel units to be installed. As usual, we begin our dynamic programming solution in a backward manner, that is, we begin by considering only component 3. For this one-stage problem we have the entire $7500 to spend, and can install $x_1 = 0, 1, 2,$ or 3 parallel units of component 3. The values of s for this one-stage problem will be the ranges in dollars that s can assume, as $x_1 = 0, 1, 2$, or 3 parallel units of component three are installed. The possible interactions result in the following one-stage table ($n = 1$).

s \ x_1	$f_1(s,x_1) = p_1(x_1)$: 0	1	2	3	$f_1^*(s)$	x_1^*
$0 \le s \le 2499$	0.00	—	—	—	0.00	0
$2500 \le s \le 3499$	—	0.60	—	—	0.60	1
$3500 \le s \le 3749$	—	—	0.75	—	0.75	2
$3750 \le s \le 7500$	—	—	—	0.85	0.85	3

Each value of $f_1(s,x_1)$ in this one-stage table is simply the probability, $p_1(x_1)$, associated with installing $x_1 = 0, 1, 2$, or 3 parallel units of component 3. Each value of $f_1^*(s)$ is identical to the corresponding value of $f_1(s,x_1)$ since there is only one value for each (s,x_1) combination. The value of x_1^* is the single value of x_1 that produces the optimal (maximum) value of the objective function, $f_1^*(s)$.

The next step in this dynamic programming problem involves moving backward one more stage, that is, considering the decision that must be made when there are $n = 2$ more stages to go, or when we must consider installing parallel units for both component 2 and component 3. The computational process for this two-stage problem becomes slightly more complicated. First, we must establish a recursion relationship for the two-stage problem that links to the optimal decision made for the one-stage problem. Remember that we are seeking to maximize the probability that the navigational system will function properly. This means that at any stage in the decision process we must seek to maximize the joint probability of the respective components functioning over all the components in the system at that stage in the decision process. However, this must be accomplished with respect to a cost limitation, which in turn, affects the number of parallel units of a component that can be installed in attempting to increase the probability of that component functioning properly. Under these conditions the recursion relationship for the two-stage problem becomes $f_2(s,x_2) = p_2(x_2) \cdot f_1^*[s - c_n(x_n)]$. Note that this recursion relationship is in a multiplicative form rather than in the additive form used in the previous examples. Although this recursion relationship may appear not to be deterministic because it involves probabilities, it is still a deterministic relationship because the state at the next stage is completely determined by the state and policy decision at the current stage.

For the two-stage problem we consider the possibility of installing $x_2 = 0, 1, 2$, or 3 parallel units of component 2. The values of s for this two-stage problem will be the ranges in dollars that s can assume, as $x_2 = 0, 1, 2$, or 3 parallel units of component 2 are installed. These ranges must be specified in terms of the dollars remaining to be spent as a function of this decision stage and the number of units being installed in parallel. The possible interactions result in the following two-stage table ($n = 2$).

s \ x_2	$f_2(s,x_2) = p_2(x_2) \cdot f_1^*[s - c_2(x_2)]$				$f_2^*(s)$	x_2
	0	**1**	**2**	**3**		
$0 \le s \le 4499$	—	0	—	—	0	0
$4500 \le s \le 5499$	0	0.48	0	—	0.48	1
$5500 \le s \le 5599$	0	0.60	0	0	0.60	1
$5600 \le s \le 5749$	0	0.60	0.528	0	0.60	1
$5750 \le s \le 5999$	0	0.68	0.528	0	0.68	1
$6000 \le s \le 6599$	0	0.68	0.528	0.576	0.68	1
$6600 \le s \le 6849$	0	0.68	0.660	0.576	0.68	1
$6850 \le s \le 6999$	0	0.68	0.748	0.576	0.748	2
$7000 \le s \le 7249$	0	0.68	0.748	0.720	0.748	2
$7250 \le s \le 7500$	0	0.68	0.748	0.816	0.816	3

Each value of $f_2(s,x_2)$ in this two-stage table is the probability, $p_2(x_2)$, associated with installing $x_2 = 0$, 1, 2, or 3 parallel units of component two times the corresponding optimal value of $f_1^*[s - c_2(x_2)]$. The optimal value of $f_1^*[s - c_2(x_2)]$ is obtained from the one-stage problem, for the appropriate values. For example, consider the computation for $x_2 = 2$, for the range ($6,850 \le s \le 6,999$). For this set of conditions:

$$
\begin{aligned}
f_2(s,x_2) &= p_2(x_2) \cdot f_1^*[s - c_2(x_2)] \\
&= p_2(x_2 = 2) \cdot f_1^*[6,999 - c_2(x_2 = 2)] \\
&= 0.88 \cdot f_1^*[6,999 - 3,100] \qquad\qquad (11\text{–}31) \\
&= 0.88 \cdot f_1^*[3,899] \\
&= 0.88 \cdot 0.85 \\
&= 0.748
\end{aligned}
$$

The other values of $f_2(s,x_2)$ in this table are computed in a similar manner. The values $f_2^*(s)$ are the optimal value of the $f_2(s,x_2)$. The value of x_2^* is the single value of x_2 that produces the optimal (maximum) value of the objective function, $f_2^*(s)$.

Proceeding to the next step, we consider the first component, or the three-stage problem. For the three-stage problem we consider the probability of installing $x_3 = 0$, 1, 2, or 3 parallel units of component 1. The value of s for this three-stage problem is the entire $7500 that would be available for spending at this decision stage, that is, we are at the last decision stage and would seek to spend the entire $7500. The possible interactions results in the following three-stage table ($n = 3$).

s \ x_3	$f_3(s,x_3) = p_3(x_3) \cdot f_2^*[s - c_3(x_3)]$				$f_3^*(s)$	x_3^*
	0	**1**	**2**	**3**		
7500	0	0.511	0.578	0.570	0.578	2

Having obtained this three-stage table our dynamic programming solution is complete. The three-stage table indicates that the optimal configuration of parallel units for the three components will result in an overall probability of 0.578 of the navigational system functioning properly. The three-stage table also indicates that $x_3^* = 2$ parallel units for component one should be installed. This will result in a cost of \$1500. Entering the two-stage table with $s = \$7500 - \$1500 = \$6000$, we observe that $x_2^* = 1$ unit for component 2 should be installed. This will result in a cost of \$2000. Next, entering the one-stage table with $s = \$7500 - \$1500 - \$2000 = \$4000$, we observe that $x_1^* = 3$ parallel units for component 3 should be installed. This will result in a cost of \$3750, with the overall cost for the entire system being \$7250, which is less than the \$7500 available for expenditure.

11.4 DYNAMIC PROGRAMMING UNDER UNCERTAINTY

Each of the previously discussed examples has involved deterministic dynamic programming situations. In such situations the state at the next stage in the decision process is completely determined by the state and policy decision that is present in the current stage. For example, in our solution of the shortest-route problem by means of dynamic programming, each state in the decision process involved movement along some branch to a specific node, from a node specified by the particular stage of the decision process. Movement from stage to stage in the decision process by means of various states was always done in terms of known (deterministic) distances.

In **probabilistic dynamic programming**, or dynamic programming under uncertainty, the state at the next stage in the decision process is not completely determined by the state-and-policy decision at the current stage of the decision process. Rather, there is a probability distribution that describes what the next state will be, with this probability distribution being determined by the state and policy decision at the current stage of the decision process.

We will now consider an example that illustrates the use of dynamic programming under uncertainty.

11.4.1 Probabilistic Lot Scheduling by Dynamic Programming

The Armadillo Candle Shop has received an order for a lot of 100 of its ''Rainbow Spectacular'' candles. Its candle-making process involves a setup cost of \$200 and a variable production cost of \$100 per lot of 100. Unfortunately, the customer is very particular and will not accept delivery of the lot of 100 candles if any of the candles do not meet the specified color, size, shape, etc. The manager of the Armadillo Candle Shop estimates that there is only a 60-percent chance of producing a perfect lot of candles in any production run.

If a lot of candles is judged to be defective by the customer it is completely worthless and must be scrapped. In this instance, the entire production process must be set up again at an additional cost of \$200.

The manager of the Armadillo Candle Shop contemplates making no more than two production runs because of other orders. If she is not able to obtain one perfect lot of 100 candles after two production runs the cost associated with lost sales and penalties will be \$1000. Her objective is to determine a policy that specifies the number of lot(s) to be produced in the production run(s) in order to minimize the total expected cost for the candle-making process.

In this probabilistic dynamic programming problem the stages are the two production runs that are possible. The decision variables $x_n(n = 1, 2)$ are the number of production lots of 100 candles that are produced at stage n. The number of acceptable lots (of size 100) that need to be produced at one of the two stages of the production process will be the state of the system. Thus, as the candle-making process begins, the state of the system must be $s = 1$ (one acceptable lot of 100 candles is required). If an acceptable lot is subsequently obtained the state of the system becomes $s = 0$, and no further production costs are incurred.

Now, let $f_n(s,x_n)$ be the minimum total expected cost for the last n stages, given that we are in state s, and select x_n as the number of lots of candles to be produced. We proceed, as usual, in a backward manner by considering first the second (last) stage of the decision process. For this one-stage problem the manufacturing cost will be $(K + \$100x_n)$ where:

$$K = \begin{cases} 0, & \text{if } x_n = 0 \\ \$200, & \text{if } x_n > 0 \end{cases} \tag{11-32}$$

This contribution to the manufacturing cost $(K + \$100x_n)$ will remain the same at both stages in the production process. Thus, if one acceptable lot is required for this stage of the manufacturing process the expression for the minimum total expected cost will be

$$f_n(1,x_n) = \underbrace{K + \$100x_n}_{\substack{\text{Manfacturing} \\ \text{cost for cur-} \\ \text{rent stage.}}} + \underbrace{(0.40)^{x_n} \cdot f^*_{n-1}(1)}_{\substack{\text{Expected penalty} \\ \text{cost for unaccept-} \\ \text{able lot(s) from} \\ \text{previous manufac-} \\ \text{turing stage.}}} + \underbrace{[1 - (0.40)^{x_n}]f^*_{n-1}(0)}_{\substack{\text{Expected penalty cost for} \\ \text{acceptable lot(s) from} \\ \text{previous manufacturing} \\ \text{stage.}}} \tag{11-33}$$

Reducing this expression we obtain

$$f_n(s,x_n) = K + \$100x_n + (0.40)^{x_n} \cdot f^*_{n-1}(1) \tag{11-34}$$

since $f^*_0(0) = 0$. Note also that $f^*_0(1) = \$1000$, the cost that is incurred at the end of the production process if no acceptable lots (of size 100) have been obtained. Using this relationship we can now construct the following one-stage table ($n = 1$).

x_1	$f_1(I,x_1) = K + 100x_1 + (0.40)^{x_1} \cdot (1000)$						
s	*0*	*1*	*2*	*3*	*4*	$f^*_1(s)$	x^*_1
0	0	—	—	—	—	0	0
1	1000	700	560	564	626	560	2

The next step in the dynamic programming solution to this problem involves moving backward one more stage, that is, considering the decision when there are two more stages to go. Herein, we employ a recursion relationship of the form:

$$f_2(s,s_2) = \min \ \{K + \$100x_2 + (0.40)^{x_2}f^*_{2-1}(1)\} \qquad x_2 = 0, 1, \ldots \tag{11-35}$$

since $f_{2-1}^*(0) = 0$. Using this recursion relationship the following two-stage table $(n = 2)$ can be constructed.

s \ x_2	$f_2(1,x_2) = K + \$100x_2 + (0.40)^{x_2} f_1^*(s)$						$f_2^*(s)$	x_2^*
	0	**1**	**2**	**3**	**4**	**5**		
1	560	524	490	536	614	705	490	2

We have now proceeded backward to the beginning of the production-scheduling process and have determined the optimal (minimum total expected cost) solution. The two-stage table indicates that the optimal solution will result in a minimum total expected cost of $490. This will be achieved by producing two lots of 100 candles on the first production run. Then, if none of these lots of candles is acceptable, two lots of candles should be produced on the second production run.

11.5 INFINITE-STATE DYNAMIC PROGRAMMING

One of the ways in which dynamic programming problems are characterized is in terms of the number of states associated with a particular stage of the decision process. The examples and illustrations considered previously in this chapter have been concerned with situations in which there were a finite number of states associated with the stages in the decision process. However, there are a number of practical situations in which the state variable s can be a continuous variable and thus take on an infinite number of values over a certain interval. We will next consider an example of such an **infinite-state dynamic programming problem.**

11.5.1 An Infinite-State Work-Force Employment Problem

The workload for the Do-Right Job Shop is very erratic, and subject to considerable seasonal variability. The manager of the Do-Right Job Shop, Mr. Edwards, has made the following estimates for his work-force requirements during the four quarters of the year, for the foreseeable future.

Quarter	Work-Force Requirements
Spring	275
Summer	225
Autumn	250
Winter	200

Mr. Edwards finds it very difficult to find machine operators to hire, and also finds that they are costly to train. Thus, he is very reluctant to lay off workers during his slack seasons. Furthermore, he is strongly opposed to overtime work on a regular basis. He has estimated that his hiring and training costs are such that the total cost of changing the level of employment from one season to the next is

$250 times the square of the difference in employment levels. He will, under no circumstances, allow his seasonal employment to fall below the respective levels shown above.

However, Mr. Edwards does not want to maintain his peak-season payroll when it is not required. Because he is running a job shop that manufactures to customer orders, however, he cannot build up inventories during slack seasons. He has thus estimated that his excess work-force cost is $1500 per person per season.

At the beginning of each season, a cost is incurred for any change in the employment level from the previous period and for any idleness from the previous period. We will assume that fractional levels of employment are possible, since a few employees are willing to work on a part-time basis. The cost data shown above apply proportionately to these part-time employees. We will further assume that there are no operators employed at the beginning of the first period, and that no charges will be made for the fourth period. We seek to determine the levels of employment for each of the seasons in order to minimize total cost.

On the basis of the work-force requirement data provided above, it is clear that employment should never go above the peak season (spring) requirement of 275 operators. Thus, spring employment will always be 275 operators, and our problem simplifies to the determination of the employment levels for the remaining three seasons. Each of these seasons becomes one stage in a dynamic programming problem formualtion. This problem actually has an indefinite number of stages, since we indicated earlier that our estimates of work-force requirements are applicable to the foreseeable future. However, each year begins an identical work-force requirement cycle. Since spring employment is always set at 275 operators, it is possible to consider only one cycle of four seasons ending with the spring season.

The decision variables for this problem $x_n(n = 1,2,3,4)$, are the employment levels at the nth stage from the end of the cycle. The spring season is the last stage in the cycle since we already know the optimal value of the decision variable for the last stage. For all other stages, the solution for the optimal employment level must consider its effect on costs in the following season. Thus, x_1, x_2, x_3, and x_4 are the employment levels for spring, winter, autumn, and summer, respectively.

The total cost for any stage depends only on the current decision x_n and the employment level in the previous season. The objective function with n stages to go, $f_n(s,x_n)$, must be the minimal total cost over the remaining stages, given that the stage is s and the initial decision is x_n. Thus, $f_n^*(s)$ is the minimum value of $f_n(s,x_n)$ over all permissible values of x_n, and x_n^* is the minimizing value of x_n.

The problem presents an interesting contrast to the previous problems. In the present problem, the number of possible states and the number of possible values of the decision variables are now infinite rather than finite. However, we can deal with the infinite state structure of our problem by expressing the total cost at any stage as a function of employment in a previous stage. Thus, the preceding employment level is all the information that is required in the current stage to determine an optimal policy for the future. We can then employ calculus to determine the optimal value of the decision variable as a function of the state of the system. At each stage of the process we seek to minimize

$$f_n(s,x_n) = 250(x_n - s)^2 + 1500(x_n - r_n) + f_{n-1}^*(x_n) \qquad (11-36)$$

where r_n is the minimum work-force requirement at the nth stage from the end.

For the one-stage problem, it is already known that $x_1^* = 275 = r_1$. We can therefore table the results for the following one-stage problem ($n = 1$).

s	$f_1^*(s)$	x_1^*
≤ 275	$250(2750 - s)^2$	275

Note that the cost of the optimal policy after the last stage of the current cycle, $f_0^*(x_0)$, is a fixed constant, since spring employment is always known; therefore, it can be omitted from further consideration. Additionally, note that $s \leq 275$, and therefore, we need not consider the second term in the recursion, since we cannot "overemploy" in the last stage of the cycle.

The two-stage problem involves finding the minimizing value of x_2 in the relationship:

$$
\begin{aligned}
f_2^*(s) &= \min f_2(s, x_2) \\
&= \min_{x_2 \geq r_2} \{250(x_2 - s)^2 + 1500(x_2 - r_2) + f_1^*(x_2)\} \qquad (11\text{-}37) \\
&= \min_{x_2 \geq 200} \{250(x_2 - s)^2 + 1500(x_2 - 200) + 250(275 - x_2)^2\}
\end{aligned}
$$

The value of x_2 that minimizes $f_2(s, x_2)$ over all values of x_2 is found by solving the equation derived by setting the function's partial derivative to zero, as follows.

$$
\frac{\partial}{\partial x_2} f_2(s, x_2) = 0 = 500(x_2 - s) + 1500 - 500(275 - x_2) \qquad (11\text{-}38)
$$

Observe that the second partial derivative of this function with respect to x_2 is

$$
\frac{\partial^2}{\partial x_2^2} f_2(s, x_2) = 1000 \qquad (11\text{-}39)
$$

and is positive for all values of x_2. We thus solve

$$
\begin{aligned}
\frac{\partial}{\partial x_2^2} f_2(s, x_2) = 0 &= 1000 x_2 + 500 s - 136{,}000 \\
&= 500(2x_2 - s - 272)
\end{aligned}
$$

and $\qquad x_2 = \dfrac{s + 272}{2}$

is the minimizing value.

We need to consider the minimization of $f_2(s, x_2)$ only over values of $x_2 \geq 200$. When $s \geq 128$, x_2 would be greater than 200, as can be seen in Equation 11-38. However, if $s \leq 128$, then

$$
\frac{\partial}{\partial x_2} f_2(s, x_2) = 500(2x_2 - s - 272)
$$

is positive for all values of $x_2 \geq 200$. Therefore, the optimal value of x_2 is

$$x_2^* = \begin{cases} \dfrac{s + 272}{2}, \text{ if } s \geq 128 \\ 200, \text{ if } s \leq 128 \end{cases} \tag{11-40}$$

We determine $f_2^*(s)$ by setting $x_2 = x_2^*$ in the $f_2(s,x_2)$ function. If $s \geq 128$:

$$f_2^* = 250\left(\frac{s + 272}{2} - s\right)^2 + 1500\left(\frac{s + 272}{2} - 200\right) \tag{11-41}$$

$$= +250\left(275 - \left[\frac{s + 272}{2}\right]\right)^2$$

$$= 62.5(272 - s)^2 + 750(s - 128) + 62.5(278 - s)^2$$

if $s < 128$:

$$f_2^* = 250(200 - s)^2 + 1500(200 - 200) + 250(275 - 200)^2$$
$$= 250(200 - s)^2 + 0 + 250(5625) \tag{11-42}$$
$$= 250(200 - s)^2 + 0 + 1{,}406{,}250$$

We can now construct the following table for the two-stage problem:

s	$f_2^*(s)$	x_2^*
≤ 128	$250(200 - s)^2 + 1{,}406{,}250$	200
$128 - 275$	$62.5(272 - s)^2 + 750(s - 128) + 62.5(278 - s)^2$	$\dfrac{s + 272}{2}$

The three-stage problem involves finding the minimizing value of x_3 in the relationship:

$$f_3^*(s) = \min_{x_3 \geq r_3} f_3(s,x_3)$$

$$= \min_{x_3 \geq r_3} \{250(x_3 - s)^2 + 1500(x_3 - r_3) = f_2^*(x_3)\} \tag{11-43}$$

$$= \min_{x_3 \geq 250_2} \{250(x_3 - s)^2 + 1500(x_3 - 250) + 62.5(272 - x_3)^2$$

$$+ 750(x_3 - 128) + 62.5(278 - x_3)^2$$

in the region $250 \leq x_3 \leq 275$.

This value of x_3 is found by setting:

$$\frac{\partial}{\partial x_3} f_3(s,x_3) = 0$$

$$\geq 500(x_3 - s) + 1500 - 125(272 - x_3) \tag{11-44}$$
$$+ 750 - 125(278 - x_3)$$
$$= 500(x_3 - s) - 125(272 - x_3)$$
$$- 125(278 - x_3) + 2250$$

Solving for x_3, we obtain

$$0 = 500x_3 - 500s - 34{,}000 + 125x_3 - 34{,}750 + 125x_3 + 2250$$
$$0 = 750x_3 - 500s - 66{,}500$$
$$0 = 250(3x_3 - 2s - 266) \tag{11-45}$$
$$3x_3 = 2s + 266$$
$$x_3 = \frac{2s + 266}{3}$$

Note further that $\quad \dfrac{\partial^2}{\partial x_3^2} f_3(s, x_3) = 750 < 0 \tag{11-46}$

and is, therefore, positive for all values of x_3. Thus, $x_3 = (2s + 266)/3$ is the desired minimizing value of $s \geq 242$.

If $s < 242$ then,

$$\frac{\partial}{\partial x_3} f_3(s, x_3) > 0 \qquad \text{for } x_3 = 250 \tag{11-47}$$

so that $x_3 = 250$ would be the minimizing value. To summarize, the optimal value of x_2 is

$$x_3^* = \begin{cases} \dfrac{2s + 266}{3} \\[2mm] 250 \text{ if } s < 242 \end{cases} \tag{11-48}$$

We proceed to determine $f_3^*(s)$ by setting $x_3 = x_3^*$ in the $f_3(s, x_3)$ function. If $s \geq 242$

$$
\begin{aligned}
f_3^*(s) &= 250\left(\frac{2s + 266}{3} - s\right)^2 + 1500\left(\frac{2s + 266}{3} - 250\right) \\
&\quad + 62.5\left[272 - \left(\frac{2s + 266}{3}\right)\right]^2 + 750\left(\frac{2s + 266}{3} - 128\right) \\
&\quad + 62.5\left[278 - \left(\frac{2s + 266}{3}\right)\right]^2 \\
&= \frac{250}{9}(266 - s)^2 + 500(2s - 484) + \frac{62.5}{9}(500 - 2s)^2 \tag{11-49} \\
&\quad + 250(2s - 118) + \frac{62.5}{9}(568 - 2s)^2 \\
&= \frac{250}{9}(266 - s)^2 + \frac{62.5}{9}[(550 - 2s)^2 + (568 - 2s)^2] \\
&\quad + 1500s - 271{,}500
\end{aligned}
$$

If $s < 242$

$$
\begin{aligned}
f_3^*(s) &= 250(250 - s)^2 + 1500(250 - 250) + 62.5(272 - 250)^2 \\
&\quad + 750(250 + 128) + 62.5(278 - 250)^2 \\
&= 250(250 - s)^2 + 0 + 30{,}250 + 91{,}500 + 49{,}000 \tag{11-50} \\
&= 250(250 - s)^2 + 170{,}750
\end{aligned}
$$

We can now construct the following table for the three-stage problem.

s	$f_3^*(s)$	x_3^*
<242	$250(250 - s)^2 + 170,750$	250
$242 - 275$	$\dfrac{250}{9}(266 - s)^2 + \dfrac{62.5}{9}[(550 - 2s)^2 + (568 - 2s)^2]$	$\dfrac{2s + 266}{3}$
x_3^*	$+1500s - 271,500$	

The four-stage problem involves finding the minimizing value of x_4 in the relationship:

$$f_4^* = \min_{x_4 \geq r_4} f_4(s, x_4)$$
$$= \min_{x_4 \geq 225} \{250(x_4 - s)^2 + 1500(x_4 - r_4) + f_3^*(x_4) + f_3^*(x_4)\} \tag{11-51}$$

Since $r_4 = 225$, we must consider the region $225 \leq x_4 \leq 275$. The expression for $f_3^*(x_4)$ will differ in the two portions, $225 \leq x_4 \leq 242$ and $242 \leq x_4 \leq 275$ of this region.

If $225 \leq x_4 \leq 242$,

$$f_4(s, x_4) = 250(x_4 - s)^2 + 1500(x_4 - 225) \tag{11-52}$$
$$+ 250(250 - x_4)^2 + 170,750$$

If $242 \leq x_4 \leq 275$,

$$f_4(s, x_4) = 250(x_4 - s)^2 + 1500(x_4 - 225) + \frac{250}{9}(266 - x_4)^2 \tag{11-53}$$
$$+ \frac{62.5}{9}[(550 - 2x_4)^2 + (568 + 2x_4)^2]$$
$$+ 1500x_4 - 271,500$$

Consider first the case where $225 \leq x_4 \leq 242$,

$$\frac{\partial}{\partial x_4} f_4(s, x_4) = 500(x_4 - s) + 1500 - 500(250 - x_4)$$
$$= 500x_4 - 500s + 1500 - 125,000 + 500x_4 \tag{11-54}$$
$$= 1000x_4 - 500s - 123,500$$
$$= 500(2x_4 - s - 247)$$

In this stage we know that $s = 275$, since spring employment is constant at a level of 275. Thus,

$$\frac{\partial}{\partial x_4} f_4(s, x_4) = 500\,(2x_4 - 275 - 247)$$
$$= 500\,(2x_4 - 522) \tag{11-55}$$
$$= 1000\,(x_4 - 261)$$

Observe now that $\partial/\partial x_4 f_4(s, x_4) < 242$. Therefore, $x_4 = 242$ is the minimizing value in the region $225 \le x_4 \le 242$.

Considering next the case in which $242 \le x_4 \le 275$,

$$\frac{\partial}{\partial x_4} f_4(s, x_4) = 500\,(x_4 - s) + 1500 - \frac{500}{9}(266 - x_4)$$
$$\qquad - \frac{250}{9}(550 - 2x_4) - \frac{250}{9}(568 - 2x_4) + 1500$$
$$= 500x_4 - 500s + 1500 - \frac{133{,}000}{9} + \frac{500x_4}{9}$$
$$\qquad + \frac{137{,}000}{9} + \frac{500x_4}{9} - \frac{142{,}000}{9} + \frac{500x_4}{9} + 1500$$
$$= \frac{4500}{9}x_4 - \frac{4500s}{9} + \frac{13{,}500}{9} - \frac{133{,}000}{9} + \frac{500x_4}{9} \tag{11-56}$$
$$\qquad - \frac{137{,}500}{9} + \frac{500x_4}{9} - \frac{142{,}000}{9} + \frac{500x_4}{9} + \frac{13{,}500}{9}$$
$$= \frac{6000}{9}x_4 - \frac{4500\,s}{9} + \frac{385{,}500}{9}$$
$$= \frac{500}{9}(12x_4 - 9s - 771)$$

Observe that

$$\frac{\partial}{\partial x_4} f_4(s, x_4) = 12 > 0 \text{ for all } x_4 \tag{11-57}$$

Thus, we can set $\dfrac{\partial}{\partial x_4} f_4(s, x_4) = 0$

and solve $12x_4 - 9s - 771 = 0$
$$12x_4 = 9s + 777 \tag{11-58}$$
$$x_4 = \frac{9s + 777}{12}$$

Since $s = 275$, $x_4 = \dfrac{9(275) + 771}{12} = \dfrac{3246}{12}$ $\tag{11-59}$

$$= 270.5$$

minimizes $f_4(s, x_4)$ over the region $242 \le x_4 \le 275$. Since $x_4 = 270.5$ is in the region that includes $x_4 = 242$, which minimizes $f_4(s, x_4)$ over the region where $x_4 \le 242$, it is clear that $x_4 = 270.5$ also minimizes $f_4(s, x_4)$ over the entire region of interest $225 \le x_4 \le 275$.

We can now compute $f_4^*(x)$ with $x_4^* = 270.5$ as

$$f_4^*(275) = 250(270.5 - 275)^2 + 1500(270.5 - 225)$$

$$+ \frac{250}{9}(266 - 270.5)^2 + \frac{62.5}{9}(550 - 2 \cdot 270.5)^2$$

$$+ \frac{62.5}{9}(568 - 2 \cdot 270.5)^2 + 1500(70.5) - 271,500$$

$$= 250(20.25) + 1500(45.5) + \frac{250}{9}(20.25) + \frac{62.5}{9}(81) \quad (11\text{-}60)$$

$$+ \frac{62.5}{9}(729) + 1500(270.5) - 271,500$$

$$= \$5,062.50 + 68,250.00 + 562.50 + 562.50 + 5062.50$$

$$+ 405,750 - 271,500$$

$$= \$213,750$$

We can now construct the following table for the four-stage problem.

s	$f_4^*(s)$	x_4^*
275	\$213,750	270.5

The optimal policy is

$$x_4^* = 270.5$$

$$x_3^* = \frac{2s + 266}{3} = \frac{2(270.5) + 266}{3} = \frac{807}{3} = 269 \quad (11\text{-}61)$$

$$x_2^* = \frac{s + 272}{2} + \frac{269 + 272}{2} = \frac{541}{2} = 270.5$$

$$x_1^* = 275$$

This policy produces an estimated employment cost per cycle of \$213,750.
We can also perform a check on the cost of our optimal policy, as follows.

	Wasted Work Force Cost		Hiring and Firing Costs		Total Employment Cost
$r_1 = 275 \quad x_1^* = 275$	1500(0)	$+$	$250(4.5)^2$	$=$	\$ 5,062.50
$r_2 = 225 \quad x_2^* = 270.5$	1500(45.5)	$+$	$250(4.5)^2$	$=$	73,312.50
$r_3 = 250 \quad x_3^* = 269$	1500(19)	$+$	$250(1.5)^2$	$=$	29,062.50
$r_4 = 200 \quad x_4^* = 270.5$	1500(70.5)	$+$	$250(1.5)^2$	$=$	106,312,50
					\$213,750.00

11.6 CASE STUDY—DYNAMIC PROGRAMMING APPLIED TO CAPITAL BUDGETING

E. R. Petersen has developed a dynamic programming model for determining an optimal capacity expansion plan for an electric power system.[1] The objective of the model is the minimization of discounted expected capital, operating, maintenance, and penalty costs for a specified planning horizon. The solution to the dynamic programming model specifies the least-cost mix in capacity between hydroelectric, thermal, and nuclear plants, the size of the plants to be added to the system, and the timing of the additions. The determination of an optimal capacity expansion plan is actually a capital-budgeting type problem, and the techniques developed by Petersen are applicable to a large class of capital-budgeting problems characterized by uncertainty. This particular problem is concerned with an electric power system composed of a number of hydroelectric, thermal, and nuclear generation plants that are connected to each customer by an extensive transmission network. The total electric demand or load on the system is a stochastic process that increases with time over the planning horizon. The model explicitly considers cost-relevant characteristics of the three alternate energy sources in determining the optimal capacity mix. For example, hydroelectric plants are characterized by high initial capital costs; however, their incremental operating cost per kilowatt hour is minimal. In contrast, thermal plants cost less to install than hydroelectric units but have a substantial fuel cost per kilowatt hour of energy output. Also, unlike hydroelectric plants, these plants can be operated continuously at maximum capacity. A specialized form of the thermal units is the peaking turbines, which, though inexpensive to install, are inefficient in their use of fuel. The units are designed for short periods of time only and are attractive from a cost standpoint for serving short-term peak requirements. The capital cost for a nuclear plant falls somewhat between the thermal and hydroelectric units. The fuel cost is substantially lower than for a conventional thermal plant.

The effect of economies of scale were considered with respect to selecting both thermal and nuclear plants for the optimal expansion plan. The average capital and fixed operating costs per kilowatt capacity decreases substantially with the size of the plant, asymptotically approaching a constant for very large installations. The fact that each type of plant has a significantly different economic life was also considered in the costing of each alternative.

To illustrate the model, Petersen presents a small example in which the optimal expansion of a hypothetical electric power system is determined. In his formulation, the state of the system at any time t is defined by a vector $\mathbf{S}_t = (H_t, T_t, N_t, P_t)$ where:

H_t is a measure of the system's hydroelectric capability at time t. (It must be noted that the number of new hydroelectric projects is limited.)

T_t is the number of megawatts of nu-

---

[1] For further details, see: E. R. Petersen, "A Dynamic Programming Model for the Expansion of Electric Power Systems," *Management Science*, vol. 20, no. 8 (December, Part II, 1973), 656–664, copyright 1973, The Institute of Management Science, reprinted by permission.

clear capacity that have been added to the initial system by time t.

N_t is the number of megawatts of nuclear capacity that have been added to the initial system by time t.

P_t is the number of megawatts of peaking turbine capacity that have been added to the initial system by time t.

A recursion relationship is defined that relates cost and expansion considerations so that the model is able to select the optimal level of each of these variables for all periods t.

In the example, a relatively small system with a 1972 peak load of 2000 megawatts is considered. The distribution of demand during the year is represented by the normalized load duration curve provided in Table 11.4. The curve describes the percentage of time the demand will be greater than or equal to a given level relative to the peak demand. The total energy demand each year is the product of peak demand, the number of hours per year, and the integral of the load duration curve. The 1972 energy demand is 10,293 gigawatt hours.

The facilities available to supply the current market are presented in Tables 11.5 and 11.6. Table 11.5 describes the existing hydroelectric capability in terms of the capacity in megawatts and the annual energy production capability in gigawatt hours. The energy ca-

TABLE 11.4   Normalized Load Duration Curve

Fraction of Time	Load Greater Than or Equal to (relative to peak)
0.025	1.000
0.050	0.845
0.150	0.780
0.250	0.728
0.350	0.682
0.450	0.642
0.500	0.604
0.550	0.580
0.600	0.562
0.650	0.504
0.700	0.465
0.750	0.425
0.850	0.410
0.950	0.350
1.000	0.292

TABLE 11.5   Existing Hydroelectric Plants

Name	Capacity, mw	Energy Capability, gwh
Hydro No. 1	100	438
Hydro No. 2	300	657
Hydro No. 3	400	2102
Hydro No. 4	100	350
Hydro No. 5	150	195
Hydro No. 6	100	788

TABLE 11.6   Existing Thermal Plants

Name	Capacity, mw	Marginal Operating Cost = ($ per mwh)
Thermal No. 1	40	$8.00
Thermal No. 2	60	8.00
Thermal No. 3	80	7.00
Thermal No. 4	90	6.00
Thermal No. 5	120	5.80
Thermal No. 6	150	5.50
Thermal No. 7	150	5.30
Thermal No. 8	180	4.80
Thermal No. 9	200	4.30
Thermal No. 10	200	4.10

pability of a hydroelectric plant is constrained by the available streamflow in the river. For each thermal plant the capacity and marginal operating cost (fuel cost) is given in Table 11.6. The energy production capability per year of a thermal plant is not limited and is equal to its capacity times the hours per year (assuming fuel supply availability).

The problem involves the planning of the expansion of the generation facilities through 1985. It is assumed that the peak demand grows at an annual rate of 8 percent and that the relative shape of the demand each year is unchanged and described by the load duration curve in Table 11.4. Due to reliability problems, it is also assumed that a reserve capacity of 15 percent of the peak load is required. Thus the objective is to specify a generation facilities expansion plan that satisfies the peak-plus-reserve load capacity and the energy production requirements at minimum present worth cost.

It is assumed that hydroelectric, nuclear, and conventional fuel thermal plants can be used to meet the growing demand. Table 11.7 presents the assumed cost characteristics for each plant type. Additionally, it is assumed that four new hydroelectric facilities are available, as shown in Table 11.8. Note that the first two hydroelectric alternatives involve the expansion of generation capacity at existing plants while the last two represent the development of new sites. For the existing plants, Table 11.8 provides the total capacity and energy capability, after expansion.

The optimal expansion plan is depicted in Table 11.9. The resulting plan initially increases the capacity of the two expandable existing hydroelectric plants, adds four new nuclear plants, and then mixes the addition of nuclear and thermal plants. Note that nuclear units are used initially, since the existing system has considerable thermal capacity allowing the nuclear plants

TABLE 11.7 Expansion Costs

	New Hydroelectric Site	Add Generations at Existing Site	Nuclear	Thermal
Capital Cost				
Fixed cost per plant ($1000)	0.	0.	20,000.	$5,000.
Variable cost per kilowatt capacity ($)	350.	100.	200.	100.
Fixed O & M costs				
Per plant ($1000)	100.	0.	300.	150.
Variable cost per kilowatt capacity ($)	1.4	1.4	2.0	1.0
Marginal operating cost per megawatt hour (S)				
Economic life (years)	50.	50.	30.	20.
Annual capital recovery factor at $ percent	0.08174	0.8174	0.08853	0.10185

TABLE 11.8 Potential Hydroelectric Expansions

Name	Capacity, mw	Energy Capability, gwh
Expand Hydroelectric No. 3	550	409
Expand Hydroelectric No. 4	280	858
Develop Hydroelectric No. 7	250	1314
Develop Hydroelectric No. 8	100	219

added to have a high utilization. Recall that nuclear plants are economic only if they have a high utilization due to their high capital but low marginal operating costs.

TABLE 11.9   Optimal Expansion Plan

Year	Plan
1972	Expand Hydroelectric No. 4
1973	Expand Hydroelectric No. 3
1974	250 mw nuclear
1975	250 mw nuclear
1976	300 mw nuclear
1977	300 mw nuclear
1978	150 mw thermal
1979	300 mw nuclear
1980	400 mw nuclear
1981	300 mw thermal
1982	450 mw nuclear
1983	400 mw nuclear
1984	450 mw thermal
Present worth cost at 8%	$477,800.000

11.7   CONCLUSION

The dynamic programming problems considered in this chapter have varied considerably in their difficulty and complexity. From these examples, it should be apparent to the student that there is no general dynamic programming algorithm in the sense of the simplex method or the branch-and-bound technique. Rather, there exists a large number of sequential decision-making problems that can be conceptualized within a dynamic programming framework. For each such problem situation, the initial problem-solving step is the structuring of the problem in a dynamic programming format. Then the problem must be separated into a series of subproblems that involve a limited number of variables that can be related in a recursive manner. Assuming that these two steps have been accomplished with a reasonable degree of skill, the analyst can then solve the problem using the general methodology of dynamic programming.

GLOSSARY OF TERMS

Backward Induction   A process in which the first stage analyzed is the final stage of the problem and solution of the problem proceeds by moving back one stage at a time until all stages in the problem are considered.

Deterministic Dynamic Programming   Or dynamic programming under certainty; involves problem situations in which the state in the next stage of the decision process is completely determined by the interaction of the state and the policy decision, with respect to the decision variable that occurs at the current stage. In deterministic dynamic programming there is no uncertainty nor probability distribution associated with what the next state in the decision process will be.

Dynamic Programming   A management science technique applicable to certain types of problems involving a sequence of decisions that are interrelated. It is a general type of problem-solving procedure that can be applied to sequential decision-making situations.

Forward Induction   A process where the first stage analyzed is the initial stage of the problem and the solution proceeds by moving forward one stage at a time until all stages in the problem are considered.

Infinite-State Dynamic Programming Problem   A dynamic programming problem in which the number of states associated with a particular stage of the decision process is infinite. In other words, it is a dynamic programming problem in which the state variable is a continuous variable and thus takes on an infinite number of values over a certain interval.

"N-Stage" Problem   In dynamic programming, the problem of finding the optimal decision that must be made when there are n more stages to go.

Principle of Optimality   An optimal policy must have the property that, regardless of the decision made to enter a particular state, the remaining decisions must constitute an optimal policy for leaving that state (Bellman 1957).

Probabilistic Dynamic Programming   Or dynamic programming under uncertainty; involves problem situations in which the state at the next stage in the decision process is not completely determined by the state-and-policy decision at the current stage of the decision process; rather, there is a probability distribution being determined by the state-and-policy decision at the current stage of the decision process.

Recursion Relationship   A relationship for the N-stage problem that links the optimal decision for the last stage considered ($m = N$) to the optimal decisions made for stages $m = N - 1, \ldots, m = 1$.

Return Function   The value associated with making decision d_n at stage n for a specific value of the input variable x_n.

Stage   One of the smaller optimization subproblems into which a dynamic programming problem is divided, which requires a standardized policy decision.

States   The various possible conditions in which the problem system may be at a point in time. The number of states may be finite or infinite for any stage of the decision process.

Transition Function   Defines, as a functional relationship, the value of the state variable at each stage and serves to interconnect the stages of the dynamic programming problem.

SELECTED REFERENCES

DYNAMIC PROGRAMMING

Beckman, Martin J. 1968. *Dynamic Programming of Economic Decisions*. Berlin, New York: Springer-Verlag Inc.

Bellman, Richard E., and Stuart E. Dreyfus. 1962. *Applied Dynamic Programming*. Princeton, N.J.: Princeton University Press.

Bellman, Richard. 1957. *Dynamic Programming*. Princeton, N.J.: Princeton University Press.

Dreyfus, Stuart E. 1965. *Dynamic Programming and the Calculus of Variations*. New York: Academic Press, Inc.

Gluss, Brian. 1972. *An Elementary Introduction to Dynamic Programming*. Boston: Allyn & Bacon, Inc.

Hadley, G. 1964. *Nonlinear and Dynamic Programming*. Reading, Mass.: Addison-Wesley Publishing Co., Inc.

Hinderer, Karl. 1970. *Foundations of Non-stationary Dynamic Programming with Discrete Time Parameters*. Berlin, New York: Springer-Verlag Inc.

Howard, Ronald A. 1960. *Dynamic Programming and Markov Processes*. Cambridge, Mass.: Massachusetts Institute of Technology Press.

Jacobson, H. Davitt, and D. Q. Mayne. 1970. *Differential Dynamic Programming*, vol. 24. New York: Elsevier-North Holland Publishing Co.

Kaufmann, A. 1967. *Graphs, Dynamic Programming and Finite Games*. New York: Academic Press, Inc.

Kaufmann, A., and R. Cruon. 1967. *Dynamic Programming: Sequential Scientific Management*. New York: Academic Press, Inc.

Nemhauser, G. L. 1966. *Introduction to Dynamic Programming*. New York: John Wiley & Sons, Inc.

Tou, Julius. 1963. *Optimum Design of Digital Control Systems Via Dynamic Programming*. New York: Academic Press, Inc.

White, D. J. 1969. *Dynamic Programming*. San Francisco: Holden-Day, Inc.

DISCUSSION QUESTIONS

1. When can the number of states be "infinite" for a particular stage of the decision process in dynamic programming?
2. Describe briefly how you determine the complete optimal solution to a N-stage dynamic programming problem once you have found the optimal solution to the n-stage problem. Does this procedure also work for dynamic programming problems under uncertainty? Why or why not?
3. How does a setup cost make a cost function nonlinear?
4. What is one of the main advantages of using a dynamic programming approach?
5. Why doesn't Table 11.1 have an entry at $i = 6$ and $n = 1$?
6. Why is the example presented in Section 11.3.3 a "deterministic" dynamic programming problem, even though it involves probabilities?
7. Explain the "infinite" stage character of the problem presented in Section 11.5.1.

PROBLEM SET

1. Mr. Hi Life has been family vacationing in Philadelphia and now is faced with a decision concerning travel back to his home in Los Angeles. Because he has small children, he must make his trip in stages. Because he has spent most of his vacation money in Philadelphia he must make the trip home using the shortest possible route. His potential travel network is shown on the following page. The distance associated with the branches of this network are as follows.

$d_{12} = 350$	$d_{25} = 400$	$d_{59} = 350$	$d_{912} = 500$
$d_{13} = 300$	$d_{26} = 410$	$d_{510} = 375$	$d_{1012} = 525$
$d_{14} = 280$	$d_{27} = 390$	$d_{511} = 360$	$d_{1112} = 515$
	$d_{28} = 380$	$d_{69} = 400$	
	$d_{35} = 350$	$d_{610} = 390$	
	$d_{36} = 375$	$d_{611} = 370$	
	$d_{37} = 360$	$d_{79} = 365$	
	$d_{38} = 380$	$d_{710} = 375$	
	$d_{45} = 400$	$d_{711} = 400$	
	$d_{46} = 425$	$d_{89} = 410$	
	$d_{47} = 390$	$d_{810} = 400$	
	$d_{48} = 370$	$d_{811} = 390$	

Determine Mr. Life's shortest route home, using dynamic programming.

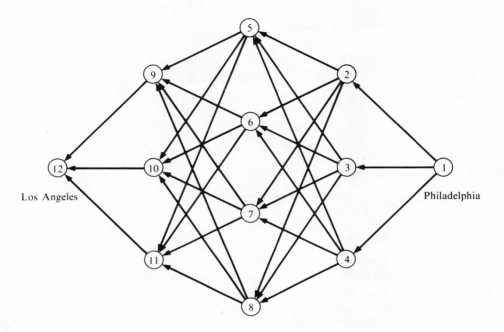

2. Find the shortest route for the following network, using dynamic programming.

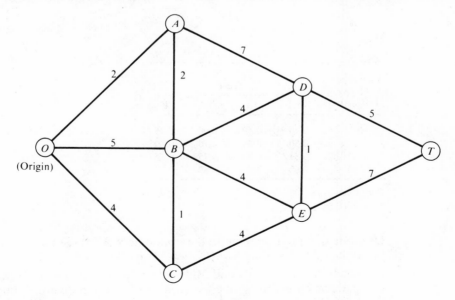

3. Several enterprising young entrepreneurs at a large Midwestern state university have secured 10 cases of a well-known beer brewed in a Western state. They are contemplating selling 7 cases (keeping 3 for themselves) to one or more of three friends. The following table gives the expected profits associated with selling various numbers of cases to the three friends.

Total Expected Profit

Number of Cases	Friend		
	Bill	Sam	Sue
0	0	0	0
1	7	5	6
2	10	11	12
3	13	13	14
4	17	18	14
5	17	19	14
6	18	19	14
7	19	19	15

Use dynamic programming to solve this problem, namely the sale of the seven cases to the three friends in a manner that maximizes the expected profit.

4. The manager of a major league baseball team is faced with a decision concerning the assigning of players from his current major league roster to one or more of four minor league affiliated teams. He wishes to do this in a manner that will enhance the probability that all four teams will win the pennant in their respect leagues. The following table gives the estimated probability that the respective teams will win their league's pennant when 0, 1, 2, or 3 players are assigned to that team.

Number of Players Assigned	Team			
	AAA	AA	A	B
0	0.40	0.50	0.60	0.75
1	0.50	0.65	0.70	0.80
2	0.55	0.70	0.75	0.85
3	0.60	0.70	0.80	0.85

Use dynamic programming to determine how the three additional players should be allocated to the four teams.

5. A tornado has struck a small Midwestern town. The mayor of the town is faced with a decision involving the assignment of six volunteer clean-up work crews to the four major sections of the town. She wishes to assign the six workers to the four areas in a way that maximizes their effectiveness. The following table gives the estimated effectiveness of the assignment of the various number of workers to the four districts (using a scale of 1-100).

Number of Workers	Area			
	1	*2*	*3*	*4*
0	0	0	0	0
1	10	20	30	5
2	15	25	40	25
3	30	30	50	30
4	35	30	50	40
5	40	35	50	40
6	50	45	60	55

Use dynamic programming to determine how many of the six workers should be assigned to each of the four precincts to maximize the total effectiveness of the clean-up campaign.

6. Bill Edwards is in the last semester (hopefully) of his undergraduate business program and must take final exams in five courses. He anticipates that he has 50 hours of study time available. He has made the following estimates of grade likelihood for these courses as a function of the study time he devotes to a course.

	Expected Grade as a Function of Study Hours			
Course	*5 hours*	*10 hours*	*15 hours*	*20 hours*
Accounting	D	C	B	A
Finance	C	B	A	A
Management science	D	C	B	A
Business policy	B	A	A	A
Management	C	B	A	A

Edwards wishes to allocate his study time to maximize the total grade points he receives for the five course (A = 5 points, B = 4 points, C = 3 points, D = 1 point). Formulate and solve using dynamic programming.

7. Ajax Manufacturing Company is faced with a forecasted demand for its product in each of the next 4 months, as shown below.

Month	Units Demanded D_n
1	3
2	4
3	3
4	5

It is trying to determine a production schedule to meet this forecasted demand. In any month the cost of production is $1.50 per unit, plus a setup cost of $2.50, which is incurred only if one or more units are produced. No more than 6 units can be produced in any time period. In addition, there is an inventory-holding cost of $0.75 per unit per period. The firm has zero inventory on hand at the beginning of month 1 and wishes to have zero inventory on hand at the end of month 4. Use dynamic programming to determine a production schedule that will meet the demand requirements at a minimum cost (production plus inventory costs).

8. Rework Problem 7, assuming that the beginning inventory is one unit, the inventory holding cost is $0.50 per unit per period, and it is desired to have a two-unit inventory on hand at the end of month 4.

9. The Sentry Company manufactures a home fire protection device, which is composed of three major electronic components. The reliability of this home fire protection device can be improved by installing several parallel units of one or more of the three major components. The following table summarizes the probability that the respective components will function properly if they consist of one, two, or three parallel units.

	Component		
	Probability of Functioning Properly		
Number of Parallel Units	1	2	3
1	0.80	0.82	0.85
2	0.88	0.90	0.95
3	0.92	0.94	0.97

The probability that the fire protection device will function properly is the product of the probabilities associated with the individual components functioning properly. The costs of installing one, two, or three parallel units for the respective components are given in the following table.

	Component		
	Cost of Installation		
Number of Parallel Units	1	2	3
1	$10	$16	$17
2	12	18	23
3	15	20	25

The manufacturer wants the fire protection device to cost not more than $50, regardless of the number of parallel units that are used. Use dynamic programming to determine how many parallel units should be installed for each of the three components in order to maximize the probability that the fire protection device will function properly.

10. The Medi-Quick Company has recently completed the design of a new diagnostic device that can be used for internal diagnosis of cancer in humans. This diagnostic device has three major components, each of which is driven by one or more power cells. The probability that any one component will not fail depends on the number of power cells assigned to it. The following table summarizes these probabilities.

Number of Power Cells	Probability of Component Reliability		
	Component 1	Component 2	Component 3
1	0.80	0.94	0.84
2	0.86	0.95	0.88
3	0.92	0.97	0.92
4	0.97	0.99	0.96

The engineers for the company would like to determine how many power cells should be assigned to each component in order to maximize the overall reliability of the diagnostic device. The costs of installing from one to four power cells for the respective components are given in the following table.

Number of Power Cells	Component		
	Cost of Installation		
	1	2	3
1	$20,000	$40,000	$30,000
2	22,000	47,000	33,000
3	24,000	53,000	35,000
4	26,000	58,000	36,000

The Medi-Quick Company feels that the overall cost of its diagnostic device should not exceed $100,000. Formulate and solve by dynamic programming.

11. Reconsider the Armadillo Candle Shop problem considered in Section 11.4.1. Assume that further production data indicates that each lot produced will likely be acceptable with probability ½. Resolve this problem.

12. As an investor you have $5000 to invest in either of two investments at the beginning of each of the next 3 years. The investments, their return, and associated probabilities are as follows.

Investment	Return	Probability (return)
A	500 (Loss of $4500)	0.3
	7500 (Gain of $2500)	0.7
B	3000 (Loss of $2000)	0.4
	8000 (Gain of $3000)	0.6

Only one investment can be made each year and the entire $5000 must be invested (any excess funds remain idle). Use dynamic programming to determine the investment policy that maximizes the expected amount of money accumulated after 3 years.

13. A soap manufacturer is trying to determine its advertising allocation for the forthcoming year. It has a $7-million advertising budget that it must spend in whole million-dollar increments on some or all of three advertising media. The following table indicates the expected market penetration for various expenditures for the three advertising media.

	Expected Market Penetration		
Millions of Dollars Spent	Media 1	Media 2	Media 3
0	0	0	0
1	0.10	0.25	0.40
2	0.15	0.35	0.45
3	0.20	0.45	0.50
4	0.25	0.55	0.60
5	0.30	0.65	0.70
6	0.35	0.75	0.80
7	0.40	0.85	0.90

Use dynamic programming to determine how to allocate the $7 million to maximize the expected market penetration for the entire campaign.

14. A state education agency has $5 million available for allocation to three local school districts for improvement in early learning skills of children. In general, the greater the allocation to as school district, the higher will be the development of early learning skills, as measured by a standardized testing instrument. Past surveys have indicated the following test score measurements for various funds allocation.

School District	Funds Allocation (millions of dollars)					
	0	1	2	3	4	5
1	30	50	60	70	80	90
2	40	60	80	85	90	95
3	45	60	75	85	95	97

Use dynamic programming to determine the optimal allocation of funds for the three school districts.

15. A trucking firm has a fleet of trucks, each of which has a capacity of 15 tons. There are three types of commercial products that may be carried in the truck. The profit and the weight associated with a unit of each of the three products are shown in the following table.

Product Type	Profit per Unit ($)	Weight per Unit (tons)
Steel ingots	10	5
Metal castings	12	3
Scrap metal	7	2

Use dynamic programming to determine the product loading combination that produces the maximum profit, subject to the truck's overall weight limitation.

Inventory Models

12.1 INTRODUCTION

Problems associated with the maintenance of inventories are present in virtually all business organizations. Small retailers, moderate-size wholesalers, and large manufacturing firms—all must establish some type of inventory control procedures. These inventory control procedures can encompass three types of inventories.

1. Raw materials.
2. Work in process, including component assemblies.
3. Finished goods (items kept in stock).

Consequently, there are numerous reasons underlying the need for the development of a comprehensive inventory policy. Among the most important of these are:

1. Raw materials inventory allows the producer to take advantage of raw material prices and to hedge against price changes.

2. Work-in-process inventory permits flexibility in plant scheduling, allows for the handling of production variations, and helps in avoiding an increase in plant capacity.
3. Finished goods inventory allows the producer to provide adequate customer service despite sales fluctuations, enables the production of the finished items in economic run sizes, and gives the customers assurance of availability.

Although the reasons for maintaining the various kinds of inventories are not mutually exclusive, the primary focus in inventory control is on finished goods inventory. Herein, inventory serves as a decoupling mechanism between fluctuations in sales and the production process. In business, the maintenance of inventories never completely succeeds in decoupling sales and production. However, inventory control policies can be developed that attempt to strike a balance between operating savings and customer goodwill, and the cost and capital requirements associated with the inventory itself. This balancing process becomes the basic problem of inventory control, and we can summarize the objectives of inventory control, as follows.

1. Adequate customer service.
2. Production efficiency.
3. Minimum capital investment in inventory.

To illustrate the basic considerations in the development of an inventory policy, consider the following examples.

EXAMPLE 1   A major Midwestern firm buys large sheets of metal, which it then cuts into smaller-size pieces according to customer orders. As a result of this "cutting to order" process a "random inventory" of various-size pieces is created. The company is interested in determining a rule that will allow it to specify exactly what size piece should be put into this random inventory as opposed to being sold for scrap. The considerations for this inventory control situation are as follows.

1. The yearly cost associated with the maintenance of the random inventory is estimated to be 13 percent of the original purchase cost of the metal. It is felt that this 13 percent can be prorated linearly over the time that a piece of material remains in the random inventory.
2. The cost (loss) associated with scrapping a piece of metal is estimated to be $0.65 per pound (original purchase cost of $1.35 per pound, salvage price of $0.70 per pound).

Herein, a balance is sought between inventory maintenance costs and scrap losses.

EXAMPLE 2   A St. Louis retail distributor of stereo equipment is experiencing difficulty in shortages of its most popular compact stereo system. The retailer purchases the compact stereo system from a Chicago wholesaler. The retailer, after an analysis of the situation, has determined that the following considerations are important.

1. Stereo customers are notoriously fickle. Consequently, the retailer feels that

being out of stock of the compact stereo system, which sells for $300, will cause a goodwill loss of at least 15 percent ($45) of the selling price.

2. The inventory holding cost is estimated by the retailer to be approximately $3 per unit remaining in inventory at the end of the month. This inventory holding cost represents the cost of warehouse space, insurance, taxes, and the cost of capital tied up in the unit.

3. The cost associated with placing an order with the wholesale distributor is estimated to be $250, consisting of $200 for the unit and $50 for the associated ordering paperwork.

Herein, a balance is sought between out-of-stock costs, ordering costs, and inventory-carrying costs.

The preceding discussion and examples indicate some of the factors and tradeoffs that must be considered in the development of inventory models. We will now attempt to consider in more detail the framework and components necessary for the derivation of various inventory models. In the subsequent discussion we will focus our attention on the control of finished goods inventory from the standpoint of overall importance in the typical manufacturing situation. However, the analytical procedures we will develop will also be relevant to distributors and retailers.

12.2 THE FRAMEWORK AND COMPONENTS OF INVENTORY MODELS

In developing the framework for **inventory model** construction, perhaps the first question is: "What inventory do we want to control?" Remembering that we are focusing our attention on finished goods inventories, one obvious answer would be: "We want to control all our finished goods inventory." However, long practical experience and many studies have shown that for the typical production process or group of items, a small number of items in the group will account for the bulk of the total inventory value. This concept, called the **ABC classification**, is one of the most widely known, yet least-exploited ideas of inventory control. In basic terms, in using an ABC classification we attempt to consider the small number of items that will account for most of the sales dollars and that are therefore the most important ones to control for effective inventory management. To illustrate the ABC classification, consider Table 12.1, which provides yearly sales volume data for 10 items. In Table 12.1 we have multiplied the annual sales in number of units by the unit cost, for each item, to determine the annual sales dollars associated with each item. These annual sales dollars have then been ranked. Now, consider Table 12.2, which presents the items ranked in order according to their annual sales dollars. Table 12.2 also indicates the cumulative annual dollar sales, and the cumulative percentage sales. Assume that we have decided to classify the first 20 percent of the 10 items in the "A" class, the next 30 percent of the 10 items in the "B" class, and the remaining 50 percent of the 10 items in the "C" class. As can be seen in Table 12.2, the "A" items would then account for approximately 60 percent of the annual sales, the "B" items would account for 25 percent of the annual sales, and the "C" items would account for the remaining 15 percent of the annual sales. Clearly, by concentrating our control efforts on the "A" items and achieving a 25-percent inventory reduction, we

TABLE 12.1 Yearly Sales Data

Sales Item	Annual Sales (no. of units)	Unit Cost	Annual Sales ($)	Rank (annual sales, $)
F-1	40,000	0.06	2,400	7
F-3	195,000	0.10	19,500	1
F-7	30,000	0.09	2,700	6
H-1	100,000	0.05	5,000	3
H-3	3,000	0.15	450	10
H-4	50,000	0.06	3,000	5
H-6	10,000	0.07	700	8
J-1	30,000	0.12	3,600	4
J-3	150,000	0.05	7,500	2
K-3	6,000	0.09	540	9

would then have a very substantial inventory reduction, even if the "C" items increased by almost 50 percent. Thus, we should initiate our inventory control procedures where it will do the most good, namely on those items that are most important from a total dollar-usage standpoint. For example, some companies have concluded that it is much easier to carry a large stock of low-value items and not maintain any sort of control records for these items. The time, effort, and expense saved is then used to very closely control the high-value items. The ideas concerning the proper degree of control can be summarized as follows.

"A" Items Very tight control, very complete and accurate records. Regular review by major decision makers.

"B" Items Less tightly controlled, good records and regular review.

"C" Items Simplest possible controls, little or no records, large inventories, periodic review, and reordering.

Inventory models are designed to improve the profitability of the firm. Thus, a major consideration in the development of inventory models is the cost structure that is appropriate for a particular situation. The major costs that affect profitability can be categorized as follows.

TABLE 12.2 ABC Classification

Sales Item	Annual Sales ($)	Cumulative Annual Sales ($)	Cumulative Annual Sales (%)	Class
F-3	19,500	19,500	43.0	A
J-3	7,500	27,000	59.4	A
H-1	5,000	32,000	70.5	B
J-1	3,600	35,600	78.4	B
H-4	3,000	38,600	85.0	B
F-7	2,700	41,300	90.9	C
F-1	2,400	43,700	96.3	C
H-6	700	44,400	97.8	C
K-3	540	44,940	99.0	C
H-3	450	45,390	100.0	C

1. The ordering or manufacturing cost.
2. The holding or storage cost.
3. Stockout or shortage cost.

The **ordering** or **manufacturing cost**, in its simplest form, is directly proportional to the amount that is ordered or produced. In this case the cost function is simply $c(x) = c \cdot x$ where c is the cost of ordering or producing one unit and x is the number of units ordered or produced. Another slightly more complicated cost structure is based on the assumption that $c(x)$ is composed of two parts: a term that is directly proportional to the amount ordered and a term K that is zero for $x = 0$ and constant for $x > 0$. In this case, if x is positive, the ordering or production cost is given by $c(x) = K + c \cdot x$. For example, assume that we have a production process for the manufacture of suitcases in which the setup cost for a production run is $1000, with each suitcase then costing $10 to manufacture. The production cost function for this situation is given by:

$$\text{Production cost:} \quad c(x) = \$1000 + \$10x \quad \text{for } x > 0 \qquad (12\text{--}1)$$

The fixed portion of the production cost in this instance would be independent of the amount produced and would include clerical and administrative costs and the costs of labor and material used in setting up the production run. In another situation involving an item ordered from a supplier we might incur a $100 cost for placing the order, and a cost of $5 for each unit being ordered. The ordering cost function for this situation would then be given by:

$$\text{Ordering Cost:} \quad c(x) = \$100 + \$5x \quad \text{for } x > 0 \qquad (12\text{--}2)$$

The fixed portion of the ordering cost in this instance would be independent of the amount ordered and would be primarily clerical and administrative in nature. Typical components of the fixed portion of the ordering cost include the costs associated with processing and expediting the purchase order, transportation, inspection, handling, and paying for the order. It should be recognized that a particular inventory model will have either a cost of manufacturing, if the item is to be produced, or a cost of **ordering**, if the item is to be purchased. Although the structure of these two cost functions is similar, the cost functions apply to two markedly different types of business operations.

The **holding** or **storage cost** is the cost associated with maintaining an inventory until it is used or sold. Holding or storage cost includes the cost of maintaining storage facilities, the cost of insuring the inventory, taxes attributed to storage, costs associated with obsolescence, and opportunity costs associated with the capital that is committed to the inventory. The opportunity cost incurred by having capital tied up in inventory rather than having it invested elsewhere is frequently the most important component of the inventory holding cost. This opportunity cost is generally equated to the largest return that the company could obtain from alternative investments. The holding or storage cost is usually related to the maximum quantity, average quantity, or excess of supply over demand for a particular time period. For example, in the previously discussed stereo equipment inventory situation, the holding cost of $3 per unit was related to the units remaining in inventory at the end of any month. In another inventory control modeling effort in which the author has participated, a metal-processing firm estimated that their *annual* inventory holding cost was approximately 13 to 15 percent of the original purchase price of the metal commodity. Thus, a common practice is to estimate the holding costs as a percentage of the unit cost of the item.

A **stockout** or **shortage cost** occurs when the demand for an item exceeds its supply. When a stockout or shortage occurs, one of two possible actions may be taken.

1. The shortage may be met by some type of "rush," "special handling," or "priority" shipment.
2. The shortage may not be able to be responded to at all.

The cost associated with a stockout or shortage is dependent on how the shortage is handled. Consider first the cost in which the demand that occurs when the inventory system is out of supply is **back-ordered**. In this case it is assumed that the demand is satisfied when the item next becomes available. From a practical standpoint, it may be very difficult to determine accurately the nature and magnitude of the back-ordering cost. A small portion of the back-ordering cost, such as the cost of notifying the customer that the item has been back-ordered and when delivery can be expected, may be fairly easy to determine. Another portion of the back-ordering cost may involve explicit costs for overtime, special clerical and administrative costs incurred for expediting, and extraordinary transportation charges. These types of costs are much more difficult to determine. Finally, a major portion of the back-ordering cost will be an implicit cost reflecting loss of customer goodwill. This is a very difficult cost to measure since it is intended to be a penalty cost that accounts for lost future sales. For example, in the previously discussed stereo equipment problem, the shortage cost, which is composed primarily of the loss of customer goodwill, can only be estimated to be 15 percent of the original purchase cost of the stereo system. In the second case in which back-ordering is not permitted, the shortage costs will be almost entirely composed of the costs associated with loss of immediate and future sales. These costs include the cost of notifying the customer, the loss in profit from the sale, and the future loss of customer goodwill.

The shortage cost may also be dependent on the size of the shortage and the length of time for which the shortage occurs. For example, customers may have specific penalty clauses, based on shortage amounts and times, written into purchase contracts. However, in other instances the shortage cost may be a fixed amount regardless of the number of units that are not available or the period of time over which the shortage exists.

In our subsequent discussion concerning the construction of inventory models we will focus on determining optimal inventory policies using the criterion of minimizing the total cost, composed of some combination of the costs described above. We will seek to find answers to two questions.

1. *When* should the inventory be replenished, or when should an order be placed or a new lot be manufactured?
2. *How much* should we order or produce?

We will divide our discussion of inventory models into classifications according to whether the demand for a certain time period is known (**deterministic demand**) or whether it is a random variable having unknown demand described by some probability distribution (**stochastic** or **nondeterministic** or **probabilistic demand**). Our previous example dealing with the cutting of metal sheets would be an example of stochastic demand, described by some probability distribution. Conversely, the previous example concerning stereo equipment would be an example of deterministic demand, assuming that the stereo retailer ordered a fixed amount of the items on a regular basis (for example, purchased 100 units per month from the wholesaler).

A final classification procedure that we shall employ in subsequent work relates to how the inventory is reviewed, continuously or periodically. Under **continuous review**, an order is placed immediately when the stock level falls below the prescribed **reorder point**. This type of inventory system is also often referred to as an **order-point system**. Under **periodic review**, the inventory level is checked at discrete intervals and orders are placed at this time, assuming that they are needed. Obviously, under periodic review, the inventory level may dip below the reorder point prior to the periodic review being made. For a deterministic problem situation, the continuous review (fixed-reorder quantity) inventory system and the periodic review (fixed-reorder time) system are equivalent. Herein, an order of a certain size is made during continuous review when the inventory level falls to zero, or equivalently, at the review time, when an order of a certain size is made if the inventory level is zero. However, when the demand on the inventory system can only be described in probabilistic terms, the two review systems produce quite different results.

12.3   DETERMINISTIC MODELS

To begin our study of inventory models we will consider a collection of models for which the rate of demand for items kept in stock in the system is assumed to be known with certainty and is constant over time. Such deterministic models are often fairly severe abstractions of the real world, since demand can rarely be predicted with certainty. However, the discussion of deterministic models is still of importance and interest because such deterministic models provide the foundation for developing an understanding of more complicated inventory systems. Finally, in many instances the results obtained from these deterministic models are very useful to the inventory manager in spite of the simplifying assumptions that are made.

12.3.1   Simple Lot-Size Model: Constant Demand, No Stockouts

Perhaps the most common and simplest inventory problem faced by a wide variety of manufacturers, wholesalers, and retailers is that of controlling the inventory of a given item at a single location, under the assumption that the demand for the item is a constant a units per time period. For this model, inventory items are assumed to be depleted continuously at the known constant rate and then replenished by the arrival, or production, of an "economic lot size" of new items. Thus, it is further assumed that items are produced, or ordered in equal numbers, Q at a time, and all Q items arrive simultaneously when they are ordered. Inventory shortages are assumed not to occur in this situation, and the only costs to be considered are the setup cost or ordering cost K, incurred at the time of production or ordering, a production or purchasing cost of c dollars per item, and an inventory holding cost of h dollars per item per unit of time. The question to be answered is "How much should be ordered?" The correct number to be ordered balances the *number* of orders placed in a unit of time against the *size* of the orders placed. When these costs are balanced properly, the total cost is minimized and the resulting amount produced or ordered is called the **economic lot-size** or **economic ordering quantity** (EOQ).

This particular inventory situation can be described graphically as shown in Fig. 12.1.

The costs associated with this model are obtained as follows.

1. The production (or ordering) costs per **cycle** (i.e., cycle = Q/a) is given by:

$$\text{Production (or ordering) cost per cycle} = \begin{cases} 0 & \text{if } Q = 0 \\ K + cQ & \text{if } Q > 0 \end{cases} \qquad (12\text{-}3)$$

2. The holding cost per cycle is determined as a function of the average inventory level during a cycle. From Fig. 12.1 it can be seen that the inventory varies from Q to 0 during a cycle. Thus, the average inventory level is $(Q + 0)/2 = Q/2$ items per unit of time, and the corresponding average holding cost is $hQ/2$ per unit of time. Each cycle is of length Q/a, so the holding cost per cycle is given by:

$$\text{Holding cost per cycle} = \frac{hQ^2}{2a} \qquad (12\text{-}4)$$

3. The total cost per cycle is now simply the sum of the ordering, or production costs, plus the holding costs, and is given by:

$$\text{Total cost per cycle} = K + cQ + \frac{hQ^2}{2a} \qquad (12\text{-}5)$$

4. The total costs per unit of time, TC, is given by:

$$TC = \text{total cost per unit of time} = \frac{K + cQ + hQ^2/2a}{Q/a} \qquad (12\text{-}6)$$

$$= \frac{aK}{Q} + ac + \frac{hQ}{2}$$

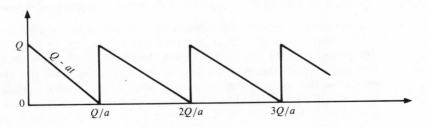

FIGURE 12.1 **Simple Lot-Size Model—Constant Demand, No Stockouts**

Now, from classical calculus it is evident that the value of Q, say Q^*, which minimizes TC, is found by solving

$$\frac{dTC}{dQ} = \frac{-aK}{Q^2} + \frac{h}{2} = 0$$

so that $Q^* = \sqrt{\frac{2aK}{h}}$ (12-7)

Furthermore, since $d^2TC/dQ^2 > 0$, we know that Equation 12–7 is a minimum. The result given by Equation 12–7 is the economic lot-size formula.

Similarly, the time t^* that is required for this economic lot size to be depleted is given by:

$$t^* = \frac{Q^*}{a} = \sqrt{\frac{2K}{ah}}$$ (12-8)

Let us now consider these results applied to a typical problem situation.

EXAMPLE   *Application of the EOQ Formula.*   A Texas-based manufacturer of electronic calculators orders its semiconductor components from Japan. Its monthly usage of semiconductor components is 10,000, and its ordering cost is $1000. Inventory holding costs are estimated to be $0.05 per unit per month. The economic lot size for this situation is given by:

$$Q^* = \sqrt{\frac{2aK}{h}} = \sqrt{\frac{2(10,000)(1,000)}{0.05}}$$

$$= \sqrt{400,000,000} = 20,000$$ (12-9)

The time required for this economic lot size to be depleted is

$$t^* = \frac{Q^*}{a} = \frac{20,000 \text{ units}}{10,000/\text{units/month}} = 2 \text{ months}$$ (12-10)

Thus, this company should place an order for 20,000 semiconductor components every 2 months.

12.3.2 Simple Lot-Size Model: Constant Demand, Shortages Allowed

The inventory problem discussed in the previous section becomes slightly more complicated when shortages are permitted to occur. However, there are many situations in which it is economically desirable to allow for shortages. Permitting shortages allows the manufacturer or retailer to increase the cycle time, thereby spreading the setup or ordering costs over a longer time period. Allowing shortages may also be desirable where the unit value of the inventory, and hence the inventory holding cost, is high. An example of this situation would be a recreational vehicle dealer who typically will not maintain an inventory of all the expensive (>$10,000) recreational vehicles that are sold. Rather, the dealer will order the particular recreational vehicle that the customer wants at the time of the sale.

Assume now that we allow shortages and that they are costed at \$4 for each unit of demand unfilled for one unit of time. Graphically, this situation can be summarized as in Fig. 12.2.

The costs associated with this model are obtained as follows.

1. The production (or ordering) cost per cycle is given by:

$$\text{Production (or ordering) cost per cycle} = \begin{cases} 0 & \text{if } Q = 0 \\ K + cQ & \text{if } Q > 0 \end{cases} \quad (12\text{–}11)$$

2. The holding cost per cycle is obtained in the following manner. From Fig. 12.2 it can be seen that the inventory level ranges from S to 0 over the time period S/a. Thus, the average inventory level during this time period is $(S + 0)/2 = S/2$, and the corresponding inventory holding cost is $hS/2$. Similarly, the holding cost for the period of time for which the inventory level is positive, or the holding cost per cycle, is given by:

$$\text{Holding cost per cycle} = \frac{hS}{2} \frac{S}{a} = \frac{hS^2}{2a} \quad (12\text{–}12)$$

3. The shortage cost per cycle is obtained in the following manner. From Fig. 12.2 it can be seen that the shortage level ranges from 0 to $(Q - S)$ and thus, the average shortage level is $(Q - S)/2$ per unit of time. Shortages occur for the time period $(Q - S)/a$. The corresponding shortage cost, where each shortage is priced at a cost of u dollars for each unit of demand unfilled for one unit of time, is $u(Q - S)/2$ per unit of time. Similarly, the total shortage cost for the period of time for which shortages exist, or the shortage cost per cycle, is given by:

$$\text{Shortage cost per cycle} = \frac{u(Q - S)}{2} \frac{(Q - S)}{a} = \frac{u(Q - S)^2}{2a} \quad (12\text{–}13)$$

4. The total cost per cycle is now simply the sum of the ordering or production costs, plus the holding costs, plus the shortage costs, and is given by:

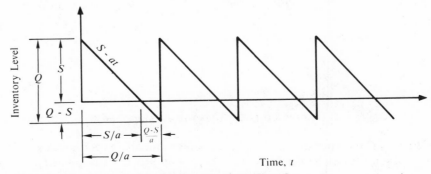

FIGURE 12.2 Simple Lot-Size Model—Shortages Allowed

$$\text{Total cost per cycle} = K + cQ + \frac{hS^2}{2a} + \frac{u(Q-S)^2}{2a} \qquad (12\text{-}14)$$

5. The total cost per unit of time, TC, is given by:

$$\text{Total cost per unit of time} = TC \;=\; \frac{K + cQ + \dfrac{hS^2}{2a} + \dfrac{u(Q-S)^2}{2a}}{Q/a} \qquad (12\text{-}15)$$

$$= \frac{aK}{Q} + ac + \frac{hS^2}{2Q} + \frac{u(Q-S)^2}{2Q}$$

Note that, in this function, we must solve for two unknowns (S and Q). The optimum values S^* and Q^* are found by solving the two partial derivatives:

$$\frac{\partial TC}{\partial S} = \frac{hS}{Q} - \frac{u(Q-S)}{Q} = 0 \qquad (12\text{-}16)$$

$$\frac{\partial TC}{\partial Q} = \frac{-aK}{Q^2} - \frac{hS^2}{2Q} + \frac{u(Q-S)}{Q} - \frac{u(Q-S)^2}{2Q^2} = 0 \qquad (12\text{-}17)$$

Solving Equations 12–16 and 12–17 simultaneously we obtain

$$S^* = \sqrt{\frac{2aK}{h}}\sqrt{\frac{u}{u+h}} \qquad (12\text{-}18)$$

$$Q^* = \sqrt{\frac{2aK}{h}}\sqrt{\frac{u+h}{u}} \qquad (12\text{-}19)$$

Furthermore, since it can be shown that $\partial^2 TC/\partial Q^2 > 0$ and $\partial^2 TC/\partial S^2 > 0$, Equations 12–18 and 12–19 are minima.

The time t^* that is required for the economic lot size to be depleted is given by:

$$t^* = \frac{Q^*}{a} = \sqrt{\frac{2K}{ah}}\sqrt{\frac{u+h}{u}} \qquad \text{(Cycle time)} \qquad (12\text{-}20)$$

The maximum shortage that can occur is given by:

$$Q^* - S^* = \sqrt{\frac{2aK}{u}}\sqrt{\frac{h}{u+h}} \qquad \text{(Maximum shortage)} \qquad (12\text{-}21)$$

Finally, the fraction of time that no shortage exists is given by:

$$\frac{S^*/a}{Q^*/a} = \frac{u}{u+h} \qquad (12\text{-}22)$$

Let us now consider these results applied to a typical problem situation.

EXAMPLE   The owner of a mobile home sales company experiences a constant demand of 40 units per month for mobile homes and incurs an ordering cost of $250 every time she places a new order with the factory. The inventory-holding costs are estimated to be $25 per unit per month, and a shortage cost of $100 is incurred for each mobile home demand that cannot be met. The economic lot size for this situation is determined as follows.

$$Q^* = \sqrt{\frac{2aK}{h}}\sqrt{\frac{u+h}{u}} = \sqrt{\frac{2(40)(250)}{25}}\sqrt{\frac{125}{100}} \tag{12-23}$$
$$= 31.61 \text{ (use 32)}$$

$$S^* = \sqrt{\frac{2aK}{h}}\sqrt{\frac{u}{u+h}} = \sqrt{\frac{2(40)(250)}{25}}\sqrt{\frac{100}{125}} \tag{12-24}$$
$$= 25.16 \text{ (use 25)}$$

$$t^* = \frac{Q^*}{a} = \frac{32}{40} = 0.800 \text{ months} \qquad \text{(Cycle time)} \tag{12-25}$$

$$Q^* - S^* = 32 - 25 = 7 \text{ units} \qquad \text{(Maximum shortage)} \tag{12-26}$$

Finally, the fraction of time that no shortage exists is

$$\frac{u}{u+h} = \frac{100}{100+25} = 0.80 \qquad \begin{array}{l}(i.e., \text{ no shortage exists for 0.80 of the} \\ \text{cycle time, or for } 0.80 \times 0.800 \text{ month} \\ = 0.64 \text{ month)}\end{array} \tag{12-27}$$

12.3.3 Uniform Replenishment Rate: Constant Demand, No Shortages

Let us now consider an inventory situation in which units are supplied to inventory at a uniform rate over time, rather than in an economic lot size at various points in time. Specifically, this inventory system has a uniform replenishment rate p that must be larger than, or equal to, the constant demand rate a. Graphically, this situation can be portrayed as is shown in Fig. 12.3. Observe in Fig. 12.3 that the inventory cycle is composed of two parts:

1. The length of time t_p required to produce a lot. During this time period there is a net inflow of $p - a$ units into inventory.

2. The length of time t_d required to deplete the inventory that has been built up during t_p. During this time period there is a net outflow of a units from inventory.

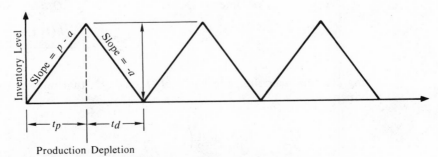

FIGURE 12.3 **Uniform Replenishment Rate Inventory Model**

The inventory level reaches its maximum value just as production is completed. This inventory level is then drawn down to a zero level, and the production cycle is again initiated.

The costs associated with this model are obtained as follows.

1. The production (or ordering) cost per cycle is given by:

$$\text{Production (or ordering) cost per cycle} = \begin{cases} 0 & \text{if } Q = 0 \\ K + cQ & \text{if } Q > 0 \end{cases} \quad (12\text{--}28)$$

2. The holding cost per cycle is obtained in the following manner. From Fig. 12.3 the inventory level is increased by $(p - a)$ units each unit of time. The length of time required to produce a lot $t_p = Q/p$. Thus, the maximum inventory level at the end of t_p will be

$$t_p(p - a) = \frac{Q}{p}(p - a) = Q\left(1 - \frac{a}{p}\right) \quad (12\text{--}29)$$

Now, the average inventory level will be

$$\frac{Q}{2}\left(1 - \frac{a}{p}\right) \quad (12\text{--}30)$$

and the holding cost per cycle will be given by:

$$\text{Holding cost per cycles} = \frac{Q^2}{2a}\left(1 - \frac{a}{p}\right) \cdot h \quad (12\text{--}31)$$

3. The total cost per cycle is now simply the sum of the production (or ordering) costs and the holding costs, and is given by:

$$K + cQ + \frac{Q^2}{2a}\left(1 - \frac{a}{p}\right) \cdot h \quad (12\text{--}32)$$

4. The total cost per unit of time TC is given by:

$$TC = \begin{array}{l}\text{total cost per unit} \\ \text{of time}\end{array} = \frac{K + cQ + \frac{Q^2}{2a}\left(1 - \frac{a}{p}\right) \cdot h}{Q/a} \quad (12\text{--}33)$$

$$= \frac{Ka}{Q} + ca + \frac{hQ\left(1 - \frac{a}{p}\right)}{2}$$

Using classical calculus, the value of Q, say Q^*, that minimizes TC is found by solving:

$$\frac{dTC}{dQ} = \frac{-aK}{Q^2} + \frac{h}{2}\left(1 - \frac{a}{p}\right) \quad (12\text{--}34)$$

so that
$$Q^* = \sqrt{\frac{2aK}{h}\left(\frac{p}{p - a}\right)} \qquad (12\text{-}35)$$

The length of time required to produce a lot is:

$$t_p^* = \frac{Q^*}{p} \qquad (12\text{-}36)$$

The length of time required to deplete the maximum on hand inventory is:

$$t_d^* = \frac{Q^*}{a}\left(1 - \frac{a}{p}\right) \qquad (12\text{-}37)$$

The length of a cycle is then given by:

$$t_c^* = t_p^* + t_d^* = \frac{Q^*}{a} \qquad (12\text{-}38)$$

Let us now consider these results applied to a typical problem situation.

EXAMPLE   The Gearing Machine Works manufactures a complete line of pistons that are supplied directly to its customers from a factory warehouse. One particular piston has a known and constant demand rate of 2000 units per year. The fixed cost of the setup for each production run is $100, and the inventory holding cost is $2 per unit per year. The production rate is 8000 units per year. The economic lot size for this situation is determined as follows.

$$Q^* = \sqrt{\frac{2aK}{h}\left(\frac{p}{p - a}\right)} = \sqrt{\frac{2(2000)(100)}{2}\left(\frac{8000}{8000 - 2000}\right)} \qquad (12\text{-}39)$$
$$= 516$$

The length of time required to produce a lot is

$$t_p^* = \frac{Q^*}{p} = \frac{516}{8000} = 0.065 \text{ year} \qquad (12\text{-}40)$$

The length of time required to deplete the maximum on hand inventory is

$$t_d^* = \frac{Q^*}{a}\left(1 - \frac{a}{p}\right) = \frac{516}{2000}\left(1 - \frac{2000}{8000}\right) \qquad (12\text{-}41)$$
$$= 0.194 \text{ year}$$

The length of the cycle is given by:

$$t_c^* = t_p^* + t_d^* = \frac{Q^*}{a} = \frac{516}{2000} = 0.259 \text{ year} \qquad (12\text{-}42)$$

12.3.4 Quantity Discounts: No Shortages

The deterministic inventory control models previously considered have been developed under the assumption that the unit cost of an item was independent of the quantity produced, or ordered. However, in many businesses and industries, **quantity discounts** are provided as an incentive for the purchase of larger quantities of products. Fortunately, the basic EOQ model can be modified for application to a situation in which quantity discounts are offered.

The general procedure for determining the economic lot size when quantity discounts are offered will now be illustrated using the data shown in Table 12.3. For this situation assume that the annual demand is for 10,000 units, the annual holding costs are 20 percent of the unit costs, and the ordering costs are $100 per order. No shortages are to be allowed.

To begin our evaluation of this inventory problem we compute an optimum economic lot size for each discount category, using Equation 12–7.

$$Q_A^* = \sqrt{\frac{2(10,000)(100)}{(0.20)(10)}} = 1000 \tag{12–43}$$

$$Q_B^* = \sqrt{\frac{2(10,000)(100)}{(0.20)(9.80)}} = 1010 \tag{12–44}$$

$$Q_C^* = \sqrt{\frac{2(10,000)(100)}{(0.20)(9.50)}} = 1025 \tag{12–45}$$

Note that the economic order quantities resulting from the three evaluations of Equation 12–7 are nearly the same, since the only difference is the slight change in the inventory holding cost (denominator) of the models. However, we observe that Q_B^* and Q_C^* are not sufficiently large to qualify for the discount that is possible. For those Q^* that are too small for the discount being offered, we adjust the order quantity upward to the nearest order quantity that will permit the quantity discount to be realized. In our current problem, these values become

$$Q_B^* = 1500 \tag{12–46}$$
$$Q_C^* = 2500 \tag{12–47}$$

If the calculated value of Q^* for a given unit cost is larger than the maximum order quantity required to receive this unit cost, this Q^* need not be considered any further, as it cannot lead to an optimal solution.

Now, in the quantity discount model the total annual cost will vary according

TABLE 12.3 Sample Data, Quantity Discounts

Discount Category	Order Size	Discount per Order,%	Unit Cost per Item, c
A	0 to 1499	0	$10.00
B	1500 to 2499	2	9.80
C	2500+	5	9.50

TABLE 12.4 Total Annual Costs, Quantity Discounts

Discount Category	Unit Cost per Item, c	Economic Order Quantity	Annual Inventory Holding Cost	Annual Ordering Cost	Annual Purchase Cost	Total Annual Cost
A	$10.00	1000	$1000	$1000	$100,000	$102,000
B	9.80	1500	1470	667	98,000	100,137
C	9.50	2500	2375	400	95,000	99,875

to the order quantity decision and the associated unit cost. The expression for the total annual cost in the quantity discount model is

$$\text{Total annual cost} = TC = \frac{aK}{Q} + \frac{hQ}{2} + ac \qquad (12\text{--}48)$$

Observe that this is the same expression for the total annual cost that we obtained for the derivation of the simple economic lot-size model (Equation 12–5). However, the order quantity situation is unlike the simple economic lot-size model in which we ignored the annual purchase cost of the item because it was constant and never affected by the inventory order quantity. Thus, we must now apply the total annual cost expression given by Equation 12–48 using the appropriate unit costs shown in Table 12.3. These computations are summarized in Table 12.4. As can be seen in Table 12.4, a decision to order 2500 units at the 5-percent discount rate will result in the minimum-cost solution. The higher discount rate possible for this order size more than offsets the higher inventory holding costs incurred.

12.3.5 Anticipated Price Change

Consider next a simple inventory system of the type described earlier in Section 12.3.1 in which we are informed that at some future time t_1 there will be a unit cost increase. Obviously, just prior to the date of the anticipated cost increase, the firm might want to place a special large order Q'. This inventory situation is shown graphically in Fig. 12.4.

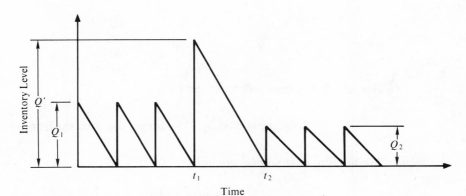

FIGURE 12.4 Anticipated Price Changes Inventory Model

For this situation the following notation will be employed.

c_1 = cost per unit before cost increase.
c_2 = cost per unit after cost increase.
p = inventory holding cost percentage per unit of time.
K = reorder cost.
t_1 = time when special order is placed (just prior to cost increase).
t_2 = time when inventory of special-order stock is depleted.
Q' = quantity ordered just prior to cost increase.
a = constant demand rate over time T.
Q_1 = optimal order quantity prior to cost increase.
Q_2 = optimal order quantity after cost increase.

We further assume that all of the variables noted above, with the exception of Q', have known values. Observe that the inventory holding cost = $h = cp$.

We begin our analysis of this inventory-modeling situation by observing that the time interval $t_2 - t_1 = Q'/a$. Now, if a special large order is placed:

1. Reordering cost = K during the interval from t_1 to t_2 (12-49)

2. Inventory holding cost $= \dfrac{hQ'}{2}\dfrac{Q'}{a}$ (12-50)

    $= \dfrac{c_1 p Q'}{2}\dfrac{Q'}{a}$ during the interval from t_1 to t_2 (12-51)

3. Purchase cost = $Q'c_1$ during the interval from t_1 to t_2

Thus, the total cost of placing a special order Q' during the time interval from t_1 to t_2 is given by:

$$\text{Total cost of placing an order for } Q' = K + \left(\frac{c_1 p Q'}{2}\right)\left(\frac{Q'}{a}\right) + Q'c_1 \quad (12\text{-}52)$$

Now, if no special order is placed during the time period t_1 to t_2, the firm will simply place orders of size:

$$Q_2^* = \sqrt{\frac{2Ka}{c_2 p}} \quad (12\text{-}53)$$

The reordering cost will be given by:

$$\text{Reordering cost} = \frac{KQ'}{Q_2}\text{during the interval from } t_1 \text{ to } t_2 \quad (12\text{-}54)$$

The holding cost will be given by:

$$\text{Holding cost} = \left(\frac{c_2 p Q_2}{2}\right)\left(\frac{Q'}{a}\right)\text{during the interval from } t_1 \text{ to } t_2 \quad (12\text{-}55)$$

The purchase cost will be given by:

$$\text{Purchase cost} = Q'c_2 \text{ during the interval from } t_1 \text{ to } t_2 \qquad (12\text{-}56)$$

Thus, the total cost of placing orders of size Q_2 during t_1 to t_2 is given by:

Total cost of placing orders of size Q_2 during t_1 to t_2 $\qquad (12\text{-}57)$

$$= \frac{KQ'}{Q_2} + \frac{c_2 p \, Q_2 Q'}{2a} + Q'c_2$$

Now, the savings possible from placing a large special order is equal to the difference in total costs given by Equation 12-57 − Equation 12-52. Thus, the possible savings is given by:

Savings that are due to a large special order $= SO = \dfrac{KQ'}{Q_2} + \dfrac{c_2 p Q_2 Q'}{2a} + Q'c_2 - K - \dfrac{c_1 p(Q')^2}{2a} - Q'c_1$

$$(12\text{-}58)$$

By differential calculus, the value of Q' that will maximize the savings that are due to a large special order is given by:

$$\frac{d}{dQ'}(SO) = Q' = Q_2 + \left[\frac{c_2 - c_1}{c_1} \right] \left[Q_2 + \left(\frac{a}{p} \right) \right] \qquad (12\text{-}59)$$

To illustrate these results consider the following problem situation.

EXAMPLE *Anticipated Price Change.* A manufacturer of lawn fertilizer is currently buying potassium at \$0.50 per pound, but anticipates that next month the price of potassium will increase to \$0.75 per pound. Potassium is used in the production of lawn fertilizer at the constant rate of 500 pounds per month. The inventory-holding cost, on an annual basis, is 20 percent of the cost of the potassium being carried in inventory. The ordering cost for an order is \$25.

If no special order were to be placed, the firm would order in lot sizes given by:

$$Q_2 = \sqrt{\frac{2Ka}{c_2 p}} = \sqrt{\frac{2 \cdot 25(12 \cdot 500)}{(0.75)(0.20)}} \qquad (12\text{-}60)$$

$$= 1414.20 \simeq 1414 \text{ pounds}$$

However, to take advantage of the anticipated price change, the firm should place a large special order of a size given by:

$$Q' = Q_2 + \left[\frac{c_2 - c_1}{c_1} \right] \left[Q_2 + \left(\frac{a}{p} \right) \right] \qquad (12\text{-}61)$$

$$= 1414 + \left[\frac{0.75 - 0.50}{0.50} \right] \left[1414 + \frac{6000}{0.20} \right]$$

$$= 17{,}121 \text{ pounds}$$

By placing the large special order, the savings realized will be given by:

$$
\begin{aligned}
\text{Savings} &= \frac{KQ'}{Q_2} + \frac{c_2 p Q_2 Q'}{2a} + Q'c_2 - K - \frac{c_1 p (Q)^2}{2a} - Q'c_1 \\[2mm]
&= \frac{(25)(17,121)}{1414} + \frac{(0.75)(0.20)(1414)(17,121)}{2(6000)} \\[2mm]
&\quad + (17,121)(0.75) - 25 - \frac{(0.50)(0.20)(17,121)^2}{2(6000)} - 17,121(0.50) \\[2mm]
&= 303 + 303 + 12,841 - 25 - 244 - 8561 = \$4617
\end{aligned}
\tag{12-62}
$$

12.4 PROBABILISTIC MODELS

We will now consider a more difficult type of inventory control problem in which the exact demand for an item is not known for certain in advance and therefore can only be described in probabilistic terms. Inventory models having this characteristic are called "probabilistic" or "stochastic" models. Inventory control problems having probabilistic demands often require a great deal of advanced mathematical analysis for solution. Consequently, we shall attempt to limit our discussion to probabilistic demand situations in which solutions can be derived using a reasonable level of mathematical rigor. It should also be emphasized that even when probabilistic demands exist, the inventory manager is still concerned with two basic decisions, namely "order timing" and "order size." Likewise, the relevant costs are still the ordering cost, the inventory holding cost, and the costs associated with shortages.

12.4.1 Reorder Point Model: Normal Demand During Leadtime

Consider an inventory control situation that can be described graphically as shown in Fig. 12.5. In Fig. 12.5 we can observe that there is a base **safety stock**, SS, and a cost associated with carrying this amount of inventory. For this situation we are concerned with the determination of the order point, or the point in time at which an economic order quantity of size $Q^* = \sqrt{2ak/h}$ is placed. Note that this determination of the order point is assumed not to affect the optimum order

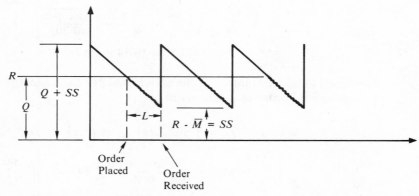

FIGURE 12.5 Reorder Point Model

quantity. This assumption ignores the effect that the selection of the order point may have with respect to carrying costs. Second, we assume that the demand rate a is constant over the "overlap" period, which is the period of time when new stock has been received but there is still old stock on hand. Third, we assume that the **lead time**, L, is also a constant but that M, the demand during the lead time, is normally distributed.

Based on the situation shown in Fig. 12.5, and the assumptions and characteristics noted above, the inventory model for this situation can be derived as follows. We seek to determine R^* the optimum reorder point, in terms of the number of units remaining in inventory at which time an order of size Q^* is placed. Recall that the amount demanded during the lead time was assumed to be a random variable. Thus, there will be $R - M$ units that are unsold at the point in time at which Q^* units are received. The time of overlap can now be expressed as $(R - M)/a$. Now, the costs of possible overage, or underage, during the lead time must be determined as a function of the probability of M. This situation is shown in Fig. 12.6. In Fig. 12.6, if M exceeds R, and there is a shortage cost, u, associated with each unit of lost sales, the cost of underage (shortage) $= u(M - R)$. If R exceeds M, and the inventory carrying cost per unit is h, the cost of overage $= [Q \cdot (R - M)/a] \cdot h = (Qh/a)(R - M)$. The total cost for this situation is given by:

Total cost = Expected cost of overage and expected cost of underage

$$\text{Total cost} = \int_{-\infty}^{R} \frac{Qh}{a}(R - M)f(M)dM + \int_{R}^{\infty} u(M - R)f(M)dM$$

$$= \frac{Q}{a}hR\int_{-\infty}^{R} f(M)dM - \frac{Q}{a}hR\int_{-\infty}^{R} Mf(M)dM \tag{12-63}$$

$$+ u\int_{R}^{\infty} Mf(M)dM - uR\int_{R}^{\infty} f(M)dM$$

$$= \frac{Q}{a}hR[F(R)] - \frac{Q}{a}h\left[\mathop{E}_{-\infty}^{R}(M)\right]$$

$$+ u\left[\mathop{E}_{R}^{\infty}(M)\right] - uR[G(R)]$$

where
$$F(R) + G(R) = 1 \tag{12-64}$$
$$G(R) = 1 - F(R)$$

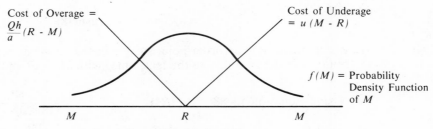

Cost of Overage = $\frac{Qh}{a}(R - M)$

Cost of Underage $= u(M - R)$

$f(M)$ = Probability Density Function of M

M R M

Demand During Lead Time

FIGURE 12.6   Cost During Lead Time, L

$$\left[\underset{-\infty}{\overset{R}{E}} (M) \right] = \text{the partial expectation of } M \text{ for values of } M \text{ from } -\infty \text{ to } R.$$

$$\left[\underset{R}{\overset{+\infty}{E}} (M) \right] = \text{the partial expectation of } M \text{ for values of } M \text{ from } R \text{ to } +\infty.$$

Furthermore, since $\overline{M} = \left[\underset{-\infty}{\overset{+\infty}{E}} (M) \right]$ (12–65)

$$\underset{R}{\overset{\infty}{E}} (M) = \overline{M} - \underset{-\infty}{\overset{R}{E}} (M)$$

Rearranging Equation 12–63 we obtain

$$\left(\frac{Q}{a}h + u \right)\left[RF(R) \right] - \left(\frac{Qh}{a} + u \right) \underset{-\infty}{\overset{R}{E}} (M) + u(\overline{M} - R)$$ (12–66)

To find the minimum of this total cost expression we take the derivative and set it equal to zero.

$$\frac{d \text{ Total cost}}{dR} = \left(\frac{Qh}{a} + u \right)\left[F(R) - Rf(R) \right] - \left(\frac{Qh}{a} + u \right)Rf(R) - u$$

$$= \left(\frac{Qh}{a} + u \right)F(R) - u = 0$$ (12–67)

Solving, we obtain $\quad F(R^*) = \dfrac{u}{\dfrac{Qh}{a} + u}$ (12–68)

The term $F(R^*)$ is interpreted as: Set R^* so that there is $u/(u + Qh/a)$ probability of M being equal to or less than R^*. To illustrate the preceding results, consider the following example.

EXAMPLE *Probabilistic (Normal) Demand.* A transmission rebuilder experiences a yearly demand of 200 units for a particular type of Chevrolet transmission. He has an inventory holding cost of $25 per unit per year, and a shortage cost of $50 per unit. Based on his reordering cost of $20 per order he has determined the economic order quantity to be:

$$Q^* = \sqrt{\frac{2aK}{h}} = \sqrt{\frac{2 \cdot 200 \cdot 20}{25}}$$ (12–69)

$$= \sqrt{320} = 17.9 \text{ (use 18)}$$

He wishes to develop an order-point system based on the assumption of a normal distribution of demand during the lead time, with $M = 10$ and $\sigma_M = 2$.

Using Equation 12–68: $\quad F(R^*) = \dfrac{u}{\dfrac{Qh}{a} + u} = \dfrac{50}{\dfrac{(18)(20)}{200} + 50}$ (12–70)

$$= 0.97$$

Now, we seek to find Z, the number of standard deviations we must go from the mean demand, $\overline{M}$, before the probability is $F(R^*)$ that the demand, M, is equal to or less than R^*. The situation we must consider is shown in Fig. 12.7. As can be seen in Fig. 12.7, the optimum order point, R^*, is given by:

$$R^* = \overline{M} \pm Z\sigma_M \begin{pmatrix} \text{Use } + Z\sigma_M \text{ if } F(R^*) > 0.50 \\ \text{Use } - Z\sigma_M \text{ if } F(R^*) < 0.50 \end{pmatrix} \tag{12-71}$$

For $F(R^*) = 0.97, Z = 1.88$ (from a standardized normal table). Thus, the optimum reorder point is

$$\begin{aligned} R^* = \overline{M} + Z\sigma_M &= 10 + 1.88(2) \\ &= 10 + 3.76 = 13.76 \text{ (use 14)} \end{aligned} \tag{12-72}$$

With an order point set at 14 units, we should not run out of units during the lead time 97 percent of the time.

The recommended inventory decision is to order 18 units whenever the inventory level reaches the reorder point of 14 units. Since the mean demand expected during the lead time is $\overline{M} = 10$ units, the safety stock $= SS = R^* - \overline{M} = 14 - 10 = 4$ units serves as a buffer, and these four units can be expected to prevent stockouts during the lead time, 97 percent of the time. The anticipated annual costs for this reorder point system are as follows.

$$\text{Reordering cost} = \left(\frac{a}{Q}\right) \cdot K = \frac{200}{18}(20) \quad = \$222.22 \tag{12-73}$$

$$\begin{aligned} \text{Inventory holding cost} \\ \text{(Normal inventory)} \end{aligned} = \left(\frac{Q}{2}\right)h = \frac{18}{2}(25) = \quad 225.00 \tag{12-74}$$

$$\begin{aligned} \text{Inventory holding cost} &= SS \cdot h = 4(25) \quad = \underline{100.00} \\ \text{(Safety stock)} & \qquad\qquad\qquad\qquad \$547.22 \end{aligned} \tag{12-75}$$

If the transmission rebuilder could have assumed that demand were a constant 200 units, $Q^* = 18$, $R^* = 200/18 = 12$ units, and the total annual cost of $\$222.22 + \$225.00 = \$447.22$ would be expected. However, since the demand pattern is considered to be uncertain, the transmission rebuilder must pay for this uncertainty by maintaining a safety stock of four units, which costs an additional $\$100$ yearly.

As we evidenced in the previous example, the safety stock absorbs variations in demand and/or variations in supply lead time. Obviously, the larger the safety stock, the smaller is the risk of running out of inventory. The inventory control problem thus becomes one of setting the safety stock at a level such that the risk of a stockout is acceptably low. Herein, a common managerial practice involves

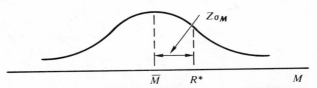

FIGURE 12.7 Normal Distribution of M, Demand During Lead Time

the determination of a service level that guarantees that average stockouts will not exceed some predefined level.

From our previous example involving normal demand during the replenishment lead time, the safety stock was computed as:

$$\text{Safety stock:} \quad SS = R^* - \overline{M} = Z\sigma_M \tag{12-76}$$

Thus, for a specified distribution (i.e., the normal distribution in this situation) and a known value of σ_M, the safety stock can be determined for various service levels using the data of the previous example, as shown in Table 12.5. Within Table 12.5 the probability of a stockout, or conversely, the service level determines the value of Z that is employed in the computation of the required safety stock using Equation 12–76. In general, the safety stock requirement can be computed as:

$$\text{Safety stock:} \quad SS = n\sigma_M \tag{12-77}$$

where n = safety factor based on the service level
required and the probability distribution being
used to describe demand during the lead time.

12.4.2 Payoff Table Analysis

When the probability for demand is discrete and has a finite number of possible demand values, a **payoff table analysis** can be performed. To illustrate a payoff table analysis, consider the following situation. The Agrico Fertilizer Company produces a liquid fertilizer in 1000-gallon batches. A typical customer orders from 1 to 5 batches every 3 months, and since the production process for the liquid fertilizer is continuous the production decision (number of batches in a production run) must be made prior to the receipt of an order. Although Agrico can list the possible alternatives resulting from demands ranging from 1000 to 5000 gallons, the exact demand distribution is uncertain.

The manufacturing costs for the production process are $100 per 1000 gallons, and the fertilizer sells for $500 per 1000 gallons. If shortages occur Agrico must buy a similar liquid fertilizer from a competitor in order to satisfy customer demand. This substitute liquid fertilizer will cost Agrico $750 per 1000 gallons. The liquid fertilizer is a highly volatile, unstable chemical and cannot be stored safely for any long period of time. Consequently, any production run that is not completely sold is chemically neutralized with an attendant salvage value of $50 per 1000 gallons.

TABLE 12.5   Required Safety Stock at Various Service Levels

Probability of a Stockout	Service Level (%)	Required Safety Stock: $SS = Z\sigma_M$
0.25	75	$SS = 0.674(2) = 1.348$
0.20	80	$SS = 0.842(2) = 1.684$
0.15	85	$SS = 1.036(2) = 2.072$
0.10	90	$SS = 1.282(2) = 2.564$
0.05	95	$SS = 1.645(2) = 3.290$
0.001	99.9	$SS = 3.090(2) = 6.180$

This problem situation can be treated as a single-period inventory model since customer orders are received once every 3 months and no inventory is maintained. Thus, production setup costs are fixed, regardless of the size of the production run, and can be ignored. Since no inventory is maintained, no inventory carrying costs are incurred. Consequently, this single-period inventory problem can be couched in terms of maximizing the profits, or payoffs, associated with a particular size of order rather than minimizing the ordering and inventory-holding costs.

We will now proceed to determine the profits associated with the various demand and order size possibilities. Let

$$p = \text{selling price per 1000 gallons} = \$500$$

$$c = \text{cost of manufacturing per 1000 gallons} = \$100$$

$$d = \text{cost of outside purchase per 1000 gallons} = \$750$$

$$s = \text{salvage value per 1000 gallons} = \$50$$

$$Q = \text{production quantity}$$

$$D = \text{demand quantity}$$

The profit (payoff) equations can be written as a function of three possible demand situations.

1. If $Q = D$

$$\text{Payoff } (P) = (\text{sales}) - (\text{production cost})$$
$$= \$500 \cdot D - \$100 \cdot Q \tag{12–78}$$

2. If $Q < D$

$$\text{Payoff } (P) = (\text{sales}) - (\text{production cost}) - (\text{shortage cost})$$
$$= \$500 \cdot D - \$100 \cdot Q - \$750(D - Q) \tag{12–79}$$
$$= -\$250 \cdot D + \$650 \cdot Q$$

3. If $Q > D$

$$\text{Payoff } (P) = (\text{sales}) - (\text{production cost}) + (\text{salvage value})$$
$$= \$500 \cdot D - \$100 \cdot Q + \$50 \cdot (Q - D) \tag{12–80}$$
$$= \$450 \cdot D - \$ 50 \cdot Q$$

These three profit equations can now be used to compute Agrico's profits under all combinations of order quantities and demands. These profit computations are summarized in Table 12.6. Note that the profits shown in Table 12.6 are conditional, based on specific order size (Q) – demand (D) possibilities.

In order to make a decision concerning the order quantity we must make an assessment of the probability distribution for demand. Assume that an analysis of orders for the last 5 years indicates a demand pattern as shown in Table 12.7.

TABLE 12.6 Conditional Payoff Table—Agrico Fertilizer Company

Possible Order Quantity Q(×1000)	Potential Demand D(×1000)	Sales ($500 · D)	Production Cost ($100 · Q)	Shortage Cost $750(D − Q)	Salvage Value $50(Q − D)	Total Profit (P)
1	1	$ 500	$100	$ 0	0	$ 400
	2	1000	100	750	0	150
	3	1500	100	1500	0	−100
	4	2000	100	2250	0	−350
	5	2500	100	3000	0	−600
2	1	500	200	0	50	350
	2	1000	200	0	0	800
	3	1500	200	750	0	550
	4	2000	200	1500	0	300
	5	2500	200	2250	0	50
3	1	500	300	0	100	300
	2	1000	300	0	50	750
	3	1500	300	0	0	1200
	4	2000	300	750	0	950
	5	2500	300	1500	0	700
4	1	500	400	0	150	250
	2	1000	400	0	100	700
	3	1500	400	0	50	1150
	4	2000	400	0	0	1600
	5	2500	400	750	0	1350
5	1	500	500	0	200	200
	2	1000	500	0	150	650
	3	1500	500	0	100	1100
	4	2000	500	0	50	1550
	5	2500	500	0	0	2000

TABLE 12.7 Demand Distribution—Agrico Fertilizer Company

Demand D(×1000)	Probability of Demand, D
1	0.20
2	0.20
3	0.30
4	0.20
5	0.10

We can now compute the expected profit associated with each order quantity by multiplying the conditional profits by their associated probabilities. These expected profits are as follows.

$$\text{Expected profit } (Q = 1000) = 0.2(400) + 0.2(150) + 0.3(-100)$$
$$+ 0.2(-350) + 0.1(-600) \tag{12–81}$$
$$= -\$50$$

$$\text{Expected profit } (Q = 2000) = 0.2(350) + 0.2(800) + 0.3(550) \\ + 0.2(300) + 0.1(50) \tag{12-82}$$

$$= \$460$$

$$\text{Expected profit } (Q = 3000) = 0.2(300) + 0.2(750) + 0.3(1200) \\ + 0.2(950) + 0.1(700) \tag{12-83}$$

$$= \$830$$

$$\text{Expected profit } (Q = 4000) = 0.2(250) + 0.2(700) + 0.3(1150) \\ + 0.2(1600) + 0.1(1350) \tag{12-84}$$

$$= \$990$$

$$\text{Expected profit } (Q = 5000) = 0.2(200) + 0.2(650) + 0.3(1100) \\ + 0.2(1550) + 0.1(2000) \tag{12-85}$$

$$= \$1010$$

Consequently, our payoff table analysis indicates that Agrico Fertilizer Company should produce in $Q = 5000$-gallon batches in order to maximize profits for its single-period inventory situation. Note once again that a payoff table analysis is applicable to discrete demand situations having a finite number of possible demand values.

12.4.3 Marginal Analysis

In the previous section of this chapter we considered the use of a payoff table analysis for a single-period inventory problem in which demand could be described by a discrete distribution having a finite number of possible values. Unfortunately, there are many inventory situations in which demand must be described by a continuous probability distribution. Thus, a payoff table analysis is not possible. Instead, we must resort to a **marginal** or **incremental analysis**. Marginal analysis will now be illustrated by means of an example.

EXAMPLE Consider Tred-Mart Stores, Inc., which is contemplating its fall order of 21-in. color television sets for its 25 Arizona outlets. Based on historical experience, management of Tred-Mart Stores, Inc. has concluded that yearly demand for the 21-in. color television set can be described by a normal distribution with mean $u = 2000$ sets and standard deviation $\sigma = 200$ sets.

Incremental analysis approaches the "order size" problem by considering the cost and/or loss associated with either stocking or not stocking additional units. Tred-Mart Stores, Inc. has determined that each television set will cost \$350; can be sold for \$400; and if not sold at the end of one year, will have a "mark down" value of \$310. Based on these considerations, the "loss" associated with stocking one additional unit when it is not needed is the original cost minus the salvage value, or \$350 − \$310 = \$40. Conversely, the "loss" associated with not stocking one additional unit when it is needed is the selling price minus the original cost, or \$400 − \$350 = \$50. These two types of losses can be written in general as:

$$L_+ = c - s \tag{12-86}$$

$$L_- = p - c \qquad\qquad (12\text{-}87)$$

where

$L_+ =$ loss associated with stocking one additional unit and finding it could not be sold.

$L_- =$ loss associated with not stocking one additional unit and finding it could be sold.

$c =$ cost per unit.

$s =$ salvage value per unit.

$p =$ selling price per unit.

To determine the expected value of the losses we must multiply the possible losses by the probabilities associated with these possible losses. The general expressions for the expected losses can be written as:

$$EL_+ = L_+ \cdot P(D \le Q^*) \qquad\qquad (12\text{-}88)$$

$$EL_- = L_- \cdot P(D > Q^*) \qquad\qquad (12\text{-}89)$$

where

$$D = \text{demand}$$

$$Q^* = \text{optimal order quantity}$$

Using a marginal analysis we would then want to equate the expected loss associated with having an additional unit to the expected loss associated with not having an incremental unit. Thus, the optimal order quantity will be found when:

$$L_+ \cdot P(D \le Q^*) = L_- \cdot P(D > Q^*) \qquad\qquad (12\text{-}90)$$

Furthermore, we know that:

$$P(D > Q^*) = 1 - P(D \le Q^*) \qquad\qquad (12\text{-}91)$$

Substituting Equation 12–91 into Equation 12–90 we obtain

$$L_+ \cdot P(D \le Q^*) = L_- \cdot [1 - P(D < Q^*)]$$

$$L_+ \cdot P(D \le Q^*) = L_- - [L_- \cdot P(D \le Q^*)] \qquad (12\text{-}92)$$

$$[L_+ \cdot P(D \le Q^*)] + [L_- \cdot P(D \le Q^*)] = L_-$$

$$P(D \le Q^*) = \frac{L_-}{L_+ + L_-}$$

We previously determined our losses to be

$$L_+ = c - s = \$350 - \$310 = \$40 \qquad\qquad (12\text{-}93)$$

$$L_- = p - c = \$400 - \$350 = \$50 \qquad\qquad (12\text{-}94)$$

Thus, Equation 12–92 can be evaluated as:

$$P(D \leq Q^*) = \frac{L_-}{L_+ + L_-} = \frac{50}{40 + 50} = 0.56 \tag{12-95}$$

Now, we can determine the optimal order quantity for Q^* by considering the probability distribution for demand, which is predicted to be normal with mean $u = 2000$ and $\sigma = 200$. We seek to find a Q^*, using a normal distribution having a mean $u = 2000$ and standard deviation $\sigma = 200$, such that:

$$P(D \leq Q^*) = 0.56 \tag{12-96}$$

Referring to a standardized normal table, we observe that 0.56 of the area under the normal curve is obtained for a Z value of 0.15. Thus, we can compute Q^* as:

$$\begin{aligned} Q^* &= u + Z\sigma \\ &= 2000 + (0.15)(200) \\ &= 2030 \text{ units} \end{aligned} \tag{12-97}$$

Thus, Tred-Mart Stores, Inc. should order 2030 units of 21-in. color television sets under this assumed set of demand conditions.

12.5 MATERIAL REQUIREMENTS PLANNING

A **material requirements planning** (MRP) system is a production/inventory-control information system that utilizes data from various organizational sources to determine the time-phased demand for end products and then uses this end-product demand to calculate the time phasing of the demand for component parts and raw materials. Inherent in the use of an MRP system is the fact that the end product is an assembly composed of components, whose demand is thus **dependent**. This is in contrast to an **independent** demand situation for which inventories should be controlled by the use of order-point and economic-order quantity equations. Thus, an MRP system is a logical means of examining a finished product, exploding it into its component parts, and specifying the lead times at which the component parts should be incorporated into the assembled product. An MRP system is typically used to determine how much of the components of a company's finished product should be ordered, and when over time these components should be ordered. MRP systems are useful in managing dependent-demand items, in production planning, scheduling, and inventory control. A graphic representation of the MRP process is shown in Fig. 12.8.

Referring to Fig. 12.8 and our previous discussion, it should be emphasized that there are a number of factors that are required prior to attempting to develop and implement an MRP system. Key factors are:

1. The production process must involve end products that are composed of assemblies, subassemblies, or component parts.
2. An accurate bill-of-materials must exist for each **end item** and its associated components, and it must be in a form that will allow it to be structured in a computerized file.
3. Accurate inventory status information must be available for each item and its

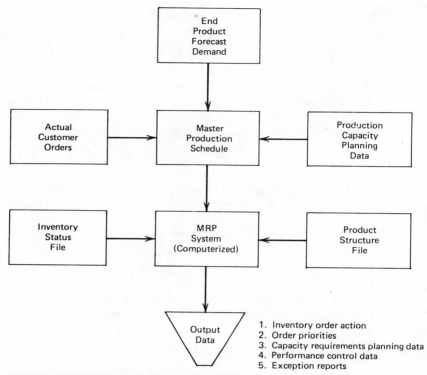

FIGURE 12.8   Material Requirements Planning Process

associated components, and it must be in a form that will allow it to be structured in a computerized file.

4.   The overall production plan for all end items must be expressed in the form of a master production schedule, which is then adhered to throughout the production process.

5.   The company must have available a computer for use in making the computations required in MRP and for maintaining the MRP data files. Experience in developing and implementing other large-scale computer systems is also useful.

When these requirements are present MRP can be very useful to a company for improving efficiency in:

1.   Inventory control.
2.   Priority planning and expediting.
3.   Providing data for capacity requirements planning.

Material requirements planning has become very widely used during the last decade, primarily as a result of improvements in computer technology—and the dissemination of reports concerning its successful utilization. It has become a way of life for industries involved in fabrication and assembly, such as transportation equipment and consumer appliances. It has received particular emphasis from the membership of the American Production and Inventory Control Society (APICS).

12.5.1 Product Structure File

The product structure file, also called the **bill-of-materials** file, contains up-to-date, accurate information on every assembly, subassembly, component, part, or raw material item required to produce an end product. This means that the bill-of-materials must be carefully structured, according to the actual manufacturing process, from the product-end-item level down to the assembly, component, and raw-material level. The bill-of-materials is much more than just a parts list, and its structuring requires careful attention. Information on each part in the end product, such as part number, quantity required per end item, description, and use in next higher assembly, is required. The bill of materials is structured in levels, with each **level** representing a stage in the manufacturing process.

To illustrate the bill-of-materials concept let us trace through the development of a product structure file for a simple product. Consider the Roll-Ease Company, which manufactures a metal office chair whose construction is as shown in Fig. 12.9.

The product structure for the Roll-Ease metal office chair is shown in the tree diagram of Fig. 12.10. The bill-of-materials file for the metal office chair would appear as follows.

Bill-of-Materials: Roll-Ease Metal Office Chair

Metal Office Chair	Part No. 0001
Seat and Back Assembly	Part No. 1001 (1)
Legs Assembly	Part No. 1002 (1)
Roller Assembly	Part No. 1003 (3)
Seat and Back Assembly	Part No. 1001
Padding Kit	Part No. 2001 (1)
Formed Frame	Part No. 2002 (1)
Legs Assembly	Part No. 1002

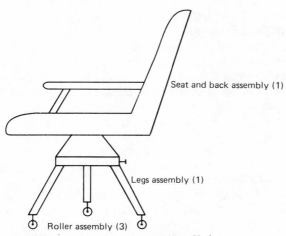

FIGURE 12.9 **Roll-Ease Metal Office Chair**

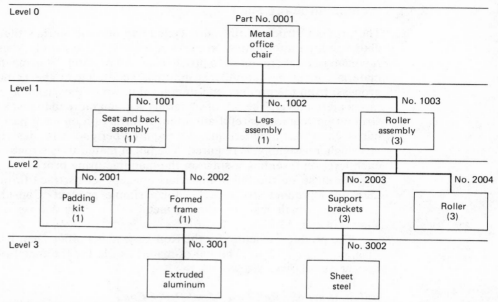

FIGURE 12.10   Product Structure Tree Diagram for Roll-Ease Metal Office Chair

Roller Assembly	Part No. 1003
Support Brackets	Part No. 2003 (3)
Rollers	Part No. 2004 (4)
Formed Frame	Part No. 2002
Extruded Aluminum	Part No. 3001
Support Brackets	Part No. 2003
Sheet Steel	Part No. 3002

Note the hierarchial nature of this bill-of-material. It begins at level 0, the end product level at which one metal office chair is produced. This end product is assigned Part No. 0001, with the first 0 in this 4-digit number specifying that it is a finished product (end item) and the final 1 specifying its unique part number. Within the bill of material we observe that this end product is composed of one seat and back assembly, one legs assembly, and three roller assemblies. Each of these assemblies now has a 1 as the first digit in its part number indicating that we have moved down one level in the manufacturing process. Moving down to level 2, we observe that the seat and back assembly has two lower-level components (i.e., padding kit and formed frame), the legs assembly has no lower-level component (i.e., it is a directly purchased component), and the roller assembly has two lower-level components (i.e., support brackets and rollers). Moving finally to level 3 we see that the formed frame is made of extruded aluminum while the support brackets are made of sheet steel.

It is important to emphasize that the product structure file must be accurate. The MRP system utilizes the product structure file to develop lower-level schedules for all assemblies, subassemblies, components, and raw materials. Thus, the accuracy of the product structure file is essential to production planning and scheduling. If a lower-level component is missing, a shortage will occur, while if the quantity specified for an item is too large, an unnecessary work-in-process inventory will be created.

12.5.2 Inventory Status File

The **inventory status file** contains up-to-date, accurate information on every assembly, subassembly, component, part, or raw-material item required to produce an end product. As with the bill-of-materials file, all inventory items must be uniquely defined. This is done using the same part-numbering system as is used for the bill-of-materials file. All end products carry the storage addresses (commonly called **pointers**) of the respective bill of materials in their inventory status records. Thus, the inventory status file and the bill-of-materials file are linked for purposes of computation of requirements.

The inventory status file contains information about every part number that is to be controlled by the MRP system. It contains the part number, the lead time for purchasing the item or producing it from its components, the gross requirements, scheduled receipts (open orders), quantity on hand, and planned-order releases. This basic information is all that is required for MRP processing. However, in many MRP systems the inventory status files may contain additional data such as scrap rates and change orders.

To illustrate the format of the inventory record output from an MRP system, let us return to our example concerning the manufacturing of the Roll-Ease metal office chair. The inventory record for this end product is shown in Table 12.8.

TABLE 12.8 Inventory Record—Metal Office Chair

Item: Part No. 0001 (manufactured) Lead Time: 1 week Metal Office Chair	Week											
	1	2	3	4	5	6	7	8	9	10	11	12
Gross Requirements		100		100		75		75		150		50
Scheduled Receipts		75		75		100		100		100		50
On Hand (50)	50	25	25	0	0	25	25	50	50	0	0	0
Planned-Order Releases	75		75		100		100		100		50	

Table 12.8 indicates that planning is to be done for 12 weeks into the future. The weeks indicated across the top of the report are the time periods, or **time buckets**, of the planning horizon.

The numbers in the "**Gross Requirements**" row of Table 12.8 indicate the quantity of the item that will be disbursed, or issued, out of inventory to go into some higher-level assembly or to supply the demand for the item as an end product (i.e., in this instance we are considering the end product). In our example Roll-Ease plans to ship 100 finished metal chairs in weeks 2 and 4, 75 finished metal chairs in weeks 6 and 8, 150 finished metal chairs in week 10, and 50 finished metal chairs in week 12. The numbers in the "Scheduled Receipts" row indicate the quantity of metal chairs that are scheduled to be completed and to go into inventory in each week of the planning horizon. In our example Roll-Ease anticipates receipts of 75 metal chairs in weeks 2 and 4, 100 metal chairs in weeks 6 and 8, and 50 metal chairs in week 10. The numbers in the "On Hand" row indicate the planned inventory level in each week of the planning horizon. In our example Roll-Ease has a beginning inventory of 50 metal chairs. In week 1 there are no requirements and no receipts of metal chairs. Thus, the balance, or "On Hand" at the end of week 1 is $50 + 0 - 0 = 50$. Note that this is simply the well-known **perpetual inventory** approach: Quantity available (next period) equals quantity on hand (current period) plus scheduled receipts (current period) minus anticipated demand (current period). In week 2, however, there are scheduled receipts of 75 metal chairs and gross requirements of 100 metal chairs. Thus, the "On Hand" at the end of week 2 is $50 + 75 - 100 = 25$. The "On Hand" quantities for the remaining weeks in the planning horizon are computed in similar fashion. The "Planned-Order Release" row indicates the week (time bucket) an order must be released so that it will be received in the week (time bucket) indicated in the "Scheduled Receipts" row. Note that the metal chair has a 1-week lead time, so that "Planned-Order Releases" must be time-phased backwards one week to be available in the week indicated in the "Scheduled Receipts" row. This procedure is referred to as **lead time offsetting**.

The example presented above should make it clear that the inventory status file must be maintained in an up-to-date and accurate manner. The "Planned-Order Releases" that are the output of the MRP system cannot be accurately computed, and time phased, unless all inventory transactions are posted in an accurate and timely manner.

12.5.3   Master Production Schedule

The aggregate demand for end products is initially forecasted over a number of time periods. This end product demand is then scheduled over these time periods in the form of a **master production schedule**. The master production schedule expresses the overall production plan for all end-product demand, taking into account actual customer orders and production capacity planning information. It may also allow for an accumulation or a depletion of inventory, based upon expected marketing action. In determining the master production schedule a planning horizon that includes the cumulative procurement and production lead times for all of the components of the finished product is used. In practice a planning horizon composed of several 1-week time increments is employed. It is important to note that this master production schedule is developed from both end-item forecasts and actual customer orders. It also must be done in a realistic manner that takes into consideration available production capacity planning data. Master production scheduling is *only* done at the end-product level, and it then becomes the driving force for the MRP system.

12.5.4   The Material Requirements Planning System

The MRP system is generally a set of computer programs (i.e., commercially available software packages) that accesses as input the master production schedule, product structure data, and inventory status data. It then performs all of the calculations necessary to obtain or produce all of the component items at the proper time so that the end-product items in the master production schedule can be produced as required. Thus, the end-product items in the master production schedule are **exploded** through all levels of their bills of materials to arrive at the gross requirement of all components necessary for the end product.

The processing logic of an MRP system is designed to produce an output report that is a detailed schedule for the release of each component for either production or purchase. It utilizes *level-by-level processing*, beginning at the zero level, or end product, and working downward to the raw materials requirements. To illustrate this process refer to Table 12.9, which shows the relationship between the inventory records for the roller components of our metal office chair. The linkage between the three inventory records shown in Table 12.9 is between the end-item planned-order release and the component gross requirements. This linkage must also be correctly time phased because the components must be available at the time the end item is released for production.

The explosion of requirements from the master production schedule down through the various component levels is guided by the logical linkage of inventory records, and their associated time phasing. At each level the **net requirements** are computed using the relationship:

TABLE 12.9   Relationships Between Inventory Records for Three Levels of Production of the Metal Office Chair

(Level 0)
Item: Part No. 0001 (manufactured)
Lead time: 1 week
Metal office chair

	1	2	3	4	5	6	7	8	9	10	11	12
Gross requirements										150		
Scheduled receipts										100		
On hand (50)									50	0		
Planned-order releases[a]									100			

[a] *Note:* The planned-order releases of 100 metal office chairs must be multiplied by 3 to arrive at the gross requirements of the roller assembly because there are 3 roller assemblies

lead time offset
(1 week)

(Level 1)
Item: Part No. 1003
Lead time: 2 weeks
Roller assembly

	1	2	3	4	5	6	7	8	9	10	11	12
Gross requirements									300			
Scheduled receipts									150			
On hand								150	0			
Planned-order releases							150					

lead time offset
(2 weeks)

(Level 2)
Item: Part No. 2003
Lead time: 3 weeks
Support brackets

	1	2	3	4	5	6	7	8	9	10	11	12
Gross requirements							150					
Scheduled receipts							125					
On hand						25	0					
Planned-order releases				125								

lead time offset (3 weeks)

$$\text{Net requirements} = \text{Gross requirements} - \text{Available inventory} \quad (12\text{-}98)$$

Obviously, if the available inventory is equal to, or exceeds, the gross requirements for an item, then the net requirements for the item is zero.

Initially, the computed net requirements for the end item are covered by the planned-order releases for the end item. The quantity and timing of planned-order releases for the end items then are used to determine the component gross requirements at the next lower level. This procedure is then repeated for successively lower levels, down to the raw materials requirement.

Focusing on weeks 9 and 10 in Table 12.9, we observe that in week 10 we need scheduled receipts of 100 to be added to the on-hand inventory of 50 in order to be able to satisfy the gross requirements (demand) of 150. Offsetting this scheduled receipt of 100 units by the 1-week lead time for the end-item results in a planned-order release of 100 for week 9 for the end item.

This planned-order release of 100 metal chairs is then multiplied by 3 (i.e., there are three roller assemblies per metal chair) to arrive at a gross requirement of 300 roller assemblies in week 9. Assuming an on-hand balance of 150 items at the end of week 8, we need scheduled receipts of 150 to be added to our on-hand inventory in order to be able to satisfy the gross requirements (demand) of 300. Offsetting this scheduled receipt of 150 units by the 2-week lead time for the roller assembly results in a planned-order release of 150 for week 7, for the roller assembly.

This planned-order release of 150 roller assemblies then becomes the gross requirements for the support bracket in week 7. Assuming an on-hand balance of 25 support brackets at the end of week 6, we need scheduled receipts of 125 to be added to the on-hand inventory to be able to satisfy the gross requirements (demand) of 150. Offsetting this scheduled receipt of 125 units by the 3-week lead time for the support bracket results in planned-order release of 125 for week 4, for the support bracket.

The process of moving from gross requirements to net requirements to planned-order releases down to the lowest level of the production process is the most important characteristic of an MRP system. To generate a planned order correctly, the MRP system must determine

1. The starting date of the planned-order release.
2. The **due date** of the planned-order receipt.
3. The planned-order quantity.

The *timing* of these planned-orders is usually determined in a straightforward manner, using the lead time associated with a particular component. However, the determination of the planned-order release quantity may not be simply a matter of setting it equal to the net requirement. For example, a component may be used in more than one higher-level assembly or in more than one end item. A typical MRP system will sum all of the net requirements at one level and set them equal to the planned-order releases at that level and to the gross requirements at the next lower level. Then, at this point in the material requirements planning process, one of a number of possible **lot-sizing**, or **ordering, rules** may be applied. These lot-sizing, or ordering, rules are designed to balance inventory-holding costs against ordering or production setup costs, and are determined independently of the MRP system. Thus, it is important to note that MRP is not exactly an inventory control system and that the crucial question of how much to order must be answered using cost data external to the MRP system. Orlicky has suggested that there are at least nine approaches to lot sizing that may be used in MRP systems, including:[1]

1. Fixed-order quantity
2. Economic order quantity (EOQ)
3. Lot for lot
4. Fixed-period requirements
5. Period order quantity (POQ)
6. Least-unit cost (LUC)
7. Least-total cost (LTC)
8. Part-period balancing (PPB)
9. Wagner-Whitin dynamic programming algorithm

Two approaches have been employed to actually implement MRP systems. These approaches are

1. **Regenerative approach**
2. **Net-change approach**

Under the *regenerative approach*, every end item in the master production schedule is exploded periodically, on the basis of the latest master production schedule requirements. Thus, every active bill-of-materials is retrieved, the status of every inventory item is recomputed, and a voluminous amount of output is produced. Regenerative MRP systems are designed for low-frequency replanning (i.e., a weekly or longer cycle) and employ batch-processing techniques. In a *net-change approach* to MRP, only part of the master production schedule is exploded at any one time. Thus, the entire requirements for all components are not recalculated periodically; instead, only additions and subtractions from the master schedule are entered. The effect of explosions down to lower levels is then limited to the end item triggering the explosion. A net-change MRP system is used for high-frequency replanning, and it is typically run once a day.

12.5.5 Output of the Material Requirements Planning System

A material requirements planning system produces a voluminous amount of output, which may be in a variety of formats, at the discretion of the user. While the specific format of the output varies widely by user, there are six broad categories of output information that are typically produced:[2]

1. Outputs for inventory order action—based primarily on planned orders becoming mature for release in the current time period.
2. Outputs for replanning order priorities—used for rescheduling when the open-order due date and the date of actual need have diverged.
3. Outputs to help safeguard priority integrity—used to relate problems of item inventory status to the master production schedule.
4. Outputs for capacity requirements planning—based on the use of quantities and due dates of both open- and planned-shop order as input to the capacity-requirements-planning (loading) system.

---

[1] J. Orlicky, *Material Requirements Planning* (New York: McGraw-Hill Book Company, 1975), pp. 120–138.
[2] Orlicky, *Material Requirements Planning*, pp. 142–144.

5. Outputs to aid in performance control—used to measure deviations that enable management to monitor the performance of inventory planners, buyers, vendors, and the shop, as well as financial or cost performance.
6. Outputs reporting errors, incongruities, or out-of-bound situations—exception reports indicate to the user that data is invalid or inconsistent.

12.5.6 Advantages and Disadvantages of Material Requirements Planning

Since its inception around 1960 material requirements planning has become widely used throughout American industry. Many of its users have become strong advocates of the MRP approach. Among the advantages indicated for MRP are

1. Reduction in finished goods and work-in-process inventories.
2. Better customer service, including greater reliability of delivery promise dates, reduction in loss sales, expediting of due dates for orders.
3. Better planning, including improvement in the planning and timing of design changes, reduction of lead times, and improvement in keeping priorities of work items up to date.
4. Facilitates capacity requirements planning, including better equipment utilization, better scheduling of maintenance, and increased identification of bottlenecks in various work centers.
5. Minimization of shortages of component parts.
6. Provides for the *exact* explosion of end-product needs into component parts needs.
7. Provides a large amount of useful time-phased data, which facilitates future planning efforts.
8. Reacts quickly to the dynamic change inherent in production systems.
9. Fully utilizes the power of the digital computer in considering a large-scale and complex manufacturing problem.

In spite of the number of advantages afforded by material requirements planning systems, such systems are not without some inherent disadvantages. Among the disadvantages indicated for material requirements planning are

1. A computer must be available to perform the necessary computations and to manipulate the data files.
2. MRP applies only to products that are assembled from component parts.
3. Bills-of-materials and inventory status files must be completely and accurately determined for all products in the MRP system.
4. A valid master schedule must be determined.
5. Accurate data must be available from the shop floor and various inventory locations.
6. Users must be able to interpret and use the output from the system.
7. The plan resulting from the MRP system must be adhered to.

Note that most of the disadvantages attributed to MRP systems relate to the assumptions and requirements that must be met before a MRP system can be utilized.

12.6 CASE STUDY—INVENTORY CONTROL IN DOUGHNUT MAKING

The single-period inventory model is concerned with goods having a characteristically short shelf life. B. A. Pasternak has described an application of this classic model to doughnut making.[3] The purpose of the application was to provide the corporate management of a highly decentralized chain of doughnut shops with needed insight into a crucial business area: how modifications in pricing structure could induce individual store managers to make production decisions that were more closely aligned with the firm's objectives.

The company derived its profit from a markup on the raw ingredients it sold to each store along with an administrative fee markup designed to cover the cost of store rent, advertising, etc. The current policy was for the markup on the ingredient sales to approximately equal the administrative fee markup. The company was interested in improving the policy by changing the pricing of the ingredient and/or the administrative fee.

Since the operation of a doughnut shop was conducive to modeling as a single-commodity business, the one-commodity single-period inventory model was employed in determining the optimal production policy. The relevant parameters for the model were the net unit selling price, the net unit production cost, the net unit goodwill cost due to shortage, and the unit salvage value. It must be pointed out that the relevant costs and revenues for the doughnut shop manager and the company were not the same. This was due to the fact that the net unit selling price was lower for the store manager than

the company because the company charged a markup in the administrative fee and because the net unit production cost was higher for the store manager than for the company due to the markup on ingredients sold to store managers by the company. It should be mentioned that the goodwill cost resulting from shortages was at least as large for the company as for the individual store manager. Thus, the optimal policies for the two parties based on the model were different. The analysis assumed that the store manager would produce the optimal quantity specified by the model using the parameters that were relevant to the store manager's situation. The parameters of interest were defined as follows.

p is the net unit selling price (from the company's standpoint).

c is the net unit production cost (from the company's standpoint).

g is the unit goodwill cost due to stockouts (from the company's standpoint).

s is the unit salvage value.

a is the per-unit administrative fee markup charged by the company on sales.

b is the per-unit ingredient price markup charged by the company.

d is the difference between the company's and the manager's per-unit goodwill cost due to stockout.

D is the daily demand for the product.

The optimal production quantity from the company's point of view was the smallest value of Q such that the probability of the daily demand D being

[3] For further details, see: Barry Alan Pasternak, "Filling Out the Doughnuts: The Single Period Inventory Model in Corporate Pricing Policy," *Interfaces*, vol. 10 (October 1980), 96–100, copyright 1980, The Institute of Management Sciences, reprinted by permission.

less than or equal to Q was greater than $(p - c + g)/(p - s + g)$. However, from the store manager's standpoint, the effective unit selling price was equal to $p - a$, the unit production cost was equal to $c + b$, and the goodwill cost equalled $g - d$. Thus the optimal production quantity from the manager's position was the smallest value of Q such that the same probability exceeded $(p - c + g - (a + b + d))/(p - s + g - (a + d))$. Based on this framework the following conclusions were reached. The manager's optimal production quantity was less than the company's optimal production quantity, and the total profit earned by both the manager and the company increased as the manager's optimal production quantity increased to the company's optimal production quantity. Thus, any change in the company's pricing policy that would increase the manager's optimal quantity to more nearly the company's optimal quantity would result in an increase in the combined expected profit of the company and the manager. If such a change in pricing policy was effected so that the manager's expected profit remained constant, then the company's expected profit would be in-creased. Such a change could be effected by the company lowering the markup charged on ingredients while simultaneously raising the markup charged on the administrative fee. However, in order for the company's profit not to decline, the increase in the administrative fee markup must be greater than the decrease in the ingredients' markup. The normal distribution was used to describe the probability distribution for demand D, with the values of μ and σ calculated from past sales histories. These parameters were then used to derive formulas for the expected profit of the manager and expected profit of the company.

The major finding of the analysis was that a reduction in the ingredients' price markup, b, to zero coupled with an increase in the administrative fee markup, a, of an amount slightly greater than b could, in general, increase the company's expected profit by 1 to 2 percent, while causing no reduction in the manager's expected profit. On the basis of the results, the company subsequently decided to modify the markup on ingredient prices as part of a revision in the manager's compensation agreement.

12.7 CONCLUSION

In this chapter we have examined inventory decision models under both deterministic and probabilistic demand situations. In each instance we have examined several inventory models that can be developed for various situations. It should be stressed that a large number of potential inventory models are possible, and we have considered only a few of the more prominent inventory models in this chapter. Thus, the key consideration in inventory model development is the careful establishment of the appropriate demand and cost considerations.

Also, we have considered inventory control in a modeling context in this chapter. In many business situations inventory control is a part of a large computerized systems effort. Among the notable inventory control systems that have been successfully implemented in several companies are **IMPACT** and Material Requirements Planning. IMPACT is an inventory control system that is commercially available from IBM in the form of a computer software package. It has been successfully used by several large grocery wholesalers. Material Requirements Planning is a system that considers both production planning and inventory control within a complex manufacturing environment. This system has also been successfully utilized by a number of manufacturing concerns. In summary, much of the work in inventory control involves a systems effort which, in turn, incorporates models such as those discussed in this chapter.

GLOSSARY OF TERMS

ABC Classification   A procedure used in inventory control in which an attempt is made to consider the small number of items that will account for most of the sales and that are therefore the most important ones to control for effective inventory management.

Back-Order Demand   Demand for an item when the inventory system is out of supply. This demand is satisfied when the item next becomes available.

Bill-of-Materials   A sequential list of all the assemblies, subassemblies, components, and raw materials that go into a finished product. The bill-of-materials will also identify the quantity of each needed to make the end item.

Continuous Review Inventory System   An inventory system in which an order is placed immediately when the stock level falls below the prescribed reorder point.

Cycle   The period of time between the placement of two consecutive orders.

Dependent Demand   Demand that is dependent upon requirements generated by higher-level subassemblies and assemblies. Such dependent demand can be calculated rather than forecasted.

Deterministic Inventory Models   Inventory models for which the rate of demand for items kept in stock in the system is assumed to be known with certainty.

Due Date   Calendar date at which an order is to be completed.

Economic Ordering Quantity (EOQ)   Or economic lot size; the amount of an item that is produced or ordered in the single-lot-size model so that total cost is minimized.

End Item   Finished product, that is, product sold in completed form.

Explosion   Extension of the bill-of-materials into the total of each of the components required to manufacture an assembly or subassembly.

Gross Requirements   The total requirements for a particular component, not taking into account any inventory of that component.

Holding (Storage) Cost   The cost associated with maintaining an inventory until it is used or sold.

IMPACT   An inventory control system that is commercially available from IBM in the form of a computer software package.

Independent Demand   Demand that is customer related and consequently must be forecasted.

Inventory Models   Models associated with the maintenance and control of inventories in business organizations.

Inventory Status File   A file that contains up-to-date, accurate information on every assembly, subassembly, component, part, or raw material item required to produce an end product.

Lead Time   The elapsed time between placement of an order and receipt of the order.

Lead Time Offsetting   The procedure whereby the planned order release for a product is time phased backwards according to the lead time specified for the product so that the product is available when needed.

Level   Structure associated with an assembled end product: Level 0, for example, is the final assembled product; Level 1 is all the major assemblies that go into the end product; and so forth, on down to the lowest level, which is the raw materials.

Lot-Sizing or Ordering Rules   Rules designed to balance inventory holding costs for a component against ordering or setup costs, which operate independently of the MRP system to determine the lot size for a component.

Marginal or Incremental Analysis   An inventory control method that can be used for inventory situations in which demand must be described by a continuous probability distribution.

Master Production Schedule   A high-level schedule that indicates the end products and the time periods in which they are to be manufactured. It becomes the basis for the detailed, time-phased scheduling of components.

Material Requirements Planning   A system that considers both production planning and inventory control within a complex manufacturing environment.

Net-Change Approach   An approach to material requirements planning in which updating occurs as each requirement change occurs.

Net Requirements   The actual manufacturing or purchasing requirements for a particular component. The net requirements for a component are generally computed by deducting the available inventory from the gross requirements.

Ordering Cost   The cost associated with placing an order.

Ordering (Manufacturing) Cost   The cost that is directly associated with the number of items ordered or manufactured.

Order-Point System   An inventory system in which a perpetual inventory is maintained and reviewed continuously. Replenishment orders are then placed when the inventory level drops below the predefined reorder point.

Payoff Table Analysis   A payoff table analysis may be used when the probability distribution for demand is discrete and has a finite number of possible demand values. In using the payoff table one seeks to maximize the profit associated with a particular size of order rather than minimizing the ordering and inventory-holding costs.

Periodic Review Inventory System   An inventory system in which inventory levels are checked at discrete intervals; replenishment orders are placed at these times, if necessary.

Perpetual Inventory   An inventory system in which each inventory transaction is recorded and a new balance is computed as each inventory transaction occurs.

Pointers   Storage addresses of the bills-of-materials for the end products.

Probabilistic Inventory Models or Stochastic Inventory Models   Models in which the exact demand for an item is not known for certain in advance and therefore can only be described in probabilistic terms.

Quantity Discount   A discount on the total purchase price, provided as an incentive for the purchase of larger quantities of product.

Regenerative Approach   An approach to material requirements planning in which updating occurs on a periodic basis (usually 1 week or longer).

Reorder Point   The inventory level at which a replenishment order is placed in an order-point inventory system.

Safety Stock   In probabilistic models, it is the amount of items in stock used as a "buffer" to prevent stockouts during the lead time.

Stockout (Shortage) Cost   The cost that occurs when the demand for an item exceeds it supply.

Time Buckets   The weekly time periods that comprise the planning horizon in a material requirements planning system.

SELECTED REFERENCES

INVENTORY
MODELS

Bowman, E. H., and R. B. Fetter. 1961. *Analysis for Production Management*. Homewood, Ill.: Richard D. Irwin, Inc.

Buchan, J., and E. Koenisberg. 1963. *Scientific Inventory Management*. Englewood Cliffs, N.J.: Prentice-Hall, Inc.

Brown, R. G. 1967. *Decision Rules for Inventory Management*. New York: Holt, Rinehart & Winston, Inc.

Buffa, E. S., and W. H. Taubert. 1972. *Production-Inventory Systems: Planning and Control*. Homewood, Ill.: Richard D. Irwin, Inc.

Fetter, R. B., and W. C. Dalleck. 1961. *Decision Models for Inventory Management*. Homewood, Ill.: Richard D. Irwin, Inc.

Greene, J. H. 1974. *Production and Inventory Control*. Homewood, Ill.: Richard D. Irwin, Inc.

Hadley, G., and T. M. Whitin. 1963. *Analysis of Inventory Systems*. Englewood Cliffs, N.J.: Prentice-Hall, Inc.

Hanssman, F. 1962. *Operations Research in Production and Inventory Control*. New York: John Wiley & Sons, Inc.

Holt, C. C., F. Modigliani, J. F. Muth, and H. A. Simon. 1960. *Production Planning, Inventories, and Work Force*. Englewood Cliffs., N. J.: Prentice-Hall, Inc.

Lewis, C. D. 1970. *Scientific Inventory Control*. New York: Elsevier–North Holland Publishing Company, Inc.

Magee, J. F., and David M. Boodman. 1967. *Production Planning and Inventory Control*. New York: McGraw-Hill Book Company.

Naddor, E. 1966. *Inventory Systems*. New York: John Wiley & Sons, Inc.

Niland, P. 1970. *Production Planning, Scheduling, and Inventory Control*. New York: Macmillan Publishing Company, Inc.

Orlicky, J. A. 1975. *Material Requirements Planning*. New York: McGraw-Hill Book Company.

Plossl, G. W., and O. W. Wright. 1967. *Production and Inventory Control: Principles and Techniques*. Englewood Cliffs, N.J.: Prentice-Hall, Inc.

Starr, M. K., and D. W. Miller. 1962. *Inventory Control: Theory and Practice*. Englewood Cliffs, N.J.: Prentice-Hall, Inc.

Tersine, R. J. 1976. *Materials Management and Inventory Systems*. New York: Elsevier–North Holland Publishing Company, Inc.

Wagner, H. M. 1962. *Statistical Management of Inventory Systems*. New York: John Wiley & Sons, Inc.

Whitin, T. M. 1957. *The Theory of Inventory Management*. Princeton, N.J.: Princeton University Press.

Wight, O. W. 1974. *Production and Inventory Management in the Computer Age*. Boston: Cahners Publishing Company, Inc.

DISCUSSION QUESTIONS

1. What is the "opportunity cost" of inventory?
2. From a solely administrative standpoint, would you prefer shortages in inventory being solved by "special handling" or by "back ordering"?
3. Why are the continuous review inventory system and periodic review system equivalent for a deterministic problem situation?
4. Describe in detail what the EOQ means.
5. Why does the cycle time equal Q/a time units within the single-lot size model? How would you define the cycle time verbally?
6. Name at least two situations for which you think it is feasible to allow "shortages" in an inventory system.
7. What would be the effect of a smaller replenishment rate than demand rate in a uniform replenishment rate inventory system?
8. What modification is made in the total cost function of the EOQ model when we consider quantity discounts to be valid?
9. For what type of situation would you have a probabilistic inventory model, even though demand is known with certainty?
10. Do you think a normally distributed demand during the lead time in a probabilistic inventory model is a realistic assumption? Why or why not?
11. Is $F(R^*)$ (Section 12.4.1) a cumulative probability? Why or why not? What relationship exists between $F(R^*)$ and the standardized Z-values?
12. Does there exist some relationship between $F(R^*)$ and the safety stock with respect to possible stockouts? If so, what relationship?
13. Describe briefly how safety stocks are determined when various service levels are given a priori and have to be met.
14. For what type of situation is a payoff table analysis appropriate?
15. When is marginal analysis appropriate? Describe briefly what it does.
16. What is material requirements planning?
17. To what type of production planning and scheduling situation is material requirements planning (MRP) applicable?
18. What are the primary assumptions and requirements for an MRP system?
19. What are the major inputs to an MRP system?
20. What are some of the advantages of an MRP system?
21. What are some of the disadvantages of an MRP system?
22. What is the "inventory status file" and how is it used?
23. What is the "product structure file" and how is it used?
24. What is the "master production schedule" and how is it used?
25. What is the "bill-of-materials" and how is it exploded?
26. Why has the use of MRP accelerated in recent years?

PROBLEM SET

1. Given the following cost and demand parameters

$$K = 10,000$$
$$h = 0.50$$
$$a = 7,500$$

compute Q^* and t^*.

2. In the Boom Fireworks Factory the demand for roman candles is 2000 units per month, and the items are withdrawn continuously and uniformly. The setup cost each time a production run is made is $150, and the production cost is $1 per roman candle. The inventory holding cost is $0.10 per roman candle per month. No shortages are allowed. Determine Q^* and t^*.

3. The Van Dyke Brewery experiences a constant annual demand for its beer of 100,000 cases. The setup cost each time a production run is made is 1000, and the holding cost is $25 per case per month. No shortages are allowed. Determine Q^* and t^*.

4. Given the following cost and demand parameters

    $$K = 10,000$$
    $$h = 0.50$$
    $$u = 0.10$$
    $$a = 7,500$$

    compute Q^*, S^*, t^*, and the difference $Q^* - S^*$.

5. The Dusty Spoke Bicycle Shop has a monthly demand for 60 bikes. Each time a bike order is placed to the factory, an ordering cost of $25 is incurred. The inventory-holding cost for the bicycle shop is $1 per month per bicycle, and the shortage cost is estimated to be $5 per unit. Compute Q^*, S^*, and t^*.

6. The Tred-Rite Shoe Store sells 250 pairs of shoes monthly. Its ordering costs from the shoe factory is $15 per order. Each pair of shoes incurs an inventory-holding cost of $0.75 per month. Each time a customer cannot be fitted with a desired pair of shoes, a shortage cost of $2 is incurred. Compute Q^*, S^*, and t^*.

7. Given the following cost and demand parameters

    $$K = \$500$$
    $$h = \$50 \text{ per unit per year}$$
    $$a = 15,000 \text{ units per year}$$
    $$p = 25,000 \text{ units per year}$$

    Compute Q^*, t_p^*, t_d^*, and t_c^*.

8. The Slurpy Soup Company produces chicken noodle soup on a production line that has an annual capacity of 100,000 cans. The annual demand for the chicken soup is estimated to be 75,000 cans, and it is felt that this annual demand rate is constant throughout the year. When chicken soup is manufactured, the cleaning and setup of the production line costs approximately $500. The annual inventory holding cost is estimated to be $0.25 per can per year. What is the appropriate production lot size?

9. The Auto-Bright Company produces car wax on a production line having a monthly capacity of 10,000 cans. Its annual demand for auto wax is 100,000 cans, on a uniform basis. The setup cost associated with the production of car wax is $250 per production run. The monthly inventory holding cost is estimated to be $0.50 per can of car wax. What is the appropriate production lot size?

10. Assume that the following quantity discount schedule is appropriate.

Order Size	Discount	Unit Cost ($)
0 to 99	0	50.00
100 to 249	3%	48.50
250+	5%	47.50

If the annual demand for the item under consideration is 1000 units, the ordering cost is $50 per order, and the annual inventory holding cost is 25 percent of the unit cost of the item, compute the economic order quantity.

11. Handy Man Hardware Wholesalers, Inc., orders power mowers from a major Midwestern manufacturer. The following quantity discount schedule applies to 21-in. self-propelled, electric-start rotary power mowers.

Order Size	Discount (%)	Unit Cost ($)
0 to 99	0	90.00
100 to 199	1	89.10
200 to 399	3	87.30
400+	5	85.50

Its annual demand is 1000 units; its holding cost per year is 10 percent of the unit cost; and its ordering cost is $10 per order. Determine the economic order quantity for this situation.

12. The Speedy Boat Rental Company operates a boat rental concession at the Lake of the Ozarks. The company uses gasoline at the rate of 5000 gallons per month. The purchase cost associated with obtaining the gasoline is $25, and the inventory holding cost is 1 percent of the unit cost. The cost of the gasoline is 50 cents per gallon for a purchase of 1 to 5000 gallons, 45 cents per gallon for a purchase of 5001 to 10,000 gallons, and 40 cents per gallon for a purchase of 10,001 gallons or more. Assuming that shortages are not allowed, how much gasoline should the company order?

13. Given the following cost and demand parameters for an anticipated price change inventory modeling situation, compute the optimal lot size to be ordered in anticipation of the price change, and the savings to be expected from making this special large purchase.

$$c_1 = \$5.00$$
$$c_2 = \$10.00$$
$$a = 500 \text{ per units per year}$$
$$p = 0.25$$
$$K = \$5.00$$

14. The owner of a fast-food restaurant has been told that the price of hamburger buns

is going to increase from $3.00 per case to $3.50 per case within a month's time. The firm's current usage of hamburger buns is 30 cases per month, and its annual inventory-holding cost is 20 percent of the purchase cost of the buns. Ordering costs are $5.00 per order. What lot size should be ordered in anticipation of the price change? What savings will result from this order?

15. The River City Daily News publishes a daily evening newspaper. Unfortunately, it faces an increase in its cost of newsprint. Its current cost is $2.50 per 1000 lb, and its increased cost will be $3.50 per 1000 lb. It uses newsprint at the rate of 300,000 lb yearly, with an inventory-holding cost of 15 percent of the cost of the newsprint. The ordering cost for ordering newsprint is $50 per order. What lot size (1000-lb units) should be ordered in anticipation of the price change? What savings will result from this order?

16. Given a normal demand during the lead time of $\overline{M} = 15$ units with $\sigma_M = 3$, and the following cost and demand parameters,

$$a = 100 \text{ units per year}$$
$$h = \$15 \text{ per unit per year}$$
$$u = \$25 \text{ per unit}$$
$$K = \$10 \text{ per order}$$

compute Q^*, $F(R^*)$, R^*, and determine the reordering cost, inventory-holding cost (normal inventory), and the inventory-holding cost (safety stock).

17. A large farm implement company experiences an annual demand for 300 tractors. However, this demand exhibits some variability such that the lead time demand follows a normal distribution with $\overline{M} = 30$ units and $\sigma_M = 10$. The holding cost is $50 per unit per year, the shortage cost is $100 per unit, and the order cost is $25 per order. Compute Q^*, $F(R^*)$, R^*, and determine the reordering cost, the inventory-holding cost (normal inventory), and the inventory-holding cost (safety stock).

18. Ajax Distributors is a liquor wholesaler in the Los Angeles area. It is currently experiencing a yearly demand of 1000 cases for a particular brand of Scotch. The inventory holding cost is $10 per case per year, the shortage cost is $15 per case, and the order cost is $25 per order. It estimates that it has 2 weeks' lead time on its orders for Scotch.

(a) What is the economic order quantity for Ajax Distributors? What is the reorder point for Ajax Distributors if it assumes a constant demand of 20 cases per week?

(b) Assume that Ajax Distributors feels that its demand over the lead time is normally distributed with mean $\overline{M} = 15$ and $\sigma_M = 3$. What is the optimum reorder point for this situation?

(c) What is the safety stock under the revised order point as specified in item (b)? What is the annual safety stock holding cost?

(d) Assume that Ajax Distributors feels that its demand over the lead time is normally distributed with mean $\overline{M} = 20$ and standard deviation $\sigma_M = 5$. If it feels that it can allow a 0.3 probability of a stockout during a given order cycle, what is the reorder point and safety stock?

(e) What is the annual safety stock holding cost for the safety stock determined in item (d)?

19. Referring to the Agrico Fertilizer Company example, assume that a change in the manufacturing process makes the following cost profit parameters applicable.

$$p = \$500 \text{ per } 1000 \text{ gallons}$$

$$c = \$400 \text{ per } 1000 \text{ gallons}$$

$$d = \$800 \text{ per } 1000 \text{ gallons}$$

$$s = \$50 \text{ per } 1000 \text{ gallons}$$

The demand distribution for the liquid fertilizer remains the same as that shown in Table 12.6. What is the recommended order quantity and associated expected profit under this new set of conditions?

20. Assume that we have computed the following conditional profit table.

	Demand, D		
Order Quantity, Q	500	1000	1500
500	200	100	0
1000	100	50	−25
1500	−50	0	100

The probability of demand D is given by $P(D = 500) = 0.4$, $P(D = 1000) = 0.3$, $P(D = 1500) = 0.3$. Determine the optimum-order quantity and expected profit for this situation.

21. Dominic's Pizzeria orders its pizza sauce from a wholesaler on a monthly basis. Each 5-gallon jar of pizza sauce costs $10 and ultimately results in $15 profit. Any pizza sauce unused at the end of a month is badly deteriorated and has only a $3 per 5-gallon jug salvage value. Dominic's Pizzeria uses an average of fifty 5-gallon jugs of pizza sauce monthly, and this usage pattern is normally distributed with a standard deviation of $\sigma = 5$. Use incremental analysis to determine the optimum-order quantity of pizza sauce for Dominic's Pizzeria.

22. The True-to-Life Poster Company makes political posters and is contemplating its cardboard order for the forthcoming election year. In previous election years it has used 20,000 cardboard sheets, with this demand being normally distributed with a standard deviation of $\sigma = 5000$ sheets. It buys its cardboard sheets in various colors for $0.50 per sheet, and if the sheets are sold as a finished poster, they bring $1.25 each. The salvage value of the cardboard sheets remaining after the election is $0.25 per sheet. What is the optimum-order quantity of cardboard sheets for the True-to-Life Poster Company?

III

Stochastic Models

Waiting Line Models

13.1 INTRODUCTION

Waiting lines, or **queues**, are a common occurrence both in everyday life and in a variety of business and industrial situations. The formation of waiting lines occurs whenever the demand for service from a facility exceeds the capacity of that facility.

Examples of common waiting-line situations are presented below in Table 13.1.

If the demands to be placed on a service facility were known in advance and could be accurately predicted, it would be a relatively simple chore to schedule the service facility in an efficient manner. However, it is often very difficult to predict accurately when units will arrive for service and/or how much time will be required to provide the needed service. Consequently, **waiting-line**, or **queueing theory** can be categorized by the following characteristics.

1. Customers, or arrivals, that require service.
2. Uncertainty concerning the demand and the timing of the demand of the customers.
3. Service facilities, or servers, that perform the service operation.

TABLE 13.1 Common Waiting-Line Situations

Situation	Arrivals	Servers	Service Mechanism
Doctor's office	Patients	Doctor and nurses	Medical care
Movie theater box office	Movie patrons	Ticket seller	Ticket selling
Traffic intersection	Automobiles	Traffic signal	Movement through intersection
Port	Ship	Dock workers	Unloading and loading ships
Garage	Automobiles	Repairmen	Repair automobile
Registrar's office	Prospective students	Registration clerks	Registration of students
Pizza restaurant	Hungry people	Pizza makers	Make and serve pizzas
Airport	Airplanes	Runways, gates, and terminal	Airplane arrivals and departures

4. Uncertainty concerning the time duration of the service operation.
5. Uncertainty concerning the behavior of the customers as they arrive for service and/or wait in the queue.

Based on these five characteristics the objective of queueing theory becomes the provision of an adequate but not excessive service facility. Providing too much service to the extent that the service facility is often **idle** or empty represents an incurrence of unnecessary costs, namely the direct cost of idle employees, or the loss associated with poor employee morale resulting from being idle. Conversely, excessive waiting has a cost in terms of customer frustration and loss of goodwill. Thus, the goal of waiting-line modeling is the achievement of an economic balance between the cost of the service and the cost associated with the wait required for that service. The relationship between the level of service provided, the cost of the service, the cost associated with the wait required for that service, and the total expected cost (i.e., the sum of the service cost and the waiting cost) is shown graphically in Fig. 13.1.

Before we proceed to explore some of the more common types of queueing models, we should note that there is virtually an infinite number of such models that can be derived. This is true because of the uncertainty that exists, both for the arrivals and for the operation of the service facility. Since these two stochastic elements of queueing models can be described by a myriad of probability distributions, an extremely large number of queueing models results. New types of queueing models are being derived constantly; consequently, we shall attempt to survey only some of the more important and useful results that have been obtained. Our focus will be on the applicability of the results of queueing theory, rather than on its rigorous mathematical framework. We will now proceed to discuss the basic structure of waiting-line models, using an example to enhance our understanding.

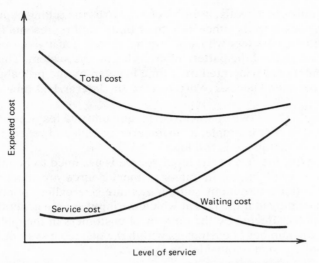

FIGURE 13.1   **Service Level-Cost Relationships-Queueing Analysis**

13.2   THE BASIC STRUCTURE OF QUEUEING MODELS

The First Federated Bank is located in the small town of Knob Noster, Missouri. The bank's main facilities are located in a 5500-square-foot, one-story brick building, which was built in 1890. Because of crowded conditions in the main facility, the bank of Knob Noster has hired a management science professor from a local university as a consultant to determine whether or not to build a drive-in banking facility next to its main bank.

In preparing a consultant report for the First Federated Bank of Knob Noster the professor began by providing a basic overview of the alternative queueing models that might be developed. His description of these alternative queueing models was subdivided into three major elements, according to the diagram shown in Fig. 13.2.

13.2.1   The Input Process

The **input process** for a queueing model is concerned with the manner in which items or customers enter into or arrive at the queueing system. This input process is usually described in terms of two characteristics.

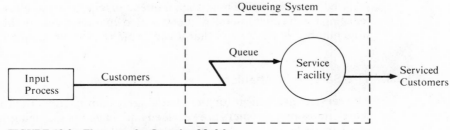

FIGURE 13.2   **Elements of a Queueing Model**

1. The source of arrivals, usually referred to as the **calling population**. The size of the input source is either infinite or finite, and represents the total number of potential customers who will require service for a given period of time.
2. A description of the pattern of arrivals into the system. This pattern by which customers are generated over time is given by the probability distribution of time between successive arrivals, or the **interarrival time**.

In addition to these two characteristics, any unusual features of the input process must be noted. For example, a customer may **balk** and refuse to enter the queueing system if the queue is too long.

Generally, the size of the input source is assumed to be infinite, because the calculations involving an infinite-size input source are much easier than those involving a finite-size input source. A finite-size calling population assumption should be employed if the rate at which the input source generates new customers is significantly affected by the number of customers in the queueing system. For this case, the number of customers within the queueing system affects the number of potential customers outside the system.

13.2.2   The Queue Discipline

The **queue discipline** specifies the order in which customers entering the queueing system are served. Common types of queue disciplines are

1. First-come, first-served. Customers are serviced in the order in which they enter the queue. Standing in line to purchase tickets at a movie theater is an example of a first-come, first-served queue discipline.
2. Last-come, first-served. Customers are serviced in the reverse order in which they enter the queue. An elevator in which people move to the rear as they enter is an example of a last-come, first-served queue discipline.
3. Random. In this queue discipline there is no order of service. Question and answer sessions in televised news conferences often appear to be a random queue discipline.
4. Priority. In this queue discipline there is a predefined rule that determines the order of service. For example, people with chronic respiratory problems may be selected first in the general population of a city for a flu inoculation.

As with the input source, any unusual circumstance concerning the queue discipline should be specified as a part of its general characteristics. For example, the queue discipline may be such that customers tend to become impatient. If this happens, the customers will tend to leave the queueing system before they are selected to be served. Thus, such a queue discipline must allow for the process of **reneging** by the customers. A queue is also characterized by the maximum permissible number of customers that it can contain and can be either finite or infinite.

13.2.3   The Service Mechanism

The **service mechanism** for the queueing system is concerned with the manner in which items or customers are serviced and leave the queueing system. The service mechanism is usually described in terms of two characteristics.

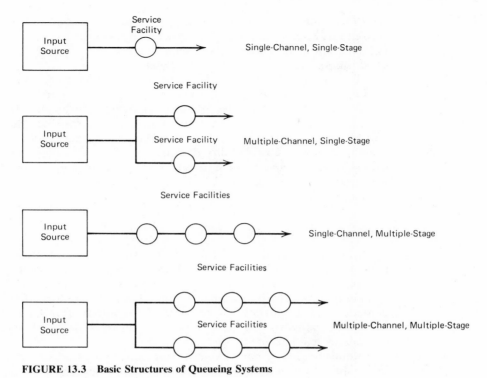

FIGURE 13.3   Basic Structures of Queueing Systems

1. The number and configuration of service facilities or service channels.
2. A description of the pattern of services. This involves a description of the time to complete a service and of the number of individuals whose requirements are satisfied at each service event.

The service mechanism may consist of a single-service facility, or multiple-service facilities. A queueing system with multiple-service facilities arranged in parallel is called a **multiple-channel** queueing system. A queueing system with multiple-service facilities arranged in series is called a **multiple-stage** queueing system. Thus, the number of **channels** in a queueing system refers to the number of parallel service facilities available for servicing arrivals. The number of **stages** in a queueing system refers to the number of sequential service steps each individual arrival must pass through.

Queueing systems can be categorized into four basic structures, according to the type of service facility present. Each of these four categories is shown graphically in Fig. 13.3.

An example of a **single-channel, single-stage** queueing system would be a small grocery store with only one checkout station. An example of a **multiple-channel, single-stage** queueing system would be a large grocery store with several checkout stations. An example of a **single-channel, multiple-stage** queueing system would be a dentist's office in which a patient was first treated by a dental hygienist and then treated by the dentist. If there were several dental hygienists and several dentists in the office, this would be an example of a **multiple-channel, multiple-stage** queueing system.

Variations of these basic queueing systems do exist, but will not be considered in this book because of their complexity. Indeed, we will restrict our queueing analyses in this chapter to single-channel and multiple-channel, **single-stage** queueing systems.

The time needed for completing the service is referred to as the **service time** or **holding time**. This service time is generally dependent upon the customer's service requirement, but it may also be partially dependent on the state of the service mechanism. For example, the servers may tend to speed up their service if they perceive that many customers are waiting. A queueing model must also have a specification of the probability distribution of the service times for each server. Commonly, the same service time probability distribution is used for all servers. An exponential service time distribution, or a constant service time distribution, is often appropriate.

13.2.4 Waiting-Line Analysis

In the previous sections of this chapter we have examined some of the basic features of waiting-line models. From this preliminary discussion it should be apparent that a myriad of waiting-line models are possible. Many of the possible waiting-line models that can be developed prove quite formidable in terms of the mathematical sophistication required for their solution. Consequently, most waiting-line analysis proceeds along the basis of using simple models as approximations to real systems.

Returning to our bank example, the consultant studied similar drive-in banking facilities and determined that the following conditions were most descriptive of the situation. A single waiting line of customers (which could be empty at various times) forms in front of a single-service facility (drive-in bank teller). This service facility could contain either one or two servers (tellers) to handle the customers who typically spend some time in the waiting line (queue). The consultant further concluded that the number of customer arrivals was Poisson distributed while the customer service times were exponentially distributed.

13.2.5 Waiting-Line Notation

The development of queueing models is greatly facilitated by the use of a standardized set of terminology and notation. Thus, in the remainder of this chapter we shall employ the following standard terminology and notation.

λ = Mean **arrival rate** of customers into the queueing system (expected number or average number of arrivals into the queueing system) per unit of time.

μ = Mean **service rate** for the queueing system (expected number or average number of customers completing service) per unit of time.

$\frac{1}{\lambda}$ = Expected interarrival time.

$\frac{1}{\mu}$ = Expected service completion time.

s = Number of servers (parallel service channels) in the queueing system.

ρ = Utilization factor for the service facility = $\lambda/\mu s$.

L = Expected number of customers in the queueing system.

L_q = Expected queue length.
W = Expected waiting time in the queueing system (including service time).
W_q = Expected waiting time in the queue (excluding service time).

Traditionally in queueing theory, the arrival process, the service process, and the number of servers are represented using a shorthand notation. This notation consists of three symbols, indicating

arrival process/service process/number servers, where:

M = Arrivals or services having Poisson or exponential probability distributions.
D = Arrivals having a deterministic arrival rate.
G = Services having a general probability distribution.

For example, a queueing system in which the number of arrivals is described by a Poisson probability distribution, the service time is described by an exponential distribution, and there is a single server, would be characterized as *M/M/*1.

13.3   THE *M/M/*1 QUEUEING MODEL

In attempting to make a recommendation to the bank, the consultant first attempted to analyze the situation as an *M/M/*1 queueing model.[1] There are four basic assumptions for the *M/M/*1 queueing model.

1. The probability that a customer arrival will occur or that a customer service will be completed during a time interval Δt is dependent only on the length of Δt. Thus, the events occurring prior to the beginning of the time interval or the starting point of the time interval have no effect on the probability of occurrence.
2. There is a positive probability that an arrival or service will occur in a nonzero time interval.
3. If the time interval is made sufficiently small, no more than one arrival can occur and no more than one service can be completed.
4. Only one waiting line is formed.

Further, assume that we are given a particular time interval T that can be divided into k small time intervals Δt that are sufficiently small so that the first three assumptions given above are satisfied. Letting p denote the probability (fixed, i.e., $p = \lambda T/k$) of an arrival during the small time interval Δt, then the probability of n arrivals during the k small time intervals will be given by the Poisson distribution:

$$P(n|k, p) = \frac{e^{-\lambda T}(\lambda T)^n}{n!} \tag{13-1}$$

---

[1] In this section of the chapter we will present only the important results for the *M/M/*1 queueing model. The complete set of derivations for the *M/M/*1 queueing model is presented in Appendix 13.1, at the end of the chapter.

The major relationships for the $M/M/1$ queueing system can then be summarized as follows.

Probability that the queueing system is empty:

= probability that there are 0 units in the queueing system

$= P_0 = 1 - (\lambda/\mu)$ $\qquad\qquad$ (13–2)

Probability that the queueing system is busy:

= probability that there are n or more units in the queueing system

$= P_n = \left(\dfrac{\lambda}{\mu}\right)^n P_0$ $\qquad\qquad$ (13–3)

Expected number in the queueing system:

$= L = \dfrac{\lambda}{\mu - \lambda}$ $\qquad\qquad$ (13–4)

Expected number in the queue:

$= L_q = \dfrac{\lambda^2}{\mu(\mu - \lambda)}$ $\qquad\qquad$ (13–5)

Expected waiting time in the queueing system:

$= W = \dfrac{1}{\mu - \lambda}$ $\qquad\qquad$ (13–6)

Expected waiting time in the queue:

$= W_q = \dfrac{\lambda}{\mu(\mu - \lambda)}$ $\qquad\qquad$ (13–7)

The probabilities associated with various times between services are given by:

$P[T$ or fewer time units between services (given μ)]

$= P(T \leq t) = 1 - e^{-\mu T}$ $\qquad\qquad$ (13–8)

$P[$more than T time units between services (given μ)]

$= P(T > t) = e^{-\mu T}$ $\qquad\qquad$ (13–9)

The waiting-line probabilities for the single-server case are computed as:

$P(W' > t) = e^{-\mu(1 - (\lambda/\mu))t}$ $\qquad (t \geq 0)$ $\qquad\qquad$ (13–10)

$P(W'_q > t) = \dfrac{\lambda}{\mu} e^{-\mu(1 - (\lambda/\mu))t}$ $\qquad (t \geq 0)$ $\qquad\qquad$ (13–11)

13.3.1 Applications of the $M/M/1$ Queueing Model

Let us now return to the situation involving the addition of a drive-in banking facility for the First Federated Bank. We will attempt to analyze this situation, using the various results previously obtained for the $M/M/1$ queueing model.

From observations made at random times during one week of bank operations, the consultant has estimated that the mean arrival rate for the drive-in banking facility will likely be $\lambda = 30$ customers per hour and that the mean service rate for the facility will likely be $\mu = 60$ customers per hour. Both arrivals and services are assumed to be Poisson distributed. He decides to begin his analysis by computing the probabilities of various number of arrivals during 1-minute,

5-minute, and 10-minute intervals, using the general results obtained earlier, namely,

$$P[n|k,p] = \frac{e^{-\lambda T}(\lambda T)^n}{n!} \tag{13-12}$$

These computations are summarized in Table 13.2. Next, the utilization factor for the queueing system is computed, using

$$\rho = \frac{\lambda}{\mu s} = \frac{30}{60(1)} = 0.50 \tag{13-13}$$

The probability that the queueing system is idle is given by:

$$\begin{aligned} P_0 &= 1 - \left(\frac{\lambda}{\mu}\right) = 1 - \left(\frac{30}{60}\right) \\ &= 0.50 \end{aligned} \tag{13-14}$$

The probabilities associated with various numbers of customers being in the queueing system are given by:

$$P_n = \left(\frac{\lambda}{\mu}\right)^n P_0 \tag{13-15}$$

Computational results for $n = 1, 2, \ldots, 5$ are shown in Table 13.3. The expected number of customers in the queueing system is given by:

$$\begin{aligned} L &= \frac{\lambda}{\mu - \lambda} \\ &= \frac{30}{60 - 30} = 1 \text{ person} \end{aligned} \tag{13-16}$$

The expected number of customers in the queue is given by:

$$\begin{aligned} L_q &= \frac{\lambda^2}{\mu(\mu - \lambda)} \\ &= \frac{(30)^2}{60(60 - 30)} = \frac{1}{2} \text{ person} \end{aligned} \tag{13-17}$$

TABLE 13.2 Probability of *n* Arrivals for Various Values of *T*, Given λ = 30 Arrivals per Hour

Number of Arrivals, n	$T = {}^1/_{60}$: $\dfrac{e^{-30(1/60)}(30 \cdot {}^1/_{60})^n}{n!}$	$T = {}^5/_{60}$: $\dfrac{e^{-30(5/60)}(30 \cdot {}^5/_{60})^n}{n!}$	$T = {}^{10}/_{60}$: $\dfrac{e^{-30(10/60)}(30 \cdot {}^{10}/_{60})^n}{n!}$
0	0.606	0.082	0.007
1	0.303	0.205	0.034
2	0.076	0.256	0.084
3	0.013	0.214	0.140
4	0.002	0.133	0.174
5	0.000	0.067	0.174

TABLE 13.3 Probability of n Customers in Queueing System, Given $\lambda = 30$, $\mu = 60$

Number of Customers in System, n	$P_n = (^{30}/_{60})^n(0.50)$
1	0.250
2	0.125
3	0.063
4	0.031
5	0.015

The expected waiting time in the queueing system is given by:

$$W = \frac{1}{\mu - \lambda}$$

$$= \frac{1}{60 - 30} = 0.033 \text{ hour} \qquad (13\text{-}18)$$

The expected waiting time in the queue is given by:

$$W_q = \frac{\lambda}{\mu(\mu - \lambda)}$$

$$= \frac{30}{60(60 - 30)} = 0.0167 \text{ hour} \qquad (13\text{-}19)$$

The probabilities associated with various times between services are given by:

$$P(T \leq t) = 1 - e^{-\mu T}$$
$$P(T > t) = e^{-\mu T} \qquad (13\text{-}20)$$

Computational results for $T = 1$ minute ($^1/_{60}$ hour), $^2/_{60}$ hour, $^3/_{60}$ hour, $^4/_{60}$ hour, $^5/_{60}$ hour, $^8/_{60}$ hour, and 10 minutes ($^1/_6$ hour) are shown in Table 13.4. Assuming that $n > 0$ (i.e., customers are in the system), the probability that the waiting time (including service time) will be greater than 5 minutes ($^1/_{12}$ hour) is computed as:

TABLE 13.4 Probabilities—Time Between Services

T	$P(T \leq t) = 1 - e^{-\mu T}$	$P(T > t) = e^{-\mu T}$
$^1/_{60}$	0.633	0.367
$^2/_{60}$	0.865	0.135
$^3/_{60}$	0.951	0.049
$^4/_{60}$	0.982	0.018
$^5/_{60}$	0.993	0.007
$^8/_{60}$	0.998	0.002
$^1/_6$	1.000	0.000

$$P\left(W' > t = \frac{5}{60}\right) = e^{-\mu(1 - (\lambda/\mu))t}$$

$$= e^{-60[1 - (30/60)](5/60)} \tag{13-21}$$

$$= e^{-2.5} = 0.082$$

Finally, assuming that $n > 0$ (i.e., customers are in the system) the probability that the waiting time (excluding service time) will be greater than 5 minutes ($^1/_{12}$ hour) is given by:

$$P\left(W'_q > t = \frac{5}{60}\right) = \left(\frac{\lambda}{\mu}\right) e^{-\mu(1 - (\lambda/\mu))t}$$

$$= \left(\frac{30}{60}\right) e^{-60[1 - (30/60)](1/12)} \tag{13-22}$$

$$= \frac{1}{2} e^{-2.5}$$

$$= 0.041$$

While reasonably confident that the customer arrival rate will be $\lambda = 30$ customers per hour, the consultant is also interested in measuring the sensitivity of the operating characteristics of the $M/M/1$ queueing system assuming that the customer arrival rate might vary. Thus, the consultant next decides to compute the major operating characteristics at values of $\lambda = 25$, 30 (already done), 35, 40, 45, and 50 customers per hour, with the mean service rate for the facility being held constant at $\mu = 60$ customers per hour.

Using the relationships previously derived and discussed for the $M/M/1$ queueing system, the consultant computed the data shown in Table 13.5.

From the data shown in Table 13.5 the sensitivity of the $M/M/1$ queueing model to possible changes in the customer arrival rate can be measured. For example, assume that the actual customer arrival rate is $\lambda = 45$ customers per hour, or 50 percent higher than originally predicted. In this instance, the probability of the facility being idle drops from $P_0 = 0.50$ (for $\lambda = 30$) to $P_0 = 0.25$ (for $\lambda = 45$), or decreases by one-half. The expected number of customers in the queueing system increases from $L = 1$ to $L = 3$, or triples. The expected number of customers in the queue increases from $L_q = 0.50$ to $L_q = 2.25$, or some $4^1/_2$ times.

TABLE 13.5 Operating Characteristics of $M/M/1$ Queueing System for Various Customer Arrival Rates

Customer Arrival Rate, λ	Probability of Idle System, P_0	Expected Number of Customers in Queueing System, L	Expected Number of Customers in the Queue, L_q	Expected Waiting Time in the Queueing System, W	Expected Waiting Time in the Queue, W_q
25	0.58	0.71	0.30	0.029 hr	0.012 hr
30	0.50	1	0.50	0.033 hr	0.016 hr
35	0.42	1.4	0.82	0.040 hr	0.023 hr
40	0.33	2	1.33	0.050 hr	0.033 hr
45	0.25	3	2.25	0.066 hr	0.050 hr
50	0.16	5	4.16	0.100 hr	0.083 hr

The expected waiting time in the queueing system increases from $W = 0.033$ hour to $W = 0.066$ hour, or doubles. Finally, the expected waiting time in the queue increases from $W_q = 0.016$ hour to $W_q = 0.050$ hour, or triples. Similar comparisons could be made for other values of λ. From these comparisons it is evident that this modeling situation is very sensitive to the customer arrival rate. These results indicate the importance of trying to accurately measure the queueing model parameters, such as the customer arrival rate λ, prior to making operating characteristic computations.

As a final part of the analysis, the consultant is interested in investigating two alternative computerized ledger systems for the drive-in banking facility. Under the first alternative, arrivals and services will be as indicated in the previous analysis. Under the second alternative the mean service rate for the facility will increase to $\mu = 90$ customers per hour. The average hourly cost associated with the ill will caused by a customer waiting is thought to be $10. The operating cost for the first ledger system is $50 per hour while the operating cost for the second ledger system is $60 per hour. The consultant is considering the question of which computerized ledger system to recommend.

For System 1:

$\lambda = 30$ arrivals per hour.
$\mu = 60$ services per hour.
$W = 0.033$ hour.

$$
\begin{aligned}
\text{Average hourly cost of ill will} = \\
30(0.033 \text{ hr})(\$10 \text{ per hour}) = \$\ 9.90 \\
\text{Hourly operating cost} = \underline{50.00} \\
\text{Total hourly cost} = \$59.90
\end{aligned}
\tag{13-23}
$$

For System 2:

$\lambda = 30$ arrivals per hour.
$\mu = 90$ services per hour.

$$
W = \frac{1}{\mu - \lambda} = \frac{1}{90 - 30} = 0.0167 \text{ hour}
$$

$$
\begin{aligned}
\text{Average hourly cost of ill will} = \\
30(0.0167 \text{ hr})(\$10 \text{ per hour}) = \$\ 4.95 \\
\text{Hourly operating cost} = \underline{60.00} \\
\text{Total hourly cost} = \$64.95
\end{aligned}
\tag{13-24}
$$

Thus, the first computerized ledger system is preferable to the second computerized leger system, in spite of the fact that the second computerized ledger system would provide a 50-percent faster mean service rate.

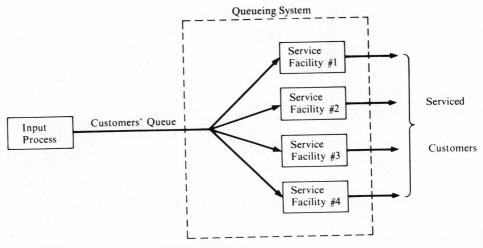

FIGURE 13.4   A *M/M/s* = 4 Queueing System

13.4   The *M/M/s* QUEUEING MODEL

A logical extension of the *M/M/*1 queueing model is the *M/M/s* queueing model or the multiple channel waiting line with Poisson arrivals and exponential service time. It should be apparent that many queueing systems are comprised of more than one server, and thus the *M/M/s* queueing model is of practical importance. A typical *M/M/s* queueing system, with $s = 4$ service facilities, is shown in Fig. 13.4. For this queueing system it is assumed that customers arrive at a mean arrival rate, λ, and then are serviced on a "first-in, first-out" basis at any of the s service facilities that are available. It is further assumed that only one queue forms, and each of the s service facilities has the same mean service rate, μ.

For this queueing model we will not go through the lengthy and complex derivations of its steady-state conditions.[2] Rather they will be stated without proof, and their use will then be demonstrated. The basic relationships for the *M/M/s* queueing model are as follows.

Probability that the queueing system is empty

= probability that there are 0 units in the queueing system

= P_0

$$= \frac{1}{\left[\sum_{n=0}^{s-1} \frac{\left(\frac{\lambda}{\mu}\right)^n}{n!} + \frac{\left(\frac{\lambda}{\mu}\right)^s}{s!} \frac{1}{1 - (\lambda/s\mu)} \right]} \qquad (13\text{--}25)$$

---

[2] The reader interested in such derivations should consult; Harvey M. Wagner, *Principles of Operations Research* (Englewood Cliffs, N.J.: Prentice-Hall, Inc., 1975), pp. 880–82.

Probability that the queueing system is busy:

= probability that there are n or more units in the queueing system

= P_n

$$= \begin{cases} \dfrac{\left(\dfrac{\lambda}{\mu}\right)^n}{n!} P_0, & \text{if } 0 \le n \le s \\[4ex] \dfrac{\left(\dfrac{\lambda}{\mu}\right)^n}{s!\, s^{n-s}} P_0, & \text{if } n \ge s \end{cases} \tag{13-26}$$

Expected number in the queue $= L_q = \dfrac{\left(\dfrac{\lambda}{\mu}\right)^s \left(\dfrac{\lambda}{\mu s}\right) P_0}{s!\left(1 - \dfrac{\lambda}{\mu s}\right)^2}$ $\qquad$ (13-27)

Expected number in the queueing system $= L = L_q + \dfrac{\lambda}{\mu}$ $\qquad$ (13-28)

Expected waiting time in the queue $= W_q = \dfrac{L_q}{\lambda}$ $\qquad$ (13-29)

Expected waiting time in the queueing system $= W = W_q + \dfrac{1}{\mu}$ $\qquad$ (13-30)

The waiting-time probabilities for the multiple-server case can be computed as:[3]

$$P(W' > t) = e^{-\mu t} \left[1 + \frac{P_0 \left(\dfrac{\lambda}{\mu}\right)^s}{s!\left(1 - \dfrac{\lambda}{\mu s}\right)} \left(\frac{1 - e^{-\mu t(s - 1 - (\lambda/\mu))}}{s - 1 - \dfrac{\lambda}{\mu}} \right) \right] \tag{13-31}$$

$$P(W_q' > t) = [1 - P(W_q' = 0)]e^{-s\mu[1 - (\lambda/\mu s)]t} \tag{13-32}$$

where $\qquad P(W_q' = 0) = \displaystyle\sum_{n=0}^{s-1} P_n$ $\qquad$ (13-33)

13.4.1 Application of the *M*/*M*/*s* Queueing Model

Returning to our example concerning the analysis of a drive-in bank facility, let us consider the situation in which a single line of cars arrives at the facility at a mean arrival rate of $\lambda = 30$ customers per hour. The service facility now is to be comprised of two tellers, each of whom can provide service at $\mu = 40$ customers per hour.

For this $M/M/s = 2$ queueing system, the following computations are appropriate. First, the utilization factor for this queueing system is computed, using

---

[3] When $s - 1 - (\lambda/\mu) = 0$, $[1 - e^{-\mu t}(s - 1 - (\lambda/\mu))]/(s - 1 - (\lambda/\mu))$ should be replaced by μt.

$$\rho = \frac{\lambda}{s\mu}$$

$$= \frac{30}{(2)(40)} = \frac{30}{80} = 0.375 \tag{13-34}$$

The probability that the queueing system is idle is given by:

$$P_0 = \frac{1}{\left[\displaystyle\sum_{n=0}^{1} \frac{(30/40)^n}{n!} + \frac{(30/40)^2}{2!} \frac{1}{1 - (30/2 \cdot 40)} \right]}$$

$$= \frac{1}{\left[\dfrac{(30/40)^0}{0!} + \dfrac{(30/40)^1}{1!} + \dfrac{(30/40)^2}{2!} \dfrac{1}{1 - (30/80)} \right]} \tag{13-35}$$

$$= \frac{1}{\left[1 + 0.75 + \dfrac{9}{32} \cdot \dfrac{8}{5} \right]}$$

$$= \frac{1}{[1 + 0.75 + 0.45]} = \frac{1}{[2.2]} = 0.45$$

The probabilities associated with various numbers of customers being in the queueing system are calculated as:

$$P_n = \begin{cases} \dfrac{\left(\dfrac{\lambda}{\mu}\right)^n}{n!} P_0, & \text{if } 0 \le n < 2 \\[3ex] \dfrac{\left(\dfrac{\lambda}{\mu}\right)^n}{s!\, s^{n-s}} P_0, & \text{if } n \ge 2 \end{cases} \tag{13-36}$$

Computational results for $n = 1, 2, \ldots, 5$ are presented in Table 13.6. The expected number of customers in the queue is given by:

$$L_q = \frac{\left(\dfrac{\lambda}{\mu}\right)^s \left(\dfrac{\lambda}{\mu s}\right) P_0}{s!\left(1 - \dfrac{\lambda}{\mu s}\right)^2}$$

$$\frac{\left(\dfrac{30}{40}\right)^2 \left(\dfrac{30}{40 \cdot 2}\right) (0.45)}{(2 \cdot 1)\left(1 - \dfrac{30}{40 \cdot 2}\right)^2} \tag{13-37}$$

$$\frac{\left(\dfrac{9}{16}\right)\left(\dfrac{3}{8}\right)(0.45)}{2\left(\dfrac{5}{8}\right)^2}$$

$$= 0.12 \text{ person}$$

TABLE 13.6 **Probability of *n* Customers in Queueing System, Given λ = 30, μ = 40, s = 2**

Number of Customers in System, n	P_n
1	0.338
2	0.126
3	0.046
4	0.018
5	0.007

The expected number of customers in the queueing system is given by:

$$L = L_q + \frac{\lambda}{\mu}$$

$$= 0.12 + \frac{30}{40} \tag{13-38}$$

$$= 0.87 \text{ person}$$

The expected waiting time in the queue is given by:

$$W_q = \frac{L_q}{\lambda}$$

$$= \frac{0.12}{30} \tag{13-39}$$

$$= 0.0040 \text{ hour}$$

The expected waiting time in the queueing system is given by:

$$W = W_q + \frac{1}{\mu}$$

$$= 0.0040 + \frac{1}{40} \tag{13-40}$$

$$= 0.0290 \text{ hour}$$

Assuming that $n > 0$ (i.e., customers are in the system), the probability that the waiting time (including service time) will be greater than 5 minutes ($^1/_{12}$ hour) can be computed as:

$$P[W' > t = {}^5/_{60}] = e^{-\mu t} \left[1 + \frac{P_0 \left(\frac{\lambda}{\mu} \right)^s}{s! \left(1 - \frac{\lambda}{\mu s} \right)} \left(\frac{1 - e^{-\mu t(s - 1 - (\lambda/\mu))}}{s - 1 - \frac{\lambda}{\mu}} \right) \right]$$

$$= e^{-40(1/12)} \left[1 + \frac{0.45 \left(\frac{30}{40} \right)^2}{2 \cdot 1 \left(1 - \frac{30}{40 \cdot 2} \right)} \left(\frac{1 - e^{-40(1/12)(2 - 1 - (30/40))}}{2 - 1 - \frac{30}{40}} \right) \right]$$

$$= e^{-3.33} \left[1 + \frac{0.253}{1.25} (2.25) \right]$$

$$= e^{-3.33} [1.45] \tag{13-41}$$

$$= 0.03583 [1.45] = 0.0520$$

The probability that the waiting time (excluding service time) will be greater than 5 minutes ($^1/_{12}$ hour) is given by:

$$P[W_q' > t = {}^5/_{60}] = [1 - P(W_q' = 0)] e^{-s\mu[1 - (\lambda/\mu s)]t}$$

$$= \left[1 - \sum_{n=0}^{1} P_n \right] e^{-2(40)[1 - (30/40 \cdot 2)](1/12)}$$

$$= [1 - (0.45 + 0.338)] e^{-80(5/8)(1/12)} \tag{13-42}$$

$$= [1 - (0.788)] e^{-4.17}$$

$$= (0.212)(0.0155) = 0.0032$$

Again, in this situation, the consultant is interested in measuring the sensitivity of the analysis to possible changes in the customer arrival rate; and, thus, next decides to compute the major operating characteristics for this *M/M/2* queueing system at values of $\lambda = 25$, 30 (already done), 35, 40, 45, and 50 customers per hour, with the mean service rate for the facility being held constant at $\mu = 40$ customers per hour for each of the two tellers.

Using the relationships previously derived and discussed for the *M/M/2* queueing system, the consultant computed the data shown in Table 13.7.

From the data shown in Table 13.7 the sensitivity of the *M/M/2* queueing model to possible changes in the customer arrival rate can be measured. For example, assume that the actual customer arrival rate is $\lambda = 45$ customers per hour, or 50 percent higher than originally predicted. In this instance the probability of the facility being idle drops from $P_0 = 0.45$ (for $\lambda = 30$) to $P_0 = 0.28$ (for $\lambda = 45$), a decrease of about 40 percent. The expected number of customers in the queueing system increases from $L = 0.87$ to $L = 1.65$, an increase of 90 percent. The expected number of customers in the queue increases from $L_q = 0.12$ to $L_q = 0.52$, an increase of 333 percent. The expected waiting time in the queueing system increases from $W = 0.0290$ hours to $W = 0.0423$ hours, an increase of about 46 percent. Finally, the expected waiting time in the queue increases from $W_q = 0.0040$ hour to $W_q = 0.0173$ hour, an increase of about 330 percent. Similar comparisons could be made for other values of λ. Again, these results indicate the sensitivity of this modeling situation to the customer arrival rate, and reinforce the need for accurately measuring the customer arrival rate λ prior to making operating characteristic computations. A comparison of the results shown in Table 13.7 for the *M/M/2* queueing model for similar results presented in Table 13.5 for the

TABLE 13.7 Operating Characteristics of M/M/2 Queueing System for Various Customer Arrival Rates

Customer Arrival Rate, λ	Probability of Idle System, P_0	Expected Number of Customers in Queueing System, L	Expected Number of Customers in the Queue, L_q	Expected Waiting Time in the Queueing System, W (Hour)	Expected Waiting Time in the Queue, W_q (Hour)
25	0.53	0.70	0.07	0.0273	0.0023
30	0.45	0.87	0.12	0.0290	0.0040
35	0.39	1.09	0.21	0.0320	0.0070
40	0.33	1.33	0.33	0.0360	0.0110
45	0.28	1.65	0.52	0.0423	0.0173
50	0.23	2.05	0.80	0.0517	0.0267

$M/M/1$ queueing model indicates that the $M/M/2$ queueing model is generally not quite as sensitive to changes in the customer arrival rate as is the $M/M/1$ queueing model.

13.4.2 Comparison of the M/M/1 and M/M/2 Queueing Models

A final step in the consultant's analysis is comparison of the steady-state conditions for the $M/M/1$ and the $M/M/2$ queueing models, using best estimates of the customer arrival rate (i.e., $\lambda = 30$ arrivals per hour for both models) and the customer service rate (i.e., $\mu = 60$ services per hour for the $M/M/1$ model and $\mu = 80$ services per hour for the $M/M/2$ model). A summary of the steady-state conditions is presented in Table 13.8. The consultant has previously concluded that the average hourly cost associated with the ill will caused by a customer waiting is $10, and now learns from bank officials that the hourly cost of each bank teller is $3. The consultant's economic comparison of the two queueing systems is as follows.

System 1 (M/M/1 Queueing System):

$\lambda = 30$ arrivals per hour.
$\mu = 60$ services per hour.
$W = 0.033$ hour.

$$\text{Average hourly cost of ill will} = 30(0.033 \text{ hr})(\$10 \text{ per hour})$$
$$= \$ 9.90$$

$$\text{Hourly operating cost (1 teller)} = \$ 3.00$$
$$\text{Total hourly cost} = \$12.90$$

(13–43)

System 2 (M/M/s = 2 Queueing System):

$\lambda = 30$ arrivals per hour.
$\mu = 80$ services per hour.
$W = 0.0277$ hour.

TABLE 13.8 Comparison of Steady-State Results from Queueing Models for Bank Drive-In Facility

Result	s = 1	s = 2
ρ	0.50	0.375
P_0	0.50	0.45
P_1	0.25	0.338
P_2	0.125	0.126
P_5	0.015	0.007
L	1.0 person	0.87 person
L_q	0.5 person	0.12 person
W	0.033 hour	0.0290 hour
W_q	0.0167 hour	0.0040 hour
$P(W' > {}^1/_{12}$ hour$)$	0.082	0.052
$P(W_q' > {}^1/_{12}$ hour$)$	0.041	0.0032

$$
\begin{aligned}
\text{Average hourly cost of ill will} \quad &= 30(0.0290 \text{ hr})(\$10 \text{ per hour}) \\
&= \$\ 8.70 \\
\text{Hourly operating cost (2 tellers)} &= \$\ 6.00 \\
\text{Total hourly cost} &= \overline{\$14.70}
\end{aligned}
$$

(13–44)

On the basis of this comparison of the two alternative queueing systems, the consultant recommended that the bank build a single-server drive-in banking facility that could serve an average of 60 customers per hour.

13.5 THE *M/M/s* QUEUEING MODEL: FINITE QUEUE ALLOWED

In our earlier discussion of the queue discipline (Section 13.2.2) we mentioned that queues are sometimes characterized as having a finite length. This means that the number of customers in the queueing system is not permitted to exceed some specified number (e.g., specified as N). An example of this type of queueing system would be a motel with a certain number of rooms, say N. Assuming that this motel had a policy of sending customers to another motel when it became full, a finite queue would result, and any customer arriving after the queue was full would be refused entry into the system. This type of system is also an example of balking, in which arriving customers leave whenever they find too many customers (N) ahead of them in the system and are not willing to incur a long wait.

For this type of queueing system we will again simply state the structural relationships without reviewing their lengthy and complicated derivation. First, it should be noted that the mean arrival rate for the system becomes zero at a certain time, that is,

$$
\lambda_n = \begin{cases} \lambda, & \text{for } n = 0, 1, 2, \ldots, N - 1 \\ 0, & \text{for } n \geq N \end{cases}
$$

(13–45)

For the single-server case ($s = 1$):

$$P_0 = \frac{1}{\sum_{n=0}^{N} \left(\frac{\lambda}{\mu}\right)^n}$$

$$= \frac{1 - \dfrac{\lambda}{\mu}}{1 - \left(\dfrac{\lambda}{\mu}\right)^{N+1}} \tag{13-46}$$

$$P_n = \left(\frac{1 - \dfrac{\lambda}{\mu}}{1 - \left(\dfrac{\lambda}{\mu}\right)^{N+1}}\right)\left(\frac{\lambda}{\mu}\right)^n \qquad \text{for } n = 0, 1, 2, \ldots, N \tag{13-47}$$

$$L = \sum_{n=1}^{N} nP_n$$

$$= \frac{\left(\dfrac{\lambda}{\mu}\right)}{1 - \left(\dfrac{\lambda}{\mu}\right)} - \frac{(N + 1)\left(\dfrac{\lambda}{\mu}\right)^{N+1}}{1 - \left(\dfrac{\lambda}{\mu}\right)^{N+1}} \tag{13-48}$$

$$L_q = L - (1 - P_0) \tag{13-49}$$

$$W = \frac{L}{\bar{\lambda}} \tag{13-50}$$

$$W_q = \frac{L_q}{\bar{\lambda}} \tag{13-51}$$

where
$$\bar{\lambda} = \sum_{n=0}^{\infty} \lambda_n P_n$$

$$= \sum_{n=0}^{N-1} \lambda P_n \tag{13-52}$$

$$= \lambda(1 - P_N)$$

For the multiple-server case ($1 < s \leq N$):

$$P_0 = \frac{1}{\left[1 + \displaystyle\sum_{n=1}^{s} \frac{\left(\dfrac{\lambda}{\mu}\right)^n}{n!} + \frac{\left(\dfrac{\lambda}{\mu}\right)^s}{s!} \displaystyle\sum_{n=s+1}^{N} \left(\dfrac{\lambda}{s\mu}\right)^{n-s}\right]} \tag{13-53}$$

$$
P_n = \begin{cases} \dfrac{\left(\dfrac{\lambda}{\mu}\right)^n}{n!} P_0, & \text{for } n = 1, 2, \ldots, s \\[3em] \dfrac{\left(\dfrac{\lambda}{\mu}\right)^n}{s!\,s^{n-s}} P_0, & \text{for } n = s, s+1, \ldots, N \\[3em] 0, & \text{for } n > N \end{cases}
\tag{13-54}
$$

$$
L_q = \frac{P_0 \left(\dfrac{\lambda}{\mu}\right)^s \left(\dfrac{\lambda}{s\mu}\right)}{s!\left(1 - \dfrac{\lambda}{s\mu}\right)^2} \left[1 - \left(\frac{\lambda}{s\mu}\right)^{N-s} - (N-s)\left(\frac{\lambda}{s\mu}\right)^{N-s}\left(1 - \frac{\lambda}{s\mu}\right) \right]
\tag{13-55}
$$

$$
L = \sum_{n=0}^{s-1} nP_n + L_q + s\left(1 - \sum_{n=0}^{s-1} P_n\right)
\tag{13-56}
$$

W and W_q are computed from L and L_q in the same manner as indicated earlier for the single-server case.

The utilization factor for this queueing system is given by the usual relationship:

$$
\rho = \frac{\lambda}{\mu s}
\tag{13-57}
$$

13.5.1 Application of the *M/M/s* Queueing Model: Finite Queue Allowed[4]

Grady Coolidge Auditorium for the Performing Arts has two ticket sellers who answer phone calls and take incoming ticket reservations. In addition, two callers can be put on hold until one of the two ticket sellers is available to take the call. If all four phone lines are busy (both ticket sellers and both "hold" lines), it is assumed that the potential customer will become discouraged and thus business will be lost. The calling process is Poisson at a mean rate of two per minute. The ticket reservation service time process follows an exponential distribution with a mean of $1/3$ minute.

For this situation we have a $M/M/s = 2$ queueing system with the queue length limited to $N = 4$. Additionally, $\lambda = 2$ and $\mu = 3$.

The probability that the queueing system is idle (i.e., the customer will immediately get to talk to a ticket seller) is given by:

$$
P_0 = \frac{1}{\left[1 + \displaystyle\sum_{n=1}^{s} \frac{\left(\dfrac{\lambda}{\mu}\right)^n}{n!} + \frac{\left(\dfrac{\lambda}{\mu}\right)^s}{s!} \displaystyle\sum_{n=s+1}^{N} \left(\frac{\lambda}{s\mu}\right)^{n-s} \right]}
$$

---

[4] Hand computations for finite queue problems can become tedious. Consequently, tables that simplify the computational burden have been published. See: L. G. Peck and R. N. Hazelwood, *Finite Queueing Tables* (New York: John Wiley & Sons, Inc., 1958).

$$P_0 = \cfrac{1}{\left[1 + \cfrac{\left(\frac{2}{3}\right)^1}{1} + \cfrac{\left(\frac{2}{3}\right)^2}{2 \cdot 1} + \cfrac{\left(\frac{2}{3}\right)^2}{2 \cdot 1}\left[\left(\frac{2}{3 \cdot 2}\right)^1 + \left(\frac{2}{3 \cdot 2}\right)^2 \right] \right]} \qquad (13\text{-}58)$$

$$= \frac{1}{[1 + {}^2/_3 + {}^2/_9 + {}^8/_{81}]} = \frac{1}{[1 + {}^{80}/_{81}]} = \frac{1}{[1.9877]}$$

$$= 0.503$$

The probabilities associated with the other possible number of customers are computed as follows.

$$n = 1: \qquad P_1 = \frac{\left(\frac{\lambda}{\mu}\right)^1}{1!} P_0 \qquad (13\text{-}59)$$

$$\frac{({}^2/_3)^1}{1!}(0.503) = (0.667)(0.503) = 0.336$$

$$n = 2: \qquad P_2 = \frac{\left(\frac{\lambda}{\mu}\right)^2}{2 \cdot 1} P_0 \qquad (13\text{-}60)$$

$$= \frac{({}^2/_3)^2}{2 \cdot 1}(0.503) = ({}^2/_9)(0.503) = 0.112$$

$$n = 3: \qquad P_3 = \frac{\left(\frac{\lambda}{\mu}\right)^3}{2!2^{3-2}} P_0 \qquad (13\text{-}61)$$

$$= \frac{({}^2/_3)^3}{2!2^1}(0.503) = ({}^2/_{27})(0.503) = 0.037$$

$$n = 4: \qquad P_4 = \frac{\left(\frac{\lambda}{\mu}\right)^4}{2!2^2} P_0 \qquad (13\text{-}62)$$

$$= \frac{({}^2/_3)^4}{2!4}(0.503) = 0.012$$

The expected number of customers in the queue is given by:

$$L_q = \frac{P_0\left(\frac{\lambda}{\mu}\right)^2 \rho}{s!(1 - \rho)^2}[1 - \rho^{N-s} - (N - s)\rho^{N-s}(1 - \rho)] \qquad (13\text{-}63)$$

$$= \frac{0.503\left(\frac{2}{3}\right)^2\left(\frac{2}{3 \cdot 2}\right)}{2!\left(1 - \frac{2}{3 \cdot 2}\right)^2}\left[1 - \left(\frac{2}{3 \cdot 2}\right)^{4-2} - (4 - 2)\left(\frac{2}{3 \cdot 2}\right)^{4-2}\left(1 - \frac{2}{3 \cdot 2}\right)\right]$$

$$= 0.0838[0.7407]$$

$$= 0.0610 \text{ customer}$$

The expected number of customers in the queueing system is computed as:

$$L = \sum_{n=0}^{s-1} nP_n + L_q + s\left(1 - \sum_{n=0}^{s-1} P_n\right)$$

$$= (1)(0.336) + 0.061 + 2(1 - 0.503 - 0.336) \qquad (13\text{-}64)$$

$$= 0.336 + 0.061 + 0.322 = 0.719 \text{ customer}$$

The expected waiting time in the system (including service time) is computed as:

$$W = \frac{L}{\overline{\lambda}} \qquad (13\text{-}65)$$

where $\quad \overline{\lambda} = \lambda(1 - P_N)$

$$= 2(1 - 0.012) = 1.976 \text{ customers/minute} \qquad (13\text{-}66)$$

Thus $\quad W = \dfrac{L}{\overline{\lambda}} = \dfrac{0.719}{1.976} = 0.3639 \qquad (13\text{-}67)$

The expected waiting time in the queue (excluding service time) is given by:

$$W_q = \frac{L_q}{\overline{\lambda}} = \frac{0.0610}{1.976} = 0.0309 \text{ minute} \qquad (13\text{-}68)$$

Finally, the utilization rate for this queueing system is simply:

$$\rho = \frac{\lambda}{\mu s} = \frac{2}{3 \cdot 2} = 0.333 \qquad (13\text{-}69)$$

Let us now examine the sensitivity of this queueing system to possible changes in the service time process. To do this we will compute the operating characteristics for this queueing situation for values of $\mu = 2$, 3 (already done), and 4 customers per minute, with the mean customer arrival rate for the facility being held constant at $\lambda = 2$ customers per minute, and the queue length being limited to $N = 4$.

Using the relationships previously presented and discussed for the $M/M/s = 2$ queueing model having a finite queue length of $N = 4$, we can compute the data shown in Table 13.9.

The data shown in table 13.9 indicates the sensitivity of this queueing model to changes in the customer service rate. For example, assume that the customer service rate increases from $\mu = 3$ customers per minutes to $\mu = 4$ customers per minute, or an increase of $1/3$. For this assumed change, the probability of the system being idle will increase from $P_0 = 0.503$ to $P_0 = 0.601$, a change of 19 percent. The expected number of customers in the queueing system will change from $L = 0.719$ to $L = 0.5262$, a decrease of 27 percent. The expected number of customers in the queue will change from $L_q = 0.061$ to $L_q = 0.0282$, a decrease of 54 percent. The expected waiting time in the queueing system will change from $W = 0.3639$ minutes to $W = 0.2643$ minutes, a decrease of 27 percent. Finally, the expected waiting time in the queue changes from 0.0309 minutes to 0.0142 minutes, a decrease of 54 percent. In summary then, this sensitivity analysis indicates

TABLE 13.9   Operating Characteristics of $M/M/2$ (Finite Queue Length, $N = 4$) Queueing Model for Various Customer Service Rates

Customer Service Rate, μ	Probability of Idle System, P_0	Expected Number of Customers in Queueing System, L	Expected Number of Customers in Queue, L_q	Expected Waiting Time in the Queueing System, W (minute)	Expected Waiting Time in the Queue, W_q (minute)
2	0.347	1.1330	0.1740	0.5922	0.0909
3	0.503	0.719	0.061	0.639	0.0309
4	0.601	0.5262	0.0282	0.2643	0.0142

that the probability of the system being idle, the expected number of customers in the queueing system, and the expected waiting time in the queueing system are not particularly sensitive to the change in the mean customer service rate. These values decrease by 19 to 27 percent for a $33\frac{1}{3}$-percent increase in the mean customer service rate. However, the expected number of customers in the queue and the expected waiting time in the queue are rather sensitive to the change in the mean customer service rate. These values decrease by about 54 percent for a $33\frac{1}{3}$-percent increase in the mean customer service rate.

13.6   THE $M/M/s$ QUEUEING MODEL: LIMITED INPUT SOURCE

Another variation of the $M/M/s$ queueing model that has a number of significant applications concerns the situation in which the input source is limited, or the size of calling population is finite. If we denote the size of the calling population as N, then when the number of customers in the queueing system is $n(n = 0, 1, 2, \ldots, N)$, there can be only $(N - n)$ possible customers remaining in the calling population. The most common application of the queueing model has been to the machine-servicing problem in which one or more repair operators are assigned the responsibility for maintaining a certain group of N machines. In this situation, the N machines are the calling population. Each machine is considered to be a customer within the queueing system when it is idle and waiting to be repaired or when it is being repaired. Conversely, it is considered to be outside the queueing system when it is running.

For this type of queueing model, the steady-state conditions can be stated as follows. For the single-server case ($s = 1$):

$$\lambda_n = \begin{cases} (N - n)\lambda, & \text{for } n = 0, 1, 2, \ldots, N \\ 0, & \text{for } n \geq N \end{cases} \tag{13-70}$$

$$\mu_n = \mu, \quad \text{for } n = 1, 2, \ldots, N \tag{13-71}$$

$$P_0 = \frac{1}{\displaystyle\sum_{n=0}^{N} \left[\frac{N!}{(N - n)!} \left(\frac{\lambda}{\mu} \right)^n \right]} \tag{13-72}$$

$$P_n = \frac{N!}{(N-n)!}\left(\frac{\lambda}{\mu}\right)^n P_0, \quad \text{for } n = 1, 2, \ldots, N \quad (13\text{-}73)$$

$$L_q = \sum_{n=1}^{N} (n-1)P_n$$
$$= N - \frac{\lambda + \mu}{\lambda}(1 - P_0) \quad (13\text{-}74)$$

$$L = \sum_{n=0}^{N} nP_n = L_q + (1 - P_0)$$
$$= N - \frac{\mu}{\lambda}(1 - P_0) \quad (13\text{-}75)$$

$$W = \frac{L}{\overline{\lambda}} \quad (13\text{-}76)$$

$$W_q = \frac{L_q}{\overline{\lambda}} \quad (13\text{-}77)$$

$$\text{where} \quad \overline{\lambda} = \sum_{n=0}^{\infty} \lambda_n P_n = \sum_{n=0}^{N} (N-n)\lambda P_n \quad (13\text{-}78)$$
$$= \lambda(N - L)$$

For the multiple-server case ($s > 1$):

$$\lambda_n = \begin{cases} (N-n)\lambda, & \text{for } n = 0, 1, 2, \ldots, N \\ 0, & \text{for } n \geq N \end{cases} \quad (13\text{-}79)$$

$$\mu_n = \mu, \quad \text{for } n = 1, 2, \ldots, N \quad (13\text{-}80)$$

$$P_0 = \frac{1}{\left[\displaystyle\sum_{n=0}^{s-1} \frac{N!}{(N-n)!n!}\left(\frac{\lambda}{\mu}\right)^n + \sum_{n=s}^{N} \frac{N!}{(N-n)s!s^{n-s}}\left(\frac{\lambda}{\mu}\right)^n \right]} \quad (13\text{-}81)$$

$$P_n = \begin{cases} P_0 \dfrac{N!}{(N-n)!n!}\left(\dfrac{\lambda}{\mu}\right)^n, & \text{if } 0 \leq n \leq s \\[2mm] P_0 \dfrac{N!}{(N-n)!s!s^{n-s}}\left(\dfrac{\lambda}{\mu}\right)^n, & \text{if } s \leq n \leq N \\[2mm] 0, & \text{if } n > N \end{cases} \quad (13\text{-}82)$$

$$L_q = \sum_{n=s}^{N} (n-s)P_n \quad (13\text{-}83)$$

$$L = \sum_{n=0}^{s-1} nP_n + L_q + s\left[1 - \sum_{n=0}^{s-1} P_n\right] \quad (13\text{-}84)$$

W and W_q are computed from L and L_q in the same manner as indicated earlier for the single-server case.

13.6.1 Application of the $M/M/s$ Queueing Model: Limited Input Source

The Tiehold Company currently performs its preventive maintenance by having each repairman service three machines. The average number of machine breakdowns is three per day while the repairman can repair four machines per day. The company feels that the value of lost time is approximately $150 per machine per day.

For this situation we have an $M/M/1$ queueing system with a limited input source, namely $N = 3$ machines. Under steady-state conditions, the probability that this sytem is idle is given by:

$$P_o = \frac{1}{\sum\limits_{n=0}^{N}\left[\frac{N!}{(N-n)!}\left(\frac{\lambda}{\mu}\right)^n\right]}$$

$$= \frac{1}{[{}^{3!}/_{3!}({}^3/_4)^0] + [{}^{3!}/_{2!}({}^3/_4)^1] + [{}^{3!}/_{1!}({}^3/_4)^2] + [{}^{3!}/_{0!}({}^3/_4)^3]} \tag{13-85}$$

$$= \frac{1}{[1 + {}^9/_4 + {}^{54}/_{16} + {}^{162}/_{64}]}$$

$$= {}^1/_{9.1563} = 0.1092$$

The probabilities associated with the other number of machines in the system are computed as follows.

$$n = 1: \quad P_1 = \frac{N!}{(N-n)!}\left(\frac{\lambda}{\mu}\right)^n P_0$$

$$= \frac{3!}{(3-1)!}({}^3\!/\!4)^1(0.1092) \tag{13-86}$$

$$= 0.2457$$

$$n = 2: \quad P_2 = \frac{3!}{(3-2)!}({}^3\!/\!4)^2(0.1092) \tag{13-87}$$

$$= \$0.3686$$

$$n = 3: \quad P_3 = \frac{3!}{(3-3)!}({}^3\!/\!4)^3(0.1092)$$

$$= 0.2764 \tag{13-88}$$

The expected number of machines in the queue is given by:

$$L_q = N - \frac{\lambda + \mu}{\lambda}(1 - P_0)$$

$$= 3 - \frac{3+4}{3}(1 - 0.1092) \tag{13-89}$$

$$= 3 - {}^7/_3(0.8908)$$

$$= 3 - 2.0785 = 0.9215 \text{ machine}$$

The expected number of machines in the queueing system (waiting or being serviced) is computed as:

$$L = N - \frac{\mu}{\lambda}(1 - P_0)$$

$$= 3 - {}^4/_3(1 - 0.1092) \qquad (13\text{--}90)$$

$$= 3 - 1.1877 = 1.8123 \text{ machines}$$

The mean arrival rate is

$$\overline{\lambda} = \lambda(N - L) \qquad (13\text{--}91)$$

$$= 3(3 - 1.8123) = 3.5631 \text{ machines per day}$$

The expected waiting time in the queueing system (including service time) is computed as:

$$W = \frac{L}{\overline{\lambda}} = \frac{1.8123}{3.5631} = 0.5086 \text{ day} \qquad (13\text{--}92)$$

The expected waiting time in the queue is given by:

$$W_q = \frac{L_q}{\overline{\lambda}} = \frac{0.9215}{3.5631} = 0.2586 \text{ day} \qquad (13\text{--}93)$$

Based on a lost-time cost of $150 per machine per day, the waiting cost for this queueing system would be:

3 machines per day (average arrival rate) × 0.2586 day (average waiting time in the queue) × $150 per machine per day = $116.37   (13–94)

Let us now examine the sensitivity of our previous solution to the number of machines that can be repaired by a repairman each day. To do this, we will allow the service rate to be $\mu = 3$, 4 (already done), and 5 machine repairs per day, with the number of machine breakdowns per day being held constant at $\lambda = 3$ per day.

Using the relationships previously presented and discussed for the $M/M/1$ limited input source ($N = 3$) queueing model, the results shown in Table 13.10 can be computed.

The data presented in Table 13.10 indicates that this model is only moderately sensitive to changes in the mean customer service rate. For example, assume that the machine repair rate decreases from $\lambda = 4$ machines per day to $\lambda = 3$ machines per day, a decrease of 25 percent. If this change occurs, the expected number of customers in the queueing system increases from $L = 1.8123$ machines to $L = 2.1250$ machines, an increase of 17 percent. The expected number of customers in the queue increases from $L_q = 0.9215$ machine to $L_q = 1.1250$ machines, an increase of 22 percent. The expected waiting time in the queueing system increases from $W = 0.5086$ day to $W = 0.8095$ day, an increase of 59 percent. Finally, the expected waiting time in the queue increases from $W_q = 0.2586$ day to $W_q = 0.4762$ day, an increase of 84 percent. In summary, this sensitivity analysis

TABLE 13.10   **Operating Characteristics of the M/M/1 (Limited Source, N = 3), Queueing Model for Various Customer Service Rates**

Customer Service Rate, μ	Probability of Idle System, P_0	Expected Number of Customers in Queueing System, L	Expected Number of Customers in Queue, L_q	Expected Waiting Time In the Queueing System, W	Expected Waiting Time In the Queue, W_q
3	0.0625	2.1250 machines	1.1250 machines	0.8095 day	0.4762 day
4	0.1092	1.8123 machines	0.9215 machine	0.5086 day	0.2586 day
5	0.1598	1.6010 machines	0.7596 machine	0.3815 day	0.1810 day

indicates that the probability of the system being idle, the expected number of customers in the queueing system, and the expected number of customers in the queue are not very sensitive to the change in the mean customer service rate. These values increase by 17 to 22 percent for a 25-percent decrease in the mean customer arrival rate. However, the expected waiting time in the queueing system and the expected waiting time in the queue are more sensitive to the decrease in the mean customer service rate. These values increase by 59 to 84 percent for a 25-percent decrease in the mean customer service rate.

13.7 CASE STUDY—QUEUEING THEORY APPLIED TO TRAFFIC FLOW

L. Shaw has developed a queueing theory model for the controlled merging of vehicles entering an expressway ramp.[5] The traffic situation considered is illustrated in Fig. 13.5. Note that there are two parallel roads, one "fast" and the other "slow," that are connected by a ramp on which vehicles from the slow road may be allowed to merge onto the fast road. Frequently this situation occurs when a freeway or expressway is accompanied by a service road. It is advantageous then to restrict the ramp flow in the event that an accident or congestion has caused a traffic jam downstream from the ramp. Such a course of action will facilitate the dissipation of the traffic jam; of course, this is accomplished at the expense of inconvenience to a few vehicles, which are refused access to the fast road and thus must continue traveling on the slow road. The policy is especially appropriate in the case where the fast road contains numerous high-priority vehicles. For instance, multipassenger buses might be allowed unrestricted access at the upstream ramp, while private cars would have control-limited access to the ramp. Under such a scheme, traffic signals release one ramp vehicle at a time. Previously, the rate of release has been determined either off-line, according to prior time-of-day traffic studies, or on-line, in response to downstream sensors of traffic conditions. In this particular application, the decision to permit a ramp vehicle to enter the fast road is a function of its arrival at time t when the jam is in state $w(t)$, where $w(t)$ represents the time required until all those vehicles presently stopped will be moving again at normal speeds. Such a scheme called

[5] For further details, see: Leonard Shaw, "On Optimal Ramp Control of Traffic Jam Queues," *IEEE Transactions on Automatic Control*, vol. Ac-17, no. 5 (October 1972), 630–636.

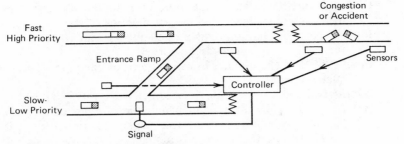

FIGURE 13.5   Ramp-Connected Roads. © **1972 IEEE**

for the development of a vehicle arrival model so that the future evolution of the traffic jam could be predicted for each possible control policy. Also, a queueing theory approach was used to describe the time required for each vehicle to start up and leave the jam so the growth and dissipation of the traffic jam could be accurately modeled.

The basic analysis permits only two choices with respect to ramp flow: unrestricted, or completely blocked. At each time t_n when a vehicle moves downstream past the ramp mouth (having come either from the ramp or from upstream), the controller will decide whether to restrict future ramp vehicles from entering the fast road. If the decision is "no restriction," then the next arrival, from either road, will initiate a new decision problem at t_{n+1}. If "restriction" is decided, future ramp vehicles will be diverted to the service road until after the next arrival from upstream on the fast road, at which time a new decision will be required. The optimal on-off controller for this stochastic problem minimizes the mean sum of the number of cars stopped in the jam and the number of cars diverted from the ramp.

13.8   CONCLUSION

In this chapter we have attempted to present some of the more basic and useful queueing models. As noted previously, there is an infinite number of such models that could be developed, and many of these models would require a great deal of mathematical sophistication. We have attempted to present those models which are fundamental to a basic understanding of queueing theory. The reader who is more interested in this area of management science should consult one or more of the references given at the end of this chapter. Also, it should be noted that simulation often affords a practical means of investigating more complex queueing models. We shall consider simulation in detail in a later chapter.

GLOSSARY OF TERMS

Arrival Rate (λ)   The average number of customers arriving in the queueing system per unit of time.

Balking   The situation in which arriving customers leave whenever they find too many customers ahead of them in the system because they are not willing to incur a long wait.

Calling Population   The input source for the queueing system.

Channel   A single-service facility or a series of service facilities.

Idle   Term that characterizes a queueing system when there are no items to be serviced or customers to be served.

Input Process   The manner in which items or customers enter into or arrive at the queueing system.

Interarrival Time   The time between two arrivals.

M/M/1   A queueing system in which the number of arrivals is described by a Poisson probability distribution, the service time is described by an exponential distribution, and there is a single server.

M/M/s   A queueing system in which the number of arrivals is described by a Poisson probability distribution, the service time is described by an exponential distribution, and there are multiple servers.

Multiple-Channel, Multiple-Stage Queueing System   A queueing system characterized by several parallel series of service facilities, each of which provides an identical sequence of servicing operations.

Multiple-Channel Queueing System   A queueing system with multiple-service facilities arranged in parallel.

Multiple-Channel, Single-Stage Queueing System   A queueing system in which service facilities providing identical services are arranged in parallel.

Multiple-Stage Queueing System   A queueing system with multiple-service facilities arranged in series.

Queue or Waiting Line   One or more units (people, machines, computer programs, etc.) waiting for service.

Queue Discipline   A rule specifying the order in which customers entering the queueing system are served.

Queueing or Waiting Line Theory   A body of knowledge concerned with the arrival of customers at one or more service facilities where the demand and timing of the demand of the customers, the time duration of the servicing operations, and the behavior of the customers as they arrive for service and/or wait in the queue are characterized by uncertainty. The objective of queueing theory is the provision of an adequate but not excessive service facility.

Reneging   A situation in which a customer in the queue becomes impatient and leaves the queue before being selected for service.

Service Mechanism   The manner in which items or customers are serviced and leave the queueing system.

Service Rate (μ)   The average number of customers served in the queueing system per unit of time.

Service Time or Holding Time   The time required for completion of a service.

Single-Channel, Multiple-Stage Queueing System   A queueing system in which several service facilities, each providing a different service, are arranged in a single series.

Single-Channel, Single-Stage Queueing System   A queueing system containing a single-service facility.

Stages   The number of sequential service steps that each individual arrival must pass through in a queueing system.

Steady-State Condition   The condition of a queueing system when the start up conditions no longer affect the operating characteristics of the system.

Utilization Factor The fraction of time the queueing system is busy, computed as the ratio of the arrival rate to the service rate.

SELECTED REFERENCES

WAITING-LINE MODELS

Beckman, P. 1968. *Introduction to Elementary Queueing Theory and Telephone Traffic.* Boulder, Col.: Golem Press.

Benes, V. E. 1963. *General Stochastic Processes in the Theory of Queues.* Reading, Mass.: Addison-Wesley Publishing Company, Inc.

Cohen, J. W. 1969. *The Single-Server Queue.* Amsterdam: Elsevier-North Holland Publishing Company.

Cooper, R. B. 1972. *Introduction to Queueing Theory.* New York: Macmillan Publishing Company, Inc.

Cox, D. R., and W. L. Smith. 1961. *Queues.* New York: John Wiley & Sons, Inc.

Gross, D., and C. M. Harris. 1971. *Fundamentals of Queueing Theory.* New York: Wiley-Interscience.

Jaiswal, N. K. 1968. *Priority Queues.* New York: Academic Press, Inc.

Lee, A. M. 1966. *Applied Queueing Theory.* New York: St. Martin's Press.

Prabu, N. U. 1965. *Queues and Inventories: A Study of Their Basic Stochastic Processes.* New York: John Wiley & Sons, Inc.

Riordan, J. 1962. *Stochastic Service Systems.* New York: John Wiley & Sons, Inc.

Saaty, T. L. 1961. *Elements of Queueing Theory.* New York: McGraw-Hill Book Company.

DISCUSSION QUESTIONS

1. What does an "infinite" input source mean in queueing theory? When is a finite-size calling population assumption appropriate?
2. Give a practical example of an infinite queue.
3. What kinds of queue discipline would you encounter the most in real-world situations?
4. How can you find the probability density function of customer arrivals and customer service times?
5. What is the main characteristic of the exponential distribution?
6. What do we mean by the "utilization factor" for the service facility? Is it true that when the utilization factor is larger than 100 percent the queue length grows infinitely? Why or why not?
7. What do we mean by "steady-state" results (expected number of customers in the system, etc.) in queueing theory?
8. Does the result, "the expected number of customers in the queue $= 1/2$," make any sense? Why or why not?
9. Why is accurate measurement of customer arrival times and customer service times so important in queueing theory?
10. Why would you expect the $M/M/s$ queueing model generally not to be as sensitive to changes in the customer arrival rate as is the $M/M/1$ queueing model?
11. In what type of queueing models could "balking" occur?
12. What do we mean by a "limited input source" queueing model?
13. What is meant by "reneging"?

PROBLEM SET

1. Police Car 54 is assigned to an outlying area of the Ninth Precinct of St. Louis. The precinct captain complains that the car is always arriving late to the scene of its calls, claiming that the car's officers, Larksy and Futch, are taking too many coffee breaks. The officers, however, defend their position by arguing that they have too many calls to answer, and they suggest that an additional car be assigned to their patrol area of the Ninth Precinct.

   Based on your knowledge of the queueing theory, develop some quantitative measures for this situation. You may assume that the number of police calls is Poisson distributed and that the service time for police calls is exponentially distributed. Your preliminary analysis indicates that the rate of calls to the car has a mean of 10 per hour and that the mean service rate for the car is 15 calls per hour. In particular, you are interested in answering the following.
   (a) What are the probabilities associated with $n = 0,1,2,3,4,5$ arrivals during 15-minute, 30-minute, and 60-minute time intervals?
   (b) What is the utilization factor for this queueing system?
   (c) What is the probability that the queueing system is idle?
   (d) What are the probabilities associated with $n = 1,2,3,4,5$ calls being in the queueing system?
   (e) What is the expected number of calls in the queueing system?
   (f) What is the expected number of calls in the queue?
   (g) How long are people waiting or being serviced on the average?
   (h) How long are people waiting on the average?

2. A drive-in restaurant has a single order window. Customers arrive at the restaurant according to a Poisson input process at a mean arrival rate of 30 per hour. Customer orders can be prepared at an average rate of 40 orders per hour. Determine L, L_q, W, and W_q for this queueing system.

3. The jobs to be processed on a particular computer arrive according to a Poisson input process at a mean arrival rate of 12 per hour. Suppose that the computer loses its core storage and that 15 minutes is required to restore the core storage. What is the probability that the number of new jobs that arrive during this time period is
   (a) Zero
   (b) One
   (c) Three
   (d) Six or more

4. A large Midwestern railroad finds that it must steam clean its cars once a year. It is considering two alternatives for its steam-cleaning operation. Under alternative 1, the railroad would operate two steam-cleaning booths, operating in parallel, at a total annual cost of $50,000. The service time distribution under this alternative is exponential with a mean of 5 hours. Under alternative 2, the railroad would operate one large steam-cleaning booth at a total annual cost of $100,000. However, the service time distribution under this alternative would be exponential with a mean of 3 hours. Under both alternatives, the railroad cars arrive according to a Poisson input process with an arrival rate of one car every 8 hours. The cost of an idle hour is thought to be $10 per hour. Assume that the steam-cleaning booths

operate (8 hours per day) $\times$ (250 days per year) = 2000 hours per year. Which alternative should the railroad choose?

5. Assume that you are being asked to analyze a $M/M/2$ queueing system. This system has an exponential interarrival time distribution with a mean of 1 hour, and an exponential service-time distribution with a mean of $1/3$ hour. You begin your analysis of the system at 8:00 A.M., at which time a customer has just arrived.

   (a) Determine the probability that the number of arrivals between 8:00 and 9:00 A.M. will be zero. One. Two. Three. Three or less.

   (b) What is the probability that the next arrival will come before 8:30 A.M.? Between 8:30 and 10:00 A.M.? After 10:30 A.M.?

   (c) Assume that both servers are busy at 9:00 A.M. What is the probability that neither server will have completed service by 9:15 A.M.? Before 10:00 A.M.? Before 9:05 A.M.?

6. A plumbing company receives 50 calls per day for plumbing repairs. On the average a single plumber can make five plumbing repairs per day. The plumbing company advertises that it will complete any plumbing repair within 24 hours of receiving the service call. How many plumbers should the plumbing company have?

   $$\rho = \frac{\lambda}{s\mu} = \frac{56}{5(5)} = 1 \qquad s = 10$$

7. During the period from 7:00 to 8:00 A.M. the arrivals of cars at a single toll station on the Goose Neck bridge average 40 cars per hour, according to a Poisson input process. The toll station has an exponential service time distribution, with a mean service-time rate of 60 cars per hour. What is the probability of having five or fewer cars in the queue at the toll station?

8. The number of customers arriving at a single checkout stand in a small grocery store follows a Poisson process. The checkout stand services the customers according to an exponential distribution.

   (a) For this $M/M/1$ queueing system, assume that the expected service rate is 12 customers per minute. Compare L, L_q, W, and W_q for cases where the mean arrival rate is 5 customers per minute, 10 customers per minute, and 11.5 customers per minute.

   (b) Now assume that there are two checkout stands and the expected service rate is 12 customers per minute. Make the same comparisons as you did for part (a).

9. Discount Tires is opening a small branch store in Tempe, Arizona, and is attempting to make a decision concerning how much space to provide for waiting customers (cars to be serviced). It estimates that customers will arrive according to a Poisson input process at a mean rate of one every 15 minutes. The length of time for servicing a customer has an exponential distribution with a mean of 10 minutes. If the waiting area is full, the customer will take his tire business elsewhere. Compute and compare the probabilities associated with the loss of potential customers if: (a) Zero, (b) One, (c) Five, and (d) 10 waiting spaces (not including the customer being serviced) were to be provided.

10. The Last Chance gasoline station in Ajo, Arizona, is located at the top of a mountain pass and has a single curved driveway that, because of limited space allows only two cars to be in the station at once. Thus, one car can be obtaining gasoline and one car can be waiting to obtain gasoline. Elmira Chance, the owner of the gasoline station, has studied a number of alternative physical arrangements for her gasoline station and has concluded that she has two feasible alternatives.

Alternative 1. She can slightly enlarge her driveway, moving the pump to one end, to permit three cars total in the station (i.e., one being serviced and two waiting). The capital costs for this arrangement are estimated to be equivalent to an additional operating cost of $1.00 per hour.

Alternative 2. She can completely rearrange the station, allowing for two pumps to provide service. Under this arrangement it would be possible to have four cars total in the station (i.e., two being serviced and two waiting). The capital costs for this arrangement are estimated to be equivalent to an additional operating cost of $0.50 per hour, and an additional attendant would also be required at a cost of $2.00 per hour.

Ms. Chance estimates that cars arrive at a rate of 15 per hour (Poisson distributed) and that a pump can service cars at the rate of 10 per hour (exponentially distributed). Should Ms. Chance keep her station as it currently is or should she adopt one of the two alternatives, assuming that her profit per customer averages $1.50?

11. Ace Typewriter Service Company has a typewriter service contract with a major Midwestern university. Under this contract it must pay a penalty of $25 per day per machine for any typewriter that is inoperative. Past experience indicates that requests for typewriter repairs average four per day. The repair operator who services the university can repair an average of six typewriters per day. Each repair operator has responsibility for servicing four typewriters.
    (a) What is the expected daily penalty cost under these conditions?
    (b) What would be the expected daily penalty cost if Ace decided to assign two repair operators to the university?
    (c) Suppose some new service equipment could be purchased that would allow the current repair operator to repair an average of eight typewriters per day. How much would this equipment be worth daily to Ace Typewriter Service Company?

12. The Hot Job Shop is contemplating the installation of a new group of automatic milling machines and is uncertain as to how many to order. It plans on using a single operator to maintain and service the group of milling machines. It anticipates that the service requirements will average three per hour, which the operator can service at a rate of five per hour. The company desires to maintain a 90-percent production rate, on an average basis. What number of milling machines (maximum possible) should be ordered for the desired production rate to be achieved?

13. Compute P_0, L, L_q, W, and W_q for Problem 13–1, for customer arrival rates of $\lambda = 5$, and $\lambda = 14$. Compare these results to those previously obtained. What do they indicate?

14. Compute P_0, L, L_q, W, and W_q for Problem 13–2, for customer service rates of $\mu = 35$, and $\mu = 45$. Compare these results to those previously obtained. What do they indicate?

15. The arrivals of customers (cars) at a large drive-in banking facility are Poisson distributed at a rate of $\lambda = 1.0$ car per minute. The drive-in bank facility has three tellers, each of which can service customers at a rate of $\mu = 0.6$ cars per minute. Determine the operating characteristics for this queueing system, that is, determine P_0, L, L_q, W, and W_q.

16. Compute P_0, L, L_q, and W_q for Problem 13–15 assuming that only two tellers are available. Repeat these computations for the situation in which four tellers are available. What do these results indicate?

17. A small barber shop currently has two barbers, and it can service a total of five customers. Arrivals at this barber shop are Poisson distributed at a mean rate of four persons per hour. The barbers can cut hair at the rate of six persons per hour. Determine L, L_q, W, and W_q for this queueing system.

18. Assume that a third barber could be added to the shop but that the number of seats for waiting customers cannot be changed. Assuming that the arrival and service rates do not change, recompute L, L_q, W and W_q. What does this increase in the number of barbers do to the operating characteristics of this queueing system?

19. The Dependable Brake Shop currently has four mechanics who perform brake repairs. However, if customers come to the shop for repairs and find no mechanic available they typically will take their business elsewhere. Thus, the manager of the brake shop is anticipating the addition of a fifth mechanic. At present, customer arrivals average three per hour and each mechanic can perform a brake repair job in an average of 1 hour. Each mechanic is paid $8 per hour, and each brake job produces $10 of revenue. Should the additional mechanic be hired?

20. A typewriter repair company has a contract to perform preventive maintenance on the typewriters at a major university. On an average day, five typewriters will require repairs. Each service operator can repair eight typewriters each day if necessary, but each is responsible for performing preventive maintenance on only five typewriters. Under the terms of its contract, the typewriter repair company is required to forfeit (pay the university) $200 per day for each typewriter that is not operating because of needed repairs. Compute the waiting time cost for this queueing system.

APPENDIX 13.1 DERIVATION OF THE *M/M/*1 QUEUEING MODEL

The relationships for the $M/M/1$ queueing model can be derived in the following manner. First, it can be shown that the probability of n arrivals during the k small time intervals Δt of time interval T will be given by the binominal distribution:

$$P(n|k,p) = \frac{k!}{(k-n)!n!}p^n(1-p)^{k-n} \qquad (13\text{-}95)$$

Now, when $n = 0$:

$$P(n=0|k,p) = \frac{k!}{(k-0)!0!}p^0(1-p)^{k-0} \qquad (13\text{-}96)$$

$$= (1-p)^k$$

$$= \left(1 - \frac{\lambda T}{k}\right)^k$$

Taking logarithms (base e) of both sides of Equation 13–96 we obtain

$$\log_e[P(n = 0|k,p)] = k \log_e\left(1 - \frac{\lambda T}{k}\right) \qquad (13\text{–}97)$$

Using a Taylor's series exhansion:

$$k \log_e\left(1 - \frac{\lambda T}{k}\right) = -\lambda T - \left(\frac{\lambda^2}{2k}\right) - \left(\frac{\lambda^3}{3k^2}\right) - \cdots$$

$$\simeq -\lambda T \qquad (\text{for } k \gg 0) \qquad (13\text{–}98)$$

Thus, $\log_e[P(n = 0|k,p)] = -\lambda T \qquad (\text{for } k \gg 0) \qquad (13\text{–}99)$

Upon taking antilogs we obtain

$$P(n = 0|k,p) = e^{-\lambda T} \qquad (\text{for large } k) \qquad (13\text{–}100)$$

which can also be expressed as:

$$P(n = 0|k,p) = \frac{e^{-\lambda T}(\lambda T)^0}{0!} \qquad (13\text{–}101)$$

since $(\lambda T)^0 = 1$ and $0! = 1$ $\qquad (13\text{–}102)$

Thus, the probability of $n = 0$ arrivals during the time interval $T = k\,\Delta T$ is given by a Poisson distribution.

Proceeding, the probability of $(n - 1)$ arrivals during the k small intervals will again be given by the binomial distribution:

$$P(n - 1|k,p) = \frac{k!}{[k - (n - 1)]!(n - 1)!}p^{n-1}(1 - p)^{k-(n-1)} \qquad (13\text{–}103)$$

Next, we form the following ratio.

$$\frac{P(n|k,p)}{P(n - 1|k,p)} = \frac{[k!/(k - n)!n!]p^n(1 - p)^{k-n}}{k!/[1 - (n - 1)]!(n - 1)!p^{n-1}(1 - p)^{k-(n-1)}}$$

$$= \frac{[k - (n - 1)]!(n - 1)!}{(k - n)!n!}p(1 - p)^{-1}$$

$$\doteq \frac{k - n - 1}{n}p(1 - p)^{-1} \qquad (13\text{–}104)$$

$$= \frac{kp - np - p}{n(1 - p)} \qquad (\text{since } kp = \lambda T)$$

$$= \frac{\lambda T - n \cdot p - p}{n(1 - 0)} \qquad (\text{for } p \text{ a very small value})$$

$$\simeq \frac{\lambda T}{n}$$

Now, $P(n|k,p) = \dfrac{\lambda T}{n} P(n - 1|k,p) \qquad (13\text{–}105)$

Thus, when $n = 1$,

$$P(n = 1|k,p) = \frac{\lambda T}{1} P(n = 0|k,p) \qquad (13\text{-}106)$$

$$P(n = 1|k,p) = \frac{\lambda T}{1} \frac{e^{-\lambda T}(\lambda T)^0}{0!}$$

$$= \frac{e^{-\lambda T}(\lambda T)^1}{1!} \qquad (13\text{-}107)$$

Thus, the probability of $n = 1$ arrivals during the time interval $T = k\Delta t$ is also given by a Poisson distribution.

Using the same inductive process we can show that the probabilities of $n = 2$, 3, . . . arrivals during the time interval $T = k\Delta t$ will also be given by the Poisson distribution. This general result is

$$P(n|k,p) = P[n \text{ arrivals during an interval of length } T = k\Delta t \text{ (given } \lambda)]$$

$$= \frac{e^{-\lambda T}(\lambda T)^n}{n!} \qquad (13\text{-}108)$$

Thus, the number of arrivals during a time interval T has a Poisson distribution for the $M/M/1$ queueing model. Using a similar inductive process we can also show that the probability that n customers will be served (assuming that the queue is nonempty) by the service facility during a time interval T is given by the Poisson probability distribution having the form:

$$P[n \text{ services during an interval of length } T = k \cdot \Delta t \text{ (given } \mu)] \qquad (13\text{-}109)$$

$$= \frac{e^{-\mu T}(\mu T)^n}{n!}$$

Using the results obtained above we can next show that the interarrival time or the service time for the $M/M/1$ queueing model has an exponential distribution. Let $f(t)$ denote the probability density function for either the interarrival time or the service time. Then,

$$P[\text{one arrival within } T \text{ units of time after a prior arrival}]$$

$$= \int_{t=0}^{t=T} f(t)dt \qquad (13\text{-}110)$$

and $\quad P[\text{no arrivals within } T \text{ units of time after a prior arrival}]$

$$= 1 - \int_{t=0}^{t=T} f(t)dt \qquad (13\text{-}111)$$

We previously determined in Equation 13–101 that the probability of zero arrivals during a time interval T is given by the Poisson distribution. Thus, we can equate Equations 13–101 and 13–111 to obtain

$$1 - \int_{t=0}^{t=T} f(t)dt = e^{-\lambda T} \qquad (13\text{-}112)$$

Differentiating both sides of Equation 13–112 we obtain

$$f(t) = \lambda e^{-\lambda t} \tag{13-113}$$

which is the probability density function for the exponential distribution. Similarly, we could obtain the probability density function for the service time as:

$$f(t) = \mu e^{-\mu t} \tag{13-114}$$

This again is an exponential probability density function. Additionally, using the cumulative probabilities for the exponential distribution, and letting the random variable T represent either *interarrival* or *service* time, we can compute the probability that T or fewer units of time will elapse between the arrivals of customers as:

$P[T$ or fewer time units between arrivals (given λ)]
$$= P(T \le t) = 1 - e^{-\lambda T} \quad (t \ge 0) \tag{13-115}$$

The probability that more than T units of time will elapse between arrivals of customers is given by:

$P[$more than T time units between arrivals (given λ)]
$$= P(T > t) = e^{-\lambda T} \tag{13-116}$$

Similarly, the probability that T or fewer units of time will elapse between the servicing of customers (assuming a nonempty queue) is given by:

$P[T$ or fewer time units between services (given μ)]
$$= P(T \le t) = 1 - e^{-\mu T} \tag{13-117}$$

Finally, the probability that more than T units of time will elapse between the servicing of customers (assuming a nonempty queue) is given by:

$P[$more than T time units between services (given μ)]
$$= P(T > t) = e^{-\mu T} \tag{13-118}$$

Using the results obtained above let us now derive the basic relationships that apply to the $M/M/1$ queueing model. Our first consideration is that of determining the probability of having n units in the system at time t. The following notation and assumptions will be employed.

$P_n(t) =$ The probability of having n units in the system at time t.

$\Delta t =$ The time interval of concern. Δt is a time interval so small that $(\Delta t)^2 \to 0$. During Δt no more than one customer can arrive, and no more than one customer can be serviced.

$\lambda \Delta t =$ Probability of an arrival during any period Δt.

$\mu\Delta t$ = Probability of a service during any period Δt (conditional probability based upon the occurrence that there is a customer in the system to be served).

Since Δt is a very small interval we will assume that the probability of more than one change during time period Δt is zero (i.e., the probability of two or more services or arrivals or a service and an arrival is zero). Thus,

$$P(\text{no change in the system}) = 1 - \lambda\Delta t - \mu\Delta t \qquad (13\text{-}119)$$

Starting with various numbers of customers in the system at time t, we can reach a state in which there are n customers in the system by one of four events occurring. These events are summarized in Table 13.11.

For the four mutually exclusive and collectively exhaustive events:

$$
\begin{aligned}
P(\text{Event } a) &= P_n(t) \cdot P(0 \text{ arrivals}) \cdot P(0 \text{ services}) \\
&= P_n(t) \cdot (1 - \lambda\Delta t) \cdot (1 - \mu\Delta t) \\
&= P_n(t) \cdot [1 - \lambda\Delta t - \mu\Delta t + \lambda\mu(\Delta t)^2] \qquad (13\text{-}120) \\
&= P_n(t) \cdot (1 - \lambda\Delta t - \mu\Delta t) \qquad \text{since } (\Delta t)^2 \to 0
\end{aligned}
$$

$$
\begin{aligned}
P(\text{Event } b) &= P_{n-1}(t) \cdot P(1 \text{ arrival}) \cdot P(0 \text{ services}) \\
&= P_{n-1}(t) \cdot (\lambda\Delta t) \cdot (1 - \mu\Delta t) \\
&= P_{n-1}(t) \cdot [\lambda\Delta t - \lambda\mu(\Delta t)^2] \qquad (13\text{-}121) \\
&= P_{n-1}(t) \cdot (\lambda\Delta t) \qquad \text{since } (\Delta t)^2 \to 0
\end{aligned}
$$

$$
\begin{aligned}
P(\text{Event } c) &= P_{n+1}(t) \cdot P(0 \text{ arrival}) \cdot P(1 \text{ services}) \\
&= P_{n+1}(t) \cdot (1 - \lambda\Delta t) \cdot (\mu\Delta t) \\
&= P_{n+1}(t) \cdot [\mu\Delta t - \lambda\mu(\Delta t)^2] \qquad (13\text{-}122) \\
&= P_{n+1}(t) \cdot (\mu\Delta t) \qquad \text{since } (\Delta t)^2 \to 0
\end{aligned}
$$

$$P(\text{Event } d) = 0 \text{ (since we cannot have more than one arrival or service during } \Delta t) \qquad (13\text{-}123)$$

TABLE 13.11 Number of Units in Queueing System

Event	Number of Units in System at Time t	Number of Arrivals	Number of Services	Number of Units in System at Time $t + \Delta t$
(a)	n	0	0	n
(b)	$n - 1$	1	0	n
(c)	$n + 1$	0	1	n
(d)	$n - y$ or $n + y$	y	y	n

Summing the probabilities derived for these four events we obtain

$$P_n(t + \Delta t) = P_n(t) [1 - \lambda\Delta t - \mu\Delta t] + P_{n-1}(t)[\lambda\Delta t] + P_{n+1}(t)[\mu\Delta t]$$

$$\frac{P_n(t + \Delta t) - P_n(t)}{\Delta t} = -(\lambda + \mu)P_n(t) + \lambda P_{n-1}(t) + \mu P_{n+1}(t) \qquad (13\text{-}124)$$

Rearranging terms and letting $\Delta t \to 0$, we obtain

$$\frac{dP_n(t)}{dt} = \lambda P_{n-1}(t) - (\lambda + \mu)P_n(t) + \mu P_{n+1}(t) \qquad (13\text{-}125)$$

At steady-state or equilibrium: $\dfrac{dP_n(t)}{dt} = 0 \qquad (13\text{-}126)$

Therefore, $0 = \lambda P_{n-1}(t) - (\lambda + \mu)P_n(t) + \mu P_{n+1}(t)$

$$P_{n+1}(t) = \frac{-\lambda}{\mu} P_{n-1}(t) + \frac{(\lambda + \mu)}{\mu} P_n(t) \qquad (13\text{-}127)$$

or $P_{n+1} = \dfrac{-\lambda}{\mu}P_{n-1} + \dfrac{(\lambda + \mu)}{\mu}P_n$

Now, refer back to Equation 13-124,

$$P_n(t + \Delta t) = P_n(t)(1 - \lambda\Delta t - \mu\Delta t) + P_{n-1}(t)(\lambda\Delta t) + P_{n+1}(t)(\mu\Delta t)$$

Assume that we want to investigate the situation for $P_0(t + \Delta t)$. In this situation $n = 0$, and $P_{n-1}(t) = 0$. Thus, we obtain

$$P_0(t + \Delta t) = P_0(t)(1 - \lambda\Delta t - \mu\Delta t) + P_1(t)(\mu\Delta t) \qquad (13\text{-}128)$$

Subtracting $P_0(t)$ from both sides and dividing by Δt, we obtain

$$\frac{P_0(t + \Delta t) - P_0(t)}{\Delta t} = -(\lambda + \mu)P_0(t) + \mu P_1(t) \qquad (13\text{-}129)$$

With $n = 0$, a customer service is impossible and thus $\mu P_0(t) = 0$. Therefore,

$$\frac{P_0(t + \Delta t) - P_0(t)}{\Delta t} = -\lambda P_0(t) - \mu P_1(t) \qquad (13\text{-}130)$$

In equilibrium: $\dfrac{P_0(t + \Delta t) - P_0(t)}{\Delta t} = 0 = \dfrac{dP_0(t)}{dt} \qquad (13\text{-}131)$

as $\Delta t \to 0$. Therefore:

$$-\lambda P_0(t) + \mu P_1(t) = 0$$

or $-\lambda P_0 + \mu P_1 = 0 \qquad (13\text{-}132)$

and $P_1 = \dfrac{\lambda}{\mu}P_0$

Substituting back into Equation 13–127 with $n = 1$, we obtain

$$P_{n+1} = \frac{-\lambda}{\mu}P_{n-1} + \frac{\lambda + \mu}{\mu}P_n$$

$$P_2 = \frac{-\lambda}{\mu}P_0 + \frac{\lambda + \mu}{\mu}P_1$$

$$P_2 = \frac{-\lambda}{\mu}P_0 + \frac{\lambda + \mu}{\mu}\left(\frac{\lambda}{\mu}P_0\right) \qquad (13\text{–}133)$$

$$P_2 = \left(\frac{-\lambda\mu}{\mu^2} + \frac{\lambda^2 + \lambda\mu}{\mu^2}\right)P_0$$

$$P_2 = \frac{\lambda^2}{\mu^2}P_0 = \left(\frac{\lambda}{\mu}\right)^2 P_0$$

Continuing this process, we can obtain the general expression:

$$P_n = \left(\frac{\lambda}{\mu}\right)^n P_0 \qquad (13\text{–}134)$$

where $\quad P_0 = 1 - \left(\frac{\lambda}{\mu}\right) \qquad (13\text{–}135)$

since λ/μ is the probability that the system is nonempty. The term $\rho = \lambda/\mu$ is referred to as the utilization factor for the service facility. Note that if the mean arrival rate λ is less than the mean service rate μ then $\rho = \lambda/\mu < 1$. If the opposite situation is present, then $\rho \geq 1$, and the queue length grows without bound ($\rightarrow\infty$). In the following development, we will assume that $\rho < 1$.

We can now determine the operating characteristics of the *M/M/1* queueing model as follows. First, the expected number of customers in the system L is

$$L = \sum_{n=0}^{\infty} nP_n$$

$$= \sum_{n=0}^{\infty} nP_0\left(\frac{\lambda}{\mu}\right)^n$$

$$= \sum_{n=0}^{\infty} n\left[1 - \left(\frac{\lambda}{\mu}\right)\right]\left(\frac{\lambda}{\mu}\right)^n \qquad (13\text{–}136)$$

$$= \left[1 - \left(\frac{\lambda}{\mu}\right)\right]\sum_{n=0}^{\infty} n\left(\frac{\lambda}{\mu}\right)^n$$

$$= \left[1 - \left(\frac{\lambda}{\mu}\right)\right]\left[0 \cdot \left(\frac{\lambda}{\mu}\right)^0 + 1\left(\frac{\lambda}{\mu}\right)^1 + 2\left(\frac{\lambda}{\mu}\right)^2 + \cdots\right]$$

Now, the term $[0 + 1(\lambda/\mu)^1 + 2(\lambda/\mu)^2 + \cdots]$ is a convergent geometric series that sums to $(\lambda/\mu)/[1 - (\lambda/\mu)]^2$. Thus,

$$L = \frac{[1 - (\lambda/\mu)](\lambda/\mu)}{[1 - (\lambda/\mu)]^2} \qquad (13\text{–}137)$$

$$= \frac{\lambda}{\mu - \lambda}$$

Second, the expected number in the queue L_q is

$$L_q = \sum_{n=1}^{\infty} (n - 1)P_n = \sum_{n=1}^{\infty} nP_n - \sum_{n=1}^{\infty} P_n$$

$$= L - 1(1 - P_0)$$

$$= \left(\frac{\lambda}{\mu - \lambda} \right) - \left(1 - \left[1 - \frac{\lambda}{\mu} \right] \right) \qquad (13\text{--}138)$$

$$= \left(\frac{\lambda}{\mu - \lambda} \right) - \left(\frac{\lambda}{\mu} \right) = \frac{\mu\lambda - \mu\lambda + \lambda^2}{\mu(\mu - \lambda)}$$

$$= \frac{\lambda^2}{\mu(\mu - \lambda)}$$

Third, the expected time in the system W is

$$W = \text{expected time in the queueing system}$$
$$= \text{expected number in the system/arrival rate} \qquad (13\text{--}139)$$

$$= \frac{L}{\lambda} = \frac{\dfrac{\lambda}{\mu - \lambda}}{\lambda} = \frac{1}{\mu - \lambda}$$

Fourth, the expected waiting time in the queue W_q is

$$W_q = \text{expected waiting time in the queue}$$
$$= \text{expected waiting time in the queueing system-expected service time}$$

$$= W - \frac{1}{\mu} \qquad (13\text{--}140)$$

$$= \left[\frac{1}{(\mu - \lambda)} \right] - \left[\frac{1}{\mu} \right] = \frac{\lambda}{\mu(\mu - \lambda)}$$

When $\lambda \geq \mu$, so that the mean arrival rate exceeds the mean service rate, the above "steady-state" results no longer hold (since the summation originally used for computing P_0 is no longer convergent). In this instance, the queue would theoretically grow infinitely long.

For the case in which $\lambda < \mu$, we can derive the probability distribution for waiting time. Thus, let W' be a random variable denoting the waiting time in the system (including service time) for a random arrival assuming that the service discipline is first-in, first out. The probability that this waiting time is greater than some arbitrary value is given by:

$$P(W' > t) = e^{-\mu(1 - (\lambda/\mu))t} \qquad (t \geq 0) \qquad (13\text{--}141)$$

In some situations we may be interested in only the waiting time until service begins. Thus, let the random variable W'_q be the waiting time in the queue (excluding service time) for a random arrival assuming that the service discipline is first-in, first-out. If this arrival finds *no* customers in the queueing system, he begins to be served immediately. Thus,

$$P(W'_q = 0) = P_0 = 1 - \frac{\lambda}{\mu} \qquad (13\text{--}142)$$

If, however, he finds $n > 0$ customers in the queueing system, then the probability that the waiting time in the system (excluding service time) is greater than some arbitrary value is given by:

$$P(W'_q > t) = \frac{\lambda}{\mu} e^{-\mu} \left(1 - \frac{\lambda}{\mu}\right) t \qquad (t \geq 0) \qquad (13\text{--}143)$$

Markov Processes

14.1 INTRODUCTION

Markov process models deal with the behavior of dynamic systems over time. Such behavior is referred to as a **stochastic process**. A stochastic process is defined to be an indexed collection (family) of random variables $[X_t]$, where the index t runs over a given set T. Thus, for each t contained in the index set T, X_t is a random variable. The index set T is often composed of nonnegative integers, and X_t is taken to be some measurable characteristic of interest at time t. For example, the stochastic process X_1, X_2, X_3, X_4 could represent bank deposits made in each of four successive weeks. The random variable X_t represents the **state** of the stochastic process at time t. If T is a countable set, the stochastic process is said to be a **discrete time** process. If T is an open or closed interval of the real line, the stochastic process is said to be a **continuous time** process. The set of possible values that the random variable $\{X_t, t \varepsilon T\}$ may assume is called the **state space** of the stochastic process.

The evolution of the system over time frequently involves a series of repeated trials where the state or outcome of the system at any particular trial cannot be determined with certainty. Herein, a set of transition probabilities is employed to describe the manner in which the system makes a transition from one time period, or trial, to another. Thus, we will be interested in the probability associated with the system being in a particular state at a given time period.

Markov process models have been used extensively in marketing to study "brand switching," the phenomenon of a consumer purchasing brand A in one period and then purchasing brand B in the following period. Markovian analysis has been employed in the study of equipment maintenance and failure problems. Markov chains have also been used in analyzing accounts receivables to estimate the amount of accounts receivable that will ultimately become bad debts, and in studying stock-market price movements. The study of Markov process models is somewhat similar to the study of inventory models and waiting-line models in that it can quickly become very complex and difficult because of the nature of the underlying stochastic processes. Consequently, we shall focus our study of Markov processes on those reasonably simple situations that have been shown to have practical business application.

14.2 THE STRUCTURE OF MARKOV PROCESSES

A **Markov process**, or **Markov chain**, is a stochastic process that is defined as follows.

DEFINITION
A stochastic process $\{X_n, n = 0, 1, 2, \ldots\}$, *with a finite or countable state space, is said to have a Markov chain structure if* $P\{X_{n+1} = j \mid X_0 = i_0, X_1 = i_1, \ldots, X_{n-1} = i_{n-1}, X_n = i\} = P\{X_{n+1} = j \mid X_n = i\}$, *for all* i, j, *and for* n = 0, 1, \ldots

A Markov process is a stochastic process for which the occurrence of a future state depends only on the immediately preceding state. Thus, for a Markov process, given that the present state is known, the conditional probability of the next state is independent of the states prior to the present state.

A Markov process is described by its state space, which is the list of possible outcomes at a point in time, and its *time structure*. The state space is considered to be finite, with size equal to N. Additionally, we seek to relate the uncertainty about the state at one point in time to the uncertainty about the state at other points in time. The **Markovian property** defined above is equivalent to stating that the conditional probability of any future state ($X_{n+1} = j$), given any past state ($X_0 = i_0, \ldots, X_{n-1} = i_{n-1}$) and the present state ($X_n = i$), is *independent* of the past state and depends only on the present state of the process.

The conditional probabilities $P\{X_{n+1} = j \mid X_n = i\}$ are denoted as **transition probabilities**. If, for each i and j, $1 \le i, j \le N$, $P\{X_{n+1} = j \mid X_n = i\} = P\{X_1 = j \mid X_0 = i\}$ for all $n = 0, 1, \ldots$, then the (one-step) transition probabilities are defined as being **stationary** and are denoted simply as p_{ij}. Stationary transition probabilities thus do not change over time, and for each i, j, and $n(n = 0, 1, 2, \ldots)$ $P\{X_{t+n} = j \mid X_t = i\} = P\{X_n = j \mid X_0 = i\}$, for all $t = 0, 1, \ldots$. These conditional probabilities are denoted simply as $p_{ij}{}^{(n)}$ and are called n-step transition probabilities. These conditional probabilities state that the random variable X, starting in state i, will be in state j after exactly n time units. The transition probabilities, P_{ij}, must satisfy the properties:

$$0 \le p_{ij} \le 1 \qquad 1 \le i, j \le N \tag{14-1}$$

$$\sum_{j=1}^{N} p_{ij} = 1, \qquad i = 1, 2, \ldots N \tag{14-2}$$

Note that we allow for the possibility of the same state being occupied after a transition; the probabilities p_{ij}, $i = 1, 2, \ldots, N$ are not necessarily zero.

The N^2 transition probabilities that describe a Markov process are conveniently represented by an $N \times N$ **transition probability matrix P** having elements p_{ij}, in matrix form as:

$$
\mathbf{P} = \begin{array}{c|cccc}
\text{State} & 1 & 2 & \cdots & N \\
\hline
1 & p_{11} & p_{12} & \cdots & p_{1N} \\
2 & p_{21} & p_{22} & \cdots & p_{2N} \\
\cdot & \cdot & \cdot & \cdot & \cdot \\
\cdot & \cdot & \cdot & \cdot & \cdot \\
\cdot & \cdot & \cdot & \cdot & \cdot \\
N & p_{N1} & p_{N2} & \cdots & p_{NN}
\end{array}
$$

$$
\mathbf{P} = \{p_{ij}\} = \begin{bmatrix}
p_{11} & p_{12} & \cdots & p_{1N} \\
p_{21} & p_{22} & \cdots & p_{2N} \\
\cdot & \cdot & \cdot & \cdot \\
\cdot & \cdot & \cdot & \cdot \\
\cdot & \cdot & \cdot & \cdot \\
p_{N1} & p_{N2} & \cdots & p_{NN}
\end{bmatrix}
$$

(14–3)

A complete formal definition of a finite-state Markov property (chain) can now be given. A stochastic process $\{X_n\}$, $n = 0, 1, \ldots$, is a finite-state Markov process if it has the following.

1. A finite number of states N.
2. The Markovian property.
3. Stationary transition probabilities.
4. A set of initial probabilities $P\{X_0 = i\}$ for all i.

EXAMPLE   Let us now consider an example to illustrate the structure of a Markov process. A certain small Midwestern college town has three pizzerias, and we are interested in analyzing the market share and customer loyalty associated with these three pizzerias. To make this analysis we focus on the collective Saturday night eating habits of a social fraternity at the college. We will assume that the membership of the fraternity will choose to eat at one of the three pizzerias each Saturday night.

The particular pizzeria that is selected by the fraternity group in any one week is the state of the system in that time period. There is a finite number of possible states for this Markov process, namely three, which are the three pizzerias.

The fraternity makes its weekly selection of the pizzerias on Saturday afternoon. Assume that we have observed the selection process for 6 months (26 weeks). According to the Markovian property, we need to express these weekly data in probabilistic form. The Markovian property will be equivalent to stating that the conditional probability of any future state, given any past state and the present state $X_t = i$, will be *independent* of the past state and will depend only on the present state of the process.

Suppose that in reviewing the data we discover that the conditional probabilities shown in Table 14.1 are appropriate for the pizzeria selection process. These conditional probabilities are associated with the transition from a particular pizzeria (state) in a given time period to a particular pizzeria (state) in a following time period. They are thus the transition probabilities for the Markov process. Note that an important property of this table of transition probabilities is that the sum of the entries in each row is 1.0. For example, given that Pizzeria A is selected in the current week, then Pizzerias A, B, or C must be selected in the following week and the entries in the first row of Table 14.1 provide the probabilities associ-

TABLE 14.1 Conditional Selection Probabilities—Three Pizzerias

Current Selection	Selection Next Week		
	Pizzeria A	Pizzeria B	Pizzeria C
Pizzeria A	0.5	0.3	0.2
Pizzeria B	0.4	0.2	0.4
Pizzeria C	0.3	0.3	0.4

ated with each of these future events. Note further that the transition probabilities do not change over time. They are stationary and can be used to determine which pizzeria will be selected next Saturday, given that we know which pizzeria has been selected this Saturday.

The set of transition probabilities given in Table 14.1 has one row and one column for each state of the process. Using our previously introduced notation, the (one-step) transition matrix is given by:

$$\mathbf{P} = \begin{bmatrix} p_{11} & p_{12} & p_{13} \\ p_{21} & p_{22} & p_{23} \\ p_{31} & p_{32} & p_{33} \end{bmatrix} = \begin{bmatrix} 0.5 & 0.3 & 0.2 \\ 0.4 & 0.2 & 0.4 \\ 0.3 & 0.3 & 0.4 \end{bmatrix} \tag{14-4}$$

The diagonal elements in this (one-step) transition matrix can be interpreted as measures of "pizzeria loyalty" in that they represent the probability of a repeat selection of the same pizzeria. Conversely, the off-diagonal elements represent the "pizzeria switching" characteristics of the fraternity. Finally, it is obvious that we have defined a set of initial probabilities $P\{X_0 = i\}$ for all i as the first column in Table 14.1. Thus, we have accounted for the four properties necessary for the definition of the finite-state Markov process.

14.3 PROBABILITY ANALYSIS USING MARKOV CHAINS

The transition matrix can next be used to determine the probability of being in a certain state after n steps, given some specified initial state S_i. To illustrate this type of probability analysis, consider the transition matrix developed for our pizzeria example. Suppose that the fraternity has just eaten at Pizzeria B (step $n = 0$), and we are interested in determining the probability that the fraternity will eat at Pizzeria A 2 weeks in the future (step $n = 2$).

The desired probability can be determined by means of classical probability theory. Enumerating the various outcomes we can construct a tree diagram as shown in Fig. 14.1. Tabulating and summing the probabilities illustrated in the tree diagram, we obtain the results shown in Table 14.2. Thus, our analysis indicates that given that Pizzeria B is selected at time $n = 0$, the probability that Pizzeria A will be selected at time $n = 2$ is 0.40.

This same result can be obtained using Markov chains directly. Let us first define $\mathbf{V}_i^n$ as the probability vector that describes the probabilities of possible outcomes in n future steps (time periods) if the present state (time $n = 0$) is S_i. Consider now the probability vector $\mathbf{V}_2^1$ associated with time $n = 1$, and state $S_2 = $ (selection of Pizzeria B). For state S_2, $\mathbf{V}_2^1 = (0.4 \quad 0.2 \quad 0.4)$. This probability vector indicates that, if the present state is S_2, the probability that the next state is

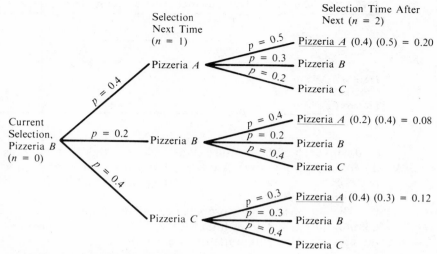

FIGURE 14.1   Tree Diagram—Pizzeria Example

S_1 is $p_{21} = 0.4$, is S_2 is $p_{22} = 0.2$, is S_3 is $p_{23} = 0.4$. Thus, the vector $\mathbf{V}_2^1$ indicates the probabilities of outcomes for the next step, time $n = 1$, given a specified present state at the present time, $n = 0$. Our problem can now be couched in terms of determining $\mathbf{V}_2^2$, the probability vector that will contain the probabilities of all possible selections at time $n = 2$, given that the current selection is state S_2 (Pizzeria B). This computation is made by multiplying $\mathbf{V}_2^1$ and the transition probability matrix $\mathbf{P}$. We thus obtain

$$\mathbf{V}_2^2 = \mathbf{V}_2^1 \cdot \mathbf{P} = (0.4 \quad 0.2 \quad 0.4) \begin{bmatrix} 0.5 & 0.3 & 0.2 \\ 0.4 & 0.2 & 0.4 \\ 0.3 & 0.3 & 0.4 \end{bmatrix}$$

$$= [(0.4)(0.5) + (0.2)(0.4) + (0.4)(0.3) \quad (0.4)(0.3) + (0.2)(0.2)$$
$$+ (0.4)(0.3) \quad (0.4)(0.2) + (0.2)(0.4) + (0.4)(0.4)]$$
$$= [0.40 \quad 0.28 \quad 0.32]$$

$$(14-5)$$

The vector $\mathbf{V}_2^2$ indicates that, if the present state is S_2 at $n = 0$, two time periods later ($n = 2$), the probability of being in state S_1 is 0.40, in state S_2 is 0.28 and in

TABLE 14.2   Summary of Results—Tree Diagram

Selection at Time n = 1		Selection at Time n = 2		Probability Pizzeria A Selected
State	Probability	State	Probability	
Pizzeria A	0.4	Pizzeria A	0.5	(0.4)(0.5) = 0.20
Pizzeria B	0.2	Pizzeria A	0.4	(0.2)(0.4) = 0.08
Pizzeria C	0.4	Pizzeria A	0.3	(0.4)(0.3) = 0.12
				Total 0.40

state $S_3 = 0.32$. The first term is exactly the same as we obtained earlier in our tree diagram analysis.

The above example indicates that the following relationships hold

$$\mathbf{V}_i^0 = [p_{i1}p_{i2} \cdots p_{ii} \cdots p_{in}] \quad \text{and} \quad p_{ii} = 1.0, p_{i \neq j} = 0.0 \quad (14\text{-}6)$$

At time $n = 0$, we know what the state is, and thus there is a probability of 1 that state i exists.

$$\mathbf{V}_i^1 = \mathbf{V}_i^0\mathbf{P} = [p_{i1}p_{i2} \cdots p_{in}] \quad (14\text{-}7)$$

At time $n = 1$, $\mathbf{V}_i^1$ is given by the ith row in the transition matrix $\mathbf{P}$.

$$\mathbf{V}_i^2 = \mathbf{V}_i^1\mathbf{P} \quad (14\text{-}8)$$

At time $n = 2$, $\mathbf{V}_i^2$ is given by the product of the probability vector $\mathbf{V}_i^1$ and the transition matrix $\mathbf{P}$. Thus, the following general results obtain

$$\mathbf{V}_i^3 = \mathbf{V}_i^2\mathbf{P} = (\mathbf{V}_i^1\mathbf{P}) \cdot \mathbf{P} = \mathbf{V}_i^1\mathbf{P}^2 \quad (14\text{-}9)$$
$$\mathbf{V}_i^4 = \mathbf{V}_i^3\mathbf{P} = (\mathbf{V}_i^1\mathbf{P}^2) \cdot \mathbf{P} = \mathbf{V}_i^1\mathbf{P}^3 \quad (14\text{-}10)$$
$$\mathbf{V}_i^n = \mathbf{V}_i^{n-1}\mathbf{P} = (\mathbf{V}_i^1\mathbf{P}^{n-2})\mathbf{P} = \mathbf{V}_i^1\mathbf{P}^{n-1} \quad (14\text{-}11)$$

In summary then, the probabilities associated with various states n time periods in the future can be determined from the probability vector $\mathbf{V}_i^1$ and some power of the transition matrix $\mathbf{P}$.

14.4 THE CHAPMAN-KOLMOGOROV EQUATIONS

We have previously discussed the transition probability, p_{ij}, and we are now concerned with the use of the transition probability when the process is in state i and the probability that the process will be in state j after n periods is desired. This can be accomplished by use of the **Chapman-Kolmogorov equations**. First, let us define the n-step transition probability as $p_{ij}^{(n)}$. The Chapman-Kolmogorov equations can then be written as:

$$p_{ij}^{(n)} = \sum_{k=0}^{M} p_{ik}^r p_{kj}^{(n-r)}, \quad \text{for all } i, j, n, \text{ and } 0 \leq r \leq n \quad (14\text{-}12)$$

The left-hand side of these equations represents the probability that the process goes from state i to state j in n steps. The right-hand side of these equations indicates the conditional probability that starting from state i, the process goes to state k from r steps and then on to state j in $(n - r)$ steps. Since the right-hand side is summed over all possible k, this summation must yield $p_{ij}^{(n)}$.

If we now let $\mathbf{P}^{(n)}$ denote the matrix of n step transition probabilities $p_{ij}^{(n)}$, then Equation 14-12 can be rewritten as:

$$\mathbf{P}^{(n)} = \mathbf{P} \cdot \mathbf{P}^{(n-1)} = \mathbf{P} \cdot \mathbf{P} \cdot \mathbf{P}^{(n-2)} = \cdots = \mathbf{P}^n \quad (14\text{-}13)$$

where the dot represents matrix multiplication. Thus, $\mathbf{P}^{(n)}$ can be calculated simply by multiplying the matrix $\mathbf{P}$ by itself n times.

EXAMPLE 1   To illustrate how the Chapman-Kolmogorov equations are used, consider the problem of determining the probability of selection of Pizzeria A at a time $n = 3$, given that it has currently been selected.

$$\mathbf{V}_1^1 = (0.5 \quad 0.3 \quad 0.2) \tag{14-14}$$

$$\mathbf{V}_1^3 = \mathbf{V}_1^1 \mathbf{P}^2$$
$$= (0.5 \quad 0.3 \quad 0.2) \cdot \mathbf{P}^2 \tag{14-15}$$

Using the results of Equation 14–13, we can compute $\mathbf{P}^2$ as:

$$\mathbf{P}^2 = \begin{bmatrix} 0.5 & 0.3 & 0.2 \\ 0.4 & 0.2 & 0.4 \\ 0.3 & 0.3 & 0.4 \end{bmatrix} \begin{bmatrix} 0.5 & 0.3 & 0.2 \\ 0.4 & 0.2 & 0.4 \\ 0.3 & 0.3 & 0.4 \end{bmatrix} = \begin{bmatrix} 0.43 & 0.27 & 0.30 \\ 0.40 & 0.28 & 0.32 \\ 0.39 & 0.27 & 0.34 \end{bmatrix} \tag{14-16}$$

Therefore, $$\mathbf{V}_1^3 = (0.5 \quad 0.3 \quad 0.2) \begin{bmatrix} 0.43 & 0.27 & 0.30 \\ 0.40 & 0.28 & 0.32 \\ 0.39 & 0.27 & 0.34 \end{bmatrix} = (0.413 \quad 0.273 \quad 0.314)$$
$$\tag{14-17}$$

Within this vector the probability associated with the selection of Pizzeria A is the probability associated with the first state, namely 0.413. Observe also that the matrix $\mathbf{P}^n$ gives the probabilities of being in any given state at time n given all possible starting states. Thus, in the matrix $\mathbf{P}^2$ that was computed above, the first row gives the probabilities at time $n = 2$ associated with a starting state S_1; the second row gives the probabilities at time $n = 2$ associated with a starting state S_2; and the third row gives the probabilities at time $n = 2$ associated with a starting state S_3.

For small values of n, the n-step transition matrix can be calculated using the simple matrix multiplication procedure described in Chapter 2 and shown above. For large values of n, this computation becomes very tedious, and round-off errors may be a problem.

EXAMPLE 2   In the above example we computed the two-step transition matrix. Using the results shown in Equation 14–13, the four-step transition matrix could be obtained as:

$$\mathbf{P}^{(4)} = \mathbf{P} \cdot \mathbf{P}^{(3)} = \mathbf{P} \cdot \mathbf{P} \cdot \mathbf{P}^{(2)} = \mathbf{P}^{(2)} \cdot \mathbf{P}^{(2)}$$

$$= \begin{bmatrix} 0.43 & 0.27 & 0.30 \\ 0.40 & 0.28 & 0.32 \\ 0.39 & 0.27 & 0.34 \end{bmatrix} \begin{bmatrix} 0.43 & 0.27 & 0.30 \\ 0.40 & 0.28 & 0.32 \\ 0.39 & 0.27 & 0.34 \end{bmatrix}$$

$$= \begin{bmatrix} 0.4099 & 0.2727 & 0.3174 \\ 0.4088 & 0.2728 & 0.3184 \\ 0.4083 & 0.2727 & 0.3190 \end{bmatrix} \tag{14-18}$$

14.5 THE LONG-RUN BEHAVIOR OF MARKOV PROCESSES

Given that the system or process being modeled as a Markov chain has certain properties, it is then possible to analyze its long-run behavior to determine the probabilities of outcomes after **steady-state conditions** have been reached. For example, after the Markov process has been in operation for a long time period (many steps), a given outcome will tend to occur a fixed percent of the time. However, for a Markov chain to reach steady-state conditions, the chain must be **ergodic**. An ergodic Markov chain has the property that it is possible to go from one state to any other state, in a finite number of steps, regardless of the present state.

The transition matrix describing a Markov process can be checked to see whether or not it describes an ergodic chain simply by checking to see if it is possible to move from every starting state or present state to all other states. As an example, consider the following transition matrix.

EXAMPLE 1

$$
\begin{array}{c}
\text{Future States} \\[4pt]
\begin{array}{cc}
 & \begin{array}{cccc} 1 & 2 & 3 & 4 \end{array} \\
\begin{array}{r}\text{Present} \\ \text{States}\end{array}
\begin{array}{c} 1 \\ 2 \\ 3 \\ 4 \end{array}
\left[\begin{array}{cccc}
1/3 & 1/3 & 0 & 1/3 \\
0 & 1/2 & 1/4 & 1/4 \\
1/4 & 0 & 2/4 & 1/4 \\
0 & 0 & 1/3 & 2/3
\end{array}\right]
\end{array}
\end{array}
\tag{14-19}
$$

Note that, from state 1, it is possible to go directly to every other state except state 3. For state 3 it is possible to go from state 1 to state 2 and from state 2 to state 3. Therefore, it is possible to go from state 1 to any other state. Checking the other states we observe that it is always possible to get to state 1, as follows.

State 2 Go to state 3 or state 4, then from state 3 to state 1, or from state 4 to state 3 to state 1.

State 3 Go directly to state 1.

State 4 Go to state 3, then from state 3 to state 1.

Since we have shown that it is possible to go from state 1 to all other states, and to go from all other states to state 1, we have shown that this is a transition matrix for an ergodic chain.

A special type of ergodic chain that is of interest is the **regular** chain. A regular chain is defined as a chain having a transition matrix $\mathbf{P}$ that for some power of $\mathbf{P}$ has only positive probability values (i.e., no zeroes). Thus, all regular chains must be ergodic chains, but not all ergodic chains must be regular. The easiest way to check an ergodic chain to see if it is regular is to continue squaring the transition matrix until all zeroes are removed, or until a pattern is observed indicating that at least one zero will never be removed. To illustrate this property consider the transition matrix used previously, in which we will now use an "X" to indicate the presence of a positive probability element. Thus, we have

EXAMPLE 2

$$
\mathbf{P}^{(1)} = \begin{bmatrix}
X & X & 0 & X \\
0 & X & X & X \\
X & 0 & X & X \\
0 & 0 & X & X
\end{bmatrix}
\tag{14-20}
$$

$$
\mathbf{P}^{(2)} = \begin{bmatrix}
X & X & X & X \\
X & X & X & X \\
X & X & X & X \\
X & 0 & X & X
\end{bmatrix}
\tag{14-21}
$$

$$\mathbf{P}^{(3)} = \begin{bmatrix} X & X & X & X \\ X & X & X & X \\ X & X & X & X \\ X & X & X & X \end{bmatrix} \tag{14-22}$$

Thus the third power of the transition matrix becomes a matrix having only positive probability elements (i.e., all X's), and we have a regular chain.

It should be emphasized that not all ergodic chains will be regular. To illustrate this fact consider the following transition matrix.

EXAMPLE 3

$$\mathbf{P}^1 = \begin{bmatrix} 0 & X & X & X & 0 \\ X & 0 & 0 & 0 & X \\ X & 0 & 0 & 0 & X \\ X & 0 & 0 & 0 & X \\ 0 & X & X & X & 0 \end{bmatrix} \tag{14-23}$$

$$\mathbf{P}^2 = \begin{bmatrix} X & 0 & 0 & 0 & X \\ 0 & X & X & X & 0 \\ 0 & X & X & X & 0 \\ 0 & X & X & X & 0 \\ X & 0 & 0 & 0 & X \end{bmatrix} \tag{14-24}$$

$$\mathbf{P}^3 = \begin{bmatrix} 0 & X & X & X & 0 \\ X & 0 & 0 & 0 & X \\ X & 0 & 0 & 0 & X \\ X & 0 & 0 & 0 & X \\ 0 & X & X & X & 0 \end{bmatrix} \tag{14-25}$$

$$\mathbf{P}^4 = \begin{bmatrix} X & 0 & 0 & 0 & X \\ 0 & X & X & X & 0 \\ 0 & X & X & X & 0 \\ 0 & X & X & X & 0 \\ X & 0 & 0 & 0 & X \end{bmatrix} \tag{14-26}$$

Thus, $\mathbf{P}$ raised to an even power will give the result shown as $\mathbf{P}^2$ or $\mathbf{P}^4$, while $\mathbf{P}$ raised to an odd power will give the original matrix. All these matrices will have some nonpositive elements, and are *not regular*. However, if we examine $\mathbf{P}^1$ we see that we can move in the following manner.

State 1   State 1 to states 2, 3, or 4.
State 2   State 2 to state 1 or 5.
State 3   State 3 to state 1 or 5.
State 4   State 4 to state 1 or 5.
State 5   State 5 to states 2, 3, or 4. From states 2, 3, or 4 to state 1.

Thus, the transition matrix is *ergodic* but *not regular*.

14.5.1   Determination of Steady-State Conditions

Earlier, in Section 14.4, we computed the four-step transition matrix for the pizzeria selection example using the Chapman-Kolmogorov equations. Since the one-step transition matrix for this example had all positive probability values, it is clearly a transition matrix for a regular ergodic chain. Now, the determination of steady-state conditions in a regular ergodic chain can be accomplished most readily by computing $\mathbf{P}^n$ for larger values of n. To illustrate, consider the eight-step transition probabilities given by the matrix:

$$\mathbf{P}^8 = \mathbf{P}^4 \cdot \mathbf{P}^4 = \begin{bmatrix} 0.4099 & 0.2727 & 0.3174 \\ 0.4088 & 0.2728 & 0.3184 \\ 0.4083 & 0.2727 & 0.3190 \end{bmatrix} \begin{bmatrix} 0.4099 & 0.2727 & 0.3174 \\ 0.4088 & 0.2728 & 0.3184 \\ 0.4083 & 0.2727 & 0.3190 \end{bmatrix}$$

$$= \begin{bmatrix} 0.4090 & 0.2727 & 0.3183 \\ 0.4090 & 0.2727 & 0.3183 \\ 0.4090 & 0.2727 & 0.3183 \end{bmatrix} \tag{14-27}$$

Note the interesting fact that as n becomes larger, the values of the p_{ij} move to a fixed limit and each probability vector $\mathbf{V}_i^n$ tends to become equal for all values of i. Thus, each of the four rows of $\mathbf{P}^8$ has identical entries, implying that the probability of being in state j 8 weeks in the future is independent of the pizzeria initially selected. Therefore, these results indicate that there is a limiting probability that the system will be in state j after a large, but finite, number of transitions, and this probability is independent of the initial state of the system.

The results illustrated above can be generalized in the following manner. For a regular ergodic Markov chain:

$$\lim_{n \to \infty} p_{ij}^{(n)} = \pi_j \tag{14-28}$$

and this limit is independent of i. The π_j's are referred to as the **steady-state probabilities** of the Markov chain, and are the probabilities associated with finding the process in state j after a large number of transitions. The value π_j is independent of the initial probability distribution that was defined over all the states. The π_j's satisfy the following steady-state equations:

$$\pi_j > 0 \tag{14-29}$$

$$\sum_{j=1}^{M} \pi_j = 1 \tag{14-30}$$

$$\pi_j = \sum_{i=1}^{M} \pi_i p_{ij}, \quad \text{for } j = 1, \dots, M \tag{14-31}$$

These steady-state equations consist of $(M + 1)$ equations in M unknowns. The steady-state equations can be solved for the M unknowns by discarding any one of the $(M + 1)$ equations except the equation $\sum_{j=1}^{M} \pi_j = 1$. The equation $\sum_{j=1}^{M} \pi_j = 1$ cannot be discarded since, if it was, the remaining m equations would be satisfied by $\pi_j = 0$ for all j.

EXAMPLE 1   Considering our pizzeria selection problem, the steady-state equations can be expressed as:

$$1 = \pi_1 + \pi_2 + \pi_3$$

$$\pi_1 = 0.5\pi_1 + 0.4\pi_2 + 0.3\pi_3$$

$$\pi_2 = 0.3\pi_1 + 0.2\pi_2 + 0.3\pi_3 \qquad (14\text{-}32)$$

$$\pi_3 = 0.2\pi_1 + 0.4\pi_2 + 0.4\pi_3$$

Discarding the last equation and making the appropriate algebraic manipulations, we obtain

$$\pi_1 + \quad \pi_2 + \quad \pi_3 = 1.0$$

$$-0.5\pi_1 + 0.4\pi_2 + 0.3\pi_3 = 0 \qquad (14\text{-}33)$$

$$0.3\pi_1 - 0.8\pi_2 + 0.3\pi_3 = 0$$

Solving these three equations simultaneously, we obtain

$$\pi_1 = 0.4090$$

$$\pi_2 = 0.2727$$

$$\pi_3 = \underline{0.3183} \qquad (14\text{-}34)$$

$$\overline{1.0000}$$

Observe that the values of the π_j's are the same as the elements that were obtained earlier for the eight-step transition matrix (see Equation 14-27). Interpreting the results of our steady-state computations we can assert that, after many weeks, or in the long run, Pizzeria A will be selected 40.9 percent of the time; Pizzeria B will be selected 27.27 percent of the time; and Pizzeria C will be selected 31.83 percent of the time.

14.6   FIRST PASSAGE TIMES

In addition to determining the n-step transition probabilities it is quite often important to be able to determine the transition times for the Markov chain. Transition time information is usually defined in terms of the number of transitions made as the process goes from state i to state j for the first time. This length of time is defined to be the **first passage time** associated with going from state i to state j. We will denote the first passage time in going from state i to state j as T_{ij}. When $j = i$, this first passage time is called the **recurrence time** for state i, and is simply the number of transitions until the process returns to the initial state i.

EXAMPLE 1   As an example of first passage times consider a record store that maintains inventory records for a certain best-selling album. The ending inventories for an 8-week period are as follows.

$$I_1 = 8$$
$$I_2 = 6$$
$$I_3 = 5$$
$$I_4 = 7 \qquad (14\text{-}35)$$
$$I_5 = 5$$
$$I_6 = 8$$

$$I_7 = 6$$
$$I_8 = 2$$

For these ending inventories the first passage time in going from state 8 to state 5 is 2 weeks, from state 8 to state 7 is 3 weeks, and the recurrence time of state 8 is 5 weeks, while the recurrence time of state 5 is 2 weeks.

EXAMPLE 2 If the probability of the process going from state i to state j is eventually 1 (perhaps in a large number of steps), then the corresponding first passage time T_{ij} is a random variable having an associated probability distribution. Otherwise, T_{ij} is infinitely large. To illustrate, consider first the following one-step transition matrix.

$$
\mathbf{P}^1 =
\begin{array}{c}
\text{States} \\
1 \\
2 \\
3
\end{array}
\begin{array}{ccc}
1 & 2 & 3 \\
\left[\begin{array}{ccc}
\frac{1}{4} & \frac{3}{4} & 0 \\
0 & \frac{1}{3} & \frac{2}{3} \\
\frac{1}{2} & \frac{1}{2} & 0
\end{array}\right]
\end{array}
\tag{14-36}
$$

EXAMPLE 3 For this process the first passage time between any two states is a random variable since the probability of eventually getting to a given state is always 1. Consider next the following one-step transition matrix.

$$
\mathbf{P}^1 =
\begin{array}{c}
\text{States} \\
1 \\
2 \\
3
\end{array}
\begin{array}{ccc}
1 & 2 & 3 \\
\left[\begin{array}{ccc}
\frac{1}{4} & \frac{3}{4} & 0 \\
0 & 1 & 0 \\
\frac{1}{2} & \frac{1}{2} & 0
\end{array}\right]
\end{array}
\tag{14-37}
$$

For this process the first passage times T_{11} and T_{13} are not random variables since the process will eventually go to state 2 and then it will never return. Likewise, T_{21}, T_{23}, T_{31}, and T_{33} are not random variables. However, T_{12} and T_{32} are random variables since the system will eventually get to state 2.

If the first passage time T_{ij} is a random variable, let $g_{ij}^{(n)}$ denote the probability that the first passage time from state i to j is equal to n. It can be shown that the probabilities satisfy the following recursive relationships.

$$
\begin{aligned}
g_{ij}^{(1)} &= p_{ij}^{(1)} = p_{ij} \\
g_{ij}^{(2)} &= p_{ij}^{(2)} - g_{ij}^{(1)} p_{jj} \\
&\cdot \qquad \cdot \\
&\cdot \qquad \cdot \\
&\cdot \qquad \cdot \\
g_{ij}^{(n)} &= p_{ij}^{(n)} - g_{ij}^{(1)} p_{jj}^{(n-1)} - g_{ij}^{(2)} p_{jj}^{(n-2)} \cdots - g_{ij}^{(n-1)} p_{jj}
\end{aligned}
\tag{14-38}
$$

The one-step transition probabilities can thus be used to compute recursively the probability of a first passage time from state i to state j in n steps. Using the one-step transition probabilities from our pizzeria example, the probability distribution of the first passage time in going from state 1 to state 3 is determined as follows.

$$
g_{13}^{(1)} = p_{13}^{(1)} = 0.2
\tag{14-39}
$$

$$g_{13}^{(2)} = p_{13}^{(2)} - g_{13}^{(2)}p_{33}$$
$$= 0.3 - 0.2(0.4) \tag{14-40}$$
$$= 0.22$$

.

.

.

For fixed i and j, the $g_{ij}^{(n)}$ are nonnegative numbers for which:

$$\sum_{n=1}^{\infty} g_{ij}^{(n)} \leq 1 \tag{14-41}$$

When this sum holds as a strict inequality, the process initially in state i may never reach state j. When this sum holds as a strict equality, $g_{ij}^{(n)}$ $(n = 1, 2, \ldots)$ is the probability distribution for the first passage time T_{ij}, which is a random variable. When $i = j$ and

$$\sum_{n=1}^{\infty} g_{ii}^{(n)} = 1 \tag{14-42}$$

then state i is called a **recurrent state** since once the process is in state i, it must return to state i.

An **absorbing state** is a special case of a recurrent state for which the one-step transition probability p_{ii} equals 1. The process can never leave an absorbing state once it enters it.

A **transient state** occurs for the situation in which:

$$\sum_{n=1}^{\infty} g_{ii}^{(n)} < 1 \tag{14-43}$$

In this case, once the process is in state i, there is a strictly positive probability that it will never return to state i.

EXAMPLE 4   To illustrate the various types of states that can occur consider the following one-step transition matrix.

$$\mathbf{P}^1 = \begin{array}{c} \\ 1 \\ 2 \\ 3 \\ 4 \\ 5 \end{array} \begin{array}{c} \text{States} \quad 1 \quad\; 2 \quad\; 3 \quad\; 4 \quad 5 \\ \left[\begin{array}{ccccc} \frac{1}{3} & \frac{2}{3} & 0 & 0 & 0 \\ \frac{5}{6} & \frac{1}{6} & 0 & 0 & 0 \\ 0 & 0 & 1 & 0 & 0 \\ 0 & 0 & \frac{1}{2} & \frac{1}{2} & 0 \\ 1 & 0 & 0 & 0 & 0 \end{array}\right] \end{array} \tag{14-44}$$

In this Markov process the states 1 and 2 are recurrent, although, strictly speaking, this assertion must be verified by showing that:

$$\sum_{n=1}^{\infty} g_{11}^{(n)} = 1 \tag{14-45}$$

$$\sum_{n=1}^{\infty} g_{22}^{(n)} = 1 \qquad (14\text{--}46)$$

It should be cautioned that this verification is often time-consuming and tedious. Consequently, an alternative criterion is employed, namely that of showing that there exists a value of n for which $p_{ij}^{(n)} > 0$ for all i and j. For this matrix $p_{ij}^{(2)}$ is positive for i and j equal to 1 and 2, and thus states 1 and 2 are recurrent.

For the same Markov process it is apparent that state 3 is an absorbing state (and also a recurrent state) because once the process enters state 3, it will never leave state 3, since $p_{33} = 1$. States 4 and 5 are transient states. For state 4, the probability is $1/2$ that the process will go to state 3 on the first step, and once the process is in state 3 it will stay in state 3. For state 5, it is apparent that once the process leaves state 5 it cannot return.

Denoting the expected value of the first passage time from state i to state j as u_{ij}, this expected value is given by:

$$u_{ij} = \sum_{n=1}^{\infty} n g_{ij}^{(n)}, \qquad \text{if} \qquad \sum_{n=1}^{\infty} g_{ij}^{(n)} = 1 \qquad (14\text{--}47)$$

$$u_{ij} = \infty, \qquad \text{if} \qquad \sum_{n=1}^{\infty} g_{ij}^{(n)} < 1 \qquad (14\text{--}48)$$

In general, if the first passage times are random variables, that is, whenever $\sum_{n=1}^{\infty} g_{ij}^{(n)} = 1$, then the u_{ij} will uniquely satisfy the system of linear equations given by:

$$u_{ij} = 1 + \sum_{k \neq j} p_{ik} u_{kj} \qquad (14\text{--}49)$$

For our pizzeria example, the equation given by Equation 14–49 can be employed to determine the expected first passage times from state $i = 1$ to state $j = 3$. Using Equation 14–49 we form the simultaneous linear equations:

$$
\begin{aligned}
&u_{13} = 1 + p_{11} u_{13} + p_{12} u_{23} \\
\text{or} \quad &u_{23} = 1 + p_{21} u_{13} + p_{22} u_{23} \\
&u_{13} = 1 + 0.5 u_{13} + 0.3 u_{23} \\
&u_{23} = 1 + 0.4 u_{13} + 0.2 u_{23}
\end{aligned}
\qquad (14\text{--}50)
$$

The solution to this system of two simultaneous equations is

$$
\begin{aligned}
u_{13} &= 3.92 \text{ weeks} \\
u_{23} &= 3.21 \text{ weeks}
\end{aligned}
\qquad (14\text{--}51)
$$

Thus, the **expected first passage time** from state 1 to state 3 is 3.92 weeks; and as a result of solving these two equations simultaneously, we also obtain the expected first passage time from state 2 to state 3 as 3.21 weeks.

When $j = i$, the expected first passage time is referred to as the **expected**

recurrence time. The recurrent state is termed **null recurrent** if $u_{ii} = \infty$ and is termed **positive recurrent** if $u_{ii} < \infty$. In a finite-state Markov chain, such as we are considering in our pizzeria example, there are no null recurrent states (i.e., there are only positive recurrent states). Thus, the steady-state probabilities we computed earlier (Equation 14–34) are equal to the reciprocal of the expected recurrence time, that is,

$$\pi_j = \frac{1}{u_{jj}} \quad \text{for } j = 1, 2, \ldots, M \tag{14–52}$$

Using this result, we can easily compute the expected recurrence time for $j = i = 3$ (state 3) as:

$$u_{33} = \frac{1}{\pi_3} = \frac{1}{0.3183} = 3.14 \text{ weeks} \tag{14–53}$$

14.7 ANALYSIS OF ABSORBING MARKOV CHAINS

In the previous section of the chapter we discussed the concept of an absorbing state in a Markov chain. Recall that an absorbing state is a state having a zero probability of being left once entered. Once the absorbing state is entered the process either stops completely or stops and is then reinitiated from some other state. A Markov chain can be shown to be an **absorbing Markov chain** if:

1. It has at least one absorbing state.
2. And it is possible to move from every nonabsorbing state to at least one absorbing state in a finite number of steps.

EXAMPLE 1 To illustrate the properties of absorbing Markov chains consider the following problem situation. A Phoenix tennis pro, Sancho Margolies, is in the process of analyzing his tennis pupils as a Markov process (Margolies studied OR as a student at Arizona State University). Considering the instruction of a single tennis student over a several-week period, each week of instruction can be considered as a trial of a Markov process with the student existing in one of four states.

State 1 Championship tournament caliber.
State 2 "Washout"—switch to another sport.
State 3 Daily instruction and practice needed.
State 4 Twice daily instruction and practice needed.

Thus, the status of a tennis pupil can be evaluated by using a Markov analysis to identify the state of the system for a particular week or time period in the future.

Margolies has kept historical records concerning the progress, or lack thereof, of his former pupils. From this historical information, the following transition matrix has been developed.

$$\mathbf{P} = \begin{bmatrix} 1 & 0 & 0 & 0 \\ 0 & 1 & 0 & 0 \\ 0.3 & 0.1 & 0.5 & 0.1 \\ 0.2 & 0.2 & 0.2 & 0.4 \end{bmatrix} \tag{14–54}$$

In this transition matrix the transition probabilities are defined as follows.

p_{ij} = probability of a tennis student in state i in one week moving to state j in the following week.

For example, there is a 0.3 probability that a student in state 3 (daily instruction and practice needed) will move to state 1 (championship tournament caliber) in the following week. Note also that there are two absorbing states for this Markov process. Once a tennis student makes a transition to state 1 (championship tournament caliber) the probability of moving to any other state is zero. Similarly, once a tennis student moves to state 2 ("washout"—switch to another sport) the probability of a move to any other state is zero. Thus, all the tennis students will eventually be absorbed into either states 1 or 2, the absorbing states.

When we are confronted with a Markov process having absorbing states, we cannot compute the steady-state probabilities associated with the various states in the manner shown in Section 14.5.2 because the process must eventually end up in one of the absorbing states. However, several kinds of interesting information can be obtained from the analysis of absorbing Markov chains. Thus, we can determine

1. The probability of absorption by any given absorbing state.
2. The expected number of steps before the process is absorbed.
3. The expected number of times the process is in any given nonabsorbing state.

To perform the analysis of absorbing Markov chains we begin by rearranging the transition probability matrix into four submatrices.

$$\mathbf{P} = \left[\begin{array}{c|c} \mathbf{I} & \mathbf{0} \\ \hline \mathbf{A} & \mathbf{N} \end{array} \right] \qquad (14\text{--}55)$$

The submatrices all contain probability elements but individually none of them are transition matrices. Assuming that there are r absorbing states, s nonabsorbing states, and $r + s = t$ total states, then the four submatrices can be described as follows.

I An r-by-r identity matrix defining the probabilities of staying within an absorbing state once it is reached.

0 An r-by-s null matrix indicating the probabilities of going from an absorbing state to a nonabsorbing state.

A An s-by-r matrix containing the probabilities of going from a nonabsorbing state to an absorbing state.

N An s-by-s matrix showing the probabilities of going from a nonabsorbing state to another nonabsorbing state.

EXAMPLE 2 For the example cited above, the transition probability matrix can be structured into the four submatrices just defined, as follows.

$$\mathbf{P} = \left[\begin{array}{cc|cc} 1 & 0 & 0 & 0 \\ 0 & 1 & 0 & 0 \\ \hline 0.3 & 0.1 & 0.5 & 0.1 \\ 0.2 & 0.2 & 0.2 & 0.4 \end{array} \right] = \left[\begin{array}{c|c} \mathbf{I} & \mathbf{0} \\ \hline \mathbf{A} & \mathbf{N} \end{array} \right] \qquad (14\text{--}56)$$

Using the submatrix **N** from the subdivided transition matrix, a **fundamental matrix F** can be calculated using the following formula.

$$\mathbf{F} = (\mathbf{I} - \mathbf{N})^{-1} \qquad (14\text{-}57)$$

For a given starting state, the fundamental matrix **F** indicates the expected number of times a process is in each nonabsorbing state before it is absorbed. The submatrix **N** indicates the probabilities of going from any nonabsorbing state to any other nonabsorbing state in exactly one step. The submatrix $\mathbf{N}^n$ would provide the same information for n steps. Since the submatrix **N** is composed of decimal numbers, p_{ij}, where $0 \leq p_{ij} \leq 1$, as n becomes large, $\mathbf{N}^n$ will contain elements all approaching zero. To find the expected number of steps before the process is absorbed requires the summation of the expected number of times the process is in each nonabsorbing state. The expected number of times the process will be in nonabsorbing state j is given by:

Expected number of times in nonabsorbing state j = (1 × probability of being in nonabsorbing state j at beginning) + (1 × probability of being in state j after 1 step) + (1 × probability of being in state j after 2 steps) + · · ·

$$\begin{aligned} &= 1\mathbf{N}^0 + 1\mathbf{N}^1 + 1\mathbf{N}^2 + 1\mathbf{N}^3 + \cdots \\ &= \mathbf{N}^0 + \mathbf{N}^1 + \mathbf{N}^2 + \mathbf{N}^3 + \cdots \end{aligned} \qquad (14\text{-}58)$$

Now, it can be shown that this series behaves like an algebraic power series, as follows.

$$\mathbf{N}^0 + \mathbf{N}^1 + \mathbf{N}^2 + \mathbf{N}^3 + \cdots = (\mathbf{I} - \mathbf{N})^{-1} \qquad (14\text{-}59)$$

which is the result shown above as the equation for the fundamental matrix.

EXAMPLE 3 Using the data from our tennis example, the computation of the fundamental equation is as follows.

$$(\mathbf{I} - \mathbf{N}) = \begin{bmatrix} 1 & 0 \\ 0 & 1 \end{bmatrix} - \begin{bmatrix} 0.5 & 0.1 \\ 0.2 & 0.4 \end{bmatrix} = \begin{bmatrix} 0.5 & -0.1 \\ -0.2 & 0.6 \end{bmatrix} \qquad (14\text{-}60)$$

Next, this matrix is inverted to obtain

$$\mathbf{F} = (\mathbf{I} - \mathbf{N})^{-1} = \begin{bmatrix} 2.14 & 0.36 \\ 0.71 & 1.79 \end{bmatrix} \qquad (14\text{-}61)$$

To interpret the results given by the fundamental matrix, recall that the nonabsorbing states are states 3 and 4. As indicated previously, the expected number of steps before absorption is simply the sum of the times the process is in each nonabsorbing state. These summations are shown in Table 14.3.

To compute the **probability of absorption** by any of the absorbing states, we employ the following relationship.

$$\text{Probability of absorption} = \mathbf{FA} = (\mathbf{I} - \mathbf{N})^{-1} \cdot \mathbf{A} \qquad (14\text{-}62)$$

TABLE 14.3   Computation of Expected Steps Before Absorption

Beginning State	*Expected Steps Before Absorption*
S_3	$2.14 + 0.36 = 2.50$
S_4	$0.71 + 1.79 = 2.50$

Recall that the submatrix **A** contains the probabilities of going from any nonabsorbing state to an absorbing state. Let i define some specified nonabsorbing state; let j signify some given absorbing state; and let k be any nonabsorbing state. As indicated previously:

P(going from nonabsorbing state i to absorbing state j in one step)
$$= \mathbf{A} \tag{14-63}$$

Now, P(going from nonabsorbing state i to absorbing state j in two steps) = probability of going from i to k in one step × probability of going from k to j in one step summed over all values of $k = \mathbf{N}^1\mathbf{A}$ (14-64)

Similarly, P(going from nonabsorbing state i to absorbing state j in three steps) $= \mathbf{N}^2\mathbf{A}$ (14-65)

$$\vdots$$

P(going from nonabsorbing state to absorbing state j in n steps) $= \mathbf{N}^{n-1}\mathbf{A}$ (14-66)

Thus, the probability of going from nonabsorbing state i to absorbing state j is given by the convergent power series:

P(going from nonabsorbing state i to absorbing state j)

$$= \mathbf{A} + \mathbf{NA} + \mathbf{N}^2\mathbf{A} + \mathbf{N}^3\mathbf{A} + \cdots$$
$$= \mathbf{1A} + \mathbf{NA} + \mathbf{N}^2\mathbf{A} + \mathbf{N}^3\mathbf{A} + \cdots \tag{14-67}$$
$$= (\mathbf{1} + \mathbf{N} + \mathbf{N}^2 + \mathbf{N}^3 + \cdots)\mathbf{A}$$
$$= (\mathbf{I} - \mathbf{N})^{-1}\mathbf{A}$$

which is the result shown above as Equation 14–62.

Returning to our tennis example:

EXAMPLE 4   Probability of absorption $= (\mathbf{I} - \mathbf{N})^{-1} \cdot \mathbf{A}$

$$= \begin{bmatrix} 2.14 & 0.36 \\ 0.71 & 1.79 \end{bmatrix} \begin{bmatrix} 0.3 & 0.1 \\ 0.2 & 0.2 \end{bmatrix} = \begin{bmatrix} 0.71 & 0.29 \\ 0.57 & 0.43 \end{bmatrix} \tag{14-68}$$

The first row of the absorption probability matrix gives the probabilities that a tennis player beginning in state 3 will end up in each of the absorbing states. We observe that there is a 0.71 probability that a player beginning in state 3 will end up in state 1 (championship tournament caliber) and a 0.29 probability that a player beginning in state 3 will end up in state 2 (''washout''—switch to another sport). The second row of the absorption matrix indicates the probabilities that a tennis player beginning in state 4 will end up in each of the absorbing states. Thus, there is a 0.57 probability that a player beginning in state 4 will end up in state 1 and a 0.43 probability that a player beginning in state 4 will end up in state 2.

Assume that Sancho currently has 100 tennis students, with 40 students being in state S_3, and 60 students being in state S_4. We can employ the absorption matrix to determine how many of these students will eventually go to states 1 and 2 respectively. Denoting the present composition of the tennis students as the vector **T**:

$$\begin{array}{cc} S_3 & S_4 \\ \mathbf{T} = (40 & 60) \end{array} \tag{14-69}$$

The final composition of the tennis students, denoted as **T**′, will be

$$\mathbf{T}' = \mathbf{T} \cdot \text{probability of absorption}$$

$$= \begin{array}{cc} S_3 & S_4 \\ (40 & 60) \end{array} \begin{array}{c} S_3 \\ S_4 \end{array} \begin{array}{cc} S_1 & S_2 \\ \left[\begin{array}{cc} 0.71 & 0.29 \\ 0.57 & 0.43 \end{array}\right] \end{array} \tag{14-70}$$

$$= \begin{array}{cc} S_1 & S_2 \\ (62.6 & 37.4) \end{array}$$

Thus, of the current 100 tennis students, 62.6 (say 63) will eventually become of ''championship tournament caliber'' while 37.4 (say 37) will eventually ''wash out.''

14.8 APPLICATIONS OF MARKOV PROCESS MODELS

EXAMPLE 1   Let us now consider some decision-making situations involving the application of Markov process models. Initially, let us consider a decision-making situation involving a high-speed printer, which is an essential part of a computerized management information system used to prepare daily financial statements for an automobile parts manufacturer. A management science analyst has been working with the computer system operations staff and has determined that the observed condition of the printer output after a particular day of operation can be categorized into one of three states.

State	Condition of Printer Output
1	Excellent
2	Acceptable, but of marginal quality
3	Unacceptable, blurry and unreadable

Furthermore, the management science analyst has determined a transition matrix that describes the behavior of the printer over time, under the assumption this behavior is a stochastic process described by a finite-state Markov chain. This transition matrix is given by:

	To State		
From State	1	2	3
1	0	$7/8$	$1/8$
2	0	$3/4$	$1/4$
3	0	0	1

$$(14\text{--}71)$$

By observation of this transition matrix it is apparent that state 3 is an absorbing state. Thus, over time the printer will enter state 3 and will remain there. At this point in time, unacceptable reports will be produced. Thus, a decision will have to be made with respect to replacing or repairing the printer. Further analysis has indicated that the following expected costs are appropriate for the various states.

State	Expected Cost
1	$0
2	$1000 (Cost of illegible reports)
3	$5000 (Cost of illegible reports, plus cost of repairing printer)

Now, assume that we are interested in trying to determine the cost associated with a maintenance policy decision that requires that the printer be repaired or replaced when it enters state 3. The stochastic process that results from this sytem having such a maintenance policy is also a finite-state Markov chain, but it now has a transition matrix given by:

	To State		
From State	1	2	3
1	0	$7/8$	$1/8$
2	0	$3/4$	$1/4$
3	1	0	0

$$(14\text{--}72)$$

Assume that we are interested in evaluating the cost associated with this maintenance policy. Using the transition matrix given by Equation 14–72, and the results shown earlier in Section 14.5.1, the steady-state equations can be expressed as:

$$1 = \pi_1 + \pi_2 + \pi_3$$

$$\pi_1 = 1\pi_3$$

$$(14\text{--}73)$$

$$\pi_2 = {}^7\!/_8\,\pi_1 + {}^3\!/_4\,\pi_2$$

$$\pi_3 = {}^1\!/_8\,\pi_1 + {}^1\!/_4\,\pi_2$$

Solving these equations simultaneously, we obtain

$$
\begin{aligned}
\pi_1 &= {}^2\!/_{11} = 0.1818 \\
\pi_2 &= {}^7\!/_{11} = 0.6364 \\
\pi_3 &= \underline{{}^2\!/_{11} = 0.1818} \\
&\quad\; {}^{11}\!/_{11} = 1.0000
\end{aligned}
\tag{14-74}
$$

These results indicate that over the long run, the printer will be in state 1, 18.18 percent of the time; in state 2, 63.64 percent of the time; and in state 3, 18.18 percent of the time. Hence, the long run expected average cost for the particular maintenance policy will be given by:

$$
\begin{aligned}
\$0\,\pi_1 &\quad + \$1000\,\pi_2 \quad + \$5000\,\pi_3 \quad = \\
\$0(0.1818) &+ \$1000(0.6364) + \$5000(0.1818) = \$\;636.40 + \$909.00 \\
&\qquad\qquad\qquad\qquad\qquad\qquad\quad = \$1545.40
\end{aligned}
\tag{14-75}
$$

EXAMPLE 2   Another area in which Markov process models have proven useful is that of credit or accounts receivable control. Thus, let us consider another decision-making situation in which a credit card company is attempting to determine a more effective set of credit-control policies. This company has traditionally classified all its accounts receivable into one of the following four categories.

Accounts Receivable Category (states)	Status of Accounts Receivable
1	Paid in full
2	Bad debt
3	0–30 days late
4	31–120 days late

Based on a historical analysis of the weekly transition pattern for its accounts receivable, the company has developed the following transition matrix.

$$
\mathbf{P} = \begin{array}{c}
 \\ \text{From} \\ A|R \\ \text{Category} \\ \text{(state)}
\end{array}
\begin{array}{c}
\text{To } A|R \text{ Cateogry (state)} \\
\begin{array}{cccc}
1 & 2 & 3 & 4
\end{array} \\
\begin{array}{c}
1 \\ 2 \\ 3 \\ 4
\end{array}
\left[\begin{array}{cccc}
1 & 0 & 0 & 0 \\
0 & 1 & 0 & 0 \\
0.4 & 0.2 & 0.2 & 0.2 \\
0.3 & 0.3 & 0.3 & 0.1
\end{array}\right]
\end{array}
\tag{14-76}
$$

From this transition matrix it can be seen, for example, that the probability of a customer accounts receivable moving from the "0–30 days late" state to the "paid in full" state in the next week is 0.4. Note also that this transition matrix has two absorbing states, namely states 1 and 2. Thus, all the accounts receivable dollars will eventually be absorbed into either the "paid in full" or "bad debt" category.

Suppose further that the credit-card company is interested in predicting the amount of money that eventually will be paid and the amount of money that will be lost as bad debts. Using the transition matrix given by 14–76, and the results presented previously in Section 14.7, we can initially subdivide the transition probability matrix into four submatrices, as follows.

$$
\mathbf{P} = \begin{bmatrix} 1 & 0 & 0 & 0 \\ 0 & 1 & 0 & 0 \\ 0.4 & 0.2 & 0.2 & 0.2 \\ 0.3 & 0.3 & 0.3 & 0.1 \end{bmatrix} = \begin{bmatrix} \mathbf{I} & \mathbf{O} \\ \mathbf{A} & \mathbf{N} \end{bmatrix} \tag{14-77}
$$

Then, using the submatrices **I** and **N** from the subdivided transition matrix, the fundamental matrix **F** can be calculated as:

$$
\begin{aligned}
\mathbf{F} &= (\mathbf{I} - \mathbf{N})^{-1} \\
&= \left(\begin{bmatrix} 1 & 0 \\ 0 & 1 \end{bmatrix} - \begin{bmatrix} 0.2 & 0.2 \\ 0.3 & 0.1 \end{bmatrix} \right)^{-1} \\
&= \begin{pmatrix} 0.8 & -0.2 \\ -0.3 & 0.9 \end{pmatrix}^{-1} \\
&= \begin{bmatrix} 1.365 & 0.303 \\ 0.455 & 1.212 \end{bmatrix}
\end{aligned} \tag{14-78}
$$

Since we are interested in predicting the amount of money that eventually will be paid and that eventually will be lost as bad debts, we must next compute the probability of absorption for states 1 and 2. To do this we employ the relationship:

$$
\text{Probability of absorption} = \mathbf{FA} = (\mathbf{I} - \mathbf{N})^{-1} \cdot \mathbf{A} \tag{14-79}
$$

$$
\begin{aligned}
&= \begin{bmatrix} 1.365 & 0.303 \\ 0.455 & 1.212 \end{bmatrix} \begin{bmatrix} 0.4 & 0.2 \\ 0.3 & 0.3 \end{bmatrix} \\
&= \begin{bmatrix} 0.637 & 0.363 \\ 0.546 & 0.454 \end{bmatrix}
\end{aligned}
$$

The first row of the absorption probability matrix gives the probabilities that an accounts receivable dollar beginning in state 3 ("0–30 days late") eventually will end up in absorbing states 1 and 2, respectively. The second row of the absorption probability matrix gives the probabilities that an accounts receivable dollar beginning in state 4 ("31–120 days late") eventually will end up in absorbing states 1 and 2, respectively.

Now, let us assume that the credit card company has $1 million of accounts receivables outstanding in state 3 ("0–30 days late") and $500,000 of accounts receivables outstanding in state 4 ("31–120 days late"). We can employ the absorption probability matrix to determine how many of these dollars will eventually go to states 1 and 2 respectively. Denoting the present composition of the accounts receivable dollars as the vector **T**:

$$
\begin{array}{cc}
S_3 & S_4 \\
\end{array}
$$
$$
\mathbf{T} = (\$1,000,000 \quad \$500,000) \tag{14-80}
$$

The final composition of the accounts receivable dollars, denoted as **T′**, will be

$$
\mathbf{T'} = \mathbf{T} \cdot \text{Probability of absorption}
$$

$$
= (\$1,000,000 \quad \$500,000) \; \begin{array}{c} S_3 \\ S_4 \end{array} \begin{bmatrix} S_1 & S_2 \\ 0.637 & 0.363 \\ 0.546 & 0.454 \end{bmatrix}
$$

$$
= \begin{array}{cc} S_1 & S_2 \\ (\$910,000 & \$590,000) \end{array} \tag{14-81}
$$

Thus, if the credit card company currently has $1.5 million of outstanding accounts receivable, divided as indicated by Equation 14–80, it can expect that eventually $910,000 will be collected while $590,000 will become bad debts.

Numerous other applications of Markov process models have been reported. Other Markov process applications include the scheduling of hospital admissions, analyses of stock-market price movements, management of recreational facilities, and the determination of expected payout for life insurance policies.

14.9 CASE STUDY—A MARKOVIAN ANALYSIS OF A GERIATRIC WARD

The cost effectiveness of a geriatric re-socialization program initiated at a California mental hospital was evaluated by Jack Meredith using Markov chains to model the movement of patients into, through, and out of the program. The alternative patient states in the study were defined as follows.

State 1 In the geriatric resocialization program (GRP).

State 2 In one of the hospital wards.

State 3 In a home, but placed from GRP.

State 4 In a home, but placed directly from a ward.

State 5 Dead.

Various analyses were used to determine first passage and recurrence times, long-term trends, and stay times and costs until death. In addition, long-run effects of contemplated program modifications were considered.[1]

The probabilities of movement between the designated states for a 1-month period, and the associated costs, are provided in Table 14.4.

The redistributed data in Table 14.4 was also used to obtain the long-run trend of the typical patient by calculating the probabilities associated with finding the process in state j after a large number of transitions. The resultant steady-state probabilities for the

[1] For more details, see: Jack Meredith, "A Markovian Analysis of a Geriatric Ward," *Management Science,* vol. 19, no. 6 (February 1973), 604–612, copyright 1973, The Institute of Management Sciences, reprinted by permission.

TABLE 14.4 One-Month Transition and Cost Matrix

	GRP	Ward	Home (G)	Home (W)	Dead	Cost, $
GRP	0.854	0.028	0.112	0.000	0.006	$682
Ward	0.013	0.978	0.000	0.003	0.006	655
Home (G)	0.025	0.000	0.969	0.000	0.006	226
Home (W)	0.000	0.025	0.000	0.969	0.006	226
Dead	0.000	0.000	0.000	0.000	1.000	0

Markov chain were as follows: 0.12, 0.34, 0.42, 0.12. From these results it was concluded that the chances of a patient being in one of the hospital wards was approximately 1 in 3, while the probability of being in a home was 1 in 2. The long-term expected monthly cost of a patient was found by multiplying the row vector of steady-state probabilities by the column vector of monthly costs specified in Table 14.4 (with the state of death omitted). This vector multiplication specified an expected monthly cost of $426 per patient.

The original transition matrix depicted in Table 14.4 was used to compute the expected stay times (before death). The expected stay times and associated costs are given in Table 14.5. The numbers indicate the amount of time a patient can expect to spend in each state, depending on the initial state, before dying. It is interesting to note the rather minimal effect the initial state has on the time the patient spends in other states; it primarily impacts on the time the patient spends in the initial state. The results indicated that a patient who is a candidate for the GRP program (i.e., in cohort "ward") can expect to spend 1.5 years in GRP, 6.5 years in the hospital wards, 5 years out on placement from GRP, and 0.5 year on placement from the wards before dying; while patients in GRP can expect to spend 40 percent more time on home placement and only half as much time in the wards as their ward counterparts. (Note that the stay times were not usually concurrent but rather consisted of a number of visits back and forth between states; the numbers given, then, were the total times spent in each of the states.) The expected time spent in all states prior to death was determined by summing the stay times across all states from each state and turned out to be 14 years regardless of starting state. The expected stay times in Table 14.5 were used to compute the total expected, undiscounted cost of treating a patient until death by multiplying the stay times matrix in Table 14.5 times the cost vector of Table 14.4. The results are indicated in the right-hand column of Table 14.5. It should be pointed out that the null probabilities in the table resulted from the assumption that movement through two states within a

TABLE 14.5 Expected Stay Time (Months) and Cost Matrix

	GRP	Ward	Home (G)	Home (W)	Cost, $
GRP	26	38	95	4	$64,950
Ward	17	77	63	7	77,800
Home (G)	21	31	109	3	59,900
Home (W)	14	62	51	38	70,250

TABLE 14.6 First Passage and Recurrence Times Matrix, in Months

	GRP	Ward	Home (G)	Home (W)
GRP	9	156	45	411
Ward	133	3	179	255
Home (G)	33	189	2	444
Home (W)	167	33	212	9

period of 1 month is not feasible. The remaining probabilities were determined from hospital records.

By temporarily ignoring the low-probability state of death and distributing its probability of 0.006 among the other states, the expected recurrence and first passage times were calculated and are presented in Table 14.6. Note that the typical expected recurrence times were less than a year, while expected first passage times were usually greater than the remaining lifetime of the patient except for placements from GRP, which averaged about 4 years, and readmissions from home placements, which averaged about 3 years.

The study also considered the long-run expected costs of treating the same patients without the benefit of GRP, which were found to be significantly higher. In addition, a program modification designed to double the number of placements from GRP was subjected to examination. The program modification was found to effectively reduce the long-run costs of treating patients in GRP by about $8000 and that of a patient in any other state by about $5000 until death. Both of these analyses were conducted by modifying the form of the original transition probability matrix.

In summary, this study illustrated how a Markovian model was employed to evaluate the cost-effectiveness of a hospital program as well as the effect it had on patient's release prognoses.

14.10 CONCLUSION

In this chapter we have presented the fundamental concepts involved in Markov process models and have presented a number of examples of their application. In these examples, and in the problem set at the end of this chapter, we have illustrated some of the numerous physical, economics, and business situations that can be mathematically modeled by a Markov chain. We observed that Markov modeling was very helpful in providing decision-making information in processes involving a sequence of repeated trials with a finite number of outcomes (states) possible at each trial. We were primarily concerned with the long-run behavior of Markov processes, and in determining the steady-state conditions that define the probabilities of each of the states occurring after a number of steps, or time periods, have elapsed. We also indicated how to compute and utilize the first passage time, and concluded our work in this area with an analysis of absorbing Markov chains.

GLOSSARY OF TERMS

Absorbing Markov Chain   A Markov chain that has at least one absorbing state, and it is possible to move from every nonabsorbing state to at least one absorbing state in a finite number of steps.

Absorbing State   A state having a zero probability of being left once it is entered.

Chapman-Kolmogorov Equations   Equations used in a Markovian analysis to determine the probability that the process will be in state j after n periods, given the process is currently in state i.

Continuous Time Process A stochastic process $[X_t]$, where t runs over a given set T defined to be an open or closed interval of the real number line.

Discrete Time Process A stochastic process $[X_t]$, where t runs over a countable set T.

Ergodic Markov Chain A Markov chain possessing the property that it is possible to go from one state to any other state in a finite number of steps, regardless of the present state.

Expected First Passage Time The expected value of the first passage time.

Expected Recurrence Time The expected value of the first passage time when $j = i$.

First Passage Time The length of time (number of transitions) as the process goes from state i to state j for the first time.

Fundamental Matrix A matrix employed in analyzing absorbing Markov chains to determine the expected number of times a process is in each nonabsorbing state before it is absorbed.

Markov Chain or Markov Process A stochastic process for which the occurrence of a future state depends only on the immediately preceding state; thus, for a Markov process, given that the present state is known, the conditional probability of the next state is independent of the states prior to the present state.

Markovian Property The property that states that the conditional probability of any future state, given any past state and the present state, is independent of the past state and depends only on the present state of the process.

Markov Process Models A class of management science models that deals with the behavior of dynamic systems over time.

Null Recurrent State A recurrent state whose expected recurrence time is infinity.

Positive Recurrent State A recurrent state whose expected recurrence time is less than infinity.

Probability of Absorption The probability of going from a nonabsorbing state i to an absorbing state j.

Recurrence Time The number of transitions until the process returns to the initial state i.

Recurrent State A state possessing the property that once the process is in the state, it must return to that state.

Regular Chain A special type of ergodic chain that has a transition matrix **P** that for some power of **P** has only positive probability values (i.e., no zeros).

State The condition of the stochastic process, represented by the random variable X_t, at time t.

State Space of a Stochastic Process The set of possible values that the random variable $\{X_t, t \in T\}$ may assume.

Stationary Transition Probabilities Transition probabilities that do not change over time.

Steady-State Conditions Conditions characterizing a Markov process that has been in operation for a long time, where a given outcome will tend to occur a fixed percent of the time.

Steady-State Probabilities (π_j) The probabilities associated with finding the Markov process in state j after a large number of transitions, where the value π_j is independent of the initial probability distribution that was defined over all the states.

Stochastic Process An indexed collection of random variables $[X_t]$, where the index t runs over a given set T and X_t is taken to be some measurable characteristic of interest at time t.

Transient State A state possessing the property that once the process is in the state, there is a strictly positive probability that it will never return to that state.

Transition Probabilities Conditional probabilities used in stochastic processes to describe the manner in which the system makes a transition from one time period to another.

Transition Probability Matrix A matrix of transition probabilities.

SELECTION REFERENCES

MARKOV PROCESSES

Bhat, U. N. 1972. *Elements of Applied Stochastic Processes*. New York: John Wiley & Sons, Inc.

Chung, K. L. 1960. *Markov Chain with Stationary Transition Probabilities*. Berlin: Springer-Verlag.

Clark, A. Bruce, and Ralph L. Disney. 1970. *Probability and Random Processes for Engineers and Scientists*. New York: John Wiley & Sons, Inc.

Derman, C., and M. Klein. 1959. *Probability and Statistical Inference for Engineers*. New York: Oxford University Press.

Howard, Ronald A. 1971. *Dynamic Probabilistic Models*. (Vol. 1: Markov Models). New York: John Wiley & Sons, Inc.

Kemeny, J. G., J. L. Snell, and G. L. Thompson. 1959. *Finite Markov Chains*. New York: D. Van Nostrand Company.

Parzen, E. 1960. *Modern Probability Theory and Its Applications*. New York: John Wiley & Sons, Inc.

Parzen, E. 1962. *Stochastic Processes*. San Francisco: Holden-Day, Inc.

Ross, S. M. 1972. *Introduction to Probability Models*. New York: Academic Press, Inc.

DISCUSSION QUESTIONS

1. Could we also consider an "infinite"-state stochastic process in a Markov chain structure? Why or why not?
2. Do you think the assumption of "stationary" transition probabilities is realistic? Why or why not?
3. Are the transition probability matrices always square matrices? Why or why not?
4. What is the difference in objective when doing a probability analysis using Markov chains compared to using the Chapman-Kolmogorov equations?
5. What problem could occur when using the Chapman-Kolmogorov equations for large n?
6. Suppose you are given some transition matrix. How can you determine if it describes a regular chain?
7. Could you determine steady-state conditions for a nonregular ergodic chain? Why or why not?
8. When is the "first passage time" a random variable, and when is it not?
9. What is the difference between a "recurrent" and an "absorbing" state? Describe briefly how you can tell in your transition matrix which states are recurrent and which are not.
10. Why is the expected value of the first passage time from state k to state 1 infinite, when the summation over all n of $g(n)_{1k}$ is strictly less than one?

11. Describe the mathematical condition for which a recurrent state is null recurrent.
12. Judge this statement: The steady-state probabilities are zero for null recurrent states.
13. Suppose you have a transition matrix in which one or more absorbing states occur. How would you calculate the probabilities of going from any nonabsorbing state to any other nonabsorbing state in, let us say, 5 steps?
14. What does the fundamental matrix **F** calculate?
15. Give some examples of practical applications of Markovian analysis.
16. What is a necessary condition for a Markov chain to reach steady-state conditions?

PROBLEM SET

1. Bill and Betty have tied the first set of their tennis match at 6 games each, and are going to play a 9-point "tie breaker" to break the tie (i.e., the first player winning 5 points wins the tie breaker and the set). Bill has a probability of 0.6 of winning any one point, and Betty has a probability of 0.4 of winning any one point. Represent this situation as a Markov chain and form the transition matrix.

2. A marketing research firm has just completed a survey of consumer buying habits with respect to three brands of coffee. It estimates that at the present time, 40 percent of the customers buy Brand A, 20 percent of the customers buy Brand B, and 40 percent of the customers buy Brand C. Additionally, the marketing research firm has analyzed its survey data and has determined that the following brand-switching matrix is appropriate for the three brands of coffee.

$$
\begin{array}{c}
\text{Brand Just} \\
\text{Purchased}
\end{array}
\quad
\begin{array}{cc}
& \text{Brand Next Purchased} \\
& \begin{array}{ccc} A & B & C \end{array} \\
\begin{array}{c} A \\ B \\ C \end{array} &
\begin{bmatrix}
0.5 & 0.4 & 0.1 \\
0.2 & 0.6 & 0.2 \\
0.3 & 0.3 & 0.5
\end{bmatrix}
\end{array}
$$

What will be the expected distribution of customers two time periods later?

3. A machine-failure transition matrix has been determined as follows.

$$
\mathbf{P} = \begin{bmatrix}
0.7 & 0.1 & 0.2 \\
0.5 & 0.2 & 0.3 \\
0.1 & 0.4 & 0.5
\end{bmatrix}
$$

Compute the four-step transition matrix.

4. For each of the transition matrices given, compute $\mathbf{P}^2$ and $\mathbf{P}^3$. Determine if they are regular chains.

(a)
$$
\begin{bmatrix}
0.4 & 0.2 & 0.4 \\
0 & 0 & 1 \\
1 & 0 & 0
\end{bmatrix}
$$

(b)
$$
\begin{bmatrix}
0 & 1 & 0 \\
0.8 & 0 & 0.2 \\
0 & 1 & 0
\end{bmatrix}
$$

(c) $\begin{bmatrix} 0.3 & 0 & 0.7 \\ 0.6 & 0.4 & 0 \\ 1 & 0 & 0 \end{bmatrix}$

5.   For each of the transition matrices given, determine if it is ergodic and/or regular.

   (a) $\begin{bmatrix} 0 & 0.5 & 0.5 & 0 \\ 0.7 & 0 & 0 & 0.3 \\ 0.2 & 0 & 0 & 0.8 \\ 0 & 0.4 & 0.6 & 0 \end{bmatrix}$

   (b) $\begin{bmatrix} 0 & 1 & 0 \\ 0.6 & 0 & 0.4 \\ 0 & 1 & 0 \end{bmatrix}$

   (c) $\begin{bmatrix} 0 & 0.8 & 0.2 \\ 0 & 0 & 1 \\ 0.3 & 0.7 & 0 \end{bmatrix}$

   (d) $\begin{bmatrix} 0.7 & 0 & 0.3 & 0 \\ 0 & 0.8 & 0 & 0.2 \\ 0.4 & 0 & 0.6 & 0 \\ 0 & 0.3 & 0 & 0.7 \end{bmatrix}$

6.   Formulate and solve the steady-state equations for the Markov process with the following one-step transition probabilities.

$$\mathbf{P} = \begin{bmatrix} 0.2 & 0.6 & 0.2 \\ 0.1 & 0.1 & 0.8 \\ 0.5 & 0.3 & 0.2 \end{bmatrix}$$

7.   Formulate and solve the steady-state equations for the Markov process with the following one-step transition probabilities.

$$\mathbf{P} = \begin{bmatrix} 0 & 0.5 & 0.3 & 0.2 \\ 0.2 & 0.4 & 0.1 & 0.3 \\ 0.8 & 0.2 & 0 & 0 \\ 0 & 0 & 1 & 0 \end{bmatrix}$$

8.   Given the following one-step transition matrix, determine the nature of its states.

$$\begin{bmatrix} 1 & 0 & 0 & 0 \\ 0 & \frac{1}{2} & \frac{1}{2} & 0 \\ 0 & \frac{3}{4} & \frac{1}{4} & 0 \\ 0 & 0 & 0 & 1 \end{bmatrix}$$

9.   Given the following one-step transition matrix, determine the nature of its states.

$$\begin{bmatrix} 0 & 0 & \frac{1}{3} & \frac{2}{3} \\ 0 & 1 & 0 & 0 \\ 1 & 0 & 0 & 0 \\ 1 & 0 & 0 & 0 \end{bmatrix}$$

10.   Calculate the expected first passage time from state 2 to state 3 if the one-step stationary transition probabilities are given by:

$$\begin{array}{cc} \text{States} & \begin{array}{ccc} 1 & 2 & 3 \end{array} \\ \mathbf{P}^1 = \begin{array}{c} 1 \\ 2 \\ 3 \end{array} & \begin{bmatrix} 0.8 & 0.1 & 0.1 \\ 0.2 & 0.5 & 0.3 \\ 0.4 & 0.2 & 0.4 \end{bmatrix} \end{array}$$

11. Calculate the expected first passage time from state 1 to state 2 if the one-step stationary transition probabilities are given by:

$$\begin{array}{cc} \text{States} & \begin{array}{ccc} 1 & 2 & 3 \end{array} \\ \mathbf{P}^1 = \begin{array}{c} 1 \\ 2 \\ 3 \end{array} & \begin{bmatrix} 0.3 & 0.3 & 0.4 \\ 0.2 & 0.2 & 0.6 \\ 0.5 & 0.1 & 0.4 \end{bmatrix} \end{array}$$

12. Calculate the expected recurrence times for all states using the one-step stationary transition matrix given by:

$$\begin{array}{cc} \text{States} & \begin{array}{cc} 1 & 2 \end{array} \\ \mathbf{P}^1 = \begin{array}{c} 1 \\ 2 \end{array} & \begin{bmatrix} 0.2 & 0.8 \\ 0.5 & 0.5 \end{bmatrix} \end{array}$$

13. Calculate the expected recurrence times for all states using the one-step stationary transition matrix given by:

$$\begin{array}{cc} \text{States} & \begin{array}{ccc} 1 & 2 & 3 \end{array} \\ \mathbf{P}^1 = \begin{array}{c} 1 \\ 2 \\ 3 \end{array} & \begin{bmatrix} 0.1 & 0.6 & 0.3 \\ 0.2 & 0.2 & 0.6 \\ 0.8 & 0.1 & 0.1 \end{bmatrix} \end{array}$$

14. A soccer team has a 0.7 probability of winning its game next week if it wins its game today, and a 0.4 probability of losing its game next week if its loses its game today.
    (a) Determine the one-step transition matrix for this Markov process.
    (b) Determine the steady-state probabilities.

15. A St. Louis meteorologist has determined that the following Markov process transition matrix describes the behavior of the daily weather in St. Louis.

		Tomorrow's Weather		
		Sunny	Cloudy	Rainy
Today's	Sunny	0.6	0.3	0.1
Weather	Cloudy	0.4	0.3	0.3
	Rainy	0.2	0.3	0.5

Note that the meteorologist is assuming that the states of the weather are mutually exclusive.
    (a) If it is sunny today, what is the probability that the first rainy weather will occur n days ($n \gg 0$) from now?
    (b) If it is cloudy today, what is the expected number of days until the next rainy weather?

16. Joe College likes to spend his Friday evenings tipping a few beers with the boys at three local taverns. Joe has his first beer at tavern 1 and then uses a random walk to choose his next tavern. His behavior can be described by the following Markov process transition matrix.

$$
\begin{array}{c}
\text{Next Beer} \\
\begin{array}{cc}
\text{Tavern} & \begin{array}{ccc} 1 & 2 & 3 \end{array} \\
\begin{array}{c}\text{Current}\\\text{Beer}\end{array}
\begin{array}{c} 1 \\ 2 \\ 3 \end{array}
\left[\begin{array}{ccc}
0.7 & 0.1 & 0.2 \\
0 & 0.4 & 0.6 \\
0.3 & 0.2 & 0.5
\end{array}\right]
\end{array}
\end{array}
$$

(a) Assume that it takes Joe many beers to become convinced to go home for some sleep. What is the probability that he decides to go home while in tavern 1, 2, 3?

(b) What is the expected number of beers before Joe gets to tavern 3, assuming that he starts in tavern 1?

17. Given the following transition matrix with states 1 and 2 as absorbing states,

$$
\mathbf{P} = \begin{array}{c}
\begin{array}{ccccc} & S_1 & S_2 & S_3 & S_4 \end{array} \\
\begin{array}{c} S_1 \\ S_2 \\ S_3 \\ S_4 \end{array}
\left[\begin{array}{cccc}
1 & 0 & 0 & 0 \\
0 & 1 & 0 & 0 \\
0.4 & 0.3 & 0.2 & 0.1 \\
0.2 & 0.4 & 0.1 & 0.3
\end{array}\right]
\end{array}
$$

What is the probability that an item beginning in states 3 and 4 ends up in the absorbing states? That is, determine the structure of the absorption matrix.

18. Friendly Finance Company categorizes its loans into five categories, as follows.

Category 1: Loan paid in full.
Category 2: Loan defaulted (bad debt).
Category 3: Loan payment late (0–30 days).
Category 4: Loan payment late (31–90 days).
Category 5: Loan payment late (91 + days).

From past historical data, the company has derived the following transition matrix as being descriptive of the behavior of its loan categories on a weekly basis.

$$
\mathbf{P} = \begin{array}{c}
\begin{array}{cccccc} & S_1 & S_2 & S_3 & S_4 & S_5 \end{array} \\
\begin{array}{c} S_1 \\ S_2 \\ S_3 \\ S_4 \\ S_5 \end{array}
\left[\begin{array}{ccccc}
1 & 0 & 0 & 0 & 0 \\
0 & 1 & 0 & 0 & 0 \\
0.4 & 0.2 & 0.1 & 0.2 & 0.1 \\
0.3 & 0.4 & 0.1 & 0.1 & 0.1 \\
0.2 & 0.4 & 0.1 & 0.1 & 0.2
\end{array}\right]
\end{array}
$$

(a) Compute the expected number of steps before absorption for states S_3, S_4, and S_5.

(b) Compute the matrix that contains the probabilities of absorption associated with states S_1 and S_2.

(c) If the company currently has $10,000 of outstanding loans in state S_3, $20,000 of outstanding loans in state S_4, and $15,000 of outstanding loans in state S_5, what is the expected amount to eventually be collected, and what is the expected amount to eventually be written off as a bad debt?

19. The Desert Cactus Firm grows and sells for transportation saguaro cacti. It currently has in stock some 2000 cacti in various stages of growth. Of this number, some 500 are too small for transplanting, while the remaining 1500 are available for sale. The operation of this cacti farm can be viewed as a year-time-period Markov chain, with the following four states.

State 1 Sold and transplanted.
State 2 Loss-disease, stolen, too big to transplant.
State 3 Too small for sale.
State 4 Satisfactory size but not sold.

The Desert Cactus Farm has determined that the following transition matrix is appropriate for its yearly operations.

$$
\mathbf{P} = \begin{array}{c} \\ S_1 \\ S_2 \\ S_3 \\ S_4 \end{array}
\begin{array}{cccc}
S_1 & S_2 & S_3 & S_4 \\
\left[\begin{array}{cccc}
1 & 0 & 0 & 0 \\
0 & 1 & 0 & 0 \\
0.5 & 0.1 & 0.1 & 0.3 \\
0.6 & 0.1 & 0 & 0.3
\end{array}\right]
\end{array}
$$

How many of the Desert Cactus Farm's currently available 2000 cacti will eventually be sold, and how many will be lost?

20. As an investor you own 500 shares of a speculative stock whose daily price changes are described by the following one-step transition matrix.

$$
\mathbf{P} = \begin{array}{c} \\ -10\% \\ \text{No Change} \\ +10\% \end{array}
\begin{array}{ccc}
-10\% & \text{No Change} & +10\% \\
\left[\begin{array}{ccc}
0.4 & 0.4 & 0.2 \\
0.1 & 0.6 & 0.3 \\
0.1 & 0.4 & 0.5
\end{array}\right]
\end{array}
$$

Today there was no change in the price of the stock. However, because of other financial commitments you must sell your stock within 4 days. Will it likely be to your advantage to sell after 1 day? 2 days? 3 days? 4 days? Why or why not?

21. The New Machine Works has been experiencing considerable down time on its automatic milling machines. It currently has 10 automatic milling machines. Assume that the "running versus down time" process can be described by a Markov chain, and that the probability of the system being in a running state or a down-time state is dependent upon the state of the system in the previous period. Based on historical data, the following transition probability matrix has been derived.

Previous Period—States	Current Period–States	
	Running Time	*Down Time*
Running Time	0.8	0.2
Down Time	0.4	0.6

(a) If the set of 10 milling machines is currently running, what is the probability that the set of machines will experience down time in the next period?
(b) What are the steady-state probabilities of the set of milling machines being in the running-time state and the down-time state?
(c) If the New Machine Works has 8 milling machines running and 2 milling machines being repaired, what is the expected number of machines that will be running in the long run?

Simulation Modeling

15.1 INTRODUCTION

Simulation modeling is one of the most powerful management science techniques available for the analysis and study of today's increasingly complex management systems. Thus, the verb "simulate," which means "to take on the characteristics of reality," has become an important term in management science. Although most of the decision-making techniques that we have previously discussed in this book are designed to lead to a single "optimal" solution, it should be apparent that there are many complex problems for which a single "optimal" solution cannot be determined. Management science techniques, such as linear programming, that result in the determination of a single "best" answer are referred to as **analytical** techniques. Simulation, conversely, is an **experimental** technique that usually results in a series of answers, any one of which may be acceptable to the manager. In general, simulation modeling is employed for problem situations whose complexity precludes the use of an analytical problem-solving technique.

Lack of resources may also be present in the problem formulation phase of a management science study, and such a lack may necessitate the use of simulation modeling. For example, we may lack the facilities necessary for the physical testing of a particular system, and may thus be forced to simulate the system's physical characteristics. Additionally, the scope of the managerial problem may require the structuring of a model that is simply too big to be solved by a management science technique, such as linear programming, using available computer resources.

An excellent operational definition of simulation has been provided by Naylor, et al. (1966, p. 3):

> Simulation is a numerical technique for conducting experiments on a digital computer, which involves certain types of mathematical and logical models that describe the behavior of a business or economical system (or some component thereof) over extended periods of real time.

Embodied in this definition is a summary of the basic approach used in building a simulation model. First, simulation is a technique that involves setting up a model of a real situation and then performing repetitive experiments on the model. Second, the model will be conveniently represented using a logical or mathematical structure. Third, the repetitive experiments will be made using a digital computer and, in general, will take place over extended periods of time during which the system will be subjected to dynamic and stochastic stimuli. Finally, the results of the application of the simulation technique may not be optimal in a purely analytical sense, but rather, the combined judgment of the manager and analyst may be required to choose between the alternative results that are produced by the various experiments. Indeed, evaluation of the simulation test results will often cause the analyst to restructure the original simulation and perform additional simulation experiments. A summary of the conceptual approach of simulation is presented in Fig. 15.1

As evidenced in Fig. 15.1, the practice of simulation is a classic application of the principles of the scientific method that were discussed earlier in Chapter 1. As such, the practice of simulation may be subdivided into five procedural steps, along the general guidelines of the scientific method.

1. Problem formulation as a result of observation of the form and structure of the system.
2. Simulation model design involving hypothesis specification and analysis of the interactions among the variables of the system.

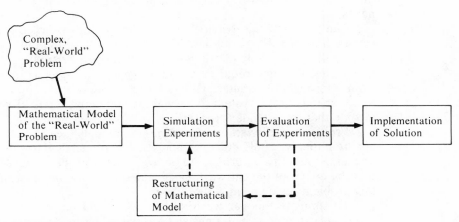

FIGURE 15.1 The Conceptual Approach of Simulation

3. Computerization of the simulation model and preliminary hypothesis testing and analysis.
4. Analysis and validation of the simulation model output data with subsequent model modification and refinement.
5. Implementation of the results of the simulation solution.

Simulation modeling has long been an important tool for the physical scientist. For example, chemical engineers have routinely simulated new or modified chemical processes through the operation of a pilot plant. Similarly, airplane flight has been simulated in a wind tunnel, and civil engineers have simulated the behavior of entire rivers through various physical means. The most dramatic use of simulation in modern times was that performed by National Aeronautics and Space Administration scientists and engineers with respect to the simulation testing of the problems and hazards of space flight to the moon prior to actually undertaking it in the manned spacecraft.

With the development of the high-speed digital computer, simulation has become one of the most important tools of the business analyst. Although simulation may be an imprecise technique, and may require a large amount of modeling and computer time, it is nevertheless of great value in many instances in which the problem to be considered is ill-structured and complex. Its flexibility and versatility make it one of the most important tools available to the management scientist.

15.2 A SIMULATION EXAMPLE

Before we proceed to an in-depth examination of simulation modeling, we will find it useful and instructive to consider a very simple simulation example. This example illustrates the basic concepts of the simulation model, without becoming enmeshed in the complexity that may actually arise in a real-world simulation study.

The owner of the Bright-Shine Car Wash is contemplating hiring a second attendant for the car wash. At present, the car wash facility consists of a single set of three gasoline pumps (premium, regular, unleaded) at which a customer can purchase gas, and a small car wash at which the customer can have a car wash. The price of the car wash is dependent on the amount of gasoline purchased. The entire facility is currently operated by a single attendant, but a recent increase in business has created the need for a study to determine if a second attendant is necessary.

The owner of the Bright-Shine Car Wash has observed the operation of the car wash for a 5-day period and has determined that the time between arrivals of customers is uniformly distributed from 1 through 20 minutes. He has also determined that the time required to service each customer is uniformly distributed from 1 through 10 minutes. He would like to determine the average time a customer spends in the system (both waiting and being serviced) and the percentage of time that the attendant is idle.

From our earlier study of waiting-line models (see Chapter 13), it should be apparent that we could utilize an analytical approach and develop a single-channel queueing model to determine an answer to this problem. Instead, let us assume that the owner of the car wash has decided to adopt an experimental approach to this problem, using a simulation model.

To simulate this car wash system we would need to be able to generate a series of customer arrival times and a series of associated customer service times.

For simplicity, assume that we can treat both customer arrival times and customer service times in terms of whole minutes. Then, one means of generating a series of customer arrival times would be to number consecutively 20 paper slips, place these slips in a hat, shake the hat vigorously, and then draw out slips of paper randomly (i.e., each slip of paper is replaced after each drawing). A similar process involving 10 slips of paper could be employed to generate a series of customer service times.

As a set of customer arrival times and customer service times is generated, the problem becomes one of keeping track of a set of relevant information. Table 15.1 presents one set of information that could result from the simulation of a series of 25 customer arrivals and services.

As seen in Table 15.1, a set of customer interarrival times and a set of customer service times are first generated, using the simple mechanical procedure described above. Next, a clock mechanism is devised—and it is used to keep track of the customer arrival time, the time at which a service (car wash) begins, and the time at which a service ends. The time the customer is in the system (sum of the waiting time plus the service time) is then calculated by subtracting the

TABLE 15.1   Bright-Shine Car Wash Simulation Data

Customer	Inter-arrival Time (min)	Service Time (min)	Clock Arrival Time	Clock Service Time Start	Clock Service Time End	Customer Waiting Time (min)	Attendant Idle Time (min)
1	—	8	0:00	0:00	0:08	8	0
2	3	7	0:03	0:08	0:15	12	0
3	12	4	0:15	0:15	0:19	4	0
4	2	1	0:17	0:19	0:20	3	0
5	3	5	0:20	0:20	0:25	5	0
6	12	9	0:32	0:32	0:41	9	7
7	5	3	0:37	0:41	0:44	7	0
8	8	5	0:45	0:45	0:50	5	1
9	7	8	0:52	0:52	0:60	8	2
10	4	1	0:56	0:60	1:01	5	0
11	1	6	0:57	1:01	1:07	10	0
12	8	1	1:05	1:07	1:08	3	0
13	1	6	1:06	1:08	1:14	8	0
14	14	3	1:20	1:20	1:23	3	6
15	5	2	1:25	1:25	1:27	2	2
16	18	3	1:43	1:43	1:46	3	16
17	4	6	1:47	1:47	1:53	6	1
18	2	4	1:49	1:53	1:57	8	0
19	8	7	1:57	1:57	2:04	7	0
20	6	5	2:03	2:04	2:09	6	0
21	18	6	2:21	2:21	2:27	6	12
22	1	2	2:22	2:27	2:29	7	0
23	12	6	2:34	2:34	2:40	6	5
24	6	1	2:40	2:40	2:41	1	0
25	10	5	2:50	2:50	2:55	5	9
					Totals:	147	61

Note: Average time customer in system $= {}^{147}/_{25} = 5.9$ minutes.
Percent of time attendant is idle $= {}^{61}/_{175} = 35$ percent.

customer arrival time from the time at which the service ends. The time that the attendant is idle is computed as the difference between the time when one service ends and the next service begins.

For the 25-customer simulation shown in Table 15.1, the average time a customer is in the system is 5.9 minutes. Additionally, the attendant is idle 35 percent of the time. In this simple simulation example we have ignored the starting conditions for the problem and have assumed that the car wash is idle when the first customer arrives. Also, we have not attempted to use a large sample size, as would be required to achieve statistical significance for this problem situation. Both of these aspects of simulation modeling will be discussed in detail in a later section of this chapter. In spite of the rudimentary nature of this example, it does provide an indication of the manner in which simulation can be used to analyze a particular problem situation.

15.3   CASE STUDY—THE PRACTICE OF SIMULATION MODELING

To further enhance our understanding of simulation modeling, let us now consider a more complex and detailed simulation case study. The Star Metals Corporation was a midwestern-based metals distributor engaged in the warehousing and distribution of aluminum, stainless steel, carbon steel, nickel, copper, and other metals.[1] The majority of the firm's orders required the cutting, shearing, or sawing of a metal commodity to a particular customer's specification. As each piece of material was cut to a particular specification, one or two pieces of scrap material resulted, as can be seen in Fig. 15.2.

15.3.1   Problem Formulation

Before a simulation model is actually designed, two basic questions must be asked and answered by the analyst as an integral part of the problem formulation. These questions are

1. What is the intended purpose and use of the simulation model? That is, what problem will the simulation model be used to investigate?

2. What are the requirements for precision and accuracy that the simulation model must satisfy?

The basic question concerning the intended purpose and use of the simulation model was answered as follows. The resulting piece(s) of scrap material could be either maintained in "random inventory" or sold for their salvage value. The salvage value was somewhat less than the original cost of the metal commodity. However, if the scrap pieces were maintained in random inventory, there was no assurance that they could eventually be used to fill a customer's order. The basic decision problem, therefore, was one of balancing the cost of maintaining the random inventory against the incremental cost associated with the loss incurred from scrapping at less than original cost. Management of the company was hopeful of determining a decision rule that would specify a lower bound for the size of pieces to be maintained in random inventory, that is, they were seeking to determine a specific rule that would allow them to make a decision

---

[1] The name of the participating company has been altered to protect its proprietary interest. All the information and data presented in the case, however, are real.

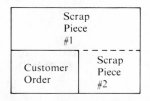

a. One Piece of Scrap Resulting From Cut.   b. Two Pieces of Scrap Resulting From Cut.

FIGURE 15.2   Typical Stock-Cutting Examples

concerning the scrapping of the pieces that resulted from the production process.

The management science staff of the firm had decided that this problem was particularly amenable to analysis by means of simulation modeling. The decision was reached because of several factors. First, the mathematical complexity of the "stock cutting" problem precluded its formulation by more analytical means, such as integer programming. Second, even if the problem could be formulated in an integer-programming format, it was doubtful if it could be solved because of its size and complexity, that is, efficient computer codes were not available. Third, it was felt that simulation afforded a particularly flexible means of testing a large number of scrap decision rules.

The basic question concerning model precision and accuracy was answered as follows. First, a decision was made to attempt to develop a simulated set of inventory conditions for a single shape and type of metal, namely, *Monel plate*. The decision to consider this particular metal type and shape classification was predicated upon the following factors.

1. The salvage value of Monel plate at the time of the study was relatively high ($0.65-per-pound salvage value).

2. The firm had a considerable volume of business in Monel plate. Thus, control of Monel plate scrap

inventory was of major economic importance.

3. Customers' orders for Monel plate rarely called for stock sizes. Instead, orders normally required some cutting or shearing, and thus generated scrap pieces.

The company essentially felt that Monel plate was very representative of the literally thousands of items that it sold (i.e., items composed of different combinations of metals, shapes, sizes, and thicknesses). Second, a decision was made that a decision rule stated in whole (integer) inches was acceptable. Accuracy for the model was thus defined in simple terms, namely, that of a decision rule stated in whole inch measurements, with the decision parameter being total cost, composed of the scrap loss and the inventory carrying cost.

15.3.2   Simulation Model Design

Actual simulation model design begins with the specification of a hypothesis or hypotheses. Hypothesis testing is very nearly self-explanatory. In essence, the analyst must specify some basic beliefs he wishes to prove or disprove; these are his hypotheses. Once his hypotheses have been defined, he must then attack the system itself. Mize and Cox (1968, pp. 142–46) have suggested that all systems can be analyzed in terms of the following common features.

1. Components (containing any num-

ber of elements greater than zero).
2. Variables (both external and internal).
3. Parameters.
4. Relationships (both cause and effect) among components and variables.

Components are defined as those entities of a system that are to be independently identified and whose collective performance determines the output of the system. **Variables** are defined as those attributes of the system that take on different values under different conditions or in different system states. The variables that are commonly employed in business and economic studies are used in a fashion that relates various components to each other. They are typically classified as **exogenous** variables, **status** variables, and **endogenous** variables (Naylor 1966, pp. 10–11). Exogenous variables are the input or independent variables and are usually predetermined. The status variables are used to describe the state of the system and its components at a point in time. The status variables interact with both the exogenous and endogenous variables of the system, according to the functional and structural relationships of the system. The endogenous variables are the dependent or output variables of the system, and are generated from the interaction of the system's exogenous and status variables. **Parameters** are those attributes of a system that do not change during the simulation because of anything that occurred during the simulation. They are essentially fixed and can be changed only at the command of the analyst. Finally, we have the **relationships** in a system that are the connections between components, variables, and parameters that control the changes of state in the system. Relationships can assume the following forms.

1. Structural relationships—those that link components and their attributes together.
2. Functional relationships—those that determine the behavior of a component or components as a function of the state of all the components and as a function of the values of the external, controllable, and independent variables in the system.
3. Sequential relationships—those that pertain to events within a performing system that are related only by time dependence.

The basic hypothesis employed in the simulation study was that there was a specific decision rule for Monel plate that could be employed to minimize the total cost composed of the scrap loss and the inventory-carrying cost. The major components of the system were as follows.

1. The customer order frequency distributions.
2. The random inventory-generating process.
3. The cost determination process.

Each of these major components of the system will now be discussed in greater detail.

Customer Order Frequency Distributions. Customer order frequency distributions were constructed for three exogenous or input variables. These exogenous variables were as follows.

1. Type of material (e.g., $\frac{1}{4}$-in. Monel plate, hot-rolled both sides).
2. Width of material (e.g., 20-in. width).
3. Length of material (e.g., 20-in. length).

The frequency distributions were constructed from sales data (a random sample of 400 orders) that were provided by the firm and are shown in Table 15.2.

Note that, in this instance, the input variables were probabilistic in nature and were defined by discrete probability distributions. The random numbers associated with the random variables, which are also shown in Table 15.2, were used in the Monte Carlo order generation process that will be described in detail later in this chapter.

The Random Inventory Generating Process. The second component of the model was designed to evaluate relationships involving the status variables of the system, the pieces of metal in the random inventory. The random-size pieces in this inventory were the status variables of the model. Questions asked concerning these status variables, as each customer's order was generated were

1. Can the customer's order be cut from a piece of material residing in random inventory, or must it be cut from a piece of standard-size stock?
2. As a result of cutting a piece of material to a customer's specification, what are the size(s) of the remaining piece(s) of material?
3. Should the new random piece be put in random inventory, or should it be sold immediately for its salvage value?
4. As a result of adding and subtracting pieces from random inventory, what is the new random inventory?

In answering Question 1 above, it was necessary to sequentially search the existing random inventory. In this search process, a heuristic procedure was employed. Searching was terminated whenever a scrap piece was located that was 1 inch larger, or more, on both dimensions than the size of the

piece required for the customer's order.

The customer orders that activated the decision stage of the model were, in turn, generated by a Monte Carlo process, using the input variables of the first stage of the model. The customer orders were thus randomly generated from the discrete distributions shown in Table 15.2, using the Monte Carlo process to be described later.

The Cost Determination Process. The final component of the decision model was used to determine the values of the endogenous variables. The endogenous variables were the various costs associated with the operation of the random inventory system. Thus, if a particular scrap decision rule caused a scrap piece to be sold for its salvage value, an incremental salvage loss was computed. The incremental salvage loss was computed by multiplying the weight of the piece sold for salvage by the incremental salvage loss per pound. The incremental salvage loss per pound was a constant value (parameter), based on the prevailing prices for Monel plate at the time of the study.

If, however, a particular scrap decision rule resulted in a scrap piece being placed in random inventory, an inventory-carrying cost was computed. For those scrap pieces that remained in the scrap inventory for the entire year, a yearly inventory cost was computed by multiplying the weight of the scrap piece by the firm's yearly inventory-carrying cost per pound. For those scrap pieces that remained in the random inventory for a portion of a year, the firm's yearly inventory-carrying cost was adjusted to represent the portion of the year, and the computation of the inventory cost proceeded in the same manner as previously described.

Both salvage-loss costs and inventory-carrying costs were accumulated during the simulation run. These costs were added to obtain a total scrap cost

TABLE 15.2 Customer Order Frequency Distributions for Monel Plate

a. Material *Type (thickness)* *Standard Inventory Number*	*Frequency (%)*	*Random Number*
9	4	1–4
13	3	5–7
17	1	8
20	2	9–10
25	40	11–50
52	10	51–60
56	40	61–100

b. Width (in.)	*Frequency (%)*	*Random Number*
2	12	1–12
3	7	13–19
4	18	20–37
5	10	38–47
6	7	48–54
7	2	55–56
8	12	47–68
9	3	69–71
10	3	72–74
11	9	75–83
12	2	84–85
13	4	86–89
14	1	90
17	2	91–92
20	1	93
24	1	94
36	3	95–97
38	1	98
48	2	99–100

c. Length (in.)	*Frequency (%)*	*Random Number*
4	3	1–3
5	27	4–30
6	4	31–34
7	3	35–37
8	5	38–42
9	1	43
10	3	44–46
11	8	47–54
12	12	55–66
13	3	67–69
14	2	70–71
17	2	72–73
18	1	74
19	5	75–79
24	1	80
33	2	81–82
36	2	83–84
37	1	85
40	1	86

TABLE 15.2   Continued

c. Length (in.)	Frequency (%)	Random Number
42	1	87
44	1	88
46	4	89–92
48	1	93
59	1	94
60	1	95
62	1	96
95	1	97
96	3	98–100

for a particular decision rule. The total scrap cost was the basic decision variable in the minimization process. A hypothesis was made that the total cost curve would be unimodal in shape. The unimodal shape was believed to be a result of an increase in incremental salvage losses with an increase in the size of scrap decision rules and a decrease in inventory-carrying costs with an increase in the size of scrap decision rules, and conversely. The hypothesized cost curves can be seen in Fig. 15.3.

Input parameters (constants) for the model included

1. Purchase cost for Monel plate ($1.35 per lb).
2. Salvage value for Monel plate ($0.70 per lb).
3. Annual inventory-carrying cost for Monel plate (13 percent of purchase cost).

Relationships between the components, variables, and parameters of the system were expressed as mathematical and logical statements.

15.3.3   Computerization of the Simulation Model

Computerization of the simulation model requires the same basic steps, with the possible exception of a choice of a computer code, that other mathematical models require. As suggested by Naylor, et al. (1966, pp. 37–39), the activities required in the construction of a computer program for a simulation model include

1. Flowcharting of model logic.
2. Computer coding.
   (a) General purpose languages.
   (b) Special purpose languages.
3. Error checking.
4. Data input and starting conditions.
5. Data generation.
6. Output reports.

The need for flowcharting of the basic logic of the simulation model cannot be overemphasized, as it is not uncommon for simulation models to become extremely large and complex. A good flowchart serves to outline the logical sequence of events to be carried out by the computer within a specific sequential time frame.

Once the simulation model's logic has been outlined by means of the flowchart we are ready to write the actual computer code that will be used to make simulation runs or tests on the computer. Two coding alternatives are available. We can either write our program in a general purpose language, such as FORTRAN, PL/1, ALGOL, or BASIC, or we can use one of the special purpose simulation languages, such

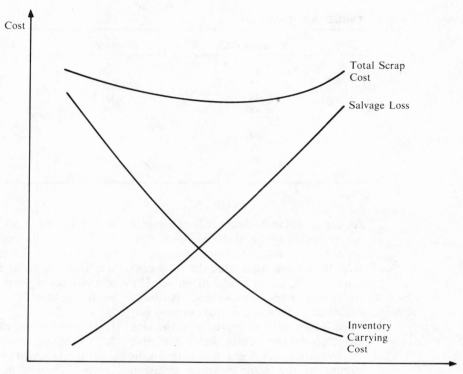

FIGURE 15.3 **Hypothesized Cost Curves**

as GPSS,[2] SIMSCRIPT,[3] GASP,[4] SIMPAC,[5] DYNAMO,[6] or PROGRAM SIMULATE.[7] Use of a special purpose simulation language may have certain advantages, including

1. Less programming time may be required.
2. Error checking is easier.

Use of special purpose languages, how-ever, may not be desirable because they reduce the programming flexibility of the analyst and may result in in-creased computer running times.

Error checking is required during coding and is nothing more than the traditional "debugging" required for all computer programs. Selection of data input and specification of starting con-ditions are related to the previous data collection effort. In essence, the start-

[2] *General Purpose Simulation II*, Program Library, Reference 7090-CS-13X, IBM Corporation.

[3] H. M. Markowitz, Bernard Hausner, and H. W. Karr, *SIMSCRIPT: A Simulation Programming Language*, The RAND Corporation RM-3310 (Santa Monica, Calif., November 1962).

[4] Philip J. Kiviat, *GASP—A General Activity Simulation Program*, Project No. 90. 17-019 (2), Applied Research Laboratory, United States Steel (Monroeville, Pa., July 1963).

[5] *SIMPAC Users Manual*, TM 602/000/00, Systems Development Corporation (Santa Monica, Calif., April 1962).

[6] Alexander L. Pugh, *DYNAMO User's Manual* (Cambridge, Mass.: The M.I.T. Press, 1963).

[7] Charles C. Holt, et al., *PROGRAM SIMULATE: A User's and Programmer's Manual*, Social Systems Research Institute, University of Wisconsin (Madison, Wisc., May 1964).

ing model parameters, input, data, etc., must be defined and coded in a fashion similar to the computer program itself.

For the Star Metals Company, the simulation model was programmed in FORTRAN IV, because of the flexibility it afforded. The general programming logic employed can be summarized as follows.

1. An initial random inventory matrix was created by running the simulation model without making cost calculations, for a 3-month period.
2. Sixty-four hundred customer orders, representing 4 years' sales activity, were simulated using a Monte Carlo random number generating subroutine and the discrete frequency distributions shown in Table 15.2.
3. Each order was then tested against the decision section of the model. This section first provided for searching the on-hand random inventory for a piece of material equal to or larger than the piece required to fill the customer's order. If a random piece having the required characteristics was found, the customer's order was cut from it and one or two new random pieces were created. The dimensions of the new pieces were then tested against the scrap decision rule and were accordingly either scrapped or put into random inventory. Depending on the result, a scrap loss, an inventory-carrying cost, or perhaps both resulted. This latter situation occurred when only one of the two new random pieces was scrapped.
4. If no random stock satisfying the customer's order was available, the customer's order was cut from standard inventory stock. Again, one or two new random pieces were created and tested against the scrap decision rule.
5. Scrapping a piece of random stock or using it to fill a customer's order resulted in its being deleted from the random inventory. Likewise, the cutting of either standard stock inventory or random inventory to fill a customer order resulted in adding two new pieces to the random inventory *if and only if* the new pieces passed the scrap decision rule. Thus, random inventory was subject to constant fluctuation throughout the simulation run.
6. Four types of data were printed out as the result of each simulation run.
    (a) Total inventory-carrying cost.
    (b) Total scrap-loss cost.
    (c) Total Cost = total inventory-carrying cost + total scrap-loss cost.
    (d) M = number of standard stock pieces cut during simulation run.

A simplified flowchart of the programming logic of the simulation model is presented in Fig. 15.4.

The model was used to test each of 21 decision rules, and the results of the simulation testing are summarized in Table 15.3. The test results have been plotted, and are shown in Fig. 15.5. The three cost curves are shown as discontinuous curves, since the various scrap decision rules were defined in terms of "families" of decision rules. For example, a discontinuity in the cost curves is evidenced between the "2-inch family" of scrap decision rules and the "4-inch family" of scrap decision rules.

15.3.4 Analysis and Validation of Output Data

The primary emphasis in the field of simulation has been on model design and computerization. Relatively little work has been done on the analysis and validation of simulation output data.

TABLE 15.3 Scrap Inventory Cost Simulation Test Results

Size of Scrap Decision Rule, in.	Inventory Cost,[a] $	Scrap Cost, $	Total Cost,[a] $
2 × 2	30604	0.20	30604
2 × 4	30147	5.10	30152
2 × 6	29793	10.90	29805
2 × 8	29593	87.80	29681
2 × 12	29386	377.79	29764
2 × 16	29113	610.00	29723
4 × 4	32576	391.00	32967
4 × 6	29931	634.00	30565
4 × 8	27717	1287.00	29004
4 × 12	26810	3355.00	30165
4 × 16	24911	6036.00	30947
6 × 6	26403	2160.00	28563
6 × 8	21075	5301.00	26376[b]
6 × 12	19206	10107.00	29313
6 × 16	15613	16101.00	31714
8 × 8	21202	5740.00	26942
8 × 12	19438	10245.00	29683
8 × 16	17560	21769.00	39329
12 × 12	19824	23246.00	43071
12 × 16	17600	40098.00	57698
16 × 16	18124	42485.00	60968

[a]Rounded to the nearest whole dollar.
[b]Minimum.

Often the analyst spends so much time and effort in model design and computerization that he has little time left for analysis and validation of his results. In addition, analysis and validation of a computer simulation model introduces pragmatic, theoretical, statistical, and philosophical difficulties. As a result, there is widespread disagreement as to the appropriate techniques to use in analyzing data generated by simulation experiments.[8]

One method for analyzing and validating simulation output involves statistical tests, such as analysis of variance, multiple comparison, or spectral analysis. Another procedure involves asking the question: Have we adequately described the actual physical situation through our simulation? In answering this question, the management scientist will often want to consider one or more of the following factors (Mize and Cox 1968, p. 155).

1. *Reproduction of past data.* All simulation experiments should reproduce the underlying probability distributions with a high degree of accuracy.

2. *Reasonableness of results.* The validity of a simulation model can often be tested by performing several manual calculations and examining the model's resultant behavior.

3. *Completeness of results.* A final check of the model should be made to see that no important factor has been omitted.

---

[8] See for example: R. W. Conway, "Some Tactical Problems in Digital Simulation," *Management Science*, Vol. 10, no. 2 (October 1963), 38–49.

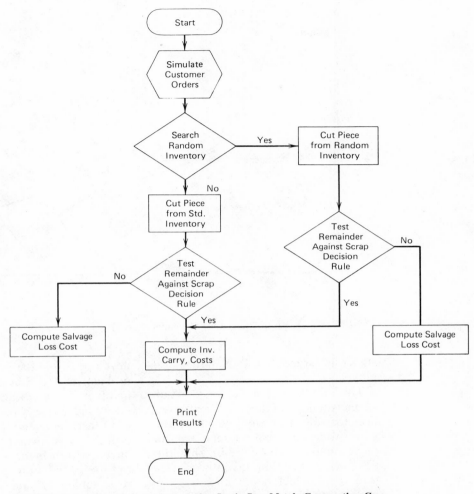

FIGURE 15.4   Flowchart of Programming Logic-Star Metals Corporation Case

In summary, the final measure of the value of a simulation model is determined by how closely it predicts the behavior of the physical system or managerial process being examined. If possible, one should attempt to compare simulation results with actual data. If this is not possible, as is often the case, one must resort to validation methods such as those suggested above.

In the Star Metals case the evaluation of the simulation results, as presented in Table 15.3 and Fig. 15.5, was relatively straightforward.

From Fig. 15.5, it can been seen that the total cost minimization of $26,376 occurs when a 6- × 8-in. scrap decision rule is employed. Within the "6-in. family" of scrap decision rules, the total cost curve rises rapidly on either side of the 6- × 8-in. scrap decision rule. It is interesting to note that an 8- × 8-in. scrap decision rule produces a total cost of $26,942, which is close to the total cost minimization that occurs for the 6- × 8-in. scrap decision rule. Again, however, within the "8-in. family" of scrap decision rules, the total cost curve rises rapidly as a scrap deci-

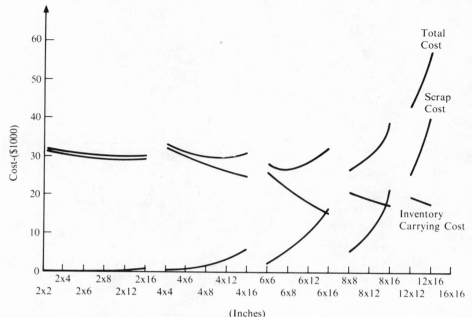

FIGURE 15.5   Scrap Inventory Cost Simulation

sion rule larger than 8- × 8-in. is employed.

The simulation model tests results strongly indicated that the "best" scrap decision rule to be employed for Monel plate was one that stated that any piece smaller than 6- × 8-in. should be scrapped rather than inventoried. This rule was selected on the basis of minimizing the *total* cost, where the total cost was composed of scrap cost and an inventory-carrying cost.[9]

Validation of the simulation model developed for the inventory control problem of the Star Metals Company involved consideration of all the factors discussed above. Chi-square goodness-of-fit tests indicated that the underlying probability distributions were reproduced with a high degree of accuracy by the simulation experiments. The reasonableness and completeness of the simulation results were confirmed by lengthy discussion with the firm's management.

15.4   THE MONTE CARLO METHOD

In our discussion of the simulation methodology employed in the Star Metals Company case, we noted that the Monte Carlo method was used to generate random samples of customer orders for Monel plate. In performing simulation experiments we may often want to take a random sample or samples from some probability distribution describing a population in order to make inferences or

[9] A more detailed description of this simulation modeling effort can be found in: Robert E. Markland, "A Simulation Model for Determining Scrap Decision Rules in the Metal Processing Industry," *Production and Inventory Management*, 11: no. 1 (First Quarter 1970), 29–35.

generalizations about the population. The random sample is thus used as exogenous input to the aggregate simulation model. This random sampling process is commonly referred to as the **Monte Carlo Method**, and it consists of first generating random numbers and then generating random observations from a given probability distribution using these random numbers. The Monte Carlo method traces its origin to the work of Von Neumann and Ulan in the late 1940s.

The Monte Carlo method involves the artificial generation of experience or data by the use of a **random number generator** and the cumulative probability distribution being considered. The random number generator may be a mechanical device, such as numbered slips of paper in a hat, a table of random digits, or a computer subroutine. The cumulative probability distribution being sampled may have been derived from past empirical data, or it may have resulted from a recent set of statistical experiments. Alternatively, it can be a known theoretical distribution. The **random numbers** that are generated are then used to artificially reproduce the expected experience that would be produced by the probability distribution in question.

15.4.1 Generating Random Numbers

In discussing the generation of random numbers we will attempt to use terminology that is fairly consistent with that commonly used by practitioners in the field. Thus, we will refer to a random variable uniformly distributed over the interval, a to b, as a random number. Such a random variable has a uniform probability density function, which can be graphed as shown in Fig. 15.6. A random number is thus a number drawn as a random sample from the uniform probability distribution shown in Fig. 15.6. Each random number, corresponding to a value of x, will lie between a and b and will be uniformly distributed over the range between a and b. This means that any random number we select will have an equally likely probability of being chosen, namely $1/(b-a)$.

In practice, we usually desire to generate a sequence of random numbers. Four alternative methods have been used by practitioners to generate sequences of random numbers. They are

1. Manual methods.
2. Library tables.
3. Analog computer methods.
4. Digital computer methods.

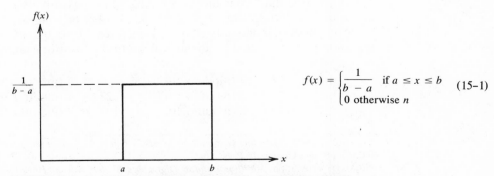

$$f(x) = \begin{cases} \dfrac{1}{b-a} & \text{if } a \le x \le b \\ 0 \text{ otherwise } n \end{cases} \quad (15\text{--}1)$$

FIGURE 15.6 Probability Density Function for the Uniform Distribution

Manual methods are extremely simple to employ but are of little practical value when anything other than a very short sequence of random numbers is needed. Such manual methods include coin flipping, dice rolling, card shuffling, roulette wheels, and the drawing of prenumbered slips of paper or balls out of a container. These methods may be useful for short demonstrations of how to obtain random numbers, but are of little value otherwise. They also have the disadvantage that it is impossible to reproduce a sequence of numbers generated by such devices.

Several library tables of random numbers are in existence. The earliest was prepared by Tippett[10] in 1927, and many others have appeared since that time. The RAND Corporation library table is probably the table most frequently employed today.[11] Library tables offer the advantage that the random numbers they produce can be readily reproduced. However, their use is awkward and slow, and when they are used in conjunction with a digital computer they must be either stored internally in memory, or externally on tape, disk, or cards, and read when random numbers are required.

Analog computers have also been used to generate random numbers, and indeed the RAND Corporation's library table was originally generated by an analog computer. Analog generation methods are much faster than either manual methods or library tables, but they again have the handicap of not being reproducible.

When digital computers are used to generate random numbers, several alternative procedures are possible. Tocher (1963) suggests three: external provision, internal generation by a random physical process, and internal generation of sequences of digits by a recurrence relation. External provision involves recording of the random number tables on magnetic tape and subsequently using them as direct input to the digital computer. Internal generation by a random physical process usually requires a special adjunct to the digital computer, such as an electronic valve circuit that produces "thermal noise" that can be tracked. The major shortcoming of this method is that its results are not reproducible and thus cannot be checked. The third alternative involves generation of **pseudorandom numbers** by repeatedly transforming an arbitrary set of numbers. At the present time, most computer codes for generating random numbers do so by means of this third alternative. Thus, the sequence of numbers that is produced is reproducible in a manner such that a "reasonable" statistical test will show no significant departure from randomness. Typical ways of generating pseudorandom numbers include the **additive**, **multiplicative**, and **mixed congruential methods**.

A congruential procedure is a recursive process involving a congruent relationship. Two integer numbers x and y are said to be **congruent modulo m** (m also being an integer), if and only if, there is an integer k such that $(x - y) = km$. Thus, the quantity $(x - y)$ must be an integral multiple of m. For example, letting $m = 10$, we can state

$$
\begin{array}{ll}
2 \equiv 2 \ (\text{modulo } 10) & \qquad 7 \equiv 7 \ (\text{modulo } 10) \\
22 \equiv 2 \ (\text{modulo } 10) & \qquad 27 \equiv 7 \ (\text{modulo } 10) \\
192 \equiv 2 \ (\text{modulo } 10) & \qquad 197 \equiv 7 \ (\text{modulo } 10)
\end{array}
\tag{15-2}
$$

[10] L.H.C. Tippett, "Random Sampling Numbers," *Tracts for Computers*, no. 15 (Cambridge, England: Cambridge University Press, 1927).

[11] RAND Corporation, *A Million Random Digits with 100,000 Normal Deviates* (New York: The Free Press, 1955).

To find the value of, say, 253 (modulo 10), we would calculate the integer *remainder* of 253 divided by 10, which is 3.

The multiplicative congruential method will now be explained in order to demonstrate this type of approach. The multiplicative congruential method derives the $(n + 1)$st random number, x_{n+1}, from the nth random number x_n by using the recurrence relation:

$$x_{n+1} \equiv Kx_n \text{ (modulo } m) \tag{15-3}$$

where K and m are positive integers $(K < m)$. This recurrence relationship indicates that, to obtain the random number x_{n+1}, we take the last random number x_n, multiply it by the constant K, and take the result modulo m (i.e., divide Kx_n by m and treat the remainder as x_{n+1}). The first random number x_1 is obtained by selecting any large integer for x_0 and then applying the recurrence relation given by Equation 15-3. For example, suppose we set $x_0 = 1$, $K = 7$, and $m = 10$ (modulo 10). We can now generate a set of integers, as follows.

$$x_0 \equiv 1$$

$$x_1 \equiv \frac{(7)(1)}{10} \equiv \frac{(0 + 7)}{10} \equiv 7$$

$$x_2 \equiv \frac{(7)(7)}{10} \equiv \frac{(40 + 9)}{10} \equiv 9$$

$$x_3 \equiv \frac{(7)(9)}{10} \equiv \frac{(60 + 3)}{10} \equiv 3 \tag{15-4}$$

$$x_4 \equiv \frac{(7)(3)}{10} \equiv \frac{(20 + 1)}{10} \equiv 1$$

$$x_5 \equiv \frac{(7)(1)}{10} \equiv \frac{(0 + 7)}{10} \equiv 7$$

Thus, the sequence 1, 7, 9, 3, 1, 7, 9, 3, . . . is obtained. Obviously, this is not a valid sequence of random numbers, because only 4 of the 10 possible digits (0, 1, . . . , 9) are ever generated, and the sequence is cyclic with periodicity of length 4. To generate a sequence of random numbers, we need a starting number or **seed** x_0, a multiplier K, and a modulus (m). However, for any pseudorandom number generator only a finite number of integers will be generated before the sequence begins to repeat itself. The period, or length of the sequence, is dependent upon the modulus that is chosen and the particular computer that is employed. The statistical properties of the sequence of numbers that is generated are dependent upon the choice of the seed and the multiplier. In general, the choice of x_0, K, and m are made to create the maximum period and minimum degree of correlation for the pseudorandom numbers that are needed.

One combination of x_0, K, and m that has produced good results and, consequently, has been used frequently is

$$K = 5^{13} = 1,220,703,125$$
$$m = (2^{31} - 1) = 2,147,483,647 \tag{15-5}$$

so that:

$$x_{n+1} \equiv 1,220,703,125x_n \text{ modulo } (2^{31} - 1) \tag{15-6}$$

where x_0, the seed, can be any integer in the range:

$$1 \leq x_0 \leq 2,147,483,647 \tag{15-7}$$

The resulting sequence of pseudorandom numbers will have a period of length 2,147,483,646, with each number in this range appearing once and only once.

Note once again that numbers generated by the multiplicative congruential method are pseudorandom, since they are predictable and reproducible, given a specific value of K, m, and x_0. This is often advantageous, as we may need to experiment under different sets of conditions using *exactly* the same sequence of randomly generated events.

15.4.2 Generating Random Observations

Once we have generated our sequence of random (really, pseudorandom) numbers we must consider the question of how to generate a corresponding sequence of random observations from a given probability distribution. To draw an artificial sample randomly from some population described by a probability distribution, we proceed according to the following steps.

1. Plot the data being considered as a cumulative probability distribution function. The values of the variable of interest are plotted on the x axis (abscissa), and the cumulative probabilities, from 0 to 1, are plotted on the y axis (ordinate).
2. Using a random number generator determine a random decimal number between 0 and 1.
3. Using this random decimal number, project horizontally from the corresponding point on the y axis to the intersection on the cumulative probability distribution curve.
4. Project downward from this point of intersection on the cumulative probability distribution curve to the x axis.
5. The value of x so determined is then the sample value. These steps are then repeated until a specified sample size requirement has been met.

For discrete distributions the procedure is very simple. Suppose we have been given the set of data (shown in Table 15.4) representing the probabilities associated with various sales quantities.

The cumulative probability distribution for this set of data is shown in Fig. 15.7. Now, assume that we have generated five random decimal numbers: 0.92, 0.08, 0.37, 0.62, and 0.45. Using this cumulative probability distribution and the steps outlined previously, we would then obtain the results shown in Table 15.5.

TABLE 15.4 Sales Data

Sales Quantities	Probability	Cumulative Probability
0	0.10	0.10
1	0.20	0.30
2	0.30	0.60
3	0.30	0.90
4	0.10	1.00

TABLE 15.5 Monte Carlo Generated Sales Data

Sales Order	Random Decimal Number	Generated Sales Quantity
1	0.92	4
2	0.08	0
3	0.37	2
4	0.62	3
5	0.45	2

For continuous probability distributions, the procedure is more complicated, but essentially the same. The first step is to construct the cumulative distribution function $F(x) = P(X \leq x)$, where x is the random variable of interest. This can be done by writing the equation for this function by graphically plotting the cumulative distribution function, or by developing a table giving the value of x for uniformly spaced values of $F(x)$ from 0 to 1. Next, a random decimal number between 0 and 1 must be generated. Finally, we set $P(X \leq x)$ equal to the random decimal number and solve for x (Mize and Cox 1968, pp. 76–93; Naylor, et al. 1966, pp. 68–120).

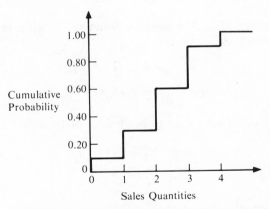

FIGURE 15.7 Discrete Cumulative Distribution Function

To illustrate this process for a continuous distribution consider Fig. 15.8. Figure 15.8 is a graphical plot of a continuous cumulative distribution function. Assume that we have generated the random decimal number 0.58. Using the procedure outlined previously, this results in the generation of a value of 3 for the random variable X, as shown by the arrows in Fig. 15.8.

As noted above, for certain distributions we can use the approach involving writing the equation for the distribution. To illustrate this approach consider the exponential distribution that has a cumulative distribution function given by:

$$P\{X \leq x\} = 1 - e^{-\theta x}, \quad \text{for } x \geq 0 \tag{15-8}$$

where $1/\theta$ = the mean of the distribution

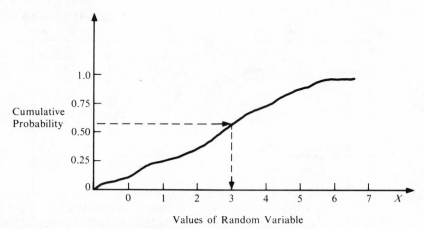

FIGURE 15.8   Continuous Cumulative Distribution Function

We proceed by setting this function equal to a random decimal number between 0 and 1, as follows.

$$1 - e^{-\theta x} = \text{R.N.} \tag{15-9}$$

Since the complement of such a random number is itself a random number, an equivalent relationship is

$$e^{-\theta x} = (1 - \text{R.N.})$$

$$\text{or} \quad e^{-\theta x} = (\text{R.N.}) \tag{15-10}$$

Then, taking the natural logarithm of both sides of Equation 15-10, we obtain

$$ln\ (e^{-\theta x}) = ln\ (\text{R.N.})$$
$$-\theta x = ln\ (\text{R.N.})$$
$$x = \frac{ln\ (\text{R.N.})}{-\theta} \tag{15-11}$$

Thus, x is a random observation from the exponential distribution with a mean of $1/\theta$.

The normal distribution is an important and widely used continuous distribution. Fortunately, there exists a simple technique for generating a random observation from the normal distribution. This technique is based upon the central limit theorem, which states that, if we take n samples from a distribution with mean u, and variance σ^2, then the sum of the n samples is asymptotically normally distributed with mean nu and variance $n\sigma^2$ (when n is large). Now, a random decimal number has a uniform distribution from 0 to 1 with a mean of $1/2$ and a standard deviation of $1/\sqrt{12}$. Therefore, the central limit theorem implies that the sum of n random decimal numbers has approximately a normal distribution with mean $n/2$ and standard deviation $\sqrt{n/12}$. Thus, if $(\text{R.N.})_1, (\text{R.N.})_2, \ldots, (\text{R.N.})_n$ are a sample of n random decimal numbers, then,

$$x = \frac{\sigma}{\sqrt{n/12}} \sum_{i=1}^{n} (\text{R.N.})_i + u - \frac{n}{2} \frac{\sigma}{\sqrt{n/12}} \qquad (15\text{-}12)$$

is a random observation from an approximately normal distribution with mean u and standard deviation σ. In using this approximation, a sample size of $n = 12$ is often employed because it eliminates the square-root terms from Equation 15-12. This approximation has been found to be very good, even for small values of n. Various other techniques for generating random observations from a normal distribution have also been developed (Shannon 1975, pp. 360-62).

15.5 TIME FLOW MECHANISMS IN SIMULATION

Most simulation studies involve the performance of a dynamic system over a period of time. Consequently, one of the most important considerations in simulation language selection and model design is that of the time flow mechanism to be employed. The time flow mechanism that is employed in a simulation study is used to increment the time status of the system and to facilitate the synchronization of the events that occur during the simulation process. Thus, the time flow mechanism is an integral part of simulation model design, as it causes the various events to occur in the proper order and with the proper time interval between successive events.

Two basic time flow mechanisms are available for use in simulation model design. They are known as **fixed-time incrementing** and **next-event incrementing**. The mechanisms are also referred to as **fixed-time step incrementation** and **next-event step incrementation**, respectively.

Using a fixed-time incrementing method a two-step process is employed. Assume that we begin at a given point in time with the system in its initial state. The first step in the time incrementing process is to advance time by a small fixed amount, Δt. We thus add Δt to a register that serves as the master clock for the system to record this passage of time. Then, as the second step in the time incrementing process we update the system in terms of determining what events occurred during this elapsed time Δt and measure the state of the simulation system. These two steps are then repeated for the entire time period needed for the simulation run. The fixed-time incrementing method can be illustrated as shown in Fig. 15.9. As seen in Fig. 15.9 the values of simulation time, T_1, $T_2, \ldots, T_5$, are not dependent upon the actual event occurrence times, e_1, $e_2, \ldots, e_6$. The arrows in Fig. 15.9 indicate the time values at which time is updated and the events of the simulation appear to occur.

Next-event incrementing involves a variable time incrementing process in which the simulation process continues running until an event occurs. When an event occurs, changes in the system are recorded. Thus, the master clock for the simulation system is incremented by a variable amount rather than a fixed amount, throughout the simulation run. The next-event time incrementing method can be illustrated as shown in Fig. 15.10. As seen in Fig. 15.10, the values of simulation time, $T_1, T_2, \ldots, T_5$, are entirely dependent on the actual event occurrence times, $e_1, e_2, \ldots, e_6$. The arrows in Fig. 15.10 again indicate the time values at which time is updated, and correspond to time at which the events of the simulation actually occur.

There is no easy way to determine the proper or best time flow mechanism to

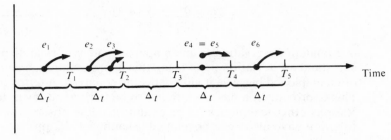

Initial
State, $T = 0$

FIGURE 15.9   Fixed-Time Incrementing

be employed in a particular simulation study. In general, if the system being analyzed involves a continuous flow of information, or events considered in an aggregate rather than individual sense, a **continuous change model** is appropriate. Continuous change models use fixed-time incrementing mechanisms. Conversely, if the system being analyzed involves a consideration of individual events, a **discrete change model** is warranted. Discrete change models use next-event time incrementing mechanisms. Unfortunately, many systems can be described by either type of simulation model, and the subsequent choice of a time incrementing mechanism is a question that must be answered by the analyst.

The choice of a particular time flow mechanism to be used in a simulation model will have a significant effect on the computer run time required for the tracking of the events and the updating of the master clock. Also, the choice of Δt in a fixed-time incrementing mechanism can have a critical influence on the simulation results, since it can cause two nonsimultaneous events to have occurred at the same point in time (see, for example, events e_2 and e_3 in Fig. 15.9). Thus, the next-event time incrementing procedure has the advantage of processing events as simultaneously occurring only when they do have identical occurrence times (see, for example, events e_4 and e_5 in Fig. 15.10).

The problems involved in the choice of a time flow mechanism have been investigated by Conway, Johnson, and Maxwell,[12] and Lave.[13] Shannon (1975, p. 114) indicates that a fixed-time incrementing method should be used when:

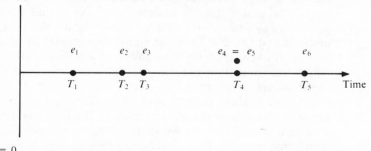

Initial
State, $T = 0$

FIGURE 15.10   Next Event Incrementing

---

[12] R. W. Conway, B. M. Johnson, and W. L. Maxwell, "Some Problems of Digital Systems Simulation," *Management Science* (October 1959).
[13] Roy E. Lave, "Timekeeping for Simulation," *The Journal of Industrial Engineering* (July 1967).

1. Events occur in a regular and fairly equally spaced manner.
2. A large number of events occur during some simulated time T and the mean length of events is short.
3. The exact nature of the significant events are not well known, such as the early part of a study.

Alternatively, he indicates that a next-event timekeeping method should be used when:

1. The system is static and no events occur for long periods of time. This will result in savings in computer time.
2. No knowledge of the size of the time increment to be used is available.
3. Events occur unevenly in time and/or the mean length of events is long.

When programming is done with a general purpose computer language, either time incrementing method can be employed. Some special purpose simulation languages may restrict the user to one method or the other.

15.6 DESIGN OF SIMULATION EXPERIMENTS

One of the most difficult tasks encountered in using a simulation modeling approach to the solution of a particular management science problem concerns the design of the appropriate simulation experiment. This task basically concerns the specification of a plan for obtaining and analyzing a set of data. The cost and quality of this information will be dependent upon the design of the simulation experiment that is employed. The experimental design that is used in a simulation experiment allows the analyst to gather the information needed to make valid inferences about the problem being investigated.

The design of simulation experiments is a complex and difficult area of study. A complete discussion of this topic is beyond the scope of this survey textbook. Thus, in this chapter we will attempt to consider some of the more salient aspects of the design of computer simulation experiments. Hopefully, this material will provide the reader with a background and an understanding of the terminology required for a more extensive study of this area. Several outstanding textbooks have been written dealing with the problems of constructing and analyzing experiments. Notable among these are books by Bartee,[14] Cochran and Cox,[15] Dixon and Massey,[16] and Hicks.[17] In addition, Naylor[18] has published an excellent monograph containing papers from a symposium in simulation experiment design. The more interested reader is referred to these sources for additional and ad-

---

[14] E. M. Bartee, *Engineering Experimental Design Fundamentals,* (Englewood Cliffs, N.J.: Prentice-Hall, Inc., 1968).

[15] W. G. Cochran, and G. M. Cox, *Experimental Designs,* (New York: John Wiley & Sons, Inc., 1957).

[16] W. J. Dixon, and E. J. Massey, Jr., *Introduction to Statistical Analysis* (New York: McGraw-Hill Book Company, 1957).

[17] C. R. Hicks, *Fundamental Concepts in the Design of Experiments* (New York: Holt, Rinehart & Winston, Inc., 1973).

[18] Thomas H. Naylor (ed.), *The Design of Computer Simulation Experiments,* (Durham, N.C.: The Duke University Press, 1969).

vanced material on this topic. The material that follows assumes a basic background in probability and statistics on the part of the reader.

The design of simulation experiments is largely based upon the statistical experimental design procedures that are used in physical experimentation. As a result, management scientists have generally tried to adopt known statistical experimental design procedures for simulation studies. It should be noted that such procedures may not be very appropriate for simulation studies for a number of reasons. First, most physical experiments involve some type of well-defined hypothesis that can be tested using standard statistical tests. Simulation experiments, however, usually are concerned with determining some sort of optimum condition, and statistical hypothesis testing may be more difficult in this instance. Second, many standard statistical testing procedures are based on the assumption that the separate observations of the variables being measured are uncorrelated and drawn from a normal distribution having the same parameters. In many simulation experiments we create multidimensional time series data that is correlated and not necessarily normal. Third, in physical experiments variability is beyond the control of the experimenter, while in simulation experiments, variability is typically designed as an important feature of the model. This variability must then be considered in the statistical analysis of the output results. In summary, it should be cautioned that, while much of the design of simulation experiments is based on standard statistical techniques, consideration should be given to the particular technique being employed and its underlying assumptions.

Simulation studies are generally complex and lengthy, involving a very large number of factors (independent variables), factor levels, and responses (dependent variables). Thus, tradeoffs in experimental design must be made in order to stay within cost and time resource boundaries. Depending on resource limitations and the purpose of the simulation study, Shannon (1975, p. 150) suggests that three broad types of analysis may be warranted.

1. A comparison of the means and variances of alternatives.
2. An analysis of the importance or effect of different independent variables.
3. A search for the optimal values of a set of variables.

Each of these types of experimentation will now be discussed.

15.6.1 Single-Factor Experimental Design

A comparison of the means and variances of alternatives involves **single-factor experimental design**. Herein, the modeler is concerned with measuring the response (dependent variable) as a function of a single factor (independent variable). Since variability will naturally be present, replication is necessary for accuracy and precision in the results. This replication has a cost in terms of computer time and analysis effort. Thus, there are a number of important considerations that affect the cost, accuracy, and precision of the simulation results. Among these considerations are the starting conditions and equilibrium, the determination of the sample size, and variance reduction techniques.

Most simulation models are designed with the objective of measuring equilibrium or steady-state operating conditions. Unfortunately, the inherent variability in most simulation models causes there to be a transient condition at the beginning of the simulation run. This transient condition is likely to be very atypical of the normal operating condition for the system being studied. For example, you will recall that we did not begin our inventory simulation run with zero random inventory present because this would be a very atypical condition. Now, there are a number of ways in which we can reduce the biasing effect of the initial transient period, including

1. Exclude a part of the early results produced during the simulation run.
2. Use a long enough time period for the simulation run to make insignificant the results obtained from the transient period at the beginning of the run.
3. Select the initial starting conditions so that they represent the actual steady-state conditions.

Each of these procedures has advantages and disadvantages in terms of cost and accuracy. It is not generally possible to completely determine when equilibrium has been reached. Often, the modeler will find it useful to make one or more pilot runs and examine the output, and then try to select a method for achieving equilibrium. Among suggestions made by other researchers are

1. Truncate the series of measurements until the first of the series is neither the maximum nor the minimum of the remaining set.[19]
2. Examine the sequence of observations from the simulation run. If the number of observations in which the output value is greater than the average value for the sequence is the same as the number of observations in which the output value is less than the average value for the sequence, then steady-state conditions may exist (Emshoff and Sisson 1970).
3. Compute a moving average for the output values, and when this moving average no longer changes over time, equilibrium may have been achieved (Emshoff and Sisson 1970).

A second important consideration is that of sample size. Herein, the analyst must decide on the sample size required to achieve statistical significance for a given expenditure for experimentation. Again, it is very difficult to consider all the approaches to sample size determination in this chapter. In general two approaches to sample size determination are used.

1. The sample size is determined prior to and independently of the operation of the model.
2. The sample size is determined during the operation of the model as a function of the results generated from the operation of the model.

Using the first approach the assumption is often made that the responses of the model are independent and normally distributed. Then, a confidence limit approach to determining the required sample size is used. For example, suppose that we are interested in determining the sample size based on a confidence interval for the mean. Suppose that we seek to determine an estimate $\bar{x}$ of the true population mean u, such that:

---

[19] Conway, R. W., "Some Tactical Problems in Digital Simulation," *Management Science*, 10, no. 2 (October 1963), 42.

$$P\{u - \epsilon \leq \bar{x} \leq u + \epsilon\} = 1 - \alpha \qquad (15\text{--}13)$$

where
$\bar{x}$ = sample mean
u = population mean
ϵ = tolerable error of the estimate
$1 - \alpha$ = probability that the interval $u \pm \epsilon$ contains $\bar{x}$.

Under the assumption of normality of the sampling distribution of $\bar{x}$, the required sample size can be shown to be

$$n = \frac{Z_{\alpha/2}^2 \sigma^2}{\epsilon^2} \qquad (15\text{--}14)$$

where
$Z_{\alpha/2}^2$ = standard normal deviate for $\alpha/2$
σ = population standard deviation
ϵ = tolerable error of the mean

To use this formula we must know σ, $Z_{\sigma/2}$, and ϵ. These values are estimated or determined as a result of a short pilot experiment.

Using the second approach to sample size determination, we compute the confidence intervals for the output values as they are generated during a simulation run and then terminate the run when a predefined confidence interval objective has been met. This approach involves setting an automatic stopping rule for the simulation. Two basic approaches can be used (Shannon 1975, p. 197).

1. Run the simulation in two stages. First, run a sample of size n and collect the resulting statistical information. Use these results to estimate n^*, using a statistical procedure such as that described above. If $n^* < n$, the run has been completed. If $n^* > n$, extend the run by $n^* - n$.
2. Specify a minimum n, and take a sample. Calculate the sample standard deviation s for this sample. Then, compute the quantity:

$$d = \frac{(s)t_{1-\alpha, n-1}}{\sqrt{n}} \qquad (15\text{--}15)$$

where
s = sample standard deviation
$t_{1-\alpha,\ n-1}$ = t statistic for $1 - \alpha$, $n - 1$ degrees of freedom
n = sample size

The quantity d is then compared to ϵ, and the simulation is terminated when $d \leq \epsilon$ for the first time.

A third major consideration is that of variance reduction. Since considerable computer time is usually required for simulation experimentation, the modeler should seek to gain as much and as precise information as is possible from a given sample size. This has led to the development of **variance reduction techniques** for increasing the precision of estimates for a fixed sample size or decreasing the sample size required to obtain a fixed degree of precision. Again, we will not attempt to survey this extensive area of study but will briefly discuss some of the basic techniques used for variance reduction.

To illustrate the idea of variance reduction consider the exponential distribution with a parameter $\theta = 2$. The probability density function for this exponential distribution is

$$f(x) = \frac{1}{\theta} e^{-x/\theta} = \frac{1}{2} e^{-x/2} \qquad (15-16)$$

The cumulative distribution function for this exponential distribution is

$$F(x) = 1 - e^{-x/2} \qquad (15-17)$$

Furthermore for this distribution, the mean $u = 1/\theta = 1/2$ is known.

Assume now that we do not know the value of the mean of the distribution and wish to estimate the value by using simulation. Using a straightforward simulation approach, sometimes referred to as a *crude* Monte Carlo approach, we would simply generate random observations from the exponential distribution having the properties specified above, and then use the average of these observations as an estimate of the mean. As determined earlier, Equation 15–11, the random observations would be given by:

$$x_i = \frac{-\ln (\text{R.N.})_i}{\theta}, \qquad \text{for } i = 1, 2, \ldots, n \qquad (15-18)$$

Assume that we proceed to generate 10 random decimal numbers and then use Equation 15–18 to compute 10 random observations. These results are summarized in Table 15.6. Then, the sum and mean of these 10 random observations is

$$\text{Sum} = 1.787$$
$$\text{Mean} = 1.787/10 = 0.179 \qquad (15-19)$$

Thus, the sample mean is 0.179, as opposed to the true mean, which is 0.500. This indicates that our crude Monte Carlo sampling procedure has not produced a very good estimate.

TABLE 15.6 Crude Monte Carlo Example

i	*Random Number* $(R.N.)_i$	*Random Observation* $x_i = \dfrac{-\ln (R.N.)_i}{2}$
1	0.75	0.144
2	0.73	0.157
3	0.29	0.618
4	0.67	0.200
5	0.81	0.105
6	0.87	0.069
7	0.57	0.281
8	0.93	0.036
9	0.73	0.157
10	0.96	0.020

TABLE 15.7   Complementary Random Number Example

i	Random Number $(R.N.)_i$	Random Observation	Complementary Random Number $(1-R.N.)_i$	Random Observation
1	0.75	0.144	0.25	0.693
2	0.73	0.157	0.27	0.651
3	0.29	0.618	0.71	0.171
4	0.67	0.200	0.33	0.550
5	0.81	0.105	0.19	0.833
6	0.87	0.069	0.13	0.020
7	0.57	0.281	0.43	0.422
8	0.93	0.036	0.07	1.333
9	0.73	0.157	0.27	0.650
10	0.96	0.020	0.04	1.605

Instead, let us now proceed to use the method of **complementary random numbers**. This method is a special case of the method of antithetic variates. The basic idea is to have two estimators of each random observation, with the first estimator x_1 having a negative correlation with the second estimator x_2. The combined average of the pairs of estimators will then tend to be closer to the mean. Using complementary random numbers we employ a random decimal number and the complement of this random decimal number to generate pairs of random observations and then compute an average from these pairs of random observations. This process is summarized in Table 15.7.

Then, the sum and mean of these paired random observations is

$$\text{Sum} = 9.715$$
$$\text{Mean} = 9.715/20 = 0.486$$

(15–20)

Thus, by using the method of complementary random number we have improved our estimate of the mean from 0.179 to 0.486. This latter estimate is very close to the true mean value of 0.500.

Other variance reduction techniques include stratified sampling, importance sampling, Russian roulette, splitting, and correlated sampling. The reader interested in learning more about these variance reduction methods is referred to the references given at the end of this chapter.

15.6.2   Multifactor Experimental Design

Multifactor experimental design involves situations in which two or more factors are of interest to the modeler. One design procedure used in multifactor experiments is to vary the levels of one factor at a time while keeping all other factors constant. This requires making a series of computer runs, whose number is given by:

$$N = pq^k$$

(15–21)

where k = number of factors (independent variables)
p = number of replications
q = number of factor levels

The number of replications required at each factor level is usually 10 or more. Thus, for a small number of factors and factor levels, a large number of computer runs may be required.

Reducing the number of computer runs required in a multifactor experiment requires the use of **full factorial experimental designs**, or, more often, **fractional factorial experimental designs**. The basic principles and methods of constructing factorial designs include those by Cochran and Cox[20] and Hicks.[21] The results obtained from either full factorial experiments or fractional experiments are then analyzed using analysis of variance techniques.[22]

To illustrate a symmetrical full factorial experiment, consider Table 15.8. In Table 15.8, we have two factors, A and B, which are each measured at two levels, using 5 replications. Note that this results in 10 measurements of factor A at each level and 10 measurements of factor B at each level. Additionally, we obtain a measurement of the AB interaction effect, as seen in the analysis of variance summary.

Fractional factorial designs are particularly useful for reducing the number of computer experiments that must be made. With a full factorial design the number of combinations to be tested can become large if more than a very few variables are tested. Additionally, higher-order interactions become numerous and are hard to analyze. If we are not interested in some of the higher-order interactions, then a large portion of the necessary information can be obtained by running only a fraction ($1/2$, $1/4$, or $1/8$) of the total combinations possible. Such a design is called a fractional factorial experiment. A problem, called **aliasing**, may exist when a fractional factorial design is used. Aliasing occurs when a statistic that measures one effect also measures another effect, and the two effects cannot be separated. Fortunately, tables of suggested fractional factorial experiments can be found in Cochran and Cox[23] and Davis.[24] The reader is referred to the sources for actual designs. Quite often, the modeler will use a fractional factorial design during the

TABLE 15.8 Symmetrical, Full Factorial Design (Two Factors, Two Levels)

			Analysis of Variance	
Factors	*A Level 1*	*A Level 2*	*Source*	*Degrees of Freedom*
B Level 1	XXXXX	XXXXX	A effect	1
			B effect	1
B Level 2	XXXXX	XXXXX	$A B$ interaction	1
Total			Error	16
				19

Replications

[20] W. G. Cochran, and G. M. Cox, *Experimental Designs* (New York: John Wiley & Sons, Inc., 1957).

[21] C. R. Hicks, *Fundamental Concepts in the Design of Experiments* (New York: Holt, Rinehart & Winston, Inc. 1973).

[22] John Neter, and William Wasserman, *Applied Linear Statistical Models* (Homewood, Ill.: Richard G. Irwin, Inc. 1974).

[23] Cochran and Cox, *Experimental Designs*.

[24] O. L. Davis, ed., *The Design and Analysis of Industrial Experiments* (New York: Hafner Publishing Company, 1963).

early stage of a study to explore the effect of a large number of variables. On the basis of this analysis, the number of variables of interest can often be reduced. Then, a full factorial design can be used for a more detailed analysis.

15.6.3   Sequential Search Procedures

In many simulation projects the objective may be that of determining the values or levels of the factors or independent variables that will yield the optimal (maximum or minimum) values of the responses or dependent variables. Given this objective, a **response surface methodology** is often an appropriate procedure. The theory and application of response surface methodology is rigorously discussed in a number of textbooks, including those by Cochran and Cox,[25] Davis,[26] Himmelblau,[27] and Saaty and Bram.[28] Again, this is a complex and extensive area of study and we will attempt only to provide a brief introduction to its potential use in simulation modeling.

The basic idea of a response surface involves a response variable, y, and several independent variables $(x_1, x_2, \ldots, x_n)$. The response surface is expressed as

$$y = f(x_1, x_2, \ldots, x_n) \qquad (15\text{--}22)$$

where the independent variables are assumed to be numerically measurable and continuous. Examples of two-dimensional response surfaces are shown in Fig. 15.11. In the two examples shown in Fig. 15.11 the solid lines are contours, or equal response lines, that connect the values of x_1 and x_2 that yield the same value of y. In the "rising ridge surface" the contours increase in value as we move upward and to the right in the x_1, x_2 plane. In the "minimax or saddle surface" there is one point, called the **saddle point**, from which the contours decrease in one direction while increasing in the other direction.

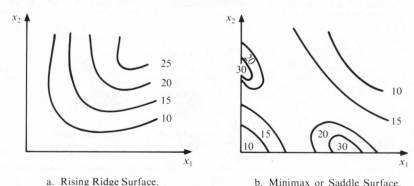

a. Rising Ridge Surface.   b. Minimax or Saddle Surface.

FIGURE 15.11   Two-Dimensional Response Surfaces

[25] *Experimental Design.*

[26] *The Design and Analysis of Industrial Experiments.*

[27] David M. Himmelblau, *Applied Nonlinear Programming* (New York: McGraw-Hill Book Company, 1972).

[28] Thomas L. Saaty, and Joseph Bram, *Nonlinear Mathematics* (New York: McGraw-Hill Book Company, 1964).

Response surface methodology involves the use of a series of small experiments utilizing full or fractional factorial designs. Quite often the **path of steepest ascent** is employed. Herein, the modeler conducts a simple experiment over a small area of the response surface. This small area is then considered to be a plane, and a first-order polynomial is used to fit the data that resulted from the initial experiment. This first-order polynomial is given by:

$$y = a_0 + a_1 x_1 + a_2 x_2 + \cdots + a_n x_n \tag{15-23}$$

From this equation, the modeler decides in which direction to move to conduct the next experiment. Since the optimum value of the response surface is desired, the direction chosen should be that which leads to the highest point of the response surface the fastest. This is then the path of steepest ascent. Note that this method does not indicate how far to move for conducting successive experiments, but indicates only the direction in which movement should occur.

To illustrate the method of steepest ascent consider the example shown in Fig. 15.12. Suppose that the modeler has run a small experiment in the neighborhood of point A. Using the data from this experiment the modeler can then compute a_0, a_1, and a_2, which then defines the response surface. The signs of a_0, a_1, and a_2 will determine the slope of the response surface and the direction of the greatest slope, or ascent, up the response surface. In Fig. 15.12 this is in the direction of the arrow marked with a B, which is at right angles to the contour lines. A second experiment is then conducted at some distance from A in this direction, and the response surface is again measured. Using this process, the modeler will obtain points of higher and higher response. As the optimum area is reached, the process becomes more difficult as higher order polynomials are required to describe the response surface. Consequently, other experimental designs are used when the area near the optimum is reached. Some useful designs for fitting second-order response surfaces are **central composite** or **rotatable designs**. The reader is referred to the references previously given for a more extensive discussion of these complicated designs.

15.7 USE OF A SPECIAL-PURPOSE SIMULATION LANGUAGE: AN EXAMPLE

Most simulation modeling work is performed using a digital computer. As noted previously, digital simulation modeling involves the use of both general and spe-

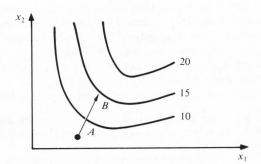

FIGURE 15.12 Gradient Search Example

cial purpose simulation languages. Earlier, in Section 15.3.3, we discussed general and special purpose simulation languages, and indicated some of the advantages and disadvantages of each. The use of a general purpose simulation language, FORTRAN IV, was then illustrated in the Star Metals Corporation case study. Let us now consider a simulation modeling example in which a special-purpose simulation language was found to be appropriate.

The simulation modeling effort arose in the context of a study[29] of the regional economy of the St. Louis, Missouri, Standard Metropolitan Statistical Area (SMSA). The objective of this study was to analyze this regional economy and to evaluate the prospective benefits of various locally conceived policies to engender economic renewal.

Structuring of the model to describe this regional economy focused on the operation of the local market for labor. In doing so it identified the important factors affecting the supply of labor, most of which were demographic, and the important determinants of demand, most of which were derived from the demand for the area's exports.

The demographic sector of the model specified the most important elements contributing to the supply of labor, namely: births, deaths, and migration. Births and deaths were projected on the basis of fertility and mortality rates. Migration was used as an equilibrating mechanism that balanced the demand for and the supply of labor. Migration was made dependent upon the unemployment rate in the St. Louis SMSA in relation to the unemployment rate in the United States, as a whole.

The employment sector of the model specified the most important elements contributing to the demand for labor using an "export base theory" of employment.[30] Thus, certain of the region's industries are viewed as selling the majority of their output outside the St. Louis SMSA. These "export" industries were the first major category in the employment sector. The second major category was "business serving" employment that was modeled to respond to the growth in other productive activities in the area. The final major category of the employment sector was "household serving" employment that was modeled to respond linearly to population growth.

Figure 15.13 depicts the primary linkages between the demographic and employment sectors of the model. It illustrates the principal role of migration and the unemployment rate in balancing population and employment levels.

The mathematical description of the model structure shown in Fig. 15.13 resulted in some 270 equations, which were nonlinear and recursive in nature. These equations involved variables that were continuous in value, but discrete over time. The mathematical structure (nonlinear and continuous equations) and size (≈ 270 equations) of this model precluded solution by any analytical method. Thus, a simulation approach was suggested. The choice between a general purpose and special-purpose simulation language was dictated by the fact that the model variables were continuous in value but discrete over time. On this basis the DYNAMO language was selected as being most appropriate.

The **DYNAMO** simulation language was developed at the Massachusetts In-

[29] A complete description of this research may be found in: Robert E. Markland and Peter J. Grandstaff, "Modeling Demographic-Employment Interactions In An Urban Economy," *Simulation* (February 1975), 33–43.

[30] R. W. Pfouts, ed., *The Techniques of Urban Economic Analysis* (Trenton, N.J.: Chandler-Davis Publishing Company, 1960).

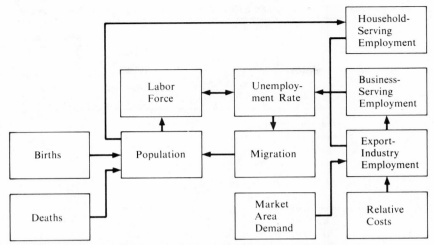

FIGURE 15.13 **Linkages Between Demographic and Employment Sectors**

stitute of Technology and utilizes first-order difference equations to approximate the continuous functions.[31] The state variables and output variables in a time dynamic simulation model are described in DYNAMO by level equations and rate equations, respectively. The state variables (levels) describe the state or condition of the system at a given time. The rate variables (rates) describe how the states change with the passage of time. Auxiliary equations, which are components of the rate equations, completely describe the function of rate equations. The auxiliary equations provide for the feedback control of the rates.

This model, programmed in DYNAMO, has been used to conduct a number of simulation experiments. One use of the model was to simulate various scenarios for the local economy, as they were suggested by local politicians, planners, and academicians. Three typical simulated scenarios were

1. No extraordinary events affect the local economy and no major policy actions are taken.
2. Local employment in motor-vehicle production decreases by 15 percent during 1970–79.
3. A concerted, sustained effort succeeds in reducing the indices of St. Louis' relative wages by 10 percent over a 15-year period.

The simulation output produced by DYNAMO is voluminous, as it is possible to track the value of each of the model variables, over time. Table 15.9 presents some comparisons concerning the levels and rates of changes of important variables in 10-year intervals for the three simulation experiments discussed above. Population did not grow rapidly in any of the three experiments. The experiment involving a reduction in the area's relative wage levels produced the best results with respect to improvement over time, of the variables of interest. The worst results were produced for the second simulation experiment, which involved a

---

[31] Alexander L. Pugh, *DYNAMO User's Manual* (Cambridge Mass.: M.I.T. Press, 1963).

TABLE 15.9 St. Louis SMSA Economy: Variable Levels and Changes

Output Data	Simulation Run		
	Baseline Case	Drop in Automobile Employment	Drop in Relative Cost of Labor
Initially, $T = 0$, 1970:			
Population, thousands	2370	2370	2370
Unemployment rate, %	5.5	5.5	5.5
Per-capita income, dollars	4200	4200	4200
After 10 years, $T = 10$, 1980:			
Population increase, %	5	4	5
Net migration, thousands	−56	−64	−45
Unemployment rate, %	5.8	6.0	5.4
Per-capita income increase, %	16	16	15
Export employment increase, %	−1	−3	4
Total employment increase, %	7	6	9
After 20 years, $T = 20$, 1990:			
Population increase, %	3	2	7
Unemployment rate, %	6.0	6.2	4.7
Per-capita income increase, %	35	35	35
Export employment increase, %	5	2	25

decline in automobile manufacturing, one of the area's most important export industries.

In addition to providing a voluminous and detailed tabular output DYNAMO affords the modeler an opportunity of obtaining plots of the simulation results. An example of such a plot is shown in Fig. 15.14. Figure 15.14 presents a plot of the migration and population variables for the "baseline" simulation experiment summarized in Table 15.9. Time is plotted vertically and the horizontal axes are labeled for the two variables. Thus, in Fig. 15.14 the vertical numbering (0, 10, and 20) indicates the passage of time over the 20-year span of the experiment, and the horizontal numbering, extending from 2200.T to 2500.T [T for thousand] indicates the range of the population (P) axis from 2,200,000 to 2,500,000 persons. The −30.T to 10.T labels indicate the range of the number of migrants (M) on net account from −30,000 to 10,000. This figure depicts that population of the area will grow moderately, according to the results of the simulation experiment. In 1980, the time of the next census, the graphical results suggest that the residents in the area may number 100,000 more than in 1970. Throughout the decade, however, net outmigration takes place at a level averaging about 5000 persons per year.

This simulation model has been used to conduct a number of other simulation experiments involving the identification of potential industrial sectors and industries that have particular importance to the aggregate growth of the region. Recent use of the model has concentrated on a series of simulation experiments involving an integrated set of beneficial policy actions, including faster growth in local federal employment, a decline in the area's relative wage levels, and growth in the area's transportation equipment production sector.

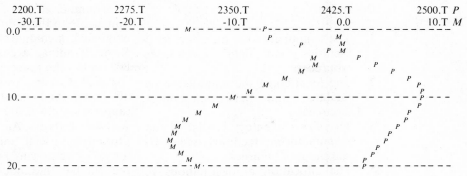

FIGURE 15.14   Population and Migration Changes—Baseline Run

15.8   CASE STUDY—WAREHOUSE LOCATION PLANNING

This case study involved a comprehensive simulation-modeling approach to the problem of locating warehousing facilities in a fashion that would minimize the cost associated with operating a multiproduct, multisource, multidestination distribution system. The simulation model described in this case study was designed, tested, and implemented within the actual production/distribution environment of the Ralston Purina Company, St. Louis, Missouri.

In order to facilitate our discussion, consider the following three-stage production-distribution network, given a company with m facilities (sources), located throughout the United States. These manufacturing facilities produce p various types of products that are then transported to c customers (destinations), either directly from the manufacturing facilities, or indirectly through any of w field warehouses (sources). All products are not necessarily produced at each manufacturing facility, nor necessarily stored at each warehousing facility. In addition, product movement may also occur between manufacturing facilities or between field warehouses. Finally, there is no stipulation that all types of products

must be shipped between all sources and all destinations.

The general location-allocation problem may now be stated as follows.

Given

1. The geographical location of each customer.
2. The product requirements of each customer, which are assumed not to be affected by the choice of facility through which shipments to that customer are routed.
3. A set of *transportation costs* associated with a movement of a particular product from sources to destinations, which are assumed to be linear functions of the distances traveled.
4. A set of *warehousing costs* associated with each source (manufacturing facility or field warehouse).
5. A set of *penalty costs* associated with either a delay or inability in satisfying a customer's order.
6. Possible inventory capacity restrictions at the manufacturing facilities and field warehouses.
7. Possible production capacity restrictions at the manufacturing facilities.

Determine

1. The number of manufacturing facilities and field warehouses (sources).
2. The location of the manufacturing facilities and field warehouses (sources).
3. The size (inventory levels) of the manufacturing facilities and field warehouses (sources).
4. The allocation of destinations to sources, for delivery purposes.

This must be done in a fashion that optimizes (minimizes) the resultant total cost of distribution. In the case study described herein, attention centered on the determination of the number and location of the warehousing facilities.

The purpose of any distribution system is to link production activity with consumer demand. Accordingly, goods are produced and distributed according to the demand of the consumers—the driving force in the distribution system. Therefore, the key to the analysis of any distribution system is the identification of the end-customer, or marketing-distribution unit. This identification is critical for two reasons. First, such marketing-distribution units are geographic subdivisions that contain certain demographic characteristics, which influence the marketing effort and hence the distribution pattern for that unit. Second, it was necessary from a practical viewpoint to define some type of geo-reference system for the end-customer that could be used to reduce or delimit the massive number of end-customers that are typically present in a geographic area such as the United States.[32] Consequently, our initial efforts entailed the definition of a suitable geo-reference system for the United States.

A number of geo-reference systems applicable to the United States were in existence, including the Rand McNally Basic Trading Areas (approximately 500 units), the Sales Management Metropolitan County Areas (approximately 300 units), the Picadid Key City System (approximately 2500 units), and the Railway Express Agency System (approximately 3600 units). Each of the above systems was rejected for use in the simulation model because of the large number of units required. The geo-reference system ultimately adopted for the simulation model utilized 137 "demand analysis areas" in the United States (including Hawaii and Alaska). These 137 demand analysis areas were defined as a result of three factors.

1. A consolidation of the 600 ZIP Code Sectional Center Areas, with the elimination of all split counties.
2. A matching of the consolidated ZIP Code Sectional Center Areas with the 200 major United States television markets, as defined by the American Research Bureau.
3. A matching of the known distribution patterns of 10 major United States food chains with the areas resulting from the first two factors considered above.

Such a system has a number of desirable features—the major ones being that the ZIP code was widely understood, was an integral part of the end-customer's mailing address, and provided a convenient entry port to the company's management information system. The geo-reference system described above was thus employed in a manner that reduced the original 20,000 end-customers in the distribution system to 137 demand analysis areas within which all customer shipment data was aggregated.

---

[32] The distribution system that was the subject of this study originally had some 20,000 end-customers.

The second major consideration in the design of the simulation model was the recreation of the product flows. An "industrial dynamics" format, based on the work of Jay Forrester,[33] was employed as a dynamic feedback-control mechanism in which product flow was the major control parameter. However, unlike Forrester, we considered the interactions and interrelationships between the *multiple* product flows present in the distribution system that was the subject of our analysis.

The production-distribution system was divided into three interconnected sectors. These sectors were

1. Wholesale sector (based on demand analysis areas)
2. Production sector
3. Distribution sector

Within each of the three sectors of the model, three sets of variables were considered.

1. *Levels*—quantities of product that were measurable when the system was at steady state (for example, inventory levels).
2. *Flows*—quantities of product required during a specified time period (for example, units of product demanded per month at the wholesale level).
3. *Delays*—a system characteristic that causes a delay in flow (for example, the shipping delay from manufacturing facility to wholesaler).

The interrelationships between the three sectors of the simulation model is presented in terms of the model variables in Fig. 15.15.

To facilitate an understanding of the discussion that follows, it is first necessary to define the variables and their corresponding indices, which will subsequently be utilized in the derivation of the simulation model. Thus, let the indices for the model variables be defined as follows in Exhibit A.

EXHIBIT A

c	$= 1, \ldots, C$	Customers
m	$= 1, \ldots, M$	Manufacturing facilities (plants)
p	$= 1, \ldots, P$	Products
t	$= 1, \ldots, T$	Time periods
w	$= 1, \ldots, W$	Warehouses (field warehouses).

Using these indices, let the model variables be defined as follows.

$SMW^t_{p,m,w}$	Amount of product p shipped from manufacturing facility m to field warehouse w in time period t.
$SMC^t_{p,m,c}$	Amount of product p shipped from manufacturing facility m to customer c in time period t.
$SWC^t_{p,w,c}$	Amount of product p shipped from field warehouse w to customer c in time period t.
SWW^t_{p,w,w^*}	Amount of product p shipped from field warehouse w to field warehouse w^* in time period t.
SMM^t_{p,m,m^*}	Amount of product p shipped from manufacturing facility m to manufacturing facility m^* in time period t.
$CMW_{p,m,w}$	Per-unit cost of shipping product p from manufacturing facility m to field warehouse w (constant over time).

[33] Jay Forrester, *Industrial Dynamics* (Cambridge, Mass.: The M.I.T. Press, 1961).

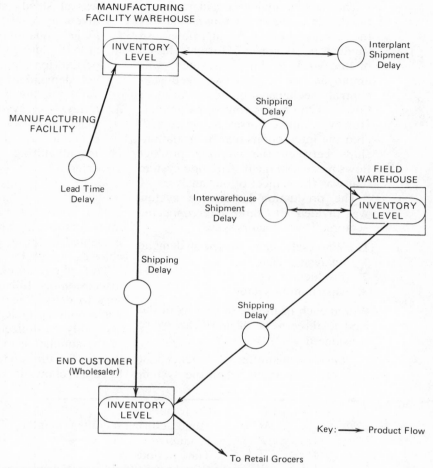

FIGURE 15.15 Interrelationships between Model Sectors

$CMC_{p,m,c}$	Per-unit cost of shipping product p from manufacturing facility m to customer c (constant over time).
$CWC_{p,w,c}$	Per-unit cost of shipping product p from field warehouse w to customer c (constant over time).
CWW_{p,w,w^*}	Per-unit cost of shipping product p from field warehouse w to field warehouse w^* (constant over time).
CMM_{p,m,m^*}	Per-unit cost of shipping product p from manufacturing facility m to manufacturing facility m^* (constant over time).
$IW_{p,w}^t$	Inventory of product p at field warehouse w in time period t.
$IM_{p,m}^t$	Inventory of product p at manufacturing facility warehouse m in time period t.
$ICW_{p,w}$	Inventory capacity for product p at field warehouse w (constant over time).

$ICM_{p,m}$	Inventory capacity for product p at manufacturing facility warehouse m (constant over time).
$PM_{p,m}^t$	Production of product p at manufacturing facility m in time period t.
$PCM_{p,m}$	Production capacity for product p at manufacturing facility m (constant over time).
FCM_m	Fixed cost of operating manufacturing facility warehouse m over $t = 1, \ldots T$.
FCW_w	Fixed cost of operating field warehouse w over $t = 1, \ldots, T$.
$VCM_{p,m}$	Variable unit warehousing cost for product p in manufacturing facility warehouse m.
$VCW_{p,w}$	Variable unit warehousing cost for product p in field warehouse w.
$X_m = \begin{Bmatrix} 1 \\ 0 \end{Bmatrix}$	If manufacturing facility warehouse m is utilized; otherwise.
$Y_w = \begin{Bmatrix} 1 \\ 0 \end{Bmatrix}$	If field warehouse w is utilized; otherwise.
$D_{c,p}^t$	Demand of customer c for product p in time period t.
$BC_{c,p}^t$	Backordering cost for customer c for product p in time period t.
$OC_{c,p}^t$	Order shifting cost for customer c for product p in time period t.

On the basis of the above specification of variables, the mathematical structure of the simulation model can now be defined by the following equations and contraints. Let *customer demand* (product flow) be defined by the following set of equations.

$$D_{c,p}^t = \Sigma_{m=1}^M SMC_{p,m,c}^t + \Sigma_{w=1}^W SWC_{p,w,c}^t \tag{15-24}$$

$c = 1, \ldots, C; p = 1, \ldots, P; t = 2, \ldots, T$

Let *manufacturing facility inventory levels* be defined by the following set of equations.

$$IW_{p,w}^t = IW_{p,w}^{t-1} + \Sigma_{m=1}^M SMW_{p,m,w}^{t-1} + \Sigma_{\substack{w=1 \\ w \neq w^*}}^W SWW_{p,w,w^*}^{t-1} - \Sigma_{\substack{w^*=1 \\ w^* \neq w}}^W SWW_{p,w,*,w}^{t-1}$$
$$- \Sigma_{c=1}^C SWC_{p,w,c}^{t-1} \tag{15-25}$$

$c = 1, \ldots, C; p = 1, \ldots, P; t = 2, \ldots, T$

Let *manufacturing facility inventory levels* be defined by the following set of equations.

$$IM_{p,m}^t = IM_{p,m}^{t-1} + PM_{p,m,}^t + \Sigma_{\substack{m=1 \\ m \neq m^*}}^M SMM_{p,m,m^*}^{t-1} - \Sigma_{\substack{m^*=1 \\ m^* \neq m}}^M \tag{15-26}$$

$$SMM_{p,m^*,m}^{t-1} - \Sigma_{w=1}^W SMW_{p,m,w}^{t-1} - \Sigma_{c=1}^C SMC_{p,m,c}^t$$

$c = 1, \ldots, C; p = 1, \ldots, P; t = 2 \ldots, T$

Furthermore we must constrain *production and inventory capacities* as follows.

$$IW^t_{p,w} \leq ICW_{p,w} \qquad \text{over all } p,w,t$$

(Field warehouse inventory capacity cannot be exceeded)

(15–27)

$$IM^t_{p,m} \leq ICM_{p,m} \qquad \text{over all } p,m,t$$

(Manufacturing facility warehouse inventory capacity cannot be exceeded)

(15–28)

$$PM^t_{p,m} \leq PCM_{p,m} \qquad \text{over all } p,m,t$$

(Manufacturing facility production capacity cannot be exceeded)

(15–29)

Finally, we seek to minimize the *total cost of distribution*, defined as follows.

$$
\begin{aligned}
\text{Minimize } Z = \; & \Sigma_{t=1}^{T} \Sigma_{p=1}^{P} \Big[\Sigma_{m=1}^{M} \Sigma_{w=1}^{W} SMW^t_{p,m,w} \, CMW_{p,m,w} \\
& + \Sigma_{m=1}^{M} \Sigma_{c=1}^{C} SMC^t_{p,m,c} \, CMC_{p,m,c} + \Sigma_{w=1}^{W} \Sigma_{c=1}^{C} SWC^t_{p,w,c} \, CWC_{p,w,c} \\
& + \Sigma_{\substack{w=1 \\ w \neq w^*}}^{W} SWW^t_{p,w,w^*} \, CWW_{p,w,w^*} - \Sigma_{\substack{w^*=1 \\ w^* \neq w}}^{W} SWW^t_{p,w^*,w} \, CWW_{p,w^*,w} \\
& - \Sigma_{\substack{m=1 \\ m \neq m^*}}^{M} SMM^t_{p,m,m^*} \, CMM_{p,m,m^*} - \Sigma_{\substack{m^*=1 \\ m^* \neq m}}^{M} SMM^t_{p,m^*,m} \, CMM_{p,m^*,m} \\
& + \Sigma_{m=1}^{M} VCM_{p,m} \, X_m (\Sigma_{w=1}^{W} SMW^t_{p,m,w} + \Sigma_{c=1}^{C} SMC^t_{p,m,c} \\
& + \Sigma_{\substack{m=1 \\ m \neq m^*}}^{M} SMM^t_{p,m,m^*} + \Sigma_{\substack{m^*=1 \\ m^* \neq m}}^{M} SMM^t_{p,m^*,m}) + \Sigma_{w=1}^{W} VCW_{p,w} \, Y_w \\
& (\Sigma_{c=1}^{C} SWC^t_{p,w,c} + \Sigma_{\substack{w^*=1 \\ w \neq w^*}}^{W} SWW^t_{p,w,w^*} + \Sigma_{\substack{w^*=1 \\ w^* \neq w}}^{W} SWW^t_{p,w^*,w}) \\
& + \Sigma_{c=1}^{C} BC^t_{c,p} + \Sigma_{c=1}^{C} OC^t_{c,p} \Big] + \Sigma_{m=1}^{M} FCM_m + \Sigma_{w=1}^{W} FCW_w
\end{aligned}
$$

(15–30)

subject to Equations 15–24, 15–25, 15–26; Constraints 15–27, 15–28, 15–29, with all product flows being zero or positive.

Several comments concerning the problem formulation presented above are in order. First, observe that the entire model is constructed within an industrial dynamics framework, with the product flows and inventory levels being defined by sets of first-order-difference equations. In reality, we were attempting to model a closed-loop, continuous flow system. The interactions between the variables and parameters of this system were also continuous, and were theoretically defined by a series of differential equations involving continuous time integrals. How-

ever, since we were constrained to use of a digital computer, we utilized a series of first-order-difference equations as discrete approximations to the continuous time integrals. The delay factor employed within these difference equations was assumed to be 1 month—that is, the length of the time period t was specified as 1 month. This determination would generally be based upon the company's reporting system, and the desired application of the model.

Second, note the size, detail, and complexity of the model. It explicitly considered flows of product directly from manufacturing facilities to end-customers, from manufacturing facility to manufacturing facility, and from warehouse to warehouse. In addition, we allowed for inventories at manufacturing facilities as well as at field warehouses, and included two types of penalty costs.

Finally, witness that the size of the problem, as formulated above, and the inherent nonlinearities in its objective function precluded the application of purely analytical techniques, such as linear or integer programming. Nonlinearities were present in two major segments of the objective function—the transportation costs associated with the various product movements, and the warehousing costs associated with storage and handling at the various warehousing facilities. In general, we used the simulation model itself to describe and account for these nonlinearities. Specifically, the transportation cost associated with a particular shipment was simulated as a function of the weight of the shipment, the method of shipment employed, and the distance involved in the movement. This procedure provided a close approximation to the transportation cost, which was a (strictly) concave function of shipment volume. The warehousing cost was composed of a fixed-charge element and a variable element, which was again a (strictly) concave function of the volume of shipments through a particular warehouse. The fixed-cost element of warehousing cost was approximated from existing company data and included such items as negotiation, bookkeeping, and administration costs. The variable cost element was approximated linearly. This approximation was considered satisfactory over the range of volumes of shipment encountered in actually testing the model, particularly when the ease of adding or deleting the space used in a public warehouse was noted.

The basic structure of the simulation model was modular in nature and was organized as follows.[34]

1. Data Base Module—a series of COBOL subroutines used to create and update the data base.
2. Computational Module—a series of FORTRAN IV subroutines used to recreate the product flows, perform the simulation experiments, and compute the costs associated with alternative warehousing networks.
3. Retrieval Module—a series of FORTRAN IV subroutines used for random accessing between the data base and the main program.

The data base was generated from the company's existing management information system and was composed of customer demand, shipment, and production data for the 27-month period of January 1968 through March 1970. This data base was maintained on a disk file and accessed when required by a series of retrieval subroutines. The computational module, the major component of the total model, will be described in detail below.

The computational module utilized the retrieval subroutines to recreate the actual product flows from which alternative warehousing configurations were tested. Initially, a series of input arrays for the particular simulation run were specified. These included the following.

1. Manufacturing Facility/Field Warehouse Location Array—a variable array of the geographic coordinates (latitude and longitude) of each manufacturing facility and field warehouse to be included in the

---

[34] More details concerning the development of the simulation model can be found in: Robert E. Markland, "Analyzing Geographically Discrete Warehousing Networks by Computer Simulation," *Decision Sciences,* vol. 4, no. 2 (April 1973), published by the American Institute for Decision Sciences.

simulation run, which was altered for each simulation run.

2. End-Customer Location Array—a constant array of the geographic coordinates for each end-customer (demand analysis area) in the section of the United States encompassed by the model.

3. Transportation Rate Array—a constant array of the transportation rates associated with all possible moves between sources and destinations. *Note*: Transportation rates were specified in terms of cost per unit distance (cost per mile) for a particular mode of transportation (rail or truck) and freight class.

4. Fixed and Variable Inventory Cost Array—a set of four constant arrays containing the fixed and variable costs associated with manufacturing facility warehouses and field warehouses.

5. Inventory Capacity Arrays—a set of two constant arrays specifying the inventory capacities at the manufacturing facility warehouse and field warehouses.

6. Production Capacity Array—a constant array specifying the production capacities at the manufacturing facilities.

7. Product Availability Array—a variable zero-one decision matrix specifying the availability of each product at each facility, which was altered for each simulation run.[35]

8. Initial Inventory Availability Array—a constant array of the initial inventory available at the various facilities for the various products. This array was determined for various points in time by analysis of actual inventory data.

In addition to these arrays, the cost of order shifting and backordering were also specified, and the probability distributions subsequently used for simulating the source of shipments (manufacturing facilities or field warehouses), mode of shipment (truck or rail), and freight class of shipment were initialized. These costs and probability distributions were again determined empirically by using actual data for the time period spanned by the model.

Having specified the basic parameters for the model, each simulation run was begun by initializing the time period loop, i.e., set $t = 1$. This was followed by an adjustment of the inventory levels at the manufacturing facility warehouses and field warehouses, using Equations 15–25 and 15–26. Inventory capacities and production capacities were then checked, using Constraints 15–27, 15–28, and 15–29. Additionally, all facilities were searched for backordered quantities, and any backorders in existence were filled from existing inventories prior to initialization of the customer demand (order) loop.

The customer demand (order) loop was next initialized, i.e., demand for customer $c = 1$ was simulated. A customer demand or order was composed of a request for a certain amount of one or more products, with customer demand data again being obtained by a retrieval subroutine. This in turn required the initialization of the product loop, i.e., set $p = 1$. Within the product loop the simulation proceeded by determination of the "source of shipment"—that is, by determination of whether the product was shipped from a manufacturing facility or field warehouse—on the basis of previously specified probability distributions. Having determined that the order was to be supplied by a field warehouse (manufacturing facility warehouse), the

---

[35] Note that a "zero" in the "product availability array" effectively initialized the corresponding initial inventory level in the "initial inventory availability array" to zero.

location of the nearest field warehouse (manufacturing facility warehouse) having the product available was ascertained, using a simple heuristic search procedure.

> Facility Search Heuristic: Search possible facilities in order of increasing distance from the end-customer placing the order. If order is for a field warehouse, search all field warehouses first, then search all manufacturing warehouses. Do the opposite if the order is for a manufacturing facility warehouse. If the order is satisfied by a field warehouse (manufacturing facility warehouse) which is not the closest to the end-customer, compute a cost of order shifting which represents the customer's loss in goodwill from having his shipment delayed. If the order cannot be satisfied at any facility, create a backorder and compute a backordering cost which represents the customer's loss in goodwill from his demand not being satisfied. Utilize the same process for the situation in which the order can partially be satisfied at a facility, i.e., move from facility to facility, in order of increasing distance, until the order is completely satisfied or a backorder is requested.

Once the location of the source of shipment had been ascertained, the "mode of shipment" (truck or rail) was simulated for previously determined probability distributions. The railroad or highway mileage between the source and destination of the shipment was then computed using a program that converted geographic coordinates to Cartesian coordinates, and Cartesian coordinates to linear distances. Finally, the cost associated with the shipment was computed by multiplying the distance involved in the move by the cost per unit distance, where cost per unit distance was a function of the product type, mode of shipment, and freight class.

Having determined the source, destination, and amount of the product being shipped, we again adjusted the inventories at the facility or facilities involved and computed the variable cost of inventorying at the facility or facilities involved. We then accumulated the inventory and transportation costs associated with the product shipment, and we looped back through the same process for products ($p = 2, \ldots, P$) for the first customer's order.

This process was then repeated for customer orders, $c = 2, \ldots, C$, and for time periods, $t = 2, \ldots, T$, for all products. After all time periods had been simulated we computed and accumulated the fixed costs associated with maintaining inventories at the various facilities. The final step in the program involved printing of a series of reports that summarized the costs associated with each facility, and in total, for a particular simulation run.

Simulation experiments were conducted to answer two major strategic questions.

1. What is the optimum field warehouse configuration, in terms of the number and location of field warehouses, given that the optimum configuration must be some subset of the currently existing network?[36]

2. What is the optimum inventory

---

[36] We adopted a "drop" strategy because management was primarily concerned with consolidating or closing the existing warehouses. In addition, an "add" strategy could have required the consideration of routes or facilities for which cost information was not readily available.

level for the currently existing field warehouse network?

The simulation experiments were conducted using a prototype geographical area of the United States that included 29 demand analysis areas. This consisted of all, or a portion of, 10 Midwestern states. Accordingly, the simulation experiments were restricted to interaction between the customers, manufacturing facilities, and field warehouse within these areas. The field warehouses were located in Chicago, Illinois; East Peoria, Illinois; Fostoria, Ohio; Indianapolis, Indiana; and Milwaukee, Wisconsin. The manufacturing facilities and their associated warehouses were located in Battle Creek, Michigan; Cincinnati, Ohio; Clinton, Iowa; and Davenport, Iowa.

Using the prototype described above, 32 field warehouse location patterns were simulated and tested in order to answer the first of the two strategic questions. Each location pattern was one of the possible combination of 5, 4, 3, 2, 1, or 0 field warehouses that could be chosen from the existing 5 field warehouse network.[37] Using the same prototype, the second strategic question was investigated by simulating the behavior of the existing distribution system (5 field warehouses and 4 plant warehouses) under 11 hypothetical inventory levels.

A summary of simulation test results for the first strategic question is presented in Table 15.10. For warehouse configurations having more than one combination (e.g., there are 10 possible 2-warehouse combinations that can be chosen from among 5 possible warehouse locations), only the minimum cost combination is shown. As can be seen from Table 15.10, the lowest total

distribution cost was obtained for a 3-warehouse configuration.

Examining the optimum warehouse configuration, it was apparent that the warehousing costs for the 3-warehouse configuration were reduced from those produced for the existing 5-warehouse configuration, simply because less warehouses were employed. However, the optimum (minimum total cost of distribution) network resulted primarily from a configuration in which total transportation costs were minimized. Basically, about 60 to 70 percent of the total cost of distribution was composed of transportation costs. Thus, the warehousing configuration that minimized this component of the total cost of distribution also minimized the total cost of distribution itself. The penalty costs associated with the various warehousing configurations were not of major importance. Indeed, the optimum warehousing configuration (three warehouses) had a relatively high set of penalty costs ($13,000). However, penalty costs cannot be completely ignored despite their relatively small magnitude, because they are a reflection of the service level being provided by the distribution system.

A summary of simulation test results for the second strategic question is presented in Table 15.11. As can be seen from Table 15.11, an 85-percent inventory level produced the optimum (minimum) total cost of distribution. It should be noted that all of the inventory levels shown in Table 15.11 were defined on the basis of a hypothetical 100-percent inventory level. The 100-percent inventory level was defined as the case in which any source can supply any product and in which the amount demanded at a particular facility never exceeds the inventory capacity of that

---

[37] Each field-warehouse-location pattern was generated by use of the previously described product availability array.

TABLE 15.10 Distribution Cost Summary (Three-Month Period) Alternative Warehouse Locations ($000)

Type of Cost	Five Field Warehouses	Four[a] Field Warehouses	Three[a] Field Warehouses	Two[a] Field Warehouses	One[a] Field Warehouses	Zero Field Warehouses
Transportation Costs[b]						
Mfg. Facility → Customer	$514	$530	$525	$567	$574	$665
Mfg. Facility → Field Warehouse	36	30	20	17	10	0
Field Warehouse → Customer	60	51	42	20	28	0
Subtotal	610	611	587	604	612	665
Warehousing Costs						
Field Warehouses	30	25	16	13	6	0
Mfg. Facility Warehouses	303	304	310	313	316	320
Subtotal	333	329	326	326	322	320
Penalty Costs						
Order Shifting Costs	12	8	9	7	5	22
Backordering Costs	4	2	4	4	3	4
Subtotal	16	10	13	11	8	26
Total Distribution Cost	$959	$950	$926	$941	$942	$1011

[a] Minimum cost combination for the particular warehouse configuration.
[b] Transportation costs associated with interplant and interwarehouse shipments are not shown, for the sake of brevity. They were of small magnitude and did not vary significantly between the various simulation runs.

TABLE 15.11 Distribution Cost Summary (Three-Month Period) Alternative Inventory Levels ($000)

| Type of Cost | Inventory Level | | | | | | | | | | |
	100%	95%	90%	85%[a]	80%	75%	70%	65%	60%	55%	50%
Transportation Costs[b]											
Mfg. Facility → Customer	$ 460	660	594	543	559	575	613	638	694	736	761
Mfg. Facility → Field Warehouse	147	45	40	36	41	36	38	39	41	43	44
Field Warehouse → Customer	235	64	50	58	58	58	61	71	60	50	52
Subtotal	842	769	684	637	658	669	713	748	795	829	857
Warehousing Costs											
Field Warehouse	318	28	27	26	26	25	25	24	24	24	23
Mfg. Facility Warehouses	71	303	304	305	306	307	308	309	310	310	312
Subtotal	389	331	331	331	332	332	333	333	334	334	335
Penalty Costs											
Order Shifting Costs	0	11	9	11	12	11	12	13	14	15	16
Backordering Costs	0	3	3	3	3	3	3	3	3	4	4
Subtotal	0	14	12	14	15	14	15	16	17	19	20
Total Distribution Cost	$1231	1114	1027	982	1005	1015	1061	1097	1146	1182	1212

[a] Minimum cost inventory level.
[b] Transportation costs associated with interplant and interwarehouse shipments are not shown for the sake of brevity. They were of small magnitude and did not vary significantly between the various simulation runs.

facility. The 100-percent inventory level case nominally represents a situation in which a 100-percent service level to customers is provided, and all of the other cases represent situations in which the service level is reduced. Finally, it should be stressed that the simulation results dealing with the second strategic question are largely theoretical, as the actual service level provided by the existing warehouse network was unknown.

The production and inventory control aspects of the simulation experiments were also considered but were of relatively minor importance. In no instance were inventory capacity constraints at either the field warehouses or the plant warehouses exceeded. Likewise, the production capacities of the plants were not exceeded in any of the simulation experiments. One obvious extension of the present work would be to test the effect of beginning the simulation experiments with differing inventory levels.

Validation of the operation and output of the simulation model described in this paper was an elusive task, as is the case for most simulation models. Statistical validation of the output was irrelevant, since the model was not employed in a statistical sense. Furthermore, actual historical data comparable to that produced by the simulation experiment were not available. As a result of these factors, model validity was largely considered in terms of: Have we adequately described the distribution system we are trying to model? This meant that we were constrained to use of tests of reasonableness and tests of completeness, and in this regard we re-

ceived user and management support as to the model's accuracy in describing the physical distribution system. In addition, an independent audit of the costs associated with operating the various field warehouses used in our prototype supported the findings of our simulation experiments.

This case has described the design and application of a dynamic simulation model to the problem of determining an optimum warehousing configuration within the context of a total physical distribution system. The application of a simulation methodology to this problem offered four major advantages.

1. It allowed great flexibility in terms of modeling the complex aspects of the problem.
2. It enabled consideration of the total size of the problem.
3. The dynamic structure of the physical distribution system was accurately described.
4. The inherent nonlinearities of the distribution system's cost function were adequately considered.

Using the simulation methodology described herein, we were able to analyze all possible warehouse network configurations that could result from a reduction of the present warehouse network. In attacking this question, we were able to define a globally optimum three-warehouse configuration. Additionally, the simulation methodology was used to analyze the costs resulting from various inventory levels. The results for this question were much more theoretical but were, nevertheless, of considerable value to management.

15.9 CONCLUSION

A simulation-modeling effort generally encompasses total systems design. This occurs because more and more frequently, business studies involve complex systems composed of large numbers of variables, each interacting with the other according to (complicated) performance rules. Consequently, complex systems must be analyzed as a whole and not as sums of their component parts, because, if total systems interactions are not considered, it is very easy to suboptimize. By suboptimize, we mean the process in which modules of a system are analyzed and locally optimized, often in a fashion that does not produce an optimized total system. Thus, as the scope of business studies has broadened, the concomitant effect has been to transfer the consideration of such problems from purely analytical methods to the experimental methods of simulation. In fact, it is common to find the terms "systems simulation" and "simulation" used interchangeably.

There have been numerous applications of simulation modeling in a wide variety of business and managerial situations. A study of the nonacademic members of the Operations Research Society of America indicated that simulation had the third highest value of all the management science techniques being used by practitioners.[38] Simulation modeling offers the basic advantage of being a highly flexible experimental tool that can be applied to complex, ill-structured, total systems problems. Additionally, it can be employed in instances where purely analytical models would be very difficult to design and implement. Simulation modeling also allows for compression of time, and systems or processes with long time frames may thus be analyzed rapidly using simulation. In some instances simulation may be the only way of studying a system without changing the system. For example, we could simulate the effect of making a change in a physical distribution system without actually incurring the cost and possible system disruption from making such a change. Finally, the analyst and manager may gain valuable insights from designing and implementing a simulation model. Quite often, the importance of specific variables will become apparent during a simulation study.

Although simulation modeling is a very important and useful management science tool, it should not be regarded as a panacea and used indiscriminately. Simulation models are inherently time consuming and costly to construct and run on digital computers. Additionally, simulation results may be imprecise and very hard to validate. Finally, simulation provides only statistical estimates rather than exact results. Thus, the judgments of the analyst and the manager are required to compare alternatives and to select a course of action.

In summary, simulation modeling is more of an art than a science. Nevertheless, it is a very flexible and useful tool for the management scientist who can master the art of simulation modeling.

GLOSSARY OF TERMS

Additive, Multiplicative, and Mixed Congruential Methods   Methods for generating pseudorandom numbers.

Aliasing   A problem that may result when a fractional factorial design is used; it occurs when a statistic that measures one effect also measures another effect, and the two effects cannot be separated.

Analytical Techniques   Management science techniques that result in the determination of a single "best" answer (e.g., linear programming).

---

[38] R. E. Shannon, and W. E. Biles, "The Utility of Certain Topics to Operations Research Practitioners," *Operation Research,* vol. 18, no. 4 (July–August 1970).

Central Composite or Rotatable Designs   Experimental designs for fitting second-order response surfaces.

Complementary Random Number   Given a random number $R.N.$, its complement is defined as $1 - R.N.$

Components   The entities of a system that are to be independently identified and whose collective performance determines the output of the system.

Congruent Modulo m   Two integer numbers x and y are said to be congruent modulo m (where m is an integer) if, and only if, there is an integer k such that $(x - y) = km$.

Continuous Change Model   A simulation model that uses a fixed-time incrementing time flow mechanism and is appropriate if the system being analyzed involves a continuous flow of information or events considered in an aggregate rather than in an individual sense.

Discrete Change Model   A simulation model that uses a next-event incrementing time flow mechanism and is appropriate if the system being analyzed involves a consideration of individual events.

DYNAMO   A special-purpose simulation language that uses first-order difference equations to model continuous relationships.

Endogenous Variables   The dependent or output variables of the system that are generated from the interaction of the system's exogenous and status variables.

Exogenous Variables   The input or independent variables of the system that are usually predetermined.

Experimental Techniques   Management science techniques that usually result in a series of answers any one of which may be acceptable to the decision maker.

Fixed-Time Incrementing or Fixed-Time Step Incrementation   A simulation process in which the system clock is advanced a fixed-time increment.

Fractional Factorial Experimental Design   An experimental design where some factor-level combinations are excluded from the experiment.

Full Factorial Experimental Design   An experimental design where all factor-level combinations are included in the experiment.

Monte Carlo Method   A sampling process used to randomly select sample values from a probability distribution.

Multifactor Experimental Design   An experimental design used to model a situation in which the effect of two or more factors on the response variable is of interest.

Next-Event Incrementing or Next-Event Step Incrementation   A simulation process in which the system clock is advanced to the time of the next event when that event occurs.

Parameters   Those attributes of the system that do not change during the simulation.

Path of Steepest Ascent   A direction that leads to the highest point of a response surface the fastest.

Pseudorandom Numbers   A sequence of numbers that is reproducible, predictable, and that occurs randomly, which is generated by some mathematical process.

Random Number   A random variable uniformly distributed over the unit interval 0 to 1.

Random Number Generator   A mechanical device or computer subroutine that generates the random numbers used in the Monte Carlo Method.

Relationships The connections between components, variables, and parameters that control the changes of state in the system.

Response Surface The response surface is expressed as $y = f(x_1, x_2, \ldots, x_m)$, where the independent variables are assumed to be numerically measurable and continuous.

Response Surface Methodology A procedure that can be used when the objective of the simulation project is to determine the values or levels of the factors or independent variables which will yield the optimal value of the response or dependent variable.

Saddle Point A point in a two-dimensional response surface from which the contours decrease in one direction while increasing in the other direction.

Seed A starting number used to generate a sequence of pseudorandom numbers.

Simulation Modeling A numerical technique for conducting experiments on a digital computer, which involves certain types of mathematical and logical models that describe the behavior of a business or economic system over extended periods of real time.

Single-Factor Experimental Design An experimental design in which the modeler is concerned with measuring the response as a function of a single factor.

Status Variables Variables used to describe the state of the system and its components at a point in time. The status variables interact with both the exogenous and endogenous variables of the system according to the functional and structural relationships of the system.

Stratified Sampling, Importance Sampling, Russian Roulette, Splitting and Correlated Sampling Different variance reduction techniques used in simulation.

Time Flow Mechanism An integral part of simulation model design, as it causes the various events to occur in the proper order and with the proper time interval between successive events.

Transient Conditions The variability in the output of a simulation experiment that results from the initial starting conditions.

Validation of the Simulation Model The determination of how closely the simulation model predicts the behavior of the physical system or managerial process being examined.

Variables Those attributes of the system that take on different values under different conditions or in different system states.

Variance Reduction Techniques Techniques for increasing the precision of estimates for a fixed sample size or for decreasing the sample size required to obtain a fixed degree of precision.

SELECTED REFERENCES

SIMULATION MODELING

Bonini, Charles P. 1963. *Simulation of Information and Decision Systems in the Firm.* Englewood Cliffs, N.J.: Prentice-Hall, Inc.

Chorafas, D. N. 1965. *Systems and Simulation.* New York, Academic Press, Inc.

Emshoff, James R., and Roger L. Sisson. 1970. *Design and Use of Computer Simulation Models.* New York: Macmillan Publishing Company, Inc.

Gordon, Geoffrey. 1978. *System Simulation.* Englewood Cliffs, N.J.: Prentice-Hall, Inc.

Hammersley, J. M., and D. C. Handscomb. 1964. *Monte Carlo Methods.* London: Methuen; New York: John Wiley & Sons, Inc.

Hoggatt, Austin C., and Frederick E. Balderstron, eds. 1963. *Symposium on Simulation*

Models: Methodology and Applications to the Behavioral Sciences. Cincinnati: Southwestern Publishing Company.

Korn, Granino A. 1966. *Random Process Simulation and Measurements*. New York: McGraw-Hill Book Company.

Meier, Robert C., William T. Newell, and Harold L. Pazer. 1969. *Simulation in Business and Economics*. Englewood Cliffs, N.J.: Prentice-Hall, Inc.

Mihram, G. Arthur. 1972. *Simulation: Statistical Foundations and Methodology*. New York: Academic Press, Inc.

Mize, Joe H., and J. Grady Cox. 1968. *Essentials of Simulation*. Englewood Cliffs, N.J. Prentice-Hall, Inc.

Naylor, Thomas H. 1971. *Computer Simulation Experiments with Models of Economic Systems*. New York: John Wiley & Sons, Inc.

Naylor, Thomas H., Joseph L. Balintfy, Donald S. Burdick, and Kong Chu. 1966. *Computer Simulation Techniques*. New York: John Wiley & Sons, Inc.

Schmidt, J. W., and R. E. Taylor. 1970. *Simulation and Analysis of Industrial Systems*. Homewood, Ill.: Richard D. Irwin, Inc.

Shannon, Robert E. 1975. *Systems Simulation*. Englewood Cliffs, N.J.: Prentice-Hall, Inc.

Smith, Wilfred Nye, Elmer E. Estey, and Ellsworth F. Vines, 1968. *Integrated Simulation*. Cincinnati: Southwestern Publishing Company.

Thorelli, Hans, B., and R. L. Graves. 1964. *International Operations Simulation*. New York: The Free Press.

Tocher, K. D. 1963. *The Art of Simulation*. Princeton, N.J.: D. Van Nostrand & Company.

RAND Corporation. 1955. *A Million Random Digits with 100,000 Normal Deviates*. Santa Monica, Calif.: The Free Press.

Watson, Hugh J. 1981. *Computer Simulation in Business*. New York: John Wiley & Sons, Inc.

DISCUSSION QUESTIONS

1. What is the main difference between experimental techniques (such as simulation) and analytical techniques (such as linear programming)?
2. When is simulation an appropriate technique to use?
3. What is the difference between a constant and a parameter?
4. Why is "flowcharting" so important in the computerization of the simulation model?
5. What are the advantages and disadvantages of a special-purpose simulation language?
6. What area in the field of simulation is still relatively "vague"?
7. When would it be appropriate to use statistical tests for validating the simulation output?
8. Are observations generated randomly in the Monte Carlo Method?
9. Why do you want to use a uniform distribution for generating random numbers? Why do the random numbers have to lie between 0 and 1?
10. What is the difference between a set of "random numbers" and a set of "pseudorandom numbers"?
11. Judge this statement: A pseudorandom number generator is able to generate an infinite number of random integers.
12. What is the difference between the uniformly generated random numbers and the random numbers generated via some probability function?
13. Why do you think a "small sample" for $(R.N.)_i$ in Equation 15–12 would give an approximately normally distributed random x?

14. What is the difference between a "fixed-time incrementing" and a "next-event incrementing" time flow mechanism?
15. Why do continuous change models use fixed-time incrementing time flow mechanisms?
16. When would you expect transient conditions to occur in a simulation run? What implications do transient conditions cause?
17. What do we mean by a "pilot" experiment, and what is it used for?
18. What are "variance reduction techniques" used for? Name two such techniques.
19. Describe in detail the situation for which a "fractional factorial experiment" is appropriate.
20. What problem does "aliasing" cause?
21. Discuss "response surface methodology."
22. Name some advantages of using the DYNAMO simulation language.

PROBLEM SET

1. Use the multiplicative congruential method to obtain a sequence of 10 random numbers such that $x_{n+1} \equiv 13x_n$ (modulo 10) and $x_0 = 7$.

2. Use the multiplicative congruential method to obtain a sequence of 10 random numbers such that $x_{n+1} \equiv 5x_n$ (modulo 3) and $x_0 = 4$.

3. Generate 10 random observations from each of the following probability distributions.
   (a) $P(x = k) = 0.20, 0.10, 0.05, 0.30, 0.20,$ and 0.15 for $k = 1, 2, 3, 4, 5,$ and 6, respectively.
   (b) The uniform distribution between 0 and 50.
   (c) The distribution whose probability density function is

   $$f(x) = \begin{cases} e^{-x}, & \text{if } 0 \le x \le \infty \\ 0, & \text{otherwise} \end{cases}$$

   (d) The distribution whose probability density function is

   $$f(x) = \begin{cases} 3x^2, & \text{if } 0 \le x \le 1 \\ 0, & \text{otherwise} \end{cases}$$

   (e) The distribution of the sum of two dice.

4. Generate five random observations from each of the following probability distributions.
   (a) The normal distribution with mean = 6 and standard deviation = 3 (*Hint:* Use the Central Limit Theorem and 12 random numbers to obtain each observation).
   (b) The exponential distribution with mean = 5.

5. The Beanbody Coal Company operates a barge terminal at the Mississippi River port of St. Louis. This facility has a single dock that can be used to unload coal from barges. A management science analyst for the company has gathered the following data with respect to barge arrivals and unloadings.

Time Between Arrivals of Successive Barges (hour)	Avg. t	Frequency	Time Required to Unload Barge (hour)	Frequency
0 to 3.99	2	20	0 to 5.99	10
4.00 to 7.99	6	30	6.00 to 9.99	20
8.00 to 11.99	10	20	10.00 to 14.99	40
12.00 to 15.99	14	10	15.00 to 24.99	20
16.00 to 19.99	18	10	25.00 to 50.00	10
20.00 to 24.00	22	10		

The barges are unloaded on a first-come, first-served basis and the facility operates on a 24-hour basis, 7 days a week. Simulate the arrival and unloading of 30 barges. Compute the average waiting time in the system, and the percentage of the time the system is idle.

6. Jane Williams is about to open a keymaking shop in a suburban shopping center. She will make the keys and is contemplating hiring another keymaker to handle anticipated business. She has observed the operation of a similar keymaking shop in another shopping center and has determined the following set of data.

Time Between Customer Arrivals (min)	Avg. t btwn. arrivals	Assigned random val. Frequency		Time Required for Customer Service (min)	Avg. t for cust. service	Assigned rand. no. Frequency	
0 to 0.99	.5	07	1-7	0 to 2.99	1.5	20	1-20
1.00 to 2.99	2	15	8-22	3.00 to 5.99	4.5	40	21-60
3.00 to 5.99	4.5	40	23-62	6.00 to 9.99	8	25	61-85
6.00 to 14.99	10.5	20	63-82	10.00 to 14.99	12.5	10	86-95
15.00 to 29.99	22.5	10	83-92	15.00 to 30.00	22.5	05	96-100
30.00 to 60.00	45	08	93-100				

The customers are served on a first-come, first-served basis. The shop operates from 8:00 A.M. to 8:00 P.M., 6 days a week. Simulate the arrival and servicing of 25 customers. Compute the average waiting time in the system and the percentage of time the store is idle.

7. Simulate 50 plays of the game of craps, using the following set of rules.
   (a) The player throws two dice one or more times until an event occurs that determines a win or a loss.
   (b) If the first throw results in a sum of 7 or 11, or, alternatively, if the first sum is 4, 5, 6, 8, 9, or 10, and the same sum reappears *before* a sum of 7 has appeared, the player *wins*.
   (c) If the first throw results in a sum of 2, 3, or 12, or, alternatively, if the first sum is 4, 5, 6, 8, 9, or 10, and a sum of 7 appears *before* the first sum reappears, the player *loses*.
   From your simulated 50 plays of the game, compute the probability of winning.

8. A traveling salesperson wishes to go from San Francisco to New York in the year 1870. The salesperson is contemplating making this trip in three stages. For each stage there is an associated probability distribution for the destination cities

associated with the stage. The three stages and their associated probability distributions are as follows.

Stage 1
San Francisco → Salt Lake City   P(arrival) = 0.9
San Francisco → Denver   P(arrival) = 0.8
San Francisco → Albuquerque   P(arrival) = 0.7

Stage 2
Salt Lake City → St. Louis   P(arrival) = 0.8
Salt Lake City → Chicago   P(arrival) = 0.7
Denver   → St. Louis   P(arrival) = 0.9
Denver   → Chicago   P(arrival) = 0.7
Albuquerque   → St. Louis   P(arrival) = 0.6
Albuquerque   → Chicago   P(arrival) = 0.8

Stage 3
Chicago   → New York   P(arrival) = 0.9
St. Louis → New York   P(arrival) = 0.7

Using these probability distributions, simulate 25 trips from San Francisco to New York; and from these results, estimate the probability of arriving in New York.

9. Fleece Rental Company rents U-Haul trailers and is trying to determine the number of trailers to have available. From historical records they have determined the following probability distributions.

Number of Trailers Rented Daily	*1*	*2*	*3*	*4*	*5*
Probability	0.20	0.20	0.30	0.15	0.15

Length of Rental (days)	*1*	*2*	*3*	*4*
Probability	0.35	0.30	0.20	0.15

Fleece makes $25 net profit per day for each trailer rented. If there is a demand for a trailer, and no trailer is available, the goodwill loss is $50. If a trailer is in inventory but not used, the daily storage cost is $5. Simulate 15 days of operation, starting with three trailers in inventory. For each day, determine the number of trailers on hand, and for each trailer required and available, the day when it is due back. Assume that trailers are immediately available when they are returned. Determine the net profit after 15 days of operations.

10. The Ace Job Shop receives a varying number of orders each day, and the orders vary in the time required to process them. The firm is interested in determining how many machines to have in its shop to minimize the combined cost of machine idle time and order waiting time. The firm has collected the following data.

Probability Distribution	
Number of Orders (days)	
Number of Orders	**Probability**
1	0.10
2	0.15
3	0.25
4	0.40
5	0.10

Probability Distribution	
Day Required per Order	
Days/Order	**Probability**
1	0.10
2	0.20
3	0.30
4	0.30
5	0.10

Cost per day of idle machine time = $15
Cost per day for a backorder = $10

Simulate 25 days of this company's operations, and determine how many machines it should have in its shop.

11. The Ajax Machinery Company has been having trouble with its milling machines, which have been experiencing a high failure rate. The milling machines have three critical parts that are subject to failure. The company has been replacing these parts, one at a time, as failure occurs. However, a proposal has been made to replace all three parts when any one of them fails.

    The pertinent data for this problem are as follows. For each part, the operating time to failure follows an approximately normal distribution with a mean of 200 hours and a standard deviation of 50 hours. The milling machine must be shut down for 1 hour to replace one part, or 2 hours to replace all three parts. The cost associated with the replacement process is $25.00 per part plus $50.00 per hour. Simulate the operations of the two alternative policies of 2000 hours of simulated time. Which policy should be adopted?

12. Assume that you are offered the chance to play a game in which you could repeatedly flip an unbiased coin until the difference between the number of heads tossed and the number of tails tossed is four. You would be required to pay $1 for each flip of the coin, but you would receive $10 at the end of the game. Use simulation to show whether or not you should play this game.

13. A small shoe retailer experiences daily demand for pairs of shoes according to the following probability distribution.

Daily Demand for Pairs of Shoes	Probability of Demand
25	0.05
30	0.10
40	0.20
50	0.25
60	0.25
70	0.10
80	0.05

The retailer's ordering rule involves placing an order to replenish back to 100 pairs of shoes whenever the inventory falls below 40 pairs of shoes. The lead time for filling an order is given by the following probability distribution.

Lead Time	Probability
1 day	0.10
2 days	0.30
3 days	0.20
4 days	0.30
5 days	0.10

Inventory-holding costs are estimated by the retailer to be $0.10 for each pair of shoes held in inventory at the start of a day. A shortage cost of $0.25 is incurred for each pair of shoes that must be backordered. The inventory-ordering cost is $5, regardless of the number of pairs of shoes ordered.

(a) Simulate 25 days of retailing operations and estimate the mean daily cost of this inventory policy as it currently exists. Assume that the beginning inventory is 100 pairs of shoes.

(b) Repeat the simulation experiment with a replenishment back to 200 pairs of shoes whenever the inventory falls to 60 pairs of shoes. Assume that the beginning inventory is 100 pairs of shoes.

(c) Which inventory policy is better? Why?

14. As a college student you are responsible for all of your educational expenses. Over the past 3 years you have studied your monthly income and expenditure patterns and have developed the following set of information.

Monthly Income	P(Monthly Income)	Monthly Expenditures	P(Monthly Expenditures)
$250	0.20	$400	0.20
500	0.30	600	0.40
1000	0.40	1000	0.30
1500	0.10	1200	0.10

(a) Simulate the monthly pattern of income and expenditures for the 12 months of your senior year in college. Assume that you begin with $1000 in the bank. What is your balance at the end of the 12-month period?

(b) What is your highest monthly balance during the year? What is your average monthly balance for the year?

15. The First National Bank of Ajo, Arizona, has just purchased a new automatic check-sorting machine. The manufacturer of this check sorter has indicated that there are three identical transistorized circuits within the machine that are subject to failure. The company is contemplating what replacement policy to follow for the transistorized circuits. It calculates that it will cost $25 per hour to replace a faulty circuit, and that 1 hour is required to replace one circuit, while all three circuits can be replaced in 2 hours. The cost of each circuit is estimated to be $15. The probability distribution of the time between failures for the individual circuits is as follows.

Hours Between Failure (one circuit)	Probability
1500	0.05
1750	0.25
2000	0.50
2500	0.15
3000	0.05

The probability distribution of the time for the three circuits taken as a group is as follows.

Hours Between Failure (three circuits)	Probability
3000	0.10
3750	0.50
5000	0.30
7500	0.10

Design and run a simulation experiment to determine the best replacement policy for this bank.

16. Consider the following time network problem in which the probabilities of selecting a route at each stage in the network are also indicated.

(a) Simulate 20 trips from the origin to the destination, and compute the average trip time required.

(b) Using the method of complementary numbers, repeat part (a).

17. A certain type of bearing is subjected to high stress and temperature. As a result its mean time to failure is exponentially distributed with parameter $\theta = 1$. Assume now that we do not know the mean of this distribution and wish to estimate it by simulation. Use the method of complementary random numbers, with a sample size of $n = 20$, to estimate the mean time to failure for this situation.

18. Consider the probability distribution whose probability density function is

$$f(x) = \begin{cases} 3x^2, & \text{if } 0 \le x \le 1 \\ 0, & \text{otherwise} \end{cases}$$

For each of the following cases, generate 20 observations and calculate the resulting estimate of the mean of this distribution.

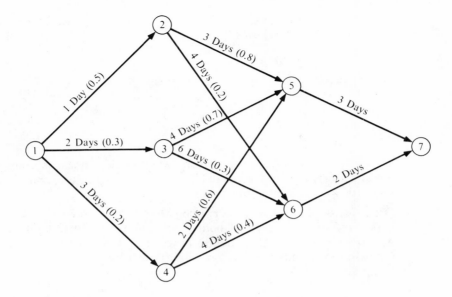

(a) Using a crude Monte Carlo method.

(b) Using the method of complementary random numbers.

19. Lexington County Council has formed a committee to investigate its operating procedures. Data collected and analyzed for the past 5 years (60 months) indicated that the disposition of bills at the beginning of each month (with associated probability) was in one of four states: (1) in committee, (2) on the floor of the County Council, (3) passed by the County Council, or (4) rejected by the County Council. The investigative committee determined that 65 percent of the bills in committee for 1 month were still in committee the following month, with the remaining 35 percent having moved onto the floor of the County Council. Of those bills on the floor of the County Council at the beginning of the month, by the end of the month 20 percent were sent back to committee, 40 percent were still on the floor, 15 percent were rejected, and 25 percent were passed.

Simulate the monthly progress of five separate bills from their start in committee until they are either passed or rejected. For each bill, determine whether or not it was passed or rejected, and how many months it was in progress.

20. The coach of a college soccer team has eight forwards on the team. The coach wishes to evaluate how injuries might affect the availability of forwards. A major injury to a forward, which has a probability of occurring in any game equal to 0.03, will put the injured player out of action for the remainder of the season. No more than one major injury can occur in a single game.

A minor injury causes a player to be removed from the game and miss only one additional game. The probability distribution of minor injuries per game is as follows.

Number of Minor Injuries	Probability of Occurrence
0	.250
1	.450
2	.210
3	.060
4	.025
5	.005

The injury pattern over the season, which is 15 games, is completely random. Simulate the 15-game season and determine the high, low, and average number of forwards available over the season.

21. Dr. I. M. Hipp, an eye doctor, opens her office at 8:30 A.M. She has scheduled patients to arrive every half hour from 8:30 A.M. until 12:00 noon and from 1:30 P.M. until 5:00 P.M. All patients, however, do not arrive exactly on time. The following table indicates the probability distribution for being early, on time, or being late.

Arrival for Appointment	Probability of Arrival
15 minutes early	0.10
10 minutes early	0.15
5 minutes early	0.20
On Time	0.20
5 minutes late	0.20
10 minutes late	0.10
15 minutes late	0.05

The following table indicates the probability distribution for the length of time required to complete the appointment.

Length of Time to Complete Appointment	Probability of Completion Time
15 minutes	0.05
20 minutes	0.10
25 minutes	0.15
30 minutes	0.30
35 minutes	0.15
40 minutes	0.10
45 minutes	0.10
60 minutes	0.05

(a) Simulate, for a 1-day period, the arrival times of patients and their appointment durations.

(b) Determine, for each patient, the waiting time, the starting time of treatment, and the ending time of treatment.

(c) Determine the average waiting time, the average treatment time, and the percentage of time that Dr. Hipp is idle.

(d) How much time did the doctor have for lunch?

(e) At what time did the office close?

22. Aqua Tech, Inc., is developing a new water separator for use on diesel-powered automobiles. The company can utilize either of two research and development strategies for this new water separator, and it has made the following time estimates (with associated probabilities).

Research and Development Time	Research and Development Strategy	
	No. 1	No. 2
6 months	0.20	0.15
12 months	0.40	0.45
18 months	0.35	0.37
24 months	0.05	0.03

If Aqua Tech, Inc., utilizes research and development strategy 1, it will need a $1 million capital investment and the water separator will have a variable cost per unit of $80.00. If Aqua Tech, Inc., utilizes research and development strategy 2, it will need a $1.5 million capital investment and the water separator will have a variable cost per unit of $60.00. The water separator will ultimately be sold to automobile manufacturers at an expected price of $100.00. The expected sales for the water separator are directly dependent on the time required for research and development, since a number of other firms are also developing water separators. Aqua Tech, Inc., has made the following estimates of expected sales volumes (with associated probabilities).

Expected Sales Volume (units)	Research and Development Time			
	6 mo	12 mo	18 mo	24 mo
2,000,000	0.20	0.37	0.48	0.59
2,500,000	0.75	0.60	0.50	0.40
3,000,000	0.05	0.03	0.02	0.01

Simulate 15 trials for each research and development strategy. What is Aqua Tech's profit for each research and development strategy. What should Aqua Tech, Inc., do?

23. Mr. Jeter is a cotton farmer in Bamberg, South Carolina. Based on past experience he has made the following assessment of cotton prices, yields in bales per acre, and farming costs in dollar per acre.

Cotton Prices ($ per bale)	Probability	Yields (bales per acre)	Probability	Costs ($ per acre)	Probability
10	.05	4	.10	20	.03
15	.20	6	.20	25	.15
17	.25	8	.40	40	.40
19	.30	10	.20	50	.39
21	.15	12	.10	60	.03
25	.05				

Assuming that cotton prices, yields, and costs are independent, simulate 25 computations of the expected profit per acre.

24. Given the random observations .923, .658, .207 on [0,1] generate the appropriate random observations from:
(a) The probability distribution where:

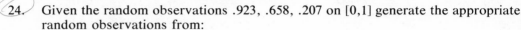

y	1	2	3	4
$p(y)$	$\frac{1}{8}$	$\frac{2}{8}$	$\frac{3}{8}$	$\frac{2}{8}$

(b) The uniform distribution on [0,10].

(c) The distribution $f(x) = \begin{cases} \frac{1}{2}x, & \text{if } 0 \leq x \leq 2 \\ 0, & \text{elsewhere} \end{cases}$

25. Generate five (5) random observations from each of the following probability distributions.
(a) $P(x = k) = .30, .07, .10, .20, .13, .05, .10, .05$ for $k = 1, \ldots, 8$, respectively
(b) The uniform distribution between 100 and 150.
(c) The distribution whose probability distribution function is

$$f(x) = \begin{cases} \frac{1}{2}(x - 4), & \text{if } 4 \leq x \leq 6 \\ 0, & \text{otherwise} \end{cases}$$

26. Consider the probability distribution whose probability density function is

$$f(x) = \begin{cases} 3e^{-3x}, & x > 0 \\ 0, & x \leq 0 \end{cases}$$

Use the crude Monte Carlo method to generate five observations given that:

$$f(x) = \begin{cases} 1 - e^{-3x}, & x > 0 \\ 0, & \text{elsewhere} \end{cases}$$

27. A small sports store experiences daily demand for No. 6 shotgun shells according to the following probability distribution.

Daily Demand for Boxes of 50 Shells	Probability of Demand
15	0.10
20	0.10
25	0.15
30	0.40
35	0.20
40	0.05

The manager's ordering rule is to place an order to replenish back to 150 boxes whenever the inventory falls below 70 boxes. The lead time for filling an order is given by the following probability distribution.

Lead Time	Probability
1 day	0.10
2 days	0.40
3 days	0.40
4 days	0.10

Inventory-holding costs are estimated to be $0.05 for each box of shells held in inventory at the start of a day. A shortage cost of $0.50 is incurred for each box that must be backordered. The inventory-ordering cost is $15.00 regardless of the number of boxes ordered.

(a) Simulate 20 days of operations for this sports store and estimate the mean daily cost of the inventory policy. Assume beginning inventory is 80 boxes of shells.

(b) Comment on the cost efficiency of this inventory policy. Are improvements possible?

(c) Repeat the simulation with a replenishment back to 150 boxes of shells whenever the inventory falls below 90 boxes.

Decision Analysis

16.1 INTRODUCTION

Decision analysis, or **decision theory**, is a probabilistic management science methodology that is useful in situations in which the decision maker has several alternative courses of action but is also faced with an uncertain future set of possible events. For example, consider the decision-making situation encountered by the manager of a ski resort. He would generally want to try to be certain that he has large quantities of ski equipment for rental and plenty of food and drink available for the ski season. However, if particularly bad skiing weather (i.e., no snow) were anticipated, he would certainly want to reduce both his ski equipment and food and drink inventories. Unfortunately, the ski manager would have to make these inventory decisions prior to the start of the ski season and without knowledge concerning the likely snow conditions for the ski season. A decision-making problem such as this would generally be suited for a decision theory or decision analysis approach for solution.

As noted above, decision analysis is primarily concerned with improving the decision process of managers under conditions of uncertainty. In many decision-making situations, managers assume certainty in terms of the data used to make a decision. In spite of this assumption of certainty, the decision-making process may still be very complex. Capital budgeting is an example of an area in which certainty assumptions are often employed, but which still requires a complex analysis.

In this chapter we will be concerned primarily with the process of decision making under uncertainty. This will, in turn, necessitate the assessment or specification of the probabilities associated with various events, or occurrences. Traditionally, two approaches to probability assessment have been employed, namely:

1. **Objective (classical) probabilities,** based on the historically observed, long-run, relative frequency of a particular event.
2. **Subjective (Bayesian) probabilities,** based on a personal assessment of the likely occurrence of a particular event.

The objective, or classical, approach has long been dominant in scientific research and engineering analysis where reliable, measurable, objective evidence is commonly available. The subjective, or Bayesian, approach has come into prominence in business decision making because of the lack of reliable objective evidence. Additionally, the subjectively oriented decision maker feels that it is very important for him, or her, to interject personal preferences or feelings into the decision-making process. This is an attitude often espoused by the business decision maker, and the use of subjective probabilities may facilitate this desire.

We will be concerned primarily with the subjective approach, or philosophy, of probability assessment in this chapter. As the reader may be aware, a long and vigorous controversy between the objective and subjective approaches to probability estimation has occurred. It is not our intention to dwell on this controversy, although it should be noted that the subjective approach has become increasingly popular in business decision-making situations.

16.2 THE GENERAL FRAMEWORK FOR DECISION ANALYSIS

The first step in using a decision analysis approach for a given problem situation is to list the courses of action, or **decision alternatives,** that may be of importance to the decision maker. Care should be taken to include all possible alternatives that the decision maker has available. The number of possible alternatives may be large in some cases, but in most situations only a reasonable number of alternatives will be required. It should also be stressed that these decision alternatives are strictly under the control of the decision maker, that is, the decision maker determines what courses of action are possible.

The second step in applying decision theory requires the decision maker to develop an exhaustive list of possible future events. Again, care should be taken to include all possible future events that might occur, even though the decision maker will likely be very unsure as to which specific event will occur. These future events are referred to as **states of nature**, and it is assumed that the states of nature are mutually exclusive and collectively exhaustive. Obviously, the states of nature are not under the control of the decision maker, and there may be a great deal of uncertainty with respect to their occurrence.

The third step in decision analysis involves the specification of the outcomes resulting from selecting a certain decision alternative and then having a particular state of nature occur. This interaction is usually referred to as the **payoff** for the decision alternative–state of nature combination. It should be recognized that the determination of these payoffs may be a difficult task, but the decision maker should attempt to use all of the information available in completing this task. The payoffs may be expressed in terms of profits, losses, revenues, costs, utilities, or any other appropriate measurement parameter. The payoff estimates are presented in terms of the interaction of the decision alternatives and the states of nature in the form of a **payoff table**.

To illustrate the definition of decision alternatives, the specification of the states of natures, and the development of the payoff table, consider the following example. The Great Western Land Development Company owns 5000 acres of land near Show Low, Arizona, and is contemplating the development of the land as recreational homesites. The company feels that it has three possible decision alternatives.

Decision Alternative 1   Develop a "small" amount of acreage, approximately 500 acres.

Decision Alternative 2   Develop a "medium" amount of acreage, approximately 2,500 acres.

Decision Alternative 3   Develop a "large" amount of acreage, approximately 5,000 acres.

The company is thus faced with decisions concerning whether to develop a small portion ($\simeq$ 10 percent) of its land, about half of its land, or virtually all of its land. Given these three decision alternatives the company feels that three states of nature are likely to occur.

State of Nature 1   Low customer demand for recreational property.
State of Nature 2   Moderate customer demand for recreational property.
State of Nature 3   High customer demand for recreational property.

The company has analyzed the interactions between the three decision alternatives and the three states of nature and has developed the profit payoff table seen in Table 16.1.

TABLE 16.1   Table of Profit Payoffs—Great Western Land Company

	States of Nature		
Decision Alternatives	*Low Customer Demand*	*Moderate Customer Demand*	*High Customer Demand*
Develop "small" acreage	$3,500,000	$ 3,000,000	$ 2,700,000
Develop "medium" acreage	1,000,000	12,500,000	12,400,000
Develop "large" acreage	−500,000	−250,000	25,000,000

This payoff table indicates that the company will, in general, make profits on its land development. Exceptions occur in the cases in which it develops a "large" acreage and then experiences "low" or "moderate" customer demand. Herein, losses are incurred as a result of overbuilding. Note also that profits are reduced for the case in which the company develops "medium" acreage and then "low" or "high" customer demand occurs. If "medium" acreage is developed and "low" demand occurs, overbuilding has again occurred and a diminution of profits is the result. If "medium" acreage is developed and "high" demand occurs, profits will again be reduced because the company will incur larger than expected sales-related costs (i.e., showing of properties, hiring more sales personnel, and increased correspondence and paperwork).

Given this payoff table, the decision maker would generally be interested in maximizing the profits expected over all states of nature. However, as can be observed, there is no single decision alternative that can be selected that will maximize the profits for all states of nature. Thus, the next question is how can the decision maker best utilize the payoff table information to make a decision? Herein, there are a number of decision-making criteria that may be employed. The appropriateness of a specific decision-making criterion is, in turn, dependent on the type of decision-making situation that is encountered.

16.2.1   Types of Decision-Making Situations

Two basic types of decision-making situations are typically encountered by a manager. Each situation involves a varying degree of uncertainty with respect to the decision-making situation. The two basic types of decision-making situations are as follows.

1.   **Decision making under certainty.**
2.   **Decision making under uncertainty or risk.**

In decision-making situations involving certainty the state of nature is known with certainty for each decision alternative. Thus, the payoff for each alternative can be easily determined and the decision maker can make an optimal decision simply by selecting the largest payoff available. Consequently, there is no need to further discuss decision making under certainty.

In decision-making situations involving uncertainty or risk, more than one state of nature exists for each alternative, and the probability associated with each state of nature given each alternative can generally be estimated. This type of decision-making situation is that which is most frequently encountered by business managers. This is the area of decision making to which decision theory is commonly applied. Consequently, our subsequent discussion will consider this area of decision making in detail.

16.3   DECISION MAKING UNDER UNCERTAINTY

Decision making under uncertainty involves probability data being available for the various states of nature. While multiple states of nature are possible, and the decision maker cannot be sure which state of nature will occur, probability estimates can be made for the likelihood of all the states of nature. If we let

$$\theta_j = \text{the state of nature, } j$$
$$P(\theta_j) = \text{the probability of occurrence of state of nature } \theta_j$$
$$N = \text{the number of possible states of nature; } j = 1, 2, \ldots, N$$

then $P(\theta_j) \geq 0$ for all states of nature, j (16–1)

$$\sum_{j=1}^{N} P(\theta_j) = 1 \tag{16–2}$$

The probability of occurrence of state of nature j, $P(\theta_j)$, can be determined subjectively by analyzing historical data or by consulting some external source (e.g., probabilities concerning weather conditions available from a weather bureau). Once this has been done, three criteria can be employed for decision making under uncertainty. These criteria are

1. Expected value
2. Expected loss
3. Expected opportunity loss

16.3.1   Expected Value

Let us assume that the decision maker must select an action a_i from a set A of possible actions. If the decision maker decides to use the expected-value criterion, he would compute the expected value associated with each decision alternative. The **expected value (EV) of a decision alternative,** a_i, is given by:

$$EV(a_i) = \sum_{j=1}^{N} P(\theta_j) \, V(a_i, \theta_j) \tag{16–3}$$

where $V(a_i, \theta_j) = $ the value associated with decision alternative a_i and state of nature θ_j

Thus, the expected value of a decision alternative is equal to the sum of the probabilities associated with the states of nature times the associated values of the decision alternatives and states of nature.

Using the payoff data of our previous land development example, let us assume that the company's management has determined, based on lengthy historical records, that there is a 0.2 probability associated with "low" customer demand for recreational property, a 0.5 probability associated with "moderate" customer demand, and a 0.3 probability associated with "high" customer demand. Using these probabilities, and the payoff estimates shown earlier in Table 16.1, the expected values for the three decision alternatives can be calculated as follows.

$$EV(a_1) = \sum_{j=1}^{3} P(\theta_j) \, V(a_1, \theta_j)$$
$$= 0.2(3,500,000) + 0.5(3,000,000) + 0.3(2,700,000) \tag{16–4}$$
$$= \$3,010,000$$

$$EV(a_2) = \sum_{j=1}^{3} P(\theta_j) \, V(a_2, \theta_j)$$
$$= 0.2(1,000,000) + 0.5(12,500,000) + 0.3(12,400,000) \qquad (16\text{-}5)$$
$$= \$10,170,000$$

$$EV(a_3) = \sum_{j=1}^{3} P(\theta_j) \, V(a_3, \theta_j)$$
$$= 0.2(-500,000) + 0.5(-250,000) + 0.3(25,000,000) \qquad (16\text{-}6)$$
$$= \$7,275,000$$

Under the expected-value decision criterion we see that Decision Alternative 2—develop a "medium" amount of acreage, approximately 2500 acres—should be selected as it produces the largest expected value (\$10,170,000) among the three alternatives.

Note that use of the expected-value decision criterion is based upon a constant set of probabilities for the occurrence of the states of nature. If the probabilities associated with the states of nature change, then a different decision alternative may become preferable. For example, assume that the probabilities associated with the three states of nature become

$$P(\theta_1) = 0.8$$
$$P(\theta_2) = 0.1 \qquad (16\text{-}7)$$
$$P(\theta_3) = 0.1$$

Using these probabilities, the expected values for the three decision alternatives are as follows.

$$EV(a_1) = 0.8(3,500,000) + 0.1(3,000,000) + 0.1(2,700,000)$$
$$= \$3,370,000 \qquad (16\text{-}8)$$
$$EV(a_2) = 0.8(1,000,000) + 0.1(12,500,000) + 0.1(12,400,000)$$
$$= \$3,290,000 \qquad (16\text{-}9)$$
$$EV(a_3) = 0.8(-500,000) + 0.1(-250,000) + 0.1(25,000,000)$$
$$= \$2,075,000 \qquad (16\text{-}10)$$

The best decision alternative is now Decision Alternative 1: Develop a "small" amount of acreage, approximately 500 acres.

16.3.2 Expected Loss

A second method for selecting an alternative a_i from a set A of possible actions involves the determination of a loss function, $l(a_i, \theta_j)$. This loss function is defined for each combination of a_i and θ_j and is generally measured in monetary terms. The general expression for the loss function is given by:

$$l(a_i, \theta_j) = -V(a_i, \theta_j) \qquad (16\text{-}11)$$

The loss function of our land development problem is easily computed from the data given in Table 16.1. This loss function is shown in Table 16.2. In Table 16.2 note that gains or profits appear as negative values while losses appear as positive values.

TABLE 16.2   Loss Function—Great Western Land Company

	States of Nature		
Decision Alternative	θ_1: Low Customer Demand	θ_2: Medium Customer Demand	θ_3: High Customer Demand
a_1: Develop "small" acreage	−$3,500,000	−$3,000,000	−$2,700,000
a_2: Develop "medium" acreage	−1,000,000	−12,500,000	−12,400,000
a_3: Develop "large" acreage	500,000	250,000	−25,000,000

The expected-loss criterion uses the probabilities of the states of nature as weights for the loss values. The **expected loss (EL) of a decision alternative**, a_i, is given by:

$$EL(a_i) = \sum_{j=1}^{N} P(\theta_j)l(a_i,\theta_j) \qquad (16\text{-}12)$$

Using our previous estimates of the probabilities associated with the three demand levels (states of nature), namely $P(\theta_1) = 0.2$, $P(\theta_2) = 0.5$, $P(\theta_3) = 0.3$, the expected losses for the three decision alternatives are

$$\begin{aligned} EL(a_1) &= 0.2(-3,500,000) + 0.5(-3,000,000) + 0.3(-2,700,000) \\ &= -\$3,010,000 \end{aligned} \qquad (16\text{-}13)$$

$$\begin{aligned} EL(a_2) &= 0.2(-1,000,000) + 0.5(-12,500,000) + 0.3(-12,400,000) \\ &= -\$10,170,000 \end{aligned} \qquad (16\text{-}14)$$

$$\begin{aligned} EL(a_3) &= 0.2(500,000) + 0.5(250,000) + 0.3(-25,000,000) \\ &= -\$7,275,000 \end{aligned} \qquad (16\text{-}15)$$

Remembering that negative loss values signify gains, we would seek to minimize the expected loss or maximize the expected gain. Thus, we would again select decision alternative 2: Develop a "medium" amount of acreage.

16.3.3   Expected Opportunity Loss

A third method for selecting an alternative a_i from a set A of possible actions involves the determination of an opportunity loss or regret function, $R(a_i,\theta_j)$. The general expression for this opportunity loss or regret function is given by:

$$R(a_i,\theta_j) = |V^*(\theta_j) - V(a_i,\theta_j)| \qquad (16\text{-}16)$$

where:

$R(a_i,\theta_j)$ = opportunity loss or regret associated with decision alternative a_i and state of nature θ_j.

$V^*(\theta_j)$ = best payoff under state of nature, θ_j.

$V(a_i, \theta_j)$ = payoff associated with decision alternative a_i and state of nature θ_j.

The opportunity loss function for our land development problem can be computed by applying Equation 16–16 to the data of Table 16.1. The opportunity loss function is shown in Table 16.3.

TABLE 16.3   Opportunity Loss Function—Great Western Land Company

	State of Nature		
Decision Alternative	θ_1: *Low Customer Demand*	θ_2: *Medium Customer Demand*	θ_3: *High Customer Demand*
a_1: Develop "small" acreage	$ 0	$ 9,500,000	$22,300,000
a_2: Develop "medium" acreage	2,500,000	0	12,600,000
a_3: Develop "large" acreage	4,000,000	12,750,000	0

Having computed the opportunity loss table, the expected opportunity loss criterion uses the probabilities of the states of nature as weights for the opportunity loss values. The **expected opportunity loss (EOL) of a decision alternative**, a_i, is then computed as:

$$EOL(a_i) = \sum_{j=1}^{N} P(\theta_j)R(a_i, \theta_j) \qquad (16\text{–}17)$$

Using our previous estimates of the probabilities associated with the three demand levels (states of nature) namely $P(\theta_1) = 0.2$, $P(\theta_2) = 0.5$, and $P(\theta_3) = 0.3$, the expected opportunity losses for the three decision alternatives are

$$\begin{aligned} EOL(a_1) &= 0.2(0) + 0.5(9,500,000) + 0.3(22,300,000) \\ &= \$11,440,000 \end{aligned} \qquad (16\text{–}18)$$

$$\begin{aligned} EOL(a_2) &= 0.2(2,500,000) + 0.5(0) + 0.3(12,600,000) \\ &= \$4,280,000 \end{aligned} \qquad (16\text{–}19)$$

$$\begin{aligned} EOL(a_3) &= 0.2(4,000,000) + 0.5(12,750,000) + 0.3(0) \\ &= \$7,175,000 \end{aligned} \qquad (16\text{–}20)$$

Since we would seek to minimize the expected opportunity loss, we would again select Decision Alternative 2: Develop a "medium" amount of acreage, as it produces the smallest expected opportunity loss.

From our use of the three decision criteria we observe that the same decision alternative is always selected. This will always be the case for decision making under risk, and while any one of these alternative criteria can be applied, the expected value criterion is most widely used for decision making under uncertainty.

16.4   DECISION MAKING UNDER UNCERTAINTY— GAMING APPROACHES

In certain situations involving decision making under uncertainty it may be possible to employ decision criteria that do not require the estimation of the probabilities associated with the occurrence of the states of nature. These criteria are essentially those that are employed in **game theory**.[1] Game theory is an analytical approach to decision making involving a conflict situation between two or more decision makers, or between a decision maker and "nature," which is assumed to be an aggressive opponent. While game theory has not been widely employed in business and managerial decision-making situations, it is useful to briefly consider some decision criteria based on game theory. Three such decision-making criteria can be employed, including

1. Minimax decision procedure
2. Maximax decision procedure
3. Minimax regret decision procedure

16.4.1   Minimax Decision Procedure

The **minimax decision procedure** is the most conservative criterion that can be employed. It is based on the fundamental notion that "nature" is an aggressive opponent that is actively trying to outwit, or defeat, the decision maker. To utilize the minimax decision criterion the decision maker examines the loss table (e.g., Table 16.2) and determines the *maximum* loss that would occur under each decision alternative. Arraying these losses, he then selects the *minimum* loss among them.

To demonstrate the application of the minimax decision procedure refer back to the loss function for our land development example that was presented as Table 16.2. This table is reproduced as Table 16.4, along with an extra column that indicates the maximum loss associated with each decision alternative.

TABLE 16.4   Minimax Decision Criterion—Great Western Land Company

| | State of Nature | | | |
Decision Alternative	θ_1: *Low Customer Demand*	θ_2: *Medium Customer Demand*	θ_3: *High Customer Demand*	*Maximum Loss*
a_1: Develop "small" acreage	−$3,500,000	−$ 3,000,000	−$ 2,700,000	−$2,700,000
a_2: Develop "medium" acreage	−1,000,000	−12,500,000	−12,400,000	−1,000,000
a_3: Develop "large" acreage	500,000	250,000	−25,000,000	500,000

In the final column of Table 16.4 the minimum value among the maximum losses, −$2,700,000, is circled. (Remember that a negative loss really represents a gain.) The minimax criterion can thus be stated in terms of selecting

---

[1] Detailed discussions of game theory can be found in: R. Duncan Luce, and Howard Raiffa, *Games and Decisions* (New York: John Wiley & Sons, Inc., 1957); and G. Owen, *Game Theory* (Philadelphia: W. B. Saunders, 1968).

$$\text{Minimum}_{a_i} \quad \text{maximum}_{\theta_j} [l(a_i, \theta_j)] = -\$2,700,000 \qquad (16\text{-}21)$$
$$\text{(Decision alternative } a_1)$$

It should also be noted that the reverse of the minimax procedure, namely the maximin procedure, can be employed to produce the same selection for a table of payoffs such as that presented earlier as Table 16.1. Using this approach the decision maker first lists the *minimum* payoff that is possible for each decision alternative. He then selects the decision alternative that produces the maximum payoff from this group. The reader should verify that the maximin procedure selects the same decision alternative as does the minimax procedure.

16.4.2 Maximax Decision Procedure

The **maximax decision procedure** affords the decision maker an aggressive, or optimistic, criterion. Using this criterion, the decision maker first arrays the *maximum* payoffs possible under the various decision alternatives. The decision that maximizes these maximum payoffs is then selected.

To illustrate the application of the maximax decision procedure refer back to the payoff table for our land development problem that was presented as Table 16.1. This table is reproduced as Table 16.5, and includes an extra column that indicates the maximum payoff associated with each decision alternative.

TABLE 16.5 Maximax Decision Criterion—Great Western Land Company

	State of Nature			
Decision Alternative	θ_1: *Low Customer Demand*	θ_2: *Medium Customer Demand*	θ_3: *High Customer Demand*	*Maximum Payoff*
a_1: Develop "small" acreage	$3,500,000	$ 3,000,000	$ 2,700,000	$ 3,500,000
a_2: Develop "medium" acreage	1,000,000	12,500,000	12,400,000	12,500,000
a_3: Develop "large" acreage	−500,000	−250,000	25,000,000	(25,000,000)

In the final column of Table 16.5, the maximum value among the maximum payoffs, $25,000,000, is circled. The maximax criteria can thus be stated in terms of selecting

$$\text{Maximum}_{a_i} \quad \text{maximum}_{\theta_j} [V(a_i, \theta_j)] = \$25,000,000 \qquad (16\text{-}22)$$
$$\text{(Decision alternative } a_3)$$

The reverse of the maximax procedure, namely the minimin procedure, can be employed to produce the same selection for a table of losses such as that presented earlier as Table 16.2. Using this decision criterion the decision maker selects the minimum among the minimum losses for various decision alternatives. Again, the reader should apply the minimin decision procedure to Table 16.2 to show that it results in the selection of the same decision alternative as does the maximax procedure.

16.4.3 Minimax Regret Decision Procedure

The **minimax regret decision procedure** employs the opportunity loss function, such as was presented previously in Table 16.3. Assuming that the decision maker has determined an opportunity loss function, the minimax regret decision procedure proceeds with the identification of the maximum opportunity loss or maximum regret for each decision alternative. The final selection is then made as the minimum of the maximum regret values.

To demonstrate the application of the minimax regret decision procedure refer back to the opportunity loss table for our land development problem that was presented as Table 16.3. This table is reproduced as Table 16.6 and includes an extra column that indicates the maximum regret associated with each decision alternative.

TABLE 16.6 Minimax Regret Decision Procedure—Great Western Land Company

| | State of Nature | | | |
Decision Alternatives	θ_1: Low Customer Demand	θ_2: Medium Customer Demand	θ_3: High Customer Demand	Maximum Regret
a_1: Develop "small" acreage	\$ 0	\$ 9,500,000	\$22,300,000	\$22,300,000
a_2: Develop "medium" acreage	2,500,000	0	12,600,000	(12,600,000)
a_3: Develop "large" acreage	4,000,000	12,750,000	0	12,750,000

In the final column of Table 16.6, the minimum value among the maximum regrets, \$12,600,000, is circled. The minimax regret decision procedure can thus be stated in terms of selecting.

$$\begin{array}{cc} \text{Minimum} & \text{maximum } [R(a_i,\theta_j)] = \$12,600,000 \\ a_i & \theta_j \qquad \text{(Decision alternative } a_2) \end{array} \qquad (16\text{–}23)$$

The reader will observe that application of the three gaming criteria for decision making under uncertainty does not lead to the selection of the same alternative. This is to be expected since the minimax procedure is a pessimistic approach, while the maximax procedure is an optimistic approach; and the minimax regret procedure focuses on minimizing losses from a marginal perspective. Since each of the decision procedures approaches uncertainty from a different viewpoint, different courses of action are selected.

16.5 DECISION MAKING UNDER UNCERTAINTY— BAYESIAN APPROACHES

Our previous discussions involving decision making under uncertainty have involved situations in which the decision maker must select a decision alternative based on very limited information. We have seen that such decisions are affected by the preliminary or prior probability estimates for the states of nature. In order to arrive at the best decision that is possible the decision maker may often want to obtain additional current information about the probabilities of occurrence associated with the various states of nature. Then, it may be possible to use this new information to update or revise the prior probabilities thus improving the quality of the final decision.

For example, reconsider our land development example and assume that it is now possible to conduct a market survey concerning the public's buying intentions with respect to this land development at a cost of $10,000. Analysis of the market survey data results in four possible consumer responses.

1. No interest in buying land.
2. Mild interest in buying land.
3. Considerable interest in buying land.
4. Enthusiastic interest in buying land.

Past market surveys of a similar nature have indicated the following frequency data is appropriate. Observe in Table 16.7 that the cell frequencies have been converted into probabilities (shown in brackets). The values shown in brackets in each cell are interpreted as conditional probabilities, with the conditioning being dependent upon the state of nature. For example, given that the state of nature is θ_1: low customer demand, then the cell probability $[\frac{5}{120} = 0.045]$ is the conditional probabilility that the buyer interest category is no. 4, "enthusiastic interest."

TABLE 16.7 Market Survey Data—Buyer Interest Frequencies Converted into Conditional Probabilities

	State of Nature		
Buyer Interest Category	θ_1: Low Customer Demand	θ_2: Medium Customer Demand	θ_3: High Customer Demand
1. No interest	$60[\frac{60}{120} = 0.50]$	$50[\frac{50}{500} = 0.10]$	$0[\frac{0}{380} = 0.0]$
2. Mild interest	$40[\frac{40}{120} = 0.33]$	$100[\frac{100}{500} = 0.20]$	$30[\frac{30}{380} = 0.079]$
3. Considerable interest	$15[\frac{15}{120} = 0.125]$	$250[\frac{250}{500} = 0.50]$	$100[\frac{100}{380} = 0.263]$
4. Enthusiastic interest	$5[\frac{5}{120} = 0.045]$	$100[\frac{100}{500} = 0.20]$	$250[\frac{250}{380} = 0.658]$
Totals	$120[\frac{120}{1000} = 0.12]$	$500[\frac{500}{1000} = 0.50]$	$380[\frac{380}{1000} = 0.38]$

Let us now proceed to consider how information such as that summarized in Table 16.7 may be used in the decision-making process. First, observe that this frequency data has been determined by an "experimental" process. In this case the experiment consists of surveying a group of people with respect to their interest in buying recreational land. Thus, let X denote the information made available by experimentation assumed to have been done by random sampling. The decision maker wants to choose a decision rule that will enable him or her to specify the action to take as a function of the possible values of the random variable X. We will denote the decision function as $d_k[x]$ so that if the random variable X takes on the value x, then $a_i = d_k[x]$ would be the action chosen to be taken by the decision maker. The decision function is also a random variable, and the loss associated with taking a particular action is dependent upon the distribution of this random variable. Thus, we can define a risk function to give the expected value of the loss, for a true state of nature θ_j. This risk function is

$$R(d_k, \theta_j) = EV[l(d_k[X], \theta_j)] \tag{16-24}$$

Let us now illustrate the use of this decision function by applying it to our land development example, using the frequency data shown in Table 16.7. Suppose we want to evaluate the following decision rule, d_1. If a buyer's interest response is no. 1 or no. 2, take action a_1; if a buyer's interest response is no. 3, take action a_2; and if the buyer's interest response is no. 4, take action a_3. Thus, the decision function can be defined as:

$$\begin{array}{llll}
d_1[x] = a_1 & \text{for } x = 1 & \text{or} & x = 2 \\
d_1[x] = a_2 & \text{for } x = 3 & & \\
d_1[x] = a_3 & \text{for } x = 4 & &
\end{array} \tag{16-25}$$

Next, using the risk function given by Equation 16–24 we compute

$$\begin{aligned}
R(d_1, \theta_1) &= -3{,}500{,}000[0.50 + 0.33] - 1{,}000{,}000[0.125] \\
&\quad + 500{,}000[0.045] + 10{,}000 \\
&= -2{,}905{,}000 - 125{,}000 + 22{,}500 + 10{,}000 \\
&= -\$2{,}997{,}500
\end{aligned} \tag{16-26}$$

$$\begin{aligned}
R(d_1, \theta_2) &= -3{,}000{,}000[0.10 + 0.20] - 12{,}500{,}000[0.50] \\
&\quad + 250{,}000[0.20] + 10{,}000 \\
&= -900{,}000 - 6{,}250{,}000 + 50{,}000 + 10{,}000 \\
&= -\$7{,}090{,}000
\end{aligned} \tag{16-27}$$

$$\begin{aligned}
R(d_1, \theta_3) &= -2{,}700{,}000[0.0 + 0.079] - 12{,}400{,}000[0.263] \\
&\quad - 25{,}000{,}000[0.658] + 10{,}000 \\
&= -213{,}300 - 3{,}261{,}200 - 16{,}450{,}000 + 10{,}000 \\
&= -\$19{,}924{,}500
\end{aligned} \tag{16-28}$$

Note that, in the evaluation of the risk function, $10,000 represents the cost (loss) associated with determining buyer interest. Observe also it will, in general, be very difficult if not impossible to define an "optimal" decision function that will minimize the risk for every value of θ. Thus, the above approach by itself is inadequate, and the decision maker must seek a more robust approach. Consequently, we will next discuss Bayesian approaches to decision making under uncertainty.

16.5.1 Bayes' Decision Procedure Without Data

In many decision-making situations the decision maker may have some intuitive feeling concerning the probability of occurrence of each state of nature. In this instance, the probability distribution of the state of nature θ_j is called the **prior distribution of θ_j**. Prior distributions are often based on previous experience and/or the subjective or intuitive feelings of the decision maker. The procedure for decision making that makes use of such subjective probabilities is referred to as the **Bayes' decision procedure without data**.

Using the Bayes' decision procedure without data, the decision maker employs the prior distribution to obtain the expected loss for each decision alternative, and then selects the decision action that produces the smallest expected loss. The expected loss, $E[l(a_i, \theta_j)]$, is computed with respect to the prior distribution, which is defined for all the possible states of nature, as follows.

$$E[l(a_i, \theta)] = \begin{cases} \sum_{j=1}^{N} P(\theta_j) l(a_i, \theta_j), & \text{if } \theta_j \text{ is discrete} \\ \int_{-\infty}^{+\infty} l(a_i, x) P_\theta(x) dx, & \text{if } \theta \text{ is continuous} \end{cases}$$
(16-29)

Returning to our land development situation, suppose that the company's management has made the following three subjective probability estimates for the states of nature:

$$P(\theta_1) = 0.1$$
$$P(\theta_2) = 0.5$$
$$P(\theta_3) = 0.4$$
(16-30)

The losses associated for the interactions between the various decision alternatives and the various states of nature were determined previously and summarized in Table 16.2. Thus, for this problem situation, the expected losses for the three decision alternatives can be computed using the prior distribution of θ as:

$$\begin{aligned} E[l(a_1, \theta)] &= 0.1(-3,500,000) + 0.5(-3,000,000) + 0.4(-2,700,000) \\ &= -\$2,930,000 \end{aligned}$$
(16-31)

$$\begin{aligned} E[l(a_2, \theta)] &= 0.1(-1,000,000) + 0.5(-12,500,000) + 0.4(-12,400,000) \\ &= -\$11,310,000 \end{aligned}$$
(16-32)

$$\begin{aligned} E[l(a_3, \theta)] &= 0.1(500,000) + 0.5(250,000) + 0.4(-25,000,000) \\ &= -\$9,825,000 \end{aligned}$$
(16-33)

Thus, the Bayes' decision procedure using the subjective prior distribution of θ would lead to the selection of decision alternative a_2 because it has the minimum expected loss. Using this decision criterion the Great Western Land Company should develop a "medium" acreage project.

16.5.2 Bayes' Decision Procedure With Data

Recall that in using the Bayes' decision procedure without data, we selected the course of action a_i that minimized the expected loss with respect to the prior distribution of the state of nature θ_j. Suppose that we now have additional (experimental) data. Thus, we know more about the state of nature θ_j, and we can use this additional data with the prior distribution of θ_j to obtain an updated distribution of θ_j as a function of the random variable X. This updated distribution of θ_j as a function of X is called the **posterior distribution of θ_j**, and is the conditional distribution of θ_j, given $X = x$. If θ_j and X are discrete, then the posterior distribution is denoted by:[2]

$$h_\theta(\theta_j | X = x) \qquad (16\text{-}34)$$

To calculate $h_\theta(\theta_j | X = x)$, we first define

$$g_X(x) = \text{marginal distribution of } X$$
$$f_{X\theta}(x, \theta_j) = \text{joint distribution of } X \text{ and } \theta$$

Now, $f_{X\theta}(x, \theta_j)$ can be written in terms of known distributions as follows.

$$f_{X\theta}(x, \theta_j) = Q_X(x | \theta = \theta_j)P(\theta_j) \qquad (16\text{-}35)$$

where:
$$\theta_j = \text{state of nature}$$
$$X = \text{random variable related to } \theta_j$$
$$P(\theta_j) = \text{prior distribution of } \theta$$
$$Q_X(x | \theta = \theta_j) = \text{conditional distribution of } \theta, \text{ given } X = x$$

Also, the distribution $g_X(x)$, which is the marginal distribution of the random variable X evaluated at $X = x$ can be expressed as:

$$g_X(x) = \sum_{j=1}^{N} Q_X(x | \theta = \theta_j)P(\theta_j) \qquad (16\text{-}36)$$

Thus,
$$\begin{aligned}
h_\theta(\theta_j | X = x) &= \frac{f_{X\theta}(x, \theta_j)}{g_X(x)} \\
&= \frac{Q_X(x | \theta = \theta_j)P(\theta_j)}{\sum_{j=1}^{N} Q_X(x | \theta = \theta_j)P(\theta_j)}
\end{aligned} \qquad (16\text{-}37)$$

We can now use the posterior distribution of θ to compute the expected losses for various decision alternatives, as:

$$E[l(a_i, \theta)] = \sum_{j=1}^{N} h_\theta(\theta_j | X = x)l(a_j, \theta_j), \qquad i = 1, 2, \ldots, m \qquad (16\text{-}38)$$

Under the **Bayes' decision procedure with data**, the decision maker would simply choose the action that results in the smallest expected loss, as computed using Equation 16–38.

To illustrate these computations let us return to our land development example. Assume that a particular consumer has been put in buyer interest category 4, "enthusiastic interest." Recall that the prior distribution of the state of nature (extent of customer demand) was subjectively estimated to be:

---

[2] We shall consider only this case in this chapter. The reader interested in the cases in which θ and/or X are continuous variables may consult: Frederick S. Hillier, and Gerald J. Lieberman, *Operations Research* (San Francisco: Holden-Day, Inc., 1980), pp. 619–25.

$$P\{\theta = \theta_1\} = 0.10$$
$$P\{\theta = \theta_2\} = 0.50 \qquad (16\text{-}39)$$
$$P\{\theta = \theta_3\} = 0.40$$

We now seek to calculate the posterior distribution:

$$h_\theta(\theta_j | X = 4) = \frac{Q_X(4 | \theta = \theta_j) P(\theta_j)}{\sum\limits_{j=1}^{N} Q_X(4 | \theta = \theta_j) P(\theta_j)} \qquad (16\text{-}40)$$

For this problem, $Q_X(4 | \theta = \theta_j)$ is the probability that consumer response will be classified into category 4, enthusiastic interest, given that extent of customer demand is θ_j. These values can be obtained directly from the fourth row of Table 16.7 as:

$$Q_X(4 | \theta = \theta_1) = 0.045$$
$$Q_X(4 | \theta = \theta_2) = 0.200 \qquad (16\text{-}41)$$
$$Q_X(4 | \theta = \theta_3) = 0.658$$

The denominator of the expression for the posterior distribution is the marginal distribution of the random variable X evaluated at $X = x$. It is computed as:

$$\begin{aligned}
\sum_{j=1}^{N} Q_X(4 | \theta = \theta_j) \cdot P(\theta_j) &= Q_X(4 | \theta = \theta_1) \cdot P\{\theta = \theta_1\} \\
&\quad + Q_X(4 | \theta = \theta_2) \cdot P\{\theta = \theta_2\} \\
&\quad + Q_X(4 | \theta = \theta_3) \cdot P\{\theta = \theta_3\} \\
&= (0.045)(0.10) + (0.200)(0.50) \\
&\quad + (0.658)(0.40) \\
&= 0.3677
\end{aligned} \qquad (16\text{-}42)$$

Using the result obtained in Equation 16–42, the desired posterior distribution can be computed as:

$$h_\theta(\theta_1 | X = 4) = \frac{(0.045)(0.10)}{0.3677} = 0.0122$$

$$h_\theta(\theta_2 | X = 4) = \frac{(0.200)(0.50)}{0.3677} = 0.2719 \qquad (16\text{-}43)$$

$$h_\theta(\theta_3 | X = 4) = \frac{(0.658)(0.40)}{0.3677} = 0.7159$$

The posterior distributions for the other categories given the state of nature can be computed similarly. These values are summarized in Table 16.8. The posterior distribution of θ_j can now be employed with the Bayes' procedure to select that action that minimizes the expected loss, given $X = x$. Again, assume that the consumer's response has resulted in assignment to buyer interest category 4. The expected loss with respect to the posterior distribution of θ, given $X = 4$, for each of the actions is determined as follows.

$$E[l(a_1,\theta)] = 0.0122(-3,500,000) + 0.2719(-3,000,000)$$
$$+ 0.7159(-2,700,000) + 10,000$$
$$= -42,700 - 815,700 - 1,932,930 + 10,000 \qquad (16\text{-}44)$$
$$= -\$2,781,330$$

$$E[l(a_2,\theta)] = 0.0122(-1,000,000) + 0.2719(-12,500,000)$$
$$+ 0.7519(-12,400,000) + 10,000$$
$$= -12,200 - 3,398,750 - 9,323,560 + 10,000 \qquad (16\text{-}45)$$
$$= -\$12,724,510$$

$$E[l(a_3,\theta)] = 0.0122(500,000) + 0.2719(250,000)$$
$$+ 0.7519(-25,000,000) + 10,000$$
$$= 6,100 + 67,975 - 18,797,500 + 10,000 \qquad (16\text{-}46)$$
$$= -\$18,713,425$$

TABLE 16.8   Posterior Distribution of θ_j

	State of Nature		
Buyer Interest Category	θ_1: *Low Customer Demand*	θ_2: *Medium Customer Demand*	θ_3: *High Customer Demand*
1. No interest	0.5000	0.5000	0.0000
2. Mild interest	0.2004	0.6077	0.1919
3. Considerable interest	0.0339	0.6800	0.2861
4. Enthusiastic interest	0.0122	0.2719	0.7159

The Bayes' procedure using the posterior distribution would select action a_3, since this minimizes the expected loss. Thus, using this decision criterion the Great Western Land Company should develop a "large" acreage project. Referring back to Section 16.4.4 you will recall that when the Bayes' procedure was employed without prior data, or without experimentation, the best action was to develop a "medium" acreage project. Thus, the process of obtaining the additional information at a cost of $10,000, has changed the course of action that should be taken by the decision maker.

16.5.3   Expected Value of Sample Information

In the land development problem, Great Western Land Company now has selected a decision alternative involving the development of a "large" acreage project. This decision has been reached on the basis of a Bayes' procedure employing sample information gained at a cost of $10,000. As a part of its analysis the company is interested in the value of this information compared to the cost associated with obtaining it. The value of such information in decision analysis is typically measured by computing the **expected value of sample information** (EVSI), defined as:

$$EVSI = \left|\left[\begin{array}{c}\text{Expected value of the} \\ \text{optimal decision with} \\ \text{sample information}\end{array}\right] - \left[\begin{array}{c}\text{Expected value of the} \\ \text{optimal decision with-} \\ \text{out sample information}\end{array}\right]\right| \qquad (16\text{-}47)$$

The expected value of the optimal decision with sample information is determined in the following manner. It has been shown previously that if the marketing research data is classified in category 4, then the optimal Bayes' action is a_3, with a corresponding loss of $-\$18,713,425$. Using the same computational procedure, the optimal Bayes' actions can be determined for cases in which the marketing research data is classified in categories 1, 2, or 3. The results of these computations are summarized in Table 16.9. Note that the final column of Table 16.9 indicates the values of the function $Q_X(x)$, which is the marginal distribution of the random variable X evaluated at $X = x$. These values were obtained using Equation 16–42. The values for the expected losses shown in Table 16.9 depend on the outcome of the experiment, that is, the classification category. Consequently, the aggregate measurement of the effectiveness of the experiment, or the expected value of the optimal decision with sample information, is determined by computing the weighted sum of the expected losses using the respective marginal probabilities of the random variables X. This value is given by:

Expected value of the optimal decision with sample information

$$
\begin{aligned}
&= -6,740,000(0.1000) - 10,166,210(0.1646) \\
&\quad - 12,071,540(0.3677) - 18,713,425(0.3677) \\
&= -674,000 - 1,673,358 - 4,438,705 - 6,880,926 \\
&= -\$13,666,989
\end{aligned}
\tag{16–48}
$$

TABLE 16.9 Summary of Optimal Bayes' Actions, Expected Losses, and Marginal Distribution—Great Western Land Company

Classification Category	Optimal Bayes' Action	Expected Loss	Marginal Distribution $\sum_{j=1}^{N} Q_X(x\|\theta = \theta_j)P(\theta_j)$
1	a_1	$-\$\ 6,740,000$	0.1000
2	a_2	$-\$10,166,210$	0.1646
3	a_3	$-\$12,071,540$	0.3677
4	a_4	$-\$18,713,425$	0.3677

Previously, in Section 16.5.1, we determined an optimal Bayes' action without data. This led to an expected loss of $-\$11,310,000$. This value is the expected value of the optimal decision without sample information. We can now compute the expected value of sample information as:

$$
\begin{aligned}
EVSI &= \left\| \begin{bmatrix} \text{Expected value of the} \\ \text{optimal decision with} \\ \text{sample information} \end{bmatrix} - \begin{bmatrix} \text{Expected value of the} \\ \text{optimal decision with-} \\ \text{out sample information} \end{bmatrix} \right\| \\
&= |(-\$13,666,989) - (\$11,310,000)| \\
&= \$2,356,989
\end{aligned}
\tag{16–49}
$$

Thus, the Great Western Land Company should be willing to pay up to $2,356,989 for market research (sample information). This expected value of sample information of $2,356,989 is, of course, dependent upon the survey frequency data being as indicated in Table 16.7.

Recall from Section 16.5, that we defined a decision procedure d_1. The weighted expected loss for this decision procedure is given by:

$$\begin{bmatrix} \text{Weighted expected} \\ \text{loss for decision} \\ \text{procedure } d_1 \end{bmatrix} = \begin{aligned} &(-2,997,500)(0.10) - (7,090,000)(0.50) \\ &(-19,924,500)(0.40) \\ &= -299,750 - 3,545,000 - 7,969,800 \\ &= -\$11,814,550 \end{aligned} \qquad (16\text{-}50)$$

Thus, by obtaining the sample information, that is, using an optimal Bayes' procedure, an expected savings can be realized. This expected savings is

$$\text{Expected savings} = \left| \begin{bmatrix} \text{Expected value of the} \\ \text{optimal decision with} \\ \text{sample information} \end{bmatrix} - \begin{bmatrix} \text{Weighted expected} \\ \text{loss of decision} \\ \text{procedure } d_1 \end{bmatrix} \right|$$

$$= |(-\$13,666,989) - (\$11,814,550)|$$
$$= \$1,852,439 \qquad (16\text{-}51)$$

16.5.4 Expected Value of Perfect Information

In the previous section of this chapter we have measured the value of the data obtained by sampling or experimentation. For our land development problem, this information was seen to have considerable value to the decision maker. However, it should be recognized that in other situations such information may be costly or nearly impossible to obtain. Furthermore, this sample or experimental data will always be imperfect because it has been obtained by sampling. Thus, the decision maker may be interested in the question: What if I could obtain perfect information concerning the states of nature? The value of such information in decision theory is measured by computing the **expected value of perfect information**.

From our loss table, Table 16.2, it is apparent that if one knew that there would be "low" customer demand, then action a_1, develop "small" acreage, should be taken. However, if one knew there would be "medium" customer demand, then action a_2, develop "medium" acreage, should be taken. Finally, if one were certain that there would be "high" customer demand, then action a_3, develop "large" acreage should be initiated. Now, we know the prior probabilities of each of these states of nature. We can thus reason that if we were able to obtain perfect information, the prior probability would correspond to the probability that the perfect information would tell us that θ_j was the true state of nature. Thus, we can use these prior probabilities to compute the *expected value of perfect information* (EVPI) as:

$$EVPI = \sum_{j=1}^{N} P(\theta_j) R(a_i^*, \theta_j) \qquad (16\text{-}52)$$

where $R(a_i^*, \theta_j)$ = opportunity loss, or regret, associated with the best decision alternative a_i^* and state of nature θ_j

Our calculations in Section 16.3.3 indicated that alternative a_2 was the best course of action in terms of minimizing the opportunity loss. Using Equation 16–52 we can compute the expected value of perfect information as:

$$EVPI = \sum_{j=1}^{3} P(\theta_j)R(a_2, \theta_j)$$

$$= 0.1(2,500,000) + 0.5(0) + 0.4(12,600,000)$$

$$= \$5,290,000$$

(16–53)

This value indicates that, if we can obtain perfect information, we could then expect an increase in the expected value equal to \$5,290,000. Thus, the company should never pay more than \$5,290,000 for information, no matter how perfect such information may be.

Observe further that the expected value of perfect information is the same as the minimum expected opportunity loss computed using the prior probabilities, $P(\theta_1) = 0.1$, $P(\theta_2) = 0.5$, $P(\theta_3) = 0.4$, namely,

$$EOL(a_1) = 0.1(0) + 0.5(9,500,000) + 0.4(22,300,000)$$
$$= \$13,670,000$$

(16–54)

$$EOL(a_2) = 0.1(2,500,000) + 0.5(0) + 0.4(12,600,000)$$
$$= \$5,290,000 \quad \text{(Minimum)}$$

(16–55)

$$EOL(a_3) = 0.1(4,000,000) + 0.5(12,750,000) + 0.4(0)$$
$$= \$6,775,000$$

(16–56)

Alternatively, using the prior probabilities the expected loss with perfect information available about the state of nature can be computed as:

$$\text{Expected loss with perfect information} = 0.1(-3,500,000)$$
$$+ 0.5(-12,500,000)$$
$$+ 0.4(-25,000,000)$$
$$= -\$16,600,000$$

(16–57)

Since the Bayes' solution (without any data) provided for an expected value of $-\$11,310,000$, the expected value of perfect information can also be computed as:

$$EVPI = \left| \begin{bmatrix} \text{Expected loss with} \\ \text{perfect information} \end{bmatrix} - \begin{bmatrix} \text{Expected value of the} \\ \text{optimal decision without} \\ \text{sample information} \end{bmatrix} \right|$$

$$= |(-\$16,600,000) - (-\$11,310,000)|$$

(16–58)

$$= \$5,290,000$$

16.5.5 Efficiency of Information

The efficiency of the information obtained by sampling or experimentation may be compared to perfect information, under the assumption that perfect information has an efficiency of 100 percent. Under this assumption, the **efficiency of information**, E_I, is computed as:

$$E_I = \frac{\text{EVSI}}{\text{EVPI}} \times 100 \qquad\qquad (16\text{--}59)$$

For our land development example:

$$E_I = \frac{\text{EVSI}}{\text{EVPI}} \times 100 = \frac{\$2,356,989}{\$5,290,000} \times 100 = 45 \text{ percent}$$

Thus, the information obtained from the marketing research firm is 45 percent as efficient as perfect information. In this case, the rather low efficiency rate ($<$50 percent) might cause the company to seek other types of information. However, in making such a decision the cost of obtaining different information would also need to be considered.

16.6   DECISION TREES

A graphical method for performing a decision analysis is available through the use of **decision trees**. A decision tree approach can be used as an alternative to the analytical methods presented earlier in this chapter. To illustrate the decision tree procedure, consider Fig. 16.1, which is the decision tree for the Great Western Land Company problem.

The construction of a decision tree proceeds according to the natural, or chronological, order that is followed in the decision-making process. In the current problem, the decision maker must first decide whether or not to obtain market research information. This initial node, node A, is marked $\square$ as a square, indicating that it is a decision node. Assume first that the decision maker decides not to obtain the market research data and, in this case, moves down the "Do not obtain data" path and arrives at the node, node B, having branches marked

1. Develop "small" acreage
2. Develop "medium" acreage
3. Develop "large" acreage

Node B is again a decision node. Thus, the decision maker must then choose one of these branches on which to proceed. Choosing any one of these branches and proceeding, the decision maker will arrive at a node, (node 1, 2, or 3) having branches marked

1. "Low" customer demand
2. "Medium" customer demand
3. "High" customer demand

Nodes 1, 2, and 3 are chance nodes, marked $\bigcirc$ as circles. Continuation down the branches out of these nodes is a chance event. Depending on the outcome of this chance event, a terminating point is then reached.

Assume instead that the decision maker chooses to obtain market research data and, in this case, moves down the "Obtain data" path and arrives at the chance node, node 16, having branches marked

1. No interest

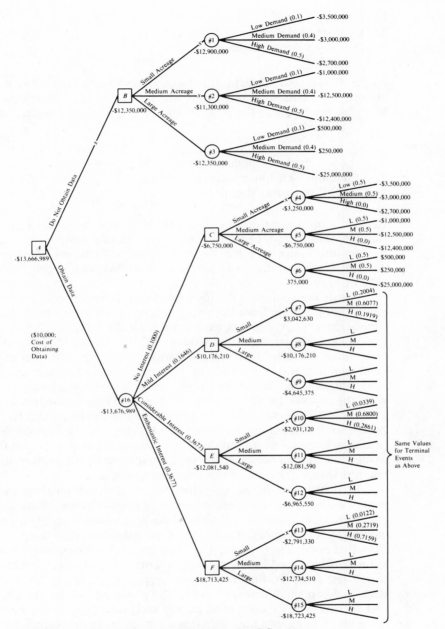

FIGURE 16.1   Decision Tree—Great Western Land Company

2. Mild interest
3. Considerable interest
4. Enthusiastic interest

At this point, the branch on which movement continues is a chance event. Depending on the outcome of this chance event, the decision maker will arrive at a node (node *C, D, E,* or *F*) having branches marked

1. Develop "small" acreage
2. Develop "medium" acreage
3. Develop "large" acreage

Nodes *C, D,* and *E* again are decision nodes. The decision maker must then choose one of these branches on which to proceed. Choosing any one of these branches and proceeding, he or she will arrive at a node (nodes 4–15) with branches marked

1. "Low" customer demand (*L*)
2. "Medium" customer demand (*M*)
3. "High" customer demand (*H*)

Continuation down these branches is, of course, a chance event. Depending on the outcome of this chance event, a terminating point is then reached. In this manner the entire tree has been constructed in terms of actions, events, and choices. Note that the lower part of the tree has been slightly compressed for the sake of brevity.

Let us now consider the losses shown for the terminal events. For the terminal events resulting from the initial choice of not obtaining data, the payoffs are simply the expected losses associated with the terminal events. These expected losses were tabulated earlier in Table 16.2. For example, if we do not obtain data, then make a choice to develop a "small" acreage, and then experience "low" customer demand, the resultant terminal event will have an expected loss of − $3,500,000. For the terminal events resulting from the initial choice of obtaining data, the payoffs are again simply the expected losses associated with the terminal events. For example, if we do obtain data, this data indicates no interest, we decide to develop a small acreage, and there is low customer demand, then the resultant terminal event will have an expected loss of −$3,500,000. The payoffs associated with all the other terminal events can be determined in similar fashion, and are shown for each of these terminal events.

Evaluation of the decision tree begins with the terminal events, whose expected losses have been determined as indicated above. Working backward from each terminal event to the nearest node (a chance node), an expected loss is computed for the node based on the probabilities associated with the branches from that node. These probabilities are the probabilities associated with a state of nature, as indicated by the terminal event, being chosen, given the path followed to the last fork. To illustrate, consider the chance node for the "do not obtain data, develop small acreage" path. The expected loss for the chance node at the end of this path is computed as the weighted sum of the probabilities of the branches leading into this node times the losses of the terminal events associated with these branches. The probabilities associated with the branches are simply the prior probabilities of the terminal events. Thus, the expected loss for this node can be computed as:

$$EL(\text{chance node 1}) = (0.1)(-\$3,500,000) + (0.5)(-\$3,000,000)$$
$$+ (0.4)(-\$2,700,000) \tag{16-60}$$
$$= -\$2,930,000$$

The expected losses at chance nodes 2 and 3 are computed in the same fashion. Continuing to work backward we next seek to evaluate the decision node at the end of the "do not obtain data" path. Since we are now dealing with a decision fork, no probabilities are involved, and the loss associated with this node is just the minimum loss over all the branches associated with that node. These losses were just computed. Thus, the loss for decision node B is determined as:

$$L(\text{decision node } B) = \text{minimum } \{-\$2,930,000; \, -\$11,310,000; \\ - \$9,825,000\} \\ = -\$11,310,000 \tag{16-61}$$

Thus, at this decision fork, the best action to take is to develop a large acreage. The other two actions can now be eliminated, and this is shown by the X through the branches "develop small acreage," and "develop medium acreage."

Consider now the portion of the tree for which we do obtain data. Initially, let us evaluate the chance node (chance node 4) at the end of the "obtain data, no interest, small acreage" path. We must again work backward from the terminal events to this chance node, computing an expected loss using the probabilities associated with the branches from that node. These probabilities are the posterior probabilities associated with various customer demands, given that the market survey indicates no interest (see Table 16.8). The expected loss for the chance node at the end of this path is computed as the weighted sum of the (posterior) probabilities of the branches leading into this node times the losses of the terminal events associated with these branches. Thus, the expected loss for this node can computed as:

$$EL(\text{chance node 4}) = (0.5)(-\$3,500,000) + (0.5)(-\$3,000,000) \\ + (0.0)(-\$2,700,000) \\ = -\$3,250,000 \tag{16-62}$$

The expected losses at chance nodes 5 through 15 are computed in the same manner, using the appropriate posterior probabilities from Table 16.8. Working backward we observe that we next encounter the decision nodes C, D, E, and F. The loss associated with each of these decisions nodes is just the minimum loss over all the branches associated with that node. These losses were just computed for these branches. Thus, the losses for the four decision nodes can be determined as:

$$L(\text{decision node } C) = \text{minimum } \{-\$3,250,000; \\ -\$6,750,000; \$375,000\} \\ = -\$6,750,000 \tag{16-63}$$
$$L(\text{decision node } D) = \text{minimum } \{-\$3,042,630; \\ -\$10,176,210; \\ -\$4,545,375\} \\ = -\$10,176,210 \tag{16-64}$$
$$L(\text{decision node } E) = \text{minimum } \{-\$2,431,120; \\ -\$12,081,540; \\ -\$6,965,550\} \\ = -\$12,081,540 \tag{16-65}$$

$$L(\text{decision node } F) = \text{minimum } \{-\$2,791,330;$$
$$-\$12,734,510;$$
$$-\$18,723,425\} \tag{16-66}$$
$$= -\$18,723,425$$

Now at each of these four decision nodes we can eliminate those actions (branches) that do not produce the minimum loss. This is again indicated by an X on the appropriate branches.

Continuing to work backward we next encounter chance node 16. The loss associated with this node is the expected loss weighted with respect to the probabilities associated with the branches leading back to it. These probabilities are the unconditional, or marginal, probabilities that the market research result indicated by the branch is obtained, given the path followed to the decision node. These marginal probabilities were computed earlier, and summarized in Table 16.9. Using these marginal probabilities, and the losses just determined for decision nodes $B, C, D,$ and E, we can compute the expected loss for chance node 16 as:

$$EL(\text{chance node } 16) = 0.1000(-\$6,750,000) + 0.1646(-\$10,176,210)$$
$$+0.3677(-\$12,081,540) + 0.3677(-\$18,723,425)$$
$$= -\$675,000 - \$1,675,004 - \$4,442,382 \tag{16-67}$$
$$-\$6,884,603$$
$$= -\$13,676,989$$

We are now able to evaluate decision node A. The loss for this node is simply the minimum of the loss of the two branches leading into it, namely,

$$L(\text{decision node } A) = \text{minimum } \{[-\$12,350,000],$$
$$[-\$13,676,989 + \$10,000]\} \tag{16-68}$$
$$= -\$13,666,989 \quad \text{(i.e., gain of } \$13,666,989)$$

Note that, in computing this minimum, we must add in the $10,000 cost of obtaining the market research data to the respective branch. Having computed this minimum, the "do not obtain data" branch is eliminated, and the optimal decision procedure indicates that the "obtain data" branch should be followed, resulting in an expected loss of $-\$13,666,989$. This expected loss is, of course, identical to the expected loss obtained earlier in Section 16.5.2.

In summary, the decision tree approach affords the decision maker with a graphical approach to decision analysis. The calculations made using the decision tree approach are identical to those made previously using an analytical approach. A possible advantage of the decision tree approach is that it may offer the management science analyst an excellent means of presenting the results of the analysis, that is, a graphical approach may facilitate the presentation and implementation of the decision analysis results to management.

16.7 UTILITY THEORY

In all of the examples considered previously in this chapter we have made decisions using various criteria involving expected loss (or profits) expressed in monetary terms. However, there may be decision situations in which such criteria involving expected monetary payoffs (losses) are inappropriate. To illustrate this phenomenon consider the following set of paired alternatives.

$A_1 =$ You receive a $10,000 gift, tax free, with certainty;

or

$A_2 =$ You receive a $22,000 gift, tax free, if on the flip of a fair coin it comes up heads. However, if it comes up tails, you receive nothing.

$B_1 =$ You lose $500, with certainty;

or

$B_2 =$ You lose $10,000, with a probability of $1/100$. You have a $99/100$ probability of losing nothing.

For each set of alternatives you must choose one alternative, that is, either A_1 or A_2 and either B_1 or B_2.

Based on individual preferences, most people would probably choose alternative A_1, even though the expected monetary value of alternative A_2 is given by:

$$EMV(\text{alternative } A_2) = 1/2(\$22,000) + 1/2(0)$$
$$= \$11,000 \tag{16-69}$$

Thus, alternative A_2 should be chosen if you want to maximize the expected monetary value.

Considering the second set of alternatives, most people would probably choose alternative B_1 even though the expected monetary loss of alternative B_2 is given by:

$$EML(\text{alternative } B_2) = 1/100(-\$10,000) + 99/100(0)$$
$$= -\$100 \tag{16-70}$$

Thus, alternative B_2 should be chosen if you want to maximize the expected monetary loss.

As noted above, it is apparent that most people would choose alternatives A_1 and B_1 rather than the alternatives that maximize the expected monetary value or minimize the expected monetary loss. Therefore, it is reasonable to suggest that many people may not always make decisions with respect to monetary values. The question now is, does this invalidate our previous discussion in this chapter? The answer is that it does not, but that it suggests an alternative criterion for decision making. Under this alternative criterion, the decision maker attempts to optimize expected **utility** rather than expected monetary value. The concept of utility and its measurement can be traced to the pioneering work of John Von Neumann and Oskar Morgenstern, as contained in their work titled, *Theory of Games and Economic Behavior* (1944). Using utility theory, the decision maker attempts to transform monetary values into an appropriate scale that measures the decision maker's preference, including a willingness to take or avoid risk. The scale is referred to as the **utility scale**, and it becomes the appropriate measure of the consequences of selecting an action, given a state of nature.

16.7.1   Constructing a Utility Function

The Von Neumann-Morgenstern **utility function** is measured on an **interval**, or **cardinal, scale.** An interval scale is characterized by the lack of a specified origin and by the specification of an arbitrary unit for making measurements using the scale. A thermometer is an example of a device that employs interval measurement. Thus, using the interval scale of a Fahrenheit thermometer, the freezing and boiling points of water are specified at 32° and 212°, respectively.

Suppose now that we are interested in constructing a utility function for a decision-making situation involving the payoffs from a series of research and development projects. In Table 16.10 we present a monetary payoff table for a series of four research and development projects, given four possible states of nature.

TABLE 16.10   Payoff Table—Research and Development Projects ($ Millions)

	States of Nature		
R & D Project	*θ₁: Low Commercial Development*	*θ₂: Medium Commercial Development*	*θ₃: High Commercial Development*
1	5	7	12
2	1	4	7
3	3	5	7
4	4	6	9

Assume that we are interested in determining a utility function for all the monetary values that represent payoffs to the decision maker in this situation. The Von Neumann-Morgenstern approach to specifying a utility function involves computing the utility for a number of points between the values shown in the monetary payoff tables, and then using these computed values to sketch out the entire utility function.

Construction of the utility function for the payoff table proceeds according to the following steps.

1.   We determine the highest monetary payoff, $P_{max} = 12$, and the lowest monetary payoff, $P_{min} = 1$, in the payoff table. For these two payoff values we arbitrarily assign the utility indices of 1 and 0. That is,

$$U(\$12,000,000) = 1 \qquad U(\$1,000,000) = 0 \qquad (16\text{--}71)$$

The selection of the utility values of 1 and 0 is arbitrary, and we can use any two indices for which the index of the larger monetary payoff exceeds the index of the smaller monetary payoff. We have thus determined two points on the utility function.

2.   Next, we determine a **certainty equivalent** that represents a monetary payoff for which the decision maker is indifferent to receiving the uncertain payoffs P_1 and P_2, each with probability 0.5, and the option of receiving the certainty equivalent with certainty. For our present problem situation, assume that we have discussed the situation at length with the company's vice-president for research and development and that he has indicated that he has a certainty equivalent of $5,500,000 compared to receiving a payoff of $P_1 = \$12,000,000$ with probability of 0.5 and a payoff of $P_2 = \$1,000,000$ with probability 0.5. Now, since the vice-president for research and development is indifferent to the riskless payoff of $P_1 = \$12,000,000$ and $P_2 = \$1,000,000$, it then follows that the utility associated with the certainty equivalent of $5,500,000 must be equal to the expected utility associated with $P_1 = \$12,000,000$ and $P_2 = \$1,000,000$. Thus,

$$
\begin{aligned}
U(5.5) &= 0.5 \cdot U(12) + 0.5 \cdot U(1) \\
&= 0.5(1) + 0.5(0) \\
&= 0.5
\end{aligned}
\tag{16-72}
$$

Thus, we have determined a third point on our utility function.

3. We now repeat Step 2 a number of times until enough points have been determined to establish a smooth utility function curve. We can arbitrarily select monetary payoff values to determine the utility of the certainty equivalent, as long as the monetary payoff values have known utility indices. Note that we had to use P_{max} and P_{min} to establish the third point on the utility function. Once the third point is established, it can then be used with either P_{max} or P_{min} to establish a fourth point, and so forth. In Table 16.11 we present a set of six points for which monetary payoffs and associated utility indices have been determined.

TABLE 16.11 **Monetary Payoffs and Associated Utility Indices**

Point	Monetary Payoff (certainty equivalent)	Utility Index
1	$12,000,000	1.00
2	1,000,000	0.00
3	5,500,000	0.50
4	3,000,000	0.25
5	9,000,000	0.75

4. From the data shown in Table 16.11, the utility function is then drawn. This utility function is shown in Fig. 16.2.

Based on the utility function shown in Fig. 16.2, it is now possible to replace the payoffs shown in Table 16.10 by utility indices. The utility table constructed using the utility function shown in Fig. 16.2 is presented in Table 16.12.

TABLE 16.12 **Utility Table for Research and Development Projects**

R&D Project	State of Nature		
	θ_1: Low Commercial Development	θ_2: Medium Commercial Development	θ_3: High Commercial Development
1	0.44	0.57	1.00
2	0.00	0.35	0.57
3	0.25	0.40	0.57
4	0.35	0.53	0.73

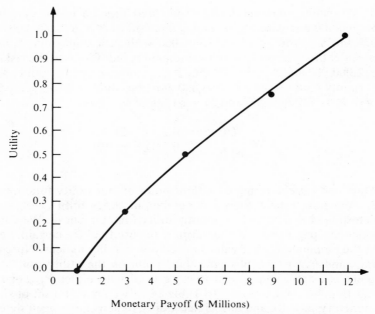

Monetary Payoff ($ Millions)

FIGURE 16.2   Utility Function—Research and Development Example

16.7.2   Using the Utility Function

Once the utility function and utility table have been determined, they can be employed in decision making in the same manner that monetary values were used previously in this chapter. For example, let us assume that the vice-president for research and development has subjectively determined that there is a 0.3 probability associated with "low" commercial development, a 0.5 probability associated with medium commercial development, and a 0.2 probability associated with high commercial development.

Using these probabilities and the monetary payoffs shown earlier in Table 16.10, the expected monetary values for the four research and development projects can be calculated as follows.

$$
\begin{aligned}
EMV(\text{R\&D Project 1}) &= 0.3(\$5,000,000) + 0.5(\$7,000,000) \\
&\quad + 0.2(\$2,000,000) \\
&= \$5,400,000
\end{aligned}
\tag{16-73}
$$

$$
\begin{aligned}
EMV(\text{R\&D Project 2}) &= 0.3(\$1,000,000) + 0.5(\$4,000,000) \\
&\quad + 0.2(\$7,000,000) \\
&= \$3,700,000
\end{aligned}
\tag{16-74}
$$

$$
\begin{aligned}
EMV(\text{R\&D Project 3}) &= 0.3(\$3,000,000) + 0.5(\$5,000,000) \\
&\quad + 0.2(\$7,000,000) \\
&= \$4,800,000
\end{aligned}
\tag{16-75}
$$

$$
\begin{aligned}
EMV(\text{R\&D Project 4}) &= 0.3(\$4,000,000) + 0.5(\$6,000,000) \\
&\quad + 0.2(\$9,000,000) \\
&= \$6,000,000
\end{aligned}
\tag{16-76}
$$

Now, using these same probabilities and the utilities shown in Table 16.12, the expected utilities for the four research and development projects can be calculated as follows.

$$EU(\text{R\&D Project 1}) = 0.3(0.44) + 0.5(0.57) + 0.2(1.00) = 0.617 \qquad (16\text{-}77)$$

$$EU(\text{R\&D Project 2}) = 0.3(0.00) + 0.5(0.35) + 0.2(0.57) = 0.289 \qquad (16\text{-}78)$$

$$EU(\text{R\&D Project 3}) = 0.3(0.25) + 0.5(0.40) + 0.2(0.57) = 0.389 \qquad (16\text{-}79)$$

$$EU(\text{R\&D Project 4}) = 0.3(0.35) + 0.5(0.53) + 0.2(0.73) = 0.5160 \qquad (16\text{-}80)$$

From these two sets of computations we see that, based on expected monetary value, the decision maker would select research and development project 4. However, based on expected utility, the decision maker would select research and development project 1. In this example the construction of the utility function and the utility table implicitly allow the decision maker to insert his or her risk preference for possible monetary payoff into the decision process. The optimal decision made when risk preference is taken into consideration is quite different than that which would be made if only monetary payoffs are considered.

16.8 CASE STUDY—DECISION ANALYSIS APPLIED TO LIVER DISEASE DIAGNOSIS

Daniel Peña Sanchez De Rivera has developed a decision analysis model for the diagnosis and treatment of undifferentiated liver disease with jaundice.[3] The differential diagnosis of a jaundiced patient whose disease does not become clear after routine (nonrisky) exploration and laboratory tests is considered. This is viewed as an extremely difficult problem by the medical community. The difficulty can be attributed to the fact that there are six possible liver diseases that mimic each other very closely.

1. Cholestatic hepatitis (HC)
2. Primary biliary cirrhosis (CBP)
3. Choledocho lithiasis (CL)
4. Carcinoma of bile ducts (CBD)
5. Carcinoma of the papilla of Vater (CPV)
6. Carcinoma of head of pancreas (CHP)

Differential diagnosis was considered essential in the first place since the treatment required for hepatitis and cirrhosis was medical, whereas the treatment for the other diseases was surgical. Secondly, the prognosis in the case of carcinoma depended on its rapid identification, so that any delay before surgical intervention increased the patient's risk. Another important consideration was that the differential diagnosis of these diseases cannot, in general, be based merely on those sources of information with minimum mortality risk such as laboratory tests and radiology. Thus, it was often necessary to apply tests that have a significant risk of mortality (i.e., tests such as liver bi-

[3] For further details, see: Daniel Peña Sanchez De Rivera, "A Decision Analysis Model for a Serious Medical Problem," *Management Science*, vol. 26, no. 7 (July 1980), 707–718, copyright 1980, The Institute of Management Sciences, reprinted by permission.

opsy and percutaneous transhepatic cholangiography). A final consideration was that the results of treatment in patients with carcinoma (of the bile ducts or of the head of the pancreas) was poor and there was no general agreement among doctors as to the usefulness of surgery, especially in the case of older patients. The problem situation outlined above was conducive to a decision analysis approach. An interesting feature of the decision model was that it incorporated the patient's preference for consequences in determining the best treatment in each case. The preference structure for the problem was defined over the remaining life of the patient. Two kinds of preference structures were considered: linear preferences, and decreasing risk aversion. The patient with linear preferences selected that treatment which maximized his life expectancy. On the other hand, risk aversion implied that the patient would prefer a treatment T_1 with expected life E_1 to another treatment T_2 with expected life E_2, even if E_1 were less than E_2, if the probability distribution of death in the short run with T_1

was sufficiently lower than with T_2. Perhaps the major contribution of this paper was that it demonstrated the usefulness of length of life as a criterion for summarizing the relevant effects of a medical policy.

The model was built on the following assumptions: (1) the patient has one and only one of the six possible diseases; (2) the doctor can use two risky tests before applying treatment: liver biopsy (LB) and percutaneous transhepatic cholangiography (PTC); (3) the treatments available are divided into two groups: medical and surgical. The basic structure of the model is presented in Fig. 16.3. Note that the first decision the doctor had to make was whether or not to collect more information using one of the two risky tests. If a test was applied, one of several mutually exclusive and exhaustive results occurred. When the test results became known, the doctor revised his probability assessment over the diseases, taking account of the likelihood of the result obtained according to Bayes' rule. Note that the doctor, before selecting the treatment, had the choices of using

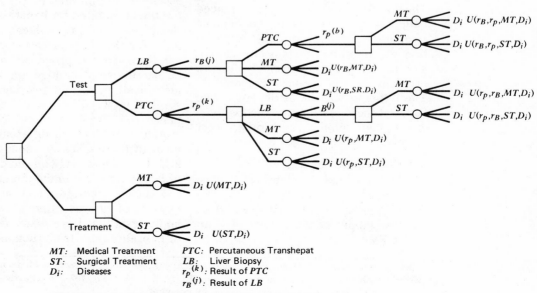

MT: Medical Treatment	*PTC*: Percutaneous Transhepat
ST: Surgical Treatment	*LB*: Liver Biopsy
D_i: Diseases	$r_p^{(k)}$: Result of *PTC*
	$r_B^{(j)}$: Result of *LB*

FIGURE 16.3 Structure of the Decision Analysis Model

both tests sequentially, one of them alone, or no test at all. The final consequence for the patient depended on the test used, the treatment applied (which incorporated patient preferences), and the real disease the patient had. The analysis of this problem required the following data: (1) the a priori probability for each disease; (2) the likelihoods of the test results, given the disease; and (3) the preference structure over the consequences. With these inputs, the model was used to select the strategy that maximized expected utility.

The author of this paper advocated the use of decision analysis in the study of serious medical problems based on the following considerations.

1. Decisions analysis offers a systematic methodology for the structuring and analysis of complex problems in which differences in expert opinions can be understood and to some extent resolved through the explicit introduction of subjective probability preferences.
2. The approach may be effective in training new doctors.
3. The methodology provides a guide to hospitals on the kinds of information to collect systematically and their relative importance as far as decisions are concerned.
4. The approach can be easily linked to automatic diagnosis programs that have been developed over the last two decades.

16.9 CONCLUSION

Decision analysis, or decision theory, has become an important tool for the management scientist. Its use requires the management scientist to delineate alternative courses of action and possible states of nature. Then, payoffs resulting from the interaction of the courses of action and the states of nature must be specified. Finally, the decision maker attempts to define probabilities for the various states of nature occurring. Given that these types of data are available, decision analysis affords an excellent problem solving methodology. Furthermore, we have seen how experimental or sample data can also be employed to refine or improve the decision analysis. Additionally, the graphical approach to decision analysis, through the use of decision trees, was discussed and illustrated. Finally, it should be stressed that decision analysis is particularly useful for applications involving broad, complicated problems involving risk or uncertainty such as are commonly found in corporate planning, new venture analysis, product development and introduction, research and development, and real estate ventures.

GLOSSARY OF TERMS

Bayes' Decision Procedure With Data A decision-making procedure in which the decision maker selects the decision alternative that results in the smallest expected loss, computed by using the posterior distribution.

Bayes' Decision Procedure Without Data A decision-making procedure that makes use of subjective prior probabilities; the decision maker employs the prior distribution to obtain the expected loss for each decision alternative and then selects the decision action that produces the smallest expected loss.

Certainty Equivalent Represents a monetary payoff for which the decision maker is indifferent to receiving the uncertain payoffs P_1 and P_2, each with probability 0.50, and the option of receiving the certainty equivalent with certainty.

Decision Alternatives   The possible courses of action the decision maker can take.

Decision Analysis or Decision Theory   A probability-oriented management science methodology that is useful in situations in which a decision maker is faced with several alternative courses of action but is also confronted with an uncertain future set of possible events.

Decision Making under Certainty   A decision-making situation in which the state of nature is known with certainty for each decision alternative.

Decision Making under Uncertainty   A decision-making situation in which more than one state of nature exists for each alternative and in which the probability associated with each state of nature can generally be estimated.

Decision Tree   A graphical method for performing a decision analysis.

Efficiency of Information   The efficiency of the information obtained by sampling or experimentation as compared to perfect information, assuming that perfect information has an efficiency of 100 percent.

Expected Loss (EL) of a Decision Alternative   The sum of the probabilities associated with the states of nature times the associated loss values of the decision alternatives and states of nature.

Expected Opportunity Loss (EOL) of a Decision Alternative   The sum of the probabilities associated with the states of nature times the associated opportunity loss values of the decision alternatives and states of nature.

Expected Value (EV) of a Decision Alternative   The sum of the probabilities associated with the states of nature times the associated values of the decision alternatives and states of nature.

Expected Value of Perfect Information   A measure of the value of "perfect" information concerning the states of nature in decisions theory assuming such information could be obtained.

Expected Value of Sample Information   The expected value of the optimal decision with sample information minus the expected value of the optimal decision without sample information.

Game Theory   An analytical approach to decision making involving a conflict situation between two or more decision makers, or between a decision maker and "nature," that is assumed to be an aggressive opponent. Game theory employs decision criteria that do not require the estimation of the probabilities associated with the occurrence of the states of nature.

Interval Scale or Cardinal Scale   A scale characterized by the lack of specified origin and by the specification of an arbitrary unit for making measurements using the scale.

Maximax Decision Procedure   A decision criterion in game theory in which the decision maker arrays the "maximum" payoffs possible under the various decision alternatives and then selects the decision alternative that "maximizes" the maximum payoffs.

Minimax Decision Procedure   A decision criterion in game theory where the decision maker determines the "maximum" loss that would occur under each decision alternative and then selects the decision alternative that is associated with the "minimum" loss among the maximum losses.

Minimax Regret Decision Procedure   A decision criterion in game theory where the decision maker identifies the "maximum" opportunity loss or "maximum" regret for each decision alternative and then selects the decision alternative associated with the "minimum" maximum regret value.

Objective (Classical) Probabilities   Probabilities that are based on the historically observed, long-run, relative frequency of a particular event.

Payoff   The outcome for a decision alternative–state of nature combination that results from selecting a certain decision alternative and then having a particular state of nature occur.

Payoff Table   A tabular representation of the payoff estimates in terms of the interaction of the decision alternatives and the states of nature.

Posterior Distribution of the State of Nature θ_j   A revised probability distribution of θ_j computed by updating the prior distribution of θ_j by means of additional (experimental) data.

Prior Distribution of the State of Nature θ_j   The probability distribution of the state of nature θ_j, where the probability of occurrence of each state of nature is determined by some intuitive feeling of the decision maker or is based upon the previous experience of the decision maker.

States of Nature   All possible future events that might occur; it is assumed that these events are mutually exclusive and collectively exhaustive.

Subjective (Bayesian) Probabilities   Probabilities that are based on a personal assessment of the likely occurrence of a particular event.

Utility Function   A function that depicts the dependent relation of utility upon monetary payoff.

Utility Scale   A scale that measures the decision maker's preference, including a willingness to take or avoid risk.

Utility Theory   A body of knowledge that suggests a utility-based criterion for decision making where the decision maker attempts to optimize expected utility rather than expected monetary value.

SELECTED REFERENCES

DECISION
ANALYSIS

Chernoff, H., and L. E. Moses. 1959. *Elementary Decision Theory*. New York: John Wiley & Sons, Inc.

Hadley, G. 1967. *Introduction to Probability and Statistical Decision Theory*. San Francisco: Holden-Day, Inc.

Luce, R. D., and H. Raiffa. 1957. *Games and Decisions*. New York: John Wiley & Sons, Inc.

Martin, J. J. 1967. *Bayesian Decision Problems and Markov Chains*. New York: John Wiley & Sons, Inc.

Newman, J. W. 1971. *Management Applications of Decision Theory*. New York: Harper & Row Publishers, Inc.

Pratt, J. W., H. Raiffa, and R. O. Schlaifer. 1965. *Introduction to Statistical Decision-Theory*. New York: McGraw-Hill Book Company.

Raiffa, H. 1968. *Decision Analysis*. Reading, Mass: Addison-Wesley Publishing, Inc.

Schlaiffer, R. O. 1969. *Analysis of Decisions Under Uncertainty*. New York: McGraw-Hill Book Company.

Schlaiffer, R. O. 1961. *Introduction to Statistics for Business Decisions*. New York: McGraw-Hill Book Company.

Weiss, L. 1961. *Statistical Decision Theory*. New York: McGraw-Hill Book Company.

Winkler, R. L. 1972. *Introduction to Bayesian Inference and Decision*. New York: Holt, Rinehart & Winston, Inc.

DISCUSSION QUESTIONS

1. What is the difference between "classical" and "Bayesian" probabilities?
2. Consider the states of nature for the Great Western Land Development Company example. Suppose you are able to influence "demand" to some degree via strong marketing actions. Would you still consider demand as being a state of nature? Why or why not?
3. Can the "state of nature" be a continuous variable? Why or why not?
4. Why would you expect game theory not to be widely employed in managerial decision-making situations? When do you think game theory may be an appropriate technique to use?
5. What is the difference between the Bayes' decision procedure without data and the Bayes' decision procedure with data?
6. Is a "posterior distribution" relevant in a Bayes' decision procedure without data? Why or why not?
7. What is the "expected value of sample information" dependent upon? What is it used for?
8. Describe how you calculate the "weighted expected loss for a decision procedure d_i"?
9. What does the "expected value of perfect information" tell us?
10. Why is the expected value of perfect information equal to the minimum expected opportunity loss computed using the prior probabilities?
11. What is the difference between an "expected value" approach and a "decision tree" approach in decision making?
12. In what type of situations would the "utility" approach be appropriate?
13. Suppose we could "shift up" the utility scale by some constant C. Is this going to change anything with respect to a possible future utility-based decision? Why or why not?
14. Can decision making based on expected utility yield different results compared to decision making based on expected monetary value? Why or why not?

PROBLEM SET

1. Suppose that you are a decision maker faced with four decision alternatives and four states of nature. On the basis of your analysis of the problem environment you have developed the following payoff table.

Decision Alternative	State of Nature			
	θ_1	θ_2	θ_3	θ_4
a_1	15	10	9	6
a_2	12	11	11	8
a_3	9	11	13	9
a_4	7	12	13	13

Additionally, you have available a considerable amount of historical data that has enabled you to make the following probability estimates for the occurrence of the states of nature.

$$P(\theta_1) = 0.4$$
$$P(\theta_2) = 0.2$$
$$P(\theta_3) = 0.1$$
$$P(\theta_4) = 0.3$$

(a) Using an expected value decision criterion, which decision alternative should be selected?
(b) Using an expected loss decision criterion show that the same decision alternative as in part (a) above should be selected.
(c) Using an expected opportunity loss decision criterion show that the same decision alternative as in parts (a) and (b) above should be selected.
(d) If the probabilities associated with the states of nature change to:

$$P(\theta_1) = 0.1$$
$$P(\theta_2) = 0.3$$
$$P(\theta_3) = 0.4$$
$$P(\theta_4) = 0.2$$

does the selection of the optimum decision alternative also change?

2.   Suppose that a decision maker having four decision alternatives and four states of nature has developed the following payoff table.

Decision Alternative	State of Nature			
	θ_1	θ_2	θ_3	θ_4
a_1	15	13	12	9
a_2	12	11	9	10
a_3	9	10	7	12
a_4	7	10	8	12

You may assume that the decision maker knows nothing concerning the probability of occurrence of the various states of nature.
(a) Using a minimax decision procedure, which decision alternative should be selected?
(b) Using a maximax decision procedure, which decision alternative should be selected?
(c) Using a minimax regret decision procedure, which decision alternative should be selected?
(d) Assume that the decision maker is able to make the following subjective estimates of the probability of occurrence of the states of nature.

$$P(\theta_1) = 0.3$$
$$P(\theta_2) = 0.2$$
$$P(\theta_3) = 0.2$$
$$P(\theta_4) = 0.3$$

What decision alternative should be selected using a Bayes' decision procedure without data?

3. Harry is comtemplating his return from the Midwest to his prestigious East Coast university following the Christmas vacation. He has three modes of transportation, namely: airplane, railroad, or bus. Although not concerned with the cost of the trip, being independently wealthy, he is concerned with minimizing the time required to make the trip. Unfortunately, the time requirement for the trip, according to the mode of transportation, is subject to the vagaries of the weather. Since he is a management science student, Harry has decided to use decision theory to analyze the situation. Initially, he has developed the following transit time (hours) table.

Decision Alternative	State of Nature		
	θ_1: Good Weather	θ_2: Fair Weather	θ_3: Bad Weather
a_1: Plane	2	4	20
a_2: Train	8	10	12
a_3: Bus	10	12	16

Harry has also made a subjective estimate of the probability of occurrence of the three states of nature. These estimates are

$$P(\theta_1) = 0.2$$
$$P(\theta_2) = 0.3$$
$$P(\theta_3) = 0.5$$

What mode of transportation should Harry select?

4. Babs' Sporting Goods Store in suburban St. Louis is contemplating its seasonal order of new tennis equipment. Management of the store must decide whether to order a high, medium, or low amount of tennis equipment prior to the beginning of the tennis season, since the delivery time for the equipment is approximately 2 months. Sales of tennis equipment are a function of the tennis conditions in the area throughout the season. Subjective estimates that seasonal tennis playing conditions will be excellent, good, or poor, are 0.6, 0.3, and 0.1, respectively. The expected profit for each action and state of nature is given in the following table.

Decision Alternative	State of Nature		
	θ_1: Excellent Season	θ_2: Good Season	θ_3: Poor Season
a_1: Large order	$5000	$4000	$200
a_2: Medium order	4000	3000	500
a_3: Small order	2000	1000	750

(a) What decision alternative should Babs' Sporting Goods select, assuming that a Bayes' decision procedure without data is employed?
(b) The local weather bureau has compiled extensive actual data related to seasonal weather predictions. These data have been compiled in probabilistic form as indicated in the following table.

Forecasted Weather Is	*Actual Weather Is*		
	Excellent	*Good*	*Poor*
Excellent	0.7	0.2	0.1
Good	0.2	0.6	0.2
Poor	0.1	0.2	0.7

This data is provided free of charge by the weather bureau. What are the optimal Bayes' actions, given the various weather forecasts?
(c) What is the expected value of the optimal decision with the same data?
(d) What is the expected value of the sample information for this situation?
(e) What is the expected value of perfect information for this situation?
(f) What is the efficiency of information for this situation?

5. Bright Lites Movie Company is contemplating the production of a feature length documentary concerning the building of the Alaska oil pipeline. It can either produce and sell the film, or it can produce and lease the film. Under either arrangement, the film can go into limited distribution, United States distribution, or worldwide distribution. The profits expected to accrue to Bright Lites Movie Company for this situation are summarized in the following table.

Decision Alternative	*State of Nature*		
	θ_1: *Limited Distribution*	θ_2: *U.S. Distribution*	θ_3: *Worldwide Distribution*
a_1: Produce and sell	−$100,000	$1,000,000	$3,000,000
a_2: Produce and lease	100,000	900,000	3,000,000

Bright Lites Movie Company has made subjective estimates concerning the probability of the film's distribution. These estimates are

$$P(\theta_1: \text{Limited Distribution}) = 0.2$$
$$P(\theta_2: \text{U.S. Distribution}) = 0.5$$
$$P(\theta_3: \text{Worldwide Distribution}) = 0.3$$

(a) What decision alternative should Bright Lites Movie Company select, assuming that a Bayes' decision procedure without data is employed?
(b) Bright Lites Movie Company can purchase a market research study that will indicate public interest with respect to the three levels of distribution. Previous studies of a similar nature have indicated the following results.

Public Interest	State of Nature		
	θ_1: *Limited Distribution*	θ_2: *U.S. Distribution*	θ_3: *Worldwide Distribution*
Enthusiastic	0.2	0.4	0.7
Lukewarm	0.3	0.4	0.2
Negative	0.5	0.2	0.1

The cost of obtaining such data is $20,000. What are the optimal Bayes' actions, given the various expressions of public interest?

(c) What is the expected value of the optimal decision with the sample information?

(d) What is the expected value of the sample information for this situation?

(e) What is the expected value of perfect information for this problem?

(f) What is the efficiency of information for this problem?

6. The Cactus Land Company owns 10,000 acres of land in southeastern Arizona that may contain valuable uranium deposits. The company is faced with a decision whether to explore extensively for uranium, to lease the land, or to sell the land. For each of these three alternatives three states of nature may exist: θ_1, a large uranium deposit; θ_2, a small uranium deposit; θ_3, no uranium deposit. The possible profits for the various alternatives and the various states of nature are shown in the following table.

Decision Alternative	State of Nature		
	θ_1: *Large Uranium Deposit*	θ_1: *Small Uranium Deposit*	θ_3: *No Uranium Deposit*
Explore extensively	$10,000,000	$4,000,000	−$500,000
Lease land	5,000,000	2,000,000	750,000
Sell land	1,000,000	1,000,000	1,000,000

The Cactus Land Company has made (prior) subjective estimates concerning the probabilities of finding the various sizes of uranium deposits. These estimates are

$$P(\theta_1: \text{Large uranium deposit}) = 0.3$$
$$P(\theta_2: \text{Small uranium deposit}) = 0.3$$
$$P(\theta_3: \text{No uranium deposit}) = 0.4$$

(a) What decision alternative should the Cactus Land Company choose, assuming that a Bayes' decision procedure without data is employed?

(b) The Cactus Land Company can have a geologic study made of its land holdings. This study will cost $10,000 and will lead to four possible land classifications:

(1) Uranium deposits highly likely.
(2) Uranium deposits possible.

(3)   Uranium deposits unlikely.
(4)   Uranium deposits virtually impossible.

Based on previous studies of a similar nature the following probability information is obtained.

Geologic Classification	State of Nature		
	θ_1: Large Uranium Deposit	θ_2: Small Uranium Deposit	θ_3: No Uranium Deposit
Uranium deposits highly likely	0.6	0.3	0.1
Uranium deposits possible	0.2	0.5	0.1
Uranium deposits unlikely	0.1	0.1	0.1
Uranium deposits impossible	0.1	0.1	0.7

What are the optimal courses of action, given the various geologic classifications?
(c) What is the expected value of the optimal decision with the sample information?
(d) What is the expected value of the sample information for this situation?
(e) What is the expected value of perfect information for this problem?
(f) What is the efficiency of information for this problem?

7.   A revolutionary new process has been developed for the manufacture of golf balls. These golf balls are packaged in sets of three, and the manufacturer will sell a package of golf balls to a sporting goods wholesaler for $1.50. However, in order to become a distributor of these revolutionary new golf balls, the wholesaler must agree to one of two promotional actions.

1—Sell the package of golf balls for $2.50, agreeing to refund the entire purchase price if one or more of the golf balls is found to be defective.
2—Sell the package of golf balls for $2.00, agreeing to refund $0.50 for each golf ball found to be defective.

(a) Determine the loss table for this problem situation.
(b) The wholesaler has determined the following set of information related to the number of defectives based upon testing 60 randomly selected test boxes.

Quality of Test Ball	State of Nature			
	θ_1: 0 Defective	θ_2: 1 Defective	θ_3: 2 Defective	θ_4: 3 Defective
Good	11	10	7	3
Bad	4	6	7	12
Total	15	16	14	15

Testing does not cost the wholesaler anything. A priori, the wholesaler assumed that the probabilities associated with the states of nature were as follows.

$$P(\theta_1: \ 0 \text{ defective}) = 0.25$$
$$P(\theta_2: \ 1 \text{ defective}) = 0.30$$
$$P(\theta_3: \ 2 \text{ defective}) = 0.20$$
$$P(\theta_4: \ 3 \text{ defective}) = 0.25$$

What is the optimal Bayes' action before examining the test ball?

(c) What are the optimal Bayes' actions given the two measures of quality of the test balls?

(d) What is the expected value of the optimal decision with the sample information?

(e) What is the expected value of the sample information for this problem?

(f) What is the expected value of perfect information for this problem?

(g) What is the efficiency of information for this problem?

8. Work Problem 4 using a decision tree approach.

9. Work Problem 5 using a decision tree approach.

10. Work Problem 6 using a decision tree approach.

11. Work Problem 7 using a decision tree approach.

12. Consider the following table, which presents monetary payoffs for a series of three real estate projects, given three states of nature.

Real Estate Project	State of Nature		
	θ_1: Poor Market	θ_2: Average Market	θ_3: Good Market
Apartment complex	$1,000,000	$3,000,000	$5,000,000
Shopping center	5,000,000	11,000,000	18,000,000
Office building	30,000,000	50,000,000	100,000,000

Discussions with a real estate entrepreneur who is considering investing in these three projects suggest that she is initially indifferent to receiving a certain payoff of $60,000,000 compared to receiving a payoff of $P_1 = \$100,000,000$ with probability of 0.5 and a payoff of $P_2 = \$1,000,000$ with probability of 0.5. Continue this process, using your own set of certainty equivalents and determine a set of corresponding utility indices (determine at least five points).

13. Use the utility indices you determined in Problem 12 to draw a utility function. Then, construct a utility table to replace the payoff table for Problem 12. Assume that the real estate entrepreneur has estimated that there is a 0.2 probability associated with a "poor" market, a 0.5 probability associated with an "average" market, and a 0.3 probability associated with a "good" market. Determine the estimated monetary values and the estimated utilities for the three real estate projects. What is the best decision based on an expected monetary value decision criterion? What is the best decision based on an expected utility decision criterion?

14. Consider the following table, which presents the monetary payoffs associated with three farming plans, given three states of nature.

Farming Plan	State of Nature		
	θ_1: Bad Weather	θ_2: Average Weather	θ_3: Ideal Weather
Plant small acreage	−$10,000	$15,000	$25,000
Plant half of acreage	− 50,000	25,000	50,000
Plant entire acreage	− 100,000	40,000	90,000

Conversations with the farmer have led to the following assessment of his monetary payoffs and associated utility indices.

Point	Monetary Payoff $\left(\begin{array}{c}Certainty\\Equivalent\end{array}\right)$	Utility Index
1	−$100,000	0.00
2	90,000	1.00
3	55,000	0.50
4	75,000	0.75
5	25,000	0.25

Use these utility indices to construct a utility function. Then determine a utility table to replace the payoff table shown above.

15. Assume that the farmer in the previous problem has consulted his Farmer's Almanac and has estimated that there is a 0.25 probability associated with "bad" weather, a 0.50 probability associated with "average" weather, and a 0.25 probability associated with "ideal" weather. Determine the estimated monetary values and the estimated utilities for the three farming plans. What is the best decision based on an expected monetary value decision criterion? What is the best decision based on an expected utility decision criterion?

16. A saleswoman has two prospects, to which she has made sales in the past. The saleswoman's estimates of the payoff functions and her utility functions for the two prospects are as follows.

Prospect 1:

Payoff	Probability	$	U($)
$25	0.10	$25	0
100	0.70	100	0.50
250	0.20	200	0.65
		250	1.00

Prospect 2:

Payoff	Probability	$	U($)
$0	0.20	0	0
100	0.40	50	0.10
300	0.40	100	0.30
		200	0.60
		300	1.00

Determine the expected monetary value and the expected utility for each prospect and indicate which prospect should be preferred for each of the two decision criteria.

17. Suppose that another saleswoman has made a similar analysis and has arrived at identical payoff functions for the two prospects. However, she has a single utility function which is applicable to both prospects. This utility function is as follows.

$	$U(\$)$
0	0.00
25	0.10
50	0.20
100	0.30
200	0.50
250	0.65
300	0.80
500	1.00

On an expected utility basis, which prospect should be preferred for this saleswoman?

IV

Synthesis

Implementation of Management Science

17.1 INTRODUCTION

In this textbook we have attempted to consider the major topical areas of management science. To achieve this objective much of our discussion has necessarily been of a quantitative nature. Obviously, the competent management science professional must have a strong background and a firm understanding of the mathematical techniques that form the framework of management science. However, we do not want to leave the student of management science with the impression that management science is nothing more than a collection of mathematical exercises. Indeed, the mathematical analysis required in a typical management science study is often only a small portion of the total effort required for the study's completion. Consequently, in this final chapter we shall attempt to review some of the important aspects of implementing management science.

Recall from our introductory remarks in Chapter 1 that the methodology of management science proceeds according to the following steps.

1. Analysis of the system and problem formulation.
2. Model formulation based on the analysis of the system.
3. Model and hypothesis testing.
4. Model conclusions and implementation.

In this chapter we will examine in more detail the final important step in the methodology of management science; **implementation**. Unlike our previous discussions, this material will not be mathematical. Rather, we shall focus on the people and the human relations aspects of management science. As we begin our discussion we must stress that there is no universal process or guaranteed procedure for the implementation of management science. Thus, we shall attempt only to provide a few reasonable and practical guidelines for the management scientist to follow. Overriding this future discussion should be the understanding that the key to conducting management science successfully is the mature judgment of the analyst, a characteristic that is gained with experience. In this regard, it is important for the management scientist to recognize that the results of the study provide only one input to the decision maker, or manager. Although this input may be very important, it will most likely not be the only input on which the manager must base a decision.

There is no hard evidence as to what constitutes a "typical" management science study. In a survey of the *Fortune* "top 500" corporations in the United States, Turban[1] found that the average duration of management science projects was about 10 months. The duration of individual projects varied from 1 to 80 months.

He also determined that an average of 2.5 people are assigned to a typical management science project. This suggests that most management science projects require a team effort. Projecting his findings we might conclude that a typical management science project lasting about 10 months and utilizing an average of 2.5 people could be expected to require about 2 man-years of effort to complete.

Turban also considered the question of how many management science projects are successfully implemented. First, he asked a general question concerning the percentage of projects that were implemented, and then he asked a specific question about the implementation of each project that was considered in the study. With respect to the general question concerning implementation he found that almost 65 percent of all management science projects were implemented to a major degree. Considering specific project implementation Turban determined that over 55 percent of all management science projects were implemented successfully.[2]

The implementation of management science models may create a source of conflict between the management scientist and the operating manager. The professionally oriented management scientist tends to emphasize the quality of the modeling effort. The most important considerations are the development of a rigorous, powerful, and mathematically sophisticated model. Elegant computerization of the model is also a favored characteristic of the modeling process. The approach and the philosophy of the management scientist are readily understandable, given that the likelihood of his or her promotion and professional recognition and stature are closely related to the quality of the modeling effort.

The operating manager, however, tends to view models as a device for evaluating various decision alternatives. The operating manager must recognize that a problem requiring a decision exists, search for possible courses of action, evaluate these courses of action, and select the alternative that he or she believes will satisfy the need. The model therefore comes to be judged by the manager from a pragmatic viewpoint. From a managerial viewpoint the best and most effective

---

[1] Efraim Turban, "A Sample Survey of Operations Research Activities at the Corporate Level," *Operations Research*, 20: no. 3 (May–June 1972), 708–721.

[2] Ibid.

model is one that is valid, relevant, and cost-effective. The model is **valid** if its results can be depended upon; it is **relevant** if it effectively addresses the problem under consideration; and it is **cost-effective** if it suggests operating improvements that exceed the costs of developing and applying the model. The manager is also keenly interested in obtaining the model's output in a timely manner.

The conflict that may arise from the differing viewpoints of the manager and management scientist is apparent from the discussion above. One manifestation is that the management scientist tends to seek out problems that will enhance his or her professional reputation and skills. Unfortunately, such problems may not be those that are considered to be most important from the viewpoint of the operating manager. Thus, the management scientist may become more interested in implementing solutions to problems that advance the state of the art but that do very little with respect to real-world management problems.

A second manifestation of the potential conflict between the manager and the management scientist arises with respect to the successful completion of the modeling effort. Quite often, the management scientist may view his or her professional responsibility as demanding that the modeling effort be 100 percent completed. The operating manager, however, may be willing to implement the results achieved with 75 to 85 percent of the modeling effort completed. Again, the professional and technological orientation of the management scientist may not be in accord with the pragmatic approach of the manager. In summary, conflicts of modeling criteria are among the most important potential barriers to the implementation of management science.

17.2 THE IMPLEMENTATION PROBLEM

As management science has evolved in business, government, and military organizations over the last three decades, there has been a constant debate concerning its successful implementation.[3] In its early development, management science was perhaps oversold by zealous practitioners. As such, management science was suggested as a panacea or "cure all" for numerous corporation problems. Early emphasis was on modeling and improving various operations of the firm. As a result of the successful utilization of management science techniques for solving specific, small operating problems, the tendency was to seek problems of an ever-increasing magnitude to which management science could be applied. This philosophy led to the development of large, complex models of the entire corporation. As Hayes and Nolan[4] have noted, the type of reasoning used in this evolution to a corporate model had the following steps.

1. Assuming that the company can develop a model for a single plant function, such as plant operations, then the company should be able to develop a model for all plant functions.

---

[3] Much of the material in this section is drawn from an earlier paper: Robert E. Markland and Robert J. Newett, "A Subjective Taxonomy for Evaluating the Stages of Management Science Research," *Interfaces*, 2: no. 2 (January 1972), 31-9, copyright 1972, The Institute of Management Sciences, reprinted by permission.

[4] For an excellent discussion of the evolution of such a corporate modeling approach see: Robert H. Hayes, and Richard L. Nolan, "What Kind of Corporate Modeling Functions are Best?" *Harvard Business Review*, 52: no. 3 (May–June 1974), 102-12.

2. Assuming that the company can develop a model for all the functions of one plant, it should be able to develop a model that encompasses all of its plants.
3. By adding a "corporate functions" sector to the model that encompasses all of the plants, a corporate model emerges.

One notable example of the failure of such an approach occurred in a large, vertically integrated wood products company. This company successfully utilized a linear programming model in the improvement of the performance of one of its saw mills in the early 1960s. It then utilized the same approach for other plants, and ultimately tried to implement an extremely complicated linear programming model of its entire vertically integrated operation. However, this attempt was unsuccessful and led to abandonment of large-scale management science modeling efforts by this company. A comparable situation occurred within a major oil company, where a large-scale simulation model became intractable and unwieldy, and was abandoned as an unsuccessful attempt was made to implement it as a large-scale planning device. The author is also familiar with a network-modeling study that was abandoned after 2 years of effort by a large chemical company because the corporate managers could not delay any further making critical distribution decisions. Similar examples of management science implementation failures, although seldom found in published literature, are often the subject of conversation and discussion at professional meetings.

During the 1960s and 1970s a large body of theoretical management science knowledge was accumulated. At the same time, however, many practitioners were expressing considerable doubt concerning the future viability of management science activities within large organizations. This doubt was based on the pervasive question of, "To what extent has the implementation of management science research been successful?"

During this same time period the implementation dilemma was discussed, debated, and assessed by professional societies, such as The Institute of Management Science (TIMS), the Operations Research Society of American (ORSA), and the American Institute for Decision Sciences (AIDS), and by academicians, researchers, and managers. A vast body of research on the problems associated with implementation has resulted and been reported in various forms. One body of this previous research has been devoted to surveying and categorizing the types of techniques that have been utilized for management science work within large corporations. Several surveys of this nature were discussed earlier in Chapter 1. A considerably larger segment of research has focused attention on the problems associated with implementation. As an example of this type of study, Grayson[5] has indicated the following reasons for the failure to utilize management science.

1. Shortage of time required to make the management science study.
2. Inaccessibility of data required for the management science study.
3. Resistance to change by the organization and its managers.
4. Long response time required for the management science study.
5. Invalidating simplifications that are often present in the management science study.

---

[5] C. Jackson Grayson, Jr., "Management Science and Business Practice," *Harvard Business Review*, 51, no. 4 (July–August 1973), 41–8.

In summary, then, a constant theme of the research dealing with the implementation of management science has been that the implementation problem has not been resolved, and in many instances has not even been satisfactorily analyzed.

17.2.1 Defining Implementation

In attempting to analyze the implementation problem, it is probably useful to begin by attempting to develop a working definition of "successful implementation." At the user's end of the spectrum, successful implementation is most usually thought of in terms of the usefulness of the model and its attendant solution. Herein, the user's main concern is that the model's output is useful, timely, and relevant. A different concept of successful implementation is likely to be held by the management science analyst and the manager of the management science staff or group. These individuals are inclined to equate successful implementation with the selling of the study and its results to operating management. Indeed, many would contend that the practicing management scientist needs to be both a technical expert and a master of the "art of persuasion." Furthermore, a revealing observation is that, in much of the published information on the subject, implementation is obliquely discussed in terms of "effective communication with operating personnel," with an emphasis being placed on the "selling" aspects of "communicating."

Churchman and Schainblatt, in their classic study of the dialectic of implementation that exists between the researcher and manager developed four concepts of the manager-researcher relationship that can be used to analyze implementation. However, in spite of the intellectual sophistication of the Churchman-Schainblatt paper, they advocate a rather straightforward definition of implementation in which they state:

> We shall use the term "implementation" to refer to the manner in which the manager may come to use the results of scientific effort. The "problem of implementation" is the problem of determining what activities of the scientist and manager are most appropriate to bring about an effective relationship.[6]

This definition indicates that Churchman and Schainblatt are simply suggesting that successful implementation occurs whenever a viable working relationship is established between the researcher and the user. Another approach to this definitional problem has been made by Huysmans (1970, p. 1) who offers a provisional working definition of implementation, indicating

> We will say that an operations research recommendation is implemented if the manager or managers affected by the recommendation adopt the research in essence and continue to use it as long as the conditions underlying the research apply.

We would propose to modify these definitions slightly, and suggest that successful implementation should be defined as the establishment of a viable working relationship that is maintained for a reasonable time period between the user and analyst, and during which controls for the continuous review and scrutiny of the

---

[6] C. N. Churchman, and A. H. Schainblatt, "The Researcher and The Manager: A Dialectic of Implementation," *Management Science* 2, no. 4 (February 1965), B69–87.

research's recommended solution are developed and utilized. This expanded definition embodies both the necessary technical model validity and the required communications link between analyst and user. Additionally, a control mechanism is made an integral part of the definition, because only by continuous review can one be sure that communication concerning validity is really taking place. Finally, it includes the important premise that the working relationship that is established between the analyst and user must exist over time instead of occurring at a point in time.

Implementation of the results of a management science study inherently involves change in the operating environment of an organization. In many cases, the decisions made as a result of a management science study can have a significant effect on several functional areas of a company. For example, the author has participated in a management science study that led to a change in the company's distribution system. This distribution system change then required changes in the company's marketing efforts, production planning and scheduling, inventory control procedures, and warehouse locations.

Since change is inherent in the implementation of management science, the analyst must be aware of the critical importance of the working relationship that is established with the user. The user of the results of the management science study is the decision maker who is responsible for managing the change that will occur. Thus, the decision maker's role in the study must be active rather than passive. This means that the management scientist must seek to involve the user, or manager, in all phases and all aspects of the study. From the user's perspective it is important that this involvement be truly active, and the user should plan on making a specific time commitment in order to actively participate in the project.

17.2.2 A Procedure for Evaluating Implementation

Having developed a working definition for implementation it is necessary next to develop an evaluation procedure for studying the implementation success or failure of individual projects. Such an evaluation procedure was developed a few years ago by the author, in cooperation with the management science staff of the Ralston Purina Company, St. Louis, Missouri.

We began by attempting to survey those implementation factors that were considered to be important by previous researchers. Second, we sought to consider the factors affecting implementation success as they were perceived by the members of the management science staff at Ralston Purina. This approach to isolating the factors affecting successful implementation blended both the academic and the pragmatic.

We next considered the important matter of timing, and its influence on the success or failure of a management science project. For example, a factor that might have a significant influence on the success of a project in the early stage of that project might have little or no influence on the success of the same project in a later stage of its life. Additionally, the evaluation criteria should be measured at a number of important junctures of the project's life, and reasons for changes in the measurement of the evaluation criteria should be noted and analyzed.

In order to incorporate timing into the evaluation methodology, we defined a "project life chronology" by restructuring the taxonomy proposed by Rubenstein, et al.,[7] for the evolution of management science activities within the large corporation. Our project life chronology included six "life phases" defined as follows:

1. *Prebirth Phase.* This phase occurs when either the operating manager or the management science manager perceives a possibly useful management science project. During this phase no formal project exists, but small, informal projects may be in progress within the operating division.
2. *Introductory Phase.* This phase begins with operating management granting a charter for a specific management science activity. As a result, specific resources are allocated to the activity.
3. *Transitional Phase.* This phase is characterized by an emphasis being placed on results by operating and top management. During this phase the management science team is necessarily results-oriented, toward project definition and model construction and solution.
4. *Maturity Phase.* This phase is signaled by the acceptance of the study by operating management as a decision-making aid. Continued modeling and analytical efforts by the management science team are likely during this phase, but the intensity of commitment of resources is probably diminishing.
5. *Death Phase.* During this phase, all project activities are formally completed by agreement between the user and the management science manager. If the study is considered successful, this phase may involve the "systematizing" or "computerizing" of its results on a recurring basis for the operating manager.
6. *Resurrection Phase.* This phase occurs when a previously "dead" project is resurrected for any of a number of reasons (e.g., a new manager becomes interested in a dead project, or software permitting the solution of a previously unsolvable problem becomes available).

The two major features of our proposed taxonomy were combined to form an "ideal implementation evaluation grid," shown as Table 17.1. Within the grid framework shown in Table 17.1, we evaluated the importance of each implementation criterion over time and assigned an "ideal" value of 1.0 to each implementation criterion judged to be of extreme importance during any particular life phase. If an implementation criterion did not have an entry of 1.0 during some life phase, this did not necessarily imply that it was of no importance. Rather, we focused our appraisal on those implementation factors having the greatest importance at various time junctures.

This ideal implementation evaluation grid was then employed to quantitatively appraise the life stages of various management science projects in a subjective manner. A scale value of 0.0 was considered as representing a completely "negative" measure of implementation success, while the scale value of 1.0 was considered as representing a completely "positive" or "ideal" measure of implementation success. The scale value of 0.5 denoted a "neutral" value of implementation success in which the project was unaffected by a particular factor.

---

[7] A. H. Rubenstein, et al., "Some Organizational Factors Related to Effectiveness of Management Science Groups in Industry," *Management Science*, 13, no. 8 (April 1967), B508–18.

TABLE 17.1 "Ideal" Implementation Evaluation Grid

Implementation Criteria	Life Phases					
	Prebirth	Introductory	Transitional	Maturity	Death	Resurrection
1. Managerial						
a. Top mgmt.—interest		1.0	1.0			1.0
b. Operating mgmt.—involvment	1.0	1.0	1.0	1.0	1.0	1.0
c. Operations research mgmt.—managerial skill	1.0	1.0			1.0	1.0
2. Operations research/ MS Team						
a. Technical ability		1.0	1.0			
b. Project management skills		1.0	1.0	1.0		
c. Results orientation		1.0	1.0	1.0		
d. Communicative ability	1.0	1.0	1.0	1.0		
3. Project						
a. Technical feasibility	1.0	1.0	1.0			
b. Economic feasibility		1.0	1.0	1.0		
c. Operational feasibility		1.0	1.0	1.0		1.0
Summation	4.0	10.0	9.0	6.0	2.0	4.0

17.2.3 Case Studies—Evaluating Implementation

The implementation evaluation grid described above was subsequently employed as an appraisal device for two management science projects that were judged to have been successful by the cooperating company. Both projects had evolved over a period of time in excess of 2½ years and were characterized by the establishment of a strong working relationship between the user organization and the management science team. Additionally, both projects resulted in the delivery of model output to the user which was subsequently employed in a decision-making context. Each of these projects will now be discussed as case studies illustrating the process of evaluating implementation.

CASE STUDY 1: DISTRIBUTION SYSTEM SIMULATION MODEL

The simulation-modeling problem arose in the context of a management science effort directed at improving the aggregate distribution system of the Consumer Products Division of the company. This division was responsible for the production and marketing of breakfast cereals, seafood products, pet foods, and poultry products. It sought to provide service to all of its national marketing areas from a series of manufacturing plants, mixing points, and warehouses. Meeting this objective created the problem of defining a total distribution system that would minimize the inclusive costs of distributing all products to the market while maintaining a satisfactory level of customer service.

The model that was developed to

TABLE 17.2 Implementation Evaluation Grid for Distribution System Simulation Model

	Life Phases[a]					
Implementation Criteria	1/67 Prebirth	1/69 Introductory	1/70 Transitional	6/70 Maturity	Death	Resurrection
1. Managerial						
a. Top mgmt.—interest		0.7	0.5			
b. Operating mgmt.—involvement	0.8	0.8	0.7	0.8		
c. Operations research mgmt.—managerial skill	0.8	0.7				
2. Operations research/ MS team						
a. Technical ability		0.9	0.7			
b. Project management skills		0.8	0.7	0.7		
c. Results orientation		0.7	0.8	0.7		
d. Communicative ability	0.7	0.8	0.8	0.7		
3. Project						
a. Technical feasibility	0.8	0.8	0.5	0.6		
b. Economic feasibility		0.5	0.6	0.7		
c. Operational feasibility		0.5	0.7	0.8		
Summation	3.1	7.2	6.0	4.4		
Percent of "ideal" summation	77.5	72.0	66.7	73.3		

[a]The dates indicated are starting dates.

meet this objective was designed to simulate the product flows and inventory levels of the division, over time, throughout approximately 150 "demand analysis areas" of the United States.[8] The continuous flow aspects of the model were defined by an industrial dynamics methodology that incorporated a three-echelon model (production sector, distribution sector, and wholesale sector) and utilized a series of first-order difference equations as discrete approximations to the continuous time product flow integrals.

A quantitative appraisal of the importance of the various implementation factors over the project's life phases is presented in Table 17.2. Although the values shown in Table 17.2 are obviously the results of subjective judgments, the importance of operating management's continuing involvement throughout the project's life is apparent, as is the effect of continual communication efforts on the part of the management science team. Furthermore, the values shown in the grid reflect the importance of the technical aspects of the project during its early life phases. The lack of major interest by top management can also be discerned, as well as the fact that the organizational skills of the management science manager are most important during the

[8] A detailed discussion of this model can be found in: Robert E. Markland, "Analyzing Geographically Discrete Warehousing Networks by Computer Simulation," *Decision Sciences*, 4, no. 2 (April 1973), 216–36.

first two phases of the project's life. Additionally, the decrease, over time, in the importance of economic feasibility can be contrasted to the increasing importance, over time, of operating feasibility. Finally, the gradual erosion of the management science team's importance, over time, is manifested in the grid.

The major conclusions drawn from this first case study of implementation were

- The continuing involvement of the management of the operating division was a very important contributory factor to implementation success.

- The communicative ability of the management science team was of major importance in each life phase.

- Top management interest had little impact on the successful implementation of the project.

- The technical feasibility of the project decreased in importance over time, while the project's economic feasibility and operational feasibility assumed greater importance.

CASE STUDY 2: LARGE LINEAR PROGRAMMING MODEL

The linear programming model that was the subject of the second evaluation was developed for the Checkerboard Farms Division of the company's agricultural products group. This division had responsibility for the production, processing, and marketing of whole ice-pack broilers (chickens) to 45 national markets. (In a later year this operation was sold.)

Since the selling price and feed costs for broilers were affected by commodity price fluctuations, the basic objective of this study was to derive a planning model, with a 15- to 27-month time horizon, which could be used to maximize broiler production (i.e., specify the number of pounds of a particular grade of broiler to be produced monthly). The operating division provided the basic model inputs, which consisted of forecasts of broiler selling prices and feed costs, for the duration of the planning horizon. These data were then utilized in the construction and solution of a 925-row by 3800-column linear programming model.

A quantitative appraisal of the importance of the various implementation factors over the project's life phases is presented in Table 17.3. As reflected in the grid, there was a low level of top management interest and operating management involvement in the project until the very late life phases. Conversely, the high degree of involvement of the management science manager, as reflected in his managerial skill, was also apparent from the examination of the grid values. The positive aspect of the technical ability of the management science team was also evident, as was the importance of the choice of a linear programming methodology to satisfy technical feasibility requirements. The grid indicated a very moderate concern for economic feasibility and a marked lack of concern for operational feasibility. The breakdown in communications, during the "transitional" phase of the project's life, could also be detected. Finally, the overall skills of the management science team throughout the project's life were very discernible.

The major conclusions resulting from this second case study of implementation were

- The low level of top management interest and operating management

TABLE 17.3 Implementation Evaulation Grid for Large Linear Programmming Model

Implementation Criteria	Life Phases[a]					
	10/67 Prebirth	1/68 Introductory	6/68 Transitional	10/68 Maturity	5/69 Death	6/70 Resurrection
1. Managerial						
a. Top mgmt.—interest		0.2	0.6			0.9
b. Operating mgmt.—involvement	0.2	0.2	0.6	0.3	0.7	0.6
c. Operations research mgmt.—managerial skill	0.8	0.6			0.7	0.8
2. Operations research/ MS team						
a. Technical ability		0.9	0.8			
b. Project management skills		0.8	0.7	0.7		
c. Results orientation		0.8	0.8	0.9		
d. Communicative ability	0.8	0.8	0.4	0.6		
3. Project						
a. Technical feasibility	0.9	0.9	0.8			
b. Economic feasibility		0.6	0.6	0.6		
c. Operational feasibility		0.8	0.8	0.8		0.5
Summation	2.7	6.4	5.6	3.9	1.4	2.8
Percent of "ideal" summation	67.5	64.0	62.2	65.0	70.0	70.0

[a]The dates indicated are starting dates.

involvement created a number of implementation "roadblocks," which were overcome primarily by the results orientation of the management science team.

- The choice of linear programming as an analytical tool greatly enhanced project implementation from a technical standpoint.
- A lack of concern for the project's operational feasibility during its early life phases had a negative effect, and this led to project redirection toward operational feasibility during later project life.
- The management science manager's skills were required both early and late during the project's life, primarily in a communicative capacity.
- Top management interest was the major factor leading to resurrection of the project.

In summary, the empirical case studies reported above have suggested several implications concerning the factors most significant to the successful implementation of management science research. Although these implications are certainly not offered as necessary and sufficient conditions for successful implementation, the evaluation procedure that has been suggested might well serve as a framework for evaluating data concerning the implementation question.

Northwestern University, under the leadership of Professor Albert H. Rubenstein,[9] has been conducting a continuing investigation of management science practices in industry. These studies have led to the identification of 10 factors that seem to determine the success or failure of management science groups. These factors are

1. The level of managerial support including the extent of managerial understanding and acceptance of the need for management science activities.
2. The organizational location of the management science activity.
3. The adequacy of the resources allocated to the activity.
4. The receptivity of the client as manifested in the charter granted to the management science group to select projects, gather data, and implement results.
5. The strength of opposition to the management science activity within the organization.
6. The reputation of the management science activity within the organization.
7. The general perception of the level of success of the management science activity within the organization.
8. The organizational and technical capability of the management science group.
9. The relevance and practicability of the projects undertaken by the management science group.
10. The influence that the management science group and its leadership could exert within the organization.

The Northwestern University studies tended to agree with our research in that they also concluded that the relationships among the management science group, operating management, and top management were most critical to the success or failure of the management science activity. They also stressed that the ultimate success of a management science group is determined by the production of successful results. This suggests that it may be desirable for the management science group to initially select a few short-term, high-return projects and attempt to successfully complete them in a short time period. In this manner the credibility and capability of the management science group will be enhanced and more project requests will likely result.

17.2.4 Control Aspects of Implementation

Given that implementation of a management science study proceeds over a reasonably long period of time, a need may arise for the establishment of some type of review and control system. The basic reason for establishing such a control system is to monitor the implemented model's output and to make sure that this output continues to produce valid and relevant information for the decision-making process. In this regard, it should be recognized that a number of changes can occur that may affect the validity of a model's output.

First, the criteria used to develop the measure of effectiveness (i.e., objective function) for the original model may change. For example, instead of simply

[9] Albert H. Rubenstein, et al., "Some Organizational Factors Related to the Effectiveness of Management Science Groups in Industry, *Management Science,* 13, no. 8 (April 1967), B508–18.

maximizing profit, the decision maker may find it necessary to instead minimize the utilization of some increasingly scarce resource.

Second, there may be a drastic change in the variables that were controllable in the original model. For example, changes in discrimination laws may preclude work-force reductions that were suggested by the solution resulting from the original model formulation.

Third, it is very likely for some of the model constraints to change over time. Advances in processing technology, changes in resource availabilities, and increased governmental regulations, all can have a significant effect on constraint relationships in a modeling context.

Finally, the structure of the modeling environment may change markedly. For example, a distribution system model based on rail transportation would have to be drastically altered if the company purchased a truck fleet to service part of its distribution needs.

Because of the dynamic environment in which managerial decisions are made, effective control systems for implemented management science modeling efforts are necessary. If such control systems are not instituted as a part of the implementation process, it is likely that the model's output will cause decisions to be made based on an incorrect set of conditions. Thus, a feedback control mechanism should be an integral part of the implementation process in management science work. Quite often a feedback control system will involve the use of a digital computer. The development of decision-making management information systems in which management science models are integrated is a rapidly developing area of interest. This topic will be discussed more fully in a later section of this chapter.

17.3 THE "TEAM" APPROACH TO MANAGEMENT SCIENCE

In the technical literature concerning the practice of management science there has been considerable discussion of the desirability of an interdisciplinary approach to management science studies. However, most management science groups in business, and in governmental, military, and industrial organizations, tend to be rather small in number. Most management science groups are composed of persons with training in mathematics, statistics, engineering (typically industrial, mechanical, or electrical), business administration, and economics. Often, one or more will hold a doctoral degree, and most of the group will have master's degrees. Thus, it is apparent that the management science group itself will typically not tend to have broad interdisciplinary skills.

Rather than advocating an interdisciplinary approach to management science that is often unattainable because of personnel limitations, we would suggest that a "team" approach be employed. A **team approach** involves utilizing a variety of skills and backgrounds within the organization, including those of the management science staff and operating personnel. Shycon[10] has suggested that the team consist of the following types of individuals.

1. *One or more management scientists.* Persons with skills and experience in applying management science to real-world management problems. These in-

---

[10] Harvey N. Shycon, "All Around the Model," *Interfaces,* 2: no. 3. (May 1972), 33–5.

dividuals should have a practical applications orientation and strong analytical ability.

2. *One or more computer scientists.* These persons should be a blend of analyst, model builder, and computer programmer. They are, however, much more than simply programmers, and indeed may be management scientists with a particular facility for using the computer to manipulate data and solve problems.

3. *One or more broad, nontechnical individuals.* These persons should know the company and its organization well, so that the operating problem can be interpreted for the management scientist. They can also assist in data collection, in obtaining the cooperation of operating personnel, and in facilitating the implementation of the results of the study.

4. *One or more persons from the area being studied.* These individuals will have an intimate, direct knowledge of the operating problem being studied. They will be called upon by the management scientist to provide data, to interpret proposed solutions, and to actually see that the model continues to serve as a decision-making tool over time.

The team approach to management science utilizes the diverse backgrounds of numerous individuals throughout the organization. Although the management scientist assumes the key leadership role in the team's efforts, other members of the team provide valuable insights concerning the model's applicability to the real-world problem being analyzed. Thus, it is necessary for the efforts of all the members of the team to be integrated into a single effort that all the members of the team understand and agree is worthwhile.

17.4   MANAGING THE MANAGEMENT SCIENCE STAFF

As noted previously, the management science staff in any organization may be highly variable in size and location. Large companies may have sizeable groups with 25 or more individuals, while the management science staff in a small company may be composed of only 5 or 6 professionals. Depending upon the size and organizational structure of the company, management science activities may occur at both the corporate level (**centralized**) and within the operating divisions (**decentralized**). The management science staff may find itself reporting to the controller, the director of data processing, a financial vice-president, a manufacturing vice-president, or a research and development manager. Thus, no standard pattern with respect to the size and location of the management science staff has evolved.

A few comments can be made concerning the management of the management science staff. First, it is obvious that size alone is not a good indicator of the productivity of the staff. The quality of the management science staff should be stressed rather than its size. A small group of talented and dedicated management scientists is likely to have a greater impact on the organization than a large group that is less professionally oriented.

Second, it is apparent the manager of the management science staff must encourage and foster an attitude of professional responsibility. This means that the manager should encourage professional activities, attendance at professional meetings, writing and delivering of papers and speeches, and continued education.

Likewise, the management science manager must seek to make sure that the management science staff adheres to high professional standards and does not engage in excessive organizational politics.

Third, it must be recognized that management science is virtually always a staff activity. It exists only as a service to some user. Thus, the orientation and philosophy of the management science staff must be toward providing a useful service. Herein, the management science manager must be careful not to undertake more projects than can be accomplished within a reasonable period of time. Likewise, the management science manager should attempt to cooperate with the user in the selection of projects to be worked on. Often, projects of a less interesting technical nature, but with a greater real-world payoff, will be most desirable from the operating manager's perspective. The successful manager of a management science staff will recognize this fact and will adopt a viewpoint that is compatible with the user's desires.

17.5 INFORMATION SYSTEMS AND MANAGEMENT SCIENCE

In recent years the rapid development of the high-speed digital computer has facilitated the provision of more accurate and timely information for managerial decision making. Many organizations have spent enormous sums of money to design and implement formal systems for collecting, analyzing, and reporting information to managers. Such computerized systems are called **management information systems**. The study of the design and implementation of management information systems has become a major field of research and academic interest. While it is not feasible or practical to consider management information systems to any great extent in this chapter, it is useful to briefly discuss the interface between management information systems and management science models.

Management information systems can be classified according to the output they provide the user. Beginning with a **data base**, which is usually a large, computerized set of raw data, various hardware and software systems are utilized to make a transformation of the raw data into information that can be used by managers in making decisions. The three types of management information systems that usually result are

1. Control report management information systems
2. Interactive inquiry management information systems
3. Decision-making management information systems

The **control report management information system** merely transforms the raw data contained in the data base into various types of summary reports that can then be used for control purposes. Typical reports that are produced by this type of management information system are

1. Profit and loss statements
2. Balance sheets
3. Pro forma income statements
4. Inventory level reports
5. Daily production summaries

All these types of reports involve the transformation of the data base into historical or status reports involving some aspect of the corporation's activities.

The **interactive inquiry management information system** creates reports that enable the manager to access the possible consequences of future events or conditions. Quite often this type of management information is implemented in a **time-sharing computer environment**. In such an environment, the manager can interact with the computer (i.e., with the information system that has been computerized) by asking various questions that probe the future consequences of various decisions and actions. These questions are usually referred to as "what if" questions. Typical questions that might be posed within such a system are

1. How will profitability be affected by a price increase for a particular product line?
2. How will the cash flow for a particular division be affected by opening a major new plant facility?
3. Can cost savings be realized by the divestiture of a particular operating division?

The reports generated from an interactive inquiry management information system tend to be projections based on various assumptions, and often weighted by probabilistic information. Quite often, simple mathematical or statistical model are an integral part of such management information systems.

The **decision-making management information system** represents the evolution in which the management science model is embedded within the information system itself. In this type of management information system, the manager receives a report that indicates the consequences of future events and suggests or recommends a course of action. Virtually any of the management science models or techniques we have discussed in this book would be suitable for incorporation in a decision-making management information system. For example, inventory control models are commonly structured into information systems and used to make decisions concerning when and how much to manufacture of a particular product. Similarly, the author has worked with the installation of a large logistics-planning information system in which a transportation algorithm is employed for making commodity purchasing and allocation decisions for multiple plants, origins, and destinations for a major United States food manufacturer.[11] The logistics planning system was developed using teleprocessing for interactive communication between the widely scattered production plants and the large central computer system (IBM 370/155) located at the company's headquarters in St. Louis, Missouri. The major components of this decision-making management information system are shown in Fig. 17.1.

This logistics planning system allowed the company to make rapid and accurate decisions concerning the purchasing of its raw materials and the allocation of its end products. Interactive teleprocessing was employed to facilitate rapid communication between the widely scattered production facilities, at which the basic logistics decisions were made, and the central computer facility, which contained the data base and mathematical model (transportation algorithm) used to determine the optimum logistics decisions employed at the plants.

---

[11] Details concerning this system may be found in: Robert E. Markland, "Logistics Planning, Using Teleprocessing," *Journal of Systems Management*, 20: no. 10 (October 1973), 32–6.

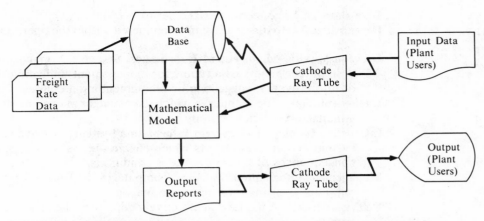

FIGURE 17.1   Logistics Planning System. Reprinted from Journal of Systems Management

In summary, management science is becoming much more important in the development of management information systems. The mathematical models that are developed as a part of the methodology of management science can be employed both to transform the raw data base into useful information and to enable managers to use this transformed information to make better decisions. The increased use of management science models within management information systems is necessary for obtaining the maximum benefit from both the information system development effort and the management science project.

17.6   CONCLUSION

It has been over 30 years since operations research or management science was introduced as a means of decision making in business, industrial, governmental, and military organizations. Since that time a number of important contributions and achievements can be attributed to practitioners of operations research or management science. However, there still are many situations in which management science is not being utilized to its fullest potential because of various operational, organizational, or administrative problems. Most of the problems revolve about the implementation of the technical results produced by the management scientist. Thus, to be a truly successful management science practitioner one must not only have a firm understanding of the tools and techniques of field but must also be able to effectively utilize the findings of other disciplines, particularly those of the behavioral sciences, in achieving implementation.

GLOSSARY OF TERMS

Centralized Activities   Activities conducted at the corporate level.

Control Report Management Information System   A management information system that transforms the raw data contained in the data base into various types of summary reports which can then be used for control purposes.

Cost-Effective Model   A model that suggests operating improvements which decrease operating costs by an amount that exceeds the cost of developing and applying the model.

Data Base   A large, computerized set of raw data.

Decentralized Activities   Activities conducted within the operating divisions of the firm.

Decision-Making Management Information System   A management information system that generates a report for management indicating the consequences of future events, suggesting or recommending a course of action.

Implementation   The manner in which the manager may come to use the results of a management science study.

Interactive Inquiry Management Information System   A management information system that creates reports which enable the manager to assess the possible consequences of future events or conditions.

Management Information Systems   Computerized systems for collecting, analyzing, and reporting information to managers.

Relevant Model   A model that effectively addresses the problem under consideration.

"Team" Approach to Management Science   An approach that involves utilizing a variety of skills and backgrounds within the organization, including those of the management science staff and operating personnel.

Time-Sharing Computer Environment   An environment in which the manager can interact with the computer by asking various questions that probe the future consequences of various decisions and actions.

Valid Model   A model whose results can be depended upon.

SELECTED REFERENCES

IMPLEMENTATION OF MANAGEMENT SCIENCE

Ackoff, Russell, and Patrick Rivett. 1963. *A Manager's Guide to Operations Research*. New York: John Wiley & Sons, Inc.

Bennis, Warren G. 1966. *Changing Organizations*. New York: McGraw-Hill Book Company, Inc.

Huysmans, Jan H.B.M. 1970. *The Implementation of Management Science*. New York: John Wiley & Sons, Inc.

Lerner, Robert N. 1965. *The Management of Improvement*. New York: Reinhold Publishing Company.

Miller, David W., and Martin K. Starr. 1969. *Executive Decisions and Operations Research*. Englewood Cliffs, N.J.: Prentice-Hall, Inc.

Schuchman, Abe. 1963. *Scientific Decision Making in Business*. New York: Holt, Rinehart & Winston, Inc.

Singh, J. 1972. *Great Ideas of Operations Research*. New York: Dover Publishing.

DISCUSSION QUESTIONS

1. Why might the implementation of management science models create a source of conflict between the management scientist and operating manager?
2. Develop a comprehensive working definition of "successful implementation."
3. Why is a "working relationship" between the analyst and the user so important once the results of a management science study are implemented?
4. What is the importance of a "project life chronology" with respect to an evaluation procedure for implementation?
5. How is an "ideal implementation evaluation grid framework" used?

6. When may the establishment of some "control system" become necessary with respect to the implementation of a management science study?
7. Name four possible changes that may affect the validity of a model's output.
8. What do we mean by a "team" approach to management science? What is the main advantage of this approach?
9. Describe briefly the difference between "control report," "interactive inquiry," and "decision making" management information systems.

Appendices

Probability Theory and Statistics Review

Probability theory and statistics are utilized in several places in this textbook, most notably for decision analysis, waiting line models, Markov processes, simulation, and PERT analysis. Consequently, in this appendix we provide a brief review of probability theory and statistics. Most students will probably have had some exposure to probability theory and statistics in a previous course. This appendix is meant primarily as a "refresher" for those students who have been exposed to comparable materials elsewhere. For an in-depth treatment of probability theory and statistics, the references at the end of this appendix should be consulted.

BASIC CONCEPTS AND DEFINITIONS

As a starting point for our review of probability and statistics we define the more important terms used in the material that follows.

In doing statistical work a **sample** is drawn from a **universe** or **population**. The universe can be **finite** or **infinite**. A finite universe might be the number of students in a class, whereas an infinite universe might be the set of all prime numbers. If we selected a sample of five students from the class, with the selection process based strictly on chance, then we would have a *random sample*. In describing the universe, we speak of its **parameters**, which are the characteristics of the universe. In describing the sample, we speak of its **statistics**, which are the characteristics of the sample drawn from the universe. It is necessary to distinguish between parameters and statistics, so a notational system is employed. This notation, for the mean and variance (terms to be defined later) is as follows:

Universe (Population)	Sample
μ = population mean (parameter)	x = sample mean (statistic)
σ^2 = population variance (parameter)	s^2 = sample variance (statistic)

When we select a set of sample data, we perform an **experiment**, which is a predetermined process the results of which are subject to chance. The result of an experiment is referred to as an **outcome**, and the number of outcomes of an experiment can be either finite or infinite, depending on the experiment. The

sample space is then the set of all possible outcomes of an experiment. An **event** is a subset of outcomes from the sample space.

To illustrate these definitions, consider the experiment of drawing a ball from an urn containing six balls, numbered 1 to 6. The sample space for this experiment consists of the six balls, namely:

$$S = \{1, 2, 3, 4, 5, 6\}$$

Thus, the outcomes of this experiment are finite (since there are six balls in the urn) and discrete (since the outcomes are "countable" integers). One possible event for this experiment is the selection of a ball marked "3."

PRINCIPLES OF PROBABILITY THEORY

Probability theory can be viewed as the study of **random phenomenon**. A random (or chance) phenomenon is an empirical phenomenon characterized by the property that an observation under a given set of circumstances does not always lead to the same observed outcome but rather to different outcomes in such a way that there is **statistical regularity**. This means that numbers exist between 0 and 1 that represent the relative frequency with which the different possible outcomes may be observed in a series of observations of independent occurrences of the phenomenon. Now, a **random event** is one whose relative frequency of occurrence, in a very long sequence of observations of randomly selected samples in which the event may occur, approaches a stable limiting value as the number of observations is increased to infinity. The limiting value of the relative frequency is called the **probability of the random event**.

This **relative frequency** or **objective** interpretation of probability can be illustrated as follows. If an experiment is performed n times under the same conditions and there are x outcomes, $x < n$, in which an event, E, occurs, then an estimate of the probability of that event, E, is the ratio x/n. Furthermore, the estimate of the probability of an event x/n approaches as a limit the true probability of the event, when n increases without limit, that is,

$$P(\text{Event } E) = \lim_{n \to \infty} \frac{x}{n}$$

In other situations, probabilities are often assigned to events without any experimentation being done. For example, a sportscaster may quote the odds on a football game, or a researcher may state that there is an 80% chance of her research leading to a new product. In these instances, **subjective probabilities** are employed, and are not based on the measurement of the relative frequency with which an event has occurred.

Although there can be different approaches to defining probability, a number of principles of probability can be stated without strictly defining probability. These principles of probability theory can be stated as follows:

1. The probability of each event in the sample space occurring is positive or zero.

$$P(E) \geq 0 \quad \text{for every event } E$$

2. The sum of the probabilities of all possible outcomes in the sample space is 1.

$$P(S) = 1.0 \text{ where } S \text{ is the sample space}$$

For example, in a coin-flipping experiment, the sample space consists of two outcomes: $S = \{Heads, Tails\}$. The probability of each outcome is $\frac{1}{2}$; thus:

$$P(S) = P(Heads) + P(Tails) = \tfrac{1}{2} + \tfrac{1}{2} = 1.0$$

3. The probability of an impossible event, called the **null set**, is zero.

$$P(Null\ Set) = P(\phi) = 0$$

4. The probability of an event, E, is equal to the sum of the probabilities of the outcomes belonging to event E. If $O_{i \to n}$ are the outcomes in event E, then

$$P(E) = P(0_1) + P(0_2) + \cdots + P(0_n)$$

For example, assume that we are tossing a six-sided die, and that event $E = \{3, 6\}$. In this instance, $P(3) = \frac{1}{6}$ and $P(6) = \frac{1}{6}$, and $P(E) = \frac{1}{6} + \frac{1}{6} = \frac{2}{3}$.

5. The **union** $E \cup F$ is defined as consisting of the outcomes that belong to at least one of the events E or F. The **intersection** $E \cap F$ is defined as consisting of the outcomes that belong to both event E and event F. The **addition law** of probability states that the probability of a union between events E and F ($E \cup F$) is given by

$$P(E \cup F) = P(E) + P(F) - P(E \cap F)$$

In the die-tossing experiment if $E = \{1, 6\}$ and $F = \{3, 6\}$, then $P(E) = \frac{2}{6} = \frac{1}{3}$, $P(F) = \frac{2}{6} = \frac{1}{3}$, $P(E \cap F) = P(6) = \frac{1}{6}$. Thus

$$P(E \cup F) = \tfrac{1}{3} + \tfrac{1}{3} - \tfrac{1}{6} = \tfrac{3}{6} = \tfrac{1}{2}$$

6. Events are called **mutually exclusive** if one and only of them can occur. If E and F are mutually exclusive events, then $P(E \cap F) = 0$. Therefore, the addition law for mutually exclusive events can be written as

$$P(E \cup F) = P(E) + P(F) \qquad \text{if } E \text{ and } F \text{ are mutually exclusive events}$$

For example, in the die-tossing experiment if $E = \{1, 6\}$, and $F = \{3\}$, then E and F are mutually exclusive events and $P(E \cup F) = P(E) + P(F) = \frac{1}{3} + \frac{1}{6} = \frac{1}{2}$. Additionally, two, or more events, are said to be mutually exclusive and **exhaustive** if they do not intersect but do take up the entire sample space. For example, in the die-tossing experiment if event $E = \{1, 2\}$ and event $F = \{3, 4, 5, 6\}$, then E and F are mutually exclusive and exhaustive. Notationally, this condition is represented as

$$E \cap F = \phi$$
$$E \cup F = S$$

7. The **conditional probability** law denotes the probability of occurrence of event E given the occurrence of event F. The conditional probability of E given that F has occurred is written as $P(E|F)$ and is defined as

$$P(E|F) = \frac{P(E \cap F)}{P(F)} \quad \text{if } P(F) > 0$$

For example, consider a family with two children and assume that each child is as likely to be a boy as it is to be a girl. What is the conditional probability that the older child will be a boy given that the younger child is a boy? Let E be the event that the older child is a boy, let F be the event that the younger child is a boy, and let $E \cap F$ be the event that both children are boys. The desired conditional probability is

$$P(E|F) = \frac{P(E \cap F)}{P(F)} = \frac{(1/2 \cdot 1/2)}{1/2} = \frac{1/4}{1/2} = 1/2$$

8. The **multiplication law** of probability can be obtained by manipulating the formula for the conditional probability, and can be written as

$$P(E \cap F) = P(E|F) \cdot P(F)$$

It should also be mentioned that $P(E \cap F)$ is often called the **joint** or **compound** probability of E and F. When the occurrence of event F has an effect on the occurrence of event E, we say that they are **dependent** events. For example, suppose that a box contains three black balls and two red balls. Let event F be the event "first ball drawn is black" and let E be the event "second ball drawn is red," where the balls are not replaced after being drawn. In this instance, E and F are clearly dependent events. The probability that the first ball drawn is black, $P(F) = 3/(3 + 2) = 3/5$ and the conditional probability that the second ball drawn is red given that the first ball drawn is black, $P(E|F) = 2/(2 + 2) = 1/2$. Then, the desired joint probability is computed as

$$P(E \cap F) = P(E|F) \cdot P(F) = 1/2 \cdot 3/5 = 3/10$$

9. Two or more events are said to be **independent** if the occurrence of one event has no effect on the probability of the occurrence of the other events. Thus, if two events E and F are independent, the conditional probability is

$$P(E|F) = P(E)$$

and the multiplication law can be written as

$$P(E \cap F) = P(E) \cdot P(F) \quad \text{if } E \text{ and } F \text{ are independent}$$

For example, if the probability that A will be alive in 10 years is 0.7 and the probability that B will be alive in 10 years is 0.8, then the probability that both A and B will be alive in 10 years is

$$P(A \cap B) = P(A) \cdot P(B) = (0.7) \cdot (0.8) = 0.56$$

BAYES' THEOREM

As discussed in the previous section, in the usual sense of conditional probability we seek the probability of some event E given that an event F has occurred. Generally, events F and E are sequenced in that order, over time, and event E is an end effect for which event F is a possible cause. For example, we might seek to determine the conditional probability $P(E|F)$, where E is the event "10 defective parts are produced" and F is the event "machine no. 6 is used." Consider, instead, the situation in which we know, *after the fact*, that 10 defective parts were produced but we do not know which machine was used. How can we now determine the probability that some particular event F is the cause of a known end effect E. Such probabilities are given by Bayes' theorem (or law), which is defined as

$$P(F_i|E) = \frac{P(F_i)\, P(E|F_i)}{\sum_{i=1}^{n} P(F_i)\, P(E|F_i)}$$

where:

F_i = a set of n mutually exclusive and exhaustive events

E = a known end effect or the outcome of an experiment

$P(F_i)$ = the prior probability for event i

$P(E|F_i)$ = the conditional probability of end effect, E, given the occurrence of F_i

Observe that $P(E|F_i)$ is a conditional probability defined in terms of the discussion in the previous section. The computed probability $P(F_i|E)$ is also a conditional probability, but it reverses the sequence of events and is called the **posterior** probability.

To illustrate the application of Bayes' theorem, consider the following situation. The "Golf World" store receives its sets of golf clubs from three sporting goods companies. The Zilson Company supplies 20% of the stock, the Malding Company supplies 40% of the stock, and the McMartin Company supplies 40% of the stock. Based on previous experience, "Golf World" can predict the percentage of the stock that will be defective for each of the three suppliers. In this regard, Zilson Company produces 3% defective products; Malding Company produces 2% defective products; and McMartin Company produces 4% defective products. Given that one set of golf clubs from a day's shipment is defective, we seek to determine the probabilities associated with it having come from each of the three companies.

The prior and conditional probabilities for this situation are as follows:

Prior Probabilities	Conditional Probabilities
$P(F_1) = 0.20$	$P(E|F_1) = 0.03$
$P(F_2) = 0.40$	$P(E|F_2) = 0.02$
$P(F_3) = 0.40$	$P(E|F_3) = 0.04$

Given these probabilities, we can then apply Bayes' theorem to determine the posterior probabilities associated with a defective set of golf clubs having come from each of the three companies. Using Bayes' theorem,

$$P(F_1|E) = \frac{P(F_1)\,P(E|F_1)}{P(F_1)\,P(E|F_1) + P(F_2)\,P(E|F_2) + P(F_3)\,P(E|F_3)}$$

$$= \frac{(0.20)\,(0.03)}{(0.20)\,(0.03) + (0.40)\,(0.02) + (0.40)\,(0.04)}$$

$$= \frac{0.006}{0.030} = 0.20$$

$$P(F_2|E) = \frac{P(F_2)\,P(E|F_2)}{P(F_1)\,P(E|F_1) + P(F_2)\,P(E|F_2) + P(F_3)\,P(E|F_3)}$$

$$= \frac{(0.40)\,(0.02)}{(0.20)\,(0.03) + (0.40)\,(0.02) + (0.40)\,(0.04)}$$

$$= \frac{0.008}{0.030} = 0.267$$

$$P(F_3|E) = \frac{P(F_3)\,P(E|F_3)}{P(F_1)\,P(E|F_1) + P(F_2)\,P(E|F_2) + P(F_3)\,P(E|F_3)}$$

$$= \frac{(0.40)\,(0.04)}{(0.20)\,(0.03) + (0.40)\,(0.02) + (0.40)\,(0.04)}$$

$$= \frac{0.016}{0.030} = 0.533$$

COMBINATORIAL ANALYSIS

In obtaining probabilities of complicated events, an enumeration of all possible cases may be difficult or time-consuming. Hence, use is often made of basic principles known as **combinatorial analysis**. The so-called **fundamental principle of combinatorial analysis** states that if one event can happen in any one of n_1 ways and if when this has occurred another event can happen in any one of n_2 ways, then the number of ways in which both events can happen in the specified order is $n_1 \cdot n_2$. To illustrate, if there are three candidates for governor and four candidates for lieutenant governor, the two positions can be filled in $3 \cdot 4 = 12$ ways.

In counting sample points, we may be concerned with the order of arrangement of the objects being counted. Herein, a **permutation** of n different objects taken r at a time is an **arrangement** of r out of the n objects with attention given to the order of arrangement. The number of permutations of n objects taken r at a time is denoted by $_nP_r$, $P(n,r)$, or $P_{n,r}$ and is given by

$$_nP_r = n(n-1)(n-2)\ldots(n-r+1) = \frac{n!}{(n-r)!}$$

where factorial n, denoted by $n!$ is defined as $n! = n(n-1)(n-2)\ldots 1$, and $0! \equiv 1$. For example, the number of permutations of the letters a, b, c, d taken two at a time is

$$4P2 = \frac{4!}{(4-2)!} = \frac{4 \cdot 3 \cdot 2 \cdot 1}{2 \cdot 1} = 12$$

In some instances we may not be interested in the order of arrangement of the objects being counted. Herein, a **combination** of n different objects taken r at a time is a **selection** of r out of the n objects with no attention given to the order of arrangement. The number of combinations of n objects taken r at a time is denoted by $_nC_r$, $C(n, r)$, or $\binom{n}{r}$, and is given by

$$_nC_r = \frac{n(n-1) \ldots (n-r+1)}{r!} = \frac{n!}{r!(n-r)!} = \frac{_nP_r}{r!}$$

For example, the number of combinations of the letters a, b, c, d taken two at a time is

$$_4C_2 = \frac{4!}{2!(4-2)!} = \frac{4 \cdot 3 \cdot 2 \cdot 1}{(2 \cdot 1)(2 \cdot 1)} = \frac{12}{2} = 6$$

DESCRIPTIVE STATISTICS

One very important element of statistics concerns the description of a set of data. To illustrate, consider Table A.1 that summarizes monthly sales information for the World Cup Soccer Store for the last three years.

TABLE A.1   Monthly Sales-World Cup Soccer Store ($000)

60.5	40.2	37.7
20.9	70.5	41.6
32.7	41.6	50.9
62.7	80.2	41.5
52.6	60.7	76.5
30.7	51.2	47.9
47.8	61.5	52.5
52.9	52.7	61.5
61.5	45.6	51.9
43.9	51.6	47.5
71.5	65.7	41.3
28.9	56.8	55.6

Looking at this table, we would probably find it difficult to make any generalization about the monthly sales pattern. Thus, some method for generalizing about a set of data is needed.

This situation can be greatly improved by grouping the data into a **frequency distribution**. To begin this process we must tabulate the monthly sales figures into several class intervals, as shown in Table A.2.

Using Table A.2, we can now observe some characteristics of the data that were very hard to determine from Table A.1. For example, we see that the monthly sales tend to cluster between $40,000 per month to $65,000 per month, and that there were very few months with either extremely high or extremely low sales. To obtain a more graphical representation, the frequency distribution data can be plotted in a **histogram** (see Figure A.1).

TABLE A.2 Frequency Distribution-Monthly Sales Data

Class Limits ($000)	Frequency (No. of Observations)
20.1–25.0	1
25.1–30.0	1
30.1–35.0	2
35.1–40.0	1
40.1–45.0	6
45.1–50.0	4
50.1–55.0	7
55.1–60.0	3
60.1–65.0	6
65.1–70.0	1
70.1–75.0	2
75.1–80.0	1
80.1–85.0	1

This histogram provides a clearer interpretation of the data, and again highlights the fact that monthly sales tend to be in the range of $40,000 to $65,000.

In addition to the histogram, there are several statistical measurements that can be used to describe or specify distributions. Two important classes of statistical measurement concern the central tendency and variability of a distribution.

As noted previously, we often employ a random sample from the population to estimate the measure of the central tendency of the population. When this is done, we then calculate the arithmetic **mean**, **x**, of the sample as

$$\mathbf{x} = \frac{\sum_{i=1}^{n} x_i}{n} = \frac{x_1 + x_2 + x_3 + \cdots + x_n}{n}$$

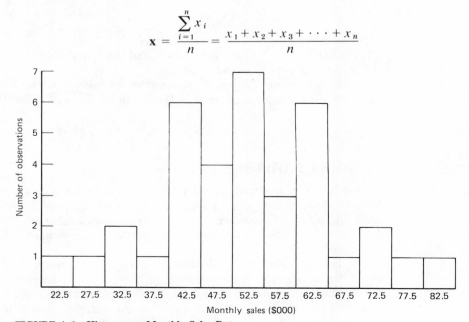

FIGURE A.1 Histogram—Monthly Sales Data

where the x_i are the individual observations, numbered from 1 to n, and n is the total number of observations. Thus, for our monthly sales data example, we calculate **x** from Table A.1 as follows:

$$\mathbf{x} = \frac{60.5 + 20.9 + 32.7 + \cdots + 55.6}{36} = 51.45$$

This value, $\mathbf{x} = 51.45$, is the estimate of the population mean of the underlying distribution of monthly sales.

Two other measurements of central tendency are sometimes used, to describe data. The first is the **median**, which is that point which divides the frequency distribution, or area under the histogram, into two equal parts. The second is the **mode**, which is the most frequently occurring value in a frequency distribution.

The random sample selected from the population can also be used to estimate the variability of the population. Herein, the sample **variance** is utilized, and is computed as

$$s^2 = \frac{\sum_{i=1}^{n}(x_i - \mathbf{x})^2}{n - 1} = \frac{\sum_{i=1}^{n} x_i^2 - n\mathbf{x}^2}{n - 1}$$

Therefore, for our monthly sales data example, we calculate s^2 from Table A-1 as follows:

$$s^2 = \frac{(60.5 - 51.45)^2 + (20.9 - 51.45)^2 + \cdots + (55.6 - 51.45)^2}{35}$$

$$= \frac{6180.99}{35} = 176.60$$

This value, $s^2 = 176.60$, is the estimate of the population variance of the underlying distribution of monthly sales.

Another commonly used measure of variability is the **standard deviation**, which is simply the square root of the variance. Thus, for the data of Table A.1,

$$s = \sqrt{s^2} = \sqrt{176.60} = 13.28$$

RANDOM VARIABLES

Earlier, we indicated that probability theory can be viewed as the study of random phenomenon. In studying a population, we often measure some population characteristic by using a **random variable**. A **random variable** is a numerically valued function whose value is determined by a random experiment (i.e., is defined over a sample space).

It is very important to distinguish between two types of random variables: those that are discrete and those that are continuous. A **discrete** random variable is one in which the number of its values is finite or **countably infinite**. By countably infinite we mean that the values of the random variable may be placed in a one-to-one correspondence with the positive integers, 0, 1, 2, . . . , $+\infty$. An example of a discrete random variable would be the number of heads appearing in 10 flips of a coin.

A **continuous** random variable assumes values that are on an interval of the real line. Thus, the number of values that a continuous random variable may assume is infinite. An example of a continuous random variable is the weight of male students in a class.

DISCRETE PROBABILITY DISTRIBUTION

A discrete probability distribution can be described by a **probability mass function**, which assigns probability to the values of the discrete random variable as follows:

$$p(x) = P(X = x) \qquad \text{where } x \text{ is a discrete random variable}$$

In addition the probability mass function must satisfy the following two conditions:

1. All of the probabilities of the discrete random variable are positive or zero.

$$0 \leq p(x) \leq 1.0 \qquad -\infty < x < \infty$$

2. The sum of all the probabilities for the discrete random variable must equal 1.0.

$$\Sigma p(x) = 1.0$$

To illustrate a simple discrete distribution consider the familiar experiment of tossing one die. The discrete probability distribution for this experiment is given in the following table:

x	_1_	_2_	_3_	_4_	_5_	_6_
$p(x)$	1/6	1/6	1/6	1/6	1/6	1/6

This discrete probability distribution can also be plotted as shown in Figure A.2.

The **cumulative distribution**, which is the probability that the random variable X has a value less than or equal to x, is defined for a discrete random variable as

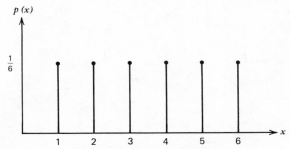

FIGURE A.2   Discrete Probability Distribution

$$F(x) = P(X \le x)$$

For example, in the die-tossing experiment, assume that we want to determine the probability that one toss of a die will result in a face value of 3 or less. The cumulative probability is

$$F(2) = P(X \le 2) = P(x = 1) + P(x = 2)$$
$$= \frac{1}{6} + \frac{1}{6} = \frac{2}{6} = \frac{1}{3}$$

Graphically, the cumulative distribution of $F(x)$ for the die-tossing experiment is a step function, which can be plotted as shown in Figure A.3.

The expected value, $E(x)$, of a discrete random variable, x, is defined by

$$E(x) = \sum_x x \cdot p(x)$$

To illustrate, consider the following sales levels and their associated probabilities

Sales x	p(x)
0	0.05
1	0.25
2	0.20
3	0.30
4	0.20

The expected value of sales is computed as

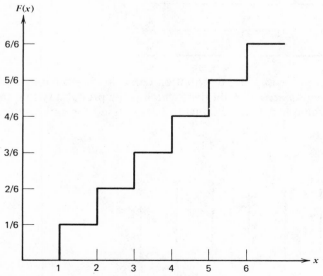

FIGURE A.3   **Cumulative Discrete Distribution**

$$E(x) = (0)(0.05) + (1)(0.25) + (2)(0.20) + (3)(0.30) + (4)(0.20)$$
$$= 0.00 + 0.25 + 0.40 + 0.90 + 0.80 = 2.35$$

The variance, $V(x)$, of a discrete random variable is defined by

$$V(x) = E(x^2) - [E(x)]^2$$

Thus, the variance is the weighted average of the deviations from the expected values, squared. The square root of the variance is the standard deviation. To illustrate, consider the sales demand data. The following table summarizes the computation of the variance and the standard deviation.

Sales x	x^2	$p(x)$	$xp(x)$	$x^2p(x)$
0	0	0.05	0.00	0.00
1	1	0.25	0.25	0.25
2	4	0.20	0.40	0.80
3	9	0.30	0.90	2.70
4	16	0.20	0.80	3.20
			$E(x) = \overline{2.35}$	$E(x^2) = \overline{6.95}$

Thus,

$$V(x) = E[x^2] - [E(x)]^2$$
$$= 6.95 - (2.35)^2$$
$$= 6.95 - 5.52 = 1.43$$

Standard Deviation $= \sqrt{1.43} = 1.19$

DISCRETE UNIFORM DISTRIBUTION

The **discrete uniform distribution** is described by the probability mass function:

$$p(x) = 1/n, \qquad x = 1, 2, \ldots, n$$

where n is the number of outcomes in the sample space. Thus, for any possible value of the discrete random variable x between 1 and n, the probability of the outcome, x, is the same, namely $1/n$.

The expected value and variance for the discrete uniform distribution are given by

$$E(x) = \frac{n + 1}{2}$$

$$V(x) = \frac{n^2 - 1}{12}$$

To illustrate, recall that the possible outcomes of the roll of a six-sided die are the integers 1, 2, 3, 4, 5, and 6. Thus, the expected value and variance of this random variable are

$$E(x) = \frac{6 + 1}{2} = 3.5$$

$$V(x) = \frac{n^2 - 1}{12} = \frac{6^2 - 1}{12} = \frac{35}{12}$$

BINOMIAL DISTRIBUTION

In an experiment that produces binomial random variables, the key elements are

1. The experiment is composed of n trials.
2. In each trial, there are only two possible outcomes of the experiment: "success" or "failure."
3. The probability of a "success" is the same for each trial, and is denoted as p. Likewise, the probability of "failure" is the same for each trial, and is denoted as $1 - p = q$.
4. The n trials in the experiment are independent.
5. The random variable is defined to be the number of successes in the n trials.

The binomial random variable delineated according to the above elements is often generated by a Bernoulli process. A simple example of a Bernoulli process is an experiment where a fair coin is flipped 25 times. This experiment consists of 25 Bernoulli trials, in which each trial (i.e., flip of the coin) has two outcomes, heads (e.g., success) and tails (e.g., failure). The probability of success is ½ for each of the 25 trials (i.e., $p = $ ½) and the probability of failure is $1 - p = q = $ ½. The flips of the coins (trials) are obviously independent.

The **binomial probability distribution** is described by the probability mass function:

$$p(x) = \binom{n}{x} p^x q^{n-x}, \qquad \text{where } q = 1 - p$$

$$\text{where } \binom{n}{x} = \frac{n!}{x! \, (n - x)!}$$

Observe that the form of the binomial probability distribution depends on the parameters n and p.

To illustrate the binomial probability distribution, consider a family of three children, and assume that we are interested in determining the probability that exactly two of the children are boys. Assuming that either sex is equally likely to occur in each birth, and that the births (i.e., trials) are independent, let the event "boy" represent a success. The probability of a success in a single trial is $p = 0.5$, and there are three trials. The probability of exactly $x = 2$ successes in the three trials is given by

$$P(x = 2) = \binom{3}{2} (0.50)^2 (0.50)^{3-2}$$

$$= \frac{3!}{2!(3 - 2)!} (0.50)^2 (0.50) = 0.375$$

The expected value or mean number of successes for a binomial experiment consisting of n trials (i.e., the binomial random variable, x) is defined as

$$E(x) = np$$

The variance of the binomial random variable, x, is

$$V(x) = npq$$

To illustrate, suppose that we know that 25% of all college professors exercise regularly. Assume that we select 25 college professors at random. The expected number of exercisers from the 25 college professors selected would be given by

$$E(x) = np = (25)\ (0.25) = 6.25$$

The variance of the expected number of exercisers is

$$V(x) = npq = (25)(0.25)(0.25) = 1.56$$

POISSON DISTRIBUTION

The **Poisson distribution** is defined by the probability mass function:

$$p(x) = \frac{\lambda^x e^{-x}}{x!}$$

where: x = a Poisson random variable

$\lambda = np$ = the expected value, or mean, where p is extremely small, and n is very large

$e = 2.71828$

Note that since p is very small, it is close to 0. Thus, as p approaches 0, q approaches 1.

The expected value and variance of a Poisson random variable, x, are defined as follows:

$$E(x) = \lambda = np$$
$$V(x) = npq$$
$$= np\ (1) = np = \lambda$$

To illustrate the use of the Poisson distribution, consider the following example. Customers arrive at the checkout counter of a drugstore at an average rate of 20 customers per hour (i.e., $\lambda = 20$). Assume that we want to determine the probability that 30 customers will arrive at the checkout counter in an hour. This probability is given by

$$p(x = 30) = \frac{(20)^{30}\ e^{-20}}{30!} = 0.0083$$

The Poisson distribution is tabulated for specific values of x and λ in Table 4 in Appendix C.

CONTINUOUS PROBABILITY DISTRIBUTION

A continuous probability distribution can be described by a **probability density function**. The probability density function of the continuous random variable x, denoted by $f(x)$, must satisfy the following two conditions:

1. $0 \le f(x) \le 1.0,$ $-\infty < x < +\infty$

2. $\int_{-\infty}^{+\infty} f(x) \, dx = 1.0$

The first condition indicates that the probability of any value of the random variable must be nonnegative, whereas the second condition indicates that the sum of the sample space defined by $f(x)$ equals 1.0. The second condition is obtained by integrating $f(x)$, which determines the area under the curve (area = 1.0) mapped by $f(x)$, as shown in Figure A.4.

To illustrate a probability density function, consider the situation in which we have a queueing problem involving a bank teller in which arrivals occur between 0 and 5 minutes. Furthermore, assume that the probability density function of the time of an arrival has been defined as

$$f(x) = x/12.5, \qquad 0 \le x \le 5$$

Figure A.5 presents a graph of this probability density function. Observe that the area under this probability density function is 1.0.

The **cumulative density function** for a continuous random variable is defined as

$$F(x) = P(X \le x) = \int_{-\infty}^{x} f(x) \, dx$$

Integrating the function $f(x)$ in the defined range determines the area under the curve up to x, which corresponds to the probability that the random variable X is less than or equal to x.

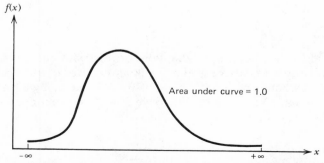

FIGURE A.4   **Probability Density Function-Continuous Random Variable**

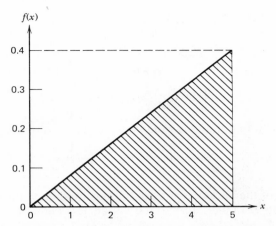

FIGURE A.5   Probability Density Function Example

From our previous example, the probability that the time of arrival is less than or equal to x years is

$$F(x) = \int_0^x \left(\frac{x}{12.5}\right) dx$$

Integrating, we obtain

$$F(x) = \frac{x^2}{25}, \qquad 0 \le x \le 5$$

The graph of this cumulative density function is shown in Figure A.6.

The expected value of a continuous random variable, x, is defined as

$$E(x) = \int_x xf(x) \, dx$$

As an illustration of the expected value of a continuous random variable, consider the probability density function for our queueing example:

$$f(x) = x/12.5, \qquad 0 \le x \le 5$$

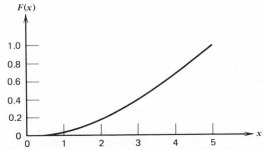

FIGURE A.6   Cumulative Density Function Example

The expected value is computed as

$$\int_0^5 x\left(\frac{x}{12.5}\right) dx = \int_0^5 \left(\frac{x^2}{12.5}\right) dx$$

$$= \left[\frac{x^3}{37.5}\right]_0^5 = 3.333$$

The variance of a continuous random variable, x, is defined as

$$V(x) = \int_x x^2 f(x)\, dx - [E(x)]^2$$

As an illustration of the variance of a continuous random variable, consider once again our queueing example. Herein, the variance is computed as

$$V(x) = \int_0^5 x^2 \left(\frac{x}{12.5}\right) dx - [E(x)]^2$$

$$= \int_0^5 \left(\frac{x^3}{12.5}\right) dx - [3.333]^2$$

$$= \left[\frac{x^4}{50}\right]_0^5 - 11.11$$

$$= 12.50 - 11.11 = 1.49$$

CONTINUOUS UNIFORM DISTRIBUTION

The **continuous uniform distribution** is defined by the probability density function:

$$f(x) = \frac{1}{b - a}, \qquad a \le x \le b$$

Thus, the continuous uniform distribution is analogous to the discrete uniform distribution except that there are an infinite number of values in the range of the continuous uniform distribution, and the probability of any one value is zero.

The expected value and variance of the continuous uniform distribution are given by

$$E(x) = \frac{a + b}{2}$$

$$V(x) = \frac{(b - a)^2}{12}$$

For example, consider a continuous uniform distribution over the range (0 to 50). The probability density function and cumulative density function for this distribution are shown below in Figure A.7.
The expected value and variance for this continuous uniform distribution are

$$E(x) = \frac{a + b}{2} = \frac{0 + 50}{2} = 25$$

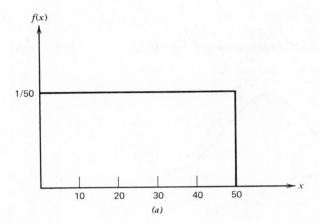

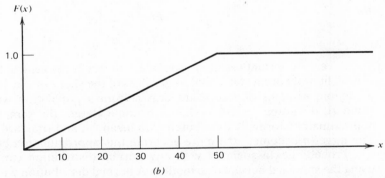

FIGURE A.7 Probability Density Function and Cumulative Density Function. (a) Probability Density Function. (b) Cumulative Density Function.

$$V(x) = \frac{(b-a)^2}{12} = \frac{(50-0)^2}{12} = \frac{2500}{12} = 208.33$$

THE NORMAL DISTRIBUTION

The **normal distribution** is probably the most important distribution encountered in statistics, because it approximates the probability distributions of a number of physical phenomena in the real world. Examples of random variables that are approximated by the normal distribution are the height and weight of people, the diameters of drive shafts produced by a metal lathe, the IQ of people, the life of bearings, and the grades on an examination.

The probability density function of the normal distribution is

$$f(x) = \frac{e^{-(x-\mu)^2/2\sigma^2}}{\sigma\sqrt{2\pi}}$$

where μ and σ^2 are the mean and variance of the random variable x, and $e = 2.71828$, and $\pi = 3.14159$.

The normal distribution appears as shown below in Figure A.8.

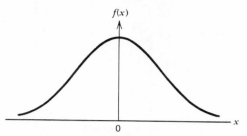

FIGURE A.8   Normal Distribution

From Figure A.8 note that the normal distribution is a continuous curve that is symmetrical about the dependent axis.

The mean and variance of the normal random variable x are given by

$$E(x) = \mu$$
$$V(x) = \sigma^2$$

A very important result of probability theory is the **central limit theorem**. The central limit theorem states that, regardless of the shape of the original population, if random samples of size n are drawn from a population with mean, μ, and standard deviation, σ, then when n becomes large, the sample mean **x** will be approximately normally distributed with mean, μ, and standard deviation, $\sigma/\sqrt{n}$. The larger n becomes, the more accurate this approximation becomes.

Probabilities associated with any normal distribution can be computed by using the **standard normal distribution**. A normal distribution with $\mu = 0$ and $\sigma = 1$ is called a standard normal distribution. A normally distributed random variable x can be converted to a **standardized normal random variable**, Z, for specific values of x, using

$$Z = \frac{x - \mu}{\sigma}$$

The form of the standard normal distribution is illustrated below in Figure A.9. As indicated in Figure A.9, for any normal deviation, 68.27% of the values of Z lie within one standard deviation of the mean, 95.45% of the values of Z lie within two standard deviations of the mean, and 99.73% of the values of Z lies within three standard deviations of the mean.

Probabilities for the standard normal distribution are presented in Table 3 in Appendix C. Each entry in Table 3 is the area under the normal curve that lies under the segment between the mean and Z standard deviations from the mean. Since the normal distribution is symmetric about its mean (which is zero in this case), and the total area under the curve is one (one-half to the left of zero, and one-half to the right of zero), the probability that Z is in any interval may be determined by using this table as the following example demonstrates.

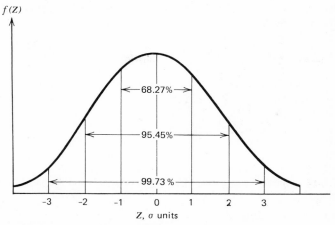

FIGURE A.9   Standard Normal Distribution

Assume that we have purchased a new bearing for the drive shaft on a piece of production equipment. According to the manufacturer's specifications, the life expectancy of this new bearing is 500 workdays (i.e., 8-hour days) with a standard deviation of 50 workdays. Initially, assume that we are interested in determining the probability that this new bearing will last up to 600 workdays. The desired probability is shown below in Figure A.10. To find the desired probability we first compute the value of Z as

$$Z = \frac{x - \mu}{\sigma} = \frac{600 - 500}{50} = \frac{100}{50} = 2$$

Referring to Table 3 in Appendix C we see that the area under the normal curve from the mean to $Z = 2.0$ is 0.4772. However, since the normal curve is symmetrical we must add to this area, the area under the normal curve to the left of the mean, or to the left of $Z = 0.0$. This area by symmetry is 0.5000. Thus, the desired probability is

$$P(x \leq 600) = 0.5000 + 0.4772 = 0.9772$$

Assume next that we are interested in determining the probability that this new bearing will last between 350 and 550 workdays. The desired probability is shown

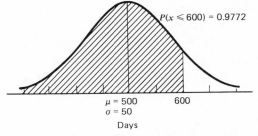

FIGURE A.10   Probability—Bearing Will Last up to 600 Workdays

below in Figure A.11. This probability corresponds to the sum of the two areas shown in Figure A.11.

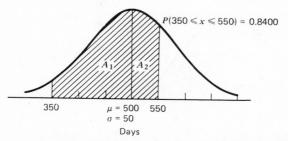

FIGURE A.11   Probability—Bearing Will Last Between 350 and 550 Workdays

For area A_2, the value of Z is

$$Z = \frac{550 - 500}{50} = 1.0$$

From Table 3, the corresponding probability is 0.3413. For area A_1, the value of Z is

$$Z = \frac{350 - 500}{50} = -3.0$$

From Table 3 (disregarding the negative sign, since the normal curve is symmetrical) the corresponding probability is 0.4987. Thus, the desired probability is

$$P(350 \le x \le 550) = A_1 + A_2 = 0.4987 + 0.3413$$
$$= 0.8400$$

Finally, assume that we are interested in determining the probability that the new bearing will last less than 450 workdays. The desired probability is shown below in Figure A.12.

To find the desired probability, we first compute the value of Z as

$$Z = \frac{x - \mu}{\sigma} = \frac{450 - 500}{50} = \frac{-50}{50} = -1$$

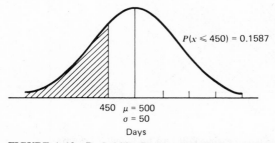

FIGURE A.12   Probability-Bearing Will Last Less Than 450 Workdays

From Table 3 (disregarding the negative sign, since the normal curve is symmetrical) the corresponding probability is 0.3413. However, since the normal curve is symmetrical we must first add to this area the area to the right of the mean, or the right of $Z = 0.00$ (i.e., area to the right of the mean = 0.5000). Then, this total area must be subtracted from 1.0 to obtain the desired probability, namely:

$$P(x \leq 450) = 1.0 - 0.3413 - 0.5000$$
$$= 0.1587.$$

EXPONENTIAL DISTRIBUTION

The **exponential distribution** is defined by the probability density function:

$$f(x) = \lambda e^{-\lambda x}$$

where λ is a parameter of the distribution and $e = 2.71828$.

The exponential distribution is frequently used to model the distribution of a random variable that represents service time; the time required to buy stamps in a post office, the time required to have four tires balanced, the time spent in a dentist's chair having teeth cleaned, and so forth.

The probability density function for the exponential distribution has the form shown in Figure A.13.

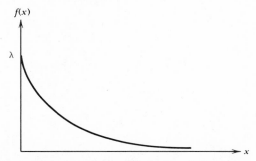

FIGURE A.13   Exponential Distribution

The expected value and variance of the exponential distribution are given by

$$E(x) = \frac{1}{\lambda}$$

$$V(x) = \frac{1}{\lambda^2}$$

The cumulative density function for the exponential distribution is also widely used and has the following form:

$$F(x) = 1 - e^{-\lambda x}$$

To faciliate working with the exponential distribution, the values of e^x and e^{-x} for a range of values of x have been computed and appear as Table 5 in Appendix C.

SELECTED REFERENCES

PROBABILITY AND STATISTICS

Chou, Y. 1975. *Statistical Analysis*. New York: Holt, Rinehart and Winston.

Harnett, Donald L. 1970. *Introduction to Statistical Methods*. Reading, Mass.: Addison-Wesley Publishing Company, Inc.

Mansfield, Edwin. 1980. *Statistics For Business and Economics*. New York: W. W. Norton & Company.

Mendenhall, William, and James E. Reinmuth. 1978. *Statistics for Management and Economics*. Belmont, Calif.: Wadsworth Publishing Company, Inc.

Neter, John, and William Wasserman. 1973. *Fundamental Statistics for Business and Economics*. Boston: Allyn & Bacon.

Parzen, Emanuel. 1960. *Modern Probability Theory*. New York: John Wiley & Sons, Inc.

Pfaffenberger, Roger C., and James H. Patterson. 1977. *Statistical Methods for Business and Economics*. Homewood, Ill.: Richard D. Irwin, Inc.

Spurr, William A., and Charles P. Bonini. 1973. *Statistical Analysis for Business Decisions*. Homewood, Ill.: Richard D. Irwin, Inc.

B Calculus Review

In several sections of this textbook we have employed calculus. However, our use of calculus has been of an expository nature in that it has been used to derive various relationships or to explain certain concepts. Thus, we have not made a knowledge of calculus a prerequisite to *applying* any of the management science techniques described herein. These techniques can be used as they are, and the calculus derivations are presented only for explanatory purposes.

In this appendix we will attempt to provide a brief calculus review. This review is intended to be for the more interested reader, and is not meant to be mandatory for an understanding of the textbook material. For an in-depth treatment of calculus, the references at the end of this appendix should be consulted.

The study of calculus is usually divided into two distinct parts, which are, in turn, related. Initial study in calculus is generally concerned with **differentiation**. Differential calculus is concerned with the slope, or rate of change of a function at any given point on that function. To illustrate, consider the curve plotted in Fig. B.1. Considering Fig. B.1, assume that we are interested in determining the slope of this function at an arbitrarily selected point "*a*." We will denote the corresponding x and y values at "*a*" as x_0 and $f(x_0)$, respectively. Now, the rate of change of the function $y = f(x)$ with respect to x at the point "*a*" is equal to the slope of the line tangent to the curve at that point. The **derivative** of the function $f(x_0)$ with respect to x_0, is the slope of the tangent to the curve at x_0. The derivative measures the instantaneous rate of change of $f(x_0)$ with respect to x_0.

To determine the derivative at point "*a*" differential calculus proceeds by the determination of a series of successively better approximations to the tangent line.

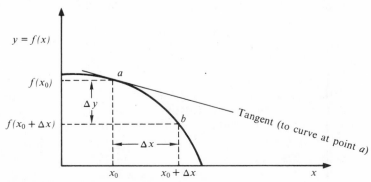

FIGURE B.1   Differentiation Example

To illustrate, assume that we move a small distance along the curve to point "b," as shown in Fig. B.1. Now, the slope of the straight line "$a - b$" is given by:

$$\frac{\Delta y}{\Delta x} = \frac{f(x_0) - f(x_0 + \Delta x)}{\Delta x}$$

As Δx approaches zero, the slope of the line "$a - b$" can be seen to approach the slope of the tangent to the curve at point "a." At the limit at which Δx approaches zero, the slopes will be equal and we can state:

$$\lim_{\Delta x \to 0} \frac{\Delta y}{\Delta x} = \lim_{\Delta x \to 0} \frac{f(x_0) - f(x_0 + \Delta x)}{\Delta x} = \text{slope of the tangent}$$
$$\text{to the curve at point "}a\text{."}$$

In calculus notation this slope, or derivative, is expressed as:

$$\frac{df(x)}{dx} \quad \text{or} \quad \frac{dy}{dx} \quad \text{or} \quad f'(x)$$

In this case we have determined the **first derivative** of the function $f(x)$ with respect to the point x_0. Higher derivatives of a function may also exist. For example, the second derivative of a function is denoted as:

$$\frac{d^2f(x)}{dx^2} \quad \text{or} \quad f''(x)$$

and represents the rate of change of the slope of the function. Thus, the second derivative is simply the derivative of the slope of the function.

In Chapter 10, we illustrated the use of derivatives for finding the maximum or minimum points of a function. This was accomplished by setting the first derivative of the function equal to zero and solving for the value x. The second derivative was then used to determine whether the function was a maximum or a minimum.

In Chapter 10, and elsewhere, we also employed **partial derivatives**. Partial differentiation involves determining the rate of change, or slope, between two variables when the dependent variable z is a function of two or more variables, e.g., $z = f(x,y)$. Thus, in partial differentiation, the dependent variable z and a chosen independent variable are treated as constants and differentiation proceeds. In this process the partial derivative of the function z with respect to x is denoted as:

$$\frac{\partial z}{\partial x} \quad \text{or} \quad \frac{\partial f(x,y)}{\partial x}$$

A function having n independent variables will thus have n partial derivatives.

A number of rules, or derivative formulas, are in existence. Among the more important derivative formulas are the following.

1. $y = a; \dfrac{dy}{dx} = 0$

2. $y = x; \dfrac{dy}{dx} = 1$

3. $y = ax + b; \dfrac{dy}{dx} = a$

4. $y = x^n; \dfrac{dy}{dx} = nx^{n-1}$

5. $y = e^x; \dfrac{dy}{dx} = e^x$

6. $y = [f(x) \pm g(x) \pm \cdots]; \dfrac{dy}{dx} = \dfrac{df(x)}{dx} \pm \dfrac{dg(x)}{dx} \pm \cdots$

7. $y = f(x) \cdot g(x); \dfrac{dy}{dx} = \dfrac{f(x)\, dg\,(x)}{dx} + \dfrac{g(x)\, df\,(x)}{dx}$

8. $y = \dfrac{f(x)}{g(x)}; \dfrac{dy}{dx} = \dfrac{g(x)[df/dx] - f(x)[dg(x)/dx]}{[g(x)]^2}$

9. $y = \log_e x; \dfrac{dy}{dx} = \dfrac{1}{x}$

10. $y = \log_a u; \dfrac{dy}{dx} = \dfrac{\log_a e}{u}\dfrac{du}{dx}$ (where u is a function of x)

11. $y = a^x; \dfrac{dy}{dx} = a^x \log_e a$

12. $y = au; \dfrac{dy}{dx} = a\dfrac{du}{dx}$ (where u is a function of x)

13. $y = [f(x)]^n; \dfrac{dy}{dx} = n[f(x)]^{n-1}\dfrac{df(x)}{dx}$

14. $y = e^{f(x)}; \dfrac{dy}{dx} = e^{f(x)}\dfrac{d[f(x)]}{dx}$

15. $y = u^v; \dfrac{dy}{dx} = vu^{v-1}\dfrac{du}{dx} + u^v \log_e u \dfrac{dv}{dx}$ (where u and v are functions of x)

The second major area of study in calculus is that of **integration**. Integral calculus is concerned with the process of finding the area under a curve, that is, the area between a curve and the x axis, or abscissa. To illustrate, consider the curve plotted in Fig. B.2. In Fig. B.2 assume that we are interested in determining

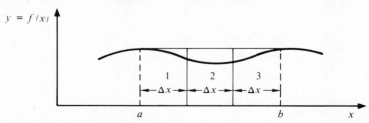

FIGURE B.2   **Integration Example**

the area under the curve $y = f(x)$ between points "a" and "b." We can approximate this area by summing the area under the three rectangles indicated. This sum is given by:

$$\sum_{i=1}^{3} f(x_i)\ \Delta x$$

where $f(x_i)$ is the height of rectangle i and Δx is the width of each rectangle. In this example, this approximation will obviously overestimate the area under the curve between "a" and "b," since the height of each approximating rectangle exceeds the average height of the curve it attempts to approximate. However, as Δx becomes smaller, approaching zero ($\Delta x \rightarrow 0$), the approximation improves. At the limit at which Δx approaches zero, we can state

$$\lim_{\Delta x \rightarrow 0} f(x_i)\ dx = \qquad \text{(Area between } a \text{ and } b \text{ under the curve } y = f(x)\text{)}$$

This limit is written notationally as the **integral**:

$$\int_{a}^{b} f(x)\ dx$$

where the term dx denotes the independent variable of interest.

A number of rules, or integration formulas, are in existence. Among the more important integration formulas are the following.

1. $\displaystyle\int_{a}^{b} dx = [x]_a^b = b - a$

2. $\displaystyle\int_{a}^{b} k\ dx = [kx]_a^b = (b - a)k$

3. $\displaystyle\int_{a}^{b} kf(x)\ dx = k \int_{a}^{b} f(x)\ dx$

4. $\displaystyle\int_{a}^{b} (u + v)\ dx = \int_{a}^{b} u\ dx + \int_{a}^{b} v\ dx$ (where u and v are functions of x)

5. $\displaystyle\int_{a}^{b} x^n\ dx = \left[\frac{x^{n+1}}{n+1}\right]_a^b = \left[\frac{b^{n+1}}{n+1}\right] - \left[\frac{a^{n+1}}{n+1}\right]$

6. $\displaystyle\int_{a}^{b} \frac{1}{x}\ dx = [(\log_e x]_a^b = \log_e b - \log_e a$

7. $\displaystyle\int_{a}^{b} \log_e x\ dx = [x \log_e x - x]_a^b$

8. $\displaystyle\int_{a}^{b} [f(x) \pm g(x)]\ dx = \int_{a}^{b} f(x)\ dx \pm \int_{a}^{b} g(x)\ dx$

9. $\displaystyle\int_{a}^{b} e^{cx}\ dx = \left[\frac{1}{c} e^{cx}\right]_a^b$

10. $\displaystyle\int_a^b xe^{cx}\,dx = \left[\frac{1}{c^2}e^{cx}(1-cx)\right]_a^b$

11. $\displaystyle\int_a^b u\,dv = \left[uv - \int v\,du\right]_a^b$ (where u and v are functions of x)

SELECTED REFERENCES

CALCULUS   Anderson, Chaney, and R. C. Pierce, Jr. 1975. *Elementary Calculus for Business, Economics, and Social Sciences.* Boston: Houghton Mifflin Company.

—XXBeer, Gerald A. 1978. *Applied Calculus for Business and Economics.* Cambridge, Mass.: Winthrop Publishers, Inc.

Childress Robert L. 1972. *Calculus for Business and Economics.* Englewood Cliffs, N.J.: Prentice-Hall, Inc.

Freund, John E. 1975. *College Mathematics With Business Applications.* Englewood Cliffs, N.J.: Prentice-Hall, Inc.

Goldstein, Larry J., David C. Lay, and David I. Schneider. 1980. *Calculus and Its Applications.* Englewood Cliffs, N.J.: Prentice-Hall, Inc.

Lial, Margaret L., and Charles D. Miller. 1980. *Essential Calculus with Applications.* Glenview, Ill.: Scott, Foresman and Company.

Leithold, Louis. 1978. *Essentials of Calculus For Business and Economics.* New York: Harper & Row, Publishers.

Whipkey, Kenneth L., and Mary N. Whipkey. 1972. *The Power of Calculus.* New York: John Wiley & Sons, Inc.

C Tables

Appendix C consists of the following tables:

1. Greek Alphabet
2. Glossary of Common Mathematical Symbols
3. Standard Normal Distribution
4. Poisson Distribution—Individual Terms
5. Exponential Functions
6. Random Numbers (1,000 Random Numbers)
7. Random Normal Numbers, $\mu = 0$, $\sigma = 1$ (900 Random Normal Numbers)
8. Powers, Roots, and Factorials of Numbers

TABLE 1 Greek Alphabet

A	α	Alpha	N	ν	Nu
B	β	Beta	Ξ	ξ	Xi
Γ	γ	Gamma	O	o	Omicron
Δ	δ	Delta	Π	π	Pi
E	ϵ	Epsilon	P	ρ	Rho
Z	ζ	Zeta	Σ	σ	Sigma
H	η	Eta	T	τ	Tau
Θ	θ	Theta	Y	υ	Upsilon
I	ι	Iota	Φ	ϕ	Phi
K	κ	Kappa	X	χ	Chi
Λ	λ	Lambda	Ψ	ψ	Psi
M	μ	Mu	Ω	ω	Omega

TABLE 2   Glossary of Common Mathematical Symbols

Symbol	Name or Meaning	Symbol	Name or Meaning
$+$	Plus or positive	$P(E)$	Probability of E
$-$	Minus or negative	$\approx$ or $\leftrightarrow$	Is equivalent to
$\pm$	Plus or minus; Positive or negative	$\not\approx$	Is not equivalent to
$\mp$	Minus or plus; Negative or positive	$f(x)$, $F(x)$,	Function of x
		Δy	Increment of y
$\times$	Multiplied by	$\doteq$ or $\rightarrow$	Approaches as a limit
$\div$	Divided by	Σ	Summation of
$=$	Equals	∞	Infinity
$\neq$, $\not\equiv$	Does not equal	dy	Differential of y
$\equiv$	Identical with, identically equal to	$\dfrac{dy}{dx}$ or $f'(x)$	Derivative of $y = f(x)$ with respect to x
$\not\equiv$	Not identical with, is not identically equal to	$\dfrac{d^2y}{dx^2}$ or $f''(x)$	Second derivative of $y = f(x)$ with respect to x
$\cong$	Equals approximately; Congruent	$\dfrac{d^ny}{dx^n}$ or $f^{(n)}(x)$	nth derivative of $y = f(x)$ with respect to x
$>$	Greater than		
$<$	Less than	$\dfrac{\partial z}{\partial x}$	Partial derivative of z with respect to x
$\geqq$	Greater than or equal to		
$\leqq$	Less than or equal to	$\dfrac{\partial^2 z}{\partial x\,\partial y}$	Second partial derivative of z with respect to y and x
$\sim$	Similar to		
$\therefore$	Therefore	$\int$	Integral of
$\lvert a \rvert$	Absolute value of a	$\int_a^b$	Integral between the limits a and b
$n!$	n factorial; $n! = 1 \cdot 2 \cdot 3 \cdots n$		
$0!$	Zero factorial, $0! = 1$	$\log$ or $\log_{10}$	Common logarithm
$\sqrt{}$	Square root	$\ln$ or $\log_e$	Natural logarithm; Napierian logarithm
$\sqrt[n]{}$	nth root	e or ϵ	Base (2.718) of natural system of logarithms
a^n	nth power of a		
$\displaystyle\sum_{i=1}^{n} a_i$	$\displaystyle\sum_{i=1}^{n} a_i = a_1 + a_2 + \cdots + a_n$	π	Pi (3.1416)
		$\rightarrow$ or $\Rightarrow$	Implies; *implication*
$\varnothing$	The null set; the empty set	R^{-1}	The *inverse* of relation R

TABLE 3   Standard Normal Distribution

The table below gives the area under the standardized normal curve from 0 to Z, as shown by the shaded portion of the following figure.

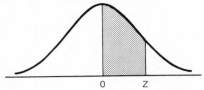

Examples: If Z is the standardized normal random variable, then:

$P(0 \leq Z \leq 1.25) = 0.3944$
$P(Z \geq 1.25) = 0.5000 - 0.3944 = 0.1056$
$P(Z \leq 1.25) = 0.5000 + 0.3944 = 0.8944$
$P(Z \leq -1.25) = 0.1056$ (by symmetry)

Z	.00	.01	.02	.03	.04	.05	.06	.07	.08	.09
0.0	.0000	.0040	.0080	.0120	.0160	.0199	.0239	.0279	.0319	.0359
0.1	.0398	.0438	.0478	.0517	.0557	.0596	.0636	.0675	.0714	.0753
0.2	.0793	.0832	.0871	.0910	.0948	.0987	.1026	.1064	.1103	.1141
0.3	.1179	.1217	.1255	.1293	.1331	.1368	.1406	.1443	.1480	.1517
0.4	.1554	.1591	.1628	.1664	.1700	.1736	.1772	.1808	.1844	.1879
0.5	.1915	.1950	.1985	.2019	.2054	.2088	.2123	.2157	.2190	.2224
0.6	.2257	.2291	.2324	.2357	.2389	.2422	.2454	.2486	.2518	.2549
0.7	.2580	.2612	.2642	.2673	.2704	.2734	.2764	.2794	.2823	.2852
0.8	.2881	.2910	.2939	.2967	.2995	.3023	.3051	.3078	.3106	.3133
0.9	.3159	.3186	.3212	.3238	.3264	.3289	.3315	.3340	.3365	.3389
1.0	.3413	.3438	.3461	.3485	.3508	.3531	.3554	.3577	.3599	.3621
1.1	.3643	.3665	.3686	.3708	.3729	.3749	.3770	.3790	.3810	.3830
1.2	.3849	.3869	.3888	.3907	.3925	.3944	.3962	.3980	.3997	.4015
1.3	.4032	.4049	.4066	.4082	.4099	.4115	.4131	.4147	.4162	.4177
1.4	.4192	.4207	.4222	.4236	.4251	.4265	.4279	.4292	.4306	.4319
1.5	.4332	.4345	.4357	.4370	.4382	.4394	.4406	.4418	.4429	.4441
1.6	.4452	.4463	.4474	.4484	.4495	.4505	.4515	.4525	.4535	.4545
1.7	.4554	.4564	.4573	.4582	.4591	.4599	.4608	.4616	.4625	.4633
1.8	.4641	.4649	.4656	.4664	.4671	.4678	.4686	.4693	.4699	.4706
1.9	.4713	.4719	.4726	.4732	.4738	.4744	.4750	.4756	.4761	.4767
2.0	.4772	.4778	.4783	.4788	.4793	.4798	.4803	.4808	.4812	.4817
2.1	.4821	.4826	.4830	.4834	.4838	.4842	.4846	.4850	.4854	.4857
2.2	.4861	.4864	.4868	.4871	.4875	.4878	.4881	.4884	.4887	.4890
2.3	.4893	.4896	.4898	.4901	.4904	.4906	.4909	.4911	.4913	.4916
2.4	.4918	.4920	.4922	.4925	.4927	.4929	.4931	.4932	.4934	.4936
2.5	.4938	.4940	.4941	.4943	.4945	.4946	.4948	.4949	.4951	.4952
2.6	.4953	.4955	.4956	.4957	.4959	.4960	.4961	.4962	.4963	.4964
2.7	.4965	.4966	.4967	.4968	.4969	.4970	.4971	.4972	.4973	.4974
2.8	.4974	.4975	.4976	.4977	.4977	.4978	.4979	.4979	.4980	.4981
2.9	.4981	.4982	.4982	.4983	.4984	.4984	.4985	.4985	.4986	.4986
3.0	.49865	.4987	.4987	.4988	.4988	.4989	.4989	.4989	.4990	.4990
4.0	.4999683									

TABLE 4 Poisson Distribution—Individual Terms

The Poisson probability function is given by:

$$f(x; \lambda) = \frac{\lambda^x e^{-\lambda}}{x!} \text{ for } \lambda > 0, x = 0, 1, 2, \ldots$$

The following table contains the individual terms of $f(x; \lambda)$ for specified values of x and λ.

x	0.01	0.02	0.03	0.04	0.05	0.06	0.07	0.08	0.09	0.10	0.15	x
0	.990	.980	.970	.961	.951	.942	.932	.923	.914	.905	.861	0
1	.010	.020	.030	.038	.048	.057	.065	.074	.082	.090	.129	1
2				.001	.001	.002	.002	.003	.004	.005	.010	2

x	0.20	0.25	0.30	0.40	0.50	0.60	0.70	0.80	0.90	1.0	1.1	1.2	1.3	1.4	1.5	1.6	1.7	1.8	1.9	2.0	x
0	.819	.779	.741	.670	.607	.549	.497	.449	.407	.368	.333	.301	.273	.247	.223	.202	.183	.165	.150	.135	0
1	.164	.195	.222	.268	.303	.329	.348	.359	.366	.368	.366	.361	.354	.345	.335	.323	.311	.298	.284	.271	1
2	.016	.024	.033	.054	.076	.099	.122	.144	.165	.184	.201	.217	.230	.242	.251	.258	.264	.268	.270	.271	2
3	.001	.002	.003	.007	.013	.020	.028	.038	.049	.061	.074	.087	.100	.113	.126	.138	.150	.161	.171	.180	3
4				.001	.002	.003	.005	.008	.011	.015	.020	.026	.032	.039	.047	.055	.063	.072	.081	.090	4
5							.001	.001	.002	.003	.004	.006	.008	.011	.014	.018	.022	.026	.031	.036	5

x	2.1	2.2	2.3	2.4	2.5	2.6	2.7	2.8	2.9	3.0	3.1	3.2	3.3	3.4	3.5	3.6	3.7	3.8	3.9	4.0	x
0	.122	.111	.100	.091	.082	.074	.067	.061	.055	.050	.045	.041	.037	.033	.030	.027	.025	.022	.020	.018	0
1	.257	.244	.231	.218	.205	.193	.181	.170	.160	.149	.140	.130	.122	.113	.106	.098	.091	.085	.079	.073	1
2	.270	.268	.265	.261	.257	.251	.245	.238	.231	.224	.216	.209	.201	.193	.185	.177	.169	.162	.154	.147	2
3	.189	.197	.203	.209	.214	.218	.220	.222	.224	.224	.224	.223	.221	.219	.216	.212	.209	.205	.200	.195	3
4	.099	.108	.117	.125	.134	.141	.149	.156	.162	.168	.173	.178	.182	.186	.189	.191	.193	.194	.195	.195	4
5	.042	.048	.054	.060	.067	.074	.080	.087	.094	.101	.107	.114	.120	.126	.132	.138	.143	.148	.152	.156	5
6	.015	.017	.021	.024	.028	.032	.036	.041	.045	.050	.056	.061	.066	.072	.077	.083	.088	.094	.099	.104	6
7	.004	.005	.007	.008	.010	.012	.014	.016	.019	.022	.025	.028	.031	.035	.039	.042	.047	.051	.055	.060	7
8	.001	.002	.002	.002	.003	.004	.005	.006	.007	.008	.010	.011	.013	.015	.017	.109	.022	.024	.027	.030	8
9			.001	.001	.001	.001	.002	.002	.003	.003	.004	.005	.006	.007	.008	.009	.010	.012	.013	9
10							.001	.001	.001	.001	.002	.002	.002	.003	.003	.004	.005	.005	10

TABLE 4   Poisson Distribution—Individual Terms (Continued)

λ

x	4.1	4.2	4.3	4.4	4.5	4.6	4.7	4.8	4.9	5.0	5.1	5.2	5.3	5.4	5.5	5.6	5.7	5.8	5.9	6.0	x
0	.017	.015	.014	.012	.011	.010	.009	.008	.007	.007	.006	.006	.005	.005	.004	.004	.003	.003	.003	.002	0
1	.068	.063	.058	.054	.050	.046	.043	.040	.036	.034	.031	.029	.026	.024	.022	.021	.019	.018	.016	.015	1
2	.139	.132	.125	.119	.112	.106	.100	.095	.089	.084	.079	.075	.070	.066	.062	.058	.054	.051	.048	.045	2
3	.190	.185	.180	.174	.169	.163	.157	.152	.146	.140	.135	.129	.124	.119	.113	.108	.103	.098	.094	.089	3
4	.195	.194	.193	.192	.190	.188	.185	.182	.179	.175	.172	.168	.164	.160	.156	.152	.147	.143	.138	.134	4
5	.160	.163	.166	.169	.171	.173	.174	.175	.175	.175	.175	.175	.174	.173	.171	.170	.168	.166	.163	.161	5
6	.109	.114	.119	.124	.128	.132	.136	.140	.143	.146	.149	.151	.154	.156	.157	.158	.159	.160	.160	.161	6
7	.064	.069	.073	.078	.082	.087	.091	.096	.100	.104	.109	.113	.116	.120	.123	.127	.130	.133	.135	.138	7
8	.033	.036	.039	.043	.046	.050	.054	.058	.061	.065	.069	.073	.077	.081	.085	.089	.092	.096	.100	.103	8
9	.015	.017	.019	.021	.023	.026	.028	.031	.033	.036	.039	.042	.045	.049	.052	.055	.059	.062	.065	.069	9
10	.006	.007	.008	.009	.010	.012	.013	.015	.016	.018	.020	.022	.024	.026	.029	.031	.033	.036	.039	.041	10
11	.002	.003	.003	.004	.004	.005	.006	.006	.007	.008	.009	.010	.012	.013	.014	.016	.017	.019	.021	.023	11
12	.001	.001	.001	.001	.002	.002	.002	.003	.003	.003	.004	.005	.005	.006	.007	.007	.008	.009	.010	.011	12
13					.001	.001	.001	.001	.001	.001	.002	.002	.002	.002	.003	.003	.004	.004	.005	.005	13
14											.001	.001	.001	.001	.001	.001	.001	.002	.002	.002	14
15																	.001	.001	.001	.001	15

λ

x	6.1	6.2	6.3	6.4	6.5	6.6	6.7	6.8	6.9	7.0	7.1	7.2	7.3	7.4	7.5	8.0	8.5	9.0	9.5	10.0	x
0	.002	.002	.002	.002	.002	.001	.001	.001	.001	.001	.001	.001	.001	.001	.001						0
1	.014	.013	.012	.011	.010	.009	.008	.008	.007	.006	.006	.005	.005	.005	.004	.003	.002	.001	.001		1
2	.042	.039	.036	.034	.032	.030	.028	.026	.024	.022	.021	.019	.018	.017	.016	.011	.007	.005	.003	.002	2
3	.085	.081	.077	.073	.069	.065	.062	.058	.055	.052	.049	.046	.044	.041	.039	.029	.021	.015	.011	.008	3
4	.129	.125	.121	.116	.112	.108	.103	.099	.095	.091	.087	.084	.080	.076	.073	.057	.044	.034	.025	.019	4
5	.158	.155	.152	.149	.145	.142	.138	.135	.131	.128	.124	.120	.117	.113	.109	.092	.075	.061	.048	.038	5
6	.160	.160	.159	.159	.157	.156	.155	.153	.151	.149	.147	.144	.142	.139	.137	.122	.107	.091	.076	.063	6
7	.140	.142	.144	.145	.146	.147	.148	.149	.149	.149	.149	.149	.148	.147	.146	.140	.129	.117	.104	.090	7
8	.107	.110	.113	.116	.119	.121	.124	.126	.128	.130	.132	.134	.135	.136	.137	.140	.138	.132	.123	.113	8
9	.072	.076	.079	.082	.086	.089	.092	.095	.098	.101	.104	.107	.110	.112	.114	.124	.130	.132	.130	.125	9
10	.044	.047	.050	.053	.056	.059	.062	.065	.068	.071	.074	.077	.080	.083	.086	.099	.110	.119	.124	.125	10
11	.024	.026	.029	.031	.033	.035	.038	.040	.043	.045	.048	.050	.053	.056	.059	.072	.085	.097	.107	.114	11
12	.012	.014	.015	.016	.018	.019	.021	.023	.025	.026	.028	.030	.032	.034	.037	.048	.060	.073	.084	.095	12
13	.006	.007	.007	.008	.009	.010	.011	.012	.013	.014	.015	.017	.018	.020	.021	.030	.040	.050	.062	.073	13
14	.003	.003	.003	.004	.004	.005	.005	.006	.006	.007	.008	.009	.009	.010	.011	.017	.024	.032	.042	.052	14
15	.001	.001	.001	.002	.002	.002	.002	.003	.003	.003	.004	.004	.005	.005	.006	.009	.014	.019	.027	.035	15
16			.001	.001	.001	.001	.001	.001	.001	.001	.002	.002	.002	.002	.003	.005	.007	.011	.016	.022	16
17									.001	.001	.001	.001	.001	.001	.001	.002	.004	.006	.009	.013	17
18																.001	.002	.003	.005	.007	18
19																	.001	.001	.002	.004	19
20																		.001	.001	.002	20

TABLE 5   Exponential Functions

x	e^x	e^{-x}	x	e^x	e^{-x}
0.00	1.0000	1.0000	0.45	1.5683	0.6376
0.01	1.0101	0.9900	0.46	1.5841	0.6313
0.02	1.0202	0.9802	0.47	1.6000	0.6250
0.03	1.0305	0.9704	0.48	1.6161	0.6188
0.04	1.0408	0.9608	0.49	1.6323	0.6126
0.05	1.0513	0.9512	0.50	1.6487	0.6065
0.06	1.0618	0.9418	0.51	1.6653	0.6005
0.07	1.0725	0.9329	0.52	1.6820	0.5945
0.08	1.0833	0.9231	0.53	1.6989	0.5886
0.09	1.0942	0.9139	0.54	1.7160	0.5827
0.10	1.1052	0.9048	0.55	1.7333	0.5769
0.11	1.1163	0.8958	0.56	1.7507	0.5712
0.12	1.1275	0.8869	0.57	1.7683	0.5655
0.13	1.1388	0.8780	0.58	1.7860	0.5599
0.14	1.1503	0.8693	0.59	1.8040	0.5543
0.15	1.1618	0.8607	0.60	1.8221	0.5488
0.16	1.1735	0.8521	0.61	1.8404	0.5433
0.17	1.1853	0.8436	0.62	1.8589	0.5379
0.18	1.1972	0.8353	0.63	1.8776	0.5326
0.19	1.2092	0.8269	0.64	1.8965	0.5273
0.20	1.2214	0.8187	0.65	1.9155	0.5220
0.21	1.2337	0.8106	0.66	1.9348	0.5168
0.22	1.2461	0.8025	0.67	1.9542	0.5117
0.23	1.2586	0.7945	0.68	1.9739	0.5066
0.24	1.2712	0.7866	0.69	1.9937	0.5016
0.25	1.2840	0.7788	0.70	2.0138	0.4965
0.26	1.2969	0.7710	0.71	2.0340	0.4916
0.27	1.3100	0.7633	0.72	2.0544	0.4867
0.28	1.3231	0.7558	0.73	2.0751	0.4819
0.29	1.3364	0.7482	0.74	2.0959	0.4771
0.30	1.3499	0.7408	0.75	2.1170	0.4723
0.31	1.3634	0.7334	0.76	2.1383	0.4677
0.32	1.3771	0.7261	0.77	2.1598	0.4630
0.33	1.3910	0.7189	0.78	2.1815	0.4584
0.34	1.4049	0.7118	0.79	2.2034	0.4538
0.35	1.4191	0.7046	0.80	2.2255	0.4493
0.36	1.4333	0.6977	0.81	2.2479	0.4448
0.37	1.4477	0.6907	0.82	2.2705	0.4404
0.38	1.4623	0.6839	0.83	2.2933	0.4360
0.39	1.4770	0.6770	0.84	2.3164	0.4317
0.40	1.4918	0.6703	0.85	2.3396	0.4274
0.41	1.5068	0.6636	0.86	2.3632	0.4231
0.42	1.5220	0.6570	0.87	2.3869	0.4189
0.43	1.5373	0.6505	0.88	2.4109	0.4148
0.44	1.5527	0.6440	0.89	2.4351	0.4106

TABLE 5 Exponential Functions (Continued)

x	e^x	e^{-x}	x	e^x	e^{-x}
0.90	2.4596	0.4066	2.80	16.445	0.0608
0.91	2.4843	0.4025	2.85	16.288	0.0578
0.92	2.5093	0.3985	2.90	18.174	0.0550
0.93	2.5345	0.3945	2.95	19.106	0.0523
0.94	2.5600	0.3906	3.00	20.086	0.0498
0.95	2.5857	0.3867	3.05	21.115	0.0474
0.96	2.6117	0.3829	3.10	22.198	0.0450
0.97	2.6379	0.3790	3.15	23.336	0.0429
0.98	2.6645	0.3753	3.20	24.533	0.0408
0.99	2.6912	0.3716	3.25	25.790	0.0389
1.00	2.7183	0.3678	3.30	27.113	0.0369
1.05	2.8577	0.3499	3.35	28.503	0.0351
1.10	3.0042	0.3329	3.40	29.964	0.0333
1.15	3.1582	0.3166	3.45	31.500	0.0317
1.20	3.3201	0.3012	3.50	33.115	0.0302
1.25	3.4903	0.2865	3.55	34.813	0.0287
1.30	3.6693	0.2625	3.60	36.598	0.0273
1.35	3.8574	0.2592	3.65	38.475	0.0260
1.40	4.0552	0.2466	3.70	40.447	0.0247
1.45	4.2631	0.2346	3.75	42.521	0.0235
1.50	4.4817	0.2231	3.80	44.701	0.0224
1.55	4.7115	0.2122	3.85	46.993	0.0213
1.60	4.9530	0.2019	3.90	49.402	0.0202
1.65	5.2070	0.1921	3.95	51.935	0.0193
1.70	5.4739	0.1821	4.00	54.598	0.0183
1.75	5.7546	0.1738	4.05	57.397	0.0174
1.80	6.0496	0.6153	4.10	60.340	0.0166
1.85	6.3593	0.1572	4.15	63.434	0.0158
1.90	6.6850	0.1496	4.20	66.686	0.0150
1.95	7.0287	0.1423	4.25	70.105	0.0143
2.00	7.3891	0.1353	4.30	73.700	0.0136
2.05	7.7679	0.1287	4.35	77.478	0.0129
2.10	8.1662	0.1224	4.40	81.451	0.0123
2.15	8.5849	0.1165	4.45	85.627	0.0117
2.20	9.0250	0.1108	4.50	90.017	0.0111
2.25	9.4877	0.1054	4.55	94.632	0.0107
2.30	9.9742	0.1003	4.60	99.844	0.0101
2.35	10.486	0.0954	4.65	104.58	0.0096
2.40	11.023	0.0907	4.70	109.95	0.0091
2.45	11.588	0.0863	4.75	115.58	0.0087
2.50	12.182	0.0821	4.80	121.51	0.0082
2.55	12.807	0.0781	4.85	127.74	0.0078
2.60	13.464	0.0743	4.90	134.29	0.0074
2.65	14.154	0.0707	4.95	141.17	0.0070
2.70	14.880	0.0672	5.00	148.41	0.0067
2.75	15.643	0.0639			

TABLE 5 Exponential Functions (Concluded)

x	e^x	e^{-x}	x	e^x	e^{-x}
5.10	164.02	0.0061	7.60	1998.2	0.0005
5.20	181.27	0.0055	7.70	2208.3	0.0005
5.30	200.34	0.0050	7.80	2440.6	0.0004
5.40	221.41	0.0045	7.90	2697.3	0.0004
5.50	244.69	0.0041	8.00	2981.0	0.0003
5.60	270.43	0.0037	8.10	3294.5	0.0003
5.70	298.87	0.0033	8.20	3641.0	0.0003
5.80	330.30	0.0030	8.30	4023.9	0.0002
5.90	365.04	0.0027	8.40	4447.1	0.0002
6.00	403.43	0.0025	8.50	4914.8	0.0002
6.10	445.86	0.0022	8.60	5431.7	0.0002
6.20	492.75	0.0020	8.70	6002.9	0.0002
6.30	544.57	0.0018	8.80	6634.2	0.0002
6.40	601.85	0.0017	8.90	7332.0	0.0001
6.50	665.14	0.0015	9.00	8103.1	0.0001
6.60	735.10	0.0014	9.10	8955.3	0.0001
6.70	812.41	0.0012	9.20	9897.1	0.0001
6.80	897.85	0.0011	9.30	10938	0.0001
6.90	992.27	0.0010	9.40	12088	0.0001
7.00	1096.6	0.0009	9.50	13360	0.0001
7.10	1212.0	0.0008	9.60	14765	0.0001
7.20	1339.4	0.0007	9.70	16318	0.0001
7.30	1480.3	0.0007	9.80	18034	0.0001
7.40	1636.0	0.0006	9.90	19930	0.0001
7.50	1808.0	0.0006	10.00	22026	0.0000

TABLE 6   Random Numbers (1000 Random Numbers)

71120	20048	30087	00092	29765	77762	98690	92278	65456	62229	84269	45548	14865	79255	41743	37160	47268	49170	69602
75082	24072	95501	54780	69172	22011	9512	58973	68226	78595	57535	37856	09319	15206	07359	07297	77553	99644	99882
02494	16026	97993	24612	65728	72859	45602	17876	96838	20146	49326	14645	43933	31790	95343	85946	57592	72036	13885
34981	84923	03904	71102	91478	08947	30380	01752	37089	06767	06797	79879	18102	89697	75265	44318	88518	32246	96809
90638	72547	64302	09963	81058	96682	50565	33255	44441	67349	04119	18576	74378	79082	05091	18806	67012	32815	93780
67342	60032	54111	84376	56155	63622	76339	85428	25521	84271	75931	97146	99493	22642	40408	38672	68358	62098	57361
85281	95442	05117	71720	60126	02341	72915	16418	42269	05852	54687	75455	60542	84156	60060	02950	77159	36400	23967
16205	81523	43290	26035	66599	92248	66024	65910	01243	14268	74420	18099	38817	70008	70690	94069	28201	22584	81691
86886	86097	34601	32731	84977	26885	23791	00785	90586	36447	03405	92409	23807	11159	52687	15696	19986	78650	92028
44313	37623	26924	22934	95283	34190	17534	97491	27140	85417	68236	40661	29843	13105	10040	42294	63404	99776	28011
70086	68409	79681	62406	82159	77232	23954	48636	76228	19642	31799	14017	97909	61296	86595	67906	28081	57332	91256
31547	67978	23944	31866	67355	22907	31243	81295	06577	07810	87661	55675	45100	69522	11224	41647	48865	18365	70401
57118	09097	40515	61217	02660	66113	11594	74544	42916	86600	33359	20746	24249	58773	34397	77426	54981	33050	03470
23364	08958	43468	80182	89879	96886	22613	63705	78710	98914	85096	20342	56191	54064	18659	25378	84335	77607	06622
41269	88015	56664	47847	77102	98007	00146	18814	11568	00077	96348	77390	97207	86730	45516	92521	45480	40191	31827
29237	88978	70735	23604	05007	60580	05005	84808	63797	19508	42871	81658	04102	89691	01225	00126	89731	37252	15930
60306	18464	68031	42007	39758	60484	86104	70924	50613	65357	36619	31505	59455	73182	03992	65313	55946	47858	83635
71087	73804	03046	54033	96783	95349	22496	76829	58514	59615	31064	49849	19517	68455	35076	94356	50450	53489	66887
19915	17505	25799	97245	32426	33111	06827	42957	96301	91189	80426	61850	47268	26952	36298	75219	24630	70806	03164
81724	61870	35700	57366	22895	20392	32684	12570	81264	74447	15307	21815	93130	62438	36457	56798	12677	64878	75174
67140	26272	53367	83758	22236	77456	48358	93041	23016	00730	97233	76822	85836	23612	69151	02390	91983	30385	54459
52387	29586	97931	21305	46451	03690	39509	03846	67492	70338	14601	54561	95956	84686	44509	04881	28703	28290	11405
13821	80281	57289	21207	11635	68958	03236	98786	63592	92477	82531	62894	34578	41421	37323	51146	70964	65473	54156
35676	26656	38846	93173	09419	22937	76059	49921	14996	40682	09130	88636	49646	00151	54090	23174	52236	04843	58937

10031	29748	88211	61529	75277	97899	09899	78302	80724	79620	51206	90651	83052	82455	47259	41458	23413	67355	93413	54286
84993	21385	63365	87724	56058	46835	76484	37385	35952	79240	51872	98071	21574	46799	86629	98581	11823	83708	95844	21684
67509	09898	51806	21748	64234	89674	59931	52521	75742	81765	08909	17570	25235	93280	32567	55878	42163	50071	20956	75098
61979	95995	18151	44955	06364	33592	44275	63316	81418	18667	79236	07409	31326	21271	45691	82701	84985	65598	28718	81928
33106	61279	69716	66788	73282	38593	72020	84785	60524	00075	55735	33731	00769	01034	99285	86403	24851	71476	05192	87863
80451	91936	27558	37920	79499	35713	98780	71265	38566	90011	92975	47747	49704	68494	63628	65321	19271	27732	92955	08135
12215	00071	90488	42288	39331	55394	78380	71734	24985	04298	00922	66851	92806	55174	95788	78158	06852	37694	64490	47692
05738	05201	79559	30544	67235	28509	65938	39047	40839	93609	94101	22120	85811	15781	22385	92274	52179	82609	26041	12764
42213	38405	50509	57409	89872	22542	26408	55563	95710	74189	83739	34737	54764	15950	02823	73385	14898	28920	39438	76345
03123	31634	31689	85432	57386	75428	36092	37692	01323	67814	00373	83808	99486	42645	60496	79167	30534	70700	49397	60078
15896	54669	84946	17654	41405	89546	64625	81836	09393	19826	34422	28094	58760	99715	69450	19261	90515	69735	03777	95046
36277	62246	46983	21683	07252	48366	24925	14251	61179	38808	82237	44145	24735	51108	84028	44196	08923	55772	54319	23965
54918	13825	88683	07672	47886	18265	07300	07614	36270	51924	85110	43340	94050	74238	98975	25706	63462	49416	25340	07293
15694	28526	29907	22703	67051	97978	84403	24618	88080	06914	48760	30336	43174	86013	27513	90959	98138	70192	37911	95738
33228	37718	27257	24078	99155	78226	76955	57693	53563	02142	30784	65420	15467	04015	84889	73195	75168	92251	76989	31674
97137	97757	12305	94018	53358	73988	63705	16334	24652	00907	83573	93269	07461	05339	64887	41264	63605	10245	89028	41690
50506	25392	97799	58262	69382	91934	27162	35563	68911	93401	40205	00617	41856	45586	96809	70575	52171	77849	97553	84675
30066	18320	39328	71083	72544	95511	20167	61402	86909	68831	30800	65324	14739	00513	70428	17947	73829	81445	24208	12246
55603	23400	39967	29201	15499	30187	41626	78075	93812	60193	16850	59361	04516	92842	16409	62872	29552	11455	02766	13496
56081	15018	85377	77102	94212	71354	80215	39105	12692	24205	31007	68188	30070	66721	29694	77680	98828	93844	73614	97084
19979	46117	96888	66272	25639	57382	13545	64828	67058	18895	09851	89049	45631	72342	23364	89109	24373	44261	46202	78863
57358	34377	90038	30830	74634	70335	50305	68808	60103	41343	07126	70668	59873	23219	00460	93786	58571	07351	16967	35640
61136	46053	26091	42066	17573	26837	02866	75662	28173	88083	74933	56852	66715	88620	31283	90112	59121	43717	30216	87840
55088	39969	44019	04394	30191	41597	77860	92782	55949	00659	00405	96502	75362	83652	23654	89051	21416	27039	69489	73577
16061	34166	60450	55200	87150	26095	72222	98476	58839	85347	82528	27043	19507	66360	73648	66328	35135	13849	66880	76639
57911	57715	25090	31104	60809	84915	62207	09006	94174	83984	56338	82172	85985	76360	84296	18536	52548	48461	17836	70864

TABLE 7 Random Normal Numbers, $\mu = 0$, $\sigma = 1$. (900 Random Normal Numbers)

1.085	0.480	-1.114	0.834	-0.006	-1.272	1.719	-0.354	0.936	1.573	-0.036	-0.123	0.436	0.178	-0.824	0.224	0.077	0.768
-0.493	-1.369	1.027	0.350	0.437	-0.883	-0.915	-0.169	1.638	0.641	-0.050	-0.171	-1.055	0.677	0.487	-0.650	-0.744	0.764
1.531	1.502	1.355	0.304	-0.208	-0.446	0.731	0.062	1.125	0.645	-1.130	-0.003	0.677	-0.435	-0.051	-0.573	0.657	0.163
-0.662	-0.647	0.958	1.363	0.056	1.110	-0.442	0.820	1.207	-0.528	-0.562	-1.325	0.251	1.540	0.090	0.559	-1.288	0.477
1.174	-0.491	1.988	0.257	1.284	0.923	-1.472	0.646	-0.247	-0.930	-0.569	0.217	1.352	-0.637	0.499	0.914	-0.083	0.278
1.346	0.354	-1.342	-0.223	-1.402	-0.811	-0.330	1.144	0.695	1.449	-0.313	0.039	-1.276	1.857	-0.174	-0.280	-2.170	-0.797
0.225	0.336	0.245	-0.222	0.180	1.171	0.071	-1.018	1.030	-2.318	-0.892	-1.377	0.174	-0.092	-1.214	1.271	0.070	-1.051
0.242	-2.032	1.088	-0.822	1.275	0.191	0.884	-1.112	1.815	-0.094	-1.341	-0.492	-1.427	1.463	0.155	-0.081	-1.679	-0.723
0.894	-0.179	-0.411	-1.045	1.190	-1.365	-1.679	-0.344	0.169	1.318	0.364	-0.700	-0.148	0.535	0.772	0.083	1.326	2.010
1.738	-0.468	0.210	-0.848	2.296	0.951	-0.341	-0.861	0.275	0.180	1.313	-1.333	2.009	0.195	-1.462	0.241	-1.105	1.034
0.393	-0.202	1.478	-1.128	-1.974	-0.350	-1.762	0.254	0.379	0.814	-0.342	1.336	0.099	-0.420	-0.582	-2.063	-0.104	-0.702
-0.457	-0.619	-0.017	-0.716	0.875	-0.695	0.458	0.982	-1.212	0.607	-1.388	0.101	-0.757	-1.111	1.437	-0.227	-1.737	0.812
-0.067	0.104	-1.625	-0.384	0.399	0.552	-0.217	-0.637	1.872	1.006	1.452	-0.184	0.625	0.381	0.684	1.418	-0.009	-1.350
0.370	-0.147	-0.631	0.161	0.220	0.089	-0.260	0.503	-0.936	0.523	-0.484	0.397	0.487	0.379	1.312	0.601	0.137	0.946
0.724	-0.425	-0.260	0.273	0.019	0.678	-1.082	0.569	-1.141	-0.270	-0.794	-1.175	0.140	0.271	-0.468	-1.887	-0.178	1.900
1.928	-0.718	-0.672	0.369	-0.457	0.140	-1.032	0.789	0.814	0.264	-1.014	-1.858	-1.048	-0.496	-0.377	-0.191	0.228	0.772
-1.022	1.046	1.035	-1.072	0.598	1.362	1.603	1.456	0.550	-0.178	-0.618	0.451	0.356	1.588	-0.077	-0.393	-0.400	-1.114
0.930	-0.996	-0.177	-0.507	0.056	-0.707	-1.399	-0.075	-0.250	0.165	0.983	-0.080	-1.153	-0.903	-0.167	0.485	0.246	1.626
0.905	1.354	-0.281	-1.332	1.847	-1.058	-0.200	0.612	-0.843	2.117	-0.560	-0.222	-1.016	-0.333	-2.183	-0.514	-0.465	-0.558
0.085	0.356	0.813	1.120	1.968	1.383	-0.899	-1.004	1.581	0.563	-0.533	-0.683	1.385	-1.004	-0.598	0.715	-0.098	-0.156
0.716	0.334	0.255	1.578	-0.524	-0.247	-0.531	1.621	-0.109	-0.548	0.841	-0.107	-0.266	-1.156	0.176	2.337	1.839	-0.595
-1.895	-0.327	-0.740	0.835	1.491	1.248	-0.071	-0.910	1.020	-2.206	-0.600	1.921	0.776	1.036	-0.210	0.583	-0.093	-0.238
-0.377	-0.178	-0.897	-0.255	0.196	0.131	1.571	1.071	-0.038	-1.338	0.047	0.881	-0.682	0.456	0.960	1.745	-1.277	-0.389
0.701	-0.708	2.124	-0.775	-1.164	-2.277	-1.455	-0.708	-0.224	-0.807	0.744	0.315	1.230	0.053	0.460	-0.823	-0.028	1.715

−1.164	0.655	0.724	0.254	−1.281	−0.589	0.067	0.546	1.581	0.584	0.518	0.829	0.446	−2.163	−0.870	1.296	−0.602	−0.104
0.584	−0.453	0.367	−0.125	0.214	−1.357	−0.589	0.688	0.561	−0.903	0.457	1.088	0.960	−0.117	−1.129	−0.418	−0.192	0.040
−0.434	1.668	0.579	−0.808	0.755	0.931	−0.082	1.634	1.960	−1.946	−1.286	−0.178	−1.170	0.325	0.647	−1.424	−0.926	2.095
−0.536	−0.223	0.949	−0.629	−0.164	0.846	−1.012	−1.637	1.086	0.841	0.503	0.824	0.176	0.362	−1.515	0.884	0.127	0.072
0.024	0.697	−0.871	1.643	0.015	0.025	0.085	0.919	0.309	0.906	0.099	−0.053	−0.820	−0.746	−0.527	−0.829	0.962	1.044
1.053	−1.685	−1.168	−0.700	−0.088	−1.834	−1.264	−1.595	0.062	−0.239	−0.159	0.109	−0.912	0.326	−1.238	−0.832	−1.362	1.148
1.421	−0.422	1.834	0.695	−0.790	1.030	−0.471	−0.012	−3.160	−2.022	2.131	0.289	−1.792	1.962	−0.432	0.667	−1.726	0.581
−0.939	−0.502	−0.025	1.246	−0.346	−2.560	−0.884	0.898	2.199	−0.806	1.432	2.529	−0.092	−0.390	0.165	0.522	0.053	−0.397
−0.032	−1.853	1.157	−0.567	1.051	−0.719	0.211	−0.573	0.762	−1.895	1.272	−0.066	−1.377	−0.217	−0.108	−0.350	1.220	1.539
−0.800	0.662	0.341	−0.203	−0.728	−0.497	−0.410	−1.071	0.210	0.474	−0.762	0.671	−0.153	0.052	−1.848	0.031	0.083	−1.226
0.876	0.241	0.557	−0.057	1.249	0.116	0.092	−0.179	1.287	1.124	1.982	−1.031	1.138	1.054	−0.592	0.706	−0.989	0.756
−0.820	1.144	−0.109	−2.463	−0.022	−0.808	−3.382	−0.417	−1.197	0.939	−0.781	−0.880	1.116	0.486	−0.814	1.780	1.439	−1.004
−0.644	−0.306	0.495	−1.690	0.515	−1.132	−0.868	0.757	−0.373	0.869	−0.276	−0.521	0.463	0.111	−0.924	−0.580	−0.141	0.067
−0.288	−0.722	0.584	−0.946	−1.018	1.342	−0.339	−0.053	−0.309	−1.076	1.337	0.462	2.925	1.749	0.728	−1.144	−1.169	0.605
−0.382	−1.657	0.433	−1.378	−1.440	1.875	0.293	0.820	−0.009	1.178	−1.042	0.549	1.309	−0.711	−2.144	1.380	−0.026	1.309
−0.492	−0.599	0.382	−2.068	0.496	−1.210	1.180	−1.894	0.585	−1.234	1.551	1.283	−1.514	−1.323	0.237	−0.655	−1.029	−1.062
−2.125	0.024	−0.168	−0.036	−0.905	−1.527	0.536	−0.403	1.592	−0.115	0.144	−1.733	1.387	−0.075	−0.290	0.169	−0.433	0.316
0.277	−0.152	1.247	0.759	−1.271	0.371	0.636	0.147	−1.805	−1.201	1.824	−1.831	0.009	0.105	0.177	0.332	0.569	−0.670
0.336	0.573	1.152	1.421	−1.169	−1.003	−0.179	−0.327	0.639	1.828	−0.256	0.718	1.408	−0.646	−1.401	−0.624	−0.151	−0.074
0.732	−1.043	−0.862	1.119	0.894	1.922	−0.509	2.155	−0.768	0.359	2.116	−0.294	−1.294	−1.130	0.006	−0.096	0.337	−0.883
0.212	0.825	1.855	0.080	−1.522	−0.217	−0.891	−0.365	0.344	−1.159	0.218	1.988	1.083	2.913	−0.516	−1.415	−0.969	0.974
0.583	0.062	1.017	1.598	1.202	0.278	−0.796	0.216	0.408	0.784	0.388	−0.520	0.787	−2.193	−2.814	1.147	0.986	−1.366
0.715	−2.383	−0.599	0.027	−0.252	−1.833	0.363	−0.933	−0.082	−0.239	−1.972	−0.838	3.123	−1.063	−1.675	0.382	−0.677	0.296
0.541	−0.500	−0.155	1.784	1.862	−1.725	−0.763	−0.583	−0.568	−0.591	0.601	−0.923	−2.537	−0.247	−0.821	1.145	−1.774	−0.781
1.056	−2.216	0.251	1.347	0.351	0.486	0.541	0.557	0.571	−0.576	−0.366	−2.672	−0.762	−0.237	0.084	0.354	1.938	1.728
−2.683	−0.394	−0.417	1.260	−0.914	0.749	1.051	−1.157	0.017	0.569	−0.284	0.082	0.945	0.542	0.444	−1.014	−0.232	0.207

TABLE 8   Powers, Roots, and Factorials of Numbers

$$(n = 1, 2, \ldots, 25)$$

n	n^2	n^3	n^4	n^5	$\sqrt{n}$	$\sqrt[3]{n}$	$n!$
1	1	1	1	1	1.000	1.000	1
2	4	8	16	32	1.414	1.260	2
3	9	27	81	243	1.732	1.442	6
4	16	64	256	1024	2.000	1.587	24
5	25	125	625	3125	2.236	1.710	120
6	36	216	1296	7776	2.449	1.817	720
7	49	343	2401	16807	2.646	1.913	5040
8	64	512	4096	32768	2.828	2.000	40320
9	81	729	6561	59049	3.000	2.080	3.6288×10^5
10	100	1000	10000	100000	3.162	2.154	3.6288×10^6
11	121	1331	14641	161051	3.316	2.224	3.9917×10^7
12	144	1728	20736	248832	3.464	2.289	4.7900×10^8
13	169	2197	28561	371293	3.605	2.351	6.2270×10^9
14	196	2744	38416	537824	3.741	2.410	8.1178×10^{10}
15	225	3375	50625	759375	3.873	2.466	1.3077×10^{12}
16	256	4096	65536	1048576	4.000	2.520	2.0923×10^{13}
17	289	4913	83521	1419857	4.123	2.571	3.5569×10^{14}
18	324	5832	104976	1889568	4.243	2.621	6.4024×10^{15}
19	361	6859	130321	2476099	4.359	2.668	1.2165×10^{17}
20	400	8000	160000	3200000	4.472	2.714	2.4329×10^{18}
21	441	9261	194481	4084101	4.583	2.759	5.1091×10^{19}
22	484	10648	234256	5153632	4.690	2.802	1.1240×10^{21}
23	529	12167	279841	6436343	4.796	2.843	2.5852×10^{22}
24	676	13824	331776	7962624	4.899	2.884	6.2045×10^{23}
25	625	15625	390625	9765625	5.000	2.924	1.5511×10^{25}

ANSWERS TO
EVEN-NUMBERED PROBLEMS

CHAPTER 2 • FUNDAMENTALS OF LINEAR ALGEBRA

2. $f(x) = 2x - 1$

4. See the following plots.

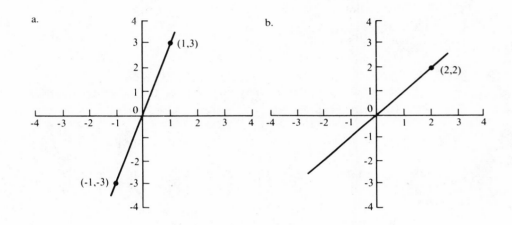

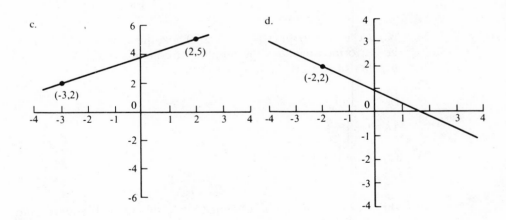

6. (a) $f(x) = \$10 + \$2.50x$, where x = number of units produced
   (b) $f(x) = \$50 + \$10x$, where x = number of units bought
   (c) $f(y) = \$1000 + \$250y$, where y = number of years
   (d) $f(y) = \$1000 - \$250y$, where y = number of years
   (e) $f(x) = \$1500 + \$.50x$, where x = number of bushels of corn sold.

8.   Let: a = number of bushels of oranges sold
            b = number of bushels of apples sold
            c = number of bushels of pears sold

    Mr. X: $\$3a + \$4b + \$6c \le \$50$
    Mr. Y: $\$3a + \$4b + \$6c \le \$75$

10.   Used car lot inventory

	Chevrolets	Fords	Plymouths
Sam's lot	25	22	19
Asa's lot	33	42	15

12. $20x_1 + 10x_2 + 5x_3 = 100$
    $40x_1 + 50x_2 \qquad = 200$
    $10x_1 + 20x_2 + 10x_3 = 300$

14.   No, $[A] + [C]$, the indicated matrix addition is not possible since $[A]$ and $[C]$ are not conformable (i.e., they do not have the same dimensions).

16.   (a) $2[A] = \begin{bmatrix} 2 & -6 \\ 10 & -4 \end{bmatrix}$ (c) $[A] + 2[B] = \begin{bmatrix} 5 & -1 \\ -9 & 6 \end{bmatrix}$

    (b) $-3[B] = \begin{bmatrix} -6 & -3 \\ 21 & -12 \end{bmatrix}$ (d) $\frac{1}{2}[B] - 3[A] = \begin{bmatrix} -2 & 9.5 \\ -18\frac{1}{2} & 8 \end{bmatrix}$

18.   (a) $[AB] = \begin{bmatrix} 2 & -1 \\ 1 & 3 \\ -3 & 5 \end{bmatrix} \begin{bmatrix} 1 & 0 & -2 \\ 2 & 3 & 1 \end{bmatrix} = \begin{bmatrix} 0 & -3 & -5 \\ 7 & 9 & 1 \\ 7 & 15 & 11 \end{bmatrix}$

    (b) $[BA] = \begin{bmatrix} 1 & 0 & -2 \\ 2 & 3 & 1 \end{bmatrix} \begin{bmatrix} 2 & -1 \\ 1 & 3 \\ -3 & 5 \end{bmatrix} = \begin{bmatrix} 8 & -11 \\ 4 & 12 \end{bmatrix}$

20.   No. $[A]$ is (2×2) and $[B]$ is (3×2). Thus, the matrix multiplication $[A] \cdot [B]$ cannot be performed because the number of columns (i.e., 2) in $[A]$ does not equal the number of rows (i.e., 3) in $[B]$.

22. $[A]^3 = \begin{bmatrix} 13 & 14 \\ 14 & 13 \end{bmatrix}$

24. $[A^{-1}] = \begin{bmatrix} \frac{5}{6} & -\frac{2}{3} \\ -\frac{1}{6} & \frac{1}{3} \end{bmatrix}$

26.   (a)   The inverse is: $\begin{bmatrix} 1/a & 0 & 0 \\ 0 & 1/b & 0 \\ 0 & 0 & 1/c \end{bmatrix}$

    (b)   No inverse can be obtained since this (3×3) square matrix has only two linearly independent rows (columns).

28. $\mathbf{x} = \begin{bmatrix} x_1 \\ x_2 \end{bmatrix} = \begin{bmatrix} \frac{5}{4} \\ \frac{1}{4} \end{bmatrix}$

30. $\mathbf{x} = \begin{bmatrix} x_1 \\ x_2 \\ x_3 \\ x_4 \end{bmatrix} = \begin{bmatrix} -20 \\ 12 \\ -2 \\ -10 \end{bmatrix}$

32. $[-1 \quad 2] \cdot \begin{bmatrix} 3 & 1 \\ 6 & 2 \end{bmatrix} = [9 \quad 3]$, which has rank = 1.

34. (a) Rank of $[\mathbf{A}]$ = rank of $[\mathbf{A}|\mathbf{b}]$ = n = 2
        ∴ consistent and unique solution.

    (b) Rank of $[\mathbf{A}]$ = rank of $[\mathbf{A}|\mathbf{b}]$ = $1 \neq n$
        ∴ consistent and infinite number of solutions.

    (c) Rank of $[\mathbf{A}]$ = $2 \neq$ rank of $[\mathbf{A}|\mathbf{b}]$ = 3
        ∴ inconsistent.

36. Rank of $[\mathbf{A}]$ = rank of $[\mathbf{A}|\mathbf{b}]$ = $2 \neq n$
    ∴ consistent and infinite number of solutions.

38. Set $x_1 = 0$:
    $x_1 = 0$
    $x_2 = {}^3/_{11}$ (Feasible, nondegenerate)
    $x_3 = {}^5/_{11}$

    Set $x_2 = 0$:
    $x_1 = {}^6/_{17}$
    $x_2 = 0$ (Feasible, nondegenerate)
    $x_3 = {}^8/_{17}$

    Set $x_3 = 0$:
    $x_1 = -10$
    $x_2 = 8$ (Infeasible)
    $x_3 = 0$

40. Set $x_1 = 0$:
    $x_1 = 0$
    $x_2 = -2$ (Infeasible)
    $x_3 = 1$
    $x_4 = 3$

    Set $x_2 = 0$:
    $x_1 = {}^2/_3$
    $x_2 = 0$ (Feasible, nondegenerate)
    $x_3 = {}^2/_3$
    $x_4 = 2$

    Set $x_3 = 0$:
    $x_1 = 2$
    $x_2 = 4$ (Feasible, degenerate)
    $x_3 = 0$
    $x_4 = 0$

    Set $x_4 = 0$:
    $x_1 = 2$
    $x_2 = 4$ (Feasible, degenerate)
    $x_3 = 0$
    $x_4 = 0$

42. Set $x_1 = 0$:
    $x_1 = 0$
    $x_2 = -9$ (Infeasible)
    $x_3 = 9$

    Set $x_2 = 0$:
    $x_1 = 9$
    $x_2 = 0$ (Feasible, degenerate)
    $x_3 = 0$

    Set $x_3 = 0$:
    $x_1 = 9$
    $x_2 = 0$ (Feasible, degenerate)
    $x_3 = 0$

44. (a) Convex set
    (b) Nonconvex set
    (c) Convex set
    (d) Nonconvex set

CHAPTER 3 • INTRODUCTION TO LINEAR PROGRAMMING

2.

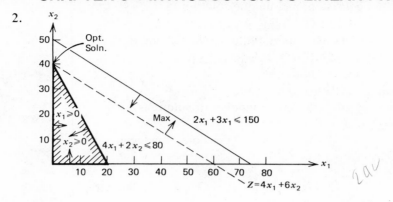

(a)   The optimal solution is $x_1 = 0$ and $x_2 = 40$; Max $Z = 240$.

(b)   There are three extreme points: $x_1 = 0$, $x_2 = 0$, $Z = 0$; $x_1 = 20$, $x_2 = 0$, $Z = 80$; and $x_1 = 0$, $x_2 = 40$, and $Z = 240$.

(c)   The redundant constraint is $2x_1 + 3x_2 \le 150$.

4.   (a)

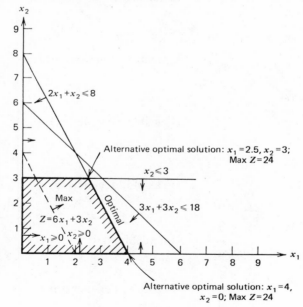

(b)   The problem has more than one optimal solution. The alternative optimal solutions are: $x_1 = 2.5$, $x_2 = 3$, Max $Z = 24$; $x_1 = 4$, $x_2 = 0$, Max $Z = 24$. All points lying on the line segment connecting these alternative optimal extreme point solutions are also optimal solutions to the linear programming problem.

(c)   This problem contains a redundant constraint: $3x_1 + 3x_2 \le 18$.

6.

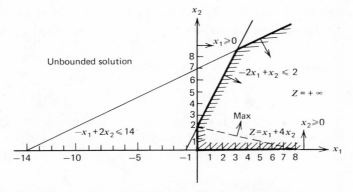

8. Inconsistent constraint set—no feasible solution.

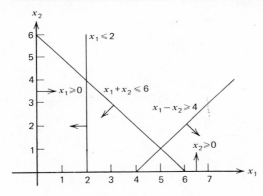

10.

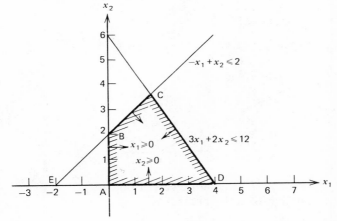

(a)

Extreme point	Value of	
	x_1	x_2
A	0	0
B	0	2
C	$8/5$	$18/5$
D	4	0
E	-2	0

(b) A, B, C, D. Yes, E, but E is not an extreme point of the feasible region.

(c)

Feasible Extreme Points	Objective Function Values
A	$Z = 0$
B	$Z = 8$
C	$Z = {}^{88}/_5$
D	$Z = 8$

(d) The optimal solution is $x_1 = {}^8/_5$, $x_2 = {}^{18}/_5$, which yields an objective function value of $Z = {}^{88}/_5$ (extreme point C).

12.

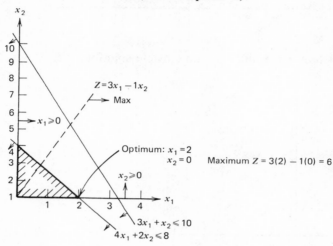

13. $Z = 3x_1 - 1x_2$ Max

$x_1 \geqslant 0$

Optimum: $x_1 = 2$
$x_2 = 0$ Maximum $Z = 3(2) - 1(0) = 6$

$x_2 \geqslant 0$

$3x_1 + x_2 \leqslant 10$
$4x_1 + 2x_2 \leqslant 8$

14.

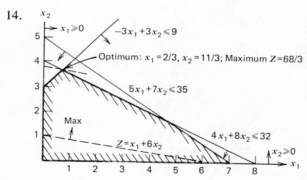

$x_1 \geqslant 0$ $-3x_1 + 3x_2 \leqslant 9$

Optimum: $x_1 = 2/3$, $x_2 = 11/3$; Maximum $Z = 68/3$

$5x_1 + 7x_2 \leqslant 35$

Max

$4x_1 + 8x_2 \leqslant 32$

$Z = x_1 + 6x_2$

$x_2 \geqslant 0$

16. Let: x_1 – number of hanging flowerpot holders;
x_2 – number of wall hangings.

Maximize (sales) $Z = \$3x_1 + \$4x_2$

subject to:
$$17x_1 + 5x_2 \leq 150 \text{ (Rope A)}$$
$$109x_1 + 13x_2 \leq 210 \text{ (Rope B)}$$
$$3x_1 + 18x_2 \leq 130 \text{ (Rope C)}$$
$$6x_1 + 8x_2 \leq 190 \text{ (Rope D)}$$

with $x_1 \geq 0, x_2 \geq 0$

18. Let: x_1 = number of "competition" soccer balls;
x_2 = number of "professional" soccer balls.

Minimize (production cost) $Z = $ (2 hours)($5.50 per hour)$x_1$
  $+$ (4 hours)($8.50 per hour)$x_1$ $+$ (3 hours)($5.50 per hour)$x_2$
  $+$ (6 hours)($8.50 per hour)$x_2 = \$45.00x_1 + \$67.50x_2$

subject to: $\quad 2x_1 + 3x_2 \leq 80$ (Semiskilled hours)
$\qquad\qquad 4x_1 + 6x_2 \leq 150$ (Skilled hours)
$\qquad\qquad 1x_1 \qquad\;\; \geq 15$ ("Competition" balls)
$\qquad\qquad\qquad 1x_2 \geq 10$ ("Professional" balls)

with $\quad x_1 \geq 0, x_2 \geq 0$ (implicitly, from third and fourth constraints).

20. Let: $\;x_1 -$ number of pounds of ingredient no. 1;
$\qquad\;\; x_2 -$ number of pounds of ingredient no. 2;
$\qquad\;\; x_3 -$ number of pounds of ingredient no. 3;
$\qquad\;\; x_4 -$ number of pounds of ingredient no. 4.

Minimize (production cost) $Z = \$28.00x_1 + \$35.00x_2 + \$52.00x_3 + \$26.00x_4$

subject to:

$$\left.\begin{array}{l} x_1 \qquad\qquad\qquad \leq 22 \text{ (lb)} \\ \qquad x_2 \qquad\qquad\; \leq 18 \text{ (lb)} \\ \qquad\qquad x_3 \qquad\; \leq 20 \text{ (lb)} \\ \qquad\qquad\qquad x_4 \leq 24 \text{ (lb)} \end{array}\right\} \text{ supplies}$$

$$\left.\begin{array}{l} 0.55x_1 - 0.45x_2 - 0.45x_3 - 0.45x_4 \geq 0 \\ 0.40x_1 - 0.60x_2 - 0.60x_3 - 0.60x_4 \leq 0 \\ -0.10x_1 + 0.90x_2 - 0.10x_3 - 0.10x_4 \geq 0 \\ -0.10x_1 - 0.10x_2 + 0.90x_3 - 0.10x_4 \geq 0 \\ -0.25x_1 + 0.75x_2 + 0.75x_3 - 0.25x_4 \leq 0 \\ -0.50x_1 - 0.50x_2 - 0.50x_3 + 0.50x_4 \leq 0 \end{array}\right\} \begin{array}{l} \text{Mixing} \\ \text{requirements} \end{array}$$

$\qquad x_1 + \qquad x_2 + \qquad x_3 + \qquad x_4 \geq 25$ (Total requirement)

with $\quad x_1 \geq 0, x_2 \geq 0, x_3 \geq 0, x_4 \geq 0$.

22. Let: $\;x_{ij} -$ number of barrels of crude stock $i; i =$
$\qquad\qquad$ 1, 2, 3, 4, used in oil brand $j; j = 1, 2, 3$.

$i = 1 -$ crude stock no. 1 $\qquad j = 1 -$ "regular" brand oil
$i = 2 -$ crude stock no. 2 $\qquad j = 2 -$ "multigrade" brand oil
$i = 3 -$ crude stock no. 3 $\qquad j = 3 -$ "premium" brand oil
$i = 4 -$ crude stock no. 4

Maximize (profit) $Z = (\$8.50 - \$7.10)x_{11} + (\$9.00 - \$7.10)$
  $x_{12} + (\$10.00 - \$7.10)x_{13} + (\$8.50 - \$8.50)x_{21} + (\$9.00 -$
  $\$8.50)x_{22} + (\$10.00 - \$8.50)x_{23} + (\$8.50 - \$7.70)x_{31} +$
  $(\$9.00 - \$7.70)x_{32} + (\$10.00 - \$7.70)x_{33} + (\$8.50 - \$9.00)x_{41} + (\$9.00 -$
  $\$9.00)x_{42} + (\$10.00 - \$9.00)x_{43}$

subject to:

$$\left.\begin{array}{l} -\;5x_{11} + 15x_{21} + \;\;5x_{31} + 30x_{41} \geq 0 \\ -15x_{12} + \;\;5x_{22} - \;\;5x_{32} + 20x_{42} \geq 0 \\ -30x_{13} - 10x_{23} - 20x_{33} + \;\;5x_{43} \geq 0 \end{array}\right\} \begin{array}{l} \text{Viscosity} \\ \text{requirement} \\ \text{constraints} \end{array}$$

$$\left.\begin{array}{l} x_{11} + x_{12} + x_{13} \leq 1000 \\ x_{21} + x_{22} + x_{23} \leq 1100 \\ x_{31} + x_{32} + x_{33} \leq 1200 \\ x_{41} + x_{42} + x_{43} \leq 1100 \end{array}\right\} \begin{array}{l} \text{Supply availability} \\ \text{constraints} \end{array}$$

$$x_{11} + x_{21} + x_{31} + x_{41} \geq 2000 \quad \Big\} \text{ Demand}$$
$$x_{12} + x_{22} + x_{32} + x_{42} \geq 1500 \quad \Big\} \text{ requirement}$$
$$x_{13} + x_{23} + x_{33} + x_{43} \geq 750 \quad \Big] \text{ constraints}$$

with $x_{11} \geq 0, x_{12} \geq 0, x_{13} \geq 0, x_{21} \geq 0, x_{22} \geq 0,$
$x_{23} \geq 0, x_{31} \geq 0, x_{32} \geq 0, x_{33} \geq 0, x_{41} \geq 0,$
$x_{42} \geq 0, x_{43} \geq 0.$

24. Let: x_1 – number of women's magazine ads used;
    x_2 – number of radio ads used;
    x_3 – number of television ads used;
    x_4 – number of newspaper ads used.

Maximize (advertising effectiveness) $Z = 1{,}505{,}000x_1 +$
$2{,}948{,}000x_2 + 6{,}960{,}000x_3 + 3{,}280{,}000x_4$

subject to:

$\$1000x_1 + \$1500x_2 + \$3500x_3 + \$500x_4 \leq \$100{,}000$ (Total spending limit)

$$x_1 \geq 10 \quad \Big\} $$
$$x_2 \geq 5 \quad \Big\} \text{ Minimum number of}$$
$$x_3 \geq 3 \quad \Big\} \text{ advertisements}$$
$$x_4 \geq 15 \quad \Big] \text{ required constraints}$$

with $x_1 \geq 0, x_2 \geq 0, x_3 \geq 0, x_4 \geq 0$ (implicitly from last four constraints).

26. Let: x_1 – percentage used – recommendation no. 1
    x_2 – percentage used – recommendation no. 2
    x_3 – percentage used – recommendation no. 3

Minimize (cost) $Z = 15x_1 + 30x_2 + 20x_3$ ($ million)

subject to:
$$60x_1 + 40x_2 + 50x_3 \geq 50 \quad \Big\} \text{ Desired reduction}$$
$$75x_1 + 60x_2 + 40x_3 \geq 60 \quad \Big\} \text{ in emission}$$
$$60x_1 + 90x_2 + 80x_3 \geq 70 \quad \Big] \text{ rate constraints}$$

$$x_1 + x_2 + x_3 = 1.00$$

with $x_1 \geq 0, x_2 \geq 0, x_3 \geq 0.$

28. Let: x_{ij} – gallons of paint manufactured at plant
    $i(i = 1, 2)$ and shipped to contractor
    $j(j = 1, 2, 3).$

Minimize cost Production + Shipping)
$Z = $ blending-plant no. 1
$[(x_{11} + x_{12} + x_{13})(0.10 \text{ hr/gal})(\$3.80/\text{hr}) +$ tinting-plant no. 1
$(x_{11} + x_{12} + x_{13})(0.25 \text{ hr/gal})(\$3.20/\text{hr}) +$ blending-plant no. 2
$(x_{21} + x_{22} + x_{23})(0.15 \text{ hr/gal})(\$4.00/\text{hr}) +$ tinting-plant no. 2
$(x_{21} + x_{22} + x_{23})(0.20 \text{ hr/gal})(\$3.10/\text{gal}) + 1.80x_{11} + 2.00x_{21} + 2.60x_{12}$
$+ 2.20x_{22} + 2.10x_{13} + 2.25x_{23} = 2.98x_{11} + 3.78x_{12} + 3.28x_{13} + 3.22x_{21}$
$+ 3.42x_{22} + 3.47x_{23}$

subject to:

Order size constraints: $x_{11} + x_{21} =\ \ 750$
$$x_{12} + x_{22} = 1500$$
$$x_{13} + x_{23} = 1500$$

Blending constraints:

$(x_{11} + x_{12} + x_{13})(0.10\ \text{hr/gal}) \leq 300$ (plant no. 1)
$(x_{21} + x_{22} + x_{23})(0.15\ \text{hr/gal}) \leq 600$ (plant no. 2)

Tinting constraints:

$(x_{11} + x_{12} + x_{13})(0.25\ \text{hr/gal}) \leq 360$ (plant no. 1)
$(x_{21} + x_{22} + x_{23})(0.20\ \text{hr/gal}) \leq 720$ (plant no. 2)

with $\quad x_{ij} \geq 0$ for all i and j.

30. Let: x_i — bags of blend of tea used, $i = 1, 2, 3, 4$.
$$(x_i \geq 0)$$

Maximize (profits) $Z = (0.05 - 0.03)x_1 + (0.05 - 0.02)x_2$
$$+ (0.05 - 0.04)x_3 + (0.05 - 0.01)x_4$$

subject to:

Average oiliness coefficient: $2x_1 + 4x_2 + 1x_3 + 6x_4 \leq 4(5000)$

Average bitterness coefficient: $6x_1 + 5x_2 + 4x_3 + 2x_4 \leq 5(5000)$

Total sales constraint: $x_1 + x_2 + x_3 + x_4 = 5000$

Tea bag availability constraints $\begin{cases} x_1 \leq 2000 \\ x_2 \leq 2000 \\ x_3 \leq 1000 \\ x_4 \leq 3000 \end{cases}$

Indonesian tea limit constraint: $x_2 \leq 0.30(5000)$

with $\quad x_1 \geq 0, x_2 \geq 0, x_3 \geq 0, x_4 \geq 0$.

32. Let: x_{ij} — the number of majority students from neighborhood i ($i = 1, 2, 3, 4$)
bused to high school j ($j = 1, 2$).
y_{ij} — the number of minority students from neighborhood i ($i = 1, 2, 3, 4$)
bused to high school j ($j = 1, 2$).

Minimize (total busing miles) $Z = 1.7x_{11} + 1.7y_{11} + 2.6x_{21}$
$$+ 2.6y_{21} + 2.5x_{31} + 2.5y_{31} + 2.6x_{41} + 2.6y_{41} + 1.3x_{12}$$
$$+ 1.3y_{12} + 2.3x_{22} + 2.3y_{22} + 2.7x_{32} + 2.7y_{32}$$

(*Note:* omit $3.2x_{42} + 3.2y_{42}$ from the objective function because of the requirement that no student be bused more than three miles, that is, $3.2 > 3.0$.)

subject to:

$\left. \begin{array}{l} x_{11} + x_{12} = (.90)(2200) = 1980 \\ x_{21} + x_{22} = (.80)(2100) = 1680 \\ x_{31} + x_{32} = (.50)(1500) =\ \ 750 \\ x_{41} + x_{42} = (.30)(1800) =\ \ 540 \end{array} \right\}$ Majority students in each neighborhood

$$y_{11} + y_{12} = (.10)(2200) = 220$$
$$y_{21} + y_{22} = (.20)(2100) = 420$$
$$y_{31} + y_{32} = (.50)(1500) = 750$$
$$y_{41} + y_{42} = (.70)(1800) = 1260$$

Minority students in each neighborhood

$$y_{11} + y_{21} + y_{31} + y_{41} \geq 0.25(x_{11} + y_{11} + x_{21}$$
$$+ y_{21} + x_{31} + y_{31} + x_{41} + y_{41})$$
$$y_{11} + y_{21} + y_{31} + y_{41} \leq 0.50(x_{11} + y_{11} + x_{21}$$
$$+ y_{21} + x_{31} + y_{31} + x_{41} + y_{41})$$
$$y_{12} + y_{22} + y_{32} \geq 0.25(x_{12} + y_{12} + x_{22} + y_{22}$$
$$+ x_{32} + y_{32})$$
$$y_{12} + y_{22} + y_{32} \leq 0.50(x_{12} + y_{12} + x_{22} + y_{22}$$
$$+ x_{32} + y_{32})$$

Integration requirement constraints

$$0.75(y_{11} + y_{21} + y_{31} + y_{41}) - 0.25(x_{11} + x_{21}$$
$$+ x_{31} + x_{41}) \geq 0$$
$$0.50(y_{11} + y_{21} + y_{31} + y_{41}) - 0.50(x_{11} + x_{21}$$
$$+ x_{31} + x_{41}) \leq 0$$
$$0.75(y_{12} + y_{22} + y_{32}) - 0.25(x_{12} + x_{22} + x_{32})$$
$$\geq 0$$
$$0.50(y_{12} + y_{22} + y_{32}) - 0.50(x_{12} + x_{22} + x_{32})$$
$$\leq 0$$

Integration requirement constraints in standard form

$$x_{11} + y_{11} + x_{21} + y_{21} + x_{31} + y_{31} \leq 2200$$
(since $x_{41} = 540$, $y_{41} = 1260$)
$$x_{12} + y_{12} + x_{22} + y_{22} + x_{32} + y_{32} \leq 4000$$

High school capacity constraints

with $x_{ij} \geq 0, y_{ij} \geq 0$ for all i and j.

34.   Let x_{ij} – the number of tons of cargo i allocated to compartment j; $i = 1, \ldots, 4$; $j = 1, \ldots, 3$.

Maximize (total profit) $Z = \$125 \left(\sum_{j=1}^{3} x_{1j} \right) + \$160 \left(\sum_{j=1}^{3} x_{2j} \right)$

$+ \$130 \left(\sum_{j=1}^{3} x_{3j} \right) + \$110 \left(\sum_{j=1}^{3} x_{4j} \right)$

subject to:

$$x_{11} + x_{12} + x_{13} \leq 20$$
$$x_{21} + x_{22} + x_{23} \leq 18$$
$$x_{31} + x_{32} + x_{33} \leq 22$$
$$x_{41} + x_{42} + x_{43} \leq 10$$

Cargo weight constraints

$$x_{11} + x_{21} + x_{31} + x_{41} \leq 15$$
$$x_{12} + x_{22} + x_{32} + x_{42} \leq 20$$
$$x_{13} + x_{23} + x_{33} + x_{43} \leq 12$$

Weight capacity constraints

$$\frac{x_{11} + x_{21} + x_{31} + x_{41}}{\displaystyle\sum_{i=1}^{4} \sum_{j=1}^{3} x_{ij}} = {}^{15}/_{47} \text{ or } 0.319$$

$$\frac{x_{12} + x_{22} + x_{32} + x_{42}}{\displaystyle\sum_{i=1}^{4} \sum_{j=1}^{3} x_{ij}} = {}^{20}/_{47} \text{ or } 0.426$$

Proportional
weight
constraints

$$\frac{x_{13} + x_{23} + x_{33} + x_{43}}{\displaystyle\sum_{i=1}^{4} \sum_{j=1}^{3} x_{ij}} = {}^{12}/_{47} \text{ or } 0.255$$

$$500x_{11} + 800x_{21} + 600x_{31} + 400x_{41} \leq 10000$$
$$500x_{12} + 800x_{22} + 600x_{32} + 400x_{42} \leq 16000$$
$$500x_{13} + 800x_{23} + 600x_{33} + 400x_{43} \leq 12000$$

Space
capacity
constraints

with $\quad x_{ij} \geq 0; i = 1, \ldots, 4; j = 1, \ldots, 3.$

36.

Month	Production Hours Required	Taco Slingers Required	Number Quitting (20%/Month)	Number Remaining End of Month	Slingers Required
January	1000	10	2	13 − 2 = 11	0
February	1000	10	2	11 − 2 = 9	1
March	1000	10	2	9 − 2 + 1 = 8	2
April	1500	15	3	8 − 3 + 2 = 7	8
May	1500	15	3	7 − 3 + 8 = 12	3
June	1500	15	3	12 − 3 + 3 = 12	3

Let x_{ij} = the number of taco slingers hired in month i
and put to work on a regular basis in month j.

Minimize (total personnel cost) $Z = [(5)(400) + 1000]x_{12}$
$+ [(4)(400) + 50 + 1000]x_{13} + [(4)(400) + 1000]x_{23}$
$[(3)(400) + 100 + 1000]x_{14} + [(3)(400) + 50 + 1000]x_{24}$
$+ [(3)(400) + 1000]x_{34} + [(2)(400) + 150 + 1000]x_{15}$
$[(2)(400) + 100 + 1000]x_{25} + [(2)(400) + 50 + 1000]x_{35}$
$+ [(2)(400) + 1250]x_{45} + [400 + 200 + 1000]x_{16}$
$+ [400 + 150 + 1000]x_{26} + [400 + 100 + 1000]x_{36}$
$+ [400 + 50 + 1250]x_{46} + [400 + 1250]x_{56}$
$= 3000x_{12} + 2650x_{13} + 2600x_{23} + 2300x_{14} + 2250x_{24}$
$+ 2200x_{34} + 1950x_{15} + 1900x_{25} + 1850x_{35} + 2050x_{45}$
$+ 1600x_{16} + 1550x_{26} + 1500x_{36} + 1700x_{46} + 1650x_{56}$

subject to:

$$x_{12} + x_{13} + x_{14} + x_{15} + x_{16} \leq 4$$
$$x_{23} + x_{24} + x_{25} + x_{26} \leq 4$$
$$x_{34} + x_{35} + x_{36} \leq 4$$
$$x_{45} + x_{46} \leq 4$$
$$x_{56} \leq 4$$

Maximum
monthly
hiring
allowed

$$x_{12} = 1$$
$$x_{13} + x_{23} = 2$$
$$x_{14} + x_{24} + x_{34} = 8$$
$$x_{15} + x_{25} + x_{35} + x_{45} = 3$$
$$x_{16} + x_{26} + x_{36} + x_{46} + x_{56} = 3$$

$\left.\vphantom{\begin{matrix}1\\2\\3\\4\\5\end{matrix}}\right\}$ Monthly hiring requirements

with $\quad x_{ij} \geq 0 \quad$ for all i and j.

38.   Let x_{ij} – the number of acres in section i to be planted with crop j; $i = 1, 2, 3$; $j = 1, 2, 3$.

Minimize (total labor cost) $Z = \$120 x_{11} + \$225 x_{12} + \$168 x_{13}$
$$+ \$210 x_{21} + \$160 x_{22} + \$160 x_{23} + \$162 x_{31} + \$143 x_{32} + 168 x_{33}$$

subject to:

$$x_{11} + x_{12} + x_{13} \leq 200$$
$$x_{21} + x_{22} + x_{23} \leq 500$$
$$x_{31} + x_{32} + x_{33} \leq 260$$

$\left.\vphantom{\begin{matrix}1\\2\\3\end{matrix}}\right\}$ Land availability constraints

$$x_{11} + x_{21} + x_{31} \geq 225$$
$$x_{12} + x_{22} + x_{32} \geq 160$$
$$x_{13} + x_{23} + x_{33} \geq 275$$

$\left.\vphantom{\begin{matrix}1\\2\\3\end{matrix}}\right\}$ Demand requirement constraints

with $\quad x_{ij} \geq 0$; $i = 1, 2, 3$; $j = 1, 2, 3$.

40.   Let: x_1 – the number of "Clamp" systems manufactured.
               x_2 – the number of "Vise" systems manufactured.
               x_3 – the number of "Clamp" systems subcontracted.
               x_4 – the number of "Vise" systems subcontracted.

Maximize (total profit) $Z = \$45 x_1 + \$50 x_2 + \$30 x_3 + \$25 x_4$

subject to:

$$x_1 + x_3 \geq 14000$$
$$x_2 + x_4 \geq 11500$$

$\left.\vphantom{\begin{matrix}1\\2\end{matrix}}\right\}$ Demand requirement constraints

$$0.15 x_1 + 0.17 x_2 \leq 2400$$
$$0.12 x_1 + 0.15 x_2 \leq 2700$$
$$0.10 x_1 + 0.14 x_2 \leq 3000$$

$\left.\vphantom{\begin{matrix}1\\2\\3\end{matrix}}\right\}$ Production hour availability constraints

$$x_3 + x_4 \leq 10000 \quad \text{(Subcontracting availability constraint)}$$

with $\quad x_1, x_2, x_3, x_4 \geq 0$.

42.   Let: x_j – the proportion of funds to be invested in the jth investment alternative; $j = 1, \ldots, 7$.

$j = 1$ – Public utility stocks
$j = 2$ – Public utility bonds
$j = 3$ – Government securities
$j = 4$ – Industrial stocks
$j = 5$ – Industrial bonds
$j = 6$ – Municipal bonds
$j = 7$ – Real estate trust

Maximize (total return on the portfolio) $Z = 0.08x_1$
$+ 0.10x_2 + 0.07x_3 + 0.11x_4 + 0.12x_5 + 0.09x_6 + 0.15x_7$

subject to:

$x_1 + x_2 \leq 0.50$	(Public utility securities constraint)
$x_4 + x_5 \leq 0.50$	(Industrial securities constraint)
$x_4 \leq 0.10$	(Industrial stock constraint)
$x_7 \leq 0.07$	(Real estate trust constraint)
$x_2 \geq 0.35$	(Public utility bonds constraint)
$x_3 \geq 0.25$	(Government securities constraint)

$x_1 + x_2 + x_3 + x_4 + x_5 + x_6 + x_7 = 1.0$

with $x_j \geq 0; j = 1, \ldots, 7.$

44.

Org. Behavior Paper		Financial Management Test		Quant. Methods Test	
No. of Hours	*Grade*	*No. of Hours*	*Grade*	*No. of Hours*	*Grade*
0	70	0	60	0	40
4	85	5	80	10	70
8	100	10	100	20	100

1 hour of study is worth 3.75 points	1 hour of study is worth 4.00 points	1 hour of study is worth 3.00 points

Let: x_j — the number of hours devoted to course j; $j = 1, 2, 3.$

$j = 1$ — Organizational behavior
$j = 2$ — Financial management
$j = 3$ — Quantitative methods

Maximize (overall grade point average) $Z = (0.50/0.95)(70 + 3.75x_1) + (0.25/0.95)(60 + 4.00x_2) + (0.20/0.95)(40 + 3.00x_3)$
$= 1.9725x_1 + 1.052x_2 + 0.633x_3 + 61.04$

subject to:

$\left. \begin{array}{l} x_1 \geq 0.0 \\ x_2 \geq 2.5 \\ x_3 \geq 10.0 \end{array} \right\}$ Lower bound constraints on study time by course

$\left. \begin{array}{l} x_1 \leq 8.0 \\ x_2 \leq 10.0 \\ x_3 \leq 20.0 \end{array} \right\}$ Upper bound constraints on study time by course

$x_1 + x_2 + x_3 \leq 20.0$ (Total study time availability constraint)

with $x_j \geq 0; j = 1, 2, 3.$

46.   Let: x_{ij} — the number of acres planted of crop i in
season j; $i = 1, 2, 3$; $j = 1, 2$.
y_{ij} — the size of herd i in season j; $i = 1, 2,$; $j = 1, 2$.
z_j — the number of unused manhours in season j; $j = 1, 2$.

Maximize (profit) $Z = (\$350 - \$4)(x_{11} + x_{12}) + (\$250 - \$2)(x_{21}$
$+ x_{22}) + (\$400 - \$1)(x_{31} + x_{32}) + (\$450 - \$250)(y_{11} + y_{12})$
$+ (\$200 - \$125)(y_{21} + y_{22}) + \$2.35z_1 + \$3.50z_2$
$= \$346x_{11} + \$346x_{12} + \$248x_{21} + \$248x_{22} + \$399x_{31} + \$399x_{32}$
$+ \$200y_{11} + \$200y_{12} + \$75y_{21} + \$75y_{22} + \$2.35z_1 + \$3.50z_2$

subject to:

$4x_{11} + 4x_{12} + 2x_{21} + 2x_{22} + 1x_{31} + 1x_{32}$
$+ 250y_{11} + 250y_{12} + 125y_{21} + 125y_{22} \leq 25000$ (Investment constraint)

$x_{11} + x_{12} + x_{21} + x_{22} + x_{31} + x_{32}$
$+ 2y_{11} + 2y_{12} + y_{21} + y_{22} \leq 300$ (Acreage availability constraint)

$20x_{11} + 15x_{21} + 0x_{31} + 30y_{11}$
$+ 20y_{21} + z_1 = 1500$ (Fall/winter labor availability constraint)

$40x_{12} + 35x_{22} + 50x_{32} + 15y_{12}$
$+ 10y_{22} + z_2 = 5000$ (Spring/summer labor availability constraint)

$x_{31} = 0$ (Season constraint for peaches)

$y_{11} + y_{12} \leq 50$ (Cow herd size constraint)
$y_{21} + y_{22} \leq 100$ (Pig herd size constraint)

with $x_{ij} \geq 0$; $i = 1, 2, 3$; $j = 1, 2$
$y_{ij} \geq 0$; $i = 1, 2$; $j = 1, 2$
$z_j \geq 0$; $j = 1, 2$.

48.   Let: x_{ij} — the number of gallons of diesel fuel from
company j to be purchased in city i; $i = 1, \ldots, 4$;
$j = 1, \ldots, 3$.

Minimize (fuel purchasing cost) $Z = 0.80x_{11} + 0.90x_{12}$
$+ 0.92x_{13} + 0.87x_{21} + 0.75x_{22} + 0.70x_{23} + 0.75x_{31} + 0.70x_{32}$
$+ 0.92x_{33} + 0.90x_{41} + 0.85x_{42} + 0.80x_{43}$

subject to:

$\left.\begin{array}{l} x_{11} + x_{12} + x_{13} = 350{,}000 \\ x_{21} + x_{22} + x_{23} = 400{,}000 \\ x_{31} + x_{32} + x_{33} = 450{,}000 \\ x_{41} + x_{42} + x_{43} = 500{,}000 \end{array}\right\}$ Demand requirement constraints

$\left.\begin{array}{l} x_{11} + x_{21} + x_{31} + x_{41} \leq 450{,}000 \\ x_{12} + x_{22} + x_{32} + x_{42} \leq 700{,}000 \\ x_{13} + x_{23} + x_{33} + x_{43} \leq 800{,}000 \end{array}\right\}$ Supply availability constraints

with $x_{ij} \geq 0$; $i = 1, \ldots, 4$; $j = 1, \ldots, 3$.

50.

Resource	Products			Resource Availability
	A	*B*	*C*	
Machine 1	4	3	2	180
Machine 2	2	5	4	155
Machine 3	1	2	5	160

Profit: $35. $45. $40.

Let: x_j — the number of units of product j to be manufactured; $j = 1, 2, 3$.

Maximize (total profit) $Z = \$35x_1 + \$45x_2 + \$40x_3$

subject to:

$$\left.\begin{array}{l} 4x_1 + 3x_2 + 2x_3 \leq 180 \\ 2x_1 + 5x_2 + 4x_3 \leq 155 \\ 1x_1 + 2x_2 + 5x_3 \leq 160 \end{array}\right\} \text{Resource availability constraints}$$

with $x_j \geq 0$; $j = 1, 2, 3$.

52. Let: x_{ijk} — the number of units produced in month i by production type j, and shipped in month k; $i = 1, \ldots, 6$; $j = 1, 2$; $k = 1, \ldots, 6$; $i \leq k$.

Minimize (Total production and inventory costs) Z

$$\left.\begin{array}{l} = 8(x_{111} + x_{112} + x_{113} + x_{114} + x_{115} + x_{116} \\ \quad + x_{212} + x_{213} + x_{214} + x_{215} + x_{216} \\ \quad + x_{313} + x_{314} + x_{315} + x_{316} \\ \quad + x_{414} + x_{415} + x_{416} \\ \quad + x_{515} + x_{516} \\ \quad + x_{616}) \end{array}\right\} \begin{array}{l}\text{Regular time}\\\text{production}\\\text{costs}\end{array}$$

$$\left.\begin{array}{l} + 10(x_{121} + x_{122} + x_{123} + x_{124} + x_{125} + x_{126} \\ \quad + x_{222} + x_{223} + x_{224} + x_{225} + x_{226} \\ \quad + x_{323} + x_{324} + x_{325} + x_{326} \\ \quad + x_{424} + x_{425} + x_{426} \\ \quad + x_{525} + x_{526} \\ \quad + x_{626}) \end{array}\right\} \begin{array}{l}\text{Overtime}\\\text{production}\\\text{costs}\end{array}$$

$$\left.\begin{array}{l} + 2\left[\displaystyle\sum_{j=1}^{2} (x_{1j2} + x_{2j3} + x_{3j4} + x_{4j5} + x_{5j6})\right] \\ \\ + 4\left[\displaystyle\sum_{j=1}^{2} (x_{1j3} + x_{2j4} + x_{3j5} + x_{4j6})\right] \\ \\ + 6\left[\displaystyle\sum_{j=1}^{2} (x_{1j4} + x_{2j5} + x_{3j6})\right] \\ \\ + 8\left[\displaystyle\sum_{j=1}^{2} (x_{1j5} + x_{2j6})\right] \\ \\ + 10\left[\displaystyle\sum_{j=1}^{2} x_{1j6}\right] \end{array}\right\} \begin{array}{l}\text{Inventory}\\\text{holding}\\\text{costs}\end{array}$$

subject to:

$$\sum_{i=1}^{6} \sum_{j=1}^{2} \sum_{k=1}^{6} x_{ijk} = 16000 \qquad \text{(Constraint to ensure no ending inventory)}$$
$$(i \le k)$$

$$\left.\begin{array}{l} \sum_{k \ge i}^{6} x_{i1k} \le 1700; \ i = 1, \ldots, 6 \\[2em] \sum_{k \ge i}^{6} x_{i2k} \le 1100; \ i = 1, \ldots, 6 \end{array}\right\} \quad \begin{array}{l} \text{Production capacity} \\ \text{constraints} \end{array}$$

$$\left.\begin{array}{l} \sum_{j=1}^{2} x_{1j1} \ge 1000 \\[2em] \sum_{j=1}^{2} (x_{1j2} + x_{2j2}) \ge 4000 \\[2em] \sum_{j=1}^{2} (x_{1j3} + x_{2j3} + x_{3j3}) \ge 3000 \\[2em] \sum_{j=1}^{2} (x_{1j4} + x_{2j4} + x_{3j4} + x_{4j4}) \ge 2000 \\[2em] \sum_{j=1}^{2} (x_{1j5} + x_{2j5} + x_{3j5} + x_{4j5} + x_{5j5}) \ge 3500 \\[2em] \sum_{j=1}^{2} (x_{1j6} + x_{2j6} + x_{3j6} + x_{4j6} + x_{5j6} + x_{6j6}) \ge 2500 \end{array}\right\} \quad \begin{array}{l} \text{Shipment} \\ \text{requirement} \\ \text{constraints} \end{array}$$

with $x_{ijk} \ge 0; \ i = 1, \ldots, 6; \ j = 1, 2; \ k = 1, \ldots, 6; \ i \le k$

54.   Let: $x_{ij} = \begin{cases} 1, & \text{if route } i \text{ to } j \text{ is taken;} \\ 0, & \text{otherwise.} \end{cases}$

Minimize (total distance traveled) $Z = 50x_{12} + 75x_{13} + 60x_{14}$
$\qquad + 50x_{21} + 90x_{23} + 120x_{24} + 75x_{31} + 90x_{32} + 135x_{34} + 60x_{41}$
$\qquad + 120x_{42} + 135x_{43}$

subject to:

$$\left.\begin{array}{l} x_{12} + x_{13} + x_{14} = 1 \\ x_{21} + x_{23} + x_{24} = 1 \\ x_{31} + x_{32} + x_{34} = 1 \\ x_{41} + x_{42} + x_{43} = 1 \end{array}\right\} \quad \begin{array}{l} \text{Constraints that ensure one} \\ \text{route is taken from each city.} \end{array}$$

$$\left.\begin{array}{l} x_{21} + x_{31} + x_{41} = 1 \\ x_{12} + x_{32} + x_{42} = 1 \\ x_{13} + x_{23} + x_{43} = 1 \\ x_{14} + x_{24} + x_{34} = 1 \end{array}\right\} \quad \begin{array}{l} \text{Constraints that ensure one} \\ \text{route is taken to each city.} \end{array}$$

$$x_{12} + x_{21} \leq 1$$
$$x_{13} + x_{31} \leq 1$$
$$x_{14} + x_{41} \leq 1$$
$$x_{23} + x_{32} \leq 1$$
$$x_{24} + x_{42} \leq 1$$
$$x_{34} + x_{43} \leq 1$$

Constraints that ensure a feasible routing to and from all four cities is achieved.

with $\quad x_{ij} \geq 0; i = 1, \ldots, 4; j = 1, \ldots, 4.$

CHAPTER 4 • THE SIMPLEX METHOD

(*Note:* For problems 2 to 10, the optimal solution(s) is(are) indicated in each table of basic solutions by an asterisk; also, the variables that are set equal to zero to obtain a given basic solution are indicated by the use of parentheses around the zero values.)

2.

	Basic Solutions			Feasible/ Nonfeasible	Value of Objective Function
x_1	x_2	x_3	x_4		
(0)	(0)	7	10	Feasible	0
(0)	$-7/3$	(0)	$44/3$	Nonfeasible	$-7/3$
(0)	5	22	(0)	Feasible	10*
$7/2$	(0)	(0)	$13/2$	Feasible	$7/2$
10	(0)	-13	(0)	Nonfeasible	-20
6.2	1.9	(0)	(0)	Feasible	10*

4.

	Basic Solutions			Feasible/ Nonfeasible	Value of Objective Function
x_1	x_2	x_3	x_4		
(0)	(0)	90	60	Feasible	0
(0)	30	(0)	-30	Nonfeasible	150
(0)	20	30	(0)	Feasible	100*
45	(0)	(0)	-120	Nonfeasible	135
15	(0)	60	(0)	Feasible	45
-15	40	(0)	(0)	Nonfeasible	155

6.

	Basic Solutions			Feasible/ Nonfeasible	Value of Objective Function
x_1	x_2	x_3	x_4		
(0)	(0)	-10	-8	Nonfeasible	0
(0)	2	(0)	-6	Nonfeasible	14
(0)	8	30	(0)	Feasible	56
5	(0)	(0)	7	Feasible	15
$8/3$	(0)	$-14/3$	(0)	Nonfeasible	8
$30/13$	$70/65$	(0)	(0)	Feasible	14.46*

8.

		Basic Solutions			Feasible/ Nonfeasible	Value of Objective Function
x_1	x_2	x_3	x_4	x_5		
(0)	(0)	−10	−12	−12	Nonfeasible	0
(0)	5	(0)	2	18	Nonfeasible	10
(0)	6	2	(0)	24	Feasible	12*
(0)	2	−6	−8	(0)	Nonfeasible	4
2	(0)	(0)	−8	−10	Nonfeasible	8
6	(0)	20	(0)	−6	Nonfeasible	24
12	(0)	50	12	(0)	Feasible	48
−.66	6.66	(0)	(0)	27.33	Nonfeasible	10.67
1.285	1.78	(0)	−5.86	(0)	Nonfeasible	8.70
1.8	1.2	16.4	(0)	(0)	Feasible	21.60

10.

		Basic Solutions			Feasible/ Nonfeasible	Value of Objective Function
x_1	x_2	x_3	x_4	x_5		
(0)	(0)	(0)	−9	11	Nonfeasible	0
(0)	(0)	$9/5$	(0)	$64/5$	Feasible	5.4
(0)	(0)	−11	−64	(0)	Nonfeasible	−33
(0)	3	(0)	(0)	−1	Nonfeasible	18
(0)	$11/4$	(0)	$−3/4$	(0)	Nonfeasible	16.50
(0)	$64/23$	$3/23$	(0)	(0)	Feasible	17.09
$9/7$	(0)	(0)	(0)	$59/7$	Feasible	2.57*
$11/2$	(0)	(0)	$59/2$	(0)	Feasible	11
$64/17$	(0)	$−295/85$	(0)	(0)	Nonfeasible	−2.88
$3/22$	$236/88$	(0)	(0)	(0)	Feasible	16.363

12. $x_1 = 0$
$x_2 = 5$
$x_3 = 22$ Maximum $Z = 10$
$x_4 = 0$

14. $x_1 = 0$
$x_2 = 20$
$x_3 = 30$ Maximum $Z = 100$
$x_4 = 0$

16. $x_1 = 2$
$x_2 = 0$
$x_3 = 0$ Maximum $Z = 6$
$x_4 = 4$

18. $x_1 = {}^{16}/_7$
$x_2 = 0$
$x_3 = 0$ Maximum $Z = {}^{80}/_7$
$x_4 = {}^{76}/_7$

20. $x_1 = 2$
    $x_2 = 12$
    $x_3 = 10$ Maximum $Z = 66$
    $x_4 = 0$
    $x_5 = 0$

22. $x_1 = {}^{16}/_5$
    $x_2 = {}^9/_5$
    $x_3 = 0$ Minimum $Z = 15{}^2/_5$
    $x_4 = 0$

24. $x_1 = {}^3/_2$
    $x_2 = 0$
    $x_3 = 0$ Minimum $Z = {}^9/_2$
    $x_4 = 6$
    $x_5 = 0$

26. $x_1 = 5$
    $x_2 = 0$
    $x_3 = 12$
    $x_4 = 25$ Maximum $Z = 70$
    $x_5 = 0$
    $x_6 = 0$

28. $x_1 = {}^3/_2$
    $x_2 = {}^7/_4$
    $x_3 = 0$ Maximum $Z = 9\,{}^1/_2$
    $x_4 = 6\,{}^1/_4$
    $x_5 = 0$

30. $x_1 = 2$
    $x_2 = 2$
    $x_3 = 0$
    $x_4 = 0$
    $x_5 = 0$ Minimum $Z = 18$
    $x_6 = 0$
    $x_7 = 4$
    $x_8 = 0$

32. $x_1 = 12$
    $x_2 = 0$
    $x_3 = 0$ Maximum $Z = 48$
    $x_4 = 0$
    $x_5 = 2$

34. (a) Let $x_3 = x_3' - x_3''$

    Maximize $Z = 3x_1 + 4x_2 + \ 6x_3' - \ 6x_3'' + 0x_4 - Mx_5 + 0x_6 - Mx_7$

    subject to: $\quad 2x_1 + 3x_2 \qquad\qquad\quad + 1x_4 \qquad\qquad\qquad = 30$
    $\qquad\qquad\quad 5x_1 + 2x_2 + \ 3x_3' - \ 3x_3'' \qquad\quad + 1x_5 \qquad\qquad = 40$
    $\qquad\qquad\quad 8x_1 \qquad\quad + 10x_3' - 10x_3'' \qquad\qquad\qquad - 1x_6 + \ 1x_7 = 40$

    with $\quad x_1, x_2, x_3', x_3'', x_4, x_5, x_6, x_7 \geq 0$

    (b) Initial simplex tableau:

c_j			3	4	6	-6	0	-M	0	-M
	Variables in Basis	*Solution Values,*								
c_b		x_b	a_1	a_2	a_3	a_3''	a_4	a_5	a_6	a_7
0	x_4	30	2	3	0	0	1	0	0	0
-M	x_5	40	5	2	3	-3	0	1	0	0
-M	x_7	40	8	0	⑩	-10	0	0	-1	1
	Z_j	-80M	-13M	-2M	-13M	13M	0	-M	M	-M
	$c_j - Z_j$		3 + 13M	4 + 2M	6 + 13M	-6 - 13M	0	0	-M	0

Initial basic feasible solution: $x_1 = 0$
$x_2 = 0$
$x_3' = 0$
$x_3'' = 0$ $\quad Z = -80M$
$x_4 = 30$
$x_5 = 40$
$x_6 = 0$
$x_7 = 40$

(c) First iteration:

c_j			3	4	6	-6	0	-M	0	-M
	Variables in Basis	*Solution Values,*								
c_b		x_b	a_1	a_2	a_3'	a_3''	a_4	a_5	a_6	a_7
0	x_4	30	2	3	0	0	1	0	0	0
-M	x_5	28	$^{26}/_{10}$	2	0	0	0	1	$^{3}/_{10}$	$-^{3}/_{10}$
6	x_3'	4	⑧/₁₀	0	1	-1	0	0	$-^{1}/_{10}$	$^{1}/_{10}$
	Z_j	24 - 28M	4.8 - 2.6M	-2M	6	-6	0	-M	-0.6 - 0.3M	0.6 + 0.3M
	$c_j - Z_j$		2.6M - 1.8	4 + 2M	0	0	0	0	0.6 + 0.3M	-1.3M - 0.6

Second iteration:

c_j			3	4	6	-6	0	-M	0	-M
	Variables in Basis	*Solution Values,*								
c_b		x_b	a_1	a_2	a_3'	a_3''	a_4	a_5	a_6	a_7
0	x_4	20	0	3	$-^{20}/_8$	$^{20}/_8$	1	0	$^{1}/_4$	$-^{1}/_4$
-M	x_5	15	0	2	$-^{26}/_8$	$^{26}/_8$	0	1	$^{5}/_8$	$-^{5}/_8$
3	x_1	5	1	0	$^{10}/_8$	$-^{10}/_8$	0	0	$-^{1}/_8$	$^{1}/_8$
	Z_j	15 - 15M	3	-2M	3.25M + 3.75	-3.25M - 3.75	0	0	-0.625M - 0.375	0.625M + 0.375
	$c_j - Z_j$		0	4 + 2M	-3.25M + 2.25	3.25M - 2.25	0	-M	0.625M + 0.375	-1.625M - 0.375

36. (a) Minimize $Z = 1x_1 - 3x_2 + 3x_3 + 0x_4 + Mx_5 + 0x_6 + Mx_7 + Mx_8$

   subject to:
   $$-2x_1 + 1x_2 + 1x_3 - 1x_4 + 1x_5 = 18$$
   $$1x_1 + 1x_2 + 3x_3 - 1x_6 + 1x_7 = 36$$
   $$-1x_1 + 3x_2 + 1x_3 + 1x_8 = 24$$

   with $x_1, x_2, x_3, x_4, x_5, x_6, x_7, x_8 \geq 0$

(b) Initial simplex tableau:

		c_j	1	-3	3	0	M	0	M	M
c_b	Variables in Basis	Solution Values, x_b	a_1	a_2	a_3	a_4	a_5	a_6	a_7	a_8
M	x_5	18	-2	1	1	-1	1	0	0	0
M	x_7	36	1	1	3	0	0	-1	1	0
M	x_8	24	-1	③	1	0	0	0	0	1
	Z_j	$78M$	$-2M$	$5M$	$5M$	$-M$	M	$-M$	M	M
	$c_j - Z_j$		$1 + 2M$	$-3 - 5M$	$3 - 5M$	M	0	M	0	0

Initial basic feasible solution:
$$x_1 = 0$$
$$x_2 = 0$$
$$x_3 = 0$$
$$x_4 = 0$$
$$x_5 = 18$$ $Z = 78M$
$$x_6 = 0$$
$$x_7 = 36$$
$$x_8 = 24$$

(c) First iteration:

		c_j	1	-3	3	0	M	0	M	M
c_b	Variables in Basis	Solution Values, x_b	a_1	a_2	a_3	a_4	a_5	a_6	a_7	a_8
M	x_5	10	$-5/3$	0	$2/3$	-1	1	0	0	$-1/3$
M	x_7	28	$4/3$	0	⑧/₃	0	0	-1	1	$-1/3$
-3	x_2	8	$-1/3$	1	$1/3$	0	0	0	0	$1/3$
	Z_j	$38M - 24$	$-M/3 + 1$	-3	$10M/3 - 1$	$-M$	M	$-M$	M	$-2M/3 - 1$
	$c_j - Z_j$		$M/3$	0	$4 - 10M/3$	M	0	M	0	$1 + 5M/3$

Second iteration:

	c_j		*1*	*−3*	*3*	*0*	*M*	*0*	*M*	*M*
c_b	Variables in Basis	Solution Values, x_b	a_1	a_2	a_3	a_4	a_5	a_6	a_7	a_8
M	x_5	3	-2	0	0	-1	1	$1/4$	$-1/4$	$-1/4$
3	x_3	$21/2$	$1/2$	0	1	0	0	$-3/8$	$3/8$	$-1/8$
-3	x_2	$4/2$	$-1/2$	1	0	0	0	$1/8$	$-1/8$	$3/8$
	Z_j	$3M + 1/8$	$-2M + 3$	-3	3	$-M$	M	$M/4 - 3/2$	$-M/4 + 3/2$	$-M/4 - 3/2$
	$c_j - Z_j$		$2M - 2$	0	0	M	0	$3/2 - M/4$	$5M/4 - 3/2$	$5M/4 + 3/2$

38. (a) Let $x_4 = x_4' - x_4''$

$$\text{Min } Z = 2x_1 - 1x_2 + 4x_3 - 3x_4' + 3x_4'' + Mx_5 + 0x_6 + 0x_7 + 0x_8 + 0x_9 + Mx_{10}$$

s.t.
$$1x_1 + 2x_2 + 4x_3 + 2x_4' - 2x_4'' + 1x_5 = 8$$
$$1x_2 + 3x_4' - 3x_4'' + 1x_6 = 10$$
$$1x_1 + 1x_3 - 2x_4' + 2x_4'' + 1x_7 = 5$$
$$2x_1 + 4x_2 - 3x_3 + 1x_4' - 1x_4'' + 1x_8 = 15$$
$$2x_1 + 4x_2 - 3x_3 + 1x_4' - 1x_4'' - 1x_9 + 1x_{10} = 5$$

with $x_1, x_2, x_3, x_4', x_4'', x_5, x_6, x_7, x_8, x_9, x_{10} \geq 0$

(b) Initial simplex tableau:

	c_j		*2*	*−1*	*4*	*−3*	*3*	*M*	*0*	*0*	*0*	*0*	*M*
c_b	Variables in Basis	Solution Values, x_b	a_1	a_2	a_3	a_4'	a_4''	a_5	a_6	a_7	a_8	a_9	a_{10}
M	x_5	8	1	2	4	2	-2	1	0	0	0	0	0
0	x_6	10	0	1	0	3	-3	0	1	0	0	0	0
0	x_7	5	1	0	1	-2	2	0	0	1	0	0	0
0	x_8	15	2	4	-3	1	-1	0	0	0	1	0	0
M	x_{10}	5	2	④	-3	1	-1	0	0	0	0	-1	1
	Z_j	$13M$	$3M$	$6M$	M	$3M$	$-3M$	M	0	0	0	$-M$	M
	$c_j - Z_j$		$2 - 3M$	$-1 - 6M$	$4 - M$	$-3 - 3M$	$3 + 3M$	0	0	0	0	M	0

Initial basic feasible solution:

$x_1 = 0$	$x_8 = 15$
$x_2 = 0$	$x_9 = 0$
$x_3 = 0$	$x_{10} = 5$
$x_4' = 0$	$Z = 13M$
$x_4'' = 0$	
$x_5 = 8$	
$x_6 = 10$	
$x_7 = 5$	

(c) First iteration:

			c_j	2	−1	4	−3	3	M	0	0	0	0	M
c_b	Variables in Basis	Solution Values, $\mathbf{x}_b$		$\mathbf{a}_1$	$\mathbf{a}_2$	$\mathbf{a}_3$	$\mathbf{a}_4'$	$\mathbf{a}_4''$	$\mathbf{a}_5$	$\mathbf{a}_6$	$\mathbf{a}_7$	$\mathbf{a}_8$	$\mathbf{a}_9$	$\mathbf{a}_{10}$
M	x_5	22/4		0	0	(22/4)	6/4	−6/4	1	0	0	0	2/4	−2/4
0	x_6	35/4		−2/4	0	3/4	11/4	−11/4	0	1	0	0	1/4	−1/4
0	x_7	5		1	0	1	−2	2	0	0	1	0	0	0
0	x_8	10		0	0	0	0	0	0	0	0	1	1	−1
−1	x_2	5/4		2/4	1	−3/4	1/4	−1/4	0	0	0	0	−1/4	1/4
	Z_j	22M/4 − 5/4		−2/4	−1	22M/4 + 3/4	6M/4 − 1/4	−6M/4 + 1/4	M	0	0	0	2M/4 + 1/4	−2M/4 − 1/4
	$c_j − Z_j$			10/4	0	−22M/4 + 13/4	−6M/4 − 11/4	6M/4 + 11/4	0	0	0	0	−2M/4 − 1/4	6M/4 + 1/4

Second iteration:

			c_j	2	−1	4	−3	3	M	0	0	0	0	M
c_b	Variables in Basis	Solution Values, $\mathbf{x}_b$		$\mathbf{a}_1$	$\mathbf{a}_2$	$\mathbf{a}_3$	$\mathbf{a}_4'$	$\mathbf{a}_4''$	$\mathbf{a}_5$	$\mathbf{a}_6$	$\mathbf{a}_7$	$\mathbf{a}_8$	$\mathbf{a}_9$	$\mathbf{a}_{10}$
4	x_3	1		0	0	1	6/22	−6/22	4/22	0	0	0	2/22	−2/22
0	x_6	8		−2/4	0	0	112/44	−112/44	−3/22	1	0	0	2/11	−2/11
0	x_7	4		1	0	0	−25/11	25/11	−4/22	0	1	0	−2/22	2/22
0	x_8	10		0	0	0	0	0	0	0	0	1	1	−1
−1	x_2	2		2/4	1	0	10/22	−10/22	3/22	0	0	0	−4/22	4/22
	Z_j	2		−2/4	−1	4	14/22	−14/22	13/22	0	0	0	12/22	−12/22
	$c_j − Z_j$			6/4	0	0	−80/22	80/22	M − 13/22	0	0	0	−12/22	M + 12/22

40. Optimal simplex tableau:

c_b	Variables in Basis	Solution Values, x_b	c_j 6 a_1	3 a_2	0 a_3	0 a_4	0 a_5
6	x_1	4	1	$1/2$	$1/2$	0	0
0	x_4	6	0	$3/2$	$-3/2$	1	0
0	x_5	3	0	1	0	0	1
	Z_j	24	6	3	3	0	0
	$c_j - Z_j$		0	0	-3	0	0

↑
Alternative optima indicated

Alternative optimal solution (obtained from introducing x_2 into the basis):

$x_1 = 5/2$
$x_2 = 3$
$x_3 = 0$ $Z = 24$
$x_4 = 3/2$
$x_5 = 0$

42. Optimal simplex tableau:

c_b	Variables in Basis	Solution Values, x_b	c_j 2 a_1	8 a_2	0 a_3	M a_4	0 a_5	M a_6	0 a_7	M a_8
2	x_1	$32/6$	1	0	0	0	$-4/6$	$4/6$	$1/3$	$-1/3$
0	x_3	$110/6$	0	0	1	-1	$-19/6$	$19/6$	$4/3$	$-4/3$
8	x_2	$10/6$	0	1	0	0	$1/6$	$-1/6$	$-1/3$	$1/3$
	Z_j	$144/6$	2	8	0	0	0	0	-2	2
	$c_j - Z_j$		0	0	0	M	0	M	2	$M - 2$

↑
Alternative optima indicated

Alternative optimal solution (obtained from introducing x_5 into the basis):

$x_1 = 12$ $x_6 = 0$
$x_2 = 0$ $x_7 = 0$
$x_3 = 50$ $x_8 = 0$
$x_4 = 0$
$x_5 = 10$ $Z = 24$

44. Optimal simplex tableau:

c_b	Variables in Basis	c_j Solution Values, x_b	3 a_1	-2 a_2	0 a_3	0 a_4
0	x_3	$23/3$	0	$1/3$	1	$-1/3$
3	x_1	$7/6$	1	$-2/3$	0	$1/6$
	Z_j	$7/2$	3	-2	0	$1/2$
	$c_j - Z_j$		0	0	0	$-1/2$

↑
Alternative optima indicated

Alternative optimal solution (obtained from introducing x_2 into the basis):

$x_1 = 33/2$
$x_2 = 23$ $Z = 7/2$
$x_3 = 0$
$x_4 = 0$

46. Initial simplex tableau:

c_b	Variables in Basis	c_j Solution Values, x_b	-2 a_1	3 a_2	0 a_3	0 a_4
0	x_3	5	1	0	1	0
0	x_4	6	2	-3	0	1
	Z_j	0	0	0	0	0
	$c_j - Z_j$		-2	3	0	0

↑
Unbounded solution indicated

48. Final simplex tableau:

| c_b | Variables in Basis | Solution Values, x_b | c_j | 3 | 1 | 0 | $-M$ | 0 | $-M$ |
				a_1	a_2	a_3	a_4	a_5	a_6
0	x_5	9		0	$13/2$	$-3/2$	$3/2$	1	-1
3	x_1	5		1	$5/2$	$-1/2$	$1/2$	0	0
	Z_j	15		3	$15/2$	$-3/2$	$3/2$	0	0
	$c_j - Z_j$			0	$-13/2$	$3/2$	$-M - 3/2$	0	$-M$

↑
Unbounded solution indicated

50. Final simplex tableau:

| c_b | Variables in Basis | Solution Values, x_b | c_j | 4 | -3 | 5 | 2 | 0 | 0 | 0 | $-M$ |
				a_1	a_2	a_3	a_4	a_5	a_6	a_7	a_8
0	x_5	92		26	-14	0	33	1	9	0	0
0	x_7	70		23	-4	0	29	0	7	1	-1
5	x_3	10		3	-1	1	3	0	1	0	0
	Z_j	50		15	-5	5	15	0	5	0	0
	$c_j - Z_j$			-11	2	0	-13	0	-5	0	$-M$

↑
Unbounded solution indicated

52. Final simplex tableau:

| c_b | Variables in Basis | Solution Values, x_b | c_j | 2 | 3 | 0 | $-M$ | 0 | 0 |
				a_1	a_2	a_3	a_4	a_5	a_6
$-M$	x_4	2		0	-1	-1	1	0	-1
0	x_5	4		0	1	0	0	1	-1
2	x_1	2		1	0	0	0	0	1
	Z_j	$4 - 2M$		2	M	M	$-M$	0	$M + 2$
	$c_j - Z_j$			0	$3 - M$	$-M$	0	0	$-M - 2$

Since no $c_j - Z_j$ value is positive, the solution appears to be optimal. However, since the artificial variable x_4, which should have been driven to zero, is present as a positive (i.e., $x_4 = 2$) basic variable in the solution, *no feasible solution exists.*

54. Final simplex tableau:

c_b	Variables in Basis	Solution Values, x_b	c_j	1 a_1	3 a_2	0 a_3	$-M$ a_4	0 a_5	$-M$ a_6
$-M$	x_4	4		-2	0	-1	1	-1	1
3	x_2	3		-3	1	0	0	-1	1
	Z_j	$9 - 4M$		$2M - 9$	3	M	$-M$	$M - 3$	$3 - M$
	$c_j - Z_j$			$8 - 2M$	0	$-M$	0	$3 - M$	-3

Since no $c_j - Z_j$ value is positive, the solution appears to be optimal. However, since the artificial variable x_4, which should have been driven to zero, is present as a positive (i.e., $x_4 = 4$) basic variable in the solution, *no feasible solution exists.*

56. Final simplex tableau:

c_b	Variables in Basis	Solution Values, x_b	c_j	3 a_1	7 a_2	0 a_3	$-M$ a_4	0 a_5	$-M$ a_6
$-M$	x_4	5		-2	0	-1	1	-1	1
7	x_2	5		-3	1	0	0	-1	1
	Z_j	$35 - 5M$		$-21 + 2M$	7	$+M$	$-M$	$+M - 7$	$-M + 7$
	$c_j - Z_j$			$24 - 2M$	0	$-M$	0	$-M + 7$	-7

Since no $c_j - Z_j$ value is positive, the solution appears to be optimal. However, since the artificial variable x_4, which should have been driven to zero, is present as a positive (i.e., $x_4 = 5$) basic variable in the solution, *no feasible solution exists.*

(*Note:* For problems 58–96, solutions were obtained by using the linear programming code appearing in the *Instructor's Manual*. For these problems, the solution values of the decision variables that are greater than zero are provided along with the optimal value of the objective function.)

58. See the answer to problem 3–16 for formulation.

$x_1 = 1.087$ $x_2 = 7.041$ Maximum $Z = \$31.43$

60. See the answer to problem 3–18 for formulation.

$x_1 = 15.0$ $x_2 = 10.0$ Minimum $Z = \$1350.00$

62. See the answer to problem 3–20 for formulation.

$x_1 = 11.25$ $x_2 = 2.5$ $x_3 = 2.5$ $x_4 = 8.75$
Minimum $Z = \$760.00$

64. See the answer to problem 3–22 for formulation.

$x_{11} = 998.5$ $x_{13} = 1.454$ $x_{22} = 1100.0$ $x_{31} = 1001.5$
$x_{32} = 198.54$ $x_{42} = 201.46$ $x_{43} = 898.54$ Maximum $Z = \$3910.00$

66. See the answer to problem 3–24 for formulation.

$x_1 = 10.0$ $x_2 = 5.0$ $x_3 = 3.0$ $x_4 = 144.0$
Maximum $Z = 522,989.75$

68. See the answer to problem 3–26 for formulation.

$x_1 = 0.5333$ $x_2 = 0.0667$ $x_3 = 0.400$ Minimum $Z = \$18$
(million)

70. See the answer to problem 3–28 for formulation.

$x_{11} = 750.0$ $x_{13} = 690.0$ $x_{22} = 1500.0$ $x_{23} = 810.0$
Minimum $Z = \$12,438.90$

72. See the answer to problem 3–30 for formulation.

$x_1 = 1750.0$ $x_2 = 1500.0$ $x_4 = 1750.0$ Maximum $Z = \$150.00$

74. See the answer to problem 3–32 for formulation.

$x_{12} = 1980.0$ $x_{21} = 660.0$ $x_{22} = 1020.0$ $x_{31} = 750.0$
$x_{41} = 540.0$ $y_{12} = 220.0$ $y_{22} = 420.0$ $y_{31} = 390.0$
$y_{32} = 360.0$ $y_{41} = 1260.0$ Minimum $Z = 16,389.988$ Total Busing
Miles

76. See the answer to problem 3–34 for formulation.

$x_{13} = 6.9483$ $x_{22} = 18.00$ $x_{31} = 14.977$ $x_{32} = 2.00$
$x_{33} = 5.0235$ Maximum $Z = \$6608.60$

78. See the answer to problem 3–36 for formulation.

$x_{12} = 1.0$ $x_{23} = 2.0$ $x_{14} = 2.0$ $x_{24} = 2.0$
$x_{34} = 4.0$ $x_{15} = 1.0$ $x_{45} = 2.0$ $x_{56} = 3.0$
Minimum $Z = \$37,100.00$

80. See the answer to problem 3–38 for formulation.

$x_{11} = 200.0$ $x_{23} = 275.0$ $x_{31} = 25.0$ $x_{32} = 160.0$
Minimum $Z = \$94,930.00$

82. See the answer to problem 3–40 for formulation.

$x_1 = 11750.00$ $x_2 = 3750.0$ $x_3 = 2250.0$ $x_4 = 7750.0$
Maximum $Z = \$977,500.06$

84. See the answer to problem 3–42 for formulation.

$x_2 = 0.35$ $x_3 = 0.25$ $x_5 = 0.33$ $x_7 = 0.07$
Maximum $Z = 0.1026$

86. See the answer to problem 3–44 for formulation.

$x_1 = 7.5$ $x_2 = 2.5$ $x_3 = 10.0$
Maximum $Z = 61.04 + 23.75 = 84.79$ (Grade Point Average)

88. See the answer to problem 3–46 for formulation.

$x_{11} = 75.0$ $x_{12} = 106.30$ $y_{12} = 50.0$ Maximum $Z = \$72,712.44$

90. See the answer to problem 3–48 for formulation.

$x_{11} = 350,000$ $x_{23} = 400,000$ $x_{32} = 450,000$ $x_{42} = 100,000.$
$x_{43} = 400,000$ Maximum $Z = \$1,280,000$

92. See the answer to problem 3–50 for formulation.

$x_1 = 34.17$ $x_3 = 21.67$ Maximum $Z = \$2062.50$

94. See the answer to problem 3–52 for formulation.

$x_{111} = 300.0$ $x_{112} = 1200.0$ $x_{113} = 200.0$ $x_{212} = 1700.0$
$x_{313} = 1700.0$ $x_{414} = 1000.0$ $x_{415} = 700.0$ $x_{515} = 1700.0$
$x_{616} = 1700.0$ $x_{121} = 700.0$ $x_{222} = 1100.0$ $x_{323} = 1100.0$
$x_{424} = 1000.0$ $x_{525} = 1100.0$ $x_{626} = 800.0$ Minimum $Z = \$144,200.00$

96. See the answer to problem 3–54 for formulation.

$x_{12} = 1.0$ $x_{23} = 1.0$ $x_{34} = 1.0$ $x_{41} = 1.0$
Minimum $Z = 335.0$ Miles

CHAPTER 5 • DUALITY AND SENSITIVITY ANALYSIS

2. Minimize $Z_y = 7y_1 + 10y_2$

   subject to:
   $$2y_1 + 1y_2 \geq 1$$
   $$-3y_1 + 2y_2 \geq 2$$

   with $y_1 \geq 0, y_2 \leq 0$

4. Maximize $Z_x = 18x_1 + 12x_2 + 16x_3$

   subject to:
   $$6x_1 + 2x_2 + 2x_2 \leq 5$$
   $$3x_1 + 4x_2 + 8x_3 \leq 4$$

   with $x_1 \geq 0, x_2 \geq 0, x_3 \geq 0$

6. Maximize $Z_x = 7x_1 + 5x_2 + 8x_3$

   subject to:
   $$3x_1 + 2x_2 \quad\quad \leq 2$$
   $$2x_1 \quad\quad + 4x_3 \leq 3$$
   $$5x_1 + x_2 + 3x_3 \leq 5$$

   with $x_1 \geq 0, x_2 \geq 0, x_3 \geq 0$

8. Minimize $Z_y = -12y_1 + 10y_2 + 15y_3$

   subject to:
   $$-3y_1 \quad\quad + 2y_3 = 1$$
   $$-2y_1 - 1y_2 + 1y_3 \geq -3$$
   $$4y_1 \quad\quad - 3y_3 \geq 5$$
   $$2y_1 + 4y_2 \quad\quad \geq -1$$

   with $y_1 \geq 0$, y_2 unrestricted in sign, $y_3 \geq 0$

10. Maximize $Z_x = -12x_1 + 10x_2 + 18x_3$

subject to:
$$-1x_1 \qquad + \quad 1x_3 \le -2$$
$$3x_1 + 2x_2 \qquad \le \quad 4$$
$$-2x_1 + 1x_2 - 2x_3 = \quad 3$$

with $x_1 \ge 0, x_2 \ge 0, x_3$ unrestricted in sign

12. (a) Maximize $Z_x = 5x_1 - 3x_2$

subject to:
$$2x_1 - 6x_2 \le -20$$
$$6x_1 - 2x_2 \le \quad 2$$
$$-6x_1 + 2x_2 \le \quad -2$$
$$-4x_1 + 1x_2 \le \quad 0$$

with $x_1 \ge 0, x_2 \ge 0$

(b) Minimize $Z_y = -20y_1 + 2y_2' - 2y_2''$

subject to:
$$2y_1 + 6y_2' - 6y_2'' - 4y_3 \ge \quad 5$$
$$-6y_1 - 2y_2' + 2y_2'' + 1y_3 \ge -3$$

with $y_1 \ge 0, y_2' \ge 0, y_2'' \ge 0, y_3 \ge 0$

14. (a) Minimize $Z_x = 2x_1 - 5x_2 - 3x_3$

subject to:
$$2x_1 - 4x_2 + 3x_3 \ge -14$$
$$- 1x_2 + 1x_3 \ge \quad 10$$
$$1x_2 - 1x_3 \ge -10$$
$$4x_1 \qquad - 2x_3 \ge \quad -6$$

with $x_1 \ge 0, x_2 \ge 0, x_3 \ge 0$

(b) Maximize $Z_y = -14y_1 + 10y_2' - 10y_2'' - 6y_3$

subject to:
$$2y_1 \qquad + 4y_3 \le \quad 2$$
$$-4y_1 - 1y_2' + 1y_2'' \qquad \le -5$$
$$3y_1 + 1y_2' - 1y_2'' - 2y_3 \le -3$$

with $y_1 \ge 0, y_2' \ge 0, y_2'' \ge 0, y_3 \ge 0$

16.

		Optimal Values of	
	Primal Variables		*Corresponding Dual Variables*
Basic:	$x_2 = 5.0$ (2nd primal decision variable)	Nonbasic: $y_4 =$	0 (2nd dual surplus variable)
	$x_3 = 22.0$ (1st primal slack variable)	$y_1 =$	0 (1st dual decision variable)
Nonbasic: $x_1 =$	0 (1st primal decision variable)	Basic:	$y_3 =$ 0 (1st dual surplus variable)
$x_4 =$	0 (2nd primal slack variable)		$y_2 = 1.0$ (2nd dual decision variable)

18.

Optimal Values of

Primal Variables	Corresponding Dual Variables

Basic: $y_1 = 2.0$ (1st primal decision variable)

$y_2 = 2.0$ (2nd primal decision variable)

$y_5 = 4.0$ (3rd primal surplus variable)

Nonbasic: $y_3 = 0$ (1st primal surplus variable)

$y_4 = 0$ (2nd primal surplus variable)

Nonbasic: $x_4 = 0$ (1st dual slack variable)

$x_5 = 0$ (2nd dual slack variable)

$x_3 = 0$ (3rd dual decision variable)

Basic: $x_1 = {}^2/_3$ (1st dual decision variable)

$x_2 = {}^1/_2$ (2nd dual decision variable)

20.

Optimal Values of

Primal Variables	Corresponding Dual Variables

Basic: $y_1 = 2.5$ (1st primal decision variable)

$y_2 = 2.0$ (2nd primal decision variable)

$y_4 = 4.5$ (1st primal surplus variable)

Nonbasic: $y_3 = 0$ (3rd primal decision variable)

$y_5 = 0$ (2nd primal surplus variable)

$y_6 = 0$ (3rd primal surplus variable)

Nonbasic: $x_4 = 0$ (1st dual slack variable)

$x_5 = 0$ (2nd dual slack variable)

$x_1 = 0$ (1st dual decision variable)

Basic: $x_6 = 1.75$ (3rd dual slack variable)

$x_2 = 1.00$ (2nd dual decision variable)

$x_3 = 0.75$ (3rd dual decision variable)

22. Dual formulation:

Minimize $Z = 5y_1 + 1y_2$

subject to: $\quad -1y_2 \geq 2$

$\quad 1y_1 + 1y_2 \geq 1$

with $\quad y_1 \geq 0, y_2 \geq 0$

Final tableau:

c_b	Variables in Basis	Solution Values, $\mathbf{x}_b$	c_j	5	1	0	M	0	M
				$\mathbf{a}_1$	$\mathbf{a}_2$	$\mathbf{a}_3$	$\mathbf{a}_4$	$\mathbf{a}_5$	$\mathbf{a}_6$
M	y_4	2		0	-1	-1	1	0	0
5	y_1	1		1	1	0	0	-1	1
	Z_j	$2M + 5$		5	$5 - M$	$-M$	M	-5	5
	$c_j - Z_j$			0	$M - 4$	M	0	5	$M - 5$

Since no $c_j - Z_j$ value is negative, the solution to the dual problem appears to be optimal. However, since the artificial variable y_4, which should have been driven to zero, is present as a positive (i.e., $y_4 = 2$) basic variable in the dual solution, the dual problem has *no feasible solution*.

24. Dual formulation:

Minimize $Z = -10y_1 - 6y_2$

subject to: $-2y_1 - 3y_2 \geq 3$
$-5y_1 - 1y_2 \geq 1$

with $y_1 \geq 0$, $y_2 \geq 0$

Initial tableau:

c_b	Variables in Basis	c_j Solution Values, x_b	-10 a_1	-6 a_2	0 a_3	M a_4	0 a_5	M a_6
M	y_4	3	-2	-3	-1	1	0	0
M	y_6	1	-5	-1	0	0	-1	1
	Z_j	$4M$	$-7M$	$-4M$	$-M$	M	$-M$	M
	$c_j - Z_j$		$7M - 10$	$4M - 6$	M	0	M	0

Since no $c_j - Z_j$ value is negative, the solution to the dual problem appears to be optimal. However, since the artificial variables y_4 and y_6, which should have been driven to zero, are present as positive (i.e., $y_4 = 3$ and $y_6 = 1$) basic variables in the dual solution, the dual problem has *no feasible solution*.

26. Dual formulation:

Minimize $Z = 20y_1 + 21y_2 - 5y_3$

subject to: $4y_1 + 7y_2 - 1y_3 \geq 3$
$4y_1 + 3y_2 \qquad \geq 5$

with $y_1 \geq 0$, $y_2 \geq 0$, $y_3 \geq 0$

Final tableau:

c_b	Variables in Basis	c_j Solution Values, x_b	20 a_1	21 a_2	-5 a_3	0 a_4	M a_5	0 a_6	M a_7
21	y_2	$5/3$	$4/3$	1	0	0	0	$-1/3$	$1/3$
-5	y_3	$26/3$	$16/3$	0	1	1	-1	$-7/3$	$7/3$
	Z_j	$-25/3$	$4/3$	21	-5	-5	5	$14/3$	$-14/3$
	$c_j - Z_j$		$56/3$	0	0	5	$M - 5$	$-14/3$	$M + 14/3$

$\uparrow$
Unbounded solution indicated

28. Dual formulation:

Minimize $Z = -1y_1 - 3y_2$

subject to: $-1y_1 + 3y_2 \geq 1$
$1y_1 - 1y_2 \geq 3$

with $y_1 \geq 0$, $y_2 \geq 0$

Final tableau:

		c_j	-1	-3	0	M	0	M
c_b	*Variables in Basis*	*Solution Values,* x_b	a_1	a_2	a_3	a_4	a_5	a_6
-3	y_2	2	0	1	$-1/2$	$1/2$	$-1/2$	$1/2$
-1	y_1	5	1	0	$-1/2$	$1/2$	$-3/2$	$3/2$
	Z_j	-11	-1	-3	2	-2	3	-3
	$c_j - Z_j$		0	0	-2	$M+2$	-3	$M+3$

↑
Unbounded solution indicated

30. (a) and (b)

			Optimal Values of		
	Primal Variables			*Corresponding Dual Variables*	

Basic: $x_2 = 0.33$ (2nd primal decision variable)

$x_3 = 0.67$ (3rd primal decision variable)

$x_4 = 1496.7$ (1st primal slack variable)

$x_7 = 2.83$ (2nd primal surplus variable)

$x_9 = 8.33$ (3rd primal surplus variable)

$x_{11} = 8.33$ (4th primal surplus variable)

$x_{13} = 0$ (5th primal surplus variable)

Nonbasic: $x_1 = 0$ (1st primal decision variable)

$x_5 = 0$ (1st primal slack variable)

$x_{15} = 0$ (2nd primal slack variable)

Nonbasic: $y_8 = 0$ (2nd dual slack variable)

$y_9 = 0$ (3rd dual slack variable)

$y_1 = 0$ (1st dual decision variable)

$y_3 = 0$ (3rd dual decision variable)

$y_4 = 0$ (4th dual decision variable)

$y_5 = 0$ (5th dual decision variable)

$y_6' = 0$ (6th dual decision variable)

Basic: $y_7 = 0.03$ (1st dual slack variable)

$y_2 = 0.0012$ (2nd dual decision variable)

$y_6'' = 0.108$ (7th dual decision variable)

(c) Economic interpretation of the primal problem: The primal problem seeks to determine the quantities of the various ingredients that should be blended to meet the established standards for the dog food, while minimizing the cost of the dog food. Note that the objective function expresses the total cost of the blend in dollar units.

(d) Economic interpretation of the dual problem: Inasmuch as the objective function of the primal problem is in dollar units, its dual counterpart must also be in dollars. Consider that the right-hand-side constants in the primal are physical units of the respective nutrients, so that the dual decision variables with which they appear in the dual objective function must be in units of dollars per unit of the respective nutrients. In other words, the dual decision variables denote the imputed values of the various nutrients. In this light, each dual constraint may be interpreted to mean that the total value imputed to the nutrients contained in one unit of every ingredient should be no greater than the price of that ingredient. Actually, common sense prohibits the purchase of the jth ingredient if its price exceeds the imputed value of its nutrient content because a person would not be getting his money's worth. Therefore, the optimal solution will only specify the purchase of those ingredients for which the imputed values of their respective nutrient contents are exactly equal to their respective prices.

The objective of the dual program is to maximize the total imputed value of minimum nutrient requirements, subject to aforementioned constraints.

32.   (a) and (b)

Primal problem decision variable key:

$x_1 = x_{11}$	$x_6 = x_{21}$	$x_{11} = x_{31}$	$x_{16} = y_1$
$x_2 = x_{12}$	$x_7 = x_{22}$	$x_{12} = x_{32}$	$x_{17} = y_2$
$x_3 = x_{13}$	$x_8 = x_{23}$	$x_{13} = x_{33}$	$x_{18} = y_3$
$x_4 = x_{14}$	$x_9 = x_{24}$	$x_{14} = x_{34}$	$x_{19} = y_4$
$x_5 = x_{15}$	$x_{10} = x_{25}$	$x_{15} = x_{35}$	$x_{20} = y_5$

	Optimal Values of	
	Primal Variables	**Corresponding Dual Variables**
Basic:	x_1 = 100000 (1st primal decision variable)	Nonbasic: $y_{16} = 0$ (1st dual surplus variable)
	x_2 = 100000 (2nd primal decision variable)	$y_{18} = 0$ (2nd dual surplus variable)
	x_3 = 100000 (3rd primal decision variable)	$y_{20} = 0$ (3rd dual surplus variable)
	x_4 = 100000 (4th primal decision variable)	$y_{22} = 0$ (4th dual surplus variable)
	x_5 = 100000 (5th primal decision variable)	$y_{24} = 0$ (5th dual surplus variable)
	x_6 = 38680 (6th primal decision variable)	$y_{26} = 0$ (6th dual surplus variable)
	x_7 = 320300 (7th primal decision variable)	$y_{28} = 0$ (7th dual surplus variable)
	x_9 = 403500 (9th primal decision variable)	$y_{32} = 0$ (9th dual surplus variable)
	x_{11} = 50000 (11th primal decision variable)	$y_{36} = 0$ (11th dual surplus variable)
	x_{13} = 50000 (13th primal decision variable)	$y_{40} = 0$ (13th dual surplus variable)
	x_{16} = 311300 (16th primal decision variable)	$y_{46} = 0$ (16th dual surplus variable)
	x_{20} = 9000 (20th primal decision variable)	$y_{54} = 0$ (20th dual surplus variable)

Primal Variables	Corresponding Dual Variables
$x_{42} = 50000$ (12th primal slack variable)	$y_{12} = 0$ (17th dual decision variable)
$x_{44} = 50000$ (14th primal slack variable)	$y_{14} = 0$ (19th dual decision variable)
$x_{45} = 50000$ (15th primal slack variable)	$y_{15} = 0$ (20th dual decision variable)
Nonbasic: $x_8 = 0$ (8th primal decision variable)	$y_{30} = 0$ (8th dual surplus variable)
$x_{10} = 0$ (10th primal decision variable)	$y_{34} = 1.00$ (10th dual surplus variable)
$x_{12} = 0$ (12th primal decision variable)	$y_{38} = 0.024$ (12th dual surplus variable)
$x_{14} = 0$ (14th primal decision variable)	$y_{42} = 1.060$ (14th dual surplus variable)
$x_{15} = 0$ (15th primal decision variable)	$y_{44} = 1.00$ (15th dual surplus variable)
$x_{17} = 0$ (17th primal decision variable)	$y_{48} = 0.064$ (17th dual surplus variable)
$x_{18} = 0$ (18th primal decision variable)	$x_{50} = 0$ (18th dual surplus variable)
$x_{19} = 0$ (19th primal decision variable)	$y_{52} = 0.06$ (19th dual surplus variable)
$x_{21} = 0$ (1st primal slack variable)	$y_1' = 1.124$ (1st dual decision variable)
$x_{22} = 0$ (1st primal surplus variable)	$y_1'' = 0$ (2nd dual decision variable)
$x_{24} = 0$ (2nd primal slack variable)	$y_2' = 1.124$ (3rd dual decision variable)
$x_{25} = 0$ (2nd primal surplus variable)	$y_2'' = 0$ (4th dual decision variable)
$x_{27} = 0$ (3rd primal slack variable)	$y_3' = 1.06$ (5th dual decision variable)
$x_{28} = 0$ (3rd primal surplus variable)	$y_3'' = 0$ (6th dual decision variable)
$x_{30} = 0$ (4th primal slack variable)	$y_4' = 1.06$ (7th dual decision variable)
$x_{31} = 0$ (4th primal surplus variable)	$y_4'' = 0$ (8th dual decision variable)
$x_{33} = 0$ (5th primal slack variable)	$y_5' = 1.00$ (9th dual decision variable)
$x_{34} = 0$ (5th primal surplus variable)	$y_5'' = 0$ (10th dual decision variable)
$x_{36} = 0$ (6th primal slack variable)	$y_6 = 0.101$ (11th dual decision variable)
$x_{37} = 0$ (7th primal slack variable)	$y_7 = 0.032$ (12th dual decision variable)
$x_{38} = 0$ (8th primal slack variable)	$y_8 = 0.095$ (13th dual decision variable)
$x_{39} = 0$ (9th primal slack variable)	$y_9 = 0.030$ (14th dual decision variable)
$x_{40} = 0$ (10th primal slack variable)	$y_{10} = 0.090$ (15th dual decision variable)
$x_{41} = 0$ (11th primal slack variable)	$y_{11} = 0.043$ (16th dual decision variable)
$x_{43} = 0$ (13th primal slack variable)	$y_{13} = 0.040$ (18th dual decision variable)

34.   (a) and (b)

Primal problem decision variable key:

$x_1 = x_{111}$	$x_6 = x_{213}$	$x_{11} = x_{121}$	$x_{16} = x_{223}$
$x_2 = x_{112}$	$x_7 = x_{214}$	$x_{12} = x_{122}$	$x_{17} = x_{224}$
$x_3 = x_{113}$	$x_8 = x_{313}$	$x_{13} = x_{123}$	$x_{18} = x_{323}$
$x_4 = x_{114}$	$x_9 = x_{314}$	$x_{14} = x_{124}$	$x_{19} = x_{324}$
$x_5 = x_{212}$	$x_{10} = x_{414}$	$x_{15} = x_{222}$	$x_{20} = x_{424}$

Optimal Values of

Primal Variables		Corresponding Dual Variables	
Basic:	$x_1 = 3000$ (1st primal decision variable)	Nonbasic: $y_{17} = 0$	(1st dual slack variable)
	$x_5 = 3000$ (5th primal decision variable)	$y_{21} = 0$	(5th dual slack variable)
	$x_6 = 0$ (6th primal decision variable)	$y_{22} = 0$	(6th dual slack variable)
	$x_7 = 0$ (7th primal decision variable)	$y_{23} = 0$	(7th dual slack variable)
	$x_8 = 3000$ (8th primal decision variable)	$y_{24} = 0$	(8th dual slack variable)
	$x_{10} = 3000$ (10th primal decision variable)	$y_{26} = 0$	(10th dual slack variable)
	$x_{11} = 0$ (11th primal decision variable)	$y_{27} = 0$	(11th dual slack variable)
	$x_{15} = 1000$ (15th primal decision variable)	$y_{31} = 0$	(15th dual slack variable)
	$x_{18} = 2000$ (18th primal decision variable)	$y_{34} = 0$	(18th dual slack variable)
	$x_{20} = 2000$ (20th primal decision variable)	$y_{36} = 0$	(20th dual slack variable)
	$x_{25} = 2000$ (5th primal slack variable)	$y_5 = 0$	(5th dual decision variable)
	$x_{26} = 1000$ (6th primal slack variable)	$y_6 = 0$	(6th dual decision variable)
	$x_{31} = 0$ (9th primal slack variable)	$y_9'' = 0$	(10th dual decision variable)
	$x_{34} = 0$ (10th primal slack variable)	$y_{10}'' = 0$	(12th dual decision variable)
	$x_{37} = 0$ (11th primal slack variable)	$y_{11}'' = 0$	(14th dual decision variable)
	$x_{40} = 0$ (12th primal slack variable)	$y_{12}'' = 0$	(16th dual decision variable)
Nonbasic:	$x_2 = 0$ (2nd primal decision variable)	Basic: $y_{18} = 50$	(2nd dual slack variable)
	$x_3 = 0$ (3rd primal decision variable)	$y_{19} = 50$	(3rd dual slack variable)
	$x_4 = 0$ (4th primal decision variable)	$y_{20} = 50$	(4th dual slack variable)
	$x_9 = 0$ (9th primal decision variable)	$y_{25} = 0$	(9th dual slack variable)
	$x_{12} = 0$ (12th primal decision variable)	$y_{28} = 50$	(12th dual slack variable)

Optimal Values of	
Primal Variables	*Corresponding Dual Variables*
$x_{13} = 0$ (13th primal decision variable)	$y_{29} = 50$ (13th dual slack variable)
$x_{14} = 0$ (14th primal decision variable)	$y_{30} = 50$ (14th dual slack variable)
$x_{16} = 0$ (16th primal decision variable)	$y_{32} = 0$ (16th dual slack variable)
$x_{17} = 0$ (17th primal decision variable)	$y_{33} = 0$ (17th dual slack variable)
$x_{19} = 0$ (19th primal decision variable)	$y_{35} = 0$ (19th dual slack variable)
$x_{21} = 0$ (1st primal slack variable)	$y_1 = 1000$ (1st dual decision variable)
$x_{22} = 0$ (2nd primal slack variable)	$y_2 = 1000$ (2nd dual decision variable)
$x_{23} = 0$ (3rd primal slack variable)	$y_3 = 1050$ (3rd dual decision variable)
$x_{24} = 0$ (4th primal slack variable)	$y_4 = 1100$ (4th dual decision variable)
$x_{27} = 0$ (7th primal slack variable)	$y_7 = 50$ (7th dual decision variable)
$x_{28} = 0$ (8th primal slack variable	$y_8 = 100$ (8th dual decision variable)
$x_{29} = 0$ (1st primal surplus variable)	$y_9' = 2500$ (9th dual decision variable)
$x_{32} = 0$ (2nd primal surplus variable)	$y_{10}' = 2500$ (11th dual decision variable)
$x_{35} = 0$ (3rd primal surplus variable)	$y_{11}' = 2550$ (13th dual decision variable)
$x_{38} = 0$ (4th primal surplus variable)	$y_{12}' = 2600$ (15th dual decision variable)

36. (a) and (b)

Optimal Values of	
Primal Variables	*Corresponding Dual Variables*
Basic: $x_1 = 4.0$ (1st primal decision variable)	Nonbasic: $y_4 = 0$ (1st dual slack variable)
$x_2 = 1.0$ (2nd primal decision variable)	$y_5 = 0$ (2nd dual slack variable)
$x_6 = 0$ (2nd primal slack variable)	$y_2'' = 0$ (3rd dual decision variable)
$x_7 = 12.0$ (2nd primal surplus variable)	$y_3 = 0$ (4th dual decision variable)
Nonbasic: $x_3 = 0$ (1st primal slack variable)	$y_1 = 1.0$ (1st dual decision variable)
$x_4 = 0$ (1st primal surplus variable)	$y_2' = 3.5$ (2nd dual decision variable)

38. Initial dual simplex tableau:

c_b	Variables in Basis	c_j Solution Values, y_b	7 a_1	5 a_2	1 a_3	0 a_4	0 a_5	0 a_6
0	y_4	-7	-5	0	3	1	0	0
0	y_5	-4	0	-2	5	0	1	0
0	y_6	3	1	-3	0	0	0	1
	Z_j	0	0	0	0	0	0	0
	$c_j - Z_j$		7	5	1	0	0	0

Optimal tableau:

c_b	Variables in Basis	c_j Solution Values, y_b	7 a_1	5 a_2	1 a_3	0 a_4	0 a_5	0 a_6
7	y_1	$7/5$	1	0	$-3/5$	$-1/5$	0	0
5	y_2	2	0	1	$-5/2$	0	$-1/2$	0
0	y_6	$38/5$	0	0	$-69/10$	$1/5$	$-3/2$	1
	Z_j	$99/5$	7	5	$-167/10$	$-7/5$	$-5/2$	0
	$c_j - Z_j$		0	0	$177/10$	$7/5$	$5/2$	0

40. Initial dual simplex tableau:

c_b	Variables in Basis	c_j Solution Values, x_b	-4 a_1	-2 a_2	-3 a_3	0 a_4	0 a_5	0 a_6
0	x_4	-7	-1	-2	-1	1	0	0
0	x_5	-5	-2	0	-3	0	1	0
0	x_6	-9	0	-3	-1	0	0	1
	Z_j	0	0	0	0	0	0	0
	$c_j - Z_j$		-4	-2	3	0	0	0

Optimal tableau:

c_b	Variables in Basis	c_j — Solution Values, x_b	-4 a_1	-2 a_2	-3 a_3	0 a_4	0 a_5	0 a_6
0	x_6	$2/3$	$7/6$	0	0	$-3/2$	$1/6$	1
-3	x_3	$5/3$	$2/3$	0	1	0	$-1/3$	0
-2	x_2	$8/3$	$1/6$	1	0	$-1/2$	$1/6$	0
	Z_j	$-31/3$	$-7/3$	-2	-3	1	$2/3$	0
	$c_j - Z_j$		$-5/3$	0	0	-1	$-2/3$	0

42. Initial dual simplex tableau:

c_b	Variables in Basis	c_j — Solution Values, x_b	4 a_1	2 a_2	1 a_3	0 a_4	0 a_5	0 a_6
0	x_4	-10	-2	-4	-5	1	0	0
0	x_5	-3	-3	1	-6	0	1	0
0	x_6	-12	-5	-2	-1	0	0	1
	Z_j	0	0	0	0	0	0	0
	$c_j - Z_j$		4	2	1	0	0	0

Optimal tableau:

c_b	Variables in Basis	c_j — Solution Values, x_b	4 a_1	2 a_2	1 a_3	0 a_4	0 a_5	0 a_6
1	x_3	$26/23$	0	$16/23$	1	$-5/23$	0	$2/23$
0	x_5	$237/23$	0	$137/23$	0	$-27/23$	1	$-3/23$
4	x_1	$50/23$	1	$6/23$	0	$1/23$	0	$-5/23$
	Z_j	$226/23$	4	$40/23$	1	$-1/23$	0	$-18/23$
	$c_j - Z_j$		0	$6/23$	0	$1/23$	0	$18/23$

44. (a) Produce 2 $2/3$ units of toy no. 2
    Produce 2 $2/3$ units of toy no. 3
    No alternative optimal production schedules are possible

(b) $y_1 = {}^7/_9$, $y_2 = {}^8/_9$, $y_3 = 0$

(c) $y_4 = {}^7/_2$, $y_6 = 0$, $y_8 = 0$

(d)

Machine	Shadow Price
A	$7/9
B	$8/9
C	$0

(e) $3.50, every unit of toy no. 1 that is produced under the present set of circumstances will cost the company $3.50.

46. (a) Optimal production schedule:

    0 units — product no. 1

    12 units — product no. 2

    21 units — product no. 3

    No alternative optimal production schedules exist.

(b) Marginal value of an additional hour of time on machine no. 1 = $7.50. range for b_1:

$$\begin{bmatrix} {}^1/_3 & -{}^1/_3 & 0 \\ -{}^1/_6 & {}^2/_3 & 0 \\ -{}^2/_3 & -{}^1/_3 & 1 \end{bmatrix} \begin{bmatrix} 90 + \delta_1 \\ 54 \\ 93 \end{bmatrix} \geq \begin{bmatrix} 0 \\ 0 \\ 0 \end{bmatrix}$$

$30 + \delta_1/3 - 18 \geq 0 \rightarrow 12 + \delta_1/3 \geq 0 \rightarrow \delta_1/3 \geq -12 \rightarrow \delta_1 \geq -36$

$-15 - \delta_1/6 + 36 \geq 0 \rightarrow 21 - \delta_1/6 \geq 0 \rightarrow \delta_1/6 \leq 21 \rightarrow \delta_1 \leq 126$

$-60 - 2\delta_1/3 - 18 + 93 \geq 0 \rightarrow -15 - 2\delta_1/3 \geq 0 \rightarrow 2\delta_1/3 \leq 15 \rightarrow \delta_1 \leq {}^{45}/_2$

$\therefore -{}^3/_6 \leq \delta_1 \leq {}^{45}/_2$ $(90 - 36) \leq b_1' \leq (90 + {}^{45}/_2)$

                        $54 \leq b_1' \leq 112 \, {}^1/_2$

(c) Opportunity cost associated with product no. 1 = $12.50. Each unit of product no. 1 that is forced into production will cost the company $12.50.

(d) Yes, this would change the optimum production schedule because the marginal value for product no. 1 would become $43.00 − $42.50 = $0.50. Thus, this variable (x_1) would enter the basis resulting in a change in the optimum production plan.

(e) Range for c_2:

$-{}^{75}/_6 - \delta_2/3 \leq 0 \rightarrow \delta_2 \geq -{}^{75}/_2$

$-{}^{45}/_6 - \delta_2/3 \leq 0 \rightarrow \delta_2 \geq -{}^{45}/_2$

$-10 + \delta_2/3 \leq 0 \rightarrow \delta_2 \leq 30$

$\therefore -{}^{45}/_2 \leq \delta_2 \leq 30$ $(40 - {}^{45}/_2) \leq c_2' \leq (40 + 30)$

                        $({}^{35}/_2) \leq c_2' \leq 70$

(f) Dual decision variables: $y_1 = 7.5$

                             $y_2 = 10$

                             $y_3 = 0$

(g) Marginal value = $55 (contribution margin) − [4 hours on machine no. 1 ($7.50/hour marginal cost on machine no. 1) + 2 hours on machine no. 2 ($10.00/hour marginal cost on machine no. 2) + 3 hours on machine no. 3 ($0.00/hour marginal cost on machine no. 3)] = $55.00 − $30.00 − $20.00 − $0.00 = $5.00

Therefore, this new product should be produced because it has a positive marginal value of $5.00.

48. (a) Let: x_1 — number of units of feed no. 1 used

x_2 — number of units of feed no. 2 used

Primal problem: Minimize $Z_x = \$0.05x_1 + \$0.03x_2$

subject to:
$$20x_1 + 30x_2 \geq 200$$
$$40x_1 + 25x_2 \geq 350$$
$$30x_1 + 45x_2 \geq 430$$

$x_1 \geq 0,\ x_2 \geq 0$

Initial tableau:

c_b	Variables in Basis	Solution Values, $\mathbf{x}_b$	c_j / $\mathbf{a}_1$	$\mathbf{a}_2$	$\mathbf{a}_3$	$\mathbf{a}_4$	$\mathbf{a}_5$	$\mathbf{a}_6$	$\mathbf{a}_7$	$\mathbf{a}_8$
			0.05	*0.03*	*0*	*+M*	*0*	*+M*	*0*	*+M*
$+M$	x_4	200	20	30	-1	1	0	0	0	0
$+M$	x_6	350	40	25	0	0	-1	1	0	0
$+M$	x_8	430	30	45	0	0	0	0	-1	1
	Z_j	980	90M	100M	$-M$	$+M$	$-M$	$+M$	$-M$	$+M$
	$c_j - Z_j$		$0.05 - 90M$	$0.03 - 100M$	$+M$	0	$+M$	0	$+M$	0

Optimal tableau:

c_b	Var. in Basis	Solution Values, $\mathbf{x}_b$	$\mathbf{a}_1$	$\mathbf{a}_2$	$\mathbf{a}_3$	$\mathbf{a}_4$	$\mathbf{a}_5$	$\mathbf{a}_6$	$\mathbf{a}_7$	$\mathbf{a}_8$
		c_j	*0.05*	*0.03*	*0*	*+M*	*0*	*+M*	*0*	*+M*
0.03	x_2	6.381	0	1	0	0	0.029	-0.029	-0.038	0.038
0.05	x_1	4.762	1	0	0	0	-0.043	0.043	0.024	-0.024
0	x_3	86.67	0	0	1	-1	0	0	-0.667	0.667
	Z_j	0.429	0.05	0.03	0	0	-0.0013	$+0.0013$	0	0
	$c_j - Z_j$		0	0	0	0	$+0.0013$	$M - 0.0013$	0	0

Optimal values for primal variables:

$x_1 = 4.762$
$x_2 = 6.381$ Minimum $Z_x = \$0.43$

(b) Shadow prices: nutrient no. 1 — 0

nutrient no. 2 — 0.0013

nutrient no. 3 — 0

(c) Third feed cost $0.02 per pound:

Marginal value of third feed = (35 units of nutrient A × 0.00 marginal value for nutrient A) + (30 units of nutrient B × 0.0013 – marginal value of nutrient B) + (50 units of nutrient C × 0.00 – marginal value for nutrient C) = $0.039 per pound.

∴. Third feed should be used and will change the optimal mix of feeds.

New solution:
$x_1 = 0$
$x_2 = 0$ Minimum $Z_x = \$0.23$
$x_3 = 11.67$

(d) Equivalent to adding a row:

$20x_1 + 30x_2 \geq 250$
$20(4.762) + 30(6.381) \geq 250$
$94.4 + 191.43 \geq 250$
$\qquad 285.83 \geq 250$

∴. Solution does not change.

50. (a) $x_1 = 13{,}333.33$ (fertilizer 1)
$x_2 = \quad 3{,}333.33$ (fertilizer 2)
$x_3 = \qquad 0.0$ (fertilizer 3)

There are no alternate optimal solutions to the problem since the $c_j - Z_j$ values associated with the nonbasic variables all are less than zero.

(b) $y_1 = {}^{460}/_3$, $y_2 = 0$, $y_3 = {}^{280}/_3$

(c) $y_4 = 0$, $y_6 = 0$, $y_8 = 5$

(d)

Raw Ingredient	Shadow Price
nitrite	$153.00
phosphate	$ 0.0
potash	$ 93.33

(e) The opportunity cost associated with fertilizer no. 3 is $5.00.

52. (a) $x_1 = 200$ acres (Tomatoes)
$x_2 = 400$ acres (Corn)
$x_3 = \quad 0$ acres (Cabbages)

There are no alternate optimal solutions to this problem, since the $c_j - Z_j$ values associated with the nonbasic variables in the optimal solution are all less than zero.

(b) $y_1 = 100$, $y_2 = 0$, $y_3 = 0$, $y_4 = 100$

(c) $y_5 = 0$, $y_7 = 0$, $y_9 = 390$

(d)

Resource	Shadow Price
Labor	$100
Water	$0
Fertilizer	$0

(e)

Crop	Opportunity Cost
Tomatoes	$0
Corn	$0
Cabbages	$380

54. (a) $x_1 = $ 4 (Large-sized trucks)
$x_2 = $ 5 (Medium-sized trucks)
$x_3 = $ 10 (Large-sized trucks)

There are no alternate optimal solutions to this problem, since the $c_j - Z_j$ values associated with the nonbasic variables in the optimal solution are all greater than zero.

(b) $y_1 = 0$, $y_2 = 25,000$, $y_3 = 20,000$, $y_4 = 10,000$, $y_5 = 0$, $y_6 = 0$

(c) $y_7 = 0$, $y_8 = 0$, $y_9 = 0$

(d)

Resource	Shadow Price
Purchasing funds	$0
Storage space	$0
Maintenance facilities	$0

(e)

Truck Size	Opportunity Cost
Large	$0
Medium	$0
Small	$0

CHAPTER 6 • GOAL PROGRAMMING

(*Note:* The solutions to problems 2, 4, 6, 8, and 10 were obtained with the use of Sang M. Lee's Linear Optimization for Management Code; a listing of this code can be found in *Goal Programming for Decision Analysis*, Philadelphia, Pennsylvania: Auerbach Publishers, 1972.)

2. Let: x_j = number of hours line j is in operation; $j = 1, 2$.
$j = 1 - $ "line A"
$j = 2 - $ "line B"

Minimize $Z = P_1 d_1^- + P_2 d_4^+ + 3P_3 d_2^- + 2P_3 d_3^- + 2P_4 d_2^+ + 3P_4 d_3^+$

subject to: $3x_1 + 2x_2 + d_1^- - d_1^+ = 228$ (Production goal constraint)
$x_1 \qquad + d_2^- - d_2^+ = 40$ (Operation time goal constraint $-$ line A)
$x_2 + d_3^- - d_3^+ = 40$ (Operation time goal constraint $-$ line B)
$d_2^+ + d_4^- - d_4^+ \qquad = 5$ (Overtime operation goal constraint $-$ line A)

with $x_j \geq 0, j = 1, 2; d_1^-, d_1^+, d_2^-, d_2^+, d_3^-, d_3^+, d_4^-, d_4^+ \geq 0$

where d_1^- = underachievement of the production goal
d_1^+ = production in excess of the production goal
d_2^- = underutilization of regular working hours $-$ line A

d_2^+ = overtime operation for line A
d_3^- = underutilization of regular working hours − line B
d_3^+ = overtime operation for line B
d_4^- = difference between the actual overtime operation of line A and the maximum desired overtime operation of line A
d_4^+ = overtime operation of line A in excess of the maximum desired overtime operation of line A

Computer solution:

$x_1 = 45$ $d_1^- = 0$ $d_2^- = 0$ $d_3^- = 0$ $d_4^- = 0$
$x_2 = 46.5$ $d_1^+ = 0$ $d_2^+ = 5$ $d_3^+ = 6.5$ $d_4^+ = 0$

Summary of goal achievement:

Priority	Underachievement
4	29.5
3	0
2	0
1	0

The goals that were assigned priorities 1, 2, and 3 were exactly achieved: the production goal was exactly satisfied, the overtime operation of line A was limited to five hours and the underutilization of regular working hours for both lines was avoided. However, both of the lines did utilize overtime operation that, when weighted by the differential weights assigned to overtime operation, yielded an underachievement figure of 29.5 for the fourth priority goal [2(5) + 3(6.5) = 29.5].

4.   Let: x_j = number of units of food type j that are included in the diet menu
           $j = 1$ − "cottage cheese"
           $j = 2$ − "fruit"
           $j = 3$ − "yogurt"
           $j = 4$ − "bread"
           $j = 5$ − "carob candy bar"

Minimize $Z = P_1 d_5^- + P_2 d_1^- + P_3 d_2^- + P_4 d_4^- + P_5 d_3^-$

subject to: $2.00x_1 + 0.10x_2 + 1.10x_3 + 0.08x_4 + 0.75x_5 \leq 25$
                                  (Budget constraint)

               $225x_1 + 200x_2 + 175x_3 + 150x_4 + 400x_5 \leq 10{,}000$
                                  (Calorie intake constraint)

           $0.15x_1 + 0.25x_2 + 0.15x_3 + 0.05x_4 + 0.08x_5 \geq 9.5$
                                  (Protein consumption constraint)

               $x_1 + d_1^- = 100$ (Cottage cheese goal constraint)
               $x_2 + d_2^- = 100$ (Fruit goal constraint)
               $x_3 + d_3^- = 100$ (Yogurt goal constraint)
               $x_4 + d_4^- = 100$ (Bread goal constraint)
               $x_5 + d_5^- = 100$ (Carob candy bar constraint)

with $x_j \geq 0, j = 1, \ldots, 5; d_j^- \geq 0, j = 1, \ldots, 5$

where d_j^- = underachievement of the aspiration level for food type j, which was set to an arbitrarily large value, that is, 100. Note that the minimization of d_j^- has the effect of maximizing the value of x_j subject to the constraints specified and the prioritization of d_j^-.)

Computer solution:

$x_1 = 0$	$d_1^- = 100$
$x_2 = 35.714$	$d_2^- = 64.286$
$x_3 = 0$	$d_3^- = 100$
$x_4 = 0$	$d_4^- = 100$
$x_5 = 7.142$	$d_5^- = 92.857$

Summary of goal achievement:

Priority	Underachievement
5	100
4	100
3	64.286
2	100
1	92.857

The underachievement figures for the five prioritized goals cannot be interpreted literally, since the aspiration levels for the goals were set to arbitrarily large values. However, it can be concluded that the resultant diet included Sally's first and third choice foods (carob candy bars and fruit), since the underachievement figures associated with the priority levels were less than the arbitrarily assigned values of 100.

6.   Let: x_j = number of acres planted in crop j; $j = 1, \ldots, 4$.

(a)   Linear programming formulation and solution:

Maximize $Z = 253x_1 + 443x_2 + 284x_3 + 516x_4$

subject to: $x_1 + x_2 + x_3 + x_4 \leq 200$ (Acreage availability constraint)
$30x_1 + 45x_2 + 35x_3 + 60x_4 \leq 10{,}000$ (Labor hour availability constraint)
$-x_1 + x_2 - x_3 + x_4 \leq 0$ (Rotational and market outlet constraint)

with $x_j \geq 0, j = 1, \ldots, 4$

Computer solution:

$x_1 = 0$
$x_2 = 0$
$x_3 = 100$
$x_4 = 100$

Maximum $Z = 80{,}000$ (Total Gross Margin)

(b)   Goal programming formulation and solution:

Minimize $Z = P_1d_1^- + P_2d_2^-$

subject to: $253x_1 + 443x_2 + 284x_3 + 516x_4 + d_1^- - d_1^+ = 103,200$
(Gross margin goal constraint)
$x_1 + x_2 + x_3 + x_4 + d_2^- = 200$ (Acreage goal constraint)
$30x_1 + 45x_2 + 35x_3 + 60x_4 \leq 10,000$ (Labor hour availability constraint)
$-x_1 + x_2 - x_3 + x_4 \leq 0$ (Rotational and market outlet constraint)

with $x_j \geq 0, j = 1, \ldots, 4; d_1^-, d_1^+, d_2^- \geq 0$

where d_1^- = underachievement of the target gross margin level (Note that the aspiration level for the gross margin goal constraint was set to the highest possible value, that is, 516×200.)

d_1^+ = overachievement of the target gross margin level (Note that this deviational variable will be forced to assume a value of zero due to the structure of the acreage goal constraint.)

d_2^- = underutilization of available acreage

Computer solution:

$x_1 = 0$ $x_3 = 100$ $d_1^- = 23,200$ $d_2^- = 0$
$x_2 = 0$ $x_4 = 100$ $d_1^+ = 0$

Note that the goal programming formulation in part (b) yielded the same solution as the linear programming formulation in part (a). Total gross margin achieved was 80,000 and there was no underutilization of available acreage.

(c)   Goal programming formulation and solution:

Minimize $Z = P_1 d_1^- + P_2 d_2^- + 5P_2 d_2^+$

subject to: $253x_1 + 443x_2 + 284x_3 + 516x_4 + d_1^- - d_1^+ = 103,200$
(Gross margin goal constraint)
$x_1 + x_2 + x_3 + x_4 + d_2^- - d_2^+ = 200$ (Acreage goal constraint)
$30x_1 + 45x_2 + 35x_3 + 60x_4 \leq 10,000$ (Labor hour availability constraint)
$-x_1 + x_2 - x_3 + x_4 \leq 0$ (Rotational and market outlet constraint)

with $x_j \geq 0; j = 1, \ldots, 4; d_1^-, d_1^+, d_2^-, d_2^+ \geq 0$

where d_1^- = underachievement of the target gross margin level
d_1^+ = overachievement of the target gross margin level
d_2^- = underutilization of available acreage
d_2^+ = overutilization of available acreage

Computer solution:

$x_1 = 133.33$ $x_3 = 0$ $d_1^- = 10,402.32$ $d_2^- = 0$
$x_2 = 133.33$ $x_4 = 0$ $d_1^+ = 0$ $d_2^+ = 66.67$

For this particular goal programming formulation, total gross margin achieved was 92,797.68, and the farmer acquired additional acreage to achieve this gross margin level.

(d) Comparison:

The solution in part (c) provided the higher total gross margin level; however, to obtain this higher level, the farmer was forced to acquire 66.67 additional acres of land.

8. Let: x_j = number of units produced of product j

$$j = 1 - \text{``product A''}$$
$$j = 2 - \text{``product B''}$$

Minimize $Z = P_1(d_1^- + d_2^-) + P_2(d_3^+ + d_4^+ + d_5^+) + P_3(d_6^- - d_6^+)$

subject to:
$$x_1 + d_1^- - d_1^+ = 7 \text{ (Production goal constraint } - \text{ product A)}$$
$$x_2 + d_2^- - d_2^+ = 10 \text{ (Production goal constraint } - \text{ product B)}$$
$$7x_1 + 5x_2 + d_3^- - d_3^+ = 95 \text{ (Material usage goal constraint)}$$
$$3x_1 - 5x_2 + d_4^- - d_4^+ = 125 \text{ (Labor hour usage goal constraint)}$$
$$6x_1 + 4x_2 + d_5^- - d_5^+ = 110 \text{ (Equipment hour usage goal}$$
$$\text{constraint)}$$
$$30x_1 + 25x_2 + d_6^- - d_6^+ = 550 \text{ (Profit goal constraint)}$$

with $x_j \geq 0, \; j = 1, 2; \; d_i^-, d_i^+ \geq 0, \; i = 1, \ldots, 6$

where d_1^- = underachievement of the desired minimum production level for product A

d_1^+ = overachievement of the desired minimum production level for product A

d_2^- = underachievement of the desired minimum production level for product B

d_2^+ = overachievement of the desired minimum production level for product B

d_3^- = amount by which material usage remains below the desired maximum material usage level

d_3^+ = amount by which material usage exceeds the desired maximum material usage level

d_4^- = amount by which labor hour usage remains below the desired maximum labor hour usage level

d_4^+ = amount by which labor hour usage exceeds the desired maximum labor hour usage level

d_5^- = amount by which equipment hour usage remains below the desired maximum equipment usage level

d_5^+ = amount by which equipment hour usage exceeds the desired maximum equipment usage level

d_6^- = underachievement of the target profit level

d_6^+ = overachievement of the target profit level

Computer solution:

$x_1 = 7$	$d_1^- = 0$	$d_2^- = 0$	$d_3^- = 0$	$d_4^- = 54$	$d_5^- = 28$	$d_6^- = 90$
$x_2 = 10$	$d_1^+ = 0$	$d_2^+ = 0$	$d_3^+ = 4$	$d_4^+ = 0$	$d_5^+ = 0$	$d_6^+ = 0$

Summary of goal achievement:

Priority	Underachievement
1	0
2	4
3	90

The highest priority objectives of manufacturing at least 7 units of product A and 10 units of product B were satisfied. One of the second highest priority goals was not achieved: the material usage level exceeded the maximum desired material usage level by 4 units. Also, the resultant profit fell short of the specified aspiration level by $90.

10. Let: x_j = number of pairs of ski type j produced; $j = 1, \ldots, 7$.

Minimize $Z = d_1^- + 2d_2^- + d_3^- + 2d_4^- + d_5^- + d_6^- + d_7^-$

subject to: $3x_1 + \quad 3x_2 + \quad 2x_3 + \quad 7x_4 + \quad 5x_5 + \quad 5x_6 + \quad 3x_7 \le 600$
(Resource availability constraint $-$ resource 1)
$\qquad 2x_1 + \quad 2x_2 + \quad 1x_3 + \quad 3x_4 + \quad 4x_5 + \quad 2x_6 + \quad 2x_7 \le 350$
(Resource availability constraint $-$ resource 2)
$\qquad 5x_1 + \quad 5x_2 + \quad 4x_3 + \quad 4x_4 + \quad 3x_5 + \quad 2x_6 + \quad 1x_7 \le 450$
(Resource availability constraint $-$ resource 3)
$\qquad 3x_1 + \quad 2x_2 + \quad 3x_3 + \quad 3x_4 + \quad 2x_5 + \quad 2x_6 + \quad 1x_7 \le 300$
(Resource availability constraint $-$ resource 4)
$100x_1 + 125x_2 + 275x_3 + 275x_4 + 350x_5 + 250x_6 + 125x_7 \ge 30{,}000$
(Profit constraint)

subject to: $x_1 + d_1^- - d_1^+ = 10$ (Sales forecast goal constraint-type 1)
$\qquad x_2 + d_2^- - d_2^+ = 40$ (Sales forecast goal constraint-type 2)
$\qquad x_3 + d_3^- - d_3^+ = 40$ (Sales forecast goal constraint-type 3)
$\qquad x_4 + d_4^- - d_4^+ = 40$ (Sales forecast goal constraint-type 4)
$\qquad x_5 + d_5^- - d_5^+ = 30$ (Sales forecast goal constraint-type 5)
$\qquad x_6 + d_6^- - d_6^+ = 30$ (Sales forecast goal constraint-type 6)
$\qquad x_7 + d_7^- - d_7^+ = 30$ (Sales forecast goal constraint-type 7)

with $x_j \ge 0, j = 1, \ldots, 7; d_j^-, d_j^+ \ge 0, j = 1, \ldots, 7$

where d_j^- = underachievement of the sales forecast for ski type j; $j = 1, \ldots, 7$
$\qquad d_j^+$ = overachievement of the sales forecast for ski type j; $j = 1, \ldots, 7$

Computer solution (weighted linear goal programming formulation):

$x_1 = 0$ $\qquad d_1^- = 10$
$x_2 = 33.06$ $\qquad d_2^- = 6.94$
$x_3 = 15.55$ $\qquad d_3^- = 24.45$
$x_4 = 26.694$ $\qquad d_4^- = 13.306$
$x_5 = 8.571$ $\qquad d_5^- = 21.429$
$x_6 = 30.0$ $\qquad d_6^- = 0$
$x_7 = 30.0$ $\qquad d_7^- = 0$

Summary of results

The sales forecasts for ski types 6 and 7 only were achieved. The failure to meet the sales forecasts for the other ski types, especially ski types 2 and 4, will result in a loss of goodwill for the company. Note that Minimum $Z = 10 + 2(6.94) + 24.45 + 2(13.306) + 21.429 + 0 + 0 = 96.37$.

CHAPTER 7 • THE TRANSPORTATION AND ASSIGNMENT PROBLEMS

2.

Allocation, Route	Cost
16,000 barrels, $R_1 \rightarrow S_4$	$ 960,000
6,000 barrels, $R_2 \rightarrow S_1$	360,000
12,000 barrels, $R_2 \rightarrow S_3$	480,000
2,000 barrels, $R_2 \rightarrow S_4$	160,000
4,000 barrels, $R_3 \rightarrow S_1$	200,000
10,000 barrels, $R_3 \rightarrow S_2$	500,000
Totals 50,000 barrels	$2,660,000

4.

Allocation, Route	Cost	
25 units, $O_1 \rightarrow D_1$	$ 50	
15 units, $O_1 \rightarrow D_3$	30	
20 units, $O_2 \rightarrow D_3$	60	*Note:* There
15 units, $O_2 \rightarrow D_4$	30	are alternative
25 units, $O_2 \rightarrow D_5$	125	optimal solu-
50 units, $O_3 \rightarrow D_2$	150	tions to this
5 units, $O_3 \rightarrow D_5$	30	problem.
30 units, $O_3 \rightarrow D_6$	60	
30 units, $O_4 \rightarrow D_5$	150	
Totals 215 units	$685	

6.   Same answer as problem 4

8.   Same answer as problem 4

10.

Allocation, Route	Cost
40 units, $O_1 \rightarrow D_2$	$ 40
15 units, $O_2 \rightarrow D_4$	45
35 units, $O_2 \rightarrow D_5$	35
30 units, $O_3 \rightarrow D_1$	60
10 units, $O_3 \rightarrow D_2$	30
10 units, $O_3 \rightarrow D_3$	50
10 units, $O_3 \rightarrow D_4$	40
30 units, $O_4 \rightarrow D_3$	60
Totals 180 units	$360

12.   Same answer as problem 10

14.   Same answer as problem 10

16.   Same answer as problem 10

18.

Allocation, Route	Cost
4(1000 barrels), $R_1 \rightarrow S_2$	$ 280
3(1000 barrels), $R_1 \rightarrow S_3$	150
17(1000 barrels), $R_1 \rightarrow S_4$	1020
20(1000 barrels), $R_2 \rightarrow S_1$	1200
10(1000 barrels), $R_2 \rightarrow S_3$	400
16(1000 barrels), $R_3 \rightarrow S_2$	800
Totals 70(1000 barrels)	$3,850

20.

Allocation, Route	Cost
15 units, $DC_1 \rightarrow APA_2$	$120.00
5 units, $DC_1 \rightarrow APA_4$	50.00
25 units, $DC_2 \rightarrow APA_1$	312.50
20 units, $DC_2 \rightarrow APA_4$	240.00
5 units, $DC_3 \rightarrow APA_1$	55.00
5 units, $DC_3 \rightarrow APA_3$	57.50
Totals 75 units	$835.00

22.

Allocation, Route	Cost
30 units, $O_1 \rightarrow D_4$	$150
0 units, $O_2 \rightarrow D_4$	0
20 units, $O_2 \rightarrow D_5$	120
20 units, $O_2 \rightarrow D_6$	160
10 units, $O_3 \rightarrow D_6$	70
50 units, $O_4 \rightarrow D_1$	250
20 units, $O_4 \rightarrow D_2$	80
10 units, $O_4 \rightarrow D_3$	90
0 units, $O_4 \rightarrow D_4$	0
Totals 160 units	$920

24.

Allocation, Route	Cost
20 units, $P_1 \rightarrow SM_1$	$ 60
30 units, $P_1 \rightarrow SM_2$	30
0 units, $P_1 \rightarrow SM_5$	0
10 units, $P_2 \rightarrow SM_2$	20
35 units, $P_2 \rightarrow SM_3$	35
10 units, $P_3 \rightarrow SM_1$	40
50 units, $P_3 \rightarrow SM_4$	200
20 units, $P_3 \rightarrow SM_6$	20
60 units, $P_4 \rightarrow SM_5$	120
Totals 235 units	$525

26.

Allocation, Route	Cost
20 units, $O_1 \rightarrow D_3$	\$ 140
30 units, $O_1 \rightarrow D_4$	150
20 units, $O_2 \rightarrow D_1$	160
20 units, $O_2 \rightarrow D_5$	120
20 units, $O_2 \rightarrow D_6$	160
20 units, $O_3 \rightarrow D_6$	140
50 units, $O_4 \rightarrow D_1$	250
40 units, $O_4 \rightarrow D_2$	160
0 units, $O_1 \rightarrow D_6$	0
Totals 220 units	\$1280

28.

Allocation, Route	Cost
30 units, $S_1 \rightarrow D_4$	\$ 150
50 units, $S_1 \rightarrow D_5$	500
10 units, $S_2 \rightarrow D_1$	150
70 units, $S_2 \rightarrow D_3$	1750
0 units, $S_2 \rightarrow D_4$	0
200 units, $S_3 \rightarrow D_2$	4000
25 units, $S_3 \rightarrow D_4$	375
70 units, $S_4 \rightarrow D_1$	350
Totals 455 units	\$7275

30.

Allocation, Route	Cost
18 units, $O_1 \rightarrow D_4$	\$1080
2 units, $O_1 \rightarrow$ Slack	0
5 units, $O_2 \rightarrow D_1$	300
12 units, $O_2 \rightarrow D_3$	480
5 units, $O_2 \rightarrow$ Slack	0
5 units, $O_3 \rightarrow D_1$	250
10 units, $O_3 \rightarrow D_2$	50
Totals 50 units	\$2610

32.

Allocation, Route	Cost
3,500 units, $O_1 \rightarrow D_1$	\$ 35,000
2,500 units, $O_1 \rightarrow D_2$	22,500
0 units, $O_1 \rightarrow D_3$	0
4,000 units, $O_1 \rightarrow D_4$	12,000
7,000 units, $O_2 \rightarrow D_3$	126,000
500 units, $O_2 \rightarrow D_5$	5,500
1,000 units, $O_3 \rightarrow D_5$	6,000
3,500 units, $O_3 \rightarrow D_6$	52,500
7,500 units, $O_3 \rightarrow D_7$	0
Totals 29,500 units	\$259,500

34.

Allocation, Route		Cost
55 units, Los Angeles	→ Cleveland	$ 1,100
100 units, Los Angeles	→ Reno	2,000
45 units, Los Angeles	→ Tampa	1,350
75 units, Dallas	→ New York	3,000
15 units, San Francisco	→ New York	750
20 units, San Francisco	→ Cleveland	500
70 units, San Francisco	→ Slack	0
150 units, Denver	→ Tampa	5,250
Totals 530 units		$13,950

36.

Allocation, Route		Cost	
5(100,000 bushels), Moscow	→ Corn	150	(100 rubles)
20(100,000 bushels), Moscow	→ Wheat	500	(100 rubles)
75(100,000 bushels), Minsk	→ Barley	1,875	(100 rubles)
0(100,000 bushels), Minsk	→ Wheat	0	(100 rubles)
100(100,000 bushels), Kiev	→ Wheat	2,000	(100 rubles)
35(100,000 bushels), Volgograd	→ Corn	1,750	(100 rubles)
5(100,000 bushels), Volgograd	→ Wheat	250	(100 rubles)
40(100,000 bushels), Dummy	→ Barley	3,200	(100 rubles)
Totals 280(100,000 bushels)		9,725	(100 rubles)

38.

Allocation, Route		Cost
40 truckloads, North Wilkesboro	→ Raleigh	$ 8,000
0 truckloads, North Wilkesboro	→ Asheville	0
15 truckloads, Boone	→ Charlotte	3,000
15 truckloads, Boone	→ Burlington	5,250
20 truckloads, Hendersonville	→ Burlington	7,000
5 truckloads, Hendersonville	→ Asheville	1,750
30 truckloads, Dummy	→ Asheville	21,000
Totals 125 truckloads		$46,000

Note: All dummy routes prices at $700/truckload.

40.

	Allocation, Route		Cost
	50 cartons, Plant 1	→ Distribution Center 1	$ 3,750
	75 cartons, Plant 2	→ Department Store 1	9,000
	50 cartons, Plant 2	→ Department Store 3	6,500
(Transshipment)	35 cartons, Plant 3	→ Plant 2	1,575
(Transshipment)	50 cartons, Distribution Center 1	→ Department Store 2	5,000
			$25,825

Note: Net shipments from Plant 2 = −35 + 75 + 50 = +90 cartons

42.

	Allocation, Route		Cost
	25 truckloads, Boise	→ Sacramento	$ 1,500
	75 truckloads, Denver	→ Albuquerque	3,375
	5 truckloads, Omaha	→ Albuquerque	300
	45 truckloads, Omaha	→ Tampa	5,625
(Transshipment)	50 truckloads, Albuquerque	→ Houston	3,000
			$13,800

Note: Net shipments to Albuquerque = +75 + 5 − 50 = 30 truckloads

44.

Assignment		Time
Sue	→ Job 6	5 hours
Alice	→ Job 3	3 hours
Elton	→ Job 1	5 hours
Janet	→ Job 4	4 hours
Bill	→ Job 5	3 hours
Yvonne	→ Job 2	2 hours
		22 hours

46.

Assignment	Revenue, ($, hundreds)
Customer 1 → Car 6	16
Customer 2 → Car 4	17
Customer 3 → Car 2	15
Customer 4 → Car 5	14
Customer 5 → Car 3	15
Dummy → Car 1	0
	77

48.

Assignment	Time, hours
Mechanic 1 → Job 4	4
Mechanic 2 → Job 6	4
Mechanic 3 → Job 5	4
Mechanic 4 → Job 3	1
Mechanic 5 → Job 7	7
Mechanic 6 → Job 2	1
Mechanic 7 → Job 1	3
	24 hours

CHAPTER 8 • NETWORK MODELS

2.

Flow Assignments

4 to path 1→2→4→7
4 to path 1→3→6→7
4 to path 1→3→5→7
1 to path 1→2→4→5→7
1 to path 1→2→5→7
14 = Maximum flow

4.   **Flow Assignments**

     2 to path $1 \rightarrow 2 \rightarrow 4 \rightarrow 7 \rightarrow 9$
     2 to path $1 \rightarrow 3 \rightarrow 6 \rightarrow 8 \rightarrow 9$
     2 to path $1 \rightarrow 3 \rightarrow 8 \rightarrow 9$
     2 to path $1 \rightarrow 5 \rightarrow 9$
     2 to path $1 \rightarrow 2 \rightarrow 5 \rightarrow 9$
     <u>2</u> to path $1 \rightarrow 2 \rightarrow 4 \rightarrow 7 \rightarrow 5 \rightarrow 9$

     12 = Maximum flow

6.   **Flow Assignments**

     14 to path *Oilfield* $\rightarrow A \rightarrow D \rightarrow G \rightarrow$ *Refinery*
     15 to path *Oilfield* $\rightarrow B \rightarrow E \rightarrow G \rightarrow$ *Refinery*
     18 to path *Oilfield* $\rightarrow C \rightarrow F \rightarrow H \rightarrow$ *Refinery*
     5 to path *Oilfield* $\rightarrow A \rightarrow B \rightarrow E \rightarrow G \rightarrow H \rightarrow$ *Refinery*
     2 to path *Oilfield* $\rightarrow C \rightarrow B \rightarrow D \rightarrow E \rightarrow G \rightarrow H \rightarrow$ *Refinery*
     <u>1</u> to path *Oilfield* $\rightarrow A \rightarrow D \rightarrow E \rightarrow G \rightarrow$ *Refinery*

     55 = Maximum flow

Note: There is an alternative optimal solution to this problem.

8.   **Flow Assignments**

     5 to path *Sydney* $\rightarrow 1 \rightarrow$ *Beargrass Zoo*
     3 to path *Sydney* $\rightarrow 3 \rightarrow$ *Beargrass Zoo*
     1 to path *Sydney* $\rightarrow 1 \rightarrow 3 \rightarrow$ *Beargrass Zoo*
     <u>1</u> to path *Sydney* $\rightarrow 2 \rightarrow$ *Beargrass Zoo*

     10 = Maximum flow

10.   Shortest Route: $O \rightarrow C \rightarrow B \rightarrow A \rightarrow E \rightarrow T$
           Length = 8 days

12.   Shortest Route: $O \rightarrow C \rightarrow F \rightarrow G \rightarrow T$
     Distance = 19 (hundred miles)

14.   Shortest Route: Center 1 $\rightarrow$ Center 5 $\rightarrow$ Center 7 $\rightarrow$ Center 9 $\rightarrow$ Center 10
           Distance = 10.2 miles
     or

     Shortest Route: Center 1 $\rightarrow$ Center 4 $\rightarrow$ Center 5 $\rightarrow$ Center 7 $\rightarrow$ Center 9 $\rightarrow$ Center 10
           Distance = 10.2 miles

16.   Shortest Route: Entrance (1) $\rightarrow 4 \rightarrow 6 \rightarrow 8 \rightarrow$ Exit (11)
           Distance = 2.4 miles

18.   Resurface now, year 0, and at the end of year 2 or 3, for a minimum total cost of $55,000.

20.   Minimum spanning tree = 12 days (time).

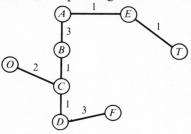

22. Minimum spanning tree = 4500 miles (length).

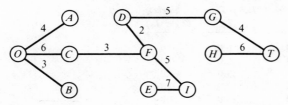

24. Minimum spanning tree = 33 miles (length).

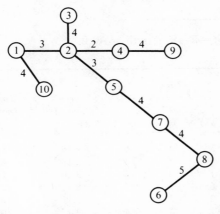

26. Minimum spanning tree = 993 miles (length).

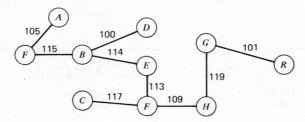

28.

Event Number	Earliest Time, T_E	Latest Time, T_L	Slack $(T_L - T_E)$
1	0.0	0.0	0.0
2	5.0	7.0	2.0
3	2.0	2.0	0.0
4	4.0	6.0	2.0
5	6.0	9.0	3.0
6	8.0	8.0	0.0
7	9.0	11.0	2.0
8	11.0	11.0	0.0
9	10.0	12.0	2.0
10	16.0	16.0	0.0

Critical path 1→3→6→8→10; length = 16.0.

30.

Event Number	Earliest Time, T_E	Latest Time, T_L	Slack $(T_L - T_E)$
1	0.0	0.0	0.0
2	6.0	6.0	0.0
3	13.0	13.0	0.0
4	19.0	19.0	0.0
5	16.0	18.0	2.0
6	25.0	25.0	0.0
7	32.0	32.0	0.0
8	40.0	40.0	0.0

Critical path: 1→2→3→4→6→7→8; length = 40.0.

32. (a)

Activities		Time Estimates			Expected Elapsed Time, t_e	Standard Deviation $\sigma_{t,e}$	Variance $\sigma_{t,e}^2$
Predecessor Event	Successor Event	a	m	b			
1	2	3	4	6	4.16	0.5	0.25
1	3	1	2	4	2.17	0.5	0.25
2	3	1	3	5	3.00	0.67	0.45
2	4	6	8	12	8.33	1.0	1.00
3	4	2	3	5	3.17	0.5	0.25
3	5	1	2	4	2.17	0.5	0.25
4	6	4	5	9	5.50	0.83	0.69
5	6	4	6	11	6.50	1.17	1.37

(b)

Event Number	Earliest Time, T_E Expected Value	Variance	Latest Time, T_L Expected Value	Variance	Slack $(T_L - T_E)$
1	0	0	0	1.94	0
2	4.16	0.25	4.16	1.69	0
3	7.16	0.70	9.33	1.19	2.17
4	12.50	1.25	12.50	0.69	0
5	9.33	0.95	11.50	1.37	2.17
6	18.0	1.94	18.0	0	0

Critical path: 1→2→4→6; length = 18.0 weeks

(c) Probability (meeting scheduled completion time of 16 weeks)

$$= P\left(Z \geq \frac{18.0 - 16.0}{\sqrt{1.94}}\right)$$

$$= P\left(Z \geq \frac{2.0}{1.393}\right) = P(Z \geq 1.436)$$

$$= 0.0749$$

34. (a) Critical path: $A{\to}C{\to}D{\to}H{\to}I$; length $= 30$ days
     Total project completion cost $= \$2{,}705$ (Regular basis)

    (b)

Activity	Days Shortened by Crash Program	Incremental Cost per Day
$A \to C$	2	\$150
$C \to D$	2	\$175
$D \to H$	3	\$200
$H \to I$	3	\$200

1. Crash activities $A{\to}C$ by two days and activity $C{\to}D$ by two days at an added cost of $2(\$150) + 2(\$175) = \$650$. This would reduce the total project completion time along path $A{\to}C{\to}D{\to}H{\to}I$ to the desired 26 days. Note also, that path $A{\to}C{\to}D{\to}G{\to}I$ (originally 28 days in length) would be reduced to $28 - 2 - 2 = 24$ days (i.e., below the desired completion time) by the crashing of activity $A{\to}C$ by two days, and the crashing of activity $C{\to}D$ by two days.

2. Path $A{\to}B{\to}E{\to}H{\to}I$ (29 days) is now the critical path, and is above the desired 26 days.

Activity	Days Shortened by Crash Program	Incremental Cost per Day
$A \to B$	1	\$100
$B \to E$	2	\$125
$E \to H$	2	\$175
$H \to I$	3	\$200

Thus, crash activity $A{\to}B$ by one day and activity $B{\to}E$ by two days at an added cost of $1(\$100) + 2(\$125) = \$350$. This would reduce the total project completion time along path $A{\to}B{\to}E{\to}H{\to}I$ to the desired 26 days. Note also, that path $A{\to}B{\to}D{\to}H{\to}I$ (originally 27 days in length) would be reduced to $27 - 1 = 26$ days (i.e., the desired completion time) by the crashing of activity $A{\to}B$ by one day.

3. Path $A{\to}C{\to}E{\to}H{\to}I$ (which has been crashed to 27 days) is now the critical path, and is above the desired 26 days.

Activity	Days Shortened by Crash Program	Incremental Cost per Day
$A \to C$	2	\$150 (already crashed)
$C \to E$	1	\$225
$E \to H$	2	\$175
$H \to I$	3	\$200

Thus, crash activity $C \rightarrow E$ by one day at an added cost of \$225. This would reduce the total project completion time along path $A \rightarrow C \rightarrow E \rightarrow H \rightarrow I$ to $27 - 1 = 26$ days (i.e., the desired completion time).

Path	Activity Shortened	Amount	Added Cost
$A \rightarrow C \rightarrow D \rightarrow H \rightarrow I$	$A \rightarrow C$	2 days	\$ 300
	$C \rightarrow D$	2 days	350
$A \rightarrow C \rightarrow D \rightarrow G \rightarrow I$	$A \rightarrow C$	2 days	—
$A \rightarrow B \rightarrow E \rightarrow H \rightarrow I$	$A \rightarrow B$	1 day	100
	$B \rightarrow E$	2 days	250
$A \rightarrow B \rightarrow D \rightarrow H \rightarrow I$	$A \rightarrow B$	1 day	—
$A \rightarrow C \rightarrow E \rightarrow H \rightarrow I$	$C \rightarrow E$	1 day	225
			\$1,225

Total project completion cost $= \$2,705 + \$1,225 = \$2,930$

CHAPTER 9 • INTEGER PROGRAMMING

2. $x_1 = 1, x_2 = 1$ Maximum $Z = 3.7$

4. Let: x_{ij} – the number of a particular type of auditing personnel $j(j = 1,2,3)$; assigned to a particular job $i(i = 1,2,3)$.

Minimize (total audit cost) $Z = \$2500(x_{11} + x_{21} + x_{31}) + \$1500(x_{12} + x_{22} + x_{32}) +$
$\$ 500(x_{13} + x_{23} + x_{33})$

subject to: $5.0x_{11} + 3.0x_{12} + 1.0x_{13} \geq 20.0$ (Hours – Job 1)
$4.0x_{21} + 2.5x_{22} + 0.5x_{23} \geq 15.0$ (Hours – Job 2)
$4.5x_{31} + 2.0x_{32} + 1.5x_{33} \geq 18.0$ (Hours – Job 3)

$x_{11} + \quad x_{21} + \quad x_{31} \leq 15$ (Senior auditors available)
$x_{12} + \quad x_{22} + \quad x_{32} \leq 20$ (Junior auditors available)
$x_{13} + \quad x_{23} + \quad x_{33} \leq 25$ (Clerks available)

$x_{ij} \leq 3$, all i and j

with: $x_{ij} \geq 0$, all i and j
x_{ij} integer, all i and j

Optimal solution: $x_{11} = 3 \qquad x_{21} = 2 \qquad x_{31} = 3$
$x_{12} = 1 \qquad x_{22} = 3 \qquad x_{32} = 0$ Minimum $Z = \$28,500$
$x_{13} = 2 \qquad x_{23} = 0 \qquad x_{33} = 3$

6. Let: x_{ij} – number of games scheduled on court $i(i = 1,2)$ of game $j(j = 1,2,3)$.

Maximize (total hours scheduled) $Z = 1.0x_{11} + 0.75x_{12} + 1.25x_{21} + 1.33x_{22}$

subject to: $1.0x_{11} + 0.75x_{12} \leq 12$ hours (Availability, indoors)
$1.25x_{21} + 1.33x_{22} \leq 14$ hours (Availability, outdoors)

$x_{11} \geq 2.0$ games per day
$x_{12} \geq 3.0$ games per day
$x_{21} \geq 2.0$ games per day
$x_{22} \geq 3.0$ games per day
$x_{12} - 2.0x_{11} \geq 0 \Big\}$ at least twice as many racquetball games
$x_{22} - 2.0x_{21} \geq 0 \Big\}$ as handball games

with: x_{ij} integer, all i and j

Optimal solution: $x_{11} = 2 \quad x_{21} = 3$ Maximum $Z = 24.81$ hours
$\qquad\qquad\qquad\quad x_{12} = 13 \quad x_{22} = 7$

8. $x_1 = 0, x_2 = 2, x_3 = 2$ Maximum $Z = 14$

10.   Let: x_j – number of units of ingredient $j (j = 1,2,3)$ used.

Minimize (cost) $Z = \$1.10x_1 + \$1.25x_2 + \$1.00x_3$

subject to: $30x_1 + 35x_2 + 17x_3 \geq 100$ (Reg., Vitamin A)
$\qquad\qquad\quad 20x_1 + 40x_2 + 11x_3 \geq 200$ (Reg., Vitamin B)
$\qquad\qquad\quad 17x_1 + 31x_2 + 9x_3 \geq 160$ (Reg., Vitamin C)
$\qquad\qquad\quadx_1 \qquad\qquad\qquad\geq 1$
$\qquad\qquad\qquad\qquad x_2 \qquad\qquad\geq 1$
$\qquad\qquad\qquad\qquad\qquad\quad x_3 \geq 1$

with: x_1, x_3 integers

Optimal solution: $x_1 = 1, x_2 = 4.323, x_3 = 1$
$\qquad\qquad\qquad\quad$ Minimum $Z = \$7.50$

12.   Optimal routing: $A \to D \to B \to C \to E \to A$ Cost $= 610$

14.   **Optimum Sequence**   **Changeover Time**

Red to yellow	14 hours
Yellow to green	8 hours
Green to blue	12 hours
Blue to red	15 hours
	49 hours

16.

Allocation, Route	**Cost**
25 units, $O_1 \to D_1$	$ 50
25 units, $O_1 \to D_3$	50
10 units, $O_2 \to D_3$	30
15 units, $O_2 \to D_4$	30
45 units, $O_2 \to D_5$	225
30 units, $O_3 \to D_2$	90
30 units, $O_3 \to D_6$	60
30 units, $O_3 \to D_7$	0
20 units, $O_4 \to D_2$	40
15 units, $O_4 \to D_5$	75
Total 275 units	$650

18. $x_1 = 2, x_2 = 1$ Maximum $Z = 10$

20. $x_1 = 0, x_2 = 1, x_3 = 1, x_4 = 1$ Maximum $Z = 16$

22. Let $x_{ij} = 0, 1$ — the assignment of applicant i to machine j.

Maximize (overall applicants' ability) Z
$$= 30x_{11} + 60x_{12} + 60x_{21} + 50x_{22} + 50x_{31} + 50x_{32} + 55x_{41} + 45x_{42} + 40x_{51} + 35x_{52}$$
$$+ 25x_{61} + 70x_{62}$$

subject to:
$$x_{11} + x_{12} \le 1$$
$$x_{21} + x_{22} \le 1$$
$$x_{31} + x_{32} \le 1 \quad \text{(Each applicant can be assigned}$$
$$x_{41} + x_{42} \le 1 \quad \text{to only one machine type.)}$$
$$x_{51} + x_{52} \le 1$$
$$x_{61} + x_{62} \le 1$$

$$x_{11} + x_{21} + x_{31} + x_{41} + x_{51} + x_{61} \le 3 \quad \text{(No more than three appli-}$$
$$x_{12} + x_{22} + x_{32} + x_{42} + x_{52} + x_{62} \le 3 \quad \begin{array}{l}\text{cants can be assigned to} \\ \text{any one machine type.)}\end{array}$$

$$x_{21} + x_{31} + x_{61} \ge 1 \quad \text{(At least one female applicant must be}$$
$$x_{22} + x_{32} + x_{62} \ge 1 \quad \text{assigned to each machine type.)}$$

with: $x_{ij} = 0, 1$ and integer, for all i and j.

Optimal solution:
$x_{11} = 0$	$x_{12} = 1$
$x_{21} = 1$	$x_{22} = 0$
$x_{31} = 0$	$x_{32} = 1$
$x_{41} = 1$	$x_{42} = 0$
$x_{51} = 1$	$x_{52} = 0$
$x_{61} = 0$	$x_{62} = 1$

Maximum $Z = 335$

24. Let: $x_{ij} = 0, 1$ for $i = 1, 2, \ldots, 5; j = 1, 2, \ldots, 4$ represent the construction of plant i in year j.

Minimize (total construction cost) $= \$100,000x_{11} + \$125,000x_{12} + \$110,000x_{13}$
$$+ \$130,000x_{14}$$
$$+ \$150,000x_{21} + \$125,000x_{22} + \$175,000x_{23}$$
$$+ \$140,000x_{24}$$
$$+ \$125,000x_{31} + \$110,000x_{32} + \$100,000x_{33}$$
$$+ \$170,000x_{34}$$
$$+ \$175,000x_{41} + \$200,000x_{42} + \$220,000x_{43}$$
$$+ \$250,000x_{44}$$
$$+ \$140,000x_{51} + \$105,000x_{52} + \$155,000x_{53}$$
$$+ \$135,000x_{54}$$

subject to:
$$x_{13} = 0$$
$$x_{14} = 0 \quad \text{(Plant } A \text{ must be constructed in year 1 or 2.)}$$

$$x_{23} = 0$$
$$x_{24} = 0 \quad \text{(Plant } B \text{ must be constructed in year 1 or 2.)}$$

$$\$100,000x_{11} + \$125,000x_{12} + \$110,000x_{13} + \$130,000x_{14} + \$150,000x_{21}$$
$$+ \$125,000x_{22}$$
$$+ \$175,000x_{23} + \$140,000x_{24} + \$125,000x_{31} + \$110,000x_{32}$$
$$+ \$100,000x_{33}$$
$$+ \$170,000x_{34} + \$175,000x_{41} + \$200,000x_{42} + \$220,000x_{43}$$
$$+ \$250,000x_{44}$$

$$+ \$140{,}000x_{51} + \$105{,}000x_{52} + \$155{,}000x_{53} + \$135{,}000x_{54}$$
$$\leq \$500{,}000 \text{ (total company spending limit)}$$

$$
\begin{array}{lll}
x_{41} = x_{51} & \text{or} & x_{41} - x_{51} = 0 \\
x_{42} = x_{52} & \text{or} & x_{42} - x_{52} = 0 \quad \text{(Plants } D \text{ and } E \text{ must be built in the} \\
x_{43} = x_{53} & \text{or} & x_{43} - x_{53} = 0 \quad \quad \text{same year.)} \\
x_{44} = x_{54} & \text{or} & x_{44} - x_{54} = 0
\end{array}
$$

with: $x_{ij} = 0$, 1 and integer, for all i and j

Optimal solution:

$$
\begin{array}{llll}
x_{11} = 0 & x_{12} = 0 & x_{13} = 0 & x_{14} = 0 \\
x_{21} = 0 & x_{22} = 0 & x_{23} = 0 & x_{24} = 0 \\
x_{31} = 1 & x_{32} = 0 & x_{33} = 0 & x_{34} = 0 \\
x_{41} = 0 & x_{42} = 0 & x_{43} = 1 & x_{44} = 0 \\
x_{51} = 0 & x_{52} = 0 & x_{53} = 1 & x_{54} = 0
\end{array}
$$

(Minimum $Z = \$500{,}000$)

26.   Let: $x_j =$ the number of type j Christmas cakes to be baked; $j = 1, \ldots, 3$

$$
\begin{array}{l}
j = 1 - \text{``Fudge/Walnut''} \\
j = 2 - \text{``Angel Food''} \\
j = 3 - \text{``Cherry Berry''}
\end{array}
$$

Let: $y_1 = \begin{cases} 1 \text{ if honey is substituted for sugar} \\ 0, \text{ otherwise} \end{cases}$

Let: $y_2 = \begin{cases} 1 \text{ if margarine is substituted for butter} \\ 0, \text{ otherwise} \end{cases}$

Maximize (profit) $Z = 5.25x_1 + 5.89x_2 + 5.75x_3$

subject to: $3.00x_1 + 3.75x_2 + 2.75x_3 \leq 500$ (Flour supply constraint)

$$
\left.
\begin{array}{l}
1.00x_1 + 1.25x_2 + 1.75x_3 \leq 425 + My_1 \\
0.75x_1 + 1.50x_2 + 1.375x_3 \leq 424 + M(1 - y_1)
\end{array}
\right\}
\begin{array}{l}
\text{either sugar} \\
\text{or honey sup-} \\
\text{ply constraint}
\end{array}
$$

$$
\left.
\begin{array}{l}
0.75x_1 + 0.50x_2 + 0.875x_3 \leq 300 + My_2 \\
0.625x_1 + 0.75x_2 + 0.75x_3 \leq 299 + M(1 - y_2)
\end{array}
\right\}
\begin{array}{l}
\text{either butter} \\
\text{or marg. sup-} \\
\text{ply constraint}
\end{array}
$$

with $x_j \geq 0, j = 1, \ldots, 3; y_1, y_2 = 0$ or 1; M is a very large constant.

28.   Let: $x_j = \begin{cases} 1 \text{ if investment } j \text{ is selected} \\ 0, \text{ otherwise} \end{cases}; j = 1, \ldots, 10$

Maximize $Z = 4.0x_1 + 8.1x_2 + 9.3x_3 + 4.7x_4 + 5.0x_5 + 7.0x_6$
$$+ 7.5x_7 + 3.0x_8 + 5.5x_9 + 6.3x_{10}$$

subject to: $125x_1 + 235x_2 + 320x_3 + 155x_4 + 500x_5 + 450x_6$
$$+ 100x_7 + 85x_8 + 175x_9 + 425x_{10} \leq 1150 \quad \text{(Budget constraint)}$$
$$x_3 \leq x_5 \quad \text{or} \quad x_3 - x_5 \leq 0 \quad \text{(Contingency constraint)}$$
$$x_7 + x_8 + x_9 + x_{10} \leq 2 \quad \text{(Diversification constraint)}$$

with $x_j = 0$ or 1; $j = 1, \ldots, 10$

30.   Let: $x_{ij} =$ the amount to be shipped from warehouse i to customer j; $i = 1, \ldots,$
        $5; j = 1, \ldots, 5.$

$$y_i = \begin{cases} 1 \text{ if warehouse } i \text{ is leased} \\ 0, \text{ otherwise} \end{cases}; i = 1, \ldots, 5$$

General notation:

Minimize $Z = \sum_{i=1}^{5} \sum_{j=1}^{5} (o_i + t_{ij})x_{ij} + \sum_{i=1}^{5} l_i y_i$

subject to: $\sum_{i=1}^{5} x_{ij} = d_j; j = 1, \ldots, 5$ (Demand requirement constraints)

$\left. \sum_{j=1}^{5} x_{ij} - y_i \left(\sum_{j=1}^{5} d_j \right) \le 0; i = 1, \ldots, 5 \right\}$ Constraints that ensure that $y_i = 1$ if $\sum_{j=1}^{5} x_{ij} > 0$

with $x_{ij} \ge 0; i = 1, \ldots, 5; j = 1, \ldots, 5; y_i = 0$ or $1, i = 1, \ldots, 5.$

Rewritten:

Minimize $Z = (.50 + .75)x_{11} + (.50 + .71)x_{12} + (.50 + .80)x_{13}$
$+ (.50 + .50)x_{14} + (.50 + .76)x_{15} + (.55 + .82)x_{21}$
$+ (.55 + .89)x_{22} + (.55 + .75)x_{23} + (.55 + .65)x_{24}$
$+ (.55 + .75)x_{25} + (.45 + .77)x_{31} + (.45 + .65)x_{32}$
$+ (.45 + .85)x_{33} + (.45 + .45)x_{34} + (.45 + .65)x_{35}$
$+ (.57 + .71)x_{41} + (.57 + .65)x_{42} + (.57 + .95)x_{43}$
$+ (.57 + .80)x_{44} + (.57 + .59)x_{45} + (.48 + .68)x_{51}$
$+ (.48 + .55)x_{52} + (.48 + .99)x_{53} + (.48 + .82)x_{54}$
$+ (.48 + .89)x_{55} + 500y_1 + 515y_2 + 530y_3 + 498y_4 + 505y_5$

subject to: $\sum_{i=1}^{5} x_{i1} = 100$ (Demand requirement constraint − customer 1)

$\sum_{i=1}^{5} x_{i2} = 200$ (Demand requirement constraint − customer 2)

$\sum_{i=1}^{5} x_{i3} = 350$ (Demand requirement constraint − customer 3)

$\sum_{i=1}^{5} x_{i4} = 400$ (Demand requirement constraint − customer 4)

$\sum_{i=1}^{5} x_{i5} = 175$ (Demand requirement constraint − customer 5)

$\sum_{j=1}^{5} x_{1j} - 1225y_1 \le 0$ (Constraint that ensures $y_1 = 1$ if $\sum_{j=1}^{5} x_{1j} > 0$)

$\sum_{j=1}^{5} x_{2j} - 1225y_2 \le 0$ (Constraint that ensures $y_2 = 1$ if $\sum_{j=1}^{5} x_{2j} > 0$)

$\sum_{j=1}^{5} x_{3j} + 1225y_3 \le 0$ (Constraint that ensures $y_3 = 1$ if $\sum_{j=1}^{5} x_{3j} > 0$)

$\sum_{j=1}^{5} x_{4j} - 1225y_4 \le 0$ (Constraint that ensures $y_4 = 1$ if $\sum_{j=1}^{5} x_{4j} > 0$)

$$\sum_{j=1}^{5} x_{5j} - 1225y_5 \leq 0 \text{ (Constraint that ensures } y_5 = 1 \text{ if } \sum_{j=1}^{5} x_{5j} > 0)$$

with $\quad x_{ij} \geq 0; i = 1, \ldots, 5; j = 1, \ldots, 5; y_i = 0 \text{ or } 1, i = 1, \ldots, 5.$

32. Let: $\quad y_j = \begin{cases} 1 \text{ if site } j \text{ is selected} \\ 0, \text{ if otherwise} \end{cases}; j = 1, \ldots, 8$

    Let: $\quad x_{ij} = \begin{cases} 1 \text{ if district } i \text{ is assigned to site } j \\ 0, \text{ otherwise} \end{cases}; \begin{array}{l} i = 1, \ldots, 5 \\ j = 1, \ldots, 8 \end{array}$

General notation:

Minimize (total distance) $Z = \sum_{i=1}^{5} \sum_{j=1}^{8} d_{ij} x_{ij}$

subject to: $\quad \sum_{j=1}^{8} x_{ij} = 1; i = 1, \ldots, 5 \quad$ (Constraint ensures that district i is assigned exactly one fire station)

$\sum_{i=1}^{5} x_{ij} \leq 5y_j; j = 1, \ldots, 8 \quad$ (Constraint ensures that districts are assigned to a site only if site is selected)

$n_j - \sum_{i=1}^{5} p_i x_{ij} = 0; j = 1, \ldots, 8 \quad$ (Constraint is used to tally the number of people assigned to site j if site j is selected)

$n_j \leq 40000y_j; j = 1, \ldots, 8 \quad$ (Constraint ensures the number of people assigned to site j is less than 40000 if j is selected and 0 if j is not selected)

$\sum_{j=1}^{8} c_j(n_j)y_j \leq B \quad$ (Budget constraint)

with $\quad x_{ij} = 0 \text{ or } 1, i = 1, \ldots, 5; j = 1, \ldots, 8; y_j = 0 \text{ or } 1, j = 1, \ldots, 8$

Rewritten:

Minimize $Z = \quad (2x_{11} + 3x_{12} + 4x_{13} + 5x_{14} + 7x_{15} + 7x_{16} + 8x_{17} + 11x_{18})$

$+ (7x_{21} + 2x_{22} + 1x_{23} + 2x_{24} + 4x_{25} + 7x_{26} + 7x_{27} + 8x_{28})$

$+ (6x_{31} + 4x_{32} + 7x_{33} + 7x_{34} + 1x_{35} + 1x_{36} + 3x_{37} + 5x_{38})$

$+ (10x_{41} + 6x_{42} + 9x_{43} + 5x_{44} + 3x_{45} + 7x_{46} + 2x_{47} + 2x_{48})$

$+ (11x_{51} + 9x_{52} + 11x_{53} + 10x_{54} + 6x_{55} + 5x_{56} + 2x_{57} + 4x_{58})$

$$\text{subject to:} \quad \sum_{j=1}^{8} x_{ij} = 1$$

$$\sum_{j=1}^{8} x_{2j} = 1$$

$$\sum_{j=1}^{8} x_{3j} = 1$$

$$\sum_{j=1}^{8} x_{4j} = 1$$

$$\sum_{j=1}^{8} x_{5j} = 1$$

$$\sum_{i=1}^{5} x_{i1} \le 5y_1$$

$$\sum_{i=1}^{5} x_{i2} \le 5y_2$$

$$\sum_{i=1}^{5} x_{i3} \le 5y_3$$

$$\sum_{i=1}^{5} x_{i4} \le 5y_4$$

$$\sum_{i=1}^{5} x_{i5} \le 5y_5$$

$$\sum_{i=1}^{5} x_{i6} \le 5y_6$$

$$\sum_{i=1}^{5} x_{i7} \le 5y_7$$

$$\sum_{i=1}^{5} x_{i8} \le 5y_8$$

$$n_1 - (5000x_{11} + 2000x_{21} + 2500x_{31} + 4500x_{41} + 3000x_{51}) = 0$$
$$\vdots$$
$$n_8 - (5000x_{18} + 2000x_{28} + 2500x_{38} + 4500x_{48} + 3000x_{58}) = 0$$
$$\vdots$$
$$n_1 \le 40000y_1$$
$$\vdots$$
$$n_8 \le 40000y_8$$

$$50000y_1 + 40n_1 + 55000y_2 + 50n_2 + 60000y_3 + 35n_3$$
$$+ 45000y_4 + 45n_4 + 58000y_5 + 38n_5 + 48000y_6 + 35n_6$$
$$+ 50000y_7 + 45n_7 + 52000y_8 + 40n_8 \leq 1,000,000.$$

with $x_{ij} = 0$ or 1, $i = 1, \ldots, 5$; $j = 1, \ldots, 8$; $y_j = 0$ or 1, $j = 1, \ldots, 8$

34.   Let: $x_j = \begin{cases} 1 \text{ if employee } j \text{ is selected for the team} \\ 0, \text{ otherwise} \end{cases}$; $j = 1, \ldots, 7$

$y = \begin{cases} 1 \text{ if Joe Score is selected for the team} \\ 0, \text{ otherwise} \end{cases}$

Maximize (total height) $Z = 7x_1 + 5x_2 + 7x_3 + 1x_4 + 3x_5 + 5x_6 + 4x_7$

subject to: $x_1 + x_2 + x_3 + x_4 + x_5 + x_6 + x_7 = 5$ (Constraint to ensure a five-man team)

$x_3 + x_4 \geq 1$ (Constraint to ensure at least one forward starts)
$x_1 + x_2 \geq 1$ (Constraint to ensure at least one center starts)
$x_1 + x_2 \leq 2$ (Constraint to ensure no more than two centers start)
$x_5 + x_6 + x_7 \geq 1$ (Constraint to ensure at least one guard starts)

$\left.\begin{array}{l} x_3 + 100y \leq 0 \\ x_7 - 100(1 - y) \leq 0 \end{array}\right\}$ Constraints that ensure either Joe Score or Nick Toss is held in reserve.

with $x_j = 0$ or 1, $j = 1, \ldots, 7$; $y = 0$ or 1.

CHAPTER 10 • NONLINEAR PROGRAMMING

2. (a) Global maximum at -4 and $+4$ (c) Global maximum at $+5$
        Global minimum at 0 Global minimum at -5

  (b) Global maximum at -2 (d) Global maximum at -3
        Global minimum at $+2$ Global minimum at $+3$

4. See the following graph.

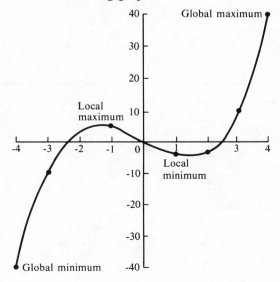

6. Local maximum at $x_1 = 2$, $x_2 = 0$

8. **Kuhn-Tucker conditions:**

(1a) $4 - \lambda_1(2x_1 - 4) \leq 0$
(1b) $3 - \lambda_1(2x_2 - 2) \leq 0$
(2a) $x_1[4 - \lambda_1(2x_1 - 4)] = 0$
(2b) $x_2[3 - \lambda_1(2x_2 - 2)] = 0$
(3) $x_1^2 - 4x_1 + x_2^2 - 2x_2 - 3 \leq 0$
(4) $\lambda_1(x_1^2 - 4x_1 + x_2^2 - 2x_2 - 3) = 0$
(5) $x_1 \geq 0$, $x_2 \geq 0$
(6) $\lambda_1 \geq 0$

10. Optimal Product Mix: $x_1 = 80$, $x_2 = 0$, Maximum profits = \$773

12. $x_1 = 4.955$, $x_2 = 2.045$, $\lambda_1 = 8.405$, Minimum $Z = 21.63$

14. $x_1 = 0.75$, $x_2 = 1.25$, Maximum $Z = 3.13$

16. $x_1 = 11.111$, $x_2 = 27.778$, Maximum $Z = 211.118$

CHAPTER 11 ● DYNAMIC PROGRAMMING

2. Shortest Route: $O \rightarrow A \rightarrow B \rightarrow D \rightarrow T$ Length = 13

4. Assign first player to AA team
   Assign second player to AAA team
   Assign third player to A team

   Probability (all four teams will win pennant) = 0.1706

6.

Course	Assigned Study Hours	Expected Grade	Grade Points
Accounting	20	A	5
Finance	10	B	4
Management Science	10	C	3
Business policy	5	B	4
Management	5	C	3
			19 points

8.

Month	Production
1	6
2	0
3	4
4	6
Total	16

Total cost = \$35
Total cost per month = \$8.75

10.

Component	Number of Power Cells Assigned	Cost	Probability of Functioning Properly
1	3	$ 24,000	0.92
2	1	40,000	0.94
3	4	36,000	0.96
		$100,000	

Maximum overall reliability $= 0.92 \times 0.94 \times 0.96 = 0.8302$

12. Investment B should be used each year.
Maximum expected profit $= \$2,200$
Total accumulation $= \$5,000 + \$2,200 = \$7,200$

14.

School District	Allocation	Test Score
1	$1 million	50
2	$2 million	80
3	$2 million	75
	$5 million	205

CHAPTER 12 • INVENTORY MODELS

2. $Q^* = 2,449$ candles $t^* = 1.2245$ months

4. $Q^* = 42,425$ units $X^* = 7,071$ units $t^* = 5.66$ $Q^* - S^* = 35,355$ units

6. $Q^* = 117.3$ pairs (Use 117) $S^* = 85$ pairs $t^* = 0.4692$ months

8. $Q^* = 34,641$ cans

10. Lowest cost economic order quantity $= 250$ units
Lowest cost $= \$49,184$

12. Lowest cost economic order quantity $= 15,000$ gals. per month
Lowest cost (monthly) $= \$2038$

14. $Q_2 = 72$ cases $Q' = 384$ cases   Savings $= \$117.67$

16. $Q^* = 11.54$ units (use 12) $F(R^*) = 0.933$
$R^* = 19.44$ units (use 20)

Reordering cost	$ 83.33
Inv. holding cost (normal inventory)	90.00
Inv. holding cost (safety stock)	75.00
Total	$248.33

18. (a) $Q^* = 70.71$ cases (use 71)
$R^* = 40$ cases

(b) $F(R^*) = 0.95$

(c) Safety stock $= 5$ cases
Annual safety stock holding cost $= \$50$ per year

(d) $R^* = 22.625$ cases (use 23)
$SS = 2.625$ cases (use 3)

(e) Annual safety stock holding cost = $30 per year

20. Optimum economic order quantity = 500 units
Expected profit ($Q^* = 500$) = $110

22. $Q^* = 23,350$ cardboard sheets

CHAPTER 13 ● WAITING LINE MODELS

2. $L = 3$ orders, $Lq = 2.25$ orders, $W = 0.10$ hours, $Wq = 0.075$ hours

4. Alternative 1 should be chosen, since the total annual cost for this alternative will be approximately $60,500 compared to a total annual cost of $112,500 for alternative 2.

6. Eleven plumbers necessary.

8. (a) $\theta = 12$ customers per minute, $s = 1$

	$\lambda = 5\ cust/min$	$\lambda = 10\ cust/min$	$\lambda = 11.5\ cust/min$
L	0.714 cust.	5 cust.	23 cust.
Lq	0.298 cust.	4.17 cust.	22.04 cust.
W	0.143 min.	0.5 min.	2.0 min.
Wq	0.0595 min.	0.417 min.	1.917 min.

(b) $\mu = 12$ customers per minute, $s = 2$

	$\lambda = 5\ cust/min$	$\lambda = 10\ cust/min$	$\lambda = 11.5\ cust/min$
L	0.4359 cust.	1.0085 cust.	1.2443 cust.
Lq	0.0189 cust.	0.1752 cust.	0.2860 cust.
W	0.087 min.	0.1008 min.	0.1083 min.
Wq	0.0038 min.	0.0175 min.	0.025 min.

10. Keep station as is, since neither alternative will reduce waiting time enough to offset additional operating expenses and capital costs.

12. $N = 4$ milling machines needed.

14.

$\lambda = 30$ per hour $\mu = 35$ per hour (decrease by 5)	$\lambda = 30$ per hour $\mu = 45$ per hour (increase by 5)
$P_0 = 0.1429$	$P_0 = 0.333$
$L = 6.0$ orders (increases by 100 percent)	$L = 2.0$ orders (decreases by 33 percent)
$Lq = 5.14$ orders (increases by 128 percent)	$Lq = 1.333$ orders (decreases by 41 percent)
$W = 0.2$ hours (increases by 100 percent)	$W = 0.0677$ hours (decreases by 33 percent)
$Wq = 0.1714$ hours (increases by 128 percent)	$Wq = 0.0444$ hours (decreases by 41 percent)

16.

$\lambda = 1$ car per minute	$\lambda = 1$ car per minute
$\mu = 0.6$ car per minute	$\mu = 0.6$ car per minute
$s = 2$ tellers	$s = 4$ tellers

$P_0 = 0.091$	$P_0 = 0.1859$
$L = 5.429$ cars	$L = 1.74$ cars
$Lq = 3.763$ cars	$Lq = 0.073$ cars
$W = 5.43$ mins.	$W = 1.74$ mins.
$Wq = 3.763$ mins.	$Wq = 0.073$ mins.

Results indicate worse queueing system performance with two tellers and better queueing system performance with four tellers.

18. $P_0 = 0.5124$
$Lq = 0.0078$ cust.
$L = 0.674$ cust.
$Wq = 0.002$ hrs.
$W = 0.169$ hrs.

All operating characteristics of the queueing system decrease.

20. Waiting time cost (queueing system) = \$436.90
Waiting time cost (queue) = \$311.30

CHAPTER 14 • MARKOV PROCESSES

2. Brand $A = 0.36$ (36 percent)
Brand $B = 0.36$ (36 percent)
Brand $C = 0.28$ (28 percent)

4.

(a)
$$\mathbf{P}^2 = \begin{bmatrix} 0.56 & 0.08 & 0.36 \\ 0.1 & 0 & 0 \\ 0.4 & 0.2 & 0.4 \end{bmatrix} \text{ (Not regular)}$$

(b)
$$\mathbf{P}^2 = \begin{bmatrix} 0.8 & 0 & 0.2 \\ 0 & 1 & 0 \\ 0.8 & 0 & 0.2 \end{bmatrix} \text{ (Not regular)}$$

$$\mathbf{P}^3 = \begin{bmatrix} 0.584 & 0.112 & 0.304 \\ 0.4 & 0.2 & 0.4 \\ 0.56 & 0.08 & 0.36 \end{bmatrix} \text{ (Regular)}$$

$$\mathbf{P}^3 = \begin{bmatrix} 0 & 1 & 0 \\ 0.8 & 0 & 0.2 \\ 0 & 1 & 0 \end{bmatrix} \text{ (Not regular)}$$

(c)
$$\mathbf{P}^2 = \begin{bmatrix} 0.79 & 0 & 0.21 \\ 0.42 & 0.16 & 0.42 \\ 0.3 & 0 & 0.7 \end{bmatrix} \text{ (Not regular)}$$

$$\mathbf{P}^3 = \begin{bmatrix} 0.447 & 0 & 0.553 \\ 0.642 & 0.064 & 0.294 \\ 0.79 & 0 & 0.21 \end{bmatrix} \text{ (Not regular)}$$

6. $\pi_1 = 0.2857$
$\pi_2 = 0.3214$
$\pi_3 = 0.3929$

8. From state 1: Cannot leave.
From state 2: Can move to State 3.
From state 3: Can move to State 2. $\therefore$ Not ergodic.
From state 4: Cannot leave.

10. Expected first passage time from state 2 to state 3 $= u_{23} = 5$.

12. $u_{11} = 2.6$, $u_{22} = 1.63$

14. (a)

		Next Week	
		Win	Lose
This Week	Win	0.7	0.3
	Lose	0.6	0.4

   (b) $\pi_1 = \frac{2}{3}$
   $\pi_2 = \frac{1}{3}$

16. (a) $\pi_1 = 0.40$ (Probability that Joe decides to go home while in tavern 1)
   $\pi_2 = 0.20$ (Probability that Joe decides to go home while in tavern 2)
   $\pi_3 = 0.40$ (Probability that Joe decides to go home while in tavern 3)

   (b) Expected number of beers from tavern 1 to tavern 3 = 3.88.

18. (a)

Beginning State	Expected Steps Before Absorption
S_3	$1.162 + 0.278 + 0.180 = 1.620$
S_4	$0.147 + 1.162 + 0.163 = 1.472$
S_5	$0.163 + 0.180 + 1.292 = 1.635$

   (b)

	S_1	S_2
Probability of absorption $= S_3$	0.5842	0.4158
S_4	0.4400	0.5600
S_5	0.3783	0.6217

   (c)

	S_1	S_2
$T' =$	($20,316	$24,684)

20.

	Probability		
	GIVEN: STARTED AT STATE 2 (NO CHANGE)		
Day	−10%	NO CHANGE	+10%
1	0.1	0.6	0.3
2	0.13	0.52	0.35
3	0.139	0.504	0.357
4	0.1417	0.5008	0.3575

Sell after day 2, since the profit probability is increasing at a decreasing rate.

CHAPTER 15 ● SIMULATION MODELING

2. $x_{n+1} \equiv 5x_n$ (modulo 3) with $x_0 = 4$

   $x_1 = 2$ $x_6 = 1$
   $x_2 = 1$ $x_7 = 2$
   $x_3 = 2$ $x_8 = 1$
   $x_4 = 1$ $x_9 = 2$
   $x_5 = 2$ $x_{10} = 1$

4. (a) $\mu = 6$, $\sigma = 3$

$$x = \frac{3}{\sqrt{\frac{12}{12}}} \sum_{i=1}^{12} RN_i + 6 - \frac{12}{2}\left(\frac{3}{\sqrt{\frac{12}{12}}}\right)$$

$$= 3\sum_{i=1}^{12} RN_i - 12$$

$\sum_{i=1}^{12} RN_i$	$x = 3\sum_{i=1}^{12} RN_i - 12$
6.77	$x = 3(6.77) - 12 = 20.31 - 12 = 8.31$
3.04	$x = 3(3.04) - 12 = 9.12 - 12 = -2.88$
5.84	$x = 3(5.84) - 12 = 17.52 - 12 = 5.52$
2.51	$x = 3(2.51) - 12 = 7.53 - 12 = -4.47$
5.12	$x = 3(5.12) - 12 = 15.36 - 12 = 3.36$

(b) Mean $= 1/\theta = 5$, $\theta = 1/5$.

$$x = \frac{\ln(1 - RN)_i}{-\theta}$$

RN_i	$x = -5\ln(1 - RN_i)$
0.093	$x = -5\ln(1 - 0.93)\ = -5\ln(0.907) = -5(-0.097) = 0.485$
0.835	$x = -5\ln(1 - 0.835) = -5\ln(0.165) = -5(-1.807) = 9.035$
0.534	$x = -5\ln(1 - 0.534) = -5\ln(0.466) = -5(-0.763) = 3.815$
0.212	$x = -5\ln(1 - 0.212) = -5\ln(0.788) = -5(-0.238) = 1.190$
0.201	$x = -5\ln(1 - 0.201) = -5\ln(0.799) = -5(-0.224) = 1.120$

Note: The following answers are dependent upon the generation and use of random numbers. Thus, they should be considered as approximate answers, and your answer may vary from those shown below.

6. Average waiting time in the system $\simeq$ 20 minutes.
    Percentage of time store is idle $\simeq$ 29 percent.

8. Expected Probability of arrival $\simeq 0.47$.

10. Based on the simulated number of orders received over 25 days ($\simeq$ 75) and the total number of machine days required to process these orders ($\simeq$210), the company would need to have nine machines. With nine machines, the Ace Job Shop will have 25 days in which a machine is idle (total cost of idle machine time = $375), and 33 days in which there is a back order (total cost of back ordering = $330).

12. Based on 50 plays of this game, you would lose $\simeq$ $175 or $\simeq$ $3.50 per play of the game.

14. (a) Ending monthly balance $\simeq$ $2400.

    (b) Highest monthly balance $\simeq$ $2400.
         Lowest monthly balance $\simeq$ $800.
         Average monthly balance $\simeq$ $1763.

16. (a) Average trip time $\simeq 8.5$ days.
     (b) Average trip time $\simeq 7.7$ days.

18. $r = $ random number $= P\{X \le x\} = \int_0^x 3t^3 dt$
     $= [t^3]_0^x = x^3$
     $\therefore x = \sqrt[3]{r}$, use $n = 20$ observations.
     (a) By crude Monte Carlo method, mean $\simeq 0.75$
     (b) By complementary random numbers, mean $\simeq 0.76$

20. High: 8 forwards
     Low: 3 forwards
     Average: 6.2 forwards

     Note: There were no major injuries in the simulated 15 game season.

22. Research and development Strategy no. 1: Average yearly profit = \$43 million
                                               Yearly profit range: \$39 million −
                                               \$49 million

     Research and development Strategy no. 2: Average yearly profit = \$86.5 million
                                               Yearly profit range: \$78.5 million −
                                               \$98.5 million

     Aqua Tech, Inc., can expect higher profit with Research and Development Strategy no. 2.

24. (a)

Observation	Random Observation	Generated Value
1	0.923	4
2	0.658	3
3	0.207	2

(b) Cumulative distribution function:
$$F(x) = \begin{cases} 0 & , \ x < 0 \\ x/10 & , \ 0 \le x \le 10 \\ 1 & , \ x > 10 \end{cases}$$

Random Observation	Generated Value
0.923	9.23
0.658	6.58
0.207	2.07

(c) Cumulative distribution function:
$$F(x) = \begin{cases} 0 & , \ x < 0 \\ {}^1/_4 x^2 & , \ 0 \le x \le 2 \\ 1 & , \ x > 2 \end{cases}$$

Random Observation	Generated Value
0.923	1.921
0.658	1.622
0.207	0.643

26. $x = \dfrac{\ln[\mathrm{RN}_i]}{-3}$

Observation	Random Number	Generated Value for x
1	0.111	0.7327
2	0.459	0.2596
3	0.987	0.0044
4	0.334	0.3655
5	0.285	0.4184

CHAPTER 16 • DECISION ANALYSIS

2. (a) a_1, a_2 (minimax loss = -9)
   (b) a_1 (maximax payoff = 15)
   (c) a_2 (minimax regret = 3)
   (d) a_1 (minimum expected loss = -12.2)
4. (a) a_1 (minimum expected loss = $-\$4220$)
   (b)

Weather Forecast	Optimal Bayes' Action	Expected Loss
Excellent	a_1	$-\$4782$
Good	a_1	$-\$4139$
Poor	a_1	$-\$2918$

   (c) Expected value of the optimal decision with sample data = $-\$4222$.
   (d) Expected value of the sample information = $|-\$4222 - \$4220| = \$2$.
   (e) Expected value of perfect information = $\$55$.
   (f) Efficiency of information, $E_I = {}^2\!/_{55} = 0.036 \simeq 4$ percent.
6. (a) a_1 (minimum expected loss = $-\$4,000,000$).
   (b)

Geologic Classification	Optimal Bayes' Action	Expected Loss
Uranium deposits highly likely	a_1	$-\$6,885,500$
Uranium deposits possible	a_1	$-\$4,710,000$
Uranium deposits unlikely	a_1	$-\$3,990,000$
Uranium deposits impossible	a_2	$-\$1,227,750$

   (c) Expected value of the optimal decision with sample information = $-\$4,128,440$.
   (d) Expected value of the sample information = $|-\$4,128,440 - \$4,000,000| = \$128,440$.
   (e) Expected value of perfect information = $\$600,000$.
   (f) Efficiency of information, $E_I = \$128,440/600,000 = 0.214 \simeq 21$ percent.
8. The decision tree analysis should produce results that parallel those obtained for problem 15–4. Thus, the expected loss at the initial decision node = $-\$4,222$.

10. The decision tree analysis should produce results that parallel those obtained for problem 15–6. Thus, the expected loss at the initial decision node = −$4,128,440.

12. *Note:* Answers will vary according to the set of certainty equivalents you select. A typical answer might be:

Point	Monetary (Certainty Payoff Equivalent)	Utility Index
1	$1,000,000	0.00
2	100,000,000	1.00
3	60,000,000	0.50
4	40,000,000	0.25
5	80,000,000	0.75

14. Utility Function—see following graph.

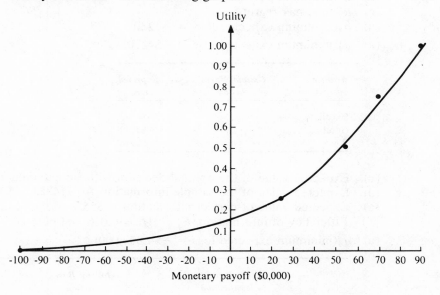

UTILITY TABLE

Farming Plan	State of Nature		
	θ_1: BAD WEATHER	θ_2: AVERAGE WEATHER	θ_3: IDEAL WEATHER
Plant small acreage	0.12	0.20	0.25
Plant half of acreage	0.05	0.25	0.47
Plant entire acreage	0.00	0.37	1.00

16. EMV(Prospect 1) = $122.50
EMV(Prospect 2) = $160.00* (Optimal decision—expected monetary value)

EU(Prospect 1) = 0.55* (Optimal decision—expected utility)
EU(Prospect 2) = 0.52

Index